Current Law

Legislation Citator

STATUTE CITATOR 2015

STATUTORY INSTRUMENT CITATOR 2015

Current Law

Legislation Citator

STATUTE CITATOR 2015

STATUTORY INSTRUMENT CITATOR 2015

SWEET & MAXWELL

 THOMSON REUTERS

Published in 2016 by Thomson Reuters (Professional) UK Limited, trading as
Sweet & Maxwell, Friars House, 160 Blackfriars Road, London, SE1 8EZ
(Registered in England & Wales, Company No.1679046.
Registered Office and address for service: 2nd floor, 1 Mark Square, Leonard
Street, London EC2A 4EG).

Computerset by Sweet & Maxwell.

Printed and bound by CPI Group (UK) Ltd, Croydon, CR0 4YY.

For further information on our products and services, visit
http://www.sweetandmaxwell.co.uk.

No natural forests were destroyed to make this product: only farmed timber
was used and replanted.
A CIP catalogue record for this book is available from the British Library.

Orders to: Sweet & Maxwell, PO Box 1000, Andover, SP10 9AF.
Tel: 0845 600 9355.
Email: TRLUKI.orders@thomsonreuters.com.

ISBN: 978-0-414-05344-1

PREFACE

The Sweet & Maxwell Current Law Service

The Current Law Service began in 1947 and provides a comprehensive guide to developments in case law, primary legislation and secondary legislation in the United Kingdom and mainland Europe. The Current Law service presently consists of the Monthly Digest and the Yearbook, Current Law Statutes Annotated and the Bound Volumes, European Current Law, Current Law Week, the Case Citator and the Legislation Citator.

The Legislation Citator

The Legislation Citator comprises the Statute Citator and the Statutory Instrument Citator and has been published annually in this format since 2005.The Citators list all amendments, modifications, repeals, etc. to primary and secondary legislation made in the years indicated.

Updates to these Citators are available in Current Law Statutes Annotated. This Volume of Legislation Citator contains the Statute Citator 2015 and the Statutory Instrument Citator 2015.

The Statute Citator

The material within the Statute Citator is arranged in chronological order and the following information is provided:

(i)   Statutes passed during the specified period;
(ii) Statutes affected during the specified period by Statute or Statutory Instrument;
(iii) Statutes judicially considered during the specified period;
(iv) Statutes repealed and amended during the specified period; and
(v)   Statutes under which Statutory Instruments have been made during this period.

The Statutory Instrument Citator

The material within the Statutory Instrument Citator is arranged in chronological order and the following information is provided:

(i)   Statutory Instruments amended, repealed, modified, etc. By Statute passed or Statutory Instrument issued during the specified period;
(ii) Statutory Instruments judicially considered during the specified period;
(iii) Statutory Instruments consolidated during the specified period; and
(iv) Statutory Instruments made under the powers of any Statutory Instrument issued during this period.

How to Use the Legislation Citator

The following example entries of the Statute and Statutory Instrument Citators indicate how to determine developments which have occurred to the piece of legislation in which you are interested. Entries to the Citators are arranged chronologically.

Statute Citator

7. Business Rates Supplement Act 2009	— Chapter number, name of Act and year
Commencement Orders: SI 2009/2892 Art.2	— Commencement orders bringing provisions into force
Royal Assent July 02, 2009	— Date of Royal Assent
s.12, enabling SI 2009/2542	— Statutory Instruments made under the powers of s.1 of the Act
s.2. see *R. v Brown* [2009] Crim. L.R. 43	— Case judicially considering s.2
s.3, amended: 2010 c.3 s.2	— s.3 amended by Act (s.2 of Ch.3 of 2010) and two SIs
s.3, enabling: SI 2009/82; SI 2010/70	
s.4, repealed: 2010 c.3 Sch.4	— s.4 repealed by Sch.4 of Ch.3 of 2010
s.4A added: SI 2009/42	— s.4A added by SI number 42 of 2009

SI Citator

3264 Agriculture (Cross compliance) Regulations 2009	— Number, name and year of SI
Reg.2, amended: SI 2010/65 Art.2	— reg.2 amended by art.2 of SI number 65 of 2010
Reg.3, revoked: 2010 c.23 Sch.15	— reg.3 revoked by Sch.15 of Ch.23 of 2010
Reg.4, see *R. v Smith* [2010] C.O.D. 54	— Case judicially considering reg.4

CONTENTS

CURRENT LAW

STATUTE CITATOR 2015

PART 4

This is Part 4 of the Current Law Statute Citator 2015 and is up to date to March 10, 2016 (Orders and Acts received).

 (i) Statutes passed between January 1, 2015 and March 10, 2016;
 (ii) Amendments, modifications and repeals made to existing Statutes during this period;
 (iii) Statutes judicially considered during this period;
 (iv) Statutes under which Statutory Instruments have been made during this period.

Definitions of legislative effects:

"added"   : new provisions are inserted by subsequent legislation

"amended"   : text of legislation is modified by subsequent legislation

"applied"   : brought to bear, or exercised by subsequent legislation

"consolidated" : used where previous Acts in the same subject area are brought together in subsequent legislation, with or without amendments

"disapplied" : an exception made to the application of an earlier enactment

"enabling"   : giving power for the relevant SI to be made

"referred to" : direction from other legislation without specific effect or application

"repealed"   : rescinded by subsequent legislation

"restored"   : reinstated by subsequent legislation (where previously repealed/ revoked)

"substituted" : text of provision is completely replaced by subsequent legislation

"varied"   : provisions modified in relation to their application to specified areas or circumstances, however the text itself remains unchanged

ACTS OF THE SCOTTISH PARLIAMENT

2000

asp 4. Adults with Incapacity (Scotland) Act 2000
    s.6, amended: SSI 2015/157 Sch.1 para.4
    s.7, enabling: SSI 2015/260
    s.9, amended: SSI 2015/157 Sch.1 para.4
    s.86, enabling: SSI 2015/260

asp 7. Ethical Standards in Public Life etc (Scotland) Act 2000
    s.22, amended: SSI 2015/402 Sch.1 para.4
    Sch.3, amended: 2015 asp 1 s.17, SSI 2015/157 Sch.1 para.5

asp 11. Regulation of Investigatory Powers (Scotland) Act 2000
    s.24, enabling: SSI 2015/33, SSI 2015/34
    s.27, enabling: SSI 2015/32

2001

asp 7. Convention Rights (Compliance) (Scotland) Act 2001
    s.12, enabling: SSI 2015/330, SSI 2015/423
    s.14, enabling: SSI 2015/423

asp 8. Regulation of Care (Scotland) Act 2001
    s.73, enabling: SSI 2015/62

2002

asp 5. Community Care and Health (Scotland) Act 2002
    s.1, enabling: SSI 2015/154
    s.2, enabling: SSI 2015/154
    s.5, enabling: SSI 2015/202
    s.23, enabling: SSI 2015/154, SSI 2015/202
    s.27, enabling: SSI 2015/179

asp 6. Protection of Wild Mammals (Scotland) Act 2002
    s.9, amended: SSI 2015/338 Sch.2 para.6

asp 10. Fur Farming (Prohibition) (Scotland) Act 2002
    s.2, amended: SSI 2015/338 Sch.2 para.7

asp 11. Scottish Public Services Ombudsman Act 2002
    s.3, enabling: SSI 2015/286
    s.14, amended: 2015 asp 5 s.13
    s.16H, added: 2015 asp 5 s.13
    s.18, amended: 2015 asp 5 s.13
    s.19, amended: 2015 asp 5 s.13
    s.20, amended: 2015 asp 5 s.13
    s.23, amended: 2015 asp 5 s.13
    Sch.2 Part 2 para.22A, added: 2015 asp 1 s.17
    Sch.2 Part 2 para.25ZB, added: SSI 2015/286 Art.2

asp 13. Freedom of Information (Scotland) Act 2002
    Sch.1 Part 2 para.7B, added: 2015 asp 1 s.17

asp 17. Debt Arrangement and Attachment (Scotland) Act 2002
    s.7, enabling: SSI 2015/149, SSI 2015/216
    s.62, enabling: SSI 2015/216

2003

asp 1. Local Government in Scotland Act 2003
    Part 2, repealed: 2015 asp 6 Sch.5
    s.16, amended: SSI 2015/157 Sch.1 para.6
    s.57, amended: 2015 asp 6 Sch.4 para.7
    s.57, repealed: 2015 asp 6 Sch.5

asp 2. Land Reform (Scotland) Act 2003
    s.29, amended: SSI 2015/271 Art.4
    s.33, amended: 2015 asp 6 s.36
    s.33, repealed: 2015 asp 6 s.36
    s.33, substituted: 2015 asp 6 s.36
    s.34, amended: 2015 asp 6 s.37
    s.34, enabling: SSI 2015/400
    s.35, amended: 2015 asp 6 s.38
    s.36, amended: 2015 asp 6 s.39
    s.36, enabling: SSI 2015/400
    s.37, amended: 2015 asp 6 s.40, Sch.4 para.8
    s.37, enabling: SSI 2015/400
    s.38, amended: 2015 asp 6 s.41, Sch.5
    s.38, repealed: 2015 asp 6 Sch.5

s.39, amended: 2015 asp 6 s.42
s.39, enabling: SSI 2015/400
s.39A, added: 2015 asp 6 s.43
s.40, repealed: 2015 asp 6 Sch.5
s.41, amended: 2015 asp 6 s.44
s.41, enabling: SSI 2015/400
s.44, amended: 2015 asp 6 s.45
s.44A, added: 2015 asp 6 s.46
s.48, enabling: SSI 2015/400
s.49, enabling: SSI 2015/400
s.50, amended: 2015 asp 6 s.47
s.50, repealed: 2015 asp 6 Sch.5
s.51, amended: 2015 asp 6 s.48, s.51,
s.52, Sch.4 para.8
s.51, repealed: 2015 asp 6 s.48 , Sch.5
s.51A, added: 2015 asp 6 s.49
s.51A, enabling: SSI 2015/400
s.51B, added: 2015 asp 6 s.50
s.51B, enabling: SSI 2015/400
s.51C, added: 2015 asp 6 s.51
s.52, amended: 2015 asp 6 s.52, s.53,
Sch.4 para.8
s.52, repealed: 2015 asp 6 Sch.5
s.52, enabling: SSI 2015/400
s.56, amended: 2015 asp 6 s.54
s.57, amended: 2015 asp 6 s.55
s.60, amended: 2015 asp 6 s.53, s.56
s.60A, added: 2015 asp 6 s.57
s.61, amended: 2015 asp 6 s.58, Sch.5
s.62, amended: 2015 asp 6 s.59, Sch.5
s.62, repealed: 2015 asp 6 Sch.5
s.63, enabling: SSI 2015/400
s.67A, added: 2015 asp 6 s.60
s.67B, added: 2015 asp 6 s.61
s.68, amended: 2015 asp 6 Sch.4 para.8
s.71, amended: 2015 asp 6 s.62
s.72, amended: 2015 asp 6 s.63
s.73, amended: 2015 asp 6 s.64
s.73, repealed: 2015 asp 6 s.64
s.74, amended: 2015 asp 6 s.65
s.75, amended: 2015 asp 6 s.66
s.76, amended: 2015 asp 6 s.67
s.81, amended: 2015 asp 6 s.68
s.88, amended: 2015 asp 6 s.69
s.89, amended: 2015 asp 6 s.70
s.92, amended: 2015 asp 6 s.71
s.94, amended: 2015 asp 6 s.72
s.97B, added: 2015 asp 6 s.74
s.97ZA, added: 2015 asp 6 s.73
s.97Z1, added: 2015 asp 6 s.75

s.98, amended: 2015 asp 6 Sch.4 para.8,
Sch.5
s.98, enabling: SSI 2015/400
**asp 3. Water Environment and Water
Services (Scotland) Act 2003**
s.1, varied: SSI 2015/270 Reg.2
s.2, varied: SSI 2015/270 Reg.2
s.2, enabling: SSI 2015/323
s.8, enabling: SSI 2015/211
s.9, enabling: SSI 2015/211
s.10, enabling: SSI 2015/211
s.11, amended: 2015 asp 1 Sch.1 para.8
s.19, enabling: SSI 2015/211
s.25, enabling: SSI 2015/270
s.36, enabling: SSI 2015/211, SSI
2015/270
**asp 4. Public Appointments and Public
Bodies etc (Scotland) Act 2003**
Sch.2, amended: 2015 asp 1 s.17
asp 7. Criminal Justice (Scotland) Act 2003
s.16, amended: 2015 asp 9 s.54
s.16A, added: 2015 asp 9 s.55
s.17B, added: 2015 asp 9 s.56
s.17E, added: 2015 asp 9 s.57
s.18A, added: 2015 asp 9 s.58
s.18B, added: 2015 asp 9 s.59
s.22, repealed: 2015 asp 12 Sch.1 para.2
s.88, amended: 2015 asp 9 s.59
asp 8. Building (Scotland) Act 2003
s.1, enabling: SSI 2015/218
s.35, amended: SSI 2015/271 Art.3
s.54, enabling: SSI 2015/218
asp 9. Title Conditions (Scotland) Act 2003
s.38, enabling: SSI 2015/239
**asp 13. Mental Health (Care and Treatment)
(Scotland) Act 2003**
Part 5, substituted: 2015 asp 9 s.7
Part 6, substituted: 2015 asp 9 s.8
s.1, amended: 2015 asp 9 s.53
s.19, amended: 2015 asp 9 s.36
s.21, enabling: SSI 2015/334
s.24, amended: 2015 asp 9 s.31
s.24, substituted: 2015 asp 9 s.31
s.30, amended: SSI 2015/157 Sch.1
para.7
s.36, amended: 2015 asp 9 s.4, s.11
s.36, repealed: 2015 asp 9 s.29
s.38, amended: 2015 asp 9 s.4
s.38, repealed: 2015 asp 9 s.4
s.40, amended: 2015 asp 9 s.4
s.42, amended: 2015 asp 9 s.4

s.43, amended: 2015 asp 9 s.7
s.43, substituted: 2015 asp 9 s.7
s.44, amended: 2015 asp 9 s.5, s.11
s.44, repealed: 2015 asp 9 s.29
s.46, amended: 2015 asp 9 s.5
s.47, repealed: 2015 asp 9 s.29
s.56, amended: 2015 asp 9 s.8
s.56, substituted: 2015 asp 9 s.8
s.58, repealed: 2015 asp 9 s.29
s.64, amended: 2015 asp 9 s.1
s.65, amended: 2015 asp 9 s.1
s.71A, added: 2015 asp 9 s.11
s.87A, added: 2015 asp 9 s.2
s.101, amended: 2015 asp 9 s.21
s.124, amended: 2015 asp 9 s.3
s.124A, added: 2015 asp 9 s.13
s.127, amended: 2015 asp 9 s.9, s.10
s.127, repealed: 2015 asp 9 s.9
s.128, amended: 2015 asp 9 s.10
s.136, amended: 2015 asp 9 s.12, s.34
s.153A, added: 2015 asp 9 s.50
s.157, repealed: 2015 asp 9 s.51
s.160, amended: 2015 asp 9 s.51
s.189, amended: 2015 asp 9 s.21
s.193, amended: 2015 asp 9 s.60
s.198, amended: 2015 asp 9 s.52
s.200, amended: 2015 asp 9 s.60
s.213, amended: 2015 asp 9 s.21
s.218A, added: 2015 asp 9 s.48
s.221, amended: 2015 asp 9 s.9
s.221, repealed: 2015 asp 9 s.9
s.224, amended: 2015 asp 9 s.9, s.10, s.60
s.224, repealed: 2015 asp 9 s.9
s.230, amended: 2015 asp 9 s.6
s.245, amended: 2015 asp 9 s.30
s.250, amended: 2015 asp 9 s.23
s.251, repealed: 2015 asp 9 s.22
s.253, repealed: 2015 asp 9 s.22
s.255, repealed: 2015 asp 9 s.24
s.256, amended: 2015 asp 9 s.24
s.256, repealed: 2015 asp 9 s.24
s.257, amended: 2015 asp 9 s.23, s.24
s.257, repealed: 2015 asp 9 s.24
s.257A, added: 2015 asp 9 s.25
s.259A, added: 2015 asp 9 s.27
s.261A, added: 2015 asp 9 s.28
s.264, amended: 2015 asp 9 s.14, SSI 2015/364 Reg.3
s.266, repealed: 2015 asp 9 s.15
s.267, amended: 2015 asp 9 s.15
s.267, substituted: 2015 asp 9 s.15

s.268, amended: 2015 asp 9 s.14, s.16, SSI 2015/364 Reg.3
s.268, repealed: 2015 asp 9 s.16
s.269, amended: 2015 asp 9 s.16
s.270, repealed: 2015 asp 9 s.15
s.271, amended: 2015 asp 9 s.15, s.16
s.271, substituted: 2015 asp 9 s.15
s.271A, added: 2015 asp 9 s.16
s.271A, enabling: SSI 2015/364
s.272, amended: 2015 asp 9 s.15
s.273, amended: 2015 asp 9 s.16
s.273, substituted: 2015 asp 9 s.18
s.276A, added: 2015 asp 9 s.26
s.289, amended: 2015 asp 9 s.32
s.290, amended: 2015 asp 9 s.32
s.291A, added: 2015 asp 9 s.29
s.295A, added: 2015 asp 9 s.19
s.299, amended: 2015 asp 9 s.20
s.299, repealed: 2015 asp 9 s.20
s.303, amended: 2015 asp 9 s.33
s.309, amended: 2015 asp 9 s.33
s.309A, amended: 2015 asp 9 s.32
s.310, amended: 2015 asp 9 s.33
s.318, repealed: 2015 asp 9 s.22
s.320, repealed: 2015 asp 9 s.24
s.326, amended: 2015 asp 9 s.16, s.36
s.326, enabling: SSI 2015/334
s.329, amended: 2015 asp 9 s.6, s.22, s.53, s.60, SSI 2015/157 Sch.1 para.7
Sch.2 Part 2 para.7, amended: 2015 asp 9 s.35
Sch.2 Part 3 para.10, enabling: SSI 2015/334
Sch.2 Part 3 para.13A, repealed: 2015 asp 9 s.21
Sch.3 para.1A, added: 2015 asp 9 s.35

2004

asp 3. Vulnerable Witnesses (Scotland) Act 2004
s.25, enabling: SSI 2015/244
asp 8. Antisocial Behaviour etc (Scotland) Act 2004
s.40, amended: SSI 2015/150 Sch.1 para.7
s.40A, amended: 2015 asp 12 Sch.1 para.3
s.40A, repealed: 2015 asp 12 Sch.1 para.3

s.112, amended: SSI 2015/402 Sch.1
para.5

asp 9. Local Governance (Scotland) Act 2004
s.11, enabling: SSI 2015/7
s.12, enabling: SSI 2015/7
s.16, enabling: SSI 2015/7

2005

asp 5. Fire (Scotland) Act 2005
s.41E, amended: 2015 asp 6 Sch.4 para.9
s.41J, amended: 2015 asp 6 Sch.4 para.9

**asp 6. Further and Higher Education
(Scotland) Act 2005**
s.17, varied: SSI 2015/153 Sch.1 para.21
s.23N, amended: SSI 2015/153 Sch.1
para.3
s.34, enabling: SSI 2015/153
s.35, amended: SSI 2015/153 Sch.1
para.3
Sch.2B para.17, amended: SSI 2015/153
Sch.1 para.3
Sch.2B para.18, enabling: SSI 2015/153

asp 7. Gaelic Language (Scotland) Act 2005
s.10, repealed: 2015 asp 1 Sch.1 para.9

**asp 8. Prohibition of Female Genital
Mutilation (Scotland) Act 2005**
s.3, amended: 2015 c.9 s.70
s.4, amended: 2015 c.9 s.70
s.6, amended: 2015 c.9 s.70

**asp 10. Charities and Trustee Investment
(Scotland) Act 2005**
s.7, enabling: SSI 2015/148, SSI
2015/153
s.19, enabling: SSI 2015/148, SSI
2015/153

asp 12. Transport (Scotland) Act 2005
s.40, enabling: SSI 2015/133
s.52, enabling: SSI 2015/133

**asp 14. Management of Offenders etc
(Scotland) Act 2005**
s.10, enabling: SSI 2015/431
s.21, repealed: SSI 2015/39 Sch.1 para.7
s.24, enabling: SSI 2015/429

**asp 15. Environmental Assessment (Scotland)
Act 2005**
s.3, amended: SSI 2015/271 Art.5

asp 16. Licensing (Scotland) Act 2005
Part 3, substituted: 2015 asp 10 s.59
s.2, repealed: 2015 asp 10 s.54

s.4, amended: 2015 asp 10 s.41
s.6, amended: 2015 asp 10 s.42
s.7, amended: 2015 asp 10 s.55
s.9A, added: 2015 asp 10 s.56
s.14, amended: 2015 asp 10 s.57
s.22, amended: 2015 asp 10 s.43
s.23, amended: 2015 asp 10 s.43, s.55
s.28, amended: 2015 asp 10 Sch.2 para.4
s.29, amended: 2015 asp 10 Sch.2 para.4
s.30, amended: 2015 asp 10 s.55
s.33, amended: 2015 asp 10 s.44, s.49
s.33, substituted: 2015 asp 10 s.49
s.33A, added: 2015 asp 10 s.49
s.34, repealed: 2015 asp 10 s.49
s.35, amended: 2015 asp 10 Sch.2 para.4
s.36, amended: 2015 asp 10 s.45
s.37, amended: 2015 asp 10 s.45, Sch.2
para.4
s.39, amended: 2015 asp 10 s.45
s.39A, amended: 2015 asp 10 s.45
s.39B, added: 2015 asp 10 s.45
s.40A, amended: 2015 asp 10 s.59
s.40A, repealed: 2015 asp 10 s.59
s.40A, substituted: 2015 asp 10 s.59
s.44, amended: 2015 asp 10 s.50
s.48, amended: 2015 asp 10 s.59
s.48, repealed: 2015 asp 10 s.59
s.49, amended: 2015 asp 10 Sch.2 para.4
s.57, amended: 2015 asp 10 Sch.2 para.4
s.73, amended: 2015 asp 10 s.46
s.73A, added: 2015 asp 10 s.46
s.74, amended: 2015 asp 10 s.46, s.60
s.77, amended: 2015 asp 10 s.60
s.78, amended: 2015 asp 10 s.46, s.60
s.83, amended: 2015 asp 10 s.47, s.51
s.84, amended: 2015 asp 10 s.48
s.84A, amended: 2015 asp 10 s.48, s.60
s.84B, added: 2015 asp 10 s.58
s.104A, added: 2015 asp 10 s.53
s.105, repealed: 2015 asp 10 s.53
s.105, substituted: 2015 asp 10 s.53
s.129, repealed: 2015 asp 10 s.52
s.134, amended: 2015 asp 10 s.62
s.134, substituted: 2015 asp 10 s.62
s.134ZA, added: 2015 asp 10 s.61
s.146, amended: 2015 asp 10 s.56
s.147, amended: 2015 asp 10 s.59
Sch.5 Part 1, amended: 2015 asp 10 s.45,
s.49
Sch.5 Part 2, amended: 2015 asp 10 s.47,
s.48

2006

asp 1. Housing (Scotland) Act 2006
 s.28B, enabling: SSI 2015/403
 s.28C, enabling: SSI 2015/403
 s.174, enabling: SSI 2015/144
 Sch.2 para.8, enabling: SSI 2015/369
 Sch.5 para.5, amended: SSI 2015/271
 Art.6

asp 10. Police, Public Order and Criminal Justice (Scotland) Act 2006
 s.60, amended: SSI 2015/338 Sch.2 para.9
 s.95, amended: SSI 2015/338 Sch.2 para.9
 s.96, amended: SSI 2015/338 Sch.2 para.9
 s.96, substituted: SSI 2015/338 Sch.2 para.9
 s.96A, added: SSI 2015/338 Sch.2 para.9

asp 11. Animal Health and Welfare (Scotland) Act 2006
 s.43, amended: SSI 2015/338 Sch.2 para.10

asp 16. Scottish Commission for Human Rights Act 2006
 s.14, amended: SSI 2015/402 Sch.1 para.6
 s.14, enabling: SSI 2015/356

2007

asp 3. Bankruptcy and Diligence etc (Scotland) Act 2007
 s.114, amended: SSI 2015/150 Sch.1 para.9

asp 4. Adoption and Children (Scotland) Act 2007
 s.104, enabling: SSI 2015/5
 s.114, enabling: SSI 2015/5

asp 8. Transport and Works (Scotland) Act 2007
 s.12, amended: SI 2015/1682 Sch.1 para.11
 s.14, enabling: SSI 2015/328
 s.28, enabling: SSI 2015/328

asp 12. Aquaculture and Fisheries (Scotland) Act 2007
 s.26, enabling: SSI 2015/113
 s.27, enabling: SSI 2015/113

s.29, enabling: SSI 2015/113
s.43, enabling: SSI 2015/113

asp 14. Protection of Vulnerable Groups (Scotland) Act 2007
 s.46, amended: SSI 2015/330 Art.4
 s.46, repealed: SSI 2015/330 Art.4 , SSI 2015/423 Art.4
 s.49, amended: SSI 2015/330 Art.4, SSI 2015/423 Art.4
 s.51, amended: SSI 2015/330 Art.4, SSI 2015/423 Art.4
 s.51, repealed: SSI 2015/330 Art.4
 s.52, substituted: SSI 2015/330 Art.4, SSI 2015/423 Art.4
 s.52A, repealed: SSI 2015/330 Art.4
 s.52ZA, added: SSI 2015/423 Art.4
 s.53, amended: SSI 2015/330 Art.4, SSI 2015/423 Art.4
 s.53, repealed: SSI 2015/330 Art.4 , SSI 2015/423 Art.4
 s.57A, added: SSI 2015/330 Art.4, SSI 2015/423 Art.4
 s.57A, repealed: SSI 2015/330 Art.4
 s.70, enabling: SSI 2015/223
 s.97, amended: SSI 2015/153 Sch.1 para.4

2008

asp 5. Public Health etc (Scotland) Act 2008
 s.6, amended: SSI 2015/157 Sch.1 para.8
 s.8, amended: SSI 2015/157 Sch.1 para.8

asp 6. Judiciary and Courts (Scotland) Act 2008
 s.37, enabling: SSI 2015/120
 s.62, enabling: SSI 2015/224
 Sch.3 para.3, enabling: SSI 2015/53

2009

asp 1. Scottish Parliamentary Pensions Act 2009
 Sch.1 Part N para.75, amended: 2015 c.8 Sch.4 para.43
 Sch.1 Part P para.91, amended: 2015 c.8 Sch.4 para.43

asp 9. Sexual Offences (Scotland) Act 2009
 s.44, amended: SSI 2015/153 Sch.1 para.5

asp 12. Climate Change (Scotland) Act 2009
s.10, amended: SSI 2015/197 Art.2
s.10, enabling: SSI 2015/197
s.11, amended: SSI 2015/197 Art.3
s.12, enabling: SSI 2015/197
s.13, enabling: SSI 2015/189
s.20, enabling: SSI 2015/189
s.46, enabling: SSI 2015/347
s.88, enabling: SSI 2015/159
s.88A, enabling: SSI 2015/159
s.96, enabling: SSI 2015/159, SSI 2015/189, SSI 2015/197, SSI 2015/347
Sch.1A para.3, enabling: SSI 2015/159
Sch.1A para.4, enabling: SSI 2015/159

2010

asp 2. Schools (Consultation) (Scotland) Act 2010
Sch.2 para.1, amended: 2015 asp 6 Sch.4 para.10
Sch.2 para.2, amended: 2015 asp 6 Sch.4 para.10
Sch.2 para.3, amended: 2015 asp 6 Sch.4 para.10
Sch.2 para.4, amended: 2015 asp 6 Sch.4 para.10
Sch.2 para.5, amended: 2015 asp 6 Sch.4 para.10
Sch.2 para.10, amended: 2015 asp 6 Sch.4 para.10

asp 5. Marine (Scotland) Act 2010
s.5, enabling: SSI 2015/193
s.85, enabling: SSI 2015/302, SSI 2015/437
s.86, enabling: SSI 2015/302, SSI 2015/437
s.88, enabling: SSI 2015/302, SSI 2015/303, SSI 2015/437
s.92, enabling: SSI 2015/437

asp 8. Public Services Reform (Scotland) Act 2010
s.14, enabling: SSI 2015/39
s.15, enabling: SSI 2015/39
s.51, amended: SSI 2015/157 Sch.1 para.10
s.105, amended: SSI 2015/157 Sch.1 para.10
s.115, amended: 2015 asp 6 Sch.4 para.11

s.134, enabling: SSI 2015/234
Sch.5, amended: SSI 2015/39 Art.3, SSI 2015/157 Sch.1 para.10
Sch.8, amended: 2015 asp 1 s.17, SSI 2015/39 Art.3
Sch.19, amended: 2015 asp 1 s.17
Sch.20, amended: 2015 asp 1 s.17

asp 9. Control of Dogs (Scotland) Act 2010
s.5, amended: SSI 2015/338 Sch.2 para.12
s.11, amended: SSI 2015/338 Sch.2 para.12

asp 13. Criminal Justice and Licensing (Scotland) Act 2010
s.47, repealed: 2015 asp 12 Sch.1 para.5
s.153, amended: SSI 2015/338 Sch.2 para.13
s.204, enabling: SSI 2015/388
s.206, enabling: SSI 2015/177, SSI 2015/336
Sch.1 para.2, enabling: SSI 2015/225
Sch.1 para.6A, added: SSI 2015/388 Art.2
Sch.7 para.66, repealed: 2015 asp 9 s.49

2011

asp 1. Children's Hearings (Scotland) Act 2011
s.19, amended: SSI 2015/402 Sch.1 para.7
s.152, enabling: SSI 2015/20
s.162, amended: SSI 2015/402 Sch.1 para.7
s.177, enabling: SSI 2015/21
s.195, enabling: SSI 2015/20, SSI 2015/21

asp 8. Property Factors (Scotland) Act 2011
s.3, enabling: SSI 2015/217
s.30, enabling: SSI 2015/217

asp 9. Reservoirs (Scotland) Act 2011
s.1, enabling: SSI 2015/90
s.2, enabling: SSI 2015/90, SSI 2015/315
s.9, enabling: SSI 2015/90, SSI 2015/315
s.10, enabling: SSI 2015/90
s.13, varied: SSI 2015/63 Art.7
s.14, enabling: SSI 2015/90, SSI 2015/315
s.23, enabling: SSI 2015/315
s.24, enabling: SSI 2015/315

s.27, enabling: SSI 2015/92
s.28, enabling: SSI 2015/90
s.30, enabling: SSI 2015/90
s.114, enabling: SSI 2015/63, SSI 2015/90, SSI 2015/92, SSI 2015/315
s.116, enabling: SSI 2015/43, SSI 2015/63, SSI 2015/314

asp 11. Certification of Death (Scotland) Act 2011

s.4, enabling: SSI 2015/163
s.18, enabling: SSI 2015/162
s.19, enabling: SSI 2015/165
s.28, enabling: SSI 2015/164
s.32, enabling: SSI 2015/115

asp 12. Public Records (Scotland) Act 2011

s.2, enabling: SSI 2015/335
Sch.1, amended: 2015 asp 1 s.17, SSI 2015/39 Sch.1 para.8, SSI 2015/157
Sch.1 para.11, SSI 2015/335 Art.2

asp 14. Private Rented Housing (Scotland) Act 2011

s.41, enabling: SSI 2015/326

2012

asp 5. Land Registration etc (Scotland) Act 2012

s.27, repealed: SSI 2015/265 Art.2
s.27, enabling: SSI 2015/265
s.48, enabling: SSI 2015/265
s.110, enabling: SSI 2015/265
s.116, enabling: SSI 2015/265

asp 8. Police and Fire Reform (Scotland) Act 2012

s.46, amended: 2015 asp 6 Sch.4 para.12
s.47, amended: 2015 asp 6 Sch.4 para.12

2013

asp 1. Social Care (Self-directed Support) (Scotland) Act 2013

s.15, enabling: SSI 2015/319
s.22, enabling: SSI 2015/319
s.24, amended: SSI 2015/157 Sch.1 para.12

asp 8. Forth Road Bridge Act 2013

s.7, enabling: SSI 2015/190

asp 11. Land and Buildings Transaction Tax (Scotland) Act 2013

s.24, enabling: SSI 2015/126
s.25, amended: SSI 2015/123 Art.2
s.27, amended: SSI 2015/93 Art.2, SSI 2015/123 Art.3
s.27, enabling: SSI 2015/93, SSI 2015/123
s.33, amended: SSI 2015/123 Art.4
s.46, enabling: SSI 2015/322
s.58, amended: SSI 2015/123 Art.5
s.65, amended: SSI 2015/123 Art.6
s.67, enabling: SSI 2015/71
s.68, enabling: SSI 2015/123
s.70, enabling: SSI 2015/108
Sch.5 Part 4 para.11, substituted: SSI 2015/123 Art.8
Sch.6 para.1, amended: SSI 2015/93 Art.2
Sch.6 para.2, amended: SSI 2015/93 Art.2
Sch.9 para.1, substituted: SSI 2015/93 Art.2
Sch.10A, added: SSI 2015/123 Sch.1
Sch.13A, added: SSI 2015/93 Art.2
Sch.16A, added: SSI 2015/93 Art.2
Sch.19 Part 2 para.3, enabling: SSI 2015/126
Sch.20, amended: SSI 2015/123 Art.6

asp 12. Post-16 Education (Scotland) Act 2013

s.22, enabling: SSI 2015/153
s.23, enabling: SSI 2015/82

asp 14. Scottish Independence Referendum Act 2013

s.9, enabling: SSI 2015/368

2014

asp 1. Victims and Witnesses (Scotland) Act 2014

s.1A, added: SSI 2015/444 Reg.2
s.3A, added: SSI 2015/444 Reg.3
s.3B, added: SSI 2015/444 Reg.4
s.3E, added: SSI 2015/444 Reg.5
s.3G, added: SSI 2015/444 Reg.6
s.3H, added: SSI 2015/444 Reg.7
s.3I, added: SSI 2015/444 Reg.8
s.3J, added: SSI 2015/444 Reg.9
s.4, amended: SSI 2015/444 Reg.10
s.5, amended: SSI 2015/444 Reg.11

s.8, amended: 2015 asp 12 Sch.1 para.6,
SSI 2015/444 Reg.12
s.9A, added: SSI 2015/444 Reg.13
s.9D, added: SSI 2015/444 Reg.14
s.27A, added: SSI 2015/444 Reg.15
s.29A, added: SSI 2015/444 Reg.16
s.32, amended: SSI 2015/444 Reg.17
s.34, enabling: SSI 2015/200

asp 2. Landfill Tax (Scotland) Act 2014
s.11, enabling: SSI 2015/151
s.12, varied: SSI 2015/109 Art.3
s.13, enabling: SSI 2015/45, SSI
2015/127
s.14, enabling: SSI 2015/45
s.15, enabling: SSI 2015/3, SSI 2015/152
s.18, enabling: SSI 2015/3, SSI 2015/152
s.19, enabling: SSI 2015/3, SSI 2015/152
s.20, enabling: SSI 2015/3, SSI 2015/152
s.22, enabling: SSI 2015/3
s.23, enabling: SSI 2015/3
s.25, enabling: SSI 2015/3, SSI 2015/152
s.30, enabling: SSI 2015/3
s.32, enabling: SSI 2015/3
s.37, enabling: SSI 2015/3
s.39, varied: SSI 2015/109 Art.3
s.43, enabling: SSI 2015/17, SSI
2015/109

**asp 3. Regulatory Reform (Scotland) Act
2014**
s.7, enabling: SSI 2015/271
s.20, enabling: SSI 2015/383
s.21, enabling: SSI 2015/383
s.22, enabling: SSI 2015/383
s.23, enabling: SSI 2015/383
s.24, enabling: SSI 2015/383
s.25, enabling: SSI 2015/383
s.26, enabling: SSI 2015/383
s.27, enabling: SSI 2015/383
s.28, enabling: SSI 2015/383
s.29, enabling: SSI 2015/383
s.30, enabling: SSI 2015/383
s.31, enabling: SSI 2015/383
s.32, enabling: SSI 2015/383
s.53, enabling: SSI 2015/383
s.58, enabling: SSI 2015/383
s.59, enabling: SSI 2015/383
s.61, enabling: SSI 2015/52
Sch.1, amended: 2015 asp 1 s.17, Sch.1
para.10, SSI 2015/271 Art.8

**asp 5. Marriage and Civil Partnership
(Scotland) Act 2014**

s.9, enabling: SSI 2015/371
s.10, amended: SSI 2015/371 Art.5
s.11, enabling: SSI 2015/371
s.36, enabling: SSI 2015/14

asp 6. Budget (Scotland) Act 2014
Part 2, repealed: 2015 asp 2 s.8
s.4, amended: SSI 2015/138 Art.2
s.7, enabling: SSI 2015/138
Sch.1, amended: SSI 2015/138 Art.3
Sch.2, amended: SSI 2015/138 Art.4

**asp 8. Children and Young People (Scotland)
Act 2014**
s.47, enabling: SSI 2015/268
s.99, enabling: SSI 2015/268
s.102, enabling: SSI 2015/61, SSI
2015/104, SSI 2015/317
Sch.1 para.20, added: SSI 2015/157
Sch.1 para.13
Sch.2 para.14, added: SSI 2015/157
Sch.1 para.13
Sch.3 para.15, added: SSI 2015/157
Sch.1 para.13
Sch.4 para.25, added: SSI 2015/157
Sch.1 para.13

**asp 9. Public Bodies (Joint Working)
(Scotland) Act 2014**
s.9, enabling: SSI 2015/88, SSI
2015/222, SSI 2015/266, SSI 2015/321
s.12, enabling: SSI 2015/66, SSI
2015/432
s.17, enabling: SSI 2015/66, SSI
2015/432
s.69, enabling: SSI 2015/66, SSI
2015/432
s.70, enabling: SSI 2015/157
s.72, enabling: SSI 2015/44

asp 10. Tribunals (Scotland) Act 2014
s.27, enabling: SSI 2015/404
s.32, enabling: SSI 2015/381
s.83, enabling: SSI 2015/116
Sch.1 Part 1 para.5, amended: SSI
2015/404 Reg.2
Sch.1 Part 2 para.13, amended: SSI
2015/404 Reg.2
Sch.3 Part 1 para.1, enabling: SSI
2015/381
Sch.3 Part 2 para.5, enabling: SSI
2015/381
Sch.3 Part 2 para.6, enabling: SSI
2015/381

Sch.3 Part 2 para.7, enabling: SSI 2015/381
Sch.5 Part 2 para.5, enabling: SSI 2015/381
Sch.5 Part 2 para.6, enabling: SSI 2015/381
Sch.5 Part 2 para.7, enabling: SSI 2015/381

asp 11. Bankruptcy and Debt Advice (Scotland) Act 2014
s.57, enabling: SSI 2015/54

asp 12. Procurement Reform (Scotland) Act 2014
s.4, amended: SSI 2015/446 Sch.6 para.2
s.11, amended: SSI 2015/446 Sch.6 para.2
s.41, amended: SSI 2015/446 Sch.6 para.2
s.45, enabling: SSI 2015/331, SSI 2015/411
Sch.1 Part 1 para.13B, added: 2015 asp 1 s.17
Sch.1 Part 3 para.34A, added: SSI 2015/271 Art.7
Sch.1 Part 3 para.43, amended: SSI 2015/271 Art.7

asp 14. Housing (Scotland) Act 2014
s.28, enabling: SSI 2015/252
s.101, enabling: SSI 2015/252
s.102, enabling: SSI 2015/144, SSI 2015/430
s.104, enabling: SSI 2015/122, SSI 2015/272, SSI 2015/349, SSI 2015/430

asp 16. Revenue Scotland and Tax Powers Act 2014
s.11, enabling: SSI 2015/16
s.32, enabling: SSI 2015/132
s.39, enabling: SSI 2015/184
s.50, enabling: SSI 2015/132
s.51, enabling: SSI 2015/184
s.52, enabling: SSI 2015/184
s.53, enabling: SSI 2015/184
s.54, enabling: SSI 2015/184
s.55, enabling: SSI 2015/184
s.56, enabling: SSI 2015/184
s.74, enabling: SSI 2015/130
s.81, enabling: SSI 2015/130
s.111, enabling: SSI 2015/131
s.112, enabling: SSI 2015/131
s.138, enabling: SSI 2015/38
s.142, enabling: SSI 2015/37

s.217, enabling: SSI 2015/128
s.220, enabling: SSI 2015/128
s.222, enabling: SSI 2015/36
s.225, enabling: SSI 2015/283
s.245, enabling: SSI 2015/129
s.249, enabling: SSI 2015/184
s.260, enabling: SSI 2015/18, SSI 2015/110
Sch.2 Part 3 para.22, enabling: SSI 2015/187
Sch.2 Part 3 para.23, enabling: SSI 2015/187
Sch.2 Part 4 para.32, enabling: SSI 2015/187
Sch.3 para.3, enabling: SSI 2015/130

asp 17. Disabled Persons Parking Badges (Scotland) Act 2014
s.6, enabling: SSI 2015/9
s.7, enabling: SSI 2015/8

asp 18. Courts Reform (Scotland) Act 2014
s.23, enabling: SSI 2015/120
s.39, enabling: SSI 2015/228
s.41, enabling: SSI 2015/213
s.51, amended: SSI 2015/77 Art.5
s.103, enabling: SSI 2015/227, SSI 2015/228, SSI 2015/283, SSI 2015/296, SSI 2015/312, SSI 2015/408, SSI 2015/419
s.104, enabling: SSI 2015/176, SSI 2015/227, SSI 2015/283, SSI 2015/296, SSI 2015/312, SSI 2015/351, SSI 2015/356, SSI 2015/419, SSI 2015/424
s.105, enabling: SSI 2015/246
s.106, enabling: SSI 2015/246, SSI 2015/387
s.107, enabling: SSI 2015/261, SSI 2015/262, SSI 2015/263, SSI 2015/264, SSI 2015/379, SSI 2015/383
s.133, enabling: SSI 2015/213
s.137, enabling: SSI 2015/150, SSI 2015/338, SSI 2015/402
s.138, enabling: SSI 2015/12, SSI 2015/77, SSI 2015/247, SSI 2015/336, SSI 2015/378
Sch.4 Part 2 para.3, amended: SSI 2015/405 Art.2
Sch.4 Part 2 para.3, enabling: SSI 2015/405

asp 19. Historic Environment Scotland Act 2014
s.9, enabling: SSI 2015/238

s.27, enabling: SSI 2015/239, SSI
2015/271
s.31, enabling: SSI 2015/31, SSI
2015/196

2015

asp 1. Food (Scotland) Act 2015
Royal Assent, January 13, 2015
s.61, enabling: SSI 2015/100, SSI
2015/433
s.63, enabling: SSI 2015/99
asp 2. Budget (Scotland) Act 2015
Royal Assent, March 11, 2015
s.4, amended: SSI 2015/434 Reg.2
s.7, enabling: SSI 2015/434
Sch.1, amended: SSI 2015/434 Reg.3
Sch.2, amended: SSI 2015/434 Reg.4
**asp 3. Community Charge Debt (Scotland)
Act 2015**
Royal Assent, March 25, 2015
**asp 4. Legal Writings (Counterparts and
Delivery) (Scotland) Act 2015**
Royal Assent, April 01, 2015
s.6, enabling: SSI 2015/242
asp 5. Welfare Funds (Scotland) Act 2015
Royal Assent, April 08, 2015
s.14, enabling: SSI 2015/428

**asp 6. Community Empowerment (Scotland)
Act 2015**
Royal Assent, July 24, 2015
s.145, enabling: SSI 2015/344, SSI
2015/358, SSI 2015/399
**asp 7. Scottish Elections (Reduction of Voting
Age) Act 2015**
Royal Assent, July 24, 2015
**asp 8. Prisoners (Control of Release)
(Scotland) Act 2015**
Royal Assent, August 04, 2015
s.3, enabling: SSI 2015/409
asp 9. Mental Health (Scotland) Act 2015
Royal Assent, August 04, 2015
s.61, enabling: SSI 2015/361, SSI
2015/417
**asp 10. Air Weapons and Licensing
(Scotland) Act 2015**
Royal Assent, August 04, 2015
s.88, enabling: SSI 2015/382
**asp 11. British Sign Language (Scotland) Act
2015**
Royal Assent, October 22, 2015
**asp 12. Human Trafficking and Exploitation
(Scotland) Act 2015**
Royal Assent, November 04, 2015
asp 13. Harbours (Scotland) Act 2015
Royal Assent, December 02, 2015

ACTS OF THE NORTHERN IRELAND ASSEMBLY

14 Geo. 6 (1950)

**29. Employment and Training Act
(Northern Ireland) 1950**
s.1A, added: SI 2015/2006 Art.132

10 & 11 Eliz. 2 (1961-62)

**14. Electoral Law Act (Northern Ireland)
1962**
Sch.5 Part IV para.21, amended: SI
2015/566 Art.2
Sch.5 Part IV para.26, amended: SI
2015/566 Art.2

Sch.10, amended: SI 2015/566 Sch.1,
Sch.2, Sch.3, Sch.4, Sch.5, Sch.6, Sch.7,
Sch.8, Sch.9, Sch.10

1970

32. Equal Pay Act (Northern Ireland) 1970
s.6A, amended: 2015 c.19 Sch.1 para.2
s.6A, repealed: 2015 c.19 Sch.1 para.2
s.6AB, amended: 2015 c.19 Sch.1 para.3

2000

**4. Child Support, Pensions and Social
Security Act (Northern Ireland) 2000**

s.59, repealed: SI 2015/2006 Sch.12 Part 1

s.60, amended: SI 2015/2006 Sch.2 para.44, Sch.3 para.12, Sch.12 Part 1

s.61, repealed: SI 2015/2006 Sch.12 Part 1

s.69, repealed: SI 2015/2006 Sch.12 Part 1

Sch.6 para.3, repealed: SI 2015/2006 Sch.12 Part 1

Sch.7, repealed: SI 2015/2006 Sch.12 Part 1

Sch.7 para.6, amended: SI 2015/2006 Sch.11 para.10

Sch.7 para.20, amended: SI 2015/2006 Sch.11 para.11

2001

17. Social Security Fraud Act (Northern Ireland) 2001

s.1, repealed: SI 2015/2006 Sch.12 Part 1

s.2, repealed: SI 2015/2006 Sch.12 Part 1

s.4, amended: SI 2015/2006 Sch.12 Part 1

s.4, repealed: SI 2015/2006 Sch.12 Part 1

s.5, repealed: SI 2015/2006 Sch.12 Part 1

s.5A, amended: SI 2015/2006 Sch.2 para.46, Sch.9 para.44, Sch.12 Part 1

s.5A, repealed: SI 2015/2006 Sch.12 Part 8

s.5B, amended: SI 2015/2006 Art.115, Art.117, Art.118, Art.119, Sch.2 para.47, Sch.3 para.14, Sch.12 Part 1, Sch.12 Part 11

s.5B, repealed: SI 2015/2006 Art.119 , Sch.12 Part 1

s.5C, amended: SI 2015/2006 Art.115

s.5C, repealed: SI 2015/2006 Sch.12 Part 11

s.6, amended: SI 2015/2006 Art.117, Art.118, Sch.2 para.48, Sch.3 para.15, Sch.12 Part 1

s.6, repealed: SI 2015/2006 Sch.12 Part 1

s.7, amended: SI 2015/2006 Art.115, Sch.2 para.49, Sch.7 para.12, Sch.12 Part 11

s.7, repealed: SI 2015/2006 Sch.7 para.12 , Sch.12 Part 1

s.8, amended: SI 2015/2006 Art.115, Sch.2 para.50, Sch.12 Part 11

s.8, repealed: SI 2015/2006 Sch.12 Part 1

s.9, amended: SI 2015/2006 Sch.2 para.51, Sch.9 para.45, Sch.12 Part 1

s.10, amended: SI 2015/2006 Art.117, Art.118, Sch.2 para.52, Sch.3 para.16, Sch.12 Part 11

s.10, repealed: SI 2015/2006 Sch.12 Part 1

s.12, amended: SI 2015/2006 Sch.12 Part 1, Sch.12 Part 11

s.13, repealed: SI 2015/2006 Sch.12 Part 1

2002

10. Social Security Act (Northern Ireland) 2002

s.5, repealed: SI 2015/2006 Sch.12 Part 1

s.6, repealed: SI 2015/2006 Sch.12 Part 1

Sch.1 para.6, repealed: SI 2015/2006 Sch.12 Part 1

Sch.1 para.8, repealed: SI 2015/2006 Sch.12 Part 1

Sch.1 para.9, repealed: SI 2015/2006 Sch.12 Part 1

14. State Pension Credit Act (Northern Ireland) 2002

s.1, amended: SI 2015/2006 Art.81, Sch.4 para.2, Sch.4 para.3

s.2, amended: SI 2015/2006 Art.80

s.3A, added: SI 2015/2006 Sch.4 para.4

s.4, amended: SI 2015/2006 Sch.2 para.53

s.7, amended: SI 2015/2006 Sch.4 para.5

s.12, amended: SI 2015/2006 Sch.4 para.6

s.15, repealed: SI 2015/2006 Sch.12 Part 1

s.17, amended: SI 2015/2006 Art.80, Sch.4 para.7, Sch.12 Part 1

s.19, amended: SI 2015/2006 Art.81

Sch.1 Part I para.3, repealed: SI 2015/2006 Sch.12 Part 9

Sch.1 Part II para.8, repealed: SI 2015/2006 Sch.12 Part 9

Sch.2 Part I para.2, repealed: SI 2015/2006 Sch.12 Part 1

Sch.2 Part II para.9, repealed: SI
2015/2006 Sch.4 para.8
Sch.2 Part III para.24, repealed: SI
2015/2006 Sch.12 Part 1

2007

**2. Welfare Reform Act (Northern Ireland)
2007**

s.1, amended: SI 2015/2006 Art.56,
Art.58, Art.59, Art.60, Art.67, Sch.3
para.18, Sch.12 Part 1
s.1, repealed: SI 2015/2006 Sch.12 Part 1
s.1A, added: SI 2015/2006 Art.57
s.1A, amended: SI 2015/2006 Sch.3
para.21, Sch.12 Part 1
s.1B, added: SI 2015/2006 Art.58
s.1B, amended: SI 2015/2006 Sch.3
para.21
s.1B, repealed: SI 2015/2006 Sch.12 Part
1
s.1C, added: SI 2015/2006 Art.60
s.1C, repealed: SI 2015/2006 Sch.12 Part
5
s.2, amended: SI 2015/2006 Sch.3
para.19, Sch.5 para.6, Sch.12 Part 1
s.3, amended: SI 2015/2006 Sch.3
para.21, Sch.12 Part 1
s.4, repealed: SI 2015/2006 Sch.12 Part 1
s.11, substituted: SI 2015/2006 Art.63
s.13, amended: SI 2015/2006 Art.61
s.15, amended: SI 2015/2006 Art.60
s.16, amended: SI 2015/2006 Art.60
s.16A, added: SI 2015/2006 Art.62
s.16A, repealed: SI 2015/2006 Sch.12
Part 5
s.18, amended: SI 2015/2006 Sch.3
para.21
s.19, amended: SI 2015/2006 Art.63
s.20, amended: SI 2015/2006 Sch.3
para.21
s.23, repealed: SI 2015/2006 Sch.12 Part
1
s.24, amended: SI 2015/2006 Art.63,
Sch.12 Part 1
s.24, repealed: SI 2015/2006 Sch.12 Part
5
s.25, amended: SI 2015/2006 Art.57,
Art.63

s.26, amended: SI 2015/2006 Art.57,
Sch.12 Part 1
s.26, repealed: SI 2015/2006 Sch.12 Part
5
s.27, amended: SI 2015/2006 Sch.3
para.20
s.27, repealed: SI 2015/2006 Sch.12 Part
1
s.29, repealed: SI 2015/2006 Sch.12 Part
1
s.38, repealed: SI 2015/2006 Sch.12 Part
1
s.39, repealed: SI 2015/2006 Art.123
s.42, repealed: SI 2015/2006 Sch.12 Part
1
s.44, repealed: SI 2015/2006 Sch.12 Part
9
s.45, repealed: SI 2015/2006 Sch.12 Part
11
s.48, repealed: SI 2015/2006 Sch.12 Part
8
s.50, repealed: SI 2015/2006 Sch.12 Part
7
s.57, amended: SI 2015/2006 Sch.12 Part
1
Sch.1 Part 1, repealed: SI 2015/2006
Sch.12 Part 1
Sch.1 Part 1 para.1, amended: SI
2015/2006 Sch.2 para.54, Sch.3 para.21
Sch.1 Part 1 para.1, repealed: SI
2015/2006 Sch.12 Part 1
Sch.1 Part 1 para.3, amended: SI
2015/2006 Sch.3 para.21
Sch.1 Part 2, repealed: SI 2015/2006
Sch.12 Part 1
Sch.2 para.4A, added: SI 2015/2006
Art.60
Sch.2 para.4B, added: SI 2015/2006
Art.67
Sch.2 para.6, amended: SI 2015/2006
Sch.3 para.21, Sch.12 Part 1
Sch.2 para.7, amended: SI 2015/2006
Sch.3 para.21
Sch.2 para.8, repealed: SI 2015/2006
Sch.12 Part 1
Sch.2 para.10A, amended: SI 2015/2006
Art.63
Sch.2 para.10B, added: SI 2015/2006
Art.63
Sch.2 para.10ZA, added: SI 2015/2006
Art.63

Sch.2 para.11, repealed: SI 2015/2006
Sch.12 Part 1
Sch.2 para.12, repealed: SI 2015/2006
Sch.12 Part 1
Sch.2 para.13, amended: SI 2015/2006
Art.63
Sch.3 para.1, repealed: SI 2015/2006
Sch.12 Part 1
Sch.3 para.2, repealed: SI 2015/2006
Sch.12 Part 1
Sch.3 para.3, repealed: SI 2015/2006
Sch.12 Part 1
Sch.3 para.4, repealed: SI 2015/2006
Sch.12 Part 1 , Sch.12 Part 8 , Sch.12
Part 10 , Sch.12 Part 12
Sch.3 para.10, repealed: SI 2015/2006
Sch.12 Part 8
Sch.3 para.12, repealed: SI 2015/2006
Sch.12 Part 1
Sch.4, repealed: SI 2015/2006 Sch.12
Part 1
Sch.4 para.7, amended: SI 2015/2006
Art.57
Sch.5 para.2, repealed: SI 2015/2006
Sch.12 Part 1
Sch.5 para.6, repealed: SI 2015/2006
Sch.12 Part 1
Sch.7 para.1, repealed: SI 2015/2006
Sch.12 Part 7 , Sch.12 Part 8
Sch.7 para.2, repealed: SI 2015/2006
Sch.12 Part 7
Sch.7 para.4, repealed: SI 2015/2006
Sch.12 Part 7

2008

1. Pensions Act (Northern Ireland) 2008
Sch.1 Part 5 para.23, repealed: SI
2015/2006 Sch.12 Part 1
**9. Mesothelioma, etc., Act (Northern
Ireland) 2008**
s.4, amended: SI 2015/2006 Sch.11
para.13
s.5, amended: SI 2015/2006 Sch.11
para.14
s.10, amended: SI 2015/2006 Sch.11
para.15
**10. Child Maintenance Act (Northern
Ireland) 2008**
s.3, amended: SI 2015/2006 Art.130

s.35, repealed: SI 2015/2006 Sch.12 Part
1
Sch.2 para.3, amended: SI 2015/2006
Art.126
Sch.4 para.2, repealed: SI 2015/2006
Sch.12 Part 12

2010

**13. Welfare Reform Act (Northern Ireland)
2010**
s.1, repealed: SI 2015/2006 Sch.12 Part 3
, Sch.12 Part 4
s.2, repealed: SI 2015/2006 Sch.12 Part 1
s.3, repealed: SI 2015/2006 Sch.12 Part 1
s.4, repealed: SI 2015/2006 Sch.12 Part
1, Sch.12 Part 2
s.8, amended: SI 2015/2006 Art.64
s.8, repealed: SI 2015/2006 Sch.12 Part 1
, Sch.12 Part 2 , Sch.12 Part 5
s.9, repealed: SI 2015/2006 Sch.12 Part 1
s.10, repealed: SI 2015/2006 Sch.12 Part
5
s.13, repealed: SI 2015/2006 Sch.12 Part
8
s.15, repealed: SI 2015/2006 Art.79
s.18, repealed: SI 2015/2006 Art.106
s.20, repealed: SI 2015/2006 Sch.12 Part
3
s.23, repealed: SI 2015/2006 Sch.12 Part
4
s.25, amended: SI 2015/2006 Art.60,
Sch.7 para.14
s.26, amended: SI 2015/2006 Sch.7
para.15, Sch.12 Part 2
s.26, repealed: SI 2015/2006 Sch.7
para.15 , Sch.12 Part 2 , Sch.12 Part 3 ,
Sch.12 Part 4
s.27, repealed: SI 2015/2006 Sch.12 Part
3
s.28, repealed: SI 2015/2006 Sch.12 Part
1
s.29, repealed: SI 2015/2006 Sch.12 Part
1
s.30, repealed: SI 2015/2006 Sch.12 Part
1
Sch.1, repealed: SI 2015/2006 Sch.12
Part 2
Sch.2, repealed: SI 2015/2006 Sch.12
Part 1

Sch.3 Part 1 para.1, repealed: SI 2015/2006 Sch.12 Part 11
Sch.3 Part 1 para.2, repealed: SI 2015/2006 Sch.12 Part 1
Sch.3 Part 1 para.6, repealed: SI 2015/2006 Sch.12 Part 11
Sch.4 Part 1, repealed: SI 2015/2006 Sch.12 Part 1
Sch.4 Part 3, amended: SI 2015/2006 Sch.12 Part 1, Sch.12 Part 2, Sch.12 Part 3

16. Debt Relief Act (Northern Ireland) 2010
Sch.1 para.4, repealed: 2015 c.26 s.116

2015

1. Work and Families Act (Northern Ireland) 2015
Royal Assent, January 08, 2015
2. Human Trafficking and Exploitation (Criminal Justice and Support for Victims) Act (Northern Ireland) 2015
Royal Assent, January 13, 2015

3. Off-street Parking (Functions of District Councils) Act (Northern Ireland) 2015
Royal Assent, March 12, 2015
4. Budget Act (Northern Ireland) 2015
Royal Assent, March 12, 2015
5. Pensions Act (Northern Ireland) 2015
Royal Assent, June 23, 2015
Sch.12 Part 1 para.44, repealed: SI 2015/2006 Art.102
6. Ombudsman and Commissioner for Complaints (Amendment) Act (Northern Ireland) 2015
Royal Assent, July 20, 2015
7. Budget (No.2) Act (Northern Ireland) 2015
Royal Assent, July 24, 2015
8. Reservoirs Act (Northern Ireland) 2015
Royal Assent, July 24, 2015
9. Justice Act (Northern Ireland) 2015
Royal Assent, July 24, 2015
10. Children's Services Co-operation Act (Northern Ireland) 2015
Royal Assent, December 09, 2015

ACTS OF THE PARLIAMENT OF ENGLAND, WALES & THE UNITED KINGDOM

57 Geo. 3 (1817)

97. Duchy of Lancaster Act 1817
s.25A, added: SI 2015/1560 Art.2

3 & 4 Will. 4 (1833)

85. Saint Helena Act 1833
s.112, enabling: SI 2015/213, SI 2015/218, SI 2015/824, SI 2015/825, SI 2015/826, SI 2015/1380, SI 2015/1381, SI 2015/1382, SI 2015/1383, SI 2015/1527, SI 2015/1528, SI 2015/1772, SI 2015/1898, SI 2015/1899

1 & 2 Vict. (1837-38)

110. Judgments Act 1838
s.17, see *Involnert Management Inc v Aprilgrange Ltd* [2015] EWHC 2834

(Comm), [2015] 5 Costs L.R. 813 (QBD (Comm)), Leggatt LJ; see *Novoship (UK) Ltd v Mikhaylyuk* [2014] EWCA Civ 908, [2015] Q.B. 499 (CA (Civ Div)), Longmore LJ

6 & 7 Vict. (1843)

73. Solicitors Act 1843
see *Wilsons Solicitors LLP v Bentine* [2015] EWCA Civ 1168, [2015] 6 Costs L.O. 779 (CA (Civ Div)), Arden LJ

8 & 9 Vict. (1845)

109. Gaming Act 1845
s.18, see *Ivey v Genting Casinos UK Ltd (t/a Crockfords Club)* [2014] EWHC 3394 (QB), [2015] L.L.R. 98 (QBD), Mitting J

16

10 & 11 Vict. (1847)

27. Harbours, Docks, and Piers Clauses Act 1847
    s.53, varied: SSI 2015/6 Art.3
    s.62, varied: SSI 2015/6 Art.3
    s.63, varied: SSI 2015/6 Art.3
    s.65, varied: SSI 2015/6 Art.3
89. Town Police Clauses Act 1847
    s.28, amended: 2015 c.20 Sch.23 para.45

17 & 18 Vict. (1854)

33. Public Statues (Metropolis) Act 1854
    s.V, repealed: 2015 c.20 s.27

20 & 21 Vict. (1857)

81. Burial Act 1857
    s.25, see *R. (on the application of*
    Plantagenet Alliance Ltd) v Secretary of
    State for Justice [2014] EWHC 1662
    (QB), [2015] 3 All E.R. 261 (DC),
    Hallett LJ

24 & 25 Vict. (1861)

100. Offences against the Person Act 1861
    s.18, see *Attorney General's Reference*
    (No.26 of 2015) [2015] EWCA Crim
    1119, [2015] 2 Cr. App. R. (S.) 53 (CA
    (Crim Div)), Pitchford LJ; see *R. v*
    Brookes (Dominic) [2015] EWCA Crim
    11, [2015] 1 Cr. App. R. (S.) 56 (CA
    (Crim Div)), Pitchford LJ
    s.20, see *Attorney General's Reference*
    (No.26 of 2015) [2015] EWCA Crim
    1119, [2015] 2 Cr. App. R. (S.) 53 (CA
    (Crim Div)), Pitchford LJ; see *R. v Peet*
    (Graham) [2014] EWCA Crim 2800,
    [2015] 1 Cr. App. R. (S.) 48 (CA (Crim
    Div)), Sharp LJ; see *R. v Pisano*
    (Ricardo) [2014] EWCA Crim 2519,
    [2015] 1 Cr. App. R. (S.) 33 (CA (Crim
    Div)), Jackson LJ

s.23, see *Criminal Injuries Compensation*
Authority v First-tier Tribunal (Social
Entitlement Chamber) [2014] EWCA Civ
1554, [2015] Q.B. 459 (CA (Civ Div)),
Lord Dyson MR

31 & 32 Vict. (1868)

45. Sea Fisheries Act 1868
    repealed: 2015 c.20 Sch.23 para.31

33 & 34 Vict. (1870)

35. Apportionment Act 1870
    see *Hartley v King Edward VI College*
    [2015] EWCA Civ 455, [2015] I.C.R.
    1143 (CA (Civ Div)), Elias LJ
    s.2, see *Hartley v King Edward VI*
    College [2015] EWCA Civ 455, [2015]
    I.C.R. 1143 (CA (Civ Div)), Elias LJ; see
    Marks & Spencer Plc v BNP Paribas
    Securities Services Trust Co (Jersey) Ltd
    [2015] UKSC 72, [2015] 3 W.L.R. 1843
    (SC), Lord Neuberger PSC
    s.7, see *Hartley v King Edward VI*
    College [2015] EWCA Civ 455, [2015]
    I.C.R. 1143 (CA (Civ Div)), Elias LJ
71. National Debt Act 1870
    s.5, varied: 2015 c.11 s.124

34 & 35 Vict. (1871)

lxxvii. Hampstead Heath Act 1871
    see *R. (on the application of Heath &*
    Hampstead Society) v City of London
    [2014] EWHC 3868 (Admin), [2015]
    P.T.S.R. 987 (QBD), Lang J
56. Dogs Act 1871
    see *Chief Constable of Warwickshire v*
    Young [2014] EWHC 4213 (Admin),
    (2015) 179 J.P. 49 (QBD (Admin)),
    Hickinbottom J

38 & 39 Vict. (1875)

17. Explosives Act 1875
    s.31, amended: SI 2015/1553 Reg.75

55. Public Health Act 1875
s.164, see *Naylor v Essex CC* [2014]
EWHC 2560 (Admin), [2015] J.P.L. 217
(QBD (Admin)), John Howell QC

39 & 40 Vict. (1876)

70. Sheriff Courts (Scotland) Act 1876
see *J&E Shepherd v Letley* [2015] CSIH
87 (IH (2 Div)), The Lord Justice Clerk
(Carloway)

44 & 45 Vict. (1881)

**60. Newspaper Libel and Registration Act
1881**
s.1, amended: 2015 c.20 Sch.23 para.3
s.7, repealed: 2015 c.20 Sch.23 para.2
Sch.A, repealed: 2015 c.20 Sch.23 para.2

45 & 46 Vict. (1882)

61. Bills of Exchange Act 1882
Part IVA, added: 2015 c.26 s.13
s.52, amended: 2015 c.26 s.13
s.74B, repealed: 2015 c.26 s.13
s.76, varied: SI 2015/623 Reg.58
s.77, varied: SI 2015/623 Reg.58
s.78, varied: SI 2015/623 Reg.58
s.87, amended: 2015 c.26 s.13
**72. Revenue, Friendly Societies, and
National Debt Act 1882**
s.19, repealed: 2015 c.11 s.124
**77. Citation Amendment (Scotland) Act
1882**
s.3, see *B v D* [2015] CSOH 24, 2015
S.L.T. 217 (OH), Lord Jones

46 & 47 Vict. (1883)

3. Explosive Substances Act 1883
s.4, amended: 2015 c.2 s.1

47 & 48 Vict. (1884)

**23. National Debt (Conversion of Stock) Act
1884**
repealed: 2015 c.11 s.124
s.1, varied: 2015 c.11 s.124
62. Revenue Act 1884
s.11, see *Shenken v Phoenix Life Ltd*
[2015] CSOH 96, [2015] W.T.L.R. 1833
(OH), Lord Tyre

49 & 50 Vict. (1886)

29. Crofters Holdings (Scotland) Act 1886
see *MacLachlan v Bruce* 2015 S.L.T.
(Land Ct) 23 (Land Ct), D J Houston; see
Sorbie v Kennedy 2015 S.L.T. (Land Ct)
17 (Land Ct), Lord McGhie
s.2, see *Lands Improvement Holdings
Landmatch Sarl v Cole* 2015 S.L.T.
(Land Ct) 137 (Land Ct), Lord
Minginish; see *Sorbie v Kennedy* 2015
S.L.T. (Land Ct) 17 (Land Ct), Lord
McGhie
s.11, see *MacLachlan v Bruce* 2015
S.L.T. (Land Ct) 23 (Land Ct), D J
Houston
38. Riot (Damages) Act 1886
s.2, see *Mitsui Sumitomo Insurance Co
(Europe) Ltd v Mayor's Office for
Policing and Crime* [2014] EWCA Civ
682, [2015] Q.B. 180 (CA (Civ Div)),
Lord Dyson MR
s.7, see *Mitsui Sumitomo Insurance Co
(Europe) Ltd v Mayor's Office for
Policing and Crime* [2014] EWCA Civ
682, [2015] Q.B. 180 (CA (Civ Div)),
Lord Dyson MR

50 & 51 Vict. (1887)

54. British Settlements Act 1887
enabling: SI 2015/213, SI 2015/218, SI
2015/823, SI 2015/824, SI 2015/825, SI
2015/826, SI 2015/1380, SI 2015/1381,
SI 2015/1382, SI 2015/1383, SI
2015/1527, SI 2015/1528, SI 2015/1772,
SI 2015/1898, SI 2015/1899

51 & 52 Vict. (1888)

2. National Debt (Conversion) Act 1888
repealed: 2015 c.11 s.124
s.2, varied: 2015 c.11 s.124

53 & 54 Vict. (1890)

37. Foreign Jurisdiction Act 1890
enabling: SI 2015/823
39. Partnership Act 1890
s.1, see *Connaught Income Fund Series 1
(In Liquidation) v Capita Financial
Managers Ltd* [2014] EWHC 3619
(Comm), [2015] 1 All E.R. (Comm) 751
(QBD (Comm)), Judge Mackie QC
s.9, see *Kommalage v Sayanthakumar*
[2014] EWCA Civ 1832, [2015] 2
B.C.L.C. 131 (CA (Civ Div)), Davis LJ
s.10, see *Northampton Regional
Livestock Centre Co Ltd v Cowling*
[2015] EWCA Civ 651, [2015] 4 Costs
L.O. 477 (CA (Civ Div)), Arden LJ
s.38, see *Connaught Income Fund Series
1 (In Liquidation) v Capita Financial
Managers Ltd* [2014] EWHC 3619
(Comm), [2015] 1 All E.R. (Comm) 751
(QBD (Comm)), Judge Mackie QC

54 & 55 Vict. (1891)

37. Fisheries Act 1891
repealed: 2015 c.20 Sch.23 para.31

55 & 56 Vict. (1892)

43. Military Lands Act 1892
s.14, enabling: SI 2015/1467, SI
2015/1492
54. Allotments (Scotland) Act 1892
repealed: 2015 asp 6 Sch.5

1893

**44. Sheriff Courts Consignations (Scotland)
Act 1893**
s.2A, added: SSI 2015/402 Sch.1 para.1

57 & 58 Vict. (1894)

44. Heritable Securities (Scotland) Act 1894
see *Westfoot Invesments Ltd v European
Property Holdings Inc* 2015 S.L.T. (Sh
Ct) 201 (Sh Ct (Lothian) (Edinburgh)),
Sheriff T Welsh, QC
s.5, see *Westfoot Invesments Ltd v
European Property Holdings Inc* 2015
S.L.T. (Sh Ct) 201 (Sh Ct (Lothian)
(Edinburgh)), Sheriff T Welsh, QC
s.5A, see *Westfoot Invesments Ltd v
European Property Holdings Inc* 2015
S.L.T. (Sh Ct) 201 (Sh Ct (Lothian)
(Edinburgh)), Sheriff T Welsh, QC

61 & 62 Vict. (1898)

35. Vexatious Actions (Scotland) Act 1898
repealed: SI 2015/700 Sch.1 para.1

6 Edw. 7 (1906)

25. Open Spaces Act 1906
s.9, see *Naylor v Essex CC* [2014]
EWHC 2560 (Admin), [2015] J.P.L. 217
(QBD (Admin)), John Howell QC
s.10, see *Naylor v Essex CC* [2014]
EWHC 2560 (Admin), [2015] J.P.L. 217
(QBD (Admin)), John Howell QC
41. Marine Insurance Act 1906
s.17, amended: 2015 c.4 s.14
s.18, repealed: 2015 c.4 s.21
s.33, amended: 2015 c.4 s.10
s.34, repealed: 2015 c.4 s.10
s.60, see *Suez Fortune Investments Ltd v
Talbot Underwriting Ltd* [2015] EWHC
42 (Comm), [2015] 1 Lloyd's Rep. 651
(QBD (Comm)), Flaux J
s.84, varied: 2015 c.4 Sch.1 para.12
55. Public Trustee Act 1906
s.2, amended: 2015 c.20 Sch.6 para.2

7 Edw. 7 (1907)

24. Limited Partnerships Act 1907
   s.4, varied: SI 2015/1882 Reg.9
   s.6, varied: SI 2015/1882 Reg.9
   s.7, varied: SI 2015/1882 Reg.9
   s.9, varied: SI 2015/1882 Reg.9
   s.10, varied: SI 2015/1882 Reg.9
51. Sheriff Courts (Scotland) Act 1907
   Appendix 1., amended: SSI 2015/176
   Sch.1, SSI 2015/227 r.8, Sch.2, SSI
   2015/283 r.3, SSI 2015/312 r.4, Sch.2,
   SSI 2015/419 r.5
   s.3, see *Auchnie v Auchnie* 2015 S.C. 320
   (IH (2 Div)), The Lord Justice Clerk
   (Carloway); see *H v H* [2015] CSIH 10,
   2015 Fam. L.R. 34 (IH (Ex Div)), Lady
   Paton; see *J&E Shepherd v Letley* [2015]
   CSIH 87 (IH (2 Div)), The Lord Justice
   Clerk (Carloway)
   s.7, see *Boyd v Fortune* 2015 S.C.L.R.
   361 (IH), Lord Brodie
   s.27, see *H v H* [2015] CSIH 10, 2015
   Fam. L.R. 34 (IH (Ex Div)), Lady Paton
   s.28, see *Auchnie v Auchnie* 2015 S.C.
   320 (IH (2 Div)), The Lord Justice Clerk
   (Carloway); see *H v H* [2015] CSIH 10,
   2015 Fam. L.R. 34 (IH (Ex Div)), Lady
   Paton
   s.34, see *Lormor Ltd v Glasgow City
   Council* 2015 S.C. 213 (IH (Ex Div)),
   Lady Paton
   Sch.1 Part 1 para.2, amended: SSI
   2015/227 r.8
   Sch.1 Part 1 para.3, repealed: SSI
   2015/419 r.5
   Sch.1 Part 3 para.1, amended: SSI
   2015/227 r.8
   Sch.1 Part 11 para.7, amended: SSI
   2015/419 r.5
   Sch.1 Part 11 para.8, amended: SSI
   2015/419 r.5
   Sch.1 Part 15 paraA.1, added: SSI
   2015/227 r.8
   Sch.1 Part 15A, added: SSI 2015/227 r.8
   Sch.1 Part 17 para.1, amended: SSI
   2015/296 r.2
   Sch.1 Part 17 para.2, amended: SSI
   2015/227 r.8
   Sch.1 Part 21 para.3, amended: SSI
   2015/176 r.2

Sch.1 Part 26 para.1, amended: SSI
2015/227 r.7
Sch.1 Part 26 para.1, repealed: SSI
2015/419 r.5
Sch.1 Part 26 para.1A, added: SSI
2015/227 r.7
Sch.1 Part 26 para.2, substituted: SSI
2015/227 r.7
Sch.1 Part 26 para.3, amended: SSI
2015/227 r.7
Sch.1 Part 28 para.3A, amended: SSI
2015/419 r.5
Sch.1 Part 28 para.8, amended: SSI
2015/227 r.8
Sch.1 Part 29 para.19, substituted: SSI
2015/419 r.5
Sch.1 Part 30 para.4, amended: SSI
2015/419 r.5
Sch.1 Part 30 para.8, amended: SSI
2015/419 r.5
Sch.1 Part 31 para.1, repealed: SSI
2015/419 r.5
Sch.1 Part 31 para.2, repealed: SSI
2015/419 r.5
Sch.1 Part 31 para.2A, repealed: SSI
2015/419 r.5
Sch.1 Part 31 para.3, repealed: SSI
2015/419 r.5
Sch.1 Part 31 para.9, amended: SSI
2015/419 r.5
Sch.1 Part 31 para.10, amended: SSI
2015/419 r.5
Sch.1 Part 31 para.11, repealed: SSI
2015/419 r.5
Sch.1 Part 33A para.74, substituted: SSI
2015/419 r.5
Sch.1 Part 33 para.21, substituted: SSI
2015/312 r.4
Sch.1 Part 33 para.81, substituted: SSI
2015/419 r.5
Sch.1 Part 33 para.86, amended: SSI
2015/419 r.5
Sch.1 Part 36, amended: SSI 2015/227
r.8
Sch.1 Part 36, repealed: SSI 2015/227 r.8
Sch.1 Part 36 paraC.1, substituted: SSI
2015/227 r.8
Sch.1 Part 36 paraE.1, substituted: SSI
2015/227 r.8
Sch.1 Part 36 paraF.1, amended: SSI
2015/227 r.8

Sch.1 Part 36 paraK.1, substituted: SSI
2015/227 r.8
Sch.1 Part 36A, added: SSI 2015/227 r.8
Sch.1 Part 36B, added: SSI 2015/227 r.8
Sch.1 Part 42 para.2, amended: SSI
2015/424 r.2
Sch.1 Part 48 para.1, substituted: SSI
2015/85 r.3
Sch.1 Part 50 para.5, amended: SSI
2015/419 r.5
Sch.1 Part 50 para.6, repealed: SSI
2015/419 r.5
Sch.1 Part 53, added: SSI 2015/176 r.2

1 & 2 Geo. 5 (1911)

49. Small Landholders (Scotland) Act 1911
s.26, amended: 2015 asp 6 Sch.4 para.1
57. Maritime Conventions Act 1911
s.8, see *CDE SA v Sure Wind Marine Ltd*
[2015] EWHC 720 (Admlty), [2015] 2
Lloyd's Rep. 268 (QBD (Admlty)), Jervis
Kay QC, Admiralty Registrar
**99. Great Yarmouth Port and Haven Act
1911**
s.35, repealed: SI 2015/1395 Art.12
s.36, repealed: SI 2015/1395 Art.12

4 & 5 Geo. 5 (1914)

47. Deeds of Arrangement Act 1914
repealed: 2015 c.20 Sch.6 para.1
59. Bankruptcy Act 1914
s.25, see *Omni Trustees Ltd, Re* [2015]
EWHC 2697 (Ch), [2015] B.C.C. 906
(Ch D)

5 & 6 Geo. 5 (1914-15)

90. Indictments Act 1915
Royal Assent, December 23, 2015
s.2, enabling: SI 2015/1490
s.3, see *R. v Clarke (Dean)* [2015]
EWCA Crim 350, [2015] 2 Cr. App. R. 6
(CA (Crim Div)), Lord Thomas LCJ

7 & 8 Geo. 5 (1918)

40. Income Tax Act 1918
s.37, see *Routier v Revenue and Customs
Commissioners* [2014] EWHC 3010
(Ch), [2015] P.T.S.R. 60 (Ch D), Rose J

9 & 10 Geo. 5 (1919)

50. Ministry of Transport Act 1919
s.17, amended: 2015 c.7 s.17
97. Land Settlement (Scotland) Act 1919
Part III, repealed: 2015 asp 6 Sch.5
Sch.1, repealed: 2015 asp 6 Sch.5

10 & 11 Geo. 5 (1920)

**lviii. Brodick Lamlash Lochranza and
Whiting Bay Piers Order Confirmation Act
1920**
repealed: SSI 2015/6 Sch.3
50. Mining Industry Act 1920
repealed: 2015 c.20 Sch.23 para.4

12 & 13 Geo. 5 (1922)

52. Allotments (Scotland) Act 1922
repealed: 2015 asp 6 Sch.5

15 & 16 Geo. 5 (1925)

19. Trustee Act 1925
s.41, repealed: 2015 c.20 Sch.6 para.2
s.57, see *Portman Estate, Re* [2015]
EWHC 536 (Ch), [2015] W.T.L.R. 871
(Ch D), Birss J
s.61, see *Schubert Murphy v Law Society*
[2014] EWHC 4561 (QB), [2015]
P.N.L.R. 15 (QBD), Mitting J
20. Law of Property Act 1925
s.40, see *Nata Lee Ltd v Abid* [2014]
EWCA Civ 1652, [2015] 2 P. & C.R. 3
(CA (Civ Div)), Moore-Bick LJ
s.43, amended: 2015 c.20 Sch.6 para.2
s.53, see *Nata Lee Ltd v Abid* [2014]
EWCA Civ 1652, [2015] 2 P. & C.R. 3
(CA (Civ Div)), Moore-Bick LJ

s.62, see *Tower Hamlets LBC v Bromley LBC* [2015] EWHC 1954 (Ch), [2015] B.L.G.R. 622 (Ch D), Norris J; see *Wood v Waddington* [2015] EWCA Civ 538, [2015] 2 P. & C.R. 11 (CA (Civ Div)), Richards LJ

s.146, see *Barratt v Robinson* [2015] L. & T.R. 1 (UT (Lands)), Martin Rodger QC

s.149, see *Southward Housing Co-operative Ltd v Walker* [2015] EWHC 1615 (Ch), [2015] 2 P. & C.R. 13 (Ch D), Hildyard J

s.198, amended: 2015 c.7 Sch.5 para.21

21. Land Registration Act 1925

see *Nugent v Nugent* [2013] EWHC 4095 (Ch), [2015] Ch. 121 (Ch D (Bristol)), Morgan J

s.69, see *Swift 1st Ltd v Chief Land Registrar* [2015] EWCA Civ 330, [2015] Ch. 602 (CA (Civ Div)), Moore-Bick LJ

s.83, see *Swift 1st Ltd v Chief Land Registrar* [2015] EWCA Civ 330, [2015] Ch. 602 (CA (Civ Div)), Moore-Bick LJ

s.114, see *Swift 1st Ltd v Chief Land Registrar* [2015] EWCA Civ 330, [2015] Ch. 602 (CA (Civ Div)), Moore-Bick LJ

23. Administration of Estates Act 1925

s.9, see *Mitchell v Watkinson* [2014] EWCA Civ 1472, [2015] L. & T.R. 22 (CA (Civ Div)), Arden LJ

28. Administration of Justice Act 1925

s.22, repealed: 2015 c.20 Sch.6 para.1

71. Public Health Act 1925

s.76, see *Jones v First Great Western Ltd* [2014] EWCA Civ 301, [2015] R.T.R. 3 (CA (Civ Div)), Arden LJ

90. Rating and Valuation Act 1925

s.68, see *Woolway (Valuation Officer) v Mazars LLP* [2015] UKSC 53, [2015] A.C. 1862 (SC), Lord Neuberger PSC

16 & 17 Geo. 5 (1926)

11. Law of Property (Amendment) Act 1926

s.3, amended: 2015 c.20 Sch.6 para.2

16. Execution of Diligence (Scotland) Act 1926

s.4, see *B v D* [2015] CSOH 24, 2015 S.L.T. 217 (OH), Lord Jones

s.6, repealed: SI 2015/700 Sch.1 para.2

28. Mining Industry Act 1926

s.20, repealed: 2015 c.20 Sch.23 para.6

42. Workmen's Compensation Act, 1926. 1926

repealed: SI 2015/584 Art.2

61. Judicial Proceedings (Regulation of Reports) Act 1926

s.1, see *Cooper-Hohn v Hohn* [2014] EWHC 2314 (Fam), [2015] 1 F.L.R. 19 (Fam Div), Roberts J

17 & 18 Geo. 5 (1927)

lxvii. Littlehampton Harbour and Arun Drainage Outfall Act 1927

s.3, amended: SI 2015/1387 Art.3

s.36, repealed: SI 2015/1387 Art.3

s.70, amended: SI 2015/1387 Art.20

36. Landlord and Tenant Act 1927

s.18, see *Van Dal Footwear Ltd v Ryman Ltd* [2009] EWCA Civ 1478, [2010] 1 W.L.R. 2015 (CA (Civ Div)), Sir Anthony May PQBD

s.19, see *Tindall Cobham 1 Ltd v Adda Hotels* [2014] EWCA Civ 1215, [2015] 1 P. & C.R. 5 (CA (Civ Div)), Longmore LJ

18 & 19 Geo. 5 (1928)

8. Rating and Valuation Act 1928

see *Tunnel Tech Ltd v Reeves (Valuation Officer)* [2015] EWCA Civ 718, [2015] P.T.S.R. 1490 (CA (Civ Div)), Sir Terence Etherton C

19. Agricultural Produce (Grading and Marking) Act 1928

repealed: 2015 c.20 Sch.23 para.33

20 & 21 Geo. 5 (1930)

25. Third Parties (Rights against Insurers) Act 1930

see *Harlequin Property (SVG) Ltd v Wilkins Kennedy* [2015] EWHC 1122 (TCC), [2015] B.L.R. 469 (QBD (TCC)), Coulson J

s.1, see *International Energy Group Ltd v Zurich Insurance Plc UK* [2015] UKSC 33, [2015] 2 W.L.R. 1471 (SC), Lord Neuberger PSC

21 & 22 Geo. 5 (1931)

40. Agricultural Produce (Grading and Marking) Amendment Act 1931
    repealed: 2015 c.20 Sch.23 para.33
41. Agricultural Land (Utilisation) Act 1931
    s.24, repealed: 2015 asp 6 Sch.5

22 & 23 Geo. 5 (1931-32)

12. Destructive Imported Animals Act 1932
    s.2, enabling: SI 2015/613
    s.10, amended: 2015 c.20 Sch.13 para.1

23 & 24 Geo. 5 (1932-33)

12. Children and Young Persons Act 1933
    s.1, amended: 2015 c.9 s.66
    s.12C, amended: SI 2015/664 Sch.4 para.1
    s.25, enabling: SI 2015/1757
    s.39, see *R. (on the application of JC) v Central Criminal Court* [2014] EWCA Civ 1777, [2015] 1 W.L.R. 2865 (CA (Civ Div)), Moore-Bick LJ; see *R. v Cornick (William)* [2014] EWHC 3623 (QB), [2015] E.M.L.R. 9 (QBD), Coulson J
    s.39, amended: 2015 c.2 s.79
    s.39A, added: 2015 c.2 s.79
    s.44, see *R. (on the application of JC) v Central Criminal Court* [2014] EWCA Civ 1777, [2015] 1 W.L.R. 2865 (CA (Civ Div)), Moore-Bick LJ; see *R. v Cornick (William)* [2014] EWHC 3623 (QB), [2015] E.M.L.R. 9 (QBD), Coulson J
    Sch.1, amended: 2015 c.30 Sch.5 para.1
    Sch.1A, added: 2015 c.2 Sch.15 para.1
36. Administration of Justice (Miscellaneous Provisions) Act 1933

see *Serious Fraud Office v Evans* [2014] EWHC 3803 (QB), [2015] 1 W.L.R. 3526 (QBD), Fulford LJ
    s.2, amended: 2015 c.20 s.82
    s.2, repealed: 2015 c.20 s.82
    s.2, enabling: SI 2015/1490

24 & 25 Geo. 5 (1933-34)

41. Law Reform (Miscellaneous Provisions) Act 1934
    see *Bianco v Bennett* [2015] EWHC 626 (QB), [2015] I.L.Pr. 24 (QBD), Warby J
49. Whaling Industry (Regulation) Act 1934
    s.2, amended: SI 2015/664 Sch.4 para.2
    s.3, amended: SI 2015/664 Sch.4 para.2
    s.4, amended: SI 2015/664 Sch.4 para.2
    s.6, amended: SI 2015/664 Sch.4 para.2
    s.8, amended: SI 2015/664 Sch.4 para.2
56. Incitement to Disaffection Act 1934
    s.4, repealed: SI 2015/700 Sch.1 para.3

26 Geo. 5 & Edw. 8 (1935-36)

6. Public Order Act 1936
    s.8, repealed: SI 2015/700 Sch.1 para.4
49. Public Health Act 1936
    s.276, varied: SI 2015/462 Reg.8
    s.289, varied: SI 2015/462 Reg.8
    s.294, varied: SI 2015/462 Reg.8

1 Edw. 8 & 1 Geo. 6 (1936-37)

37. Children and Young Persons (Scotland) Act 1937
    s.12, see *B v Murphy* [2015] HCJAC 14, 2015 S.L.T. 214 (HCJ), The Lord Justice Clerk (Carloway); see *M v Locality Reporter, Glasgow* [2015] CSIH 58, 2015 S.L.T. 543 (IH (2 Div)), The Lord Justice Clerk (Carloway); see *S, Petitioner* 2015 S.C.L.R. 33 (IH (Ex Div)), Lady Smith
67. Factories Act 1937
    s.47, see *McDonald v Department for Communities and Local Government* [2015] A.C. 1128 (SC), Lord Neuberger PSC

1 & 2 Geo. 6 (1937-38)

**lxv. Island of Arran Piers Order
Confirmation Act 1938**
    repealed: SSI 2015/6 Sch.3

2 & 3 Geo. 6 (1938-39)

21. Limitation Act 1939
    see *Van Heeren v Cooper* [2014] EWHC
    4797 (Ch), [2015] B.P.I.R. 953 (Ch D),
    Stuart Isaacs QC
75. Compensation (Defence) Act 1939
    s.18, amended: 2015 asp 6 Sch.4 para.2
**82. Personal Injuries (Emergency
Provisions) Act 1939**
    s.1, enabling: SI 2015/555
    s.2, enabling: SI 2015/555

3 & 4 Geo. 6 (1939-40)

**42. Law Reform (Miscellaneous Provisions)
(Scotland) Act 1940**
    s.3, see *Bell v Alliance Medical Ltd*
    [2015] CSOH 34, 2015 S.C.L.R. 676
    (OH), Lord Boyd of Duncansby; see *STV
    Central Ltd v Semple Fraser LLP* [2015]
    CSIH 35, 2015 S.L.T. 313 (IH (Ex Div)),
    Lady Paton

8 & 9 Geo. 6 (1944-45)

7. British Settlements Act 1945
    enabling: SI 2015/213, SI 2015/218, SI
    2015/823, SI 2015/824, SI 2015/825, SI
    2015/826, SI 2015/1380, SI 2015/1381,
    SI 2015/1382, SI 2015/1383, SI
    2015/1527, SI 2015/1528, SI 2015/1772,
    SI 2015/1898, SI 2015/1899
**28. Law Reform (Contributory Negligence)
Act 1945**
    s.1, see *Jackson v Murray* [2015] UKSC
    5, [2015] 2 All E.R. 805 (SC), Lady Hale
    DPSC

9 & 10 Geo. 6 (1945-46)

36. Statutory Instruments Act 1946
    see *R. (on the application of Williams) v
    Secretary of State for Energy and
    Climate Change* [2015] EWHC 1202
    (Admin), [2015] J.P.L. 1257 (QBD
    (Admin)), Lindblom J
45. United Nations Act 1946
    s.1, enabling: SI 2015/218, SI 2015/1380,
    SI 2015/1381, SI 2015/1382, SI
    2015/1383, SI 2015/1772, SI 2015/1899,
    SI 2015/2014
80. Atomic Energy Act 1946
    s.6, repealed: 2015 c.20 Sch.23 para.14
    s.15, amended: 2015 c.20 Sch.23 para.15
    s.16, amended: 2015 c.20 Sch.23 para.15
    s.19, repealed: 2015 c.20 Sch.23 para.15
    s.20, amended: 2015 c.20 Sch.23 para.15
    Sch.1, repealed: 2015 c.20 Sch.23
    para.14

10 & 11 Geo. 6 (1946-47)

41. Fire Services Act 1947
    s.26, enabling: SI 2015/579, SI
    2015/1014, SSI 2015/140, SSI 2015/173
**42. Acquisition of Land (Authorisation
Procedure) (Scotland) Act 1947**
    s.1, repealed: 2015 asp 6 Sch.5
44. Crown Proceedings Act 1947
    s.10, see *W v Advocate General for
    Scotland* [2015] CSOH 111, 2015 S.L.T.
    537 (OH), Lord Pentland
48. Agriculture Act 1947
    s.80, amended: 2015 asp 1 Sch.1 para.1

11 & 12 Geo. 6 (1947-48)

**17. Requisitioned Land and War Works Act
1948**
    s.14, amended: 2015 c.7 Sch.5 para.22
29. National Assistance Act 1948
    s.21, see *Milton Keynes Council v
    Scottish Ministers* [2015] CSOH 156,
    2015 S.L.T. 843 (OH), Lord Armstrong;
    see *R. (on the application of Cushnie) v
    Secretary of State for Health* [2014]
    EWHC 3626 (Admin), [2015] P.T.S.R.

384 (QBD (Admin)), Singh J; see *R. (on the application of Kent CC) v Secretary of State for Health* [2015] EWCA Civ 81, [2015] 1 W.L.R. 1221 (CA (Civ Div)), Lord Dyson MR; see *R. (on the application of SG) v Haringey LBC* [2015] EWHC 2579 (Admin), (2015) 18 C.C.L. Rep. 444 (QBD (Admin)), John Bowers QC; see *R. (on the application of Whapples) v Birmingham CrossCity Clinical Commissioning Group* [2015] EWCA Civ 435, [2015] P.T.S.R. 1398 (CA (Civ Div)), Underhill LJ

s.21, amended: SI 2015/914 Sch.1 para.2

s.22, enabling: SI 2015/720, SSI 2015/64, SSI 2015/65

s.24, see *R. (on the application of Cornwall Council) v Secretary of State for Health* [2015] UKSC 46 (SC), Lady Hale DPSC; see *R. (on the application of Kent CC) v Secretary of State for Health* [2015] EWCA Civ 81, [2015] 1 W.L.R. 1221 (CA (Civ Div)), Lord Dyson MR

s.24, amended: SI 2015/914 Sch.1 para.3

s.29, see *R. (on the application of Robson) v Salford City Council* [2015] EWCA Civ 6, [2015] P.T.S.R. 1349 (CA (Civ Div)), Richards LJ

s.32, amended: SI 2015/914 Sch.1 para.4

s.33, amended: SI 2015/914 Sch.1 para.5

s.47, amended: SI 2015/914 Sch.1 para.6

s.48, amended: SI 2015/914 Sch.1 para.7

s.56, amended: SI 2015/914 Sch.1 para.8

s.64, amended: SI 2015/914 Sch.1 para.9

s.66, repealed: SI 2015/914 Sch.1 para.10

45. Agriculture (Scotland) Act 1948

s.86, amended: 2015 asp 6 Sch.4 para.3

56. British Nationality Act 1948

s.5, see *Romein v Advocate General for Scotland* 2015 S.L.T. 32 (OH), Lord Brailsford

12, 13 & 14 Geo. 6 (1948-49)

25. Tenancy of Shops (Scotland) Act 1949

s.1, see *Select Service Partner Ltd v Network Rail Infrastructure Ltd* 2015 S.L.T. (Sh Ct) 116 (Sh Ct (Lothian) (Edinburgh)), Sheriff N M P Morrison, QC

29. Consular Conventions Act 1949

s.2, see *C's Executors, Applicants* 2015 S.L.T. (Sh Ct) 67 (Sh Ct (Glasgow)), Sheriff J N McCormick

42. Lands Tribunal Act 1949

s.3, see *Balfour v Keeper of the Registers of Scotland* 2015 S.L.T. (Lands Tr) 185 (Lands Tr (Scot)), R A Smith, QC

s.3, enabling: SSI 2015/199

67. Civil Aviation Act 1949

s.8, enabling: SI 2015/236, SI 2015/1769

s.57, enabling: SI 2015/1769

s.59, enabling: SI 2015/1769

s.61, enabling: SI 2015/1769

s.63, enabling: SI 2015/1769

74. Coast Protection Act 1949

Sch.4 para.7, substituted: SI 2015/523 Reg.2

Sch.4 para.9, substituted: SI 2015/523 Reg.2

Sch.4 para.17A, substituted: SI 2015/523 Reg.2

Sch.4 para.18, substituted: SI 2015/523 Reg.2

Sch.4 para.21, substituted: SI 2015/523 Reg.2

Sch.4 para.30, substituted: SI 2015/523 Reg.2

Sch.4 para.33, substituted: SI 2015/523 Reg.2

Sch.4 para.35, substituted: SI 2015/523 Reg.2

Sch.4 para.45, substituted: SI 2015/523 Reg.2

Sch.4 para.48, substituted: SI 2015/523 Reg.2

Sch.4 para.91, substituted: SI 2015/523 Reg.2

Sch.4 para.113, enabling: SI 2015/523

76. Marriage Act 1949

s.27, enabling: SI 2015/207

s.27A, enabling: SI 2015/207

s.27B, enabling: SI 2015/207

s.28D, enabling: SI 2015/123

s.28G, enabling: SI 2015/123, SI 2015/207

s.28H, enabling: SI 2015/123

s.31, enabling: SI 2015/159, SI 2015/207

s.35, enabling: SI 2015/207

s.55, enabling: SI 2015/207

s.57, enabling: SI 2015/207

s.65A, added: 2015 c.20 s.99
s.74, enabling: SI 2015/159, SI 2015/177,
SI 2015/207
s.76, enabling: SI 2015/207
88. Registered Designs Act 1949
s.35ZB, amended: 2015 c.15 Sch.6 para.1
s.35ZB, repealed: 2015 c.15 Sch.6 para.1
s.36, enabling: SI 2015/169
**97. National Parks and Access to the
Countryside Act 1949**
s.91, amended: 2015 c.20 Sch.22 para.1

14 Geo. 6 (1950)

38. Allotments (Scotland) Act 1950
repealed: 2015 asp 6 Sch.5

14 & 15 Geo. 6 (1950-51)

**vi. Island of Arran Piers Order
Confirmation Act 1951**
repealed: SSI 2015/6 Sch.3
35. Pet Animals Act 1951
see *Kent v Arun DC* [2015] EWHC 2295
(Admin), [2015] L.L.R. 753 (QBD
(Admin)), McGowan J
s.2, see *Kent v Arun DC* [2015] EWHC
2295 (Admin), [2015] L.L.R. 753 (QBD
(Admin)), McGowan J

15 & 16 Geo. 6 & 1 Eliz. 2 (1951-52)

**12. Judicial Offices (Salaries, &c.) Act
1952**
repealed: SI 2015/700 Sch.1 para.5
44. Customs and Excise Act 1952
s.275, see *R. (on the application of
Eastenders Cash & Carry Plc) v Revenue
and Customs Commissioners* [2015] A.C.
1101 (SC), Lord Neuberger PSC
52. Prison Act 1952
see *R. (on the application of King) v
Secretary of State for Justice* [2015]
UKSC 54, [2015] 3 W.L.R. 457 (SC),
Lord Neuberger PSC
s.16A, amended: 2015 c.2 s.16
s.37, amended: 2015 c.2 Sch.9 para.2,
2015 c.20 s.84

s.37, repealed: 2015 c.20 s.84
s.40CA, added: 2015 c.9 s.78
s.40CB, added: 2015 c.9 s.79
s.43, amended: 2015 c.20 s.84
s.43, substituted: 2015 c.2 s.38
s.47, amended: 2015 c.2 s.16, Sch.9
para.3
s.47, substituted: 2015 c.2 Sch.9 para.3
s.47, enabling: SI 2015/1638
s.49, amended: 2015 c.2 Sch.9 para.4
s.52, amended: 2015 c.2 s.38, Sch.10
para.28, 2015 c.20 s.84
67. Visiting Forces Act 1952
Sch.1 para.1, amended: 2015 c.9 Sch.4
para.1

1 & 2 Eliz. 2 (1952-53)

14. Prevention of Crime Act 1953
s.1, see *R. v Akhtar (Itzaz Nafeez)* [2015]
EWCA Crim 176, [2015] 1 W.L.R. 3046
(CA (Crim Div)), Sir Brian Leveson
PQBD
s.1, amended: 2015 c.2 s.28
s.1ZA, added: 2015 c.2 s.28
20. Births and Deaths Registration Act 1953
s.14, see *JB v KS (Contact: Parental
Responsibility)* [2015] EWHC 180
(Fam), [2015] 2 F.L.R. 1180 (Fam Div),
Hayden J
s.34A, added: 2015 c.20 s.98
s.39, amended: 2015 c.20 s.98
s.39A, amended: 2015 c.20 s.98
37. Registration Service Act 1953
s.20, enabling: SI 2015/207
**47. Emergency Laws (Miscellaneous
Provisions) Act 1953**
s.5, repealed: 2015 asp 6 Sch.5

2 & 3 Eliz. 2 (1953-54)

32. Atomic Energy Authority Act 1954
Sch.3, amended: 2015 c.20 Sch.23
para.15
56. Landlord and Tenant Act 1954
s.23, amended: 2015 c.26 s.35
s.24, see *Siemens Hearing Instruments
Ltd v Friends Life Ltd* [2014] EWCA Civ

382, [2015] 1 All E.R. (Comm) 1068
(CA (Civ Div)), Black LJ
s.27, see *Waaler v Hounslow LBC* [2015]
UKUT 17 (LC), [2015] L. & T.R. 24 (UT
(Lands)), Siobhan McGrath
s.41, amended: 2015 c.26 s.36
s.43ZA, added: 2015 c.26 s.35
s.66, enabling: SI 2015/1
s.69, amended: 2015 c.20 Sch.13 para.6

**64. Transport Charges &c
(Miscellaneous Provisions) Act 1954**
s.6, enabling: SI 2015/1105, SI
2015/1404, SI 2015/1573

68. Pests Act 1954
s.1, amended: 2015 c.20 Sch.22 para.2
s.8, enabling: SI 2015/1427

70. Mines and Quarries Act 1954
Sch.4, repealed: 2015 c.20 Sch.23 para.5

4 & 5 Eliz. 2 (1955-56)

**60. Valuation and Rating (Scotland) Act
1956**
s.6, see *WH Smith Plc v Assessor for
Lanarkshire Valuation Joint Board*
[2015] R.V.R. 120 (LVAC), The Lord
President (Gill)
s.6A, enabling: SSI 2015/50
s.13, enabling: SSI 2015/51
s.42, enabling: SSI 2015/51

69. Sexual Offences Act 1956
see *Attorney General's Reference (No.21
of 2015)* [2015] EWCA Crim 953, [2015]
2 Cr. App. R. (S.) 41 (CA (Crim Div)),
Hallett LJ
s.14, see *R. v Clifford (Frank Maxwell)*
[2014] EWCA Crim 2245, [2015] 1 Cr.
App. R. (S.) 32 (CA (Crim Div)), Treacy
LJ; see *R. v DO* [2014] EWCA Crim
2202, [2015] 1 Cr. App. R. (S.) 41 (CA
(Crim Div)), Pitchford LJ; see *R. v Dunn
(Christopher)* [2015] EWCA Crim 724,
[2015] 2 Cr. App. R. 13 (CA (Crim
Div)), Laws LJ

5 & 6 Eliz. 2 (1957)

11. Homicide Act 1957
s.2, see *R. v Brennan (Michael James)*
[2014] EWCA Crim 2387, [2015] 1
W.L.R. 2060 (CA (Crim Div)), Davis LJ;
see *R. v Golds (Mark Richard)* [2014]
EWCA Crim 748, [2015] 1 W.L.R. 1030
(CA (Crim Div)), Elias LJ
s.3, see *R. v Gurpinar (Mustafa)* [2015]
EWCA Crim 178, [2015] 1 W.L.R. 3442
(CA (Crim Div)), Lord Thomas LCJ

36. Cheques Act 1957
s.3, varied: SI 2015/623 Reg.58

56. Housing Act 1957
see *Tower Hamlets LBC v Bromley LBC*
[2015] EWHC 1954 (Ch), [2015]
B.L.G.R. 622 (Ch D), Norris J

6 & 7 Eliz. 2 (1957-58)

30. Land Powers Defence Act 1958
s.12, amended: 2015 c.7 Sch.5 para.25
s.17, amended: 2015 c.7 Sch.5 para.26

**33. Disabled Persons (Employment) Act
1958**
s.3, amended: SI 2015/914 Sch.1 para.11

51. Public Records Act 1958
s.1, amended: SI 2015/1897 Sch.1 para.1
s.2, amended: SI 2015/1897 Sch.1 para.1
s.2, enabling: SI 2015/2042
s.3, amended: SI 2015/1897 Sch.1 para.1
s.4, amended: SI 2015/1897 Sch.1 para.1
s.5, amended: SI 2015/1897 Sch.1 para.1
s.6, amended: SI 2015/1897 Sch.1 para.1
s.7, amended: SI 2015/1897 Sch.1 para.1
s.8, amended: SI 2015/1897 Sch.1 para.1
Sch.1 Part 2, amended: 2015 c.7 Sch.1
para.68
Sch.1 para.7, amended: SI 2015/1897
Sch.1 para.1

53. Variation of Trusts Act 1958
see *V v T* [2014] EWHC 3432 (Ch),
[2015] W.T.L.R. 173 (Ch D), Morgan J
s.1, see *Allfrey v Allfrey* [2015] EWHC
1717 (Ch), [2015] W.T.L.R. 1117 (Ch
D), Jeremy Cousins QC; see *V v T*
[2014] EWHC 3432 (Ch), [2015]
W.T.L.R. 173 (Ch D), Morgan J

69. Opencast Coal Act 1958

s.41, amended: 2015 asp 6 Sch.4 para.4
Sch.8 para.10, amended: 2015 asp 6
Sch.4 para.4, Sch.5

7 & 8 Eliz. 2 (1958-59)

56. Rights of Light Act 1959
  s.2, amended: 2015 c.7 Sch.5 para.28
  s.3, amended: 2015 c.7 Sch.5 para.29
  s.7, amended: 2015 c.7 Sch.5 para.30
57. Street Offences Act 1959
  s.1, amended: 2015 c.9 s.68
  Sch.1 Part 2 para.2, amended: 2015 c.9
  Sch.4 para.2
  Sch.1 Part 2 para.3, amended: 2015 c.9
  Sch.4 para.2
  Sch.1 Part 3 para.5, amended: 2015 c.9
  Sch.4 para.2
  Sch.1 Part 4 para.9, amended: 2015 c.9
  Sch.4 para.2
  Sch.1 Part 4 para.9, repealed: 2015 c.9
  Sch.4 para.2
  Sch.1 Part 4 para.10, amended: 2015 c.9
  Sch.4 para.2
  Sch.1 Part 4 para.10, repealed: 2015 c.9
  Sch.4 para.2
  Sch.1 Part 4 para.11, amended: 2015 c.9
  Sch.4 para.2
**70. Town and Country Planning (Scotland)
Act 1959**
  s.26, repealed: 2015 asp 6 Sch.5

8 & 9 Eliz. 2 (1959-60)

30. Occupiers Liability (Scotland) Act 1960
  s.2, see *Shepherd v Travelodge Hotels
  Ltd* 2015 Rep. L.R. 2 (OH), Lord Boyd of
  Duncansby; see *Wilkinson v Hjaltland
  Housing Association Ltd* 2015 Rep. L.R.
  62 (Sh Ct (Grampian) (Lerwick)), Sheriff
  P Mann
33. Indecency with Children Act 1960
  see *R. v Dunn (Christopher)* [2015]
  EWCA Crim 724, [2015] 2 Cr. App. R.
  13 (CA (Crim Div)), Laws LJ
  s.1, see *R. v DO* [2014] EWCA Crim
  2202, [2015] 1 Cr. App. R. (S.) 41 (CA
  (Crim Div)), Pitchford LJ
65. Administration of Justice Act 1960

s.12, see *C (A Child), Re* [2015] EWFC
79, [2015] Med. L.R. 531 (Fam Ct), Sir
James Munby PFD; see *R. (on the
application of Yam) v Central Criminal
Court* [2014] EWHC 3558 (Admin),
[2015] 3 W.L.R. 1050 (DC), Elias LJ; see
*R. (on the application of Yam) v Central
Criminal Court* [2015] UKSC 76 (SC),
Lord Neuberger JSC

9 & 10 Eliz. 2 (1960-61)

33. Land Compensation Act 1961
  s.5, see *Elitestone Ltd v National Grid
  Gas Plc* [2015] UKUT 452 (LC), [2015]
  R.V.R. 392 (UT (Lands)), PR Francis
  FRICS
  s.6, see *JS Bloor (Wilmslow) Ltd v
  Homes and Communities Agency* [2015]
  EWCA Civ 540, [2015] R.V.R. 292 (CA
  (Civ Div)), Jackson LJ
  s.14, see *JS Bloor (Wilmslow) Ltd v
  Homes and Communities Agency* [2015]
  EWCA Civ 540, [2015] R.V.R. 292 (CA
  (Civ Div)), Jackson LJ
  s.16, see *JS Bloor (Wilmslow) Ltd v
  Homes and Communities Agency* [2015]
  EWCA Civ 540, [2015] R.V.R. 292 (CA
  (Civ Div)), Jackson LJ
  s.17, see *Edwards v Rhondda Cynon Taff
  CBC* [2015] R.V.R. 25 (UT (Lands)), PR
  Francis
  Sch.1, see *JS Bloor (Wilmslow) Ltd v
  Homes and Communities Agency* [2015]
  EWCA Civ 540, [2015] R.V.R. 292 (CA
  (Civ Div)), Jackson LJ
34. Factories Act 1961
  s.176, amended: SI 2015/51 Sch.5
39. Criminal Justice Act 1961
  see *Campbell (David) v HM Advocate*
  [2015] HCJAC 28, 2015 S.L.T. 232
  (HCJ), Lord Eassie
  s.23, amended: 2015 c.2 Sch.9 para.6
  s.38, amended: 2015 c.2 Sch.9 para.7
58. Crofters (Scotland) Act 1961
  see *MacLachlan v Bruce* 2015 S.L.T.
  (Land Ct) 23 (Land Ct), D J Houston
60. Suicide Act 1961
  s.2, see *R. (on the application of AM) v
  General Medical Council* [2015] EWHC

2096 (Admin), [2015] Med. L.R. 453
(DC), Elias LJ; see *R. (on the
application of Nicklinson) v Ministry of
Justice* [2015] A.C. 657 (SC), Lord
Neuberger PSC

62. Trustee Investments Act 1961
    s.11, amended: 2015 c.20 Sch.13 para.6

10 & 11 Eliz. 2 (1961-62)

**9. Local Government (Financial Provisions
etc.) (Scotland) Act 1962**
    s.3A, added: 2015 asp 6 s.140

19. West Indies Act 1962
    s.5, enabling: SI 2015/1767
    s.7, enabling: SI 2015/1767

44. Finance Act 1962
    s.33, enabling: SI 2015/623

46. Transport Act 1962
    s.13, amended: SI 2015/1682 Sch.1
    para.4

1963

**11. Agriculture (Miscellaneous Provisions)
Act 1963**
    s.23, repealed: 2015 c.20 Sch.23 para.34

33. London Government Act 1963
    see *Tower Hamlets LBC v Bromley LBC*
    [2015] EWHC 1954 (Ch), [2015]
    B.L.G.R. 622 (Ch D), Norris J
    s.23, see *Tower Hamlets LBC v Bromley
    LBC* [2015] EWHC 1954 (Ch), [2015]
    B.L.G.R. 622 (Ch D), Norris J

37. Children and Young Persons Act 1963
    s.37, enabling: SI 2015/1757
    s.39, enabling: SI 2015/1757
    s.57, amended: 2015 c.2 s.79

51. Land Compensation (Scotland) Act 1963
    s.22, see *Steel v Scottish Ministers* 2015
    S.L.T. (Lands Tr) 81 (Lands Tr (Scot)),
    Lord McGhie

1964

14. Plant Varieties and Seeds Act 1964
    s.16, enabling: SI 2015/1953, SSI
    2015/395, SSI 2015/396

    s.36, enabling: SI 2015/1953, SSI
    2015/395, SSI 2015/396

28. Agriculture and Horticulture Act 1964
    s.22, repealed: 2015 c.20 Sch.23 para.34
    s.23, amended: 2015 c.20 Sch.22 para.3

40. Harbours Act 1964
    see *R. (on the application of Powell) v
    Brighton Marina Co Ltd* [2015] EWCA
    Civ 650, [2015] J.P.L. 1301 (CA (Civ
    Div)), Arden LJ
    s.14, enabling: SI 2015/1384, SI
    2015/1387, SI 2015/1390, SI 2015/1395,
    SSI 2015/4, SSI 2015/6, SSI 2015/298
    s.15, enabling: SI 2015/2003
    s.40A, enabling: SI 2015/573, SI
    2015/1656
    Sch.3 Part I para.7, repealed: 2015 asp 13
    s.2
    Sch.4 Part I para.1, amended: 2015 asp
    13 s.2

75. Public Libraries and Museums Act 1964
    s.2, repealed: SI 2015/850 Art.3
    s.7, see *R. (on the application of Draper)
    v Lincolnshire CC* [2014] EWHC 2388
    (Admin), [2015] P.T.S.R. 769 (QBD
    (Admin)), Collins J

81. Diplomatic Privileges Act 1964
    s.2, see *Al-Malki v Reyes* [2015] EWCA
    Civ 32, [2015] I.C.R. 931 (CA (Civ
    Div)), Lord Dyson MR

84. Criminal Procedure (Insanity) Act 1964
    see *R. v Chinegwundoh (Harold)* [2015]
    EWCA Crim 109, [2015] 1 W.L.R. 2818
    (CA (Crim Div)), Sir Brian Leveson
    PQBD
    s.4, see *R. v Chinegwundoh (Harold)*
    [2015] EWCA Crim 109, [2015] 1
    W.L.R. 2818 (CA (Crim Div)), Sir Brian
    Leveson PQBD
    s.4A, see *R. v Jagnieszko (Tomasz)*
    [2008] EWCA Crim 3065, [2015]
    M.H.L.R. 99 (CA (Crim Div)), Hallett
    LJ; see *R. v Wells (Marc Martin)* [2015]
    EWCA Crim 2, [2015] 1 W.L.R. 2797
    (CA (Crim Div)), Sir Brian Leveson
    PQBD
    s.5, see *R. v Chinegwundoh (Harold)*
    [2015] EWCA Crim 109, [2015] 1
    W.L.R. 2818 (CA (Crim Div)), Sir Brian
    Leveson PQBD

1965

2. Administration of Justice Act 1965
Sch.1, amended: 2015 c.20 Sch.6 para.2
12. Industrial and Provident Societies Act 1965
see *Southward Housing Co-operative Ltd v Walker* [2015] EWHC 1615 (Ch), [2015] 2 P. & C.R. 13 (Ch D), Hildyard J
49. Registration of Births, Deaths and Marriages (Scotland) Act 1965
s.21, enabling: SSI 2015/180
s.27, enabling: SSI 2015/180
s.27A, enabling: SSI 2015/162, SSI 2015/166
s.54, enabling: SSI 2015/180
51. National Insurance Act 1965
s.36, amended: SI 2015/457 Art.8
s.37, varied: SI 2015/457 Art.8
56. Compulsory Purchase Act 1965
see *Saunders v Caerphilly CBC* [2015] EWHC 1632 (Ch), [2015] 2 P. & C.R. 20 (Ch D (Cardiff)), Judge Milwyn Jarman QC
Part I, varied: SI 2015/781 Art.9
s.7, see *Elitestone Ltd v National Grid Gas Plc* [2015] UKUT 452 (LC), [2015] R.V.R. 392 (UT (Lands)), PR Francis FRICS
s.7, varied: SI 2015/23 Sch.11 para.4, SI 2015/780 Sch.9 para.4, SI 2015/781 Sch.2 para.4
s.8, varied: SI 2015/23 Sch.11 para.5, SI 2015/780 Sch.9 para.5, SI 2015/781 Sch.2 para.5
s.9, varied: SI 2015/23 Sch.11 para.6, SI 2015/780 Sch.9 para.6
s.11, amended: SI 2015/780 Sch.9 para.7
s.11, varied: SI 2015/23 Sch.11 para.7
s.20, varied: SI 2015/23 Sch.11 para.8, SI 2015/780 Sch.9 para.8
s.22, varied: SI 2015/23 Sch.11 para.9, SI 2015/780 Sch.9 para.9
Sch.1 para.10, varied: SI 2015/23 Sch.11 para.6, SI 2015/780 Sch.9 para.6
Sch.2 para.2, varied: SI 2015/23 Sch.11 para.6, SI 2015/780 Sch.9 para.6
Sch.4 para.2, varied: SI 2015/23 Sch.11 para.6, SI 2015/780 Sch.9 para.6

Sch.4 para.7, varied: SI 2015/23 Sch.11 para.6, SI 2015/780 Sch.9 para.6
64. Commons Registration Act 1965
see *R. (on the application of Littlejohns) v Devon CC* [2015] EWHC 730 (Admin), [2015] Q.B. 869 (QBD (Admin)), Lang J
s.1, see *R. (on the application of Littlejohns) v Devon CC* [2015] EWHC 730 (Admin), [2015] Q.B. 869 (QBD (Admin)), Lang J

1966

19. Law Reform (Miscellaneous Provisions) (Scotland) Act 1966
s.8, amended: SSI 2015/150 Sch.1 para.1
36. Veterinary Surgeons Act 1966
s.5A, amended: SI 2015/2073 Reg.3
s.5B, amended: SI 2015/2073 Reg.4
s.5CA, amended: SI 2015/2073 Reg.6
s.5CCA, added: SI 2015/2073 Reg.7
s.5CD, amended: SI 2015/2073 Reg.8
s.5CE, amended: SI 2015/2073 Reg.9
s.5D, amended: SI 2015/2073 Reg.10
s.5ZBA, added: SI 2015/2073 Reg.5
s.6, amended: SI 2015/2073 Reg.11
s.19, enabling: SI 2015/772
s.27, amended: SI 2015/2073 Reg.12
Sch.1A para.1, amended: SI 2015/2073 Reg.13
Sch.1A para.3, amended: SI 2015/2073 Reg.13
Sch.1A para.5, amended: SI 2015/2073 Reg.13
Sch.1A para.5, substituted: SI 2015/2073 Reg.13
Sch.1B para.4, amended: SI 2015/2073 Reg.14
Sch.1B para.5, amended: SI 2015/2073 Reg.14

1967

7. Misrepresentation Act 1967
s.2, see *Salt v Stratstone Specialist Ltd (t/a Stratstone Cadillac Newcastle)* [2015] EWCA Civ 745, [2015] C.T.L.C. 206 (CA (Civ Div)), Longmore LJ
s.3, substituted: 2015 c.15 Sch.4 para.1

8. Plant Health Act 1967
s.2, enabling: SI 2015/610, SI 2015/1723,
SI 2015/1827, SSI 2015/10
s.3, enabling: SI 2015/382, SI 2015/610,
SI 2015/741, SI 2015/1723, SI
2015/1827, SSI 2015/10
s.4, enabling: SI 2015/610, SSI 2015/10
s.4A, enabling: SI 2015/382
s.5, enabling: SI 2015/741

9. General Rate Act 1967
s.115, see *Woolway (Valuation Officer) v
Mazars LLP* [2015] UKSC 53, [2015]
A.C. 1862 (SC), Lord Neuberger PSC

10. Forestry Act 1967
s.7C, amended: 2015 asp 6 s.98
s.7C, repealed: 2015 asp 6 s.98
s.32, amended: SI 2015/475 Sch.1 Part 1
s.37, repealed: SI 2015/475 Sch.1 Part 1
s.38, amended: SI 2015/475 Sch.1 Part 1
s.38, repealed: SI 2015/475 Sch.1 Part 1

13. Parliamentary Commissioner Act 1967
s.4, enabling: SI 2015/214
Sch.2, amended: 2015 c.7 Sch.1 para.69,
2015 c.20 Sch.14 para.32, 2015 c.26
Sch.1 para.23, SI 2015/214 Art.2, SI
2015/850 Art.3, SI 2015/978 Sch.1 Part
1, SI 2015/1682 Sch.1 para.4
Sch.4, amended: 2015 c.20 Sch.6 para.22

**45. Uniform Laws on International Sales Act
1967**
s.1, amended: SI 2015/1726 Sch.1 para.1

50. Farm and Garden Chemicals Act 1967
repealed: 2015 c.20 Sch.23 para.24

58. Criminal Law Act 1967
s.3, see *Metcalf v Crown Prosecution
Service* [2015] EWHC 1091 (Admin),
[2015] 2 Cr. App. R. 25 (DC), Burnett LJ

77. Police (Scotland) Act 1967
s.17, see *Carmichael v Harvie* [2015]
HCJAC 81, 2015 S.L.T. 670 (HCJ), Lord
Drummond Young
s.44, see *Carmichael v Harvie* [2015]
HCJAC 81, 2015 S.L.T. 670 (HCJ), Lord
Drummond Young

80. Criminal Justice Act 1967
s.9, amended: 2015 c.20 s.80
s.9, repealed: 2015 c.20 s.80
s.66, repealed: 2015 c.2 Sch.10 para.29
Sch.3 Part I, amended: 2015 c.20 Sch.23
para.34

83. Sea Fisheries (Shellfish) Act 1967

s.1, enabling: SI 2015/1346, SSI 2015/28,
SSI 2015/30
s.3, amended: SI 2015/664 Sch.4 para.3
s.7, amended: SI 2015/664 Sch.4 para.3
s.7, enabling: SSI 2015/28, SSI 2015/30
s.12, enabling: SI 2015/751
Sch.1 para.6, enabling: SI 2015/1346

84. Sea Fish (Conservation) Act 1967
s.1, enabling: SI 2015/1791, SI
2015/2076, SSI 2015/183
s.3, enabling: SI 2015/1791
s.4, see *R. v JC* [2015] EWCA Crim 210,
[2015] L.L.R. 380 (CA (Crim Div)),
Davis LJ
s.4, enabling: SI 2015/647
s.5, enabling: SI 2015/441, SI 2015/2076
s.6, enabling: SI 2015/441, SI 2015/2076,
SSI 2015/183
s.11, amended: SI 2015/664 Sch.4 para.4
s.15, amended: SI 2015/664 Sch.4 para.4
s.15, enabling: SI 2015/647, SI
2015/1791
s.16, amended: SI 2015/664 Sch.4 para.4
s.20, enabling: SI 2015/647, SI
2015/1791, SI 2015/2076, SSI 2015/183

87. Abortion Act 1967
s.1, see *Doogan v Greater Glasgow and
Clyde Health Board* [2015] A.C. 640
(SC), Lady Hale DPSC
s.4, see *Doogan v Greater Glasgow and
Clyde Health Board* [2015] A.C. 640
(SC), Lady Hale DPSC

88. Leasehold Reform Act 1967
s.2, see *Jewelcraft Ltd v Pressland* [2015]
EWCA Civ 1111, [2015] H.L.R. 48 (CA
(Civ Div)), Patten LJ
s.19, amended: 2015 c.7 Sch.5 para.32
s.28, amended: 2015 c.20 Sch.13 para.6

1968

ii. Brighton Marina Act 1968
see *R. (on the application of Powell) v
Brighton Marina Co Ltd* [2015] EWCA
Civ 650, [2015] J.P.L. 1301 (CA (Civ
Div)), Arden LJ
s.5, see *R. (on the application of Powell)
v Brighton Marina Co Ltd* [2015] EWCA
Civ 650, [2015] J.P.L. 1301 (CA (Civ
Div)), Arden LJ

s.23, see *R. (on the application of Powell) v Brighton Marina Co Ltd* [2015] EWCA Civ 650, [2015] J.P.L. 1301 (CA (Civ Div)), Arden LJ

s.40, see *R. (on the application of Powell) v Brighton Marina Co Ltd* [2015] EWCA Civ 650, [2015] J.P.L. 1301 (CA (Civ Div)), Arden LJ

2. Provisional Collection of Taxes Act 1968

s.1, amended: 2015 c.11 s.115

14. Public Expenditure and Receipts Act 1968

s.5, enabling: SI 2015/117

Sch.3 para.1, enabling: SI 2015/117

19. Criminal Appeal Act 1968

see *R. v Gray (Dean Andrew)* [2014] EWCA Crim 2372, [2015] 1 Cr. App. R. (S.) 27 (CA (Crim Div)), Hallett LJ

s.23, see *R. v Vowles (Lucinda)* [2015] EWCA Crim 45, [2015] 1 W.L.R. 5131 (CA (Civ Div)), Lord Thomas LCJ

s.50, amended: 2015 c.9 Sch.4 para.3

20. Court Martial Appeals Act 1968

s.49, enabling: SI 2015/1814

27. Firearms Act 1968

s.1, see *R. v Antoine (Jordan)* [2014] EWCA Crim 1971, [2015] 1 Cr. App. R. 8 (CA (Crim Div)), Davis LJ; see *R. v Goldsborough (Paul)* [2015] EWCA Crim 1278, [2015] 1 W.L.R. 4921 (CA (Crim Div)), Treacy LJ; see *R. v Yong (Matthew)* [2015] EWCA Crim 852, [2015] 2 Cr. App. R. 15 (CA (Crim Div)), Treacy LJ

s.3, amended: 2015 asp 10 Sch.2 para.1

s.3, repealed: 2015 asp 10 Sch.2 para.1

s.5, see *R. v Antoine (Jordan)* [2014] EWCA Crim 1971, [2015] 1 Cr. App. R. 8 (CA (Crim Div)), Davis LJ; see *R. v Goldsborough (Paul)* [2015] EWCA Crim 1278, [2015] 1 W.L.R. 4921 (CA (Crim Div)), Treacy LJ; see *R. v Rhodes (John)* [2015] EWCA Crim 155, [2015] 2 Cr. App. R. 16 (CA (Crim Div)), Sir Brian Leveson PQBD; see *R. v Withers (Zoe)* [2015] EWCA Crim 132, [2015] 1 Cr. App. R. (S.) 64 (CA (Crim Div)), Beatson LJ; see *R. v Yong (Matthew)* [2015] EWCA Crim 852, [2015] 2 Cr. App. R. 15 (CA (Crim Div)), Treacy LJ

s.10, amended: SI 2015/1782 Sch.6 para.1

s.10, repealed: SI 2015/1782 Sch.6 para.1

s.16, see *R. v Smith (Owen)* [2014] EWCA Crim 2163, [2015] 1 W.L.R. 937 (CA (Crim Div)), Davis LJ

s.16A, see *Rodger (Alan) v HM Advocate* 2015 J.C. 215 (HCJ), Lord Eassie

s.17, see *R. v Yusuf (Samir)* [2014] EWCA Crim 1586, [2015] 1 Cr. App. R. (S.) 4 (CA (Crim Div)), Elias LJ

s.21, see *R. v Antoine (Jordan)* [2014] EWCA Crim 1971, [2015] 1 Cr. App. R. 8 (CA (Crim Div)), Davis LJ

s.21A, amended: 2015 asp 10 Sch.2 para.1

s.22, repealed: 2015 asp 10 Sch.2 para.1

s.23, repealed: 2015 asp 10 Sch.2 para.1

s.24, amended: 2015 asp 10 Sch.2 para.1

s.24ZA, amended: 2015 asp 10 Sch.2 para.1

s.27, see *Lomax v Chief Constable of the Police Service of Scotland* 2015 S.L.T. (Sh Ct) 14 (Sh Ct (South Strathclyde) (Dumfries)), Sheriff Principal B A Lockhart

s.32, amended: SI 2015/611 Art.2

s.35, amended: SI 2015/611 Art.3

s.43, enabling: SI 2015/611

s.44, see *Lomax v Chief Constable of the Police Service of Scotland* 2015 S.L.T. (Sh Ct) 14 (Sh Ct (South Strathclyde) (Dumfries)), Sheriff Principal B A Lockhart

s.51A, see *R. v Antoine (Jordan)* [2014] EWCA Crim 1971, [2015] 1 Cr. App. R. 8 (CA (Crim Div)), Davis LJ; see *R. v Withers (Zoe)* [2015] EWCA Crim 132, [2015] 1 Cr. App. R. (S.) 64 (CA (Crim Div)), Beatson LJ

s.57, see *R. v Yong (Matthew)* [2015] EWCA Crim 852, [2015] 2 Cr. App. R. 15 (CA (Crim Div)), Treacy LJ

s.57, amended: 2015 asp 10 Sch.2 para.1

Sch.1 para.6A, added: 2015 c.2 Sch.10 para.30

Sch.1 para.8, amended: 2015 c.2 Sch.10 para.30

Sch.4 Part 1, amended: 2015 asp 10 Sch.2 para.1

Sch.4 Part 2, amended: 2015 asp 10
Sch.2 para.1
Sch.4 Part 2, substituted: 2015 asp 10
Sch.2 para.1
Sch.4 Part 3, added: 2015 asp 10 Sch.2
para.1
Sch.6 Part I, amended: 2015 asp 10 Sch.2
para.1
Sch.6 Part II para.7, amended: 2015 asp
10 Sch.2 para.1
Sch.6 Part II para.8, amended: 2015 asp
10 Sch.2 para.1

29. Trade Descriptions Act 1968
s.2, repealed: 2015 c.20 Sch.23 para.34
s.26, amended: 2015 c.15 Sch.6 para.3
s.27, repealed: 2015 c.15 Sch.6 para.4
s.28, repealed: 2015 c.15 Sch.6 para.5
s.29, repealed: 2015 c.15 Sch.6 para.6
s.30, repealed: 2015 c.15 Sch.6 para.7
s.33, repealed: 2015 c.15 Sch.6 para.8
s.40, amended: 2015 c.15 Sch.6 para.9
s.40, repealed: 2015 c.15 Sch.6 para.9
Sch.1 para.3, repealed: 2015 c.20 Sch.23
para.34

**46. Health Services and Public Health Act
1968**
s.45, amended: SI 2015/914 Sch.1
para.13
s.46, repealed: SI 2015/914 Sch.1 para.14

47. Sewerage (Scotland) Act 1968
s.1, enabling: SSI 2015/79

48. International Organisations Act 1968
s.1, enabling: SI 2015/1884, SSI
2015/421

49. Social Work (Scotland) Act 1968
see *Ansari v Aberdeen City Council*
[2015] CSOH 168 (OH), Lord Glennie
s.6B, amended: SSI 2015/157 Sch.1
para.1
s.12, see *Milton Keynes Council v
Scottish Ministers* [2015] CSOH 156,
2015 S.L.T. 843 (OH), Lord Armstrong
s.12A, amended: SSI 2015/157 Sch.1
para.1
s.86, see *Milton Keynes Council v
Scottish Ministers* [2015] CSOH 156,
2015 S.L.T. 843 (OH), Lord Armstrong
s.87, amended: SSI 2015/157 Sch.1
para.1

54. Theatres Act 1968
s.1, repealed: 2015 asp 10 s.74

s.12, repealed: 2015 asp 10 s.74
s.15, amended: 2015 asp 10 s.74
s.15, repealed: 2015 asp 10 s.74
s.18, amended: 2015 asp 10 s.74
Sch.1, repealed: 2015 asp 10 s.74

59. Hovercraft Act 1968
s.2, amended: SSI 2015/150 Sch.1 para.2

60. Theft Act 1968
s.8, see *Campbell (David) v HM
Advocate* [2015] HCJAC 28, 2015 S.L.T.
232 (HCJ), Lord Eassie

64. Civil Evidence Act 1968
see *Rogers v Hoyle* [2014] EWCA Civ
257, [2015] Q.B. 265 (CA (Civ Div)),
Arden LJ
s.3, see *Rogers v Hoyle* [2014] EWCA
Civ 257, [2015] Q.B. 265 (CA (Civ
Div)), Arden LJ
s.12, repealed: SI 2015/914 Sch.1 para.15

65. Gaming Act 1968
see *Revenue and Customs Commissioners
v IFX Investment Co Ltd* [2015] S.T.C.
294 (UT (Tax)), Norris J; see *Revenue
and Customs Commissioners v Rank
Group Plc* [2015] UKSC 48, [2015] 1
W.L.R. 3472 (SC), Lord Neuberger PSC;
see *Ritz Hotel Casino Ltd v Daher*
[2014] EWHC 2847 (QB), [2015] 4 All
E.R. 222 (QBD), Judge Seys-Llewellyn
QC
s.31, see *Revenue and Customs
Commissioners v Rank Group Plc* [2015]
UKSC 48, [2015] 1 W.L.R. 3472 (SC),
Lord Neuberger PSC

73. Transport Act 1968
s.9, amended: 2015 c.20 Sch.8 para.9
s.10, amended: 2015 c.20 s.49, Sch.8
para.2, Sch.8 para.3
s.16, amended: 2015 c.20 Sch.8 para.9
s.20, amended: 2015 c.20 Sch.8 para.4
s.23A, amended: 2015 c.20 Sch.8 para.5
s.95, enabling: SI 2015/502
s.97D, amended: SI 2015/502 Reg.2
Sch.5 Part II para.2, amended: 2015 c.20
Sch.8 para.9
Sch.5 Part III para.11, amended: 2015
c.20 Sch.8 para.9

77. Sea Fisheries Act 1968
s.10, amended: SI 2015/664 Sch.4 para.5

1969

**22. Redundant Churches and Other
Religious Buildings Act 1969**
s.1, enabling: SI 2015/908
46. Family Law Reform Act 1969
s.22, enabling: SI 2015/1834, SI
2015/2048
**57. Employers Liability (Compulsory
Insurance) Act 1969**
see *Campbell v Peter Gordon Joiners Ltd*
[2015] CSIH 11, 2015 S.C. 453 (IH (Ex
Div)), Lord Brodie
s.1, see *Campbell v Peter Gordon Joiners
Ltd* [2015] CSIH 11, 2015 S.C. 453 (IH
(Ex Div)), Lord Brodie
s.2, see *Broni v Ministry of Defence*
[2015] EWHC 66 (QB), [2015] 1 Costs
L.R. 111 (QBD), Supperstone J
s.3, amended: 2015 c.20 Sch.13 para.6
s.5, see *Campbell v Peter Gordon Joiners
Ltd* [2015] CSIH 11, 2015 S.C. 453 (IH
(Ex Div)), Lord Brodie
58. Administration of Justice Act 1969
s.12, amended: 2015 c.2 s.63
s.12, repealed: 2015 c.2 s.63
s.16, amended: 2015 c.2 s.63

1970

9. Taxes Management Act 1970
s.3, see *Barton v Secretary of State for
Scotland* [2015] CSIH 92 (IH (Ex Div)),
Lady Smith
s.7A, added: 2015 c.11 Sch.7 para.42
s.8, see *R. (on the application of Higgs) v
Revenue and Customs Commissioners*
[2015] UKUT 92 (TCC), [2015] S.T.C.
1600 (UT (Tax)), Barling J
s.9, see *R. (on the application of Higgs) v
Revenue and Customs Commissioners*
[2015] UKUT 92 (TCC), [2015] S.T.C.
1600 (UT (Tax)), Barling J
s.9A, see *Norman v Revenue and
Customs Commissioners* [2015] UKFTT
303 (TC), [2015] S.F.T.D. 868 (FTT
(Tax)), Judge Thomas
s.12ZA, added: 2015 c.11 Sch.7 para.43
s.28A, amended: 2015 c.11 Sch.7 para.44
s.28C, amended: 2015 c.33 Sch.8 para.25

s.28G, added: 2015 c.11 Sch.7 para.45
s.29, see *Burgess v Revenue and Customs
Commissioners* [2015] UKUT 578
(TCC), [2015] B.T.C. 533 (UT (Tax)),
Judge Roger Berner; see *Hargreaves v
Revenue and Customs Commissioners*
[2015] S.T.C. 905 (UT (Tax)), Nugee J;
see *Martin v Revenue and Customs
Commissioners* [2015] UKUT 161
(TCC), [2015] S.T.C. 2490 (UT (Tax)),
Warren J; see *Norman v Revenue and
Customs Commissioners* [2015] UKFTT
303 (TC), [2015] S.F.T.D. 868 (FTT
(Tax)), Judge Thomas; see *R. (on the
application of Hely-Hutchinson) v
Revenue and Customs Commissioners*
[2015] EWHC 3261 (Admin), [2015]
B.T.C. 37 (QBD (Admin)), Whipple J
s.29, amended: 2015 c.11 Sch.7 para.46
s.29A, added: 2015 c.11 Sch.7 para.47
s.33, see *Tindale v Revenue and Customs
Commissioners* [2015] S.T.C. 139 (UT
(Tax)), Judge Timothy Herrington
s.34, see *Burgess v Revenue and Customs
Commissioners* [2015] UKUT 578
(TCC), [2015] B.T.C. 533 (UT (Tax)),
Judge Roger Berner; see *R. (on the
application of Higgs) v Revenue and
Customs Commissioners* [2015] UKUT
92 (TCC), [2015] S.T.C. 1600 (UT
(Tax)), Barling J
s.34, amended: 2015 c.11 Sch.7 para.48
s.36, see *Burgess v Revenue and Customs
Commissioners* [2015] UKUT 578
(TCC), [2015] B.T.C. 533 (UT (Tax)),
Judge Roger Berner; see *R. (on the
application of Higgs) v Revenue and
Customs Commissioners* [2015] UKUT
92 (TCC), [2015] S.T.C. 1600 (UT
(Tax)), Barling J
s.42, amended: 2015 c.11 Sch.7 para.49
s.49F, see *Ali v Revenue and Customs
Commissioners* [2015] UKFTT 464 (TC),
[2015] B.P.I.R. 1348 (FTT (Tax)), Judge
Richard Thomas
s.50, see *Norman v Revenue and Customs
Commissioners* [2015] UKFTT 303 (TC),
[2015] S.F.T.D. 868 (FTT (Tax)), Judge
Thomas
s.54, see *Ali v Revenue and Customs
Commissioners* [2015] UKFTT 464 (TC),

[2015] B.P.I.R. 1348 (FTT (Tax)), Judge
Richard Thomas; see *Southern Cross
Employment Agency Ltd v Revenue and
Customs Commissioners* [2015] UKUT
122 (TCC), [2015] S.T.C. 1933 (UT
(Tax)), Newey J
s.55, amended: 2015 c.11 Sch.18 para.11
s.59A, repealed: 2015 c.11 Sch.7 para.50
s.59AA, added: 2015 c.11 Sch.7 para.51
s.59B, amended: 2015 c.11 Sch.7 para.52
s.59D, amended: 2015 c.33 s.38
s.59E, amended: 2015 c.33 Sch.3 para.2
s.73, see *Currie v Revenue and Customs
Commissioners* [2015] S.F.T.D. 51 (FTT
(Tax)), Judge Anne Redston
s.74, see *Drown v Revenue and Customs
Commissioners* [2015] W.T.L.R. 775
(FTT (Tax)), Judge Barbara Mosedale
s.77, see *Drown v Revenue and Customs
Commissioners* [2015] W.T.L.R. 775
(FTT (Tax)), Judge Barbara Mosedale
s.98C, amended: 2015 c.11 Sch.17
para.3, Sch.17 para.8, Sch.17 para.11,
Sch.17 para.13, Sch.17 para.15, Sch.17
para.18
s.100, amended: 2015 c.11 s.18
s.107A, amended: 2015 c.11 Sch.7
para.53
s.113, enabling: SI 2015/171, SI
2015/1927
s.118, see *Raftopoulou v Revenue and
Customs Commissioners* [2015] UKUT
579 (TCC), [2015] B.T.C. 532 (UT
(Tax)), Judge Roger Berner
s.118, amended: 2015 c.11 Sch.7 para.54
Sch.1A, see *Spring Salmon & Seafood
Ltd v Revenue and Customs
Commissioners* [2015] S.T.C. 563 (UT
(Tax)), Warren J
Sch.1AB, see *Raftopoulou v Revenue and
Customs Commissioners* [2015] UKUT
579 (TCC), [2015] B.T.C. 532 (UT
(Tax)), Judge Roger Berner
Sch.1AB para.3A, see *Currie v Revenue
and Customs Commissioners* [2015]
S.F.T.D. 51 (FTT (Tax)), Judge Anne
Redston
Sch.1A para.9, see *Currie v Revenue and
Customs Commissioners* [2015] S.F.T.D.
51 (FTT (Tax)), Judge Anne Redston

Sch.3ZA para.1, amended: 2015 c.11
Sch.7 para.55
Sch.3ZA para.2, amended: 2015 c.11
Sch.7 para.55
Sch.3ZA para.3, amended: 2015 c.11
Sch.7 para.55
Sch.3ZA para.5, amended: 2015 c.11
Sch.7 para.55

31. Administration of Justice Act 1970
s.41, amended: 2015 c.30 Sch.5 para.11
s.44A, see *Novoship (UK) Ltd v
Mikhaylyuk* [2014] EWCA Civ 908,
[2015] Q.B. 499 (CA (Civ Div)),
Longmore LJ
Sch.9 Part I para.9A, added: 2015 c.2
s.54
Sch.9 Part I para.12C, added: 2015 c.30
Sch.5 para.11
Sch.9 Part I para.13, substituted: 2015 c.2
s.54
Sch.9 Part I para.13A, substituted: 2015
c.2 s.54
Sch.9 Part I para.13B, added: 2015 c.30
Sch.5 para.11

**34. Marriage (Registrar General's Licence)
Act 1970**
s.2, enabling: SI 2015/207
s.7, enabling: SI 2015/207
s.18, enabling: SI 2015/207

**35. Conveyancing and Feudal Reform
(Scotland) Act 1970**
see *Hoblyn v Barclays Bank Plc* 2015
S.C.L.R. 85 (IH (Ex Div)), Lady Paton;
see *Swift Advances Plc v Martin* [2015]
CSIH 65, 2015 Hous. L.R. 50 (IH), Lord
Brodie
s.19, see *Westfoot Invesments Ltd v
European Property Holdings Inc* 2015
S.L.T. (Sh Ct) 201 (Sh Ct (Lothian)
(Edinburgh)), Sheriff T Welsh, QC
s.20, see *Westfoot Invesments Ltd v
European Property Holdings Inc* 2015
S.L.T. (Sh Ct) 201 (Sh Ct (Lothian)
(Edinburgh)), Sheriff T Welsh, QC
s.24, see *Aronson v Keeper of the
Registers of Scotland* 2015 S.L.T. 122
(OH), Lord Doherty; see *Swift Advances
Plc v Martin* [2015] CSIH 65, 2015
Hous. L.R. 50 (IH), Lord Brodie; see
*Westfoot Invesments Ltd v European
Property Holdings Inc* 2015 S.L.T. (Sh

Ct) 201 (Sh Ct (Lothian) (Edinburgh)),
Sheriff T Welsh, QC
s.24A, see *Swift Advances Plc v Martin*
[2015] CSIH 65, 2015 Hous. L.R. 50
(IH), Lord Brodie; see *Westfoot
Invesments Ltd v European Property
Holdings Inc* 2015 S.L.T. (Sh Ct) 201 (Sh
Ct (Lothian) (Edinburgh)), Sheriff T
Welsh, QC
s.26, see *Aronson v Keeper of the
Registers of Scotland* 2015 S.L.T. 122
(OH), Lord Doherty
s.27, see *Aronson v Keeper of the
Registers of Scotland* 2015 S.L.T. 122
(OH), Lord Doherty

**39. Local Authorities (Goods and Services)
Act 1970**
s.1, amended: 2015 c.20 Sch.13 para.6

40. Agriculture Act 1970
s.66, enabling: SI 2015/255, SI 2015/454
s.67, enabling: SI 2015/454
s.68, enabling: SI 2015/255
s.74A, enabling: SI 2015/255, SI
2015/454
s.79, enabling: SI 2015/454
s.84, enabling: SI 2015/255, SI 2015/454
s.106, enabling: SI 2015/793

42. Local Authority Social Services Act 1970
s.7, see *H v Bexley LBC* [2015] EWHC
1843 (Admin), (2015) 18 C.C.L. Rep.
375 (QBD (Admin)), Roger Ter Haar
QC; see *R. (on the application of Smieja)
v Bexley LBC* [2014] EWHC 4113
(Admin), [2015] B.L.G.R. 112 (QBD
(Admin)), Neil Cameron QC
s.7, amended: SI 2015/914 Sch.1 para.17
Sch.1, amended: SI 2015/914 Sch.1
para.18, SI 2015/1272 Art.8

**44. Chronically Sick and Disabled Persons
Act 1970**
s.1, amended: SI 2015/914 Sch.1 para.20
s.2, see *R. (on the application of Robson)
v Salford City Council* [2015] EWCA Civ
6, [2015] P.T.S.R. 1349 (CA (Civ Div)),
Richards LJ
s.2, amended: SI 2015/914 Sch.1 para.21
s.2, repealed: SI 2015/914 Sch.1 para.21
s.20, enabling: SI 2015/59, SI 2015/779
s.21, enabling: SSI 2015/9
s.28A, amended: SI 2015/914 Sch.1
para.22

s.29, amended: SI 2015/914 Sch.1
para.23

1971

22. Animals Act 1971
s.4, amended: 2015 c.23 s.4
s.4A, added: 2015 c.23 s.4
s.5, amended: 2015 c.23 s.4
s.7, amended: 2015 c.23 s.1
s.7A, added: 2015 c.23 s.1
s.7B, added: 2015 c.23 s.2
s.7C, added: 2015 c.23 s.3
s.10, amended: 2015 c.23 s.4
s.11, amended: 2015 c.23 s.1

23. Courts Act 1971
s.52, see *Chief Constable of
Warwickshire v MT* [2015] EWHC 2303
(Admin), (2015) 179 J.P. 454 (QBD
(Admin)), Hickinbottom J; see *Chief
Constable of Warwickshire v Young*
[2014] EWHC 4213 (Admin), (2015) 179
J.P. 49 (QBD (Admin)), Hickinbottom J

29. National Savings Bank Act 1971
s.2, enabling: SI 2015/623
s.3, enabling: SI 2015/623
s.4, enabling: SI 2015/623
s.6, enabling: SI 2015/623
s.7, enabling: SI 2015/623
s.8, enabling: SI 2015/623
s.9, enabling: SI 2015/623
s.15, enabling: SI 2015/623

38. Misuse of Drugs Act 1971
s.2, enabling: SI 2015/215
s.2A, enabling: SI 2015/1027, SI
2015/1396, SI 2015/1929
s.4, see *B v HM Advocate* [2015] HCJAC
17, 2015 S.L.T. 182 (HCJ), Lord Brodie;
see *Carroll (Graham) v HM Advocate*
[2015] HCJAC 75, 2015 S.C.L. 859
(HCJ), Lord Eassie; see *Darroch (Scott
David) v HM Advocate* [2015] HCJAC
40, 2015 S.C.L. 626 (HCJ), The Lord
Justice Clerk (Carloway); see *Dunbar
(David) v HM Advocate* [2015] HCJAC
22, 2015 S.C.L. 465 (HCJ), Lord Eassie;
see *Glasgow Housing Association Ltd v
Lilley* 2015 Hous. L.R. 68 (Sh Ct
(Glasgow)), Sheriff A Y Anwar; see
Glasgow Housing Association Ltd v

Stuart 2015 Hous. L.R. 2 (Sh Ct (Glasgow)), Sheriff S Reid; see *HM Advocate v Younas (Mohammed)* 2015 S.C.L. 162 (HCJ), Lord Pentland; see *Johnston (Jacqueline) v HM Advocate* [2015] HCJAC 118 (HCJ), Lady Paton; see *Lord Advocate v Mackie* [2015] CSIH 88 (IH (2 Div)), The Lord Justice Clerk (Carloway); see *McGartland (Peter) v HM Advocate* [2015] HCJAC 23, 2015 S.C.L. 471 (HCJ), Lord Eassie; see *O'Neill v Harvie* 2015 S.L.T. 55 (HCJ), Lady Paton; see *R. v Martin (Dwain Ashley)* [2014] EWCA Crim 1940, [2015] 1 W.L.R. 588 (CA (Crim Div)), Lord Thomas LCJ; see *Stewart v Harvie* [2015] HCJAC 13 (HCJ), Lord Brodie; see *Sutherland (Alexander) v HM Advocate* [2015] HCJAC 115 (HCJ), The Lord Justice Clerk (Carloway)

s.5, see *Bowden v Harvie* [2015] HCJAC 11, 2015 S.C.L. 325 (HCJ), Lord Brodie; see *McKenzie v Murphy* 2015 S.C.L. 194 (HCJ), Lady Dorrian; see *Stewart v Dunn* [2015] HCJAC 93, 2015 S.L.T. 872 (HCJ), Lady Smith

s.7, enabling: SI 2015/231, SI 2015/232, SI 2015/704, SI 2015/891

s.7A, enabling: SI 2015/1027, SI 2015/1396, SI 2015/1929

s.10, enabling: SI 2015/231, SI 2015/891

s.16, see *Glasgow Housing Association Ltd v Lilley* 2015 Hous. L.R. 68 (Sh Ct (Glasgow)), Sheriff A Y Anwar

s.22, enabling: SI 2015/231, SI 2015/891

s.23, see *B v HM Advocate* [2015] HCJAC 17, 2015 S.L.T. 182 (HCJ), Lord Brodie; see *Borland (Robert) v HM Advocate* [2015] HCJAC 95 (HCJ), The Lord Justice Clerk (Carloway); see *Darroch (Scott David) v HM Advocate* [2015] HCJAC 40, 2015 S.C.L. 626 (HCJ), The Lord Justice Clerk (Carloway); see *Glasgow Housing Association Ltd v Lilley* 2015 Hous. L.R. 68 (Sh Ct (Glasgow)), Sheriff A Y Anwar; see *Haashi (Shirwa Abdisayed) v HM Advocate* 2015 J.C. 4 (HCJ), The Lord Justice Clerk (Carloway); see *McKenzie v Murphy* 2015 S.C.L. 194 (HCJ), Lady Dorrian; see *Skeet (Ronald)*

v HM Advocate [2015] HCJAC 66, 2015 S.C.L. 780 (HCJ), Lord Brodie; see *Stewart v Harvie* [2015] HCJAC 13 (HCJ), Lord Brodie

s.27, see *R. v Guraj (Lodvik)* [2015] EWCA Crim 305, [2015] 1 W.L.R. 4149 (CA (Crim Div)), Jackson LJ; see *R. v Kakkad (Freshkumar)* [2015] EWCA Crim 385, [2015] 1 W.L.R. 4162 (CA (Crim Div)), Pitchford LJ

s.31, enabling: SI 2015/231, SI 2015/891, SI 2015/1027, SI 2015/1396, SI 2015/1929

Sch.2 Pt II para.1, see *Carroll (Graham) v HM Advocate* [2015] HCJAC 75, 2015 S.C.L. 859 (HCJ), Lord Eassie

Sch.2 Part I para.1, amended: SI 2015/215 Art.3

48. Criminal Damage Act 1971

s.2, see *R. v Ankerson (Kenneth)* [2015] EWCA Crim 549, (2015) 179 J.P. 219 (CA (Crim Div)), Elias LJ

s.3, see *R. v Akhtar (Itzaz Nafeez)* [2015] EWCA Crim 176, [2015] 1 W.L.R. 3046 (CA (Crim Div)), Sir Brian Leveson PQBD

56. Pensions (Increase) Act 1971

s.19, amended: 2015 c.8 Sch.5 para.2

Sch.2 Part I para.4AA, added: 2015 c.8 Sch.5 para.3

58. Sheriff Courts (Scotland) Act 1971

s.2, repealed: SI 2015/700 Art.2

s.3, repealed: SI 2015/700 Art.2

s.4, repealed: SI 2015/700 Sch.1 para.6

s.32, enabling: SSI 2015/5, SSI 2015/85, SSI 2015/119

s.36B, see *Tallo v Clark* 2015 S.L.T. (Sh Ct) 181 (Sh Ct (Lothian) (Edinburgh)), Sheriff Principal M M Stephen, QC

s.38, varied: SSI 2015/378 Art.4

60. Prevention of Oil Pollution Act 1971

s.2, amended: SI 2015/664 Sch.4 para.6

s.3, amended: SI 2015/664 Sch.4 para.6

77. Immigration Act 1971

see *Amirteymour (EEA Appeals: Human Rights: United States)* [2015] UKUT 466 (IAC), [2015] Imm. A.R. 1365 (UT (IAC)), McCloskey J

s.3, see *JG (Jamaica) v Secretary of State for the Home Department* [2015] EWCA Civ 410, [2015] Imm. A.R. 1193 (CA

(Civ Div)), Jackson LJ; see *R. (on the application of Oboh) v Secretary of State for the Home Department* [2015] EWCA Civ 514, [2015] Imm. A.R. 1216 (CA (Civ Div)), Richards LJ
s.3, enabling: SI 2015/863
s.3A, enabling: SI 2015/434
s.3B, enabling: SI 2015/434
s.4, enabling: SI 2015/863
s.5, see *R. (on the application of Byczek) v Secretary of State for the Home Department* [2014] EWHC 4298 (Admin), [2015] 2 C.M.L.R. 7 (QBD (Admin)), Jay J
s.8, enabling: SI 2015/1866
s.8B, enabling: SI 2015/388, SI 2015/1994
s.24A, see *R. v Ali (Nazakat)* [2015] EWCA Crim 43, [2015] 1 Cr. App. R. 32 (CA (Crim Div)), Rafferty LJ
s.25, see *R. v Ali (Nazakat)* [2015] EWCA Crim 43, [2015] 1 Cr. App. R. 32 (CA (Crim Div)), Rafferty LJ
s.25C, amended: 2015 c.30 Sch.5 para.2
s.27, substituted: 2015 c.6 Sch.5 para.2
s.32, enabling: SI 2015/863
Sch.2 Part I para.27, amended: 2015 c.6 Sch.5 para.1
Sch.2 Part I para.27, enabling: SI 2015/859
Sch.2 Part I para.27B, amended: 2015 c.6 Sch.5 para.1
Sch.2 Part I para.27B, enabling: SI 2015/859
Sch.2 Part I para.27BA, added: 2015 c.6 Sch.5 para.1
Sch.2 Part I para.27BB, enabling: SI 2015/961
Sch.2 Part I para.27C, repealed: 2015 c.6 Sch.5 para.1
Sch.2 Pt I para.16, see *R. (on the application of Mohammed) v Secretary of State for the Home Department* [2014] EWHC 4317 (Admin), [2015] 1 W.L.R. 3349 (QBD (Admin)), Stephen Morris QC
Sch.2 para.21, see *R. (on the application of B) v Secretary of State for the Home Department* [2015] EWCA Civ 445, [2015] 3 W.L.R. 1031 (CA (Civ Div)), Lord Dyson MR

Sch.2 para.22, see *R. (on the application of B) v Secretary of State for the Home Department* [2015] EWCA Civ 445, [2015] 3 W.L.R. 1031 (CA (Civ Div)), Lord Dyson MR
Sch.2 para.29, see *R. (on the application of B) v Secretary of State for the Home Department* [2015] EWCA Civ 445, [2015] 3 W.L.R. 1031 (CA (Civ Div)), Lord Dyson MR
Sch.3, see *R. (on the application of Byczek) v Secretary of State for the Home Department* [2014] EWHC 4298 (Admin), [2015] 2 C.M.L.R. 7 (QBD (Admin)), Jay J; see *R. (on the application of Francis) v Secretary of State for the Home Department* [2014] EWCA Civ 718, [2015] 1 W.L.R. 567 (CA (Civ Div)), Moore-Bick LJ
Sch.3 para.2, see *R. (on the application of B) v Secretary of State for the Home Department* [2015] EWCA Civ 445, [2015] 3 W.L.R. 1031 (CA (Civ Div)), Lord Dyson MR; see *R. (on the application of Francis) v Secretary of State for the Home Department* [2014] EWCA Civ 718, [2015] 1 W.L.R. 567 (CA (Civ Div)), Moore-Bick LJ
Sch.3 para.5, see *R. (on the application of Byczek) v Secretary of State for the Home Department* [2014] EWHC 4298 (Admin), [2015] 2 C.M.L.R. 7 (QBD (Admin)), Jay J

1972

11. Superannuation Act 1972
s.1, enabling: SI 2015/919
s.7, enabling: SSI 2015/448
s.9, enabling: SI 2015/594, SSI 2015/98
s.10, enabling: SSI 2015/95, SSI 2015/96
s.12, enabling: SI 2015/594, SSI 2015/96, SSI 2015/98, SSI 2015/140, SSI 2015/173, SSI 2015/448
s.16, enabling: SSI 2015/140, SSI 2015/173
s.24, enabling: SSI 2015/96
Sch.1, amended: SI 2015/919 Art.2, Art.3, Art.4, Art.5

Sch.3, enabling: SI 2015/594, SSI
2015/95, SSI 2015/96, SSI 2015/448

30. Civil Evidence Act 1972

s.3, see *AB (A Child) (Temporary Leave
to Remove from Jurisdiction: Expert
Evidence), Re* [2014] EWHC 2758
(Fam), [2015] 1 F.C.R. 164 (Fam Div),
Judge Clifford Bellamy

35. Defective Premises Act 1972

s.1, see *Rendlesham Estates Plc v Barr
Ltd* [2014] EWHC 3968 (TCC), [2015] 1
W.L.R. 3663 (QBD (TCC)), Edwards-
Stuart J

41. Finance Act 1972

Sch.5, see *Revenue and Customs
Commissioners v IFX Investment Co Ltd*
[2015] S.T.C. 294 (UT (Tax)), Norris J

**59. Administration of Justice (Scotland) Act
1972**

s.1, see *Clark v TripAdvisor LLC* 2015
S.C. 368 (IH (Ex Div)), Lady Paton; see
Kirkham v Sneddon Morrison 2015
S.L.T. (Sh Ct) 184 (Sh Ct (Lothian)
(Edinburgh)), Sheriff Principal M M
Stephen, QC; see *Martin & Co (UK) Ltd
v Stenhouse* [2015] CSIH 86 (IH (Ex
Div)), Lady Paton
s.1, amended: SSI 2015/150 Sch.1 para.3

61. Land Charges Act 1972

s.1, repealed: 2015 c.20 Sch.6 para.2
s.7, repealed: 2015 c.20 Sch.6 para.2
s.17, amended: 2015 c.20 Sch.6 para.2

**62. Agriculture (Miscellaneous Provisions)
Act 1972**

s.20, enabling: SSI 2015/10

63. Industry Act 1972

Sch.3 para.1, repealed: 2015 c.20 Sch.23
para.7

65. National Debt Act 1972

s.3, enabling: SI 2015/624
s.11, enabling: SI 2015/624

66. Poisons Act 1972

s.1, repealed: 2015 c.20 Sch.21 para.1
s.2, substituted: 2015 c.20 Sch.21 para.3
s.3, substituted: 2015 c.20 Sch.21 para.4
s.3A, enabling: SI 2015/966
s.4, repealed: 2015 c.20 Sch.21 para.5
s.4A, added: 2015 c.20 Sch.21 para.6
s.4A, enabling: SI 2015/966
s.5, repealed: 2015 c.20 Sch.21 para.7
s.7, substituted: 2015 c.20 Sch.21 para.8

s.7, enabling: SI 2015/966
s.7A, added: 2015 c.20 Sch.21 para.9
s.8, substituted: 2015 c.20 Sch.21 para.10
s.9, amended: 2015 c.20 Sch.21 para.11
s.9, repealed: 2015 c.20 Sch.21 para.11
s.9A, added: 2015 c.20 Sch.21 para.12
s.9B, added: 2015 c.20 Sch.21 para.13
s.9B, enabling: SI 2015/966
s.10, substituted: 2015 c.20 Sch.21
para.14
s.10, enabling: SI 2015/966
s.11, amended: 2015 c.20 Sch.21 para.15
s.11, repealed: 2015 c.20 Sch.21 para.15
Sch.1, repealed: 2015 c.20 Sch.21 para.1
Sch.1A, added: 2015 c.20 Sch.21 para.16

68. European Communities Act 1972

s.1, amended: 2015 c.32 s.1
s.1, enabling: SI 2015/843, SI 2015/844,
SI 2015/847
s.2, see *AB v JJB (EU Maintenance
Regulation: Modification Application
Procedure)* [2015] EWHC 192 (Fam),
[2015] 2 F.L.R. 1143 (Fam Div), Sir
Peter Singer; see *AI v Advocate General
for Scotland* [2015] CSOH 95, 2015
S.L.T. 507 (OH), Lady Rae; see *R. (on
the application of Byczek) v Secretary of
State for the Home Department* [2014]
EWHC 4298 (Admin), [2015] 2
C.M.L.R. 7 (QBD (Admin)), Jay J; see
United States v Nolan [2015] UKSC 63,
[2015] 3 W.L.R. 1105 (SC), Lord
Neuberger PSC
s.2, enabling: SI 2015/11, SI 2015/16, SI
2015/19, SI 2015/21, SI 2015/63, SI
2015/81, SI 2015/88, SI 2015/97, SI
2015/98, SI 2015/102, SI 2015/139, SI
2015/168, SI 2015/180, SI 2015/191, SI
2015/209, SI 2015/219, SI 2015/310, SI
2015/323, SI 2015/347, SI 2015/348, SI
2015/349, SI 2015/350, SI 2015/355, SI
2015/356, SI 2015/363, SI 2015/385, SI
2015/386, SI 2015/398, SI 2015/399, SI
2015/412, SI 2015/419, SI 2015/422, SI
2015/430, SI 2015/446, SI 2015/469, SI
2015/483, SI 2015/486, SI 2015/542, SI
2015/575, SI 2015/609, SI 2015/627, SI
2015/639, SI 2015/660, SI 2015/663, SI
2015/668, SI 2015/719, SI 2015/782, SI
2015/786, SI 2015/787, SI 2015/810, SI
2015/814, SI 2015/821, SI 2015/829, SI

2015/852, SI 2015/855, SI 2015/860, SI
2015/862, SI 2015/903, SI 2015/910, SI
2015/912, SI 2015/979, SI 2015/980, SI
2015/1252, SI 2015/1325, SI 2015/1336,
SI 2015/1350, SI 2015/1360, SI
2015/1361, SI 2015/1391, SI 2015/1392,
SI 2015/1393, SI 2015/1394, SI
2015/1415, SI 2015/1417, SI 2015/1456,
SI 2015/1489, SI 2015/1493, SI
2015/1503, SI 2015/1504, SI 2015/1519,
SI 2015/1530, SI 2015/1546, SI
2015/1553, SI 2015/1557, SI 2015/1586,
SI 2015/1597, SI 2015/1623, SI
2015/1625, SI 2015/1629, SI 2015/1640,
SI 2015/1644, SI 2015/1658, SI
2015/1669, SI 2015/1681, SI 2015/1686,
SI 2015/1691, SI 2015/1695, SI
2015/1711, SI 2015/1731, SI 2015/1740,
SI 2015/1755, SI 2015/1768, SI
2015/1770, SI 2015/1782, SI 2015/1798,
SI 2015/1811, SI 2015/1849, SI
2015/1850, SI 2015/1864, SI 2015/1882,
SI 2015/1896, SI 2015/1911, SI
2015/1926, SI 2015/1928, SI 2015/1933,
SI 2015/1935, SI 2015/1937, SI
2015/1947, SI 2015/1968, SI 2015/1972,
SI 2015/1973, SI 2015/1980, SI
2015/1997, SI 2015/2004, SI 2015/2020,
SI 2015/2024, SI 2015/2038, SI
2015/2050, SI 2015/2059, SI 2015/2072,
SI 2015/2073, SSI 2015/1, SSI 2015/58,
SSI 2015/91, SSI 2015/103, SSI
2015/105, SSI 2015/107, SSI 2015/161,
SSI 2015/167, SSI 2015/181, SSI
2015/185, SSI 2015/188, SSI 2015/192,
SSI 2015/194, SSI 2015/211, SSI
2015/214, SSI 2015/215, SSI 2015/226,
SSI 2015/237, SSI 2015/249, SSI
2015/318, SSI 2015/320, SSI 2015/346,
SSI 2015/359, SSI 2015/376, SSI
2015/384, SSI 2015/386, SSI 2015/393,
SSI 2015/395, SSI 2015/401, SSI
2015/410, SSI 2015/438, SSI 2015/444,
SSI 2015/446
s.3, see *Caldwell v easyJet Airline Co Ltd*
2015 S.L.T. (Sh Ct) 223 (Sh Ct (Lothian)
(Edinburgh)), Sheriff T Welsh, QC; see
Dawson v Thomson Airways Ltd [2014]
EWCA Civ 845, [2015] 1 W.L.R. 883
(CA (Civ Div)), Moore-Bick LJ

Sch.2, see *AB v JJB (EU Maintenance
Regulation: Modification Application
Procedure)* [2015] EWHC 192 (Fam),
[2015] 2 F.L.R. 1143 (Fam Div), Sir
Peter Singer
Sch.2 para.1A, enabling: SI 2015/21, SI
2015/168, SI 2015/191, SI 2015/310, SI
2015/610, SI 2015/627, SI 2015/675, SI
2015/787, SI 2015/910, SI 2015/1252, SI
2015/1360, SI 2015/1361, SI 2015/1417,
SI 2015/1519, SI 2015/1553, SI
2015/1597, SI 2015/1686, SI 2015/1723,
SI 2015/1740, SI 2015/1782, SI
2015/1827, SI 2015/1867, SI 2015/1997,
SI 2015/2059, SSI 2015/26, SSI 2015/48,
SSI 2015/58, SSI 2015/103, SSI
2015/105, SSI 2015/167, SSI 2015/181,
SSI 2015/185, SSI 2015/188, SSI
2015/189, SSI 2015/192, SSI 2015/194,
SSI 2015/211, SSI 2015/214, SSI
2015/320, SSI 2015/359, SSI 2015/384,
SSI 2015/401, SSI 2015/410, SSI
2015/446

70. Local Government Act 1972
s.70, amended: 2015 c.20 Sch.13 para.6
s.80, amended: 2015 c.20 Sch.13 para.6
s.85, amended: 2015 c.20 Sch.13 para.6
s.86, amended: 2015 c.20 Sch.13 para.6
s.92, repealed: 2015 c.20 Sch.13 para.6
s.100A, see *Laporte v Commissioner of
Police of the Metropolis* [2014] EWHC
3574 (QB), [2015] 3 All E.R. 438
(QBD), Turner J
s.100D, see *R. (on the application of
Joicey) v Northumberland CC* [2014]
EWHC 3657 (Admin), [2015] P.T.S.R.
622 (QBD (Admin)), Cranston J; see *R.
(on the application of Perry) v Hackney
LBC* [2014] EWHC 3499 (Admin),
[2015] J.P.L. 454 (QBD (Admin)),
Patterson J
s.100F, see *R. (on the application of
Perry) v Hackney LBC* [2014] EWHC
3499 (Admin), [2015] J.P.L. 454 (QBD
(Admin)), Patterson J
s.100J, amended: 2015 c.20 Sch.13
para.6
s.100J, repealed: 2015 c.20 Sch.13 para.6
s.101, see *R. (on the application of
Couves) v Gravesham BC* [2015] EWHC
504 (Admin), [2015] J.P.L. 1193 (QBD

(Admin)), Ouseley J; see *R. (on the application of Pemberton International Ltd) v Lambeth LBC* [2014] EWHC 1998 (Admin), [2015] J.P.L. 42 (QBD (Admin)), Lewis J
s.101, amended: 2015 c.20 Sch.13 para.6
s.122, see *R. (on the application of Maries) v Merton LBC* [2014] EWHC 2689 (Admin), [2015] P.T.S.R. 295 (QBD (Admin)), King J
s.138A, added: 2015 c.27 s.1
s.138C, added: 2015 c.27 s.2
s.146A, amended: 2015 c.20 Sch.13 para.6
s.175, amended: 2015 c.20 Sch.13 para.6
s.176, amended: 2015 c.20 Sch.13 para.6
s.223, amended: 2015 c.20 Sch.13 para.6
s.224, amended: 2015 c.20 Sch.13 para.6
s.225, amended: 2015 c.20 Sch.13 para.6
s.228, repealed: 2015 c.20 Sch.13 para.6
s.229, amended: 2015 c.20 Sch.13 para.6
s.230, amended: 2015 c.20 Sch.13 para.6
s.231, amended: 2015 c.20 Sch.13 para.6
s.232, amended: 2015 c.20 Sch.13 para.6
s.233, amended: 2015 c.20 Sch.13 para.6
s.234, amended: 2015 c.20 Sch.13 para.6
s.239, amended: 2015 c.20 Sch.13 para.6
s.241, enabling: SI 2015/770
s.265A, amended: 2015 c.27 s.2
s.266, enabling: SI 2015/770
s.270, amended: 2015 c.20 Sch.13 para.6
Sch.12 Part I para.4, amended: SI 2015/5 Art.2
Sch.12 Part II para.10, amended: SI 2015/5 Art.2

1973

13. Supply of Goods (Implied Terms) Act 1973
amended: 2015 c.15 Sch.1 para.2
s.8, amended: 2015 c.15 Sch.1 para.2
s.9, amended: 2015 c.15 Sch.1 para.2
s.10, amended: 2015 c.15 Sch.1 para.2
s.10, repealed: 2015 c.15 Sch.1 para.3
s.11, amended: 2015 c.15 Sch.1 para.2
s.11A, amended: 2015 c.15 Sch.1 para.2, Sch.1 para.4
s.11A, repealed: 2015 c.15 Sch.1 para.4
s.12A, amended: 2015 c.15 Sch.1 para.2

s.12A, repealed: 2015 c.15 Sch.1 para.5
s.14, amended: 2015 c.15 Sch.1 para.2
s.14, repealed: 2015 c.15 Sch.1 para.6
s.15, amended: 2015 c.15 Sch.1 para.2, Sch.1 para.7
s.15, repealed: 2015 c.15 Sch.1 para.7
s.18, amended: 2015 c.15 Sch.1 para.2

15. Administration of Justice Act 1973
s.9, amended: SI 2015/700 Sch.1 para.7

18. Matrimonial Causes Act 1973
s.23, see *Mann v Mann* [2014] EWCA Civ 1674, [2015] 2 F.L.R. 1116 (CA (Civ Div)), Patten LJ
s.24, see *AB v CB (Financial Remedies: Variation of Trust)* [2015] EWCA Civ 447, [2015] C.P. Rep. 34 (CA (Civ Div)), Jackson LJ; see *Birch v Birch* [2015] EWCA Civ 833, [2015] 3 F.C.R. 249 (CA (Civ Div)), Gross LJ; see *Joy v Joy-Morancho* [2015] EWHC 2507 (Fam), [2015] 5 Costs L.O. 629 (Fam Div), Sir Peter Singer; see *Quan v Bray* [2014] EWHC 3340 (Fam), [2015] 2 F.L.R. 546 (Fam Div), Coleridge J
s.24A, see *Birch v Birch* [2015] EWCA Civ 833, [2015] 3 F.C.R. 249 (CA (Civ Div)), Gross LJ
s.25, see *Quan v Bray* [2014] EWHC 3340 (Fam), [2015] 2 F.L.R. 546 (Fam Div), Coleridge J; see *Thiry v Thiry* [2014] EWHC 4046 (Fam), [2015] 2 F.L.R. 743 (Fam Div), Sir Peter Singer; see *Vince v Wyatt* [2015] UKSC 14, [2015] 1 W.L.R. 1228 (SC), Lady Hale DPSC; see *WA v Executors of the Estate of HA, Deceased* [2015] EWHC 2233 (Fam), [2015] W.T.L.R. 1471 (Fam Div), Moor J
s.31, see *Birch v Birch* [2015] EWCA Civ 833, [2015] 3 F.C.R. 249 (CA (Civ Div)), Gross LJ; see *Mann v Mann* [2014] EWCA Civ 1674, [2015] 2 F.L.R. 1116 (CA (Civ Div)), Patten LJ
s.37, see *Ahmed v Mustafa* [2014] EWCA Civ 277, [2015] 1 F.L.R. 139 (CA (Civ Div)), Moore-Bick LJ

26. Land Compensation Act 1973
Pt I., see *Dickinson v Network Rail Infrastructure Ltd* [2015] R.V.R. 19 (UT (Lands)), Sir Keith Lindblom P

s.29, see *Rapose v Wandsworth LBC*
[2015] UKUT 172 (LC), [2015] R.V.R.
388 (UT (Lands)), Martin Rodger QC
s.30, amended: SI 2015/1514 Reg.2, SI
2015/1878 Reg.2
s.30, enabling: SI 2015/1514, SI
2015/1878
s.33, see *R. (on the application of
Mahoney) v Secretary of State for
Communities and Local Government*
[2015] EWHC 589 (Admin), [2015]
R.V.R. 237 (QBD (Admin)), Lindblom J
s.33C, see *Rapose v Wandsworth LBC*
[2015] UKUT 172 (LC), [2015] R.V.R.
388 (UT (Lands)), Martin Rodger QC
s.37, see *Rapose v Wandsworth LBC*
[2015] UKUT 172 (LC), [2015] R.V.R.
388 (UT (Lands)), Martin Rodger QC
s.38, see *Rapose v Wandsworth LBC*
[2015] UKUT 172 (LC), [2015] R.V.R.
388 (UT (Lands)), Martin Rodger QC
s.38, amended: SI 2015/914 Sch.1
para.24
s.41, varied: SI 2015/781 Sch.2 para.2
s.44, varied: SI 2015/23 Sch.11 para.2, SI
2015/129 Sch.6 para.2, SI 2015/318
Sch.6 para.2, SI 2015/780 Sch.9 para.2
s.52, amended: 2015 c.7 Sch.5 para.33
s.58, varied: SI 2015/23 Sch.11 para.2, SI
2015/129 Sch.6 para.2, SI 2015/780
Sch.9 para.2, SI 2015/781 Sch.2 para.2

35. Employment Agencies Act 1973
s.13, repealed: 2015 c.20 Sch.13 para.6

43. Hallmarking Act 1973
s.9, amended: 2015 c.15 Sch.6 para.10
s.9, repealed: 2015 c.15 Sch.6 para.10

**45. Domicile and Matrimonial Proceedings
Act 1973**
s.5, see *Chai v Peng* [2014] EWHC 3518
(Fam), [2015] 2 F.L.R. 424 (Fam Div),
Bodey J; see *Tan v Choy* [2014] EWCA
Civ 251, [2015] 1 F.L.R. 492 (CA (Civ
Div)), Sir Brian Leveson PQBD
Sch.1 para.9, see *Tan v Choy* [2014]
EWCA Civ 251, [2015] 1 F.L.R. 492
(CA (Civ Div)), Sir Brian Leveson
PQBD

51. Finance Act 1973
s.56, enabling: SI 2015/639, SI 2015/777,
SI 2015/802, SI 2015/1431, SI
2015/1669, SI 2015/1996, SSI 2015/392

**52. Prescription and Limitation (Scotland)
Act 1973**
see *Highlands and Islands Airports Ltd v
Shetland Islands Council* [2015] CSIH
30, 2015 S.C. 588 (IH (1 Div)), The Lord
President (Gill)
s.6, see *Cumbernauld Housing
Partnership Ltd v Davies* [2015] CSIH
22, 2015 S.C. 532 (IH (Ex Div)), Lord
Brodie; see *Highlands and Islands
Airports Ltd v Shetland Islands Council*
[2015] CSIH 30, 2015 S.C. 588 (IH (1
Div)), The Lord President (Gill); see
*Perth and Kinross Council v Scottish
Water Ltd* [2015] CSOH 138, 2015
S.L.T. 788 (OH), Lord Stewart
s.9, see *Highlands and Islands Airports
Ltd v Shetland Islands Council* [2015]
CSIH 30, 2015 S.C. 588 (IH (1 Div)),
The Lord President (Gill)
s.10, see *Cumbernauld Housing
Partnership Ltd v Davies* [2015] CSIH
22, 2015 S.C. 532 (IH (Ex Div)), Lord
Brodie
s.14, amended: SI 2015/1392 Reg.3, SI
2015/1972 Reg.2
s.17, see *Mitchell v Advocate General for
Scotland* [2015] CSOH 2, 2015 S.L.T. 92
(OH), Lord Tyre
s.18, see *Mitchell v Advocate General for
Scotland* [2015] CSOH 2, 2015 S.L.T. 92
(OH), Lord Tyre
s.19A, see *A v N* [2015] CSIH 26, 2015
S.L.T. 289 (IH (Ex Div)), Lord Menzies;
see *Ferguson v J & A Lawson (Joiners)
Ltd* 2015 S.C. 243 (IH (Ex Div)), Lady
Paton
s.22, see *Mitchell v Advocate General for
Scotland* [2015] CSOH 2, 2015 S.L.T. 92
(OH), Lord Tyre
Sch.1, see *Cumbernauld Housing
Partnership Ltd v Davies* [2015] CSIH
22, 2015 S.C. 532 (IH (Ex Div)), Lord
Brodie
Sch.1 para.2, see *Cumbernauld Housing
Partnership Ltd v Davies* [2015] CSIH
22, 2015 S.C. 532 (IH (Ex Div)), Lord
Brodie

56. Land Compensation (Scotland) Act 1973

s.5, see *Steel v Scottish Ministers* 2015
S.L.T. (Lands Tr) 81 (Lands Tr (Scot)),
Lord McGhie
s.25, see *Steel v Scottish Ministers* 2015
S.L.T. (Lands Tr) 81 (Lands Tr (Scot)),
Lord McGhie
s.50, see *Steel v Scottish Ministers* 2015
S.L.T. (Lands Tr) 81 (Lands Tr (Scot)),
Lord McGhie

60. Breeding of Dogs Act 1973
s.1, amended: 2015 c.20 Sch.23 para.36
s.1, repealed: 2015 c.20 Sch.23 para.35 ,
Sch.23 para.36

63. Government Trading Funds Act 1973
s.1, enabling: SI 2015/41, SI 2015/473
s.2, enabling: SI 2015/41
s.2A, enabling: SI 2015/41
s.2AA, enabling: SI 2015/41
s.2C, enabling: SI 2015/41
s.6, enabling: SI 2015/41, SI 2015/473

65. Local Government (Scotland) Act 1973
s.56, amended: 2015 asp 6 s.86
s.73, amended: 2015 asp 6 Sch.4 para.5
s.99, amended: 2015 asp 6 Sch.4 para.5
s.102, amended: 2015 asp 6 Sch.4 para.5
s.103J, amended: SSI 2015/402 Sch.1
para.2
Sch.27 Part II para.16, repealed: 2015 asp
6 Sch.5
Sch.27 Part II para.54, repealed: 2015 asp
6 Sch.5
Sch.27 Part II para.58, repealed: 2015 asp
6 Sch.5

1974

3. Slaughterhouses Act 1974
s.16, amended: SI 2015/1782 Sch.6
para.2

7. Local Government Act 1974
Part IIA, added: 2015 c.22 s.1
s.25, repealed: 2015 c.20 Sch.13 para.6
s.26, see *R. (on the application of ER) v
Commissioner for Local Administration
in England (Local Government
Ombudsman)* [2014] EWCA Civ 1407,
[2015] E.L.R. 36 (CA (Civ Div)), Moore-
Bick LJ
s.26C, repealed: 2015 c.20 Sch.13 para.6
s.28, amended: 2015 c.22 s.2

s.34, see *R. (on the application of ER) v
Commissioner for Local Administration
in England (Local Government
Ombudsman)* [2014] EWCA Civ 1407,
[2015] E.L.R. 36 (CA (Civ Div)), Moore-
Bick LJ

23. Juries Act 1974
s.1, amended: 2015 c.2 s.68
s.3, amended: 2015 c.2 s.68
s.15A, added: 2015 c.2 s.69
s.20, substituted: 2015 c.2 s.71
s.20A, added: 2015 c.2 s.71
s.20B, added: 2015 c.2 s.72
s.20C, added: 2015 c.2 s.73
s.20D, added: 2015 c.2 s.74
s.22, amended: 2015 c.2 s.77
Sch.1 Part II para.6A, added: 2015 c.2
s.77

24. Prices Act 1974
Sch.1 para.3, repealed: 2015 c.15 Sch.6
para.11
Sch.1 para.7, repealed: 2015 c.15 Sch.6
para.11
Sch.1 para.9, repealed: 2015 c.15 Sch.6
para.11
Sch.1 para.14, amended: 2015 c.15 Sch.6
para.11
Sch.1 para.15, added: 2015 c.15 Sch.6
para.11

37. Health and Safety at Work etc Act 1974
s.1, amended: SI 2015/374 Art.2
s.3, amended: 2015 c.20 s.1
s.3, enabling: SI 2015/1583
s.5, repealed: SI 2015/374 Art.2
s.11, amended: 2015 c.20 s.1
s.15, amended: SI 2015/1682 Sch.1
para.4
s.15, enabling: SI 2015/21, SI 2015/51,
SI 2015/398, SI 2015/430, SI 2015/483,
SI 2015/1393, SI 2015/1917
s.18, amended: SI 2015/1682 Sch.1
para.4
s.28, amended: 2015 c.20 Sch.13 para.6
s.43, enabling: SI 2015/363, SI 2015/430,
SI 2015/483
s.43A, amended: SI 2015/1682 Sch.1
para.4
s.50, amended: SI 2015/1682 Sch.1
para.4
s.53, enabling: SI 2015/1583

s.80, enabling: SI 2015/21, SI 2015/51,
SI 2015/483
s.82, amended: 2015 c.20 s.1
s.82, enabling: SI 2015/21, SI 2015/51,
SI 2015/363, SI 2015/398, SI 2015/483,
SI 2015/1583
Sch.3 para.1, enabling: SI 2015/51, SI
2015/398, SI 2015/430, SI 2015/483
Sch.3 para.4, enabling: SI 2015/430
Sch.3 para.6, enabling: SI 2015/51
Sch.3 para.7, enabling: SI 2015/51
Sch.3 para.8, enabling: SI 2015/51, SI
2015/398
Sch.3 para.9, enabling: SI 2015/51, SI
2015/398
Sch.3 para.10, enabling: SI 2015/51
Sch.3 para.11, enabling: SI 2015/51
Sch.3 para.12, enabling: SI 2015/51
Sch.3 para.14, enabling: SI 2015/51, SI
2015/398
Sch.3 para.15, enabling: SI 2015/51, SI
2015/398, SI 2015/483, SI 2015/1917
Sch.3 para.16, enabling: SI 2015/51, SI
2015/398, SI 2015/483
Sch.3 para.18, enabling: SI 2015/51
Sch.3 para.20, enabling: SI 2015/51, SI
2015/483
Sch.3 para.21, enabling: SI 2015/51
Sch.3A para.1, amended: SI 2015/664
Sch.4 para.7
39. Consumer Credit Act 1974
see *Grace v Black Horse Ltd* [2014]
EWCA Civ 1413, [2015] 3 All E.R. 223
(CA (Civ Div)), Lord Dyson MR; see
NRAM Plc v McAdam [2014] EWHC
4174 (Comm), [2015] 2 All E.R. 340
(QBD (Comm)), Burton J; see *NRAM
Plc v McAdam* [2015] EWCA Civ 751,
[2015] E.C.C. 30 (CA (Civ Div)),
Longmore LJ; see *Swift Advances Plc v
Okokenu* [2015] C.T.L.C. 302 (CC
(Central London)), Judge Hand QC; see
Welcome Financial Service Ltd, Re
[2015] EWHC 815 (Ch), [2015] 2 All
E.R. (Comm) 992 (Ch D (Companies
Ct)), Rose J; see *Wood v Capital
Bridging Finance Ltd* [2015] EWCA Civ
451, [2015] E.C.C. 17 (CA (Civ Div)),
Patten LJ

s.8, see *NRAM Plc v McAdam* [2014]
EWHC 4174 (Comm), [2015] 2 All E.R.
340 (QBD (Comm)), Burton J
s.8, amended: SI 2015/910 Sch.1 para.2
s.12, see *Scotland v British Credit Trust
Ltd* [2014] EWCA Civ 790, [2015] 1 All
E.R. 708 (CA (Civ Div)), Moore-Bick LJ
s.16B, see *Payne, Re* [2015] EWHC 968
(Ch), [2015] B.P.I.R. 933 (Ch D), John
Male QC; see *Wood v Capital Bridging
Finance Ltd* [2015] EWCA Civ 451,
[2015] E.C.C. 17 (CA (Civ Div)), Patten
LJ
s.55C, amended: SI 2015/910 Sch.1
para.2
s.56, see *Scotland v British Credit Trust
Ltd* [2014] EWCA Civ 790, [2015] 1 All
E.R. 708 (CA (Civ Div)), Moore-Bick LJ
s.60, amended: SI 2015/910 Sch.1 para.2
s.61A, amended: SI 2015/910 Sch.1
para.2
s.66A, amended: SI 2015/910 Sch.1
para.2
s.74, see *Payne, Re* [2015] EWHC 968
(Ch), [2015] B.P.I.R. 933 (Ch D), John
Male QC
s.75, see *Scotland v British Credit Trust
Ltd* [2014] EWCA Civ 790, [2015] 1 All
E.R. 708 (CA (Civ Div)), Moore-Bick LJ
s.75A, amended: SI 2015/910 Sch.1
para.2
s.77, see *Welcome Financial Service Ltd,
Re* [2015] EWHC 815 (Ch), [2015] 2 All
E.R. (Comm) 992 (Ch D (Companies
Ct)), Rose J
s.77A, see *NRAM Plc v McAdam* [2014]
EWHC 4174 (Comm), [2015] 2 All E.R.
340 (QBD (Comm)), Burton J; see
NRAM Plc v McAdam [2015] EWCA Civ
751, [2015] E.C.C. 30 (CA (Civ Div)),
Longmore LJ
s.77B, amended: SI 2015/910 Sch.1
para.2
s.78, see *Welcome Financial Service Ltd,
Re* [2015] EWHC 815 (Ch), [2015] 2 All
E.R. (Comm) 992 (Ch D (Companies
Ct)), Rose J
s.106, see *Welcome Financial Service
Ltd, Re* [2015] EWHC 815 (Ch), [2015] 2
All E.R. (Comm) 992 (Ch D (Companies
Ct)), Rose J

s.127, see *NRAM Plc v McAdam* [2015] EWCA Civ 751, [2015] E.C.C. 30 (CA (Civ Div)), Longmore LJ

s.129, see *NRAM Plc v McAdam* [2015] EWCA Civ 751, [2015] E.C.C. 30 (CA (Civ Div)), Longmore LJ; see *Welcome Financial Service Ltd, Re* [2015] EWHC 815 (Ch), [2015] 2 All E.R. (Comm) 992 (Ch D (Companies Ct)), Rose J

s.135, see *NRAM Plc v McAdam* [2015] EWCA Civ 751, [2015] E.C.C. 30 (CA (Civ Div)), Longmore LJ

s.139, see *Welcome Financial Service Ltd, Re* [2015] EWHC 815 (Ch), [2015] 2 All E.R. (Comm) 992 (Ch D (Companies Ct)), Rose J

s.140A, see *Axton v GE Money Mortgages Ltd* [2015] EWHC 1343 (QB), [2015] E.C.C. 29 (QBD), Swift J; see *Scotland v British Credit Trust Ltd* [2014] EWCA Civ 790, [2015] 1 All E.R. 708 (CA (Civ Div)), Moore-Bick LJ; see *Swift Advances Plc v Okokenu* [2015] C.T.L.C. 302 (CC (Central London)), Judge Hand QC; see *Welcome Financial Service Ltd, Re* [2015] EWHC 815 (Ch), [2015] 2 All E.R. (Comm) 992 (Ch D (Companies Ct)), Rose J

s.140B, see *Axton v GE Money Mortgages Ltd* [2015] EWHC 1343 (QB), [2015] E.C.C. 29 (QBD), Swift J; see *Scotland v British Credit Trust Ltd* [2014] EWCA Civ 790, [2015] 1 All E.R. 708 (CA (Civ Div)), Moore-Bick LJ; see *Welcome Financial Service Ltd, Re* [2015] EWHC 815 (Ch), [2015] 2 All E.R. (Comm) 992 (Ch D (Companies Ct)), Rose J

s.142, see *Welcome Financial Service Ltd, Re* [2015] EWHC 815 (Ch), [2015] 2 All E.R. (Comm) 992 (Ch D (Companies Ct)), Rose J

s.161, amended: 2015 c.15 Sch.6 para.13
s.162, repealed: 2015 c.15 Sch.6 para.14
s.163, repealed: 2015 c.15 Sch.6 para.15
s.164, repealed: 2015 c.15 Sch.6 para.16
s.165, repealed: 2015 c.15 Sch.6 para.17
s.189, see *Payne, Re* [2015] EWHC 968 (Ch), [2015] B.P.I.R. 933 (Ch D), John Male QC

s.189, amended: SI 2015/910 Sch.1 para.2
Sch.1, amended: 2015 c.15 Sch.6 para.18

40. Control of Pollution Act 1974
s.57, repealed: 2015 c.20 Sch.13 para.10
s.63, repealed: 2015 c.20 Sch.13 para.11
s.68, amended: 2015 c.20 Sch.22 para.4
s.69, repealed: 2015 c.20 Sch.13 para.12
s.71, enabling: SI 2015/227
s.73, amended: 2015 c.20 Sch.13 para.13
s.104, amended: 2015 c.20 Sch.13 para.15
Sch.1, repealed: 2015 c.20 Sch.13 para.14

47. Solicitors Act 1974
see *Assaubayev v Michael Wilson and Partners Ltd* [2014] EWCA Civ 1491, [2015] C.P. Rep. 10 (CA (Civ Div)), Aikens LJ
s.1B, repealed: SI 2015/401 Sch.1 para.2
s.9, repealed: SI 2015/401 Sch.1 para.3
s.10, amended: SI 2015/401 Sch.1 para.4
s.10A, repealed: SI 2015/401 Sch.1 para.5
s.13, repealed: SI 2015/401 Sch.1 para.6
s.13A, repealed: SI 2015/401 Sch.1 para.8
s.13B, amended: SI 2015/401 Sch.1 para.9
s.13ZA, repealed: SI 2015/401 Sch.1 para.7
s.17A, repealed: SI 2015/401 Sch.1 para.10
s.20, see *Assaubayev v Michael Wilson and Partners Ltd* [2014] EWCA Civ 1491, [2015] C.P. Rep. 10 (CA (Civ Div)), Aikens LJ
s.24, see *Assaubayev v Michael Wilson and Partners Ltd* [2014] EWCA Civ 1491, [2015] C.P. Rep. 10 (CA (Civ Div)), Aikens LJ
s.28, amended: SI 2015/401 Sch.1 para.11
s.28, repealed: SI 2015/401 Sch.1 para.11
s.31, amended: SI 2015/401 Sch.1 para.12
s.41, see *Law Society of England and Wales v Shah* [2015] EWHC 2711 (Ch), [2015] 1 W.L.R. 2094 (Ch D), Tim Kerr QC
s.47, repealed: SI 2015/401 Sch.1 para.13

s.49, see *Brett v Solicitors Regulation Authority* [2014] EWHC 2974 (Admin), [2015] P.N.L.R. 2 (DC), Lord Thomas LCJ

s.50, see *Law Society of England and Wales v Shah* [2015] EWHC 2711 (Ch), [2015] 1 W.L.R. 2094 (Ch D), Tim Kerr QC

s.70, see *Edwin Coe LLP v Aidiniantz* [2014] EWHC 3994 (QB), [2015] 1 Costs L.O. 129 (QBD), Judge Richard Seymour QC; see *Eurasian Natural Resources Corp Ltd v Dechert LLP* [2014] EWHC 3389 (Ch), [2015] 1 W.L.R. 4621 (Ch D), Roth J; see *Garcha v Charity Commission for England and Wales* [2014] EWHC 2754 (Ch), [2015] W.T.L.R. 453 (Ch D), Norris J; see *Vlamaki v Sookias & Sookias (A Firm)* [2015] EWHC 3334 (QB), [2015] 6 Costs L.O. 827 (QBD), Walker J; see *Wilsons Solicitors LLP v Bentine* [2015] EWCA Civ 1168, [2015] 6 Costs L.O. 779 (CA (Civ Div)), Arden LJ

s.87, amended: SI 2015/401 Sch.1 para.14

Sch.1 Pt II, see *Law Society (Solicitors Regulation Authority), Re* [2015] EWHC 166 (Ch), [2015] 1 W.L.R. 4064 (Ch D), Iain Purvis QC; see *Williams v Law Society of England and Wales* [2015] EWHC 2302 (Ch), [2015] 1 W.L.R. 4982 (Ch D), Sir William Blackburne

Sch.1 Part I para.1, repealed: SI 2015/401 Sch.1 para.15

Sch.1 Pt II para.6, see *Law Society v Elsdon* [2015] EWHC 1326 (Ch), [2015] W.T.L.R. 1601 (Ch D), Newey J; see *Williams v Law Society of England and Wales* [2015] EWHC 2302 (Ch), [2015] 1 W.L.R. 4982 (Ch D), Sir William Blackburne

Sch.1 Pt II para.9, see *Law Society (Solicitors Regulation Authority), Re* [2015] EWHC 166 (Ch), [2015] 1 W.L.R. 4064 (Ch D), Iain Purvis QC

Sch.1 para.16, see *Law Society of England and Wales v Shah* [2015] EWHC 2711 (Ch), [2015] 1 W.L.R. 2094 (Ch D), Tim Kerr QC

53. Rehabilitation of Offenders Act 1974

see *R. (on the application of T) v Chief Constable of Greater Manchester* [2015] A.C. 49 (SC), Lord Neuberger JSC

s.1, amended: 2015 c.2 Sch.12 para.1

s.4, enabling: SI 2015/317, SSI 2015/329

s.7, enabling: SI 2015/317, SSI 2015/329

s.10, enabling: SI 2015/317, SSI 2015/329

Sch.2 para.4, enabling: SI 2015/317

Sch.2 para.6, enabling: SI 2015/317

Sch.3 para.9, added: 2015 c.2 s.19

1975

22. Oil Taxation Act 1975

s.1, amended: 2015 c.11 s.52

Sch.2 para.17, amended: 2015 c.11 s.52

23. Reservoirs Act 1975

see *R. (on the application of Heath & Hampstead Society) v City of London* [2014] EWHC 3868 (Admin), [2015] P.T.S.R. 987 (QBD), Lang J

s.4, see *R. (on the application of Heath & Hampstead Society) v City of London* [2014] EWHC 3868 (Admin), [2015] P.T.S.R. 987 (QBD), Lang J

s.10, see *R. (on the application of Heath & Hampstead Society) v City of London* [2014] EWHC 3868 (Admin), [2015] P.T.S.R. 987 (QBD), Lang J

s.19, see *R. (on the application of Heath & Hampstead Society) v City of London* [2014] EWHC 3868 (Admin), [2015] P.T.S.R. 987 (QBD), Lang J

24. House of Commons Disqualification Act 1975

Sch.1 Part I, amended: SI 2015/700 Sch.1 para.8

Sch.1 Part II, amended: SI 2015/1682 Sch.1 para.4

Sch.1 Part III, amended: 2015 c.19 Sch.1 para.4, 2015 c.26 Sch.1 para.24, 2015 c.30 s.40

25. Northern Ireland Assembly Disqualification Act 1975

Sch.1 Part I, amended: SI 2015/700 Sch.1 para.9

Sch.1 Part III, amended: 2015 c.20 Sch.6 para.22, 2015 c.30 s.40

26. Ministers of the Crown Act 1975

s.1, enabling: SI 2015/1376, SI
2015/1526, SI 2015/1897, SI 2015/2013
s.2, enabling: SI 2015/1897

30. Local Government (Scotland) Act 1975
s.7B, enabling: SSI 2015/47
s.37, enabling: SSI 2015/47

35. Farriers (Registration) Act 1975
s.7, amended: SI 2015/2072 Reg.2
s.9, amended: SI 2015/2072 Reg.2
s.15, amended: SI 2015/2072 Reg.2
Sch.1 Part I para.1, amended: 2015 c.20
Sch.13 para.3

**47. Litigants in Person (Costs and Expenses)
Act 1975**
s.1, enabling: SSI 2015/398

**51. Salmon and Freshwater Fisheries Act
1975**
s.30, amended: SI 2015/10 Reg.18
s.39, amended: SI 2015/10 Reg.18
Sch.2 para.14A, see *R. (on the
application of Mott) v Environment
Agency* [2015] EWHC 314 (Admin),
[2015] Env. L.R. 27 (QBD (Admin)),
Judge David Cooke
Sch.4 Part I para.1, amended: SI
2015/664 Sch.4 para.8

52. Safety of Sports Grounds Act 1975
s.1, enabling: SI 2015/661, SI 2015/1374,
SI 2015/1556, SI 2015/1807
s.18, enabling: SI 2015/661, SI
2015/1556, SI 2015/1807

60. Social Security Pensions Act 1975
s.59, enabling: SI 2015/671

**63. Inheritance (Provision for Family and
Dependants) Act 1975**
see *Ilott v Mitson* [2015] EWCA Civ 797,
[2015] 2 F.L.R. 1409 (CA (Civ Div)),
Arden LJ; see *Kaur v Dhaliwal* [2014]
EWHC 1991 (Ch), [2015] 2 F.C.R. 40
(Ch D), Barling J; see *Lim v Walia*
[2014] EWCA Civ 1076, [2015] Ch. 375
(CA (Civ Div)), Arden LJ; see *Seals v
Williams* [2015] EWHC 1829 (Ch),
[2015] 4 Costs L.O. 423 (Ch D), Norris J;
see *Williams v Seals* [2014] EWHC 3708
(Ch), [2015] W.T.L.R. 339 (Ch D),
David Richards J
s.1, see *Williams v Seals* [2014] EWHC
3708 (Ch), [2015] W.T.L.R. 339 (Ch D),
David Richards J

s.2, see *Dellal v Dellal* [2015] EWHC
907 (Fam), [2015] W.T.L.R. 1137 (Fam
Div), Mostyn J; see *Wright v Waters*
[2014] EWHC 3614 (Ch), [2015]
W.T.L.R. 353 (Ch D), Judge Behrens
s.3, see *Ilott v Mitson* [2015] EWCA Civ
797, [2015] 2 F.L.R. 1409 (CA (Civ
Div)), Arden LJ; see *Wright v Waters*
[2014] EWHC 3614 (Ch), [2015]
W.T.L.R. 353 (Ch D), Judge Behrens
s.9, see *Lim v Walia* [2014] EWCA Civ
1076, [2015] Ch. 375 (CA (Civ Div)),
Arden LJ
s.10, see *Dellal v Dellal* [2015] EWHC
907 (Fam), [2015] W.T.L.R. 1137 (Fam
Div), Mostyn J

65. Sex Discrimination Act 1975
s.20A, see *Deer v University of Oxford*
[2015] EWCA Civ 52, [2015] I.C.R.
1213 (CA (Civ Div)), Sullivan LJ

76. Local Land Charges Act 1975
amended: 2015 c.7 Sch.5 para.2
s.3, substituted: 2015 c.7 Sch.5 para.3
s.4, repealed: 2015 c.7 Sch.5 para.4
s.5, amended: 2015 c.7 Sch.5 para.5
s.5, repealed: 2015 c.7 Sch.5 para.5
s.6, amended: 2015 c.7 Sch.5 para.6
s.8, amended: 2015 c.7 Sch.5 para.7
s.9, amended: 2015 c.7 Sch.5 para.8
s.9, repealed: 2015 c.7 Sch.5 para.8
s.10, amended: 2015 c.7 Sch.5 para.9
s.10, repealed: 2015 c.7 Sch.5 para.9
s.12, amended: 2015 c.7 Sch.5 para.10
s.13, amended: 2015 c.7 Sch.5 para.11
s.13A, repealed: 2015 c.7 Sch.5 para.12
s.14, amended: 2015 c.7 Sch.5 para.13
s.15, amended: 2015 c.7 Sch.5 para.14
s.16, amended: 2015 c.7 Sch.5 para.15
s.19, amended: 2015 c.7 Sch.5 para.16
Sch.1, amended: 2015 c.7 Sch.5 para.31

1976

30. Fatal Accidents Act 1976
see *Bianco v Bennett* [2015] EWHC 626
(QB), [2015] I.L.Pr. 24 (QBD), Warby J;
see *Brownlie v Four Seasons Holdings
Inc* [2015] EWCA Civ 665, [2015] C.P.
Rep. 40 (CA (Civ Div)), Arden LJ; see
Docherty v Secretary of State for

Business Innovation and Skills [2015] CSOH 149, 2015 S.L.T. 858 (OH), Lord Boyd of Duncansby

35. Police Pensions Act 1976

s.1, enabling: SI 2015/2057, SSI 2015/174

36. Adoption Act 1976

s.6, see *FAS v Secretary of State for the Home Department* [2015] EWHC 622 (Fam), [2015] 3 All E.R. 1001 (Fam Div), Mostyn J

55. Agriculture (Miscellaneous Provisions) Act 1976

s.7, amended: 2015 c.20 Sch.22 para.5

57. Local Government (Miscellaneous Provisions) Act 1976

s.44, amended: 2015 c.20 Sch.13 para.6

s.53, amended: 2015 c.20 s.10

s.55, amended: 2015 c.20 s.10

s.55A, added: 2015 c.20 s.11

s.63, see *Jones v First Great Western Ltd* [2014] EWCA Civ 301, [2015] R.T.R. 3 (CA (Civ Div)), Arden LJ

63. Bail Act 1976

s.5B, enabling: SI 2015/1490

s.7, see *R. (on the application of BG) v Chief Constable of the West Midlands* [2014] EWHC 4374 (Admin), (2015) 179 J.P. 93 (QBD (Admin)), Fulford LJ

76. Energy Act 1976

s.9, repealed: 2015 c.20 Sch.23 para.16

80. Rent (Agriculture) Act 1976

s.5, repealed: 2015 c.20 Sch.13 para.6

86. Fishery Limits Act 1976

s.2, amended: SI 2015/664 Sch.4 para.9

s.2, enabling: SI 2015/648

s.6, enabling: SI 2015/648

Sch.2 para.7, repealed: 2015 c.20 Sch.23 para.32

1977

3. Aircraft and Shipbuilding Industries Act 1977

repealed: 2015 c.20 Sch.23 para.8

5. Social Security (Miscellaneous Provisions) Act 1977

s.12, enabling: SI 2015/208

s.24, enabling: SI 2015/208

7. Nuclear Industry (Finance) Act 1977

s.3, repealed: 2015 c.20 Sch.23 para.18

15. Marriage (Scotland) Act 1977

s.3, amended: SSI 2015/371 Art.4

s.3, enabling: SSI 2015/313

s.3A, added: SI 2015/396 Sch.1 para.2

s.4, amended: SI 2015/396 Sch.1 para.4

s.5, amended: SSI 2015/371 Art.3

s.6, amended: SI 2015/396 Sch.1 para.5

s.6A, added: SI 2015/396 Sch.1 para.6

s.19, amended: SI 2015/396 Sch.1 para.7

s.26, amended: SI 2015/396 Sch.1 para.8

Sch.1A, added: SI 2015/396 Sch.1 para.3

32. Torts (Interference with Goods) Act 1977

s.4, see *Environment Agency v Churngold Recycling Ltd* [2014] EWCA Civ 909, [2015] Env. L.R. 13 (CA (Civ Div)), Moses LJ

33. Price Commission Act 1977

s.16, repealed: 2015 c.15 Sch.6 para.85

37. Patents Act 1977

see *Samsung Electronics Co Ltd v Apple Retail UK Ltd* [2014] EWCA Civ 250, [2015] R.P.C. 3 (CA (Civ Div)), Moore-Bick LJ

s.1, see *Lantana Ltd v Comptroller-General of Patents, Designs and Trade Marks* [2014] EWCA Civ 1463, [2015] R.P.C. 16 (CA (Civ Div)), Arden LJ

s.14, see *Teva UK Ltd v AstraZeneca AB* [2014] EWHC 2873 (Pat), (2015) 142 B.M.L.R. 94 (Ch D (Patents Ct)), Sales J

s.21, see *Icahn School of Medicine at Mount Sinai's SPC Application* [2015] R.P.C. 21 (IPO), L Cullen

s.37, see *Future New Developments Ltd v B&S Patente Und Marken GmbH* [2014] EWHC 1874 (IPEC), [2015] F.S.R. 15 (IPEC), Judge Hacon

s.60, see *Actavis UK Ltd v Eli Lilly & Co* [2015] EWCA Civ 555, [2015] Bus. L.R. 1068 (CA (Civ Div)), Longmore LJ; see *Warner-Lambert Co LLC v Actavis Group PTC EHF* [2015] EWCA Civ 556, [2015] R.P.C. 25 (CA (Civ Div)), Arden LJ

s.64, see *Environmental Defence Systems Ltd v Synergy Health Plc* [2014] EWHC 1306 (IPEC), [2015] F.S.R. 6 (IPEC), Judge Hacon

s.75, see *Rovi Solutions Corp v Virgin Media Ltd* [2014] EWHC 1793 (Pat), [2015] R.P.C. 5 (Ch D), Mann J

s.76, see *Teva UK Ltd v AstraZeneca AB* [2014] EWHC 2873 (Pat), (2015) 142 B.M.L.R. 94 (Ch D (Patents Ct)), Sales J

s.125, see *Eli Lilly & Co Ltd v Human Genome Sciences Inc* [2014] EWHC 2404 (Pat), [2015] R.P.C. 8 (Ch D (Patents Ct)), Warren J

42. Rent Act 1977

see *Queensbridge Investment Ltd v 61 Queens Gate Freehold Ltd* [2015] L. & T.R. 8 (UT (Lands)), Martin Rodger QC; see *Swanbrae Ltd v Ryder* [2015] UKUT 69 (LC), [2015] L. & T.R. 33 (UT (Lands)), Martin Rodger QC

s.14, repealed: 2015 c.20 Sch.13 para.6

s.45, see *Swanbrae Ltd v Ryder* [2015] UKUT 69 (LC), [2015] L. & T.R. 33 (UT (Lands)), Martin Rodger QC

s.137, see *Swanbrae Ltd v Ryder* [2015] UKUT 69 (LC), [2015] L. & T.R. 33 (UT (Lands)), Martin Rodger QC

43. Protection from Eviction Act 1977

see *Sims v Dacorum BC* [2015] A.C. 1336 (SC), Lord Neuberger PSC

s.3, see *R. (on the application of N) v Lewisham LBC* [2015] A.C. 1259 (SC), Lord Neuberger PSC

s.3A, see *R. (on the application of N) v Lewisham LBC* [2015] A.C. 1259 (SC), Lord Neuberger PSC

45. Criminal Law Act 1977

s.1, see *Papachristos v Serious Fraud Office* [2014] EWCA Crim 1863, [2015] Lloyd's Rep. F.C. 88 (CA (Crim Div)), Fulford LJ; see *R. v Chapman (Scott Derek)* [2015] EWCA Crim 539, [2015] Q.B. 883 (CA (Crim Div)), Lord Thomas LCJ

s.39, amended: 2015 c.2 Sch.11 para.1

s.48, enabling: SI 2015/1490

48. Housing (Homeless Persons) Act 1977

s.17, see *Haile v Waltham Forest LBC* [2015] UKSC 34, [2015] A.C. 1471 (SC), Lord Neuberger PSC

50. Unfair Contract Terms Act 1977

see *Barclays Bank Plc v Grant Thornton UK LLP* [2015] EWHC 320 (Comm),

[2015] 2 B.C.L.C. 537 (QBD (Comm)), Cooke J

s.1, amended: 2015 c.15 Sch.4 para.3

s.2, see *Barclays Bank Plc v Grant Thornton UK LLP* [2015] EWHC 320 (Comm), [2015] 2 B.C.L.C. 537 (QBD (Comm)), Cooke J

s.2, amended: 2015 c.15 Sch.4 para.4

s.3, amended: 2015 c.15 Sch.4 para.5

s.4, repealed: 2015 c.15 Sch.4 para.6

s.5, repealed: 2015 c.15 Sch.4 para.7

s.6, amended: 2015 c.15 Sch.4 para.8

s.6, repealed: 2015 c.15 Sch.4 para.8

s.7, amended: 2015 c.15 Sch.4 para.9

s.7, repealed: 2015 c.15 Sch.4 para.9

s.9, repealed: 2015 c.15 Sch.4 para.10

s.12, repealed: 2015 c.15 Sch.4 para.11

s.13, amended: 2015 c.15 Sch.4 para.12

s.14, amended: 2015 c.15 Sch.4 para.13

s.15, amended: 2015 c.15 Sch.4 para.14

s.15, repealed: 2015 c.15 Sch.4 para.14

s.16, amended: 2015 c.15 Sch.4 para.15

s.17, amended: 2015 c.15 Sch.4 para.16

s.18, repealed: 2015 c.15 Sch.4 para.17

s.19, repealed: 2015 c.15 Sch.4 para.18

s.20, amended: 2015 c.15 Sch.4 para.19

s.20, repealed: 2015 c.15 Sch.4 para.19

s.21, amended: 2015 c.15 Sch.4 para.20

s.22, repealed: 2015 c.15 Sch.4 para.21

s.25, amended: 2015 c.15 Sch.4 para.22

s.25, repealed: 2015 c.15 Sch.4 para.22

s.26, amended: 2015 c.15 Sch.4 para.23

s.27, amended: 2015 c.15 Sch.4 para.24

s.27, repealed: 2015 c.15 Sch.4 para.24

s.28, repealed: 2015 c.15 Sch.4 para.25

Sch.1, amended: 2015 c.15 Sch.4 para.26

Sch.1 para.1, amended: 2015 c.15 Sch.4 para.26

Sch.1 para.2, amended: 2015 c.15 Sch.4 para.26

Sch.1 para.3, amended: 2015 c.15 Sch.4 para.26

Sch.2, amended: 2015 c.15 Sch.4 para.27

1978

29. National Health Service (Scotland) Act 1978

see *M v State Hospitals Board for Scotland* 2015 S.C. 112 (IH (2 Div)), The Lord Justice Clerk (Carloway)

s.10ZA, amended: SSI 2015/157 Sch.1 para.2

s.13, amended: SSI 2015/157 Sch.1 para.2

s.26, enabling: SSI 2015/219

s.34, enabling: SSI 2015/219

s.69, enabling: SSI 2015/160

s.70, enabling: SSI 2015/86

s.73, enabling: SSI 2015/86

s.74, enabling: SSI 2015/86

s.75A, enabling: SSI 2015/333

s.85B, enabling: SSI 2015/102

s.105, enabling: SSI 2015/86, SSI 2015/102, SSI 2015/160, SSI 2015/219, SSI 2015/333

s.106, enabling: SSI 2015/219

s.108, amended: SSI 2015/157 Sch.1 para.2

s.108, enabling: SSI 2015/86

Sch.1 Part I para.8A, amended: SSI 2015/157 Sch.1 para.2

Sch.5 para.8A, amended: SSI 2015/157 Sch.1 para.2

Sch.7A Part II para.17, amended: SSI 2015/157 Sch.1 para.2

Sch.11 para.2, enabling: SSI 2015/86

Sch.11 para.2A, enabling: SSI 2015/86, SSI 2015/333

30. Interpretation Act 1978

see *EAD Solicitors LLP v Abrams* [2015] B.C.C. 882 (EAT), Langstaff J

s.6, see *Ottimo Property Services Ltd v Duncan* [2015] I.C.R. 859 (EAT), Judge Eady QC; see *Scottish Legal Aid Board v Lavery* 2015 S.L.T. (Sh Ct) 35 (Sh Ct (Glasgow)), Sheriff A D Miller

s.7, see *Provincial Real Estate Burton Ltd v Virk (Valuation Officer)* [2015] R.V.R. 191 (VT), Graham Zellick QC

s.14A, enabling: SI 2015/441, SI 2015/541, SI 2015/647, SI 2015/648, SI 2015/787, SI 2015/810, SI 2015/1556, SI 2015/1587, SI 2015/1675, SI 2015/1695

s.16, see *Wight v Keeper of the Registers of Scotland* 2015 S.L.T. (Lands Tr) 195 (Lands Tr (Scot)), R A Smith, QC

Sch.1, amended: 2015 c.7 Sch.5 para.34, SI 2015/700 Sch.1 para.10

31. Theft Act 1978

s.3, see *Beaumont v Ferrer* [2014] EWHC 2398 (QB), [2015] P.I.Q.R. P2 (QBD (Manchester)), Kenneth Parker J

33. State Immunity Act 1978

s.2, see *London Steam Ship Owners Mutual Insurance Association Ltd v Spain* [2015] EWCA Civ 333, [2015] 2 Lloyd's Rep. 33 (CA (Civ Div)), Moore-Bick LJ; see *PCL v Regional Government of X* [2015] EWHC 68 (Comm), [2015] 1 W.L.R. 3948 (QBD (Comm)), Hamblen J

s.4, see *Benkharbouche v Embassy of Sudan* [2015] EWCA Civ 33, [2015] 3 W.L.R. 301 (CA (Civ Div)), Lord Dyson MR

s.12, see *PCL v Regional Government of X* [2015] EWHC 68 (Comm), [2015] 1 W.L.R. 3948 (QBD (Comm)), Hamblen J

s.16, see *Benkharbouche v Embassy of Sudan* [2015] EWCA Civ 33, [2015] 3 W.L.R. 301 (CA (Civ Div)), Lord Dyson MR

36. House of Commons (Administration) Act 1978

s.1, amended: 2015 c.24 s.1

s.2, amended: 2015 c.24 s.2

Sch.1 para.1A, added: 2015 c.24 Sch.1 para.2

Sch.1 para.2, amended: 2015 c.24 Sch.1 para.3

Sch.1 para.3, amended: 2015 c.24 Sch.1 para.4

Sch.1 para.5, amended: 2015 c.24 Sch.1 para.5

Sch.1 para.5, repealed: 2015 c.24 Sch.1 para.5

Sch.1 para.6, amended: 2015 c.24 Sch.1 para.6

40. Rating (Disabled Persons) Act 1978

s.8, amended: SI 2015/914 Sch.1 para.25

47. Civil Liability (Contribution) Act 1978

see *Chief Constable of Hampshire v Southampton City Council* [2014] EWCA Civ 1541, [2015] C.P. Rep. 13 (CA (Civ

Div)), Jackson LJ; see *Schubert Murphy
v Law Society* [2014] EWHC 4561 (QB),
[2015] P.N.L.R. 15 (QBD), Mitting J
s.1, see *South West SHA v Bay Island
Voyages* [2015] EWCA Civ 708, [2015]
2 Lloyd's Rep. 652 (CA (Civ Div)), Laws
LJ; see *WH Newson Holding Ltd v IMI
Plc* [2015] EWHC 1676 (Ch), [2015] 1
W.L.R. 4881 (Ch D), Rose J
s.10, see *Chief Constable of Hampshire v
Southampton City Council* [2014] EWCA
Civ 1541, [2015] C.P. Rep. 13 (CA (Civ
Div)), Jackson LJ

1979

2. Customs and Excise Management Act 1979

s.24, amended: SI 2015/664 Sch.2 para.1
s.50, amended: SI 2015/664 Sch.2 para.1
s.53, amended: SI 2015/664 Sch.2 para.1
s.56, amended: SI 2015/664 Sch.2 para.1
s.57, amended: SI 2015/664 Sch.2 para.1
s.58E, amended: SI 2015/664 Sch.2
para.1
s.60A, enabling: SI 2015/368
s.63, amended: SI 2015/664 Sch.2 para.1
s.64, amended: SI 2015/664 Sch.2 para.1
s.66, amended: SI 2015/664 Sch.2 para.1
s.68, amended: SI 2015/664 Sch.2 para.1
s.68A, amended: SI 2015/664 Sch.2
para.1
s.93, enabling: SI 2015/368
s.100, amended: SI 2015/664 Sch.2
para.1
s.102, amended: SI 2015/664 Sch.2
para.1
s.118A, enabling: SI 2015/3, SI
2015/942, SI 2015/1650
s.129, amended: SI 2015/664 Sch.2
para.1
s.136, amended: SI 2015/664 Sch.2
para.1
s.139, see *R. (on the application of
Eastenders Cash & Carry Plc) v Revenue
and Customs Commissioners* [2015] A.C.
1101 (SC), Lord Neuberger PSC
s.141, amended: SI 2015/664 Sch.5
para.1

s.144, see *R. (on the application of
Eastenders Cash & Carry Plc) v Revenue
and Customs Commissioners* [2015] A.C.
1101 (SC), Lord Neuberger PSC
s.158, amended: SI 2015/664 Sch.2
para.1
s.159, amended: SI 2015/664 Sch.2
para.1
s.167, amended: SI 2015/664 Sch.2
para.1
s.168, amended: SI 2015/664 Sch.2
para.1
s.170, amended: SI 2015/664 Sch.2
para.1
s.170B, amended: SI 2015/664 Sch.2
para.1
Sch.1 para.1, amended: SI 2015/664
Sch.2 para.1

3. Customs and Excise Duties (General Reliefs) Act 1979

s.13, amended: SI 2015/664 Sch.2 para.2
s.13C, amended: SI 2015/664 Sch.2
para.2
s.15, amended: SI 2015/664 Sch.2 para.2
s.15, repealed: SI 2015/664 Sch.2 para.2

4. Alcoholic Liquor Duties Act 1979

Part VIA, added: 2015 c.11 s.54
s.4, amended: 2015 c.11 s.54
s.5, amended: 2015 c.11 s.53
s.17, amended: SI 2015/664 Sch.2 para.3
s.25, amended: SI 2015/664 Sch.2 para.3
s.36, amended: 2015 c.11 s.53
s.37, amended: 2015 c.11 s.53
s.62, amended: 2015 c.11 s.53
s.88A, enabling: SI 2015/1516
s.88B, enabling: SI 2015/1516
s.88C, amended: 2015 c.11 s.54
s.88C, enabling: SI 2015/1516
s.88E, enabling: SI 2015/1516, SI
2015/1921
s.88F, added: 2015 c.11 s.54
s.88I, enabling: SI 2015/1516
s.90, amended: 2015 c.11 s.54
Sch.1, amended: 2015 c.11 s.53
Sch.2B, added: 2015 c.11 s.54
Sch.2A para.5, amended: SI 2015/664
Sch.2 para.3
Sch.2A para.6, amended: SI 2015/664
Sch.2 para.3
Sch.2A para.7, amended: SI 2015/664
Sch.2 para.3

5. Hydrocarbon Oil Duties Act 1979
s.10, amended: SI 2015/664 Sch.2 para.4
s.13, amended: SI 2015/664 Sch.2 para.4
s.13AB, amended: SI 2015/664 Sch.2
para.4
s.14, amended: SI 2015/664 Sch.2 para.4
s.14D, amended: SI 2015/664 Sch.2
para.4
s.20AA, enabling: SI 2015/550, SI
2015/943
s.24, enabling: SI 2015/36
s.24A, amended: SI 2015/664 Sch.2
para.4
s.24A, enabling: SI 2015/36
Sch.4, enabling: SI 2015/36

7. Tobacco Products Duty Act 1979
s.6A, added: 2015 c.11 s.56
Sch.1, amended: 2015 c.11 s.55

10. Public Lending Right Act 1979
s.3, enabling: SI 2015/7

17. Vaccine Damage Payments Act 1979
s.1, enabling: SI 2015/47
s.2, varied: SI 2015/47 Art.3
s.2, enabling: SI 2015/47

21. Forestry Act 1979
s.2, amended: 2015 c.20 Sch.22 para.6

33. Land Registration (Scotland) Act 1979
s.9, see *Aronson v Keeper of the
Registers of Scotland* 2015 S.L.T. 122
(OH), Lord Doherty; see *Balfour v
Keeper of the Registers of Scotland* 2015
S.L.T. (Lands Tr) 185 (Lands Tr (Scot)),
R A Smith, QC; see *Campbell-Gray v
Keeper of the Registers of Scotland* 2015
S.L.T. (Lands Tr) 147 (Lands Tr (Scot)),
R A Smith, QC; see *Mathers v Keeper of
the Registers of Scotland* 2015 S.L.T.
(Lands Tr) 109 (Lands Tr (Scot)), R
Smith QC; see *Mirza v Salim* 2015 S.C.
31 (IH (Ex Div)), Lady Paton; see
Rivendale v Clark [2015] CSIH 27, 2015
S.C. 558 (IH (Ex Div)), Lord Brodie; see
*Wight v Keeper of the Registers of
Scotland* 2015 S.L.T. (Lands Tr) 195
(Lands Tr (Scot)), R A Smith, QC
s.25, see *Balfour v Keeper of the
Registers of Scotland* 2015 S.L.T. (Lands
Tr) 185 (Lands Tr (Scot)), R A Smith,
QC; see *Campbell-Gray v Keeper of the
Registers of Scotland* 2015 S.L.T. (Lands
Tr) 147 (Lands Tr (Scot)), R A Smith,

QC; see *Mathers v Keeper of the
Registers of Scotland* 2015 S.L.T. (Lands
Tr) 109 (Lands Tr (Scot)), R Smith QC;
see *Wight v Keeper of the Registers of
Scotland* 2015 S.L.T. (Lands Tr) 195
(Lands Tr (Scot)), R A Smith, QC

38. Estate Agents Act 1979
s.3, amended: 2015 c.15 Sch.6 para.20
s.9, repealed: 2015 c.15 Sch.6 para.21
s.11, repealed: 2015 c.15 Sch.6 para.22
s.11A, repealed: 2015 c.15 Sch.6 para.23
s.26, amended: 2015 c.15 Sch.6 para.24
s.27, repealed: 2015 c.15 Sch.6 para.25
Sch.2 Part II para.14, amended: 2015
c.15 Sch.6 para.26

**41. Pneumoconiosis etc (Workers
Compensation) Act 1979**
s.1, enabling: SI 2015/503
s.7, enabling: SI 2015/503

**46. Ancient Monuments and Archaeological
Areas Act 1979**
s.1, enabling: SSI 2015/230, SSI
2015/328
s.1B, enabling: SSI 2015/230
s.1E, enabling: SSI 2015/231
s.2, enabling: SSI 2015/229
s.3A, enabling: SSI 2015/229
s.3C, enabling: SSI 2015/229, SSI
2015/231
s.4B, enabling: SSI 2015/231
s.4D, enabling: SSI 2015/231, SSI
2015/328
s.9C, enabling: SSI 2015/231
s.9CB, enabling: SSI 2015/231, SSI
2015/328
s.23B, enabling: SSI 2015/231
s.60, enabling: SSI 2015/229
Sch.1 Part I para.1, enabling: SSI
2015/229
Sch.1 Part I para.2, enabling: SSI
2015/229
Sch.1 Part I para.3, enabling: SSI
2015/229
Sch.1 Part II para.11, enabling: SSI
2015/229
Sch.1A para.1, enabling: SSI 2015/232

53. Charging Orders Act 1979
s.3, see *Veluppillai v Veluppillai* [2015]
EWHC 3095 (Fam), [2015] 6 Costs L.O.
735 (Fam Div), Mostyn J

54. Sale of Goods Act 1979

Part VA, repealed: 2015 c.15 Sch.1
para.27
s.1, amended: 2015 c.15 Sch.1 para.9
s.11, amended: 2015 c.15 Sch.1 para.10
s.12, amended: 2015 c.15 Sch.1 para.11
s.13, see *Saipol SA v Inerco Trade SA*
[2014] EWHC 2211 (Comm), [2015] 1
Lloyd's Rep. 26 (QBD (Comm)), Field J
s.13, amended: 2015 c.15 Sch.1 para.12
s.14, see *Saipol SA v Inerco Trade SA*
[2014] EWHC 2211 (Comm), [2015] 1
Lloyd's Rep. 26 (QBD (Comm)), Field J
s.14, amended: 2015 c.15 Sch.1 para.13
s.14, repealed: 2015 c.15 Sch.1 para.13
s.15, amended: 2015 c.15 Sch.1 para.14
s.15A, amended: 2015 c.15 Sch.1 para.15
s.15B, amended: 2015 c.15 Sch.1 para.16
s.15B, repealed: 2015 c.15 Sch.1 para.16
s.20, amended: 2015 c.15 Sch.1 para.17
s.25, see *Carlos Soto SAU v AP Moller-*
Maersk AS [2015] EWHC 458 (Comm),
[2015] 2 All E.R. (Comm) 382 (QBD
(Comm)), Eder J
s.29, amended: 2015 c.15 Sch.1 para.18
s.30, amended: 2015 c.15 Sch.1 para.19
s.31, amended: 2015 c.15 Sch.1 para.20
s.32, amended: 2015 c.15 Sch.1 para.21
s.33, substituted: 2015 c.15 Sch.1 para.22
s.34, substituted: 2015 c.15 Sch.1 para.23
s.35, amended: 2015 c.15 Sch.1 para.24
s.35, repealed: 2015 c.15 Sch.1 para.24
s.35A, amended: 2015 c.15 Sch.1 para.25
s.36, substituted: 2015 c.15 Sch.1 para.26
s.50, see *Lakatamia Shipping Co Ltd v Su*
[2014] EWHC 3611 (Comm), [2015] 1
Lloyd's Rep. 216 (QBD (Comm)), Cooke
J
s.51, amended: 2015 c.15 Sch.1 para.28
s.52, amended: 2015 c.15 Sch.1 para.29
s.53, see *Saipol SA v Inerco Trade SA*
[2014] EWHC 2211 (Comm), [2015] 1
Lloyd's Rep. 26 (QBD (Comm)), Field J
s.53, amended: 2015 c.15 Sch.1 para.30
s.53A, amended: 2015 c.15 Sch.1 para.31
s.54, see *Saipol SA v Inerco Trade SA*
[2014] EWHC 2211 (Comm), [2015] 1
Lloyd's Rep. 26 (QBD (Comm)), Field J
s.54, substituted: 2015 c.15 Sch.1 para.32
s.55, amended: 2015 c.15 Sch.1 para.33
s.58, substituted: 2015 c.15 Sch.1 para.34
s.61, amended: 2015 c.15 Sch.1 para.35

s.61, repealed: 2015 c.15 Sch.1 para.35
s.62, amended: 2015 c.15 Sch.1 para.36
Sch.2 para.19, repealed: 2015 c.15 Sch.4
para.39
Sch.2 para.21, amended: 2015 c.15 Sch.4
para.39

1980

9. Reserve Forces Act 1980
Sch.2 para.2A, added: SI 2015/914 Sch.1
para.26
**27. Import of Live Fish (England and Wales)
Act 1980**
s.1, enabling: SI 2015/88
43. Magistrates Courts Act 1980
see *Letherbarrow v Warwickshire CC*
[2014] EWHC 4820 (Admin), (2015) 179
J.P. 307 (DC), Bean LJ
s.1, amended: 2015 c.2 Sch.11 para.3
s.1, repealed: 2015 c.2 Sch.11 para.3
s.11, amended: 2015 c.2 s.48, Sch.11
para.4
s.12, amended: 2015 c.20 s.80, s.81
s.12, enabling: SI 2015/1490
s.16A, added: 2015 c.2 s.48
s.22A, amended: 2015 c.2 s.52
s.32, amended: SI 2015/664 Sch.5 para.2
s.64, see *Chief Constable of*
Warwickshire v MT [2015] EWHC 2303
(Admin), (2015) 179 J.P. 454 (QBD
(Admin)), Hickinbottom J; see *Chief*
Constable of Warwickshire v Young
[2014] EWHC 4213 (Admin), (2015) 179
J.P. 49 (QBD (Admin)), Hickinbottom J
s.82, amended: 2015 c.2 Sch.12 para.3
s.108, see *Bizunowicz v Poland* [2014]
EWHC 3238 (Admin), [2015] 1 W.L.R.
2341 (QBD (Admin)), Aikens LJ; see *R.*
(on the application of Purnell) v Essex
Magistrates [2015] EWHC 333 (Admin),
[2015] 2 Cr. App. R. (S.) 4 (DC), Treacy
LJ
s.108, amended: 2015 c.2 Sch.12 para.4
s.121, amended: 2015 c.2 s.49
s.123, see *Essence Bars (London) Ltd (t/a*
Essence) v Wimbledon Magistrates'
Court [2014] EWHC 4334 (Admin),
(2015) 179 J.P. 79 (QBD (Admin)),
Wilkie J

s.123, amended: 2015 c.2 Sch.11 para.5
s.142, see *R. v Antoine (Jordan)* [2014]
EWCA Crim 1971, [2015] 1 Cr. App. R.
8 (CA (Crim Div)), Davis LJ
s.144, enabling: SI 2015/421, SI
2015/423, SI 2015/1478
s.150, amended: 2015 c.2 Sch.11 para.6
Sch.1 para.16, repealed: 2015 c.20 Sch.6
para.2

44. Education (Scotland) Act 1980
s.28A, see *J's Parents v Dumfries and*
Galloway Council 2015 S.L.T. (Sh Ct)
253 (Sh Ct (South Strathclyde)
(Dumfries)), Sheriff G Jamieson
s.28D, see *J's Parents v Dumfries and*
Galloway Council 2015 S.L.T. (Sh Ct)
253 (Sh Ct (South Strathclyde)
(Dumfries)), Sheriff G Jamieson
s.28F, see *J's Parents v Dumfries and*
Galloway Council 2015 S.L.T. (Sh Ct)
253 (Sh Ct (South Strathclyde)
(Dumfries)), Sheriff G Jamieson
s.53, enabling: SSI 2015/269
s.72, amended: SSI 2015/153 Sch.1
para.1
s.73, enabling: SSI 2015/212, SSI
2015/248
s.73B, enabling: SSI 2015/212
s.74, enabling: SSI 2015/212, SSI
2015/248
s.75A, enabling: SSI 2015/318
s.75B, enabling: SSI 2015/318

45. Water (Scotland) Act 1980
s.6, enabling: SSI 2015/79
s.10, see *Campbell Construction Group*
Ltd v Scottish Water 2015 S.L.T. (Sh Ct)
159 (Sh Ct (Glasgow)), Sheriff A F
Deutsch
s.76B, enabling: SSI 2015/346
s.76F, enabling: SSI 2015/346
s.76J, enabling: SSI 2015/346
s.101, enabling: SSI 2015/346

46. Solicitors (Scotland) Act 1980
s.20, see *B v D* [2015] CSOH 24, 2015
S.L.T. 217 (OH), Lord Jones
s.23, see *B v D* [2015] CSOH 24, 2015
S.L.T. 217 (OH), Lord Jones

**47. Criminal Appeal (Northern Ireland) Act
1980**
s.30, amended: 2015 c.9 Sch.4 para.4

51. Housing Act 1980

s.89, see *Lawal v Circle 33 Housing*
Trust [2014] EWCA Civ 1514, [2015]
H.L.R. 9 (CA (Civ Div)), Sir Terence
Etherton

**55. Law Reform (Miscellaneous Provisions)
(Scotland) Act 1980**
Sch.1 Part I, amended: SSI 2015/39
Sch.1 para.1

58. Limitation Act 1980
see *Davy v Pickering* [2015] EWHC 380
(Ch), [2015] 2 B.C.L.C. 116 (Ch D
(Cardiff)), Judge Keyser QC; see
Parissis v Blair Court (St John's Wood)
Management Ltd [2015] L. & T.R. 7 (UT
(Lands)), Judge Huskinson
s.2, see *Aspect Contracts (Asbestos) Ltd v*
Higgins Construction Plc [2015] UKSC
38, [2015] 1 W.L.R. 2961 (SC), Lord
Mance JSC; see *Tower Hamlets LBC v*
Bromley LBC [2015] EWHC 1954 (Ch),
[2015] B.L.G.R. 622 (Ch D), Norris J
s.3, see *Tower Hamlets LBC v Bromley*
LBC [2015] EWHC 1954 (Ch), [2015]
B.L.G.R. 622 (Ch D), Norris J
s.5, see *Aspect Contracts (Asbestos) Ltd v*
Higgins Construction Plc [2015] UKSC
38, [2015] 1 W.L.R. 2961 (SC), Lord
Mance JSC; see *Parissis v Blair Court*
(St John's Wood) Management Ltd
[2015] L. & T.R. 7 (UT (Lands)), Judge
Huskinson
s.9, see *Arcadia Group Brands Ltd v Visa*
Inc [2015] EWCA Civ 883, [2015] Bus.
L.R. 1362 (CA (Civ Div)), Sir Terence
Etherton C; see *Dawson v Thomson*
Airways Ltd [2014] EWCA Civ 845,
[2015] 1 W.L.R. 883 (CA (Civ Div)),
Moore-Bick LJ; see *Grace v Black*
Horse Ltd [2014] EWCA Civ 1413,
[2015] 3 All E.R. 223 (CA (Civ Div)),
Lord Dyson MR; see *Holdsworth v*
Bradford MDC [2015] R.A. 559 (VT),
Graham Zellick QC; see *HS v Leicester*
City Council [2015] R.A. 565 (VT),
Graham Zellick QC; see *Khan v Tyne*
and Wear Passenger Transport Executive
(t/a Nexus) [2015] UKUT 43 (LC),
[2015] R.V.R. 165 (UT (Lands)), Martin
Rodger QC; see *Parissis v Blair Court*
(St John's Wood) Management Ltd
[2015] L. & T.R. 7 (UT (Lands)), Judge

Huskinson; see *Saunders v Caerphilly CBC* [2015] EWHC 1632 (Ch), [2015] 2 P. & C.R. 20 (Ch D (Cardiff)), Judge Milwyn Jarman QC

s.10, see *Chief Constable of Hampshire v Southampton City Council* [2014] EWCA Civ 1541, [2015] C.P. Rep. 13 (CA (Civ Div)), Jackson LJ

s.11, see *Platt v BRB (Residuary) Ltd* [2014] EWCA Civ 1401, [2015] P.I.Q.R. P7 (CA (Civ Div)), Jackson LJ

s.12, amended: SI 2015/1392 Reg.4

s.14, see *Platt v BRB (Residuary) Ltd* [2014] EWCA Civ 1401, [2015] P.I.Q.R. P7 (CA (Civ Div)), Jackson LJ

s.14A, see *Freehold Estates Ltd v National Westminster Bank Plc* [2014] EWHC 4621 (Comm), [2015] 5 Costs L.R. 773 (QBD (Comm)), Hamblen J; see *Jacobs v Sesame Ltd* [2014] EWCA Civ 1410, [2015] P.N.L.R. 6 (CA (Civ Div)), Sullivan LJ; see *Schumann v Veale Wasbrough* [2015] EWCA Civ 441, [2015] Med. L.R. 425 (CA (Civ Div)), Longmore LJ; see *Seton House Group Ltd v Mercer Ltd* [2014] EWHC 4234 (Ch), [2015] Pens. L.R. 45 (Ch D), Judge David Cooke

s.21, see *Parissis v Blair Court (St John's Wood) Management Ltd* [2015] L. & T.R. 7 (UT (Lands)), Judge Huskinson

s.24, see *Van Heeren v Cooper* [2014] EWHC 4797 (Ch), [2015] B.P.I.R. 953 (Ch D), Stuart Isaacs QC

s.29, see *Van Heeren v Cooper* [2014] EWHC 4797 (Ch), [2015] B.P.I.R. 953 (Ch D), Stuart Isaacs QC

s.32, see *Arcadia Group Brands Ltd v Visa Inc* [2015] EWCA Civ 883, [2015] Bus. L.R. 1362 (CA (Civ Div)), Sir Terence Etherton C; see *Burrell v Clifford* [2015] EWHC 2001 (Ch), [2015] 6 Costs L.O. 719 (Ch D), Mann J; see *Grace v Black Horse Ltd* [2014] EWCA Civ 1413, [2015] 3 All E.R. 223 (CA (Civ Div)), Lord Dyson MR; see *WH Newson Holding Ltd v IMI Plc* [2015] EWHC 1676 (Ch), [2015] 1 W.L.R. 4881 (Ch D), Rose J

s.32A, see *Arcadia Group Brands Ltd v Visa Inc* [2015] EWCA Civ 883, [2015]

Bus. L.R. 1362 (CA (Civ Div)), Sir Terence Etherton C; see *Bewry v Reed Elsevier (UK) Ltd* [2014] EWCA Civ 1411, [2015] 1 W.L.R. 2565 (CA (Civ Div)), Lewison LJ

s.33B, added: SI 2015/1392 Reg.4

s.33B, repealed: SI 2015/1972 Reg.3

65. Local Government, Planning and Land Act 1980

s.2, repealed: 2015 c.20 Sch.13 para.6

s.3, enabling: SI 2015/471, SI 2015/480, SI 2015/494

s.98, repealed: 2015 c.20 Sch.13 para.6

s.99, repealed: 2015 c.20 Sch.13 para.6

s.100, amended: 2015 c.20 Sch.13 para.6

s.134, varied: 2015 c.20 s.46

s.134, enabling: SI 2015/747

s.135, varied: 2015 c.20 s.47

s.135, enabling: SI 2015/747

s.149, enabling: SI 2015/748

Sch.2 para.14, repealed: 2015 c.20 Sch.13 para.15

Sch.2 para.18, repealed: 2015 c.20 Sch.13 para.15

Sch.16 para.5BA, repealed: 2015 c.20 Sch.13 para.6

Sch.26 para.1, enabling: SI 2015/747

Sch.28 Part III para.6, amended: SI 2015/1794 Art.2

66. Highways Act 1980

see *Dorset CC v Reeves (Valuation Officer)* [2015] R.V.R. 340 (VT), MF Young

s.1, amended: 2015 c.7 Sch.1 para.2

s.2, amended: 2015 c.7 Sch.1 para.3

s.3, amended: 2015 c.7 Sch.1 para.4

s.4, amended: 2015 c.7 Sch.1 para.5

s.5, amended: 2015 c.7 Sch.1 para.6

s.6, amended: 2015 c.7 Sch.1 para.7

s.8, amended: 2015 c.7 Sch.1 para.8

s.9, amended: 2015 c.7 Sch.1 para.9

s.10, amended: 2015 c.7 Sch.1 para.10

s.10, enabling: SI 2015/1581, SI 2015/2016

s.11, amended: 2015 c.7 Sch.1 para.11

s.12, enabling: SI 2015/1581, SI 2015/2016

s.14, amended: 2015 c.7 Sch.1 para.12

s.16, amended: 2015 c.7 Sch.1 para.13

s.16, enabling: SI 2015/1901

s.18, amended: 2015 c.7 Sch.1 para.14

s.19, amended: 2015 c.7 Sch.1 para.15

s.23, amended: 2015 c.7 Sch.1 para.16

s.24, amended: 2015 c.7 Sch.1 para.17

s.26, amended: 2015 c.7 Sch.1 para.18

s.37, see *R. (on the application of Redrow Homes Ltd) v Knowsley MBC* [2014] EWCA Civ 1433, [2015] 1 W.L.R. 386 (CA (Civ Div)), Lord Dyson MR

s.38, see *R. (on the application of Redrow Homes Ltd) v Knowsley MBC* [2014] EWCA Civ 1433, [2015] 1 W.L.R. 386 (CA (Civ Div)), Lord Dyson MR

s.38, amended: 2015 c.7 Sch.1 para.19

s.41, amended: 2015 c.7 Sch.1 para.20

s.55, amended: 2015 c.7 Sch.1 para.21

s.63, amended: 2015 c.7 Sch.1 para.22

s.66, amended: 2015 c.7 Sch.1 para.23

s.69, amended: 2015 c.7 Sch.1 para.24

s.80, amended: 2015 c.7 Sch.1 para.25

s.90A, amended: 2015 c.20 Sch.10 para.14

s.90B, amended: 2015 c.20 Sch.10 para.15

s.90C, amended: 2015 c.7 Sch.1 para.26, 2015 c.20 Sch.10 para.16

s.90C, repealed: 2015 c.20 Sch.10 para.16

s.90D, amended: 2015 c.20 Sch.10 para.17

s.90E, amended: 2015 c.20 Sch.10 para.18

s.90F, amended: 2015 c.20 Sch.10 para.19

s.90FA, added: 2015 c.20 Sch.10 para.20

s.93, amended: 2015 c.7 Sch.1 para.27

s.93, repealed: 2015 c.7 Sch.1 para.27

s.95, amended: 2015 c.7 Sch.1 para.28

s.97, amended: 2015 c.7 Sch.1 para.29

s.105A, amended: 2015 c.7 Sch.1 para.30

s.105B, amended: 2015 c.7 Sch.1 para.31

s.105C, amended: 2015 c.7 Sch.1 para.32

s.105D, amended: 2015 c.7 Sch.1 para.33

s.106, amended: 2015 c.7 Sch.1 para.34

s.106, enabling: SI 2015/31, SI 2015/1124, SI 2015/1474, SI 2015/1824

s.108, amended: 2015 c.7 Sch.1 para.35

s.110, amended: 2015 c.7 Sch.1 para.36

s.112, amended: 2015 c.7 Sch.1 para.37

s.113, amended: 2015 c.7 Sch.1 para.38

s.118ZA, amended: 2015 c.20 s.23, s.25

s.119ZA, amended: 2015 c.20 s.23, s.25

s.121A, amended: 2015 c.20 s.25

s.121E, amended: 2015 c.20 s.23, s.25

s.124, amended: 2015 c.7 Sch.1 para.39

s.129, amended: 2015 c.7 Sch.1 para.40

s.137ZA, amended: SI 2015/664 Sch.3 para.1

s.146, amended: 2015 c.20 s.24

s.147, amended: 2015 c.20 s.24

s.154, amended: 2015 c.7 Sch.1 para.41

s.174, amended: 2015 c.7 Sch.1 para.42

s.175B, added: 2015 c.7 Sch.1 para.43

s.232, amended: 2015 c.7 Sch.1 para.44

s.239, amended: 2015 c.7 Sch.1 para.45

s.240, amended: 2015 c.7 Sch.1 para.46

s.245A, amended: 2015 c.7 Sch.1 para.47

s.247, amended: 2015 c.7 Sch.1 para.48

s.254, amended: 2015 c.7 Sch.1 para.49

s.260, amended: 2015 c.7 Sch.1 para.50

s.263, see *Dorset CC v Reeves (Valuation Officer)* [2015] R.V.R. 340 (VT), MF Young

s.263, amended: 2015 c.7 Sch.1 para.51

s.265, amended: 2015 c.7 Sch.1 para.52

s.266, amended: 2015 c.7 Sch.1 para.53

s.266A, amended: 2015 c.7 Sch.1 para.54

s.267, amended: 2015 c.7 Sch.1 para.55

s.271, amended: 2015 c.7 Sch.1 para.56

s.277, amended: 2015 c.7 Sch.1 para.57

s.284, amended: 2015 c.7 Sch.1 para.58

s.284A, amended: 2015 c.7 Sch.1 para.59

s.325, amended: 2015 c.20 Sch.10 para.21

s.329, amended: 2015 c.7 Sch.1 para.60

s.330, amended: 2015 c.7 Sch.1 para.61

s.331, amended: 2015 c.7 Sch.1 para.62

Sch.1 Part I para.1, amended: 2015 c.7 Sch.1 para.63

Sch.1 Part I para.2, amended: 2015 c.7 Sch.1 para.63

Sch.1 Part I para.3, amended: 2015 c.7 Sch.1 para.63

Sch.1 Part I para.4, amended: 2015 c.7 Sch.1 para.63

Sch.1 Part I para.6, amended: 2015 c.7 Sch.1 para.63

Sch.1 Part I para.7, amended: 2015 c.7 Sch.1 para.63

Sch.1 Part I para.8, amended: 2015 c.7 Sch.1 para.63

Sch.1 Part I para.9, amended: 2015 c.7 Sch.1 para.63

Sch.1 Part II para.10, amended: 2015 c.7
Sch.1 para.63
Sch.1 Part II para.11, amended: 2015 c.7
Sch.1 para.63
Sch.1 Part II para.12, amended: 2015 c.7
Sch.1 para.63
Sch.1 Part II para.13, amended: 2015 c.7
Sch.1 para.63
Sch.1 Part II para.14, amended: 2015 c.7
Sch.1 para.63
Sch.1 Part II para.15, amended: 2015 c.7
Sch.1 para.63
Sch.1 Part II para.16, amended: 2015 c.7
Sch.1 para.63
Sch.1 Part III para.17, amended: 2015 c.7
Sch.1 para.63
Sch.3 Part I, amended: 2015 c.7 Sch.1
para.64
Sch.3 Part II, amended: 2015 c.7 Sch.1
para.64
Sch.3 Part III, amended: 2015 c.7 Sch.1
para.64
Sch.5 Part I para.3, amended: 2015 c.7
Sch.1 para.65
Sch.5 Part II para.1, amended: 2015 c.7
Sch.1 para.65
Sch.5 Part II para.3, amended: 2015 c.7
Sch.1 para.65
Sch.5 Part II para.4, amended: 2015 c.7
Sch.1 para.65
Sch.5 Part II para.5, amended: 2015 c.7
Sch.1 para.65
Sch.6 Part I para.1, amended: 2015 c.20
Sch.7 para.8
Sch.6 Part I para.2, amended: 2015 c.20
Sch.7 para.8
Sch.6 Part I para.2A, amended: 2015 c.20
s.23
Sch.6 Part I para.2B, amended: 2015 c.20
s.25
Sch.6 Part I para.2ZZA, added: 2015 c.20
Sch.7 para.8
Sch.6 Part II para.4A, amended: 2015
c.20 Sch.7 para.8
Sch.6 Part II para.5, amended: 2015 c.20
Sch.7 para.8
Sch.9 para.9, amended: 2015 c.7 Sch.5
para.35
Sch.11 para.9, amended: 2015 c.7 Sch.1
para.66

Sch.11 para.15, amended: 2015 c.7 Sch.1
para.66
Sch.11 para.17, repealed: 2015 c.7 Sch.1
para.66
Sch.21 para.1, amended: 2015 c.7 Sch.1
para.67
Sch.21 para.3, amended: 2015 c.7 Sch.1
para.67
Sch.21 para.4, amended: 2015 c.7 Sch.1
para.67
Sch.21 para.6, amended: 2015 c.7 Sch.1
para.67

1981

14. Public Passenger Vehicles Act 1981
s.24, enabling: SI 2015/888
s.25, enabling: SI 2015/888
s.60, enabling: SI 2015/888, SSI
2015/420
s.68, amended: SI 2015/583 Sch.2 para.1
**18. Disused Burial Grounds (Amendment)
Act 1981**
s.2, amended: 2015 c.7 Sch.5 para.36
20. Judicial Pensions Act 1981
s.17, amended: SI 2015/182 Sch.3
para.13
Sch.1A Part I para.3, amended: 2015 c.8
Sch.4 para.1, Sch.4 para.47
22. Animal Health Act 1981
Part IIA, repealed: 2015 c.20 Sch.23
para.37
s.1, enabling: SI 2015/364, SI 2015/584,
SI 2015/751, SI 2015/1773, SI
2015/1838, SI 2015/1992, SI 2015/2023,
SSI 2015/186, SSI 2015/327
s.2, enabling: SI 2015/751
s.6, enabling: SI 2015/364
s.7, enabling: SI 2015/364, SSI 2015/327
s.8, enabling: SI 2015/364, SI 2015/584,
SI 2015/1838, SI 2015/1992, SSI
2015/186, SSI 2015/327
s.10, enabling: SI 2015/751
s.15, enabling: SI 2015/364, SI 2015/584,
SSI 2015/327
s.17, enabling: SI 2015/584
s.23, enabling: SI 2015/584
s.25, enabling: SI 2015/584, SSI
2015/327
s.28, enabling: SI 2015/364, SI 2015/584

s.28E, amended: SSI 2015/338 Sch.2
para.1

s.29, enabling: SI 2015/751

s.32, enabling: SI 2015/364, SSI
2015/327

s.34, enabling: SI 2015/364, SI 2015/751,
SSI 2015/327

s.35, enabling: SI 2015/364

s.83, enabling: SI 2015/1992, SSI
2015/186, SSI 2015/327

s.83A, enabling: SSI 2015/327

s.87, enabling: SI 2015/364, SI 2015/751,
SSI 2015/327

s.88, enabling: SI 2015/584, SI 2015/751,
SI 2015/2023

29. Fisheries Act 1981

s.24, repealed: SI 2015/664 Sch.4 para.95

s.30, enabling: SI 2015/191, SSI
2015/320

s.35, repealed: SI 2015/664 Sch.4 para.95

49. Contempt of Court Act 1981

s.1, see *A Healthcare NHS Trust v P*
[2015] EWCOP 15, [2015] C.O.P.L.R.
147 (CP), Newton J

s.2, see *A Healthcare NHS Trust v P*
[2015] EWCOP 15, [2015] C.O.P.L.R.
147 (CP), Newton J

s.4, see *Guardian News and Media Ltd v
Incedal* [2014] EWCA Crim 1861,
[2015] 1 Cr. App. R. 4 (CA (Crim Div)),
Gross LJ

s.8, amended: 2015 c.2 s.74

s.8, repealed: 2015 c.2 s.74

s.11, see *BBC, Re* [2015] A.C. 588 (SC),
Lady Hale DPSC; see *Guardian News
and Media Ltd v Incedal* [2014] EWCA
Crim 1861, [2015] 1 Cr. App. R. 4 (CA
(Crim Div)), Gross LJ; see *R. (on the
application of Yam) v Central Criminal
Court* [2014] EWHC 3558 (Admin),
[2015] 3 W.L.R. 1050 (DC), Elias LJ

s.14, see *R. (on the application of James)
v Governor of Birmingham Prison* [2015]
EWCA Civ 58, [2015] 1 W.L.R. 4210
(CA (Civ Div)), Arden LJ

s.19, see *R. (on the application of Yam) v
Central Criminal Court* [2014] EWHC
3558 (Admin), [2015] 3 W.L.R. 1050
(DC), Elias LJ

**53. Deep Sea Mining (Temporary
Provisions) Act 1981**

s.18, enabling: SI 2015/2012

54. Senior Courts Act 1981

s.2, amended: SI 2015/1885 Art.2

s.2, enabling: SI 2015/1885

s.9, see *Perry v FH Brundle* [2015]
EWHC 2737 (IPEC), [2015] B.P.I.R.
1449 (IPEC), Judge Hacon

s.18, see *R. (on the application of
Panesar) v Central Criminal Court*
[2014] EWCA Civ 1613, [2015] 1
W.L.R. 2577 (CA (Civ Div)), Patten LJ

s.19, see *Liberty Mercian Ltd v Cuddy
Civil Engineering Ltd* [2014] EWHC
3584 (TCC), [2015] B.L.R. 242 (QBD
(TCC)), Ramsey J

s.19, enabling: SI 2015/1490

s.20, see *Harms Bergung Transport und
Heavylift Gmbh & Co KG v Harms
Offshore AHT "Uranus" GmbH & Co KG*
[2015] EWHC 1269 (Admlty), [2015] 2
All E.R. (Comm) 953 (QBD (Admlty)),
Simon J

s.21, see *Bank of Tokyo-Mitsubishi UFJ
Ltd v Owners of the Sanko Mineral*
[2014] EWHC 3927 (Admlty), [2015] 2
All E.R. (Comm) 979 (QBD (Admlty)),
Teare J

s.28A, see *Hull and Holderness
Magistrates' Court v Darroch* [2014]
EWHC 4184 (Admin), (2015) 179 J.P. 64
(DC), Foskett J

s.29, see *Campbell-Brown v Central
Criminal Court* [2015] EWHC 202
(Admin), [2015] 1 Cr. App. R. 34 (DC),
Fulford LJ; see *R. (on the application of
M) v Kingston Crown Court* [2014]
EWHC 2702 (Admin), [2015] 4 All E.R.
1028 (DC), Ouseley J; see *R. (on the
application of Yam) v Central Criminal
Court* [2014] EWHC 3558 (Admin),
[2015] 3 W.L.R. 1050 (DC), Elias LJ

s.31, see *General Medical Council v
Michalak* [2015] I.C.R. 502 (EAT),
Langstaff J; see *Gibraltar Betting &
Gaming Association Ltd v Secretary of
State for Culture, Media and Sport*
[2014] EWHC 3236 (Admin), [2015] 1
C.M.L.R. 28 (QBD (Admin)), Green J;
see *R. (on the application of Torbay
Quality Care Forum Ltd) v Torbay
Council* [2014] EWHC 4321 (Admin),

[2015] B.L.G.R. 563 (QBD (Admin)),
Judge Lambert
s.31, amended: 2015 c.2 s.84, s.85
s.33, see *Big Bus Co Ltd v Ticketogo Ltd*
[2015] EWHC 1094 (Pat), [2015] Bus.
L.R. 867 (Ch D (Patents Ct)), Arnold J
s.34, see *L v R* [2015] EWCA Civ 61,
Times, April 7, 2015 (CA (Civ Div)),
Aikens LJ
s.37, see *AmTrust Europe Ltd v Trust
Risk Group SpA* [2015] EWHC 1927
(Comm), [2015] 2 Lloyd's Rep. 231
(QBD (Comm)), Andrew Smith J; see
*Cartier International AG v British Sky
Broadcasting Ltd* [2014] EWHC 3354
(Ch), [2015] 1 All E.R. 949 (Ch D),
Arnold J; see *Cruz City 1 Mauritius
Holdings v Unitech Ltd* [2014] EWHC
3131 (Comm), [2015] 1 All E.R. (Comm)
336 (QBD (Comm)), Males J; see *Law
Society of England and Wales v Shah*
[2015] EWHC 2711 (Ch), [2015] 1
W.L.R. 2094 (Ch D), Tim Kerr QC; see
*Southport Success SA v Tsingshan
Holding Group Co Ltd* [2015] EWHC
1974 (Comm), [2015] 2 Lloyd's Rep. 578
(QBD (Comm)), Phillips J; see *Warner-
Lambert Co LLC v Actavis Group PTC
EHF* [2015] EWHC 485 (Pat), [2015]
R.P.C. 24 (Ch D (Patents Ct)), Arnold J
s.51, see *Capita Translation and
Interpreting Ltd, Re* [2015] EWFC 5,
[2015] 3 All E.R. 123 (Fam Ct), Sir
James Munby PFD; see *Kommalage v
Sayanthakumar* [2014] EWCA Civ 1832,
[2015] 2 B.C.L.C. 131 (CA (Civ Div)),
Davis LJ; see *Wagenaar v Weekend
Travel Ltd (t/a Ski Weekend)* [2014]
EWCA Civ 1105, [2015] 1 W.L.R. 1968
(CA (Civ Div)), Laws LJ
s.51, amended: 2015 c.2 s.67
s.52, enabling: SI 2015/1490
s.66, enabling: SI 2015/1490
s.67, enabling: SI 2015/1490
s.69, see *Gregory v Commissioner of
Police of the Metropolis* [2014] EWHC
3922 (QB), [2015] 1 W.L.R. 4253
(QBD), Cranston J; see *Rufus v Elliott*
[2015] EWCA Civ 121, [2015] E.M.L.R.
17 (CA (Civ Div)), McCombe LJ
s.73, enabling: SI 2015/1490

s.74, enabling: SI 2015/1490
s.87, enabling: SI 2015/1490
s.121, see *Randall v Randall* [2014]
EWHC 3134 (Ch), [2015] W.T.L.R. 99
(Ch D), Deputy Master Collaco Moraes
s.142, enabling: SI 2015/329
Sch.1 para.2, amended: 2015 c.6 s.15
Sch.1 para.3, amended: 2015 c.9 Sch.4
para.5

**59. Matrimonial Homes (Family Protection)
(Scotland) Act 1981**
see *Hoblyn v Barclays Bank Plc* 2015
S.C.L.R. 85 (IH (Ex Div)), Lady Paton

61. British Nationality Act 1981
see *G (Children) (Recognition of
Brazilian Adoption), Re* [2014] EWHC
2605 (Fam), [2015] 1 F.L.R. 1402 (Fam
Div), Cobb J; see *R. (on the application
of Kaziu) v Secretary of State for the
Home Department* [2014] EWHC 832
(Admin), [2015] 1 W.L.R. 945 (QBD
(Admin)), Ouseley J
s.3, see *G (Children) (Recognition of
Brazilian Adoption), Re* [2014] EWHC
2605 (Fam), [2015] 1 F.L.R. 1402 (Fam
Div), Cobb J
s.4C, see *Romein v Advocate General for
Scotland* 2015 S.L.T. 32 (OH), Lord
Brailsford
s.6, see *R. (on the application of Amiri) v
Secretary of State for the Home
Department* [2014] EWHC 4418
(Admin), [2015] Imm. A.R. 467 (QBD
(Admin)), Jay J
s.37, enabling: SI 2015/1771
s.40, see *Pham v Secretary of State for
the Home Department* [2015] UKSC 19,
[2015] 1 W.L.R. 1591 (SC), Lord
Neuberger PSC
s.41, enabling: SI 2015/681, SI 2015/738,
SI 2015/1806
s.50, enabling: SI 2015/1615
Sch.1, see *R. (on the application of
Amiri) v Secretary of State for the Home
Department* [2014] EWHC 4418
(Admin), [2015] Imm. A.R. 467 (QBD
(Admin)), Jay J
Sch.1 para.1, see *R. (on the application of
Lakaj) v Secretary of State for the Home
Department* [2014] EWHC 4273

(Admin), [2015] Imm. A.R. 457 (QBD
(Admin)), Lewis J
Sch.3, amended: SI 2015/1771 Art.2

63. Betting and Gaming Duties Act 1981
see *Aspinalls Club Ltd v Revenue and
Customs Commissioners* [2013] EWCA
Civ 1464, [2015] Ch. 79 (CA (Civ Div)),
Moses LJ
s.26F, see *Aspinalls Club Ltd v Revenue
and Customs Commissioners* [2013]
EWCA Civ 1464, [2015] Ch. 79 (CA
(Civ Div)), Moses LJ
s.26L, amended: SI 2015/664 Sch.2
para.5
Sch.1 para.13, amended: SI 2015/664
Sch.2 para.5
Sch.1 para.14, amended: SI 2015/664
Sch.2 para.5
Sch.3 Part II para.16, amended: SI
2015/664 Sch.2 para.5

64. New Towns Act 1981
s.19, amended: SI 2015/1794 Art.3

**66. Compulsory Purchase (Vesting
Declarations) Act 1981**
s.3, amended: 2015 c.7 Sch.5 para.37
s.3, varied: SI 2015/318 Art.26, SI
2015/680 Art.23, SI 2015/781 Art.10
s.5, varied: SI 2015/318 Art.26, SI
2015/680 Art.23, SI 2015/780 Art.23, SI
2015/781 Art.10
s.7, varied: SI 2015/318 Art.26, SI
2015/680 Art.23, SI 2015/781 Art.10

67. Acquisition of Land Act 1981
s.17, amended: 2015 c.20 Sch.13 para.6
Sch.2 Part II, varied: SI 2015/23 Art.21,
SI 2015/318 Art.22

69. Wildlife and Countryside Act 1981
s.7, enabling: SI 2015/618
s.11A, enabling: SSI 2015/377
s.14, amended: 2015 c.7 s.23, s.25
s.14ZA, amended: 2015 c.7 s.25
s.14ZB, amended: 2015 c.7 s.25
s.19, amended: 2015 c.7 s.23
s.22, amended: 2015 c.7 s.25
s.22, enabling: SI 2015/1180
s.25, amended: 2015 c.7 s.23
s.26, amended: 2015 c.7 s.23
s.28E, see *Natural England v Day* [2014]
EWCA Crim 2683, [2015] 1 Cr. App. R.
(S.) 53 (CA (Crim Div)), Lord Thomas
LCJ

s.28F, see *RSPB v Secretary of State for
the Environment, Food and Rural Affairs*
[2015] EWCA Civ 227, [2015] Env. L.R.
24 (CA (Civ Div)), Jackson LJ
s.28P, see *Natural England v Day* [2014]
EWCA Crim 2683, [2015] 1 Cr. App. R.
(S.) 53 (CA (Crim Div)), Lord Thomas
LCJ
s.28P, amended: SI 2015/664 Sch.4
para.10
s.34, amended: SI 2015/664 Sch.4
para.10
s.53, see *R. (on the application of Trail
Riders' Fellowship) v Dorset CC* [2015]
UKSC 18, [2015] 1 W.L.R. 1406 (SC),
Lord Neuberger PSC
s.53, amended: 2015 c.20 Sch.7 para.2,
Sch.7 para.10
s.53B, amended: 2015 c.20 Sch.7 para.4
s.53ZA, added: 2015 c.20 Sch.7 para.3
s.54B, added: 2015 c.20 Sch.7 para.5
Sch.9A, added: 2015 c.7 s.23
Sch.9 Part I, added: 2015 c.7 s.24
Sch.9 Part I, amended: 2015 c.7 s.24
Sch.9 Part 1A, added: 2015 c.7 s.24
Sch.9 Part IB, added: 2015 c.7 s.24
Sch.9 Part IB, amended: SI 2015/1180
Art.2
Sch.13A, added: 2015 c.20 Sch.7 para.6
Sch.14, see *R. (on the application of Trail
Riders' Fellowship) v Dorset CC* [2015]
UKSC 18, [2015] 1 W.L.R. 1406 (SC),
Lord Neuberger PSC
Sch.14, amended: 2015 c.20 Sch.7
para.11
Sch.14A, added: 2015 c.20 Sch.7 para.7
Sch.14 para.1, see *R. (on the application
of Trail Riders' Fellowship) v Dorset CC*
[2015] UKSC 18, [2015] 1 W.L.R. 1406
(SC), Lord Neuberger PSC
Sch.14 para.5, amended: 2015 c.20 Sch.7
para.11
Sch.15, amended: 2015 c.20 Sch.7
para.12
Sch.15 para.13, amended: 2015 c.20
Sch.7 para.12

1982

10. Industrial Training Act 1982
s.11, enabling: SI 2015/677, SI 2015/701
s.12, enabling: SI 2015/677, SI 2015/701

16. Civil Aviation Act 1982
s.60, enabling: SI 2015/870, SI
2015/1768
s.61, enabling: SI 2015/870, SI
2015/1768, SI 2015/1769
s.78, amended: SI 2015/664 Sch.3 para.2
s.78B, amended: SI 2015/664 Sch.3
para.2
s.88, amended: SI 2015/912 Sch.5 para.8
Sch.15 para.18, repealed: 2015 c.20
Sch.23 para.9

23. Oil and Gas (Enterprise) Act 1982
Sch.3 para.37, repealed: 2015 c.20
Sch.23 para.17

27. Civil Jurisdiction and Judgments Act 1982
s.1, amended: SI 2015/1644 Reg.3
s.4B, added: SI 2015/1644 Reg.4
s.4B, varied: SI 2015/1644 Reg.25
s.6B, added: SI 2015/1644 Reg.5
s.7, amended: SI 2015/1644 Reg.6
s.9, amended: SI 2015/1644 Reg.7
s.11B, added: SI 2015/1644 Reg.8
s.12, amended: SI 2015/1644 Reg.9
s.15, amended: SI 2015/1644 Reg.10
s.16, see *Sauchiehall Street Properties One Ltd v EMI Group Ltd* 2015 Hous. L.R. 24 (Sh Ct (Glasgow)), Sheriff S Reid
s.16, amended: SI 2015/1644 Reg.11
s.18, amended: 2015 c.9 Sch.4 para.6
s.20, see *Sauchiehall Street Properties One Ltd v EMI Group Ltd* 2015 Hous. L.R. 24 (Sh Ct (Glasgow)), Sheriff S Reid
s.24, amended: SI 2015/1644 Reg.12
s.25, see *Blue Holding (1) Pte Ltd v United States* [2014] EWCA Civ 1291, [2015] 1 W.L.R. 1917 (CA (Civ Div)), Rimer LJ
s.25, amended: SI 2015/1644 Reg.13
s.27, amended: SI 2015/1644 Reg.14
s.28, amended: SI 2015/1644 Reg.15
s.32, see *Spliethoff's Bevrachtingskantoor BV v Bank of China Ltd* [2015] EWHC

999 (Comm), [2015] 2 Lloyd's Rep. 123 (QBD (Comm)), Carr J
s.32, amended: SI 2015/1644 Reg.16
s.33, amended: SI 2015/1644 Reg.17
s.48, amended: SI 2015/1644 Reg.18
s.48, varied: SI 2015/1644 Reg.25
s.48, enabling: SI 2015/913, SI
2015/1420, SSI 2015/26
s.49, amended: SI 2015/1644 Reg.19
s.50, amended: SI 2015/700 Sch.1
para.11, SI 2015/1644 Reg.20
Sch.4 para.11, see *Sauchiehall Street Properties One Ltd v EMI Group Ltd* 2015 Hous. L.R. 24 (Sh Ct (Glasgow)), Sheriff S Reid
Sch.8 para.5, see *Sauchiehall Street Properties One Ltd v EMI Group Ltd* 2015 Hous. L.R. 24 (Sh Ct (Glasgow)), Sheriff S Reid

29. Supply of Goods and Services Act 1982
Part IB, repealed: 2015 c.15 Sch.1
para.50
s.1, amended: 2015 c.15 Sch.1 para.38,
Sch.1 para.39
s.2, amended: 2015 c.15 Sch.1 para.38
s.3, amended: 2015 c.15 Sch.1 para.38
s.4, amended: 2015 c.15 Sch.1 para.38
s.4, repealed: 2015 c.15 Sch.1 para.40
s.5, amended: 2015 c.15 Sch.1 para.38
s.5A, amended: 2015 c.15 Sch.1 para.38,
Sch.1 para.41
s.6, amended: 2015 c.15 Sch.1 para.38,
Sch.1 para.42
s.7, amended: 2015 c.15 Sch.1 para.38
s.8, amended: 2015 c.15 Sch.1 para.38
s.9, amended: 2015 c.15 Sch.1 para.38
s.9, repealed: 2015 c.15 Sch.1 para.43
s.10, amended: 2015 c.15 Sch.1 para.38
s.10A, amended: 2015 c.15 Sch.1
para.38, Sch.1 para.44
s.11, amended: 2015 c.15 Sch.1 para.38
s.11A, amended: 2015 c.15 Sch.1
para.38, Sch.1 para.45
s.11B, amended: 2015 c.15 Sch.1 para.38
s.11C, amended: 2015 c.15 Sch.1 para.38
s.11D, amended: 2015 c.15 Sch.1 para.38
s.11D, repealed: 2015 c.15 Sch.1 para.46
s.11E, amended: 2015 c.15 Sch.1 para.38
s.11F, amended: 2015 c.15 Sch.1 para.38
s.11F, repealed: 2015 c.15 Sch.1 para.47

s.11G, amended: 2015 c.15 Sch.1
para.38, Sch.1 para.48
s.11H, amended: 2015 c.15 Sch.1 para.38
s.11I, amended: 2015 c.15 Sch.1 para.38
s.11J, amended: 2015 c.15 Sch.1 para.38
s.11J, repealed: 2015 c.15 Sch.1 para.49
s.11K, amended: 2015 c.15 Sch.1 para.38
s.11L, amended: 2015 c.15 Sch.1 para.38
s.12, amended: 2015 c.15 Sch.1 para.38,
Sch.1 para.51
s.13, amended: 2015 c.15 Sch.1 para.38
s.14, amended: 2015 c.15 Sch.1 para.38
s.15, amended: 2015 c.15 Sch.1 para.38
s.16, amended: 2015 c.15 Sch.1 para.38
s.18, amended: 2015 c.15 Sch.1 para.38,
Sch.1 para.52
s.18, repealed: 2015 c.15 Sch.1 para.52
Sch.1 para.1, amended: 2015 c.15 Sch.1
para.38
Sch.1 para.2, amended: 2015 c.15 Sch.1
para.38

**30. Local Government (Miscellaneous
Provisions) Act 1982**
see *R. (on the application of Bridgerow
Ltd) v Cheshire West and Chester BC*
[2014] EWHC 1187 (Admin), [2015]
P.T.S.R. 91 (QBD (Admin)), Stuart-
Smith J
s.33, amended: 2015 c.20 Sch.13 para.6
s.41, repealed: 2015 c.20 Sch.13 para.6
Sch.3 para.22, amended: SI 2015/664
Sch.4 para.11
Sch.3 para.23, amended: SI 2015/664
Sch.4 para.11

34. Forfeiture Act 1982
s.2, see *Chadwick v Collinson* [2014]
EWHC 3055 (Ch), [2015] W.T.L.R. 25
(Ch D), Judge Pelling QC

36. Aviation Security Act 1982
s.11, amended: 2015 c.6 Sch.5 para.9,
Sch.5 para.11
s.12, amended: 2015 c.6 Sch.5 para.9,
Sch.5 para.11
s.13, amended: 2015 c.6 Sch.5 para.11
s.13A, amended: 2015 c.6 Sch.5 para.11
s.14, amended: 2015 c.6 Sch.5 para.11
s.16, amended: 2015 c.6 Sch.5 para.9
s.22A, added: 2015 c.6 Sch.5 para.11
s.22A, enabling: SI 2015/930
s.24, amended: 2015 c.6 Sch.5 para.9
s.38, amended: 2015 c.6 Sch.5 para.9

41. Stock Transfer Act 1982
Sch.1 para.7, amended: 2015 c.20 Sch.13
para.6
42. Derelict Land Act 1982
s.1, repealed: 2015 c.20 Sch.22 para.7
45. Civic Government (Scotland) Act 1982
Part III, substituted: 2015 asp 10 s.76
Part IIIA, added: 2015 asp 10 s.82
s.3, amended: 2015 asp 10 s.77
s.5, amended: 2015 asp 10 s.78
s.7, amended: 2015 asp 10 s.66
s.10, amended: 2015 asp 10 s.63
s.13, amended: 2015 asp 10 s.64
s.22, repealed: 2015 asp 10 s.65
s.22, substituted: 2015 asp 10 s.65
s.28, amended: 2015 asp 10 s.67
s.28, repealed: 2015 asp 10 s.67
s.29, repealed: 2015 asp 10 s.67
s.30, repealed: 2015 asp 10 s.70
s.31, repealed: 2015 asp 10 s.68
s.33, repealed: 2015 asp 10 s.70
s.33A, added: 2015 asp 10 s.69
s.33C, added: 2015 asp 10 s.70
s.33D, added: 2015 asp 10 s.70
s.34, amended: 2015 asp 10 s.70
s.35A, added: 2015 asp 10 s.71
s.37, amended: 2015 asp 10 s.72
s.37A, added: 2015 asp 10 s.73
s.41, amended: 2015 asp 10 s.74, s.75,
s.76
s.45A, added: 2015 asp 10 s.76
s.45B, added: 2015 asp 10 s.76
s.45D, added: 2015 asp 10 s.77
s.45E, added: 2015 asp 10 s.80
s.45F, added: 2015 asp 10 s.80
s.52A, see *McMurdo (Craig McLeod) v
HM Advocate* [2015] HCJAC 37, 2015
S.L.T. 277 (HCJ), The Lord Justice Clerk
(Carloway)
Sch.1, substituted: 2015 asp 10 s.78
Sch.1 para.3, amended: 2015 asp 10 s.83
Sch.1 para.5, amended: 2015 asp 10
Sch.2 para.5
Sch.1 para.7, amended: 2015 asp 10
Sch.2 para.5
Sch.1 para.10, amended: 2015 asp 10
s.77
Sch.1 para.11, amended: 2015 asp 10
s.78
Sch.1 para.12, amended: 2015 asp 10
s.78

Sch.1 para.13, amended: 2015 asp 10
s.78
Sch.1 para.14, amended: 2015 asp 10
s.78
Sch.1 para.16A, added: 2015 asp 10 s.83
Sch.1 para.17, amended: 2015 asp 10
s.78
Sch.1 para.18, amended: 2015 asp 10
s.78
Sch.1 para.18A, added: 2015 asp 10 s.79
Sch.2 para.8, amended: 2015 asp 10 s.83
Sch.2 para.9, amended: 2015 asp 10 s.80,
s.81
Sch.2 para.9, repealed: 2015 asp 10 s.80
Sch.2 para.15, amended: 2015 asp 10
s.77
Sch.2 para.22A, added: 2015 asp 10 s.83
Sch.2 para.24A, added: 2015 asp 10 s.79

48. Criminal Justice Act 1982
s.32, amended: 2015 c.2 Sch.9 para.8
s.32, repealed: 2015 c.2 Sch.9 para.8
s.37, amended: SI 2015/664 Sch.5 para.3

53. Administration of Justice Act 1982
see *Steel v McGill's Bus Service Ltd*
[2015] CSOH 5, 2015 S.C.L.R. 617
(OH), Lady Stacey
s.8, see *Gallagher v SC Cheadle Hume
Ltd* 2015 Rep. L.R. 33 (OH), Lord Uist
s.9, see *Gallagher v SC Cheadle Hume
Ltd* 2015 Rep. L.R. 33 (OH), Lord Uist
s.12, see *Boyd v Gates (UK) Ltd* [2015]
CSOH 100, 2015 S.L.T. 483 (OH), Lord
Uist; see *Cole v Advocate General for
Scotland* [2015] CSOH 102, 2015 S.L.T.
504 (OH), Lady Stacey; see *Fraser v
Kitsons Insulation Contractors Ltd*
[2015] CSOH 135, 2015 S.L.T. 753
(OH), Lord Doherty; see *W v Advocate
General for Scotland* [2015] CSOH 111,
2015 S.L.T. 537 (OH), Lord Pentland
s.20, see *Marley v Rawlings* [2015] A.C.
129 (SC), Lord Neuberger JSC; see
Reading v Reading [2015] EWHC 946
(Ch), [2015] W.T.L.R. 1245 (Ch D),
Asplin J
s.21, see *Harte (Deceased), Re* [2015]
EWHC 2351 (Ch), [2015] W.T.L.R. 1735
(Ch D), Judge Hodge QC; see *Marley v
Rawlings* [2015] A.C. 129 (SC), Lord
Neuberger JSC; see *Reading v Reading*

[2015] EWHC 946 (Ch), [2015]
W.T.L.R. 1245 (Ch D), Asplin J

1983

2. Representation of the People Act 1983
see *Moohan, Petitioner* [2015] A.C. 901
(SC), Lord Neuberger PSC
s.2, see *Moohan, Petitioner* [2015] A.C.
901 (SC), Lord Neuberger PSC
s.2, amended: 2015 asp 7 s.1
s.3, see *Moohan, Petitioner* [2015] A.C.
901 (SC), Lord Neuberger PSC; see
Moohan, Petitioner 2015 S.C. 1 (IH (1
Div)), The Lord President (Gill)
s.7B, amended: 2015 asp 7 s.8
s.9, amended: 2015 asp 7 s.12
s.9A, amended: 2015 asp 7 s.2
s.9D, enabling: SI 2015/450, SI 2015/467
s.9E, amended: 2015 asp 7 s.3
s.10A, enabling: SI 2015/1939
s.10ZC, enabling: SI 2015/450, SI
2015/467, SI 2015/1966, SI 2015/1971
s.10ZD, enabling: SI 2015/450, SI
2015/467, SI 2015/1966, SI 2015/1971
s.13, amended: 2015 c.25 Sch.2 para.2
s.13A, amended: 2015 c.25 Sch.2 para.3
s.13AB, amended: 2015 c.25 Sch.2
para.4
s.13B, amended: 2015 c.25 Sch.2 para.5
s.13BA, amended: 2015 c.25 Sch.2
para.6
s.13BC, added: 2015 c.25 Sch.2 para.7
s.14, amended: 2015 asp 7 s.9
s.15, amended: 2015 asp 7 s.9
s.16, substituted: 2015 asp 7 s.9
s.17, amended: 2015 asp 7 s.9
s.29, enabling: SI 2015/476, SI 2015/761,
SI 2015/885
s.36, enabling: SI 2015/103, SI 2015/104
s.53, enabling: SI 2015/221, SI 2015/450,
SI 2015/467, SI 2015/1966, SI 2015/1971
s.56, amended: 2015 c.25 Sch.2 para.8
s.58, amended: 2015 c.25 Sch.2 para.9
s.87, repealed: SI 2015/664 Sch.5 para.4
s.106, see *Morrison v Carmichael* 2015
S.L.T. 675 (IH), Lady Paton
s.127, see *Erlam v Rahman* [2014]
EWHC 2766 (QB), [2015] 1 W.L.R. 231
(QBD), Supperstone J; see *Erlam v*

Rahman [2014] EWHC 2767 (QB),
[2015] 1 W.L.R. 245 (QBD),
Supperstone J
s.130, see *Erlam v Rahman* [2014]
EWHC 2767 (QB), [2015] 1 W.L.R. 245
(QBD), Supperstone J
s.131, see *Erlam v Rahman* [2014]
EWHC 2767 (QB), [2015] 1 W.L.R. 245
(QBD), Supperstone J
s.199ZA, substituted: SI 2015/1376 Sch.2
para.1
s.201, enabling: SI 2015/221, SI
2015/656
s.202, enabling: SI 2015/221
Sch.1 Part 1, amended: SI 2015/656
Sch.1
Sch.1 Part 1, amended: 2015 c.25 Sch.6
para.1
Sch.1 Part 1 para.1, substituted: SI
2015/656 Sch.2
Sch.1 Part III para.19, enabling: SI
2015/656
Sch.1 Part III para.24, enabling: SI
2015/221
Sch.1 Part III para.28, enabling: SI
2015/221
Sch.1 Part III para.32, enabling: SI
2015/221
Sch.2 para.1, enabling: SI 2015/450, SI
2015/467, SI 2015/1971
Sch.2 para.1A, enabling: SI 2015/450, SI
2015/467, SI 2015/1966, SI 2015/1971
Sch.2 para.1B, enabling: SI 2015/450, SI
2015/467, SI 2015/1971
Sch.2 para.2, enabling: SI 2015/1971
Sch.2 para.3ZA, enabling: SI 2015/450,
SI 2015/467, SI 2015/1966, SI 2015/1971
Sch.2 para.12, enabling: SI 2015/450

8. British Fishing Boats Act 1983
repealed: 2015 c.20 Sch.23 para.31
s.1, amended: SI 2015/664 Sch.4 para.12
s.4, amended: SI 2015/664 Sch.4 para.12

16. Level Crossings Act 1983
s.1, amended: SI 2015/1682 Sch.1 para.4

20. Mental Health Act 1983
see *A Local Health Board v AB* [2015]
EWCOP 31, [2015] C.O.P.L.R. 412 (CP),
Judge Parry; see *Bostridge v Oxleas
NHS Foundation Trust* [2015] EWCA
Civ 79, (2015) 18 C.C.L. Rep. 144 (CA
(Civ Div)), Sir Terence Etherton C; see

*K v Kingswood Centre Hospital
Managers* [2014] EWHC 2271 (Admin),
[2015] M.H.L.R. 68 (QBD (Admin)),
Burton J; see *NHS Trust v FG* [2015] 1
W.L.R. 1984 (CP), Keehan J; see *NM v
Kent CC* [2015] UKUT 125 (AAC),
[2015] C.O.P.L.R. 537 (UT (AAC)),
Judge Edward Jacobs; see *PJ (A Patient)
v A Local Health Board* [2015] UKUT
480 (AAC), [2015] C.O.P.L.R. 756 (UT
(AAC)), Charles J; see *R. (on the
application of Letts) v Lord Chancellor*
[2015] EWHC 402 (Admin), [2015] 1
W.L.R. 4497 (QBD (Admin)), Green J;
see *R. (on the application of N) v Walsall
MBC* [2014] EWHC 1918 (Admin),
[2015] 1 All E.R. 165 (QBD (Admin)),
Leggatt J
s.2, see *KD v A Borough Council* [2015]
UKUT 251 (AAC), [2015] C.O.P.L.R.
486 (UT (AAC)), Charles J
s.3, see *A Local Health Board v AB*
[2015] EWCOP 31, [2015] C.O.P.L.R.
412 (CP), Judge Parry; see *K v
Kingswood Centre Hospital Managers*
[2014] EWCA Civ 1332, [2015] P.T.S.R.
287 (CA (Civ Div)), Moore-Bick LJ; see
KD v A Borough Council [2015] UKUT
251 (AAC), [2015] C.O.P.L.R. 486 (UT
(AAC)), Charles J; see *R. (on the
application of Antoniou) v Central and
North West London NHS Foundation
Trust* [2013] EWHC 3055 (Admin),
[2015] 1 W.L.R. 4459 (DC), Aikens LJ;
see *R. (on the application of Wiltshire
Council) v Hertfordshire CC* [2014]
EWCA Civ 712, [2015] 2 All E.R. 518
(CA (Civ Div)), Moses LJ; see *SL v
Ludlow Street Healthcare* [2015] UKUT
398 (AAC), [2015] M.H.L.R. 390 (UT
(AAC)), Judge Jacobs
s.17, see *SL v Ludlow Street Healthcare*
[2015] UKUT 398 (AAC), [2015]
M.H.L.R. 390 (UT (AAC)), Judge Jacobs
s.17A, see *PJ (A Patient) v A Local
Health Board* [2015] UKUT 480 (AAC),
[2015] C.O.P.L.R. 756 (UT (AAC)),
Charles J
s.18, see *KD v A Borough Council* [2015]
UKUT 251 (AAC), [2015] C.O.P.L.R.
486 (UT (AAC)), Charles J

s.25, see *K v Kingswood Centre Hospital Managers* [2014] EWCA Civ 1332, [2015] P.T.S.R. 287 (CA (Civ Div)), Moore-Bick LJ; see *K v Kingswood Centre Hospital Managers* [2014] EWHC 2271 (Admin), [2015] M.H.L.R. 68 (QBD (Admin)), Burton J

s.32, see *K v Kingswood Centre Hospital Managers* [2014] EWCA Civ 1332, [2015] P.T.S.R. 287 (CA (Civ Div)), Moore-Bick LJ

s.35, see *R. (on the application of M) v Kingston Crown Court* [2014] EWHC 2702 (Admin), [2015] 4 All E.R. 1028 (DC), Ouseley J

s.37, see *R. (on the application of Wiltshire Council) v Hertfordshire CC* [2014] EWCA Civ 712, [2015] 2 All E.R. 518 (CA (Civ Div), Moses LJ; see *R. v Daniels (Jade Louise)* [2014] EWCA Crim 2009, [2015] M.H.L.R. 91 (CA (Crim Div)), Wyn Williams J; see *R. v Fox (Wayne Anthony)* [2011] EWCA Crim 3299, [2015] M.H.L.R. 12 (CA (Crim Div)), Davis LJ; see *R. v Poole (Matthew Jason)* [2014] EWCA Crim 1641, [2015] 1 W.L.R. 522 (CA (Crim Div)), Macur LJ; see *R. v Quirk (Peter)* [2014] EWCA Crim 1052, [2015] M.H.L.R. 22 (CA (Crim Div)), Davis LJ; see *R. v Vowles (Lucinda)* [2015] EWCA Crim 45, [2015] 1 W.L.R. 5131 (CA (Civ Div)), Lord Thomas LCJ; see *Secretary of State for Justice v KC* [2015] UKUT 376 (AAC), [2015] C.O.P.L.R. 804 (UT (AAC)), Charles J

s.37, amended: 2015 c.2 Sch.5 para.1

s.38, see *R. v Vowles (Lucinda)* [2015] EWCA Crim 45, [2015] 1 W.L.R. 5131 (CA (Civ Div)), Lord Thomas LCJ

s.41, see *R. (on the application of Wiltshire Council) v Hertfordshire CC* [2014] EWCA Civ 712, [2015] 2 All E.R. 518 (CA (Civ Div)), Moses LJ; see *R. v Daniels (Jade Louise)* [2014] EWCA Crim 2009, [2015] M.H.L.R. 91 (CA (Crim Div)), Wyn Williams J; see *R. v Fox (Wayne Anthony)* [2011] EWCA Crim 3299, [2015] M.H.L.R. 12 (CA (Crim Div)), Davis LJ; see *R. v Poole (Matthew Jason)* [2014] EWCA Crim

1641, [2015] 1 W.L.R. 522 (CA (Crim Div)), Macur LJ; see *R. v Quirk (Peter)* [2014] EWCA Crim 1052, [2015] M.H.L.R. 22 (CA (Crim Div)), Davis LJ; see *R. v Vowles (Lucinda)* [2015] EWCA Crim 45, [2015] 1 W.L.R. 5131 (CA (Civ Div)), Lord Thomas LCJ; see *Secretary of State for Justice v KC* [2015] UKUT 376 (AAC), [2015] C.O.P.L.R. 804 (UT (AAC)), Charles J

s.42, see *R. (on the application of Lee-Hirons) v Secretary of State for Justice* [2014] EWCA Civ 553, [2015] Q.B. 385 (CA (Civ Div)), Jackson LJ; see *R. (on the application of Wiltshire Council) v Hertfordshire CC* [2014] EWCA Civ 712, [2015] 2 All E.R. 518 (CA (Civ Div)), Moses LJ

s.45A, see *R. v Brown (Edward)* [2015] EWCA Crim 1328, [2015] 2 Cr. App. R. 31 (CA (Crim Div)), Fulford LJ; see *R. v Fox (Wayne Anthony)* [2011] EWCA Crim 3299, [2015] M.H.L.R. 12 (CA (Crim Div)), Davis LJ; see *R. v Poole (Matthew Jason)* [2014] EWCA Crim 1641, [2015] 1 W.L.R. 522 (CA (Crim Div)), Macur LJ; see *R. v Quirk (Peter)* [2014] EWCA Crim 1052, [2015] M.H.L.R. 22 (CA (Crim Div)), Davis LJ; see *R. v Vowles (Lucinda)* [2015] EWCA Crim 45, [2015] 1 W.L.R. 5131 (CA (Civ Div)), Lord Thomas LCJ

s.47, see *R. (on the application of LV) v Secretary of State for Justice* [2014] EWHC 1495 (Admin), [2015] M.H.L.R. 29 (QBD (Admin)), Irwin J; see *R. v Vowles (Lucinda)* [2015] EWCA Crim 45, [2015] 1 W.L.R. 5131 (CA (Civ Div)), Lord Thomas LCJ

s.49, see *R. (on the application of LV) v Secretary of State for Justice* [2014] EWHC 1495 (Admin), [2015] M.H.L.R. 29 (QBD (Admin)), Irwin J

s.50, amended: 2015 c.2 Sch.3 para.2

s.64D, see *PJ (A Patient) v A Local Health Board* [2015] UKUT 480 (AAC), [2015] C.O.P.L.R. 756 (UT (AAC)), Charles J

s.66, see *AF v Nottingham NHS Trust* [2015] UKUT 216 (AAC), [2015]

M.H.L.R. 347 (UT (AAC)), Judge
Wright
s.72, see *KD v A Borough Council* [2015]
UKUT 251 (AAC), [2015] C.O.P.L.R.
486 (UT (AAC)), Charles J; see *NM v
Kent CC* [2015] UKUT 125 (AAC),
[2015] C.O.P.L.R. 537 (UT (AAC)),
Judge Edward Jacobs; see *PJ (A Patient)
v A Local Health Board* [2015] UKUT
480 (AAC), [2015] C.O.P.L.R. 756 (UT
(AAC)), Charles J
s.73, see *Secretary of State for Justice v
KC* [2015] UKUT 376 (AAC), [2015]
C.O.P.L.R. 804 (UT (AAC)), Charles J
s.74, see *R. (on the application of LV) v
Secretary of State for Justice* [2014]
EWHC 1495 (Admin), [2015] M.H.L.R.
29 (QBD (Admin)), Irwin J
s.74, amended: 2015 c.2 Sch.3 para.3
s.117, see *AF v Nottingham NHS Trust*
[2015] UKUT 216 (AAC), [2015]
M.H.L.R. 347 (UT (AAC)), Judge
Wright; see *R. (on the application of
Wiltshire Council) v Hertfordshire CC*
[2014] EWCA Civ 712, [2015] 2 All E.R.
518 (CA (Civ Div)), Moses LJ
s.117B, added: SI 2015/914 Sch.1
para.28
s.135, amended: SI 2015/914 Sch.1
para.29
s.136, see *BS, Re* [2015] EWCOP 39,
(2015) 18 C.C.L. Rep. 486 (CP), Mostyn
J

23. Water Act 1983
s.3, repealed: 2015 c.20 Sch.23 para.28
s.10, amended: 2015 c.20 Sch.23 para.28
Sch.2 Part I para.3, enabling: SI
2015/751
Sch.2 Part I para.8, enabling: SI
2015/639
Sch.2 Part II para.10, enabling: SI
2015/751

40. Education (Fees and Awards) Act 1983
s.1, amended: 2015 c.20 Sch.14 para.33

**41. Health and Social Services and Social
Security Adjudications Act 1983**
s.17, amended: SI 2015/914 Sch.1
para.31
s.17, repealed: SI 2015/914 Sch.1 para.31
s.22, amended: SI 2015/914 Sch.1
para.32

s.23, amended: SI 2015/914 Sch.1
para.33

54. Medical Act 1983
s.1, amended: SI 2015/794 Art.2, Art.3
s.1, repealed: SI 2015/794 Art.3
s.1, substituted: SI 2015/794 Art.21
s.29A, enabling: SI 2015/1375
s.29B, enabling: SI 2015/1375
s.29D, enabling: SI 2015/1375
s.29J, enabling: SI 2015/1375
s.31, amended: SI 2015/794 Art.12
s.31, enabling: SI 2015/92
s.31A, amended: SI 2015/794 Art.12
s.34H, amended: SI 2015/794 Art.21
s.35A, amended: SI 2015/794 Art.15
s.35B, amended: SI 2015/794 Art.4,
Art.9, Art.12
s.35C, amended: SI 2015/794 Art.5,
Art.6, Art.21
s.35CC, amended: SI 2015/794 Art.4,
Art.22
s.35CC, enabling: SI 2015/1964
s.35D, amended: SI 2015/794 Art.5,
Art.12
s.35D, substituted: SI 2015/794 Art.5
s.35E, amended: SI 2015/794 Art.5,
Art.21
s.38, amended: SI 2015/794 Art.4, Art.12
s.38, repealed: SI 2015/794 Art.12
s.38, substituted: SI 2015/794 Art.12
s.40, see *Jasinarachchi v General
Medical Council* [2014] EWHC 3570
(Admin), [2015] Med. L.R. 277 (QBD
(Admin)), Stewart J
s.40, amended: SI 2015/794 Art.16
s.40, substituted: SI 2015/794 Art.16
s.40A, added: SI 2015/794 Art.17
s.41, amended: SI 2015/794 Art.12,
Art.19, Art.21
s.41A, amended: SI 2015/794 Art.6
s.41C, amended: SI 2015/794 Art.12
s.43, amended: SI 2015/794 Art.8
s.43, substituted: SI 2015/794 Art.8
s.44, amended: SI 2015/794 Art.4, Art.8,
Art.13, Art.21
s.44C, enabling: SI 2015/1375
s.47, amended: SI 2015/794 Art.4, Art.12
s.52B, added: SI 2015/794 Art.20
s.53, amended: SI 2015/794 Art.4
s.55, amended: SI 2015/794 Art.2, Art.21

Sch.1 Part II para.15, amended: SI
2015/794 Art.2
Sch.1 Part II para.16, amended: SI
2015/794 Art.2
Sch.1 Part III para.19A, repealed: SI
2015/794 Art.3
Sch.1 Part III para.19B, enabling: SI
2015/1964, SI 2015/1965
Sch.1 Part III para.19C, enabling: SI
2015/1964, SI 2015/1965
Sch.1 Part III para.19D, enabling: SI
2015/1964, SI 2015/1965
Sch.1 Part III para.19E, repealed: SI
2015/794 Art.3
Sch.1 Part III para.19F, added: SI
2015/794 Art.2
Sch.1 Part III para.19F, enabling: SI
2015/1967
Sch.1 Part III para.19G, added: SI
2015/794 Art.3
Sch.1 Part III para.19G, enabling: SI
2015/1964, SI 2015/1965
Sch.1 Part III para.23, amended: SI
2015/794 Art.4
Sch.1 Part III para.23, enabling: SI
2015/1965
Sch.1 Part III para.23B, amended: SI
2015/794 Art.4
Sch.1 Part III para.23B, enabling: SI
2015/1965
Sch.1 Part III para.23C, amended: SI
2015/794 Art.4
Sch.1 Part III para.23D, added: SI
2015/794 Art.4
Sch.1 Part III para.23D, amended: SI
2015/794 Art.21
Sch.1 Part III para.24, amended: SI
2015/794 Art.4
Sch.1 Part III para.25, amended: SI
2015/794 Art.4
Sch.3A para.4, amended: SI 2015/794
Art.23
Sch.3B para.3, amended: SI 2015/794
Art.23, Art.26
Sch.4, substituted: SI 2015/794 Art.7,
Art.8
Sch.4, substituted: SI 2015/794 Art.10
Sch.4 para.1, amended: SI 2015/794
Art.7, Art.8, Art.9, Art.21
Sch.4 para.1, enabling: SI 2015/1958, SI
2015/1964

Sch.4 para.2, amended: SI 2015/794
Art.8
Sch.4 para.3, amended: SI 2015/794
Art.8
Sch.4 para.3A, repealed: SI 2015/794
Art.8
Sch.4 para.5A, amended: SI 2015/794
Art.10, Art.11, Art.21
Sch.4 para.5A, enabling: SI 2015/1964
Sch.4 para.5B, amended: SI 2015/794
Art.10
Sch.4 para.5C, amended: SI 2015/794
Art.11, Art.21
Sch.4 para.5C, enabling: SI 2015/1964
Sch.4 para.7, amended: SI 2015/794
Art.13
Sch.4 para.7, repealed: SI 2015/794
Art.13
Sch.4 para.7, enabling: SI 2015/1958
Sch.4 para.7A, added: SI 2015/794
Art.14
Sch.4 para.7A, enabling: SI 2015/1964
Sch.4 para.8, amended: SI 2015/794
Art.12, Art.22, Art.24
Sch.4 para.9, amended: SI 2015/794
Art.5, Art.12
Sch.4 para.10, amended: SI 2015/794
Art.8
Sch.4 para.10A, added: SI 2015/794
Art.12
Sch.4 para.10B, amended: SI 2015/794
Art.8
Sch.4 para.11, amended: SI 2015/794
Art.12, Art.17, Art.25
Sch.4 para.12, amended: SI 2015/794
Art.12
Sch.4 para.13, amended: SI 2015/794
Art.8, Art.26

55. Value Added Tax Act 1983
s.10, see *N & M Walkingshaw Ltd v*
Revenue and Customs Commissioners
[2015] UKUT 123 (TCC), [2015] S.T.C.
1620 (UT (Tax)), Warren J
Sch.4 para.3, see *N & M Walkingshaw*
Ltd v Revenue and Customs
Commissioners [2015] UKUT 123
(TCC), [2015] S.T.C. 1620 (UT (Tax)),
Warren J
Sch.4 para.7, see *Revenue and Customs*
Commissioners v General Motors (UK)

Ltd [2015] UKUT 605 (TCC), [2015]
B.V.C. 536 (UT (Tax)), Henderson J

1984

12. Telecommunications Act 1984
s.101, amended: SI 2015/1682 Sch.1
para.4
16. Foreign Limitation Periods Act 1984
s.1, amended: SI 2015/1392 Reg.5
s.1B, added: SI 2015/1392 Reg.5
s.1B, repealed: SI 2015/1972 Reg.4
22. Public Health (Control of Disease) Act 1984
s.45F, amended: SI 2015/664 Sch.3
para.15
s.45F, repealed: SI 2015/664 Sch.3
para.15 , Sch.4 para.86
s.45O, amended: SI 2015/664 Sch.4
para.13
s.46, amended: SI 2015/914 Sch.1
para.34
s.63, amended: SI 2015/664 Sch.4
para.13
24. Dentists Act 1984
s.1, amended: 2015 c.28 Sch.1 para.1
s.1, repealed: 2015 c.28 Sch.1 para.1
s.15, amended: SI 2015/806 Art.12
s.15, repealed: SI 2015/806 Art.12
s.15A, added: SI 2015/806 Art.13
s.16, enabling: SI 2015/735
s.17, amended: SI 2015/806 Art.14
s.17, repealed: SI 2015/806 Art.14
s.19, amended: SI 2015/806 Art.15
s.21A, amended: SI 2015/806 Art.16
s.26A, enabling: SI 2015/1758
s.27, amended: SI 2015/806 Art.17
s.27A, amended: 2015 c.28 Sch.1 para.1,
SI 2015/806 Art.18
s.27B, see *Kirschner v General Dental
Council* [2015] EWHC 1377 (Admin),
[2015] Med. L.R. 317 (QBD (Admin)),
Mostyn J
s.27BA, added: SI 2015/806 Art.19
s.33, amended: 2015 c.28 Sch.1 para.1
s.36C, amended: SI 2015/806 Art.20
s.36C, repealed: SI 2015/806 Art.20
s.36CA, added: SI 2015/806 Art.21
s.36E, amended: SI 2015/806 Art.22
s.36F, amended: SI 2015/806 Art.23

s.36L, enabling: SI 2015/1758
s.36N, amended: SI 2015/806 Art.24
s.36O, amended: 2015 c.28 Sch.1 para.1,
SI 2015/806 Art.25
s.36PA, added: SI 2015/806 Art.26
s.36W, amended: 2015 c.28 Sch.1 para.1
s.50D, amended: SI 2015/806 Art.27
s.52, enabling: SI 2015/735
s.53, amended: 2015 c.28 Sch.1 para.1,
SI 2015/806 Art.28
Sch.2A para.1, amended: SI 2015/806
Art.29
Sch.2A para.2, amended: SI 2015/806
Art.29
Sch.2A para.3, amended: SI 2015/806
Art.29
Sch.2A para.4, amended: SI 2015/806
Art.29
Sch.4ZA, amended: SI 2015/806 Art.30
Sch.4A para.1, amended: SI 2015/806
Art.31
Sch.4A para.2, amended: SI 2015/806
Art.31
Sch.4A para.3, amended: SI 2015/806
Art.31
Sch.4A para.4, amended: SI 2015/806
Art.31
26. Inshore Fishing (Scotland) Act 1984
s.1, enabling: SSI 2015/435, SSI
2015/436, SSI 2015/437
s.2A, enabling: SSI 2015/435, SSI
2015/436, SSI 2015/437
27. Road Traffic Regulation Act 1984
s.1, amended: 2015 c.7 Sch.1 para.71
s.1, enabling: SI 2015/764, SI 2015/1085,
SI 2015/1218, SI 2015/1243, SI
2015/1301, SI 2015/1328, SI 2015/1538,
SI 2015/1925, SI 2015/1950, SI
2015/2017
s.2, amended: 2015 c.7 Sch.1 para.72
s.2, enabling: SI 2015/764, SI 2015/1085,
SI 2015/1218, SI 2015/1243, SI
2015/1301, SI 2015/1328, SI 2015/1538,
SI 2015/1925, SI 2015/1950, SI
2015/2017, SSI 2015/2, SSI 2015/22, SSI
2015/23, SSI 2015/24, SSI 2015/25, SSI
2015/27, SSI 2015/40, SSI 2015/42, SSI
2015/55, SSI 2015/57, SSI 2015/67, SSI
2015/68, SSI 2015/69, SSI 2015/70, SSI
2015/75, SSI 2015/76, SSI 2015/78, SSI
2015/106, SSI 2015/111, SSI 2015/112,

SSI 2015/114, SSI 2015/134, SSI
2015/135, SSI 2015/136, SSI 2015/137,
SSI 2015/147, SSI 2015/168, SSI
2015/169, SSI 2015/170, SSI 2015/171,
SSI 2015/172, SSI 2015/175, SSI
2015/178, SSI 2015/191, SSI 2015/195,
SSI 2015/204, SSI 2015/205, SSI
2015/206, SSI 2015/207, SSI 2015/253,
SSI 2015/255, SSI 2015/256, SSI
2015/259, SSI 2015/273, SSI 2015/274,
SSI 2015/275, SSI 2015/276, SSI
2015/277, SSI 2015/280, SSI 2015/281,
SSI 2015/282, SSI 2015/284, SSI
2015/285, SSI 2015/287, SSI 2015/288,
SSI 2015/289, SSI 2015/290, SSI
2015/291, SSI 2015/292, SSI 2015/293,
SSI 2015/294, SSI 2015/299, SSI
2015/300, SSI 2015/304, SSI 2015/306,
SSI 2015/307, SSI 2015/308, SSI
2015/309, SSI 2015/310, SSI 2015/316,
SSI 2015/339, SSI 2015/340, SSI
2015/341, SSI 2015/342, SSI 2015/343,
SSI 2015/352, SSI 2015/353, SSI
2015/354, SSI 2015/355, SSI 2015/357,
SSI 2015/362, SSI 2015/366, SSI
2015/367, SSI 2015/372, SSI 2015/374,
SSI 2015/385, SSI 2015/389, SSI
2015/390, SSI 2015/391, SSI 2015/394,
SSI 2015/407, SSI 2015/416, SSI
2015/418, SSI 2015/426, SSI 2015/439,
SSI 2015/440, SSI 2015/441, SSI
2015/442, SSI 2015/445, SSI 2015/449
s.4, enabling: SI 2015/1218, SI
2015/1243, SI 2015/1925, SI 2015/1950,
SI 2015/2017, SSI 2015/2, SSI 2015/22,
SSI 2015/23, SSI 2015/24, SSI 2015/25,
SSI 2015/27, SSI 2015/40, SSI 2015/42,
SSI 2015/55, SSI 2015/57, SSI 2015/67,
SSI 2015/68, SSI 2015/69, SSI 2015/70,
SSI 2015/75, SSI 2015/76, SSI 2015/78,
SSI 2015/106, SSI 2015/111, SSI
2015/112, SSI 2015/114, SSI 2015/134,
SSI 2015/135, SSI 2015/136, SSI
2015/137, SSI 2015/147, SSI 2015/168,
SSI 2015/169, SSI 2015/170, SSI
2015/171, SSI 2015/172, SSI 2015/175,
SSI 2015/178, SSI 2015/191, SSI
2015/195, SSI 2015/204, SSI 2015/205,
SSI 2015/206, SSI 2015/207, SSI
2015/253, SSI 2015/255, SSI 2015/256,
SSI 2015/259, SSI 2015/273, SSI

2015/274, SSI 2015/275, SSI 2015/276,
SSI 2015/277, SSI 2015/280, SSI
2015/281, SSI 2015/282, SSI 2015/284,
SSI 2015/285, SSI 2015/287, SSI
2015/288, SSI 2015/289, SSI 2015/290,
SSI 2015/291, SSI 2015/292, SSI
2015/293, SSI 2015/294, SSI 2015/299,
SSI 2015/300, SSI 2015/304, SSI
2015/306, SSI 2015/307, SSI 2015/308,
SSI 2015/309, SSI 2015/310, SSI
2015/316, SSI 2015/339, SSI 2015/340,
SSI 2015/341, SSI 2015/342, SSI
2015/343, SSI 2015/352, SSI 2015/353,
SSI 2015/354, SSI 2015/355, SSI
2015/357, SSI 2015/362, SSI 2015/366,
SSI 2015/367, SSI 2015/372, SSI
2015/374, SSI 2015/385, SSI 2015/389,
SSI 2015/390, SSI 2015/391, SSI
2015/394, SSI 2015/407, SSI 2015/416,
SSI 2015/418, SSI 2015/426, SSI
2015/439, SSI 2015/440, SSI 2015/441,
SSI 2015/442, SSI 2015/445, SSI
2015/449
s.5, enabling: SI 2015/1195
s.6, amended: 2015 c.7 Sch.1 para.73
s.9, amended: 2015 c.7 Sch.1 para.74
s.14, enabling: SI 2015/45, SI 2015/49,
SI 2015/56, SI 2015/71, SI 2015/148, SI
2015/149, SI 2015/150, SI 2015/151, SI
2015/152, SI 2015/153, SI 2015/154, SI
2015/155, SI 2015/156, SI 2015/157, SI
2015/158, SI 2015/160, SI 2015/161, SI
2015/163, SI 2015/164, SI 2015/166, SI
2015/167, SI 2015/245, SI 2015/248, SI
2015/249, SI 2015/250, SI 2015/251, SI
2015/252, SI 2015/254, SI 2015/256, SI
2015/258, SI 2015/260, SI 2015/262, SI
2015/268, SI 2015/271, SI 2015/272, SI
2015/273, SI 2015/274, SI 2015/276, SI
2015/278, SI 2015/279, SI 2015/280, SI
2015/281, SI 2015/282, SI 2015/283, SI
2015/284, SI 2015/285, SI 2015/290, SI
2015/291, SI 2015/292, SI 2015/294, SI
2015/296, SI 2015/297, SI 2015/298, SI
2015/299, SI 2015/306, SI 2015/308, SI
2015/309, SI 2015/311, SI 2015/331, SI
2015/332, SI 2015/333, SI 2015/334, SI
2015/516, SI 2015/517, SI 2015/519, SI
2015/520, SI 2015/525, SI 2015/526, SI
2015/528, SI 2015/529, SI 2015/530, SI
2015/535, SI 2015/536, SI 2015/538, SI

2015/540, SI 2015/553, SI 2015/554, SI
2015/556, SI 2015/557, SI 2015/558, SI
2015/586, SI 2015/679, SI 2015/684, SI
2015/685, SI 2015/686, SI 2015/688, SI
2015/689, SI 2015/690, SI 2015/691, SI
2015/695, SI 2015/696, SI 2015/697, SI
2015/702, SI 2015/703, SI 2015/707, SI
2015/708, SI 2015/709, SI 2015/711, SI
2015/712, SI 2015/713, SI 2015/714, SI
2015/715, SI 2015/724, SI 2015/734, SI
2015/736, SI 2015/739, SI 2015/745, SI
2015/753, SI 2015/756, SI 2015/757, SI
2015/762, SI 2015/763, SI 2015/765, SI
2015/834, SI 2015/835, SI 2015/837, SI
2015/849, SI 2015/976, SI 2015/984, SI
2015/986, SI 2015/1002, SI 2015/1003,
SI 2015/1004, SI 2015/1005, SI
2015/1006, SI 2015/1009, SI 2015/1011,
SI 2015/1012, SI 2015/1015, SI
2015/1017, SI 2015/1019, SI 2015/1021,
SI 2015/1022, SI 2015/1023, SI
2015/1024, SI 2015/1029, SI 2015/1030,
SI 2015/1031, SI 2015/1032, SI
2015/1033, SI 2015/1034, SI 2015/1035,
SI 2015/1036, SI 2015/1037, SI
2015/1038, SI 2015/1039, SI 2015/1040,
SI 2015/1041, SI 2015/1042, SI
2015/1043, SI 2015/1044, SI 2015/1045,
SI 2015/1046, SI 2015/1047, SI
2015/1048, SI 2015/1049, SI 2015/1050,
SI 2015/1051, SI 2015/1052, SI
2015/1053, SI 2015/1054, SI 2015/1055,
SI 2015/1056, SI 2015/1057, SI
2015/1058, SI 2015/1059, SI 2015/1060,
SI 2015/1061, SI 2015/1062, SI
2015/1063, SI 2015/1064, SI 2015/1065,
SI 2015/1066, SI 2015/1067, SI
2015/1068, SI 2015/1069, SI 2015/1070,
SI 2015/1071, SI 2015/1081, SI
2015/1082, SI 2015/1083, SI 2015/1086,
SI 2015/1087, SI 2015/1088, SI
2015/1089, SI 2015/1090, SI 2015/1091,
SI 2015/1092, SI 2015/1093, SI
2015/1094, SI 2015/1095, SI 2015/1096,
SI 2015/1100, SI 2015/1101, SI
2015/1102, SI 2015/1103, SI 2015/1104,
SI 2015/1107, SI 2015/1108, SI
2015/1109, SI 2015/1110, SI 2015/1111,
SI 2015/1112, SI 2015/1113, SI
2015/1114, SI 2015/1115, SI 2015/1116,
SI 2015/1119, SI 2015/1120, SI

2015/1121, SI 2015/1122, SI 2015/1123,
SI 2015/1125, SI 2015/1126, SI
2015/1127, SI 2015/1128, SI 2015/1129,
SI 2015/1130, SI 2015/1131, SI
2015/1132, SI 2015/1133, SI 2015/1134,
SI 2015/1135, SI 2015/1136, SI
2015/1137, SI 2015/1138, SI 2015/1139,
SI 2015/1140, SI 2015/1141, SI
2015/1142, SI 2015/1143, SI 2015/1144,
SI 2015/1145, SI 2015/1146, SI
2015/1147, SI 2015/1148, SI 2015/1149,
SI 2015/1150, SI 2015/1151, SI
2015/1152, SI 2015/1153, SI 2015/1154,
SI 2015/1155, SI 2015/1156, SI
2015/1157, SI 2015/1158, SI 2015/1159,
SI 2015/1160, SI 2015/1161, SI
2015/1162, SI 2015/1163, SI 2015/1164,
SI 2015/1165, SI 2015/1166, SI
2015/1167, SI 2015/1168, SI 2015/1169,
SI 2015/1170, SI 2015/1171, SI
2015/1172, SI 2015/1173, SI 2015/1174,
SI 2015/1175, SI 2015/1176, SI
2015/1177, SI 2015/1179, SI 2015/1181,
SI 2015/1183, SI 2015/1184, SI
2015/1185, SI 2015/1186, SI 2015/1187,
SI 2015/1188, SI 2015/1189, SI
2015/1190, SI 2015/1191, SI 2015/1192,
SI 2015/1193, SI 2015/1194, SI
2015/1195, SI 2015/1196, SI 2015/1197,
SI 2015/1198, SI 2015/1199, SI
2015/1200, SI 2015/1201, SI 2015/1202,
SI 2015/1203, SI 2015/1204, SI
2015/1205, SI 2015/1206, SI 2015/1207,
SI 2015/1208, SI 2015/1209, SI
2015/1210, SI 2015/1211, SI 2015/1212,
SI 2015/1213, SI 2015/1214, SI
2015/1215, SI 2015/1216, SI 2015/1219,
SI 2015/1220, SI 2015/1221, SI
2015/1222, SI 2015/1223, SI 2015/1225,
SI 2015/1226, SI 2015/1228, SI
2015/1229, SI 2015/1230, SI 2015/1232,
SI 2015/1233, SI 2015/1234, SI
2015/1235, SI 2015/1236, SI 2015/1237,
SI 2015/1238, SI 2015/1239, SI
2015/1240, SI 2015/1241, SI 2015/1242,
SI 2015/1244, SI 2015/1245, SI
2015/1246, SI 2015/1247, SI 2015/1248,
SI 2015/1249, SI 2015/1250, SI
2015/1251, SI 2015/1253, SI 2015/1254,
SI 2015/1255, SI 2015/1256, SI
2015/1257, SI 2015/1258, SI 2015/1259,

SI 2015/1260, SI 2015/1261, SI
2015/1262, SI 2015/1264, SI 2015/1269,
SI 2015/1271, SI 2015/1273, SI
2015/1274, SI 2015/1275, SI 2015/1276,
SI 2015/1278, SI 2015/1279, SI
2015/1282, SI 2015/1283, SI 2015/1284,
SI 2015/1285, SI 2015/1286, SI
2015/1287, SI 2015/1288, SI 2015/1289,
SI 2015/1290, SI 2015/1291, SI
2015/1292, SI 2015/1293, SI 2015/1294,
SI 2015/1295, SI 2015/1296, SI
2015/1297, SI 2015/1299, SI 2015/1300,
SI 2015/1302, SI 2015/1303, SI
2015/1304, SI 2015/1307, SI 2015/1308,
SI 2015/1313, SI 2015/1314, SI
2015/1315, SI 2015/1316, SI 2015/1322,
SI 2015/1326, SI 2015/1340, SI
2015/1341, SI 2015/1342, SI 2015/1433,
SI 2015/1434, SI 2015/1435, SI
2015/1436, SI 2015/1437, SI 2015/1440,
SI 2015/1441, SI 2015/1442, SI
2015/1443, SI 2015/1445, SI 2015/1447,
SI 2015/1448, SI 2015/1450, SI
2015/1473, SI 2015/1481, SI 2015/1535,
SI 2015/1547, SI 2015/1548, SI
2015/1549, SI 2015/1550, SI 2015/1551,
SI 2015/1585, SI 2015/1588, SI
2015/1590, SI 2015/1593, SI 2015/1594,
SI 2015/1595, SI 2015/1602, SI
2015/1604, SI 2015/1606, SI 2015/1617,
SI 2015/1618, SI 2015/1620, SI
2015/1622, SI 2015/1624, SI 2015/1626,
SI 2015/1627, SI 2015/1632, SI
2015/1633, SI 2015/1634, SI 2015/1668,
SI 2015/1671, SI 2015/1705, SI
2015/1706, SI 2015/1707, SI 2015/1712,
SI 2015/1713, SI 2015/1714, SI
2015/1716, SI 2015/1717, SI 2015/1718,
SI 2015/1719, SI 2015/1720, SI
2015/1738, SI 2015/1746, SI 2015/1787,
SI 2015/1788, SI 2015/1789, SI
2015/1907, SI 2015/1908, SI 2015/1909,
SI 2015/1910, SI 2015/1913, SI
2015/1914, SI 2015/1915, SI 2015/1942,
SI 2015/1943, SI 2015/1944, SI
2015/1993, SI 2015/2037, SI 2015/2077,
SI 2015/2078, SI 2015/2079, SI
2015/2080, SI 2015/2081, SSI 2015/2,
SSI 2015/22, SSI 2015/23, SSI 2015/24,
SSI 2015/25, SSI 2015/27, SSI 2015/40,
SSI 2015/42, SSI 2015/55, SSI 2015/57,

SSI 2015/67, SSI 2015/68, SSI 2015/69,
SSI 2015/70, SSI 2015/75, SSI 2015/76,
SSI 2015/78, SSI 2015/106, SSI
2015/111, SSI 2015/112, SSI 2015/114,
SSI 2015/134, SSI 2015/135, SSI
2015/136, SSI 2015/137, SSI 2015/147,
SSI 2015/168, SSI 2015/169, SSI
2015/170, SSI 2015/171, SSI 2015/172,
SSI 2015/175, SSI 2015/191, SSI
2015/195, SSI 2015/204, SSI 2015/205,
SSI 2015/206, SSI 2015/207, SSI
2015/253, SSI 2015/259, SSI 2015/274,
SSI 2015/275, SSI 2015/276, SSI
2015/277, SSI 2015/281, SSI 2015/282,
SSI 2015/284, SSI 2015/285, SSI
2015/287, SSI 2015/288, SSI 2015/289,
SSI 2015/290, SSI 2015/291, SSI
2015/292, SSI 2015/300, SSI 2015/304,
SSI 2015/306, SSI 2015/307, SSI
2015/308, SSI 2015/309, SSI 2015/310,
SSI 2015/316, SSI 2015/339, SSI
2015/340, SSI 2015/341, SSI 2015/342,
SSI 2015/343, SSI 2015/352, SSI
2015/353, SSI 2015/354, SSI 2015/355,
SSI 2015/357, SSI 2015/372, SSI
2015/389, SSI 2015/390, SSI 2015/391,
SSI 2015/394, SSI 2015/416, SSI
2015/418, SSI 2015/426, SSI 2015/439,
SSI 2015/440, SSI 2015/441, SSI
2015/442, SSI 2015/449
s.15, enabling: SI 2015/136, SI 2015/249,
SI 2015/684, SI 2015/1181, SI
2015/1223, SI 2015/1226, SSI 2015/106,
SSI 2015/111, SSI 2015/169, SSI
2015/300, SSI 2015/310, SSI 2015/343
s.16A, amended: 2015 c.7 Sch.1 para.75,
2015 c.20 s.74
s.16A, enabling: SI 2015/1263, SI
2015/1298, SI 2015/1306, SI 2015/1715,
SI 2015/1737, SSI 2015/178, SSI
2015/255, SSI 2015/256, SSI 2015/273,
SSI 2015/280, SSI 2015/293, SSI
2015/294, SSI 2015/299, SSI 2015/362,
SSI 2015/366, SSI 2015/367, SSI
2015/374, SSI 2015/385, SSI 2015/407,
SSI 2015/445
s.16B, amended: 2015 c.7 Sch.1 para.76
s.17, enabling: SI 2015/8, SI 2015/241,
SI 2015/392, SI 2015/405, SI 2015/408,
SI 2015/1018, SI 2015/1701
s.19, amended: 2015 c.7 Sch.1 para.77

s.23, amended: 2015 c.7 Sch.1 para.78, 2015 c.20 Sch.10 para.23

s.23, repealed: 2015 c.20 Sch.10 para.23

s.23, substituted: 2015 c.7 Sch.1 para.78

s.24, amended: 2015 c.7 Sch.1 para.79

s.37, amended: 2015 c.7 Sch.1 para.80

s.55, see *Dorset CC v Reeves (Valuation Officer)* [2015] R.V.R. 340 (VT), MF Young

s.58, amended: 2015 c.7 Sch.1 para.81

s.65, amended: 2015 c.7 Sch.1 para.82

s.69, amended: 2015 c.7 Sch.1 para.83

s.70, amended: 2015 c.7 Sch.1 para.84

s.71, amended: 2015 c.7 Sch.1 para.85

s.74B, amended: 2015 c.7 Sch.1 para.86

s.81, see *Cusick v Harvie* 2015 J.C. 72 (HCJ), The Lord Justice Clerk (Carloway)

s.82, enabling: SI 2015/1072, SI 2015/1224, SI 2015/1446, SSI 2015/332

s.83, amended: 2015 c.7 Sch.1 para.87

s.83, enabling: SI 2015/1072, SI 2015/1224, SSI 2015/332

s.84, amended: 2015 c.7 Sch.1 para.88

s.84, enabling: SI 2015/304, SI 2015/1072, SI 2015/1084, SI 2015/1178, SI 2015/1224, SI 2015/1444, SI 2015/1446, SI 2015/1708, SSI 2015/41, SSI 2015/203, SSI 2015/251, SSI 2015/267, SSI 2015/301, SSI 2015/311, SSI 2015/332, SSI 2015/345, SSI 2015/365, SSI 2015/427

s.85, amended: 2015 c.7 Sch.1 para.89

s.87, amended: 2015 c.20 s.50

s.87, repealed: 2015 c.20 s.50

s.89, see *Cusick v Harvie* 2015 J.C. 72 (HCJ), The Lord Justice Clerk (Carloway)

s.93, amended: 2015 c.7 Sch.1 para.90

s.94, amended: 2015 c.7 Sch.1 para.91

s.100, amended: 2015 c.7 Sch.1 para.92

s.101, amended: 2015 c.7 Sch.1 para.93

s.102, amended: 2015 c.7 Sch.1 para.94

s.121A, amended: 2015 c.7 Sch.1 para.95

s.122, see *Hillhead Community Council v City of Glasgow Council* [2015] CSOH 35, 2015 S.L.T. 239 (OH), Lord Bannatyne; see *Isle of Wight Council v Revenue and Customs Commissioners* [2015] S.T.C. 460 (UT (Tax)), Proudman J; see *Williams v Devon CC* [2015]

EWHC 568 (Admin), [2015] L.L.R. 624 (QBD (Admin)), Judge Cotter QC

s.122, amended: 2015 c.7 Sch.1 para.96

s.122A, enabling: SI 2015/1072, SI 2015/1084, SI 2015/1085, SI 2015/1224, SI 2015/1328

s.124, enabling: SI 2015/304, SI 2015/1446, SI 2015/1550, SI 2015/1593, SI 2015/1708, SI 2015/1746, SI 2015/1925, SI 2015/1950, SI 2015/2017, SSI 2015/41, SSI 2015/67, SSI 2015/203, SSI 2015/251, SSI 2015/267, SSI 2015/301, SSI 2015/332, SSI 2015/416, SSI 2015/426

s.124A, amended: 2015 c.7 Sch.1 para.97

s.124B, amended: 2015 c.7 Sch.1 para.98

s.130, enabling: SI 2015/1653

s.140, enabling: SI 2015/24

s.142, amended: 2015 c.7 Sch.1 para.99

Sch.6 Part III, amended: SI 2015/1653 Reg.2

Sch.6 Part IV para.4, substituted: SI 2015/1653 Reg.2

Sch.9 Part I para.1, amended: 2015 c.7 Sch.1 para.100

Sch.9 Part I para.7, repealed: 2015 c.7 Sch.1 para.100

Sch.9 Part II para.13, amended: 2015 c.7 Sch.1 para.100

Sch.9 Part II para.14, amended: 2015 c.7 Sch.1 para.100

Sch.9 Part II para.14A, added: 2015 c.7 Sch.1 para.100

Sch.9 Part II para.15, amended: 2015 c.7 Sch.1 para.100

Sch.9 Part II para.16, amended: 2015 c.7 Sch.1 para.100

Sch.9 Part III para.20, amended: 2015 c.7 Sch.1 para.100

Sch.9 Part III para.21, amended: 2015 c.7 Sch.1 para.100

Sch.9 Part IV para.27, enabling: SI 2015/136, SI 2015/304, SI 2015/1003, SI 2015/1009, SI 2015/1072, SI 2015/1104, SI 2015/1195, SI 2015/1224, SI 2015/1226, SI 2015/1274, SI 2015/1278, SI 2015/1446, SI 2015/1550, SI 2015/1593, SI 2015/1708, SI 2015/1746, SI 2015/1925, SI 2015/1950, SI 2015/2017, SSI 2015/41, SSI 2015/67, SSI 2015/203, SSI 2015/251, SSI

2015/267, SSI 2015/301, SSI 2015/332,
SSI 2015/416, SSI 2015/426
Sch.9 Pt VI para.35, see *Hillhead
Community Council v City of Glasgow
Council* [2015] CSOH 35, 2015 S.L.T.
239 (OH), Lord Bannatyne; see *Williams
v Devon CC* [2015] EWHC 568 (Admin),
[2015] L.L.R. 624 (QBD (Admin)),
Judge Cotter QC

28. County Courts Act 1984
s.53, see *L v R* [2015] EWCA Civ 61,
Times, April 7, 2015 (CA (Civ Div)),
Aikens LJ
s.60, amended: 2015 c.20 Sch.13 para.6
s.110, enabling: SI 2015/1420

39. Video Recordings Act 1984
s.9, see *R. v Dryzner (Ewa)* [2014]
EWCA Crim 2438, (2015) 179 J.P. 29
(CA (Crim Div)), Fulford LJ
s.9, amended: SI 2015/664 Sch.4 para.14
s.10, amended: SI 2015/664 Sch.4
para.14
s.16A, amended: 2015 c.15 Sch.6 para.27
s.16A, repealed: 2015 c.15 Sch.6 para.27

**42. Matrimonial and Family Proceedings
Act 1984**
see *National Crime Agency v Azam*
[2014] EWHC 3573 (QB), [2015]
Lloyd's Rep. F.C. 42 (QBD), Andrews J
Pt III., see *Abuchian v Khojah* [2014]
EWHC 3411 (Fam), [2015] 2 F.L.R. 153
(Fam Div), Mostyn J; see *M v W
(Appliction After New Zealand Financial
Agreement)* [2014] EWHC 925 (Fam),
[2015] 1 F.L.R. 465 (Fam Div),
Coleridge J
s.13, see *Abuchian v Khojah* [2014]
EWHC 3411 (Fam), [2015] 2 F.L.R. 153
(Fam Div), Mostyn J
s.16, see *Abuchian v Khojah* [2014]
EWHC 3411 (Fam), [2015] 2 F.L.R. 153
(Fam Div), Mostyn J
s.18, see *National Crime Agency v Azam*
[2014] EWHC 3573 (QB), [2015]
Lloyd's Rep. F.C. 42 (QBD), Andrews J
s.31D, enabling: SI 2015/1421
s.31F, see *S v S* [2015] EWHC 1005
(Fam), [2015] 1 W.L.R. 4592 (Fam Div),
Sir James Munby PFD; see *U (Children)
(Care Proceedings: Application for
Rehearing), Re* [2015] EWCA Civ 334,

[2015] 3 F.C.R. 46 (CA (Civ Div)),
Moore-Bick LJ
s.31G, see *K (Children) (Unrepresented
Father: Cross-Examination of Child), Re*
[2015] EWCA Civ 543, [2015] 1 W.L.R.
3801 (CA (Civ Div)), Lord Dyson MR
s.31O, enabling: SI 2015/890
s.31P, enabling: SI 2015/890

51. Inheritance Tax Act 1984
Pt III., see *Barclays Wealth Trustees
(Jersey) Ltd v Revenue and Customs
Commissioners* [2015] EWHC 2878
(Ch), [2015] B.T.C. 28 (Ch D), Mann J
s.6, amended: 2015 c.11 s.74
s.7, amended: 2015 c.33 s.9
s.8A, see *Loring v Woodland Trust*
[2014] EWCA Civ 1314, [2015] 1
W.L.R. 3238 (CA (Civ Div)), Lewison
LJ
s.8A, amended: 2015 c.33 s.9
s.8D, added: 2015 c.33 s.9
s.23, see *Routier v Revenue and Customs
Commissioners* [2014] EWHC 3010
(Ch), [2015] P.T.S.R. 60 (Ch D), Rose J
s.43, see *Barclays Wealth Trustees
(Jersey) Ltd v Revenue and Customs
Commissioners* [2015] EWHC 2878
(Ch), [2015] B.T.C. 28 (Ch D), Mann J
s.44, see *Barclays Wealth Trustees
(Jersey) Ltd v Revenue and Customs
Commissioners* [2015] EWHC 2878
(Ch), [2015] B.T.C. 28 (Ch D), Mann J
s.48, see *Barclays Wealth Trustees
(Jersey) Ltd v Revenue and Customs
Commissioners* [2015] EWHC 2878
(Ch), [2015] B.T.C. 28 (Ch D), Mann J
s.49, see *Freedman v Freedman* [2015]
EWHC 1457 (Ch), [2015] W.T.L.R. 1187
(Ch D), Proudman J
s.62A, added: 2015 c.33 Sch.1 para.2
s.64, see *Barclays Wealth Trustees
(Jersey) Ltd v Revenue and Customs
Commissioners* [2015] EWHC 2878
(Ch), [2015] B.T.C. 28 (Ch D), Mann J
s.65, see *Seddon v Revenue and Customs
Commissioners* [2015] UKFTT 140 (TC),
[2015] S.F.T.D. 539 (FTT (Tax)), Judge
Jonathan Cannan
s.66, amended: 2015 c.33 Sch.1 para.3
s.66, repealed: 2015 c.33 Sch.1 para.3

s.68, see *Seddon v Revenue and Customs Commissioners* [2015] UKFTT 140 (TC), [2015] S.F.T.D. 539 (FTT (Tax)), Judge Jonathan Cannan
s.68, amended: 2015 c.33 Sch.1 para.4
s.69, amended: 2015 c.33 Sch.1 para.5
s.71F, amended: 2015 c.33 Sch.1 para.6
s.79, amended: 2015 c.33 s.12
s.80, amended: 2015 c.33 s.13
s.81, see *Barclays Wealth Trustees (Jersey) Ltd v Revenue and Customs Commissioners* [2015] EWHC 2878 (Ch), [2015] B.T.C. 28 (Ch D), Mann J
s.82, see *Barclays Wealth Trustees (Jersey) Ltd v Revenue and Customs Commissioners* [2015] EWHC 2878 (Ch), [2015] B.T.C. 28 (Ch D), Mann J
s.104, see *Green v Revenue and Customs Commissioners* [2015] UKFTT 334 (TC), [2015] S.F.T.D. 711 (FTT (Tax)), Judge Anne Redston
s.105, see *Green v Revenue and Customs Commissioners* [2015] UKFTT 334 (TC), [2015] S.F.T.D. 711 (FTT (Tax)), Judge Anne Redston
s.142, see *Vaughan-Jones v Vaughan-Jones* [2015] EWHC 1086 (Ch), [2015] W.T.L.R. 1287 (Ch D (Manchester)), Judge Hodge QC
s.144, amended: 2015 c.33 s.14
s.153A, added: 2015 c.11 s.75
s.154, amended: 2015 c.11 s.75
s.155A, added: 2015 c.11 s.75
s.207, amended: 2015 c.33 s.12
s.224, see *Seddon v Revenue and Customs Commissioners* [2015] UKFTT 140 (TC), [2015] S.F.T.D. 539 (FTT (Tax)), Judge Jonathan Cannan
s.233, amended: 2015 c.33 s.12
s.237, amended: 2015 c.33 s.12
Sch.4 Part I para.3, amended: 2015 c.33 s.12

54. Roads (Scotland) Act 1984
see *Campbell-Gray v Keeper of the Registers of Scotland* 2015 S.L.T. (Lands Tr) 147 (Lands Tr (Scot)), R A Smith, QC
s.2, enabling: SSI 2015/15, SSI 2015/198, SSI 2015/221
s.5, enabling: SSI 2015/413, SSI 2015/415

s.7, enabling: SSI 2015/257
s.8, enabling: SSI 2015/257
s.9, enabling: SSI 2015/258
s.10, enabling: SSI 2015/257
s.12, enabling: SSI 2015/412, SSI 2015/414
s.62, enabling: SSI 2015/278, SSI 2015/373, SSI 2015/450
s.70, enabling: SSI 2015/412, SSI 2015/414
s.91, amended: SSI 2015/271 Art.2
s.151, amended: SSI 2015/271 Art.2
s.152, enabling: SSI 2015/15, SSI 2015/198, SSI 2015/221

55. Building Act 1984
s.1, amended: 2015 c.7 s.37
s.1, enabling: SI 2015/767, SI 2015/1486
s.2B, added: 2015 c.20 s.42
s.2B, enabling: SI 2015/767
s.3, enabling: SI 2015/767
s.16, enabling: SI 2015/767
s.17, enabling: SI 2015/767
s.34, enabling: SI 2015/767, SI 2015/1486
s.35, enabling: SI 2015/767
s.47, enabling: SI 2015/767
s.50, enabling: SI 2015/767
s.51, enabling: SI 2015/767
s.51A, enabling: SI 2015/767
s.52, enabling: SI 2015/767
s.54, enabling: SI 2015/767
Sch.1 para.1, enabling: SI 2015/767, SI 2015/1486
Sch.1 para.2, enabling: SI 2015/1486
Sch.1 para.4, enabling: SI 2015/767, SI 2015/1486
Sch.1 para.4A, enabling: SI 2015/767, SI 2015/1486
Sch.1 para.7, enabling: SI 2015/767, SI 2015/1486
Sch.1 para.7A, added: 2015 c.7 s.37
Sch.1 para.8, amended: 2015 c.7 s.37
Sch.1 para.8, enabling: SI 2015/767, SI 2015/1486
Sch.1 para.10, enabling: SI 2015/767, SI 2015/1486
Sch.4 para.2, enabling: SI 2015/767
Sch.4 para.3, enabling: SI 2015/767

60. Police and Criminal Evidence Act 1984
see *R. (on the application of M) v Kingston Crown Court* [2014] EWHC

2702 (Admin), [2015] 4 All E.R. 1028
(DC), Ouseley J; see *R. v*
Shanmugarajah (Prasanth) [2015]
EWCA Crim 783, [2015] 2 Cr. App. R.
14 (CA (Crim Div)), Hallett LJ
Pt II., see *Z (Children) (Application for*
Release of DNA Profiles), Re [2015]
EWCA Civ 34, [2015] 1 W.L.R. 2501
(CA (Civ Div)), Lord Dyson MR
Pt V., see *Z (Children) (Application for*
Release of DNA Profiles), Re [2015]
EWCA Civ 34, [2015] 1 W.L.R. 2501
(CA (Civ Div)), Lord Dyson MR
s.1, varied: SI 2015/1783 Sch.2 Part 1
s.2, varied: SI 2015/1783 Sch.2 Part 1
s.3, varied: SI 2015/1783 Sch.2 Part 1
s.4, varied: SI 2015/1783 Sch.2 Part 1,
Sch.2 Part 2
s.6, varied: SI 2015/1783 Sch.2 Part 1
s.7, varied: SI 2015/1783 Sch.2 Part 1
s.8, see *R. (on the application of B) v*
Huddersfield Magistrates' Court [2014]
EWHC 1089 (Admin), [2015] 1 W.L.R.
4737 (QBD (Admin)), Rafferty LJ; see
R. (on the application of Cabot Global
Ltd) v Barkingside Magistrates' Court
[2015] EWHC 1458 (Admin), [2015] 2
Cr. App. R. 26 (QBD (Admin)), Fulford
LJ; see *R. (on the application of*
Panesar) v Central Criminal Court
[2014] EWCA Civ 1613, [2015] 1
W.L.R. 2577 (CA (Civ Div)), Patten LJ
s.8, varied: SI 2015/1783 Art.18, Sch.2
Part 1
s.9, see *R. (on the application of*
Panesar) v Central Criminal Court
[2014] EWCA Civ 1613, [2015] 1
W.L.R. 2577 (CA (Civ Div)), Patten LJ
s.9, varied: SI 2015/1783 Sch.2 Part 1
s.14A, varied: SI 2015/1783 Art.6
s.14B, varied: SI 2015/1783 Art.7
s.15, see *R. (on the application of B) v*
Huddersfield Magistrates' Court [2014]
EWHC 1089 (Admin), [2015] 1 W.L.R.
4737 (QBD (Admin)), Rafferty LJ; see
R. (on the application of Cabot Global
Ltd) v Barkingside Magistrates' Court
[2015] EWHC 1458 (Admin), [2015] 2
Cr. App. R. 26 (QBD (Admin)), Fulford
LJ; see *R. (on the application of*
Chaudhary) v Bristol Crown Court

[2014] EWHC 4096 (Admin), [2015] 1
Cr. App. R. 18 (DC), Fulford LJ
s.15, varied: SI 2015/759 Art.2, SI
2015/1783 Sch.2 Part 1
s.16, see *R. (on the application of*
Chaudhary) v Bristol Crown Court
[2014] EWHC 4096 (Admin), [2015] 1
Cr. App. R. 18 (DC), Fulford LJ
s.16, varied: SI 2015/759 Art.3, SI
2015/1783 Sch.2 Part 1, Sch.2 Part 2
s.17, amended: 2015 c.2 Sch.9 para.9
s.17, varied: SI 2015/1783 Sch.2 Part 1
s.18, varied: SI 2015/1783 Art.8, Sch.2
Part 1, Sch.2 Part 2
s.19, see *R. (on the application of Cabot*
Global Ltd) v Barkingside Magistrates'
Court [2015] EWHC 1458 (Admin),
[2015] 2 Cr. App. R. 26 (QBD (Admin)),
Fulford LJ; see *Z (Children)*
(Application for Release of DNA
Profiles), Re [2015] EWCA Civ 34,
[2015] 1 W.L.R. 2501 (CA (Civ Div)),
Lord Dyson MR
s.19, varied: SI 2015/1783 Sch.2 Part 1
s.20, see *R. (on the application of Cabot*
Global Ltd) v Barkingside Magistrates'
Court [2015] EWHC 1458 (Admin),
[2015] 2 Cr. App. R. 26 (QBD (Admin)),
Fulford LJ
s.20, varied: SI 2015/1783 Sch.2 Part 1
s.21, varied: SI 2015/759 Art.4, SI
2015/1783 Sch.2 Part 1
s.22, see *Z (Children) (Application for*
Release of DNA Profiles), Re [2015]
EWCA Civ 34, [2015] 1 W.L.R. 2501
(CA (Civ Div)), Lord Dyson MR
s.22, varied: SI 2015/759 Art.5, SI
2015/1783 Sch.2 Part 1
s.24, varied: SI 2015/1783 Art.17, Sch.2
Part 1
s.24A, varied: SI 2015/1783 Sch.2 Part 1
s.26, varied: SI 2015/1783 Sch.2 Part 1
s.27, varied: SI 2015/1783 Sch.2 Part 1
s.28, see *Walker v Commissioner of*
Police of the Metropolis [2014] EWCA
Civ 897, [2015] 1 W.L.R. 312 (CA (Civ
Div)), Rimer LJ
s.28, varied: SI 2015/1783 Sch.2 Part 1
s.29, varied: SI 2015/1783 Sch.2 Part 1
s.30, varied: SI 2015/1783 Art.9, Sch.2
Part 1

s.30A, varied: SI 2015/1783 Sch.2 Part 1
s.30B, varied: SI 2015/1783 Sch.2 Part 1
s.30C, varied: SI 2015/1783 Sch.2 Part 1
s.30CA, varied: SI 2015/1783 Sch.2 Part 1
s.30D, varied: SI 2015/1783 Sch.2 Part 1
s.31, varied: SI 2015/1783 Sch.2 Part 1
s.32, varied: SI 2015/1783 Sch.2 Part 1
s.33, varied: SI 2015/1783 Sch.2 Part 1
s.34, varied: SI 2015/1783 Sch.2 Part 1
s.35, varied: SI 2015/1783 Art.10, Sch.2 Part 1
s.36, varied: SI 2015/1783 Art.11, Sch.2 Part 1, Sch.2 Part 2
s.37, amended: 2015 c.2 s.42
s.37, varied: SI 2015/1783 Sch.2 Part 1
s.37B, amended: 2015 c.2 s.18
s.37B, varied: SI 2015/1783 Sch.2 Part 1
s.37C, varied: SI 2015/1783 Sch.2 Part 1
s.37CA, varied: SI 2015/1783 Sch.2 Part 1
s.37D, varied: SI 2015/1783 Sch.2 Part 1
s.38, see *R. (on the application of BG) v Chief Constable of the West Midlands* [2014] EWHC 4374 (Admin), (2015) 179 J.P. 93 (QBD (Admin)), Fulford LJ
s.38, varied: SI 2015/1783 Sch.2 Part 1
s.39, varied: SI 2015/1783 Sch.2 Part 1, Sch.2 Part 2
s.40, varied: SI 2015/1783 Sch.2 Part 1, Sch.2 Part 2
s.40A, varied: SI 2015/1783 Sch.2 Part 1
s.41, varied: SI 2015/1783 Art.12, Sch.2 Part 1
s.42, varied: SI 2015/1783 Sch.2 Part 1, Sch.2 Part 2
s.43, varied: SI 2015/1783 Sch.2 Part 1
s.44, varied: SI 2015/1783 Sch.2 Part 1
s.45A, varied: SI 2015/1783 Sch.2 Part 1, Sch.2 Part 2
s.46, varied: SI 2015/1783 Sch.2 Part 1
s.46A, varied: SI 2015/1783 Sch.2 Part 1
s.46ZA, varied: SI 2015/1783 Sch.2 Part 1
s.47, varied: SI 2015/1783 Sch.2 Part 1
s.47A, varied: SI 2015/1783 Sch.2 Part 1
s.48, varied: SI 2015/1783 Sch.2 Part 1
s.49, varied: SI 2015/1783 Sch.2 Part 1
s.50, varied: SI 2015/1783 Art.13, Sch.2 Part 1
s.51, varied: SI 2015/1783 Sch.2 Part 1

s.53, varied: SI 2015/1783 Sch.2 Part 1
s.54, varied: SI 2015/1783 Sch.2 Part 1
s.54A, varied: SI 2015/1783 Sch.2 Part 1, Sch.2 Part 2
s.54B, varied: SI 2015/1783 Sch.2 Part 1
s.54C, varied: SI 2015/1783 Sch.2 Part 1
s.55, varied: SI 2015/1783 Art.14, Sch.2 Part 1, Sch.2 Part 2
s.55A, varied: SI 2015/1783 Sch.2 Part 1, Sch.2 Part 2
s.56, varied: SI 2015/1783 Sch.2 Part 1, Sch.2 Part 2
s.57, varied: SI 2015/1783 Sch.2 Part 1
s.58, varied: SI 2015/1783 Sch.2 Part 1, Sch.2 Part 2
s.60, varied: SI 2015/1783 Sch.2 Part 1
s.60A, varied: SI 2015/1783 Sch.2 Part 1
s.61, varied: SI 2015/1783 Sch.2 Part 1, Sch.2 Part 2
s.61A, varied: SI 2015/1783 Sch.2 Part 1
s.62, varied: SI 2015/1783 Sch.2 Part 1, Sch.2 Part 2
s.63, varied: SI 2015/1783 Sch.2 Part 1, Sch.2 Part 2
s.63A, varied: SI 2015/1783 Sch.2 Part 1
s.63B, varied: SI 2015/1783 Sch.2 Part 1, Sch.2 Part 2
s.63C, varied: SI 2015/1783 Sch.2 Part 1
s.63T, see *Z (Children) (Application for Release of DNA Profiles), Re* [2015] EWCA Civ 34, [2015] 1 W.L.R. 2501 (CA (Civ Div)), Lord Dyson MR
s.64, see *Z (Children) (Application for Release of DNA Profiles), Re* [2015] EWCA Civ 34, [2015] 1 W.L.R. 2501 (CA (Civ Div)), Lord Dyson MR
s.64, varied: SI 2015/1783 Sch.2 Part 1
s.64A, varied: SI 2015/1783 Sch.2 Part 1, Sch.2 Part 2
s.65A, amended: 2015 c.30 Sch.5 para.3
s.66, varied: SI 2015/1783 Sch.2 Part 1
s.67, varied: SI 2015/1783 Sch.2 Part 1
s.67, enabling: SI 2015/418
s.73, see *R. v M* [2014] EWCA Crim 1523, [2015] 1 W.L.R. 495 (CA (Crim Div)), Pitchford LJ
s.74, see *R. v M* [2014] EWCA Crim 1523, [2015] 1 W.L.R. 495 (CA (Crim Div)), Pitchford LJ

s.76A, see *R. v Sliogeris (Kestutis)* [2015] EWCA Crim 22, (2015) 179 J.P. 156 (CA (Crim Div)), Elias LJ

s.77, varied: SI 2015/1783 Art.15, Sch.2 Part 1

s.78, see *Barnaby v DPP* [2015] EWHC 232 (Admin), [2015] 2 Cr. App. R. 4 (DC), Fulford LJ; see *Beghal v DPP* [2015] UKSC 49 (SC), Lord Neuberger PSC; see *R. v Boardman (David)* [2015] EWCA Crim 175, [2015] 1 Cr. App. R. 33 (CA (Crim Div)), Sir Brian Leveson PQBD; see *R. v M* [2014] EWCA Crim 1523, [2015] 1 W.L.R. 495 (CA (Crim Div)), Pitchford LJ

s.81, enabling: SI 2015/1490

s.82, see *R. v Sliogeris (Kestutis)* [2015] EWCA Crim 22, (2015) 179 J.P. 156 (CA (Crim Div)), Elias LJ

s.107, varied: SI 2015/1783 Sch.2 Part 1, Sch.2 Part 2

s.110, varied: SI 2015/1783 Sch.2 Part 1

s.111, varied: SI 2015/1783 Sch.2 Part 1

s.113, varied: SI 2015/1783 Sch.2 Part 1

s.114, varied: SI 2015/1783 Sch.2 Part 1

s.114, enabling: SI 2015/1783

s.114A, varied: SI 2015/1783 Sch.2 Part 1

s.117, varied: SI 2015/1783 Sch.2 Part 1

s.118, varied: SI 2015/1783 Sch.2 Part 1

s.122, varied: SI 2015/1783 Sch.2 Part 1

Sch.1 para.7, amended: 2015 c.20 s.82

Sch.1 para.8, amended: 2015 c.20 s.82

Sch.1 para.9, amended: 2015 c.20 s.82

Sch.1 para.10, amended: 2015 c.20 s.82

Sch.1 para.12, varied: SI 2015/1783 Art.18

Sch.1 para.15A, added: 2015 c.20 s.82

Sch.2A Part I para.6, varied: SI 2015/1783 Sch.2 Part 2

Sch.2A Part III para.14, varied: SI 2015/1783 Sch.2 Part 2

Sch.2A Part IV para.16, varied: SI 2015/1783 Sch.2 Part 2

1985

4. Milk (Cessation of Production) Act 1985
repealed: 2015 c.20 Sch.23 para.39

6. Companies Act 1985

varied: SI 2015/428 Sch.1 para.2

s.36C, see *Royal Mail Estates Ltd v Maple Teesdale* [2015] EWHC 1890 (Ch), [2015] B.C.C. 647 (Ch D), Jonathan Klein

s.130, see *Vocalspruce Ltd v Revenue and Customs Commissioners* [2014] EWCA Civ 1302, [2015] S.T.C. 861 (CA (Civ Div)), Gross LJ

s.320, see *Granada Group Ltd v Law Debenture Pension Trust Corp Plc* [2015] EWHC 1499 (Ch), [2015] Bus. L.R. 1119 (Ch D), Andrews J

s.346, see *Granada Group Ltd v Law Debenture Pension Trust Corp Plc* [2015] EWHC 1499 (Ch), [2015] Bus. L.R. 1119 (Ch D), Andrews J

s.444, amended: SI 2015/664 Sch.3 para.3

s.462, varied: SI 2015/428 Sch.1 para.3

s.463, varied: SI 2015/428 Sch.1 para.4

s.464, varied: SI 2015/428 Sch.1 para.5

s.466, varied: SI 2015/428 Sch.1 para.6

s.486, varied: SI 2015/428 Sch.1 para.7

s.739, see *Granada Group Ltd v Law Debenture Pension Trust Corp Plc* [2015] EWHC 1499 (Ch), [2015] Bus. L.R. 1119 (Ch D), Andrews J

Sch.15D para.17, amended: 2015 c.15 Sch.4 para.28

Sch.15D para.17, repealed: 2015 c.15 Sch.4 para.28

Sch.15D para.25, substituted: 2015 c.15 Sch.4 para.28

Sch.15D para.37, repealed: 2015 c.20 Sch.6 para.22

21. Films Act 1985
Sch.1 para.4, enabling: SI 2015/1886

Sch.1 para.4A, amended: SI 2015/86 Art.3

Sch.1 para.4B, amended: SI 2015/86 Art.4

Sch.1 para.4C, amended: SI 2015/86 Art.5

Sch.1 para.4D, amended: SI 2015/86 Art.6

Sch.1 para.10, enabling: SI 2015/86

22. Dangerous Vessels Act 1985
s.5, amended: SI 2015/664 Sch.4 para.15

23. Prosecution of Offences Act 1985

see *R. v Gray (Dean Andrew)* [2014]
EWCA Crim 2372, [2015] 1 Cr. App. R.
(S.) 27 (CA (Crim Div)), Hallett LJ
Part II, amended: 2015 c.2 Sch.12 para.5
s.15, amended: 2015 c.2 Sch.11 para.7
s.16, see *R. (on the application of
Henderson) v Secretary of State for
Justice* [2015] EWHC 130 (Admin),
[2015] 1 Cr. App. R. 29 (DC), Burnett LJ
s.16A, see *R. (on the application of
Henderson) v Secretary of State for
Justice* [2015] EWHC 130 (Admin),
[2015] 1 Cr. App. R. 29 (DC), Burnett LJ
s.18, see *Bizunowicz v Poland* [2014]
EWHC 3238 (Admin), [2015] 1 W.L.R.
2341 (QBD (Admin)), Aikens LJ
s.19, see *Evans v Serious Fraud Office*
[2015] EWHC 263 (QB), [2015] 1
W.L.R. 3595 (QBD), Hickinbottom J; see
*Hull and Holderness Magistrates' Court
v Darroch* [2014] EWHC 4184 (Admin),
(2015) 179 J.P. 64 (DC), Foskett J; see
Quayum v DPP [2015] EWHC 1660
(Admin), (2015) 179 J.P. 390 (DC), Sir
Brian Leveson PQBD
s.19, enabling: SI 2015/12
s.19A, see *Evans v Serious Fraud Office*
[2015] EWHC 263 (QB), [2015] 1
W.L.R. 3595 (QBD), Hickinbottom J
s.19B, see *Capita Translation and
Interpreting Ltd v Luton Crown Court*
[2014] EWCA Crim 2350, (2015) 179
J.P. 36 (CA (Crim Div)), Hallett LJ
s.21A, added: 2015 c.2 s.54
s.21A, enabling: SI 2015/796
s.21C, enabling: SI 2015/796, SI
2015/1970
s.21E, enabling: SI 2015/796
s.22, see *Campbell-Brown v Central
Criminal Court* [2015] EWHC 202
(Admin), [2015] 1 Cr. App. R. 34 (DC),
Fulford LJ
s.29, enabling: SI 2015/796, SI
2015/1970

37. Family Law (Scotland) Act 1985
s.8, see *McDonald v McDonald* [2015]
CSIH 61, 2015 S.L.T. 587 (IH (Ex Div)),
Lady Smith
s.10, see *McDonald v McDonald* [2015]
CSIH 61, 2015 S.L.T. 587 (IH (Ex Div)),
Lady Smith

47. Further Education Act 1985
s.3, repealed: 2015 c.20 Sch.15 para.1
**48. Food and Environment Protection Act
1985**
s.1, amended: 2015 asp 1 Sch.1 para.2
s.1, enabling: SI 2015/300
s.2, amended: 2015 asp 1 Sch.1 para.2
s.16, repealed: SI 2015/978 Sch.1 Part 1
s.21, amended: SI 2015/664 Sch.4
para.16
s.24, enabling: SI 2015/300
s.25, amended: SI 2015/978 Sch.1 Part 1
Sch.5, repealed: SI 2015/978 Sch.1 Part 1
49. Surrogacy Arrangements Act 1985
s.2, see *JP v LP (Surrogacy
Arrangement: Wardship)* [2014] EWHC
595 (Fam), [2015] 1 All E.R. 266 (Fam
Div), Eleanor King J
50. Representation of the People Act 1985
s.15, enabling: SI 2015/221, SI 2015/654
s.22, enabling: SI 2015/803
s.27, amended: SI 2015/1376 Sch.2
para.2
51. Local Government Act 1985
s.62, see *Tower Hamlets LBC v Bromley
LBC* [2015] EWHC 1954 (Ch), [2015]
B.L.G.R. 622 (Ch D), Norris J
60. Child Abduction and Custody Act 1985
see *R, Petitioner* 2015 S.C. 310 (IH (Ex
Div)), Lady Paton
Sch.1, see *M v M* [2015] CSOH 130,
2015 S.L.T. 682 (OH), Lord Stewart
61. Administration of Justice Act 1985
Part I, substituted: SI 2015/401 Sch.1
para.17
s.9, amended: SI 2015/401 Sch.1 para.18
s.9, substituted: SI 2015/401 Sch.1
para.18
s.10A, added: SI 2015/401 Sch.1 para.19
s.15, amended: 2015 c.20 Sch.20 para.2
s.16, amended: 2015 c.20 Sch.6 para.2,
Sch.19 para.2
s.17, amended: 2015 c.20 Sch.6 para.2
s.18, amended: 2015 c.20 Sch.20 para.3
s.18, repealed: 2015 c.20 Sch.20 para.3
s.19, amended: 2015 c.20 Sch.20 para.4
s.20, repealed: 2015 c.20 Sch.20 para.5
s.24, amended: 2015 c.20 Sch.20 para.6
s.24, repealed: 2015 c.20 Sch.20 para.6
s.24A, amended: 2015 c.20 Sch.20 para.7
s.24A, repealed: 2015 c.20 Sch.20 para.7

s.26, amended: 2015 c.20 Sch.19 para.3,
Sch.20 para.8
s.26, repealed: 2015 c.20 Sch.20 para.8
s.28, amended: 2015 c.20 Sch.19 para.4
s.32, amended: 2015 c.20 s.86
s.32B, added: 2015 c.20 s.86
s.33A, amended: 2015 c.20 Sch.19 para.5
s.34, amended: 2015 c.20 Sch.19 para.6
s.39, amended: 2015 c.20 Sch.19 para.7
s.50, see *Wilby v Rigby* [2015] EWHC
2394 (Ch), [2015] W.T.L.R. 1845 (Ch
D), Judge Hodge QC
Sch.2, amended: SI 2015/401 Sch.1
para.20
Sch.2 para.1, amended: SI 2015/401
Sch.1 para.20
Sch.2 para.2, amended: SI 2015/401
Sch.1 para.20
Sch.2 para.14A, amended: SI 2015/401
Sch.1 para.20
Sch.2 para.14B, amended: SI 2015/401
Sch.1 para.20
Sch.2 para.14C, amended: SI 2015/401
Sch.1 para.20
Sch.2 para.14ZA, added: SI 2015/401
Sch.1 para.20
Sch.2 para.16, amended: SI 2015/401
Sch.1 para.20
Sch.2 para.17, amended: SI 2015/401
Sch.1 para.20
Sch.2 para.18A, amended: SI 2015/401
Sch.1 para.20
Sch.2 para.20, amended: SI 2015/401
Sch.1 para.20
Sch.2 para.21, amended: SI 2015/401
Sch.1 para.20
Sch.2 para.32, amended: SI 2015/401
Sch.1 para.20
Sch.2 para.32A, added: SI 2015/401
Sch.1 para.20
Sch.2 para.35, amended: SI 2015/401
Sch.1 para.20
Sch.3 para.2, amended: 2015 c.20 Sch.19
para.8
Sch.3 para.4, amended: 2015 c.20 Sch.20
para.9
Sch.6 para.3, amended: 2015 c.20 Sch.19
para.9
Sch.6 para.3A, amended: 2015 c.20
Sch.19 para.9, Sch.20 para.10

Sch.6 para.3A, repealed: 2015 c.20
Sch.20 para.10
Sch.6 para.4, amended: 2015 c.20 Sch.19
para.9
Sch.6 para.6, amended: 2015 c.20 Sch.20
para.10
Sch.6 para.6, repealed: 2015 c.20 Sch.20
para.10
Sch.6 para.14, amended: 2015 c.20
Sch.19 para.9

65. Insolvency Act 1985
Sch.8 para.2, repealed: 2015 c.20 Sch.6
para.2

66. Bankruptcy (Scotland) Act 1985
s.1A, enabling: SSI 2015/80
s.2, enabling: SSI 2015/80
s.5, enabling: SSI 2015/80
s.5D, enabling: SSI 2015/149
s.6, enabling: SSI 2015/80
s.7, enabling: SSI 2015/80
s.11, enabling: SSI 2015/80
s.12, see *Advocate General for Scotland v
King* 2015 S.L.T. (Sh Ct) 25 (Sh Ct
(South Strathclyde) (Stranraer)), Sheriff
Principal B A Lockhart; see *Glasgow
City Council v Chaudhry* 2015 S.L.T. (Sh
Ct) 107 (Sh Ct (Glasgow)), Sheriff
Principal C A L Scott, QC
s.19, enabling: SSI 2015/80
s.22, enabling: SSI 2015/80
s.23, enabling: SSI 2015/80
s.32, enabling: SSI 2015/80
s.40, enabling: SSI 2015/80
s.43A, enabling: SSI 2015/80
s.43B, enabling: SSI 2015/80
s.45, enabling: SSI 2015/80
s.49, enabling: SSI 2015/80
s.51, enabling: SSI 2015/80
s.54, enabling: SSI 2015/80
s.54A, enabling: SSI 2015/80
s.54C, enabling: SSI 2015/80
s.54D, enabling: SSI 2015/80
s.54E, enabling: SSI 2015/80
s.69, enabling: SSI 2015/80
s.69A, enabling: SSI 2015/80
s.71C, enabling: SSI 2015/80, SSI
2015/149
s.72, enabling: SSI 2015/80, SSI
2015/149
s.72A, enabling: SSI 2015/80
s.73, enabling: SSI 2015/80

Sch.3 Part I para.5, enabling: SSI
2015/80
Sch.3 Part I para.6, enabling: SSI
2015/80
Sch.3 Part I para.6AA, added: SI
2015/486 Reg.16
Sch.3 Part II para.9ZA, added: SI
2015/486 Reg.16
Sch.5 para.5, enabling: SSI 2015/149

67. Transport Act 1985
s.6, enabling: SSI 2015/420
s.104, amended: SI 2015/914 Sch.1
para.35
s.112G, amended: 2015 c.7 Sch.1
para.101
s.119, amended: 2015 c.20 Sch.8 para.6
s.119, repealed: 2015 c.20 Sch.8 para.6

68. Housing Act 1985
see *Begum v Birmingham City Council*
[2015] EWCA Civ 386, [2015] C.P. Rep.
32 (CA (Civ Div)), Jackson LJ; see *R.
(on the application of C) v Hackney LBC*
[2014] EWHC 3670 (Admin), [2015]
P.T.S.R. 1011 (QBD (Admin)), Turner J;
see *Southward Housing Co-operative
Ltd v Walker* [2015] EWHC 1615 (Ch),
[2015] 2 P. & C.R. 13 (Ch D), Hildyard
J; see *Waaler v Hounslow LBC* [2015]
UKUT 17 (LC), [2015] L. & T.R. 24 (UT
(Lands)), Siobhan McGrath
s.1, see *R. (on the application of C) v
Hackney LBC* [2014] EWHC 3670
(Admin), [2015] P.T.S.R. 1011 (QBD
(Admin)), Turner J
s.4, amended: 2015 c.20 Sch.13 para.6
s.12, see *R. (on the application of
Barkas) v North Yorkshire CC* [2015]
A.C. 195 (SC), Lord Neuberger PSC
s.27, see *R. (on the application of C) v
Hackney LBC* [2014] EWHC 3670
(Admin), [2015] P.T.S.R. 1011 (QBD
(Admin)), Turner J
s.80, see *Nicholas v Secretary of State for
Defence* [2015] EWCA Civ 53, [2015] 1
W.L.R. 2116 (CA (Civ Div)), Lord
Dyson MR; see *Southward Housing Co-
operative Ltd v Walker* [2015] EWHC
1615 (Ch), [2015] 2 P. & C.R. 13 (Ch D),
Hildyard J

s.85A, see *Greenwich LBC v Tuitt* [2014]
EWCA Civ 1669, [2015] H.L.R. 10 (CA
(Civ Div)), Treacy LJ
s.119, amended: 2015 c.20 s.28
s.125, see *Begum v Birmingham City
Council* [2015] EWCA Civ 386, [2015]
C.P. Rep. 32 (CA (Civ Div)), Jackson LJ
s.131, enabling: SI 2015/1349
s.176, enabling: SI 2015/1320, SI
2015/1542, SI 2015/1795
s.326, see *Clark v Manchester City
Council* [2015] UKUT 129 (LC), [2015]
L.L.R. 457 (UT (Lands)), Martin Rodger
QC

69. Housing Associations Act 1985
s.5, see *Southward Housing Co-operative
Ltd v Walker* [2015] EWHC 1615 (Ch),
[2015] 2 P. & C.R. 13 (Ch D), Hildyard J

70. Landlord and Tenant Act 1985
see *Caddick v Whitsand Bay Holiday
Park Ltd* [2015] UKUT 63 (LC), [2015]
L. & T.R. 16 (UT (Lands)), Judge Mole
QC
s.11, see *Edwards v Kumarasamy* [2015]
EWCA Civ 20, [2015] Ch. 484 (CA (Civ
Div)), Sir Terence Etherton C; see *Uddin
v Islington LBC* [2015] EWCA Civ 369,
[2015] H.L.R. 28 (CA (Civ Div)),
Pitchford LJ
s.18, see *Caddick v Whitsand Bay
Holiday Park Ltd* [2015] UKUT 63 (LC),
[2015] L. & T.R. 16 (UT (Lands)), Judge
Mole QC; see *Gateway (Leeds)
Management Ltd v Naghash* [2015]
UKUT 333 (LC), [2015] L. & T.R. 36
(UT (Lands)), Martin Rodger QC; see
Morris v Blackpool BC [2014] EWCA
Civ 1384, [2015] H.L.R. 2 (CA (Civ
Div)), Jackson LJ; see *Phillips v Francis*
[2014] EWCA Civ 1395, [2015] 1
W.L.R. 741 (CA (Civ Div)), Lord Dyson
MR
s.19, see *Anchor Trust v Corbett* [2015]
L. & T.R. 14 (UT (Lands)), Judge
Huskinson; see *Gateway (Leeds)
Management Ltd v Naghash* [2015]
UKUT 333 (LC), [2015] L. & T.R. 36
(UT (Lands)), Martin Rodger QC; see
Morris v Blackpool BC [2014] EWCA
Civ 1384, [2015] H.L.R. 2 (CA (Civ
Div)), Jackson LJ; see *Parissis v Blair*

Court (St John's Wood) Management Ltd
[2015] L. & T.R. 7 (UT (Lands)), Judge
Huskinson; see *Phillips v Francis* [2014]
EWCA Civ 1395, [2015] 1 W.L.R. 741
(CA (Civ Div)), Lord Dyson MR; see
Waaler v Hounslow LBC [2015] UKUT
17 (LC), [2015] L. & T.R. 24 (UT
(Lands)), Siobhan McGrath
s.20, see *Anchor Trust v Corbett* [2015]
L. & T.R. 14 (UT (Lands)), Judge
Huskinson; see *Phillips v Francis* [2014]
EWCA Civ 1395, [2015] 1 W.L.R. 741
(CA (Civ Div)), Lord Dyson MR
s.27A, see *Caddick v Whitsand Bay
Holiday Park Ltd* [2015] UKUT 63 (LC),
[2015] L. & T.R. 16 (UT (Lands)), Judge
Mole QC; see *Gateway (Leeds)
Management Ltd v Naghash* [2015]
UKUT 333 (LC), [2015] L. & T.R. 36
(UT (Lands)), Martin Rodger QC; see
*Parissis v Blair Court (St John's Wood)
Management Ltd* [2015] L. & T.R. 7 (UT
(Lands)), Judge Huskinson
s.29, see *Caddick v Whitsand Bay
Holiday Park Ltd* [2015] UKUT 63 (LC),
[2015] L. & T.R. 16 (UT (Lands)), Judge
Mole QC
s.30, see *Morris v Blackpool BC* [2014]
EWCA Civ 1384, [2015] H.L.R. 2 (CA
(Civ Div)), Jackson LJ; see *Phillips v
Francis* [2014] EWCA·Civ 1395, [2015]
1 W.L.R. 741 (CA (Civ Div)), Lord
Dyson MR
s.38, see *Caddick v Whitsand Bay
Holiday Park Ltd* [2015] UKUT 63 (LC),
[2015] L. & T.R. 16 (UT (Lands)), Judge
Mole QC
s.38, amended: 2015 c.20 Sch.13 para.6

72. Weights and Measures Act 1985
s.10, enabling: SI 2015/356
s.11, enabling: SI 2015/356
s.15, enabling: SI 2015/356
s.38, amended: 2015 c.15 Sch.6 para.29
s.42, repealed: 2015 c.15 Sch.6 para.30
s.79, repealed: 2015 c.15 Sch.6 para.31
s.79A, added: 2015 c.15 Sch.6 para.32
s.80, amended: 2015 c.15 Sch.6 para.33
s.81, amended: 2015 c.15 Sch.6 para.34
s.84, amended: 2015 c.15 Sch.6 para.35
s.84, repealed: 2015 c.15 Sch.6 para.35
s.86, enabling: SI 2015/356

s.94, enabling: SI 2015/356
Sch.11 para.21, amended: 2015 c.15
Sch.6 para.36

**73. Law Reform (Miscellaneous Provisions)
(Scotland) Act 1985**
s.4, see *Inverclyde Council v McCloskey
(t/a Prince of Wales Bar)* 2015 S.L.T. (Sh
Ct) 57 (Sh Ct (North Strathclyde)
(Paisley)), Sheriff Principal D L Murray
s.8, see *Mirza v Salim* 2015 S.C. 31 (IH
(Ex Div)), Lady Paton
s.9, see *Mirza v Salim* 2015 S.C. 31 (IH
(Ex Div)), Lady Paton

1986

5. Agricultural Holdings Act 1986
s.2, amended: 2015 c.20 Sch.4 para.2
s.6, amended: 2015 c.20 Sch.4 para.3
s.7, amended: 2015 c.20 Sch.4 para.4
s.7, enabling: SI 2015/950
s.8, amended: 2015 c.20 Sch.4 para.5
s.9, amended: 2015 c.20 Sch.4 para.6
s.10, amended: 2015 c.20 Sch.4 para.7
s.12, amended: 2015 c.20 Sch.4 para.8
s.13, amended: 2015 c.20 Sch.4 para.9
s.14, amended: 2015 c.20 Sch.4 para.10
s.15, amended: 2015 c.20 Sch.4 para.11
s.20, amended: 2015 c.20 Sch.4 para.12
s.25, amended: 2015 c.20 Sch.4 para.13
s.33, amended: 2015 c.20 Sch.4 para.14
s.47, amended: 2015 c.20 Sch.4 para.15
s.48, amended: 2015 c.20 Sch.4 para.16
s.66, enabling: SI 2015/327
s.74, amended: 2015 c.20 Sch.4 para.17
s.75, amended: 2015 c.20 Sch.4 para.18
s.80, amended: 2015 c.20 Sch.4 para.19
s.83, amended: 2015 c.20 Sch.4 para.20
s.84A, added: 2015 c.20 Sch.4 para.21
s.85, amended: 2015 c.20 Sch.4 para.22
s.86, amended: 2015 c.20 Sch.4 para.23
s.91, enabling: SI 2015/2082
s.96, amended: 2015 c.20 Sch.4 para.24
Sch.2, amended: 2015 c.20 Sch.4 para.25
Sch.2 para.1, amended: 2015 c.20 Sch.4
para.25
Sch.2 para.2, amended: 2015 c.20 Sch.4
para.25
Sch.2 para.3, amended: 2015 c.20 Sch.4
para.25

Sch.2 para.4, amended: 2015 c.20 Sch.4
para.25
Sch.6 Part I para.4, enabling: SI
2015/1020, SI 2015/1642, SI 2015/1745,
SI 2015/1975
Sch.8 Part I para.4A, added: SI
2015/2082 Art.2
Sch.8 Part I para.5, amended: SI
2015/2082 Art.2
Sch.8 Part I para.5A, added: SI
2015/2082 Art.2
Sch.8 Part I para.6, amended: SI
2015/2082 Art.2

14. Animals (Scientific Procedures) Act 1986
s.8, enabling: SI 2015/244
Sch.1, amended: SI 2015/1782 Sch.6
para.3

20. Horticultural Produce Act 1986
s.3, amended: 2015 c.20 Sch.22 para.8

31. Airports Act 1986
s.74, amended: SI 2015/1682 Sch.1
para.4

32. Drug Trafficking Offences Act 1986
s.1, see *Mundy v Crown Prosecution
Service* [2014] EWHC 819 (Admin),
[2015] Lloyd's Rep. F.C. 109 (QBD
(Admin)), Walker J
s.14, see *Mundy v Crown Prosecution
Service* [2014] EWHC 819 (Admin),
[2015] Lloyd's Rep. F.C. 109 (QBD
(Admin)), Walker J

**33. Disabled Persons (Services, Consultation
and Representation) Act 1986**
s.2, amended: SI 2015/914 Sch.1 para.37
s.3, amended: SI 2015/914 Sch.1 para.38
s.4, amended: SI 2015/914 Sch.1 para.39
s.8, amended: SI 2015/914 Sch.1 para.40
s.16, amended: SI 2015/914 Sch.1
para.41

38. Outer Space Act 1986
s.3, amended: 2015 c.20 s.12
s.5, amended: 2015 c.20 s.12
s.10, amended: 2015 c.20 s.12

41. Finance Act 1986
s.107, amended: 2015 c.33 s.15

44. Gas Act 1986
see *Laverty v British Gas Trading Ltd*
[2014] EWHC 2721 (Ch), [2015] 2 All
E.R. 430 (Ch D (Companies Ct)), Sir
Terence Etherton C
s.12, enabling: SI 2015/953

s.33A, enabling: SI 2015/1544
s.33AA, enabling: SI 2015/1544
s.33AB, enabling: SI 2015/1544
s.33D, enabling: SI 2015/1544
s.36, amended: 2015 c.20 s.97
s.47, enabling: SI 2015/1544

45. Insolvency Act 1986
see *Bank of Ireland Mortgage Bank v
Sheridan* [2015] NICh 12, [2015]
B.P.I.R. 1001 (Ch D (NI)), Morgan LCJ;
see *Business Environment Fleet Street
Ltd (In Administration), Re* [2014]
EWHC 3540 (Ch), [2015] 1 W.L.R. 1167
(Ch D (Companies Ct)), David Halpern
QC; see *Davy v Pickering* [2015] EWHC
380 (Ch), [2015] 2 B.C.L.C. 116 (Ch D
(Cardiff)), Judge Keyser QC; see
*Hartmann Capital Ltd (In Special
Administration), Re* [2015] EWHC 1514
(Ch), [2015] Bus. L.R. 983 (Ch D
(Companies Ct)), Newey J; see *Thomas
v Edmondson* [2014] EWHC 1494 (Ch),
[2015] 1 W.L.R. 1395 (Ch D), Asplin J;
see *Van Gansewinkel Groep BV, Re*
[2015] EWHC 2151 (Ch), [2015] Bus.
L.R. 1046 (Ch D), Snowden J
Part VI, substituted: 2015 c.26 s.124
Part VIII, amended: 2015 c.26 Sch.9
para.63
Part X, substituted: 2015 c.26 s.125
Pt IX s.281A, see *Official Receiver v
Lloyd* [2015] B.P.I.R. 374 (CC
(Norwich)), District Judge McCloughlin
Pt IX s.282, see *JSC Bank of Moscow v
Kekhman* [2015] EWHC 396 (Ch),
[2015] 1 W.L.R. 3737 (Ch D), Morgan J;
see *Mowbray (A Bankrupt), Re* [2015]
EWHC 296 (Ch), [2015] B.P.I.R. 665
(Ch D), Hildyard J; see *Munday v
Hilburn* [2014] EWHC 4496 (Ch), [2015]
B.P.I.R. 684 (Ch D), Nugee J; see *Oraki
v Bramston* [2015] EWHC 2046 (Ch),
[2015] B.P.I.R. 1238 (Ch D), Proudman
J; see *Payne, Re* [2015] EWHC 968
(Ch), [2015] B.P.I.R. 933 (Ch D), John
Male QC; see *Ridsdale v Bowles* [2015]
B.P.I.R. 1275 (CC (Bournemouth)),
District Judge Dancey
s.1, amended: 2015 c.20 Sch.6 para.20
s.2, amended: 2015 c.20 Sch.6 para.20,
2015 c.26 Sch.9 para.2

s.3, amended: 2015 c.26 Sch.9 para.3
s.3, substituted: 2015 c.26 Sch.9 para.3
s.4, amended: 2015 c.20 Sch.6 para.20,
2015 c.26 Sch.9 para.4
s.4A, amended: 2015 c.26 Sch.9 para.5
s.5, amended: 2015 c.26 Sch.9 para.6
s.6, amended: 2015 c.26 Sch.9 para.7
s.7, amended: 2015 c.20 Sch.6 para.20,
2015 c.26 Sch.9 para.8
s.11, see *Business Environment Fleet
Street Ltd (In Administration), Re* [2014]
EWHC 3540 (Ch), [2015] 1 W.L.R. 1167
(Ch D (Companies Ct)), David Halpern
QC
s.19, repealed: 2015 c.20 Sch.6 para.25
s.44, repealed: 2015 c.20 Sch.6 para.26
s.48, amended: 2015 c.26 Sch.9 para.12
s.48, repealed: 2015 c.26 Sch.9 para.12
s.49, amended: 2015 c.26 Sch.9 para.13
s.67, amended: 2015 c.26 Sch.9 para.14
s.67, repealed: 2015 c.26 Sch.9 para.14
s.68, amended: 2015 c.26 Sch.9 para.15
s.74, see *Lehman Brothers International
(Europe) (In Administration), Re* [2014]
EWHC 704 (Ch), [2015] Ch. 1 (Ch D
(Companies Ct)), David Richards J
s.87, see *PAG Management Services Ltd,
Re* [2015] EWHC 2404 (Ch), [2015]
B.C.C. 720 (Ch D), Norris J
s.91, see *PAG Management Services Ltd,
Re* [2015] EWHC 2404 (Ch), [2015]
B.C.C. 720 (Ch D), Norris J
s.92, see *PAG Management Services Ltd,
Re* [2015] EWHC 2404 (Ch), [2015]
B.C.C. 720 (Ch D), Norris J
s.92A, amended: 2015 c.26 s.136, Sch.9
para.16
s.93, amended: 2015 c.26 Sch.9 para.17
s.94, substituted: 2015 c.26 Sch.9 para.18
s.95, amended: 2015 c.26 Sch.9 para.19
s.95, repealed: 2015 c.26 Sch.9 para.19
s.96, amended: 2015 c.26 Sch.9 para.20
s.96, substituted: 2015 c.26 Sch.9 para.20
s.97, amended: 2015 c.26 Sch.9 para.21
s.98, repealed: 2015 c.26 Sch.9 para.22
s.99, amended: 2015 c.26 Sch.9 para.23
s.100, amended: 2015 c.26 Sch.9 para.24
s.101, amended: 2015 c.26 Sch.9 para.25
s.102, repealed: 2015 c.26 Sch.9 para.26
s.104A, amended: 2015 c.26 s.136, Sch.9
para.27

s.105, amended: 2015 c.26 Sch.9 para.28
s.106, substituted: 2015 c.26 Sch.9
para.29
s.107, see *Top Brands Ltd v Sharma*
[2014] EWHC 2753 (Ch), [2015] 2 All
E.R. 581 (Ch D (Birmingham)), Judge
Barker QC
s.114, amended: 2015 c.26 Sch.9 para.30
s.122, see *Salford Estates (No.2) Ltd v
Altomart Ltd* [2014] EWCA Civ 1575,
[2015] Ch. 589 (CA (Civ Div)), Sir
Terence Etherton C
s.123, see *Salford Estates (No.2) Ltd v
Altomart Ltd* [2014] EWCA Civ 1575,
[2015] Ch. 589 (CA (Civ Div)), Sir
Terence Etherton C
s.125, see *Synergi Partners Ltd, Re*
[2015] EWHC 964 (Ch), [2015] B.C.C.
333 (Ch D (Manchester)), Judge Hodge
QC
s.126, amended: 2015 c.33 Sch.8 para.27
s.127, see *Akers v Samba Financial
Group* [2014] EWCA Civ 1516, [2015]
Ch. 451 (CA (Civ Div)), Longmore LJ;
see *Wilson v SMC Properties Ltd* [2015]
EWHC 870 (Ch), [2015] 2 B.C.L.C. 173
(Ch D (Companies Ct)), Registrar Briggs
s.128, amended: 2015 c.33 Sch.8 para.28
s.130, see *Pioneer Cladding Ltd v John
Graham Construction Ltd* [2015] EWHC
1314 (QB), [2015] 5 Costs L.R. 781
(QBD (TCC)), Coulson J
s.130, amended: 2015 c.33 Sch.8 para.29
s.136, amended: 2015 c.26 Sch.9 para.31
s.137, amended: 2015 c.26 Sch.9 para.32
s.138, amended: 2015 c.26 Sch.9 para.33
s.139, amended: 2015 c.26 Sch.9 para.34
s.140, amended: 2015 c.26 Sch.9 para.35
s.141, amended: 2015 c.26 Sch.9 para.36
s.142, amended: 2015 c.26 Sch.9 para.37
s.146, substituted: 2015 c.26 Sch.9
para.38
s.151, repealed: 2015 c.20 Sch.6 para.9
s.160, amended: 2015 c.26 Sch.9 para.39
s.165, amended: 2015 c.26 s.120
s.166, amended: 2015 c.26 Sch.9 para.40
s.166, repealed: 2015 c.26 Sch.9 para.40
s.167, amended: 2015 c.26 s.120
s.168, amended: 2015 c.26 Sch.9 para.41
s.169, repealed: 2015 c.26 s.120
s.171, amended: 2015 c.26 Sch.9 para.42

s.172, amended: 2015 c.26 Sch.9 para.43
s.173, amended: 2015 c.26 Sch.9 para.44
s.174, amended: 2015 c.20 Sch.6 para.10,
2015 c.26 Sch.9 para.45
s.176, amended: 2015 c.33 Sch.8 para.30
s.176ZB, added: 2015 c.26 s.119
s.183, amended: 2015 c.33 Sch.8 para.31
s.189, see *Lehman Brothers International
(Europe) (In Administration), Re* [2014]
EWHC 704 (Ch), [2015] Ch. 1 (Ch D
(Companies Ct)), David Richards J
s.194, repealed: 2015 c.26 Sch.9 para.46
s.195, amended: 2015 c.26 Sch.9 para.47
s.201, amended: 2015 c.26 Sch.9 para.48
s.202, amended: 2015 c.26 Sch.9 para.49
s.204, amended: 2015 c.26 Sch.9 para.50
s.205, amended: 2015 c.26 Sch.9 para.51
s.208, amended: 2015 c.26 Sch.9 para.52
s.212, see *Coniston Hotel (Kent) LLP (In
Liquidation), Re* [2013] EWHC 93 (Ch),
[2015] B.C.C. 1 (Ch D (Companies Ct)),
Norris J; see *Mama Milla Ltd (In
Liquidation), Re v Sharma* [2014] EWCA
Civ 761, [2015] B.P.I.R. 590 (CA (Civ
Div)), Vos LJ; see *Top Brands Ltd v
Sharma* [2014] EWHC 2753 (Ch), [2015]
2 All E.R. 581 (Ch D (Birmingham)),
Judge Barker QC
s.213, see *Bilta (UK) Ltd (In Liquidation)
v Nazir* [2015] UKSC 23 (SC), Lord
Neuberger PSC
s.214, see *Brooks v Armstrong* [2015]
EWHC 2289 (Ch), [2015] B.C.C. 661
(Ch D (Companies Ct)), Registrar Jones
s.214, amended: 2015 c.26 s.117
s.221, see *Buccament Bay Ltd, Re* [2014]
EWHC 4776 (Ch), [2015] 1 B.C.L.C.
646 (Ch D (Companies Ct)), Nicholas
Strauss QC; see *Olympic Airlines SA, Re*
[2015] UKSC 27, [2015] 1 W.L.R. 2399
(SC), Lord Neuberger PSC
s.233, see *Laverty v British Gas Trading
Ltd* [2014] EWHC 2721 (Ch), [2015] 2
All E.R. 430 (Ch D (Companies Ct)), Sir
Terence Etherton C
s.233, amended: SI 2015/989 Art.2
s.233A, added: SI 2015/989 Art.4
s.234, see *Green v Chubb* [2015] EWHC
221 (Ch), [2015] B.C.C. 625 (Ch D
(Companies Ct)), Registrar Briggs

s.235, see *Green v Chubb* [2015] EWHC
221 (Ch), [2015] B.C.C. 625 (Ch D
(Companies Ct)), Registrar Briggs
s.236, see *Comet Group Ltd (In
Liquidation), Re* [2014] EWHC 3477
(Ch), [2015] B.P.I.R. 1 (Ch D
(Companies Ct)), John Baldwin QC; see
Green v Chubb [2015] EWHC 221 (Ch),
[2015] B.C.C. 625 (Ch D (Companies
Ct)), Registrar Briggs; see *Harvest
Finance Ltd (In Liquidation), Re* [2014]
EWHC 4237 (Ch), [2015] 2 B.C.L.C.
240 (Ch D (Companies Ct)), Registrar
Jones; see *Omni Trustees Ltd, Re* [2015]
EWHC 2122 (Ch), [2015] B.C.C. 644
(Ch D), Judge Pelling QC; see *Omni
Trustees Ltd, Re* [2015] EWHC 2697
(Ch), [2015] B.C.C. 906 (Ch D)
s.237, see *Comet Group Ltd (In
Liquidation), Re* [2014] EWHC 3477
(Ch), [2015] B.P.I.R. 1 (Ch D
(Companies Ct)), John Baldwin QC
s.238, see *Bilta (UK) Ltd (In Liquidation)
v Nazir* [2015] UKSC 23 (SC), Lord
Neuberger PSC; see *Husky Group Ltd,
Re* [2014] EWHC 3003 (Ch), [2015] 3
Costs L.O. 337 (Ch D (Birmingham)),
Judge Purle QC; see *Ovenden Colbert
Printers Ltd (In Liquidation), Re* [2013]
EWCA Civ 1408, [2015] B.C.C. 615 (CA
(Civ Div)), Elias LJ; see *Sofra Bakery
Ltd (In Liquidation), Re* [2013] EWHC
1499 (Ch), [2015] 1 B.C.L.C. 338 (Ch D
(Leeds)), Andrew Sutcliffe QC
s.239, see *Green v El Tai* [2015] B.P.I.R.
24 (Ch D (Companies Ct)), Registrar
Jones
s.240, see *Ovenden Colbert Printers Ltd
(In Liquidation), Re* [2013] EWCA Civ
1408, [2015] B.C.C. 615 (CA (Civ Div)),
Elias LJ
s.241, see *Ovenden Colbert Printers Ltd
(In Liquidation), Re* [2013] EWCA Civ
1408, [2015] B.C.C. 615 (CA (Civ Div)),
Elias LJ
s.242, see *3052775 Nova Scotia Ltd v
Henderson* [2015] CSOH 126, 2015
S.L.T. 691 (OH), Lord Jones; see *Joint
Administrators of Oceancrown Ltd v
Stonegale Ltd* [2015] CSIH 12, 2015

S.C.L.R. 619 (IH (Ex Div)), Lord
Menzies
s.246A, amended: 2015 c.26 Sch.9
para.54
s.246C, added: 2015 c.26 s.124
s.246ZA, added: 2015 c.26 s.117
s.246ZD, added: 2015 c.26 s.118
s.246ZE, added: 2015 c.26 s.122
s.248A, added: 2015 c.26 s.124
s.251, amended: 2015 c.26 s.90, s.122
s.252, see *Stella v Harris* [2014] EWHC
4492 (Ch), [2015] B.P.I.R. 926 (Ch D),
Mann J
s.256, amended: 2015 c.26 Sch.9 para.61
s.256, repealed: 2015 c.26 Sch.9 para.61
s.256A, amended: 2015 c.26 Sch.9
para.62
s.256A, repealed: 2015 c.26 Sch.9
para.62
s.257, amended: 2015 c.26 Sch.9 para.64
s.257, substituted: 2015 c.26 Sch.9
para.64
s.258, amended: 2015 c.26 Sch.9 para.65
s.258, repealed: 2015 c.26 Sch.9 para.65
s.258, substituted: 2015 c.26 Sch.9
para.65
s.259, amended: 2015 c.26 Sch.9 para.66
s.260, see *Thomas v Edmondson* [2014]
EWHC 1494 (Ch), [2015] 1 W.L.R. 1395
(Ch D), Asplin J
s.260, amended: 2015 c.26 Sch.9 para.67
s.260, repealed: 2015 c.20 Sch.6 para.2
s.261, amended: 2015 c.26 Sch.9 para.68
s.262, see *Forstater (In Bankruptcy), Re*
[2015] B.P.I.R. 21 (Ch D), Registrar
Derrett
s.262, amended: 2015 c.26 s.134, Sch.9
para.69
s.262B, amended: 2015 c.26 Sch.9
para.70
s.262C, amended: 2015 c.26 Sch.9
para.71
s.263, amended: 2015 c.20 Sch.6 para.2,
2015 c.26 Sch.9 para.72
s.263A, repealed: 2015 c.26 s.135
s.263D, repealed: 2015 c.20 Sch.6 para.2
s.265, see *Gate Gourmet Luxembourg IV
Sarl v Morby* [2015] EWHC 1203 (Ch),
[2015] B.P.I.R. 787 (Ch D), Registrar
Briggs

s.266, see *Ridsdale v Bowles* [2015]
B.P.I.R. 1275 (CC (Bournemouth)),
District Judge Dancey
s.267, see *Clarke v Cognita Schools Ltd
(t/a Hydesville Tower School)* [2015]
EWHC 932 (Ch), [2015] 1 W.L.R. 3776
(Ch D (Birmingham)), Newey J; see
*Howell v Lerwick Commercial Mortgage
Corp Ltd* [2015] EWHC 1177 (Ch),
[2015] 1 W.L.R. 3554 (Ch D), Nugee J
s.267, amended: SI 2015/922 Art.2
s.267, enabling: SI 2015/922
s.268, see *Howell v Lerwick Commercial
Mortgage Corp Ltd* [2015] EWHC 1177
(Ch), [2015] 1 W.L.R. 3554 (Ch D),
Nugee J
s.269, see *Gate Gourmet Luxembourg IV
Sarl v Morby* [2015] EWHC 1203 (Ch),
[2015] B.P.I.R. 787 (Ch D), Registrar
Briggs
s.271, see *Sands v Layne* [2014] EWHC
3665 (Ch), [2015] 2 All E.R. 332 (Ch D),
David Donaldson QC
s.276, amended: 2015 c.26 Sch.9 para.73
s.281, amended: 2015 c.2 Sch.12 para.6
s.282, amended: 2015 c.26 s.135
s.283, see *Official Receiver v Lloyd*
[2015] B.P.I.R. 374 (CC (Norwich)),
District Judge McCloughlin
s.283, amended: 2015 c.26 Sch.9 para.74
s.283A, see *Sands v Singh* [2015] EWHC
2219 (Ch), [2015] B.P.I.R. 1293 (Ch D
(Birmingham)), Judge Purle QC
s.284, see *Cadlock v Dunn* [2015] EWHC
1318 (Ch), [2015] B.P.I.R. 739 (Ch D
(Leeds)), Judge Behrens
s.286, amended: 2015 c.20 Sch.6 para.13,
2015 c.26 Sch.10 para.2
s.286, varied: 2015 c.20 Sch.6 para.13
s.287, amended: 2015 c.26 Sch.9 para.75,
Sch.10 para.3
s.287, repealed: 2015 c.26 Sch.10 para.3
s.287, substituted: 2015 c.26 Sch.10
para.3
s.288, amended: 2015 c.20 Sch.6 para.15
s.291, repealed: 2015 c.26 Sch.10 para.4
s.291A, added: 2015 c.26 s.133
s.292, amended: 2015 c.26 Sch.10 para.5
s.292, repealed: 2015 c.26 Sch.10 para.5
s.292, substituted: 2015 c.26 Sch.10
para.5

s.293, repealed: 2015 c.26 Sch.10 para.6
s.296, amended: 2015 c.26 Sch.9 para.76,
Sch.10 para.7
s.297, repealed: 2015 c.26 Sch.10 para.8
s.298, amended: 2015 c.26 Sch.9 para.77,
Sch.10 para.9
s.298, repealed: 2015 c.26 Sch.10 para.9
s.299, amended: 2015 c.26 Sch.9 para.78
s.300, amended: 2015 c.26 Sch.9 para.79
s.301, amended: 2015 c.26 Sch.9 para.80
s.303, see *Oraki v Bramston* [2015]
EWHC 2046 (Ch), [2015] B.P.I.R. 1238
(Ch D), Proudman J
s.304, see *Oraki v Bramston* [2015]
EWHC 2046 (Ch), [2015] B.P.I.R. 1238
(Ch D), Proudman J
s.305, see *Oraki v Bramston* [2015]
EWHC 2046 (Ch), [2015] B.P.I.R. 1238
(Ch D), Proudman J
s.307, see *Viscount St Davids v Lewis*
[2015] EWHC 2826 (Ch), [2015]
B.P.I.R. 1471 (Ch D), Henderson J; see
Viscount St Davids v Lewis [2015]
EWHC 831 (Ch), [2015] B.P.I.R. 907
(Ch D), Registrar Barber; see *Wood v
Baker* [2015] EWHC 2536 (Ch), [2015]
B.P.I.R. 1524 (Ch D), Judge Hodge QC
s.307, amended: 2015 c.20 Sch.6 para.16
s.307, repealed: 2015 c.20 Sch.6 para.16
s.309, see *Viscount St Davids v Lewis*
[2015] EWHC 2826 (Ch), [2015]
B.P.I.R. 1471 (Ch D), Henderson J; see
Viscount St Davids v Lewis [2015]
EWHC 831 (Ch), [2015] B.P.I.R. 907
(Ch D), Registrar Barber
s.310, see *Henry, Re* [2014] EWHC 4209
(Ch), [2015] 1 W.L.R. 2488 (Ch D),
Robert Englehart QC; see *Thomas v
Edmondson* [2014] EWHC 1494 (Ch),
[2015] 1 W.L.R. 1395 (Ch D), Asplin J
s.310A, see *Thomas v Edmondson* [2014]
EWHC 1494 (Ch), [2015] 1 W.L.R. 1395
(Ch D), Asplin J
s.314, amended: 2015 c.26 s.121, Sch.9
para.81
s.314, repealed: 2015 c.26 s.121
s.330, see *Oraki v Bramston* [2015]
EWHC 2046 (Ch), [2015] B.P.I.R. 1238
(Ch D), Proudman J
s.330, amended: 2015 c.26 Sch.9 para.82
s.331, amended: 2015 c.26 Sch.9 para.83

s.331, repealed: 2015 c.26 Sch.9 para.83
s.332, amended: 2015 c.26 Sch.9 para.84
s.333, see *Viscount St Davids v Lewis*
[2015] EWHC 2826 (Ch), [2015]
B.P.I.R. 1471 (Ch D), Henderson J; see
Wood v Baker [2015] EWHC 2536 (Ch),
[2015] B.P.I.R. 1524 (Ch D), Judge
Hodge QC
s.339, see *Tailby v HSBC Bank Plc*
[2015] B.P.I.R. 143 (Ch D), Registrar
Derrett
s.340, see *Sands v Layne* [2014] EWHC
3665 (Ch), [2015] 2 All E.R. 332 (Ch D),
David Donaldson QC
s.341, see *Sands v Layne* [2014] EWHC
3665 (Ch), [2015] 2 All E.R. 332 (Ch D),
David Donaldson QC
s.346, amended: 2015 c.33 Sch.8 para.32
s.347, amended: 2015 c.33 Sch.8 para.33
s.356, amended: 2015 c.26 Sch.9 para.85
s.370, amended: 2015 c.20 Sch.6 para.14
s.372, amended: 2015 c.20 Sch.6 para.2,
SI 2015/989 Art.3
s.372, repealed: 2015 c.20 Sch.6 para.2
s.372A, added: SI 2015/989 Art.5
s.375, see *Cadlock v Dunn* [2015] EWHC
1318 (Ch), [2015] B.P.I.R. 739 (Ch D
(Leeds)), Judge Behrens; see *Clarke v
Cognita Schools Ltd (t/a Hydesville
Tower School)* [2015] EWHC 932 (Ch),
[2015] 1 W.L.R. 3776 (Ch D
(Birmingham)), Newey J; see *Sands v
Layne* [2014] EWHC 3665 (Ch), [2015]
2 All E.R. 332 (Ch D), David Donaldson
QC
s.379, amended: 2015 c.20 Sch.6 para.2
s.379A, repealed: 2015 c.26 Sch.9
para.18
s.379C, added: 2015 c.26 s.125
s.379ZA, added: 2015 c.26 s.123
s.383A, added: 2015 c.26 s.125
s.385, amended: 2015 c.26 s.123
s.386, amended: SI 2015/486 Reg.14
s.387, amended: 2015 c.26 Sch.9 para.55
s.388, amended: 2015 c.20 Sch.6 para.2
s.389, repealed: 2015 c.20 Sch.6 para.18
s.389A, repealed: 2015 c.20 Sch.6
para.19
s.390, amended: 2015 c.20 s.17, 2015
c.26 s.115
s.390A, added: 2015 c.20 s.17

s.391, substituted: 2015 c.20 s.17, 2015
c.26 s.137
s.391, varied: 2015 c.20 s.17, 2015 c.26
s.137
s.391B, added: 2015 c.26 s.138
s.391D, added: 2015 c.26 s.139
s.391L, added: 2015 c.26 s.140
s.391N, enabling: SI 2015/2067
s.391O, added: 2015 c.26 s.141
s.391S, added: 2015 c.26 s.142
s.391T, added: 2015 c.26 s.143
s.392, repealed: 2015 c.20 Sch.6 para.21
s.411, enabling: SI 2015/443
s.412, enabling: SI 2015/443
s.414, substituted: SSI 2015/150 Sch.1
para.4
s.414, enabling: SI 2015/1819
s.415, enabling: SI 2015/1819
s.415A, amended: 2015 c.20 s.17, 2015
c.26 s.139, s.140
s.415A, repealed: 2015 c.20 Sch.6
para.22
s.415A, enabling: SI 2015/1977
s.418, enabling: SI 2015/26
s.419, amended: 2015 c.26 s.138
s.419, enabling: SI 2015/391
s.423, see *Ali v Bashir* [2014] EWHC
3853 (Ch), [2015] B.P.I.R. 211 (Ch D),
Judge Pelling QC; see *Husky Group Ltd,
Re* [2014] EWHC 3003 (Ch), [2015] 3
Costs L.O. 337 (Ch D (Birmingham)),
Judge Purle QC; see *Serious Fraud
Office v Evans* [2014] EWHC 3803 (QB),
[2015] 1 W.L.R. 3526 (QBD), Fulford LJ
s.433, amended: 2015 c.26 Sch.9 para.56
s.434B, amended: 2015 c.26 Sch.9
para.57
s.436, see *Ovenden Colbert Printers Ltd
(In Liquidation), Re* [2013] EWCA Civ
1408, [2015] B.C.C. 615 (CA (Civ Div)),
Elias LJ
Sch.A1 Part II para.6, amended: 2015
c.26 Sch.9 para.9
Sch.A1 Part II para.7, amended: 2015
c.26 Sch.9 para.9
Sch.A1 Part II para.8, amended: 2015
c.26 Sch.9 para.9
Sch.A1 Part IV para.28, amended: 2015
c.20 Sch.6 para.20
Sch.A1 Part V, substituted: 2015 c.26
Sch.9 para.9

Sch.A1 Part V, amended: 2015 c.26
Sch.9 para.9
Sch.A1 Part V para.29, amended: 2015
c.26 Sch.9 para.9
Sch.A1 Part V para.30, amended: 2015
c.26 Sch.9 para.9
Sch.A1 Part V para.31, amended: 2015
c.20 Sch.6 para.20, 2015 c.26 Sch.9
para.9
Sch.A1 Part V para.32, amended: 2015
c.26 Sch.9 para.9
Sch.A1 Part V para.33, amended: 2015
c.20 Sch.6 para.20, 2015 c.26 Sch.9
para.9
Sch.A1 Part V para.35, amended: 2015
c.26 Sch.9 para.9
Sch.A1 Part V para.36, amended: 2015
c.26 Sch.9 para.9
Sch.A1 Part V para.37, amended: 2015
c.26 Sch.9 para.9
Sch.A1 Part V para.38, amended: 2015
c.26 Sch.9 para.9
Sch.A1 Part V para.39, amended: 2015
c.20 Sch.6 para.20, 2015 c.26 Sch.9
para.9
Sch.A1 Part VI para.40, amended: 2015
c.26 Sch.9 para.9
Sch.A1 Part VI para.44, amended: 2015
c.26 Sch.9 para.9
Sch.A1 Part VI para.44, repealed: 2015
c.26 Sch.9 para.9
Sch.B1 Pt 4 para.22, see *Eiffel Steel
Works Ltd, Re* [2015] EWHC 511 (Ch),
[2015] 2 B.C.L.C. 57 (Ch D), Andrew
Hochhauser QC
Sch.B1 Part 004 para.25A, added: 2015
c.20 Sch.6 para.5
Sch.B1 Part 004 para.26, amended: 2015
c.20 Sch.6 para.6
Sch.B1 Pt 4 para.26, see *Eiffel Steel
Works Ltd, Re* [2015] EWHC 511 (Ch),
[2015] 2 B.C.L.C. 57 (Ch D), Andrew
Hochhauser QC
Sch.B1 Part 007, substituted: 2015 c.26
Sch.9 para.10
Sch.B1 Part 007, amended: 2015 c.26
Sch.9 para.10
Sch.B1 Part 007 para.49, amended: 2015
c.26 Sch.9 para.10
Sch.B1 Part 007 para.50, repealed: 2015
c.26 Sch.9 para.10

Sch.B1 Part 007 para.51, amended: 2015 c.26 Sch.9 para.10

Sch.B1 Part 007 para.52, amended: 2015 c.26 Sch.9 para.10

Sch.B1 Part 007 para.53, amended: 2015 c.26 Sch.9 para.10

Sch.B1 Part 007 para.54, amended: 2015 c.26 Sch.9 para.10

Sch.B1 Part 007 para.54, repealed: 2015 c.26 Sch.9 para.10

Sch.B1 Part 007 para.55, amended: 2015 c.26 Sch.9 para.10

Sch.B1 Part 007 para.56, amended: 2015 c.26 Sch.9 para.10

Sch.B1 Part 007 para.57, amended: 2015 c.26 Sch.9 para.10

Sch.B1 Part 007 para.58, repealed: 2015 c.26 Sch.9 para.10

Sch.B1 Part 008 para.60, substituted: 2015 c.26 s.129

Sch.B1 Part 008 para.60A, added: 2015 c.26 s.129

Sch.B1 Part 008 para.62, amended: 2015 c.26 Sch.9 para.10

Sch.B1 Part 008 para.65, amended: 2015 c.26 s.128

Sch.B1 Part 008 para.74, amended: 2015 c.26 Sch.9 para.10

Sch.B1 Part 009 para.76, amended: 2015 c.26 s.127

Sch.B1 Part 009 para.78, amended: 2015 c.26 Sch.9 para.10

Sch.B1 Part 009 para.78, repealed: 2015 c.26 Sch.9 para.10

Sch.B1 Part 009 para.79, amended: 2015 c.26 Sch.9 para.10

Sch.B1 Part 009 para.80, amended: 2015 c.26 Sch.9 para.10

Sch.B1 Part 009 para.83, amended: 2015 c.26 s.128, Sch.9 para.10

Sch.B1 Part 009 para.84, amended: 2015 c.26 Sch.9 para.10

Sch.B1 Part 010, amended: 2015 c.26 Sch.9 para.10

Sch.B1 Part 010 para.97, amended: 2015 c.26 Sch.9 para.10

Sch.B1 Part 010 para.98, amended: 2015 c.20 Sch.6 para.7, 2015 c.26 Sch.9 para.10

Sch.B1 Part 010 para.99, repealed: 2015 c.20 Sch.6 para.27

Sch.B1 Part 011 para.108, amended: 2015 c.26 Sch.9 para.10

Sch.B1 Part 011 para.108, repealed: 2015 c.26 Sch.9 para.10

Sch.B1 Part 011 para.111, amended: 2015 c.26 Sch.9 para.10

Sch.B1 Part 011 para.115, amended: 2015 c.26 s.130

Sch.B1 para.55, see *Pudsey Steel Services Ltd, Re* [2015] B.P.I.R. 1459 (Ch D), Judge Behrens QC

Sch.B1 para.59, see *Maxwell v Brookes* [2015] B.C.C. 113 (Ch D (Companies Ct)), Registrar Jones

Sch.B1 para.67, see *Business Environment Fleet Street Ltd (In Administration), Re* [2014] EWHC 3540 (Ch), [2015] 1 W.L.R. 1167 (Ch D (Companies Ct)), David Halpern QC; see *GSM Export (UK) Ltd (In Administration) v Revenue and Customs Commissioners* [2015] S.T.C. 504 (UT (Tax)), Judge Roger Berner

Sch.B1 para.72, see *Business Environment Fleet Street Ltd (In Administration), Re* [2014] EWHC 3540 (Ch), [2015] 1 W.L.R. 1167 (Ch D (Companies Ct)), David Halpern QC

Sch.B1 para.74, see *Coniston Hotel (Kent) LLP (In Liquidation), Re* [2013] EWHC 93 (Ch), [2015] B.C.C. 1 (Ch D (Companies Ct)), Norris J; see *Lehman Brothers International (Europe) (In Administration), Re* [2015] EWHC 2270 (Ch), [2015] B.P.I.R. 1162 (Ch D (Companies Ct)), David Richards QC

Sch.B1 para.75, see *Coniston Hotel (Kent) LLP (In Liquidation), Re* [2013] EWHC 93 (Ch), [2015] B.C.C. 1 (Ch D (Companies Ct)), Norris J

Sch.B1 para.76, see *Synergi Partners Ltd, Re* [2015] EWHC 964 (Ch), [2015] B.C.C. 333 (Ch D (Manchester)), Judge Hodge QC

Sch.B1 Pt 002 para.13, see *Synergi Partners Ltd, Re* [2015] EWHC 964 (Ch), [2015] B.C.C. 333 (Ch D (Manchester)), Judge Hodge QC

Sch.B1 Pt 004 para.22, see *Melodious Corp, Re* [2015] EWHC 621 (Ch), [2015]

2 All E.R. (Comm) 1139 (Ch D
(Companies Ct)), Sir Terence Etherton C
Sch.1, see *Maxwell v Brookes* [2015]
B.C.C. 113 (Ch D (Companies Ct)),
Registrar Jones
Sch.3 Part II, amended: 2015 c.26 s.120
Sch.4A, see *Official Receiver v Lloyd*
[2015] B.P.I.R. 374 (CC (Norwich)),
District Judge McCloughlin
Sch.4 Part I, repealed: 2015 c.26 s.120
Sch.4 Part I para.3, amended: 2015 c.26
s.120
Sch.4 Part II, repealed: 2015 c.26 s.120
Sch.4 Part III, repealed: 2015 c.26 s.120
Sch.4 Part III para.6A, repealed: 2015
c.26 s.120
Sch.4 Pt II para.4, see *Connaught Income
Fund Series 1 (In Liquidation) v Capita
Financial Managers Ltd* [2014] EWHC
3619 (Comm), [2015] 1 All E.R. (Comm)
751 (QBD (Comm)), Judge Mackie QC
Sch.4 Pt III para.13, see *Connaught
Income Fund Series 1 (In Liquidation) v
Capita Financial Managers Ltd* [2014]
EWHC 3619 (Comm), [2015] 1 All E.R.
(Comm) 751 (QBD (Comm)), Judge
Mackie QC
Sch.4A para.11, amended: 2015 c.26
s.135
Sch.5 Part I, repealed: 2015 c.26 s.121
Sch.5 Part II, repealed: 2015 c.26 s.121
Sch.5 Part III, repealed: 2015 c.26 s.121
Sch.6, amended: SI 2015/486 Reg.14
Sch.6 para.15, repealed: 2015 c.20 Sch.6
para.28
Sch.6 para.15AA, added: SI 2015/486
Reg.14
Sch.6 para.15C, amended: SI 2015/486
Reg.14
Sch.7, repealed: 2015 c.20 Sch.6 para.21
Sch.8 para.5A, added: 2015 c.26 s.124
Sch.8 para.8A, added: 2015 c.26 s.122
Sch.8 para.9A, added: 2015 c.26 Sch.9
para.58
Sch.8 para.10, amended: 2015 c.26 Sch.9
para.59
Sch.8 para.13A, added: 2015 c.26 s.131
Sch.9 para.10, repealed: 2015 c.26
Sch.10 para.10
Sch.9 para.11A, added: 2015 c.26 s.123

Sch.9 para.12A, added: 2015 c.26 Sch.9
para.86
Sch.9 para.13, amended: 2015 c.26 Sch.9
para.87
Sch.9 para.18A, added: 2015 c.26 s.132
Sch.9 para.24, amended: 2015 c.20 Sch.6
para.2
Sch.9 para.30, amended: 2015 c.26
Sch.10 para.11
Sch.10, amended: 2015 c.20 Sch.6
para.22, 2015 c.26 s.136, Sch.9 para.11,
Sch.9 para.53
Sch.14, amended: 2015 c.20 Sch.6 para.2
**46. Company Directors Disqualification Act
1986**
see *Official Receiver v Lloyd* [2015]
B.P.I.R. 374 (CC (Norwich)), District
Judge McCloughlin; see *Practice
Direction: Directors Disqualification
Proceedings* [2015] B.C.C. 224 (Ch D)
s.1, amended: 2015 c.26 Sch.7 para.2
s.1A, see *Harris v Secretary of State for
Business, Innovation and Skills* [2013]
EWHC 2514 (Ch), [2015] B.C.C. 283
(Ch D), Judge Simon Barker QC
s.1A, amended: 2015 c.26 Sch.7 para.3
s.2, amended: 2015 c.26 Sch.7 para.4
s.3, amended: 2015 c.26 Sch.7 para.5
s.5, amended: 2015 c.26 Sch.7 para.6
s.5A, added: 2015 c.26 s.104
s.6, see *Artistic Investment Advisers Ltd,
Re* [2014] EWHC 2963 (Ch), [2015] 1
B.C.L.C. 619 (Ch D), John Male QC; see
*Secretary of State for Business,
Innovation and Skills v Chohan* [2013]
EWHC 680 (Ch), [2015] B.C.C. 755 (Ch
D (Companies Ct)), Hildyard J
s.6, amended: 2015 c.26 s.106, Sch.7
para.7
s.7, see *Practice Direction: Directors
Disqualification Proceedings* [2015]
B.C.C. 224 (Ch D); see *Secretary of
State for Business, Innovation and Skills
v Chohan* [2013] EWHC 680 (Ch),
[2015] B.C.C. 755 (Ch D (Companies
Ct)), Hildyard J
s.7, amended: 2015 c.20 Sch.6 para.11,
2015 c.26 s.108, Sch.7 para.8
s.7, repealed: 2015 c.26 s.107
s.7, substituted: 2015 c.26 s.107
s.7A, added: 2015 c.26 s.107

s.8, amended: 2015 c.26 s.106, s.109
s.8, repealed: 2015 c.26 s.109
s.8, substituted: 2015 c.26 s.109
s.8A, see *Practice Direction: Directors Disqualification Proceedings* [2015] B.C.C. 224 (Ch D)
s.8A, amended: 2015 c.26 Sch.7 para.9
s.8A, see *Practice Direction: Directors Disqualification Proceedings* [2015] B.C.C. 224 (Ch D)
s.8A, amended: 2015 c.26 Sch.7 para.10
s.8ZA, added: 2015 c.26 s.105
s.9, repealed: 2015 c.26 s.106
s.9E, amended: SI 2015/1682 Sch.1 para.4
s.10, amended: 2015 c.26 Sch.7 para.11
s.11, amended: 2015 c.26 s.113
s.12C, added: 2015 c.26 s.106
s.15A, added: 2015 c.26 s.110
s.16, amended: 2015 c.26 Sch.7 para.12
s.17, amended: 2015 c.26 Sch.7 para.13
s.18, amended: 2015 c.26 Sch.7 para.14
s.20, amended: 2015 c.26 Sch.7 para.15
s.21, amended: 2015 c.26 Sch.7 para.16
s.22, see *Secretary of State for Business, Innovation and Skills v Chohan* [2013] EWHC 680 (Ch), [2015] B.C.C. 755 (Ch D (Companies Ct)), Hildyard J
s.22, amended: 2015 c.26 s.90, Sch.7 para.17
s.22A, repealed: 2015 c.26 Sch.7 para.18
s.22B, amended: 2015 c.26 Sch.7 para.19
s.22B, repealed: 2015 c.26 Sch.7 para.19
s.22C, repealed: 2015 c.26 Sch.7 para.20
s.22D, repealed: 2015 c.26 Sch.7 para.21
s.22E, amended: 2015 c.26 Sch.7 para.22
s.22E, repealed: 2015 c.26 Sch.7 para.22
s.22F, repealed: 2015 c.26 Sch.7 para.23
s.24, amended: 2015 c.26 s.113
Sch.1, substituted: 2015 c.26 s.106

47. Legal Aid (Scotland) Act 1986
see *Scottish Legal Aid Board v Lavery* 2015 S.L.T. (Sh Ct) 35 (Sh Ct (Glasgow)), Sheriff A D Miller
s.9, enabling: SSI 2015/13, SSI 2015/155, SSI 2015/279
s.17, see *Lord Advocate v Mackie* [2015] CSIH 88 (IH (2 Div)), The Lord Justice Clerk (Carloway)

s.18, see *B v Secretary of State for the Home Department* [2015] CSIH 43, 2015 S.C. 667 (IH (Ex Div)), Lord Brodie
s.19, see *B v Secretary of State for the Home Department* [2015] CSIH 43, 2015 S.C. 667 (IH (Ex Div)), Lord Brodie; see *McGraddie v McGraddie* [2015] UKSC 1, [2015] 1 W.L.R. 560 (SC), Lord Neuberger PSC
s.33, enabling: SSI 2015/337, SSI 2015/380
s.36, enabling: SSI 2015/337, SSI 2015/380

53. Building Societies Act 1986
Sch.11 para.4, amended: SI 2015/664 Sch.3 para.4
Sch.11 para.7, amended: SI 2015/664 Sch.3 para.4

55. Family Law Act 1986
see *G (A Child) (Same-sex Relationship: Family Life Declaration), Re* [2015] Fam. 133 (Fam Ct), Peter Jackson J
s.44, see *Solovyev v Solovyeva* [2015] 1 F.L.R. 734 (Fam Ct), Sir James Munby PFD
s.45, see *Solovyev v Solovyeva* [2015] 1 F.L.R. 734 (Fam Ct), Sir James Munby PFD
s.55, see *K v A (Marriage: Validity)* [2014] EWHC 3850 (Fam), [2015] 2 F.L.R. 461 (Fam Div), Roberts J
s.57, see *G (Children) (Recognition of Brazilian Adoption), Re* [2014] EWHC 2605 (Fam), [2015] 1 F.L.R. 1402 (Fam Div), Cobb J
s.58, see *G (Children) (Recognition of Brazilian Adoption), Re* [2014] EWHC 2605 (Fam), [2015] 1 F.L.R. 1402 (Fam Div), Cobb J
s.59, see *G (Children) (Recognition of Brazilian Adoption), Re* [2014] EWHC 2605 (Fam), [2015] 1 F.L.R. 1402 (Fam Div), Cobb J

56. Parliamentary Constituencies Act 1986
s.6B, substituted: SI 2015/1376 Sch.2 para.3

61. Education (No.2) Act 1986
s.61, repealed: 2015 c.20 Sch.15 para.2
s.62, repealed: 2015 c.20 Sch.15 para.2

64. Public Order Act 1986

see *Walker v Commissioner of Police of the Metropolis* [2014] EWCA Civ 897, [2015] 1 W.L.R. 312 (CA (Civ Div)), Rimer LJ

1987

4. Ministry of Defence Police Act 1987
s.3A, enabling: SI 2015/25
s.4, enabling: SI 2015/25
s.4A, enabling: SI 2015/25
9. Animals (Scotland) Act 1987
s.1, see *Ferguson v Ferguson* [2015] CSIH 63, 2015 S.L.T. 561 (IH (Ex Div)), Lord Eassie
12. Petroleum Act 1987
s.22, enabling: SI 2015/407, SI 2015/1406, SI 2015/1673
s.23, enabling: SI 2015/398
15. Reverter of Sites Act 1987
s.5, enabling: SI 2015/247, SI 2015/1577, SI 2015/1800
18. Debtors (Scotland) Act 1987
s.49, enabling: SSI 2015/370
s.53, amended: SSI 2015/370 Reg.2
s.53, enabling: SSI 2015/370
s.63, enabling: SSI 2015/370
s.90, enabling: SSI 2015/351
Sch.2, amended: SSI 2015/370 Sch.1
21. Pilotage Act 1987
s.1, enabling: SI 2015/132
26. Housing (Scotland) Act 1987
see *Ansari v Aberdeen City Council* [2015] CSOH 168 (OH), Lord Glennie; see *Boyle v South Lanarkshire Council* 2015 S.L.T. (Lands Tr) 189 (Lands Tr (Scot)), R A Smith, QC
s.61, see *Boyle v South Lanarkshire Council* 2015 S.L.T. (Lands Tr) 189 (Lands Tr (Scot)), R A Smith, QC
s.62, see *Boyle v South Lanarkshire Council* 2015 S.L.T. (Lands Tr) 189 (Lands Tr (Scot)), R A Smith, QC; see *Boyle v South Lanarkshire Council* 2015 S.L.T. (Lands Tr) 205 (Lands Tr (Scot)), R A Smith, QC; see *Mark v City of Edinburgh Council* 2015 S.L.T. (Lands Tr) 157 (Lands Tr (Scot)), Lord Minginish

s.65, see *Mark v City of Edinburgh Council* 2015 S.L.T. (Lands Tr) 157 (Lands Tr (Scot)), Lord Minginish
s.71, see *Boyle v South Lanarkshire Council* 2015 S.L.T. (Lands Tr) 205 (Lands Tr (Scot)), R A Smith, QC
31. Landlord and Tenant Act 1987
Pt II., see *R. (on the application of Cawsand Fort Management Co Ltd) v First-Tier Tribunal* [2014] EWHC 3808 (Admin), [2015] L. & T.R. 9 (QBD (Admin)), Hickinbottom J
s.21, see *R. (on the application of Cawsand Fort Management Co Ltd) v First-Tier Tribunal* [2014] EWHC 3808 (Admin), [2015] L. & T.R. 9 (QBD (Admin)), Hickinbottom J
s.24, see *Eaglesham Properties Ltd v Leaseholders of Flats 2, 3, 6, 7, 8 and 12 Drysdale Dwellings* [2015] UKUT 22 (LC), [2015] L. & T.R. 28 (UT (Lands)), Judge Alice Robinson; see *R. (on the application of Cawsand Fort Management Co Ltd) v First-Tier Tribunal* [2014] EWHC 3808 (Admin), [2015] L. & T.R. 9 (QBD (Admin)), Hickinbottom J
s.35, see *Rossman v Crown Estate Commissioners* [2015] UKUT 288 (LC), [2015] L. & T.R. 31 (UT (Lands)), Sir Keith Lindblom P
s.42, see *Parissis v Blair Court (St John's Wood) Management Ltd* [2015] L. & T.R. 7 (UT (Lands)), Judge Huskinson
38. Criminal Justice Act 1987
s.2, see *R. (on the application of Lord) v Director of the Serious Fraud Office* [2015] EWHC 865 (Admin), [2015] 2 Cr. App. R. 24 (DC), Davis LJ
s.12, see *R. v Jones (Nicholas John)* [2014] EWCA Crim 1762, [2015] 1 Cr. App. R. 5 (CA (Crim Div)), Pitchford LJ
43. Consumer Protection Act 1987
see *Allen v Depuy International Ltd* [2014] EWHC 753 (QB), [2015] 2 W.L.R. 442 (QBD), Stewart J
s.14, amended: SI 2015/1640 Sch.4 para.1
s.27, amended: 2015 c.15 Sch.6 para.38
s.28, repealed: 2015 c.15 Sch.6 para.39
s.29, amended: 2015 c.15 Sch.6 para.40

s.29, repealed: 2015 c.15 Sch.6 para.40
s.30, amended: 2015 c.15 Sch.6 para.41
s.31, amended: 2015 c.15 Sch.6 para.42
s.32, amended: 2015 c.15 Sch.6 para.43
s.33, amended: 2015 c.15 Sch.6 para.44
s.34, amended: 2015 c.15 Sch.6 para.45
s.44, amended: 2015 c.15 Sch.6 para.46
49. Territorial Sea Act 1987
s.4, enabling: SI 2015/827
53. Channel Tunnel Act 1987
s.11, enabling: SI 2015/785, SI 2015/856

1988

1. Income and Corporation Taxes Act 1988
see *Chappell v Revenue and Customs Commissioners* [2015] S.T.C. 271 (UT (Tax)), Simon J
Pt XV s.686, see *Gilchrist v Revenue and Customs Commissioners* [2015] Ch. 183 (UT (Tax)), David Richards J
s.18, see *Healey v Revenue and Customs Commissioners* [2015] UKUT 140 (TCC), [2015] S.T.C. 1749 (UT (Tax)), Henderson J; see *Manduca v Revenue and Customs Commissioners* [2015] UKUT 262 (TCC), [2015] S.T.C. 2002 (UT (Tax)), Rose J; see *Peninsular & Oriental Steam Navigation Co v Revenue and Customs Commissioners* [2015] UKUT 312 (TCC), [2015] S.T.C. 2393 (UT (Tax)), Proudman J; see *Versteegh Ltd v Revenue and Customs Commissioners* [2015] UKUT 75 (TCC), [2015] S.T.C. 1222 (UT (Tax)), Proudman J
s.74, see *Interfish Ltd v Revenue and Customs Commissioners* [2014] EWCA Civ 876, [2015] S.T.C. 55 (CA (Civ Div)), Lord Dyson MR
s.118, see *Hamilton & Kinneil (Archerfield) Ltd v Revenue and Customs Commissioners* [2015] UKUT 130 (TCC), [2015] S.T.C. 1852 (UT (Tax)), Warren J
s.118ZA, see *Hamilton & Kinneil (Archerfield) Ltd v Revenue and Customs Commissioners* [2015] UKUT 130 (TCC), [2015] S.T.C. 1852 (UT (Tax)), Warren J

s.118ZC, see *Hamilton & Kinneil (Archerfield) Ltd v Revenue and Customs Commissioners* [2015] UKUT 130 (TCC), [2015] S.T.C. 1852 (UT (Tax)), Warren J
s.231, see *Prudential Assurance Co Ltd v Revenue and Customs Commissioners* [2015] EWHC 118 (Ch), [2015] S.T.C. 1119 (Ch D), Henderson J
s.249, see *Gilchrist v Revenue and Customs Commissioners* [2015] Ch. 183 (UT (Tax)), David Richards J
s.348, see *Chappell v Revenue and Customs Commissioners* [2015] S.T.C. 271 (UT (Tax)), Simon J
s.349, see *Chappell v Revenue and Customs Commissioners* [2015] S.T.C. 271 (UT (Tax)), Simon J
s.353, see *Eclipse Film Partners No.35 LLP v Revenue and Customs Commissioners* [2015] EWCA Civ 95, [2015] S.T.C. 1429 (CA (Civ Div)), Sir Terence Etherton C
s.362, see *Eclipse Film Partners No.35 LLP v Revenue and Customs Commissioners* [2015] EWCA Civ 95, [2015] S.T.C. 1429 (CA (Civ Div)), Sir Terence Etherton C; see *Vaccine Research LP v Revenue and Customs Commissioners* [2015] S.T.C. 179 (UT (Tax)), Sales J
s.380, see *Degorce v Revenue and Customs Commissioners* [2015] UKUT 447 (TCC), [2015] B.T.C. 528 (UT (Tax)), Hildyard J
s.381, see *Vaccine Research LP v Revenue and Customs Commissioners* [2015] S.T.C. 179 (UT (Tax)), Sales J
s.492, see *Wintershall (E&P) Ltd v Revenue and Customs Commissioners* [2015] UKUT 334 (TCC) (UT (Tax)), Lord Glennie
s.501A, see *Wintershall (E&P) Ltd v Revenue and Customs Commissioners* [2015] UKUT 334 (TCC) (UT (Tax)), Lord Glennie
s.502, see *Wintershall (E&P) Ltd v Revenue and Customs Commissioners* [2015] UKUT 334 (TCC) (UT (Tax)), Lord Glennie

s.591A, see *John Mander Pension Scheme Trustees Ltd v Revenue and Customs Commissioners* [2015] UKSC 56, [2015] 1 W.L.R. 3857 (SC), Lord Neuberger PSC

s.591B, see *John Mander Pension Scheme Trustees Ltd v Revenue and Customs Commissioners* [2015] UKSC 56, [2015] 1 W.L.R. 3857 (SC), Lord Neuberger PSC

s.591C, see *John Mander Pension Scheme Trustees Ltd v Revenue and Customs Commissioners* [2015] UKSC 56, [2015] 1 W.L.R. 3857 (SC), Lord Neuberger PSC

s.591D, see *John Mander Pension Scheme Trustees Ltd v Revenue and Customs Commissioners* [2015] UKSC 56, [2015] 1 W.L.R. 3857 (SC), Lord Neuberger PSC

s.730A, see *Biffa (Jersey) Ltd v Revenue and Customs Commissioners* [2015] S.F.T.D. 163 (FTT (Tax)), Judge Greg Sinfield; see *Cater Allen International Ltd v Revenue and Customs Commissioners* [2015] UKFTT 232 (TC), [2015] S.F.T.D. 765 (FTT (Tax)), Judge Rachel Short

s.737A, see *Cater Allen International Ltd v Revenue and Customs Commissioners* [2015] UKFTT 232 (TC), [2015] S.F.T.D. 765 (FTT (Tax)), Judge Rachel Short

s.786, see *Versteegh Ltd v Revenue and Customs Commissioners* [2015] UKUT 75 (TCC), [2015] S.T.C. 1222 (UT (Tax)), Proudman J

s.790, see *Peninsular & Oriental Steam Navigation Co v Revenue and Customs Commissioners* [2015] UKUT 312 (TCC), [2015] S.T.C. 2393 (UT (Tax)), Proudman J

s.792, see *Peninsular & Oriental Steam Navigation Co v Revenue and Customs Commissioners* [2015] UKUT 312 (TCC), [2015] S.T.C. 2393 (UT (Tax)), Proudman J

s.799, see *Peninsular & Oriental Steam Navigation Co v Revenue and Customs Commissioners* [2015] UKUT 312

(TCC), [2015] S.T.C. 2393 (UT (Tax)), Proudman J

s.801, see *Peninsular & Oriental Steam Navigation Co v Revenue and Customs Commissioners* [2015] UKUT 312 (TCC), [2015] S.T.C. 2393 (UT (Tax)), Proudman J; see *Test Claimants in the FII Group Litigation v Revenue and Customs Commissioners* [2014] EWHC 4302 (Ch), [2015] S.T.C. 1471 (Ch D), Henderson J

Sch.D, see *Biffa (Jersey) Ltd v Revenue and Customs Commissioners* [2015] S.F.T.D. 163 (FTT (Tax)), Judge Greg Sinfield; see *Degorce v Revenue and Customs Commissioners* [2015] UKUT 447 (TCC), [2015] B.T.C. 528 (UT (Tax)), Hildyard J

Sch.15 Part I paraB.3, enabling: SI 2015/544

Sch.18, see *Gemsupa Ltd v Revenue and Customs Commissioners* [2015] UKFTT 97 (TC), [2015] S.F.T.D. 447 (FTT (Tax)), Judge Jonathan Cannan

7. Social Security Act 1988

s.13, enabling: SI 2015/917, SI 2015/1580

9. Local Government Act 1988

Sch.2 Part 1, amended: 2015 c.20 Sch.13 para.6

12. Merchant Shipping Act 1988

repealed: 2015 c.20 Sch.23 para.26

13. Coroners Act 1988

see *R. (on the application of Antoniou) v Central and North West London NHS Foundation Trust* [2013] EWHC 3055 (Admin), [2015] 1 W.L.R. 4459 (DC), Aikens LJ

s.13, see *HM Coroner for Isle of Wight v Prison Service* [2015] EWHC 1360 (Admin), [2015] Inquest L.R. 110 (DC), Bean LJ

16. Farm Land and Rural Development Act 1988

s.1, enabling: SI 2015/793

19. Employment Act 1988

s.26, repealed: 2015 c.20 Sch.14 para.34

20. Dartford-Thurrock Crossing Act 1988

s.46A, added: 2015 c.7 Sch.1 para.102

27. Malicious Communications Act 1988

s.1, amended: 2015 c.2 s.32

33. Criminal Justice Act 1988
s.36, amended: 2015 c.2 Sch.5 para.2
s.39, see *Barnaby v DPP* [2015] EWHC
232 (Admin), [2015] 2 Cr. App. R. 4
(DC), Fulford LJ
s.40, see *R. v Taylor (Christopher
Stephen)* [2014] EWCA Crim 2411,
[2015] R.T.R. 11 (CA (Crim Div)),
Fulford LJ
s.40, amended: 2015 c.2 Sch.10 para.31
s.71, see *R. v Guraj (Lodvik)* [2015]
EWCA Crim 305, [2015] 1 W.L.R. 4149
(CA (Crim Div)), Jackson LJ
s.72A, see *R. v Guraj (Lodvik)* [2015]
EWCA Crim 305, [2015] 1 W.L.R. 4149
(CA (Crim Div)), Jackson LJ
s.77, see *Sinclair v Glatt* [2015] EWHC
1673 (Admin), [2015] Lloyd's Rep. F.C.
481 (Ch D), Blake J
s.89, see *Bhandal v Revenue and
Customs Commissioners* [2015] EWHC
538 (Admin), [2015] Lloyd's Rep. F.C.
343 (QBD (Admin)), Collins J
s.133, see *Dinnell v Scottish Ministers*
[2015] CSIH 7, 2015 S.C. 429 (IH (Ex
Div)), Lord Eassie
s.133, amended: 2015 c.6 s.15
s.139, amended: 2015 c.2 s.28
s.139A, amended: 2015 c.2 s.28
s.139AZA, added: 2015 c.2 s.28
s.159, see *Guardian News and Media Ltd
v Incedal* [2014] EWCA Crim 1861,
[2015] 1 Cr. App. R. 4 (CA (Crim Div)),
Gross LJ
s.159, enabling: SI 2015/1490
35. British Steel Act 1988
s.4, amended: 2015 c.20 Sch.23 para.11
s.6, repealed: 2015 c.20 Sch.23 para.11
s.13, amended: 2015 c.20 Sch.23 para.11
Sch.3 para.10, repealed: 2015 c.20
Sch.23 para.12
36. Court of Session Act 1988
s.5, enabling: SSI 2015/26, SSI 2015/35,
SSI 2015/85, SSI 2015/119
s.26, amended: SSI 2015/338 Sch.1
para.1
s.27B, amended: SI 2015/700 Art.6
s.28, see *Scottish Ministers v Mirza* 2015
S.C. 334 (IH (Ex Div)), Lady Clark of
Calton
40. Education Reform Act 1988

s.128, repealed: 2015 c.20 Sch.14 para.35
s.129, enabling: SI 2015/1703
s.158, repealed: 2015 c.20 Sch.15 para.3
s.159, repealed: 2015 c.20 Sch.15 para.3
s.215, amended: 2015 c.15 Sch.6 para.47
s.215, repealed: 2015 c.15 Sch.6 para.47
s.219, repealed: 2015 c.20 Sch.15 para.3
41. Local Government Finance Act 1988
see *SJ&J Monk (A Firm) v Newbigin
(Valuation Officer)* [2015] EWCA Civ
78, [2015] 1 W.L.R. 4817 (CA (Civ
Div)), Arden LJ
s.43, enabling: SI 2015/229
s.44, enabling: SI 2015/106, SI 2015/229
s.46A, see *R. (on the application of
Reeves (Valuation Officer)) v Valuation
Tribunal for England* [2015] EWHC 973
(Admin), [2015] R.A. 241 (QBD
(Admin)), Holgate J
s.51, see *Tunnel Tech Ltd v Reeves
(Valuation Officer)* [2015] EWCA Civ
718, [2015] P.T.S.R. 1490 (CA (Civ
Div)), Sir Terence Etherton C
s.55, enabling: SI 2015/424
s.60, enabling: SI 2015/1905
s.62, enabling: SI 2015/655
s.64, enabling: SI 2015/539
s.65, enabling: SI 2015/539
s.66, see *Cornwall v Alexander
(Valuation Officer)* [2015] R.A. 504
(VT), Graham Zellick QC
s.74, enabling: SI 2015/27
s.97, enabling: SI 2015/628
s.99, enabling: SI 2015/628
s.143, enabling: SI 2015/27, SI 2015/106,
SI 2015/229, SI 2015/424, SI 2015/427,
SI 2015/539, SI 2015/617, SI 2015/628,
SI 2015/1759, SI 2015/2039
s.146, enabling: SI 2015/229, SI
2015/655
Sch.4A, see *UKI (Kingsway) Ltd v
Westminster City Council* [2015] UKUT
301 (LC), [2015] R.A. 433 (UT (Lands)),
Martin Rodger QC
Sch.4A para.2, see *UKI (Kingsway) Ltd v
Westminster City Council* [2015] UKUT
301 (LC), [2015] R.A. 433 (UT (Lands)),
Martin Rodger QC
Sch.4A para.4, see *R. (on the application
of Reeves (Valuation Officer)) v
Valuation Tribunal for England* [2015]

EWHC 973 (Admin), [2015] R.A. 241
(QBD (Admin)), Holgate J
Sch.4A para.8, see *UKI (Kingsway) Ltd v
Westminster City Council* [2015] UKUT
301 (LC), [2015] R.A. 433 (UT (Lands)),
Martin Rodger QC
Sch.5, see *Tunnel Tech Ltd v Reeves
(Valuation Officer)* [2015] EWCA Civ
718, [2015] P.T.S.R. 1490 (CA (Civ
Div)), Sir Terence Etherton C
Sch.5 para.1, see *Tunnel Tech Ltd v
Reeves (Valuation Officer)* [2015]
EWCA Civ 718, [2015] P.T.S.R. 1490
(CA (Civ Div)), Sir Terence Etherton C
Sch.5 para.2, see *Tunnel Tech Ltd v
Reeves (Valuation Officer)* [2015]
EWCA Civ 718, [2015] P.T.S.R. 1490
(CA (Civ Div)), Sir Terence Etherton C
Sch.5 para.3, see *Tunnel Tech Ltd v
Reeves (Valuation Officer)* [2015]
EWCA Civ 718, [2015] P.T.S.R. 1490
(CA (Civ Div)), Sir Terence Etherton C
Sch.5 para.16, amended: SI 2015/914
Sch.1 para.42
Sch.6, see *Gallagher (Valuation Officer)
v Read & Partners* [2015] UKUT 1 (LC),
[2015] R.A. 155 (UT (Lands)), PR
Francis
Sch.6 para.2, see *Bainbridge (Valuation
Officer) v Boldfield Ltd* [2015] UKUT
295 (LC), [2015] R.A. 459 (UT (Lands)),
PR Francis FRICS; see *Hardman v
British Gas Trading Ltd* [2015] UKUT
53 (LC), [2015] R.A. 254 (UT (Lands)),
Judge Mole QC; see *R3 Products Ltd v
Salt (Valuation Officer)* [2015] R.A. 1
(UT (Lands)), PD McCrea FRICS; see
*SJ&J Monk (A Firm) v Newbigin
(Valuation Officer)* [2015] EWCA Civ
78, [2015] 1 W.L.R. 4817 (CA (Civ
Div)), Arden LJ
Sch.6 para.2, enabling: SI 2015/1759
Sch.7 Part I para.5, enabling: SI
2015/135
Sch.7B Part III para.6, enabling: SI
2015/628
Sch.7B Part III para.7, enabling: SI
2015/628
Sch.7B Part III para.8, enabling: SI
2015/628

Sch.7B Part IV para.9, enabling: SI
2015/628
Sch.7B Part IV para.10, enabling: SI
2015/628
Sch.7B Part IV para.11, enabling: SI
2015/628
Sch.7B Part VII para.22, enabling: SI
2015/617, SI 2015/2039
Sch.7B Part VII para.25, enabling: SI
2015/617, SI 2015/2039
Sch.7B Part VII para.28, enabling: SI
2015/617
Sch.7B Part VIII para.33, enabling: SI
2015/628
Sch.7B Part IX para.37, enabling: SI
2015/2039
Sch.7B Part X para.39, enabling: SI
2015/353, SI 2015/354
Sch.7B Part X para.40, enabling: SI
2015/628
Sch.7B Part X para.41, enabling: SI
2015/628
Sch.7B Part X para.42, enabling: SI
2015/628
Sch.8 Part II para.4, enabling: SI
2015/1905
Sch.8 Part II para.6, enabling: SI
2015/1905
Sch.9 para.1, enabling: SI 2015/427, SI
2015/655
Sch.9 para.2, enabling: SI 2015/427, SI
2015/655
Sch.9 para.6B, added: SI 2015/982 Art.2
Sch.9 para.7, amended: SI 2015/982
Art.2

43. Housing (Scotland) Act 1988
s.24, see *Westfoot Invesments Ltd v
European Property Holdings Inc* 2015
S.L.T. (Sh Ct) 201 (Sh Ct (Lothian)
(Edinburgh)), Sheriff T Welsh, QC

45. Firearms (Amendment) Act 1988
s.11, amended: SI 2015/611 Art.4
s.11, enabling: SI 2015/611
s.17, amended: SI 2015/611 Art.5
s.17, enabling: SI 2015/611

48. Copyright, Designs and Patents Act 1988
s.7, see *ITV Broadcasting Ltd v TV
Catchup Ltd* [2015] EWCA Civ 204,
[2015] E.C.D.R. 16 (CA (Civ Div)),
Arden LJ

s.20, see *ITV Broadcasting Ltd v TV Catchup Ltd* [2015] EWCA Civ 204, [2015] E.C.D.R. 16 (CA (Civ Div)), Arden LJ; see *Omnibill (PTY) Ltd v Egpsxxx Ltd (In Liquidation)* [2014] EWHC 3762 (IPEC), [2015] E.C.D.R. 1 (IPEC), Birss J

s.28B, see *R. (on the application of British Academy of Songwriters, Composers and Authors) v Secretary of State for Business, Innovation and Skills* [2015] EWHC 1723 (Admin), [2015] Bus. L.R. 1435 (QBD (Admin)), Green J

s.51, see *Hull and Holderness Magistrates' Court v Darroch* [2014] EWHC 4184 (Admin), (2015) 179 J.P. 64 (DC), Foskett J

s.73, see *ITV Broadcasting Ltd v TV Catchup Ltd* [2015] EWCA Civ 204, [2015] E.C.D.R. 16 (CA (Civ Div)), Arden LJ

s.97, see *Phonographic Performance Ltd v Fletcher* [2015] EWHC 2562 (Ch), [2015] L.L.R. 806 (Ch D), Arnold J

s.97A, see *1967 Ltd v British Sky Broadcasting Ltd* [2014] EWHC 3444 (Ch), [2015] E.C.C. 3 (Ch D), Arnold J; see *Cartier International AG v British Sky Broadcasting Ltd* [2014] EWHC 3354 (Ch), [2015] 1 All E.R. 949 (Ch D), Arnold J

s.107, amended: SI 2015/664 Sch.4 para.17

s.107A, amended: 2015 c.15 Sch.6 para.49

s.107A, repealed: 2015 c.15 Sch.6 para.49

s.157, enabling: SI 2015/795

s.159, enabling: SI 2015/216

s.198, amended: SI 2015/664 Sch.4 para.17

s.198A, amended: 2015 c.15 Sch.6 para.50

s.198A, repealed: 2015 c.15 Sch.6 para.50

s.208, enabling: SI 2015/216

s.213, see *DKH Retail Ltd v H Young Operations Ltd* [2014] EWHC 4034 (IPEC), [2015] F.S.R. 21 (IPEC), Judge Hacon

s.229, see *DKH Retail Ltd v H Young Operations Ltd* [2014] EWHC 4034 (IPEC), [2015] F.S.R. 21 (IPEC), Judge Hacon

s.233, see *Kohler Mira Ltd v Bristan Group Ltd* [2014] EWHC 1931 (IPEC), [2015] F.S.R. 9 (IPEC), Judge Hacon

s.250, enabling: SI 2015/169

s.297, see *Hull and Holderness Magistrates' Court v Darroch* [2014] EWHC 4184 (Admin), (2015) 179 J.P. 64 (DC), Foskett J

s.297A, see *R. (on the application of Paolo) v City of London Magistrates' Court* [2014] EWHC 2011 (Admin), [2015] L.L.R. 298 (QBD (Admin)), Laws LJ

49. Health and Medicines Act 1988

s.26, enabling: SI 2015/839

50. Housing Act 1988

see *Southward Housing Co-operative Ltd v Walker* [2015] EWHC 1615 (Ch), [2015] 2 P. & C.R. 13 (Ch D), Hildyard J; see *Spielplatz Ltd v Pearson* [2015] EWCA Civ 804, [2015] H.L.R. 40 (CA (Civ Div)), Laws LJ; see *Swanbrae Ltd v Ryder* [2015] UKUT 69 (LC), [2015] L. & T.R. 33 (UT (Lands)), Martin Rodger QC

s.1, see *Spielplatz Ltd v Pearson* [2015] EWCA Civ 804, [2015] H.L.R. 40 (CA (Civ Div)), Laws LJ

s.6, enabling: SI 2015/620

s.8, enabling: SI 2015/620, SI 2015/1646

s.13, enabling: SI 2015/620

s.14, see *Swanbrae Ltd v Ryder* [2015] UKUT 69 (LC), [2015] L. & T.R. 33 (UT (Lands)), Martin Rodger QC

s.21, see *Charalambous v Ng* [2014] EWCA Civ 1604, [2015] 1 W.L.R. 3018 (CA (Civ Div)), Black LJ; see *McDonald v McDonald* [2014] EWCA Civ 1049, [2015] Ch. 357 (CA (Civ Div)), Arden LJ

s.21, amended: 2015 c.20 s.35, s.36, s.37

s.21, enabling: SI 2015/1646, SI 2015/1725

s.21A, added: 2015 c.20 s.38

s.21A, enabling: SI 2015/1646

s.21B, added: 2015 c.20 s.39

s.21B, enabling: SI 2015/1646

s.21C, added: 2015 c.20 s.40

s.22, enabling: SI 2015/620

s.34, see *Swanbrae Ltd v Ryder* [2015] UKUT 69 (LC), [2015] L. & T.R. 33 (UT (Lands)), Martin Rodger QC

s.45, enabling: SI 2015/620

s.61, amended: 2015 c.20 Sch.22 para.9

Sch.1 Part I para.12, repealed: 2015 c.20 Sch.13 para.6

Sch.1 Pt I para.9, see *Spielplatz Ltd v Pearson* [2015] EWCA Civ 804, [2015] H.L.R. 40 (CA (Civ Div)), Laws LJ

Sch.1 Pt I para.12, see *Southward Housing Co-operative Ltd v Walker* [2015] EWHC 1615 (Ch), [2015] 2 P. & C.R. 13 (Ch D), Hildyard J

Sch.2A para.7, enabling: SI 2015/620

Sch.2A para.9, enabling: SI 2015/620

Sch.10 Part II para.5, amended: SI 2015/1794 Art.4

Sch.18 para.3, amended: 2015 c.20 Sch.23 para.46

Sch.18 para.3, repealed: 2015 c.20 Sch.23 para.46

52. Road Traffic Act 1988

see *Christensen v Harvie* [2015] HCJAC 39, 2015 J.C. 277 (HCJ), Lord Brodie

Part I, substituted: 2015 c.20 s.75

Part V, amended: 2015 c.20 Sch.2 para.11, Sch.2 para.24

s.1, see *Geddes (Murray Albert) v HM Advocate* [2015] HCJAC 43, 2015 S.L.T. 415 (HCJ), The Lord Justice Clerk (Carloway)

s.1A, see *R. v Dewdney (Michael)* [2014] EWCA Crim 1722, [2015] 1 Cr. App. R. (S.) 5 (CA (Crim Div)), Treacy LJ; see *R. v Jenkins (Nathan)* [2015] EWCA Crim 105, [2015] 1 Cr. App. R. (S.) 70 (CA (Crim Div)), Treacy LJ; see *R. v Vincer (Jake Francis)* [2014] EWCA Crim 2743, [2015] 1 Cr. App. R. (S.) 51 (CA (Crim Div)), Hallett LJ

s.2, see *Crawford (Francis) v HM Advocate* [2015] HCJAC 70, 2015 S.L.T. 700 (HCJ), Lady Paton

s.2B, see *R. v Collins (Matthew Richard)* [2014] EWCA Crim 773, [2015] R.T.R. 4 (CA (Crim Div)), Rafferty LJ

s.3, see *Maclean v Murphy* [2015] HCJAC 77, 2015 S.L.T. 760 (HCJ), Lady Clark of Calton

s.3ZB, see *R. v McGuffog (Correy Rowan)* [2015] EWCA Crim 1116, [2015] R.T.R. 34 (CA (Crim Div)), Pitchford LJ

s.3ZB, amended: 2015 c.2 Sch.6 para.1

s.3ZB, repealed: 2015 c.2 Sch.6 para.1

s.3ZC, added: 2015 c.2 s.29

s.5, see *Gray v Harvie* [2015] HCJAC 33, 2015 S.C.L. 539 (HCJ), Lord Brodie; see *Lis v Poland* [2014] EWHC 3226 (Admin), [2015] R.T.R. 15 (QBD (Admin)), Blake J; see *McDougall v Murphy* [2015] HCJAC 112 (HCJ), The Lord Justice Clerk (Carloway)

s.5A, enabling: SI 2015/911

s.6, see *Carmichael v Harvie* [2015] HCJAC 81, 2015 S.L.T. 670 (HCJ), Lord Drummond Young

s.6A, see *Carmichael v Harvie* [2015] HCJAC 81, 2015 S.L.T. 670 (HCJ), Lord Drummond Young

s.7, amended: 2015 c.20 Sch.11 para.3, Sch.11 para.5

s.7, repealed: 2015 c.20 Sch.11 para.3

s.7A, amended: 2015 c.20 Sch.11 para.8

s.8, amended: 2015 c.20 Sch.11 para.1

s.8, repealed: 2015 c.20 Sch.11 para.1

s.8, substituted: 2015 c.20 Sch.11 para.1

s.11, amended: 2015 c.20 Sch.11 para.9

s.12, amended: 2015 c.20 s.73

s.12A, added: 2015 c.20 s.73

s.13, amended: 2015 c.20 s.75

s.13A, amended: 2015 c.20 Sch.10 para.24

s.14, enabling: SI 2015/242

s.15, enabling: SI 2015/402, SI 2015/574

s.31, enabling: SI 2015/706

s.41, enabling: SI 2015/142

s.44, amended: 2015 c.7 Sch.1 para.103

s.46, amended: 2015 c.20 Sch.10 para.26

s.51, amended: 2015 c.20 Sch.10 para.27

s.52, amended: 2015 c.20 Sch.10 para.25

s.64A, repealed: 2015 c.20 Sch.23 para.22

s.81, enabling: SI 2015/474

s.89, enabling: SI 2015/1797, SI 2015/2004

s.92, see *R. (on the application of Hitchen) v Oxford Magistrates' Court* [2015] EWHC 271 (Admin), (2015) 179 J.P. 268 (QBD (Admin)), Simler J

s.93, see *R. (on the application of Hitchen) v Oxford Magistrates' Court* [2015] EWHC 271 (Admin), (2015) 179 J.P. 268 (QBD (Admin)), Simler J

s.97, amended: SI 2015/583 Sch.2 para.2

s.97, enabling: SI 2015/15

s.99, amended: 2015 c.20 Sch.10 para.2

s.99A, amended: SI 2015/583 Sch.2 para.2

s.99A, repealed: SI 2015/583 Sch.2 para.2

s.100, amended: 2015 c.20 Sch.10 para.3

s.105, enabling: SI 2015/15, SI 2015/412, SI 2015/719, SI 2015/1797, SI 2015/2004

s.108, enabling: SI 2015/1797

s.123, enabling: SI 2015/952

s.124, amended: 2015 c.20 Sch.2 para.2

s.125, amended: 2015 c.20 Sch.2 para.3, Sch.2 para.17, SI 2015/583 Sch.2 para.2

s.125, repealed: 2015 c.20 Sch.2 para.3 , Sch.2 para.17

s.125, enabling: SI 2015/952

s.125A, added: 2015 c.20 Sch.2 para.18

s.125A, repealed: 2015 c.20 Sch.2 para.5, Sch.2 para.18

s.125ZA, amended: 2015 c.20 Sch.2 para.4

s.126, amended: 2015 c.20 Sch.2 para.19

s.126, repealed: 2015 c.20 Sch.2 para.6 , Sch.2 para.19

s.127, amended: 2015 c.20 Sch.2 para.7, Sch.2 para.20

s.127, repealed: 2015 c.20 Sch.2 para.7 , Sch.2 para.20

s.128, amended: 2015 c.20 Sch.2 para.8, Sch.2 para.21

s.128, repealed: 2015 c.20 Sch.2 para.8 , Sch.2 para.21

s.128B, added: 2015 c.20 Sch.2 para.9

s.129, amended: 2015 c.20 Sch.2 para.22

s.129, repealed: 2015 c.20 Sch.2 para.22

s.129, enabling: SI 2015/952

s.130, amended: 2015 c.20 Sch.2 para.23

s.130, repealed: 2015 c.20 Sch.2 para.23

s.132, enabling: SI 2015/952

s.133, amended: 2015 c.20 Sch.2 para.10

s.133A, amended: 2015 c.20 Sch.2 para.11, Sch.2 para.24

s.133A, repealed: 2015 c.20 Sch.2 para.24

s.133A, enabling: SI 2015/952

s.133B, amended: 2015 c.20 Sch.2 para.12, Sch.2 para.25

s.133B, repealed: 2015 c.20 Sch.2 para.12 , Sch.2 para.25

s.133B, enabling: SI 2015/952

s.133C, amended: 2015 c.20 Sch.2 para.13, Sch.2 para.26

s.133D, amended: 2015 c.20 Sch.2 para.14, Sch.2 para.27

s.133D, repealed: 2015 c.20 Sch.2 para.27

s.133E, added: 2015 c.20 Sch.2 para.28

s.133E, repealed: 2015 c.20 Sch.2 para.28

s.134, enabling: SI 2015/952

s.141, enabling: SI 2015/952

s.142, amended: 2015 c.20 Sch.2 para.15, Sch.2 para.29, SI 2015/583 Sch.2 para.2

s.143, see *DPP v Whittaker* [2015] EWHC 1850 (Admin), (2015) 179 J.P. 321 (DC), Beatson LJ

s.144, amended: 2015 c.20 Sch.13 para.6

s.144D, enabling: SI 2015/854

s.147, amended: 2015 c.20 s.9, Sch.3 para.2

s.147, repealed: 2015 c.20 s.9

s.148, amended: 2015 c.20 Sch.3 para.3

s.151, amended: 2015 c.20 Sch.3 para.4

s.152, amended: 2015 c.4 s.21, 2015 c.20 Sch.3 para.5

s.153, amended: 2015 c.20 Sch.3 para.6

s.160, enabling: SI 2015/854

s.161, repealed: 2015 c.20 Sch.3 para.7

s.165A, amended: SI 2015/583 Sch.2 para.2

s.170, see *Maclean v Murphy* [2015] HCJAC 77, 2015 S.L.T. 760 (HCJ), Lady Clark of Calton

s.172, see *Carmichael v Harvie* [2015] HCJAC 81, 2015 S.L.T. 670 (HCJ), Lord Drummond Young

s.172, amended: 2015 c.7 s.22

s.173, repealed: SI 2015/583 Sch.2 para.2

s.183, amended: 2015 c.20 Sch.23 para.22

s.189, enabling: SI 2015/24

s.193A, amended: 2015 c.20 s.75, SI
2015/583 Sch.2 para.2
s.195, amended: 2015 c.20 s.75, Sch.11
para.1
Sch.2A, enabling: SI 2015/854

53. Road Traffic Offenders Act 1988
s.2, amended: SI 2015/583 Sch.2 para.3
s.7, amended: 2015 c.2 Sch.11 para.9
s.8, amended: 2015 c.2 Sch.11 para.10
s.10, amended: SI 2015/583 Sch.2 para.3
s.12, enabling: SI 2015/1490
s.15, amended: 2015 c.20 Sch.11 para.10
s.20, see *Cusick v Harvie* 2015 J.C. 72
(HCJ), The Lord Justice Clerk
(Carloway)
s.24, amended: 2015 c.2 Sch.6 para.3
s.27, amended: 2015 c.2 Sch.11 para.11
s.28, see *Maclean v Murphy* [2015]
HCJAC 77, 2015 S.L.T. 760 (HCJ), Lady
Clark of Calton
s.34, amended: 2015 c.2 Sch.6 para.4
s.34A, see *McDougall v Murphy* [2015]
HCJAC 112 (HCJ), The Lord Justice
Clerk (Carloway)
s.34B, enabling: SI 2015/366
s.34BA, enabling: SI 2015/366
s.34C, enabling: SI 2015/366
s.35A, amended: 2015 c.2 s.30, Sch.1
para.11
s.35A, repealed: 2015 c.2 s.30
s.36, see *McDougall v Murphy* [2015]
HCJAC 112 (HCJ), The Lord Justice
Clerk (Carloway)
s.36, amended: 2015 c.2 Sch.6 para.5
s.37, amended: SI 2015/2004 Reg.2
s.41, amended: SSI 2015/338 Sch.2
para.2
s.41, substituted: SSI 2015/338 Sch.2
para.2
s.45, amended: 2015 c.2 Sch.6 para.6, SI
2015/733 Art.2
s.45A, amended: 2015 c.2 Sch.6 para.7,
SI 2015/733 Art.2
s.46, amended: SI 2015/583 Sch.2 para.3
s.53, amended: SI 2015/664 Sch.5 para.5
s.75, amended: SI 2015/583 Sch.2 para.3
s.76, amended: SI 2015/583 Sch.2 para.3
s.79, amended: 2015 c.20 s.80, SI
2015/583 Sch.2 para.3
s.91A, amended: SI 2015/583 Sch.2
para.3

s.91ZA, repealed: SI 2015/583 Sch.2
para.3
s.98, amended: SI 2015/583 Sch.2 para.3
Sch.1 para.4, amended: 2015 c.2 Sch.6
para.8, SI 2015/583 Sch.2 para.3
Sch.2 Part I, amended: 2015 c.20 Sch.2
para.31, Sch.23 para.22, Sch.2 para.32,
2015 c.2 s.29, Sch.6 para.9, SI 2015/583
Sch.2 para.3, SI 2015/733 Art.3
Sch.2 Part I, varied: 2015 c.2 s.29

1989

5. Security Service Act 1989
s.1, see *Liberty v Government
Communications Headquarters* [2015] 3
All E.R. 142 (IPT), Burton J
**14. Control of Pollution (Amendment) Act
1989**
s.5A, enabling: SI 2015/426
s.6, enabling: SI 2015/426
s.8, enabling: SI 2015/426
15. Water Act 1989
s.4, enabling: SI 2015/751
s.83, enabling: SI 2015/751
s.85, enabling: SI 2015/751
s.86, enabling: SI 2015/751
s.95, enabling: SI 2015/751
s.174, amended: 2015 c.20 Sch.23
para.28
26. Finance Act 1989
s.178, amended: 2015 c.11 s.115
s.178, enabling: SI 2015/411
29. Electricity Act 1989
see *Laverty v British Gas Trading Ltd*
[2014] EWHC 2721 (Ch), [2015] 2 All
E.R. 430 (Ch D (Companies Ct)), Sir
Terence Etherton C; see *Sustainable
Shetland v Scottish Ministers* [2015]
UKSC 4, [2015] 2 All E.R. 545 (SC),
Lord Neuberger PSC
s.4, see *Sustainable Shetland v Scottish
Ministers* 2015 S.C. 59 (IH (1 Div)), The
Lord President (Gill)
s.5, see *Sustainable Shetland v Scottish
Ministers* 2015 S.C. 59 (IH (1 Div)), The
Lord President (Gill); see *Trump
International Golf Club Scotland Ltd v
Scottish Ministers* [2015] CSIH 46, 2015
S.C. 673 (IH (1 Div)), The Lord

President (Gill); see *Trump International Golf Club Scotland Ltd v Scottish Ministers* [2015] UKSC 74 (SC), Lord Neuberger JSC

s.5, enabling: SI 2015/100, SI 2015/1409, SI 2015/1410, SI 2015/2040

s.6, see *Sustainable Shetland v Scottish Ministers* 2015 S.C. 59 (IH (1 Div)), The Lord President (Gill); see *Trump International Golf Club Scotland Ltd v Scottish Ministers* [2015] CSIH 46, 2015 S.C. 673 (IH (1 Div)), The Lord President (Gill); see *Trump International Golf Club Scotland Ltd v Scottish Ministers* [2015] UKSC 74 (SC), Lord Neuberger JSC

s.6C, enabling: SI 2015/1555

s.6D, enabling: SI 2015/1555

s.16, amended: 2015 c.7 s.52

s.16A, amended: 2015 c.7 s.52

s.19, amended: 2015 c.7 s.52

s.19, repealed: 2015 c.7 s.52

s.23, amended: 2015 c.7 s.52

s.32, enabling: SI 2015/1947, SSI 2015/384

s.32A, enabling: SI 2015/1947

s.32B, enabling: SI 2015/1947, SSI 2015/384

s.32BA, enabling: SI 2015/1947

s.32C, enabling: SI 2015/1947, SSI 2015/384

s.32D, enabling: SI 2015/1947, SSI 2015/384

s.32E, enabling: SI 2015/1947

s.32F, enabling: SI 2015/1947

s.32G, enabling: SI 2015/1947

s.32H, enabling: SI 2015/1947

s.32I, enabling: SI 2015/1947

s.32J, enabling: SI 2015/1947, SSI 2015/384

s.32K, enabling: SI 2015/920, SI 2015/1947, SSI 2015/384

s.32LA, enabling: SI 2015/920, SI 2015/1947

s.32M, enabling: SI 2015/1947

s.36, see *Sustainable Shetland v Scottish Ministers* 2015 S.C. 59 (IH (1 Div)), The Lord President (Gill); see *Trump International Golf Club Scotland Ltd v Scottish Ministers* [2015] CSIH 46, 2015 S.C. 673 (IH (1 Div)), The Lord

President (Gill); see *Trump International Golf Club Scotland Ltd v Scottish Ministers* [2015] UKSC 74 (SC), Lord Neuberger JSC

s.36D, added: SI 2015/374 Art.4

s.39, enabling: SI 2015/699, SI 2015/1544

s.39A, enabling: SI 2015/698, SI 2015/699, SI 2015/1544

s.39B, enabling: SI 2015/698, SI 2015/699, SI 2015/1544

s.40B, enabling: SI 2015/698

s.42A, enabling: SI 2015/699, SI 2015/1544

s.49, amended: 2015 c.20 s.97

s.60, enabling: SI 2015/698, SI 2015/699, SI 2015/1544, SI 2015/1555

Sch.3 Pt I para.3, see *Trump International Golf Club Scotland Ltd v Scottish Ministers* [2015] CSIH 46, 2015 S.C. 673 (IH (1 Div)), The Lord President (Gill)

Sch.5B, added: 2015 c.7 s.52

Sch.8, see *Trump International Golf Club Scotland Ltd v Scottish Ministers* [2015] CSIH 46, 2015 S.C. 673 (IH (1 Div)), The Lord President (Gill)

Sch.8 para.5B, added: SI 2015/374 Art.4

Sch.9, see *Trump International Golf Club Scotland Ltd v Scottish Ministers* [2015] CSIH 46, 2015 S.C. 673 (IH (1 Div)), The Lord President (Gill)

Sch.9 para.3, see *Trump International Golf Club Scotland Ltd v Scottish Ministers* [2015] CSIH 46, 2015 S.C. 673 (IH (1 Div)), The Lord President (Gill); see *Trump International Golf Club Scotland Ltd v Scottish Ministers* [2015] UKSC 74 (SC), Lord Neuberger JSC

34. Law of Property (Miscellaneous Provisions) Act 1989

see *Nata Lee Ltd v Abid* [2014] EWCA Civ 1652, [2015] 2 P. & C.R. 3 (CA (Civ Div)), Moore-Bick LJ

s.1, see *Gleeds Retirement Benefits Scheme, Re* [2014] EWHC 1178 (Ch), [2015] Ch. 212 (Ch D), Newey J

s.2, see *Ghadami v Donegan* [2014] EWHC 4448 (Ch), [2015] B.P.I.R. 494 (Ch D), Alan Steinfeld QC

37. Football Spectators Act 1989

s.22, enabling: SI 2015/212

38. Employment Act 1989

s.11, amended: 2015 c.20 s.6

s.12, amended: 2015 c.20 s.6

40. Companies Act 1989

Sch.18 para.16, repealed: 2015 c.20

Sch.23 para.9

41. Children Act 1989

see *A (Court of Protection: Delay and Costs), Re* [2015] C.O.P.L.R. 1 (CP), Peter Jackson J; see *DW (A Child) (Termination of Parental Responsibility), Re* [2014] EWCA Civ 315, [2015] 1 F.L.R. 166 (CA (Civ Div)), Arden LJ; see *K v A (Marriage: Validity)* [2014] EWHC 3850 (Fam), [2015] 2 F.L.R. 461 (Fam Div), Roberts J; see *Mohamoud v Kensington and Chelsea RLBC* [2015] EWCA Civ 780, [2015] H.L.R. 38 (CA (Civ Div)), Longmore LJ; see *M'P-P (Children) (Adoption: Status Quo), Re* [2015] EWCA Civ 584, [2015] 2 F.C.R. 451 (CA (Civ Div)), McFarlane LJ; see *R. (on the application of AM) v Havering LBC* [2015] EWHC 1004 (Admin), [2015] P.T.S.R. 1242 (QBD (Admin)), Cobb J; see *R. (on the application of N) v Lewisham LBC* [2015] A.C. 1259 (SC), Lord Neuberger PSC; see *R. v McGeough (Terence Gerard)* [2015] UKSC 62, [2015] 1 W.L.R. 4612 (SC), Lord Neuberger PSC; see *S-W (Children) (Care Proceedings: Summary Disposal at Case Management Hearing), Re* [2015] EWCA Civ 27, [2015] 1 W.L.R. 4099 (CA (Civ Div)), Sir James Munby PFD

Pt II., see *X (Deprivation of Liberty), Re* [2015] 1 W.L.R. 2454 (CP), Sir James Munby PFD

Pt III., see *R. (on the application of AM) v Havering LBC* [2015] EWHC 1004 (Admin), [2015] P.T.S.R. 1242 (QBD (Admin)), Cobb J

s.1, see *M'P-P (Children) (Adoption: Status Quo), Re* [2015] EWCA Civ 584, [2015] 2 F.C.R. 451 (CA (Civ Div)), McFarlane LJ; see *P (A Child) (Care and Placement: Appellate Review), Re* [2014] EWCA Civ 1648, [2015] 2 F.C.R. 400 (CA (Civ Div)), Moore-Bick LJ; see

R (A Child) (Adoption: Judicial Approach), Re [2014] EWCA Civ 1625, [2015] 1 W.L.R. 3273 (CA (Civ Div)), Sir James Munby PFD; see *Tower Hamlets LBC v D* [2014] EWHC 3901 (Fam), [2015] 2 F.L.R. 535 (Fam Div), Hayden J; see *W (Children) (Parental Agreement with Local Authority), Re* [2014] EWCA Civ 1065, [2015] 1 F.L.R. 949 (CA (Civ Div)), Sir James Munby PFD

s.3, see *H-B (Children) (Contact: Prohibition on Further Applications), Re* [2015] EWCA Civ 389, [2015] 2 F.C.R. 581 (CA (Civ Div)), Sir James Munby PFD

s.5, see *R (A Child) (Child Arrangements Order: Best Interests), Re* [2015] EWCA Civ 405, [2015] 2 F.C.R. 385 (CA (Civ Div)), Laws LJ

s.8, see *JM (A Child), Re* [2015] EWHC 2832 (Fam), [2015] Med. L.R. 544 (Fam Div), Mostyn J; see *JP v LP (Surrogacy Arrangement: Wardship)* [2014] EWHC 595 (Fam), [2015] 1 All E.R. 266 (Fam Div), Eleanor King J

s.11, see *R. (on the application of BG) v Chief Constable of the West Midlands* [2014] EWHC 4374 (Admin), (2015) 179 J.P. 93 (QBD (Admin)), Fulford LJ

s.17, see *R. (on the application of CO) v Surrey CC* [2014] EWHC 3932 (Admin), [2015] 2 F.L.R. 485 (QBD (Admin)), Popplewell J; see *R. (on the application of F) v Barking and Dagenham LBC* [2015] EWHC 2838 (Admin), (2015) 18 C.C.L. Rep. 754 (QBD (Admin)), Bobbie Cheema QC; see *R. (on the application of J) v Worcestershire CC* [2014] EWCA Civ 1518, [2015] 1 W.L.R. 2825 (CA (Civ Div)), Lord Dyson MR; see *R. (on the application of L) v Warwickshire CC* [2015] EWHC 203 (Admin), [2015] B.L.G.R. 81 (QBD (Admin)), Mostyn J; see *R. (on the application of Mensah) v Salford City Council* [2014] EWHC 3537 (Admin), [2015] P.T.S.R. 157 (QBD (Admin)), Lewis J

s.17A, amended: SI 2015/914 Sch.1 para.46

s.17B, amended: SI 2015/914 Sch.1
para.47
s.17ZA, amended: SI 2015/914 Sch.1
para.44
s.17ZB, enabling: SI 2015/527
s.17ZD, amended: SI 2015/914 Sch.1
para.45
s.20, see [2015] EWFC 11 (Fam Ct), Sir
James Munby PFD; see *A (Afghanistan)
v Secretary of State for the Home
Department* [2014] EWCA Civ 706,
[2015] 3 All E.R. 111 (CA (Civ Div)),
Maurice Kay LJ; see *A (Application for
Care Placement Orders: Local Authority
Failings), Re*; see *R. (on the application
of CO) v Surrey CC* [2014] EWHC 3932
(Admin), [2015] 2 F.L.R. 485 (QBD
(Admin)), Popplewell J; see *R. (on the
application of Cornwall Council) v
Secretary of State for Health* [2015]
UKSC 46 (SC), Lady Hale DPSC; see *R.
(on the application of Cunningham) v
Hertfordshire CC* [2015] EWHC 1936
(Admin), (2015) 18 C.C.L. Rep. 632
(QBD (Admin)), Hickinbottom J; see *R.
(on the application of GE (Eritrea)) v
Secretary of State for the Home
Department* [2014] EWCA Civ 1490,
[2015] 1 W.L.R. 4123 (CA (Civ Div)),
Davis LJ; see *W (Children) (Parental
Agreement with Local Authority), Re*
[2014] EWCA Civ 1065, [2015] 1 F.L.R.
949 (CA (Civ Div)), Sir James Munby
PFD
s.22C, enabling: SI 2015/495
s.23, see *R. (on the application of CO) v
Surrey CC* [2014] EWHC 3932 (Admin),
[2015] 2 F.L.R. 485 (QBD (Admin)),
Popplewell J; see *R. (on the application
of Cunningham) v Hertfordshire CC*
[2015] EWHC 1936 (Admin), (2015) 18
C.C.L. Rep. 632 (QBD (Admin)),
Hickinbottom J
s.23C, see *R. (on the application of GE
(Eritrea)) v Secretary of State for the
Home Department* [2014] EWCA Civ
1490, [2015] 1 W.L.R. 4123 (CA (Civ
Div)), Davis LJ
s.23E, enabling: SI 2015/495
s.23ZA, enabling: SI 2015/495

s.25, see *Barking and Dagenham LBC v
SS* [2014] EWHC 4436 (Fam), [2015] 2
F.L.R. 1358 (Fam Div), Hayden J
s.25, enabling: SI 2015/1883
s.25B, enabling: SI 2015/495
s.26, enabling: SI 2015/495
s.27, see *R. (on the application of C) v
Hackney LBC* [2014] EWHC 3670
(Admin), [2015] P.T.S.R. 1011 (QBD
(Admin)), Turner J; see *R. (on the
application of J) v Worcestershire CC*
[2014] EWCA Civ 1518, [2015] 1
W.L.R. 2825 (CA (Civ Div)), Lord
Dyson MR
s.31, see *B (Children) (Care
Proceedings), Re* [2015] EWFC 3, [2015]
1 F.L.R. 905 (Fam Ct), Sir James Munby
PFD; see *Bristol City Council v AA*
[2014] EWHC 1022 (Fam), [2015] 1
F.L.R. 625 (Fam Div), Baker J; see
Croydon LBC v U [2014] EWHC 823
(Fam), [2015] 1 F.L.R. 436 (Fam Div),
Keehan J; see *H (Children) (Care
Orders: Evidence), Re* [2015] EWCA Civ
115, [2015] 2 F.C.R. 305 (CA (Civ Div)),
Black LJ; see *L-K (Children) (Non-
Accidental Injuries: Fact Finding), Re*
[2015] EWCA Civ 830, [2015] 3 F.C.R.
151 (CA (Civ Div)), Elias LJ; see *Y
(Children) (Care Proceedings:
Proportionality Evaluation), Re* [2014]
EWCA Civ 1553, [2015] 2 F.L.R. 615
(CA (Civ Div)), Elias LJ
s.31A, see *S-W (Children) (Care
Proceedings: Summary Disposal at Case
Management Hearing), Re* [2015]
EWCA Civ 27, [2015] 1 W.L.R. 4099
(CA (Civ Div)), Sir James Munby PFD
s.31A, enabling: SI 2015/495, SI
2015/1818
s.32, see *H (Children) (Care
Proceedings: Appeals out of Time)*
[2015] EWCA Civ 583, [2015] 1 W.L.R.
5085 (CA (Civ Div)), McFarlane LJ; see
*M-F (Children) (Care Proceedings:
Extension of Time Limit), Re* [2014]
EWCA Civ 991, [2015] 1 W.L.R. 909
(CA (Civ Div)), Munby LJ; see *S (A
Child) (Interim Care Order: Residential
Assessment), Re* [2015] 1 W.L.R. 925

(CC (Bournemouth)), Sir James Munby
PFD
s.34, see *G (A Child) (Care Proceedings:
Authority to Refuse to Allow Contact), Re*
[2014] EWCA Civ 1173, [2015] 1 F.C.R.
345 (CA (Civ Div)), Aikens LJ; see *P (A
Child) (Conditions on Contact), Re*
[2015] EWCA Civ 170, [2015] 2 F.C.R.
67 (CA (Civ Div)), McFarlane LJ
s.34, enabling: SI 2015/1818
s.37, see *H (Children) (Care Orders:
Evidence), Re* [2015] EWCA Civ 115,
[2015] 2 F.C.R. 305 (CA (Civ Div)),
Black LJ; see *K (Children) (Contact:
Interim Care Order), Re* [2014] EWCA
Civ 1195, [2015] 1 F.L.R. 95 (CA (Civ
Div)), Ryder LJ
s.38, see *R (A Child) (Adoption: Judicial
Approach), Re* [2014] EWCA Civ 1625,
[2015] 1 W.L.R. 3273 (CA (Civ Div)),
Sir James Munby PFD; see *S (A Child)
(Interim Care Order: Residential
Assessment), Re* [2015] 1 W.L.R. 925
(CC (Bournemouth)), Sir James Munby
PFD
s.70, see *B v C (Surrogacy: Adoption)*
[2015] EWFC 17, [2015] 1 F.L.R. 1392
(Fam Ct), Theis J
s.87D, enabling: SI 2015/551
s.91, see *P (A Child) (Conditions on
Contact), Re* [2015] EWCA Civ 170,
[2015] 2 F.C.R. 67 (CA (Civ Div)),
McFarlane LJ
s.98, see *R. v McGeough (Terence
Gerard)* [2015] UKSC 62, [2015] 1
W.L.R. 4612 (SC), Lord Neuberger PSC
s.100, see *Birmingham City Council v
Riaz* [2014] EWHC 4247 (Fam), [2015] 2
F.L.R. 763 (Fam Div), Keehan J; see
Redbridge LBC v A [2015] EWHC 2140
(Fam), [2015] Fam. 335 (Fam Div),
Hayden J
s.104, enabling: SI 2015/495, SI
2015/551, SI 2015/1988
s.105, see *R. (on the application of C) v
Hackney LBC* [2014] EWHC 3670
(Admin), [2015] P.T.S.R. 1011 (QBD
(Admin)), Turner J
Sch.1, see *A (A Child) (Financial
Provision: Wealthy Parent), Re* [2014]
EWCA Civ 1577, [2015] Fam. 277 (CA

(Civ Div)), Lewison LJ; see *S (A Minor),
Re* [2014] EWHC 2225 (Fam), [2015] 2
F.L.R. 77 (Fam Div), Baker J; see
Seagrove v Sullivan [2014] EWHC 4110
(Fam), [2015] 2 F.L.R. 602 (Fam Div),
Holman J
Sch.1 para.1, see *D v R* [2014] EWHC
4306 (Fam), [2015] 2 F.L.R. 978 (Fam
Div), Holman J
Sch.2 Pt I para.2, see *R. (on the
application of L) v Warwickshire CC*
[2015] EWHC 203 (Admin), [2015]
B.L.G.R. 81 (QBD (Admin)), Mostyn J
Sch.2 Part II para.12E, enabling: SI
2015/495
Sch.2 Part II para.12F, enabling: SI
2015/495
Sch.2 Part II para.19B, enabling: SI
2015/495
Sch.2 Pt I para.3, see *R. (on the
application of AM) v Havering LBC*
[2015] EWHC 1004 (Admin), [2015]
P.T.S.R. 1242 (QBD (Admin)), Cobb J
Sch.4 Part III para.4, enabling: SI
2015/1988
Sch.5 Part II para.7, enabling: SI
2015/1988
Sch.6 Part II para.10, enabling: SI
2015/1988

**42. Local Government and Housing Act
1989**
s.8, enabling: SI 2015/881
s.20, enabling: SI 2015/881
s.21, repealed: 2015 c.20 Sch.13 para.6
s.152, repealed: 2015 c.20 Sch.13 para.6
s.190, enabling: SI 2015/881

44. Opticians Act 1989
s.1, amended: 2015 c.28 Sch.1 para.2
s.5A, amended: 2015 c.28 Sch.1 para.2
s.5C, amended: 2015 c.28 Sch.1 para.2
s.13D, amended: 2015 c.28 Sch.1 para.2
s.27, amended: SI 2015/914 Sch.1
para.48
s.36, amended: 2015 c.28 Sch.1 para.2

45. Prisons (Scotland) Act 1989
s.6A, added: SSI 2015/39 Art.2
s.7, amended: SSI 2015/39 Art.2
s.7A, added: SSI 2015/39 Art.2
s.8, repealed: SSI 2015/39 Art.2
s.14, amended: SSI 2015/39 Art.2
s.14, enabling: SSI 2015/324

s.15, amended: SSI 2015/39 Art.2
s.19, amended: SSI 2015/39 Art.2
s.19, repealed: SSI 2015/39 Art.2
s.34, amended: SSI 2015/39 Art.2
s.39, enabling: SSI 2015/324
s.42, amended: SSI 2015/39 Art.2
s.43, amended: SSI 2015/39 Art.2

1990

8. Town and Country Planning Act 1990
see *Oxfordshire CC v Secretary of State
for Communities and Local Government*
[2015] EWHC 186 (Admin), [2015]
J.P.L. 846 (QBD (Admin)), Lang J; see
*R. (on the application of Hayes) v
Wychavon DC* [2014] EWHC 1987
(Admin), [2015] J.P.L. 62 (QBD), Lang
J; see *Valentino Plus Ltd v Secretary of
State for Communities and Local
Government* [2015] EWHC 19 (Admin),
[2015] J.P.L. 707 (QBD (Admin)), Judge
Sycamore; see *West Berkshire DC v
Department for Communities and Local
Government* [2015] EWHC 2222
(Admin), [2015] B.L.G.R. 884 (QBD
(Admin)), Holgate J
Pt VII s.191, see *Shortt v Secretary of
State for Communities and Local
Government* [2014] EWHC 2480
(Admin), [2015] J.P.L. 75 (QBD
(Admin)), Hickinbottom J
s.4A, enabling: SI 2015/770
s.52, see *R. v Ahmed (Mohammed
Kamal)* [2014] EWCA Crim 1270,
[2015] 1 W.L.R. 378 (CA (Crim Div)),
Davis LJ
s.55, enabling: SI 2015/595, SI 2015/597,
SI 2015/1330
s.56, amended: 2015 c.7 Sch.4 para.3
s.57, amended: 2015 c.7 Sch.4 para.4
s.58, amended: 2015 c.7 Sch.4 para.5
s.59, enabling: SI 2015/595, SI 2015/596,
SI 2015/659, SI 2015/1635
s.60, enabling: SI 2015/596, SI 2015/659,
SI 2015/1635
s.61, enabling: SI 2015/595, SI 2015/596,
SI 2015/659
s.61A, enabling: SI 2015/595
s.61DA, added: 2015 c.7 Sch.4 para.1

s.61G, enabling: SI 2015/20
s.61I, enabling: SI 2015/20
s.61N, amended: 2015 c.2 s.92
s.61W, enabling: SI 2015/595
s.62, see *Obar Camden Ltd v Camden
LBC* [2015] EWHC 2475 (Admin),
[2015] L.L.R. 782 (QBD (Admin)),
Stewart J
s.62, amended: 2015 c.7 Sch.4 para.6
s.62, enabling: SI 2015/595
s.65, amended: 2015 c.7 Sch.4 para.7
s.65, enabling: SI 2015/595, SI
2015/1330
s.69, amended: 2015 c.7 Sch.4 para.8
s.69, enabling: SI 2015/595, SI
2015/1330
s.70, see *East Northamptonshire DC v
Secretary of State for Communities and
Local Government* [2014] EWCA Civ
137, [2015] 1 W.L.R. 45 (CA (Civ Div)),
Maurice Kay LJ; see *Lawson Builders
Ltd v Secretary of State for Communities
and Local Government* [2015] EWCA
Civ 122, [2015] P.T.S.R. 1324 (CA (Civ
Div)), Pitchford LJ; see *R. (on the
application of Hampton Bishop PC) v
Herefordshire Council* [2014] EWCA
Civ 878, [2015] 1 W.L.R. 2367 (CA (Civ
Div)), Sir Terence Etherton C; see *R. (on
the application of Perry) v Hackney LBC*
[2014] EWHC 3499 (Admin), [2015]
J.P.L. 454 (QBD (Admin)), Patterson J
s.70C, see *Wingrove v Stratford-on-Avon
DC* [2015] EWHC 287 (Admin), [2015]
P.T.S.R. 708 (QBD (Admin)), Cranston J
s.71, amended: 2015 c.7 Sch.4 para.9
s.71, enabling: SI 2015/595, SI
2015/1330
s.71A, enabling: SI 2015/660
s.73, see *Lawson Builders Ltd v Secretary
of State for Communities and Local
Government* [2015] EWCA Civ 122,
[2015] P.T.S.R. 1324 (CA (Civ Div)),
Pitchford LJ; see *R. (on the application
of Pemberton International Ltd) v
Lambeth LBC* [2014] EWHC 1998
(Admin), [2015] J.P.L. 42 (QBD
(Admin)), Lewis J
s.73A, see *Ioannou v Secretary of State
for Communities and Local Government*
[2014] EWCA Civ 1432, [2015] 1 P. &

C.R. 10 (CA (Civ Div)), Sullivan LJ; see
Lawson Builders Ltd v Secretary of State
for Communities and Local Government
[2015] EWCA Civ 122, [2015] P.T.S.R.
1324 (CA (Civ Div)), Pitchford LJ; see
Revenue and Customs Commissioners v
Patel [2015] S.T.C. 148 (UT (Tax)),
Judge Colin Bishopp
s.74, see *R. (on the application of HS2*
Action Alliance Ltd) v Secretary of State
for Transport [2014] EWCA Civ 1578,
[2015] P.T.S.R. 1025 (CA (Civ Div)),
Longmore LJ
s.74, amended: 2015 c.7 Sch.4 para.10
s.74, enabling: SI 2015/595, SI 2015/596
s.74A, added: 2015 c.7 s.29
s.74A, enabling: SI 2015/595
s.76C, enabling: SI 2015/797
s.77, see *R. (on the application of HS2*
Action Alliance Ltd) v Secretary of State
for Transport [2014] EWCA Civ 1578,
[2015] P.T.S.R. 1025 (CA (Civ Div)),
Longmore LJ
s.77, amended: 2015 c.7 Sch.4 para.11
s.77, enabling: SI 2015/595
s.78, see *R. (on the application of HS2*
Action Alliance Ltd) v Secretary of State
for Transport [2014] EWCA Civ 1578,
[2015] P.T.S.R. 1025 (CA (Civ Div)),
Longmore LJ
s.78, amended: 2015 c.7 Sch.4 para.12
s.78, enabling: SI 2015/595, SI
2015/1330
s.78A, enabling: SI 2015/1330
s.79, enabling: SI 2015/595
s.88, amended: 2015 c.7 Sch.4 para.13
s.91, amended: 2015 c.7 Sch.4 para.14
s.97, see *Portland Stone Firms Ltd v*
Dorset CC [2015] R.V.R. 170 (UT
(Lands)), Judge Huskinson
s.101, see *R. (on the application of*
Couves) v Gravesham BC [2015] EWHC
504 (Admin), [2015] J.P.L. 1193 (QBD
(Admin)), Ouseley J
s.106, see *R. (on the application of*
Couves) v Gravesham BC [2015] EWHC
504 (Admin), [2015] J.P.L. 1193 (QBD
(Admin)), Ouseley J; see *R. (on the*
application of Lady Hart of Chilton) v
Babergh DC [2014] EWHC 3261
(Admin), [2015] J.P.L. 491 (QBD

(Admin)), Sales J; see *R. (on the*
application of Midcounties Co-operative
Ltd) v Forest of Dean DC [2014] EWHC
3059 (Admin), [2015] J.P.L. 288 (QBD
(Admin)), Hickinbottom J; see *R. (on the*
application of Perry) v Hackney LBC
[2014] EWHC 3499 (Admin), [2015]
J.P.L. 454 (QBD (Admin)), Patterson J;
see *R. (on the application of Robert*
Hitchins Ltd) v Worcestershire CC
[2015] EWCA Civ 1060, [2015] P.T.S.R.
D57 (CA (Civ Div)), Richards LJ
s.106C, amended: 2015 c.2 s.92
s.107, see *Portland Stone Firms Ltd v*
Dorset CC [2015] R.V.R. 170 (UT
(Lands)), Judge Huskinson
s.108, amended: 2015 c.7 Sch.4 para.15
s.108, enabling: SI 2015/598
s.109, amended: 2015 c.7 Sch.4 para.16
s.171, see *Sanger v Newham LBC* [2014]
EWHC 1922 (Admin), [2015] 1 W.L.R.
332 (DC), Sir Brian Leveson PQBD
s.171B, see *Shortt v Secretary of State for*
Communities and Local Government
[2014] EWHC 2480 (Admin), [2015]
J.P.L. 75 (QBD (Admin)), Hickinbottom
J
s.171BA, see *Jackson v Secretary of*
State for Communities and Local
Government [2015] EWHC 20 (Admin),
[2015] 2 P. & C.R. 8 (QBD (Admin)),
Holgate J
s.171BB, see *Jackson v Secretary of State*
for Communities and Local Government
[2015] EWHC 20 (Admin), [2015] 2 P.
& C.R. 8 (QBD (Admin)), Holgate J
s.171BC, see *Jackson v Secretary of State*
for Communities and Local Government
[2015] EWHC 20 (Admin), [2015] 2 P.
& C.R. 8 (QBD (Admin)), Holgate J
s.171G, amended: SI 2015/664 Sch.4
para.18
s.171H, amended: 2015 c.7 Sch.4 para.17
s.172, see *Mohamed v Secretary of State*
for Communities and Local Government
[2014] EWHC 4045 (Admin), [2015]
J.P.L. 583 (QBD (Admin)), Gilbart J; see
Silver v Secretary of State for
Communities and Local Government
[2014] EWHC 2729 (Admin), [2015]

J.P.L. 154 (QBD (Admin)), Supperstone
J

s.173, see *Ioannou v Secretary of State
for Communities and Local Government*
[2014] EWCA Civ 1432, [2015] 1 P. &
C.R. 10 (CA (Civ Div)), Sullivan LJ; see
*Koumis v Secretary of State for
Communities and Local Government*
[2014] EWCA Civ 1723, [2015] J.P.L.
682 (CA (Civ Div)), Sullivan LJ

s.173A, see *Koumis v Secretary of State
for Communities and Local Government*
[2014] EWCA Civ 1723, [2015] J.P.L.
682 (CA (Civ Div)), Sullivan LJ

s.174, see *Ioannou v Secretary of State
for Communities and Local Government*
[2014] EWCA Civ 1432, [2015] 1 P. &
C.R. 10 (CA (Civ Div)), Sullivan LJ; see
*R. (on the application of Westminster
City Council) v Secretary of State for
Communities and Local Government*
[2015] EWCA Civ 482, [2015] L.L.R.
909 (CA (Civ Div)), Longmore LJ

s.174, varied: SI 2015/627 Sch.4 para.1

s.175, varied: SI 2015/627 Sch.4 para.2

s.176, see *Koumis v Secretary of State for
Communities and Local Government*
[2014] EWCA Civ 1723, [2015] J.P.L.
682 (CA (Civ Div)), Sullivan LJ

s.176, varied: SI 2015/627 Sch.4 para.3

s.177, see *Ioannou v Secretary of State
for Communities and Local Government*
[2014] EWCA Civ 1432, [2015] 1 P. &
C.R. 10 (CA (Civ Div)), Sullivan LJ; see
*Turner v Secretary of State for
Communities and Local Government*
[2015] EWHC 1895 (Admin), [2015]
J.P.L. 1347 (QBD (Admin)), CMG
Ockelton

s.177, varied: SI 2015/627 Sch.4 para.4

s.178, varied: SI 2015/627 Sch.4 para.5

s.179, see *R. v Ahmed (Mohammed
Kamal)* [2014] EWCA Crim 1270,
[2015] 1 W.L.R. 378 (CA (Crim Div)),
Davis LJ; see *R. v Ali (Salah)* [2014]
EWCA Crim 1658, [2015] 1 W.L.R. 841
(CA (Crim Div)), Beatson LJ; see
Sanger v Newham LBC [2014] EWHC
1922 (Admin), [2015] 1 W.L.R. 332
(DC), Sir Brian Leveson PQBD

s.179, amended: SI 2015/664 Sch.4
para.18

s.179, varied: SI 2015/627 Sch.4 para.6

s.180, varied: SI 2015/627 Sch.4 para.7

s.181, see *R. v Ahmed (Mohammed
Kamal)* [2014] EWCA Crim 1270,
[2015] 1 W.L.R. 378 (CA (Crim Div)),
Davis LJ

s.181, varied: SI 2015/627 Sch.4 para.8

s.187, amended: SI 2015/664 Sch.4
para.18

s.188, see *Sanger v Newham LBC* [2014]
EWHC 1922 (Admin), [2015] 1 W.L.R.
332 (DC), Sir Brian Leveson PQBD

s.188, varied: SI 2015/627 Sch.4 para.9

s.188, enabling: SI 2015/595

s.193, enabling: SI 2015/595

s.196, enabling: SI 2015/595

s.206, see *Distinctive Properties (Ascot)
Ltd v Secretary of State for Communities
and Local Government* [2015] EWHC
729 (Admin), [2015] J.P.L. 1083 (QBD
(Admin)), Holgate J

s.207, see *Distinctive Properties (Ascot)
Ltd v Secretary of State for Communities
and Local Government* [2015] EWHC
729 (Admin), [2015] J.P.L. 1083 (QBD
(Admin)), Holgate J

s.208, see *Distinctive Properties (Ascot)
Ltd v Secretary of State for Communities
and Local Government* [2015] EWHC
729 (Admin), [2015] J.P.L. 1083 (QBD
(Admin)), Holgate J

s.210, amended: SI 2015/664 Sch.4
para.18

s.237, amended: SI 2015/1794 Art.5

s.247, amended: 2015 c.7 Sch.1 para.104

s.248, amended: 2015 c.7 Sch.1 para.105

s.254, amended: 2015 c.7 Sch.1 para.106

s.256, amended: 2015 c.7 Sch.1 para.107

s.264, amended: 2015 c.7 Sch.4 para.18

s.266, amended: SI 2015/1794 Art.6

s.284, amended: 2015 c.2 Sch.16 para.2

s.285, see *Sanger v Newham LBC* [2014]
EWHC 1922 (Admin), [2015] 1 W.L.R.
332 (DC), Sir Brian Leveson PQBD

s.285, varied: SI 2015/627 Sch.4 para.10

s.287, amended: 2015 c.2 Sch.16 para.3

s.287, repealed: 2015 c.2 Sch.16 para.3

s.288, see *Connors v Secretary of State
for Communities and Local Government*

[2014] EWHC 2358 (Admin), [2015]
J.P.L. 196 (QBD (Admin)), Lewis J; see
*Distinctive Properties (Ascot) Ltd v
Secretary of State for Communities and
Local Government* [2015] EWHC 729
(Admin), [2015] J.P.L. 1083 (QBD
(Admin)), Holgate J; see *R. (on the
application of Oldfield) v Secretary of
State for Communities and Local
Government* [2014] EWCA Civ 1446,
[2015] Env. L.R. 9 (CA (Civ Div)),
Maurice Kay LJ; see *Silver v Secretary
of State for Communities and Local
Government* [2014] EWHC 2729
(Admin), [2015] J.P.L. 154 (QBD
(Admin)), Supperstone J; see *Venn v
Secretary of State for Communities and
Local Government* [2014] EWCA Civ
1539, [2015] 1 W.L.R. 2328 (CA (Civ
Div)), Sullivan LJ
s.288, amended: 2015 c.2 Sch.16 para.4
s.288, repealed: 2015 c.2 Sch.16 para.4
s.289, see *Distinctive Properties (Ascot)
Ltd v Secretary of State for Communities
and Local Government* [2015] EWHC
729 (Admin), [2015] J.P.L. 1083 (QBD
(Admin)), Holgate J; see *Kestrel Hydro v
Secretary of State for Communities and
Local Government* [2015] EWHC 1654
(Admin), [2015] L.L.R. 522 (QBD
(Admin)), Holgate J; see *Koumis v
Secretary of State for Communities and
Local Government* [2014] EWCA Civ
1723, [2015] J.P.L. 682 (CA (Civ Div)),
Sullivan LJ; see *Miaris v Secretary of
State for Communities and Local
Government* [2015] EWHC 2094
(Admin), [2015] 1 W.L.R. 4333 (QBD
(Admin)), John Howell QC; see *Silver v
Secretary of State for Communities and
Local Government* [2014] EWHC 2729
(Admin), [2015] J.P.L. 154 (QBD
(Admin)), Supperstone J
s.289, varied: SI 2015/627 Sch.4 para.11
s.293A, enabling: SI 2015/595
s.303, amended: 2015 c.7 Sch.4 para.19
s.303, enabling: SI 2015/1522
s.305, amended: 2015 c.7 Sch.4 para.20
s.316, enabling: SI 2015/807
s.323, enabling: SI 2015/1331
s.324, amended: 2015 c.7 Sch.4 para.21

s.333, amended: 2015 c.7 Sch.4 para.22
s.333, enabling: SI 2015/20, SI 2015/595,
SI 2015/596, SI 2015/597, SI 2015/659,
SI 2015/807, SI 2015/1330, SI
2015/1331, SI 2015/1522, SI 2015/1822
s.336, see *Timmins v Gedling BC* [2015]
EWCA Civ 10, [2015] P.T.S.R. 837 (CA
(Civ Div)), Richards LJ
s.336, amended: 2015 c.7 Sch.1 para.108,
Sch.4 para.23
Sch.1 para.5, enabling: SI 2015/595
Sch.1 para.6, enabling: SI 2015/595
Sch.1 para.7, enabling: SI 2015/595
Sch.1 para.8, enabling: SI 2015/595
Sch.4A, enabling: SI 2015/595
Sch.4B para.1, enabling: SI 2015/20
Sch.4B para.8, see *R. (on the application
of Gladman Developments Ltd) v
Aylesbury Vale DC* [2014] EWHC 4323
(Admin), [2015] J.P.L. 656 (QBD
(Admin)), Lewis J
Sch.4B para.16, amended: SI 2015/1376
Sch.2 para.4
Sch.6 para.1, enabling: SI 2015/1822
Sch.13, see *Portland Stone Firms Ltd v
Dorset CC* [2015] R.V.R. 170 (UT
(Lands)), Judge Huskinson
Sch.13 para.16, amended: 2015 c.7 Sch.1
para.109
Sch.13 para.18, amended: 2015 c.7 Sch.1
para.109

9. Planning (Listed Buildings and Conservation Areas) Act 1990

s.9, amended: SI 2015/664 Sch.4 para.19
s.20, enabling: SI 2015/1332
s.20A, enabling: SI 2015/1332
s.21, enabling: SI 2015/1332
s.43, amended: SI 2015/664 Sch.4
para.19
s.62, amended: 2015 c.2 Sch.16 para.5
s.63, amended: 2015 c.2 Sch.16 para.6
s.66, see *East Northamptonshire DC v
Secretary of State for Communities and
Local Government* [2014] EWCA Civ
137, [2015] 1 W.L.R. 45 (CA (Civ Div)),
Maurice Kay LJ; see *Gerber v Wiltshire
Council* [2015] EWHC 524 (Admin),
[2015] Env. L.R. 33 (QBD (Admin)),
Dove J; see *Obar Camden Ltd v Camden
LBC* [2015] EWHC 2475 (Admin),
[2015] L.L.R. 782 (QBD (Admin)),

Stewart J; see *R. (on the application of Forge Field Society) v Sevenoaks DC* [2014] EWHC 1895 (Admin), [2015] J.P.L. 22 (QBD (Admin)), Lindblom J; see *R. (on the application of Perry) v Hackney LBC* [2014] EWHC 3499 (Admin), [2015] J.P.L. 454 (QBD (Admin)), Patterson J
s.67, enabling: SI 2015/809
s.69, see *R. (on the application of GRA Acquisition Ltd) v Oxford City Council* [2015] EWHC 76 (Admin), [2015] P.T.S.R. 751 (QBD (Admin)), Ouseley J; see *R. (on the application of Silus Investments SA) v Hounslow LBC* [2015] EWHC 358 (Admin), [2015] B.L.G.R. 391 (QBD (Admin)), Lang J
s.72, see *East Northamptonshire DC v Secretary of State for Communities and Local Government* [2014] EWCA Civ 137, [2015] 1 W.L.R. 45 (CA (Civ Div)), Maurice Kay LJ; see *Obar Camden Ltd v Camden LBC* [2015] EWHC 2475 (Admin), [2015] L.L.R. 782 (QBD (Admin)), Stewart J; see *R. (on the application of Forge Field Society) v Sevenoaks DC* [2014] EWHC 1895 (Admin), [2015] J.P.L. 22 (QBD (Admin)), Lindblom J; see *R. (on the application of Perry) v Hackney LBC* [2014] EWHC 3499 (Admin), [2015] J.P.L. 454 (QBD (Admin)), Patterson J
s.73, enabling: SI 2015/809
s.82, enabling: SI 2015/809
s.89, enabling: SI 2015/1331
s.93, enabling: SI 2015/809, SI 2015/1331, SI 2015/1332, SI 2015/1822
Sch.3 para.1, enabling: SI 2015/1822

10. Planning (Hazardous Substances) Act 1990

s.4, enabling: SI 2015/627, SI 2015/1597
s.5, enabling: SI 2015/627, SI 2015/1359, SI 2015/1597
s.7, enabling: SI 2015/627, SI 2015/1597
s.8, enabling: SI 2015/627, SI 2015/1597
s.17, enabling: SI 2015/627, SI 2015/1597
s.21, enabling: SI 2015/627, SI 2015/1597
s.21B, enabling: SI 2015/1597
s.22, amended: 2015 c.2 Sch.16 para.7

s.23, amended: SI 2015/664 Sch.4 para.20
s.24, enabling: SI 2015/627, SI 2015/1597
s.25, enabling: SI 2015/627, SI 2015/1597
s.26A, enabling: SI 2015/627, SI 2015/1597
s.28, enabling: SI 2015/627, SI 2015/1597
s.30, enabling: SI 2015/627, SI 2015/1597
s.40, enabling: SI 2015/627, SI 2015/1597, SI 2015/1822
Sch.1 para.1, enabling: SI 2015/1822

16. Food Safety Act 1990

see *South Lanarkshire Council v GSR Distributions Ltd* 2015 S.L.T. (Sh Ct) 143 (Sh Ct (Glasgow)), Sheriff Reid
s.2, varied: SI 2015/518 Sch.1 Part 5, SI 2015/675 Sch.3 Part 4
s.6, amended: 2015 asp 1 Sch.1 para.3
s.6, enabling: SI 2015/518, SI 2015/675, SI 2015/1348, SI 2015/1507, SI 2015/1519, SI 2015/1867, SSI 2015/208, SSI 2015/363, SSI 2015/410
s.9, see *R. (on the application of Association of Independent Meat Suppliers) v Food Standards Agency* [2015] EWHC 1896 (Admin), [2015] P.T.S.R. 1383 (QBD (Admin)), Simon J; see *South Lanarkshire Council v GSR Distributions Ltd* 2015 S.L.T. (Sh Ct) 143 (Sh Ct (Glasgow)), Sheriff Reid
s.10, varied: SI 2015/518 Sch.1 para.1, SI 2015/675 Sch.3 para.1, SI 2015/1519 Sch.1 para.1
s.13, amended: 2015 asp 1 Sch.1 para.3
s.15A, added: 2015 asp 1 s.33
s.15A, enabling: SSI 2015/410
s.16, amended: 2015 asp 1 s.34
s.16, enabling: SI 2015/518, SI 2015/675, SI 2015/787, SI 2015/1348, SI 2015/1507, SI 2015/1519, SI 2015/1867, SSI 2015/48, SSI 2015/208, SSI 2015/363, SSI 2015/410
s.17, enabling: SI 2015/518, SI 2015/675, SI 2015/787, SI 2015/1348, SI 2015/1507, SI 2015/1519, SI 2015/1867, SSI 2015/48, SSI 2015/208, SSI 2015/363, SSI 2015/410

s.18, enabling: SSI 2015/410

s.20, varied: SI 2015/518 Sch.1 Part 5, SI
2015/675 Sch.3 Part 4

s.21, varied: SI 2015/675 Sch.3 Part 4

s.26, enabling: SI 2015/518, SI 2015/675,
SI 2015/787, SI 2015/1348, SI
2015/1507, SI 2015/1519, SI 2015/1867,
SSI 2015/48, SSI 2015/208, SSI
2015/363, SSI 2015/410

s.29, varied: SI 2015/518 Sch.1 Part 5, SI
2015/675 Sch.3 Part 4

s.30, varied: SI 2015/518 Sch.1 Part 5, SI
2015/675 Sch.3 Part 4

s.31, enabling: SI 2015/518, SI 2015/675,
SI 2015/1519, SI 2015/1867

s.32, varied: SI 2015/518 Sch.1 para.2, SI
2015/1519 Sch.1 para.2

s.33, amended: 2015 asp 1 Sch.1 para.3

s.33, varied: SI 2015/518 Sch.1 Part 5, SI
2015/675 Sch.3 Part 4

s.34, amended: 2015 asp 1 Sch.1 para.3

s.35, amended: 2015 asp 1 Sch.1 para.3,
SI 2015/664 Sch.4 para.21

s.35, repealed: SI 2015/664 Sch.4 para.21

s.35, varied: SI 2015/518 Sch.1 Part 5, SI
2015/675 Sch.3 Part 4

s.36, varied: SI 2015/518 Sch.1 Part 5, SI
2015/675 Sch.3 Part 4

s.37, varied: SI 2015/518 Sch.1 para.3, SI
2015/675 Sch.3 para.2, SI 2015/1519
Sch.1 para.3

s.39, varied: SI 2015/518 Sch.1 para.4, SI
2015/675 Sch.3 para.3, SI 2015/1519
Sch.1 para.4

s.40, amended: 2015 asp 1 Sch.1 para.3

s.41, substituted: 2015 asp 1 Sch.1 para.3

s.42, amended: 2015 asp 1 Sch.1 para.3

s.44, varied: SI 2015/518 Sch.1 Part 5, SI
2015/675 Sch.3 Part 4

s.45, enabling: SSI 2015/410

s.48, amended: 2015 asp 1 Sch.1 para.3

s.48, enabling: SI 2015/518, SI 2015/675,
SI 2015/787, SI 2015/1348, SI
2015/1507, SI 2015/1519, SI 2015/1867,
SSI 2015/48, SSI 2015/208, SSI
2015/363, SSI 2015/410

s.53, amended: 2015 asp 1 Sch.1 para.3

Sch.1 para.1, enabling: SSI 2015/410

Sch.1 para.4, enabling: SSI 2015/410

Sch.1 para.7, enabling: SI 2015/787

Sch.1 para.8, added: 2015 asp 1 s.34

Sch.3 para.5, repealed: 2015 c.20 Sch.23
para.25

18. Computer Misuse Act 1990

s.1, amended: 2015 c.9 Sch.4 para.7

s.2, amended: 2015 c.9 Sch.4 para.7

s.3, amended: 2015 c.9 Sch.4 para.7

s.3A, amended: 2015 c.9 s.41, s.42, Sch.4
para.7, Sch.4 para.8

s.3ZA, added: 2015 c.9 s.41

s.4, amended: 2015 c.9 s.43, Sch.4 para.9

s.5, amended: 2015 c.9 s.43

s.6, amended: 2015 c.9 Sch.4 para.10

s.9, amended: 2015 c.9 Sch.4 para.11

s.10, amended: 2015 c.9 s.44

s.10, substituted: 2015 c.9 Sch.4 para.12

s.13, amended: 2015 c.9 s.43

s.16, amended: 2015 c.9 s.44

**19. National Health Service and Community
Care Act 1990**

s.46, amended: SI 2015/914 Sch.1
para.50

s.47, amended: SI 2015/914 Sch.1
para.51

s.48, amended: SI 2015/914 Sch.1
para.52

s.67, enabling: SI 2015/642

**31. Aviation and Maritime Security Act
1990**

s.19, amended: 2015 c.6 Sch.5 para.12

s.21, amended: 2015 c.6 Sch.5 para.12,
SI 2015/664 Sch.3 para.5

s.22, amended: SI 2015/664 Sch.3 para.5

s.23, amended: SI 2015/664 Sch.3 para.5

s.24, amended: SI 2015/664 Sch.3 para.5

s.26, amended: 2015 c.6 Sch.5 para.12

s.31, amended: SI 2015/664 Sch.3 para.5

s.45, amended: 2015 c.6 Sch.5 para.12
Sch.1 para.2, repealed: 2015 c.6 Sch.5
para.10

**37. Human Fertilisation and Embryology
Act 1990**

see *Warren v Care Fertility
(Northampton) Ltd* [2014] EWHC 602
(Fam), [2015] Fam. 1 (Fam Div), Hogg J

s.3ZA, enabling: SI 2015/572

s.24, see *R. (on the application of M) v
Human Fertilisation and Embryology
Authority* [2015] EWHC 1706 (Admin),
[2015] 3 F.C.R. 374 (QBD (Admin)),
Ouseley J

s.30, see *Z (A Child) (Surrogate Father: Parental Order), Re* [2015] EWFC 73, [2015] 1 W.L.R. 4993 (Fam Ct), Sir James Munby PFD
s.31ZA, varied: SI 2015/572 Reg.11
s.31ZA, enabling: SI 2015/572
s.31ZB, varied: SI 2015/572 Reg.12
s.31ZC, varied: SI 2015/572 Reg.13
s.31ZD, varied: SI 2015/572 Reg.14
s.31ZE, varied: SI 2015/572 Reg.15
s.35A, enabling: SI 2015/572
s.45, enabling: SI 2015/572
Sch.3 para.4, varied: SI 2015/572 Reg.16
Sch.3 para.22, varied: SI 2015/572 Reg.17

40. Law Reform (Miscellaneous Provisions) (Scotland) Act 1990
s.30, see *Taylor Clark Leisure Plc v Revenue and Customs Commissioners* [2015] CSIH 32, 2015 S.C. 595 (IH (1 Div)), The Lord President (Gill)

41. Courts and Legal Services Act 1990
see *Coventry v Lawrence* [2015] A.C. 106 (SC), Lord Neuberger PSC
Part II, amended: 2015 c.20 s.87
s.53, amended: 2015 c.20 s.87
s.58, see *Pentecost v John* [2015] EWHC 1970 (QB), [2015] 4 Costs L.O. 497 (QBD), Turner J; see *Rees v Gateley Wareing (A Firm)* [2014] EWCA Civ 1351, [2015] 1 W.L.R. 2179 (CA (Civ Div)), Elias LJ
s.58A, amended: 2015 c.9 Sch.4 para.13
s.58AA, amended: 2015 c.15 Sch.8 para.37
s.75, amended: 2015 c.20 Sch.19 para.11
s.119, see *Rees v Gateley Wareing (A Firm)* [2014] EWCA Civ 1351, [2015] 1 W.L.R. 2179 (CA (Civ Div)), Elias LJ
s.119, amended: 2015 c.20 Sch.19 para.12
Sch.8, amended: 2015 c.20 Sch.19 para.13
Sch.8 Part I para.1, amended: 2015 c.20 Sch.19 para.13
Sch.8 Part I para.4, amended: 2015 c.20 Sch.19 para.13
Sch.8 Part I para.5, amended: 2015 c.20 Sch.19 para.13
Sch.8 Part I para.6A, added: 2015 c.20 Sch.19 para.13

Sch.8 Part I para.8, substituted: 2015 c.20 Sch.19 para.13
Sch.8 Part I para.9, repealed: 2015 c.20 Sch.19 para.13
Sch.8 Part I para.10, repealed: 2015 c.20 Sch.19 para.13
Sch.8 Part II para.21, amended: 2015 c.20 Sch.19 para.13
Sch.8 Part II para.22, amended: 2015 c.20 Sch.19 para.13
Sch.10 para.67, repealed: 2015 c.20 Sch.6 para.22

42. Broadcasting Act 1990
s.103B, amended: SI 2015/2052 Art.2
s.104AA, amended: SI 2015/2052 Art.3
s.200, enabling: SI 2015/904

43. Environmental Protection Act 1990
s.23, amended: SI 2015/664 Sch.4 para.22
s.33, see *R. v Jagger (Michael Edward)* [2015] EWCA Crim 348, [2015] Env. L.R. 25 (CA (Crim Div)), Treacy LJ
s.33, amended: SI 2015/664 Sch.4 para.22
s.34C, enabling: SI 2015/426
s.35, enabling: SSI 2015/101
s.46, amended: 2015 c.20 s.58
s.46A, added: 2015 c.20 s.58
s.46B, enabling: SI 2015/969
s.47ZB, amended: 2015 c.20 s.58
s.47ZB, repealed: 2015 c.20 s.58
s.52, amended: 2015 c.20 Sch.13 para.6
s.59, amended: SI 2015/664 Sch.3 para.6
s.62A, amended: SI 2015/1360 Reg.2
s.73A, amended: 2015 c.20 s.58
s.75, amended: SSI 2015/188 Reg.2
s.75, enabling: SI 2015/1417
s.78M, amended: SI 2015/664 Sch.3 para.6, Sch.4 para.22
s.80, see *R. (on the application of Bramford Royal British Legion) v Ipswich Magistrates' Court* [2014] EWHC 526 (Admin), [2015] Env. L.R. 1 (QBD (Admin)), Simler J
s.80, amended: SI 2015/664 Sch.3 para.6, Sch.4 para.22
s.82, amended: SI 2015/664 Sch.3 para.6
s.89, amended: 2015 c.7 Sch.1 para.111
s.98, amended: 2015 c.7 Sch.1 para.112
s.108, amended: 2015 asp 1 Sch.1 para.4
s.111, amended: 2015 asp 1 Sch.1 para.4

s.118, amended: SI 2015/664 Sch.3
para.6, Sch.4 para.22
s.126, amended: 2015 asp 1 Sch.1 para.4
s.140, amended: SI 2015/664 Sch.3
para.16
s.140, enabling: SI 2015/815
s.141, amended: SI 2015/664 Sch.3
para.16
s.153, amended: SI 2015/479 Art.2, SSI
2015/210 Art.2
s.153, enabling: SI 2015/479, SSI
2015/210
s.164, enabling: SSI 2015/72
Sch.15 para.14, repealed: SI 2015/374
Art.5
Sch.15 para.15, repealed: 2015 c.20
Sch.13 para.15
Sch.16 Part I, amended: SI 2015/374
Art.5

1991

22. New Roads and Street Works Act 1991

s.6, amended: 2015 c.7 Sch.1 para.114
s.12, amended: 2015 c.7 Sch.1 para.115
s.26, amended: 2015 c.7 Sch.1 para.116
s.49, amended: 2015 c.7 Sch.1 para.117
s.58, varied: SI 2015/293 Sch.1, SI
2015/328 Sch.1
s.58A, varied: SI 2015/293 Sch.1, SI
2015/328 Sch.1
s.63, amended: 2015 c.7 Sch.1 para.118
s.64, varied: SI 2015/293 Sch.1, SI
2015/328 Sch.1
s.67, enabling: SI 2015/384
s.69, varied: SI 2015/293 Sch.1, SI
2015/328 Sch.1
s.74, amended: 2015 c.7 Sch.1 para.119
s.74, varied: SI 2015/293 Sch.1, SI
2015/328 Sch.1
s.74A, amended: 2015 c.7 Sch.1 para.120
s.86, amended: 2015 c.7 Sch.1 para.121
s.88, varied: SI 2015/293 Sch.1, SI
2015/328 Sch.1
s.89, varied: SI 2015/293 Sch.1, SI
2015/328 Sch.1
s.90, varied: SI 2015/293 Sch.1, SI
2015/328 Sch.1
s.93, varied: SI 2015/293 Sch.1, SI
2015/328 Sch.1

s.106, amended: 2015 c.7 Sch.1 para.122
s.112A, enabling: SSI 2015/89
s.163, enabling: SSI 2015/89
Sch.2 para.1, amended: 2015 c.7 Sch.1
para.123
Sch.2 para.2, amended: 2015 c.7 Sch.1
para.123
Sch.2 para.3, amended: 2015 c.7 Sch.1
para.123
Sch.2 para.4, amended: 2015 c.7 Sch.1
para.123
Sch.3 para.9, amended: 2015 c.7 Sch.1
para.124

23. Children and Young Persons (Protection from Tobacco) Act 1991

s.3, amended: SI 2015/829 Reg.19

31. Finance Act 1991

s.116, enabling: SI 2015/1779
s.117, enabling: SI 2015/1779

34. Planning and Compensation Act 1991

s.23, repealed: SI 2015/664 Sch.4 para.96
Sch.3 Part I para.10, repealed: SI
2015/664 Sch.4 para.96

40. Road Traffic Act 1991

Sch.4 para.94, repealed: SI 2015/583
Sch.1 Part 1

48. Child Support Act 1991

s.8, see *D v R* [2014] EWHC 4306 (Fam),
[2015] 2 F.L.R. 978 (Fam Div), Holman
J
s.10, see *D v R* [2014] EWHC 4306
(Fam), [2015] 2 F.L.R. 978 (Fam Div),
Holman J
s.28A, see *Hakki v Secretary of State for
Work and Pensions* [2014] EWCA Civ
530, [2015] 1 F.L.R. 547 (CA (Civ Div)),
Longmore LJ
s.28I, see *Hakki v Secretary of State for
Work and Pensions* [2014] EWCA Civ
530, [2015] 1 F.L.R. 547 (CA (Civ Div)),
Longmore LJ
s.28ZD, enabling: SI 2015/338
s.34, enabling: SI 2015/338
s.39, amended: SI 2015/700 Sch.1
para.12
s.41B, enabling: SI 2015/338
s.44, see *D v R* [2014] EWHC 4306
(Fam), [2015] 2 F.L.R. 978 (Fam Div),
Holman J
s.49, repealed: SI 2015/700 Sch.1 para.12
s.49D, enabling: SI 2015/338

s.51, enabling: SI 2015/338
s.52, enabling: SI 2015/338
s.54, enabling: SI 2015/338
Sch.1 Pt I para.1, see *D v R* [2014]
EWHC 4306 (Fam), [2015] 2 F.L.R. 978
(Fam Div), Holman J
Sch.1 Part I para.5, enabling: SI
2015/338

52. Ports Act 1991
s.10, repealed: 2015 asp 13 s.1
s.11, repealed: 2015 asp 13 s.1
s.12, repealed: 2015 asp 13 s.1
s.20, amended: 2015 asp 13 s.1
s.37, repealed: 2015 asp 13 s.1

53. Criminal Justice Act 1991
see *Campbell (David) v HM Advocate*
[2015] HCJAC 28, 2015 S.L.T. 232
(HCJ), Lord Eassie
s.24, amended: 2015 c.2 Sch.12 para.7,
2015 c.30 Sch.5 para.12

**55. Agricultural Holdings (Scotland) Act
1991**
s.21, see *Governors of Robb's Trust v
Edwards* [2015] CSIH 39, 2015 S.C. 660
(IH (Ex Div)), Lord Menzies
s.23, see *Governors of Robb's Trust v
Edwards* [2015] CSIH 39, 2015 S.C. 660
(IH (Ex Div)), Lord Menzies

56. Water Industry Act 1991
s.5, amended: 2015 c.20 Sch.23 para.28
s.5, enabling: SI 2015/663
s.6, amended: 2015 c.20 Sch.23 para.28
s.36A, enabling: SI 2015/22
s.39ZA, varied: SI 2015/1469 Art.5
s.66DB, varied: SI 2015/1469 Art.5
s.66EB, varied: SI 2015/1469 Art.5
s.66J, amended: SI 2015/664 Sch.4
para.23
s.70, amended: SI 2015/664 Sch.4
para.23
s.86, amended: SI 2015/664 Sch.4
para.23
s.92, enabling: SI 2015/524
s.96ZA, varied: SI 2015/1469 Art.5
s.101A, amended: 2015 c.20 Sch.22
para.17
s.143A, enabling: SI 2015/365
s.144ZB, varied: SI 2015/1469 Art.5
s.157, enabling: SI 2015/924
s.202, amended: 2015 c.20 Sch.23
para.28

s.206, amended: 2015 c.20 Sch.23
para.28
s.213, enabling: SI 2015/22, SI 2015/365
s.219, enabling: SI 2015/1936
Sch.3 Part I para.1, repealed: 2015 c.20
Sch.23 para.28
Sch.3 Part I para.2, repealed: 2015 c.20
Sch.23 para.28
Sch.3 Part I para.5, repealed: 2015 c.20
Sch.23 para.28
Sch.3 Part I para.7, amended: 2015 c.20
Sch.23 para.28
Sch.3 Part I para.7, repealed: 2015 c.20
Sch.23 para.28
Sch.3 Part I para.8, amended: 2015 c.20
Sch.23 para.28
Sch.3 Part I para.8, repealed: 2015 c.20
Sch.23 para.28
Sch.3 Part I para.9, amended: 2015 c.20
Sch.23 para.28
Sch.4A para.8, amended: SI 2015/914
Sch.1 para.53
Sch.4A para.12, amended: 2015 c.26
Sch.2 para.20
Sch.4A para.13, amended: 2015 c.2 Sch.9
para.10
Sch.4ZA para.1, enabling: SI 2015/1936
Sch.13 Part I para.4, amended: 2015 c.20
Sch.23 para.28
Sch.15 Part I, amended: SI 2015/1682
Sch.1 para.4

57. Water Resources Act 1991
s.24, amended: SI 2015/664 Sch.4
para.24
s.25, amended: SI 2015/664 Sch.4
para.24
s.25C, amended: SI 2015/664 Sch.4
para.24
s.50, enabling: SI 2015/524
s.82, enabling: SI 2015/524
s.102, enabling: SI 2015/524
s.116, enabling: SI 2015/524
s.161D, amended: SI 2015/664 Sch.4
para.24
s.204, amended: 2015 c.20 Sch.23
para.28
s.211, amended: SI 2015/664 Sch.4
para.24
s.219, enabling: SI 2015/524
Sch.24 Part I, amended: SI 2015/1682
Sch.1 para.4

58. Statutory Water Companies Act 1991
    repealed: 2015 c.20 Sch.23 para.27
59. Land Drainage Act 1991
    s.3, enabling: SI 2015/872, SI 2015/923,
    SI 2015/1552
    s.61E, amended: 2015 c.20 Sch.22
    para.10
65. Dangerous Dogs Act 1991
    s.1, see *R. (on the application of Ali) v
    Chief Constable of Merseyside* [2014]
    EWHC 4772 (Admin), (2015) 179 J.P.
    333 (QBD (Admin)), King J
    s.1, enabling: SI 2015/138
    s.3, see *Reid v Murphy* [2015] HCJAC
    60, 2015 S.C.L. 772 (HCJ), Lady Paton
    s.4, see *R. (on the application of Ali) v
    Chief Constable of Merseyside* [2014]
    EWHC 4772 (Admin), (2015) 179 J.P.
    333 (QBD (Admin)), King J; see *Reid v
    Murphy* [2015] HCJAC 60, 2015 S.C.L.
    772 (HCJ), Lady Paton
    s.4, amended: SSI 2015/338 Sch.2 para.3
    s.4A, see *R. (on the application of Ali) v
    Chief Constable of Merseyside* [2014]
    EWHC 4772 (Admin), (2015) 179 J.P.
    333 (QBD (Admin)), King J
    s.4B, see *R. (on the application of Ali) v
    Chief Constable of Merseyside* [2014]
    EWHC 4772 (Admin), (2015) 179 J.P.
    333 (QBD (Admin)), King J
**67. Export and Investment Guarantees Act
1991**
    s.1, amended: 2015 c.26 s.11
    s.1, substituted: 2015 c.26 s.11
    s.6, amended: 2015 c.26 s.12
    s.6, repealed: 2015 c.26 s.12
    s.7, amended: 2015 c.26 s.12
    s.13, repealed: 2015 c.26 s.12

1992

3. Severn Bridges Act 1992
    s.9, enabling: SI 2015/2030
**4. Social Security Contributions and
Benefits Act 1992**
    s.1, amended: 2015 c.5 Sch.1 para.2
    s.1, enabling: SI 2015/478
    s.2, amended: 2015 c.5 s.6
    s.2, enabling: SI 2015/478, SI 2015/607

s.3, enabling: SI 2015/175, SI 2015/478,
SI 2015/543, SI 2015/784
s.5, enabling: SI 2015/577
s.7, amended: 2015 c.5 s.6
s.9, amended: 2015 c.5 s.1
s.9A, amended: 2015 c.5 s.1
s.9A, enabling: SI 2015/577
s.9B, added: 2015 c.5 s.1
s.10, amended: 2015 c.11 Sch.1 para.23
s.10ZB, amended: 2015 c.11 Sch.1
para.23
s.11, substituted: 2015 c.5 Sch.1 para.3
s.12, amended: 2015 c.5 Sch.1 para.4
s.12, repealed: 2015 c.5 Sch.1 para.4
s.12, enabling: SI 2015/478
s.13, amended: SI 2015/588 Art.2
s.13, enabling: SI 2015/478
s.18, amended: 2015 c.5 Sch.1 para.5
s.19, enabling: SI 2015/478
s.35, enabling: SI 2015/67
s.35A, amended: 2015 c.5 Sch.1 para.6
s.35A, enabling: SI 2015/342
s.35B, amended: 2015 c.5 Sch.1 para.7
s.35B, enabling: SI 2015/67
s.44, amended: SI 2015/457 Art.4
s.55A, varied: SI 2015/457 Art.4
s.55A, enabling: SI 2015/173
s.70, amended: SI 2015/1754 Reg.11
s.70, enabling: SI 2015/162, SI
2015/1754
s.73, see *Secretary of State for Work and
Pensions v Robertson* [2015] CSIH 82
(IH (Ex Div)), Lady Smith
s.80, amended: SI 2015/457 Art.7
s.90, enabling: SI 2015/496
s.108, enabling: SI 2015/87
s.109, enabling: SI 2015/87
s.113, enabling: SI 2015/496, SI
2015/545
s.119, enabling: SI 2015/478
s.122, amended: 2015 c.11 Sch.1 para.23
s.122, enabling: SI 2015/87, SI 2015/496,
SI 2015/607
s.123, enabling: SI 2015/1647, SI
2015/1857
s.126, amended: SI 2015/457 Art.16
s.135, enabling: SI 2015/1647, SI
2015/1754, SI 2015/1857
s.136, enabling: SI 2015/6, SI 2015/67,
SI 2015/389, SI 2015/1857
s.136A, enabling: SI 2015/6, SI 2015/67

s.137, enabling: SI 2015/6, SI 2015/67,
SI 2015/389, SI 2015/1647, SI
2015/1754, SI 2015/1857
s.138, enabling: SI 2015/67, SI 2015/183,
SI 2015/1662
s.142, enabling: SI 2015/1512
s.143, amended: SI 2015/914 Sch.1
para.54
s.157, amended: SI 2015/30 Art.3
s.171D, enabling: SI 2015/339
s.171ZJ, enabling: SI 2015/2065
s.171ZS, enabling: SI 2015/2065
s.171ZU, enabling: SI 2015/189
s.171ZV, enabling: SI 2015/189
s.171ZW, enabling: SI 2015/189
s.171ZZ4, enabling: SI 2015/2065
s.175, enabling: SI 2015/67, SI 2015/87,
SI 2015/162, SI 2015/173, SI 2015/175,
SI 2015/183, SI 2015/339, SI 2015/342,
SI 2015/389, SI 2015/478, SI 2015/496,
SI 2015/521, SI 2015/543, SI 2015/545,
SI 2015/577, SI 2015/607, SI 2015/784,
SI 2015/917, SI 2015/1512, SI
2015/1529, SI 2015/1580, SI 2015/1647,
SI 2015/1662, SI 2015/1754, SI
2015/1857
s.176, amended: 2015 c.5 s.1, Sch.1
para.8
Sch.1 para.6, enabling: SI 2015/175, SI
2015/521
Sch.1 para.7B, repealed: 2015 c.5 Sch.1
para.9
Sch.1 para.7B, enabling: SI 2015/478
Sch.1 para.7BB, added: 2015 c.5 Sch.1
para.9
Sch.1 para.7BB, enabling: SI 2015/478
Sch.1 para.8, repealed: 2015 c.5 Sch.1
para.9
Sch.1 para.8, enabling: SI 2015/478
Sch.4 Part I, amended: SI 2015/457 Sch.1
Sch.4 Part II, amended: SI 2015/457
Sch.1
Sch.4 Part III, amended: SI 2015/439
Art.2, SI 2015/457 Sch.1
Sch.4 Part IV, amended: SI 2015/457
Sch.1
Sch.4 Part V, amended: SI 2015/457
Sch.1
Sch.4B Part V para.13, amended: SI
2015/185 Art.2
Sch.5, varied: SI 2015/457 Art.4

Sch.5 para.7A, varied: SI 2015/457 Art.4
Sch.5A para.2, varied: SI 2015/457 Art.4
Sch.6 para.2, enabling: SI 2015/87
Sch.7 Part V para.13, varied: SI 2015/457
Art.4

5. Social Security Administration Act 1992
see *Murphy v L* [2015] HCJAC 21, 2015
S.L.T. 257 (HCJ), The Lord Justice
General (Gill)
s.1, enabling: SI 2015/437, SI 2015/1754
s.5, enabling: SI 2015/189, SI 2015/496,
SI 2015/1754, SI 2015/1857
s.12, enabling: SI 2015/1411
s.15A, enabling: SI 2015/343
s.71, enabling: SI 2015/499
s.71ZA, enabling: SI 2015/499
s.71ZD, enabling: SI 2015/499
s.75, enabling: SI 2015/499
s.78, enabling: SI 2015/499
s.115A, amended: SI 2015/202 Art.2
s.115A, enabling: SI 2015/202
s.132A, enabling: SI 2015/531
s.140B, enabling: SI 2015/1784
s.140F, enabling: SI 2015/1784
s.141, amended: 2015 c.5 Sch.1 para.20
s.141, enabling: SI 2015/588
s.142, enabling: SI 2015/588
s.143, amended: 2015 c.5 Sch.1 para.21
s.145, amended: 2015 c.5 Sch.1 para.22
s.148, enabling: SI 2015/187
s.148A, enabling: SI 2015/186
s.148AA, enabling: SI 2015/185
s.150, enabling: SI 2015/439, SI
2015/457
s.150A, enabling: SI 2015/457
s.151, enabling: SI 2015/457
s.151A, amended: SI 2015/1754 Reg.10
s.155, enabling: SI 2015/496, SI
2015/545
s.165, amended: 2015 c.5 s.7
s.179, enabling: SI 2015/828
s.182C, enabling: SI 2015/67, SI
2015/1828
s.189, enabling: SI 2015/67, SI 2015/185,
SI 2015/186, SI 2015/187, SI 2015/202,
SI 2015/343, SI 2015/437, SI 2015/439,
SI 2015/457, SI 2015/496, SI 2015/499,
SI 2015/531, SI 2015/545, SI 2015/1411,
SI 2015/1784, SI 2015/1828, SI
2015/1857
s.190, enabling: SI 2015/545

s.191, enabling: SI 2015/437, SI 2015/496, SI 2015/499, SI 2015/545, SI 2015/1857

7. Social Security Contributions and Benefits (Northern Ireland) Act 1992

s.1, amended: 2015 c.5 Sch.1 para.11

s.1, enabling: SI 2015/478

s.2, amended: 2015 c.5 s.6

s.2, enabling: SI 2015/478, SI 2015/607

s.3, amended: SI 2015/2006 Sch.12 Part 6

s.3, enabling: SI 2015/175, SI 2015/478, SI 2015/543, SI 2015/811

s.5, enabling: SI 2015/577

s.7, amended: 2015 c.5 s.6

s.9, amended: 2015 c.5 s.1

s.9A, amended: 2015 c.5 s.1

s.9A, enabling: SI 2015/577

s.9B, added: 2015 c.5 s.1

s.10, amended: 2015 c.11 Sch.1 para.24

s.10ZB, amended: 2015 c.11 Sch.1 para.24

s.11, substituted: 2015 c.5 Sch.1 para.12

s.12, amended: 2015 c.5 Sch.1 para.13

s.12, repealed: 2015 c.5 Sch.1 para.13

s.12, enabling: SI 2015/478

s.13, amended: SI 2015/588 Art.2

s.13, enabling: SI 2015/478

s.15, amended: SI 2015/588 Art.3

s.18, amended: 2015 c.5 Sch.1 para.14, SI 2015/588 Art.3

s.19, enabling: SI 2015/478

s.22, amended: SI 2015/2006 Sch.3 para.2, Sch.12 Part 1

s.22, repealed: SI 2015/2006 Sch.12 Part 1

s.30B, amended: SI 2015/2006 Sch.9 para.3, Sch.12 Part 8

s.30B, repealed: SI 2015/2006 Sch.12 Part 8

s.35, amended: SI 2015/2006 Art.68

s.35A, amended: 2015 c.5 Sch.1 para.15

s.35B, amended: 2015 c.5 Sch.1 para.16

s.44A, amended: SI 2015/2006 Sch.12 Part 1

s.64, amended: SI 2015/2006 Sch.9 para.4

s.64, repealed: SI 2015/2006 Sch.12 Part 8

s.71, repealed: SI 2015/2006 Art.95

s.94, amended: SI 2015/2006 Art.70

s.95A, added: SI 2015/2006 Art.72

s.103, amended: SI 2015/2006 Art.70

s.108, amended: SI 2015/2006 Art.70

s.109, amended: SI 2015/2006 Art.70

s.111, repealed: SI 2015/2006 Art.70

s.113, enabling: SI 2015/545

s.119, enabling: SI 2015/478

s.121, amended: 2015 c.11 Sch.1 para.24, SI 2015/2006 Sch.12 Part 1, Sch.12 Part 6

s.121, repealed: SI 2015/2006 Sch.12 Part 6

s.121, enabling: SI 2015/607

s.122, repealed: SI 2015/2006 Sch.12 Part 1

s.123, amended: SI 2015/2006 Art.64, Art.65

s.123A, added: SI 2015/2006 Art.65

s.129A, amended: SI 2015/2006 Art.75

s.133, amended: SI 2015/2006 Sch.12 Part 6

s.134, amended: SI 2015/2006 Art.77, Sch.12 Part 7

s.134, repealed: SI 2015/2006 Art.76, Sch.12 Part 7

s.135, repealed: SI 2015/2006 Sch.12 Part 7

s.136, amended: SI 2015/2006 Art.78

s.138, enabling: SI 2015/1512

s.146, amended: SI 2015/2006 Sch.3 para.3, Sch.9 para.5

s.146, repealed: SI 2015/2006 Sch.12 Part 1, Sch.12 Part 6, Sch.12 Part 8

s.160, amended: SI 2015/2006 Art.68

s.167ZA, amended: SI 2015/2006 Art.68

s.167ZB, amended: SI 2015/2006 Art.68

s.167ZL, amended: SI 2015/2006 Art.68

s.167ZU, amended: SI 2015/2006 Art.69

s.167ZW, amended: SI 2015/2006 Art.69

s.169A, added: SI 2015/2006 Art.68

s.171, repealed: SI 2015/2006 Sch.12 Part 1

s.171, enabling: SI 2015/175, SI 2015/478, SI 2015/521, SI 2015/543, SI 2015/545, SI 2015/577, SI 2015/607, SI 2015/811, SI 2015/1512

s.172, amended: 2015 c.5 s.1, Sch.1 para.17

Sch.1 para.6, enabling: SI 2015/175, SI 2015/521

Sch.1 para.7B, repealed: 2015 c.5 Sch.1 para.18

Sch.1 para.7B, enabling: SI 2015/478

Sch.1 para.7BB, added: 2015 c.5 Sch.1 para.18

Sch.1 para.7BB, enabling: SI 2015/478

Sch.1 para.8, repealed: 2015 c.5 Sch.1 para.18

Sch.1 para.8, enabling: SI 2015/478

Sch.4 Part III, amended: SI 2015/440 Art.2

Sch.4 Part V, amended: SI 2015/2006 Art.71

Sch.6 para.8, repealed: SI 2015/2006 Sch.12 Part 6

Sch.7 Part VI para.14, amended: SI 2015/2006 Art.73

Sch.7 Part VI para.20, amended: SI 2015/2006 Sch.12 Part 6

Sch.8, repealed: SI 2015/2006 Art.70

Sch.11 para.2, amended: SI 2015/2006 Art.68

Sch.11 para.9, added: SI 2015/2006 Art.68

8. Social Security Administration (Northern Ireland) Act 1992

Part V, amended: SI 2015/2006 Sch.12 Part 1

s.1, amended: SI 2015/2006 Sch.2 para.4, Sch.9 para.7

s.1, repealed: SI 2015/2006 Sch.9 para.7 , Sch.12 Part 1

s.2A, repealed: SI 2015/2006 Sch.12 Part 1

s.2F, amended: SI 2015/2006 Art.65

s.2G, amended: SI 2015/2006 Art.65

s.5, amended: SI 2015/2006 Art.103, Art.104, Art.105, Art.106, Sch.2 para.5, Sch.4 para.10, Sch.9 para.8, Sch.12 Part 1

s.5, repealed: SI 2015/2006 Art.104 , Sch.12 Part 1

s.5A, repealed: SI 2015/2006 Sch.12 Part 1

s.5B, amended: SI 2015/2006 Sch.12 Part 1

s.10, repealed: SI 2015/2006 Sch.12 Part 7

s.13A, amended: SI 2015/2006 Sch.2 para.6, Sch.4 para.11, Sch.12 Part 1

s.13A, repealed: SI 2015/2006 Sch.12 Part 1

s.60, amended: SI 2015/2006 Sch.4 para.12, Sch.5 para.5

s.69, amended: SI 2015/2006 Art.109, Art.110, Sch.9 para.9, Sch.12 Part 10

s.69, repealed: SI 2015/2006 Sch.12 Part 1 , Sch.12 Part 10

s.69A, repealed: SI 2015/2006 Sch.12 Part 1

s.69ZA, amended: SI 2015/2006 Art.110

s.69ZA, repealed: SI 2015/2006 Sch.12 Part 7

s.69ZB, added: SI 2015/2006 Art.109

s.69ZH, repealed: SI 2015/2006 Sch.12 Part 1

s.71, amended: SI 2015/2006 Sch.3 para.5, Sch.9 para.10, Sch.12 Part 1

s.72, amended: SI 2015/2006 Sch.2 para.7, Sch.12 Part 1

s.72, repealed: SI 2015/2006 Sch.12 Part 1

s.72A, amended: SI 2015/2006 Sch.2 para.8

s.73, amended: SI 2015/2006 Art.110

s.73, repealed: SI 2015/2006 Sch.12 Part 1

s.74, amended: SI 2015/2006 Art.110, Sch.2 para.9, Sch.8 para.2, Sch.12 Part 1

s.74, repealed: SI 2015/2006 Sch.12 Part 7

s.75, amended: SI 2015/2006 Sch.8 para.3

s.100, amended: SI 2015/2006 Sch.2 para.10, Sch.12 Part 1

s.100, repealed: SI 2015/2006 Sch.12 Part 1

s.101, amended: SI 2015/2006 Sch.2 para.11, Sch.12 Part 1

s.103, amended: SI 2015/2006 Sch.2 para.12, Sch.12 Part 1

s.103A, repealed: SI 2015/2006 Sch.12 Part 1

s.103B, amended: SI 2015/2006 Art.112

s.104A, repealed: SI 2015/2006 Sch.12 Part 1

s.105, amended: SI 2015/2006 Sch.12 Part 1

s.109A, amended: SI 2015/2006 Art.109, Art.115, Art.116, Sch.12 Part 1

s.109A, repealed: SI 2015/2006 Sch.12
Part 1
s.109B, amended: SI 2015/2006 Art.109,
Sch.12 Part 1
s.110, amended: SI 2015/2006 Art.113,
Sch.12 Part 1
s.110, repealed: SI 2015/2006 Sch.12
Part 1
s.110A, amended: SI 2015/2006 Art.114
s.110A, repealed: SI 2015/2006 Sch.12
Part 1
s.110ZA, added: SI 2015/2006 Art.114
s.110ZA, repealed: SI 2015/2006 Sch.12
Part 1
s.115CA, amended: SI 2015/2006 Sch.2
para.13, Sch.9 para.11
s.115CA, repealed: SI 2015/2006 Sch.12
Part 1
s.115D, amended: SI 2015/2006 Sch.12
Part 12
s.115D, repealed: SI 2015/2006 Sch.12
Part 12
s.115E, amended: SI 2015/2006 Sch.12
Part 12
s.115E, repealed: SI 2015/2006 Sch.12
Part 12
s.116, repealed: SI 2015/2006 Sch.12
Part 12
s.116B, amended: SI 2015/2006 Sch.2
para.14, Sch.9 para.12
s.116B, repealed: SI 2015/2006 Sch.12
Part 1
s.116C, amended: SI 2015/2006 Sch.9
para.13
s.116C, repealed: SI 2015/2006 Sch.12
Part 1
s.118, amended: SI 2015/2006 Sch.2
para.15, Sch.9 para.14
s.119, amended: SI 2015/2006 Sch.2
para.16, Sch.12 Part 1
s.119A, repealed: SI 2015/2006 Sch.12
Part 9
s.122, amended: SI 2015/2006 Sch.2
para.17
s.124, amended: SI 2015/2006 Sch.2
para.18
s.126, repealed: SI 2015/2006 Sch.12
Part 1
s.129, enabling: SI 2015/588
s.132, enabling: SI 2015/440, SI
2015/567

s.135, enabling: SI 2015/545
s.139, amended: SI 2015/2006 Sch.9
para.15
s.139, repealed: SI 2015/2006 Sch.12
Part 1
s.139A, amended: SI 2015/2006 Sch.3
para.6, Sch.9 para.16
s.139B, amended: SI 2015/2006 Sch.3
para.7, Sch.9 para.17, Sch.12 Part 1
s.139C, amended: SI 2015/2006 Sch.3
para.8, Sch.9 para.18
s.139D, added: SI 2015/2006 Sch.2
para.19
s.139D, amended: SI 2015/2006 Sch.3
para.9, Sch.12 Part 1
s.140, amended: SI 2015/2006 Sch.9
para.19
s.140, repealed: SI 2015/2006 Sch.12
Part 1
s.140A, amended: SI 2015/2006 Sch.9
para.20
s.140B, amended: SI 2015/2006 Sch.12
Part 1
s.140C, added: SI 2015/2006 Sch.2
para.20
s.144, repealed: SI 2015/2006 Sch.12
Part 6
s.145, amended: 2015 c.5 s.7, SI
2015/2006 Sch.2 para.21, Sch.9 para.22
s.147, repealed: SI 2015/2006 Sch.12
Part 7
s.149, amended: SI 2015/2006 Sch.2
para.22, Sch.9 para.23, Sch.12 Part 6
s.149, repealed: SI 2015/2006 Sch.12
Part 1
s.155, amended: SI 2015/2006 Sch.2
para.23, Sch.9 para.24
s.155, repealed: SI 2015/2006 Sch.12
Part 1
s.155A, repealed: SI 2015/2006 Sch.12
Part 1
s.156, amended: SI 2015/2006 Sch.2
para.24, Sch.9 para.25
s.158A, repealed: SI 2015/2006 Sch.12
Part 1
s.158B, amended: SI 2015/2006 Sch.2
para.25, Sch.3 para.10, Sch.9 para.26,
Sch.12 Part 1
s.158B, repealed: SI 2015/2006 Sch.12
Part 1

s.160, amended: SI 2015/2006 Sch.9
para.27
s.161, repealed: SI 2015/2006 Sch.12
Part 6
s.163, amended: SI 2015/2006 Sch.2
para.26, Sch.9 para.28
s.163, repealed: SI 2015/2006 Sch.12
Part 1
s.164, repealed: SI 2015/2006 Sch.12
Part 6
s.165, amended: SI 2015/2006 Art.108
s.165, repealed: SI 2015/2006 Sch.12
Part 1
s.165, enabling: SI 2015/440, SI
2015/545
s.166, amended: SI 2015/2006 Art.116
s.166, repealed: SI 2015/2006 Sch.12
Part 1
s.167, amended: SI 2015/2006 Sch.2
para.27, Sch.9 para.29, Sch.12 Part 1,
Sch.12 Part 6
s.167, enabling: SI 2015/545
Sch.4 Part I, amended: SI 2015/2006
Art.136, Sch.8 para.4, Sch.12 Part 7
Sch.4 Part I, repealed: SI 2015/2006
Sch.12 Part 7
Sch.5 paraA.1, added: SI 2015/2006
Sch.9 para.30
Sch.5 para.1, repealed: SI 2015/2006
Sch.12 Part 8
Sch.6, repealed: SI 2015/2006 Sch.12
Part 6
Sch.7 para.3, repealed: SI 2015/2006
Sch.12 Part 1

12. Taxation of Chargeable Gains Act 1992
see *Gemsupa Ltd v Revenue and Customs
Commissioners* [2015] UKFTT 97 (TC),
[2015] S.F.T.D. 447 (FTT (Tax)), Judge
Jonathan Cannan; see *Prowting 1968
Trustee One Ltd v Amos-Yeo* [2015]
EWHC 2480 (Ch), [2015] B.T.C. 33 (Ch
D), Master Clark; see *Revenue and
Customs Commissioners v Smith &
Williamson Corporate Services Ltd*
[2015] UKUT 666 (TCC), [2015] B.T.C.
539 (UT (Tax)), Warren J
Part II c.6, added: 2015 c.11 Sch.7
para.16
Part III c.V, added: 2015 c.33 s.43
Part V c.IV, added: 2015 c.11 s.44
s.1, amended: 2015 c.11 Sch.7 para.2

s.2, amended: 2015 c.11 Sch.7 para.3
s.2B, amended: 2015 c.11 Sch.7 para.4
s.2C, amended: 2015 c.11 Sch.8 para.2
s.2D, amended: 2015 c.11 Sch.8 para.3,
Sch.8 para.4
s.2E, amended: 2015 c.11 Sch.8 para.5
s.3, amended: 2015 c.11 Sch.7 para.5
s.4, amended: 2015 c.11 Sch.7 para.6
s.4B, substituted: 2015 c.11 Sch.7 para.7
s.8, see *Wintershall (E&P) Ltd v Revenue
and Customs Commissioners* [2015]
UKUT 334 (TCC) (UT (Tax)), Lord
Glennie
s.8, amended: 2015 c.11 Sch.7 para.8
s.10A, amended: 2015 c.11 Sch.7 para.9
s.13, amended: 2015 c.11 Sch.7 para.10
s.14B, added: 2015 c.11 Sch.7 para.11
s.16, amended: 2015 c.11 Sch.7 para.12
s.17, see *Price v Revenue and Customs
Commissioners* [2015] UKUT 164
(TCC), [2015] S.T.C. 1975 (UT (Tax)),
Nugee J; see *R. (on the application of
Hely-Hutchinson) v Revenue and
Customs Commissioners* [2015] EWHC
3261 (Admin), [2015] B.T.C. 37 (QBD
(Admin)), Whipple J
s.24, see *Drown v Revenue and Customs
Commissioners* [2015] W.T.L.R. 775
(FTT (Tax)), Judge Barbara Mosedale
s.25ZA, added: 2015 c.11 Sch.7 para.13
s.38, see *Blackwell v Revenue and
Customs Commissioners* [2015] UKUT
418 (TCC), [2015] B.T.C. 526 (UT
(Tax)), Newey J; see *Price v Revenue
and Customs Commissioners* [2015]
UKUT 164 (TCC), [2015] S.T.C. 1975
(UT (Tax)), Nugee J
s.45, amended: 2015 c.11 s.40
s.48A, added: 2015 c.11 Sch.7 para.14
s.49, see *Revenue and Customs
Commissioners v Morrison* [2015] S.T.C.
659 (IH (1 Div)), The Lord President
(Gill)
s.57A, amended: 2015 c.11 Sch.7 para.15
s.62, see *Drown v Revenue and Customs
Commissioners* [2015] W.T.L.R. 775
(FTT (Tax)), Judge Barbara Mosedale;
see *Vaughan-Jones v Vaughan-Jones*
[2015] EWHC 1086 (Ch), [2015]
W.T.L.R. 1287 (Ch D (Manchester)),
Judge Hodge QC

s.62, amended: 2015 c.11 Sch.7 para.17
s.66, amended: 2015 c.20 Sch.6 para.2
s.80A, added: 2015 c.11 Sch.7 para.18
s.86, amended: 2015 c.11 Sch.7 para.19
s.87, see *Bowring v Revenue and Customs Commissioners* [2015] UKUT 550 (TCC), [2015] B.T.C. 530 (UT (Tax)), Barling J
s.87, amended: 2015 c.11 Sch.7 para.20
s.90, see *Bowring v Revenue and Customs Commissioners* [2015] UKUT 550 (TCC), [2015] B.T.C. 530 (UT (Tax)), Barling J
s.97, see *Bowring v Revenue and Customs Commissioners* [2015] UKUT 550 (TCC), [2015] B.T.C. 530 (UT (Tax)), Barling J
s.116, see *DMWSHNZ Ltd v Revenue and Customs Commissioners* [2015] EWCA Civ 1036, [2015] B.T.C. 32 (CA (Civ Div)), Moore-Bick LJ
s.117, see *DMWSHNZ Ltd v Revenue and Customs Commissioners* [2015] EWCA Civ 1036, [2015] B.T.C. 32 (CA (Civ Div)), Moore-Bick LJ
s.139, amended: 2015 c.11 Sch.7 para.21
s.144ZA, see *R. (on the application of Hely-Hutchinson) v Revenue and Customs Commissioners* [2015] EWHC 3261 (Admin), [2015] B.T.C. 37 (QBD (Admin)), Whipple J
s.151, enabling: SI 2015/608, SI 2015/869, SI 2015/941, SI 2015/1370
s.151E, amended: 2015 c.33 Sch.7 para.98
s.151E, enabling: SI 2015/1960
s.159A, added: 2015 c.11 Sch.7 para.22
s.165, amended: 2015 c.11 Sch.7 para.23
s.166, amended: 2015 c.11 Sch.7 para.24
s.167, amended: 2015 c.11 Sch.7 para.25
s.167A, added: 2015 c.11 Sch.7 para.26
s.168, amended: 2015 c.11 Sch.7 para.27
s.168A, added: 2015 c.11 Sch.7 para.28
s.169H, amended: 2015 c.11 s.42
s.169K, amended: 2015 c.11 s.41
s.169L, amended: 2015 c.11 s.42
s.169LA, added: 2015 c.11 s.42
s.169S, amended: 2015 c.11 s.43
s.170, see *Gemsupa Ltd v Revenue and Customs Commissioners* [2015] UKFTT 97 (TC), [2015] S.F.T.D. 447 (FTT (Tax)), Judge Jonathan Cannan
s.171, see *DMWSHNZ Ltd v Revenue and Customs Commissioners* [2015] EWCA Civ 1036, [2015] B.T.C. 32 (CA (Civ Div)), Moore-Bick LJ; see *Gemsupa Ltd v Revenue and Customs Commissioners* [2015] UKFTT 97 (TC), [2015] S.F.T.D. 447 (FTT (Tax)), Judge Jonathan Cannan
s.171A, see *DMWSHNZ Ltd v Revenue and Customs Commissioners* [2015] EWCA Civ 1036, [2015] B.T.C. 32 (CA (Civ Div)), Moore-Bick LJ
s.187B, added: 2015 c.11 Sch.7 para.29
s.188A, added: 2015 c.11 Sch.7 para.30
s.222, amended: 2015 c.11 Sch.9 para.2
s.222A, added: 2015 c.11 Sch.9 para.3
s.223, amended: 2015 c.11 Sch.9 para.4
s.223A, added: 2015 c.11 Sch.9 para.5
s.225, amended: 2015 c.11 Sch.9 para.6
s.225A, amended: 2015 c.11 Sch.9 para.7
s.225B, amended: 2015 c.11 Sch.9 para.8
s.225E, amended: 2015 c.11 Sch.9 para.9
s.251, see *DMWSHNZ Ltd v Revenue and Customs Commissioners* [2015] EWCA Civ 1036, [2015] B.T.C. 32 (CA (Civ Div)), Moore-Bick LJ
s.253, see *Drown v Revenue and Customs Commissioners* [2015] W.T.L.R. 775 (FTT (Tax)), Judge Barbara Mosedale
s.260, amended: 2015 c.11 Sch.7 para.31
s.261, amended: 2015 c.11 Sch.7 para.32
s.261ZA, added: 2015 c.11 Sch.7 para.33
s.263AZA, amended: 2015 c.20 s.57
s.272, enabling: SI 2015/616
s.287, amended: 2015 c.11 s.125
s.288, amended: 2015 c.11 Sch.7 para.34
Sch.B1, added: 2015 c.11 Sch.7 para.36
Sch.C1, added: 2015 c.11 Sch.7 para.37
Sch.1 para.1, amended: 2015 c.11 Sch.7 para.35
Sch.1 para.2, amended: 2015 c.11 Sch.7 para.35
Sch.4ZZA, substituted: 2015 c.11 Sch.8 para.7
Sch.4ZZA, amended: 2015 c.11 Sch.8 para.12
Sch.4ZZB, added: 2015 c.11 Sch.7 para.39
Sch.4C para.4, amended: 2015 c.11 Sch.7 para.40

Sch.4ZZA para.1, substituted: 2015 c.11
Sch.7 para.38
Sch.4ZZA para.2, amended: 2015 c.11
Sch.7 para.38
Sch.4ZZA para.2, substituted: 2015 c.11
Sch.8 para.8
Sch.4ZZA para.3, amended: 2015 c.11
Sch.8 para.9
Sch.4ZZA para.4, amended: 2015 c.11
Sch.8 para.10
Sch.4ZZA para.5, amended: 2015 c.11
Sch.7 para.38, Sch.8 para.11
Sch.4ZZA para.6, amended: 2015 c.11
Sch.8 para.13
Sch.4ZZA para.6A, added: 2015 c.11
Sch.7 para.38
Sch.4ZZA para.8, added: 2015 c.11 Sch.7
para.38
Sch.5B para.1, see *East Allenheads
Estate Ltd v Revenue and Customs
Commissioners* [2015] UKFTT 328 (TC),
[2015] S.F.T.D. 908 (FTT (Tax)), Judge
Kevin Poole
Sch.9 Part I para.1, enabling: SI
2015/1790

13. Further and Higher Education Act 1992
s.16, enabling: SI 2015/1457
s.17, enabling: SI 2015/1457
s.19, amended: 2015 c.20 Sch.15 para.4
s.20, enabling: SI 2015/1458
s.21, enabling: SI 2015/1458
s.23, repealed: 2015 c.20 Sch.15 para.4
s.28, enabling: SI 2015/1464
s.31, amended: 2015 c.20 Sch.15 para.5
s.31, repealed: 2015 c.20 Sch.15 para.5
s.32, repealed: 2015 c.20 Sch.15 para.4
s.33D, repealed: 2015 c.20 Sch.15 para.6
s.34, repealed: 2015 c.20 Sch.15 para.4
s.35, repealed: 2015 c.20 Sch.15 para.4
s.36, repealed: 2015 c.20 Sch.15 para.4
s.38, repealed: 2015 c.20 Sch.15 para.4
s.49B, added: 2015 c.26 s.80
s.49B, enabling: SI 2015/1564
s.54, amended: 2015 c.20 Sch.14 para.37
s.56A, amended: 2015 c.20 Sch.15 para.7
s.58, repealed: 2015 c.20 Sch.15 para.4
s.61A, repealed: 2015 c.20 Sch.14
para.38
s.79, enabling: SI 2015/225
s.82, amended: 2015 c.20 Sch.14 para.39
s.83, amended: 2015 c.20 Sch.14 para.40

s.84, amended: 2015 c.20 Sch.15 para.4
s.88, amended: 2015 c.20 Sch.15 para.4
s.88A, amended: 2015 c.20 Sch.15 para.4
s.89, enabling: SI 2015/1564
Sch.4, enabling: SI 2015/1458
Sch.5, repealed: 2015 c.20 Sch.15 para.4

14. Local Government Finance Act 1992
s.3, see *Dwelling in London N2, Re*
[2015] R.V.R. 157 (VT), Graham Zellick
QC
s.12A, enabling: SI 2015/2068
s.12B, enabling: SI 2015/2068
s.13A, see *Morgan v Warwick DC* [2015]
R.V.R. 224 (VT), Graham Zellick QC;
see *R. (on the application of Winder) v
Sandwell MBC* [2014] EWHC 2617
(Admin), [2015] P.T.S.R. 34 (QBD
(Admin)), Hickinbottom J
s.13A, enabling: SI 2015/44
s.16, see *Wiltshire Council v Piggin*
[2014] EWHC 4386 (Admin), [2015]
R.V.R. 45 (QBD (Admin)), Davis J
s.25A, added: SI 2015/982 Art.3
s.26, amended: SI 2015/982 Art.3
s.52ZQ, amended: SI 2015/1376 Sch.2
para.5
s.80, enabling: SSI 2015/46
s.113, amended: SI 2015/1376 Sch.2
para.5
s.113, enabling: SI 2015/2041, SSI
2015/46
s.119, enabling: SSI 2015/59
Sch.1 para.4, see *Rupp v Cambridge City
Council* [2015] R.V.R. 310 (VT), S
Rehman
Sch.1 para.5, see *Rupp v Cambridge City
Council* [2015] R.V.R. 310 (VT), S
Rehman
Sch.1 para.7, amended: SI 2015/914
Sch.1 para.55
Sch.1A para.2, enabling: SI 2015/2041
Sch.1B para.2, enabling: SI 2015/44
Sch.1B para.3, enabling: SI 2015/44
Sch.1B para.4, enabling: SI 2015/44
Sch.1B para.5, enabling: SI 2015/44
Sch.1B para.6, enabling: SI 2015/44
Sch.1B para.7, enabling: SI 2015/44
Sch.2 para.1, enabling: SSI 2015/46
Sch.12 Part I para.1, enabling: SSI
2015/56, SSI 2015/125

Sch.12 Part II para.9, enabling: SSI
2015/56, SSI 2015/125
Sch.12 Part III para.10, amended: 2015
asp 6 s.140

15. Offshore Safety Act 1992
s.1, enabling: SI 2015/398

19. Local Government Act 1992
s.1, amended: 2015 asp 6 Sch.4 para.6

34. Sexual Offences (Amendment) Act 1992
s.2, amended: 2015 c.30 Sch.5 para.4

**37. Further and Higher Education
(Scotland) Act 1992**
s.24, enabling: SSI 2015/348
s.36, amended: SSI 2015/153 Sch.1
para.2
s.45, enabling: SSI 2015/209, SSI
2015/305
s.60, enabling: SSI 2015/209, SSI
2015/305
Sch.2 para.3, amended: SSI 2015/153
Sch.1 para.2
Sch.2 para.5B, amended: SSI 2015/153
Sch.1 para.2

40. Friendly Societies Act 1992
s.52, amended: SI 2015/575 Sch.1
para.19
s.62, amended: SI 2015/664 Sch.3 para.7
s.78, amended: SI 2015/664 Sch.3 para.7
s.119, amended: SI 2015/575 Sch.1
para.19
s.119, repealed: SI 2015/575 Sch.1
para.19
Sch.14 para.8, amended: SI 2015/664
Sch.3 para.7
Sch.14 para.9, amended: SI 2015/664
Sch.3 para.7
Sch.14 para.12, amended: SI 2015/664
Sch.3 para.7
Sch.14 para.15, amended: SI 2015/664
Sch.3 para.7
Sch.15 Part II para.15, amended: SI
2015/575 Sch.1 para.19
Sch.15 Part II para.15A, amended: SI
2015/575 Sch.1 para.19

42. Transport and Works Act 1992
s.1, enabling: SI 2015/780, SI 2015/781,
SI 2015/1652, SI 2015/1684, SI
2015/1876, SI 2015/2044
s.3, enabling: SI 2015/780

s.5, enabling: SI 2015/780, SI 2015/781,
SI 2015/1652, SI 2015/1684, SI
2015/1876, SI 2015/2044
s.31, amended: 2015 c.20 Sch.11 para.4,
Sch.11 para.6
s.31, repealed: 2015 c.20 Sch.11 para.6
s.31A, amended: 2015 c.20 Sch.11
para.12
s.32, repealed: 2015 c.20 Sch.11 para.2
s.32, substituted: 2015 c.20 Sch.11 para.2
s.38, amended: 2015 c.20 Sch.11 para.13
Sch.1 para.1, enabling: SI 2015/780, SI
2015/781, SI 2015/1652, SI 2015/1876,
SI 2015/2044
Sch.1 para.2, enabling: SI 2015/780, SI
2015/781, SI 2015/1876, SI 2015/2044
Sch.1 para.3, enabling: SI 2015/780, SI
2015/781, SI 2015/1684, SI 2015/1876,
SI 2015/2044
Sch.1 para.4, enabling: SI 2015/780, SI
2015/781, SI 2015/1684, SI 2015/1876,
SI 2015/2044
Sch.1 para.5, enabling: SI 2015/780, SI
2015/781, SI 2015/1684, SI 2015/2044
Sch.1 para.7, enabling: SI 2015/780, SI
2015/781, SI 2015/1684, SI 2015/1876,
SI 2015/2044
Sch.1 para.8, enabling: SI 2015/780, SI
2015/781, SI 2015/1652, SI 2015/1876,
SI 2015/2044
Sch.1 para.9, enabling: SI 2015/1876
Sch.1 para.10, enabling: SI 2015/780, SI
2015/781, SI 2015/1876, SI 2015/2044
Sch.1 para.11, enabling: SI 2015/780, SI
2015/781, SI 2015/1684, SI 2015/1876,
SI 2015/2044
Sch.1 para.12, enabling: SI 2015/1876
Sch.1 para.15, enabling: SI 2015/781, SI
2015/1652, SI 2015/2044
Sch.1 para.16, enabling: SI 2015/780, SI
2015/781, SI 2015/1684, SI 2015/1876,
SI 2015/2044
Sch.1 para.17, enabling: SI 2015/781, SI
2015/1652, SI 2015/2044

48. Finance (No.2) Act 1992
s.1, enabling: SI 2015/368

**49. Community Care (Residential
Accommodation) Act 1992**
s.2, enabling: SI 2015/642

50. Carriage of Goods by Sea Act 1992

s.1, see *Glencore International AG v
MSC Mediterranean Shipping Co SA*
[2015] EWHC 1989 (Comm), [2015] 2
Lloyd's Rep. 508 (QBD (Comm)),
Andrew Smith J

51. Protection of Badgers Act 1992

see *R. (on the application of Badger
Trust) v Secretary of State for the
Environment, Food and Rural Affairs*
[2014] EWCA Civ 1405, [2015] Env.
L.R. 12 (CA (Civ Div)), Davis LJ

s.3, see *McLintock v Harris* 2015 S.L.T.
(Sh Ct) 26 (Sh Ct (Lothian) (Jedburgh)),
Sheriff T A K Drummond, QC

**52. Trade Union and Labour Relations
(Consolidation) Act 1992**

s.24ZB, enabling: SI 2015/716

s.145E, amended: SI 2015/226 Sch.1

s.146, see *Smith v Carillion (JM) Ltd*
[2015] EWCA Civ 209, [2015] I.R.L.R.
467 (CA (Civ Div)), Elias LJ

s.156, amended: SI 2015/226 Sch.1

s.176, amended: SI 2015/226 Sch.1

s.188, see *Capital Energy Solutions v
Arnold* [2015] I.C.R. 611 (EAT),
Langstaff J; see *E Ivor Hughes
Educational Foundation v Morris* [2015]
I.R.L.R. 696 (EAT), Lewis J; see *United
States v Nolan* [2015] UKSC 63, [2015] 3
W.L.R. 1105 (SC), Lord Neuberger PSC;
see *University and College Union v
University of Stirling* [2015] UKSC 26
(SC), Lady Hale DPSC

s.189, see *E Ivor Hughes Educational
Foundation v Morris* [2015] I.R.L.R. 696
(EAT), Lewis J; see *University and
College Union v University of Stirling*
[2015] UKSC 26 (SC), Lady Hale DPSC

s.195, see *Capital Energy Solutions v
Arnold* [2015] I.C.R. 611 (EAT),
Langstaff J; see *University and College
Union v University of Stirling* [2015]
UKSC 26 (SC), Lady Hale DPSC

s.200, enabling: SI 2015/649

s.219, see *ISS Mediclean Ltd v GMB*
[2014] EWHC 4208 (QB), [2015]
I.R.L.R. 96 (QBD), Singh J

s.221, see *ISS Mediclean Ltd v GMB*
[2014] EWHC 4208 (QB), [2015]
I.R.L.R. 96 (QBD), Singh J

s.244, see *ISS Mediclean Ltd v GMB*
[2014] EWHC 4208 (QB), [2015]
I.R.L.R. 96 (QBD), Singh J

s.251B, amended: 2015 c.26 s.150

s.296, see *Smith v Carillion (JM) Ltd*
[2015] EWCA Civ 209, [2015] I.R.L.R.
467 (CA (Civ Div)), Elias LJ

Sch.A1, see *British Airline Pilots
Association v Jet2.com Ltd* [2015]
EWHC 1110 (QB), [2015] I.R.L.R. 543
(QBD), Supperstone J

53. Tribunals and Inquiries Act 1992

s.9, enabling: SI 2015/316, SSI 2015/182,
SSI 2015/250

Sch.1 Part I, amended: 2015 c.20 Sch.6
para.22

Sch.3 para.19, repealed: 2015 c.20 Sch.6
para.22

60. Sea Fish (Conservation) Act 1992

s.5, repealed: SI 2015/664 Sch.4 para.97

s.10, repealed: 2015 c.20 Sch.23 para.29

1993

3. Social Security Act 1993

s.2, varied: SI 2015/588 Art.4

s.2, enabling: SI 2015/588

**8. Judicial Pensions and Retirement Act
1993**

Part 1A, added: 2015 c.8 s.78

s.1, enabling: SI 2015/109

s.2, amended: SI 2015/182 Sch.3 para.12

s.2, enabling: SI 2015/533

s.4, amended: SI 2015/182 Sch.3 para.12

s.5, amended: SI 2015/182 Sch.3 para.12

s.8, amended: SI 2015/182 Sch.3 para.12

s.22, amended: 2015 c.8 Sch.5 para.5

s.28, amended: 2015 c.8 Sch.5 para.6

s.28A, amended: 2015 c.8 Sch.5 para.7

s.29, amended: 2015 c.8 Sch.5 para.8

s.30, enabling: SI 2015/109

Sch.1 Part I, amended: SI 2015/109 Art.2

Sch.2 Part I para.3, amended: 2015 c.8

Sch.4 para.2, Sch.4 para.48

Sch.2A para.1, amended: 2015 c.8 s.79

**9. Prisoners and Criminal Proceedings
(Scotland) Act 1993**

Pt I., see *Campbell (David) v HM
Advocate* [2015] HCJAC 28, 2015 S.L.T.
232 (HCJ), Lord Eassie

s.1, amended: 2015 asp 8 s.1, SSI
2015/409 Art.3
s.2, see *Telford (Derek) v HM Advocate*
2015 S.C.L. 136 (HCJ), The Lord Justice
Clerk (Carloway)
s.16, see *Campbell (David) v HM
Advocate* [2015] HCJAC 28, 2015 S.L.T.
232 (HCJ), Lord Eassie; see *McNeely
(James) v HM Advocate* [2015] HCJAC
45, 2015 S.L.T. 763 (HCJ), The Lord
Justice Clerk (Carloway)
s.17, see *McNeely (James) v HM
Advocate* [2015] HCJAC 45, 2015 S.L.T.
763 (HCJ), The Lord Justice Clerk
(Carloway)
s.26C, added: 2015 asp 8 s.2
Sch.5 para.6, repealed: SSI 2015/39
Sch.1 para.2

11. Clean Air Act 1993
s.2, amended: SI 2015/664 Sch.4 para.25
s.20, amended: 2015 c.20 s.15
s.20, enabling: SI 2015/1517
s.21, amended: 2015 c.20 s.15
s.21, enabling: SI 2015/307, SI
2015/1513
s.29, amended: 2015 c.20 s.15
s.30, amended: 2015 c.15 Sch.6 para.52
s.30, repealed: 2015 c.15 Sch.6 para.52
s.30, enabling: SI 2015/1796
s.31, amended: 2015 c.15 Sch.6 para.53
s.31, enabling: SI 2015/1796
s.32, amended: 2015 c.15 Sch.6 para.54
s.49, amended: 2015 c.15 Sch.6 para.55
s.56, amended: 2015 c.15 Sch.6 para.56
s.58, amended: 2015 c.15 Sch.6 para.57

12. Radioactive Substances Act 1993
s.16, amended: 2015 asp 1 Sch.1 para.5
s.17, amended: 2015 asp 1 Sch.1 para.5
s.25, amended: 2015 asp 1 Sch.1 para.5

21. Osteopaths Act 1993
s.1, amended: 2015 c.28 Sch.1 para.3
s.1, enabling: SI 2015/1906
s.6, enabling: SI 2015/693
s.35, enabling: SI 2015/693
s.37, enabling: SI 2015/693
Sch.1 Part I para.1B, enabling: SI
2015/1906
Sch.1 Part II para.34B, added: 2015 c.28
Sch.1 para.3
Sch.1 Part II para.38B, added: 2015 c.28
Sch.1 para.3

**25. Local Government (Overseas Assistance)
Act 1993**
s.1, repealed: 2015 c.20 Sch.13 para.6
**28. Leasehold Reform, Housing and Urban
Development Act 1993**
see *Westbrook Dolphin Square Ltd v
Friends Life Ltd* [2014] EWHC 2433
(Ch), [2015] 1 W.L.R. 1713 (Ch D),
Mann J
Pt I., see *Curzon v Wolstenholme* [2015]
UKUT 173 (LC), [2015] L. & T.R. 26
(UT (Lands)), Martin Rodger QC; see
*Queensbridge Investment Ltd v 61
Queens Gate Freehold Ltd* [2015] L. &
T.R. 8 (UT (Lands)), Martin Rodger QC
s.1, see *Cutter v Pry Ltd* [2015] L. & T.R.
27 (UT (Lands)), Judge Edward Cousins;
see *Merie Bin Mahfouz Co (UK) Ltd v
Barrie House (Freehold) Ltd* [2015] L. &
T.R. 21 (UT (Lands)), Sir Keith
Lindblom P; see *Wiggins v Regent
Wealth Ltd* [2014] EWCA Civ 1078,
[2015] 1 W.L.R. 1188 (CA (Civ Div)),
Moore-Bick LJ
s.2, see *Merie Bin Mahfouz Co (UK) Ltd
v Barrie House (Freehold) Ltd* [2015] L.
& T.R. 21 (UT (Lands)), Sir Keith
Lindblom P; see *Wiggins v Regent
Wealth Ltd* [2014] EWCA Civ 1078,
[2015] 1 W.L.R. 1188 (CA (Civ Div)),
Moore-Bick LJ
s.5, see *Westbrook Dolphin Square Ltd v
Friends Life Ltd* [2014] EWHC 2433
(Ch), [2015] 1 W.L.R. 1713 (Ch D),
Mann J
s.13, see *Curzon v Wolstenholme* [2015]
UKUT 173 (LC), [2015] L. & T.R. 26
(UT (Lands)), Martin Rodger QC; see
*Merie Bin Mahfouz Co (UK) Ltd v Barrie
House (Freehold) Ltd* [2015] L. & T.R.
21 (UT (Lands)), Sir Keith Lindblom P;
see *Natt v Osman* [2014] EWCA Civ
1520, [2015] 1 W.L.R. 1536 (CA (Civ
Div)), Sir Terence Etherton; see
*Queensbridge Investment Ltd v 61
Queens Gate Freehold Ltd* [2015] L. &
T.R. 8 (UT (Lands)), Martin Rodger QC;
see *Westbrook Dolphin Square Ltd v
Friends Life Ltd* [2014] EWHC 2433
(Ch), [2015] 1 W.L.R. 1713 (Ch D),
Mann J; see *Wiggins v Regent Wealth*

Ltd [2014] EWCA Civ 1078, [2015] 1
W.L.R. 1188 (CA (Civ Div)), Moore-
Bick LJ
s.19, see *Wiggins v Regent Wealth Ltd*
[2014] EWCA Civ 1078, [2015] 1
W.L.R. 1188 (CA (Civ Div)), Moore-
Bick LJ
s.21, see *Westbrook Dolphin Square Ltd*
v Friends Life Ltd [2014] EWHC 2433
(Ch), [2015] 1 W.L.R. 1713 (Ch D),
Mann J
s.24, see *Curzon v Wolstenholme* [2015]
UKUT 173 (LC), [2015] L. & T.R. 26
(UT (Lands)), Martin Rodger QC; see
Queensbridge Investment Ltd v 61
Queens Gate Freehold Ltd [2015] L. &
T.R. 8 (UT (Lands)), Martin Rodger QC
s.36, see *Merie Bin Mahfouz Co (UK) Ltd*
v Barrie House (Freehold) Ltd [2015] L.
& T.R. 21 (UT (Lands)), Sir Keith
Lindblom P; see *Queensbridge*
Investment Ltd v 61 Queens Gate
Freehold Ltd [2015] L. & T.R. 8 (UT
(Lands)), Martin Rodger QC
s.38, see *Curzon v Wolstenholme* [2015]
UKUT 173 (LC), [2015] L. & T.R. 26
(UT (Lands)), Martin Rodger QC; see
Merie Bin Mahfouz Co (UK) Ltd v Barrie
House (Freehold) Ltd [2015] L. & T.R.
21 (UT (Lands)), Sir Keith Lindblom P
s.48, see *Rossman v Crown Estate*
Commissioners [2015] UKUT 288 (LC),
[2015] L. & T.R. 31 (UT (Lands)), Sir
Keith Lindblom P
s.57, see *Rossman v Crown Estate*
Commissioners [2015] UKUT 288 (LC),
[2015] L. & T.R. 31 (UT (Lands)), Sir
Keith Lindblom P
s.70, amended: 2015 c.7 Sch.5 para.38
s.91, see *Cutter v Pry Ltd* [2015] L. &
T.R. 27 (UT (Lands)), Judge Edward
Cousins
s.97, see *Wiggins v Regent Wealth Ltd*
[2014] EWCA Civ 1078, [2015] 1
W.L.R. 1188 (CA (Civ Div)), Moore-
Bick LJ
s.101, see *Merie Bin Mahfouz Co (UK)*
Ltd v Barrie House (Freehold) Ltd [2015]
L. & T.R. 21 (UT (Lands)), Sir Keith
Lindblom P

Sch.3 Pt III para.15, see *Wiggins v*
Regent Wealth Ltd [2014] EWCA Civ
1078, [2015] 1 W.L.R. 1188 (CA (Civ
Div)), Moore-Bick LJ
Sch.9 Pt III para.5, see *Merie Bin*
Mahfouz Co (UK) Ltd v Barrie House
(Freehold) Ltd [2015] L. & T.R. 21 (UT
(Lands)), Sir Keith Lindblom P; see
Queensbridge Investment Ltd v 61
Queens Gate Freehold Ltd [2015] L. &
T.R. 8 (UT (Lands)), Martin Rodger QC

31. Road Traffic (Driving Instruction by
Disabled Persons) Act 1993
s.1, repealed: 2015 c.20 Sch.2 para.30
s.2, repealed: 2015 c.20 Sch.2 para.30
Sch.1 para.5, repealed: 2015 c.20 Sch.2
para.30
Sch.1 para.6, repealed: 2015 c.20 Sch.2
para.30
Sch.1 para.7, repealed: 2015 c.20 Sch.2
para.30

34. Finance Act 1993
s.29, amended: SI 2015/664 Sch.2 para.6
s.31, amended: SI 2015/664 Sch.2 para.6

37. Agriculture Act 1993
s.14, enabling: SI 2015/955
s.62, enabling: SI 2015/955
Sch.2 Part II para.42, enabling: SI
2015/955
Sch.2 Part II para.43, enabling: SI
2015/955
Sch.2 Part II para.44, enabling: SI
2015/955

38. Welsh Language Act 1993
s.26, enabling: SI 2015/655, SI 2015/803,
SI 2015/1597

43. Railways Act 1993
s.4, amended: SI 2015/1682 Sch.1 para.1
s.6, amended: SI 2015/1682 Sch.1 para.1
s.7, amended: SI 2015/1682 Sch.1 para.1
s.7, enabling: SI 2015/1877
s.8, amended: SI 2015/1682 Sch.1 para.1
s.9, amended: SI 2015/1682 Sch.1 para.1
s.11, amended: SI 2015/1682 Sch.1
para.1
s.12, amended: SI 2015/1682 Sch.1
para.1
s.13, amended: SI 2015/1682 Sch.1
para.1
s.13A, amended: SI 2015/1682 Sch.1
para.1

s.14, amended: SI 2015/1682 Sch.1
para.1
s.15, amended: SI 2015/1682 Sch.1
para.1
s.15A, amended: SI 2015/1682 Sch.1
para.1
s.15B, amended: SI 2015/1682 Sch.1
para.1
s.15C, amended: SI 2015/1682 Sch.1
para.1
s.16, amended: SI 2015/1682 Sch.1
para.1
s.16A, amended: SI 2015/1682 Sch.1
para.1
s.16B, amended: SI 2015/1682 Sch.1
para.1
s.16B, enabling: SI 2015/1877
s.16C, amended: SI 2015/1682 Sch.1
para.1
s.16D, amended: SI 2015/1682 Sch.1
para.1
s.16E, amended: SI 2015/1682 Sch.1
para.1
s.16F, amended: SI 2015/1682 Sch.1
para.1
s.16G, amended: SI 2015/1682 Sch.1
para.1
s.16H, amended: SI 2015/1682 Sch.1
para.1
s.16I, amended: SI 2015/1682 Sch.1
para.1
s.17, amended: SI 2015/1682 Sch.1
para.1
s.18, amended: SI 2015/1682 Sch.1
para.1
s.19, amended: SI 2015/1682 Sch.1
para.1
s.19A, amended: SI 2015/1682 Sch.1
para.1
s.20, amended: SI 2015/1682 Sch.1
para.1
s.20, enabling: SI 2015/1877
s.21, amended: SI 2015/1682 Sch.1
para.1
s.22, amended: SI 2015/1682 Sch.1
para.1
s.22A, amended: SI 2015/1682 Sch.1
para.1
s.22C, amended: SI 2015/1682 Sch.1
para.1

s.24, amended: SI 2015/1682 Sch.1
para.1
s.24, enabling: SI 2015/237, SI 2015/239,
SI 2015/1877
s.24A, added: 2015 c.20 Sch.8 para.8
s.26, amended: SI 2015/1682 Sch.1
para.1
s.30, amended: 2015 c.20 Sch.8 para.10
s.55, amended: SI 2015/1682 Sch.1
para.1
s.56, amended: SI 2015/1682 Sch.1
para.1
s.57A, amended: SI 2015/1682 Sch.1
para.1
s.57B, amended: SI 2015/1682 Sch.1
para.1
s.57C, amended: SI 2015/1682 Sch.1
para.1
s.67, amended: SI 2015/1682 Sch.1
para.1
s.68, amended: SI 2015/1682 Sch.1
para.1
s.69, amended: SI 2015/1682 Sch.1
para.1
s.71, amended: SI 2015/1682 Sch.1
para.1
s.72, amended: SI 2015/1682 Sch.1
para.1
s.73, amended: SI 2015/1682 Sch.1
para.1
s.73A, amended: SI 2015/1682 Sch.1
para.1
s.74, amended: SI 2015/1682 Sch.1
para.1
s.76, amended: SI 2015/1682 Sch.1
para.1
s.80, amended: SI 2015/1682 Sch.1
para.1
s.95, amended: SI 2015/1682 Sch.1
para.1
s.118, amended: SI 2015/1682 Sch.1
para.1
s.143, enabling: SI 2015/1877
s.145, amended: SI 2015/786 Reg.7, SI
2015/1682 Sch.1 para.1
s.145, repealed: 2015 c.20 Sch.6 para.22
s.151, enabling: SI 2015/1877
Sch.4 para.2, amended: SI 2015/1682
Sch.1 para.1
Sch.4 para.3, amended: SI 2015/1682
Sch.1 para.1

Sch.4 para.4, amended: SI 2015/1682
Sch.1 para.1
Sch.4 para.5, amended: SI 2015/1682
Sch.1 para.1
Sch.4 para.6, amended: SI 2015/1682
Sch.1 para.1
Sch.4A para.1, amended: SI 2015/1682
Sch.1 para.1
Sch.4A para.1A, amended: SI 2015/1682
Sch.1 para.1
Sch.4A para.1B, amended: SI 2015/1682
Sch.1 para.1
Sch.4A para.1C, amended: SI 2015/1682
Sch.1 para.1
Sch.4A para.1D, amended: SI 2015/1682
Sch.1 para.1
Sch.4A para.1E, amended: SI 2015/1682
Sch.1 para.1
Sch.4A para.1F, amended: SI 2015/1682
Sch.1 para.1
Sch.4A para.1G, amended: SI 2015/1682
Sch.1 para.1
Sch.4A para.1H, amended: SI 2015/1682
Sch.1 para.1
Sch.4A para.4, amended: SI 2015/1682
Sch.1 para.1
Sch.4A para.5, amended: SI 2015/1682
Sch.1 para.1
Sch.4A para.6, amended: SI 2015/1682
Sch.1 para.1
Sch.4A para.7, amended: SI 2015/1682
Sch.1 para.1
Sch.4A para.8, amended: SI 2015/1682
Sch.1 para.1
Sch.4A para.9, amended: SI 2015/1682
Sch.1 para.1
Sch.4A para.11, amended: SI 2015/1682
Sch.1 para.1
Sch.4A para.12, amended: SI 2015/1682
Sch.1 para.1
Sch.4A para.13, amended: SI 2015/1682
Sch.1 para.1
Sch.4A para.14, amended: SI 2015/1682
Sch.1 para.1
Sch.4A para.15, amended: SI 2015/1682
Sch.1 para.1
Sch.4A para.16, amended: SI 2015/1682
Sch.1 para.1
Sch.6 Part I para.7, amended: SI
2015/1682 Sch.1 para.1

Sch.6 Part I para.8, amended: SI
2015/1682 Sch.1 para.1
Sch.6 Part I para.9, amended: SI
2015/1682 Sch.1 para.1
Sch.6 Part I para.10, amended: SI
2015/1682 Sch.1 para.1

44. Crofters (Scotland) Act 1993
s.20, see *Lands Improvement Holdings
Landmatch Sarl v Cole* 2015 S.L.T.
(Land Ct) 137 (Land Ct), Lord
Minginish; see *Sorbie v Kennedy* 2015
S.L.T. (Land Ct) 17 (Land Ct), Lord
McGhie
s.23, see *MacGillivray v Crofting
Commission* 2015 S.L.T. (Land Ct) 163
(Land Ct), Lord Minginish
s.24, see *MacGillivray v Crofting
Commission* 2015 S.L.T. (Land Ct) 163
(Land Ct), Lord Minginish
s.25, see *MacGillivray v Crofting
Commission* 2015 S.L.T. (Land Ct) 163
(Land Ct), Lord Minginish
s.42, enabling: SSI 2015/105
s.46, enabling: SSI 2015/105
s.52A, see *MacGillivray v Crofting
Commission* 2015 S.L.T. (Land Ct) 163
(Land Ct), Lord Minginish
s.53, see *MacLachlan v Bruce* 2015
S.L.T. (Land Ct) 23 (Land Ct), D J
Houston
s.53A, see *Macnab v Castle Leod
Maintenance Fund Trustees* 2015 S.L.T.
(Land Ct) 53 (Land Ct), DJ Houston
s.61, see *MacGillivray v Crofting
Commission* 2015 S.L.T. (Land Ct) 163
(Land Ct), Lord Minginish
45. Scottish Land Court Act 1993
s.1, amended: SSI 2015/383 Art.13
46. Health Service Commissioners Act 1993
s.2, enabling: SI 2015/822
s.4, see *Miller v Parliamentary and
Health Service Ombudsman* [2015]
EWHC 2981 (Admin), (2015) 18 C.C.L.
Rep. 697 (QBD (Admin)), Lewis J
s.9, see *Miller v Parliamentary and
Health Service Ombudsman* [2015]
EWHC 2981 (Admin), (2015) 18 C.C.L.
Rep. 697 (QBD (Admin)), Lewis J
s.14, amended: 2015 c.29 s.1
48. Pension Schemes Act 1993

Part IV c.I, varied: SI 2015/370 Reg.7, SI
2015/372 Reg.7, SI 2015/390 Reg.7, SI
2015/432 Reg.7, SI 2015/436 Reg.7, SI
2015/848 Reg.7, SSI 2015/145 Reg.7,
SSI 2015/146 Reg.7
Part IV c.II, varied: SI 2015/370 Reg.8,
SI 2015/372 Reg.8, SI 2015/390 Reg.8,
SI 2015/432 Reg.8, SI 2015/436 Reg.8,
SI 2015/848 Reg.8, SSI 2015/145 Reg.8
Part IV c.III, varied: SI 2015/370 Reg.9,
Reg.10, SI 2015/372 Reg.9, Reg.10, SI
2015/390 Reg.9, Reg.10, SI 2015/432
Reg.9, Reg.10, SI 2015/436 Reg.9,
Reg.10, SI 2015/848 Reg.9, Reg.10, SSI
2015/145 Reg.9, Reg.10
Part IV c.IV, substituted: 2015 c.8 Sch.4
para.4
Part IV c.IV, varied: SI 2015/370 Reg.11,
SI 2015/372 Reg.11, SI 2015/390
Reg.11, SI 2015/432 Reg.11, SI
2015/436 Reg.11, SSI 2015/146 Reg.11
Part IV c.V, varied: SI 2015/370 Reg.13,
SI 2015/372 Reg.13, SI 2015/390
Reg.13, SI 2015/432 Reg.13, SI
2015/436 Reg.13
s.7, enabling: SI 2015/1452, SI
2015/1677
s.9, enabling: SI 2015/1452, SI
2015/1677
s.11, enabling: SI 2015/1452, SI
2015/1677
s.12A, enabling: SI 2015/1452, SI
2015/1677
s.12C, enabling: SI 2015/493
s.12D, enabling: SI 2015/1452, SI
2015/1677
s.15, amended: SI 2015/457 Art.5
s.15A, varied: SI 2015/182 Sch.3 para.4,
SI 2015/319 Reg.6, SI 2015/370 Reg.6,
SI 2015/372 Reg.6, SI 2015/390 Reg.6,
SI 2015/432 Reg.6, SI 2015/436 Reg.6,
SI 2015/848 Reg.6, SSI 2015/117 Reg.6,
SSI 2015/118 Reg.6, SSI 2015/145
Reg.6, SSI 2015/146 Reg.6
s.16, enabling: SI 2015/1452, SI
2015/1677
s.17, enabling: SI 2015/1452, SI
2015/1677
s.20, enabling: SI 2015/1452, SI
2015/1677

s.21, enabling: SI 2015/1452, SI
2015/1677
s.24B, enabling: SI 2015/1452
s.24C, enabling: SI 2015/1452, SI
2015/1677
s.24F, amended: 2015 c.8 Sch.4 para.5
s.25, enabling: SI 2015/1452, SI
2015/1677
s.34, enabling: SI 2015/1452, SI
2015/1677
s.36, enabling: SI 2015/1452, SI
2015/1677
s.37, enabling: SI 2015/1452, SI
2015/1677
s.37A, enabling: SI 2015/1452, SI
2015/1677
s.50, enabling: SI 2015/1452, SI
2015/1677
s.51, enabling: SI 2015/1452, SI
2015/1677
s.53, enabling: SI 2015/1452, SI
2015/1677
s.55, enabling: SI 2015/1452, SI
2015/1677
s.56, amended: 2015 c.8 Sch.4 para.6
s.56, enabling: SI 2015/1452, SI
2015/1677
s.57, enabling: SI 2015/1452, SI
2015/1677
s.61, enabling: SI 2015/1452, SI
2015/1677
s.68, amended: 2015 c.2 Sch.11 para.12
s.70, amended: 2015 c.8 s.39
s.70, varied: SI 2015/182 Sch.3 para.5, SI
2015/319 Reg.7, SSI 2015/117 Reg.7,
SSI 2015/118 Reg.7
s.71, amended: 2015 c.8 s.39
s.71, varied: SI 2015/182 Sch.3 para.5, SI
2015/319 Reg.7, SSI 2015/117 Reg.7,
SSI 2015/118 Reg.7, Reg.16
s.71, enabling: SI 2015/493
s.72, varied: SI 2015/182 Sch.3 para.5, SI
2015/319 Reg.7, SSI 2015/117 Reg.7,
SSI 2015/118 Reg.7, Reg.16
s.73, amended: 2015 c.8 Sch.4 para.7
s.74, amended: 2015 c.8 s.39
s.74, varied: SI 2015/182 Sch.3 para.5, SI
2015/319 Reg.7, SSI 2015/117 Reg.7,
SSI 2015/118 Reg.7, Reg.16

s.75, varied: SI 2015/182 Sch.3 para.5, SI
2015/319 Reg.7, SSI 2015/117 Reg.7,
SSI 2015/118 Reg.7, Reg.16
s.76, varied: SI 2015/182 Sch.3 para.5, SI
2015/319 Reg.7, SSI 2015/117 Reg.7,
SSI 2015/118 Reg.7
s.82A, added: 2015 c.8 Sch.1 para.2
s.83, amended: 2015 c.8 Sch.1 para.3,
Sch.2 para.2
s.83, varied: SI 2015/182 Sch.3 para.6, SI
2015/319 Reg.8, SSI 2015/117 Reg.8,
SSI 2015/118 Reg.8, SSI 2015/146 Reg.8
s.84, substituted: 2015 c.8 Sch.1 para.4
s.85A, added: 2015 c.8 Sch.1 para.5
s.86A, added: 2015 c.8 Sch.1 para.6
s.87, varied: SI 2015/182 Sch.3 para.7,
Sch.3 para.8, SI 2015/319 Reg.9, Reg.10,
SSI 2015/117 Reg.9, Reg.10, SSI
2015/118 Reg.9, Reg.10, SSI 2015/146
Reg.9, Reg.10
s.93, varied: SI 2015/182 Sch.3 para.9, SI
2015/319 Reg.11
s.93, substituted: 2015 c.8 Sch.4 para.8
s.93, varied: SSI 2015/117 Reg.11, SSI
2015/118 Reg.11
s.93, enabling: SI 2015/498
s.93A, enabling: SI 2015/498
s.95, amended: 2015 c.8 s.68, Sch.4
para.9
s.95, repealed: 2015 c.8 Sch.4 para.9
s.95, enabling: SI 2015/498, SI
2015/1614
s.96, amended: 2015 c.8 s.68, Sch.4
para.10
s.97, varied: SI 2015/182 Sch.3 para.9, SI
2015/319 Reg.11
s.97, amended: 2015 c.8 s.69, Sch.4
para.11
s.97, repealed: 2015 c.8 Sch.4 para.11
s.97, varied: SSI 2015/117 Reg.11, SSI
2015/118 Reg.11
s.97, enabling: SI 2015/498
s.97A, added: 2015 c.8 s.69
s.97C, added: 2015 c.8 s.69
s.97C, enabling: SI 2015/892
s.98, varied: SI 2015/182 Sch.3 para.9, SI
2015/319 Reg.11
s.98, substituted: 2015 c.8 Sch.4 para.12
s.98, varied: SSI 2015/117 Reg.11, SSI
2015/118 Reg.11

s.99, amended: 2015 c.8 s.50, Sch.4
para.13
s.99, repealed: 2015 c.8 Sch.4 para.13
s.99, enabling: SI 2015/498
s.100, amended: 2015 c.8 s.68
s.100A, added: 2015 c.8 Sch.4 para.14
s.101AA, varied: SI 2015/182 Sch.3
para.11
s.101AA, varied: SI 2015/182 Sch.3
para.11, SSI 2015/118 Reg.13, SSI
2015/145 Reg.13
s.101AB, varied: SI 2015/182 Sch.3
para.11
s.101AB, varied: SSI 2015/118 Reg.13,
SSI 2015/145 Reg.13
s.101AC, varied: SI 2015/182 Sch.3
para.11
s.101AC, varied: SSI 2015/118 Reg.13
s.101AI, varied: SI 2015/182 Sch.3
para.11
s.101AI, amended: 2015 c.8 s.60
s.101AI, varied: SSI 2015/118 Reg.13
s.101B, amended: 2015 c.8 s.82
s.101C, amended: 2015 c.8 s.82
s.101F, amended: 2015 c.8 Sch.4 para.15
s.101F, enabling: SI 2015/498
s.101G, substituted: 2015 c.8 Sch.4
para.16
s.101H, amended: 2015 c.8 Sch.4 para.17
s.101J, amended: 2015 c.8 s.50, Sch.4
para.18
s.101M, amended: 2015 c.8 Sch.4
para.19
s.101NA, added: 2015 c.8 Sch.4 para.20
s.101P, amended: 2015 c.8 Sch.4 para.21
s.101P, repealed: 2015 c.8 Sch.4 para.21
s.101Q, repealed: 2015 c.8 Sch.4 para.22
s.109, varied: SI 2015/470 Art.2
s.109, enabling: SI 2015/470
s.113, amended: 2015 c.8 s.38, Sch.2
para.3
s.113, repealed: 2015 c.8 s.38
s.113, enabling: SI 2015/482, SI
2015/498, SI 2015/879
s.124, amended: 2015 c.8 Sch.2 para.4
s.129, amended: 2015 c.8 Sch.4 para.23
s.130, amended: 2015 c.8 Sch.4 para.24
s.153, amended: 2015 c.8 Sch.4 para.25
s.155, enabling: SI 2015/1452, SI
2015/1677

s.156, enabling: SI 2015/1452, SI
2015/1677
s.179, amended: 2015 c.8 Sch.4 para.26
s.181, amended: 2015 c.8 Sch.2 para.5,
Sch.4 para.27
s.181, enabling: SI 2015/482, SI
2015/493, SI 2015/498, SI 2015/879, SI
2015/1452, SI 2015/1677
s.182, amended: 2015 c.8 s.70
s.182, enabling: SI 2015/482, SI
2015/493, SI 2015/498, SI 2015/879, SI
2015/892, SI 2015/1452, SI 2015/1614,
SI 2015/1677
s.183, enabling: SI 2015/482, SI
2015/493, SI 2015/498, SI 2015/892, SI
2015/1452, SI 2015/1677
s.185, amended: 2015 c.8 s.70
s.186, amended: 2015 c.8 s.70, Sch.1
para.7
Sch.2 Part I, enabling: SI 2015/1452, SI
2015/1677
Sch.3 paraA.1, added: 2015 c.8 Sch.1
para.8
Sch.3 para.2, enabling: SI 2015/1916
Sch.3 para.3A, repealed: 2015 c.8 Sch.1
para.9
Sch.3 para.4, repealed: 2015 c.8 Sch.1
para.9
Sch.3 para.5, amended: 2015 c.8 Sch.1
para.10

**49. Pension Schemes (Northern Ireland) Act
1993**

Part IV c.IV, substituted: 2015 c.8 Sch.4
para.50
s.20F, amended: 2015 c.8 Sch.4 para.51
s.51, enabling: SI 2015/1452, SI
2015/1677
s.52, amended: 2015 c.8 Sch.4 para.52
s.52, enabling: SI 2015/1452, SI
2015/1677
s.53, enabling: SI 2015/1452, SI
2015/1677
s.57, enabling: SI 2015/1452, SI
2015/1677
s.69, amended: 2015 c.8 Sch.4 para.53
s.89, substituted: 2015 c.8 Sch.4 para.54
s.91, amended: 2015 c.8 s.71, Sch.4
para.55
s.91, repealed: 2015 c.8 Sch.4 para.55
s.92, amended: 2015 c.8 s.71, Sch.4
para.56

s.93, amended: 2015 c.8 s.72, Sch.4
para.57
s.93, repealed: 2015 c.8 Sch.4 para.57
s.93A, added: 2015 c.8 s.72
s.93B, added: 2015 c.8 s.72
s.94, substituted: 2015 c.8 Sch.4 para.58
s.95, amended: 2015 c.8 s.53, Sch.4
para.59
s.95, repealed: 2015 c.8 Sch.4 para.59
s.96, amended: 2015 c.8 s.71
s.96A, added: 2015 c.8 Sch.4 para.60
s.97AI, amended: 2015 c.8 s.66
s.97F, amended: 2015 c.8 Sch.4 para.61
s.97G, substituted: 2015 c.8 Sch.4
para.62
s.97H, amended: 2015 c.8 Sch.4 para.63
s.97J, amended: 2015 c.8 s.53, Sch.4
para.64
s.97M, amended: 2015 c.8 Sch.4 para.65
s.97NA, added: 2015 c.8 Sch.4 para.66
s.97P, amended: 2015 c.8 Sch.4 para.67
s.97P, repealed: 2015 c.8 Sch.4 para.67
s.97Q, repealed: 2015 c.8 Sch.4 para.68
s.125, amended: 2015 c.8 Sch.4 para.69
s.126, amended: 2015 c.8 Sch.4 para.70
s.149, amended: 2015 c.8 Sch.4 para.71
s.174, amended: 2015 c.8 Sch.4 para.72
s.176, amended: 2015 c.8 s.73, Sch.4
para.73
s.176, enabling: SI 2015/1452, SI
2015/1677
s.177, enabling: SI 2015/1452, SI
2015/1677
s.178, enabling: SI 2015/1452, SI
2015/1677
s.181, amended: 2015 c.8 s.73
Sch.1 Part I para.1, enabling: SI
2015/1452, SI 2015/1677
Sch.1 Part I para.2, enabling: SI
2015/1452, SI 2015/1677
Sch.1 Part I para.5, enabling: SI
2015/1452, SI 2015/1677

1994

9. Finance Act 1994
s.12, see *TDG (UK) Ltd v Revenue and
Customs Commissioners* [2015] UKUT
167 (TCC), [2015] S.T.C. 1954 (UT
(Tax)), Rose J

s.13A, amended: 2015 c.11 s.54
s.16, see *CC&C Ltd v Revenue and Customs Commissioners* [2014] EWCA Civ 1653, [2015] 1 W.L.R. 4043 (CA (Civ Div)), Arden LJ
s.31, amended: 2015 c.11 s.57
s.41, amended: SI 2015/664 Sch.2 para.7
s.51, amended: 2015 c.33 s.47
Sch.5 para.3, amended: 2015 c.11 s.54
Sch.6 para.1, enabling: SI 2015/3, SI 2015/942
Sch.7 Part IV para.10, amended: SI 2015/664 Sch.2 para.7
Sch.7A Part I para.3, amended: SI 2015/2006 Sch.12 Part 8
Sch.7A Part I para.3, repealed: SI 2015/2006 Sch.12 Part 8

13. Intelligence Services Act 1994
s.1, see *Liberty v Government Communications Headquarters* [2015] 3 All E.R. 142 (IPT), Burton J

15. Antarctic Act 1994
s.8, enabling: SI 2015/126
s.32, enabling: SI 2015/126
s.34, enabling: SI 2015/823, SI 2015/1531

17. Chiropractors Act 1994
s.1, amended: 2015 c.28 Sch.1 para.4
s.6, enabling: SI 2015/1511
s.35, enabling: SI 2015/1511
s.37, enabling: SI 2015/1511
Sch.1 Part II para.34B, added: 2015 c.28 Sch.1 para.4
Sch.1 Part II para.38B, added: 2015 c.28 Sch.1 para.4

19. Local Government (Wales) Act 1994
Sch.17 Part II para.11, repealed: 2015 c.7 Sch.5 para.39

20. Sunday Trading Act 1994
Sch.1 para.7, amended: SI 2015/664 Sch.4 para.26
Sch.2 Part I para.3, repealed: 2015 c.15 Sch.6 para.58
Sch.2 Part I para.4A, added: 2015 c.15 Sch.6 para.58

21. Coal Industry Act 1994
s.54, enabling: SI 2015/596

22. Vehicle Excise and Registration Act 1994
s.22, enabling: SI 2015/403, SI 2015/1657
s.22A, enabling: SI 2015/1657

s.26, enabling: SI 2015/193
s.27, enabling: SI 2015/193
s.55, amended: 2015 c.2 Sch.11 para.13
s.57, enabling: SI 2015/193, SI 2015/403, SI 2015/1657
s.59, enabling: SI 2015/403, SI 2015/1657
Sch.1 Part IA, amended: 2015 c.33 s.46
Sch.1 Part IAA, added: 2015 c.33 s.46
Sch.1 Part IA para.1A, amended: 2015 c.33 s.46
Sch.1 Part IA para.1B, amended: 2015 c.11 s.58
Sch.1 Part II para.2, amended: 2015 c.11 s.58
Sch.2 para.1A, amended: 2015 c.11 s.59
Sch.2 para.20G, substituted: 2015 c.33 s.46
Sch.2 para.25, amended: 2015 c.33 s.46

23. Value Added Tax Act 1994
see *Investment Trust Companies (In Liquidation) v Revenue and Customs Commissioners* [2015] EWCA Civ 82, [2015] S.T.C. 1280 (CA (Civ Div)), Moore-Bick LJ; see *Westinsure Group Ltd v Revenue and Customs Commissioners* [2015] S.T.C. 238 (UT (Tax)), Nugee J
para.3A, see *Brambletye School Trust Ltd v Customs and Excise Commissioners* [2003] B.V.C. 2015 (V&DTr (London)), Nuala Brice
s.24, see *Airtours Holiday Transport Ltd (formerly My Travel Group) v Revenue and Customs Commissioners* [2014] EWCA Civ 1033, [2015] S.T.C. 61 (CA (Civ Div)), Moore-Bick LJ
s.25, enabling: SI 2015/1978
s.26, enabling: SI 2015/1978
s.29A, see *Colaingrove Ltd v Revenue and Customs Commissioners* [2015] UKUT 80 (TCC), [2015] S.T.C. 1725 (UT (Tax)), Hildyard J
s.30, enabling: SI 2015/1949
s.31, see *R. (on the application of Whistl UK Ltd (formerly TNT Post UK Ltd)) v Revenue and Customs Commissioners* [2014] EWHC 3480 (Admin), [2015] S.T.C. 1077 (QBD (Admin)), Kenneth Parker J

s.33, see *Currie v Revenue and Customs Commissioners* [2015] S.F.T.D. 51 (FTT (Tax)), Judge Anne Redston
s.33, enabling: SI 2015/449
s.33C, added: 2015 c.11 s.66
s.33D, varied: 2015 c.11 s.66
s.35, see *Barkas v Revenue and Customs Commissioners* [2015] S.T.C. 1341 (UT (Tax)), Judge Greg Sinfield; see *Revenue and Customs Commissioners v Patel* [2015] S.T.C. 148 (UT (Tax)), Judge Colin Bishopp
s.37, enabling: SI 2015/2015
s.41, amended: 2015 c.11 s.67
s.43, see *Taylor Clark Leisure Plc v Revenue and Customs Commissioners* [2015] S.T.C. 223 (UT (Tax)), Lord Doherty
s.43B, see *Copthorn Holdings Ltd v Revenue and Customs Commissioners* [2015] UKFTT 405 (TC) (FTT (Tax)), Judge Howard M Nowlan
s.72, amended: SI 2015/664 Sch.2 para.8
s.73, see *Hope v Ireland* [2014] EWHC 3854 (Ch), [2015] B.P.I.R. 344 (Ch D), John Male QC; see *Romasave (Property Services) Ltd v Revenue and Customs Commissioners* [2015] UKUT 254 (TCC) (UT (Tax)), Judge Roger Berner; see *Royal College of Paediatricians and Child Health v Revenue and Customs Commissioners* [2015] UKUT 38 (TCC), [2015] S.T.C. 1243 (UT (Tax)), Birss J
s.78, see *Littlewoods Retail Ltd v Revenue and Customs Commissioners* [2015] EWCA Civ 515, [2015] 3 W.L.R. 1748 (CA (Civ Div)), Arden LJ
s.78A, see *Southern Cross Employment Agency Ltd v Revenue and Customs Commissioners* [2015] UKUT 122 (TCC), [2015] S.T.C. 1933 (UT (Tax)), Newey J
s.79, see *Global Foods Ltd v Revenue and Customs Commissioners* [2015] S.F.T.D. 327 (FTT (Tax)), Judge Nicholas Aleksander
s.79, amended: 2015 c.11 s.66
s.80, see *Investment Trust Companies (In Liquidation) v Revenue and Customs Commissioners* [2015] EWCA Civ 82, [2015] S.T.C. 1280 (CA (Civ Div)),

Moore-Bick LJ; see *Isle of Wight Council v Revenue and Customs Commissioners* [2015] S.T.C. 460 (UT (Tax)), Proudman J; see *Littlewoods Retail Ltd v Revenue and Customs Commissioners* [2015] EWCA Civ 515, [2015] 3 W.L.R. 1748 (CA (Civ Div)), Arden LJ; see *Open University v Revenue and Customs Commissioners* [2015] UKUT 263 (TCC), [2015] S.T.C. 2324 (UT (Tax)), Henderson J; see *R. (on the application of Premier Foods (Holdings) Ltd) v Revenue and Customs Commissioners* [2015] EWHC 1483 (Admin), [2015] S.T.C. 2384 (QBD (Admin)), Supperstone J; see *Southern Cross Employment Agency Ltd v Revenue and Customs Commissioners* [2015] UKUT 122 (TCC), [2015] S.T.C. 1933 (UT (Tax)), Newey J; see *Taylor Clark Leisure Plc v Revenue and Customs Commissioners* [2015] CSIH 40, 2015 S.L.T. 412 (IH (Ex Div)), Lady Clark of Calton; see *Taylor Clark Leisure Plc v Revenue and Customs Commissioners* [2015] S.T.C. 223 (UT (Tax)), Lord Doherty
s.81, see *Investment Trust Companies (In Liquidation) v Revenue and Customs Commissioners* [2015] EWCA Civ 82, [2015] S.T.C. 1280 (CA (Civ Div)), Moore-Bick LJ
s.81, amended: 2015 c.20 Sch.6 para.2
s.83G, see *Romasave (Property Services) Ltd v Revenue and Customs Commissioners* [2015] UKUT 254 (TCC) (UT (Tax)), Judge Roger Berner
s.84, see *ToTel Ltd v Revenue and Customs Commissioners* [2015] S.T.C. 610 (UT (Tax)), Nugee J
s.85, see *Southern Cross Employment Agency Ltd v Revenue and Customs Commissioners* [2015] UKUT 122 (TCC), [2015] S.T.C. 1933 (UT (Tax)), Newey J
s.90, amended: 2015 c.11 s.66
s.98, see *Romasave (Property Services) Ltd v Revenue and Customs Commissioners* [2015] UKUT 254 (TCC) (UT (Tax)), Judge Roger Berner

Sch.1 para.1, amended: SI 2015/750 Art.3

Sch.1 para.4, amended: SI 2015/750 Art.3

Sch.1 para.15, enabling: SI 2015/750

Sch.3 para.1, amended: SI 2015/750 Art.4

Sch.3 para.2, amended: SI 2015/750 Art.4

Sch.3 para.9, enabling: SI 2015/750

Sch.4 para.1, see *British Credit Trust Ltd v Revenue and Customs Commissioners* [2015] S.F.T.D. 195 (FTT (Tax)), Judge Guy Brannan

Sch.4 para.5, see *French Connection Ltd v Revenue and Customs Commissioners* [2015] UKFTT 173 (TC), [2015] S.F.T.D. 587 (FTT (Tax)), Judge John Clark

Sch.4 para.6, see *French Connection Ltd v Revenue and Customs Commissioners* [2015] UKFTT 173 (TC), [2015] S.F.T.D. 587 (FTT (Tax)), Judge John Clark; see *Global Foods Ltd v Revenue and Customs Commissioners* [2015] S.F.T.D. 327 (FTT (Tax)), Judge Nicholas Aleksander

Sch.6 para.6, see *Revenue and Customs Commissioners v General Motors (UK) Ltd* [2015] UKUT 605 (TCC), [2015] B.V.C. 536 (UT (Tax)), Henderson J

Sch.7A Part II, repealed: SI 2015/2006 Sch.12 Part 8

Sch.7A Pt II Group 1, see *Colaingrove Ltd v Revenue and Customs Commissioners* [2015] UKUT 80 (TCC), [2015] S.T.C. 1725 (UT (Tax)), Hildyard J

Sch.7A Pt II Group 6, see *Astral Construction Ltd v Revenue and Customs Commissioners* [2015] UKUT 21 (TCC), [2015] S.T.C. 1033 (UT (Tax)), Judge Greg Sinfield

Sch.8, see *Caithness Rugby Football Club v Revenue and Customs Commissioners* [2015] UKFTT 378 (TC), [2015] S.F.T.D. 1078 (FTT (Tax)), Judge Christopher Staker; see *Colaingrove Ltd v Revenue and Customs Commissioners* [2015] UKUT 2 (TCC), [2015] S.T.C. 1013 (UT (Tax)), Warren J

Sch.8 Part II, amended: SI 2015/1949 Art.2, SI 2015/2006 Sch.12 Part 8

Sch.8 Part II, repealed: SI 2015/2006 Sch.12 Part 8

Sch.8 Group 5, see *Shields v Revenue and Customs Commissioners* [2015] S.T.C. 643 (UT (Tax)), Judge Greg Sinfield

Sch.8 Pt II Group 5, see *Astral Construction Ltd v Revenue and Customs Commissioners* [2015] UKUT 21 (TCC), [2015] S.T.C. 1033 (UT (Tax)), Judge Greg Sinfield; see *Barkas v Revenue and Customs Commissioners* [2015] S.T.C. 1341 (UT (Tax)), Judge Greg Sinfield; see *Longridge on the Thames v Revenue and Customs Commissioners* [2015] S.T.C. 672 (UT (Tax)), Rose J; see *Shields v Revenue and Customs Commissioners* [2015] S.T.C. 643 (UT (Tax)), Judge Greg Sinfield

Sch.9, see *Massey (t/a Hilden Park Partnership) v Revenue and Customs Commissioners* [2015] UKUT 405 (TCC) (UT (Tax)), Rose J; see *R. (on the application of Whistl UK Ltd (formerly TNT Post UK Ltd)) v Revenue and Customs Commissioners* [2014] EWHC 3480 (Admin), [2015] S.T.C. 1077 (QBD (Admin)), Kenneth Parker J; see *St Andrew's College Bradfield v Revenue and Customs Commissioners* [2015] UKFTT 34 (TC), [2015] S.F.T.D. 349 (FTT (Tax)), Judge John Walters QC

Sch.9 Part II, amended: 2015 c.11 s.66, 2015 c.20 Sch.14 para.41

Sch.9 Pt II Group 4, see *Revenue and Customs Commissioners v Rank Group Plc* [2015] UKSC 48, [2015] 1 W.L.R. 3472 (SC), Lord Neuberger PSC

Sch.9 Pt II Group 5, see *British Credit Trust Ltd v Revenue and Customs Commissioners* [2015] S.F.T.D. 195 (FTT (Tax)), Judge Guy Brannan; see *Wiltonpark Ltd v Revenue and Customs Commissioners* [2015] UKUT 343 (TCC) (UT (Tax)), Rose J

Sch.10A para.4, see *Associated Newspapers Ltd v Revenue and Customs Commissioners* [2015] UKUT 641

(TCC), [2015] B.V.C. 538 (UT (Tax)),
David Richards LJ

26. Trade Marks Act 1994

s.3, see *Canary Wharf Group Plc v
Comptroller General of Patents, Designs
and Trade Marks* [2015] EWHC 1588
(Ch), [2015] F.S.R. 34 (Ch D), Iain
Purvis QC; see *Dalsouple Societe
Saumuroise du Caoutchouc v Dalsouple
Direct Ltd* [2014] EWHC 3963 (Ch),
[2015] Bus. L.R. 464 (Ch D), Arnold J;
see *Total Ltd v YouView TV Ltd* [2014]
EWHC 1963 (Ch), [2015] F.S.R. 7 (Ch
D), Sales J

s.5, see *Dalsouple Societe Saumuroise du
Caoutchouc v Dalsouple Direct Ltd*
[2014] EWHC 3963 (Ch), [2015] Bus.
L.R. 464 (Ch D), Arnold J; see *R2 Pets
Ltd v Societe des Produits Nestle SA*
[2015] R.P.C. 18 (App Person), Ruth
Annand

s.10, see *IPC Media Ltd v Media 10 Ltd*
[2014] EWCA Civ 1439, [2015] E.C.C. 7
(CA (Civ Div)), Lord Dyson MR

s.56, see *Starbucks (HK) Ltd v British
Sky Broadcasting Group Plc* [2015]
UKSC 31, [2015] 1 W.L.R. 2628 (SC),
Lord Neuberger PSC

s.93, amended: 2015 c.15 Sch.6 para.59

s.93, repealed: 2015 c.15 Sch.6 para.59

**33. Criminal Justice and Public Order Act
1994**

s.35, see *Bates v Crown Prosecution
Service* [2015] EWHC 2346 (Admin),
(2015) 179 J.P. 540 (DC), Davis LJ

s.51, amended: 2015 c.2 Sch.11 para.14

s.60, see *R. (on the application of
Roberts) v Commissioner of Police of the
Metropolis* [2015] UKSC 79 (SC), Lady
Hale DPSC

s.103, repealed: SSI 2015/39 Sch.1 para.3

s.110, amended: SSI 2015/39 Sch.1
para.3

s.116, repealed: SSI 2015/39 Sch.1 para.3

Sch.9 para.6, repealed: 2015 c.20 s.80

Sch.10 para.64, repealed: SSI 2015/39
Sch.1 para.3

35. Sale and Supply of Goods Act 1994

Sch.2 para.5, repealed: 2015 c.15 Sch.1
para.55

37. Drug Trafficking Act 1994

s.60, amended: 2015 c.2 Sch.11 para.15

**39. Local Government etc (Scotland) Act
1994**

s.153, enabling: SSI 2015/49

Sch.13 para.6, repealed: 2015 asp 6 Sch.5

Sch.13 para.12, repealed: 2015 asp 6
Sch.5

Sch.13 para.14, repealed: 2015 c.20
Sch.23 para.34

Sch.13 para.35, repealed: 2015 asp 6
Sch.5

Sch.13 para.162, repealed: SSI 2015/39
Sch.1 para.4

**40. Deregulation and Contracting Out Act
1994**

s.37, amended: SI 2015/1682 Sch.1
para.4

s.79A, repealed: 2015 c.20 Sch.13 para.6

1995

4. Finance Act 1995

s.4, see *Revenue and Customs
Commissioners v Asiana Ltd* [2015]
S.T.C. 577 (UT (Tax)), Warren J

s.4, amended: SI 2015/2050 Reg.2

s.4, repealed: SI 2015/2050 Reg.2

**6. Civil Evidence (Family Mediation)
(Scotland) Act 1995**

see *M v M* [2015] CSOH 130, 2015
S.L.T. 682 (OH), Lord Stewart

s.1, see *M v M* [2015] CSOH 130, 2015
S.L.T. 682 (OH), Lord Stewart

**7. Requirements of Writing (Scotland) Act
1995**

s.1, see *Gyle Shopping Centre General
Partners Ltd v Marks & Spencer Plc*
2015 S.C.L.R. 171 (OH), Lord Tyre

**12. Carers (Recognition and Services) Act
1995**

s.1, amended: SI 2015/914 Sch.1 para.56

13. Road Traffic (New Drivers) Act 1995

Sch.2 para.5, repealed: SI 2015/583
Sch.1 Part 1

16. Prisoners (Return to Custody) Act 1995

s.1, amended: 2015 c.2 s.13, Sch.9
para.11

17. Health Authorities Act 1995

Sch.2 para.4, enabling: SI 2015/864

Sch.2 para.7, enabling: SI 2015/864

Sch.2 para.13, enabling: SI 2015/864
Sch.2 para.14, enabling: SI 2015/864
Sch.2 para.16, enabling: SI 2015/864
Sch.2 para.18, enabling: SI 2015/864
Sch.2 para.19, enabling: SI 2015/864
Sch.2 para.20, enabling: SI 2015/864

18. Jobseekers Act 1995
s.4, enabling: SI 2015/1647, SI
2015/1754
s.6, enabling: SI 2015/336, SI 2015/339,
SI 2015/389
s.6F, enabling: SI 2015/339
s.7, enabling: SI 2015/336, SI 2015/339,
SI 2015/382, SI 2015/389
s.12, enabling: SI 2015/67, SI 2015/389
s.17A, enabling: SI 2015/336
s.35, enabling: SI 2015/67, SI 2015/336,
SI 2015/339, SI 2015/389, SI 2015/1647,
SI 2015/1754
s.36, enabling: SI 2015/67, SI 2015/336,
SI 2015/339, SI 2015/389, SI 2015/1647,
SI 2015/1754
Sch.1 para.14, enabling: SI 2015/336

21. Merchant Shipping Act 1995
s.3, amended: SI 2015/664 Sch.4 para.27
s.15, amended: SI 2015/664 Sch.4
para.27
s.47, enabling: SI 2015/410, SI 2015/782
s.55, enabling: SI 2015/21
s.58, see *R. v Richley (Martin Vincent)*
[2015] EWCA Crim 1256, [2015] 2 Cr.
App. R. (S.) 77 (CA (Crim Div)), Treacy
LJ
s.85, enabling: SI 2015/21, SI 2015/68,
SI 2015/410, SI 2015/508, SI 2015/629,
SI 2015/782, SI 2015/1692
s.86, enabling: SI 2015/21, SI 2015/68,
SI 2015/410, SI 2015/508, SI 2015/629,
SI 2015/782
s.92, amended: SI 2015/664 Sch.4
para.27
s.98, amended: SI 2015/664 Sch.4
para.27
s.100, see *R. v Richley (Martin Vincent)*
[2015] EWCA Crim 1256, [2015] 2 Cr.
App. R. (S.) 77 (CA (Crim Div)), Treacy
LJ
s.100, amended: SI 2015/664 Sch.4
para.27
s.100B, amended: SI 2015/664 Sch.4
para.27

s.100G, amended: SI 2015/664 Sch.4
para.27
s.130, amended: SI 2015/664 Sch.4
para.88
s.131, amended: SI 2015/664 Sch.4
para.27
s.145, amended: 2015 c.2 Sch.11 para.16
s.163, amended: SI 2015/664 Sch.4
para.27
s.184, repealed: 2015 c.15 Sch.4 para.29
s.190, see *CDE SA v Sure Wind Marine
Ltd* [2015] EWHC 720 (Admlty), [2015]
2 Lloyd's Rep. 268 (QBD (Admlty)),
Jervis Kay QC, Admiralty Registrar
s.192A, amended: SI 2015/664 Sch.4
para.89
s.205, enabling: SI 2015/458
s.255B, amended: SI 2015/664 Sch.4
para.27
s.255D, amended: SI 2015/664 Sch.4
para.27
s.255E, amended: SI 2015/664 Sch.4
para.27
s.255K, amended: SI 2015/664 Sch.4
para.27
s.255R, enabling: SI 2015/172
s.269, amended: 2015 c.20 s.55
s.269, repealed: 2015 c.20 s.55
s.284, amended: SI 2015/664 Sch.4
para.27
s.284, varied: SI 2015/508 Reg.27, SI
2015/782 Reg.54
s.302, enabling: SI 2015/315, SI
2015/410, SI 2015/1431
s.306A, added: 2015 c.20 s.106
s.307, enabling: SI 2015/410, SI
2015/782
s.315, enabling: SI 2015/1893
Sch.3A para.8, amended: SI 2015/664
Sch.4 para.27
Sch.13 para.2, repealed: 2015 c.20
Sch.23 para.32
Sch.13 para.9, repealed: 2015 c.20
Sch.23 para.32
Sch.13 para.68, repealed: 2015 c.20
Sch.23 para.32

**22. Shipping and Trading Interests
(Protection) Act 1995**
s.3, amended: SI 2015/664 Sch.4 para.28
s.6, amended: SI 2015/664 Sch.4 para.28

25. Environment Act 1995

s.9, enabling: SI 2015/663
s.21, repealed: SI 2015/374 Art.6
s.42, amended: 2015 asp 1 Sch.1 para.6
s.63, enabling: SI 2015/770
s.72, amended: 2015 c.20 Sch.22 para.11
s.75, enabling: SI 2015/770
s.84, amended: 2015 c.20 Sch.13 para.7
s.84, repealed: 2015 c.20 Sch.13 para.7
s.86, amended: 2015 c.20 Sch.13 para.8
s.91, amended: 2015 c.20 Sch.13 para.8
s.96, see *Portland Stone Firms Ltd v
Dorset CC* [2015] R.V.R. 170 (UT
(Lands)), Judge Huskinson
s.97, amended: 2015 c.20 Sch.22 para.12
s.99, repealed: 2015 c.20 Sch.22 para.13
s.108, see *Environment Agency v
Churngold Recycling Ltd* [2014] EWCA
Civ 909, [2015] Env. L.R. 13 (CA (Civ
Div)), Moses LJ
s.108, repealed: SI 2015/374 Art.6
s.125, enabling: SSI 2015/73
Sch.7 para.1, enabling: SI 2015/770
Sch.7 para.2, enabling: SI 2015/770
Sch.8 para.3, amended: 2015 c.27 s.2
Sch.11 para.1, amended: 2015 c.20
Sch.13 para.8
Sch.11 para.4, amended: 2015 c.20
Sch.13 para.8
Sch.13, see *Portland Stone Firms Ltd v
Dorset CC* [2015] R.V.R. 170 (UT
(Lands)), Judge Huskinson
Sch.13 para.10, see *Portland Stone Firms
Ltd v Dorset CC* [2015] R.V.R. 170 (UT
(Lands)), Judge Huskinson
Sch.22 para.30, repealed: SI 2015/374
Art.6
Sch.22 para.195, repealed: SI 2015/664
Sch.4 para.98

26. Pensions Act 1995

Part I, substituted: 2015 c.8 Sch.2 para.14
s.10, enabling: SI 2015/498
s.23, repealed: 2015 c.8 s.44
s.34, amended: 2015 c.8 s.36
s.35, enabling: SI 2015/879
s.36, enabling: SI 2015/879
s.37, amended: 2015 c.8 Sch.2 para.7
s.38, amended: 2015 c.8 Sch.2 para.8
s.51, amended: 2015 c.8 s.41, s.42, s.43,
Sch.2 para.9
s.51A, amended: 2015 c.8 Sch.2 para.10
s.67, amended: 2015 c.8 s.45

s.67, repealed: 2015 c.8 s.45
s.67, enabling: SI 2015/493
s.67A, amended: 2015 c.8 s.45, s.60,
Sch.4 para.29
s.68, enabling: SI 2015/493, SI 2015/879
s.73, amended: 2015 c.8 Sch.2 para.11,
Sch.4 para.30
s.73A, amended: 2015 c.8 s.58
s.73B, amended: 2015 c.8 s.58, Sch.4
para.31
s.75, see *BESTrustees Plc v Corbett*
[2014] EWHC 3038 (Ch), [2015] Ch. 571
(Ch D), Birss J; see *MF Global UK Ltd
(In Special Administration), Re* [2015]
EWHC 883 (Ch), [2015] Pens. L.R. 405
(Ch D (Companies Ct)), David Richards
J
s.75, amended: 2015 c.8 Sch.2 para.12
s.87, amended: 2015 c.8 Sch.2 para.13
s.88, amended: 2015 c.8 Sch.2 para.15
s.89, amended: 2015 c.8 Sch.2 para.16
s.91, enabling: SI 2015/493
s.92, enabling: SI 2015/1452, SI
2015/1677
s.124, amended: 2015 c.8 s.45, Sch.2
para.17, Sch.4 para.32
s.124, enabling: SI 2015/493, SI
2015/879
s.125, amended: 2015 c.8 Sch.2 para.18
s.174, enabling: SI 2015/493, SI
2015/879, SI 2015/1452, SI 2015/1677
s.175, amended: 2015 c.8 s.43

**30. Landlord and Tenant (Covenants) Act
1995**

see *Reeves v Sandhu* [2015] EWHC 985
(Ch), [2015] B.P.I.R. 899 (Ch D), Mann
J; see *UK Leasing Brighton Ltd v
Topland Neptune Ltd* [2015] EWHC 53
(Ch), [2015] 2 P. & C.R. 2 (Ch D),
Morgan J
s.3, see *UK Leasing Brighton Ltd v
Topland Neptune Ltd* [2015] EWHC 53
(Ch), [2015] 2 P. & C.R. 2 (Ch D),
Morgan J
s.5, see *Tindall Cobham 1 Ltd v Adda
Hotels* [2014] EWCA Civ 1215, [2015] 1
P. & C.R. 5 (CA (Civ Div)), Longmore
LJ; see *UK Leasing Brighton Ltd v
Topland Neptune Ltd* [2015] EWHC 53
(Ch), [2015] 2 P. & C.R. 2 (Ch D),
Morgan J

s.6, see *Reeves v Sandhu* [2015] EWHC
985 (Ch), [2015] B.P.I.R. 899 (Ch D),
Mann J
s.11, see *Tindall Cobham 1 Ltd v Adda
Hotels* [2014] EWCA Civ 1215, [2015] 1
P. & C.R. 5 (CA (Civ Div)), Longmore
LJ; see *UK Leasing Brighton Ltd v
Topland Neptune Ltd* [2015] EWHC 53
(Ch), [2015] 2 P. & C.R. 2 (Ch D),
Morgan J
s.24, see *Tindall Cobham 1 Ltd v Adda
Hotels* [2014] EWCA Civ 1215, [2015] 1
P. & C.R. 5 (CA (Civ Div)), Longmore
LJ; see *UK Leasing Brighton Ltd v
Topland Neptune Ltd* [2015] EWHC 53
(Ch), [2015] 2 P. & C.R. 2 (Ch D),
Morgan J
s.25, see *Tindall Cobham 1 Ltd v Adda
Hotels* [2014] EWCA Civ 1215, [2015] 1
P. & C.R. 5 (CA (Civ Div)), Longmore
LJ; see *UK Leasing Brighton Ltd v
Topland Neptune Ltd* [2015] EWHC 53
(Ch), [2015] 2 P. & C.R. 2 (Ch D),
Morgan J

**32. Olympic Symbol etc (Protection) Act
1995**
s.8A, amended: 2015 c.15 Sch.6 para.60
s.8A, repealed: 2015 c.15 Sch.6 para.60

36. Children (Scotland) Act 1995
s.11, see *X v Y* 2015 Fam. L.R. 41 (Sh Ct
(South Strathclyde) (Dumfries)), Sheriff
D Kelly, QC; see *X v Y* 2015 Fam. L.R.
66 (Sh Ct (North Strathclyde) (Paisley)),
Sheriff SM Sinclair
s.25, see *Application for a child
protection order* 2015 S.L.T. (Sh Ct) 9
(Sh Ct (Lothian) (Edinburgh)), Sheriff W
Holligan
s.26A, enabling: SSI 2015/158
s.29, enabling: SSI 2015/156
s.44, amended: SI 2015/907 Art.2
s.44, repealed: SI 2015/907 Art.2
s.51, see *M v Locality Reporter Manager*
[2015] CSIH 56, 2015 Fam. L.R. 106 (IH
(Ex Div)), Lady Dorrian; see *P v
Locality Reporter Manager* 2015 S.C. 94
(IH (Ex Div)), Lord Eassie
s.52, see *M v Children's Reporter* 2015
S.L.T. (Sh Ct) 215 (Sh Ct (Glasgow)),
Sheriff Principal C A L Scott, QC

s.73, see *S, Petitioner* 2015 S.C.L.R. 33
(IH (Ex Div)), Lady Smith
s.93, see *P v Locality Reporter Manager*
2015 S.C. 94 (IH (Ex Div)), Lord Eassie
s.93, amended: SI 2015/907 Art.2

**39. Criminal Law (Consolidation) (Scotland)
Act 1995**
s.6, see *A v HM Advocate* [2015] HCJAC
105 (HCJ), The Lord Justice Clerk
(Carloway); see *HM Advocate v K*
[2015] HCJAC 114 (HCJ), The Lord
Justice Clerk (Carloway)
s.47, see *Lunn (Laura) v HM Advocate*
[2015] HCJAC 103 (HCJ), Lady Paton
s.49, see *Hannon (Bradley) v HM
Advocate* [2015] HCJAC 65, 2015 S.L.T.
585 (HCJ), The Lord Justice Clerk
(Carloway); see *Ross (Scott Daniel) v
HM Advocate* [2015] HCJAC 38, 2015
J.C. 271 (HCJ), The Lord Justice Clerk
(Carloway)

**40. Criminal Procedure (Consequential
Provisions) (Scotland) Act 1995**
Sch.4 para.71, repealed: SI 2015/583
Sch.1 Part 1

**42. Private International Law
(Miscellaneous Provisions) Act 1995**
see *Docherty v Secretary of State for
Business Innovation and Skills* [2015]
CSOH 149, 2015 S.L.T. 858 (OH), Lord
Boyd of Duncansby; see *Donkers v
Storm Aviation Ltd* [2014] EWHC 241
(QB), [2015] 1 All E.R. (Comm) 282
(QBD), Judge Forster QC
s.9, see *Docherty v Secretary of State for
Business Innovation and Skills* [2015]
CSOH 149, 2015 S.L.T. 858 (OH), Lord
Boyd of Duncansby
s.11, see *Allen v Depuy International Ltd*
[2014] EWHC 753 (QB), [2015] 2
W.L.R. 442 (QBD), Stewart J; see
Donkers v Storm Aviation Ltd [2014]
EWHC 241 (QB), [2015] 1 All E.R.
(Comm) 282 (QBD), Judge Forster QC
s.12, see *Allen v Depuy International Ltd*
[2014] EWHC 753 (QB), [2015] 2
W.L.R. 442 (QBD), Stewart J; see
Donkers v Storm Aviation Ltd [2014]
EWHC 241 (QB), [2015] 1 All E.R.
(Comm) 282 (QBD), Judge Forster QC

s.14, see *Docherty v Secretary of State for Business Innovation and Skills* [2015] CSOH 149, 2015 S.L.T. 858 (OH), Lord Boyd of Duncansby

43. Proceeds of Crime (Scotland) Act 1995
see *Lord Advocate v Mackie* [2015] CSIH 88 (IH (2 Div)), The Lord Justice Clerk (Carloway)
s.27, amended: SSI 2015/338 Sch.2 para.4

45. Gas Act 1995
Sch.4 para.11, repealed: 2015 c.20
Sch.23 para.17

46. Criminal Procedure (Scotland) Act 1995
see *HM Advocate v Coulson* [2015] HCJ 49, 2015 S.C.L. 606 (HCJ), Lord Burns;
see *Kinloch (Andrew) v HM Advocate* [2015] HCJAC 102, 2015 S.L.T. 876 (HCJ), The Lord Justice Clerk (Carloway); see *Scottish Legal Aid Board v Lavery* 2015 S.L.T. (Sh Ct) 35 (Sh Ct (Glasgow)), Sheriff A D Miller
Part VI, substituted: 2015 asp 9 s.46
s.8, amended: SSI 2015/150 Sch.1 para.5
s.14, see *B v HM Advocate* [2015] HCJAC 17, 2015 S.L.T. 182 (HCJ), Lord Brodie; see *HM Advocate v Sinclair (Angus Robertson)* 2015 J.C. 137 (HCJ), The Lord Justice Clerk (Carloway)
s.15A, see *Barclay v Harvie* [2015] HCJAC 110 (HCJ), The Lord Justice Clerk (Carloway)
s.19A, see *HM Advocate v Sinclair (Angus Robertson)* 2015 J.C. 137 (HCJ), The Lord Justice Clerk (Carloway)
s.19C, see *HM Advocate v Sinclair (Angus Robertson)* 2015 J.C. 137 (HCJ), The Lord Justice Clerk (Carloway)
s.27, see *Hannon (Bradley) v HM Advocate* [2015] HCJAC 65, 2015 S.L.T. 585 (HCJ), The Lord Justice Clerk (Carloway)
s.44, amended: SI 2015/907 Art.3
s.44A, amended: SSI 2015/402 Sch.1 para.3
s.52B, amended: 2015 asp 9 s.38
s.52C, amended: 2015 asp 9 s.38
s.52D, amended: 2015 asp 9 s.38, s.40
s.52F, amended: 2015 asp 9 s.38, s.40
s.52G, amended: 2015 asp 9 s.40
s.52H, amended: 2015 asp 9 s.40

s.52K, amended: 2015 asp 9 s.38
s.52L, amended: 2015 asp 9 s.38
s.52M, amended: 2015 asp 9 s.38, s.41
s.52P, amended: 2015 asp 9 s.38, s.41
s.52R, amended: 2015 asp 9 s.41
s.53, amended: 2015 asp 9 s.42
s.53A, amended: 2015 asp 9 s.42
s.53B, amended: 2015 asp 9 s.42, s.45
s.54, amended: 2015 asp 9 s.42
s.57, amended: 2015 asp 9 s.39
s.57A, amended: 2015 asp 9 s.43, SSI 2015/157 Sch.1 para.3
s.57B, amended: 2015 asp 9 s.43
s.57D, amended: 2015 asp 9 s.43
s.58, see *Johnstone v Scottish Ministers* [2015] CSOH 121, 2015 S.L.T. 743 (OH), Lord Glennie
s.59, see *Johnstone v Scottish Ministers* [2015] CSOH 121, 2015 S.L.T. 743 (OH), Lord Glennie
s.59A, amended: 2015 asp 9 s.44
s.59C, amended: 2015 asp 9 s.44
s.61A, added: 2015 asp 9 s.46
s.61B, added: 2015 asp 9 s.47
s.62, amended: SSI 2015/338 Sch.2 para.5
s.63, amended: SSI 2015/338 Sch.2 para.5
s.65, see *Ayres (James) v HM Advocate* [2015] HCJAC 98 (HCJ), The Lord Justice Clerk (Carloway); see *MacDonald (John) v HM Advocate* 2015 S.C.L. 189 (HCJ), Lord Bracadale; see *Potts (Donnie Daniel) v HM Advocate* [2015] HCJAC 124 (HCJ Appeal), Lord Brodie; see *Stewart (David) v HM Advocate* 2015 S.C.L. 380 (HCJ), Lord Brodie
s.71, see *HM Advocate v Robertson (Thomas)* 2015 S.L.T. (Sh Ct) 96 (Sh Ct (Tayside) (Falkirk)), Sheriff J K Mundy; see *O'Neill v Harvie* 2015 S.L.T. 55 (HCJ), Lady Paton
s.72, see *Dunn v Y* 2015 S.L.T. (Sh Ct) 113 (Sh Ct (Lothian) (Edinburgh)), Sheriff T Welsh, QC
s.72A, see *Dunn v Y* 2015 S.L.T. (Sh Ct) 113 (Sh Ct (Lothian) (Edinburgh)), Sheriff T Welsh, QC
s.74, see *Kerr (Alan) v HM Advocate* [2015] HCJAC 96, 2015 S.L.T. 837

(HCJ), The Lord Justice Clerk (Carloway)

s.90, see *Mackay (David) v HM Advocate* [2015] HCJAC 55, 2015 J.C. 282 (HCJ), The Lord Justice Clerk (Carloway)

s.92, see *Mackay (David) v HM Advocate* [2015] HCJAC 55, 2015 J.C. 282 (HCJ), The Lord Justice Clerk (Carloway)

s.97, see *HM Advocate v Mason (Christopher)* [2015] HCJAC 1, 2015 S.L.T. 41 (HCJ), Lord Brodie; see *Lauchlan (William Hugh) v HM Advocate* 2015 J.C. 75 (HCJ), The Lord Justice Clerk (Carloway)

s.97A, see *Tait (Connor) v HM Advocate* [2015] HCJAC 58, 2015 S.L.T. 495 (HCJ), Lord Brodie

s.106, see *Lilburn (David) v HM Advocate* [2015] HCJAC 50, 2015 S.C.L. 706 (HCJ), The Lord Justice Clerk (Carloway); see *MacKinnon (Jonathan) v HM Advocate* [2015] HCJAC 6, 2015 S.C.L. 272 (HCJ), Lady Dorrian

s.107, see *Birnie (Josh) v HM Advocate* [2015] HCJAC 54, 2015 J.C. 314 (HCJ), The Lord Justice Clerk (Carloway)

s.107A, see *HM Advocate v Mason (Christopher)* [2015] HCJAC 1, 2015 S.L.T. 41 (HCJ), Lord Brodie

s.108, amended: 2015 c.9 s.17, Sch.4 para.14

s.110, see *HM Advocate v Mason (Christopher)* [2015] HCJAC 1, 2015 S.L.T. 41 (HCJ), Lord Brodie

s.118, see *Lauchlan (William Hugh) v HM Advocate* 2015 J.C. 11 (HCJ), Lady Paton; see *Tait (Connor) v HM Advocate* [2015] HCJAC 58, 2015 S.L.T. 495 (HCJ), Lord Brodie

s.147, amended: SSI 2015/338 Sch.2 para.5

s.155, see *Strathern v Harvie* [2015] HCJAC 107 (HCJ), Lady Paton

s.156D, amended: SSI 2015/338 Sch.2 para.5

s.160, see *M v Murphy* [2015] HCJAC 8, 2015 S.C.L. 408 (HCJ), Lord Brodie

s.174, see *Wilson v Harvie* [2015] HCJAC 26, 2015 S.L.T. 260 (HCJ), Lord Brodie

s.175, amended: 2015 c.9 s.17, Sch.4 para.15

s.180, see *B v Murphy* [2015] HCJAC 14, 2015 S.L.T. 214 (HCJ), The Lord Justice Clerk (Carloway)

s.194B, see *Scottish Criminal Cases Review Commission v Swire* [2015] HCJAC 76, 2015 S.L.T. 556 (HCJ), The Lord Justice Clerk (Carloway)

s.194D, see *Scottish Criminal Cases Review Commission v Swire* [2015] HCJAC 76, 2015 S.L.T. 556 (HCJ), The Lord Justice Clerk (Carloway)

s.195, see *Simpson (Myles Gibson) v HM Advocate* [2015] HCJAC 20, 2015 S.C.L. 510 (HCJ), Lady Smith

s.200, amended: SSI 2015/338 Sch.2 para.5

s.201, amended: SSI 2015/338 Sch.2 para.5

s.207, see *GC v HM Advocate* [2015] HCJAC 47, 2015 S.C.L. 646 (HCJ), The Lord Justice Clerk (Carloway)

s.210A, see *Crawford (Francis) v HM Advocate* [2015] HCJAC 70, 2015 S.L.T. 700 (HCJ), Lady Paton

s.219, amended: 2015 c.9 s.19

s.222, amended: 2015 c.9 Sch.4 para.16

s.227A, see *Stewart v Dunn* [2015] HCJAC 93, 2015 S.L.T. 872 (HCJ), Lady Smith

s.227L, see *Stewart v Dunn* [2015] HCJAC 93, 2015 S.L.T. 872 (HCJ), Lady Smith

s.227X, see *Ross (Alistair George) v HM Advocate* [2015] HCJAC 80, 2015 S.L.T. 579 (HCJ), The Lord Justice Clerk (Carloway)

s.227Y, see *Stewart v Dunn* [2015] HCJAC 93, 2015 S.L.T. 872 (HCJ), Lady Smith

s.227Z, see *Stewart v Dunn* [2015] HCJAC 93, 2015 S.L.T. 872 (HCJ), Lady Smith

s.227ZA, see *Stewart v Dunn* [2015] HCJAC 93, 2015 S.L.T. 872 (HCJ), Lady Smith

s.234A, see *S v HM Advocate* [2015] HCJAC 64, 2015 S.L.T. 582 (HCJ), Lord Brodie

s.245J, amended: SSI 2015/338 Sch.2
para.5
s.254A, added: SSI 2015/107 Reg.2
s.254B, amended: SSI 2015/338 Sch.2
para.5
s.271, amended: 2015 asp 12 Sch.1
para.1
s.271, varied: SSI 2015/447 Art.3
s.271I, varied: SSI 2015/447 Art.3
s.271J, varied: SSI 2015/447 Art.3
s.271V, amended: SSI 2015/338 Sch.2
para.5
s.271W, amended: SSI 2015/338 Sch.2
para.5
s.271X, amended: SSI 2015/338 Sch.2
para.5
s.271Y, amended: SSI 2015/338 Sch.2
para.5
s.271Z, amended: SSI 2015/338 Sch.2
para.5
s.283, see *Walker v Dunn* [2015] HCJAC
119 (HCJ), The Lord Justice Clerk
(Carloway)
s.288AA, see *Macklin (Paul Alexander) v
HM Advocate* [2015] UKSC 77 (SC),
Lord Neuberger PSC
s.288E, varied: SSI 2015/447 Art.4
s.288F, varied: SSI 2015/447 Art.5
s.288G, enabling: SSI 2015/447
s.288ZB, see *HM Advocate v Porch
(Ross)* [2015] HCJAC 111 (HCJ), Lady
Paton
s.298, amended: SSI 2015/338 Sch.2
para.5
s.298A, amended: SSI 2015/338 Sch.2
para.5
s.299, see *Strathern v Harvie* [2015]
HCJAC 107 (HCJ), Lady Paton
s.299, amended: SSI 2015/338 Sch.2
para.5
s.300, amended: SSI 2015/338 Sch.2
para.5
s.300A, see *Murphy v L* [2015] HCJAC
21, 2015 S.L.T. 257 (HCJ), The Lord
Justice General (Gill)
s.300A, amended: SSI 2015/338 Sch.2
para.5
s.301A, amended: SSI 2015/338 Sch.2
para.5
s.303A, see *Scottish Criminal Cases
Review Commission v Swire* [2015]

HCJAC 76, 2015 S.L.T. 556 (HCJ), The
Lord Justice Clerk (Carloway)
s.303A, amended: SSI 2015/338 Sch.2
para.5
s.305, amended: SSI 2015/338 Art.2
s.305, enabling: SSI 2015/84, SSI
2015/121, SSI 2015/201, SSI 2015/245,
SSI 2015/295, SSI 2015/375, SSI
2015/443
s.307, amended: 2015 asp 9 s.53
Sch.9, amended: 2015 asp 10 Sch.2
para.2

50. Disability Discrimination Act 1995
see *McDonald v United Kingdom
(4241/12)* (2015) 60 E.H.R.R. 1 (ECHR),
Judge Ziemele (President)
s.49A, see *Secretary of State for Work
and Pensions v Robertson* [2015] CSIH
82 (IH (Ex Div)), Lady Smith

1996

8. Finance Act 1996
see *Cater Allen International Ltd v
Revenue and Customs Commissioners*
[2015] UKFTT 232 (TC), [2015]
S.F.T.D. 765 (FTT (Tax)), Judge Rachel
Short
s.42, amended: 2015 c.11 s.64, Sch.15
para.2
s.42, enabling: SI 2015/845, SI
2015/1385
s.51, enabling: SI 2015/744
s.53, enabling: SI 2015/744
s.63, amended: 2015 c.11 Sch.15 para.3
s.63A, added: 2015 c.11 Sch.15 para.4
s.63A, enabling: SI 2015/845, SI
2015/1385
s.70, amended: 2015 c.11 Sch.15 para.5
s.71, amended: 2015 c.11 Sch.15 para.6
s.71, enabling: SI 2015/846, SI
2015/1453
s.80, see *Versteegh Ltd v Revenue and
Customs Commissioners* [2015] UKUT
75 (TCC), [2015] S.T.C. 1222 (UT
(Tax)), Proudman J
s.81, see *DMWSHNZ Ltd v Revenue and
Customs Commissioners* [2015] EWCA
Civ 1036, [2015] B.T.C. 32 (CA (Civ
Div)), Moore-Bick LJ

s.84, see *Cater Allen International Ltd v Revenue and Customs Commissioners* [2015] UKFTT 232 (TC), [2015] S.F.T.D. 765 (FTT (Tax)), Judge Rachel Short; see *Versteegh Ltd v Revenue and Customs Commissioners* [2015] UKUT 75 (TCC), [2015] S.T.C. 1222 (UT (Tax)), Proudman J; see *Vocalspruce Ltd v Revenue and Customs Commissioners* [2014] EWCA Civ 1302, [2015] S.T.C. 861 (CA (Civ Div)), Gross LJ
Sch.5 Part I, amended: 2015 c.11 Sch.15 para.7
Sch.5 Part I para.2, enabling: SI 2015/846, SI 2015/1453
Sch.5 Part I para.2A, enabling: SI 2015/846, SI 2015/1453
Sch.5 Part I para.2B, added: 2015 c.11 Sch.15 para.7
Sch.5 Part I para.2B, enabling: SI 2015/846, SI 2015/1453
Sch.5 Part I para.2C, enabling: SI 2015/846, SI 2015/1453
Sch.5 Part II para.10, amended: 2015 c.11 Sch.15 para.7
Sch.5 Part IV para.16, amended: SI 2015/664 Sch.2 para.9
Sch.5 Part V para.22, amended: 2015 c.11 Sch.15 para.7
Sch.5 Part V para.23, enabling: SI 2015/846
Sch.9 para.12, see *Vocalspruce Ltd v Revenue and Customs Commissioners* [2014] EWCA Civ 1302, [2015] S.T.C. 861 (CA (Civ Div)), Gross LJ
Sch.9 para.13, see *Fidex Ltd v Revenue and Customs Commissioners* [2015] S.T.C. 702 (UT (Tax)), Barling J
Sch.9 para.15, see *Cater Allen International Ltd v Revenue and Customs Commissioners* [2015] UKFTT 232 (TC), [2015] S.F.T.D. 765 (FTT (Tax)), Judge Rachel Short
Sch.9 para.19A, see *Fidex Ltd v Revenue and Customs Commissioners* [2015] S.T.C. 702 (UT (Tax)), Barling J

14. Reserve Forces Act 1996
s.83, enabling: SI 2015/460
s.84, enabling: SI 2015/460

16. Police Act 1996

see *R. (on the application of Catt) v Association of Chief Police Officers of England, Wales and Northern Ireland* [2015] UKSC 9, [2015] A.C. 1065 (SC), Lord Neuberger PSC
s.50, enabling: SI 2015/453, SI 2015/455, SI 2015/626
s.51, enabling: SI 2015/461, SI 2015/626
s.60, enabling: SI 2015/630
s.84, enabling: SI 2015/626
s.85, enabling: SI 2015/625
s.89, see *Metcalf v Crown Prosecution Service* [2015] EWHC 1091 (Admin), [2015] 2 Cr. App. R. 25 (DC), Burnett LJ

17. Employment Tribunals Act 1996
Part IIA, added: 2015 c.26 s.150
s.4, see *Birring v Rogers (t/a Charity Link)* [2015] I.C.R. 1001 (EAT), Langstaff J
s.7, amended: 2015 c.26 s.151
s.11, see *EF v AB* [2015] I.R.L.R. 619 (EAT), Slade J
s.12A, amended: 2015 c.26 s.150
s.13, amended: 2015 c.26 s.151
s.13A, amended: 2015 c.26 s.151
s.18, amended: SI 2015/2054 Art.2
s.18, enabling: SI 2015/2054
s.19A, amended: 2015 c.26 s.150
s.21, see *Martineau v Ministry of Justice* [2015] I.C.R. 1122 (EAT), Lewis J; see *Wolfe v North Middlesex University Hospital NHS Trust* [2015] I.C.R. 960 (EAT), Judge Serota QC
s.30, see *Martineau v Ministry of Justice* [2015] I.C.R. 1122 (EAT), Lewis J
s.37ZA, added: 2015 c.2 s.65
s.41, amended: 2015 c.26 s.150
s.42, amended: 2015 c.26 s.150

18. Employment Rights Act 1996
see *Lodge v Dignity & Choice in Dying* [2015] I.R.L.R. 184 (EAT), Judge Peter Clark; see *R. (on the application of Hottak) v Secretary of State for Foreign and Commonwealth Affairs* [2015] EWHC 1953 (Admin), [2015] I.R.L.R. 827 (QBD (Admin)), Burnett LJ; see *Weldemichael v Secretary of State for the Home Department* [2015] UKUT 540 (IAC) (UT (IAC)), Judge Storey
Part IIA, added: 2015 c.26 s.153
Part VA, added: 2015 c.26 s.149

Pt X s.103A, see *Smania v Standard Chartered Bank* [2015] I.C.R. 436 (EAT), Langstaff J

s.23, see *Bear Scotland Ltd v Fulton* [2015] 1 C.M.L.R. 40 (EAT), Langstaff J; see *Sash Window Workshop Ltd v King* [2015] I.R.L.R. 348 (EAT), Simler J

s.27, see *Sash Window Workshop Ltd v King* [2015] I.R.L.R. 348 (EAT), Simler J

s.27B, enabling: SI 2015/2021

s.31, amended: SI 2015/226 Sch.1

s.43B, see *Chesterton Global Ltd (t/a Chestertons) v Nurmohamed* [2015] I.C.R. 920 (EAT), Supperstone J

s.43F, enabling: SI 2015/1407, SI 2015/1981

s.43FA, added: 2015 c.26 s.148

s.43K, see *Sharpe v Worcester Diocesan Board of Finance Ltd* [2015] EWCA Civ 399, [2015] I.C.R. 1241 (CA (Civ Div)), Arden LJ

s.43K, amended: SI 2015/491 Art.2

s.43K, enabling: SI 2015/491

s.44, see *Smith v Carillion (JM) Ltd* [2015] EWCA Civ 209, [2015] I.R.L.R. 467 (CA (Civ Div)), Elias LJ

s.48, see *McKinney v Newham LBC* [2015] I.C.R. 495 (EAT), Judge Peter Clark

s.50, amended: SSI 2015/39 Sch.1 para.5

s.50, repealed: SSI 2015/39 Sch.1 para.5

s.75A, enabling: SI 2015/552

s.75B, enabling: SI 2015/552

s.75D, enabling: SI 2015/552

s.75E, enabling: SI 2015/552

s.75F, enabling: SI 2015/552

s.75G, enabling: SI 2015/552

s.75H, enabling: SI 2015/552

s.94, see *Dhunna v Creditsights Ltd* [2014] EWCA Civ 1238, [2015] I.C.R. 105 (CA (Civ Div)), Rimer LJ; see *Smania v Standard Chartered Bank* [2015] I.C.R. 436 (EAT), Langstaff J

s.97, see *McKinney v Newham LBC* [2015] I.C.R. 495 (EAT), Judge Peter Clark

s.98, see *Evbenata v South West London and St George's Mental Health NHS Trust* [2015] I.C.R. 483 (EAT), Simler J

s.98ZD, see *Evbenata v South West London and St George's Mental Health NHS Trust* [2015] I.C.R. 483 (EAT), Simler J

s.98ZF, see *Evbenata v South West London and St George's Mental Health NHS Trust* [2015] I.C.R. 483 (EAT), Simler J

s.98ZG, see *Evbenata v South West London and St George's Mental Health NHS Trust* [2015] I.C.R. 483 (EAT), Simler J

s.120, amended: SI 2015/226 Sch.1

s.124, amended: SI 2015/226 Sch.1

s.139, see *Sefton BC v Wainwright* [2015] I.C.R. 652 (EAT), Judge Eady QC

s.186, amended: SI 2015/226 Sch.1

s.209, enabling: SI 2015/916, SI 2015/2021

s.221, see *Lock v British Gas Trading Ltd* [2015] I.R.L.R. 438 (ET), Judge Ahmed

s.227, amended: SI 2015/226 Sch.1

s.230, see *Sash Window Workshop Ltd v King* [2015] I.R.L.R. 348 (EAT), Simler J; see *Sharpe v Worcester Diocesan Board of Finance Ltd* [2015] EWCA Civ 399, [2015] I.C.R. 1241 (CA (Civ Div)), Arden LJ; see *Stack v Ajar-Tec Ltd* [2015] EWCA Civ 46, [2015] I.R.L.R. 474 (CA (Civ Div)), Moore-Bick LJ; see *Windle v Secretary of State for Justice* [2015] I.C.R. 156 (EAT), Judge Peter Clark

s.230, amended: 2015 c.26 s.149

s.236, amended: 2015 c.26 s.148, s.149, s.153

s.236, enabling: SI 2015/916

23. Arbitration Act 1996

see *Hurley Palmer Flatt Ltd v Barclays Bank Plc* [2014] EWHC 3042 (TCC), [2015] Bus. L.R. 106 (QBD (TCC)), Ramsey J; see *Shagang South-Asia (Hong Kong) Trading Co Ltd v Daewoo Logistics* [2015] EWHC 194 (Comm), [2015] 1 All E.R. (Comm) 545 (QBD (Comm)), Hamblen J

s.1, see *Union Marine Classification Services LLC v Comoros* [2015] EWHC 508 (Comm), [2015] 2 Lloyd's Rep. 49 (QBD (Comm)), Eder J s.9, see *Assaubayev v Michael Wilson and Partners Ltd* [2014] EWCA Civ 1491, [2015] C.P. Rep. 10 (CA (Civ Div)), Aikens LJ; see *BDMS Ltd v Rafael Advanced Defence Systems* [2014] EWHC 451 (Comm), [2015] 1 All E.R. (Comm) 627 (QBD (Comm)), Hamblen J; see *London Steam Ship Owners Mutual Insurance Association Ltd v Spain* [2015] EWCA Civ 333, [2015] 2 Lloyd's Rep. 33 (CA (Civ Div)), Moore-Bick LJ; see *Salford Estates (No.2) Ltd v Altomart Ltd* [2014] EWCA Civ 1575, [2015] Ch. 589 (CA (Civ Div)), Sir Terence Etherton C

s.15, see *Shagang South-Asia (Hong Kong) Trading Co Ltd v Daewoo Logistics* [2015] EWHC 194 (Comm), [2015] 1 All E.R. (Comm) 545 (QBD (Comm)), Hamblen J

s.16, see *Shagang South-Asia (Hong Kong) Trading Co Ltd v Daewoo Logistics* [2015] EWHC 194 (Comm), [2015] 1 All E.R. (Comm) 545 (QBD (Comm)), Hamblen J

s.18, see *Crowther v Rayment* [2015] EWHC 427 (Ch), [2015] Bus. L.R. 690 (Ch D), Andrew Smith J; see *Shagang South-Asia (Hong Kong) Trading Co Ltd v Daewoo Logistics* [2015] EWHC 194 (Comm), [2015] 1 All E.R. (Comm) 545 (QBD (Comm)), Hamblen J

s.24, see *Sierra Fishing Co v Farran* [2015] EWHC 140 (Comm), [2015] 1 All E.R. (Comm) 560 (QBD (Comm)), Popplewell J

s.27, see *Emirates Trading Agency LLC v Sociedade de Fomento Industrial Private Ltd* [2015] EWHC 1452 (Comm), [2015] 2 Lloyd's Rep. 487 (QBD (Comm)), Popplewell J

s.30, see *Crowther v Rayment* [2015] EWHC 427 (Ch), [2015] Bus. L.R. 690 (Ch D), Andrew Smith J; see *Union Marine Classification Services LLC v Comoros* [2015] EWHC 508 (Comm), [2015] 2 Lloyd's Rep. 49 (QBD (Comm)), Eder J

s.32, see *Toyota Tsusho Sugar Trading Ltd v Prolat S.R.L* [2014] EWHC 3649

(Comm), [2015] 1 Lloyd's Rep. 344 (QBD (Comm)), Cooke J

s.33, see *Brockton Capital LLP v Atlantic-Pacific Capital Inc* [2014] EWHC 1459 (Comm), [2015] 2 All E.R. (Comm) 350 (QBD (Comm)), Field J; see *BV Scheepswerf Damen Gorinchem v Marine Institute* [2015] EWHC 1810 (Comm), [2015] 2 Lloyd's Rep. 351 (QBD (Comm)), Flaux J; see *Lorand Shipping Ltd v Davof Trading (Africa) BV* [2014] EWHC 3521 (Comm), [2015] 2 All E.R. (Comm) 940 (QBD (Comm)), Eder J

s.42, see *PCL v Regional Government of X* [2015] EWHC 68 (Comm), [2015] 1 W.L.R. 3948 (QBD (Comm)), Hamblen J

s.44, see *Southport Success SA v Tsingshan Holding Group Co Ltd* [2015] EWHC 1974 (Comm), [2015] 2 Lloyd's Rep. 578 (QBD (Comm)), Phillips J

s.45, see *Secretary of State for Defence v Turner Estate Solutions Ltd* [2015] EWHC 1150 (TCC), [2015] B.L.R. 448 (QBD (TCC)), Coulson J

s.57, see *K v S* [2015] EWHC 1945 (Comm), [2015] 2 Lloyd's Rep. 363 (QBD (Comm)), Teare J; see *Union Marine Classification Services LLC v Comoros* [2015] EWHC 508 (Comm), [2015] 2 Lloyd's Rep. 49 (QBD (Comm)), Eder J

s.62, see *London Steam Ship Owners Mutual Insurance Association Ltd v Spain* [2015] EWCA Civ 333, [2015] 2 Lloyd's Rep. 33 (CA (Civ Div)), Moore-Bick LJ

s.66, see *Cruz City 1 Mauritius Holdings v Unitech Ltd* [2014] EWHC 3131 (Comm), [2015] 1 All E.R. (Comm) 336 (QBD (Comm)), Males J; see *Y v S* [2015] EWHC 612 (Comm), [2015] 2 All E.R. (Comm) 85 (QBD (Comm)), Eder J

s.67, see *Central Trading & Exports Ltd v Fioralba Shipping Co* [2014] EWHC 2397 (Comm), [2015] 1 All E.R. (Comm) 580 (QBD (Comm)), Males J; see *Emirates Trading Agency LLC v Sociedade de Fomento Industrial Private Ltd* [2015] EWHC 1452 (Comm), [2015] 2 Lloyd's Rep. 487 (QBD (Comm)),

Popplewell J; see *London Steam Ship Owners Mutual Insurance Association Ltd v Spain* [2015] EWCA Civ 333, [2015] 2 Lloyd's Rep. 33 (CA (Civ Div)), Moore-Bick LJ; see *Sun United Maritime Ltd v Kasteli Marine Inc* [2014] EWHC 1476 (Comm), [2015] 1 W.L.R. 1527 (QBD (Comm)), Hamblen J; see *Union Marine Classification Services LLC v Comoros* [2015] EWHC 508 (Comm), [2015] 2 Lloyd's Rep. 49 (QBD (Comm)), Eder J; see *Y v S* [2015] EWHC 612 (Comm), [2015] 2 All E.R. (Comm) 85 (QBD (Comm)), Eder J

s.68, see *Brockton Capital LLP v Atlantic-Pacific Capital Inc* [2014] EWHC 1459 (Comm), [2015] 2 All E.R. (Comm) 350 (QBD (Comm)), Field J; see *BV Scheepswerf Damen Gorinchem v Marine Institute* [2015] EWHC 1810 (Comm), [2015] 2 Lloyd's Rep. 351 (QBD (Comm)), Flaux J; see *Emirates Trading Agency LLC v Sociedade de Fomento Industrial Private Ltd* [2015] EWHC 1452 (Comm), [2015] 2 Lloyd's Rep. 487 (QBD (Comm)), Popplewell J; see *Lorand Shipping Ltd v Davof Trading (Africa) BV* [2014] EWHC 3521 (Comm), [2015] 2 All E.R. (Comm) 940 (QBD (Comm)), Eder J; see *Secretary of State for the Home Department v Raytheon Systems Ltd* [2015] EWHC 311 (TCC), [2015] Bus. L.R. 626 (QBD (TCC)), Akenhead J; see *Union Marine Classification Services LLC v Comoros* [2015] EWHC 508 (Comm), [2015] 2 Lloyd's Rep. 49 (QBD (Comm)), Eder J; see *Y v S* [2015] EWHC 612 (Comm), [2015] 2 All E.R. (Comm) 85 (QBD (Comm)), Eder J

s.69, see *Emirates Trading Agency LLC v Sociedade de Fomento Industrial Private Ltd* [2015] EWHC 1452 (Comm), [2015] 2 Lloyd's Rep. 487 (QBD (Comm)), Popplewell J; see *Maestro Bulk Ltd v Cosco Bulk Carrier Co Ltd* [2014] EWHC 3978 (Comm), [2015] 1 Lloyd's Rep. 315 (QBD (Comm)), Cooke J; see *Patel v Mussa* [2015] EWCA Civ 434, [2015] 1 W.L.R. 4788 (CA (Civ Div)), Moore-Bick LJ; see *Sun United*

Maritime Ltd v Kasteli Marine Inc [2014] EWHC 1476 (Comm), [2015] 1 W.L.R. 1527 (QBD (Comm)), Hamblen J; see *Y v S* [2015] EWHC 612 (Comm), [2015] 2 All E.R. (Comm) 85 (QBD (Comm)), Eder J

s.70, see *Frontier Agriculture Ltd v Bratt Bros (A Firm)* [2015] EWCA Civ 611, [2015] 2 Lloyd's Rep. 500 (CA (Civ Div)), Longmore LJ; see *K v S* [2015] EWHC 1945 (Comm), [2015] 2 Lloyd's Rep. 363 (QBD (Comm)), Teare J; see *Y v S* [2015] EWHC 612 (Comm), [2015] 2 All E.R. (Comm) 85 (QBD (Comm)), Eder J

s.72, see *London Steam Ship Owners Mutual Insurance Association Ltd v Spain* [2015] EWCA Civ 333, [2015] 2 Lloyd's Rep. 33 (CA (Civ Div)), Moore-Bick LJ

s.73, see *Emirates Trading Agency LLC v Sociedade de Fomento Industrial Private Ltd* [2015] EWHC 1452 (Comm), [2015] 2 Lloyd's Rep. 487 (QBD (Comm)), Popplewell J; see *Frontier Agriculture Ltd v Bratt Bros (A Firm)* [2015] EWCA Civ 611, [2015] 2 Lloyd's Rep. 500 (CA (Civ Div)), Longmore LJ; see *Sierra Fishing Co v Farran* [2015] EWHC 140 (Comm), [2015] 1 All E.R. (Comm) 560 (QBD (Comm)), Popplewell J

s.89, amended: 2015 c.15 Sch.4 para.31

s.90, substituted: 2015 c.15 Sch.4 para.32

s.91, amended: 2015 c.15 Sch.4 para.33

s.101, see *IPCO (Nigeria) Ltd v Nigerian National Petroleum Corp* [2014] EWHC 576 (Comm), [2015] 1 All E.R. (Comm) 593 (QBD (Comm)), Field J; see *Malicorp Ltd v Egypt* [2015] EWHC 361 (Comm), [2015] 1 Lloyd's Rep. 423 (QBD (Comm)), Walker J

s.103, see *IPCO (Nigeria) Ltd v Nigerian National Petroleum Corp* [2014] EWHC 576 (Comm), [2015] 1 All E.R. (Comm) 593 (QBD (Comm)), Field J; see *Malicorp Ltd v Egypt* [2015] EWHC 361 (Comm), [2015] 1 Lloyd's Rep. 423 (QBD (Comm)), Walker J

25. Criminal Procedure and Investigations Act 1996

see *R. (on the application of Nunn) v Chief Constable of Suffolk* [2015] A.C. 225 (SC), Lord Neuberger JSC
Pt III., see *R. v Quillan (Gary)* [2015] EWCA Crim 538, [2015] 1 W.L.R. 4673 (CA (Crim Div)), Lord Thomas LCJ
s.3, see *R. (on the application of Nunn) v Chief Constable of Suffolk* [2015] A.C. 225 (SC), Lord Neuberger JSC
s.7A, see *R. (on the application of Nunn) v Chief Constable of Suffolk* [2015] A.C. 225 (SC), Lord Neuberger JSC
s.8, see *R. v Boardman (David)* [2015] EWCA Crim 175, [2015] 1 Cr. App. R. 33 (CA (Crim Div)), Sir Brian Leveson PQBD
s.19, enabling: SI 2015/1490
s.20, enabling: SI 2015/1490
s.25, enabling: SI 2015/861
s.37, see *Guardian News and Media Ltd v Incedal* [2014] EWCA Crim 1861, [2015] 1 Cr. App. R. 4 (CA (Crim Div)), Gross LJ
s.69, repealed: 2015 c.20 s.80

27. Family Law Act 1996
see *E (Children) (Female Genital Mutilation: Protection Orders), Re* [2015] EWHC 2275 (Fam), [2015] 2 F.L.R. 997 (Fam Div), Holman J; see *R v R (Family Court: Procedural Fairness)* [2015] 1 W.L.R. 2743 (Fam Ct), Peter Jackson J; see *Redbridge LBC v A* [2015] EWHC 2140 (Fam), [2015] Fam. 335 (Fam Div), Hayden J
Pt IV., see *Guerroudj v Rymarczyk* [2015] EWCA Civ 743, [2015] H.L.R. 37 (CA (Civ Div)), Sir James Munby PFD
s.63, amended: 2015 c.9 Sch.4 para.17

31. Defamation Act 1996
s.2, see *Murray v Associated Newspapers Ltd* [2015] EWCA Civ 488, [2015] E.M.L.R. 21 (CA (Civ Div)), Longmore LJ
s.13, repealed: 2015 c.20 Sch.23 para.44

40. Party Wall etc Act 1996
see *Patel v Peters* [2014] EWCA Civ 335, [2015] 1 W.L.R. 179 (CA (Civ Div)), Richards LJ
s.10, see *Patel v Peters* [2014] EWCA Civ 335, [2015] 1 W.L.R. 179 (CA (Civ Div)), Richards LJ

47. Trusts of Land and Appointment of Trustees Act 1996
see *Bagum v Hafiz* [2015] EWCA Civ 801, [2015] 3 W.L.R. 1495 (CA (Civ Div)), Lord Dyson MR; see *Seagrove v Sullivan* [2014] EWHC 4110 (Fam), [2015] 2 F.L.R. 602 (Fam Div), Holman J
s.6, see *Preedy v Dunne* [2015] EWHC 2713 (Ch), [2015] W.T.L.R. 1795 (Ch D), Master Matthews
s.12, see *Preedy v Dunne* [2015] EWHC 2713 (Ch), [2015] W.T.L.R. 1795 (Ch D), Master Matthews
s.14, see *Bagum v Hafiz* [2015] EWCA Civ 801, [2015] 3 W.L.R. 1495 (CA (Civ Div)), Lord Dyson MR
s.15, see *Bagum v Hafiz* [2015] EWCA Civ 801, [2015] 3 W.L.R. 1495 (CA (Civ Div)), Lord Dyson MR

48. Damages Act 1996
s.1, see *LHS v First-Tier Tribunal (Criminal Injuries Compensation)* [2015] EWHC 1077 (Admin), [2015] P.I.Q.R. Q2 (QBD (Admin)), Jay J

52. Housing Act 1996
see *Guerroudj v Rymarczyk* [2015] EWCA Civ 743, [2015] H.L.R. 37 (CA (Civ Div)), Sir James Munby PFD; see *Haile v Waltham Forest LBC* [2015] UKSC 34, [2015] A.C. 1471 (SC), Lord Neuberger PSC; see *Sands v Singh* [2015] EWHC 2219 (Ch), [2015] B.P.I.R. 1293 (Ch D (Birmingham)), Judge Purle QC
Pt VI., see *R. (on the application of Alemi) v Westminster City Council* [2015] EWHC 1765 (Admin), [2015] P.T.S.R. 1339 (QBD (Admin)), Judge Blair QC; see *R. (on the application of Jakimaviciute) v Hammersmith and Fulham LBC* [2014] EWCA Civ 1438, [2015] 3 All E.R. 490 (CA (Civ Div)), Richards LJ
Pt VII., see *Ali v United Kingdom (40378/10)* [2015] H.L.R. 46 (ECHR), Judge Raimondi (President); see *Hussain v Waltham Forest LBC* [2015] EWCA Civ 14, [2015] 1 W.L.R. 2912 (CA (Civ Div)), Moore-Bick LJ; *Johnston v City of Westminster* [2015] EWCA Civ

554, [2015] P.T.S.R. 1557 (CA (Civ
Div)), Sullivan LJ; see *Mohamoud v
Kensington and Chelsea RLBC* [2015]
EWCA Civ 780, [2015] H.L.R. 38 (CA
(Civ Div)), Longmore LJ; see *R. (on the
application of AM) v Havering LBC*
[2015] EWHC 1004 (Admin), [2015]
P.T.S.R. 1242 (QBD (Admin)), Cobb J;
see *R. (on the application of
Jakimaviciute) v Hammersmith and
Fulham LBC* [2014] EWCA Civ 1438,
[2015] 3 All E.R. 490 (CA (Civ Div)),
Richards LJ; see *Temur v Hackney LBC*
[2014] EWCA Civ 877, [2015] 1 All E.R.
311 (CA (Civ Div)), Jackson LJ
s.17, enabling: SI 2015/1349
s.50J, amended: SI 2015/664 Sch.5
para.6
s.81, see *Barratt v Robinson* [2015] L. &
T.R. 1 (UT (Lands)), Martin Rodger QC
s.122, enabling: SI 2015/1753
s.124, see *Gorman v Newark and
Sherwood Homes* [2015] EWCA Civ
764, [2015] H.L.R. 42 (CA (Civ Div)),
Lord Dyson MR
s.160A, amended: SI 2015/1321 Art.2
s.160ZA, see *R. (on the application of
Jakimaviciute) v Hammersmith and
Fulham LBC* [2014] EWCA Civ 1438,
[2015] 3 All E.R. 490 (CA (Civ Div)),
Richards LJ
s.160ZA, enabling: SI 2015/967
s.166A, see *R. (on the application of
Alemi) v Westminster City Council*
[2015] EWHC 1765 (Admin), [2015]
P.T.S.R. 1339 (QBD (Admin)), Judge
Blair QC; see *R. (on the application of
Jakimaviciute) v Hammersmith and
Fulham LBC* [2014] EWCA Civ 1438,
[2015] 3 All E.R. 490 (CA (Civ Div)),
Richards LJ
s.172, enabling: SI 2015/967
s.175, see *Hussain v Waltham Forest
LBC* [2015] EWCA Civ 14, [2015] 1
W.L.R. 2912 (CA (Civ Div)), Moore-
Bick LJ; see *Johnston v City of
Westminster* [2015] EWCA Civ 554,
[2015] P.T.S.R. 1557 (CA (Civ Div)),
Sullivan LJ; see *Temur v Hackney LBC*
[2014] EWCA Civ 877, [2015] 1 All E.R.
311 (CA (Civ Div)), Jackson LJ

s.176, see *Temur v Hackney LBC* [2014]
EWCA Civ 877, [2015] 1 All E.R. 311
(CA (Civ Div)), Jackson LJ
s.177, see *Hussain v Waltham Forest
LBC* [2015] EWCA Civ 14, [2015] 1
W.L.R. 2912 (CA (Civ Div)), Moore-
Bick LJ; see *Temur v Hackney LBC*
[2014] EWCA Civ 877, [2015] 1 All E.R.
311 (CA (Civ Div)), Jackson LJ
s.183, see *Johnston v City of Westminster*
[2015] EWCA Civ 554, [2015] P.T.S.R.
1557 (CA (Civ Div)), Sullivan LJ
s.184, see *R. (on the application of N) v
Lewisham LBC* [2015] A.C. 1259 (SC),
Lord Neuberger PSC
s.188, see *R. (on the application of AM) v
Havering LBC* [2015] EWHC 1004
(Admin), [2015] P.T.S.R. 1242 (QBD
(Admin)), Cobb J; see *R. (on the
application of N) v Lewisham LBC*
[2015] A.C. 1259 (SC), Lord Neuberger
PSC
s.189, see *Hotak v Southwark LBC*
[2015] UKSC 30, [2015] 2 W.L.R. 1341
(SC), Lord Neuberger PSC
s.190, see *R. (on the application of AM) v
Havering LBC* [2015] EWHC 1004
(Admin), [2015] P.T.S.R. 1242 (QBD
(Admin)), Cobb J
s.191, see *Enfield LBC v Najim* [2015]
EWCA Civ 319, [2015] H.L.R. 19 (CA
(Civ Div)), Longmore LJ; see *Haile v
Waltham Forest LBC* [2015] UKSC 34,
[2015] A.C. 1471 (SC), Lord Neuberger
PSC
s.193, see *Akerman-Livingstone v Aster
Communities Ltd (formerly Flourish
Homes Ltd)* [2015] UKSC 15, [2015]
A.C. 1399 (SC), Lord Neuberger PSC;
see *Ali v United Kingdom (40378/10)*
[2015] H.L.R. 46 (ECHR), Judge
Raimondi (President); see *Haile v
Waltham Forest LBC* [2015] UKSC 34,
[2015] A.C. 1471 (SC), Lord Neuberger
PSC; see *Johnston v City of Westminster*
[2015] EWCA Civ 554, [2015] P.T.S.R.
1557 (CA (Civ Div)), Sullivan LJ; see
Mohamoud v Birmingham City Council
[2014] EWCA Civ 227, [2015] P.T.S.R.
17 (CA (Civ Div)), Moore-Bick LJ; see
Nzolameso v Westminster City Council

[2014] EWCA Civ 1383, [2015] P.T.S.R. 211 (CA (Civ Div)), Moore-Bick LJ; see *Nzolameso v Westminster City Council* [2015] UKSC 22, [2015] 2 All E.R. 942 (SC), Lady Hale DPSC; see *Poshteh v Kensington and Chelsea RLBC* [2015] EWCA Civ 711, [2015] H.L.R. 36 (CA (Civ Div)), Moore-Bick LJ; see *Temur v Hackney LBC* [2014] EWCA Civ 877, [2015] 1 All E.R. 311 (CA (Civ Div)), Jackson LJ

s.198, see *Johnston v City of Westminster* [2015] EWCA Civ 554, [2015] P.T.S.R. 1557 (CA (Civ Div)), Sullivan LJ

s.200, see *Johnston v City of Westminster* [2015] EWCA Civ 554, [2015] P.T.S.R. 1557 (CA (Civ Div)), Sullivan LJ

s.202, see *Nzolameso v Westminster City Council* [2015] UKSC 22, [2015] 2 All E.R. 942 (SC), Lady Hale DPSC; see *R. (on the application of N) v Lewisham LBC* [2015] A.C. 1259 (SC), Lord Neuberger PSC; see *Temur v Hackney LBC* [2014] EWCA Civ 877, [2015] 1 All E.R. 311 (CA (Civ Div)), Jackson LJ

s.203, see *Temur v Hackney LBC* [2014] EWCA Civ 877, [2015] 1 All E.R. 311 (CA (Civ Div)), Jackson LJ

s.204, see *Johnston v City of Westminster* [2015] EWCA Civ 554, [2015] P.T.S.R. 1557 (CA (Civ Div)), Sullivan LJ; see *Mohamoud v Kensington and Chelsea RLBC* [2015] EWCA Civ 780, [2015] H.L.R. 38 (CA (Civ Div)), Longmore LJ; see *Temur v Hackney LBC* [2014] EWCA Civ 877, [2015] 1 All E.R. 311 (CA (Civ Div)), Jackson LJ

s.206, see *Temur v Hackney LBC* [2014] EWCA Civ 877, [2015] 1 All E.R. 311 (CA (Civ Div)), Jackson LJ

s.208, see *Nzolameso v Westminster City Council* [2014] EWCA Civ 1383, [2015] P.T.S.R. 211 (CA (Civ Div)), Moore-Bick LJ; see *Nzolameso v Westminster City Council* [2015] UKSC 22, [2015] 2 All E.R. 942 (SC), Lady Hale DPSC; see *R. (on the application of AM) v Havering LBC* [2015] EWHC 1004 (Admin), [2015] P.T.S.R. 1242 (QBD (Admin)), Cobb J

s.210, see *Temur v Hackney LBC* [2014] EWCA Civ 877, [2015] 1 All E.R. 311 (CA (Civ Div)), Jackson LJ

s.213A, see *Mohamoud v Kensington and Chelsea RLBC* [2015] EWCA Civ 780, [2015] H.L.R. 38 (CA (Civ Div)), Longmore LJ; see *R. (on the application of AM) v Havering LBC* [2015] EWHC 1004 (Admin), [2015] P.T.S.R. 1242 (QBD (Admin)), Cobb J

s.220A, added: 2015 c.20 s.48

53. Housing Grants, Construction and Regeneration Act 1996

see *Ecovision Systems Ltd v Vinci Construction UK Ltd* [2015] EWHC 587 (TCC), [2015] 1 All E.R. (Comm) 1110 (QBD (TCC)), Judge Havelock-Allan QC; see *Galliford Try Building Ltd v Estura Ltd* [2015] EWHC 412 (TCC), [2015] B.L.R. 321 (QBD (TCC)), Edwards-Stuart J; see *Henia Investments Inc v Beck Interiors Ltd* [2015] EWHC 2433 (TCC), [2015] B.L.R. 704 (QBD (TCC)), Akenhead J; see *Imtech Inviron Ltd v Loppingdale Plant Ltd* [2014] EWHC 4006 (TCC), [2015] B.L.R. 183 (QBD (TCC)), Edwards-Stuart J; see *T Clarke (Scotland) Ltd v MMAXX Underfloor Heating Ltd* 2015 S.C. 233 (IH (Ex Div)), Lord Eassie

s.3, repealed: 2015 c.20 Sch.13 para.6

s.100, amended: SI 2015/914 Sch.1 para.57

s.104, see *Savoye v Spicers Ltd* [2014] EWHC 4195 (TCC), [2015] Bus. L.R. 242 (QBD (TCC)), Akenhead J

s.105, see *Savoye v Spicers Ltd* [2014] EWHC 4195 (TCC), [2015] Bus. L.R. 242 (QBD (TCC)), Akenhead J

s.108, see *Aspect Contracts (Asbestos) Ltd v Higgins Construction Plc* [2015] UKSC 38, [2015] 1 W.L.R. 2961 (SC), Lord Mance JSC; see *Hurley Palmer Flatt Ltd v Barclays Bank Plc* [2014] EWHC 3042 (TCC), [2015] Bus. L.R. 106 (QBD (TCC)), Ramsey J

s.111, see *Wilson and Sharp Investments Ltd v Harbour View Developments Ltd* [2014] EWHC 2875 (Ch), [2015] B.P.I.R. 199 (Ch D), Judge Hodge QC

55. Broadcasting Act 1996
    s.58, amended: SI 2015/904 Reg.2
    s.58A, enabling: SI 2015/904
    s.58ZA, added: SI 2015/904 Reg.3
56. Education Act 1996
    s.4, see *MA v Kensington and Chelsea*
    RLBC [2015] UKUT 186 (AAC), [2015]
    E.L.R. 326 (UT (AAC)), Judge Levenson
    s.9, see *Essex CC v TB* [2015] E.L.R. 67
    (UT (AAC)), Judge Rowland; see
    Hammersmith and Fulham LBC v L
    [2015] UKUT 523 (AAC), [2015] E.L.R.
    528 (UT (AAC)), Judge Mitchell; see
    KC v Hammersmith and Fulham LBC
    [2015] UKUT 177 (AAC), [2015] E.L.R.
    317 (UT (AAC)), Judge CG Ward; see
    MA v Kensington and Chelsea RLBC
    [2015] UKUT 186 (AAC), [2015] E.L.R.
    326 (UT (AAC)), Judge Levenson; see
    R. (on the application of Smieja) v Bexley
    LBC [2014] EWHC 4113 (Admin),
    [2015] B.L.G.R. 112 (QBD (Admin)),
    Neil Cameron QC
    s.13, amended: 2015 c.20 Sch.14 para.43
    s.15ZA, see *R. (on the application of*
    Smieja) v Bexley LBC [2014] EWHC
    4113 (Admin), [2015] B.L.G.R. 112
    (QBD (Admin)), Neil Cameron QC
    s.15ZA, amended: 2015 c.20 Sch.14
    para.44, SI 2015/1852 Art.2
    s.15ZC, amended: SI 2015/1852 Art.2
    s.29, enabling: SI 2015/902
    s.313, see *MC v Somerset CC* [2015]
    UKUT 461 (AAC) (UT (AAC)), Judge
    Ward
    s.316, see *KC v Hammersmith and*
    Fulham LBC [2015] UKUT 177 (AAC),
    [2015] E.L.R. 317 (UT (AAC)), Judge
    CG Ward; see *MA v Kensington and*
    Chelsea RLBC [2015] UKUT 186
    (AAC), [2015] E.L.R. 326 (UT (AAC)),
    Judge Levenson
    s.316A, see *KC v Hammersmith and*
    Fulham LBC [2015] UKUT 177 (AAC),
    [2015] E.L.R. 317 (UT (AAC)), Judge
    CG Ward
    s.323, see *MC v Somerset CC* [2015]
    UKUT 461 (AAC) (UT (AAC)), Judge
    Ward
    s.324, see *MC v Somerset CC* [2015]
    UKUT 461 (AAC) (UT (AAC)), Judge

Ward; see *R. (on the application of*
Smieja) v Bexley LBC [2014] EWHC
4113 (Admin), [2015] B.L.G.R. 112
(QBD (Admin)), Neil Cameron QC
    s.342, enabling: SI 2015/387, SI
    2015/728
    s.342A, enabling: SI 2015/728
    s.342B, enabling: SI 2015/728
    s.342C, enabling: SI 2015/728
    s.408, enabling: SI 2015/902, SI
    2015/1566
    s.507B, see *Hunt v North Somerset*
    Council [2015] UKSC 51, [2015] 1
    W.L.R. 3575 (SC), Lady Hale DPSC
    s.508B, see *P v East Sussex CC* [2014]
    EWHC 4634 (Admin), [2015] E.L.R. 178
    (QBD (Admin)), Timothy Straker QC
    s.537, enabling: SI 2015/902, SI
    2015/1566
    s.537A, enabling: SI 2015/902, SI
    2015/1566
    s.554, enabling: SI 2015/246, SI
    2015/247, SI 2015/831, SI 2015/832, SI
    2015/833, SI 2015/1429, SI 2015/1577,
    SI 2015/1799, SI 2015/1800, SI
    2015/1869
    s.556, enabling: SI 2015/246, SI
    2015/247, SI 2015/831, SI 2015/832, SI
    2015/833, SI 2015/1429, SI 2015/1577,
    SI 2015/1799, SI 2015/1800, SI
    2015/1869
    s.563, enabling: SI 2015/902
    s.569, enabling: SI 2015/387, SI
    2015/728, SI 2015/902, SI 2015/1566, SI
    2015/1793
    Sch.1 para.3, enabling: SI 2015/1793
    Sch.27 para.3, see *Essex CC v TB* [2015]
    E.L.R. 67 (UT (AAC)), Judge Rowland
61. Channel Tunnel Rail Link Act 1996
    Part I, amended: SI 2015/1682 Sch.1
    para.4
    s.17, amended: SI 2015/1682 Sch.1
    para.4
    s.21, amended: SI 2015/1682 Sch.1
    para.4
    s.21A, amended: SI 2015/1682 Sch.1
    para.4

1997

5. Firearms (Amendment) Act 1997
s.39, amended: SI 2015/860 Reg.2
s.39, substituted: SI 2015/860 Reg.2
8. Town and Country Planning (Scotland)
Act 1997
s.23D, enabling: SSI 2015/237
s.30, enabling: SSI 2015/235, SSI
2015/237
s.31, enabling: SSI 2015/235
s.32, enabling: SSI 2015/237, SSI
2015/249
s.40, enabling: SSI 2015/237, SSI
2015/249
s.43, enabling: SSI 2015/237
s.43A, enabling: SSI 2015/249
s.57, see *Sustainable Shetland v Scottish*
Ministers 2015 S.C. 59 (IH (1 Div)), The
Lord President (Gill)
s.75A, enabling: SSI 2015/249
s.75E, enabling: SSI 2015/249
s.135, varied: SI 2015/462 Reg.9
s.252, enabling: SSI 2015/181
s.267, enabling: SSI 2015/181, SSI
2015/233, SSI 2015/249
s.275, enabling: SSI 2015/233, SSI
2015/235, SSI 2015/237, SSI 2015/249
s.275A, enabling: SSI 2015/233, SSI
2015/249
9. Planning (Listed Buildings and
Conservation Areas) (Scotland) Act 1997
s.1A, enabling: SSI 2015/241, SSI
2015/328
s.5D, enabling: SSI 2015/233
s.9, enabling: SSI 2015/243, SSI
2015/328
s.10, enabling: SSI 2015/243
s.17, enabling: SSI 2015/243
s.23, enabling: SSI 2015/243, SSI
2015/328
s.25, enabling: SSI 2015/243
s.26, enabling: SSI 2015/243
s.28, enabling: SSI 2015/243
s.41D, enabling: SSI 2015/243
s.41I, enabling: SSI 2015/243
s.66, enabling: SSI 2015/243
s.73B, enabling: SSI 2015/240
s.82, enabling: SSI 2015/243, SSI
2015/328
Sch.3 para.1, enabling: SSI 2015/236

10. Planning (Hazardous Substances)
(Scotland) Act 1997
s.2, enabling: SSI 2015/181
s.3, enabling: SSI 2015/181
s.5, enabling: SSI 2015/181
s.6, enabling: SSI 2015/181
s.15, enabling: SSI 2015/181
s.16, enabling: SSI 2015/181
s.19, enabling: SSI 2015/181
s.22, enabling: SSI 2015/181
s.23, enabling: SSI 2015/181
s.27, enabling: SSI 2015/181
s.30, enabling: SSI 2015/181
s.39, enabling: SSI 2015/181
12. Civil Procedure Act 1997
s.1, see *Miaris v Secretary of State for*
Communities and Local Government
[2015] EWHC 2094 (Admin), [2015] 1
W.L.R. 4333 (QBD (Admin)), John
Howell QC
s.1, enabling: SI 2015/1881
s.2, enabling: SI 2015/670, SI 2015/877,
SI 2015/1569, SI 2015/1881
s.4, see *Miaris v Secretary of State for*
Communities and Local Government
[2015] EWHC 2094 (Admin), [2015] 1
W.L.R. 4333 (QBD (Admin)), John
Howell QC
16. Finance Act 1997
s.10, see *Aspinalls Club Ltd v Revenue*
and Customs Commissioners [2013]
EWCA Civ 1464, [2015] Ch. 79 (CA
(Civ Div)), Moses LJ
s.11, see *Aspinalls Club Ltd v Revenue*
and Customs Commissioners [2013]
EWCA Civ 1464, [2015] Ch. 79 (CA
(Civ Div)), Moses LJ; see *London Clubs*
Management Ltd v Revenue and Customs
Commissioners [2015] L.L.R. 363 (FTT
(Tax)), Judge Greg Sinfield
s.11, amended: 2015 c.11 s.60
s.12, enabling: SI 2015/1351
s.96, amended: SI 2015/575 Sch.1
para.20
Sch.1 Part II para.12, amended: SI
2015/664 Sch.2 para.10
27. Social Security (Recovery of Benefits)
Act 1997
Sch.1 Part I para.2, amended: 2015 c.30
Sch.5 para.13

28. Merchant Shipping and Maritime Security Act 1997
s.7, repealed: SI 2015/664 Sch.4 para.99

40. Protection from Harassment Act 1997
see *Crawford v Jenkins* [2014] EWCA
Civ 1035, [2015] 3 W.L.R. 843 (CA (Civ
Div)), Beatson LJ; see *R. (on the
application of Catt) v Association of
Chief Police Officers of England, Wales
and Northern Ireland* [2015] UKSC 9,
[2015] A.C. 1065 (SC), Lord Neuberger
PSC; see *R. v Chinegwundoh (Harold)*
[2015] EWCA Crim 109, [2015] 1
W.L.R. 2818 (CA (Crim Div)), Sir Brian
Leveson PQBD
s.1, see *Crawford v Jenkins* [2014]
EWCA Civ 1035, [2015] 3 W.L.R. 843
(CA (Civ Div)), Beatson LJ; see *Hayes v
Butters* [2014] EWHC 4557 (Ch), [2015]
Ch. 495 (Ch D), Nugee J
s.4A, see *R. v Boardman (David)* [2015]
EWCA Crim 175, [2015] 1 Cr. App. R.
33 (CA (Crim Div)), Sir Brian Leveson
PQBD
s.5, see *R. v Chinegwundoh (Harold)*
[2015] EWCA Crim 109, [2015] 1
W.L.R. 2818 (CA (Crim Div)), Sir Brian
Leveson PQBD
s.5A, see *R. v Chinegwundoh (Harold)*
[2015] EWCA Crim 109, [2015] 1
W.L.R. 2818 (CA (Crim Div)), Sir Brian
Leveson PQBD

43. Crime (Sentences) Act 1997
see *Campbell (David) v HM Advocate*
[2015] HCJAC 28, 2015 S.L.T. 232
(HCJ), Lord Eassie
s.28, see *R. (on the application of
Kaiyam) v Secretary of State for Justice*
[2015] A.C. 1344 (SC), Lord Neuberger
PSC; see *R. v Vowles (Lucinda)* [2015]
EWCA Crim 45, [2015] 1 W.L.R. 5131
(CA (Civ Div)), Lord Thomas LCJ
s.28, amended: 2015 c.2 s.11
s.31, amended: 2015 c.2 Sch.2 para.1
s.32, amended: 2015 c.2 s.11
s.32ZA, added: 2015 c.2 s.12
s.40, amended: SI 2015/583 Sch.2 para.5
Sch.1 Part II para.8, amended: 2015 c.2
Sch.1 para.12
Sch.1 Part II para.9, amended: 2015 c.2
Sch.1 para.12

Sch.1 Pt II para.6, see *Campbell (David)
v HM Advocate* [2015] HCJAC 28, 2015
S.L.T. 232 (HCJ), Lord Eassie

44. Education Act 1997
s.19, amended: 2015 c.20 s.66
s.19, repealed: 2015 c.20 s.66

48. Crime and Punishment (Scotland) Act 1997
s.9, repealed: 2015 asp 9 s.49
s.43, repealed: SSI 2015/39 Sch.1 para.6
Sch.1 para.13, repealed: SSI 2015/39
Sch.1 para.6

50. Police Act 1997
see *R. (on the application of B) v Chief
Constable of Hampshire* [2015] EWHC
1238 (Admin), [2015] 1 W.L.R. 5250
(QBD (Admin)), Jeremy Baker J
s.113A, see *R. (on the application of T) v
Chief Constable of Greater Manchester*
[2015] A.C. 49 (SC), Lord Neuberger
JSC
s.113A, amended: SSI 2015/330 Art.3,
SSI 2015/423 Art.3
s.113A, repealed: SSI 2015/330 Art.3 ,
SSI 2015/423 Art.3
s.113B, see *R. (on the application of T) v
Chief Constable of Greater Manchester*
[2015] A.C. 49 (SC), Lord Neuberger
JSC
s.113B, amended: SSI 2015/330 Art.3,
SSI 2015/423 Art.3
s.113B, repealed: SSI 2015/330 Art.3 ,
SSI 2015/423 Art.3
s.116ZA, added: SSI 2015/330 Art.3, SSI
2015/423 Art.3
s.116ZA, repealed: SSI 2015/330 Art.3
s.117, amended: SSI 2015/330 Art.3, SSI
2015/423 Art.3
s.117, repealed: SSI 2015/330 Art.3
s.126, amended: SSI 2015/330 Art.3, SSI
2015/423 Art.3
s.126ZA, added: SSI 2015/330 Art.3, SSI
2015/423 Art.3
s.126ZA, repealed: SSI 2015/330 Art.3
Sch.8A, added: SSI 2015/330 Art.3, SSI
2015/423 Art.3
Sch.8A, repealed: SSI 2015/330 Art.3

51. Sex Offenders Act 1997
s.1, see *R. (on the application of Hamill)
v Chelmsford Magistrates' Court* [2014]

EWHC 2799 (Admin), [2015] 1 W.L.R.
1798 (QBD (Admin)), Aikens LJ
53. Dangerous Dogs (Amendment) Act 1997
s.4, enabling: SI 2015/138
**68. Special Immigration Appeals
Commission Act 1997**
s.1, amended: 2015 c.2 s.66
s.2C, see *R. (on the application of
Secretary of State for the Home
Department) v Special Immigration
Appeals Commission* [2015] EWHC 681
(Admin), [2015] 1 W.L.R. 4799 (DC),
Sir Brian Leveson PQBD
s.2D, see *R. (on the application of
Secretary of State for the Home
Department) v Special Immigration
Appeals Commission* [2015] EWHC 681
(Admin), [2015] 1 W.L.R. 4799 (DC),
Sir Brian Leveson PQBD
s.2D, amended: 2015 c.6 s.47
s.5, enabling: SI 2015/867
s.7, amended: 2015 c.2 s.66
s.7B, added: 2015 c.2 s.66
s.8, amended: 2015 c.2 s.66
s.8, enabling: SI 2015/867

1998

**2. Public Processions (Northern Ireland)
Act 1998**
s.6, amended: SI 2015/235 Art.2
s.7, amended: SI 2015/235 Art.3
s.7A, added: SI 2015/235 Art.4
11. Bank of England Act 1998
s.9I, enabling: SI 2015/905, SI 2015/909
s.9L, enabling: SI 2015/905, SI 2015/909
14. Social Security Act 1998
s.9, enabling: SI 2015/339
s.10, enabling: SI 2015/339
s.15A, repealed: 2015 c.20 s.79
s.27, see *R. (on the application of Reilly)
v Secretary of State for Work and
Pensions* [2014] EWHC 2182 (Admin),
[2015] Q.B. 573 (QBD (Admin)), Lang J
s.79, enabling: SI 2015/339
s.84, enabling: SI 2015/339
17. Petroleum Act 1998
Part IA, added: 2015 c.7 s.41
s.4, enabling: SI 2015/766
s.4A, added: 2015 c.7 s.50

s.4B, amended: 2015 c.7 s.50
Sch.4 para.12, repealed: 2015 c.20
Sch.23 para.17
**20. Late Payment of Commercial Debts
(Interest) Act 1998**
see *Martrade Shipping & Transport
GmbH v United Enterprises Corp* [2014]
EWHC 1884 (Comm), [2015] 1 W.L.R. 1
(QBD (Comm)), Popplewell J
s.4, amended: SI 2015/102 Sch.6 para.1,
SI 2015/1336 Reg.2, SSI 2015/226
Reg.2, SSI 2015/446 Sch.6 para.1
s.4, repealed: SI 2015/1336 Reg.2 , SSI
2015/226 Reg.2
s.12, see *Martrade Shipping & Transport
GmbH v United Enterprises Corp* [2014]
EWHC 1884 (Comm), [2015] 1 W.L.R. 1
(QBD (Comm)), Popplewell J
23. Public Interest Disclosure Act 1998
see *Smania v Standard Chartered Bank*
[2015] I.C.R. 436 (EAT), Langstaff J
29. Data Protection Act 1998
see *Christian Institute v Lord Advocate*
[2015] CSIH 64, 2015 S.L.T. 633 (IH (2
Div)), The Lord Justice Clerk
(Carloway); see *Christian Institute v
Lord Advocate* [2015] CSOH 7, 2015
S.L.T. 72 (OH), Lord Pentland; see
*Gavin Edmondson Solicitors Ltd v Haven
Insurance Co Ltd* [2014] EWHC 3062
(QB), [2015] R.T.R. 14 (QBD (Merc)),
Judge Milwyn Jarman QC; see *Grace v
Black Horse Ltd* [2014] EWCA Civ
1413, [2015] 3 All E.R. 223 (CA (Civ
Div)), Lord Dyson MR; see *L v R* [2015]
EWCA Civ 61, Times, April 7, 2015 (CA
(Civ Div)), Aikens LJ; see *Law Society
(Solicitors Regulation Authority), Re*
[2015] EWHC 166 (Ch), [2015] 1
W.L.R. 4064 (Ch D), Iain Purvis QC; see
*R. (on the application of B) v Chief
Constable of Hampshire* [2015] EWHC
1238 (Admin), [2015] 1 W.L.R. 5250
(QBD (Admin)), Jeremy Baker J; see *R.
(on the application of C) v
Northumberland CC* [2015] EWHC 2134
(Admin), [2015] B.L.G.R. 675 (QBD
(Admin)), Simon J; see *R. (on the
application of Catt) v Association of
Chief Police Officers of England, Wales
and Northern Ireland* [2015] UKSC 9,

[2015] A.C. 1065 (SC), Lord Neuberger PSC; see *Various Claimants v McAlpine* [2015] EWHC 3543 (QB), [2015] 6 Costs L.R. 1085 (QBD), Supperstone J; see *Vidal-Hall v Google Inc* [2015] EWCA Civ 311, [2015] 3 W.L.R. 409 (CA (Civ Div)), Lord Dyson MR
s.7, see *Beggs v Scottish Information Commissioner* [2015] CSIH 17, 2015 S.C. 520 (IH (2 Div)), The Lord Justice Clerk (Carloway); see *Kololo v Commissioner of Police of the Metropolis* [2015] EWHC 600 (QB), [2015] 1 W.L.R. 3702 (QBD), Dingemans J; see *R. (on the application of C) v Northumberland CC* [2015] EWHC 2134 (Admin), [2015] B.L.G.R. 675 (QBD (Admin)), Simon J; see *Ranger v House of Lords Appointments Commission* [2015] EWHC 45 (QB), [2015] 1 W.L.R. 4324 (QBD), Knowles J
s.10, see *Mosley v Google Inc* [2015] EWHC 59 (QB), [2015] 2 C.M.L.R. 22 (QBD), Mitting J
s.13, see *Grace v Black Horse Ltd* [2014] EWCA Civ 1413, [2015] 3 All E.R. 223 (CA (Civ Div)), Lord Dyson MR; see *Vidal-Hall v Google Inc* [2015] EWCA Civ 311, [2015] 3 W.L.R. 409 (CA (Civ Div)), Lord Dyson MR
s.75, enabling: SI 2015/312
Sch.2, see *Gavin Edmondson Solicitors Ltd v Haven Insurance Co Ltd* [2014] EWHC 3062 (QB), [2015] R.T.R. 14 (QBD (Merc)), Judge Milwyn Jarman QC
Sch.3, see *Gavin Edmondson Solicitors Ltd v Haven Insurance Co Ltd* [2014] EWHC 3062 (QB), [2015] R.T.R. 14 (QBD (Merc)), Judge Milwyn Jarman QC
Sch.7 para.3, see *Ranger v House of Lords Appointments Commission* [2015] EWHC 45 (QB), [2015] 1 W.L.R. 4324 (QBD), Knowles J

30. Teaching and Higher Education Act 1998
s.22, enabling: SI 2015/54, SI 2015/181, SI 2015/1418, SI 2015/1505, SI 2015/1951

s.42, enabling: SI 2015/54, SI 2015/181, SI 2015/1418, SI 2015/1505, SI 2015/1951

31. School Standards and Framework Act 1998
s.45A, enabling: SI 2015/2033
s.45AA, enabling: SI 2015/2033
s.47, enabling: SI 2015/2033
s.47A, enabling: SI 2015/2033
s.47ZA, enabling: SI 2015/2033
s.48, enabling: SI 2015/2033
s.49, enabling: SI 2015/2033
s.69, enabling: SI 2015/1267, SI 2015/1344, SI 2015/1636, SI 2015/1804, SI 2015/2075
s.72, enabling: SI 2015/887
s.110, repealed: 2015 c.20 Sch.16 para.2
s.122, enabling: SI 2015/1599
s.138, amended: 2015 c.20 Sch.16 para.2
s.138, enabling: SI 2015/1599
Sch.26 para.6B, enabling: SI 2015/1599
Sch.26 para.13B, enabling: SI 2015/1599

32. Police (Northern Ireland) Act 1998
s.60ZA, amended: SI 2015/798 Sch.1 para.1

36. Finance Act 1998
Sch.18 Part I para.1, amended: 2015 c.33 Sch.3 para.3
Sch.18 Part II para.8, amended: 2015 c.33 s.38, Sch.3 para.3
Sch.18 Part V para.40, amended: 2015 c.33 Sch.8 para.40
Sch.18 Part IXE, added: 2015 c.11 Sch.2 para.2
Sch.18 Pt V para.41, see *Burgess v Revenue and Customs Commissioners* [2015] UKUT 578 (TCC), [2015] B.T.C. 533 (UT (Tax)), Judge Roger Berner
Sch.18 Pt V para.42, see *Burgess v Revenue and Customs Commissioners* [2015] UKUT 578 (TCC), [2015] B.T.C. 533 (UT (Tax)), Judge Roger Berner
Sch.18 Pt V para.43, see *Burgess v Revenue and Customs Commissioners* [2015] UKUT 578 (TCC), [2015] B.T.C. 533 (UT (Tax)), Judge Roger Berner
Sch.18 Pt V para.46, see *Burgess v Revenue and Customs Commissioners* [2015] UKUT 578 (TCC), [2015] B.T.C. 533 (UT (Tax)), Judge Roger Berner

37. Crime and Disorder Act 1998
   see *Birmingham City Council v Riaz*
   [2014] EWHC 4247 (Fam), [2015] 2
   F.L.R. 763 (Fam Div), Keehan J; see
   Campbell (David) v HM Advocate [2015]
   HCJAC 28, 2015 S.L.T. 232 (HCJ), Lord
   Eassie
   s.1C, see *R. v Hashi (Adam)* [2014]
   EWCA Crim 2119, [2015] 1 Cr. App. R.
   (S.) 17 (CA (Crim Div)), Treacy LJ
   s.41, amended: 2015 c.2 s.40, SI 2015/79
   Art.2
   s.41, repealed: 2015 c.2 s.40 , SI 2015/79
   Art.2
   s.41, enabling: SI 2015/79
   s.51, see *R. (on the application of Janner)
   v Westminster Magistrates' Court* [2015]
   EWHC 2578 (Admin), (2015) 179 J.P.
   465 (DC), Rafferty LJ
   s.51, amended: 2015 c.2 s.52
   s.51A, see *R. (on the application of DPP)
   v South Tyneside Youth Court* [2015]
   EWHC 1455 (Admin), [2015] 2 Cr. App.
   R. (S.) 59 (DC), Sir Brian Leveson
   PQBD; see *R. (on the application of P) v
   Derby Youth Court* [2015] EWHC 573
   (Admin), (2015) 179 J.P. 139 (DC),
   Davis LJ
   s.66B, amended: 2015 c.2 s.41
   s.66ZA, amended: 2015 c.2 s.41
   s.96, see *Mack v Dunn* [2015] HCJAC
   113 (HCJ), The Lord Justice Clerk
   (Carloway); see *R v Murphy* [2015]
   HCJAC 34, 2015 S.C.L. 577 (HCJ), Lord
   Brodie
   s.102, see *R. v Hookway (Lee)* [2015]
   EWCA Crim 931, [2015] 2 Cr. App. R.
   (S.) 43 (CA (Crim Div)), Fulford LJ
   Sch.8 para.135, see *Campbell (David) v
   HM Advocate* [2015] HCJAC 28, 2015
   S.L.T. 232 (HCJ), Lord Eassie
39. National Minimum Wage Act 1998
   see *Shannon v Rampersad (t/a Clifton
   House Residential Home)* [2015] I.R.L.R.
   982 (EAT), Judge Peter Clark
   s.1, enabling: SI 2015/621, SI 2015/1724
   s.2, enabling: SI 2015/621, SI 2015/1724
   s.3, enabling: SI 2015/621, SI 2015/1724
   s.9, enabling: SI 2015/621
   s.19A, amended: 2015 c.26 s.152
   s.19A, repealed: 2015 c.26 s.152

   s.46, amended: SI 2015/2001 Art.2
   s.51, enabling: SI 2015/621, SI
   2015/1724
41. Competition Act 1998
   Part I c.IV, substituted: 2015 c.15 Sch.8
   para.2
   Part I c.IV, substituted: 2015 c.15 Sch.8
   para.3
   s.2, see *Arcadia Group Brands Ltd v Visa
   Inc* [2015] EWCA Civ 883, [2015] Bus.
   L.R. 1362 (CA (Civ Div)), Sir Terence
   Etherton C; see *Lindum Construction Co
   Ltd v Office of Fair Trading* [2014]
   EWHC 1613 (Ch), [2015] 2 All E.R. 177
   (Ch D), Morgan J
   s.31, see *R. (on the application of
   Gallaher Group Ltd) v Competition and
   Markets Authority* [2015] EWHC 84
   (Admin), [2015] U.K.C.L.R. 209 (QBD
   (Admin)), Collins J
   s.31A, see *Skyscanner Ltd v Competition
   and Markets Authority* [2015] 3 All E.R.
   67 (CAT), Peter Freeman QC; see
   *Skyscanner Ltd v Competition and
   Markets Authority* [2015] Comp. A.R. 91
   (CAT), Peter Freeman QC
   s.37, see *Lindum Construction Co Ltd v
   Office of Fair Trading* [2014] EWHC
   1613 (Ch), [2015] 2 All E.R. 177 (Ch D),
   Morgan J
   s.46, see *Lindum Construction Co Ltd v
   Office of Fair Trading* [2014] EWHC
   1613 (Ch), [2015] 2 All E.R. 177 (Ch D),
   Morgan J
   s.47, see *Skyscanner Ltd v Competition
   and Markets Authority* [2015] 3 All E.R.
   67 (CAT), Peter Freeman QC; see
   *Skyscanner Ltd v Competition and
   Markets Authority* [2015] Comp. A.R. 29
   (CAT), Peter Freeman QC
   s.47A, see *DSG Retail Ltd v Mastercard
   Inc* [2015] CAT 7, [2015] Comp. A.R.
   199 (CAT), Roth J
   s.47A, substituted: 2015 c.15 Sch.8
   para.4
   s.47B, substituted: 2015 c.15 Sch.8
   para.5
   s.47C, added: 2015 c.15 Sch.8 para.6
   s.47D, added: 2015 c.15 Sch.8 para.7
   s.47E, added: 2015 c.15 Sch.8 para.8
   s.49, amended: 2015 c.15 Sch.8 para.9

s.49, repealed: 2015 c.15 Sch.8 para.9

s.49A, added: 2015 c.15 Sch.8 para.10

s.49B, added: 2015 c.15 Sch.8 para.11

s.49C, added: 2015 c.15 Sch.8 para.12

s.49C, enabling: SI 2015/1587

s.54, amended: SI 2015/1682 Sch.1
para.4

s.58, amended: 2015 c.15 Sch.8 para.13

s.58A, substituted: 2015 c.15 Sch.8
para.14

s.59, amended: 2015 c.15 Sch.8 para.15

s.71, amended: 2015 c.15 Sch.8 para.16

s.71, enabling: SI 2015/1587

Sch.6A, see *Skyscanner Ltd v
Competition and Markets Authority*
[2015] 3 All E.R. 67 (CAT), Peter
Freeman QC

Sch.8 Part I para.2, amended: 2015 c.15
Sch.8 para.17

Sch.8 Part I para.3B, added: 2015 c.15
Sch.8 para.17

Sch.8 para.3A, see *Skyscanner Ltd v
Competition and Markets Authority*
[2015] 3 All E.R. 67 (CAT), Peter
Freeman QC

42. Human Rights Act 1998

see *D v Commissioner of Police of the
Metropolis* [2014] EWHC 2493 (QB),
[2015] 1 W.L.R. 1833 (QBD), Green J;
see *DW (A Child) (Termination of
Parental Responsibility), Re* [2014]
EWCA Civ 315, [2015] 1 F.L.R. 166
(CA (Civ Div)), Arden LJ; see *K
(Children) (Unrepresented Father:
Cross-Examination of Child), Re* [2015]
EWCA Civ 543, [2015] 1 W.L.R. 3801
(CA (Civ Div)), Lord Dyson MR; see
Lord Advocate v Merica 2015 S.L.T. (Sh
Ct) 171 (Sh Ct (Lothian) (Edinburgh)),
Sheriff T Welsh, QC; see *McCreaner v
Ministry of Justice* [2014] EWHC 569
(QB), [2015] 1 W.L.R. 354 (QBD),
Cranston J; see *Montgomery v
Lanarkshire Health Board* [2015] UKSC
11, [2015] A.C. 1430 (SC), Lord
Neuberger PSC; see *N (An Adult) (Court
of Protection: Jurisdiction), Re* [2015]
EWCA Civ 411, [2015] 3 W.L.R. 1585
(CA (Civ Div)), Sir James Munby PFD;
see *R. (on the application of Eastenders
Cash & Carry Plc) v Revenue and*

Customs Commissioners [2015] A.C.
1101 (SC), Lord Neuberger PSC; see *R.
(on the application of Hardy) v Sandwell
MBC* [2015] EWHC 890 (Admin),
[2015] P.T.S.R. 1292 (QBD (Admin)),
Phillips J; see *R. (on the application of
Keyu) v Secretary of State for Foreign
and Commonwealth Affairs* [2014]
EWCA Civ 312, [2015] Q.B. 57 (CA
(Civ Div)), Maurice Kay LJ; see *R. (on
the application of Keyu) v Secretary of
State for Foreign and Commonwealth
Affairs* [2015] UKSC 69, [2015] 3
W.L.R. 1665 (SC), Lord Neuberger PSC;
see *R. (on the application of Lord
Carlile of Berriew QC) v Secretary of
State for the Home Department* [2015]
A.C. 945 (SC), Lord Neuberger PSC; see
*R. (on the application of Revenue and
Customs Commissioners) v HM Coroner
for Liverpool* [2014] EWHC 1586
(Admin), [2015] Q.B. 481 (DC), Gross
LJ

s.1, see *W v Ministry of Justice* [2015]
EWCA Civ 742, [2015] 3 W.L.R. 1909
(CA (Civ Div)), Lord Dyson MR

s.2, see *Breyer Group Plc v Department
of Energy and Climate Change* [2015]
EWCA Civ 408, [2015] 1 W.L.R. 4559
(CA (Civ Div)), Lord Dyson MR; see
Moohan, Petitioner 2015 S.C. 1 (IH (1
Div)), The Lord President (Gill); see *R.
(on the application of Harkins) v
Secretary of State for the Home
Department* [2014] EWHC 3609
(Admin), [2015] 1 W.L.R. 2975 (QBD
(Admin)), Aikens LJ

s.3, see *Allan v Revenue and Customs
Commissioners* [2015] UKUT 16 (TCC),
[2015] S.T.C. 890 (UT (Tax)), Barling J;
see *HM's Application for Judicial
Review, Re* [2015] M.H.L.R. 326 (QBD
(NI)), Treacy J; see *K (Children)
(Unrepresented Father: Cross-
Examination of Child), Re* [2015] EWCA
Civ 543, [2015] 1 W.L.R. 3801 (CA (Civ
Div)), Lord Dyson MR; see *R. (on the
application of Barclay) v Secretary of
State for Justice* [2015] A.C. 276 (SC),
Lord Neuberger JSC; see *Smith v
Carillion (JM) Ltd* [2015] EWCA Civ

209, [2015] I.R.L.R. 467 (CA (Civ Div)), Elias LJ; see *W v Ministry of Justice* [2015] EWCA Civ 742, [2015] 3 W.L.R. 1909 (CA (Civ Div)), Lord Dyson MR; see *Warren v Care Fertility (Northampton) Ltd* [2014] EWHC 602 (Fam), [2015] Fam. 1 (Fam Div), Hogg J; see *Z (A Child) (Surrogate Father: Parental Order), Re* [2015] EWFC 73, [2015] 1 W.L.R. 4993 (Fam Ct), Sir James Munby PFD; see *Z (Children) (Application for Release of DNA Profiles), Re* [2015] EWCA Civ 34, [2015] 1 W.L.R. 2501 (CA (Civ Div)), Lord Dyson MR

s.4, see *R. (on the application of Barclay) v Secretary of State for Justice* [2015] A.C. 276 (SC), Lord Neuberger JSC; see *R. (on the application of Bibi) v Secretary of State for the Home Department* [2015] UKSC 68, [2015] 1 W.L.R. 5055 (SC), Lord Neuberger PSC; see *R. (on the application of Mahoney) v Secretary of State for Communities and Local Government* [2015] EWHC 589 (Admin), [2015] R.V.R. 237 (QBD (Admin)), Lindblom J; see *W v Ministry of Justice* [2015] EWCA Civ 742, [2015] 3 W.L.R. 1909 (CA (Civ Div)), Lord Dyson MR

s.6, see *Cooper-Hohn v Hohn* [2014] EWHC 2314 (Fam), [2015] 1 F.L.R. 19 (Fam Div), Roberts J; see *J-M (A Child) (Contact Proceedings: Balance of Harm), Re* [2014] EWCA Civ 434, [2015] 1 F.L.R. 838 (CA (Civ Div)), Maurice Kay LJ; see *McCaffer v Lord Advocate* 2015 S.L.T. (Sh Ct) 44 (Sh Ct (Glasgow)), Sheriff A F Deutsch; see *Nicholas v Secretary of State for Defence* [2015] EWCA Civ 53, [2015] 1 W.L.R. 2116 (CA (Civ Div)), Lord Dyson MR; see *R. (on the application of JS) v Secretary of State for Work and Pensions* [2015] UKSC 16, [2015] 1 W.L.R. 1449 (SC), Lady Hale DPSC; see *R. (on the application of Roberts) v Commissioner of Police of the Metropolis* [2015] UKSC 79 (SC), Lady Hale DPSC; see *R. v Brown (Edward)* [2015] EWCA Crim 1328, [2015] 2 Cr. App. R. 31 (CA (Crim Div)), Fulford LJ; see *Southward*

Housing Co-operative Ltd v Walker [2015] EWHC 1615 (Ch), [2015] 2 P. & C.R. 13 (Ch D), Hildyard J; see *W v Ministry of Justice* [2015] EWCA Civ 742, [2015] 3 W.L.R. 1909 (CA (Civ Div)), Lord Dyson MR

s.7, see *Beggs v Scottish Ministers* [2015] CSOH 98, 2015 S.L.T. 487 (OH), Lady Stacey; see *G (A Child) (Same-sex Relationship: Family Life Declaration), Re* [2015] Fam. 133 (Fam Ct), Peter Jackson J; see *N (An Adult) (Court of Protection: Jurisdiction), Re* [2015] EWCA Civ 411, [2015] 3 W.L.R. 1585 (CA (Civ Div)), Sir James Munby PFD; see *W v Ministry of Justice* [2015] EWCA Civ 742, [2015] 3 W.L.R. 1909 (CA (Civ Div)), Lord Dyson MR

s.8, see *D v Commissioner of Police of the Metropolis* [2014] EWHC 2493 (QB), [2015] 1 W.L.R. 1833 (QBD), Green J; see *E (A Child) (Care Order: Change of Care Plan), Re* [2015] Fam. 145 (Fam Ct), Baker J; see *W v Ministry of Justice* [2015] EWCA Civ 742, [2015] 3 W.L.R. 1909 (CA (Civ Div)), Lord Dyson MR

s.9, see *W v Ministry of Justice* [2015] EWCA Civ 742, [2015] 3 W.L.R. 1909 (CA (Civ Div)), Lord Dyson MR

s.12, see *BBC, Re* [2015] A.C. 588 (SC), Lady Hale DPSC; see *Interflora Inc v Marks & Spencer Plc* [2014] EWHC 4168 (Ch), [2015] F.S.R. 13 (Ch D), Birss J; see *Merlin Entertainments LPC v Cave* [2014] EWHC 3036 (QB), [2015] E.M.L.R. 3 (QBD), Elisabeth Laing J

43. Statute Law (Repeals) Act 1998
Sch.2 para.9, repealed: 2015 c.20 Sch.23 para.32

46. Scotland Act 1998
see *Christian Institute v Lord Advocate* [2015] CSIH 64, 2015 S.L.T. 633 (IH (2 Div)), The Lord Justice Clerk (Carloway)
s.2, amended: SI 2015/1764 Art.4
s.12, enabling: SI 2015/743, SSI 2015/425
s.15, enabling: SSI 2015/350
s.29, see *Christian Institute v Lord Advocate* [2015] CSOH 7, 2015 S.L.T. 72 (OH), Lord Pentland

s.30, enabling: SI 2015/211, SI 2015/692,
SI 2015/1379, SI 2015/1764
s.35, see *Moohan, Petitioner* 2015 S.C. 1
(IH (1 Div)), The Lord President (Gill)
s.58, see *Moohan, Petitioner* 2015 S.C. 1
(IH (1 Div)), The Lord President (Gill)
s.63, enabling: SI 2015/692
s.66, amended: SI 2015/932 Art.2
s.66, enabling: SI 2015/932
s.80G, enabling: SI 2015/1810
s.100, see *Beggs v Scottish Ministers*
[2015] CSOH 98, 2015 S.L.T. 487 (OH),
Lady Stacey
s.104, enabling: SI 2015/48, SI 2015/374,
SI 2015/444, SI 2015/700, SI 2015/907
s.105, enabling: SI 2015/647
s.111, enabling: SI 2015/203
s.112, enabling: SI 2015/48, SI 2015/374,
SI 2015/444, SI 2015/647, SI 2015/700,
SI 2015/907
s.113, enabling: SI 2015/48, SI 2015/203,
SI 2015/374, SI 2015/444, SI 2015/647,
SI 2015/692, SI 2015/700, SI 2015/743,
SI 2015/907, SSI 2015/425
s.114, enabling: SI 2015/444, SI
2015/700
s.124, enabling: SI 2015/692
s.126, see *Christian Institute v Lord
Advocate* [2015] CSOH 7, 2015 S.L.T.
72 (OH), Lord Pentland
s.126, enabling: SI 2015/200
Sch.4 Part I para.4, amended: SI
2015/692 Art.3, SI 2015/1764 Art.2
Sch.5, see *Christian Institute v Lord
Advocate* [2015] CSOH 7, 2015 S.L.T.
72 (OH), Lord Pentland
Sch.5 Part II paraE.1, amended: SI
2015/1379 Art.2
Sch.5 Part II paraB.3, amended: SI
2015/692 Art.4, SI 2015/1764 Art.3
47. Northern Ireland Act 1998
s.34, enabling: SI 2015/222, SI
2015/1610, SI 2015/1939
s.84, enabling: SI 2015/566

1999

**2. Social Security Contributions (Transfer
of Functions, etc.) Act 1999**
s.4, amended: 2015 c.5 Sch.1 para.24

s.8, amended: 2015 c.5 Sch.1 para.25
s.9, enabling: SI 2015/174
s.11, enabling: SI 2015/174
s.13, enabling: SI 2015/174, SI 2015/521
s.25, enabling: SI 2015/174, SI 2015/521
Sch.3 para.12, repealed: 2015 c.5 Sch.1
para.26
Sch.9 para.3, repealed: 2015 c.5 Sch.1
para.27
Sch.9 para.7, repealed: 2015 c.5 Sch.1
para.27
8. Health Act 1999
s.44, enabling: SI 2015/864
s.60, enabling: SI 2015/794, SI 2015/806
s.62, enabling: SI 2015/794, SI 2015/806
s.63, enabling: SI 2015/864
Sch.3, enabling: SI 2015/794, SI
2015/806
**11. Breeding and Sale of Dogs (Welfare) Act
1999**
s.2, repealed: 2015 c.20 Sch.23 para.36
s.8, amended: 2015 c.20 Sch.23 para.41
s.8, repealed: 2015 c.20 Sch.23 para.41
16. Finance Act 1999
s.132, enabling: SI 2015/125, SI
2015/1378
s.133, enabling: SI 2015/2, SI 2015/125,
SI 2015/1516, SI 2015/1927
22. Access to Justice Act 1999
see *Coventry v Lawrence* [2015] A.C.
106 (SC), Lord Neuberger PSC; see
Coventry v Lawrence [2015] UKSC 50,
[2015] 1 W.L.R. 3485 (SC), Lord
Neuberger PSC; see *Rayner v Lord
Chancellor* [2015] EWCA Civ 1124,
[2015] 6 Costs L.R. 957 (CA (Civ Div)),
McCombe LJ
s.7, enabling: SI 2015/838
s.10, enabling: SI 2015/838
s.17A, enabling: SI 2015/838
s.22, see *AB (A Child) (Temporary Leave
to Remove from Jurisdiction: Expert
Evidence), Re* [2014] EWHC 2758
(Fam), [2015] 1 F.C.R. 164 (Fam Div),
Judge Clifford Bellamy
s.25, enabling: SI 2015/838
s.26, enabling: SI 2015/838
s.54, see *Patel v Mussa* [2015] EWCA
Civ 434, [2015] 1 W.L.R. 4788 (CA (Civ
Div)), Moore-Bick LJ

s.55, see *Miaris v Secretary of State for Communities and Local Government* [2015] EWHC 2094 (Admin), [2015] 1 W.L.R. 4333 (QBD (Admin)), John Howell QC
s.68, amended: SSI 2015/150 Sch.1 para.6
Sch.3 para.3B, enabling: SI 2015/838
Sch.3 para.8, enabling: SI 2015/838

23. Youth Justice and Criminal Evidence Act 1999

s.17, amended: 2015 c.30 s.46
s.25, amended: 2015 c.30 s.46
s.27, see *R. v Lubemba (Cokesix)* [2014] EWCA Crim 2064, [2015] 1 W.L.R. 1579 (CA (Crim Div)), Hallett LJ
s.29, see *R. (on the application of OP) v Secretary of State for Justice* [2014] EWHC 1944 (Admin), [2015] 1 Cr. App. R. 7 (DC), Rafferty LJ
s.33, amended: 2015 c.30 s.46
s.33BA, see *R. (on the application of OP) v Secretary of State for Justice* [2014] EWHC 1944 (Admin), [2015] 1 Cr. App. R. 7 (DC), Rafferty LJ
s.36, see *Abbas v Crown Prosecution Service* [2015] EWHC 579 (Admin), [2015] 2 Cr. App. R. 11 (DC), Hallett LJ
s.37, enabling: SI 2015/1490, SI 2015/1813
s.38, see *Abbas v Crown Prosecution Service* [2015] EWHC 579 (Admin), [2015] 2 Cr. App. R. 11 (DC), Hallett LJ
s.38, enabling: SI 2015/1490, SI 2015/1813
s.45A, added: 2015 c.2 s.78
s.49, amended: 2015 c.2 s.78
s.50, amended: 2015 c.2 s.78
s.61, enabling: SI 2015/727, SI 2015/1805
s.65, enabling: SI 2015/726, SI 2015/1813
s.68, enabling: SI 2015/818
Sch.2A, added: 2015 c.2 Sch.15 para.2
Sch.2 para.2, repealed: 2015 c.2 s.79

24. Pollution Prevention and Control Act 1999

s.2, enabling: SI 2015/324, SI 2015/918, SI 2015/934, SI 2015/1360, SI 2015/1417, SI 2015/1756, SI 2015/1849, SSI 2015/101

s.7, enabling: SI 2015/1756, SI 2015/1849, SSI 2015/74, SSI 2015/139
Sch.1, enabling: SI 2015/324, SI 2015/918, SI 2015/1360, SI 2015/1417, SI 2015/1756, SI 2015/1849, SSI 2015/101
Sch.1 Part I para.20, enabling: SI 2015/816, SI 2015/1352
Sch.1 Part II para.25, amended: SI 2015/664 Sch.4 para.90

26. Employment Relations Act 1999

s.10, see *Dhunna v Creditsights Ltd* [2014] EWCA Civ 1238, [2015] I.C.R. 105 (CA (Civ Div)), Rimer LJ
s.34, enabling: SI 2015/226

27. Local Government Act 1999

s.1, repealed: 2015 c.20 Sch.13 para.6
s.3A, repealed: 2015 c.20 s.103
s.23, repealed: 2015 c.20 Sch.22 para.14
s.28, amended: 2015 c.20 s.103

28. Food Standards Act 1999

s.17, repealed: 2015 asp 1 Sch.1 para.7
s.27, repealed: 2015 asp 1 Sch.1 para.7
s.30, repealed: 2015 asp 1 Sch.1 para.7
s.43, amended: 2015 asp 1 Sch.1 para.7
Sch.3 Part III para.16, repealed: SI 2015/978 Sch.1 Part 1

29. Greater London Authority Act 1999

s.17A, amended: SI 2015/1376 Sch.2 para.6
s.31, amended: 2015 c.7 s.33
s.199, amended: SI 2015/1682 Sch.1 para.4
s.200, amended: SI 2015/1682 Sch.1 para.4
s.228, amended: SI 2015/1682 Sch.1 para.4
s.235, amended: SI 2015/1682 Sch.1 para.4
s.235, repealed: 2015 c.20 Sch.6 para.22
s.252B, amended: SI 2015/1682 Sch.1 para.4
s.252C, amended: SI 2015/1682 Sch.1 para.4
s.333D, amended: 2015 c.20 s.29
s.333D, repealed: 2015 c.20 s.29
s.333DA, added: 2015 c.7 s.31
s.333DC, enabling: SI 2015/1540
s.333ZB, amended: 2015 c.7 s.32
s.355, amended: SI 2015/102 Sch.6 para.3

s.356, amended: SI 2015/102 Sch.6
para.4
s.358, amended: SI 2015/102 Sch.6
para.5
s.359, amended: SI 2015/102 Sch.6
para.6
s.360, amended: SI 2015/102 Sch.6
para.7
s.360, repealed: SI 2015/102 Sch.6 para.7
s.408, amended: 2015 c.7 s.31
s.409, amended: 2015 c.7 s.31
s.420, amended: 2015 c.7 s.31
Sch.6 para.3, amended: SI 2015/2032
Reg.2
Sch.6 para.10, enabling: SI 2015/2032
Sch.18 para.15, amended: SI 2015/1682
Sch.1 para.4

30. Welfare Reform and Pensions Act 1999
see *Henry, Re* [2014] EWHC 4209 (Ch),
[2015] 1 W.L.R. 2488 (Ch D), Robert
Englehart QC
s.1, enabling: SI 2015/879
s.8, enabling: SI 2015/879
s.23, enabling: SI 2015/173
s.38, amended: 2015 c.8 Sch.2 para.19
s.48, enabling: SI 2015/173
s.49, enabling: SI 2015/173
s.83, enabling: SI 2015/879
Sch.11 para.17, repealed: SI 2015/2006
Sch.12 Part 12
Sch.12 Part I para.31, repealed: 2015 c.8
Sch.1 para.11

31. Contracts (Rights of Third Parties) Act 1999
see *Canyon Offshore Ltd v GDF Suez
E&P Nederland BV* [2014] EWHC 3810
(Comm), [2015] Bus. L.R. 578 (QBD
(Comm)), Judge Mackie QC; see
*Starlight Shipping Co v Allianz Marine &
Aviation Versicherungs AG* [2014]
EWHC 3068 (Comm), [2015] 2 All E.R.
(Comm) 747 (QBD (Comm)), Flaux J
s.1, see *Charity Commission for England
and Wales v Framjee* [2014] EWHC
2507 (Ch), [2015] 1 W.L.R. 16 (Ch D),
Henderson J; see *Hurley Palmer Flatt
Ltd v Barclays Bank Plc* [2014] EWHC
3042 (TCC), [2015] Bus. L.R. 106 (QBD
(TCC)), Ramsey J; see *Starlight
Shipping Co v Allianz Marine & Aviation
Versicherungs AG* [2014] EWHC 3068

(Comm), [2015] 2 All E.R. (Comm) 747
(QBD (Comm)), Flaux J
s.8, see *Hurley Palmer Flatt Ltd v
Barclays Bank Plc* [2014] EWHC 3042
(TCC), [2015] Bus. L.R. 106 (QBD
(TCC)), Ramsey J

33. Immigration and Asylum Act 1999
s.4, see *R. (on the application of Cushnie)
v Secretary of State for Health* [2014]
EWHC 3626 (Admin), [2015] P.T.S.R.
384 (QBD (Admin)), Singh J; see *R. (on
the application of Mensah) v Salford City
Council* [2014] EWHC 3537 (Admin),
[2015] P.T.S.R. 157 (QBD (Admin)),
Lewis J
s.10, see *R. (on the application of Ahmed)
v Secretary of State for the Home
Department* [2015] UKUT 436 (IAC),
[2015] Imm. A.R. 1320 (UT (IAC)),
Judge Storey; see *R. (on the application
of Gazi (Bangladesh)) v Secretary of
State for the Home Department* [2015]
UKUT 327 (IAC), [2015] Imm. A.R.
1127 (UT (IAC)), McCloskey J; see *R.
(on the application of Khan) v Secretary
of State for the Home Department* [2014]
EWHC 2494 (Admin), [2015] 1 All E.R.
1057 (QBD (Admin)), Green J
s.19, repealed: 2015 c.6 Sch.5 para.3
s.41, enabling: SI 2015/657, SI
2015/1534
s.95, see *R. (on the application of
Cushnie) v Secretary of State for Health*
[2014] EWHC 3626 (Admin), [2015]
P.T.S.R. 384 (QBD (Admin)), Singh J;
see *R. (on the application of SG) v
Haringey LBC* [2015] EWHC 2579
(Admin), (2015) 18 C.C.L. Rep. 444
(QBD (Admin)), John Bowers QC
s.95, enabling: SI 2015/645, SI 2015/944,
SI 2015/1501
s.115, amended: SI 2015/2006 Sch.2
para.43, Sch.9 para.42, Sch.12 Part 1,
Sch.12 Part 8
s.115, repealed: SI 2015/2006 Sch.12
Part 1
s.166, enabling: SI 2015/645, SI
2015/944, SI 2015/1501
s.167, enabling: SI 2015/645, SI
2015/944, SI 2015/1501

Sch.8 para.1, enabling: SI 2015/645, SI 2015/944, SI 2015/1501
Sch.8 para.3, enabling: SI 2015/645, SI 2015/944, SI 2015/1501

2000

2. Representation of the People Act 2000
s.16A, substituted: SI 2015/1376 Sch.2 para.7
Sch.4 para.6, amended: 2015 asp 7 s.16
6. Powers of Criminal Courts (Sentencing) Act 2000
s.3B, see *R. (on the application of DPP) v South Tyneside Youth Court* [2015] EWHC 1455 (Admin), [2015] 2 Cr. App. R. (S.) 59 (DC), Sir Brian Leveson PQBD
s.3B, amended: 2015 c.2 s.53
s.3B, substituted: 2015 c.2 s.53
s.12, amended: 2015 c.2 Sch.5 para.4, Sch.12 para.9
s.18, amended: 2015 c.2 s.45
s.82A, see *R. v Rossi (Derek)* [2014] EWCA Crim 2081, [2015] 1 Cr. App. R. (S.) 15 (CA (Crim Div)), Fulford LJ
s.82A, amended: 2015 c.2 s.15
s.91, see *R. (on the application of DPP) v South Tyneside Youth Court* [2015] EWHC 1455 (Admin), [2015] 2 Cr. App. R. (S.) 59 (DC), Sir Brian Leveson PQBD; see *R. (on the application of P) v Derby Youth Court* [2015] EWHC 573 (Admin), (2015) 179 J.P. 139 (DC), Davis LJ
s.97, amended: 2015 c.2 s.15
s.97, repealed: 2015 c.2 s.15
s.100, amended: 2015 c.2 Sch.5 para.5
s.106, amended: 2015 c.2 s.15
s.107, amended: 2015 c.2 Sch.9 para.12
s.111, see *R. v O'Neill (Ricky Terence)* [2015] EWCA Crim 1181, [2015] 2 Cr. App. R. (S.) 71 (CA (Crim Div)), Treacy LJ
s.116, see *Campbell (David) v HM Advocate* [2015] HCJAC 28, 2015 S.L.T. 232 (HCJ), Lord Eassie; see *R. v Hookway (Lee)* [2015] EWCA Crim 931, [2015] 2 Cr. App. R. (S.) 43 (CA (Crim Div)), Fulford LJ

s.118, see *Attorney General's Reference (No.61 of 2014)* [2014] EWCA Crim 1933, [2015] 1 Cr. App. R. (S.) 25 (CA (Crim Div)), Treacy LJ
s.130, amended: 2015 c.2 Sch.5 para.6
s.132, amended: 2015 c.2 s.83
s.132, varied: 2015 c.30 s.10
s.133, amended: 2015 c.30 Sch.5 para.14
s.139, see *R. v De Jesus (Pedro)* [2015] EWCA Crim 1118, [2015] 2 Cr. App. R. (S.) 44 (CA (Crim Div)), Pitchford LJ
s.142, amended: 2015 c.2 Sch.12 para.10
s.143, see *R. v De Jesus (Pedro)* [2015] EWCA Crim 1118, [2015] 2 Cr. App. R. (S.) 44 (CA (Crim Div)), Pitchford LJ; see *R. v Hall (Martin Robert)* [2014] EWCA Crim 2413, [2015] R.T.R. 9 (CA (Crim Div)), Sharp LJ
s.146, amended: 2015 c.2 Sch.5 para.7
s.147, see *R. v Ketteridge (Nicholas)* [2014] EWCA Crim 1962, [2015] 1 Cr. App. R. (S.) 11 (CA (Crim Div)), Pitchford LJ
s.147A, amended: 2015 c.2 s.30, Sch.1 para.13
s.147A, repealed: 2015 c.2 s.30
s.155, see *R. v D* [2014] EWCA Crim 2340, [2015] 1 Cr. App. R. (S.) 23 (CA (Crim Div)), Sir Brian Leveson PQBD; see *R. v Thorsby (Adrian Kenneth)* [2015] EWCA Crim 1, [2015] 1 W.L.R. 2901 (CA (Crim Div)), Pitchford LJ
s.155, enabling: SI 2015/1490
s.160, amended: 2015 c.2 s.43
s.164, amended: 2015 c.2 Sch.5 para.8
Sch.1 Part I para.5, amended: 2015 c.2 s.44
Sch.1 Part I para.6A, added: 2015 c.2 s.43
Sch.1 Part I para.7, amended: 2015 c.2 s.43
Sch.1 Part I para.9, amended: 2015 c.2 s.44
Sch.1 Part II para.10, substituted: 2015 c.2 s.44
Sch.1 Part II para.13, amended: 2015 c.2 s.44
Sch.1 Part II para.13, repealed: 2015 c.2 s.44
Sch.1 Part II para.14, amended: 2015 c.2 s.44, s.45

7. Electronic Communications Act 2000
  s.8, enabling: SI 2015/5, SI 2015/235
  s.9, enabling: SI 2015/5, SI 2015/235
8. Financial Services and Markets Act 2000
  see *R. (on the application of Bluefin
  Insurance Ltd) v Financial Ombudsman
  Service Ltd* [2014] EWHC 3413
  (Admin), [2015] Bus. L.R. 656 (QBD
  (Admin)), Wilkie J; see *Secretary of
  State for Business, Innovation and Skills
  v Chohan* [2013] EWHC 680 (Ch),
  [2015] B.C.C. 755 (Ch D (Companies
  Ct)), Hildyard J
  Part XXA, added: 2015 c.8 Sch.3 para.2
  s.1B, amended: 2015 c.8 Sch.3 para.3
  s.1M, amended: 2015 c.8 Sch.3 para.4
  s.1S, amended: 2015 c.8 Sch.3 para.5
  s.21, enabling: SI 2015/352, SI 2015/853,
  SI 2015/910
  s.22, enabling: SI 2015/352, SI 2015/369,
  SI 2015/489, SI 2015/731, SI 2015/852,
  SI 2015/853, SI 2015/910, SI 2015/1557,
  SI 2015/1863
  s.24, repealed: SI 2015/664 Sch.5 para.7
  s.38, enabling: SI 2015/352, SI 2015/447,
  SI 2015/910
  s.39, amended: SI 2015/910 Sch.1 para.1
  s.55C, enabling: SI 2015/853
  s.55J, amended: SI 2015/575 Sch.1
  para.2, SI 2015/910 Sch.1 para.1, SI
  2015/1882 Reg.3
  s.55KA, added: SI 2015/575 Sch.1 para.3
  s.55PA, added: SI 2015/575 Sch.1 para.4
  s.55Z2, amended: SI 2015/486 Reg.13
  s.62A, varied: SI 2015/492 Art.8
  s.63ZA, varied: SI 2015/492 Art.7
  s.66A, amended: SI 2015/1864 Art.2
  s.71A, enabling: SI 2015/1865
  s.89A, amended: SI 2015/1755 Reg.2
  s.89A, repealed: SI 2015/1755 Reg.2
  s.89C, amended: SI 2015/1755 Reg.2
  s.89C, repealed: SI 2015/1755 Reg.2
  s.89E, repealed: SI 2015/1755 Reg.2
  s.89F, amended: SI 2015/1755 Reg.2
  s.89F, repealed: SI 2015/1755 Reg.2
  s.89J, repealed: SI 2015/1755 Reg.2
  s.89NA, added: SI 2015/1755 Reg.4
  s.89W, added: SI 2015/1755 Reg.3
  s.91, amended: SI 2015/1755 Reg.4
  s.97, amended: SI 2015/1755 Reg.4
  s.102A, amended: SI 2015/1755 Reg.5

s.102C, substituted: SI 2015/1755 Reg.5
s.103, amended: SI 2015/1755 Reg.5
s.103, repealed: SI 2015/1755 Reg.5
s.105, amended: SI 2015/575 Sch.1
para.5
s.116, amended: SI 2015/575 Sch.1
para.6
s.116, repealed: SI 2015/575 Sch.1 para.6
s.118, see *Financial Conduct Authority v
Da Vinci Invest Ltd* [2015] EWHC 2401
(Ch), [2015] Lloyd's Rep. F.C. 540 (Ch
D), Snowden J
s.129, see *Financial Conduct Authority v
Da Vinci Invest Ltd* [2015] EWHC 2401
(Ch), [2015] Lloyd's Rep. F.C. 540 (Ch
D), Snowden J
s.137FA, amended: 2015 c.8 Sch.2
para.21
s.137FB, added: 2015 c.8 Sch.3 para.6
s.137R, amended: SI 2015/910 Sch.1
para.1
s.138F, substituted: 2015 c.8 Sch.3 para.7
s.138I, amended: 2015 c.8 Sch.3 para.8
s.139A, amended: 2015 c.8 Sch.3 para.9
s.140A, amended: 2015 c.8 Sch.3 para.10
s.142W, enabling: SI 2015/547
s.142X, amended: 2015 c.8 Sch.2 para.22
s.150, see *Connaught Income Fund
Series 1 (In Liquidation) v Capita
Financial Managers Ltd* [2014] EWHC
3619 (Comm), [2015] 1 All E.R. (Comm)
751 (QBD (Comm)), Judge Mackie QC
s.165, amended: SI 2015/575 Sch.1
para.7
s.167, amended: SI 2015/575 Sch.1
para.8
s.168, amended: 2015 c.8 Sch.3 para.11
s.184, amended: SI 2015/1755 Reg.6
s.190, amended: SI 2015/575 Sch.1
para.9
s.194, amended: SI 2015/575 Sch.1
para.10, SI 2015/1882 Reg.3
s.194C, added: SI 2015/910 Sch.1 para.1
s.195B, added: SI 2015/910 Sch.1 para.1
s.198, amended: SI 2015/575 Sch.1
para.11
s.204A, amended: SI 2015/1864 Art.3
s.204A, repealed: SI 2015/1864 Art.3
s.204A, enabling: SI 2015/1864
s.213, enabling: SI 2015/1882
s.214, enabling: SI 2015/1882

s.215, amended: SI 2015/486 Reg.13
s.218A, amended: SI 2015/486 Reg.13
s.224, enabling: SI 2015/1882
s.226, see *R. (on the application of Bluefin Insurance Ltd) v Financial Ombudsman Service Ltd* [2014] EWHC 3413 (Admin), [2015] Bus. L.R. 656 (QBD (Admin)), Wilkie J
s.226, amended: SI 2015/1946 Reg.14
s.226, varied: SI 2015/1945 Reg.17
s.232A, amended: SI 2015/1946 Reg.14
s.232A, varied: SI 2015/1945 Reg.17
s.234, amended: SI 2015/1946 Reg.14
s.234, varied: SI 2015/1945 Reg.17
s.235, see *Financial Services Authority v Asset Ll Inc (t/a Asset Land Investment Inc)* [2014] EWCA Civ 435, [2015] 1 All E.R. 1 (CA (Civ Div)), Rimer LJ; see *Secretary of State for Business, Innovation and Skills v Chohan* [2013] EWHC 680 (Ch), [2015] B.C.C. 755 (Ch D (Companies Ct)), Hildyard J
s.235, enabling: SI 2015/754, SI 2015/2061
s.238, see *Connaught Income Fund Series 1 (In Liquidation) v Capita Financial Managers Ltd* [2014] EWHC 3619 (Comm), [2015] 1 All E.R. (Comm) 751 (QBD (Comm)), Judge Mackie QC
s.241, see *Connaught Income Fund Series 1 (In Liquidation) v Capita Financial Managers Ltd* [2014] EWHC 3619 (Comm), [2015] 1 All E.R. (Comm) 751 (QBD (Comm)), Judge Mackie QC
s.301E, amended: SI 2015/1755 Reg.6
s.316, amended: SI 2015/575 Sch.1 para.12
s.333B, amended: SI 2015/2013 Sch.1 para.1
s.333C, amended: SI 2015/2013 Sch.1 para.1
s.333D, amended: SI 2015/2013 Sch.1 para.1
s.333E, amended: SI 2015/2013 Sch.1 para.1
s.333F, amended: SI 2015/2013 Sch.1 para.1
s.333G, amended: SI 2015/2013 Sch.1 para.1
s.333J, amended: SI 2015/2013 Sch.1 para.1

s.333K, amended: SI 2015/2013 Sch.1 para.1
s.333L, amended: SI 2015/2013 Sch.1 para.1
s.333M, amended: SI 2015/2013 Sch.1 para.1
s.333P, amended: SI 2015/2013 Sch.1 para.1
s.333Q, amended: SI 2015/2013 Sch.1 para.1
s.333R, amended: SI 2015/2013 Sch.1 para.1
s.345A, enabling: SI 2015/61
s.347, amended: SI 2015/910 Sch.1 para.1
s.367, amended: SI 2015/575 Sch.1 para.13
s.380, amended: SI 2015/1755 Reg.4
s.381, see *Financial Conduct Authority v Da Vinci Invest Ltd* [2015] EWHC 2401 (Ch), [2015] Lloyd's Rep. F.C. 540 (Ch D), Snowden J
s.382, see *Financial Conduct Authority v Anderson* [2014] EWHC 3630 (Ch), [2015] B.P.I.R. 14 (Ch D), David Halpern QC
s.391, amended: SI 2015/1755 Reg.4
s.391A, substituted: SI 2015/1755 Reg.4
s.391B, added: SI 2015/1755 Reg.4
s.393, see *Macris v Financial Conduct Authority* [2015] EWCA Civ 490, [2015] Bus. L.R. 1141 (CA (Civ Div)), Longmore LJ
s.398, amended: SI 2015/1882 Reg.3
s.404B, amended: SI 2015/542 Sch.7 para.1
s.405, repealed: SI 2015/575 Sch.1 para.14
s.409, enabling: SI 2015/910
s.417, amended: SI 2015/575 Sch.1 para.15, SI 2015/910 Sch.1 para.1
s.422A, amended: SI 2015/1755 Reg.6
s.425, amended: SI 2015/575 Sch.1 para.16, SI 2015/910 Sch.1 para.1
s.426, enabling: SI 2015/623, SI 2015/732
s.427, enabling: SI 2015/623
s.428, enabling: SI 2015/369, SI 2015/547, SI 2015/731, SI 2015/754, SI 2015/910, SI 2015/1864, SI 2015/1865, SI 2015/1882

s.429, amended: 2015 c.8 Sch.3 para.12
Sch.1ZA Part 1 para.8, amended: 2015
c.8 Sch.3 para.13
Sch.1ZA Part 1 para.11, amended: 2015
c.8 Sch.3 para.14
Sch.1ZA Part 3 para.21, amended: 2015
c.8 Sch.3 para.15
Sch.1ZA Part 3 para.23, amended: 2015
c.8 Sch.3 para.16
Sch.2, enabling: SI 2015/732
Sch.2 Part III para.25, enabling: SI
2015/352, SI 2015/369, SI 2015/489, SI
2015/731, SI 2015/852
Sch.3 Part I para.1, amended: SI
2015/575 Sch.1 para.17, SI 2015/910
Sch.1 para.1
Sch.3 Part I para.1, repealed: SI 2015/575
Sch.1 para.17
Sch.3 Part I para.3, substituted: SI
2015/575 Sch.1 para.17
Sch.3 Part I para.3A, repealed: SI
2015/575 Sch.1 para.17
Sch.3 Part I para.4F, added: SI 2015/910
Sch.1 para.1
Sch.3 Part I para.5, amended: SI
2015/575 Sch.1 para.17, SI 2015/910
Sch.1 para.1
Sch.3 Part I para.5A, amended: SI
2015/910 Sch.1 para.1
Sch.3 Part I para.7A, amended: SI
2015/910 Sch.1 para.1
Sch.3 Part II para.13, amended: SI
2015/910 Sch.1 para.1
Sch.3 Part II para.14, amended: SI
2015/910 Sch.1 para.1
Sch.3 Part II para.15, amended: SI
2015/575 Sch.1 para.17
Sch.3 Part III para.19, amended: SI
2015/575 Sch.1 para.17, SI 2015/910
Sch.1 para.1
Sch.3 Part III para.20, amended: SI
2015/575 Sch.1 para.17, SI 2015/910
Sch.1 para.1
Sch.3 Part III para.20ZA, amended: SI
2015/910 Sch.1 para.1
Sch.3 Part III para.21, amended: SI
2015/910 Sch.1 para.1
Sch.3 Part III para.25, amended: SI
2015/910 Sch.1 para.1
Sch.6 Part 1B para.2G, amended: SI
2015/853 Art.2

Sch.12 Part I para.1, amended: SI
2015/575 Sch.1 para.18
Sch.12 Part I para.2, amended: SI
2015/575 Sch.1 para.18
Sch.12 Part I para.3, amended: SI
2015/575 Sch.1 para.18
Sch.12 Part I para.3A, added: SI
2015/575 Sch.1 para.18
Sch.12 Part I para.5A, amended: SI
2015/575 Sch.1 para.18
Sch.12 Part III para.10, amended: SI
2015/575 Sch.1 para.18
Sch.17 Part I para.1, amended: SI
2015/542 Sch.7 para.1
Sch.17 Part II para.2, substituted: SI
2015/542 Sch.7 para.1
Sch.17 Part III para.13, amended: SI
2015/542 Sch.7 para.1, SI 2015/1946
Reg.14
Sch.17 Part III para.13, varied: SI
2015/1945 Reg.17
Sch.17 Part III para.14, amended: SI
2015/542 Sch.7 para.1

11. Terrorism Act 2000
see *Ibrahim v United Kingdom
(50541/08)* (2015) 61 E.H.R.R. 9
(ECHR), Judge Ziemele (President)
s.3, enabling: SI 2015/55, SI 2015/959
s.17A, added: 2015 c.6 s.42
s.23, amended: 2015 c.6 s.42
s.41, see *Ibrahim v United Kingdom
(50541/08)* (2015) 61 E.H.R.R. 9
(ECHR), Judge Ziemele (President)
s.44, see *Beghal v DPP* [2015] UKSC 49
(SC), Lord Neuberger PSC
s.54, amended: 2015 c.2 s.1
s.123, enabling: SI 2015/906
Sch.2, amended: SI 2015/55 Art.2, SI
2015/959 Art.2
Sch.3A Part I para.1, amended: SI
2015/575 Sch.1 para.21
Sch.3A Part I para.3, amended: SI
2015/575 Sch.1 para.21
Sch.4 Part I para.11, amended: 2015 c.2
Sch.11 para.17
Sch.5 Part I para.10, enabling: SI
2015/1490
Sch.5 Part I para.11, amended: 2015 c.20
s.82
Sch.6 para.4, enabling: SI 2015/1490

Sch.6 para.6, amended: SI 2015/575
Sch.1 para.21
Sch.6A para.5, enabling: SI 2015/1490
Sch.7, see *Beghal v DPP* [2015] UKSC
49 (SC), Lord Neuberger PSC
Sch.7 para.9, amended: 2015 c.6 Sch.8
para.1
Sch.7 para.17, amended: 2015 c.6 Sch.5
para.4
Sch.8 Pt I para.8, see *Ibrahim v United*
Kingdom (50541/08) (2015) 61 E.H.R.R.
9 (ECHR), Judge Ziemele (President)
Sch.14 para.7, enabling: SI 2015/906

12. Limited Liability Partnerships Act 2000
s.5, see *Flanagan v Liontrust Investment*
Partners LLP [2015] EWHC 2171 (Ch),
[2015] Bus. L.R. 1172 (Ch D
(Companies Ct)), Henderson J
s.15, enabling: SI 2015/1695
s.17, enabling: SI 2015/1695

14. Care Standards Act 2000
see *R. (on the application of Whapples) v*
Birmingham CrossCity Clinical
Commissioning Group [2015] EWCA
Civ 435, [2015] P.T.S.R. 1398 (CA (Civ
Div)), Underhill LJ
s.1, enabling: SI 2015/541
s.4, repealed: 2015 c.20 s.93
s.5, repealed: 2015 c.20 s.93
s.12, enabling: SI 2015/551, SI 2015/839
s.15, enabling: SI 2015/551, SI 2015/839
s.16, enabling: SI 2015/551, SI 2015/839
s.22, enabling: SI 2015/541, SI
2015/1988
s.30A, repealed: 2015 c.20 s.93
s.30ZB, amended: SI 2015/664 Sch.5
para.8
s.31, enabling: SI 2015/551
s.34, enabling: SI 2015/541
s.35, enabling: SI 2015/541
s.118, enabling: SI 2015/541, SI
2015/551, SI 2015/839, SI 2015/1988
s.121, repealed: 2015 c.20 s.93

16. Carers and Disabled Children Act 2000
s.1, amended: SI 2015/914 Sch.1 para.59
s.6, amended: SI 2015/914 Sch.1 para.60
s.11, amended: SI 2015/914 Sch.1
para.61
s.11, repealed: SI 2015/914 Sch.1 para.61

17. Finance Act 2000

Sch.6 Part II para.19, amended: 2015
c.33 s.49
Sch.6 Part II para.22, enabling: SI
2015/947
Sch.6 Part II para.24B, amended: 2015
c.11 s.63
Sch.6 Part II para.24B, enabling: SI
2015/947
Sch.6 Part II para.24C, amended: 2015
c.11 s.63
Sch.6 Part II para.24D, enabling: SI
2015/947
Sch.6 Part IV para.42, amended: 2015
c.11 s.62
Sch.6 Part VI para.62, amended: 2015
c.11 s.63
Sch.6 Part VI para.62, enabling: SI
2015/947
Sch.6 Part VI para.75, repealed: 2015
c.20 Sch.6 para.2
Sch.6 Part VIII para.92, amended: SI
2015/664 Sch.2 para.11
Sch.6 Part VIII para.93, amended: SI
2015/664 Sch.2 para.11
Sch.6 Part VIII para.94, amended: SI
2015/664 Sch.2 para.11
Sch.6 Part VIII para.95, amended: SI
2015/664 Sch.2 para.11
Sch.6 Part X para.120, repealed: 2015
c.20 Sch.6 para.2
Sch.6 Part XIII para.139, amended: SI
2015/664 Sch.2 para.11
Sch.6 Part XIII para.146, enabling: SI
2015/947
Sch.22 Part IV para.24, enabling: SI
2015/788
Sch.22 Part IV para.27, enabling: SI
2015/788
Sch.22 Part IV para.28, enabling: SI
2015/788
Sch.22 Part IV para.29, enabling: SI
2015/788, SI 2015/1607
Sch.22 Part IV para.31, enabling: SI
2015/788, SI 2015/1607
Sch.22 Part IV para.36, enabling: SI
2015/788, SI 2015/1607

20. Government Resources and Accounts
Act 2000
s.4A, enabling: SI 2015/632, SI
2015/2062
s.10, enabling: SI 2015/1655

21. Learning and Skills Act 2000
s.135, amended: 2015 c.8 Sch.4 para.33
s.139A, see *R. (on the application of Smieja) v Bexley LBC* [2014] EWHC 4113 (Admin), [2015] B.L.G.R. 112 (QBD (Admin)), Neil Cameron QC
s.144, amended: 2015 c.20 Sch.14 para.45
s.144, repealed: 2015 c.20 Sch.14 para.45
Sch.9 para.85, repealed: 2015 c.20 Sch.16 para.2

22. Local Government Act 2000
s.4, repealed: 2015 c.20 s.100
s.4A, repealed: 2015 c.20 s.100
s.9HE, amended: SI 2015/1376 Sch.2 para.8
s.9HE, enabling: SI 2015/654
s.9MG, amended: SI 2015/1376 Sch.2 para.8
s.9MG, enabling: SI 2015/654
s.44, amended: SI 2015/1376 Sch.2 para.8
s.44, enabling: SI 2015/654
s.48A, repealed: SI 2015/1376 Sch.2 para.8
s.86, enabling: SI 2015/43, SI 2015/666, SI 2015/884
s.87, enabling: SI 2015/43, SI 2015/666, SI 2015/884
s.105, amended: SI 2015/1376 Sch.2 para.8
s.105, enabling: SI 2015/43, SI 2015/666, SI 2015/884

23. Regulation of Investigatory Powers Act 2000
see *Liberty v Secretary of State for Foreign and Commonwealth Affairs* [2015] 3 All E.R. 212 (IPT), Burton J;
see *R. v Brown (Edward)* [2015] EWCA Crim 1328, [2015] 2 Cr. App. R. 31 (CA (Crim Div)), Fulford LJ
s.3, amended: 2015 c.6 Sch.8 para.2
s.8, see *Liberty v Government Communications Headquarters* [2015] 3 All E.R. 142 (IPT), Burton J
s.16, see *Liberty v Government Communications Headquarters* [2015] 3 All E.R. 142 (IPT), Burton J; see *Liberty v Secretary of State for Foreign and Commonwealth Affairs* [2015] 3 All E.R. 212 (IPT), Burton J

s.18, amended: 2015 c.6 s.15
s.22, enabling: SI 2015/228
s.25, enabling: SI 2015/228
s.30, enabling: SI 2015/937
s.71, amended: 2015 c.9 s.83, Sch.4 para.18
s.71, enabling: SI 2015/926, SI 2015/927
s.78, enabling: SI 2015/937

26. Postal Services Act 2000
s.104, amended: 2015 c.6 Sch.8 para.3

27. Utilities Act 2000
s.5, amended: SI 2015/862 Reg.4
s.105, amended: 2015 c.7 s.51, SI 2015/862 Reg.5, SI 2015/1682 Sch.1 para.4
s.105, repealed: 2015 c.20 Sch.6 para.22

29. Trustee Act 2000
s.31, see *Spencer v Fielder* [2014] EWHC 2768 (Ch), [2015] 1 W.L.R. 2786 (Ch D), Sir Terence Etherton C

32. Police (Northern Ireland) Act 2000
s.3, amended: SI 2015/798 Sch.2 para.2
s.31A, amended: SI 2015/798 Sch.2 para.3
s.33A, amended: SI 2015/798 Sch.2 para.4
s.52, amended: SI 2015/798 Sch.2 para.5
s.57, amended: SI 2015/798 Sch.2 para.6
s.59, amended: SI 2015/798 Sch.2 para.7
s.60, amended: SI 2015/798 Sch.2 para.8
Sch.1 Part VI para.19A, added: SI 2015/798 Sch.2 para.9

33. Fur Farming (Prohibition) Act 2000
s.1, amended: SI 2015/664 Sch.4 para.29
s.5, enabling: SI 2015/663

36. Freedom of Information Act 2000
see *Dransfield v Information Commissioner* [2015] EWCA Civ 454, [2015] 1 W.L.R. 5316 (CA (Civ Div)), Arden LJ; see *Innes v Information Commissioner* [2014] EWCA Civ 1086, [2015] 1 W.L.R. 210 (CA (Civ Div)), Longmore LJ; see *Kennedy v Information Commissioner* [2015] A.C. 455 (SC), Lord Neuberger JSC; see *University and Colleges Admissions Service v Information Commissioner* [2015] E.L.R. 112 (UT (AAC)), Judge Nicholas Wikeley
Part III, amended: SI 2015/1897 Sch.1 para.2

s.1, see *Independent Parliamentary
Standards Authority v Information
Commissioner* [2015] EWCA Civ 388,
[2015] 1 W.L.R. 2879 (CA (Civ Div)),
Lord Dyson MR
s.2, see *Kennedy v Information
Commissioner* [2015] A.C. 455 (SC),
Lord Neuberger JSC; see *Ranger v
House of Lords Appointments
Commission* [2015] EWHC 45 (QB),
[2015] 1 W.L.R. 4324 (QBD), Knowles J
s.4, amended: SI 2015/1897 Sch.1 para.2
s.5, amended: SI 2015/1897 Sch.1 para.2
s.5, enabling: SI 2015/851
s.7, amended: SI 2015/1897 Sch.1 para.2
s.7, enabling: SI 2015/851
s.9, amended: SI 2015/1897 Sch.1 para.2
s.10, amended: SI 2015/1897 Sch.1
para.2
s.11, see *Independent Parliamentary
Standards Authority v Information
Commissioner* [2015] EWCA Civ 388,
[2015] 1 W.L.R. 2879 (CA (Civ Div)),
Lord Dyson MR; see *Innes v
Information Commissioner* [2014]
EWCA Civ 1086, [2015] 1 W.L.R. 210
(CA (Civ Div)), Longmore LJ
s.11A, amended: SI 2015/1415 Reg.21,
SI 2015/1897 Sch.1 para.2
s.11B, amended: SI 2015/1897 Sch.1
para.2
s.12, amended: SI 2015/1897 Sch.1
para.2
s.13, amended: SI 2015/1897 Sch.1
para.2
s.14, see *Dransfield v Information
Commissioner* [2015] EWCA Civ 454,
[2015] 1 W.L.R. 5316 (CA (Civ Div)),
Arden LJ
s.15, amended: SI 2015/1897 Sch.1
para.2
s.16, see *Innes v Information
Commissioner* [2014] EWCA Civ 1086,
[2015] 1 W.L.R. 210 (CA (Civ Div)),
Longmore LJ
s.19, amended: SI 2015/1415 Reg.21
s.32, see *Kennedy v Information
Commissioner* [2015] A.C. 455 (SC),
Lord Neuberger JSC
s.40, see *Ranger v House of Lords
Appointments Commission* [2015]

EWHC 45 (QB), [2015] 1 W.L.R. 4324
(QBD), Knowles J
s.45, amended: SI 2015/1897 Sch.1
para.2
s.46, amended: SI 2015/1897 Sch.1
para.2
s.47, amended: SI 2015/1897 Sch.1
para.2
s.53, see *R. (on the application of Evans)
v Attorney General* [2015] UKSC 21,
[2015] A.C. 1787 (SC), Lord Neuberger
PSC
s.53, amended: SI 2015/1897 Sch.1
para.2
s.57, see *R. (on the application of Evans)
v Attorney General* [2015] UKSC 21,
[2015] A.C. 1787 (SC), Lord Neuberger
PSC
s.63, see *Kennedy v Information
Commissioner* [2015] A.C. 455 (SC),
Lord Neuberger JSC
s.65, amended: SI 2015/1897 Sch.1
para.2
s.66, amended: SI 2015/1897 Sch.1
para.2
s.75, amended: SI 2015/1897 Sch.1
para.2
s.78, see *Kennedy v Information
Commissioner* [2015] A.C. 455 (SC),
Lord Neuberger JSC
s.82, amended: SI 2015/1897 Sch.1
para.2
s.83, amended: SI 2015/1897 Sch.1
para.2
s.84, amended: SI 2015/1897 Sch.1
para.2
s.85, amended: SI 2015/1897 Sch.1
para.2
Sch.1, see *University and Colleges
Admissions Service v Information
Commissioner* [2015] E.L.R. 112 (UT
(AAC)), Judge Nicholas Wikeley
Sch.1 Part II para.15A, repealed: 2015
c.20 Sch.13 para.6
Sch.1 Part VI, amended: 2015 c.7 s.9,
2015 c.20 Sch.21 para.1, 2015 c.26 Sch.1
para.25, 2015 c.30 s.40, SI 2015/850
Art.3, SI 2015/978 Sch.1 Part 1
Sch.1 Part VII, amended: SI 2015/978
Sch.1 Part 1, SI 2015/2006 Art.136,
Sch.12 Part 7

37. Countryside and Rights of Way Act 2000
s.55A, added: 2015 c.20 s.20
s.56, amended: 2015 c.20 s.22
s.56A, added: 2015 c.20 s.21
s.56B, added: 2015 c.20 s.22
s.78, repealed: SI 2015/664 Sch.4
para.100
s.91, repealed: 2015 c.20 Sch.22 para.15
38. Transport Act 2000
Part IV c.I, amended: SI 2015/1682 Sch.1
para.4
s.56, amended: SI 2015/17 Sch.6 para.3
s.127A, amended: SI 2015/65 Sch.1
para.5
s.127B, amended: SI 2015/65 Sch.1
para.5
s.131E, amended: SI 2015/65 Sch.1
para.5
s.131F, amended: SI 2015/65 Sch.1
para.5
s.132, amended: SI 2015/65 Sch.1 para.5
s.132A, amended: SI 2015/65 Sch.1
para.5
s.132B, amended: SI 2015/65 Sch.1
para.5
s.144, amended: 2015 c.20 Sch.11
para.17
s.167, amended: 2015 c.7 Sch.1 para.126
s.176, amended: 2015 c.7 Sch.1 para.127
s.177, amended: 2015 c.7 Sch.1 para.128
s.215, amended: SI 2015/1682 Sch.1
para.4
s.216, amended: SI 2015/1682 Sch.1
para.4
s.247, enabling: SI 2015/2022
Sch.9 para.3, amended: SI 2015/1682
Sch.1 para.4
Sch.9 para.3, repealed: 2015 c.20 Sch.6
para.22
Sch.10 Part 1 para.13, amended: SI
2015/1682 Sch.1 para.4
Sch.17, amended: SI 2015/1682 Sch.1
para.4
Sch.26 Part II, amended: SI 2015/1682
Sch.1 para.4
39. Insolvency Act 2000
s.4, repealed: 2015 c.20 Sch.6 para.20
**41. Political Parties, Elections and
Referendums Act 2000**
Part VII, varied: 2015 c.36 s.12
s.2, amended: SI 2015/1376 Sch.2 para.9

s.5, amended: 2015 c.25 Sch.6 para.3
s.6, amended: 2015 c.25 Sch.6 para.3
s.6A, amended: 2015 c.25 Sch.6 para.3
s.6F, amended: 2015 c.25 Sch.6 para.3
s.7, amended: 2015 c.25 Sch.6 para.3
s.10, amended: 2015 c.25 Sch.6 para.3
s.12, enabling: SI 2015/128, SI 2015/302
s.21, substituted: 2015 c.25 Sch.6 para.3
s.24, amended: 2015 c.25 Sch.6 para.4,
SI 2015/1982 Sch.1 para.1
s.25, amended: 2015 c.25 Sch.6 para.4
s.54, amended: SI 2015/1982 Sch.1
para.2
s.54, repealed: SI 2015/1982 Sch.1 para.2
s.71L, varied: 2015 c.36 Sch.2 para.13
s.72, amended: 2015 c.25 Sch.6 para.5
s.74, amended: 2015 c.25 Sch.6 para.5,
SI 2015/1982 Sch.1 para.3
s.87, amended: 2015 c.25 Sch.6 para.6
s.88, repealed: SI 2015/1982 Sch.1 para.4
s.105, amended: 2015 c.36 Sch.1 para.2,
Sch.1 para.5
s.106, amended: 2015 c.36 Sch.1 para.3
s.108, amended: 2015 c.36 Sch.1 para.9
s.108, repealed: 2015 c.36 Sch.1 para.9
s.109, repealed: 2015 c.36 Sch.1 para.10
s.109, varied: 2015 c.36 Sch.1 para.12
s.110, amended: 2015 c.36 Sch.1 para.11
s.110, repealed: 2015 c.36 Sch.1 para.11
s.115, amended: 2015 c.36 Sch.1 para.24
s.117, varied: 2015 c.36 Sch.1 para.20
s.120, amended: 2015 c.36 Sch.1 para.23,
Sch.2 para.2
s.120A, added: 2015 c.36 Sch.1 para.35
s.123, amended: 2015 c.36 Sch.1 para.36,
Sch.2 para.2
s.124, amended: 2015 c.36 Sch.2 para.2
s.124A, added: 2015 c.36 Sch.1 para.37
s.125, amended: 2015 c.36 Sch.1 para.38
s.127, amended: 2015 c.36 Sch.1 para.11
s.128, amended: 2015 c.36 Sch.3 para.2,
Sch.3 para.4, Sch.3 para.6
s.128, repealed: 2015 c.36 Sch.3 para.2 ,
Sch.3 para.4 , Sch.3 para.6
s.150, amended: SI 2015/1982 Sch.1
para.5
s.151, amended: SI 2015/1982 Sch.1
para.6
s.153, amended: SI 2015/1982 Sch.1
para.7

s.159A, amended: SI 2015/1376 Sch.2
para.9
s.160, amended: 2015 c.36 Sch.1 para.45,
SI 2015/1982 Sch.1 para.8
s.160, repealed: SI 2015/1982 Sch.1
para.8
Sch.1 para.3, amended: 2015 c.25 Sch.6
para.3
Sch.1 para.15, amended: 2015 c.20 s.94
Sch.1 para.16, amended: 2015 c.20 s.94
Sch.2 para.2, amended: SI 2015/1376
Sch.2 para.9
Sch.6 para.2, amended: 2015 c.36 Sch.1
para.27, SI 2015/1982 Sch.1 para.9
Sch.6 para.2, repealed: SI 2015/1982
Sch.1 para.9
Sch.6A para.2, amended: 2015 c.36 Sch.2
para.11, SI 2015/1982 Sch.1 para.10
Sch.12 para.2, amended: 2015 c.36 Sch.1
para.14
Sch.12 para.3, amended: 2015 c.36 Sch.1
para.14
Sch.13 Part I para.2, amended: 2015 c.36
Sch.1 para.18
Sch.14 para.1, amended: 2015 c.36 Sch.1
para.25
Sch.15A, added: 2015 c.36 Sch.2 para.1
Sch.15 Part I para.1, amended: 2015 c.36
Sch.1 para.29
Sch.15 Part I para.2, amended: 2015 c.36
Sch.2 para.2
Sch.15 Part I para.2, repealed: 2015 c.36
Sch.2 para.2
Sch.15 Part I para.4, amended: 2015 c.36
Sch.1 para.30
Sch.15 Part I para.5, amended: 2015 c.36
Sch.2 para.2
Sch.15 Part I para.5, repealed: 2015 c.36
Sch.2 para.2
Sch.15 Part II para.6, amended: 2015
c.36 Sch.1 para.31
Sch.15 Part II para.7, amended: 2015
c.36 Sch.1 para.32
Sch.15 Part II para.8, amended: 2015
c.36 Sch.1 para.33
Sch.15 Part III para.10, amended: 2015
c.36 Sch.1 para.34, Sch.2 para.2
Sch.19A para.1, amended: 2015 c.25
Sch.6 para.7, 2015 c.36 Sch.2 para.2
Sch.19C Part I para.1, amended: SI
2015/664 Sch.5 para.9

Sch.20, amended: SI 2015/664 Sch.4
para.30

**43. Criminal Justice and Court Services Act
2000**
s.12, see *F-D v Children and Family
Court Advisory Service* [2014] EWHC
1619 (QB), [2015] 1 F.C.R. 98 (QBD),
Judge Bidder QC
s.62, amended: 2015 c.2 s.7, Sch.2 para.2
s.62, repealed: 2015 c.2 Sch.2 para.2
s.62A, added: 2015 c.2 s.7
s.70, enabling: SI 2015/9

2001

2. Capital Allowances Act 2001
see *Senex Investments Ltd v Revenue and
Customs Commissioners* [2015] UKFTT
107 (TC), [2015] S.F.T.D. 501 (FTT
(Tax)), Judge W Ruthven Gemmell WS
Part 1 c.1A, added: 2015 c.21 Sch.1
para.2
Part 2 c.16ZA, added: 2015 c.21 Sch.1
para.8
Pt 2., see *Keyl v Revenue and Customs
Commissioners* [2015] UKUT 383
(TCC), [2015] B.T.C. 523 (UT (Tax)),
Judge Greg Sinfield
s.12, substituted: 2015 c.21 Sch.1 para.3
s.15, amended: 2015 c.21 Sch.1 para.4
s.38B, see *Keyl v Revenue and Customs
Commissioners* [2015] UKUT 383
(TCC), [2015] B.T.C. 523 (UT (Tax)),
Judge Greg Sinfield
s.45A, enabling: SI 2015/1508
s.45D, amended: SI 2015/60 Art.4
s.45D, enabling: SI 2015/60
s.45DA, amended: 2015 c.11 s.45
s.45DB, amended: 2015 c.11 s.45
s.45E, amended: SI 2015/60 Art.5
s.45E, enabling: SI 2015/60
s.45H, enabling: SI 2015/1509
s.45K, enabling: SI 2015/2047
s.51A, amended: 2015 c.33 s.8
s.51JA, added: 2015 c.21 Sch.1 para.5
s.61, amended: 2015 c.21 Sch.1 para.6
s.66B, added: 2015 c.21 Sch.1 para.7
s.70DA, amended: 2015 c.11 Sch.10
para.2
s.218, amended: 2015 c.11 Sch.10 para.3

s.229A, amended: 2015 c.11 Sch.10
para.4
s.242, amended: 2015 c.11 Sch.10 para.5
s.242, repealed: 2015 c.11 Sch.10 para.5
s.247, amended: 2015 c.21 Sch.1 para.9
s.253, amended: 2015 c.11 Sch.5 para.8
s.268D, repealed: SI 2015/2006 Sch.12
Part 8
s.281, see *Thomson v Revenue and
Customs Commissioners* [2015] S.T.C.
341 (UT (Tax)), Lord Tyre
s.360C, see *Senex Investments Ltd v
Revenue and Customs Commissioners*
[2015] UKFTT 107 (TC), [2015]
S.F.T.D. 501 (FTT (Tax)), Judge W
Ruthven Gemmell WS
s.360Z, amended: 2015 c.21 Sch.1
para.11
s.394, amended: 2015 c.21 Sch.1 para.12
s.432, substituted: 2015 c.21 Sch.1
para.13
s.437, see *Vaccine Research LP v
Revenue and Customs Commissioners*
[2015] S.T.C. 179 (UT (Tax)), Sales J
s.439A, added: 2015 c.21 Sch.1 para.14
s.450, substituted: 2015 c.21 Sch.1
para.15
s.484, amended: 2015 c.21 Sch.1 para.16
s.489, substituted: 2015 c.21 Sch.1
para.17
s.560, amended: SI 2015/575 Sch.1
para.22
Sch.A1 Part 1 para.2, amended: 2015
c.21 Sch.1 para.10
Sch.1 Part 2, amended: 2015 c.21 Sch.1
para.18
7. Elections Act 2001
Sch.Part 2 para.29, amended: SI
2015/566 Sch.12
9. Finance Act 2001
Pt 2., see *Northumbrian Water Ltd v
Revenue and Customs Commissioners*
[2015] UKUT 93 (TCC), [2015] S.T.C.
1458 (UT (Tax)), Rose J
s.17, amended: 2015 c.11 s.61, 2015 c.33
s.48
s.18, amended: 2015 c.33 s.48
s.19, see *Northumbrian Water Ltd v
Revenue and Customs Commissioners*
[2015] UKUT 93 (TCC), [2015] S.T.C.
1458 (UT (Tax)), Rose J

s.24, see *Northumbrian Water Ltd v
Revenue and Customs Commissioners*
[2015] UKUT 93 (TCC), [2015] S.T.C.
1458 (UT (Tax)), Rose J
s.24, enabling: SI 2015/1487
s.26, amended: SI 2015/664 Sch.2
para.12
s.30, enabling: SI 2015/946
s.30B, added: 2015 c.11 s.61
s.30B, enabling: SI 2015/946
s.30C, enabling: SI 2015/946
s.30D, enabling: SI 2015/946
s.37, repealed: 2015 c.20 Sch.6 para.2
s.45, enabling: SI 2015/946, SI
2015/1487
s.48, amended: 2015 c.11 s.61
Sch.6 Part 1 para.1, amended: SI
2015/664 Sch.2 para.12
Sch.6 Part 1 para.2, amended: SI
2015/664 Sch.2 para.12
Sch.6 Part 1 para.3, amended: SI
2015/664 Sch.2 para.12
Sch.6 Part 1 para.4, amended: SI
2015/664 Sch.2 para.12
Sch.6 Part 2 para.9A, amended: 2015
c.11 s.61
Sch.8 para.2, amended: 2015 c.11 s.61
Sch.8 para.11, repealed: 2015 c.20 Sch.6
para.2
12. Private Security Industry Act 2001
Sch.2 Part 1 para.2, amended: 2015 c.2
Sch.10 para.32
15. Health and Social Care Act 2001
s.49, see *R. (on the application of Forge
Care Homes Ltd) v Cardiff and Vale
University Health Board* [2015] EWHC
601 (Admin), [2015] P.T.S.R. 945 (QBD
(Admin)), Hickinbottom J
s.50, amended: SI 2015/914 Sch.1
para.63
s.55, amended: SI 2015/914 Sch.1
para.64
s.57, amended: SI 2015/914 Sch.1
para.65
s.59, amended: SI 2015/914 Sch.1
para.66
s.64, enabling: SI 2015/864
s.65, enabling: SI 2015/839
s.70, enabling: SI 2015/864

16. Criminal Justice and Police Act 2001
s.25, amended: SI 2015/664 Sch.4
para.31
s.50, see *R. (on the application of Cabot
Global Ltd) v Barkingside Magistrates'
Court* [2015] EWHC 1458 (Admin),
[2015] 2 Cr. App. R. 26 (QBD (Admin)),
Fulford LJ; see *R. (on the application of
Chaudhary) v Bristol Crown Court*
[2014] EWHC 4096 (Admin), [2015] 1
Cr. App. R. 18 (DC), Fulford LJ
s.57, amended: 2015 c.15 Sch.6 para.62
s.57, repealed: 2015 c.15 Sch.6 para.62
s.59, see *R. (on the application of
Chaudhary) v Bristol Crown Court*
[2014] EWHC 4096 (Admin), [2015] 1
Cr. App. R. 18 (DC), Fulford LJ; see *R.
(on the application of Panesar) v Central
Criminal Court* [2014] EWCA Civ 1613,
[2015] 1 W.L.R. 2577 (CA (Civ Div)),
Patten LJ; see *R. (on the application of
Panesar) v Central Criminal Court*
[2014] EWHC 2821 (Admin), [2015] 4
All E.R. 754 (DC), Lord Thomas LCJ
s.59, amended: 2015 c.20 s.82
s.65, amended: 2015 c.15 Sch.6 para.63
s.65, repealed: 2015 c.15 Sch.6 para.63
s.66, amended: 2015 c.15 Sch.6 para.64
s.66, repealed: 2015 c.15 Sch.6 para.64
Sch.1 Part 1 para.9, repealed: 2015 c.15
Sch.6 para.65
Sch.1 Part 1 para.16, repealed: 2015 c.15
Sch.6 para.65
Sch.1 Part 1 para.18, repealed: 2015 c.15
Sch.6 para.65
Sch.1 Part 1 para.19, repealed: 2015 c.15
Sch.6 para.65
Sch.1 Part 1 para.24, repealed: 2015 c.15
Sch.6 para.65
Sch.1 Part 1 para.36, repealed: 2015 c.15
Sch.6 para.65
Sch.1 Part 1 para.45, amended: 2015 c.15
Sch.6 para.65
Sch.1 Part 1 para.73BA, repealed: 2015
c.15 Sch.6 para.65
Sch.1 Part 1 para.73G, repealed: 2015
c.15 Sch.6 para.65
Sch.1 Part 1 para.73G, amended: 2015
c.15 Sch.6 para.65
Sch.1 Part 1 para.73Ji, repealed: 2015
c.15 Sch.6 para.65

Sch.1 Part 1 para.73Ki, repealed: 2015
c.15 Sch.6 para.65
Sch.1 Part 1 para.73N, repealed: 2015
c.15 Sch.6 para.65
Sch.1 Part 1 para.73O, repealed: 2015
c.15 Sch.6 para.65
Sch.1 Part 1 para.73P, added: 2015 c.15
Sch.6 para.65
Sch.2 Part 1 para.1, repealed: 2015 c.15
Sch.6 para.66
Sch.2 Part 1 para.3, amended: 2015 c.15
Sch.6 para.66
Sch.2 Part 1 para.4A, amended: 2015
c.15 Sch.6 para.66
Sch.2 Part 1 para.4B, repealed: 2015 c.15
Sch.6 para.66
Sch.2 Part 1 para.4D, added: 2015 c.15
Sch.6 para.66
Sch.2 Part 1 para.5, repealed: 2015 c.15
Sch.6 para.66
Sch.2 Part 1 para.7, repealed: 2015 c.15
Sch.6 para.66
Sch.2 Part 1 para.8, amended: 2015 c.15
Sch.6 para.66
Sch.2 Part 1 para.9A, amended: 2015
c.15 Sch.6 para.66
Sch.2 Part 1 para.9B, repealed: 2015 c.15
Sch.6 para.66
Sch.2 Part 1 para.9D, added: 2015 c.15
Sch.6 para.66

**24. Anti-terrorism, Crime and Security Act
2001**
see *R. (on the application of B) v
Secretary of State for the Home
Department* [2015] EWCA Civ 445,
[2015] 3 W.L.R. 1031 (CA (Civ Div)),
Lord Dyson MR
s.100, amended: 2015 c.7 s.22
s.100, repealed: 2015 c.7 s.22
Sch.4 Part 1 para.53F, varied: SI
2015/192 Sch.1 para.17

2002

1. International Development Act 2002
s.11, enabling: SI 2015/1702, SI
2015/1835, SI 2015/2069
9. Land Registration Act 2002

see *Nugent v Nugent* [2013] EWHC 4095
(Ch), [2015] Ch. 121 (Ch D (Bristol)),
Morgan J
s.29, see *North East Property Buyers
Litigation, Re* [2015] A.C. 385 (SC),
Lady Hale JSC
s.87, amended: 2015 c.20 Sch.6 para.2
s.87, repealed: 2015 c.20 Sch.6 para.2
s.100, amended: 2015 c.7 Sch.5 para.18
s.105, amended: 2015 c.7 s.35
s.105, substituted: 2015 c.7 s.35
s.106, amended: 2015 c.7 Sch.5 para.19
s.127, amended: 2015 c.7 s.36
s.132, see *North East Property Buyers
Litigation, Re* [2015] A.C. 385 (SC),
Lady Hale JSC
Sch.3 para.2, see *North East Property
Buyers Litigation, Re* [2015] A.C. 385
(SC), Lady Hale JSC
Sch.4, see *MacLeod v Gold Harp
Properties Ltd* [2014] EWCA Civ 1084,
[2015] 1 W.L.R. 1249 (CA (Civ Div)),
Richards LJ
Sch.4 para.2, see *MacLeod v Gold Harp
Properties Ltd* [2014] EWCA Civ 1084,
[2015] 1 W.L.R. 1249 (CA (Civ Div)),
Richards LJ
Sch.4 para.3, see *MacLeod v Gold Harp
Properties Ltd* [2014] EWCA Civ 1084,
[2015] 1 W.L.R. 1249 (CA (Civ Div)),
Richards LJ
Sch.4 para.8, see *MacLeod v Gold Harp
Properties Ltd* [2014] EWCA Civ 1084,
[2015] 1 W.L.R. 1249 (CA (Civ Div)),
Richards LJ
Sch.7 para.4, amended: 2015 c.7 Sch.5
para.20
Sch.8, see *Swift 1st Ltd v Chief Land
Registrar* [2015] EWCA Civ 330, [2015]
Ch. 602 (CA (Civ Div)), Moore-Bick LJ
Sch.8 para.1, see *Swift 1st Ltd v Chief
Land Registrar* [2015] EWCA Civ 330,
[2015] Ch. 602 (CA (Civ Div)), Moore-
Bick LJ
Sch.8 para.11, see *Swift 1st Ltd v Chief
Land Registrar* [2015] EWCA Civ 330,
[2015] Ch. 602 (CA (Civ Div)), Moore-
Bick LJ

**15. Commonhold and Leasehold Reform Act
2002**
Pt 2., see *Elim Court RTM Co Ltd v Avon
Freeholds Ltd* [2015] L. & T.R. 3 (UT
(Lands)), Martin Rodger QC
s.78, see *Elim Court RTM Co Ltd v Avon
Freeholds Ltd* [2015] L. & T.R. 3 (UT
(Lands)), Martin Rodger QC
s.79, see *Elim Court RTM Co Ltd v Avon
Freeholds Ltd* [2015] L. & T.R. 3 (UT
(Lands)), Martin Rodger QC; see *R. (on
the application of O Twelve Baytree Ltd)
v Leasehold Valuation Tribunal* [2014]
EWHC 1229 (Admin), [2015] 1 W.L.R.
276 (QBD (Admin)), Lewis J
s.84, see *R. (on the application of O
Twelve Baytree Ltd) v Leasehold
Valuation Tribunal* [2014] EWHC 1229
(Admin), [2015] 1 W.L.R. 276 (QBD
(Admin)), Lewis J
s.88, see *R. (on the application of O
Twelve Baytree Ltd) v Leasehold
Valuation Tribunal* [2014] EWHC 1229
(Admin), [2015] 1 W.L.R. 276 (QBD
(Admin)), Lewis J

16. State Pension Credit Act 2002
s.2, enabling: SI 2015/1754
s.3ZA, enabling: SI 2015/1529
s.9, enabling: SI 2015/1529
s.15, enabling: SI 2015/67
s.17, enabling: SI 2015/67, SI 2015/1529,
SI 2015/1754
s.19, enabling: SI 2015/67, SI 2015/1754

**17. National Health Service Reform and
Health Care Professions Act 2002**
s.25, amended: 2015 c.28 s.5
s.25A, enabling: SI 2015/400
s.29, see *Professional Standards
Authority for Health and Social Care v
General Medical Council* [2015] EWHC
1304 (Admin), [2015] Med. L.R. 327
(QBD (Admin)), Lang J; see
*Professional Standards Authority for
Health and Social Care v Nursing and
Midwifery Council* [2015] EWHC 1887
(Admin), (2015) 145 B.M.L.R. 168
(QBD (Admin)), Elisabeth Laing J; see
*Professional Standards Authority v
Health and Care Professions Council*
[2014] EWHC 2723 (Admin), (2015) 141
B.M.L.R. 128 (QBD (Admin)), Carr J

s.29, amended: SI 2015/794 Art.18
s.29A, added: SI 2015/794 Art.18
s.38, enabling: SI 2015/400

21. Tax Credits Act 2002
s.4, enabling: SI 2015/669
s.7, enabling: SI 2015/175, SI 2015/451
s.9, enabling: SI 2015/451
s.10, enabling: SI 2015/605
s.11, enabling: SI 2015/451
s.13, enabling: SI 2015/451
s.65, enabling: SI 2015/451, SI 2015/605,
SI 2015/669
s.67, enabling: SI 2015/451, SI 2015/605,
SI 2015/669
Sch.5 para.12, repealed: SI 2015/2006
Sch.12 Part 12

22. Employment Act 2002
Sch.6 para.7, repealed: SI 2015/2006
Sch.12 Part 12
Sch.6 para.12, repealed: SI 2015/2006
Sch.12 Part 12
Sch.6 para.14, repealed: SI 2015/2006
Sch.12 Part 12

23. Finance Act 2002
see *Vaughan-Jones v Vaughan-Jones*
[2015] EWHC 1086 (Ch), [2015]
W.T.L.R. 1287 (Ch D (Manchester)),
Judge Hodge QC
s.135, see *Garrod v Revenue and
Customs Commissioners* [2015] UKFTT
353 (TC), [2015] S.F.T.D. 952 (FTT
(Tax)), Judge Barbara Mosedale
s.136, enabling: SI 2015/171, SI
2015/873, SI 2015/878
s.140, enabling: SI 2015/623
Sch.23 Part 3 para.26, enabling: SI
2015/1960

**24. European Parliamentary Elections Act
2002**
s.7, enabling: SI 2015/220, SI 2015/459
s.16B, substituted: SI 2015/1376 Sch.2
para.10

26. Justice (Northern Ireland) Act 2002
s.46, amended: SI 2015/798 Sch.2
para.11
s.47, amended: SI 2015/798 Sch.2
para.12

28. Export Control Act 2002
s.1, enabling: SI 2015/97, SI 2015/351,
SI 2015/940, SI 2015/1625

s.2, enabling: SI 2015/97, SI 2015/351,
SI 2015/1625
s.3, enabling: SI 2015/97, SI 2015/1546,
SI 2015/1625, SI 2015/1933
s.4, enabling: SI 2015/97, SI 2015/351,
SI 2015/940, SI 2015/1546, SI 2015/1625
s.5, enabling: SI 2015/97, SI 2015/351,
SI 2015/940, SI 2015/1546, SI
2015/1625, SI 2015/1933
s.7, enabling: SI 2015/97, SI 2015/351,
SI 2015/940, SI 2015/1546, SI
2015/1625, SI 2015/1933

29. Proceeds of Crime Act 2002
see *Blue Holding (1) Pte Ltd v United
States* [2014] EWCA Civ 1291, [2015] 1
W.L.R. 1917 (CA (Civ Div)), Rimer LJ;
see *HM Advocate v Younas
(Mohammed)* 2015 S.C.L. 162 (HCJ),
Lord Pentland; see *Lord Advocate v
Mackie* [2015] CSIH 88 (IH (2 Div)),
The Lord Justice Clerk (Carloway); see
R. v Ahmad (Shakeel) [2015] A.C. 299
(SC), Lord Neuberger JSC; see *R. v Ali
(Salah)* [2014] EWCA Crim 1658, [2015]
1 W.L.R. 841 (CA (Crim Div)), Beatson
LJ; see *R. v Kakkad (Freshkumar)*
[2015] EWCA Crim 385, [2015] 1
W.L.R. 4162 (CA (Crim Div)), Pitchford
LJ; see *Serious Fraud Office v Saleh*
[2015] EWHC 2119 (QB), [2015]
Lloyd's Rep. F.C. 629 (QBD), Andrews J
Pt 2., see *National Crime Agency v Azam*
[2014] EWHC 3573 (QB), [2015]
Lloyd's Rep. F.C. 42 (QBD), Andrews J
Pt 5., see *National Crime Agency v Azam*
[2014] EWHC 3573 (QB), [2015]
Lloyd's Rep. F.C. 42 (QBD), Andrews J
s.6, see *R. v Ali (Salah)* [2014] EWCA
Crim 1658, [2015] 1 W.L.R. 841 (CA
(Crim Div)), Beatson LJ; see *R. v
Chahal (Jaspal Singh)* [2015] EWCA
Crim 816, [2015] Lloyd's Rep. F.C. 601
(CA (Crim Div)), Laws LJ; see *R. v Yu
(Jie)* [2015] EWCA Crim 1076, [2015] 2
Cr. App. R. (S.) 75 (CA (Crim Div)),
Gross LJ
s.6, amended: 2015 c.9 Sch.4 para.19
s.10, see *R. v Ali (Salah)* [2014] EWCA
Crim 1658, [2015] 1 W.L.R. 841 (CA
(Crim Div)), Beatson LJ; see *R. v
Chahal (Jaspal Singh)* [2015] EWCA

Crim 816, [2015] Lloyd's Rep. F.C. 601
(CA (Crim Div)), Laws LJ
s.10A, added: 2015 c.9 s.1
s.11, substituted: 2015 c.9 s.5
s.12, amended: 2015 c.9 s.5, Sch.4
para.20
s.13, see *R. v Beaumont (Lisa Tracey)*
[2014] EWCA Crim 1664, [2015] 1 Cr.
App. R. (S.) 1 (CA (Crim Div)),
Hamblen J; see *R. v Guraj (Lodvik)*
[2015] EWCA Crim 305, [2015] 1
W.L.R. 4149 (CA (Crim Div)), Jackson
LJ; see *R. v Kakkad (Freshkumar)*
[2015] EWCA Crim 385, [2015] 1
W.L.R. 4162 (CA (Crim Div)), Pitchford
LJ
s.13, amended: 2015 c.2 Sch.12 para.11,
2015 c.9 s.6, 2015 c.30 Sch.5 para.15
s.13, repealed: 2015 c.30 Sch.5 para.15
s.13A, added: 2015 c.9 s.7
s.14, see *R. v Guraj (Lodvik)* [2015]
EWCA Crim 305, [2015] 1 W.L.R. 4149
(CA (Crim Div)), Jackson LJ; see *R. v
Kakkad (Freshkumar)* [2015] EWCA
Crim 385, [2015] 1 W.L.R. 4162 (CA
(Crim Div)), Pitchford LJ
s.14, amended: 2015 c.9 Sch.4 para.21
s.15, see *R. v Guraj (Lodvik)* [2015]
EWCA Crim 305, [2015] 1 W.L.R. 4149
(CA (Crim Div)), Jackson LJ; see *R. v
Kakkad (Freshkumar)* [2015] EWCA
Crim 385, [2015] 1 W.L.R. 4162 (CA
(Crim Div)), Pitchford LJ
s.15, amended: 2015 c.9 Sch.4 para.22
s.16, amended: 2015 c.9 s.2
s.17, see *R. v Ali (Salah)* [2014] EWCA
Crim 1658, [2015] 1 W.L.R. 841 (CA
(Crim Div)), Beatson LJ
s.18, see *R. (on the application of
Sanjari) v Birmingham Crown Court*
[2015] EWHC 2037 (Admin), [2015] 2
Cr. App. R. 30 (DC), Lord Thomas LCJ
s.18, amended: 2015 c.9 s.2
s.18A, added: 2015 c.9 s.2
s.19, amended: 2015 c.9 Sch.4 para.23,
2015 c.30 Sch.5 para.16
s.20, amended: 2015 c.9 Sch.4 para.24,
2015 c.30 Sch.5 para.17
s.21, amended: 2015 c.9 Sch.4 para.25
s.22, amended: 2015 c.9 Sch.4 para.26
s.23, amended: 2015 c.9 s.8

s.25A, added: 2015 c.9 s.8
s.27, amended: 2015 c.9 s.9
s.28, amended: 2015 c.9 s.9
s.31, amended: 2015 c.9 s.3, Sch.4
para.27
s.32, amended: 2015 c.9 s.3, Sch.4
para.28, 2015 c.30 Sch.5 para.18
s.33, amended: 2015 c.9 s.3, Sch.4
para.29, 2015 c.30 Sch.5 para.19
s.35, amended: 2015 c.9 s.10, Sch.4
para.30
s.40, see *R. (on the application of Mills) v
Sussex Police* [2014] EWHC 2523
(Admin), [2015] 1 W.L.R. 2199 (QBD
(Admin)), Elias LJ
s.40, amended: 2015 c.9 s.11
s.41, see *Crown Prosecution Service v
Eastenders Group* [2015] A.C. 1 (SC),
Lady Hale DPSC
s.41, amended: 2015 c.9 s.11, Sch.4
para.31
s.41, enabling: SI 2015/868
s.42, amended: 2015 c.9 s.12, Sch.4
para.32
s.42, varied: SI 2015/868 Reg.5
s.47B, amended: 2015 c.9 s.13
s.47B, varied: SI 2015/868 Reg.5
s.47C, varied: SI 2015/868 Reg.5
s.47G, amended: 2015 c.9 s.13
s.47S, enabling: SI 2015/730
s.48, see *Crown Prosecution Service v
Eastenders Group* [2015] A.C. 1 (SC),
Lady Hale DPSC
s.51, amended: 2015 c.9 s.4
s.54, varied: SI 2015/868 Reg.5
s.55, amended: 2015 c.9 Sch.4 para.33,
2015 c.30 Sch.5 para.20
s.63, varied: SI 2015/868 Reg.5
s.67, amended: 2015 c.9 s.14
s.67A, amended: 2015 c.9 s.14
s.67D, varied: SI 2015/868 Reg.5
s.69, varied: SI 2015/868 Reg.5
s.75, see *R. v Moss (Eric John)* [2015]
EWCA Crim 713, [2015] Lloyd's Rep.
F.C. 397 (CA (Crim Div)), Lord Thomas
LCJ
s.76, see *R. v Ahmad (Shakeel)* [2015]
A.C. 299 (SC), Lord Neuberger JSC; see
R. v Chahal (Jaspal Singh) [2015]
EWCA Crim 816, [2015] Lloyd's Rep.
F.C. 601 (CA (Crim Div)), Laws LJ; see

R. v Eddishaw (Kevin) [2014] EWCA
Crim 2783, [2015] Lloyd's Rep. F.C. 212
(CA (Crim Div)), Jackson LJ; see *R. v
Harvey (Jack Frederick)* [2015] UKSC
73 (SC), Lord Neuberger PSC; see *R. v
McDowell (Christopher James)* [2015]
EWCA Crim 173, [2015] 2 Cr. App. R.
(S.) 14 (CA (Crim Div)), Pitchford LJ
s.77, see *R. v Lehair (Nicola)* [2015]
EWCA Crim 1324, [2015] 1 W.L.R.
4811 (CA (Crim Div)), Macur LJ
s.85, amended: 2015 c.2 Sch.11 para.18
s.87, amended: 2015 c.9 s.5
s.89, amended: 2015 c.9 Sch.4 para.34
s.89, enabling: SI 2015/1855
s.90, enabling: SI 2015/1855
s.91, enabling: SI 2015/1490
s.92, see *Lord Advocate v Mackie* [2015]
CSIH 88 (IH (2 Div)), The Lord Justice
Clerk (Carloway)
s.92, amended: 2015 c.9 Sch.4 para.35
s.97, amended: 2015 c.9 s.15
s.97A, added: 2015 c.9 s.15
s.97B, added: 2015 c.9 s.16
s.99, amended: 2015 c.9 Sch.4 para.36
s.100, amended: 2015 c.9 Sch.4 para.37
s.104, amended: 2015 c.9 Sch.4 para.38
s.105, amended: 2015 c.9 Sch.4 para.39
s.106, amended: 2015 c.9 Sch.4 para.40
s.107, amended: 2015 c.9 Sch.4 para.41
s.111, amended: 2015 c.9 s.18
s.112, amended: 2015 c.9 s.18
s.118, amended: 2015 c.9 s.19
s.118, repealed: 2015 c.9 Sch.4 para.42
s.119, see *Dunn v Y* 2015 S.L.T. (Sh Ct)
113 (Sh Ct (Lothian) (Edinburgh)),
Sheriff T Welsh, QC
s.119, amended: 2015 c.9 s.20
s.120, amended: 2015 c.9 s.20
s.121, see *Dunn v Y* 2015 S.L.T. (Sh Ct)
113 (Sh Ct (Lothian) (Edinburgh)),
Sheriff T Welsh, QC
s.121, amended: 2015 c.9 s.21, Sch.4
para.43
s.127B, amended: 2015 c.9 s.22
s.127G, amended: 2015 c.9 s.22
s.128, see *Lord Advocate v Mackie*
[2015] CSIH 88 (IH (2 Div)), The Lord
Justice Clerk (Carloway)
s.131, amended: 2015 c.9 Sch.4 para.44

s.150, see *HM Advocate v Younas
(Mohammed)* 2015 S.C.L. 162 (HCJ),
Lord Pentland
s.153, repealed: 2015 c.9 Sch.4 para.45
s.156, amended: 2015 c.9 Sch.4 para.46
s.160, see *Martin v Revenue and Customs
Commissioners* [2015] UKUT 161
(TCC), [2015] S.T.C. 2490 (UT (Tax)),
Warren J
s.160A, added: 2015 c.9 s.24
s.161, substituted: 2015 c.9 s.28
s.162, amended: 2015 c.9 s.28, Sch.4
para.47
s.163A, added: 2015 c.9 s.29
s.166, amended: 2015 c.9 s.25
s.168, amended: 2015 c.9 s.25
s.168A, added: 2015 c.9 s.25
s.171, see *Martin v Revenue and Customs
Commissioners* [2015] UKUT 161
(TCC), [2015] S.T.C. 2490 (UT (Tax)),
Warren J
s.173, amended: 2015 c.9 s.30
s.175A, added: 2015 c.9 s.30
s.177, amended: 2015 c.9 s.31
s.178, amended: 2015 c.9 s.31
s.181, amended: 2015 c.9 s.26, Sch.4
para.48
s.182, amended: 2015 c.9 s.26
s.183, amended: 2015 c.9 s.26
s.185, amended: 2015 c.9 s.32, Sch.4
para.49
s.189, amended: 2015 c.9 s.33
s.190, amended: 2015 c.9 s.33, Sch.4
para.50
s.191, amended: 2015 c.9 s.34, Sch.4
para.51
s.195B, amended: 2015 c.9 s.35
s.195G, amended: 2015 c.9 s.35
s.195S, amended: SI 2015/230 Art.2
s.199, amended: 2015 c.9 s.27
s.215, amended: 2015 c.9 s.36
s.215A, amended: 2015 c.9 s.36
s.235, amended: 2015 c.9 s.28
s.255G, added: 2015 c.9 s.23
s.266, see *National Crime Agency v
Atkinson* [2015] EWHC 1299 (QB),
[2015] Lloyd's Rep. F.C. 435 (QBD),
Coulson J; see *National Crime Agency v
Azam* [2014] EWHC 3573 (QB), [2015]
Lloyd's Rep. F.C. 42 (QBD), Andrews J;

see *Scottish Ministers v Mirza* 2015 S.C.
334 (IH (Ex Div)), Lady Clark of Calton
s.273, amended: 2015 c.9 Sch.4 para.52
s.277, amended: 2015 c.9 Sch.4 para.53
s.281, see *National Crime Agency v Robb*
[2014] EWHC 4384 (Ch), [2015] Ch. 520
(Ch D), Sir Terence Etherton C
s.282A, amended: SI 2015/798 Art.8
s.282B, amended: SI 2015/798 Art.8
s.282C, amended: SI 2015/798 Art.8
s.282CA, added: 2015 c.9 s.23
s.282D, amended: SI 2015/798 Art.8
s.282F, amended: SI 2015/798 Art.8
s.289, enabling: SI 2015/705
s.292, enabling: SI 2015/705
s.293, enabling: SSI 2015/220
s.297A, enabling: SI 2015/857, SI
2015/1854
s.304, see *National Crime Agency v Robb*
[2014] EWHC 4384 (Ch), [2015] Ch. 520
(Ch D), Sir Terence Etherton C; see
Serious Fraud Office v Saleh [2015]
EWHC 2119 (QB), [2015] Lloyd's Rep.
F.C. 629 (QBD), Andrews J
s.305, see *Serious Fraud Office v Saleh*
[2015] EWHC 2119 (QB), [2015]
Lloyd's Rep. F.C. 629 (QBD), Andrews J
s.308, amended: 2015 c.30 Sch.5 para.21
s.316, amended: 2015 c.9 Sch.4 para.54,
SI 2015/798 Art.8
s.327, see *O'Neill (William John) v HM
Advocate* [2015] HCJAC 68, 2015 S.C.L.
822 (HCJ), The Lord Justice Clerk
(Carloway); see *O'Neill (William) v HM
Advocate* 2015 S.C.L. 204 (HCJ), Lady
Smith; see *R. v GH* [2015] UKSC 24,
[2015] 1 W.L.R. 2126 (SC), Lord
Neuberger PSC; see *R. v Rogers
(Bradley David)* [2014] EWCA Crim
1680, [2015] 1 W.L.R. 1017 (CA (Crim
Div)), Treacy LJ
s.328, see *Iqbal (Malik) v HM Advocate*
[2015] HCJAC 71, 2015 S.C.L. 877
(HCJ), The Lord Justice Clerk
(Carloway); see *R. v GH* [2015] UKSC
24, [2015] 1 W.L.R. 2126 (SC), Lord
Neuberger PSC
s.329, see *R. v GH* [2015] UKSC 24,
[2015] 1 W.L.R. 2126 (SC), Lord
Neuberger PSC
s.338, amended: 2015 c.9 s.37

s.340, see *R. v Rogers (Bradley David)*
[2014] EWCA Crim 1680, [2015] 1
W.L.R. 1017 (CA (Crim Div)), Treacy LJ
s.341, amended: 2015 c.9 s.38, Sch.4
para.55
s.345, see *R. (on the application of
Chatwani) v National Crime Agency*
[2015] EWHC 1284 (Admin), [2015]
Lloyd's Rep. F.C. 473 (DC), Bean LJ
s.346, see *R. (on the application of
Chatwani) v National Crime Agency*
[2015] EWHC 1284 (Admin), [2015]
Lloyd's Rep. F.C. 473 (DC), Bean LJ
s.351, enabling: SI 2015/1490
s.352, see *R. (on the application of Mills)
v Sussex Police* [2014] EWHC 2523
(Admin), [2015] 1 W.L.R. 2199 (QBD
(Admin)), Elias LJ
s.352, amended: 2015 c.20 s.82
s.353, see *R. (on the application of Mills)
v Sussex Police* [2014] EWHC 2523
(Admin), [2015] 1 W.L.R. 2199 (QBD
(Admin)), Elias LJ
s.353, amended: 2015 c.9 s.38
s.355, enabling: SI 2015/759
s.362, enabling: SI 2015/1490
s.369, enabling: SI 2015/1490
s.375, enabling: SI 2015/1490
s.377, enabling: SI 2015/729
s.377A, enabling: SI 2015/612
s.388, amended: 2015 c.9 s.38
s.416, amended: 2015 c.9 Sch.4 para.56
s.439, enabling: SSI 2015/124
s.441, enabling: SSI 2015/124
s.443, enabling: SI 2015/1749
s.444, enabling: SI 2015/1750
s.445, enabling: SI 2015/206, SI
2015/1751, SI 2015/1752
s.447, amended: 2015 c.9 s.39
s.453, enabling: SI 2015/1853
s.459, amended: 2015 c.9 s.10, s.14, s.19,
s.32, s.36, Sch.4 para.57
s.459, enabling: SI 2015/206, SI
2015/612, SI 2015/729, SI 2015/759, SI
2015/857, SI 2015/1749, SI 2015/1750,
SI 2015/1751, SI 2015/1752, SI
2015/1853, SI 2015/1854, SI 2015/1855
Sch.2 para.3A, added: 2015 c.30 s.7
Sch.2 para.4, amended: 2015 c.30 s.7
Sch.2 para.4, repealed: 2015 c.30 s.7

Sch.2 para.8, amended: 2015 c.9 Sch.4
para.58
Sch.4 para.4, substituted: 2015 asp 12
s.15
Sch.4 para.4A, added: 2015 asp 12 s.15
Sch.9 Part 1 para.1, amended: SI
2015/575 Sch.1 para.23
Sch.9 Part 1 para.3, amended: SI
2015/575 Sch.1 para.23
Sch.10 Part 1 para.1, amended: 2015 c.9
Sch.4 para.59
Sch.11 para.37, repealed: 2015 c.30
Sch.5 para.22

30. Police Reform Act 2002
s.12, enabling: SI 2015/431
s.23, enabling: SI 2015/431
s.105, enabling: SI 2015/431
Sch.3, see *R. (on the application of
Demetrio) v Independent Police
Complaints Commission* [2015] EWHC
593 (Admin), [2015] P.T.S.R. 1268
(QBD (Admin)), Burnett LJ
Sch.3 para.19B, see *R. (on the
application of Chief Constable of West
Yorkshire) v Independent Police
Complaints Commission* [2014] EWCA
Civ 1367, [2015] P.T.S.R. 72 (CA (Civ
Div)), Beatson LJ

32. Education Act 2002
s.2, enabling: SI 2015/1227
s.19, enabling: SI 2015/883
s.20, enabling: SI 2015/883
s.23, enabling: SI 2015/883
s.24, enabling: SI 2015/2033
s.26, enabling: SI 2015/883
s.32, amended: 2015 c.20 Sch.16 para.3
s.32, repealed: 2015 c.20 Sch.16 para.3
s.34, enabling: SI 2015/883
s.35, amended: 2015 c.20 Sch.16 para.4
s.35, repealed: 2015 c.20 Sch.16 para.4
s.35, enabling: SI 2015/887
s.36, amended: 2015 c.20 Sch.16 para.5
s.36, repealed: 2015 c.20 Sch.16 para.5
s.36, enabling: SI 2015/887
s.76, enabling: SI 2015/901
s.87, enabling: SI 2015/900
s.108, enabling: SI 2015/1309, SI
2015/1596, SI 2015/1601
s.122, enabling: SI 2015/1582
s.123, enabling: SI 2015/1582
s.124, enabling: SI 2015/1582

s.136, amended: 2015 c.20 Sch.15 para.8
s.136, repealed: 2015 c.20 Sch.15 para.8
s.137, amended: 2015 c.20 Sch.15 para.8
s.137, repealed: 2015 c.20 Sch.15 para.8
s.138, repealed: 2015 c.20 Sch.15 para.8
s.141F, amended: 2015 c.2 Sch.11
para.19
s.183, amended: 2015 c.20 Sch.14
para.46
s.183, repealed: 2015 c.20 Sch.14 para.46
s.210, enabling: SI 2015/883, SI
2015/900, SI 2015/1309, SI 2015/1596,
SI 2015/1601
s.216, enabling: SI 2015/381
Sch.7 Part 2 para.9, repealed: 2015 c.20
Sch.16 para.2

**36. Tobacco Advertising and Promotion Act
2002**
s.19, enabling: SI 2015/839
s.20, enabling: SI 2015/839

38. Adoption and Children Act 2002
see *M-H (A Child) (Placement Order:
Correct Test to Dispense with Consent),
Re* [2014] EWCA Civ 1396, [2015] 2
F.L.R. 357 (CA (Civ Div)), Laws LJ; see
*M'P-P (Children) (Adoption: Status
Quo), Re* [2015] EWCA Civ 584, [2015]
2 F.C.R. 451 (CA (Civ Div)), McFarlane
LJ
s.1, see *AB v CT (Parental Order:
Consent of Surrogate Mother)* [2015]
EWFC 12 (Fam Ct), Theis J; see *B v C
(Surrogacy: Adoption)* [2015] EWFC 17,
[2015] 1 F.L.R. 1392 (Fam Ct), Theis J;
see *FAS v Secretary of State for the
Home Department* [2015] EWHC 622
(Fam), [2015] 3 All E.R. 1001 (Fam
Div), Mostyn J; see *G (A Child) (Non-
relative Carer: Joinder to Adoption
Proceedings), Re* [2014] EWCA Civ 432,
[2015] Fam. 223 (CA (Civ Div)),
Sullivan LJ; see *M (A Child) (Care
Proceedings: Long-term Foster Care),
Re* [2014] EWCA Civ 1406, [2015] 2
F.L.R. 197 (CA (Civ Div)), Black LJ; see
*M-H (A Child) (Placement Order:
Correct Test to Dispense with Consent),
Re* [2014] EWCA Civ 1396, [2015] 2
F.L.R. 357 (CA (Civ Div)), Laws LJ; see
*M'P-P (Children) (Adoption: Status
Quo), Re* [2015] EWCA Civ 584, [2015]

2 F.C.R. 451 (CA (Civ Div)), McFarlane
LJ; see *P (A Child) (Adoption: Leave to
Oppose), Re* [2015] EWCA Civ 777,
[2015] 3 F.C.R. 601 (CA (Civ Div)),
Richards LJ; see *P (A Child) (Care and
Placement: Appellate Review), Re* [2014]
EWCA Civ 1648, [2015] 2 F.C.R. 400
(CA (Civ Div)), Moore-Bick LJ; see *R
(A Child) (Adoption: Judicial Approach),
Re* [2014] EWCA Civ 1625, [2015] 1
W.L.R. 3273 (CA (Civ Div)), Sir James
Munby PFD
s.2, enabling: SI 2015/1802
s.9, enabling: SI 2015/1685, SI
2015/1802
s.21, see *D (A Child) (Non-availability of
Legal Aid), Re* [2015] 1 F.L.R. 531 (Fam
Ct), Sir James Munby PFD
s.22, see *D (A Child) (Non-availability of
Legal Aid), Re* [2015] 1 F.L.R. 531 (Fam
Ct), Sir James Munby PFD
s.24, see *G (A Child) (Non-relative
Carer: Joinder to Adoption
Proceedings), Re* [2014] EWCA Civ 432,
[2015] Fam. 223 (CA (Civ Div)),
Sullivan LJ; see *T (Children) (Placement
Order: Revocation), Re* [2014] EWCA
Civ 1369, [2015] 1 W.L.R. 3165 (CA
(Civ Div)), Russell J
s.29, see *G (A Child) (Non-relative
Carer: Joinder to Adoption
Proceedings), Re* [2014] EWCA Civ 432,
[2015] Fam. 223 (CA (Civ Div)),
Sullivan LJ
s.42, see *B v C (Surrogacy: Adoption)*
[2015] EWFC 17, [2015] 1 F.L.R. 1392
(Fam Ct), Theis J; see *FAS v Secretary
of State for the Home Department* [2015]
EWHC 622 (Fam), [2015] 3 All E.R.
1001 (Fam Div), Mostyn J
s.47, see *G (A Child) (Non-relative
Carer: Joinder to Adoption
Proceedings), Re* [2014] EWCA Civ 432,
[2015] Fam. 223 (CA (Civ Div)),
Sullivan LJ; see *P (A Child) (Adoption:
Leave to Oppose), Re* [2015] EWCA Civ
777, [2015] 3 F.C.R. 601 (CA (Civ Div)),
Richards LJ; see *W (Children)
(Adoption: Procedure: Conditions), Re*
[2015] EWCA Civ 403, [2015] 3 F.C.R.

99 (CA (Civ Div)), Sir James Munby
PFD
s.51, see *B v C (Surrogacy: Adoption)*
[2015] EWFC 17, [2015] 1 F.L.R. 1392
(Fam Ct), Theis J
s.52, see *M v Blackburn with Darwen BC*
[2014] EWCA Civ 1479, [2015] 1
W.L.R. 2441 (CA (Civ Div)), Beatson
LJ; see *M-H (A Child) (Placement
Order: Correct Test to Dispense with
Consent), Re* [2014] EWCA Civ 1396,
[2015] 2 F.L.R. 357 (CA (Civ Div)),
Laws LJ; see *P (A Child) (Adoption:
Step-parent's Application), Re* [2014]
EWCA Civ 1174, [2015] 1 W.L.R. 2927
(CA (Civ Div)), Moore-Bick LJ; see *P
(A Child) (Care and Placement:
Appellate Review), Re* [2014] EWCA Civ
1648, [2015] 2 F.C.R. 400 (CA (Civ
Div)), Moore-Bick LJ
s.66, see *G (Children) (Recognition of
Brazilian Adoption), Re* [2014] EWHC
2605 (Fam), [2015] 1 F.L.R. 1402 (Fam
Div), Cobb J
s.79, see *X (Adopted Child: Access to
Court File), Re* [2015] 1 F.L.R. 375 (Fam
Ct), Sir James Munby PFD
s.92, see *B v C (Surrogacy: Adoption)*
[2015] EWFC 17, [2015] 1 F.L.R. 1392
(Fam Ct), Theis J
s.93, see *B v C (Surrogacy: Adoption)*
[2015] EWFC 17, [2015] 1 F.L.R. 1392
(Fam Ct), Theis J
s.93, amended: SI 2015/664 Sch.4
para.32
s.95, amended: SI 2015/664 Sch.4
para.32
s.98, enabling: SI 2015/1685, SI
2015/1802
s.140, enabling: SI 2015/1685
s.144, enabling: SI 2015/1685, SI
2015/1802

40. Enterprise Act 2002
see *AXA PPP Healthcare Ltd v
Competition and Markets Authority*
[2015] EWCA Civ 492, [2015] 1 W.L.R.
4341 (CA (Civ Div)), Laws LJ; see
*Groupe Eurotunnel SA v Competition
Commission* [2015] UKSC 75, [2015]
Bus. L.R. 1573 (SC), Lord Neuberger
JSC

s.7, amended: 2015 c.26 s.37

s.12, amended: 2015 c.15 s.82

s.14, amended: 2015 c.15 s.82, Sch.8 para.19

s.15, amended: 2015 c.15 Sch.8 para.20

s.15, enabling: SI 2015/1648

s.16, amended: 2015 c.15 Sch.8 para.21

s.16, enabling: SI 2015/1643

s.22, see *AC Nielsen Co Ltd v Competition and Markets Authority* [2015] Comp. A.R. 4 (CAT), Sales J; see *Groupe Eurotunnel SA v Competition Commission* [2015] UKSC 75, [2015] Bus. L.R. 1573 (SC), Lord Neuberger JSC

s.35, see *Groupe Eurotunnel SA v Competition Commission* [2015] UKSC 75, [2015] Bus. L.R. 1573 (SC), Lord Neuberger JSC; see *Ryanair Holdings Plc v Competition Commission* [2015] EWCA Civ 83, [2015] U.K.C.L.R. 225 (CA (Civ Div)), Laws LJ

s.41, see *Ryanair Holdings Plc v Competition and Markets Authority* [2015] CAT 14, [2015] Comp. A.R. 262 (CAT), Hodge Malek QC; see *Ryanair Holdings Plc v Competition Commission* [2015] EWCA Civ 83, [2015] U.K.C.L.R. 225 (CA (Civ Div)), Laws LJ

s.86, see *Akzo Nobel NV v Competition Commission* [2014] EWCA Civ 482, [2015] 1 All E.R. 693 (CA (Civ Div)), Richards LJ

s.104, see *Ryanair Holdings Plc v Competition Commission* [2015] EWCA Civ 83, [2015] U.K.C.L.R. 225 (CA (Civ Div)), Laws LJ

s.120, see *AC Nielsen Co Ltd v Competition and Markets Authority* [2015] Comp. A.R. 4 (CAT), Sales J

s.121, enabling: SI 2015/1936

s.124, enabling: SI 2015/1936

s.129, see *Akzo Nobel NV v Competition Commission* [2014] EWCA Civ 482, [2015] 1 All E.R. 693 (CA (Civ Div)), Richards LJ

s.136, amended: SI 2015/1682 Sch.1 para.4

s.168, amended: SI 2015/1682 Sch.1 para.4

s.179, see *AXA PPP Healthcare Ltd v Competition and Markets Authority* [2015] EWCA Civ 492, [2015] 1 W.L.R. 4341 (CA (Civ Div)), Laws LJ; see *HCA International Ltd v Competition and Markets Authority* [2015] Comp. A.R. 18 (CAT), Sales J; see *HCA International Ltd v Competition and Markets Authority* [2015] Comp. A.R. 9 (CAT), Sales J

s.210, repealed: 2015 c.15 Sch.7 para.2

s.210, enabling: SI 2015/1392

s.211, amended: 2015 c.15 Sch.7 para.3

s.211, enabling: SI 2015/1727

s.212, enabling: SI 2015/1392, SI 2015/1628

s.213, amended: 2015 c.15 Sch.7 para.4

s.214, amended: 2015 c.15 Sch.7 para.5

s.217, amended: 2015 c.15 Sch.7 para.6

s.219, amended: 2015 c.15 Sch.7 para.7

s.219A, added: 2015 c.15 Sch.7 para.8

s.220, amended: 2015 c.15 Sch.7 para.9

s.223A, added: 2015 c.15 Sch.6 para.78

s.224, repealed: 2015 c.15 Sch.6 para.68

s.225, repealed: 2015 c.15 Sch.6 para.69

s.226, repealed: 2015 c.15 Sch.6 para.70

s.227, repealed: 2015 c.15 Sch.6 para.71

s.227A, repealed: 2015 c.15 Sch.6 para.72

s.227B, repealed: 2015 c.15 Sch.6 para.73

s.227C, repealed: 2015 c.15 Sch.6 para.74

s.227D, repealed: 2015 c.15 Sch.6 para.75

s.227E, repealed: 2015 c.15 Sch.6 para.76

s.227F, repealed: 2015 c.15 Sch.6 para.77

s.228, repealed: 2015 c.15 Sch.6 para.79

s.229, amended: 2015 c.15 Sch.7 para.10

s.236, repealed: 2015 c.15 Sch.6 para.80

s.244, see *Ryanair Holdings Plc v Competition Commission* [2015] EWCA Civ 83, [2015] U.K.C.L.R. 225 (CA (Civ Div)), Laws LJ

s.259, see *Thomas v Edmondson* [2014] EWHC 1494 (Ch), [2015] 1 W.L.R. 1395 (Ch D), Asplin J

s.264, repealed: 2015 c.26 s.135

s.270, repealed: 2015 c.20 Sch.6 para.22

Sch.4 Part 1 para.1, amended: 2015 c.15 Sch.8 para.23

Sch.4 Part 1 para.1A, added: 2015 c.15
Sch.8 para.24
Sch.4 Part 1 para.4, amended: 2015 c.15
Sch.8 para.25
Sch.4 Part 1 para.5, amended: 2015 c.15
Sch.8 para.25
Sch.4 Part 1 para.6, amended: 2015 c.15
Sch.8 para.26
Sch.4 Part 1 para.7, amended: 2015 c.15
Sch.8 para.27
Sch.4 Part 2, enabling: SI 2015/1648
Sch.4 Part 2 para.9, substituted: 2015
c.15 Sch.8 para.28
Sch.4 Part 2 para.11, amended: 2015 c.15
Sch.8 para.29
Sch.4 Part 2 para.13, substituted: 2015
c.15 Sch.8 para.30
Sch.4 Part 2 para.15A, added: 2015 c.15
Sch.8 para.31
Sch.4 Part 2 para.17, amended: 2015 c.15
Sch.8 para.32
Sch.4 Part 2 para.18, amended: 2015 c.15
s.82
Sch.4 Part 2 para.20A, added: 2015 c.15
Sch.8 para.33
Sch.4 Part 2 para.21A, added: 2015 c.15
Sch.8 para.34
Sch.4 Part 2 para.23, amended: 2015 c.15
Sch.8 para.35
Sch.4 Part 2 para.25, amended: 2015 c.15
Sch.8 para.36
Sch.13 Part 2, amended: SI 2015/1392
Reg.6
Sch.13 Part 2 para.13, added: SI
2015/542 Reg.20
Sch.13 Part 2 para.14, added: SI
2015/1392 Reg.6
Sch.13 Part 2 para.15, added: SI
2015/1911 Reg.18
Sch.14, amended: 2015 c.15 Sch.6
para.81, 2015 c.26 Sch.1 para.26, SI
2015/1726 Sch.1 para.3
Sch.15, amended: 2015 c.15 Sch.4
para.35, 2015 c.20 Sch.23 para.28, 2015
c.26 Sch.1 para.26, SI 2015/1726 Sch.1
para.4, SI 2015/1911 Reg.18
Sch.17 para.42, repealed: 2015 c.26 s.107
Sch.22 para.2, repealed: 2015 c.26 s.135
Sch.23 para.4, repealed: 2015 c.26 s.135
Sch.25 para.9, repealed: 2015 c.15 Sch.6
para.85

**41. Nationality, Immigration and Asylum
Act 2002**

Pt 5A., see *Chege (Section 117D: Article
8: Approach)* [2015] UKUT 165 (IAC),
[2015] Imm. A.R. 850 (UT (IAC)), Nicol
J; see *MK (Section 55: Tribunal
Options: Sierra Leone)* [2015] UKUT
223 (IAC), [2015] I.N.L.R. 563 (UT
(IAC)), McCloskey J
s.77, see *Al v Advocate General for
Scotland* [2015] CSOH 95, 2015 S.L.T.
507 (OH), Lady Rae
s.78, see *R. (on the application of Ahmed)
v Secretary of State for the Home
Department* [2015] UKUT 436 (IAC),
[2015] Imm. A.R. 1320 (UT (IAC)),
Judge Storey
s.82, see *Amirteymour (EEA Appeals:
Human Rights: United States)* [2015]
UKUT 466 (IAC), [2015] Imm. A.R.
1365 (UT (IAC)), McCloskey J; see *JG
(Jamaica) v Secretary of State for the
Home Department* [2015] EWCA Civ
410, [2015] Imm. A.R. 1193 (CA (Civ
Div)), Jackson LJ; see *KA (Afghanistan)
v Secretary of State for the Home
Department* [2015] CSIH 16, 2015 S.C.
479 (IH (Ex Div)), Lord Eassie; see
*Olatunde v Secretary of State for the
Home Department* [2015] EWCA Civ
670, [2015] 1 W.L.R. 4602 (CA (Civ
Div)), Moore-Bick LJ; see *R. (on the
application of Ahmed) v Secretary of
State for the Home Department* [2015]
UKUT 436 (IAC), [2015] Imm. A.R.
1320 (UT (IAC)), Judge Storey; see *R.
(on the application of Byczek) v Secretary
of State for the Home Department* [2014]
EWHC 4298 (Admin), [2015] 2
C.M.L.R. 7 (QBD (Admin)), Jay J; see
*TN (Afghanistan) v Secretary of State for
the Home Department* [2015] UKSC 40,
[2015] 1 W.L.R. 3083 (SC), Lord
Neuberger PSC
s.83, see *TN (Afghanistan) v Secretary of
State for the Home Department* [2015]
UKSC 40, [2015] 1 W.L.R. 3083 (SC),
Lord Neuberger PSC
s.84, see *Amirteymour (EEA Appeals:
Human Rights: United States)* [2015]

UKUT 466 (IAC), [2015] Imm. A.R.
1365 (UT (IAC)), McCloskey J
s.85, see *Amirteymour (EEA Appeals:
Human Rights: United States)* [2015]
UKUT 466 (IAC), [2015] Imm. A.R.
1365 (UT (IAC)), McCloskey J; see
*Olatunde v Secretary of State for the
Home Department* [2015] EWCA Civ
670, [2015] 1 W.L.R. 4602 (CA (Civ
Div)), Moore-Bick LJ
s.85A, see *Olatunde v Secretary of State
for the Home Department* [2015] EWCA
Civ 670, [2015] 1 W.L.R. 4602 (CA (Civ
Div)), Moore-Bick LJ
s.87, see *Amirteymour (EEA Appeals:
Human Rights: United States)* [2015]
UKUT 466 (IAC), [2015] Imm. A.R.
1365 (UT (IAC)), McCloskey J
s.92, see *R. (on the application of Ahmed)
v Secretary of State for the Home
Department* [2015] UKUT 436 (IAC),
[2015] Imm. A.R. 1320 (UT (IAC)),
Judge Storey
s.94, see *KA (Afghanistan) v Secretary of
State for the Home Department* [2015]
CSIH 16, 2015 S.C. 479 (IH (Ex Div)),
Lord Eassie; see *R. (on the application
of Brown) v Secretary of State for the
Home Department* [2015] UKSC 8,
[2015] 1 W.L.R. 1060 (SC), Lady Hale
DPSC; see *VS (India) v Secretary of
State for the Home Department* [2015]
CSOH 118, 2015 S.L.T. 651 (OH), Lord
Bannatyne
s.109, enabling: SI 2015/694
s.113, see *KA (Afghanistan) v Secretary
of State for the Home Department* [2015]
CSIH 16, 2015 S.C. 479 (IH (Ex Div)),
Lord Eassie
s.117A, see *Secretary of State for the
Home Department v Dube* [2015] UKUT
90 (IAC), [2015] Imm. A.R. 651 (UT
(IAC)), Nicol J; see *YM (Uganda) v
Secretary of State for the Home
Department* [2014] EWCA Civ 1292,
[2015] I.N.L.R. 405 (CA (Civ Div)),
Aikens LJ
s.117B, see *AM (S. 117B: Malawi)*
[2015] UKUT 260 (IAC), [2015] Imm.
A.R. 1019 (UT (IAC)), CMG Ockelton;
see *Chege (Section 117D: Article 8:*

Approach) [2015] UKUT 165 (IAC),
[2015] Imm. A.R. 850 (UT (IAC)), Nicol
J; see *Secretary of State for the Home
Department v Dube* [2015] UKUT 90
(IAC), [2015] Imm. A.R. 651 (UT
(IAC)), Nicol J
s.117D, see *Chege (Section 117D: Article
8: Approach)* [2015] UKUT 165 (IAC),
[2015] Imm. A.R. 850 (UT (IAC)), Nicol
J; see *Secretary of State for the Home
Department v Dube* [2015] UKUT 90
(IAC), [2015] Imm. A.R. 651 (UT
(IAC)), Nicol J; see *YM (Uganda) v
Secretary of State for the Home
Department* [2014] EWCA Civ 1292,
[2015] I.N.L.R. 405 (CA (Civ Div)),
Aikens LJ
s.120, see *Amirteymour (EEA Appeals:
Human Rights: United States)* [2015]
UKUT 466 (IAC), [2015] Imm. A.R.
1365 (UT (IAC)), McCloskey J
s.124, repealed: 2015 c.6 s.22
s.126, enabling: SI 2015/737
Sch.3 para.1, see *R. (on the application of
F) v Barking and Dagenham LBC* [2015]
EWHC 2838 (Admin), (2015) 18 C.C.L.
Rep. 754 (QBD (Admin)), Bobbie
Cheema QC
Sch.3 para.1, amended: SI 2015/914
Sch.1 para.67
Sch.3 para.3, see *R. (on the application of
F) v Barking and Dagenham LBC* [2015]
EWHC 2838 (Admin), (2015) 18 C.C.L.
Rep. 754 (QBD (Admin)), Bobbie
Cheema QC
Sch.3 para.7, see *R. (on the application of
Mensah) v Salford City Council* [2014]
EWHC 3537 (Admin), [2015] P.T.S.R.
157 (QBD (Admin)), Lewis J

42. Animal Health Act 2002
s.6, repealed: 2015 c.20 Sch.23 para.38
Sch.1, repealed: 2015 c.20 Sch.23
para.38

2003

**1. Income Tax (Earnings and Pensions) Act
2003**
Part 3 c.11, repealed: 2015 c.11 s.13
Part 4 c.7A, added: 2015 c.11 s.11

Pt 7., see *Tower Radio Ltd v Revenue and Customs Commissioners* [2015] UKUT 60 (TCC), [2015] S.T.C. 1257 (UT (Tax)), Newey J

Pt 7 s.420, see *Tower Radio Ltd v Revenue and Customs Commissioners* [2015] UKUT 60 (TCC), [2015] S.T.C. 1257 (UT (Tax)), Newey J

s.6, see *Murray Group Holdings Ltd v Revenue and Customs Commissioners* [2015] CSIH 77, 2015 S.L.T. 765 (IH (2 Div)), The Lord Justice Clerk (Carloway)

s.7, amended: 2015 c.11 Sch.1 para.2

s.9, see *Revenue and Customs Commissioners v Smith & Williamson Corporate Services Ltd* [2015] UKUT 666 (TCC), [2015] B.T.C. 539 (UT (Tax)), Warren J

s.11, see *Martin v Revenue and Customs Commissioners* [2015] S.T.C. 478 (UT (Tax)), Warren J

s.17, amended: 2015 c.11 Sch.1 para.3

s.30, amended: 2015 c.11 Sch.1 para.4

s.62, see *A v Revenue and Customs Commissioners* [2015] UKFTT 189 (TC), [2015] I.R.L.R. 962 (FTT (Tax)), Judge Swami Raghavan; see *Moorthy v Revenue and Customs Commissioners* [2015] I.R.L.R. 4 (FTT (Tax)), Judge Anne Redston; see *Murray Group Holdings Ltd v Revenue and Customs Commissioners* [2015] CSIH 77, 2015 S.L.T. 765 (IH (2 Div)), The Lord Justice Clerk (Carloway)

s.63, amended: 2015 c.11 Sch.1 para.5

s.63, repealed: 2015 c.11 Sch.1 para.5

s.65, repealed: 2015 c.11 s.12

s.66, amended: 2015 c.11 Sch.1 para.6

s.95, repealed: 2015 c.11 s.12

s.96, repealed: 2015 c.11 s.12

s.139, amended: 2015 c.11 s.7, s.8

s.140, amended: 2015 c.11 s.7, s.8

s.141, amended: 2015 c.11 s.9

s.142, amended: 2015 c.11 s.7, s.8

s.148, repealed: 2015 c.11 Sch.1 para.7

s.150, amended: SI 2015/1979 Art.2

s.155, amended: 2015 c.11 s.10, SI 2015/1979 Art.3

s.156, amended: 2015 c.11 s.10

s.157, repealed: 2015 c.11 Sch.1 para.8

s.158, amended: 2015 c.11 s.10

s.160, amended: 2015 c.11 s.10

s.161, amended: SI 2015/1979 Art.4

s.169, amended: 2015 c.11 Sch.1 para.9

s.169, repealed: 2015 c.11 Sch.1 para.9

s.169A, amended: 2015 c.11 Sch.1 para.10

s.169A, repealed: 2015 c.11 Sch.1 para.10

s.170, amended: 2015 c.11 s.10

s.170, enabling: SI 2015/1979

s.184, amended: 2015 c.11 Sch.1 para.11

s.188, amended: 2015 c.11 Sch.1 para.12

s.228, amended: 2015 c.8 s.54, 2015 c.11 s.14, Sch.1 para.13

s.229, amended: 2015 c.33 s.29

s.235A, added: 2015 c.33 s.29

s.236, amended: 2015 c.33 s.29

s.239, amended: 2015 c.11 Sch.1 para.14

s.239, repealed: 2015 c.11 Sch.1 para.14

s.266, amended: 2015 c.11 Sch.1 para.15

s.267, amended: 2015 c.11 Sch.1 para.16

s.269, amended: 2015 c.11 Sch.1 para.17

s.289A, enabling: SI 2015/1948

s.290, amended: 2015 c.11 Sch.1 para.18

s.290A, amended: 2015 c.11 Sch.1 para.19

s.290B, amended: 2015 c.11 Sch.1 para.20

s.290C, added: 2015 c.11 s.13

s.295A, added: 2015 c.33 s.29

s.306A, added: 2015 c.11 s.14

s.308B, added: 2015 c.8 s.54

s.318B, amended: SI 2015/346 Reg.2

s.318D, enabling: SI 2015/346

s.343, amended: SI 2015/886 Art.2

s.343, enabling: SI 2015/886

s.386, see *Allan v Revenue and Customs Commissioners* [2015] UKUT 16 (TCC), [2015] S.T.C. 890 (UT (Tax)), Barling J

s.392, see *Allan v Revenue and Customs Commissioners* [2015] UKUT 16 (TCC), [2015] S.T.C. 890 (UT (Tax)), Barling J

s.393B, amended: 2015 c.11 Sch.4 para.18

s.396, see *Allan v Revenue and Customs Commissioners* [2015] UKUT 16 (TCC), [2015] S.T.C. 890 (UT (Tax)), Barling J

s.401, see *Moorthy v Revenue and Customs Commissioners* [2015] I.R.L.R. 4 (FTT (Tax)), Judge Anne Redston

s.403, see *Moorthy v Revenue and Customs Commissioners* [2015] I.R.L.R. 4 (FTT (Tax)), Judge Anne Redston

s.406, see *Timothy James Consulting Ltd v Wilton* [2015] I.C.R. 764 (EAT), Singh J

s.423, see *Tower Radio Ltd v Revenue and Customs Commissioners* [2015] UKUT 60 (TCC), [2015] S.T.C. 1257 (UT (Tax)), Newey J

s.427, see *Tower Radio Ltd v Revenue and Customs Commissioners* [2015] UKUT 60 (TCC), [2015] S.T.C. 1257 (UT (Tax)), Newey J

s.431B, amended: SI 2015/360 Reg.2

s.471, see *Norman v Revenue and Customs Commissioners* [2015] UKFTT 303 (TC), [2015] S.F.T.D. 868 (FTT (Tax)), Judge Thomas

s.573, amended: 2015 c.11 Sch.4 para.20

s.579A, amended: 2015 c.11 Sch.4 para.22

s.579CA, amended: 2015 c.33 s.22

s.579CZA, amended: 2015 c.11 Sch.4 para.23

s.611A, added: 2015 c.11 Sch.4 para.21

s.636A, amended: 2015 c.33 s.22

s.636A, repealed: 2015 c.33 s.22

s.636AA, added: 2015 c.33 s.22

s.640A, amended: 2015 c.11 s.15

s.646B, added: 2015 c.11 Sch.4 para.17

s.677, amended: 2015 c.11 s.16, SI 2015/2006 Sch.12 Part 8

s.683, amended: 2015 c.33 s.22

s.684, amended: 2015 c.11 s.17

s.684, enabling: SI 2015/2, SI 2015/125, SI 2015/1667, SI 2015/1927

s.716B, enabling: SI 2015/171

Sch.1 Part 1, amended: 2015 c.11 s.16

Sch.1 Part 2, amended: 2015 c.11 Sch.1 para.21, 2015 c.33 s.29

Sch.6 Part 2 para.200, repealed: SI 2015/2006 Sch.12 Part 1

Sch.6 Part 2 para.233, repealed: SI 2015/2006 Sch.12 Part 1

Sch.7 Part 3 para.15, repealed: 2015 c.11 s.12

Sch.7 Part 3 para.17, amended: 2015 c.11 Sch.1 para.22

Sch.7 Part 3 para.17, repealed: 2015 c.11 Sch.1 para.22

Sch.7 Part 3 para.19, repealed: 2015 c.11 s.12

Sch.7 Part 3 para.27, amended: 2015 c.11 Sch.1 para.22

5. Community Care (Delayed Discharges etc.) Act 2003

s.1, repealed: SI 2015/914 Sch.1 para.69

s.4, amended: SI 2015/914 Sch.1 para.70

s.12, amended: SI 2015/914 Sch.1 para.71

s.14, amended: SI 2015/914 Sch.1 para.72

s.15, repealed: SI 2015/914 Sch.1 para.73

s.16, substituted: SI 2015/914 Sch.1 para.74

7. European Parliament (Representation) Act 2003

s.12, enabling: SI 2015/1982

s.13, enabling: SI 2015/1982

s.26A, substituted: SI 2015/1376 Sch.2 para.11

14. Finance Act 2003

see *Project Blue Ltd v Revenue and Customs Commissioners* [2015] S.T.C. 745 (UT (Tax)), Morgan J

s.24, enabling: SI 2015/636

s.26, enabling: SI 2015/636

s.41, enabling: SI 2015/636

s.42, see *R. (on the application of APVCO 19 Ltd) v Revenue and Customs Commissioners* [2015] EWCA Civ 648, [2015] S.T.C. 2272 (CA (Civ Div)), Black LJ

s.44, see *R. (on the application of APVCO 19 Ltd) v Revenue and Customs Commissioners* [2015] EWCA Civ 648, [2015] S.T.C. 2272 (CA (Civ Div)), Black LJ

s.45, see *Project Blue Ltd v Revenue and Customs Commissioners* [2015] S.T.C. 745 (UT (Tax)), Morgan J; see *R. (on the application of APVCO 19 Ltd) v Revenue and Customs Commissioners* [2015] EWCA Civ 648, [2015] S.T.C. 2272 (CA (Civ Div)), Black LJ

s.55, amended: 2015 c.1 s.1

s.55, repealed: 2015 c.1 s.1

s.63, amended: SI 2015/575 Sch.1 para.24

s.71A, see *Project Blue Ltd v Revenue and Customs Commissioners* [2015] S.T.C. 745 (UT (Tax)), Morgan J
s.73BA, amended: 2015 c.11 s.68
s.74, amended: 2015 c.1 Sch.1 para.2
s.75, amended: 2015 c.1 Sch.1 para.3
s.75A, see *Project Blue Ltd v Revenue and Customs Commissioners* [2015] S.T.C. 745 (UT (Tax)), Morgan J
s.75B, see *Project Blue Ltd v Revenue and Customs Commissioners* [2015] S.T.C. 745 (UT (Tax)), Morgan J
s.75C, see *Project Blue Ltd v Revenue and Customs Commissioners* [2015] S.T.C. 745 (UT (Tax)), Morgan J
s.77, amended: 2015 c.1 Sch.1 para.9
s.77A, amended: 2015 c.1 Sch.1 para.10
s.80, amended: 2015 c.1 Sch.1 para.4
s.80, repealed: 2015 c.1 Sch.1 para.4
s.81A, amended: 2015 c.1 Sch.1 para.6
s.81A, repealed: 2015 c.1 Sch.1 para.6
s.81ZA, amended: 2015 c.1 Sch.1 para.5
s.109, amended: 2015 c.1 Sch.1 para.11
s.122, amended: 2015 c.1 Sch.1 para.12
s.158, see *R. (on the application of Hely-Hutchinson) v Revenue and Customs Commissioners* [2015] EWHC 3261 (Admin), [2015] B.T.C. 37 (QBD (Admin)), Whipple J
s.195, see *Biffa (Jersey) Ltd v Revenue and Customs Commissioners* [2015] S.F.T.D. 163 (FTT (Tax)), Judge Greg Sinfield
Sch.4A para.3, amended: 2015 c.1 Sch.1 para.13
Sch.4A para.9, amended: 2015 c.11 s.68
Sch.6B para.2, amended: 2015 c.11 s.69
Sch.6B para.4, amended: 2015 c.1 Sch.1 para.7
Sch.6B para.4, repealed: 2015 c.1 Sch.1 para.7
Sch.6B para.5, amended: 2015 c.1 Sch.1 para.7
Sch.6B para.5, substituted: 2015 c.1 Sch.1 para.7
Sch.6B para.6, amended: 2015 c.1 Sch.1 para.7
Sch.6B para.6, repealed: 2015 c.1 Sch.1 para.7
Sch.7 Part 2 para.8, amended: 2015 c.1 Sch.1 para.8

Sch.9 para.4B, amended: 2015 c.1 Sch.1 para.14
Sch.9 para.12, amended: 2015 c.1 Sch.1 para.15
Sch.10 Part 4 para.27, amended: 2015 c.33 Sch.8 para.41
Sch.10 Pt 7 para.35, see *Portland Gas Storage Ltd v Revenue and Customs Commissioners* [2015] EWCA Civ 559, [2015] C.P. Rep. 35 (CA (Civ Div)), Jackson LJ
Sch.15 Part 3 para.30, amended: 2015 c.1 Sch.1 para.16
Sch.17A para.3, amended: 2015 c.1 Sch.1 para.17
Sch.17A para.3, repealed: 2015 c.1 Sch.1 para.17
Sch.17A para.4, amended: 2015 c.1 Sch.1 para.18
Sch.17A para.4, repealed: 2015 c.1 Sch.1 para.18
Sch.17A para.12A, see *Portland Gas Storage Ltd v Revenue and Customs Commissioners* [2015] EWCA Civ 559, [2015] C.P. Rep. 35 (CA (Civ Div)), Jackson LJ
Sch.19 para.7, amended: 2015 c.1 Sch.1 para.19
Sch.19 para.9, amended: 2015 c.1 Sch.1 para.20
Sch.24, see *Scotts Atlantic Management Ltd (In Liquidation) v Revenue and Customs Commissioners* [2015] UKUT 66 (TCC), [2015] S.T.C. 1321 (UT (Tax)), Warren J

17. Licensing Act 2003
Part 5A, added: 2015 c.20 Sch.17
Part 6, amended: 2015 c.20 Sch.18 para.4
s.2, amended: 2015 c.20 s.67
s.10, repealed: 2015 c.20 Sch.18 para.2
s.25, repealed: 2015 c.20 s.72
s.27, amended: 2015 c.20 Sch.6 para.2
s.51, see *R. (on the application of Akin (t/a Efe's Snooker Club)) v Stratford Magistrates' Court* [2014] EWHC 4633 (Admin), [2015] 1 W.L.R. 4829 (DC), Beatson LJ
s.53A, see *R. (on the application of Lalli) v Commissioner of Police of the Metropolis* [2015] EWHC 14 (Admin),

[2015] P.T.S.R. 1221 (QBD (Admin)),
John Howell QC
s.79, repealed: 2015 c.20 s.72
s.107, amended: 2015 c.20 s.68
s.110, repealed: 2015 c.20 s.72
s.115, amended: 2015 c.20 s.69
s.115, repealed: 2015 c.20 Sch.18 para.3
s.117, amended: 2015 c.20 Sch.18 para.4
s.117, repealed: 2015 c.20 Sch.18 para.4
s.119, repealed: 2015 c.20 Sch.18 para.5
s.121, repealed: 2015 c.20 Sch.18 para.6
s.122, amended: 2015 c.20 Sch.18 para.7
s.123, amended: 2015 c.20 Sch.18 para.8
s.124, amended: 2015 c.20 Sch.18 para.9
s.126, repealed: 2015 c.20 s.72
s.128, repealed: 2015 c.20 Sch.18 para.10
s.134, amended: 2015 c.20 Sch.18
para.11
s.136, amended: 2015 c.20 s.67, SI
2015/664 Sch.4 para.33
s.137, amended: SI 2015/664 Sch.4
para.33
s.140, amended: 2015 c.20 s.67
s.141, amended: 2015 c.20 s.67
s.143, amended: 2015 c.20 s.67
s.144, amended: 2015 c.20 s.67
s.147A, amended: 2015 c.20 s.67, SI
2015/664 Sch.4 para.33
s.148, repealed: 2015 c.20 s.70
s.153, amended: 2015 c.20 s.67
s.156, amended: SI 2015/664 Sch.4
para.33
s.157, amended: SI 2015/664 Sch.4
para.33
s.158, amended: 2015 c.20 Sch.18
para.12
s.159, amended: 2015 c.20 s.67
s.161, amended: SI 2015/664 Sch.4
para.33
s.165, amended: SI 2015/664 Sch.4
para.33
s.168, amended: SI 2015/664 Sch.4
para.33
s.193, enabling: SI 2015/1781
s.194, amended: 2015 c.20 s.67
s.197, amended: 2015 c.20 s.67
Sch.1 Part 2 para.6A, added: 2015 c.20
s.76
Sch.2 para.1, amended: 2015 c.20 s.71
Sch.2 para.2A, added: 2015 c.20 s.71
Sch.2 para.2A, enabling: SI 2015/1781

Sch.3, amended: 2015 c.20 Sch.18
para.13
Sch.5, see *Essence Bars (London) Ltd
(t/a Essence) v Wimbledon Magistrates'
Court* [2014] EWHC 4334 (Admin),
(2015) 179 J.P. 79 (QBD (Admin)),
Wilkie J
Sch.5 Part 3 para.17, amended: 2015 c.20
Sch.18 para.14
Sch.5 Part 3 para.17, repealed: 2015 c.20
Sch.18 para.14
20. Railways and Transport Safety Act 2003
Part 2, substituted: SI 2015/1682 Sch.1
para.2
s.1, repealed: 2015 c.20 s.54
s.14, repealed: 2015 c.20 s.54
s.15, amended: SI 2015/1682 Sch.1
para.2
s.15A, added: 2015 c.7 s.10
s.15A, enabling: SI 2015/1682
s.62, amended: SI 2015/1682 Sch.1
para.2
s.81, amended: SI 2015/1730 Reg.2
s.81, enabling: SI 2015/1730
s.83, amended: 2015 c.20 Sch.11 para.14
s.96, amended: 2015 c.20 Sch.11 para.16
Sch.1, substituted: SI 2015/1682 Sch.1
para.2
Sch.1 para.1, amended: SI 2015/1682
Sch.1 para.2
Sch.3 para.2, amended: SI 2015/1682
Sch.1 para.2
Sch.3 para.3, amended: SI 2015/1682
Sch.1 para.2
Sch.3 para.4, amended: SI 2015/1682
Sch.1 para.2
21. Communications Act 2003
see *Phonepayplus Ltd v Ashraf* [2014]
EWHC 4303 (Ch), [2015] Bus. L.R. 567
(Ch D), R Hollington QC
s.120, see *Phonepayplus Ltd v Ashraf*
[2014] EWHC 4303 (Ch), [2015] Bus.
L.R. 567 (Ch D), R Hollington QC
s.120, amended: 2015 c.15 s.80
s.121, see *Phonepayplus Ltd v Ashraf*
[2014] EWHC 4303 (Ch), [2015] Bus.
L.R. 567 (Ch D), R Hollington QC
s.121, amended: 2015 c.15 s.80
s.123, see *Phonepayplus Ltd v Ashraf*
[2014] EWHC 4303 (Ch), [2015] Bus.
L.R. 567 (Ch D), R Hollington QC

s.123, amended: 2015 c.15 s.80
s.127, amended: 2015 c.2 s.51
s.192, enabling: SI 2015/1648
s.193, enabling: SI 2015/1648
s.253A, varied: SI 2015/1000 Art.9
s.262, enabling: SI 2015/1000
s.402, enabling: SI 2015/1000
Sch.14 Part 3 para.11, enabling: SI
2015/1000

22. Fireworks Act 2003
s.12, amended: 2015 c.15 Sch.6 para.82
s.12, repealed: 2015 c.15 Sch.6 para.82

26. Local Government Act 2003
s.11, enabling: SI 2015/341
s.21, enabling: SI 2015/341
s.23, repealed: 2015 c.20 Sch.13 para.6
s.33, repealed: 2015 c.20 Sch.13 para.6
s.53, repealed: 2015 c.20 Sch.22 para.18
s.87, amended: 2015 c.20 s.29
s.88, amended: 2015 c.20 s.29
s.94, enabling: SI 2015/619
s.123, enabling: SI 2015/341, SI
2015/619

30. Sustainable Energy Act 2003
s.1, repealed: 2015 c.20 s.57
s.7, repealed: 2015 c.20 Sch.23 para.19

31. Female Genital Mutilation Act 2003
s.3, amended: 2015 c.9 s.70
s.3A, added: 2015 c.9 s.72
s.4, amended: 2015 c.9 s.70, s.72
s.4A, added: 2015 c.9 s.71
s.5, amended: 2015 c.9 s.72
s.5A, added: 2015 c.9 s.73
s.5B, added: 2015 c.9 s.74
s.5C, added: 2015 c.9 s.75
s.6, amended: 2015 c.9 s.70
s.8, amended: 2015 c.9 Sch.4 para.60
Sch.1, added: 2015 c.9 s.71
Sch.2, added: 2015 c.9 s.73
Sch.2 Pt 1, see *E (Children) (Female
Genital Mutilation: Protection Orders),
Re* [2015] EWHC 2275 (Fam), [2015] 2
F.L.R. 997 (Fam Div), Holman J
Sch.2 Part 1 para.2, enabling: SI
2015/1422
Sch.2 Part 1 para.14, enabling: SI
2015/1420

**32. Crime (International Co-operation) Act
2003**
Part 3 c.1, amended: 2015 c.2 s.31

Part 3 c.1, substituted: 2015 c.2 Sch.7
para.4
s.4A, amended: 2015 c.2 Sch.11 para.21
s.4B, amended: 2015 c.2 Sch.11 para.22
s.54, amended: 2015 c.2 s.31, Sch.7
para.2
s.55, amended: 2015 c.2 Sch.7 para.3, SI
2015/583 Sch.2 para.6
s.55, substituted: 2015 c.2 Sch.7 para.3
s.56, amended: 2015 c.2 s.31, Sch.7
para.5
s.56, repealed: 2015 c.2 Sch.7 para.5
s.57, amended: 2015 c.2 Sch.7 para.6
s.58, amended: 2015 c.2 Sch.7 para.7
s.63, amended: 2015 c.2 Sch.7 para.8
s.63, repealed: 2015 c.2 Sch.7 para.8
s.64, amended: 2015 c.2 Sch.7 para.9
s.64, repealed: 2015 c.2 Sch.7 para.9
s.65, amended: 2015 c.2 Sch.7 para.10
s.68, amended: 2015 c.2 Sch.7 para.11,
SI 2015/583 Sch.2 para.6
s.69, amended: 2015 c.2 Sch.7 para.12
s.70, amended: 2015 c.2 Sch.7 para.13
s.71A, added: 2015 c.2 s.31
s.72, amended: 2015 c.2 Sch.7 para.14
s.73, amended: 2015 c.2 Sch.7 para.15
s.74, amended: 2015 c.2 Sch.7 para.16,
Sch.7 para.17, Sch.7 para.18
s.74, repealed: SI 2015/583 Sch.2 para.6
Sch.3, amended: 2015 c.2 Sch.7 para.19
Sch.3A, added: 2015 c.2 Sch.7 para.20
Sch.3B, added: 2015 c.2 Sch.7 para.21
Sch.3 Part 1 para.1, amended: 2015 c.2
Sch.7 para.19
Sch.3 Part 1 para.2, amended: 2015 c.2
Sch.7 para.19
Sch.3 Part 1 para.3, amended: 2015 c.2
Sch.6 para.10, Sch.7 para.19
Sch.3 Part 1 para.5, amended: 2015 c.2
Sch.7 para.19
Sch.3 Part 1 para.6, amended: 2015 c.2
Sch.7 para.19
Sch.3 Part 2 para.7, amended: 2015 c.2
Sch.7 para.19
Sch.5 para.29, repealed: SI 2015/583
Sch.1 Part 1
Sch.5 para.30, repealed: SI 2015/583
Sch.1 Part 1
Sch.5 para.36, repealed: SI 2015/583
Sch.1 Part 1

Sch.5 para.37, repealed: SI 2015/583
Sch.1 Part 1
33. Waste and Emissions Trading Act 2003
s.11, enabling: SI 2015/1417
s.12, enabling: SI 2015/1417
s.13, enabling: SI 2015/1417
s.24, amended: 2015 c.20 Sch.13 para.6
s.24, repealed: 2015 c.20 Sch.13 para.6
37. Water Act 2003
s.4, amended: SI 2015/664 Sch.4 para.34
s.57, repealed: SI 2015/664 Sch.4
para.101
s.60, repealed: SI 2015/664 Sch.4
para.101
s.61, repealed: SI 2015/664 Sch.4
para.101
38. Anti-social Behaviour Act 2003
s.39, see *R. v Goldsborough (Paul)*
[2015] EWCA Crim 1278, [2015] 1
W.L.R. 4921 (CA (Crim Div)), Treacy LJ
s.40, amended: SI 2015/664 Sch.4
para.35
39. Courts Act 2003
s.1, see *K (Children) (Unrepresented
Father: Cross-Examination of Child), Re*
[2015] EWCA Civ 543, [2015] 1 W.L.R.
3801 (CA (Civ Div)), Lord Dyson MR
s.8, enabling: SI 2015/1506, SI
2015/1870
s.15, enabling: SI 2015/1423
s.54A, added: 2015 c.2 s.70
s.54A, amended: 2015 c.2 Sch.13 para.2
s.55, amended: 2015 c.2 s.70, Sch.13
para.2
s.56, amended: 2015 c.2 s.70
s.69, enabling: SI 2015/13, SI 2015/646,
SI 2015/1490
s.75, enabling: SI 2015/913, SI
2015/1420, SI 2015/1868
s.76, enabling: SI 2015/913, SI
2015/1420, SI 2015/1868
s.81, see *S v S* [2015] EWHC 1005
(Fam), [2015] 1 W.L.R. 4592 (Fam Div),
Sir James Munby PFD
s.92, enabling: SI 2015/576, SI 2015/687,
SI 2015/1419
s.108, enabling: SI 2015/687, SI
2015/1506, SI 2015/1870
s.109, enabling: SI 2015/1423
Sch.5 Part 1 para.2, amended: 2015 c.30
Sch.5 para.23

Sch.5 Part 3 para.7A, amended: 2015
c.30 Sch.5 para.23
Sch.5 Part 4 para.13, amended: 2015 c.30
Sch.5 para.23
Sch.5 Part 6 para.21, substituted: 2015
c.2 s.56
Sch.5 Part 6 para.22, amended: 2015 c.2
s.56
Sch.5 Part 6 para.22, repealed: 2015 c.2
s.56
Sch.5 Part 7 para.25, amended: 2015 c.2
s.56
Sch.5 Part 8 para.31, amended: 2015 c.2
s.56
Sch.5 Part 9 para.37, amended: 2015 c.2
s.56
Sch.8 para.409, repealed: 2015 c.9 Sch.4
para.61
41. Extradition Act 2003
Pt 1., see *Kandola v Germany* [2015]
EWHC 619 (Admin), [2015] 1 W.L.R.
5097 (DC), Aikens LJ
Pt 2., see *Lord Advocate v Mirza* 2015
S.L.T. (Sh Ct) 89 (Sh Ct (Lothian)
(Edinburgh)), Sheriff T Welsh, QC; see
McIntyre v United States [2014] EWHC
1886 (Admin), [2015] 1 W.L.R. 507
(DC), Lord Thomas LCJ
s.2, see *France v Charbit* [2014] EWHC
3579 (Admin), [2015] 1 W.L.R. 2359
(QBD (Admin)), Cranston J; see *Lis v
Poland* [2014] EWHC 3226 (Admin),
[2015] R.T.R. 15 (QBD (Admin)), Blake
J
s.11, see *Lagunionek (Slawomir) v Lord
Advocate* [2015] HCJAC 53, 2015 J.C.
300 (HCJ), Lord Menzies
s.12A, see *Kandola v Germany* [2015]
EWHC 619 (Admin), [2015] 1 W.L.R.
5097 (DC), Aikens LJ
s.14, see *Lagunionek (Slawomir) v Lord
Advocate* [2015] HCJAC 53, 2015 J.C.
300 (HCJ), Lord Menzies; see *Lord
Advocate v Merica* 2015 S.L.T. (Sh Ct)
171 (Sh Ct (Lothian) (Edinburgh)),
Sheriff T Welsh, QC
s.19B, see *Atraskevic v Lithuania* [2015]
EWHC 131 (Admin), [2015] 4 All E.R.
770 (DC), Aikens LJ

s.20, see *Lord Advocate v Merica* 2015
S.L.T. (Sh Ct) 171 (Sh Ct (Lothian)
(Edinburgh)), Sheriff T Welsh, QC
s.21, see *Lagunionek (Slawomir) v Lord
Advocate* [2015] HCJAC 53, 2015 J.C.
300 (HCJ), Lord Menzies; see *Lord
Advocate v Merica* 2015 S.L.T. (Sh Ct)
171 (Sh Ct (Lothian) (Edinburgh)),
Sheriff T Welsh, QC
s.21A, see *Czerwinski (Wojciech) v HM
Advocate* [2015] HCJAC 72, 2015 S.L.T.
610 (HCJ), The Lord Justice Clerk
(Carloway); see *Czerwinski (Wojciech) v
HM Advocate* [2015] HCJAC 73, 2015
S.L.T. 612 (HCJ), The Lord Justice Clerk
(Carloway); see *Miraszewski v Poland*
[2014] EWHC 4261 (Admin), [2015] 1
W.L.R. 3929 (DC), Pitchford LJ
s.25, see *Jantos (Agnieszka) v Lord
Advocate* [2015] HCJAC 32, 2015 S.C.L.
560 (HCJ), The Lord Justice Clerk
(Carloway)
s.26, see *Bizunowicz v Poland* [2014]
EWHC 3238 (Admin), [2015] 1 W.L.R.
2341 (QBD (Admin)), Aikens LJ; see
Czerwinski (Wojciech) v HM Advocate
[2015] HCJAC 72, 2015 S.L.T. 610
(HCJ), The Lord Justice Clerk
(Carloway); see *Czerwinski (Wojciech) v
HM Advocate* [2015] HCJAC 73, 2015
S.L.T. 612 (HCJ), The Lord Justice Clerk
(Carloway); see *Lagunionek (Slawomir)
v Lord Advocate* [2015] HCJAC 53, 2015
J.C. 300 (HCJ), Lord Menzies
s.27, see *Atraskevic v Lithuania* [2015]
EWHC 131 (Admin), [2015] 4 All E.R.
770 (DC), Aikens LJ; see *Bizunowicz v
Poland* [2014] EWHC 3238 (Admin),
[2015] 1 W.L.R. 2341 (QBD (Admin)),
Aikens LJ
s.30A, amended: SI 2015/992 Art.3
s.35, amended: SI 2015/992 Art.3
s.36, see *Neteczca v Governor of
Holloway Prison* [2014] EWHC 2098
(Admin), [2015] 1 W.L.R. 1337 (QBD
(Admin)), Moses LJ
s.36A, enabling: SI 2015/1490
s.36B, enabling: SI 2015/1490
s.37, amended: SI 2015/992 Art.3
s.38, amended: SI 2015/992 Art.3
s.42, amended: SI 2015/992 Art.3

s.60, see *Bizunowicz v Poland* [2014]
EWHC 3238 (Admin), [2015] 1 W.L.R.
2341 (QBD (Admin)), Aikens LJ
s.60, amended: SI 2015/992 Art.3
s.61, see *Bizunowicz v Poland* [2014]
EWHC 3238 (Admin), [2015] 1 W.L.R.
2341 (QBD (Admin)), Aikens LJ
s.61, amended: SI 2015/992 Art.3
s.69, enabling: SI 2015/992
s.71, enabling: SI 2015/992
s.73, enabling: SI 2015/992
s.74, enabling: SI 2015/992
s.77, see *R. (on the application of B) v
Westminster Magistrates' Court* [2015]
A.C. 1195 (SC), Lord Neuberger PSC
s.79, see *Lord Advocate v Mirza* 2015
S.L.T. (Sh Ct) 89 (Sh Ct (Lothian)
(Edinburgh)), Sheriff T Welsh, QC
s.81, see *Dean (Zain Taj) v Lord
Advocate* [2015] HCJAC 52, 2015 S.L.T.
419 (HCJ), Lady Paton; see *Lord
Advocate v Mirza* 2015 S.L.T. (Sh Ct) 89
(Sh Ct (Lothian) (Edinburgh)), Sheriff T
Welsh, QC; see *R. (on the application of
B) v Westminster Magistrates' Court*
[2015] A.C. 1195 (SC), Lord Neuberger
PSC
s.84, see *R. (on the application of B) v
Westminster Magistrates' Court* [2015]
A.C. 1195 (SC), Lord Neuberger PSC
s.84, enabling: SI 2015/992
s.86, enabling: SI 2015/992
s.103, see *Dean (Zain Taj) v Lord
Advocate* [2015] HCJAC 52, 2015 S.L.T.
419 (HCJ), Lady Paton
s.106, see *McIntyre v United States*
[2014] EWHC 1886 (Admin), [2015] 1
W.L.R. 507 (DC), Lord Thomas LCJ
s.107A, amended: SI 2015/992 Art.3
s.108, see *Dean (Zain Taj) v Lord
Advocate* [2015] HCJAC 52, 2015 S.L.T.
419 (HCJ), Lady Paton; see *McIntyre v
United States* [2014] EWHC 1886
(Admin), [2015] 1 W.L.R. 507 (DC),
Lord Thomas LCJ
s.108, varied: SI 2015/987 Art.4
s.117, amended: SI 2015/992 Art.3
s.118A, enabling: SI 2015/1490
s.118B, enabling: SI 2015/1490
s.124, amended: SI 2015/992 Art.3
s.133, amended: SI 2015/992 Art.3

s.134, amended: SI 2015/992 Art.3
s.194, see *Dean (Zain Taj) v Lord
Advocate* [2015] HCJAC 52, 2015 S.L.T.
419 (HCJ), Lady Paton
s.208, amended: SI 2015/992 Art.3
s.213, amended: SI 2015/992 Art.3
s.223, enabling: SI 2015/992
Sch.1 Pt 1, see *Kandola v Germany*
[2015] EWHC 619 (Admin), [2015] 1
W.L.R. 5097 (DC), Aikens LJ

42. Sexual Offences Act 2003
see *Birmingham City Council v Riaz*
[2014] EWHC 4247 (Fam), [2015] 2
F.L.R. 763 (Fam Div), Keehan J; see
Main v Scottish Ministers [2015] CSIH
41, 2015 S.C. 639 (IH (2 Div)), The Lord
Justice Clerk (Carloway); see *McNair v
Murphy* [2015] HCJAC 61, 2015 S.L.T.
673 (HCJ), Lord Brodie; see *R. (on the
application of E) v Birmingham
Magistrates' Court* [2015] EWHC 688
(Admin), [2015] 1 W.L.R. 4771 (DC),
Sir Brian Leveson PQBD; see *R. (on the
application of Grant) v Kingston Crown
Court* [2015] EWHC 767 (Admin),
[2015] 2 Cr. App. R. (S.) 11 (DC), Elias
LJ; see *R. (on the application of
Richards) v Teesside Magistrates' Court*
[2015] EWCA Civ 7, [2015] 1 W.L.R.
1695 (CA (Civ Div)), Lord Dyson MR;
see *R. v Clifford (Frank Maxwell)* [2014]
EWCA Crim 2245, [2015] 1 Cr. App. R.
(S.) 32 (CA (Crim Div)), Treacy LJ; see
R. v DO [2014] EWCA Crim 2202,
[2015] 1 Cr. App. R. (S.) 41 (CA (Crim
Div)), Pitchford LJ
Part 1, substituted: 2015 c.9 s.68
Pt 2., see *M v Chief Constable of
Hampshire* [2014] EWCA Civ 1651,
[2015] 1 W.L.R. 1176 (CA (Civ Div)),
Moore-Bick LJ; see *R. (on the
application of Hamill) v Chelmsford
Magistrates' Court* [2014] EWHC 2799
(Admin), [2015] 1 W.L.R. 1798 (QBD
(Admin)), Aikens LJ
s.6, see *Attorney General's Reference
(No.21 of 2015)* [2015] EWCA Crim 953,
[2015] 2 Cr. App. R. (S.) 41 (CA (Crim
Div)), Hallett LJ; see *R. v DO* [2014]
EWCA Crim 2202, [2015] 1 Cr. App. R.
(S.) 41 (CA (Crim Div)), Pitchford LJ

s.7, see *Attorney General's Reference
(No.21 of 2015)* [2015] EWCA Crim 953,
[2015] 2 Cr. App. R. (S.) 41 (CA (Crim
Div)), Hallett LJ; see *R. v DO* [2014]
EWCA Crim 2202, [2015] 1 Cr. App. R.
(S.) 41 (CA (Crim Div)), Pitchford LJ
s.9, see *R. v B* [2015] EWCA Crim 1295,
[2015] 2 Cr. App. R. (S.) 78 (CA (Crim
Div)), Sharp LJ
s.15, amended: 2015 c.2 s.36
s.15A, added: 2015 c.9 s.67
s.48, amended: 2015 c.9 s.68
s.49, amended: 2015 c.9 s.68
s.50, amended: 2015 c.9 s.68
s.51, amended: 2015 c.9 s.68
s.51, repealed: 2015 c.9 s.68
s.54, amended: 2015 c.9 Sch.4 para.62
s.58, see *R. v Ali (Yasir Ifran)* [2015]
EWCA Crim 1279, [2015] 2 Cr. App. R.
33 (CA (Crim Div)), Fulford LJ
s.59A, repealed: 2015 c.30 Sch.5 para.5
s.78, amended: 2015 c.9 Sch.4 para.63
s.80, see *McNair v Murphy* [2015]
HCJAC 61, 2015 S.L.T. 673 (HCJ), Lord
Brodie
s.82, see *Main v Scottish Ministers*
[2015] CSIH 41, 2015 S.C. 639 (IH (2
Div)), The Lord Justice Clerk (Carloway)
s.87, enabling: SI 2015/82, SI 2015/1523
s.88, see *Main v Scottish Ministers*
[2015] CSIH 41, 2015 S.C. 639 (IH (2
Div)), The Lord Justice Clerk (Carloway)
s.91A, see *R. (on the application of E) v
Birmingham Magistrates' Court* [2015]
EWHC 688 (Admin), [2015] 1 W.L.R.
4771 (DC), Sir Brian Leveson PQBD
s.91B, see *R. (on the application of
Hamill) v Chelmsford Magistrates' Court*
[2014] EWHC 2799 (Admin), [2015] 1
W.L.R. 1798 (QBD (Admin)), Aikens LJ
s.91C, see *R. (on the application of E) v
Birmingham Magistrates' Court* [2015]
EWHC 688 (Admin), [2015] 1 W.L.R.
4771 (DC), Sir Brian Leveson PQBD
s.91D, see *R. (on the application of
Hamill) v Chelmsford Magistrates' Court*
[2014] EWHC 2799 (Admin), [2015] 1
W.L.R. 1798 (QBD (Admin)), Aikens LJ
s.92, see *Montgomery v Harvie* [2015]
HCJAC 2, 2015 J.C. 223 (HCJ), The
Lord Justice Clerk (Carloway)

s.96B, see *M v Chief Constable of
Hampshire* [2014] EWCA Civ 1651,
[2015] 1 W.L.R. 1176 (CA (Civ Div)),
Moore-Bick LJ
s.104, see *Chief Constable of
Warwickshire v MT* [2015] EWHC 2303
(Admin), (2015) 179 J.P. 454 (QBD
(Admin)), Hickinbottom J
s.107, see *R. (on the application of
Richards) v Teesside Magistrates' Court*
[2015] EWCA Civ 7, [2015] 1 W.L.R.
1695 (CA (Civ Div)), Lord Dyson MR
s.108, see *R. (on the application of
Richards) v Teesside Magistrates' Court*
[2015] EWCA Civ 7, [2015] 1 W.L.R.
1695 (CA (Civ Div)), Lord Dyson MR
s.111, amended: SSI 2015/338 Sch.2
para.8
s.122A, see *Redbridge LBC v A* [2015]
EWHC 2140 (Fam), [2015] Fam. 335
(Fam Div), Hayden J
s.136A, amended: 2015 c.9 Sch.4
para.64, Sch.4 para.65
Sch.3 para.24A, added: 2015 c.9 Sch.4
para.66
Sch.3 para.35C, added: 2015 c.9 Sch.4
para.66
Sch.3 para.41A, see *McNair v Murphy*
[2015] HCJAC 61, 2015 S.L.T. 673
(HCJ), Lord Brodie
Sch.3 para.60, see *McHugh v Harvie*
[2015] HCJAC 86, 2015 S.C.L. 987
(HCJ), The Lord Justice Clerk
(Carloway)
Sch.3 para.92Y, added: 2015 c.9 Sch.4
para.66
Sch.5 para.63B, added: 2015 c.30 Sch.5
para.5
Sch.6 para.31, repealed: 2015 c.30 Sch.5
para.5
Sch.6 para.46, repealed: 2015 c.30 Sch.5
para.5

**43. Health and Social Care (Community
Health and Standards) Act 2003**
s.153, enabling: SI 2015/295, SSI
2015/81
s.156, varied: SI 2015/295 Reg.6
s.163, enabling: SI 2015/295
s.168, enabling: SSI 2015/81
s.195, enabling: SI 2015/295, SSI
2015/81

s.201, enabling: SI 2015/864
Sch.10 para.1, amended: 2015 c.30 Sch.5
para.26
44. Criminal Justice Act 2003
see *Hutchinson v United Kingdom
(57592/08)* (2015) 61 E.H.R.R. 13
(ECHR), Judge Raimondi (President);
see *R. v Atkinson (James)* [2014] EWCA
Crim 2010, [2015] M.H.L.R. 492 (CA
(Crim Div)), Sharp LJ; see *R. v B* [2015]
EWCA Crim 1295, [2015] 2 Cr. App. R.
(S.) 78 (CA (Crim Div)), Sharp LJ; see
R. v Hall (Robert) [2014] EWCA Crim
2046, [2015] 1 Cr. App. R. (S.) 16 (CA
(Crim Div)), Sir Brian Leveson PQBD;
see *R. v Halliwell (Ian)* [2015] EWCA
Crim 1134, [2015] 2 Cr. App. R. (S.) 64
(CA (Crim Div)), McCombe LJ; see *R. v
Khan (Gulan Ahmed)* [2015] EWCA
Crim 835, [2015] 2 Cr. App. R. (S.) 39
(CA (Crim Div)), Davis LJ
Part 12 c.5A, added: 2015 c.2 Sch.1
para.2
Part 12 c.6, amended: 2015 c.2 Sch.3
para.5
Pt 12 s.229, see *R. v Bennett (Anthony)*
[2014] EWCA Crim 2652, [2015] 1 Cr.
App. R. 16 (CA (Crim Div)), Jackson LJ
Pt 12 s.255B, see *R. (on the application
of Galiazia) v Governor of Hewell Prison*
[2014] EWHC 3427 (Admin), [2015] 1
W.L.R. 2767 (DC), Elias LJ
Pt 12 s.255C, see *R. (on the application
of Galiazia) v Governor of Hewell Prison*
[2014] EWHC 3427 (Admin), [2015] 1
W.L.R. 2767 (DC), Elias LJ
s.23A, amended: SI 2015/664 Sch.5
para.10
s.29, amended: 2015 c.2 s.46
s.30, see *Hutchinson v United Kingdom
(57592/08)* (2015) 61 E.H.R.R. 13
(ECHR), Judge Raimondi (President)
s.30, amended: 2015 c.2 s.47
s.30, enabling: SI 2015/1490
s.58, see *R. v Quillan (Gary)* [2015]
EWCA Crim 538, [2015] 1 W.L.R. 4673
(CA (Crim Div)), Lord Thomas LCJ; see
Serious Fraud Office v Evans [2014]
EWHC 3803 (QB), [2015] 1 W.L.R.
3526 (QBD), Fulford LJ

s.61, see *Serious Fraud Office v Evans*
[2014] EWHC 3803 (QB), [2015] 1
W.L.R. 3526 (QBD), Fulford LJ
s.76, see *R. v Henry (Duwayne)* [2014]
EWCA Crim 1816, [2015] 2 Cr. App. R.
1 (CA (Crim Div)), Treacy LJ
s.77, see *R. v Henry (Duwayne)* [2014]
EWCA Crim 1816, [2015] 2 Cr. App. R.
1 (CA (Crim Div)), Treacy LJ
s.78, see *R. v Henry (Duwayne)* [2014]
EWCA Crim 1816, [2015] 2 Cr. App. R.
1 (CA (Crim Div)), Treacy LJ
s.79, see *R. v Henry (Duwayne)* [2014]
EWCA Crim 1816, [2015] 2 Cr. App. R.
1 (CA (Crim Div)), Treacy LJ
s.98, see *R. v Jones (Nicholas John)*
[2014] EWCA Crim 1762, [2015] 1 Cr.
App. R. 5 (CA (Crim Div)), Pitchford LJ
s.100, see *Abbas v Crown Prosecution
Service* [2015] EWHC 579 (Admin),
[2015] 2 Cr. App. R. 11 (DC), Hallett LJ
s.101, see *R. v Bryon (Michael David)*
[2015] EWCA Crim 997, [2015] 2 Cr.
App. R. 21 (CA (Crim Div)), Jackson LJ;
see *R. v Daly (John Joseph)* [2014]
EWCA Crim 2117, (2015) 179 J.P. 114
(CA (Crim Div)), Elias LJ; see *R. v
Golds (Mark Richard)* [2014] EWCA
Crim 748, [2015] 1 W.L.R. 1030 (CA
(Crim Div)), Elias LJ; see *R. v Hunter
(Nigel)* [2015] EWCA Crim 631, [2015]
1 W.L.R. 5367 (CA (Crim Div)), Lord
Thomas LCJ; see *R. v M* [2014] EWCA
Crim 1523, [2015] 1 W.L.R. 495 (CA
(Crim Div)), Pitchford LJ; see *R. v
Wynes (Andrew Charles)* [2014] EWCA
Crim 2585, (2015) 179 J.P. 42 (CA (Crim
Div)), Bean LJ
s.103, see *R. v Bryon (Michael David)*
[2015] EWCA Crim 997, [2015] 2 Cr.
App. R. 21 (CA (Crim Div)), Jackson LJ
s.104, see *R. v Daly (John Joseph)* [2014]
EWCA Crim 2117, (2015) 179 J.P. 114
(CA (Crim Div)), Elias LJ
s.112, see *R. v Jones (Nicholas John)*
[2014] EWCA Crim 1762, [2015] 1 Cr.
App. R. 5 (CA (Crim Div)), Pitchford LJ
s.114, see *Barnaby v DPP* [2015] EWHC
232 (Admin), [2015] 2 Cr. App. R. 4
(DC), Fulford LJ; see *R. v Jagnieszko
(Tomasz)* [2008] EWCA Crim 3065,

[2015] M.H.L.R. 99 (CA (Crim Div)),
Hallett LJ; see *R. v Sliogeris (Kestutis)*
[2015] EWCA Crim 22, (2015) 179 J.P.
156 (CA (Crim Div)), Elias LJ
s.116, see *R. v Jagnieszko (Tomasz)*
[2008] EWCA Crim 3065, [2015]
M.H.L.R. 99 (CA (Crim Div)), Hallett LJ
s.118, see *Barnaby v DPP* [2015] EWHC
232 (Admin), [2015] 2 Cr. App. R. 4
(DC), Fulford LJ
s.132, enabling: SI 2015/1490
s.142, see *Attorney General's Reference
(No.61 of 2014)* [2014] EWCA Crim
1933, [2015] 1 Cr. App. R. (S.) 25 (CA
(Crim Div)), Treacy LJ; see *R. v Thames
Water Utilities Ltd* [2015] EWCA Crim
960, [2015] 1 W.L.R. 4411 (CA (Crim
Div)), Lord Thomas LCJ
s.142, amended: 2015 c.2 Sch.5 para.10
s.142A, amended: 2015 c.2 Sch.5 para.11
s.143, see *R. v Bowler (Richard)* [2015]
EWCA Crim 849, [2015] 2 Cr. App. R.
(S.) 38 (CA (Crim Div)), Laws LJ; see
R. v Laverick (Mark) [2015] EWCA
Crim 1059, [2015] 2 Cr. App. R. (S.) 62
(CA (Crim Div)), McCombe LJ; see *R. v
Thames Water Utilities Ltd* [2015]
EWCA Crim 960, [2015] 1 W.L.R. 4411
(CA (Crim Div)), Lord Thomas LCJ
s.144, amended: 2015 c.2 Sch.5 para.12
s.150, amended: 2015 c.2 Sch.5 para.13
s.151, amended: 2015 c.2 Sch.12 para.13,
2015 c.30 Sch.5 para.24
s.152, see *R. v Fernandez (Andrew Nigel)*
[2014] EWCA Crim 2405, [2015] 1 Cr.
App. R. (S.) 35 (CA (Crim Div)),
Rafferty LJ
s.152, amended: 2015 c.2 Sch.5 para.14
s.153, see *R. v Fernandez (Andrew Nigel)*
[2014] EWCA Crim 2405, [2015] 1 Cr.
App. R. (S.) 35 (CA (Crim Div)),
Rafferty LJ
s.153, amended: 2015 c.2 Sch.5 para.15
s.161A, amended: 2015 c.30 Sch.5
para.25
s.164, see *R. v Thames Water Utilities
Ltd* [2015] EWCA Crim 960, [2015] 1
W.L.R. 4411 (CA (Crim Div)), Lord
Thomas LCJ
s.164, amended: 2015 c.2 Sch.11 para.23
s.174, enabling: SI 2015/1490

s.177, see *R. v Khan (Gulan Ahmed)*
[2015] EWCA Crim 835, [2015] 2 Cr.
App. R. (S.) 39 (CA (Crim Div)), Davis
LJ
s.199, see *R. v Fairweather (David)*
[2015] EWCA Crim 1027, [2015] 2 Cr.
App. R. (S.) 56 (CA (Crim Div)), Sharp
LJ
s.200, see *R. v Khan (Gulan Ahmed)*
[2015] EWCA Crim 835, [2015] 2 Cr.
App. R. (S.) 39 (CA (Crim Div)), Davis
LJ
s.207, see *R. v Morgan (Terrence)* [2014]
EWCA Crim 2814, [2015] 1 Cr. App. R.
(S.) 49 (CA (Crim Div)), Rafferty LJ
s.212A, enabling: SI 2015/1482
s.217, see *R. v Fairweather (David)*
[2015] EWCA Crim 1027, [2015] 2 Cr.
App. R. (S.) 56 (CA (Crim Div)), Sharp
LJ
s.224A, see *R. v Fernandez (Andrew
Nigel)* [2014] EWCA Crim 2405, [2015]
1 Cr. App. R. (S.) 35 (CA (Crim Div)),
Rafferty LJ
s.224A, amended: 2015 c.2 s.5
s.226A, see *R. v DJ* [2015] EWCA Crim
563, [2015] 2 Cr. App. R. (S.) 16 (CA
(Crim Div)), Treacy LJ; see *R. v Hibbert
(Christopher Keith)* [2015] EWCA Crim
507, [2015] 2 Cr. App. R. (S.) 15 (CA
(Crim Div)), Pitchford LJ; see *R. v
Nelson (Michael)* [2014] EWCA Crim
2093, [2015] 1 Cr. App. R. (S.) 21 (CA
(Crim Div)), Treacy LJ
s.232A, amended: 2015 c.2 s.5
s.236A, amended: 2015 c.2 Sch.1 para.10
s.236A, repealed: 2015 c.2 Sch.1 para.10
s.237, amended: 2015 c.2 Sch.1 para.15
s.239, amended: 2015 c.2 Sch.3 para.6
s.239A, added: 2015 c.2 s.8
s.240A, see *R. v Thorsby (Adrian
Kenneth)* [2015] EWCA Crim 1, [2015] 1
W.L.R. 2901 (CA (Crim Div)), Pitchford
LJ
s.240ZA, see *R. (on the application of
Galiazia) v Governor of Hewell Prison*
[2014] EWHC 3427 (Admin), [2015] 1
W.L.R. 2767 (DC), Elias LJ; see *R. (on
the application of James) v Governor of
Birmingham Prison* [2015] EWCA Civ
58, [2015] 1 W.L.R. 4210 (CA (Civ

Div)), Arden LJ; see *R. v Kerrigan
(David Joseph)* [2014] EWCA Crim
2348, [2015] 1 Cr. App. R. (S.) 29 (CA
(Crim Div)), Hallett LJ; see *R. v Phillips
(Nathan David)* [2015] EWCA Crim 427,
[2015] 2 Cr. App. R. (S.) 9 (CA (Crim
Div)), Treacy LJ
s.240ZA, amended: 2015 c.2 Sch.1
para.16
s.241, see *R. (on the application of
Galiazia) v Governor of Hewell Prison*
[2014] EWHC 3427 (Admin), [2015] 1
W.L.R. 2767 (DC), Elias LJ
s.244, amended: 2015 c.2 Sch.1 para.5
s.244A, added: 2015 c.2 Sch.1 para.6
s.246, see *R. (on the application of
Galiazia) v Governor of Hewell Prison*
[2014] EWHC 3427 (Admin), [2015] 1
W.L.R. 2767 (DC), Elias LJ; see *R. (on
the application of Whiston) v Secretary of
State for Justice* [2015] A.C. 176 (SC),
Lord Neuberger PSC
s.246, amended: 2015 c.2 s.15, Sch.1
para.7
s.246A, see *R. v Hibbert (Christopher
Keith)* [2015] EWCA Crim 507, [2015] 2
Cr. App. R. (S.) 15 (CA (Crim Div)),
Pitchford LJ
s.246A, amended: 2015 c.2 s.4
s.247, amended: 2015 c.2 s.14
s.250, amended: 2015 c.2 s.15, Sch.1
para.17, Sch.2 para.4, Sch.3 para.7
s.250, enabling: SI 2015/337
s.253, amended: 2015 c.2 Sch.2 para.5
s.253, repealed: 2015 c.2 Sch.2 para.5
s.254, see *R. v Hookway (Lee)* [2015]
EWCA Crim 931, [2015] 2 Cr. App. R.
(S.) 43 (CA (Crim Div)), Fulford LJ
s.255, see *R. (on the application of
Whiston) v Secretary of State for Justice*
[2015] A.C. 176 (SC), Lord Neuberger
PSC
s.255A, amended: 2015 c.2 s.9
s.255B, amended: 2015 c.2 s.9
s.255C, amended: 2015 c.2 s.9
s.255ZA, added: 2015 c.2 s.12
s.256, repealed: 2015 c.2 s.9
s.256A, amended: 2015 c.2 s.9
s.256AA, amended: 2015 c.2 Sch.1
para.18

s.256AC, amended: 2015 c.2 Sch.12
para.14
s.256AZA, added: 2015 c.2 s.10
s.256B, amended: 2015 c.2 Sch.2 para.6
s.258, amended: 2015 c.2 Sch.1 para.19,
2015 c.9 s.10
s.260, amended: 2015 c.2 s.15, Sch.1
para.20, Sch.3 para.8
s.260, repealed: 2015 c.2 s.14
s.261, amended: 2015 c.2 s.14, Sch.1
para.21
s.261, repealed: 2015 c.2 s.14
s.263, amended: 2015 c.2 Sch.1 para.22
s.264, see *R. v Hibbert (Christopher
Keith)* [2015] EWCA Crim 507, [2015] 2
Cr. App. R. (S.) 15 (CA (Crim Div)),
Pitchford LJ
s.264, amended: 2015 c.2 Sch.1 para.23
s.265, see *R. v Hookway (Lee)* [2015]
EWCA Crim 931, [2015] 2 Cr. App. R.
(S.) 43 (CA (Crim Div)), Fulford LJ; see
R. v Phillips (Nathan David) [2015]
EWCA Crim 427, [2015] 2 Cr. App. R.
(S.) 9 (CA (Crim Div)), Treacy LJ
s.265, amended: 2015 c.2 Sch.1 para.24
s.268, amended: 2015 c.2 s.14, Sch.3
para.9
s.305, see *R. (on the application of
James) v Governor of Birmingham
Prison* [2015] EWCA Civ 58, [2015] 1
W.L.R. 4210 (CA (Civ Div)), Arden LJ
s.305, amended: 2015 c.2 Sch.5 para.16
s.325, see *M v Chief Constable of
Hampshire* [2014] EWCA Civ 1651,
[2015] 1 W.L.R. 1176 (CA (Civ Div)),
Moore-Bick LJ
s.327, amended: 2015 c.20 s.83
s.327, repealed: 2015 c.20 s.83
s.330, amended: 2015 c.2 s.10, Sch.1
para.3, 2015 c.9 s.10
s.330, enabling: SI 2015/337
s.332, see *R. v Hookway (Lee)* [2015]
EWCA Crim 931, [2015] 2 Cr. App. R.
(S.) 43 (CA (Crim Div)), Fulford LJ
Sch.3 Part 2 para.75, repealed: 2015 c.9
Sch.4 para.67
Sch.8 Part 2 para.9, amended: 2015 c.2
Sch.12 para.15
Sch.12 Part 2 para.9, amended: 2015 c.2
Sch.12 para.16

Sch.15B, see *R. v Nelson (Michael)*
[2014] EWCA Crim 2093, [2015] 1 Cr.
App. R. (S.) 21 (CA (Crim Div)), Treacy
LJ
Sch.15 Part 1 para.22A, added: 2015 c.2
s.2
Sch.15 Part 1 para.48A, added: 2015 c.2
Sch.6 para.11
Sch.15 Part 1 para.63G, added: 2015 c.30
s.6
Sch.15 Part 1 para.64, substituted: 2015
c.2 s.2
Sch.15 Part 1 para.65, substituted: 2015
c.2 s.2
Sch.15 Part 2 para.92, repealed: 2015 c.2
s.2
Sch.15 Part 2 para.92A, added: 2015 c.2
s.2
Sch.15 Part 2 para.116A, added: 2015 c.9
Sch.4 para.68
Sch.15 Part 2 para.136, amended: 2015
c.9 Sch.4 para.68
Sch.15 Part 2 para.137, amended: 2015
c.9 Sch.4 para.68
Sch.15 Part 2 para.138, amended: 2015
c.9 Sch.4 para.68
Sch.15 Part 2 para.152A, added: 2015
c.30 s.6
Sch.15 Part 2 para.153, substituted: 2015
c.2 s.2
Sch.15B Part 1 para.3A, added: 2015 c.2
s.3
Sch.15B Part 1 para.8A, added: 2015 c.2
s.3
Sch.15B Part 1 para.9, amended: 2015
c.2 s.3
Sch.15B Part 1 para.35, amended: 2015
c.9 Sch.4 para.69
Sch.15B Part 1 para.36, amended: 2015
c.9 Sch.4 para.69
Sch.15B Part 1 para.37, amended: 2015
c.9 Sch.4 para.69
Sch.15B Part 1 para.40A, added: 2015
c.2 s.3
Sch.15B Part 1 para.43A, added: 2015
c.30 s.6
Sch.15B Part 4 para.49, amended: 2015
c.2 s.3
Sch.15B Part 4 para.49A, added: 2015
c.2 s.3

Sch.16, see *R. v Khan (Gulan Ahmed)*
[2015] EWCA Crim 835, [2015] 2 Cr.
App. R. (S.) 39 (CA (Crim Div)), Davis
LJ
Sch.18A, added: 2015 c.2 Sch.1 para.4
Sch.20A para.4, amended: 2015 c.2 s.15
Sch.20A para.6, repealed: 2015 c.2 s.9
Sch.20A para.8, repealed: 2015 c.2 s.14
Sch.20A para.8A, added: 2015 c.2 s.14
Sch.20B Part 2 para.3, repealed: 2015 c.2
s.15
Sch.20B Part 4 para.34, amended: 2015
c.2 s.15, Sch.3 para.10
Sch.20B Part 4 para.37, amended: 2015
c.2 Sch.3 para.11
Sch.21, see *R. v Blackman (Alexander
Wayne)* [2014] EWCA Crim 1029,
[2015] 1 W.L.R. 1900 (CMAC), Lord
Thomas LCJ
Sch.21 para.4, see *R. v Reynolds (Jamie)*
[2014] EWCA Crim 2205, [2015] 1 Cr.
App. R. (S.) 24 (CA (Crim Div)), Lord
Thomas LCJ
Sch.21 para.4, amended: 2015 c.2 s.27
Sch.21 para.5, repealed: 2015 c.2 s.27
Sch.21 para.5A, see *R. v Dillon (Paul)*
[2015] EWCA Crim 3, [2015] 1 Cr. App.
R. (S.) 62 (CA (Crim Div)), Bean LJ
Sch.34A para.7, amended: 2015 c.9 Sch.4
para.70
Sch.34A para.13B, added: 2015 c.9 Sch.4
para.70
Sch.37, see *R. v Hookway (Lee)* [2015]
EWCA Crim 931, [2015] 2 Cr. App. R.
(S.) 43 (CA (Crim Div)), Fulford LJ

2004

**5. Planning and Compulsory Purchase Act
2004**
see *R. (on the application of Larkfleet
Homes Ltd) v Rutland CC* [2014] EWHC
4095 (Admin), [2015] P.T.S.R. 589
(QBD (Admin)), Collins J; see *Satnam
Millennium Ltd v Warrington BC* [2015]
EWHC 370 (Admin), [2015] Env. L.R.
30 (QBD (Admin)), Stewart J; see *West
Berkshire DC v Department for
Communities and Local Government*

[2015] EWHC 2222 (Admin), [2015]
B.L.G.R. 884 (QBD (Admin)), Holgate J
s.17, see *R. (on the application of
Larkfleet Homes Ltd) v Rutland CC*
[2014] EWHC 4095 (Admin), [2015]
P.T.S.R. 589 (QBD (Admin)), Collins J;
see *R. (on the application of Larkfleet
Homes Ltd) v Rutland CC* [2015] EWCA
Civ 597, [2015] P.T.S.R. 1369 (CA (Civ
Div)), Moore-Bick LJ
s.19, repealed: 2015 c.20 s.100
s.20, see *Gladman Developments Ltd v
Stafford BC* [2015] EWHC 444 (Admin),
[2015] J.P.L. 1002 (QBD (Admin)),
Supperstone J; see *IM Properties
Development Ltd v Lichfield DC* [2015]
EWHC 2077 (Admin), [2015] P.T.S.R.
1536 (QBD (Admin)), Cranston J; see *R.
(on the application of Luton BC) v
Central Bedfordshire Council* [2015]
EWCA Civ 537, [2015] 2 P. & C.R. 19
(CA (Civ Div)), Longmore LJ; see
*Samuel Smith Old Brewery (Tadcaster) v
Selby DC* [2014] EWHC 3441 (Admin),
[2015] P.T.S.R. 719 (QBD (Admin)),
Ouseley J
s.28, see *Satnam Millennium Ltd v
Warrington BC* [2015] EWHC 370
(Admin), [2015] Env. L.R. 30 (QBD
(Admin)), Stewart J
s.33A, see *Samuel Smith Old Brewery
(Tadcaster) v Selby DC* [2014] EWHC
3441 (Admin), [2015] P.T.S.R. 719
(QBD (Admin)), Ouseley J
s.37, see *R. (on the application of
Larkfleet Homes Ltd) v Rutland CC*
[2015] EWCA Civ 597, [2015] P.T.S.R.
1369 (CA (Civ Div)), Moore-Bick LJ
s.38, see *Dartford BC v Secretary of
State for Communities and Local
Government* [2014] EWHC 2636
(Admin), [2015] 1 P. & C.R. 2 (QBD
(Admin)), Patterson J; see *R. (on the
application of Cheshire East Council) v
Secretary of State for Communities and
Local Government* [2014] EWHC 2824
(Admin), [2015] J.P.L. 185 (QBD
(Admin)), Judge Stephen Davies; see *R.
(on the application of Gladman
Developments Ltd) v Aylesbury Vale DC*
[2014] EWHC 4323 (Admin), [2015]

J.P.L. 656 (QBD (Admin)), Lewis J; see
*R. (on the application of Hampton Bishop
PC) v Herefordshire Council* [2014]
EWCA Civ 878, [2015] 1 W.L.R. 2367
(CA (Civ Div)), Sir Terence Etherton C;
see *R. (on the application of Larkfleet
Homes Ltd) v Rutland CC* [2015] EWCA
Civ 597, [2015] P.T.S.R. 1369 (CA (Civ
Div)), Moore-Bick LJ
s.38A, see *R. (on the application of
Larkfleet Homes Ltd) v Rutland CC*
[2015] EWCA Civ 597, [2015] P.T.S.R.
1369 (CA (Civ Div)), Moore-Bick LJ
s.38A, enabling: SI 2015/20
s.38B, see *R. (on the application of
Larkfleet Homes Ltd) v Rutland CC*
[2015] EWCA Civ 597, [2015] P.T.S.R.
1369 (CA (Civ Div)), Moore-Bick LJ
s.38C, see *R. (on the application of
Larkfleet Homes Ltd) v Rutland CC*
[2015] EWCA Civ 597, [2015] P.T.S.R.
1369 (CA (Civ Div)), Moore-Bick LJ
s.54, enabling: SI 2015/595, SI
2015/1330
s.62, enabling: SI 2015/1598
s.63, enabling: SI 2015/1598
s.69, enabling: SI 2015/1598
s.77, enabling: SI 2015/1598
s.88, enabling: SI 2015/595
s.113, see *Abbotskerswell Parish Council
v Teignbridge DC* [2014] EWHC 4166
(Admin), [2015] Env. L.R. 20 (QBD
(Admin)), Lang J; see *Gallagher Homes
Ltd v Solihull MBC* [2014] EWCA Civ
1610, [2015] J.P.L. 713 (CA (Civ Div)),
Laws LJ; see *Gladman Developments
Ltd v Stafford BC* [2015] EWHC 444
(Admin), [2015] J.P.L. 1002 (QBD
(Admin)), Supperstone J; see
*Nottingham City Council v Calverton
Parish Council* [2015] EWHC 503
(Admin), [2015] P.T.S.R. 1130 (QBD
(Admin)), Lewis J
s.113, amended: 2015 c.2 Sch.16 para.8
s.113, repealed: 2015 c.2 Sch.16 para.8
s.121, enabling: SI 2015/340
s.122, enabling: SI 2015/20, SI 2015/340,
SI 2015/595, SI 2015/1598

6. Child Trust Funds Act 2004
s.3, amended: 2015 c.20 s.60, s.61, s.62
s.3, enabling: SI 2015/876, SI 2015/1371

s.5, enabling: SI 2015/1371
s.7, enabling: SI 2015/876
s.7A, added: 2015 c.20 s.62
s.7A, enabling: SI 2015/876
s.7B, added: 2015 c.20 s.62
s.7C, added: 2015 c.20 s.63
s.12, enabling: SI 2015/600
s.15, enabling: SI 2015/876
s.16, amended: 2015 c.20 s.60
s.20, amended: 2015 c.20 s.62
s.28, enabling: SI 2015/600, SI 2015/876,
SI 2015/1371

7. Gender Recognition Act 2004
see *G, Applicant* 2015 S.L.T. (Sh Ct) 212
(Sh Ct (Glasgow)), Sheriff J N
McCormick
s.2, see *Carpenter v Secretary of State for
Justice* [2015] EWHC 464 (Admin),
[2015] 1 W.L.R. 4111 (QBD (Admin)),
Thirlwall J
s.3, see *Carpenter v Secretary of State for
Justice* [2015] EWHC 464 (Admin),
[2015] 1 W.L.R. 4111 (QBD (Admin)),
Thirlwall J
s.4, see *MB v Secretary of State for Work
and Pensions* [2014] EWCA Civ 1112,
[2015] 1 All E.R. 920 (CA (Civ Div)),
Maurice Kay LJ
s.9, see *MB v Secretary of State for Work
and Pensions* [2014] EWCA Civ 1112,
[2015] 1 All E.R. 920 (CA (Civ Div)),
Maurice Kay LJ
s.11A, enabling: SI 2015/50
Sch.3 Part 1 para.11A, enabling: SI
2015/50

8. Higher Education Act 2004
s.11, amended: 2015 c.15 s.89
s.12, amended: 2015 c.15 s.89

11. Gangmasters (Licensing) Act 2004
s.1, enabling: SI 2015/805
s.15, amended: 2015 c.20 s.92
s.25, enabling: SI 2015/805

12. Finance Act 2004
s.60, see *Island Contract Management
(UK) Ltd v Revenue and Customs
Commissioners* [2015] UKUT 472
(TCC), [2015] B.T.C. 527 (UT (Tax)),
Rose J
s.61, see *Island Contract Management
(UK) Ltd v Revenue and Customs
Commissioners* [2015] UKUT 472

(TCC), [2015] B.T.C. 527 (UT (Tax)),
Rose J
s.62, enabling: SI 2015/125, SI 2015/429
s.66, see *JP Whitter (Waterwell Engineers) Ltd v Revenue and Customs Commissioners* [2015] UKUT 392 (TCC) (UT (Tax)), Warren J
s.70, enabling: SI 2015/429
s.71, enabling: SI 2015/125
s.150, enabling: SI 2015/673
s.167, amended: 2015 c.11 Sch.4 para.2
s.168, amended: 2015 c.33 s.22
s.169, enabling: SI 2015/673
s.172, amended: 2015 c.11 Sch.4 para.8
s.172A, amended: 2015 c.11 Sch.4 para.9
s.172B, amended: 2015 c.11 Sch.4 para.10
s.173, amended: 2015 c.11 Sch.1 para.25
s.192, amended: SI 2015/1810 Art.3
s.192A, added: SI 2015/1810 Art.4
s.206, amended: 2015 c.33 s.21
s.216, amended: 2015 c.11 Sch.4 para.4
s.216, varied: SI 2015/319 Reg.13, SI 2015/370 Reg.14, SI 2015/372 Reg.14, SI 2015/432 Reg.14, SI 2015/436 Reg.14, SI 2015/848 Reg.13, SSI 2015/117 Reg.13, SSI 2015/118 Reg.14, SSI 2015/145 Reg.14, SSI 2015/146 Reg.14
s.217, amended: 2015 c.11 Sch.4 para.5
s.219, amended: 2015 c.11 Sch.4 para.6
s.227, amended: 2015 c.33 Sch.4 para.11, SI 2015/1810 Art.7
s.227B, amended: 2015 c.33 Sch.4 para.4
s.227C, amended: 2015 c.33 Sch.4 para.4
s.227C, repealed: 2015 c.33 Sch.4 para.4
s.227D, repealed: 2015 c.33 Sch.4 para.4
s.227E, repealed: 2015 c.33 Sch.4 para.4
s.227ZA, amended: 2015 c.33 Sch.4 para.11
s.228B, added: SI 2015/80 Art.11
s.228C, added: 2015 c.33 Sch.4 para.6
s.228ZA, added: 2015 c.33 Sch.4 para.10
s.229, amended: 2015 c.33 Sch.4 para.8
s.230, amended: SI 2015/80 Art.12
s.232, amended: SI 2015/80 Art.13
s.232, repealed: SI 2015/80 Art.13
s.233, amended: SI 2015/80 Art.14
s.234, amended: SI 2015/80 Art.15
s.234, varied: SI 2015/319 Reg.14, SI 2015/370 Reg.15, SI 2015/372 Reg.15,

SI 2015/390 Reg.15, SI 2015/432 Reg.15, SI 2015/436 Reg.15, SI 2015/848 Reg.14, SSI 2015/117 Reg.14, SSI 2015/118 Reg.15, SSI 2015/145 Reg.15, SSI 2015/146 Reg.15
s.236, amended: SI 2015/80 Art.16
s.237B, amended: SI 2015/80 Art.17, SI 2015/1810 Art.7
s.237ZA, added: 2015 c.33 Sch.4 para.9
s.238, amended: 2015 c.33 Sch.4 para.2
s.238A, enabling: SI 2015/80
s.238ZA, added: 2015 c.33 Sch.4 para.3
s.250, enabling: SI 2015/1518
s.251, amended: 2015 c.33 s.21
s.251, enabling: SI 2015/606, SI 2015/673, SI 2015/1455
s.273B, amended: 2015 c.11 Sch.4 para.11
s.274A, enabling: SI 2015/667
s.280, amended: 2015 c.11 Sch.4 para.12, 2015 c.33 Sch.4 para.5, SI 2015/1810 Art.7
s.282, enabling: SI 2015/80, SI 2015/1455, SI 2015/1518
s.306, enabling: SI 2015/464
s.307, enabling: SI 2015/945
s.310C, added: 2015 c.11 Sch.17 para.1
s.311, amended: 2015 c.11 Sch.17 para.4
s.312, enabling: SI 2015/948
s.312A, amended: 2015 c.11 Sch.17 para.5
s.312A, enabling: SI 2015/948
s.313, amended: 2015 c.11 Sch.17 para.6
s.313, enabling: SI 2015/948
s.313C, amended: 2015 c.11 Sch.17 para.12
s.313C, substituted: 2015 c.11 Sch.17 para.12
s.313C, enabling: SI 2015/948
s.313ZC, added: 2015 c.11 Sch.17 para.9
s.313ZC, enabling: SI 2015/948
s.316, amended: 2015 c.11 Sch.17 para.2, Sch.17 para.7, Sch.17 para.10
s.316A, added: 2015 c.11 Sch.17 para.14
s.316B, added: 2015 c.11 Sch.17 para.16
s.316C, added: 2015 c.11 Sch.17 para.17
s.317, enabling: SI 2015/464, SI 2015/948
s.318, enabling: SI 2015/945, SI 2015/948

Sch.11 Part 2 para.8, amended: SI 2015/789 Art.2

Sch.11 Part 2 para.8A, added: SI 2015/789 Art.2

Sch.11 Part 3 para.12, amended: SI 2015/789 Art.3

Sch.11 Pt 3 para.12, see *JP Whitter (Waterwell Engineers) Ltd v Revenue and Customs Commissioners* [2015] UKUT 392 (TCC) (UT (Tax)), Warren J

Sch.11 Part 3 para.12A, added: SI 2015/789 Art.3

Sch.11 Part 4 para.13, enabling: SI 2015/789

Sch.28 Part 1 para.3, amended: 2015 c.11 Sch.4 para.13

Sch.28 Part 1 para.3, enabling: SI 2015/633

Sch.28 Part 1 para.6, amended: 2015 c.11 Sch.4 para.13

Sch.28 Part 1 para.6, enabling: SI 2015/633

Sch.28 Part 2 para.17, enabling: SI 2015/633

Sch.28 Part 2 para.20, enabling: SI 2015/633

Sch.28 Part 2 para.27AA, added: 2015 c.11 Sch.4 para.3

Sch.28 Part 2 para.27AA, enabling: SI 2015/1454

Sch.28 Part 2 para.27C, enabling: SI 2015/633

Sch.28 Part 2 para.27E, amended: 2015 c.11 Sch.4 para.13

Sch.28 Part 2 para.27FA, added: 2015 c.11 Sch.4 para.3

Sch.28 Part 2 para.27FA, enabling: SI 2015/1454

Sch.28 Part 2 para.27H, enabling: SI 2015/633

Sch.28 Part 2 para.27K, amended: 2015 c.11 Sch.4 para.13

Sch.29 Part 1 para.3, amended: 2015 c.11 Sch.4 para.14

Sch.29 Part 2 para.13, amended: 2015 c.33 s.21

Sch.29 Part 2 para.13, repealed: 2015 c.33 s.21

Sch.29 Part 2 para.15, amended: 2015 c.11 Sch.4 para.15

Sch.32, amended: 2015 c.11 Sch.4 para.7

Sch.32 para.1, amended: 2015 c.11 Sch.4 para.7

Sch.32 para.4, amended: 2015 c.11 Sch.4 para.7

Sch.32 para.14B, amended: 2015 c.11 Sch.4 para.7

Sch.32 para.14C, amended: 2015 c.11 Sch.4 para.7

Sch.32 para.16, amended: 2015 c.33 s.21

Sch.34 para.1, amended: 2015 c.33 s.22

Sch.36 Part 4 para.45A, added: 2015 c.11 Sch.4 para.19

15. Carers (Equal Opportunities) Act 2004

s.3, amended: SI 2015/914 Sch.1 para.76

s.6, repealed: SI 2015/914 Sch.1 para.77

18. Traffic Management Act 2004

Part 2, amended: 2015 c.7 Sch.1 para.134

s.1, amended: 2015 c.7 Sch.1 para.130

s.11, substituted: 2015 c.7 Sch.1 para.131

s.12, amended: 2015 c.7 Sch.1 para.132

s.15, amended: 2015 c.7 Sch.1 para.133

s.16, amended: 2015 c.7 Sch.1 para.135

s.17, amended: 2015 c.7 Sch.1 para.136

s.18, amended: 2015 c.7 Sch.1 para.137

s.19, amended: 2015 c.7 Sch.1 para.138

s.20, amended: 2015 c.7 Sch.1 para.139

s.21, amended: 2015 c.7 Sch.1 para.140

s.22, amended: 2015 c.7 Sch.1 para.141

s.23, amended: 2015 c.7 Sch.1 para.142

s.24, amended: 2015 c.7 Sch.1 para.143

s.25, amended: 2015 c.7 Sch.1 para.144

s.26, amended: 2015 c.7 Sch.1 para.145

s.30, amended: 2015 c.7 Sch.1 para.146

s.31, amended: 2015 c.7 Sch.1 para.147

s.33, amended: 2015 c.7 Sch.1 para.148, 2015 c.20 Sch.10 para.5

s.33A, added: 2015 c.20 Sch.10 para.6

s.34, amended: 2015 c.20 Sch.10 para.7

s.34, enabling: SI 2015/34, SI 2015/37, SI 2015/38, SI 2015/39, SI 2015/90, SI 2015/91, SI 2015/105, SI 2015/107, SI 2015/293, SI 2015/328, SI 2015/330

s.36, substituted: 2015 c.20 Sch.10 para.8

s.37, amended: 2015 c.20 Sch.10 para.9

s.37, enabling: SI 2015/958

s.39, amended: 2015 c.20 Sch.10 para.10

s.39, enabling: SI 2015/34, SI 2015/37, SI 2015/38, SI 2015/39, SI 2015/90, SI 2015/91, SI 2015/105, SI 2015/107, SI 2015/293, SI 2015/328, SI 2015/330

s.60, amended: 2015 c.7 Sch.1 para.149

s.61, amended: 2015 c.7 Sch.1 para.150
s.65, amended: 2015 c.7 Sch.1 para.151
s.72, enabling: SI 2015/561
s.73, enabling: SI 2015/561
s.78, enabling: SI 2015/1001
s.78A, added: 2015 c.20 s.53
s.78A, enabling: SI 2015/1001
s.85, amended: 2015 c.20 Sch.9 para.2
s.86, amended: 2015 c.20 Sch.9 para.3
s.87A, added: 2015 c.20 s.53
s.89, enabling: SI 2015/561, SI
2015/1001
s.99, enabling: SI 2015/199
Sch.8 Part 2 para.9, amended: 2015 c.20
Sch.11 para.19

19. Asylum and Immigration (Treatment of Claimants, etc.) Act 2004
s.2, see *R. v Jeyarasa (Sivaguru)* [2014]
EWCA Crim 2545, [2015] 1 Cr. App. R.
(S.) 39 (CA (Crim Div)), Coulson J
s.4, repealed: 2015 asp 12 Sch.1 para.4 ,
2015 c.30 Sch.5 para.6
s.5, repealed: 2015 c.30 Sch.5 para.6
s.12, see *B (Eritrea) v Secretary of State
for Work and Pensions* [2015] EWCA
Civ 141, [2015] 1 W.L.R. 3150 (CA (Civ
Div)), Jackson LJ
s.14, amended: 2015 c.30 Sch.5 para.6
s.14, repealed: 2015 c.30 Sch.5 para.6
s.21, amended: SI 2015/396 Sch.2 para.2,
Sch.2 para.3
s.23, amended: SI 2015/395 Sch.2 para.2,
Sch.2 para.3
Sch.3 Pt 2, see *Al v Advocate General for
Scotland* [2015] CSOH 95, 2015 S.L.T.
507 (OH), Lady Rae
Sch.3 Pt 2 para.3, see *Dudaev v Secretary
of State for the Home Department* [2015]
EWHC 1641 (Admin), [2015] 3
C.M.L.R. 37 (DC), Burnett LJ

20. Energy Act 2004
s.124, enabling: SI 2015/534
s.125A, enabling: SI 2015/534
s.125B, enabling: SI 2015/534
s.126, enabling: SI 2015/534
s.192, enabling: SI 2015/534

21. Fire and Rescue Services Act 2004
s.2, amended: 2015 c.20 Sch.22 para.16
s.2, enabling: SI 2015/435
s.3, enabling: SI 2015/435
s.4, amended: 2015 c.20 Sch.22 para.16

s.4, enabling: SI 2015/435
s.21, enabling: SI 2015/1931, SI
2015/1991
s.28, enabling: SI 2015/1524
s.34, enabling: SI 2015/590, SI
2015/1013, SSI 2015/143
s.60, enabling: SI 2015/435, SI 2015/590,
SI 2015/1013, SSI 2015/143
s.62, enabling: SI 2015/1013, SI
2015/1931, SI 2015/1991

25. Horserace Betting and Olympic Lottery Act 2004
s.28, enabling: SI 2015/85

26. Christmas Day (Trading) Act 2004
s.1, amended: SI 2015/664 Sch.4 para.36
s.3, amended: 2015 c.15 Sch.6 para.83
s.3, repealed: 2015 c.15 Sch.6 para.83

27. Companies (Audit, Investigations and Community Enterprise) Act 2004
s.18, repealed: 2015 c.26 s.38
s.18A, added: 2015 c.26 s.38
s.45, amended: SI 2015/664 Sch.3 para.8
s.66, amended: 2015 c.26 s.38
Sch.2 Part 3 para.28, repealed: 2015 c.26
Sch.7 para.24

28. Domestic Violence, Crime and Victims Act 2004
s.17, see *R. v A* [2015] EWCA Crim 177,
[2015] 2 Cr. App. R. (S.) 12 (CA (Crim
Div)), Fulford LJ
s.19, see *R. v A* [2015] EWCA Crim 177,
[2015] 2 Cr. App. R. (S.) 12 (CA (Crim
Div)), Fulford LJ
s.33, enabling: SI 2015/1817
Sch.9 para.26A, added: 2015 c.2 Sch.3
para.12

30. Human Tissue Act 2004
s.1, amended: SI 2015/865 Art.2
s.1, repealed: SI 2015/865 Art.2
s.4, amended: SI 2015/865 Art.2

31. Children Act 2004
s.11, see *Mohamoud v Kensington and
Chelsea RLBC* [2015] EWCA Civ 780,
[2015] H.L.R. 38 (CA (Civ Div)),
Longmore LJ; see *Nzolameso v
Westminster City Council* [2015] UKSC
22, [2015] 2 All E.R. 942 (SC), Lady
Hale DPSC
s.11, amended: 2015 c.2 Sch.9 para.14
s.13, amended: 2015 c.2 Sch.9 para.15

s.15, amended: 2015 c.2 Sch.9 para.16,
Sch.10 para.34
s.20, enabling: SI 2015/1792
s.23, enabling: SI 2015/1792
s.25, amended: 2015 c.2 Sch.9 para.17
s.28, amended: 2015 c.2 Sch.9 para.18
s.31, amended: 2015 c.2 Sch.9 para.19
s.33, amended: 2015 c.2 Sch.9 para.20,
Sch.10 para.35
s.65, amended: 2015 c.2 Sch.10 para.36
s.66, enabling: SI 2015/1792

**32. Armed Forces (Pensions and
Compensation) Act 2004**
s.1, enabling: SI 2015/413, SI 2015/497

33. Civil Partnership Act 2004
s.8, enabling: SI 2015/177
s.9B, enabling: SI 2015/123
s.9E, enabling: SI 2015/123, SI 2015/177
s.12, enabling: SI 2015/159, SI 2015/177
s.12A, enabling: SI 2015/123
s.21, enabling: SI 2015/177
s.34, enabling: SI 2015/117
s.36, amended: 2015 c.20 s.99
s.36, enabling: SI 2015/177
s.88A, added: SI 2015/396 Sch.3 para.2
s.89, amended: SI 2015/396 Sch.3 para.4
s.91, amended: SI 2015/396 Sch.3 para.5
s.94A, added: SI 2015/396 Sch.3 para.6
s.126, amended: SI 2015/396 Sch.3
para.7
s.135, amended: SI 2015/396 Sch.3
para.8
s.139A, added: SI 2015/395 Sch.3 para.2
s.140, amended: SI 2015/395 Sch.3
para.4
s.143A, added: SI 2015/395 Sch.3 para.5
s.160, amended: SI 2015/395 Sch.3
para.6
s.176, amended: SI 2015/395 Sch.3
para.7
s.258, enabling: SI 2015/117, SI
2015/159, SI 2015/177
Sch.10A, added: SI 2015/396 Sch.3
para.3
Sch.13A, added: SI 2015/395 Sch.3
para.3
Sch.23 Part 1 paraA.1, amended: SI
2015/395 Sch.3 para.8
Sch.23 Part 1 para.1, substituted: SI
2015/395 Sch.3 para.8

Sch.23 Part 3 para.8, amended: SI
2015/395 Sch.3 para.8
Sch.23 Part 4 para.12, amended: SI
2015/395 Sch.3 para.8
Sch.24 Part 5 para.96, repealed: SI
2015/2006 Sch.12 Part 1
Sch.24 Part 5 para.102, repealed: SI
2015/2006 Sch.12 Part 1
Sch.24 Part 6 para.107, repealed: SI
2015/2006 Sch.12 Part 1
Sch.24 Part 6 para.113, repealed: SI
2015/2006 Sch.12 Part 7
Sch.24 Part 10 para.131, repealed: SI
2015/2006 Sch.12 Part 1
Sch.27 para.50, repealed: 2015 c.15
Sch.6 para.85
Sch.27 para.62, repealed: 2015 c.15
Sch.6 para.85

34. Housing Act 2004
see *Charalambous v Ng* [2014] EWCA
Civ 1604, [2015] 1 W.L.R. 3018 (CA
(Civ Div)), Black LJ
Pt 1., see *Temur v Hackney LBC* [2014]
EWCA Civ 877, [2015] 1 All E.R. 311
(CA (Civ Div)), Jackson LJ
Pt 2., see *Clark v Manchester City
Council* [2015] UKUT 129 (LC), [2015]
L.L.R. 457 (UT (Lands)), Martin Rodger
QC; see *Urban Lettings (London) Ltd v
Haringey LBC* [2015] UKUT 104 (LC),
[2015] L.L.R. 611 (UT (Lands)), Judge
Behrens
s.56, see *R. (on the application of Regas)
v Enfield LBC* [2014] EWHC 4173
(Admin), [2015] H.L.R. 14 (QBD
(Admin)), Judge McKenna
s.61, see *Urban Lettings (London) Ltd v
Haringey LBC* [2015] UKUT 104 (LC),
[2015] L.L.R. 611 (UT (Lands)), Judge
Behrens
s.65, see *Clark v Manchester City
Council* [2015] UKUT 129 (LC), [2015]
L.L.R. 457 (UT (Lands)), Martin Rodger
QC
s.72, see *Urban Lettings (London) Ltd v
Haringey LBC* [2015] UKUT 104 (LC),
[2015] L.L.R. 611 (UT (Lands)), Judge
Behrens
s.72, amended: SI 2015/664 Sch.4
para.37

s.80, see *R. (on the application of Croydon Property Forum Ltd) v Croydon LBC* [2015] EWHC 2403 (Admin), [2015] L.L.R. 812 (QBD (Admin)), Sir Stephen Silber; see *R. (on the application of Regas) v Enfield LBC* [2014] EWHC 4173 (Admin), [2015] H.L.R. 14 (QBD (Admin)), Judge McKenna; see *R. (on the application of Rotherham Action Group Ltd) v Rotherham MBC* [2015] EWHC 1216 (Admin), [2015] P.T.S.R. 1312 (QBD (Admin)), Stewart J

s.80, enabling: SI 2015/977

s.81, see *R. (on the application of Rotherham Action Group Ltd) v Rotherham MBC* [2015] EWHC 1216 (Admin), [2015] P.T.S.R. 1312 (QBD (Admin)), Stewart J

s.95, amended: SI 2015/664 Sch.4 para.37

s.213, see *Charalambous v Ng* [2014] EWCA Civ 1604, [2015] 1 W.L.R. 3018 (CA (Civ Div)), Black LJ

s.214, see *Charalambous v Ng* [2014] EWCA Civ 1604, [2015] 1 W.L.R. 3018 (CA (Civ Div)), Black LJ

s.214, amended: 2015 c.20 s.31

s.215, see *Charalambous v Ng* [2014] EWCA Civ 1604, [2015] 1 W.L.R. 3018 (CA (Civ Div)), Black LJ

s.215, amended: 2015 c.20 s.31

s.215A, added: 2015 c.20 s.32

s.250, enabling: SI 2015/977, SI 2015/1821

s.257, see *Urban Lettings (London) Ltd v Haringey LBC* [2015] UKUT 104 (LC), [2015] L.L.R. 611 (UT (Lands)), Judge Behrens

s.263, see *Urban Lettings (London) Ltd v Haringey LBC* [2015] UKUT 104 (LC), [2015] L.L.R. 611 (UT (Lands)), Judge Behrens

Sch.4 para.1, amended: SI 2015/1693 Reg.15

Sch.4 para.3, enabling: SI 2015/1693

Sch.5 Pt 3 para.34, see *Clark v Manchester City Council* [2015] UKUT 129 (LC), [2015] L.L.R. 457 (UT (Lands)), Martin Rodger QC

Sch.10 para.3, enabling: SI 2015/14

Sch.13, enabling: SI 2015/1821

35. Pensions Act 2004

see *BESTrustees Plc v Corbett* [2014] EWHC 3038 (Ch), [2015] Ch. 571 (Ch D), Birss J; see *Hampshire v Board of the Pension Protection Fund* [2014] EWHC 4402 (Ch), [2015] 2 C.M.L.R. 17 (Ch D (Birmingham)), Judge Cooke; see *Olympic Airlines SA, Re* [2015] UKSC 27, [2015] 1 W.L.R. 2399 (SC), Lord Neuberger PSC

s.13, amended: 2015 c.8 Sch.2 para.24, SI 2015/879 Reg.25

s.17, amended: 2015 c.8 Sch.2 para.25

s.18, amended: 2015 c.8 s.70, Sch.4 para.35

s.18, repealed: 2015 c.8 Sch.4 para.35

s.23, amended: 2015 c.8 Sch.2 para.26, Sch.4 para.36

s.24, amended: 2015 c.8 Sch.4 para.37

s.38, amended: 2015 c.8 Sch.2 para.27

s.41, see *BESTrustees Plc v Corbett* [2014] EWHC 3038 (Ch), [2015] Ch. 571 (Ch D), Birss J

s.43, amended: 2015 c.8 Sch.2 para.28

s.50, see *BESTrustees Plc v Corbett* [2014] EWHC 3038 (Ch), [2015] Ch. 571 (Ch D), Birss J

s.52, amended: 2015 c.8 Sch.2 para.29

s.60, enabling: SI 2015/879

s.73, amended: 2015 c.8 Sch.4 para.38

s.90, amended: 2015 c.8 Sch.2 para.30

s.91, enabling: SI 2015/456

s.94, see *Granada UK Rental & Retail Ltd v Pensions Regulator* [2015] EWCA Civ 228, [2015] 4 All E.R. 919 (CA (Civ Div)), Arden LJ

s.103, see *Granada UK Rental & Retail Ltd v Pensions Regulator* [2015] EWCA Civ 228, [2015] 4 All E.R. 919 (CA (Civ Div)), Arden LJ

s.117, enabling: SI 2015/84

s.121, repealed: 2015 c.20 Sch.6 para.2

s.126, amended: 2015 c.8 Sch.2 para.31

s.135, amended: 2015 c.8 s.58, Sch.4 para.39

s.138, amended: 2015 c.8 s.59, Sch.4 para.40

s.178, enabling: SI 2015/66

s.221, substituted: 2015 c.8 Sch.2 para.32

s.254, amended: 2015 c.8 Sch.2 para.33

s.258, amended: 2015 c.8 Sch.2 para.34
s.259, enabling: SI 2015/879
s.286, amended: 2015 c.8 Sch.2 para.35
s.291, amended: 2015 c.8 Sch.2 para.36
s.307, amended: 2015 c.8 Sch.2 para.37
s.315, enabling: SI 2015/66, SI 2015/84,
SI 2015/879
s.318, amended: 2015 c.8 s.60, Sch.2
para.38, Sch.4 para.41
s.318, enabling: SI 2015/84, SI 2015/879
Sch.7 para.20, amended: 2015 c.8 Sch.4
para.42
Sch.7 para.32, amended: 2015 c.8 Sch.4
para.42
Sch.12 para.17, repealed: 2015 c.8 s.38
36. Civil Contingencies Act 2004
Sch.1 Part 3 para.28, substituted: 2015
c.7 Sch.1 para.152

2005

4. Constitutional Reform Act 2005
s.5, amended: 2015 c.2 s.81
s.39, amended: 2015 c.2 s.82
s.40, repealed: SI 2015/700 Sch.1 para.13
Sch.4 Part 1 para.19, repealed: 2015 c.20
Sch.6 para.2
Sch.4 Part 1 para.83, repealed: 2015 c.7
Sch.5 para.12
Sch.4 Part 1 para.84, repealed: 2015 c.7
Sch.5 para.8
Sch.11 Part 2 para.4, amended: 2015 c.20
Sch.6 para.2
Sch.14 Part 3, amended: 2015 c.20 Sch.6
para.22
**5. Income Tax (Trading and Other Income)
Act 2005**
see *Samarkand Film Partnership No.3 v
Revenue and Customs Commissioners*
[2015] UKUT 211 (TCC), [2015] S.T.C.
2135 (UT (Tax)), Nugee J
Pt 4., see *Lobler v Revenue and Customs
Commissioners* [2015] UKUT 152
(TCC), [2015] S.T.C. 1893 (UT (Tax)),
Proudman J
s.34, see *Vaccine Research LP v Revenue
and Customs Commissioners* [2015]
S.T.C. 179 (UT (Tax)), Sales J
s.86A, added: 2015 c.11 Sch.5 para.1

s.134, see *Samarkand Film Partnership
No.3 v Revenue and Customs
Commissioners* [2015] UKUT 211
(TCC), [2015] S.T.C. 2135 (UT (Tax)),
Nugee J
s.138, see *Samarkand Film Partnership
No.3 v Revenue and Customs
Commissioners* [2015] UKUT 211
(TCC), [2015] S.T.C. 2135 (UT (Tax)),
Nugee J
s.167, amended: SI 2015/374 Art.7
s.172F, amended: 2015 c.33 s.40
s.173, amended: 2015 c.33 s.41
s.272, amended: 2015 c.11 Sch.5 para.2
s.272A, added: 2015 c.33 s.24
s.274, amended: 2015 c.33 s.24
s.274A, added: 2015 c.33 s.24
s.322, amended: 2015 c.33 s.24
s.381, see *Savva v Revenue and Customs
Commissioners* [2015] UKUT 141
(TCC), [2015] S.T.C. 1873 (UT (Tax)),
Henderson J
s.382, amended: 2015 c.11 s.19
s.385, amended: 2015 c.11 s.19
s.396A, added: 2015 c.11 s.19
s.397, see *Shirley v Revenue and Customs
Commissioners* [2015] S.F.T.D. 247
(FTT (Tax)), Judge Nicholas Aleksander
s.397, amended: 2015 c.11 s.19
s.399, see *Shirley v Revenue and Customs
Commissioners* [2015] S.F.T.D. 247
(FTT (Tax)), Judge Nicholas Aleksander
s.399, amended: 2015 c.11 s.19
s.401, see *Shirley v Revenue and Customs
Commissioners* [2015] S.F.T.D. 247
(FTT (Tax)), Judge Nicholas Aleksander
s.427, see *Savva v Revenue and Customs
Commissioners* [2015] UKUT 141
(TCC), [2015] S.T.C. 1873 (UT (Tax)),
Henderson J
s.462, see *Lobler v Revenue and Customs
Commissioners* [2015] UKUT 152
(TCC), [2015] S.T.C. 1893 (UT (Tax)),
Proudman J
s.507, see *Lobler v Revenue and Customs
Commissioners* [2015] UKUT 152
(TCC), [2015] S.T.C. 1893 (UT (Tax)),
Proudman J
s.539, see *Lobler v Revenue and Customs
Commissioners* [2015] UKUT 152

(TCC), [2015] S.T.C. 1893 (UT (Tax)),
Proudman J
s.539, amended: SI 2015/1810 Art.9
s.669, amended: SI 2015/1810 Art.10
s.685A, amended: SI 2015/1810 Art.11
s.694, enabling: SI 2015/608, SI
2015/869, SI 2015/941, SI 2015/1370
s.695, enabling: SI 2015/869, SI
2015/941, SI 2015/1370
s.695A, enabling: SI 2015/869, SI
2015/941, SI 2015/1370
s.696, enabling: SI 2015/869, SI
2015/941, SI 2015/1370
s.697, enabling: SI 2015/869, SI
2015/941
s.698, enabling: SI 2015/869, SI
2015/941
s.699, enabling: SI 2015/869, SI
2015/941
s.701, enabling: SI 2015/869, SI
2015/941, SI 2015/1370
s.782A, amended: 2015 c.20 s.57
s.789, amended: SI 2015/1539 Art.2
s.789, enabling: SI 2015/1539
s.858, see *Huitson v Revenue and
Customs Commissioners* [2015] UKFTT
448 (TC) (FTT (Tax)), Judge Jonathan
Cannan
Sch.4 Part 2, amended: SI 2015/1810
Art.12

7. Finance Act 2005
Sch.10 para.32, repealed: 2015 c.11
Sch.4 para.16

9. Mental Capacity Act 2005
see *An English Local Authority v SW*
[2015] C.O.P.L.R. 29 (CP), Moylan J;
see *H, Re* [2015] EWCOP 52, [2015]
C.O.P.L.R. 660 (CP), Senior Judge
Denzil Lush; see *KD v A Borough
Council* [2015] UKUT 251 (AAC),
[2015] C.O.P.L.R. 486 (UT (AAC)),
Charles J; see *M (An Adult) (Capacity:
Consent to Sexual Relations), Re* [2014]
EWCA Civ 37, [2015] Fam. 61 (CA (Civ
Div)), Sir Brian Leveson PQBD; see *M
(Incapacitated Adult) (Best Interests
Declaration: Potential Contempt), Re*
[2015] EWCOP 3, [2015] Fam. 239 (CP),
Hayden J; see *Miles v Public Guardian*
[2015] EWHC 2960 (Ch), [2015]
C.O.P.L.R. 676 (Ch D), Nugee J; see

NHS Trust v FG [2015] 1 W.L.R. 1984
(CP), Keehan J; see *NM v Kent CC*
[2015] UKUT 125 (AAC), [2015]
C.O.P.L.R. 537 (UT (AAC)), Judge
Edward Jacobs; see *PJ (A Patient) v A
Local Health Board* [2015] UKUT 480
(AAC), [2015] C.O.P.L.R. 756 (UT
(AAC)), Charles J; see *Public Guardian
v M* [2015] C.O.P.L.R. 107 (CP), Senior
Judge Denzil Lush; see *Public Guardian
v Marvin* [2014] EWHC 47 (COP),
[2015] C.O.P.L.R. 59 (CP), Senior Judge
Denzil Lush; see *R. (on the application
of N) v Walsall MBC* [2014] EWHC 1918
(Admin), [2015] 1 All E.R. 165 (QBD
(Admin)), Leggatt J; see *Secretary of
State for Justice v KC* [2015] UKUT 376
(AAC), [2015] C.O.P.L.R. 804 (UT
(AAC)), Charles J; see *Smith
(Deceased), Re* [2014] EWHC 3926
(Ch), [2015] 4 All E.R. 329 (Ch D),
Stephen Morris QC; see *Tower Hamlets
LBC v TB* [2015] 2 F.C.R. 264 (CP),
Mostyn J; see *Walker (Deceased), Re*
[2014] EWHC 71 (Ch), [2015]
C.O.P.L.R. 348 (Ch D), Nicholas Strauss
QC
Pt 1., see *M (An Adult) (Capacity:
Consent to Sexual Relations), Re* [2014]
EWCA Civ 37, [2015] Fam. 61 (CA (Civ
Div)), Sir Brian Leveson PQBD
s.1, see *A (Court of Protection: Delay
and Costs), Re* [2015] C.O.P.L.R. 1 (CP),
Peter Jackson J; see *P v Surrey CC*
[2015] EWCOP 54, [2015] C.O.P.L.R.
747 (CP), District Judge Cushing; see
Public Guardian v Marvin [2014] EWHC
47 (COP), [2015] C.O.P.L.R. 59 (CP),
Senior Judge Denzil Lush; see *Walker
(Deceased), Re* [2014] EWHC 71 (Ch),
[2015] C.O.P.L.R. 348 (Ch D), Nicholas
Strauss QC
s.2, see *Smith (Deceased), Re* [2014]
EWHC 3926 (Ch), [2015] 4 All E.R. 329
(Ch D), Stephen Morris QC; see *Walker
(Deceased), Re* [2014] EWHC 71 (Ch),
[2015] C.O.P.L.R. 348 (Ch D), Nicholas
Strauss QC
s.3, see *M (An Adult) (Capacity: Consent
to Sexual Relations), Re* [2014] EWCA
Civ 37, [2015] Fam. 61 (CA (Civ Div)),

Sir Brian Leveson PQBD; see *Smith (Deceased), Re* [2014] EWHC 3926 (Ch), [2015] 4 All E.R. 329 (Ch D), Stephen Morris QC; see *Tower Hamlets LBC v TB* [2015] 2 F.C.R. 264 (CP), Mostyn J; see *Walker (Deceased), Re* [2014] EWHC 71 (Ch), [2015] C.O.P.L.R. 348 (Ch D), Nicholas Strauss QC

s.4, see *A NHS Foundation Trust v X* [2015] 2 F.C.R. 418 (CP), Cobb J; see *Aidiniantz, Re* [2015] EWCOP 65, [2015] C.O.P.L.R. 643 (CP), Peter Jackson J; see *NHS Trust v FG* [2015] 1 W.L.R. 1984 (CP), Keehan J; see *PAW, Re* [2015] EWCOP 57, [2015] W.T.L.R. 1785 (CP), Senior Judge Denzil Lush; see *St George's Healthcare NHS Trust v P* [2015] EWCOP 42, [2015] C.O.P.L.R. 561 (CP), Newton J

s.9, see *Miles v Public Guardian* [2015] EWHC 2960 (Ch), [2015] C.O.P.L.R. 676 (Ch D), Nugee J

s.10, see *Miles v Public Guardian* [2015] EWHC 2960 (Ch), [2015] C.O.P.L.R. 676 (Ch D), Nugee J; see *Public Guardian v M* [2015] C.O.P.L.R. 107 (CP), Senior Judge Denzil Lush

s.12, see *OL, Re* [2015] EWCOP 41, [2015] W.T.L.R. 1647 (CP), Senior Judge Denzil Lush; see *PC, Re* [2015] W.T.L.R. 465 (CP), Senior Judge Denzil Lush; see *XZ v Public Guardian* [2015] EWCOP 35, [2015] C.O.P.L.R. 630 (CP), Judge Lush

s.13, see *Miles v Public Guardian* [2015] EWHC 2960 (Ch), [2015] C.O.P.L.R. 676 (Ch D), Nugee J

s.15, see *M v N* [2015] EWCOP 76, (2015) 18 C.C.L. Rep. 603 (CP), Hayden J; see *N (An Adult) (Court of Protection: Jurisdiction), Re* [2015] EWCA Civ 411, [2015] 3 W.L.R. 1585 (CA (Civ Div)), Sir James Munby PFD; see *Rochdale MBC v KW* [2015] 2 F.C.R. 244 (CP), Mostyn J

s.16, see *M (Incapacitated Adult) (Best Interests Declaration: Potential Contempt), Re* [2015] EWCOP 3, [2015] Fam. 239 (CP), Hayden J; see *N (An Adult) (Court of Protection:*

Jurisdiction), Re [2015] EWCA Civ 411, [2015] 3 W.L.R. 1585 (CA (Civ Div)), Sir James Munby PFD; see *P, Re* [2015] EWCOP 59, [2015] C.O.P.L.R. 690 (CP), Charles J; see *PV, Re* [2015] EWCOP 22, [2015] C.O.P.L.R. 265 (CP), Senior Judge Denzil Lush

s.18, see *PV, Re* [2015] EWCOP 22, [2015] C.O.P.L.R. 265 (CP), Senior Judge Denzil Lush

s.19, see *Public Guardian v M* [2015] C.O.P.L.R. 107 (CP), Senior Judge Denzil Lush

s.21A, see *J (An Adult) (Deprivation of Liberty: Safeguards), Re* [2015] EWCOP 5, [2015] Fam. 291 (CP), Baker J; see *X (Deprivation of Liberty), Re* [2015] 1 W.L.R. 2454 (CP), Sir James Munby PFD

s.22, see *ARL, Re* [2015] EWCOP 55, [2015] W.T.L.R. 1489 (CP), Senior Judge Denzil Lush; see *MC, Re* [2015] EWCOP 32, [2015] W.T.L.R. 1057 (CP), Senior Judge Denzil Lush; see *OL, Re* [2015] EWCOP 41, [2015] W.T.L.R. 1647 (CP), Senior Judge Denzil Lush; see *PC, Re* [2015] W.T.L.R. 465 (CP), Senior Judge Denzil Lush; see *Public Guardian v Marvin* [2014] EWHC 47 (COP), [2015] C.O.P.L.R. 59 (CP), Senior Judge Denzil Lush

s.23, see *PC, Re* [2015] W.T.L.R. 465 (CP), Senior Judge Denzil Lush; see *Public Guardian v M* [2015] C.O.P.L.R. 107 (CP), Senior Judge Denzil Lush; see *XZ v Public Guardian* [2015] EWCOP 35, [2015] C.O.P.L.R. 630 (CP), Judge Lush

s.27, see *M (An Adult) (Capacity: Consent to Sexual Relations), Re* [2014] EWCA Civ 37, [2015] Fam. 61 (CA (Civ Div)), Sir Brian Leveson PQBD; see *XZ v Public Guardian* [2015] EWCOP 35, [2015] C.O.P.L.R. 630 (CP), Judge Lush

s.39, amended: SI 2015/914 Sch.1 para.79

s.39D, see *J (An Adult) (Deprivation of Liberty: Safeguards), Re* [2015] EWCOP 5, [2015] Fam. 291 (CP), Baker J

s.40, see *J (An Adult) (Deprivation of Liberty: Safeguards), Re* [2015] EWCOP 5, [2015] Fam. 291 (CP), Baker J
s.47, see *N (An Adult) (Court of Protection: Jurisdiction), Re* [2015] EWCA Civ 411, [2015] 3 W.L.R. 1585 (CA (Civ Div)), Sir James Munby PFD
s.48, see *Public Guardian v CT* [2015] C.O.P.L.R. 70 (CP), Senior Judge Denzil Lush
s.49, see *P, Re* [2015] EWCOP 59, [2015] C.O.P.L.R. 690 (CP), Charles J
s.50, enabling: SI 2015/548
s.51, enabling: SI 2015/548
s.53, amended: 2015 c.2 s.62
s.53, repealed: 2015 c.2 s.62
s.53, enabling: SI 2015/548
s.55, see *Public Guardian v CT* [2015] C.O.P.L.R. 70 (CP), Senior Judge Denzil Lush
s.55, enabling: SI 2015/548
s.56, enabling: SI 2015/548
s.58, enabling: SI 2015/899
s.63, see *PA, Re* [2015] EWCOP 38 (CP), Baker J
s.65, enabling: SI 2015/548, SI 2015/899
Sch.A1, see *J (An Adult) (Deprivation of Liberty: Safeguards), Re* [2015] EWCOP 5, [2015] Fam. 291 (CP), Baker J
Sch.A1 Pt 1 para.2, see *A Local Health Board v AB* [2015] EWCOP 31, [2015] C.O.P.L.R. 412 (CP), Judge Parry
Sch.A1 Pt 10, see *J (An Adult) (Deprivation of Liberty: Safeguards), Re* [2015] EWCOP 5, [2015] Fam. 291 (CP), Baker J
Sch.A1 Part 13 para.183, amended: SI 2015/914 Sch.1 para.80
Sch.1, enabling: SI 2015/899
Sch.1 Pt 2 para.11, see *XZ v Public Guardian* [2015] EWCOP 35, [2015] C.O.P.L.R. 630 (CP), Judge Lush
Sch.1 Pt 3 para.19, see *Miles v Public Guardian* [2015] EWHC 2960 (Ch), [2015] C.O.P.L.R. 676 (Ch D), Nugee J
Sch.3, see *PA, Re* [2015] EWCOP 38 (CP), Baker J; see *PD, Re* [2015] EWCOP 48, [2015] C.O.P.L.R. 544 (CP), Baker J
Sch.3 Pt 1 para.4, see *PA, Re* [2015] EWCOP 38 (CP), Baker J

Sch.3 Pt 1 para.5, see *PA, Re* [2015] EWCOP 38 (CP), Baker J
Sch.3 Pt 4 para.19, see *PA, Re* [2015] EWCOP 38 (CP), Baker J
Sch.3 Pt 4 para.21, see *PA, Re* [2015] EWCOP 38 (CP), Baker J
Sch.4 Pt 1 para.3, see *Public Guardian v IT* [2015] EWCOP 10, [2015] C.O.P.L.R. 225 (CP), Senior Judge Denzil Lush
Sch.6 para.31, repealed: 2015 c.20 Sch.6 para.20

11. Commissioners for Revenue and Customs Act 2005

s.8A, added: 2015 c.7 s.40
s.18, see *R. (on the application of Ingenious Media Holdings Plc) v Revenue and Customs Commissioners* [2015] EWCA Civ 173, [2015] 1 W.L.R. 3183 (CA (Civ Div)), Moore-Bick LJ; see *R. (on the application of Privacy International) v Revenue and Customs Commissioners* [2014] EWHC 1475 (Admin), [2015] 1 W.L.R. 397 (QBD (Admin)), Green J; see *R. (on the application of Revenue and Customs Commissioners) v HM Coroner for Liverpool* [2014] EWHC 1586 (Admin), [2015] Q.B. 481 (DC), Gross LJ
s.20, see *R. (on the application of Revenue and Customs Commissioners) v HM Coroner for Liverpool* [2014] EWHC 1586 (Admin), [2015] Q.B. 481 (DC), Gross LJ
Sch.4 para.49, repealed: SI 2015/2006
Sch.12 Part 12

12. Inquiries Act 2005

see *Kennedy v Information Commissioner* [2015] A.C. 455 (SC), Lord Neuberger JSC; see *R. (on the application of Keyu) v Secretary of State for Foreign and Commonwealth Affairs* [2015] UKSC 69, [2015] 3 W.L.R. 1665 (SC), Lord Neuberger PSC
s.1, see *R. (on the application of Keyu) v Secretary of State for Foreign and Commonwealth Affairs* [2015] UKSC 69, [2015] 3 W.L.R. 1665 (SC), Lord Neuberger PSC
s.9, see *Congregation of the Poor Sisters of Nazareth v Scottish Ministers* [2015]

CSOH 87, 2015 S.L.T. 445 (OH), Lord
Woolman
s.10, amended: SSI 2015/150 Sch.1
para.8
s.10, repealed: SSI 2015/150 Sch.1 para.8
14. Railways Act 2005
s.13, amended: 2015 c.20 Sch.8 para.7
s.22, amended: SI 2015/1682 Sch.1
para.3
s.23, amended: SI 2015/1682 Sch.1
para.3
s.24, amended: SI 2015/1682 Sch.1
para.3
s.25, amended: SI 2015/1682 Sch.1
para.3
s.25, enabling: SI 2015/1877
s.26, amended: SI 2015/1682 Sch.1
para.3
s.27, amended: SI 2015/1682 Sch.1
para.3
s.28, amended: SI 2015/1682 Sch.1
para.3
s.29, amended: SI 2015/1682 Sch.1
para.3
s.30, amended: SI 2015/1682 Sch.1
para.3
s.31, amended: SI 2015/1682 Sch.1
para.3
s.32, amended: SI 2015/1682 Sch.1
para.3
s.33, amended: SI 2015/1682 Sch.1
para.3
s.34, amended: SI 2015/1682 Sch.1
para.3
s.36, amended: SI 2015/1682 Sch.1
para.3
s.37, amended: SI 2015/1682 Sch.1
para.3
s.38, enabling: SI 2015/1877
s.45, amended: SI 2015/1682 Sch.1
para.3
s.51, amended: SI 2015/1682 Sch.1
para.3
Sch.1 Part 1 para.10, amended: SI
2015/1682 Sch.1 para.3
Sch.1 Part 1 para.24, amended: SI
2015/1682 Sch.1 para.3
Sch.1 Part 1 para.26, amended: SI
2015/1682 Sch.1 para.3
Sch.3 para.1, amended: SI 2015/1682
Sch.1 para.3

Sch.3 para.2, amended: SI 2015/1682
Sch.1 para.3
Sch.3 para.4, amended: SI 2015/1682
Sch.1 para.3
Sch.3 para.7, amended: SI 2015/1682
Sch.1 para.3
Sch.3 para.8, amended: SI 2015/1682
Sch.1 para.3
Sch.3 para.10, amended: SI 2015/1682
Sch.1 para.3
Sch.3 para.11, amended: SI 2015/1682
Sch.1 para.3
Sch.3 para.15, amended: SI 2015/1682
Sch.1 para.3
Sch.4 para.11, amended: SI 2015/1682
Sch.1 para.3
Sch.5 Part 6 para.16, amended: SI
2015/1682 Sch.1 para.3
Sch.10 Part 5 para.34, amended: SI
2015/1682 Sch.1 para.3
**15. Serious Organised Crime and Police Act
2005**
s.76, repealed: 2015 c.9 s.50
s.77, repealed: 2015 c.9 s.50
s.78, repealed: 2015 c.9 s.50
s.79, repealed: 2015 c.9 Sch.4 para.71
s.97, amended: 2015 c.9 s.40
s.154, repealed: 2015 c.20 Sch.11 para.1
s.172, amended: 2015 c.9 s.40
s.175, amended: 2015 c.9 Sch.4 para.72
s.178, enabling: SI 2015/188
s.179, amended: 2015 c.9 Sch.4 para.73
s.179, repealed: 2015 c.9 Sch.4 para.73
**16. Clean Neighbourhoods and Environment
Act 2005**
s.108, enabling: SI 2015/425
18. Education Act 2005
s.5, enabling: SI 2015/170, SI 2015/1639
s.11C, repealed: 2015 c.20 Sch.16 para.6
s.14, amended: 2015 c.20 Sch.16 para.6
s.14A, repealed: 2015 c.20 Sch.16 para.6
s.19, enabling: SI 2015/205
s.49, amended: 2015 c.20 Sch.16 para.6
s.92, amended: 2015 c.20 Sch.14 para.48
s.102, repealed: 2015 c.20 s.66
s.108, repealed: 2015 c.20 Sch.14 para.49
s.120, enabling: SI 2015/170, SI
2015/1639
s.122, repealed: 2015 c.20 s.66

19. Gambling Act 2005

see *Aspinalls Club Ltd v Revenue and
Customs Commissioners* [2013] EWCA
Civ 1464, [2015] Ch. 79 (CA (Civ Div)),
Moses LJ; see *Gibraltar Betting &
Gaming Association Ltd v Secretary of
State for Culture, Media and Sport*
[2014] EWHC 3236 (Admin), [2015] 1
C.M.L.R. 28 (QBD (Admin)), Green J;
see *Ivey v Genting Casinos UK Ltd (t/a
Crockfords Club)* [2014] EWHC 3394
(QB), [2015] L.L.R. 98 (QBD), Mitting
J; see *Ritz Hotel Casino Ltd v Daher*
[2014] EWHC 2847 (QB), [2015] 4 All
E.R. 222 (QBD), Judge Seys-Llewellyn
QC

Pt 17., see *Ivey v Genting Casinos UK
Ltd (t/a Crockfords Club)* [2014] EWHC
3394 (QB), [2015] L.L.R. 98 (QBD),
Mitting J

s.33, see *Ritz Hotel Casino Ltd v
Geabury* [2015] EWHC 2294 (QB),
[2015] L.L.R. 860 (QBD), Simler J

s.42, see *Ivey v Genting Casinos UK Ltd
(t/a Crockfords Club)* [2014] EWHC
3394 (QB), [2015] L.L.R. 98 (QBD),
Mitting J

s.81, see *Ritz Hotel Casino Ltd v Daher*
[2014] EWHC 2847 (QB), [2015] 4 All
E.R. 222 (QBD), Judge Seys-Llewellyn
QC

s.240, enabling: SI 2015/121

s.355, enabling: SI 2015/121

22. Finance (No.2) Act 2005

s.7, amended: SI 2015/1810 Art.13

s.17, enabling: SI 2015/485

s.18, enabling: SI 2015/485

2006

3. Equality Act 2006

see *Secretary of State for Work and
Pensions v Robertson* [2015] CSIH 82
(IH (Ex Div)), Lady Smith

11. Terrorism Act 2006

see *Guardian News and Media Ltd v
Incedal* [2014] EWCA Crim 1861,
[2015] 1 Cr. App. R. 4 (CA (Crim Div)),
Gross LJ

s.6, amended: 2015 c.2 s.1

s.17, amended: 2015 c.9 s.81, Sch.4
para.74

s.36, amended: 2015 c.6 s.45

**13. Immigration, Asylum and Nationality
Act 2006**

s.32, amended: 2015 c.6 Sch.5 para.6

s.32, enabling: SI 2015/859

s.32A, added: 2015 c.6 Sch.5 para.7

s.32B, enabling: SI 2015/961

s.34, amended: 2015 c.6 Sch.5 para.8

s.47, see *Olatunde v Secretary of State
for the Home Department* [2015] EWCA
Civ 670, [2015] 1 W.L.R. 4602 (CA (Civ
Div)), Moore-Bick LJ

s.63, enabling: SI 2015/1532, SI
2015/1533, SI 2015/1765

14. Consumer Credit Act 2006

s.51, repealed: 2015 c.15 Sch.6 para.85

15. Identity Cards Act 2006

see *Zenati v Commissioner of Police of
the Metropolis* [2015] EWCA Civ 80,
[2015] Q.B. 758 (CA (Civ Div)), Lord
Dyson MR

s.25, see *Adebayo v Harvie* [2015]
HCJAC 79, 2015 S.C.L. 855 (HCJ), Lady
Paton

**16. Natural Environment and Rural
Communities Act 2006**

s.67, see *R. (on the application of Trail
Riders' Fellowship) v Dorset CC* [2015]
UKSC 18, [2015] 1 W.L.R. 1406 (SC),
Lord Neuberger PSC

Sch.11 Part 1 para.99, repealed: 2015
c.20 Sch.22 para.7

Sch.11 Part 1 para.144, repealed: 2015
c.20 Sch.22 para.11

Sch.11 Part 1 para.164, repealed: 2015
c.20 Sch.22 para.15

**19. Climate Change and Sustainable Energy
Act 2006**

s.3, repealed: 2015 c.20 s.57

s.4, repealed: 2015 c.20 s.57

s.7, repealed: 2015 c.20 s.57

s.8, repealed: 2015 c.20 s.57

s.10, repealed: 2015 c.20 s.57

s.12, repealed: 2015 c.20 s.57

s.14, repealed: 2015 c.20 s.57

s.21, repealed: 2015 c.20 s.57

21. Childcare Act 2006

s.12, enabling: SI 2015/1562

s.13A, amended: 2015 c.26 s.74

s.13B, amended: 2015 c.26 s.74
s.18, amended: 2015 c.2 Sch.9 para.21
s.22, see *R. (on the application of Morris)
v Rhondda Cynon Taf CBC* [2015]
EWHC 1403 (Admin), [2015] E.L.R. 559
(QBD (Admin)), Patterson J
s.34, amended: 2015 c.26 s.75, s.76,
Sch.2 para.2
s.35, enabling: SI 2015/1562
s.36, amended: 2015 c.26 Sch.2 para.3
s.36, enabling: SI 2015/1562
s.37, amended: 2015 c.26 Sch.2 para.4
s.37, enabling: SI 2015/1562
s.37A, amended: 2015 c.26 Sch.2 para.5
s.39, enabling: SI 2015/1562
s.40, amended: 2015 c.26 s.75
s.43, enabling: SI 2015/1562
s.44, enabling: SI 2015/1562
s.53, amended: 2015 c.26 s.76, Sch.2
para.6
s.54, enabling: SI 2015/1562
s.55, amended: 2015 c.26 Sch.2 para.7
s.55, enabling: SI 2015/1562
s.56, amended: 2015 c.26 Sch.2 para.8
s.56, enabling: SI 2015/1562
s.56A, amended: 2015 c.26 Sch.2 para.9
s.57, amended: 2015 c.26 Sch.2 para.10
s.57A, amended: 2015 c.26 Sch.2 para.11
s.59, enabling: SI 2015/1562
s.62, enabling: SI 2015/1562
s.63, amended: 2015 c.26 s.75, Sch.2
para.12
s.63, enabling: SI 2015/1562
s.64, amended: 2015 c.26 Sch.2 para.13
s.64, enabling: SI 2015/1562
s.65, amended: 2015 c.26 Sch.2 para.14
s.65A, amended: 2015 c.26 Sch.2 para.15
s.67, enabling: SI 2015/1562
s.69, amended: 2015 c.26 Sch.2 para.16
s.69, enabling: SI 2015/1562
s.74, enabling: SI 2015/1562
s.83, enabling: SI 2015/1562
s.83A, enabling: SI 2015/1562
s.84, enabling: SI 2015/357
s.85A, added: 2015 c.26 Sch.2 para.17
s.85A, enabling: SI 2015/1562
s.89, enabling: SI 2015/1562
s.94, repealed: 2015 c.26 Sch.2 para.18
s.96, amended: 2015 c.26 s.76
s.99, amended: 2015 c.26 s.75
s.99, enabling: SI 2015/1696

s.104, enabling: SI 2015/357, SI
2015/1562, SI 2015/1696
s.105, repealed: 2015 c.26 Sch.2 para.19

22. Electoral Administration Act 2006
s.62, amended: 2015 c.25 s.17
s.74A, substituted: SI 2015/1376 Sch.2
para.12

25. Finance Act 2006
see *Kennedy v Kennedy* [2014] EWHC
4129 (Ch), [2015] B.T.C. 2 (Ch D), Sir
Terence Etherton C
s.162, repealed: 2015 c.1 Sch.1 para.21
s.173, enabling: SI 2015/801, SI
2015/804, SI 2015/1887, SI 2015/1888,
SI 2015/1889, SI 2015/1890, SI
2015/1891, SI 2015/1892, SI 2015/2007,
SI 2015/2008, SI 2015/2009, SI
2015/2011

26. Commons Act 2006
see *R. (on the application of Littlejohns)
v Devon CC* [2015] EWHC 730 (Admin),
[2015] Q.B. 869 (QBD (Admin)), Lang J
s.6, see *R. (on the application of
Littlejohns) v Devon CC* [2015] EWHC
730 (Admin), [2015] Q.B. 869 (QBD
(Admin)), Lang J
s.15, see *Naylor v Essex CC* [2014]
EWHC 2560 (Admin), [2015] J.P.L. 217
(QBD (Admin)), John Howell QC; see
*R. (on the application of Barkas) v North
Yorkshire CC* [2015] A.C. 195 (SC),
Lord Neuberger PSC; see *R. (on the
application of Newhaven Port and
Properties Ltd) v East Sussex CC* [2015]
UKSC 7, [2015] A.C. 1547 (SC), Lord
Neuberger PSC
s.26, enabling: SI 2015/1515
s.29, enabling: SI 2015/1515
s.30, enabling: SI 2015/1515
s.31, enabling: SI 2015/1515
s.35, enabling: SI 2015/1515
s.36, enabling: SI 2015/1515
Sch.3 para.2, see *R. (on the application of
Littlejohns) v Devon CC* [2015] EWHC
730 (Admin), [2015] Q.B. 869 (QBD
(Admin)), Lang J
Sch.3 para.3, see *R. (on the application of
Littlejohns) v Devon CC* [2015] EWHC
730 (Admin), [2015] Q.B. 869 (QBD
(Admin)), Lang J

28. Health Act 2006
  see *R. (on the application of Black) v
  Secretary of State for Justice* [2015]
  EWHC 528 (Admin), [2015] 1 W.L.R.
  3963 (QBD (Admin)), Singh J
  Pt 1., see *R. (on the application of Black)
  v Secretary of State for Justice* [2015]
  EWHC 528 (Admin), [2015] 1 W.L.R.
  3963 (QBD (Admin)), Singh J
  s.3, see *R. (on the application of Black) v
  Secretary of State for Justice* [2015]
  EWHC 528 (Admin), [2015] 1 W.L.R.
  3963 (QBD (Admin)), Singh J
  s.5, enabling: SI 2015/286, SI 2015/1363
  s.6, enabling: SI 2015/286
  s.8, enabling: SI 2015/939, SI 2015/1363
  s.9, enabling: SI 2015/286, SI 2015/1363
  s.10, enabling: SI 2015/286, SI
  2015/1363
  s.23, see *R. (on the application of Black)
  v Secretary of State for Justice* [2015]
  EWHC 528 (Admin), [2015] 1 W.L.R.
  3963 (QBD (Admin)), Singh J
  Sch.1 para.4, enabling: SI 2015/936, SI
  2015/939, SI 2015/1363, SI 2015/1663
  Sch.1 para.5, enabling: SI 2015/286, SI
  2015/896
  Sch.1 para.8, enabling: SI 2015/896

29. Compensation Act 2006
  see *International Energy Group Ltd v
  Zurich Insurance Plc UK* [2015] UKSC
  33, [2015] 2 W.L.R. 1471 (SC), Lord
  Neuberger PSC
  s.2, see *International Energy Group Ltd v
  Zurich Insurance Plc UK* [2015] UKSC
  33, [2015] 2 W.L.R. 1471 (SC), Lord
  Neuberger PSC
  s.3, see *International Energy Group Ltd v
  Zurich Insurance Plc UK* [2015] UKSC
  33, [2015] 2 W.L.R. 1471 (SC), Lord
  Neuberger PSC
  s.9, enabling: SI 2015/42
  s.15, enabling: SI 2015/42
  Sch.1, enabling: SI 2015/42

**31. International Development (Reporting
and Transparency) Act 2006**
  s.3, repealed: 2015 c.12 s.4

32. Government of Wales Act 2006
  s.16, enabling: SI 2015/1536
  s.59, enabling: SI 2015/814, SI
  2015/1530

  s.108, see *Recovery of Medical Costs for
  Asbestos Diseases (Wales) Bill, Re*
  [2015] UKSC 3, [2015] A.C. 1016 (SC),
  Lord Neuberger PSC
  s.109, enabling: SI 2015/204
  s.120, enabling: SI 2015/640
  s.147, amended: SI 2015/1897 Sch.1
  para.4
  s.148, amended: SI 2015/1897 Sch.1
  para.4
  s.150, enabling: SI 2015/865, SI
  2015/1353
  s.157, enabling: SI 2015/865
  Sch.7 Pt 1 para.9, see *Recovery of
  Medical Costs for Asbestos Diseases
  (Wales) Bill, Re* [2015] UKSC 3, [2015]
  A.C. 1016 (SC), Lord Neuberger PSC
  Sch.7 Part 2 para.5, amended: SI
  2015/204 Art.2

35. Fraud Act 2006
  see *Serious Fraud Office v Evans* [2014]
  EWHC 3803 (QB), [2015] 1 W.L.R.
  3526 (QBD), Fulford LJ
  s.2, see *R. v Smith (Raymond)* [2014]
  EWCA Crim 2707, [2015] 1 Cr. App. R.
  (S.) 43 (CA (Crim Div)), Pitchford LJ

36. Wireless Telegraphy Act 2006
  s.8, enabling: SI 2015/591, SI 2015/2066
  s.12, enabling: SI 2015/1334, SI
  2015/1709, SI 2015/1995
  s.13, enabling: SI 2015/1334, SI
  2015/1709, SI 2015/1995
  s.18, enabling: SI 2015/1397
  s.21, enabling: SI 2015/1399
  s.22, enabling: SI 2015/1399
  s.29, enabling: SI 2015/999, SI
  2015/1398
  s.30, enabling: SI 2015/1338, SI
  2015/1339, SI 2015/1401
  s.31, enabling: SI 2015/1400, SI
  2015/1401
  s.122, enabling: SI 2015/1334, SI
  2015/1338, SI 2015/1339, SI 2015/1397,
  SI 2015/1400, SI 2015/1401, SI
  2015/1709, SI 2015/1995
  Sch.2 para.1, enabling: SI 2015/1397
  Sch.4 para.2, amended: SI 2015/664
  Sch.5 para.11
  Sch.4 para.10, amended: 2015 c.20 s.80
  Sch.4 para.10, repealed: 2015 c.20 s.80

38. Violent Crime Reduction Act 2006
    s.27, see *DPP v Bulmer* [2015] EWHC
    2323 (Admin), [2015] 1 W.L.R. 5159
    (DC), Beatson LJ
    s.32, repealed: 2015 asp 10 Sch.2 para.3
40. Education and Inspections Act 2006
    s.15, enabling: SI 2015/1748
    s.88, amended: 2015 c.20 Sch.16 para.1
    s.88, repealed: 2015 c.20 Sch.16 para.1
    s.89, amended: 2015 c.20 Sch.16 para.1
    s.89, repealed: 2015 c.20 Sch.16 para.1
    s.114, enabling: SI 2015/224, SI
    2015/1377, SI 2015/1525, SI 2015/1762,
    SI 2015/1895, SI 2015/2010
    s.123, amended: 2015 c.20 Sch.14
    para.51
    s.124, repealed: 2015 c.20 Sch.14 para.52
    s.125, repealed: 2015 c.20 Sch.14 para.53
    s.126, repealed: 2015 c.20 Sch.14 para.54
    s.128, repealed: 2015 c.20 Sch.14 para.55
    s.129, repealed: 2015 c.20 Sch.14 para.56
    s.130, amended: 2015 c.20 Sch.14
    para.57
    s.130, repealed: 2015 c.20 Sch.14 para.57
    s.146, amended: 2015 c.2 Sch.9 para.22
    s.146, repealed: 2015 c.2 Sch.9 para.22
    s.155, enabling: SI 2015/551
    s.159, amended: 2015 c.20 Sch.14
    para.58
    s.166, enabling: SI 2015/883
    s.181, enabling: SI 2015/551, SI
    2015/883
    Sch.6 para.19, enabling: SI 2015/883
41. National Health Service Act 2006
    see *Warner-Lambert Co LLC v Actavis*
    Group PTC EHF [2015] EWHC 485
    (Pat), [2015] R.P.C. 24 (Ch D (Patents
    Ct)), Arnold J
    s.3, see *R. (on the application of*
    Whapples) v Birmingham CrossCity
    Clinical Commissioning Group [2015]
    EWCA Civ 435, [2015] P.T.S.R. 1398
    (CA (Civ Div)), Underhill LJ
    s.3B, enabling: SI 2015/415
    s.6C, enabling: SI 2015/921
    s.6E, enabling: SI 2015/415, SI
    2015/1430
    s.7, enabling: SI 2015/127, SI 2015/1728
    s.8, enabling: SI 2015/839
    s.9, enabling: SI 2015/1862
    s.25, enabling: SI 2015/1621

    s.27, enabling: SI 2015/650
    s.28, enabling: SI 2015/839, SI 2015/864,
    SI 2015/1683
    s.51, enabling: SI 2015/678
    s.56A, amended: 2015 c.20 s.96
    s.56AA, added: 2015 c.20 s.96
    s.57, amended: 2015 c.20 s.96
    s.64, amended: 2015 c.20 s.96
    s.64, enabling: SI 2015/678
    s.65LA, amended: 2015 c.20 s.96
    s.71, enabling: SI 2015/559
    s.75, enabling: SI 2015/1940
    s.83, enabling: SI 2015/1862
    s.85, enabling: SI 2015/196, SI 2015/915,
    SI 2015/1862
    s.86, enabling: SI 2015/1862
    s.89, enabling: SI 2015/196, SI 2015/915,
    SI 2015/1862
    s.90, enabling: SI 2015/196, SI
    2015/1862
    s.91, enabling: SI 2015/362, SI
    2015/1862
    s.93, enabling: SI 2015/1879
    s.94, enabling: SI 2015/196, SI 2015/915,
    SI 2015/1879
    s.97, enabling: SI 2015/1862
    s.104, enabling: SI 2015/416, SI
    2015/1728
    s.106, enabling: SI 2015/362
    s.109, enabling: SI 2015/416, SI
    2015/1728
    s.115, enabling: SI 2015/417, SI
    2015/1776
    s.116, enabling: SI 2015/417
    s.121, enabling: SI 2015/416
    s.123, enabling: SI 2015/362
    s.126, enabling: SI 2015/58, SI 2015/915
    s.129, enabling: SI 2015/58, SI 2015/915
    s.130, enabling: SI 2015/58
    s.132, enabling: SI 2015/58, SI 2015/915
    s.139, enabling: SI 2015/58
    s.145, enabling: SI 2015/58
    s.172, enabling: SI 2015/570
    s.174, enabling: SI 2015/570
    s.175, enabling: SI 2015/238, SI
    2015/2025
    s.176, enabling: SI 2015/417, SI
    2015/1728, SI 2015/1776
    s.178, enabling: SI 2015/570
    s.179, enabling: SI 2015/417

s.180, enabling: SI 2015/417, SI 2015/1776

s.181, enabling: SI 2015/1776

s.182, enabling: SI 2015/417, SI 2015/570, SI 2015/1776

s.183, enabling: SI 2015/1776

s.184, enabling: SI 2015/417, SI 2015/570, SI 2015/1776

s.187, enabling: SI 2015/839, SI 2015/1862

s.254, amended: SI 2015/914 Sch.1 para.82

s.254, repealed: SI 2015/914 Sch.1 para.82

s.261, enabling: SI 2015/233

s.262, enabling: SI 2015/233

s.263, enabling: SI 2015/233

s.264, enabling: SI 2015/233

s.265, enabling: SI 2015/233

s.266, enabling: SI 2015/233

s.272, enabling: SI 2015/58, SI 2015/196, SI 2015/233, SI 2015/238, SI 2015/362, SI 2015/415, SI 2015/416, SI 2015/417, SI 2015/559, SI 2015/570, SI 2015/650, SI 2015/839, SI 2015/864, SI 2015/915, SI 2015/921, SI 2015/1430, SI 2015/1559, SI 2015/1621, SI 2015/1683, SI 2015/1728, SI 2015/1776, SI 2015/1862, SI 2015/1879, SI 2015/1940, SI 2015/2025

s.273, enabling: SI 2015/127, SI 2015/678, SI 2015/839, SI 2015/864, SI 2015/1621, SI 2015/1728

s.275, enabling: SI 2015/921

s.278, enabling: SI 2015/864

Sch.1A Part 2 para.17, varied: SI 2015/192 Sch.1 para.18

Sch.4 Part 2 para.22, enabling: SI 2015/864

Sch.4 Part 3 para.28, enabling: SI 2015/1621

Sch.4 Part 3 para.31, amended: 2015 c.20 s.96

Sch.5 para.1, enabling: SI 2015/650

Sch.6 para.3, enabling: SI 2015/839

Sch.6 para.5, enabling: SI 2015/839, SI 2015/1559, SI 2015/1683

Sch.6 para.6, enabling: SI 2015/839

Sch.12 para.2, enabling: SI 2015/58

Sch.12 para.3, enabling: SI 2015/58, SI 2015/915

Sch.15 para.4, varied: SI 2015/192 Sch.1 para.19

Sch.20, repealed: SI 2015/914 Sch.1 para.83

42. National Health Service (Wales) Act 2006

s.3, see *R. (on the application of Forge Care Homes Ltd) v Cardiff and Vale University Health Board* [2015] EWHC 601 (Admin), [2015] P.T.S.R. 945 (QBD (Admin)), Hickinbottom J

s.12, enabling: SI 2015/509

s.19, enabling: SI 2015/509

s.71, enabling: SI 2015/631, SI 2015/1600

s.76, enabling: SI 2015/1600

s.125, enabling: SI 2015/512

s.128, enabling: SI 2015/603, SI 2015/631, SI 2015/1600

s.129, enabling: SI 2015/603, SI 2015/631, SI 2015/1600

s.130, enabling: SI 2015/603, SI 2015/631

s.131, enabling: SI 2015/631

s.182, enabling: SI 2015/507

s.187, enabling: SI 2015/509

s.203, enabling: SI 2015/507, SI 2015/509, SI 2015/512, SI 2015/603, SI 2015/631, SI 2015/1600

Sch.2 Part 1 para.7, enabling: SI 2015/509

Sch.3 Part 2 para.25, enabling: SI 2015/509

Sch.10, enabling: SI 2015/507

Sch.10 para.2, enabling: SI 2015/509

Sch.10 para.2A, enabling: SI 2015/509

Sch.10 para.3, enabling: SI 2015/509

Sch.10 para.4, enabling: SI 2015/509

Sch.15 para.2A, added: SI 2015/914

Sch.1 para.84

43. National Health Service (Consequential Provisions) Act 2006

s.4, enabling: SI 2015/1683

Sch.2 Part 2 para.8, enabling: SI 2015/1683

45. Animal Welfare Act 2006

see *Letherbarrow v Warwickshire CC* [2014] EWHC 4820 (Admin), (2015) 179 J.P. 307 (DC), Bean LJ

s.12, enabling: SI 2015/108, SI 2015/1990

s.31, see *Letherbarrow v Warwickshire CC* [2014] EWHC 4820 (Admin), (2015) 179 J.P. 307 (DC), Bean LJ

s.32, amended: SI 2015/664 Sch.4 para.38

s.49, amended: SSI 2015/338 Sch.2 para.11

46. Companies Act 2006

see *Sebry v Companies House* [2015] EWHC 115 (QB), [2015] 4 All E.R. 681 (QBD), Edis J

Part 8 c.2A, added: 2015 c.26 Sch.5 para.3

Part 12, substituted: 2015 c.26 Sch.5 para.10

Part 21A, added: 2015 c.26 Sch.3 para.1

Part 24, substituted: 2015 c.26 s.92

Pt 26., see *Apcoa Parking Holdings GmbH, Re* [2014] EWHC 3849 (Ch), [2015] 4 All E.R. 572 (Ch D (Companies Ct)), Hildyard J; see *Welcome Financial Service Ltd, Re* [2015] EWHC 815 (Ch), [2015] 2 All E.R. (Comm) 992 (Ch D (Companies Ct)), Rose J

s.9, amended: 2015 c.26 s.93, Sch.3 para.4

s.10, amended: 2015 c.26 Sch.6 para.2

s.10, repealed: 2015 c.26 Sch.6 para.2

s.12, amended: 2015 c.26 s.100, Sch.5 para.12

s.12A, added: 2015 c.26 Sch.3 para.5

s.32, amended: 2015 c.26 Sch.6 para.3

s.32, repealed: 2015 c.26 Sch.6 para.3

s.39, see *Abdelmamoud v Egyptian Association in Great Britain Ltd* [2015] EWHC 1013 (Ch), [2015] Bus. L.R. 928 (Ch D), Edward Murray

s.40, see *Credit Suisse International v Stichting Vestia Groep* [2014] EWHC 3103 (Comm), [2015] Bus. L.R. D5 (QBD (Comm)), Andrew Smith J

s.42, see *Abdelmamoud v Egyptian Association in Great Britain Ltd* [2015] EWHC 1013 (Ch), [2015] Bus. L.R. 928 (Ch D), Edward Murray

s.44, see *Elim Court RTM Co Ltd v Avon Freeholds Ltd* [2015] L. & T.R. 3 (UT (Lands)), Martin Rodger QC

s.54, enabling: SI 2015/17

s.56, enabling: SI 2015/17

s.57, enabling: SI 2015/17

s.60, enabling: SI 2015/17

s.63, amended: SI 2015/664 Sch.3 para.9

s.64, amended: SI 2015/664 Sch.3 para.9

s.65, enabling: SI 2015/17

s.66, enabling: SI 2015/17

s.82, enabling: SI 2015/17

s.84, enabling: SI 2015/17

s.94, amended: 2015 c.26 s.98

s.95, amended: 2015 c.26 s.100

s.108, amended: 2015 c.26 s.93, Sch.6 para.4

s.108, repealed: 2015 c.26 Sch.6 para.4

s.112, amended: 2015 c.26 Sch.5 para.13

s.112A, added: 2015 c.26 Sch.5 para.2

s.116, see *Burberry Group Plc v Fox-Davies* [2015] EWHC 222 (Ch), [2015] 2 B.C.L.C. 66 (Ch D (Companies Ct)), Registrar Briggs

s.117, see *Burberry Group Plc v Fox-Davies* [2015] EWHC 222 (Ch), [2015] 2 B.C.L.C. 66 (Ch D (Companies Ct)), Registrar Briggs

s.120, amended: 2015 c.26 Sch.3 para.6

s.122, amended: 2015 c.26 Sch.4 para.23

s.122, repealed: 2015 c.26 Sch.4 para.23

s.127, amended: 2015 c.26 Sch.5 para.14

s.129, amended: 2015 c.26 Sch.5 para.4

s.155, repealed: 2015 c.26 s.87

s.156, amended: 2015 c.26 s.87, SI 2015/664 Sch.3 para.9

s.156A, added: 2015 c.26 s.87

s.161, see *Abdelmamoud v Egyptian Association in Great Britain Ltd* [2015] EWHC 1013 (Ch), [2015] Bus. L.R. 928 (Ch D), Edward Murray

s.161A, added: 2015 c.26 Sch.5 para.6

s.162, amended: SI 2015/664 Sch.3 para.9

s.165, amended: SI 2015/664 Sch.3 para.9

s.167, amended: 2015 c.26 s.100, SI 2015/664 Sch.3 para.9

s.167A, added: 2015 c.26 Sch.5 para.7

s.170, amended: 2015 c.26 s.89

s.172, see *Cullen Investments Ltd v Brown* [2015] EWHC 473 (Ch), [2015] B.C.C. 539 (Ch D), Mark Anderson QC; see *Weatherford Global Products Ltd v Hydropath Holdings Ltd* [2014] EWHC 2725 (TCC), [2015] B.L.R. 69 (QBD (TCC)), Akenhead J

s.175, see *Goldtrail Travel Ltd (In Liquidation) v Aydin* [2014] EWHC 1587 (Ch), [2015] 1 B.C.L.C. 89 (Ch D), Rose J; see *Weatherford Global Products Ltd v Hydropath Holdings Ltd* [2014] EWHC 2725 (TCC), [2015] B.L.R. 69 (QBD (TCC)), Akenhead J

s.190, see *Smithton Ltd (formerly Hobart Capital Markets Ltd) v Naggar* [2014] EWCA Civ 939, [2015] 1 W.L.R. 189 (CA (Civ Div)), Arden LJ

s.243, enabling: SI 2015/842, SI 2015/1694

s.246, amended: 2015 c.26 Sch.5 para.15, SI 2015/664 Sch.3 para.9

s.251, amended: 2015 c.26 s.90

s.261, see *Cullen Investments Ltd v Brown* [2015] EWHC 473 (Ch), [2015] B.C.C. 539 (Ch D), Mark Anderson QC

s.263, see *Cullen Investments Ltd v Brown* [2015] EWHC 473 (Ch), [2015] B.C.C. 539 (Ch D), Mark Anderson QC

s.272, amended: SI 2015/664 Sch.3 para.9

s.274A, added: 2015 c.26 Sch.5 para.9

s.275, amended: SI 2015/664 Sch.3 para.9

s.276, amended: 2015 c.26 s.100, SI 2015/664 Sch.3 para.9

s.284, see *Sugarman v CJS Investments LLP* [2014] EWCA Civ 1239, [2015] 1 B.C.L.C. 1 (CA (Civ Div)), Briggs LJ

s.286, amended: 2015 c.26 Sch.5 para.16

s.311, amended: 2015 c.26 Sch.5 para.17

s.327, repealed: 2015 c.20 Sch.6 para.29

s.330, repealed: 2015 c.20 Sch.6 para.30

s.360B, amended: 2015 c.26 Sch.5 para.18

s.380, repealed: SI 2015/980 Reg.4

s.382, amended: SI 2015/980 Reg.4

s.383, amended: SI 2015/980 Reg.4

s.384, amended: SI 2015/980 Reg.4

s.386, see *Artistic Investment Advisers Ltd, Re* [2014] EWHC 2963 (Ch), [2015] 1 B.C.L.C. 619 (Ch D), John Male QC

s.394A, amended: SI 2015/980 Reg.5

s.394B, amended: SI 2015/980 Reg.5

s.396, amended: SI 2015/980 Reg.5

s.396, enabling: SI 2015/980, SI 2015/1672

s.397, substituted: SI 2015/980 Reg.5

s.399, amended: SI 2015/980 Reg.5

s.400, amended: SI 2015/980 Reg.5

s.400, repealed: SI 2015/980 Reg.5

s.401, amended: SI 2015/980 Reg.5

s.401, repealed: SI 2015/980 Reg.5

s.404, amended: SI 2015/980 Reg.5

s.404, enabling: SI 2015/980

s.405, amended: SI 2015/980 Reg.5

s.406, substituted: SI 2015/980 Reg.5

s.408, amended: SI 2015/980 Reg.5

s.408, repealed: SI 2015/980 Reg.5

s.409, enabling: SI 2015/980

s.410, repealed: SI 2015/980 Reg.5

s.410A, amended: SI 2015/980 Reg.5

s.411, amended: SI 2015/980 Reg.5

s.412, enabling: SI 2015/980

s.413, amended: SI 2015/980 Reg.5

s.414B, amended: SI 2015/980 Reg.6

s.415, amended: SI 2015/980 Reg.7

s.418, see *Serious Fraud Office v Evans* [2014] EWHC 3803 (QB), [2015] 1 W.L.R. 3526 (QBD), Fulford LJ

s.438, amended: SI 2015/664 Sch.3 para.9

s.442, amended: SI 2015/980 Reg.8

s.444, amended: SI 2015/980 Reg.8

s.444, repealed: SI 2015/980 Reg.8

s.445, repealed: SI 2015/980 Reg.8

s.448A, amended: SI 2015/980 Reg.8

s.448B, amended: SI 2015/980 Reg.8

s.449, repealed: SI 2015/980 Reg.8

s.450, repealed: SI 2015/980 Reg.8

s.451, amended: SI 2015/664 Sch.3 para.9

s.464, enabling: SI 2015/1675

s.465, amended: SI 2015/980 Reg.9

s.466, amended: SI 2015/980 Reg.9

s.467, amended: SI 2015/980 Reg.9

s.468, enabling: SI 2015/980

s.472, amended: SI 2015/980 Reg.9

s.472, repealed: SI 2015/980 Reg.9

s.473, enabling: SI 2015/980, SI 2015/1672

s.474, amended: SI 2015/980 Reg.9

s.479A, amended: SI 2015/980 Reg.10

s.479B, amended: SI 2015/980 Reg.10

s.481, amended: SI 2015/980 Reg.10

s.484, enabling: SI 2015/980

s.496, substituted: SI 2015/980 Reg.11

s.497A, substituted: SI 2015/980 Reg.11

s.512, repealed: 2015 c.20 Sch.5 para.2

s.514, amended: 2015 c.20 Sch.5 para.14
s.515, amended: 2015 c.20 Sch.5 para.15
s.516, amended: 2015 c.20 Sch.5 para.3,
Sch.5 para.16
s.517, amended: SI 2015/664 Sch.3
para.9
s.517, repealed: 2015 c.20 Sch.5 para.4
s.518, amended: 2015 c.20 Sch.5 para.5,
Sch.5 para.17
s.519, amended: 2015 c.20 s.18, Sch.5
para.6, Sch.5 para.18
s.519A, added: 2015 c.20 s.18
s.520, amended: 2015 c.20 Sch.5 para.7,
Sch.5 para.19
s.521, amended: 2015 c.20 Sch.5 para.8,
Sch.5 para.20
s.522, amended: 2015 c.20 Sch.5 para.9
s.523, amended: 2015 c.20 s.18
s.524, amended: 2015 c.20 Sch.5 para.10
s.524, repealed: 2015 c.20 Sch.5 para.10
s.525, amended: 2015 c.20 Sch.5 para.11
s.525, repealed: 2015 c.20 Sch.5 para.11
s.554, amended: 2015 c.26 Sch.5 para.19
s.555, amended: 2015 c.26 Sch.6 para.5
s.555, repealed: 2015 c.26 Sch.6 para.5
s.557, amended: SI 2015/664 Sch.3
para.9
s.558, amended: 2015 c.26 Sch.5 para.20
s.588, amended: 2015 c.26 Sch.5 para.21
s.597, amended: SI 2015/664 Sch.3
para.9
s.605, amended: 2015 c.26 Sch.5 para.22
s.616, amended: 2015 c.26 Sch.5 para.23
s.617, amended: 2015 c.26 Sch.4 para.24
s.619, amended: 2015 c.26 Sch.6 para.6
s.619, repealed: 2015 c.26 Sch.6 para.6
s.621, amended: 2015 c.26 Sch.6 para.7
s.621, repealed: 2015 c.26 Sch.6 para.7
s.625, amended: 2015 c.26 Sch.6 para.8
s.625, repealed: 2015 c.26 Sch.6 para.8
s.627, amended: 2015 c.26 Sch.6 para.9
s.627, repealed: 2015 c.26 Sch.6 para.9
s.641, amended: SI 2015/472 Reg.3
s.644, amended: 2015 c.26 Sch.6 para.10
s.644, repealed: 2015 c.26 Sch.6 para.10
s.649, amended: 2015 c.26 Sch.6 para.11
s.649, repealed: 2015 c.26 Sch.6 para.11
s.652, amended: 2015 c.26 Sch.4 para.25
s.655, amended: 2015 c.26 Sch.5 para.24
s.657, enabling: SI 2015/472
s.663, amended: 2015 c.26 Sch.6 para.12

s.663, repealed: 2015 c.26 Sch.6 para.12
s.678, see *New World Resources NV, Re*
[2014] EWHC 3143 (Ch), [2015] B.C.C.
47 (Ch D (Companies Ct)), Norris J
s.681, see *New World Resources NV, Re*
[2014] EWHC 3143 (Ch), [2015] B.C.C.
47 (Ch D (Companies Ct)), Norris J
s.689, amended: 2015 c.26 Sch.6 para.13
s.689, repealed: 2015 c.26 Sch.6 para.13
s.692, amended: SI 2015/532 Reg.3
s.707, amended: SI 2015/664 Sch.3
para.9
s.708, amended: 2015 c.26 Sch.6 para.14,
SI 2015/532 Reg.4
s.708, repealed: 2015 c.26 Sch.6 para.14
s.709, amended: SI 2015/532 Reg.5
s.720B, amended: 2015 c.26 Sch.6
para.15
s.720B, repealed: 2015 c.26 Sch.6
para.15
s.723, amended: SI 2015/532 Reg.6
s.723, substituted: SI 2015/532 Reg.6
s.724, amended: 2015 c.26 Sch.5 para.25,
SI 2015/532 Reg.7
s.728, amended: SI 2015/664 Sch.3
para.9
s.730, amended: 2015 c.26 Sch.6 para.16
s.730, repealed: 2015 c.26 Sch.6 para.16
s.733, amended: SI 2015/532 Reg.8
s.734, amended: SI 2015/532 Reg.9
s.737, enabling: SI 2015/532
s.762, amended: 2015 c.26 s.98
s.770, amended: 2015 c.26 Sch.5 para.26
s.771, amended: 2015 c.26 Sch.5 para.27
s.772, amended: 2015 c.26 Sch.5 para.28
s.779, amended: 2015 c.26 s.84
s.779, substituted: 2015 c.26 s.84
s.780, repealed: 2015 c.26 Sch.4 para.26
s.786, amended: 2015 c.26 Sch.5 para.29
s.790A, added: 2015 c.26 Sch.3 para.1
s.790M, amended: 2015 c.26 Sch.3
para.1
s.790N, added: 2015 c.26 Sch.3 para.1
s.790W, added: 2015 c.26 Sch.3 para.1
s.790ZF, added: 2015 c.26 Sch.3 para.1
s.793, see *Eclairs Group Ltd v JKX Oil &*
Gas Plc [2015] UKSC 71, [2015] Bus.
L.R. 1395 (SC), Lord Neuberger PSC
s.794, see *Eclairs Group Ltd v JKX Oil &*
Gas Plc [2015] UKSC 71, [2015] Bus.
L.R. 1395 (SC), Lord Neuberger PSC

s.813, amended: 2015 c.26 s.83
s.843, amended: SI 2015/575 Sch.1
para.25
s.858, amended: SI 2015/664 Sch.3
para.9
s.895, see *Van Gansewinkel Groep BV,
Re* [2015] EWHC 2151 (Ch), [2015] Bus.
L.R. 1046 (Ch D), Snowden J; see
Welcome Financial Service Ltd, Re
[2015] EWHC 815 (Ch), [2015] 2 All
E.R. (Comm) 992 (Ch D (Companies
Ct)), Rose J
s.980, amended: SI 2015/664 Sch.3
para.9
s.984, amended: SI 2015/664 Sch.3
para.9
s.994, see *Charterhouse Capital Ltd, Re*
[2015] EWCA Civ 536, [2015] B.C.C.
574 (CA (Civ Div)), Sir Terence Etherton
C
s.994, repealed: 2015 c.20 Sch.23 para.28
s.996, see *Thomas v Dawson* [2015]
EWCA Civ 706, [2015] B.C.C. 603 (CA
(Civ Div)), Arden LJ
s.1000, amended: 2015 c.26 s.103
s.1001, amended: 2015 c.26 s.103
s.1003, amended: 2015 c.26 s.103
s.1012, see *ELB Securities Ltd v Love*
[2015] CSIH 67, 2015 S.L.T. 721 (IH
(Ex Div)), Lady Paton
s.1014, see *ELB Securities Ltd v Love*
[2015] CSIH 67, 2015 S.L.T. 721 (IH
(Ex Div)), Lady Paton
s.1020, see *ELB Securities Ltd v Love*
[2015] CSIH 67, 2015 S.L.T. 721 (IH
(Ex Div)), Lady Paton
s.1022, see *ELB Securities Ltd v Love*
[2015] CSIH 67, 2015 S.L.T. 721 (IH
(Ex Div)), Lady Paton
s.1028A, added: 2015 c.26 Sch.4 para.27
s.1028A, amended: 2015 c.26 Sch.4
para.27
s.1028A, repealed: 2015 c.26 Sch.4
para.27
s.1031, see *ELB Securities Ltd v Love*
[2015] CSIH 67, 2015 S.L.T. 721 (IH
(Ex Div)), Lady Paton
s.1032, see *Davy v Pickering* [2015]
EWHC 380 (Ch), [2015] 2 B.C.L.C. 116
(Ch D (Cardiff)), Judge Keyser QC; see
ELB Securities Ltd v Love [2015] CSIH

67, 2015 S.L.T. 721 (IH (Ex Div)), Lady
Paton
s.1032A, added: 2015 c.26 Sch.4 para.28
s.1032A, amended: 2015 c.26 Sch.4
para.28
s.1032A, repealed: 2015 c.26 Sch.4
para.28
s.1033, amended: SI 2015/664 Sch.3
para.9
s.1039, repealed: 2015 c.26 Sch.7 para.25
s.1042, enabling: SI 2015/1695
s.1043, enabling: SI 2015/1695
s.1046, see *Teekay Tankers Ltd v STX
Offshore & Shipping Co* [2014] EWHC
3612 (Comm), [2015] 2 All E.R. (Comm)
263 (QBD (Comm)), Hamblen J
s.1054, amended: SI 2015/664 Sch.3
para.17
s.1056, see *Teekay Tankers Ltd v STX
Offshore & Shipping Co* [2014] EWHC
3612 (Comm), [2015] 2 All E.R. (Comm)
263 (QBD (Comm)), Hamblen J
s.1059A, amended: 2015 c.26 s.95
s.1068, amended: 2015 c.26 Sch.3 para.7,
Sch.5 para.30
s.1078, amended: 2015 c.26 s.93, s.98
s.1079B, added: 2015 c.26 s.101
s.1081, amended: 2015 c.26 Sch.5
para.31
s.1084A, added: 2015 c.26 s.95
s.1087, amended: 2015 c.26 s.96, s.99,
Sch.3 para.8
s.1087A, added: 2015 c.26 s.96
s.1087B, enabling: SI 2015/1694
s.1093, amended: SI 2015/664 Sch.3
para.9
s.1094, amended: 2015 c.26 Sch.5
para.32
s.1095, amended: 2015 c.26 s.102
s.1097A, added: 2015 c.26 s.99
s.1102, enabling: SI 2015/1928
s.1126, amended: 2015 c.26 Sch.3 para.9
s.1136, amended: 2015 c.26 Sch.3
para.10, Sch.5 para.33
s.1139, see *Ashley v Tesco Stores Ltd*
[2015] EWCA Civ 414, [2015] 1 W.L.R.
5153 (CA (Civ Div)), Arden LJ; see
*Teekay Tankers Ltd v STX Offshore &
Shipping Co* [2014] EWHC 3612
(Comm), [2015] 2 All E.R. (Comm) 263
(QBD (Comm)), Hamblen J

s.1157, see *Top Brands Ltd v Sharma*
[2014] EWHC 2753 (Ch), [2015] 2 All
E.R. 581 (Ch D (Birmingham)), Judge
Barker QC
s.1169, amended: 2015 c.26 s.93
s.1173, amended: SI 2015/980 Reg.12
s.1175, repealed: 2015 c.20 Sch.23 para.1
s.1193, enabling: SI 2015/17
s.1195, enabling: SI 2015/17
s.1197, enabling: SI 2015/17
s.1213, amended: SI 2015/664 Sch.3
para.9
s.1215, amended: SI 2015/664 Sch.3
para.9
s.1248, amended: SI 2015/664 Sch.3
para.9
s.1292, enabling: SI 2015/17, SI
2015/980, SI 2015/1672, SI 2015/1675,
SI 2015/1694, SI 2015/1695
s.1293, amended: 2015 c.26 s.90
s.1294, enabling: SI 2015/17
s.1296, enabling: SI 2015/17
Sch.1A, added: 2015 c.26 Sch.3 para.2
Sch.2 Part 2 para.18, repealed: 2015 c.20
Sch.6 para.22
Sch.2 Part 2 para.25, amended: 2015 c.15
Sch.4 para.37
Sch.2 Part 2 para.25, repealed: 2015 c.15
Sch.4 para.37
Sch.2 Part 2 para.33, substituted: 2015
c.15 Sch.4 para.37
Sch.5 Part 2 para.4, amended: 2015 c.26
Sch.5 para.34
Sch.5 Part 6 para.16, amended: 2015 c.26
Sch.5 para.34
Sch.8, amended: 2015 c.20 Sch.5
para.12, 2015 c.26 s.93, Sch.3 para.11,
Sch.5 para.35, SI 2015/980 Reg.13
Sch.9 Part 1, repealed: 2015 c.20 Sch.23
para.1
Sch.9 Part 2, repealed: 2015 c.20 Sch.23
para.1
Sch.11A Part 2 para.39, amended: 2015
c.15 Sch.4 para.38
Sch.11A Part 2 para.48, substituted: 2015
c.15 Sch.4 para.38
Sch.11A Part 2 para.64, repealed: 2015
c.20 Sch.6 para.22

47. Safeguarding Vulnerable Groups Act 2006
s.30, amended: SI 2015/914 Sch.1
para.86
Sch.4 Part 2 para.7, amended: SI
2015/914 Sch.1 para.87
49. Road Safety Act 2006
s.60, enabling: SI 2015/583
s.61, enabling: SI 2015/560
Sch.6 para.6, repealed: 2015 c.20 Sch.2
para.33
51. Legislative and Regulatory Reform Act 2006
s.1, enabling: SI 2015/998, SI 2015/1560,
SI 2015/2052
s.24, amended: SI 2015/1682 Sch.1
para.4
52. Armed Forces Act 2006
Part 14A, added: 2015 c.19 s.2
Part 18, amended: 2015 c.19 s.1
s.50, amended: 2015 c.2 Sch.14 para.5
s.51, amended: 2015 c.2 Sch.14 para.6
s.151, enabling: SI 2015/1812, SI
2015/1813
s.160, see *R. v Blackman (Alexander
Wayne)* [2014] EWCA Crim 1029,
[2015] 1 W.L.R. 1900 (CMAC), Lord
Thomas LCJ
s.163, enabling: SI 2015/726, SI
2015/1812
s.163A, added: 2015 c.2 Sch.14 para.2
s.218A, amended: 2015 c.2 s.5
s.224A, added: 2015 c.2 Sch.1 para.8
s.224A, amended: 2015 c.2 Sch.1 para.10
s.224A, repealed: 2015 c.2 Sch.1 para.10
s.288, enabling: SI 2015/726, SI
2015/1812
s.334, repealed: 2015 c.19 s.2
s.340A, enabling: SI 2015/2064
s.340B, enabling: SI 2015/1955
s.340C, enabling: SI 2015/1955
s.340D, enabling: SI 2015/1955
s.340E, enabling: SI 2015/2064
s.340F, enabling: SI 2015/1955
s.340G, enabling: SI 2015/1955
s.340H, enabling: SI 2015/1956
s.340I, enabling: SI 2015/1956
s.340L, enabling: SI 2015/1956
s.340M, enabling: SI 2015/1955, SI
2015/2064
s.340N, enabling: SI 2015/2064

s.365B, added: 2015 c.19 s.1
s.366, repealed: 2015 c.19 s.1
s.373, amended: 2015 c.2 Sch.14 para.7,
2015 c.19 Sch.1 para.10
s.374, amended: 2015 c.19 Sch.1 para.11
s.382, enabling: SI 2015/1766
Sch.2A, added: 2015 c.2 Sch.14 para.3
Sch.2 para.12, amended: 2015 c.9 Sch.4
para.75
Sch.2 para.14, added: 2015 c.2 Sch.14
para.8

2007

3. Income Tax Act 2007

see *Shirley v Revenue and Customs
Commissioners* [2015] S.F.T.D. 247
(FTT (Tax)), Judge Nicholas Aleksander
Part 13 c.5E, added: 2015 c.11 s.21
s.2, amended: 2015 c.11 s.21
s.10, amended: 2015 c.11 s.4
s.26, amended: 2015 c.33 s.24, SI
2015/1810 Art.5
s.30, amended: SI 2015/1810 Art.5
s.31, amended: SI 2015/1810 Art.14
s.34, amended: 2015 c.11 s.5
s.35, amended: 2015 c.11 s.5
s.35, substituted: 2015 c.11 s.5
s.37, amended: 2015 c.11 s.2
s.37, repealed: 2015 c.11 s.5
s.38, amended: 2015 c.11 s.2, SI
2015/914 Sch.1 para.88
s.43, amended: 2015 c.11 s.2
s.45, amended: 2015 c.11 s.2, s.5
s.46, amended: 2015 c.11 s.2, s.5
s.55B, amended: 2015 c.11 s.3, s.5, SI
2015/1810 Art.14
s.55C, amended: 2015 c.11 s.5, SI
2015/1810 Art.14
s.57, amended: 2015 c.11 s.5, 2015 c.33
s.3
s.57A, added: 2015 c.33 s.3
s.58, amended: SI 2015/1810 Art.14
s.128, see *Martin v Revenue and Customs
Commissioners* [2015] S.T.C. 478 (UT
(Tax)), Warren J
s.131, see *Drown v Revenue and Customs
Commissioners* [2015] W.T.L.R. 775
(FTT (Tax)), Judge Barbara Mosedale
s.152, amended: 2015 c.11 s.22

s.152, repealed: 2015 c.11 s.22
s.153, amended: 2015 c.11 s.22
s.154, amended: 2015 c.11 s.22
s.154A, added: 2015 c.11 s.22
s.154A, varied: 2015 c.11 s.22
s.155, amended: 2015 c.11 s.22
s.157, amended: 2015 c.33 Sch.5 para.2
s.162, amended: 2015 c.33 Sch.5 para.3
s.164A, added: 2015 c.33 Sch.5 para.4
s.166, amended: 2015 c.33 Sch.5 para.5
s.172, amended: 2015 c.33 Sch.5 para.6
s.172, repealed: 2015 c.33 Sch.5 para.6
s.173A, amended: 2015 c.33 Sch.5 para.7
s.173AA, added: 2015 c.33 Sch.5 para.8
s.173B, repealed: 2015 c.33 Sch.5 para.9
s.174, amended: 2015 c.33 Sch.5 para.10
s.175, see *East Allenheads Estate Ltd v
Revenue and Customs Commissioners*
[2015] UKFTT 328 (TC), [2015]
S.F.T.D. 908 (FTT (Tax)), Judge Kevin
Poole
s.175, amended: 2015 c.33 Sch.5 para.11
s.175A, added: 2015 c.33 Sch.5 para.12
s.186A, amended: 2015 c.33 Sch.5
para.13
s.192, amended: 2015 c.33 s.27
s.198A, amended: 2015 c.11 Sch.6
para.3, Sch.6 para.4, Sch.6 para.10
s.198A, repealed: 2015 c.11 Sch.6 para.4
, Sch.6 para.10
s.198B, amended: 2015 c.11 Sch.6 para.4
s.198B, repealed: 2015 c.11 Sch.6 para.4
, Sch.6 para.10
s.200, repealed: 2015 c.33 Sch.5 para.14
s.204, see *East Allenheads Estate Ltd v
Revenue and Customs Commissioners*
[2015] UKFTT 328 (TC), [2015]
S.F.T.D. 908 (FTT (Tax)), Judge Kevin
Poole
s.224, amended: 2015 c.33 Sch.5 para.15
s.241, amended: 2015 c.33 Sch.5 para.16
s.247, amended: 2015 c.33 Sch.5 para.17
s.251A, added: 2015 c.33 Sch.5 para.18
s.252A, added: 2015 c.33 Sch.5 para.19
s.257JE, enabling: SI 2015/2051
s.257JF, enabling: SI 2015/2051
s.257MQ, repealed: 2015 c.11 Sch.6
para.13
s.257MS, repealed: 2015 c.11 Sch.6
para.13
s.257MW, added: 2015 c.11 Sch.6 para.1

s.261, amended: 2015 c.33 Sch.6 para.2
s.274, amended: 2015 c.33 Sch.6 para.3
s.280B, amended: 2015 c.33 Sch.6 para.4
s.280C, added: 2015 c.33 Sch.6 para.5
s.286, amended: 2015 c.33 Sch.6 para.6
s.286, repealed: 2015 c.33 Sch.6 para.6
s.292A, amended: 2015 c.33 Sch.6 para.7
s.292AA, added: 2015 c.33 Sch.6 para.8
s.292B, repealed: 2015 c.33 Sch.6 para.9
s.293, amended: 2015 c.33 Sch.6 para.10
s.294A, added: 2015 c.33 Sch.6 para.11
s.297A, amended: 2015 c.33 Sch.6
para.12
s.297B, added: 2015 c.33 Sch.6 para.13
s.303, amended: 2015 c.33 s.27
s.309A, amended: 2015 c.11 Sch.6
para.7, Sch.6 para.8, Sch.6 para.11
s.309A, repealed: 2015 c.11 Sch.6 para.8
, Sch.6 para.11
s.309B, amended: 2015 c.11 Sch.6 para.8
s.309B, repealed: 2015 c.11 Sch.6 para.8
, Sch.6 para.11
s.311, repealed: 2015 c.33 Sch.6 para.14
s.313, amended: 2015 c.33 Sch.6 para.15
s.321, enabling: SI 2015/361
s.322, enabling: SI 2015/361
s.324, enabling: SI 2015/361
s.326, amended: 2015 c.33 Sch.6 para.16
s.326A, added: 2015 c.33 Sch.6 para.17
s.327, amended: 2015 c.33 Sch.6 para.18
s.330B, added: 2015 c.33 Sch.6 para.19
s.331A, added: 2015 c.33 Sch.6 para.20
s.399A, added: 2015 c.33 s.24
s.414, amended: SI 2015/1810 Art.14
s.415, amended: SI 2015/1810 Art.14
s.416, amended: 2015 c.11 s.20
s.428, amended: 2015 c.11 s.20
s.481, amended: 2015 c.11 s.19
s.482, amended: 2015 c.11 s.19
s.809C, amended: 2015 c.11 s.24
s.809EZA, amended: 2015 c.33 s.45
s.809EZB, amended: 2015 c.33 s.44
s.809EZDA, added: 2015 c.33 s.45
s.809EZG, amended: 2015 c.33 s.44
s.809H, amended: 2015 c.11 s.24
s.852, enabling: SI 2015/653
s.871, enabling: SI 2015/653
s.874, see *Ardmore Construction Ltd v
Revenue and Customs Commissioners*
[2015] UKUT 633 (TCC), [2015] B.T.C.
536 (UT (Tax)), Morgan J

s.888A, added: 2015 c.11 s.23
s.888A, enabling: SI 2015/2002
s.996, repealed: 2015 c.33 s.28
s.1014, amended: 2015 c.11 s.125, 2015
c.33 s.3
Sch.4, amended: 2015 c.11 s.21

5. Welfare Reform Act 2007
s.1, see *South Tyneside Council v Aitken*
[2014] EWHC 4163 (Admin), [2015]
R.V.R. 227 (QBD (Admin)), Ouseley J
s.4, enabling: SI 2015/1647, SI
2015/1754
s.8, enabling: SI 2015/437
s.17, enabling: SI 2015/67, SI 2015/389
s.22, enabling: SI 2015/437
s.24, enabling: SI 2015/67, SI 2015/339,
SI 2015/389, SI 2015/1647, SI 2015/1754
s.25, enabling: SI 2015/67, SI 2015/389,
SI 2015/437, SI 2015/1647, SI 2015/1754
s.29, enabling: SI 2015/437
Sch.2 para.1, enabling: SI 2015/339, SI
2015/437
Sch.4 para.1, enabling: SI 2015/437
Sch.4 para.7, enabling: SI 2015/437
Sch.4 para.8, enabling: SI 2015/437

**6. Justice and Security (Northern Ireland)
Act 2007**
s.9, enabling: SI 2015/1572

11. Finance Act 2007
see *Aspinalls Club Ltd v Revenue and
Customs Commissioners* [2013] EWCA
Civ 1464, [2015] Ch. 79 (CA (Civ Div)),
Moses LJ
s.11, see *Aspinalls Club Ltd v Revenue
and Customs Commissioners* [2013]
EWCA Civ 1464, [2015] Ch. 79 (CA
(Civ Div)), Moses LJ
s.107, see *European Commission v
United Kingdom (C-640/13)* [2015] Ch.
476 (ECJ (1st Chamber)), Judge Tizzano
(President)
Sch.24 Part 1 para.1, amended: 2015 c.11
Sch.7 para.56
Sch.24 Part 2 para.4, amended: 2015 c.11
Sch.20 para.2
Sch.24 Part 2 para.4A, amended: 2015
c.11 Sch.20 para.3
Sch.24 Part 2 para.4AA, added: 2015
c.11 Sch.20 para.4
Sch.24 Part 2 para.10, amended: 2015
c.11 Sch.20 para.5

Sch.24 Part 2 para.12, amended: 2015
c.11 Sch.20 para.6
Sch.24 Part 5 para.21A, amended: 2015
c.11 Sch.20 para.7
Sch.24 Part 5 para.21B, amended: 2015
c.11 Sch.20 para.8
Sch.24 Part 5 para.21C, added: 2015 c.11
Sch.7 para.56
Sch.26 para.4, enabling: SI 2015/635
Sch.26 para.5, enabling: SI 2015/635

**15. Tribunals, Courts and Enforcement Act
2007**

see *Gilchrist v Revenue and Customs
Commissioners* [2015] Ch. 183 (UT
(Tax)), David Richards J
s.7, enabling: SI 2015/1563
s.9, see *Essex CC v TB* [2015] E.L.R. 67
(UT (AAC)), Judge Rowland
s.11, see *Fairford Group Ltd Plc (In
Liquidation) v Revenue and Customs
Commissioners* [2015] S.T.C. 156 (UT
(Tax)), Simon J; see *Jordan v Revenue
and Customs Commissioners* [2015]
UKUT 218 (TCC), [2015] S.T.C. 2314
(UT (Tax)), Judge Colin Bishopp
s.13, see *Murray Group Holdings Ltd v
Revenue and Customs Commissioners*
[2015] CSIH 77, 2015 S.L.T. 765 (IH (2
Div)), The Lord Justice Clerk
(Carloway); see *Sarfraz v Disclosure
and Barring Service* [2015] EWCA Civ
544, [2015] 1 W.L.R. 4441 (CA (Civ
Div)), Lord Dyson MR; see *Secretary of
State for Work and Pensions v Robertson*
[2015] CSIH 82 (IH (Ex Div)), Lady
Smith
s.13, amended: 2015 c.2 s.83
s.14A, added: 2015 c.2 s.64
s.15, amended: 2015 c.2 s.84
s.16, amended: 2015 c.2 s.84, s.85
s.20A, added: SI 2015/700 Art.7
s.22, see *R. (on the application of
Detention Action) v First-tier Tribunal
(Immigration and Asylum Chamber)*
[2015] EWCA Civ 840, [2015] 1 W.L.R.
5341 (CA (Civ Div)), Lord Dyson MR
s.22, enabling: SI 2015/1510
s.25, see *Raftopoulou v Revenue and
Customs Commissioners* [2015] UKUT
630 (TCC), [2015] B.T.C. 535 (UT
(Tax)), Judge Roger Berner

s.29, see *Dickinson v Network Rail
Infrastructure Ltd* [2015] R.V.R. 19 (UT
(Lands)), Sir Keith Lindblom P; see *R.
(on the application of Okondu) v
Secretary of State for the Home
Department* [2015] Imm. A.R. 155 (UT
(IAC)), Green J; see *Raftopoulou v
Revenue and Customs Commissioners*
[2015] UKUT 630 (TCC), [2015] B.T.C.
535 (UT (Tax)), Judge Roger Berner
s.30, enabling: SI 2015/65
s.38, enabling: SI 2015/65
s.42, enabling: SI 2015/414
s.49, enabling: SI 2015/414
Sch.4 Pt 2 para.15, see *GO v Barnsley
MBC* [2015] UKUT 184 (AAC), [2015]
E.L.R. 421 (UT (AAC)), Judge Wright
Sch.5, enabling: SI 2015/1510
Sch.6 Part 4, amended: 2015 c.20 Sch.6
para.22
Sch.10 Part 1 para.19, repealed: 2015
c.20 Sch.6 para.22
Sch.13 para.21, repealed: 2015 c.20
Sch.6 para.2
Sch.13 para.67, repealed: 2015 c.20
Sch.23 para.32

**17. Consumers, Estate Agents and Redress
Act 2007**
s.57, repealed: 2015 c.15 Sch.6 para.85
s.58, repealed: 2015 c.15 Sch.6 para.85

**18. Statistics and Registration Service Act
2007**
s.47, enabling: SI 2015/1277

**19. Corporate Manslaughter and Corporate
Homicide Act 2007**
s.2, amended: 2015 c.2 Sch.9 para.23

21. Offender Management Act 2007
s.1, amended: 2015 c.2 Sch.9 para.25
s.3, amended: 2015 c.2 Sch.3 para.14
s.14, amended: 2015 c.2 Sch.3 para.15,
Sch.9 para.26, Sch.10 para.37

23. Sustainable Communities Act 2007
s.7, repealed: 2015 c.20 s.100

27. Serious Crime Act 2007
s.1, amended: 2015 c.9 Sch.1 para.2
s.2, amended: 2015 c.9 Sch.1 para.3
s.2A, added: 2015 c.9 Sch.1 para.4
s.3, amended: 2015 c.9 Sch.1 para.5
s.4, amended: 2015 c.9 Sch.1 para.6
s.5, amended: 2015 c.9 Sch.1 para.7
s.5A, added: 2015 c.9 s.50

s.7, amended: 2015 c.9 Sch.1 para.8
s.8, amended: 2015 c.9 Sch.1 para.9
s.9, amended: 2015 c.9 Sch.1 para.10,
Sch.4 para.76
s.10, amended: 2015 c.9 Sch.1 para.11
s.12, amended: 2015 c.9 Sch.1 para.12
s.13, amended: 2015 c.9 Sch.1 para.13
s.16, amended: 2015 c.9 Sch.4 para.77
s.17, amended: 2015 c.9 Sch.1 para.14
s.18, amended: 2015 c.9 Sch.1 para.15
s.19, amended: 2015 c.9 Sch.4 para.78
s.21, amended: 2015 c.9 s.48, Sch.4
para.79
s.22, amended: 2015 c.9 Sch.1 para.16
s.22A, added: 2015 c.9 Sch.1 para.17
s.22E, added: 2015 c.9 s.49
s.24A, added: 2015 c.9 Sch.1 para.18
s.27, amended: 2015 c.9 Sch.1 para.19
s.27A, added: 2015 c.9 Sch.1 para.20
s.29, amended: 2015 c.9 Sch.1 para.21
s.31, amended: 2015 c.9 Sch.1 para.22
s.31, repealed: 2015 c.9 Sch.1 para.22
s.32, repealed: 2015 c.9 Sch.1 para.23
s.34, amended: 2015 c.9 Sch.1 para.24
s.36, amended: 2015 c.9 Sch.4 para.80
s.36A, added: 2015 c.9 Sch.1 para.25
s.39, amended: 2015 c.9 Sch.1 para.26
s.40, amended: 2015 c.9 Sch.1 para.27
s.43, amended: 2015 c.9 Sch.1 para.28
s.45, see *R. v Ali (Nazakat)* [2015]
EWCA Crim 43, [2015] 1 Cr. App. R. 32
(CA (Crim Div)), Rafferty LJ
s.89, amended: 2015 c.9 Sch.1 para.29
s.93, repealed: 2015 c.9 Sch.1 para.30
Sch.1 Part 1 para.1, amended: 2015 c.9
s.47
Sch.1 Part 1 para.1A, added: 2015 c.30
Sch.5 para.7
Sch.1 Part 1 para.2, amended: 2015 c.30
Sch.5 para.7
Sch.1 Part 1 para.3, substituted: 2015 c.9
s.47
Sch.1 Part 1 para.4, amended: 2015 c.9
Sch.4 para.81
Sch.1 Part 1A, added: 2015 c.9 Sch.1
para.31
Sch.1 Part 1 para.11A, added: 2015 c.9
s.47
Sch.1 Part 1 para.13A, added: 2015 c.9
Sch.4 para.81

Sch.1 Part 2 para.17, amended: 2015 c.9
s.47
Sch.1 Part 2 para.19, amended: 2015 c.9
s.47
Sch.1 Part 2 para.19, substituted: 2015
c.9 Sch.4 para.81
Sch.1 Part 2 para.27A, added: 2015 c.9
s.47
Sch.3 Part 2 para.38A, added: 2015 c.9
Sch.4 para.82

**28. Local Government and Public
Involvement in Health Act 2007**
   see *R. (on the application of ER) v
   Commissioner for Local Administration
   in England (Local Government
   Ombudsman)* [2014] EWCA Civ 1407,
   [2015] E.L.R. 36 (CA (Civ Div)), Moore-
   Bick LJ
Part 5 c.1, amended: 2015 c.20 s.101
s.78, repealed: 2015 c.20 s.100
s.80, amended: SI 2015/998 Art.3
s.80A, added: SI 2015/998 Art.4
s.83, amended: SI 2015/998 Art.5, Art.8
s.84, amended: SI 2015/998 Art.6, Art.8
s.85, amended: SI 2015/998 Art.7, Art.8
s.92, enabling: SI 2015/115, SI 2015/116,
SI 2015/120, SI 2015/563
s.93, amended: SI 2015/998 Art.10
s.102, amended: SI 2015/998 Art.9
s.104, repealed: 2015 c.20 Sch.13 para.6 ,
Sch.14 para.59
s.105, repealed: 2015 c.20 s.101
s.106, repealed: 2015 c.20 s.100
s.111, repealed: 2015 c.20 s.100
s.114, repealed: 2015 c.20 s.100
s.117, amended: 2015 c.20 s.101
s.117, repealed: 2015 c.20 s.101
s.118, repealed: 2015 c.20 s.101
s.138, repealed: 2015 c.20 s.103
s.205, repealed: 2015 c.20 Sch.13 para.4
s.209, repealed: 2015 c.20 Sch.13 para.6
s.211, repealed: 2015 c.20 Sch.13 para.6
s.240, amended: 2015 c.20 Sch.13 para.6
Sch.13, repealed: 2015 c.20 Sch.13
para.6

29. Legal Services Act 2007
   Pt 6., see *R. (on the application of
   Kerman & Co LLP) v Legal Ombudsman*
   [2014] EWHC 3726 (Admin), [2015] 1
   W.L.R. 2081 (QBD (Admin)), Patterson
   J

s.3, see *R. (on the application of
Lumsdon) v Legal Services Board* [2015]
UKSC 41, [2015] 3 W.L.R. 121 (SC),
Lord Neuberger PSC
s.18, see *R. (on the application of
Kerman & Co LLP) v Legal Ombudsman*
[2014] EWHC 3726 (Admin), [2015] 1
W.L.R. 2081 (QBD (Admin)), Patterson
J
s.42, enabling: SI 2015/935
s.48, enabling: SI 2015/935
s.69, enabling: SI 2015/401
s.79, enabling: SI 2015/938
s.104, amended: 2015 c.20 Sch.19
para.15
s.132, see *R. (on the application of
Kerman & Co LLP) v Legal Ombudsman*
[2014] EWHC 3726 (Admin), [2015] 1
W.L.R. 2081 (QBD (Admin)), Patterson
J
s.194, see *Raftopoulou v Revenue and
Customs Commissioners* [2015] UKUT
630 (TCC), [2015] B.T.C. 535 (UT
(Tax)), Judge Roger Berner
s.204, enabling: SI 2015/401, SI
2015/935, SI 2015/938
Sch.2, see *Heron Bros Ltd v Central
Bedfordshire Council* [2015] EWHC
1009 (TCC), [2015] B.L.R. 514 (QBD
(TCC)), Edwards-Stuart J
Sch.2 para.4, see *P, Re* [2015] EWCOP
59, [2015] C.O.P.L.R. 690 (CP), Charles
J
Sch.5 Part 2 para.11, amended: 2015 c.20
Sch.19 para.16
Sch.14 para.3, see *Law Society v Elsdon*
[2015] EWHC 1326 (Ch), [2015]
W.T.L.R. 1601 (Ch D), Newey J
Sch.16 Part 1 para.3, repealed: SI
2015/401 Art.3
Sch.16 Part 1 para.15, repealed: SI
2015/401 Art.3
Sch.16 Part 1 para.17, repealed: SI
2015/401 Art.3
Sch.16 Part 1 para.22, repealed: SI
2015/401 Art.3
Sch.16 Part 1 para.30, repealed: SI
2015/401 Art.3
Sch.16 Part 1 para.49, repealed: SI
2015/401 Art.3

Sch.16 Part 1 para.75, repealed: SI
2015/401 Art.3
Sch.16 Part 2 para.81, repealed: SI
2015/401 Art.3
Sch.21 para.41, repealed: 2015 c.15
Sch.6 para.85
Sch.24, amended: 2015 c.20 Sch.19
para.17

30. UK Borders Act 2007

see *HA (Iraq) v Secretary of State for the
Home Department* [2014] EWCA Civ
1304, [2015] Imm. A.R. 207 (CA (Civ
Div)), Sullivan LJ; see *LC (China) v
Secretary of State for the Home
Department* [2014] EWCA Civ 1310,
[2015] Imm. A.R. 227 (CA (Civ Div)),
Moore-Bick LJ
s.2, amended: 2015 c.6 s.10
s.5, enabling: SI 2015/433, SI 2015/897
s.6, enabling: SI 2015/433, SI 2015/897
s.7, enabling: SI 2015/433
s.8, enabling: SI 2015/433
s.10, enabling: SI 2015/564
s.13, enabling: SI 2015/565
s.14, enabling: SI 2015/564, SI 2015/565
s.15, enabling: SI 2015/433
s.32, see *JG (Jamaica) v Secretary of
State for the Home Department* [2015]
EWCA Civ 215, [2015] C.P. Rep. 24
(CA (Civ Div)), Jackson LJ; see *JG
(Jamaica) v Secretary of State for the
Home Department* [2015] EWCA Civ
410, [2015] Imm. A.R. 1193 (CA (Civ
Div)), Jackson LJ; see *LC (China) v
Secretary of State for the Home
Department* [2014] EWCA Civ 1310,
[2015] Imm. A.R. 227 (CA (Civ Div)),
Moore-Bick LJ; see *R. (on the
application of Akpinar) v Upper Tribunal
(Immigration and Asylum Chamber)*
[2014] EWCA Civ 937, [2015] 1 W.L.R.
466 (CA (Civ Div)), Maurice Kay LJ; see
*Secretary of State for the Home
Department v AQ (Nigeria)* [2015]
EWCA Civ 250, [2015] Imm. A.R. 990
(CA (Civ Div)), Sullivan LJ
s.33, see *JG (Jamaica) v Secretary of
State for the Home Department* [2015]
EWCA Civ 410, [2015] Imm. A.R. 1193
(CA (Civ Div)), Jackson LJ; see *R. (on
the application of Akpinar) v Upper*

Tribunal (Immigration and Asylum Chamber) [2014] EWCA Civ 937, [2015] 1 W.L.R. 466 (CA (Civ Div)), Maurice Kay LJ

2008

1. European Communities (Finance) Act 2008
 repealed: 2015 c.32 s.2
4. Criminal Justice and Immigration Act 2008
 s.63, amended: 2015 c.2 s.37
 s.66, amended: 2015 c.2 s.37
 s.67, amended: 2015 c.2 s.37
 Sch.14 para.1, amended: 2015 c.2 s.37
 Sch.14 para.6, repealed: 2015 c.2 s.37
6. Child Maintenance and Other Payments Act 2008
 s.46, enabling: SI 2015/500
 s.53, enabling: SI 2015/500
 s.62, enabling: SI 2015/176
9. Finance Act 2008
 see *Shirley v Revenue and Customs Commissioners* [2015] S.F.T.D. 247 (FTT (Tax)), Judge Nicholas Aleksander
 s.58, see *Shiner v Revenue and Customs Commissioners* [2015] UKUT 596 (TCC), [2015] B.T.C. 534 (UT (Tax)), Mann J
 s.121, see *NHS Lothian Health Board v Revenue and Customs Commissioners* [2015] UKUT 264 (TCC), [2015] S.T.C. 2221 (UT (Tax)), Lord Tyre; see *Taylor Clark Leisure Plc v Revenue and Customs Commissioners* [2015] CSIH 40, 2015 S.L.T. 412 (IH (Ex Div)), Lady Clark of Calton; see *Taylor Clark Leisure Plc v Revenue and Customs Commissioners* [2015] S.T.C. 223 (UT (Tax)), Lord Doherty
 s.124, enabling: SI 2015/452
 s.131, amended: 2015 c.20 Sch.6 para.2
 s.136, enabling: SI 2015/1777
 Sch.36 Pt 1 para.1, see *Jordan v Revenue and Customs Commissioners* [2015] UKUT 218 (TCC), [2015] S.T.C. 2314 (UT (Tax)), Judge Colin Bishopp
 Sch.36 Part 4 para.21ZA, added: 2015 c.11 Sch.7 para.57

Sch.36 Pt 5, see *Jordan v Revenue and Customs Commissioners* [2015] UKUT 218 (TCC), [2015] S.T.C. 2314 (UT (Tax)), Judge Colin Bishopp
Sch.36 Pt 5 para.29, see *Jordan v Revenue and Customs Commissioners* [2015] UKUT 218 (TCC), [2015] S.T.C. 2314 (UT (Tax)), Judge Colin Bishopp
Sch.36 Pt 5 para.32, see *Jordan v Revenue and Customs Commissioners* [2015] UKUT 218 (TCC), [2015] S.T.C. 2314 (UT (Tax)), Judge Colin Bishopp
Sch.36 Pt 7 para.50, see *Revenue and Customs Commissioners v Tager* [2015] UKUT 40 (TCC), [2015] S.T.C. 1687 (UT (Tax)), Judge Colin Bishopp; see *Tager v Revenue and Customs Commissioners* [2015] UKUT 663 (TCC), [2015] B.T.C. 538 (UT (Tax)), Judge Colin Bishopp
Sch.36 Part 9 para.63, amended: 2015 c.11 s.105
Sch.41 para.1, amended: 2015 c.11 s.104
Sch.41 para.6, amended: 2015 c.11
Sch.20 para.10
Sch.41 para.6A, amended: 2015 c.11
Sch.20 para.11
Sch.41 para.6A, repealed: 2015 c.11
Sch.20 para.11
Sch.41 para.6AA, added: 2015 c.11
Sch.20 para.12
Sch.41 para.7, amended: 2015 c.11 s.104
Sch.41 para.13, amended: 2015 c.11
Sch.20 para.13
13. Regulatory Enforcement and Sanctions Act 2008
 s.4, enabling: SI 2015/776
 s.39, amended: SI 2015/664 Sch.5 para.12
 s.42, amended: SI 2015/664 Sch.5 para.12
 s.49, amended: SI 2015/664 Sch.4 para.39
 s.62, enabling: SI 2015/324
 s.73, amended: SI 2015/1682 Sch.1 para.4
 Sch.3, amended: 2015 c.15 Sch.1 para.54, 2015 c.20 Sch.23 para.25, Sch.23 para.34, SI 2015/776 Art.17, SI 2015/895 Reg.6, SI 2015/1726 Sch.1 para.5

Sch.5, amended: SI 2015/1682 Sch.1
para.4

14. Health and Social Care Act 2008
see *R. (on the application of Kent CC) v
Secretary of State for Health* [2015]
EWCA Civ 81, [2015] 1 W.L.R. 1221
(CA (Civ Div)), Lord Dyson MR
s.10, amended: SI 2015/664 Sch.4
para.40
s.20, amended: 2015 c.28 s.1
s.20, enabling: SI 2015/64
s.33, amended: SI 2015/664 Sch.4
para.40
s.34, amended: SI 2015/664 Sch.4
para.40
s.35, amended: SI 2015/664 Sch.4
para.91
s.35, enabling: SI 2015/64
s.86, enabling: SI 2015/64
s.87, amended: SI 2015/664 Sch.5
para.13
s.87, enabling: SI 2015/64
s.145, repealed: SI 2015/914 Sch.1
para.90
s.156, amended: SI 2015/914 Sch.1
para.91
s.156, repealed: SI 2015/914 Sch.1
para.91
s.161, enabling: SI 2015/64, SI 2015/864,
SI 2015/1479
s.167, enabling: SI 2015/864
Sch.1 para.3, enabling: SI 2015/1479
Sch.14 para.1, repealed: SI 2015/914
Sch.1 para.92
Sch.14 para.8, added: SI 2015/914 Sch.1
para.93
Sch.14 para.8, amended: SI 2015/914
Sch.1 para.93

17. Housing and Regeneration Act 2008
s.1, enabling: SI 2015/1471
s.11, amended: 2015 c.7 s.32
s.51, amended: 2015 c.7 s.31
s.53A, added: 2015 c.7 s.31
s.53A, enabling: SI 2015/1471
s.53B, enabling: SI 2015/1540
s.126, repealed: 2015 c.20 s.100
s.229, amended: SI 2015/664 Sch.5
para.14
s.320, amended: 2015 c.7 s.31
s.320, enabling: SI 2015/1471
Sch.3, amended: 2015 c.7 s.32

Sch.3 Part 1 para.1, amended: 2015 c.7
s.32

18. Crossrail Act 2008
s.22, amended: SI 2015/1682 Sch.1
para.4
s.23, amended: SI 2015/1682 Sch.1
para.4
s.30, amended: SI 2015/1682 Sch.1
para.4
s.48, enabling: SI 2015/781
s.54, amended: SI 2015/1682 Sch.1
para.4

21. Planning and Energy Act 2008
s.1, amended: 2015 c.20 s.43

**22. Human Fertilisation and Embryology
Act 2008**
see *B v C (Surrogacy: Adoption)* [2015]
EWFC 17, [2015] 1 F.L.R. 1392 (Fam
Ct), Theis J; see *JP v LP (Surrogacy
Arrangement: Wardship)* [2014] EWHC
595 (Fam), [2015] 1 All E.R. 266 (Fam
Div), Eleanor King J
s.23, see *X v Y* [2015] EWFC 13 (Fam
Ct), Theis J
s.36, see *X v Y* [2015] EWFC 13 (Fam
Ct), Theis J
s.37, see *X v Y* [2015] EWFC 13 (Fam
Ct), Theis J
s.54, see *AB v CT (Parental Order:
Consent of Surrogate Mother)* [2015]
EWFC 12 (Fam Ct), Theis J; see *JP v LP
(Surrogacy Arrangement: Wardship)*
[2014] EWHC 595 (Fam), [2015] 1 All
E.R. 266 (Fam Div), Eleanor King J; see
*X (A Child) (Parental Order: Time
Limit), Re* [2014] EWHC 3135 (Fam),
[2015] Fam. 186 (Fam Div
(Birmingham)), Sir James Munby PFD;
see *Z (A Child) (Surrogate Father:
Parental Order), Re* [2015] EWFC 73,
[2015] 1 W.L.R. 4993 (Fam Ct), Sir
James Munby PFD
s.54, varied: SI 2015/572 Reg.18

23. Children and Young Persons Act 2008
s.4, repealed: 2015 c.20 s.93

25. Education and Skills Act 2008
Part 3, substituted: 2015 c.26 s.78
Part 3, repealed: 2015 c.26 s.78
s.13, amended: 2015 c.20 Sch.14 para.61
s.66, amended: SI 2015/1852 Art.3
s.72, amended: 2015 c.20 Sch.14 para.62

s.77, repealed: 2015 c.20 Sch.14 para.63
s.87, amended: 2015 c.26 s.78
s.91, repealed: 2015 c.26 s.78
s.94, amended: 2015 c.26 s.75
s.132, amended: 2015 c.20 Sch.14
para.64

27. Climate Change Act 2008
s.26, enabling: SI 2015/775
s.27, enabling: SI 2015/775
s.81, repealed: 2015 c.20 s.57
s.90, enabling: SI 2015/776
Sch.6, enabling: SI 2015/776

29. Planning Act 2008
see *Chhokar v Secretary of State for
Communities and Local Government*
[2014] EWHC 3155 (Admin), [2015]
J.P.L. 345 (QBD (Admin)), Lang J; see
*Oxfordshire CC v Secretary of State for
Communities and Local Government*
[2015] EWHC 186 (Admin), [2015]
J.P.L. 846 (QBD (Admin)), Lang J; see
*R. (on the application of FCC
Environment (UK) Ltd) v Secretary of
State for Energy and Climate Change*
[2015] EWCA Civ 55, [2015] Env. L.R.
22 (CA (Civ Div)), Aikens LJ; see *R. (on
the application of Larkfleet Homes Ltd) v
Rutland CC* [2015] EWCA Civ 597,
[2015] P.T.S.R. 1369 (CA (Civ Div)),
Moore-Bick LJ
s.4, enabling: SI 2015/760
s.13, amended: 2015 c.2 s.92
s.14, amended: SI 2015/949 Art.2
s.14, enabling: SI 2015/949
s.22, amended: 2015 c.7 Sch.1 para.153
s.30A, added: SI 2015/949 Art.2
s.61, amended: 2015 c.7 s.26
s.65, amended: 2015 c.7 s.27
s.68, amended: 2015 c.7 s.27
s.73, amended: 2015 c.7 s.27
s.75, amended: 2015 c.7 s.27
s.88, enabling: SI 2015/462
s.102, enabling: SI 2015/462
s.103, enabling: SI 2015/1561
s.104, see *R. (on the application of FCC
Environment (UK) Ltd) v Secretary of
State for Energy and Climate Change*
[2015] EWCA Civ 55, [2015] Env. L.R.
22 (CA (Civ Div)), Aikens LJ
s.114, enabling: SI 2015/23, SI 2015/129,
SI 2015/147, SI 2015/318, SI 2015/680,

SI 2015/1317, SI 2015/1347, SI
2015/1386, SI 2015/1561, SI 2015/1570,
SI 2015/1574, SI 2015/1592, SI
2015/1832, SI 2015/1984
s.115, enabling: SI 2015/23, SI 2015/129,
SI 2015/147, SI 2015/680, SI 2015/1347,
SI 2015/1561, SI 2015/1570, SI
2015/1574, SI 2015/1832
s.117, enabling: SI 2015/129, SI
2015/147, SI 2015/1347
s.118, see *R. (on the application of
Williams) v Secretary of State for Energy
and Climate Change* [2015] EWHC 1202
(Admin), [2015] J.P.L. 1257 (QBD
(Admin)), Lindblom J
s.118, amended: 2015 c.2 s.92
s.119, enabling: SI 2015/243, SI
2015/1231, SI 2015/1270, SI 2015/1829,
SI 2015/1830
s.120, enabling: SI 2015/23, SI 2015/129,
SI 2015/147, SI 2015/318, SI 2015/680,
SI 2015/1347, SI 2015/1386, SI
2015/1561, SI 2015/1570, SI 2015/1574,
SI 2015/1592, SI 2015/1832, SI
2015/1984
s.122, see *R. (on the application of FCC
Environment (UK) Ltd) v Secretary of
State for Energy and Climate Change*
[2015] EWCA Civ 55, [2015] Env. L.R.
22 (CA (Civ Div)), Aikens LJ
s.122, enabling: SI 2015/23, SI 2015/129,
SI 2015/147, SI 2015/1347, SI 2015/1561
s.123, enabling: SI 2015/1561
s.142, enabling: SI 2015/1561
s.147, enabling: SI 2015/680
s.149A, enabling: SI 2015/1561
s.150, enabling: SI 2015/462
s.153, enabling: SI 2015/571, SI
2015/1460
s.154, enabling: SI 2015/462
s.155, enabling: SI 2015/462
s.160, amended: SI 2015/664 Sch.4
para.41
s.160, repealed: SI 2015/664 Sch.4
para.41
s.161, amended: SI 2015/664 Sch.4
para.41
s.161, repealed: SI 2015/664 Sch.4
para.41
s.170, enabling: SI 2015/462
s.203, enabling: SI 2015/1794

220

s.205, enabling: SI 2015/836
s.218, repealed: SI 2015/664 Sch.4
para.92
s.218, enabling: SI 2015/836
s.220, enabling: SI 2015/836
s.222, enabling: SI 2015/836
s.232, enabling: SI 2015/462, SI
2015/949
s.240, amended: SI 2015/949 Art.2
Sch.4, enabling: SI 2015/243, SI
2015/1231, SI 2015/1270
Sch.4 para.1, enabling: SI 2015/723, SI
2015/1280, SI 2015/1319, SI 2015/1616,
SI 2015/1742, SI 2015/1829, SI
2015/1830, SI 2015/2070, SI 2015/2071
Sch.5 Part 1 para.1, enabling: SI 2015/23,
SI 2015/129, SI 2015/147, SI 2015/1347
Sch.5 Part 1 para.2, enabling: SI 2015/23,
SI 2015/129, SI 2015/147, SI 2015/1347
Sch.5 Part 1 para.3, enabling: SI 2015/23,
SI 2015/129, SI 2015/147, SI 2015/1347
Sch.5 Part 1 para.10, enabling: SI
2015/23, SI 2015/129, SI 2015/147, SI
2015/1347
Sch.5 Part 1 para.11, enabling: SI
2015/23, SI 2015/129, SI 2015/147, SI
2015/1347
Sch.5 Part 1 para.12, enabling: SI
2015/23, SI 2015/129, SI 2015/147, SI
2015/1347
Sch.5 Part 1 para.13, enabling: SI
2015/23, SI 2015/129, SI 2015/147, SI
2015/1347
Sch.5 Part 1 para.14, enabling: SI
2015/23, SI 2015/129, SI 2015/147, SI
2015/1347
Sch.5 Part 1 para.15, enabling: SI
2015/23, SI 2015/129, SI 2015/147, SI
2015/1347
Sch.5 Part 1 para.16, enabling: SI
2015/23, SI 2015/147, SI 2015/1347
Sch.5 Part 1 para.17, enabling: SI
2015/23, SI 2015/129, SI 2015/147, SI
2015/1347
Sch.5 Part 1 para.19, enabling: SI
2015/23, SI 2015/129, SI 2015/147, SI
2015/1347
Sch.5 Part 1 para.22, enabling: SI
2015/129, SI 2015/147, SI 2015/1347
Sch.5 Part 1 para.23, enabling: SI
2015/147, SI 2015/1347

Sch.5 Part 1 para.26, enabling: SI
2015/23, SI 2015/129, SI 2015/147, SI
2015/1347
Sch.5 Part 1 para.33, enabling: SI
2015/23, SI 2015/129, SI 2015/147
Sch.5 Part 1 para.36, enabling: SI
2015/23, SI 2015/129, SI 2015/147, SI
2015/1347
Sch.5 Part 1 para.37, enabling: SI
2015/23, SI 2015/129, SI 2015/147, SI
2015/1347
Sch.6 para.2, amended: 2015 c.7 s.28
Sch.6 para.2, enabling: SI 2015/571, SI
2015/760, SI 2015/1460, SI 2015/1666
Sch.6 para.3, amended: 2015 c.7 s.28
Sch.6 para.4, amended: 2015 c.7 s.28
Sch.6 para.4, enabling: SI 2015/760
Sch.12 para.2, amended: SI 2015/949
Art.2

30. Pensions Act 2008
s.3, enabling: SI 2015/501
s.4, enabling: SI 2015/501
s.5, enabling: SI 2015/501
s.9, enabling: SI 2015/501
s.10, enabling: SI 2015/501
s.13, amended: SI 2015/468 Art.2
s.14, enabling: SI 2015/468
s.15A, enabling: SI 2015/468
s.20, amended: 2015 c.8 Sch.2 para.40
s.21, amended: 2015 c.8 Sch.2 para.41
s.23A, amended: 2015 c.8 Sch.2 para.42
s.23A, enabling: SI 2015/501
s.24, amended: 2015 c.8 Sch.2 para.43
s.25, enabling: SI 2015/501
s.26, amended: 2015 c.8 Sch.2 para.44
s.26, repealed: 2015 c.8 Sch.2 para.44
s.28, amended: 2015 c.8 Sch.2 para.45
s.29, substituted: 2015 c.8 Sch.2 para.46
s.30, amended: 2015 c.8 Sch.2 para.47
s.30, enabling: SI 2015/501
s.35, amended: 2015 c.8 Sch.2 para.48
s.38, amended: 2015 c.8 Sch.2 para.49
s.67, enabling: SI 2015/178
s.70, repealed: SI 2015/178 Art.3
s.70, enabling: SI 2015/178
s.87A, enabling: SI 2015/501
s.99, amended: 2015 c.8 Sch.2 para.50
s.99, enabling: SI 2015/501
s.142, enabling: SI 2015/652
s.144, enabling: SI 2015/178, SI
2015/468, SI 2015/501, SI 2015/652

32. Energy Act 2008
s.2, amended: 2015 c.20 s.14
s.3A, added: 2015 c.20 s.14
s.22, amended: SI 2015/664 Sch.4
para.42
s.22, repealed: SI 2015/664 Sch.4 para.42
s.23, amended: SI 2015/664 Sch.4
para.42
s.23, repealed: SI 2015/664 Sch.4 para.42
s.25, amended: SI 2015/664 Sch.4
para.42
s.43, enabling: SI 2015/35, SI 2015/1659,
SI 2015/2045
s.82I, amended: SI 2015/664 Sch.4
para.42
s.82K, amended: SI 2015/664 Sch.4
para.42
s.82L, amended: SI 2015/664 Sch.4
para.42
s.87, repealed: 2015 c.20 s.57
s.100, amended: 2015 c.7 s.51
s.100, repealed: 2015 c.7 s.51
s.100, enabling: SI 2015/143, SI
2015/145, SI 2015/197, SI 2015/477, SI
2015/1459
s.104, enabling: SI 2015/35, SI 2015/143,
SI 2015/145, SI 2015/197, SI 2015/1459,
SI 2015/1659, SI 2015/2045
s.105, amended: 2015 c.7 s.51
s.105, repealed: 2015 c.7 s.51

2009

1. Banking Act 2009
s.145, amended: SI 2015/989 Sch.1
para.4
s.204, enabling: SI 2015/488
s.259, enabling: SI 2015/488
**02. Local Government (Wales) Measure
2009**
s.8, enabling: SI 2015/604
Sch.2 para.3, repealed: 2015 c.20 s.100
4. Corporation Tax Act 2009
Part 5 c.3, amended: 2015 c.33 Sch.7
para.8
Part 7 c.4, amended: 2015 c.33 Sch.7
para.74
s.2, amended: 2015 c.11 Sch.7 para.58
s.54, see *Altus Group (UK) Ltd v Baker
Tilly Tax and Advisory Services LLP*

[2015] EWHC 12 (Ch), [2015] S.T.C.
788 (Ch D), Judge Keyser QC
s.86A, added: 2015 c.11 Sch.5 para.3
s.104A, amended: 2015 c.33 s.31
s.104D, amended: 2015 c.11 s.28
s.104E, amended: 2015 c.11 s.28
s.104G, amended: 2015 c.11 s.28
s.104H, amended: 2015 c.11 s.28
s.104J, amended: 2015 c.11 s.28
s.104K, amended: 2015 c.11 s.28
s.104M, amended: 2015 c.11 s.27
s.104WA, added: 2015 c.33 s.31
s.104Y, amended: 2015 c.11 s.28
s.133A, added: 2015 c.33 s.18
s.133M, added: 2015 c.33 s.18
s.133N, added: 2015 c.33 s.18
s.144, amended: SI 2015/374 Art.8
s.161, amended: 2015 c.33 s.40
s.162, amended: 2015 c.33 s.41
s.210, amended: 2015 c.11 Sch.5 para.4
s.306, amended: 2015 c.33 Sch.7 para.2
s.306A, added: 2015 c.33 Sch.7 para.3
s.307, amended: 2015 c.33 Sch.7 para.4
s.307, repealed: 2015 c.33 Sch.7 para.4
s.308, amended: 2015 c.33 Sch.7 para.5
s.308, repealed: 2015 c.33 Sch.7 para.5
s.310, amended: 2015 c.33 Sch.7 para.6
s.310, repealed: 2015 c.33 Sch.7 para.6
s.310, enabling: SI 2015/1961
s.313, amended: 2015 c.33 Sch.7 para.7
s.313, repealed: 2015 c.33 Sch.7 para.7
s.315, amended: 2015 c.33 Sch.7 para.9
s.315, repealed: 2015 c.33 Sch.7 para.9
s.316, substituted: 2015 c.33 Sch.7
para.10
s.317, repealed: 2015 c.33 Sch.7 para.11
s.318, amended: 2015 c.33 Sch.7 para.12
s.319, enabling: SI 2015/1541, SI
2015/1962
s.320, amended: 2015 c.33 Sch.7 para.13
s.320, repealed: 2015 c.33 Sch.7 para.13
s.320A, added: 2015 c.33 Sch.7 para.14
s.321, repealed: 2015 c.33 Sch.7 para.15
s.322, amended: 2015 c.33 Sch.7 para.16
s.322, repealed: 2015 c.33 Sch.7 para.16
s.323, amended: 2015 c.33 Sch.7 para.17
s.323A, added: 2015 c.33 Sch.7 para.18
s.324, amended: 2015 c.33 Sch.7 para.19
s.328, amended: 2015 c.33 Sch.7 para.20
s.328, repealed: 2015 c.33 Sch.7 para.20

s.328, enabling: SI 2015/1960, SI 2015/1961

s.328A, repealed: 2015 c.33 Sch.7 para.21

s.329, amended: 2015 c.33 Sch.7 para.22

s.330A, added: 2015 c.33 Sch.7 para.23

s.331, repealed: 2015 c.33 Sch.7 para.24

s.337, amended: SI 2015/575 Sch.1 para.26

s.340, amended: 2015 c.33 Sch.7 para.25

s.340, repealed: 2015 c.33 Sch.7 para.25

s.342, amended: 2015 c.33 Sch.7 para.26

s.347, repealed: 2015 c.33 Sch.7 para.27

s.349, amended: 2015 c.33 Sch.7 para.28

s.349, repealed: 2015 c.33 Sch.7 para.28

s.350, repealed: 2015 c.33 Sch.7 para.29

s.352, amended: 2015 c.33 Sch.7 para.30

s.352A, added: 2015 c.33 Sch.7 para.31

s.354, amended: 2015 c.33 Sch.7 para.32

s.358, amended: 2015 c.33 Sch.7 para.33

s.359, amended: 2015 c.33 Sch.7 para.34

s.361, amended: 2015 c.33 Sch.7 para.35

s.361, repealed: 2015 c.33 Sch.7 para.35

s.361A, repealed: 2015 c.33 Sch.7 para.36

s.361D, added: 2015 c.33 Sch.7 para.37

s.362, amended: 2015 c.33 Sch.7 para.38

s.362A, added: 2015 c.33 Sch.7 para.39

s.363, amended: 2015 c.33 Sch.7 para.40

s.372, amended: 2015 c.11 s.25

s.372, repealed: 2015 c.11 s.25

s.373, amended: 2015 c.11 s.25

s.374, repealed: 2015 c.11 s.25

s.377, repealed: 2015 c.11 s.25

s.406, amended: 2015 c.11 s.25

s.406, repealed: 2015 c.11 s.25

s.407, repealed: 2015 c.11 s.25

s.408, repealed: 2015 c.11 s.25

s.422, amended: 2015 c.33 Sch.7 para.41

s.422, repealed: 2015 c.33 Sch.7 para.41

s.424, amended: 2015 c.33 Sch.7 para.42

s.433, amended: 2015 c.33 Sch.7 para.43

s.433, repealed: 2015 c.33 Sch.7 para.43

s.435, amended: 2015 c.33 Sch.7 para.44

s.440, amended: 2015 c.33 Sch.7 para.45

s.440, repealed: 2015 c.33 Sch.7 para.45

s.441, amended: 2015 c.33 Sch.7 para.46

s.442, amended: 2015 c.33 Sch.7 para.47

s.443, repealed: 2015 c.33 Sch.7 para.48

s.450, amended: 2015 c.33 Sch.7 para.49

s.454, repealed: 2015 c.33 Sch.7 para.50

s.455, repealed: 2015 c.33 Sch.7 para.50

s.455B, added: 2015 c.33 Sch.7 para.51

s.465B, added: 2015 c.33 Sch.7 para.52

s.475, amended: 2015 c.33 Sch.7 para.53

s.475, enabling: SI 2015/1963

s.475A, added: 2015 c.33 Sch.7 para.54

s.476, amended: 2015 c.33 Sch.7 para.55

s.521F, amended: 2015 c.33 Sch.7 para.57

s.521F, repealed: 2015 c.33 Sch.7 para.57

s.540, amended: 2015 c.33 Sch.7 para.58

s.594, amended: 2015 c.33 Sch.7 para.60

s.594A, added: 2015 c.33 Sch.7 para.61

s.595, amended: 2015 c.33 Sch.7 para.62

s.595, repealed: 2015 c.33 Sch.7 para.62

s.597, amended: 2015 c.33 Sch.7 para.63

s.597, repealed: 2015 c.33 Sch.7 para.63

s.598, enabling: SI 2015/1541, SI 2015/1961, SI 2015/1962

s.599B, amended: 2015 c.33 Sch.7 para.64

s.604, amended: 2015 c.33 Sch.7 para.65

s.604, repealed: 2015 c.33 Sch.7 para.65

s.604A, added: 2015 c.33 Sch.7 para.66

s.605, repealed: 2015 c.33 Sch.7 para.67

s.606, amended: 2015 c.33 Sch.7 para.68

s.606, repealed: 2015 c.33 Sch.7 para.68

s.606, enabling: SI 2015/1960, SI 2015/1961

s.606A, repealed: 2015 c.33 Sch.7 para.69

s.607, amended: 2015 c.33 Sch.7 para.70

s.607A, added: 2015 c.33 Sch.7 para.71

s.608, repealed: 2015 c.33 Sch.7 para.72

s.612, amended: 2015 c.33 Sch.7 para.73

s.613, amended: 2015 c.33 Sch.7 para.75

s.613, repealed: 2015 c.33 Sch.7 para.75

s.614, substituted: 2015 c.33 Sch.7 para.76

s.615, amended: 2015 c.33 Sch.7 para.77

s.622, amended: 2015 c.33 Sch.7 para.78

s.625, amended: 2015 c.33 Sch.7 para.79

s.629, repealed: 2015 c.33 Sch.7 para.80

s.636, amended: SI 2015/575 Sch.1 para.26

s.653, amended: 2015 c.33 Sch.7 para.81

s.654, amended: 2015 c.33 Sch.7 para.82

s.658, amended: 2015 c.33 Sch.7 para.83

s.666, amended: 2015 c.33 Sch.7 para.84

s.671, amended: 2015 c.33 Sch.7 para.85

s.673, amended: 2015 c.33 Sch.7 para.86

s.675, amended: 2015 c.33 Sch.7 para.87

s.684, amended: 2015 c.33 Sch.7 para.88

s.689, amended: 2015 c.33 Sch.7 para.89

s.689, repealed: 2015 c.33 Sch.7 para.89

s.690, amended: 2015 c.33 Sch.7 para.90

s.691, amended: 2015 c.33 Sch.7 para.91

s.692, amended: 2015 c.33 Sch.7 para.92

s.698, repealed: 2015 c.33 Sch.7 para.93

s.698B, added: 2015 c.33 Sch.7 para.94

s.702, substituted: 2015 c.33 Sch.7 para.95

s.705, amended: 2015 c.33 Sch.7 para.96

s.705, enabling: SI 2015/1963

s.710, amended: 2015 c.33 Sch.7 para.97

s.715, amended: 2015 c.33 s.33

s.738A, added: 2015 c.21 Sch.2 para.1

s.746, amended: 2015 c.11 s.26, 2015 c.33 s.33

s.800, amended: 2015 c.33 s.33

s.816A, added: 2015 c.33 s.33

s.844, amended: 2015 c.11 s.26

s.844, repealed: 2015 c.33 s.33

s.846, amended: 2015 c.33 s.42

s.849B, added: 2015 c.11 s.26

s.849B, repealed: 2015 c.33 s.33

s.849B, varied: 2015 c.11 s.26

s.1044, see *Monitor Audio Ltd v Revenue and Customs Commissioners* [2015] UKFTT 357 (TC) (FTT (Tax)), Judge Rachel Short

s.1044, amended: 2015 c.11 s.27

s.1045, amended: 2015 c.11 s.27

s.1052, amended: 2015 c.11 s.28

s.1053, amended: 2015 c.11 s.28

s.1055, amended: 2015 c.11 s.27

s.1066, amended: 2015 c.11 s.28

s.1067, amended: 2015 c.11 s.28

s.1071, amended: 2015 c.11 s.28

s.1072, amended: 2015 c.11 s.28

s.1077, amended: 2015 c.11 s.28

s.1078, amended: 2015 c.11 s.28

s.1101, amended: 2015 c.11 s.28

s.1102, amended: 2015 c.11 s.28

s.1119, see *Pyreos Ltd v Revenue and Customs Commissioners* [2015] UKFTT 123 (TC), [2015] S.F.T.D. 517 (FTT (Tax)), Judge Kenneth Mure QC

s.1120, see *Pyreos Ltd v Revenue and Customs Commissioners* [2015] UKFTT 123 (TC), [2015] S.F.T.D. 517 (FTT (Tax)), Judge Kenneth Mure QC

s.1126, amended: 2015 c.11 s.28

s.1126A, added: 2015 c.11 s.28

s.1184, amended: 2015 c.11 s.29

s.1184, repealed: 2015 c.11 s.29

s.1200, amended: 2015 c.11 s.29

s.1202, amended: 2015 c.11 s.29

s.1202, repealed: 2015 c.11 s.29

s.1215, repealed: 2015 c.11 s.29

s.1216AB, amended: 2015 c.11 s.30

s.1216AC, amended: 2015 c.11 s.30

s.1216AD, amended: 2015 c.11 s.30

s.1216ADA, added: 2015 c.11 s.30

s.1216CB, enabling: SI 2015/1449, SI 2015/1941

s.1216CC, enabling: SI 2015/1449

s.1216CE, amended: 2015 c.11 s.31

s.1221, amended: 2015 c.11 Sch.5 para.5

s.1223, amended: 2015 c.11 Sch.2 para.3

s.1244A, added: 2015 c.11 Sch.5 para.6

s.1253A, added: 2015 c.11 Sch.5 para.7

s.1263, see *Altus Group (UK) Ltd v Baker Tilly Tax and Advisory Services LLP* [2015] EWHC 12 (Ch), [2015] S.T.C. 788 (Ch D), Judge Keyser QC

s.1310, amended: 2015 c.11 s.28, 2015 c.33 s.31

s.1325, amended: 2015 c.33 Sch.7 para.101

s.1329, repealed: 2015 c.33 Sch.7 para.101

Sch.2 Part 8 para.71, repealed: 2015 c.33 Sch.7 para.101

Sch.2 Part 10 para.99, repealed: 2015 c.33 Sch.7 para.101

Sch.3 Part 2, repealed: 2015 c.33 Sch.7 para.101

Sch.4, amended: 2015 c.11 s.29, 2015 c.33 Sch.7 para.99

10. Finance Act 2009

s.47, enabling: SI 2015/1983

s.69, repealed: 2015 c.11 s.22

s.104, enabling: SI 2015/974

s.125, varied: SI 2015/623 Reg.65

Sch.21 para.1, repealed: 2015 c.33 Sch.7 para.100

Sch.21 para.7, repealed: 2015 c.33 Sch.7 para.100

Sch.21 para.9, repealed: 2015 c.33 Sch.7 para.100

Sch.53 Part 2 para.7, amended: 2015 c.33 s.15

Sch.53 Part 2 para.9, amended: 2015 c.33
s.15
Sch.55, see *Dyson v Revenue and
Customs Commissioners* [2015] UKFTT
131 (TC), [2015] S.F.T.D. 529 (FTT
(Tax)), Judge Anne Redston
Sch.55 para.1, amended: 2015 c.11 Sch.7
para.59
Sch.55 para.4, see *Revenue and Customs
Commissioners v Donaldson* [2015]
S.T.C. 689 (UT (Tax)), Warren J
Sch.55 para.6, amended: 2015 c.11
Sch.20 para.15
Sch.55 para.6A, amended: 2015 c.11
Sch.20 para.16
Sch.55 para.6A, repealed: 2015 c.11
Sch.20 para.16
Sch.55 para.6AA, added: 2015 c.11
Sch.20 para.17
Sch.55 para.15, amended: 2015 c.11
Sch.20 para.18
Sch.55 para.17, amended: 2015 c.11
Sch.20 para.19
Sch.55 para.18, see *Revenue and
Customs Commissioners v Donaldson*
[2015] S.T.C. 689 (UT (Tax)), Warren J
Sch.56 para.1, amended: 2015 c.11 s.104,
2015 c.33 s.38
Sch.56 para.3, amended: 2015 c.11 s.104
Sch.56 para.4, amended: 2015 c.33 s.38

**11. Borders, Citizenship and Immigration
Act 2009**

s.55, see *HH (Nigeria) v Secretary of
State for the Home Department* [2015]
CSIH 33, 2015 S.C. 613 (IH (Ex Div)),
Lord Brodie; see *MK (Section 55:
Tribunal Options: Sierra Leone)* [2015]
UKUT 223 (IAC), [2015] I.N.L.R. 563
(UT (IAC)), McCloskey J; see
*Mohammed (Family Court Proceedings:
Outcome)* [2015] Imm. A.R. 182 (UT
(IAC)), Judge Storey; see *N (Anti-
Trafficking Convention: Respondent's
Duties)* [2015] UKUT 170 (IAC), [2015]
Imm. A.R. 886 (UT (IAC)), Judge Allen;
see *R. (on the application of Alladin) v
Secretary of State for the Home
Department* [2014] EWCA Civ 1334,
[2015] Imm. A.R. 237 (CA (Civ Div)),
Laws LJ

12. Political Parties and Elections Act 2009
s.38A, substituted: SI 2015/1376 Sch.2
para.13
18. Perpetuities and Accumulations Act 2009
s.5, see *Allfrey v Allfrey* [2015] EWHC
1717 (Ch), [2015] W.T.L.R. 1117 (Ch
D), Jeremy Cousins QC
**20. Local Democracy, Economic
Development and Construction Act 2009**
Part 7, repealed: 2015 c.20 s.102
s.35, repealed: 2015 c.20 Sch.13 para.6
s.59, enabling: SI 2015/69, SI 2015/70,
SI 2015/72, SI 2015/73, SI 2015/74, SI
2015/75, SI 2015/76, SI 2015/77, SI
2015/78, SI 2015/111, SI 2015/112, SI
2015/113, SI 2015/114, SI 2015/1461, SI
2015/1462, SI 2015/1858, SI 2015/1859,
SI 2015/1860, SI 2015/1861, SI
2015/1871, SI 2015/1872, SI 2015/1873,
SI 2015/1874, SI 2015/2026, SI
2015/2034, SI 2015/2036, SI 2015/2063
s.104, enabling: SI 2015/960
s.114, enabling: SI 2015/960
s.123, repealed: 2015 c.20 Sch.13 para.6
Sch.1 para.5, amended: 2015 c.20 s.95
Sch.1 para.12, amended: 2015 c.20 s.95
Sch.1 para.13, amended: 2015 c.20 s.95
21. Health Act 2009
s.4, enabling: SI 2015/1426
**22. Apprenticeships, Skills, Children and
Learning Act 2009**
Part 1 c.1, amended: 2015 c.20 Sch.1
para.6
Part 1 c.1, amended: 2015 c.20 Sch.1
para.9
Part 1 c.1, amended: 2015 c.20 Sch.1
para.10
Part 1 c.1, amended: 2015 c.20 Sch.1
para.13
Part 1 c.A1, added: 2015 c.20 Sch.1
para.1
Part 4, substituted: 2015 c.20 Sch.14
para.31
Part 4 c.1, substituted: 2015 c.20 Sch.14
para.31
Part 4 c.2, substituted: 2015 c.20 Sch.14
para.31
Part 4 c.3, amended: 2015 c.20 Sch.14
para.31
s.1, repealed: 2015 c.20 Sch.1 para.7
s.3, repealed: 2015 c.20 Sch.1 para.8

s.10, enabling: SI 2015/1733
s.11, amended: 2015 c.20 Sch.1 para.9
s.11, repealed: 2015 c.20 Sch.1 para.9
s.12, repealed: 2015 c.20 Sch.1 para.10
s.13, repealed: 2015 c.20 Sch.1 para.11
s.15, varied: SI 2015/994 Sch.1 para.5
s.18, amended: 2015 c.20 Sch.1 para.25
s.19, amended: 2015 c.20 Sch.1 para.26
s.19, repealed: 2015 c.20 Sch.1 para.26
s.20, amended: 2015 c.20 Sch.1 para.27
s.23, repealed: 2015 c.20 Sch.1 para.12
s.24, varied: SI 2015/994 Sch.1 para.6
s.25, varied: SI 2015/994 Sch.1 para.7
s.25, enabling: SI 2015/303, SI
2015/1761
s.32, repealed: 2015 c.20 Sch.1 para.14
s.38, amended: 2015 c.20 Sch.1 para.15
s.38, varied: SI 2015/994 Sch.1 para.8
s.39, amended: 2015 c.20 Sch.1 para.16
s.81, repealed: 2015 c.20 Sch.14 para.2
s.82, repealed: 2015 c.20 Sch.14 para.3
s.83, amended: 2015 c.20 Sch.1 para.17,
Sch.14 para.4
s.83A, amended: 2015 c.20 Sch.14
para.5, Sch.1 para.18
s.83A, repealed: 2015 c.20 Sch.1 para.18
, Sch.14 para.5
s.83B, amended: 2015 c.20 Sch.1
para.19, Sch.14 para.6
s.83B, repealed: 2015 c.20 Sch.1 para.19
s.84, repealed: 2015 c.20 Sch.14 para.7
s.85, repealed: 2015 c.20 Sch.14 para.8
s.86, amended: 2015 c.20 Sch.14 para.9
s.86, repealed: 2015 c.20 Sch.14 para.9
s.87, amended: 2015 c.20 Sch.14 para.10
s.87, repealed: 2015 c.20 Sch.14 para.10
s.88, amended: 2015 c.20 Sch.14 para.11
s.90, amended: 2015 c.20 Sch.1 para.20,
Sch.14 para.12
s.100, amended: 2015 c.20 Sch.14
para.13, Sch.1 para.2
s.100, repealed: 2015 c.20 Sch.14 para.13
s.101, amended: 2015 c.20 Sch.1 para.3,
Sch.14 para.14
s.101, repealed: 2015 c.20 Sch.1 para.3
s.102, amended: 2015 c.20 Sch.14
para.15
s.103, amended: 2015 c.20 Sch.14
para.16, Sch.1 para.4
s.103, repealed: 2015 c.20 Sch.14 para.16

s.105, amended: 2015 c.20 Sch.14
para.17
s.105, repealed: 2015 c.20 Sch.1 para.21
s.106, repealed: 2015 c.20 Sch.14 para.18
s.107, amended: 2015 c.20 Sch.14
para.19
s.107, repealed: 2015 c.20 Sch.14 para.19
s.108, repealed: 2015 c.20 Sch.14 para.20
s.110, repealed: 2015 c.20 Sch.14 para.21
s.111, repealed: 2015 c.20 Sch.14 para.22
s.115, amended: 2015 c.20 Sch.14
para.23
s.116, amended: 2015 c.20 Sch.14
para.24
s.117, repealed: 2015 c.20 Sch.14 para.25
s.120A, added: 2015 c.20 Sch.14 para.26
s.121, amended: 2015 c.20 Sch.14
para.27, Sch.1 para.22
s.122, amended: 2015 c.20 Sch.14
para.28
s.122, repealed: 2015 c.20 Sch.14 para.28
s.253A, added: 2015 c.26 s.79
s.253A, enabling: SI 2015/1567
s.262, amended: 2015 c.26 s.79
s.262, enabling: SI 2015/1567
s.267, amended: 2015 c.20 Sch.1 para.23
Sch.4, repealed: 2015 c.20 Sch.14
para.29
Sch.5 Part 2 para.3, amended: 2015 c.20
Sch.14 para.30
Sch.5 Part 2 para.8, repealed: 2015 c.20
Sch.14 para.30

23. Marine and Coastal Access Act 2009
see *R. (on the application of Powell) v
Brighton Marina Co Ltd* [2015] EWCA
Civ 650, [2015] J.P.L. 1301 (CA (Civ
Div)), Arden LJ
s.67, enabling: SI 2015/1431
s.73, amended: SI 2015/374 Art.9
s.73A, added: SI 2015/374 Art.9
s.74, enabling: SI 2015/663, SSI
2015/438
s.85, amended: SI 2015/664 Sch.4
para.43
s.92, amended: SI 2015/664 Sch.4
para.43
s.93, amended: SI 2015/664 Sch.5
para.15
s.98, enabling: SI 2015/1674
s.99, enabling: SI 2015/1674

s.103, amended: SI 2015/664 Sch.4
para.43
s.105, amended: SI 2015/664 Sch.4
para.43
s.140, amended: SI 2015/664 Sch.4
para.43
s.163, amended: SI 2015/664 Sch.4
para.43
s.189, enabling: SI 2015/2076
s.190, amended: SI 2015/664 Sch.4
para.43
s.199, repealed: SI 2015/664 Sch.4
para.102
s.205, repealed: SI 2015/664 Sch.4
para.102
s.220, repealed: SI 2015/664 Sch.4
para.102
s.232, amended: SI 2015/664 Sch.4
para.93
s.232, enabling: SI 2015/10
s.292, amended: SI 2015/664 Sch.4
para.43
s.292, repealed: SI 2015/664 Sch.4
para.43
s.316, enabling: SI 2015/10, SI
2015/1431, SI 2015/1674, SI 2015/2076

24. Welfare Reform Act 2009
s.50, amended: SI 2015/914 Sch.1
para.94, SSI 2015/157 Sch.1 para.9
s.51, repealed: SI 2015/583 Sch.2 para.7

25. Coroners and Justice Act 2009
s.9A, added: 2015 c.2 Sch.13 para.1
s.54, see *R. v Gurpinar (Mustafa)* [2015]
EWCA Crim 178, [2015] 1 W.L.R. 3442
(CA (Crim Div)), Lord Thomas LCJ
s.55, see *R. v Gurpinar (Mustafa)* [2015]
EWCA Crim 178, [2015] 1 W.L.R. 3442
(CA (Crim Div)), Lord Thomas LCJ
s.56, see *R. v Gurpinar (Mustafa)* [2015]
EWCA Crim 178, [2015] 1 W.L.R. 3442
(CA (Crim Div)), Lord Thomas LCJ
s.71, repealed: 2015 c.30 Sch.5 para.8
s.87, see *R. (on the application of B) v
Westminster Magistrates' Court* [2015]
A.C. 1195 (SC), Lord Neuberger PSC
s.125, see *Attorney General's Reference
(No.117 of 2014)* [2015] EWCA Crim 44,
[2015] 1 W.L.R. 3201 (CA (Crim Div)),
Pitchford LJ; see *Attorney General's
Reference (No.26 of 2015)* [2015] EWCA

Crim 1119, [2015] 2 Cr. App. R. (S.) 53
(CA (Crim Div)), Pitchford LJ
s.125, amended: 2015 c.2 Sch.5 para.17
s.131, amended: 2015 c.2 Sch.3 para.16
s.182, enabling: SI 2015/819
Sch.1 Part 1 para.1, amended: 2015 c.2
Sch.6 para.12
Sch.2 para.2, enabling: SI 2015/658, SI
2015/1491
Sch.5, see *R. (on the application of
Revenue and Customs Commissioners) v
HM Coroner for Liverpool* [2014]
EWHC 1586 (Admin), [2015] Q.B. 481
(DC), Gross LJ
Sch.6 Part 1, amended: 2015 c.2 Sch.13
para.4
Sch.6 Part 1 para.5A, added: 2015 c.2
Sch.13 para.5
Sch.6 Part 1A, added: 2015 c.2 Sch.13
para.6
Sch.6 Part 3 para.11, added: 2015 c.2
Sch.13 para.7
Sch.21 Part 9 para.93, repealed: 2015 c.2
Sch.7 para.22

26. Policing and Crime Act 2009
see *R. (on the application of James) v
Governor of Birmingham Prison* [2015]
EWCA Civ 58, [2015] 1 W.L.R. 4210
(CA (Civ Div)), Arden LJ
Part 4, amended: 2015 c.9 Sch.4 para.83
s.27, see *R. (on the application of
Bridgerow Ltd) v Cheshire West and
Chester BC* [2014] EWHC 1187
(Admin), [2015] P.T.S.R. 91 (QBD
(Admin)), Stuart-Smith J
s.34, substituted: 2015 c.9 s.51
s.35, amended: 2015 c.9 Sch.4 para.84
s.43, see *R. (on the application of James)
v Governor of Birmingham Prison* [2015]
EWCA Civ 58, [2015] 1 W.L.R. 4210
(CA (Civ Div)), Arden LJ
s.48, enabling: SI 2015/421
s.49, amended: 2015 c.9 Sch.4 para.85
s.112, enabling: SI 2015/925
s.116, enabling: SI 2015/983
Sch.5A Part 3 para.14, amended: 2015
c.2 Sch.9 para.27

2010

01. Children and Families (Wales) Measure 2010
s.48, amended: SI 2015/664 Sch.5 para.16
1. Video Recordings Act 2010
see *R. v Dryzner (Ewa)* [2014] EWCA Crim 2438, (2015) 179 J.P. 29 (CA (Crim Div)), Fulford LJ
02. Social Care Charges (Wales) Measure 2010
s.2, enabling: SI 2015/720
s.7, enabling: SI 2015/720
s.12, enabling: SI 2015/720
s.17, enabling: SI 2015/720
4. Corporation Tax Act 2010
see *European Commission v United Kingdom (C-172/13)* [2015] Ch. 394 (ECJ (Grand Chamber)), Judge Skouris (President)
Part 7A, added: 2015 c.11 Sch.2 para.1
Part 7A c.4, added: 2015 c.33 Sch.3 para.1
Part 8 c.5A, repealed: 2015 c.11 Sch.11 para.13
Part 8 c.6A, added: 2015 c.11 Sch.12 para.2
Part 8 c.7, repealed: 2015 c.11 Sch.12 para.3
Part 8 c.9, added: 2015 c.11 Sch.13 para.2
Part 8B, added: 2015 c.21 s.1
Part 8C, added: 2015 c.33 s.38
Part 14B, added: 2015 c.11 Sch.3 para.1
s.1, amended: 2015 c.11 Sch.2 para.4, Sch.3 para.2, 2015 c.21 Sch.2 para.5, 2015 c.33 s.38
s.9A, amended: 2015 c.33 s.34
s.9A, repealed: 2015 c.33 s.34
s.9B, amended: 2015 c.33 s.34
s.9B, repealed: 2015 c.33 s.34
s.17, amended: 2015 c.33 s.34
s.60, see *Hamilton & Kinneil (Archerfield) Ltd v Revenue and Customs Commissioners* [2015] UKUT 130 (TCC), [2015] S.T.C. 1852 (UT (Tax)), Warren J
s.129, amended: 2015 c.33 s.35
s.130, amended: 2015 c.33 s.35
s.133, amended: 2015 c.33 s.35

s.133, repealed: 2015 c.33 s.35
s.134A, repealed: 2015 c.33 s.35
s.269A, amended: 2015 c.33 Sch.3 para.5
s.269B, amended: 2015 c.33 s.20
s.269BA, amended: 2015 c.33 s.20
s.269BC, amended: 2015 c.33 s.20
s.269BC, repealed: 2015 c.33 s.20
s.269CN, amended: 2015 c.33 s.19
s.270, amended: 2015 c.11 Sch.14 para.2
s.270, repealed: 2015 c.11 Sch.11 para.11, Sch.14 para.2
s.307, amended: 2015 c.11 Sch.11 para.2
s.309, amended: 2015 c.11 Sch.11 para.3
s.311, amended: 2015 c.11 Sch.11 para.4
s.316, amended: 2015 c.11 Sch.11 para.5
s.317, amended: 2015 c.11 Sch.11 para.6
s.318A, added: 2015 c.11 Sch.11 para.7
s.326, amended: 2015 c.11 Sch.11 para.8
s.327, amended: 2015 c.11 Sch.11 para.9
s.328A, added: 2015 c.11 Sch.11 para.10
s.330, amended: 2015 c.11 s.48, Sch.14 para.3
s.330ZA, added: 2015 c.11 Sch.14 para.4
s.349A, varied: 2015 c.11 Sch.13 para.3
s.350, varied: 2015 c.11 Sch.13 para.4
s.356C, amended: 2015 c.11 Sch.14 para.5
s.356DB, repealed: 2015 c.11 Sch.14 para.6
s.356IB, added: 2015 c.11 Sch.14 para.7
s.356JB, amended: 2015 c.11 Sch.14 para.8
s.398D, repealed: 2015 c.33 s.36
s.658, amended: SI 2015/725 Reg.3
s.659, enabling: SI 2015/725
s.660, amended: SI 2015/725 Reg.10
s.660, enabling: SI 2015/725
s.660A, enabling: SI 2015/725
s.661CA, added: SI 2015/725 Reg.4
s.730G, amended: 2015 c.33 s.37
s.730H, amended: 2015 c.33 s.37
s.969, varied: 2015 c.11 Sch.16 para.1
s.1065, amended: 2015 c.11 Sch.1 para.26
s.1100, amended: 2015 c.11 s.19
s.1139, amended: 2015 c.11 s.115
s.1171, amended: 2015 c.11 s.125
Sch.4, amended: 2015 c.11 Sch.2 para.5, Sch.3 para.3, Sch.11 para.12, Sch.14 para.9, 2015 c.21 Sch.2 para.6, 2015 c.33 Sch.3 para.6

06. Playing Fields (Community Involvement in Disposal Decisions) (Wales) Measure 2010

s.1, enabling: SI 2015/1403

8. Taxation (International and Other Provisions) Act 2010

s.2, enabling: SI 2015/1888, SI 2015/1889, SI 2015/1890, SI 2015/1891, SI 2015/1892, SI 2015/2007, SI 2015/2008, SI 2015/2009, SI 2015/2011

s.332AA, added: SI 2015/662 Reg.2

s.346, amended: SI 2015/662 Reg.2

s.348, amended: SI 2015/662 Reg.2

s.353AA, enabling: SI 2015/662

s.371BC, amended: 2015 c.21 Sch.2 para.2, 2015 c.33 Sch.3 para.8

s.371BI, added: 2015 c.33 Sch.3 para.9

s.371UBA, added: 2015 c.33 Sch.3 para.10

s.371UD, amended: 2015 c.11 Sch.2 para.6, 2015 c.21 Sch.2 para.3

s.371UD, repealed: 2015 c.33 s.36

9. Child Poverty Act 2010

s.8B, enabling: SI 2015/83

s.24, repealed: 2015 c.20 s.100

10. Third Parties (Rights against Insurers) Act 2010

s.1, amended: 2015 c.4 Sch.2 para.4

s.4, amended: 2015 c.4 Sch.2 para.2

s.4, repealed: 2015 c.20 Sch.6 para.2

s.6, amended: 2015 c.4 Sch.2 para.3

s.19, substituted: 2015 c.4 s.19

s.19A, added: 2015 c.4 Sch.2 para.6

Sch.3, substituted: 2015 c.4 Sch.2 para.5

Sch.3 para.1A, added: 2015 c.4 Sch.2 para.5

13. Finance Act 2010

s.7, repealed: 2015 c.1 Sch.1 para.21

Sch.6 Part 1 para.7, amended: 2015 c.11 s.115

15. Equality Act 2010

see *Blackwood v Birmingham and Solihull Mental Health NHS Foundation Trust* [2015] I.C.R. 308 (EAT), Judge Eady QC; see *EAD Solicitors LLP v Abrams* [2015] B.C.C. 882 (EAT), Langstaff J; see *General Dynamics Information Technology Ltd v Carranza* [2015] I.C.R. 169 (EAT), Judge David Richardson; see *Metroline Travel Ltd v Stoute* [2015] I.R.L.R. 465 (EAT), Judge Serota QC; see *NHS Direct NHS Trust v*

Gunn [2015] I.R.L.R. 799 (EAT), Langstaff J; see *Poshteh v Kensington and Chelsea RLBC* [2015] EWCA Civ 711, [2015] H.L.R. 36 (CA (Civ Div)), Moore-Bick LJ; see *R. (on the application of Coll) v Secretary of State for Justice* [2015] EWCA Civ 328, [2015] 1 W.L.R. 3781 (CA (Civ Div)), Lord Dyson MR; see *R. (on the application of Roberts) v Commissioner of Police of the Metropolis* [2015] UKSC 79 (SC), Lady Hale DPSC; see *Timothy James Consulting Ltd v Wilton* [2015] I.C.R. 764 (EAT), Singh J

s.1, repealed: 2015 c.20 s.100

s.9, see *Chandhok v Tirkey* [2015] I.C.R. 527 (EAT), Langstaff J; see *Moore v Secretary of State for Communities and Local Government* [2015] EWHC 44 (Admin), [2015] B.L.G.R. 405 (QBD (Admin)), Gilbart J

s.13, see *EAD Solicitors LLP v Abrams* [2015] B.C.C. 882 (EAT), Langstaff J

s.15, see *Akerman-Livingstone v Aster Communities Ltd (formerly Flourish Homes Ltd)* [2015] UKSC 15, [2015] A.C. 1399 (SC), Lord Neuberger PSC; see *Hall v Chief Constable of West Yorkshire* [2015] I.R.L.R. 893 (EAT), Elisabeth Laing J; see *Swansea University Pension and Assurance Scheme Trustees v Williams* [2015] I.C.R. 1197 (EAT), Langstaff J

s.18, see *Sefton BC v Wainwright* [2015] I.C.R. 652 (EAT), Judge Eady QC

s.19, see *Edie v HCL Insurance BPO Services Ltd* [2015] I.C.R. 713 (EAT), Lewis J; see *Essop v Home Office (UK Border Agency)* [2015] EWCA Civ 609, [2015] I.C.R. 1063 (CA (Civ Div)), Sir Terence Etherton C; see *Games v University of Kent* [2015] I.R.L.R. 202 (EAT), Judge David Richardson; see *Moore v Secretary of State for Communities and Local Government* [2015] EWHC 44 (Admin), [2015] B.L.G.R. 405 (QBD (Admin)), Gilbart J; see *R. (on the application of Diocese of Menevia) v Swansea City and County Council* [2015] EWHC 1436 (Admin),

[2015] P.T.S.R. 1507 (QBD (Admin)), Wyn Williams J
s.20, see *General Dynamics Information Technology Ltd v Carranza* [2015] I.C.R. 169 (EAT), Judge David Richardson; see *P v East Sussex CC* [2014] EWHC 4634 (Admin), [2015] E.L.R. 178 (QBD (Admin)), Timothy Straker QC; see *Paulley v First Group Plc* [2014] EWCA Civ 1573, [2015] 1 W.L.R. 3384 (CA (Civ Div)), Arden LJ
s.26, see *Chawla v Hewlett Packard Ltd* [2015] I.R.L.R. 356 (EAT), Slade J; see *Timothy James Consulting Ltd v Wilton* [2015] I.C.R. 764 (EAT), Singh J
s.27, see *EAD Solicitors LLP v Abrams* [2015] B.C.C. 882 (EAT), Langstaff J
s.29, see *Campbell v Thomas Cook Tour Operations Ltd* [2014] EWCA Civ 1668, [2015] 1 W.L.R. 2007 (CA (Civ Div)), Longmore LJ; see *G, Applicant* 2015 S.L.T. (Sh Ct) 212 (Sh Ct (Glasgow)), Sheriff J N McCormick; see *R. (on the application of Hardy) v Sandwell MBC* [2015] EWHC 890 (Admin), [2015] P.T.S.R. 1292 (QBD (Admin)), Phillips J; see *R. (on the application of Hottak) v Secretary of State for Foreign and Commonwealth Affairs* [2015] EWHC 1953 (Admin), [2015] I.R.L.R. 827 (QBD (Admin)), Burnett LJ
s.35, see *Akerman-Livingstone v Aster Communities Ltd (formerly Flourish Homes Ltd)* [2015] UKSC 15, [2015] A.C. 1399 (SC), Lord Neuberger PSC
s.39, see *NHS Direct NHS Trust v Gunn* [2015] I.R.L.R. 799 (EAT), Langstaff J; see *R. (on the application of Hottak) v Secretary of State for Foreign and Commonwealth Affairs* [2015] EWHC 1953 (Admin), [2015] I.R.L.R. 827 (QBD (Admin)), Burnett LJ
s.45, see *EAD Solicitors LLP v Abrams* [2015] B.C.C. 882 (EAT), Langstaff J
s.53, see *General Medical Council v Michalak* [2015] I.C.R. 502 (EAT), Langstaff J
s.54, see *Wolfe v North Middlesex University Hospital NHS Trust* [2015] I.C.R. 960 (EAT), Judge Serota QC

s.55, see *Blackwood v Birmingham and Solihull Mental Health NHS Foundation Trust* [2015] I.C.R. 308 (EAT), Judge Eady QC
s.56, see *Blackwood v Birmingham and Solihull Mental Health NHS Foundation Trust* [2015] I.C.R. 308 (EAT), Judge Eady QC
s.83, see *Halawi v WDFG UK Ltd (t/a World Duty Free)* [2014] EWCA Civ 1387, [2015] 3 All E.R. 543 (CA (Civ Div)), Arden LJ; see *Windle v Secretary of State for Justice* [2015] I.C.R. 156 (EAT), Judge Peter Clark
s.91, see *Blackwood v Birmingham and Solihull Mental Health NHS Foundation Trust* [2015] I.C.R. 308 (EAT), Judge Eady QC
s.108, see *Ford Motor Co Ltd v Elliott* [2015] Pens. L.R. 559 (EAT), Slade J
s.118, amended: SI 2015/1392 Reg.7
s.120, see *General Medical Council v Michalak* [2015] I.C.R. 502 (EAT), Langstaff J
s.121, amended: 2015 c.19 Sch.1 para.13
s.121, repealed: 2015 c.19 Sch.1 para.13
s.123, see *McKinney v Newham LBC* [2015] I.C.R. 495 (EAT), Judge Peter Clark
s.124, see *Pereira de Souza v Vinci Construction UK Ltd* [2015] I.C.R. 1034 (EAT), Judge Serota QC
s.124, amended: 2015 c.20 s.2
s.124, repealed: 2015 c.20 s.2
s.125, repealed: 2015 c.20 s.2
s.127, amended: 2015 c.19 Sch.1 para.14
s.140AA, added: SI 2015/1392 Reg.7
s.140AA, repealed: SI 2015/1972 Reg.5
s.141, amended: 2015 c.19 Sch.1 para.15
s.149, see *Connors v Secretary of State for Communities and Local Government* [2014] EWHC 2358 (Admin), [2015] J.P.L. 196 (QBD (Admin)), Lewis J; see *Hotak v Southwark LBC* [2015] UKSC 30, [2015] 2 W.L.R. 1341 (SC), Lord Neuberger PSC; see *Hunt v North Somerset Council* [2015] UKSC 51, [2015] 1 W.L.R. 3575 (SC), Lady Hale DPSC; see *Moore v Secretary of State for Communities and Local Government* [2015] EWHC 44 (Admin), [2015]

B.L.G.R. 405 (QBD (Admin)), Gilbart J;
see *P v East Sussex CC* [2014] EWHC
4634 (Admin), [2015] E.L.R. 178 (QBD
(Admin)), Timothy Straker QC; see *R.
(on the application of Coll) v Secretary of
State for Justice* [2015] EWCA Civ 328,
[2015] 1 W.L.R. 3781 (CA (Civ Div)),
Lord Dyson MR; see *R. (on the
application of Cushnie) v Secretary of
State for Health* [2014] EWHC 3626
(Admin), [2015] P.T.S.R. 384 (QBD
(Admin)), Singh J; see *R. (on the
application of Diocese of Menevia) v
Swansea City and County Council* [2015]
EWHC 1436 (Admin), [2015] P.T.S.R.
1507 (QBD (Admin)), Wyn Williams J;
see *R. (on the application of Hottak) v
Secretary of State for Foreign and
Commonwealth Affairs* [2015] EWHC
1953 (Admin), [2015] I.R.L.R. 827
(QBD (Admin)), Burnett LJ; see *R. (on
the application of Karia) v Leicester City
Council* [2014] EWHC 3105 (Admin),
(2015) 141 B.M.L.R. 163 (QBD
(Admin)), Sir Stephen Silber; see *R. (on
the application of Robson) v Salford City
Council* [2015] EWCA Civ 6, [2015]
P.T.S.R. 1349 (CA (Civ Div)), Richards
LJ; see *R. (on the application of S) v
Director of Legal Aid Casework* [2015]
EWHC 1965 (Admin), [2015] 1 W.L.R.
5283 (QBD (Admin)), Collins J; see
*West Berkshire DC v Department for
Communities and Local Government*
[2015] EWHC 2222 (Admin), [2015]
B.L.G.R. 884 (QBD (Admin)), Holgate J
s.151, enabling: SSI 2015/83
s.153, enabling: SSI 2015/254
s.155, enabling: SSI 2015/254
s.183, amended: 2015 c.20 Sch.10
para.29
s.183, repealed: 2015 c.20 Sch.10 para.29
s.183, enabling: SI 2015/393, SI
2015/1631
s.184, repealed: 2015 c.20 Sch.10 para.30
s.185, amended: 2015 c.20 Sch.10
para.30
s.185, repealed: 2015 c.20 Sch.10 para.30
s.207, enabling: SI 2015/393, SI
2015/1631, SSI 2015/254
s.208, repealed: 2015 c.20 Sch.10 para.30

Sch.1 Pt 1 para.2, see *Wolfe v North
Middlesex University Hospital NHS Trust*
[2015] I.C.R. 960 (EAT), Judge Serota
QC
Sch.3 Pt 9 para.33, see *Campbell v
Thomas Cook Tour Operations Ltd*
[2014] EWCA Civ 1668, [2015] 1
W.L.R. 2007 (CA (Civ Div)), Longmore
LJ
Sch.19 Part 1, amended: 2015 c.2 Sch.3
para.17
Sch.19 Part 3, added: SSI 2015/83 Art.2
17. Crime and Security Act 2010
s.34, repealed: 2015 c.9 Sch.4 para.86
18. Personal Care at Home Act 2010
s.1, amended: SI 2015/914 Sch.1 para.95
20. Sunbeds (Regulation) Act 2010
s.2, amended: SI 2015/664 Sch.4 para.44
s.10, amended: SI 2015/664 Sch.4
para.94
23. Bribery Act 2010
see *Cruddas v Calvert* [2015] EWCA Civ
171, [2015] E.M.L.R. 16 (CA (Civ Div)),
Jackson LJ
24. Digital Economy Act 2010
s.17, repealed: 2015 c.20 s.56
s.42, repealed: SI 2015/664 Sch.4
para.103
27. Energy Act 2010
s.9, enabling: SI 2015/652
s.10, enabling: SI 2015/652
s.14, enabling: SI 2015/652
s.31, enabling: SI 2015/652
29. Flood and Water Management Act 2010
Sch.4 para.43, amended: SI 2015/48
Art.15
32. Academies Act 2010
s.3, enabling: SI 2015/1554
33. Finance (No.3) Act 2010
Sch.6 para.4, repealed: 2015 c.33 s.35
Sch.6 para.5, repealed: 2015 c.33 s.35
38. Terrorist Asset-Freezing etc Act 2010
s.2, see *Begg v HM Treasury* [2015]
EWHC 1851 (Admin), [2015] 1 W.L.R.
4424 (QBD (Admin)), Cranston J
s.31, amended: 2015 c.6 s.45
s.54, enabling: SI 2015/1763
40. Identity Documents Act 2010
see *Guardian News and Media Ltd v
Incedal* [2014] EWCA Crim 1861,

[2015] 1 Cr. App. R. 4 (CA (Crim Div)),
Gross LJ

2011

**1. Parliamentary Voting System and
Constituencies Act 2011**
s.13, amended: SI 2015/1376 Sch.2
para.14
s.14, amended: SI 2015/1376 Sch.2
para.14
01. Welsh Language (Wales) Measure 2011
s.26, enabling: SI 2015/996
s.27, enabling: SI 2015/996
s.39, enabling: SI 2015/996
s.150, enabling: SI 2015/996
s.156, enabling: SI 2015/985, SI
2015/1217, SI 2015/1413
Sch.6, amended: SI 2015/1682 Sch.1
para.12
5. Postal Services Act 2011
s.35, see *R. (on the application of Whistl
UK Ltd (formerly TNT Post UK Ltd)) v
Revenue and Customs Commissioners*
[2014] EWHC 3480 (Admin), [2015]
S.T.C. 1077 (QBD (Admin)), Kenneth
Parker J
s.38, see *R. (on the application of Whistl
UK Ltd (formerly TNT Post UK Ltd)) v
Revenue and Customs Commissioners*
[2014] EWHC 3480 (Admin), [2015]
S.T.C. 1077 (QBD (Admin)), Kenneth
Parker J
8. Wreck Removal Convention Act 2011
s.2, enabling: SI 2015/133
11. Finance Act 2011
Sch.16 Part 1 para.33, repealed: 2015
c.33 s.21
Sch.16 Part 1 para.42, repealed: 2015
c.33 s.22
Sch.19 Part 2 para.6, amended: 2015 c.11
s.76, 2015 c.33 Sch.2 para.1, Sch.2
para.2, Sch.2 para.3, Sch.2 para.4, Sch.2
para.5, Sch.2 para.6
Sch.19 Part 2 para.7, amended: 2015 c.11
s.76, 2015 c.33 Sch.2 para.1, Sch.2
para.2, Sch.2 para.3, Sch.2 para.4, Sch.2
para.5, Sch.2 para.6
Sch.19 Part 3 para.12, amended: 2015
c.33 s.20

Sch.19 Part 7 para.66, enabling: SI
2015/335, SI 2015/344
Sch.19 Part 7 para.67A, enabling: SI
2015/335
Sch.19 Part 8 para.70, amended: 2015
c.33 s.20
Sch.19 Part 8 para.72, amended: 2015
c.33 s.20
Sch.19 Part 8 para.73, amended: 2015
c.33 s.20
Sch.19 Part 8 para.78, amended: 2015
c.33 s.20
Sch.19 Part 8 para.80, amended: 2015
c.33 s.20
Sch.23 Part 1 para.1, enabling: SI
2015/672
Sch.23 Part 5 para.45, amended: 2015
c.11 s.105
12. European Union Act 2011
s.6, see *Wheeler v Office of the Prime
Minister* [2014] EWHC 3815 (Admin),
[2015] 1 C.M.L.R. 46 (QBD (Admin)),
Sir Brian Leveson PQBD
**13. Police Reform and Social Responsibility
Act 2011**
s.50, amended: SI 2015/1526 Sch.1
para.1
s.54, amended: SI 2015/1376 Sch.2
para.15
s.54, enabling: SI 2015/2031
s.55, amended: SI 2015/1526 Sch.1
para.1
s.58, amended: SI 2015/1376 Sch.2
para.15, SI 2015/1526 Sch.1 para.1
s.58, repealed: SI 2015/1526 Sch.1 para.1
s.58, enabling: SI 2015/665
s.65, amended: SI 2015/1526 Sch.1
para.1
s.66, amended: SI 2015/1526 Sch.1
para.1
s.70, amended: SI 2015/1526 Sch.1
para.1
s.71, amended: SI 2015/1526 Sch.1
para.1
s.75, amended: SI 2015/1526 Sch.1
para.1
s.75, enabling: SI 2015/2028
s.111, repealed: 2015 c.20 Sch.18 para.15
s.118, repealed: SI 2015/664 Sch.4
para.104

s.154, amended: SI 2015/1376 Sch.2
para.15
s.154, enabling: SI 2015/2031
Sch.16 Part 3 para.243, repealed: 2015
c.20 s.103
Sch.16 Part 3 para.377, repealed: 2015
c.20 s.102

16. Energy Act 2011
s.10, enabling: SSI 2015/386
s.42, enabling: SI 2015/799
s.43, enabling: SI 2015/962
s.44, enabling: SI 2015/962
s.45, enabling: SI 2015/962
s.46, enabling: SI 2015/962
s.47, enabling: SI 2015/962
s.48, enabling: SI 2015/962
s.49, enabling: SI 2015/962
s.50, enabling: SI 2015/962
s.51, enabling: SI 2015/962
s.52, enabling: SI 2015/962
s.74, enabling: SI 2015/609
s.75, enabling: SSI 2015/386
s.121, enabling: SI 2015/880

18. Armed Forces Act 2011
s.20, repealed: 2015 c.19 Sch.1 para.16

19. Pensions Act 2011
s.19, repealed: 2015 c.8 Sch.1 para.11
s.21, repealed: 2015 c.8 s.41
s.38, enabling: SI 2015/676

20. Localism Act 2011
see *R. (on the application of Larkfleet
Homes Ltd) v Rutland CC* [2014] EWHC
4095 (Admin), [2015] P.T.S.R. 589
(QBD (Admin)), Collins J; see *R. (on the
application of Larkfleet Homes Ltd) v
Rutland CC* [2015] EWCA Civ 597,
[2015] P.T.S.R. 1369 (CA (Civ Div)),
Moore-Bick LJ
s.5, enabling: SI 2015/973
s.81, see *R. (on the application of
Draper) v Lincolnshire CC* [2014]
EWHC 2388 (Admin), [2015] P.T.S.R.
769 (QBD (Admin)), Collins J
s.81, enabling: SI 2015/582
s.184, see *Charalambous v Ng* [2014]
EWCA Civ 1604, [2015] 1 W.L.R. 3018
(CA (Civ Div)), Black LJ
s.198, enabling: SI 2015/53, SI 2015/442
s.208, amended: 2015 c.7 s.32
s.235, enabling: SI 2015/442, SI
2015/973

21. Education Act 2011
s.30, repealed: 2015 c.20 Sch.14 para.65
s.70, repealed: 2015 c.20 Sch.14 para.65
s.72, repealed: 2015 c.20 Sch.14 para.65
Sch.13 para.10, repealed: 2015 c.20
Sch.16 para.2
Sch.16 para.45, repealed: 2015 c.20 s.102
Sch.18 para.4, repealed: 2015 c.20
Sch.14 para.65
Sch.18 para.6, repealed: 2015 c.20
Sch.14 para.65

**23. Terrorism Prevention and Investigation
Measures Act 2011**
s.2, amended: 2015 c.6 s.17
s.3, amended: 2015 c.6 s.20
s.4, amended: 2015 c.6 s.20
s.20, amended: 2015 c.6 s.45
s.20, repealed: 2015 c.6 s.45
s.23, amended: 2015 c.6 s.17
Sch.1 Part 1 para.1, amended: 2015 c.6
s.16
Sch.1 Part 1 para.1, repealed: 2015 c.6
s.16
Sch.1 Part 1 para.2, amended: 2015 c.6
s.17
Sch.1 Part 1 para.6A, added: 2015 c.6
s.18
Sch.1 Part 1 para.10A, added: 2015 c.6
s.19
Sch.3 para.2, amended: SSI 2015/338
Sch.2 para.14
Sch.3 para.4, amended: SSI 2015/338
Sch.2 para.14

24. Public Bodies Act 2011
s.1, enabling: SI 2015/475, SI 2015/850,
SI 2015/978
s.6, enabling: SI 2015/475, SI 2015/850,
SI 2015/978
s.35, enabling: SI 2015/475, SI 2015/850,
SI 2015/978
Sch.1, amended: 2015 c.7 s.54, SI
2015/475 Sch.1 Part 1, SI 2015/850
Art.3, SI 2015/978 Sch.1 Part 1

25. Charities Act 2011
see *Kennedy v Information Commissioner*
[2015] A.C. 455 (SC), Lord Neuberger
JSC
s.3, see *Human Dignity Trust v Charity
Commission for England and Wales*
[2015] W.T.L.R. 789 (FTT (GRC)),
Judge Alison McKenna

s.73, enabling: SI 2015/198
s.139, enabling: SI 2015/322
s.144, amended: SI 2015/321 Art.3
s.145, amended: SI 2015/321 Art.4
s.145, enabling: SI 2015/321
s.174, enabling: SI 2015/321
s.176, enabling: SI 2015/322
s.347, enabling: SI 2015/321, SI 2015/322
Sch.3 para.4, enabling: SI 2015/210, SI 2015/1894

2012

3. Public Services (Social Value) Act 2012
s.1, amended: SI 2015/102 Sch.6 para.8
s.1, repealed: SI 2015/102 Sch.6 para.8
5. Welfare Reform Act 2012
s.4, enabling: SI 2015/336, SI 2015/546
s.6, enabling: SI 2015/1362, SI 2015/1754
s.7, enabling: SI 2015/1362, SI 2015/1754
s.8, enabling: SI 2015/67, SI 2015/1649, SI 2015/1754
s.9, enabling: SI 2015/1754
s.10, enabling: SI 2015/1754
s.11, enabling: SI 2015/1647, SI 2015/1754
s.12, enabling: SI 2015/1754
s.18, enabling: SI 2015/89
s.19, enabling: SI 2015/1754
s.22, enabling: SI 2015/89, SI 2015/1754
s.24, enabling: SI 2015/1754
s.26, enabling: SI 2015/1754
s.27, enabling: SI 2015/1754
s.28, enabling: SI 2015/1754
s.32, enabling: SI 2015/1362, SI 2015/1754
s.37, enabling: SI 2015/1754
s.40, enabling: SI 2015/67, SI 2015/1647, SI 2015/1649
s.41, enabling: SI 2015/89
s.42, enabling: SI 2015/67, SI 2015/89, SI 2015/336, SI 2015/345, SI 2015/546, SI 2015/1362, SI 2015/1647, SI 2015/1649, SI 2015/1754, SI 2015/1780
s.96, see *R. (on the application of JS) v Secretary of State for Work and Pensions*

[2015] UKSC 16, [2015] 1 W.L.R. 1449 (SC), Lady Hale DPSC
s.131, enabling: SI 2015/46, SI 2015/124
s.132, enabling: SI 2015/124
s.133, enabling: SI 2015/46, SI 2015/124
s.150, enabling: SI 2015/32, SI 2015/33, SI 2015/101, SI 2015/634, SI 2015/740, SI 2015/1537
Sch.1 para.3, enabling: SI 2015/1754
Sch.1 para.4, enabling: SI 2015/67, SI 2015/345, SI 2015/1754
Sch.1 para.7, enabling: SI 2015/546
Sch.6 para.1, enabling: SI 2015/339, SI 2015/1362, SI 2015/1647, SI 2015/1780
6. Consumer Insurance (Disclosure and Representations) Act 2012
s.2, repealed: 2015 c.4 s.14
s.11, repealed: 2015 c.4 s.21
7. Health and Social Care Act 2012
s.76, amended: SI 2015/102 Sch.6 para.9
s.83, enabling: SI 2015/190
s.118, enabling: SI 2015/2018
s.120, enabling: SI 2015/2018
s.150, enabling: SI 2015/190, SI 2015/2018
s.251A, added: 2015 c.28 s.2
s.251A, enabling: SI 2015/1439
s.251B, added: 2015 c.28 s.3
s.251C, added: 2015 c.28 s.4
s.251C, amended: SI 2015/1438 Reg.4
s.251C, varied: SI 2015/1470 Sch.1
s.251C, enabling: SI 2015/1470
s.304, enabling: SI 2015/190, SI 2015/2018
s.306, enabling: SI 2015/409
Sch.5 para.172, repealed: 2015 c.20 s.102
9. Protection of Freedoms Act 2012
see *Makdessi v Cavendish Square Holdings BV* [2015] UKSC 67, [2015] 3 W.L.R. 1373 (SC), Lord Neuberger PSC; see *Z (Children) (Application for Release of DNA Profiles), Re* [2015] EWCA Civ 34, [2015] 1 W.L.R. 2501 (CA (Civ Div)), Lord Dyson MR
s.25, enabling: SI 2015/1739
s.40, enabling: SI 2015/982
s.41, enabling: SI 2015/982
s.44, enabling: SI 2015/982
s.48, enabling: SI 2015/240
s.51, enabling: SI 2015/240

s.56, see *ParkingEye Ltd v Beavis* [2015]
EWCA Civ 402, [2015] R.T.R. 27 (CA
(Civ Div)), Moore-Bick LJ
s.109, repealed: 2015 c.30 Sch.5 para.9
s.120, enabling: SI 2015/587
Sch.4, see *ParkingEye Ltd v Beavis*
[2015] EWCA Civ 402, [2015] R.T.R. 27
(CA (Civ Div)), Moore-Bick LJ
Sch.4 para.1, see *Makdessi v Cavendish
Square Holdings BV* [2015] UKSC 67,
[2015] 3 W.L.R. 1373 (SC), Lord
Neuberger PSC
Sch.9 Part 10 para.136, repealed: 2015
c.30 Sch.5 para.9
Sch.9 Part 10 para.138, repealed: 2015
c.30 Sch.5 para.9
Sch.9 Part 10 para.140, repealed: 2015
c.30 Sch.5 para.9
Sch.9 Part 10 para.141, repealed: 2015
c.30 Sch.5 para.9

**10. Legal Aid, Sentencing and Punishment
of Offenders Act 2012**
see *Coventry v Lawrence* [2015] UKSC
50, [2015] 1 W.L.R. 3485 (SC), Lord
Neuberger PSC; see *Hartmann Capital
Ltd (In Special Administration), Re*
[2015] EWHC 1514 (Ch), [2015] Bus.
L.R. 983 (Ch D (Companies Ct)), Newey
J; see *K (Children) (Unrepresented
Father: Cross-Examination of Child), Re*
[2015] EWCA Civ 543, [2015] 1 W.L.R.
3801 (CA (Civ Div)), Lord Dyson MR;
see *King's Lynn and West Norfolk BC v
Bunning* [2013] EWHC 3390 (QB),
[2015] 1 W.L.R. 531 (QBD), Blake J; see
*R v R (Family Court: Procedural
Fairness)* [2015] 1 W.L.R. 2743 (Fam
Ct), Peter Jackson J; see *R. (on the
application of Ben Hoare Bell Solicitors)
v Lord Chancellor* [2015] EWHC 523
(Admin), [2015] 1 W.L.R. 4175 (QBD
(Admin)), Beatson LJ; see *R. (on the
application of Letts) v Lord Chancellor*
[2015] EWHC 402 (Admin), [2015] 1
W.L.R. 4497 (QBD (Admin)), Green J;
see *R. (on the application of Public Law
Project) v Secretary of State for Justice*
[2014] EWHC 2365 (Admin), [2015] 1
W.L.R. 251 (DC), Moses LJ; see *R. (on
the application of Rights of Women) v
Lord Chancellor* [2015] EWHC 35

(Admin), [2015] 2 F.L.R. 823 (QBD
(Admin)), Fulford LJ; see *R. v Hibbert
(Christopher Keith)* [2015] EWCA Crim
507, [2015] 2 Cr. App. R. (S.) 15 (CA
(Crim Div)), Pitchford LJ
s.1, see *R. (on the application of Ben
Hoare Bell Solicitors) v Lord Chancellor*
[2015] EWHC 523 (Admin), [2015] 1
W.L.R. 4175 (QBD (Admin)), Beatson
LJ
s.2, see *R. (on the application of Ben
Hoare Bell Solicitors) v Lord Chancellor*
[2015] EWHC 523 (Admin), [2015] 1
W.L.R. 4175 (QBD (Admin)), Beatson
LJ
s.2, enabling: SI 2015/325, SI 2015/882,
SI 2015/898, SI 2015/1369, SI
2015/1416, SI 2015/1678, SI 2015/2049
s.9, see *R. (on the application of Ben
Hoare Bell Solicitors) v Lord Chancellor*
[2015] EWHC 523 (Admin), [2015] 1
W.L.R. 4175 (QBD (Admin)), Beatson
LJ; see *R. (on the application of Public
Law Project) v Secretary of State for
Justice* [2014] EWHC 2365 (Admin),
[2015] 1 W.L.R. 251 (DC), Moses LJ;
see *R. (on the application of Rights of
Women) v Lord Chancellor* [2015]
EWHC 35 (Admin), [2015] 2 F.L.R. 823
(QBD (Admin)), Fulford LJ
s.10, see *Q v Q* [2015] 1 W.L.R. 2040
(Fam Ct), Sir James Munby PFD; see *R.
(on the application of Gudanaviciene) v
Director of Legal Aid Casework* [2014]
EWCA Civ 1622, [2015] 1 W.L.R. 2247
(CA (Civ Div)), Lord Dyson MR; see *R.
(on the application of Public Law
Project) v Secretary of State for Justice*
[2014] EWHC 2365 (Admin), [2015] 1
W.L.R. 251 (DC), Moses LJ; see *R. (on
the application of Rights of Women) v
Lord Chancellor* [2015] EWHC 35
(Admin), [2015] 2 F.L.R. 823 (QBD
(Admin)), Fulford LJ; see *R. (on the
application of S) v Director of Legal Aid
Casework* [2015] EWHC 1965 (Admin),
[2015] 1 W.L.R. 5283 (QBD (Admin)),
Collins J
s.11, enabling: SI 2015/1414, SI
2015/1571, SI 2015/2005

s.12, see *R. (on the application of Rights of Women) v Lord Chancellor* [2015] EWHC 35 (Admin), [2015] 2 F.L.R. 823 (QBD (Admin)), Fulford LJ

s.12, enabling: SI 2015/1416, SI 2015/1678

s.13, enabling: SI 2015/1369, SI 2015/2049

s.14, see *Brown v Haringey LBC* [2015] EWCA Civ 483, [2015] H.L.R. 30 (CA (Civ Div)), Richards LJ; see *King's Lynn and West Norfolk BC v Bunning* [2013] EWHC 3390 (QB), [2015] 1 W.L.R. 531 (QBD), Blake J

s.14, enabling: SI 2015/326, SI 2015/838, SI 2015/1416

s.15, enabling: SI 2015/1369, SI 2015/2049

s.16, see *Brown v Haringey LBC* [2015] EWCA Civ 483, [2015] H.L.R. 30 (CA (Civ Div)), Richards LJ; see *King's Lynn and West Norfolk BC v Bunning* [2013] EWHC 3390 (QB), [2015] 1 W.L.R. 531 (QBD), Blake J

s.18, see *Brown v Haringey LBC* [2015] EWCA Civ 483, [2015] H.L.R. 30 (CA (Civ Div)), Richards LJ

s.18, enabling: SI 2015/1369

s.19, see *King's Lynn and West Norfolk BC v Bunning* [2013] EWHC 3390 (QB), [2015] 1 W.L.R. 531 (QBD), Blake J

s.21, enabling: SI 2015/838, SI 2015/1369, SI 2015/1416, SI 2015/2049

s.22, enabling: SI 2015/838, SI 2015/1408, SI 2015/2005

s.23, enabling: SI 2015/710, SI 2015/838, SI 2015/1416, SI 2015/1678

s.25, enabling: SI 2015/1678

s.27, enabling: SI 2015/1678

s.30, enabling: SI 2015/1678

s.41, see *R. (on the application of Public Law Project) v Secretary of State for Justice* [2014] EWHC 2365 (Admin), [2015] 1 W.L.R. 251 (DC), Moses LJ

s.41, enabling: SI 2015/325, SI 2015/326, SI 2015/710, SI 2015/838, SI 2015/882, SI 2015/898, SI 2015/1369, SI 2015/1408, SI 2015/1414, SI 2015/1416, SI 2015/1571, SI 2015/1678, SI 2015/2005, SI 2015/2049

s.42, see *K (Children) (Unrepresented Father: Cross-Examination of Child), Re* [2015] EWCA Civ 543, [2015] 1 W.L.R. 3801 (CA (Civ Div)), Lord Dyson MR

s.44, see *R. (on the application of Whitston) v Secretary of State for Justice* [2014] EWHC 3044 (Admin), [2015] 1 Costs L.R. 35 (QBD (Admin)), William Davis J

s.46, see *R. (on the application of Whitston) v Secretary of State for Justice* [2014] EWHC 3044 (Admin), [2015] 1 Costs L.R. 35 (QBD (Admin)), William Davis J

s.48, see *R. (on the application of Whitston) v Secretary of State for Justice* [2014] EWHC 3044 (Admin), [2015] 1 Costs L.R. 35 (QBD (Admin)), William Davis J

s.77, enabling: SI 2015/1480

s.85, enabling: SI 2015/664

s.102, amended: 2015 c.2 Sch.9 para.29

s.103, amended: 2015 c.2 Sch.9 para.30

s.103, enabling: SI 2015/569

s.128, amended: 2015 c.2 s.11, Sch.1 para.25

s.149, enabling: SI 2015/664

s.151, enabling: SI 2015/504

Sch.1 Pt 1, see *R. (on the application of Ben Hoare Bell Solicitors) v Lord Chancellor* [2015] EWHC 523 (Admin), [2015] 1 W.L.R. 4175 (QBD (Admin)), Beatson LJ; see *R. (on the application of Public Law Project) v Secretary of State for Justice* [2014] EWHC 2365 (Admin), [2015] 1 W.L.R. 251 (DC), Moses LJ

Sch.1 Part 1 para.6, amended: SI 2015/914 Sch.1 para.96

Sch.1 Part 1 para.6, repealed: SI 2015/914 Sch.1 para.96

Sch.1 Pt 1 para.9, see *JM (A Child), Re* [2015] EWHC 2832 (Fam), [2015] Med. L.R. 544 (Fam Div), Mostyn J

Sch.1 Pt 1 para.12, see *R. (on the application of Rights of Women) v Lord Chancellor* [2015] EWHC 35 (Admin), [2015] 2 F.L.R. 823 (QBD (Admin)), Fulford LJ

Sch.1 Part 1 para.15A, added: 2015 c.9 Sch.4 para.87

Sch.1 Pt 1 para.21, see *R. (on the application of Sisangia) v Director of Legal Aid Casework* [2014] EWHC 3706 (Admin), [2015] 1 W.L.R. 1891 (QBD (Admin)), Dingemans J
Sch.1 Part 1 para.32, amended: 2015 c.30 Sch.5 para.10
Sch.1 Part 1 para.32A, added: 2015 c.30 s.47
Sch.1 Part 1 para.38, amended: 2015 c.9 Sch.4 para.87
Sch.1 Part 1 para.45A, added: 2015 c.6 s.1
Sch.1 Part 3 para.6, amended: 2015 c.9 Sch.4 para.88
Sch.1 Part 3 para.8, amended: 2015 c.9 Sch.4 para.88
Sch.1 Part 3 para.13, amended: 2015 c.30 s.47
Sch.1 Pt 3 para.21, see *R. (on the application of Sisangia) v Director of Legal Aid Casework* [2014] EWHC 3706 (Admin), [2015] 1 W.L.R. 1891 (QBD (Admin)), Dingemans J
Sch.1 Part 3 para.22A, added: 2015 c.6 s.1
Sch.2 para.3, see *R. (on the application of Sisangia) v Director of Legal Aid Casework* [2014] EWHC 3706 (Admin), [2015] 1 W.L.R. 1891 (QBD (Admin)), Dingemans J
Sch.3 para.3, enabling: SI 2015/1571
Sch.13 Part 2 para.8, repealed: 2015 c.2 s.30
Sch.13 Part 2 para.12, repealed: 2015 c.2 s.30
Sch.24 para.21, see *R. (on the application of Sisangia) v Director of Legal Aid Casework* [2014] EWHC 3706 (Admin), [2015] 1 W.L.R. 1891 (QBD (Admin)), Dingemans J
Sch.27 para.7, repealed: SI 2015/583 Sch.1 Part 1

11. Scotland Act 2012
s.20, repealed: 2015 c.20 Sch.11 para.1
s.25, enabling: SI 2015/2000
s.29, enabling: SI 2015/637
s.31, enabling: SI 2015/638
s.36, see *Macklin (Paul Alexander) v HM Advocate* [2015] UKSC 77 (SC), Lord Neuberger PSC

s.42, enabling: SI 2015/599, SI 2015/683
s.44, enabling: SI 2015/682

14. Finance Act 2012
see *R. (on the application of APVCO 19 Ltd) v Revenue and Customs Commissioners* [2015] EWCA Civ 648, [2015] S.T.C. 2272 (CA (Civ Div)), Black LJ
s.26, varied: SI 2015/1983 Reg.4
s.26, enabling: SI 2015/1999
s.27, varied: SI 2015/1983 Reg.4
s.30, enabling: SI 2015/1983, SI 2015/1999
s.129, amended: SI 2015/1959 Reg.2
s.129, enabling: SI 2015/1959
s.213, repealed: 2015 c.1 Sch.1 para.21
s.221, enabling: SI 2015/2056
Sch.3 para.2, repealed: 2015 c.11 s.27
Sch.6 Part 3 para.11, repealed: 2015 c.33 Sch.5 para.20
Sch.6 Part 3 para.13, repealed: 2015 c.33 Sch.5 para.20
Sch.6 Part 3 para.15, repealed: 2015 c.33 Sch.6 para.22
Sch.6 Part 3 para.17, repealed: 2015 c.33 Sch.6 para.22
Sch.7 Part 1 para.12, repealed: 2015 c.33 Sch.5 para.20
Sch.7 Part 1 para.16, repealed: 2015 c.33 Sch.5 para.20
Sch.8 para.9, repealed: 2015 c.33 Sch.6 para.22
Sch.8 para.14, repealed: 2015 c.33 Sch.6 para.22
Sch.8 para.21, repealed: 2015 c.33 Sch.6 para.21
Sch.17 Part 1 para.13, amended: SI 2015/1959 Reg.3
Sch.17 Part 2 para.35A, added: SI 2015/1959 Reg.4
Sch.17 Part 3 para.37, enabling: SI 2015/1959
Sch.20 Part 3 para.38, repealed: 2015 c.33 s.36
Sch.24 Part 1 para.37, amended: SI 2015/664 Sch.2 para.13
Sch.35 para.2, repealed: 2015 c.1 Sch.1 para.21
Sch.35 para.5, repealed: 2015 c.1 Sch.1 para.21

19. Civil Aviation Act 2012
Sch.6 para.4, amended: 2015 c.20 Sch.6
para.22, SI 2015/1682 Sch.1 para.4
**20. Prisons (Interference with Wireless
Telegraphy) Act 2012**
s.4, amended: 2015 c.2 Sch.9 para.31
21. Financial Services Act 2012
s.85, amended: 2015 c.8 Sch.3 para.17
s.87, amended: 2015 c.26 s.20
s.93, enabling: SI 2015/369
s.107, amended: 2015 c.15 Sch.6 para.84
s.107, repealed: 2015 c.15 Sch.6 para.84
23. Small Charitable Donations Act 2012
s.1, amended: SI 2015/2027 Art.3
s.4, amended: SI 2015/2027 Art.4
s.6, amended: SI 2015/2027 Art.5
s.9, amended: SI 2015/2027 Art.6
s.14, enabling: SI 2015/2027

2013

**3. Prevention of Social Housing Fraud Act
2013**
s.4, amended: 2015 c.30 Sch.5 para.27
Sch.1 para.2, repealed: 2015 c.30 Sch.5
para.27
Sch.1 para.5, repealed: 2015 c.30 Sch.5
para.27
Sch.1 para.9, repealed: 2015 c.30 Sch.5
para.27
Sch.1 para.14, repealed: 2015 c.9 Sch.4
para.89
Sch.1 para.22, repealed: 2015 c.9 Sch.4
para.89
Sch.1 para.26, repealed: 2015 c.30 Sch.5
para.27
Sch.1 para.30, repealed: 2015 c.30 Sch.5
para.27
**5. European Union (Croatian Accession and
Irish Protocol) Act 2013**
s.4, enabling: SI 2015/694
**6. Electoral Registration and
Administration Act 2013**
s.13, enabling: SI 2015/1520
s.25, amended: SI 2015/1376 Sch.2
para.16
s.25, enabling: SI 2015/1520
Sch.5 Part 2 para.6, varied: SI 2015/1520
Art.3

Sch.5 Part 7 para.28, enabling: SI
2015/1520
11. Prisons (Property) Act 2013
s.2, enabling: SI 2015/771
15. Antarctic Act 2013
s.18, enabling: SI 2015/823, SI
2015/1531
16. Welfare Benefits Up-rating Act 2013
s.1, enabling: SI 2015/30, SI 2015/567
s.2, enabling: SI 2015/567
**17. Jobseekers (Back to Work Schemes) Act
2013**
see *R. (on the application of Reilly) v
Secretary of State for Work and Pensions*
[2014] EWHC 2182 (Admin), [2015]
Q.B. 573 (QBD (Admin)), Lang J
18. Justice and Security Act 2013
see *R. (on the application of K) v
Secretary of State for the Home
Department* [2014] EWCA Civ 151,
[2015] 1 W.L.R. 125 (CA (Civ Div)),
Richards LJ
19. Groceries Code Adjudicator Act 2013
s.9, enabling: SI 2015/722
20. Succession to the Crown Act 2013
s.5, enabling: SI 2015/894
22. Crime and Courts Act 2013
see *McIntyre v United States* [2014]
EWHC 1886 (Admin), [2015] 1 W.L.R.
507 (DC), Lord Thomas LCJ
s.4, amended: SI 2015/798 Art.3
s.11, amended: SI 2015/798 Sch.2
para.14
s.44, see *R. v Khan (Gulan Ahmed)*
[2015] EWCA Crim 835, [2015] 2 Cr.
App. R. (S.) 39 (CA (Crim Div)), Davis
LJ
s.47, enabling: SI 2015/868
s.58, enabling: SI 2015/925
s.59, enabling: SI 2015/230, SI 2015/733,
SI 2015/798, SI 2015/925, SI 2015/1489
s.60, enabling: SI 2015/964
s.61, enabling: SI 2015/813, SI 2015/964,
SI 2015/1837
Sch.1 Part 1 para.6A, added: SI 2015/798
Sch.2 para.15
Sch.5 Part 4 para.11, amended: SI
2015/798 Sch.1 para.2
Sch.9 Part 3 para.82, repealed: 2015 c.15
Sch.6 para.85

Sch.19 Part 1, amended: SI 2015/798
Art.9
Sch.22 para.8, repealed: 2015 c.20
Sch.11 para.15
Sch.22 para.14, repealed: 2015 c.20
Sch.11 para.15
Sch.24 para.2, enabling: SI 2015/798
Sch.24 para.3, enabling: SI 2015/798
Sch.24 para.5, enabling: SI 2015/798
Sch.24 para.7, enabling: SI 2015/798
Sch.25 Part 1 para.3, enabling: SI
2015/798
Sch.25 Part 1 para.4, enabling: SI
2015/798
Sch.25 Part 1 para.7, enabling: SI
2015/798
Sch.25 Part 2 para.10, enabling: SI
2015/798
Sch.25 Part 2 para.11, enabling: SI
2015/798
Sch.25 Part 2 para.14, enabling: SI
2015/798

**24. Enterprise and Regulatory Reform Act
2013**

s.17, see *Chesterton Global Ltd (t/a
Chestertons) v Nurmohamed* [2015]
I.C.R. 920 (EAT), Supperstone J
s.52, amended: SI 2015/1682 Sch.1
para.4
s.53, amended: SI 2015/1682 Sch.1
para.4
s.92, enabling: SI 2015/989
s.93, enabling: SI 2015/989
s.94, enabling: SI 2015/989
s.95, enabling: SI 2015/989
s.97, see *Chandhok v Tirkey* [2015]
I.C.R. 527 (EAT), Langstaff J
s.100, enabling: SI 2015/641, SI
2015/1558
s.103, enabling: SI 2015/641, SI
2015/1558
Sch.4 Part 1 para.16, amended: SI
2015/1682 Sch.1 para.4
Sch.4 Part 3 para.35, amended: SI
2015/16 Reg.2
Sch.4 Part 3 para.35, repealed: SI
2015/16 Reg.2
Sch.4 Part 3 para.48, amended: SI
2015/16 Reg.2
Sch.4 Part 3 para.51, repealed: SI
2015/16 Reg.2

Sch.19 para.20, repealed: 2015 c.26
Sch.10 para.12
25. Public Service Pensions Act 2013
s.1, enabling: SI 2015/57, SI 2015/94, SI
2015/182, SI 2015/319, SI 2015/370, SI
2015/372, SI 2015/390, SI 2015/432, SI
2015/436, SI 2015/445, SI 2015/465, SI
2015/466, SI 2015/568, SI 2015/581, SI
2015/589, SI 2015/592, SI 2015/594, SI
2015/601, SI 2015/602, SI 2015/622, SI
2015/755, SI 2015/848, SI 2015/871, SI
2015/1016, SSI 2015/19, SSI 2015/60,
SSI 2015/87, SSI 2015/94, SSI 2015/95,
SSI 2015/97, SSI 2015/117, SSI
2015/118, SSI 2015/141, SSI 2015/142,
SSI 2015/145, SSI 2015/146, SSI
2015/325, SSI 2015/448
s.2, enabling: SI 2015/94, SI 2015/182,
SI 2015/319, SI 2015/370, SI 2015/372,
SI 2015/390, SI 2015/432, SI 2015/436,
SI 2015/445, SI 2015/568, SI 2015/589,
SI 2015/592, SI 2015/602, SI 2015/622,
SI 2015/871, SI 2015/1016, SSI 2015/60,
SSI 2015/117, SSI 2015/118, SSI
2015/145, SSI 2015/146
s.3, enabling: SI 2015/57, SI 2015/94, SI
2015/182, SI 2015/319, SI 2015/370, SI
2015/372, SI 2015/390, SI 2015/432, SI
2015/436, SI 2015/445, SI 2015/465, SI
2015/568, SI 2015/581, SI 2015/589, SI
2015/592, SI 2015/594, SI 2015/601, SI
2015/602, SI 2015/622, SI 2015/755, SI
2015/848, SI 2015/871, SI 2015/1016,
SSI 2015/95, SSI 2015/117, SSI
2015/118, SSI 2015/145, SSI 2015/146
s.4, enabling: SI 2015/94, SI 2015/182,
SI 2015/390, SI 2015/445, SI 2015/622
s.5, enabling: SI 2015/57, SI 2015/94, SI
2015/182, SI 2015/445, SSI 2015/60
s.7, enabling: SI 2015/57, SI 2015/94, SI
2015/445, SI 2015/465, SI 2015/622, SSI
2015/60
s.8, enabling: SI 2015/94, SI 2015/182,
SI 2015/445, SI 2015/622
s.9, enabling: SI 2015/769
s.11, enabling: SI 2015/94
s.12, enabling: SI 2015/57, SI 2015/94,
SI 2015/182, SI 2015/445, SI 2015/465,
SI 2015/622
s.14, enabling: SI 2015/94

s.18, enabling: SI 2015/94, SI 2015/182,
SI 2015/445, SI 2015/568, SI 2015/589,
SI 2015/592, SI 2015/622, SI 2015/1016,
SSI 2015/95

s.25, enabling: SI 2015/94, SI 2015/445,
SI 2015/581

s.37, enabling: SI 2015/94

s.41, enabling: SI 2015/4

Sch.1 para.2, enabling: SI 2015/580, SI
2015/1483

Sch.2 para.2, enabling: SI 2015/182

Sch.2 para.3, enabling: SSI 2015/60

Sch.2 para.4, enabling: SI 2015/592, SSI
2015/97

Sch.2 para.5, enabling: SI 2015/94, SSI
2015/94

Sch.2 para.6, enabling: SI 2015/589, SI
2015/622, SI 2015/848, SI 2015/871, SI
2015/1016, SSI 2015/19, SSI 2015/141

Sch.2 para.7, enabling: SI 2015/445, SSI
2015/142, SSI 2015/325

Sch.3, enabling: SI 2015/57, SI 2015/94,
SI 2015/182, SI 2015/445, SI 2015/465,
SI 2015/581, SI 2015/589, SI 2015/592,
SI 2015/594, SI 2015/601, SI 2015/602,
SI 2015/622, SI 2015/755, SI 2015/871,
SI 2015/1016, SSI 2015/95

Sch.5 para.1, amended: 2015 c.8 s.80

Sch.5 para.18, enabling: SI 2015/592

Sch.5 para.20, enabling: SI 2015/622

Sch.5 para.21, enabling: SI 2015/622

Sch.7 para.1, varied: SI 2015/622 Sch.2
para.32, Sch.2 para.33, SSI 2015/19
Sch.2 para.32, Sch.2 para.33

Sch.7 para.1, enabling: SI 2015/182, SI
2015/445, SI 2015/589, SI 2015/1016

Sch.7 para.2, enabling: SI 2015/182, SI
2015/445, SI 2015/589, SI 2015/1016

Sch.7 para.5, enabling: SI 2015/182, SI
2015/445, SI 2015/589, SI 2015/1016

26. Defamation Act 2013

s.1, see *Ames v Spamhaus Project Ltd*
[2015] EWHC 127 (QB), [2015] 1
W.L.R. 3409 (QBD), Warby J; see
Cooke v MGN Ltd [2014] EWHC 2831
(QB), [2015] 1 W.L.R. 895 (QBD), Bean
J

s.11, see *Rufus v Elliott* [2015] EWCA
Civ 121, [2015] E.M.L.R. 17 (CA (Civ
Div)), McCombe LJ; see *Yeo v Times
Newspapers Ltd* [2014] EWHC 2853

(QB), [2015] 1 W.L.R. 971 (QBD),
Warby J

29. Finance Act 2013

s.99, amended: 2015 c.11 s.70

s.102, amended: 2015 c.11 s.71

s.110, amended: 2015 c.11 s.72

s.159, amended: 2015 c.11 s.73

s.159, varied: 2015 c.11 s.73

s.159A, added: 2015 c.11 s.73

s.161, amended: 2015 c.11 s.73

s.194, see *R. (on the application of
APVCO 19 Ltd) v Revenue and Customs
Commissioners* [2015] EWCA Civ 648,
[2015] S.T.C. 2272 (CA (Civ Div)),
Black LJ

s.206, amended: 2015 c.11 s.115

s.217, enabling: SI 2015/463, SI
2015/2053

s.222, amended: 2015 c.33 s.50

s.222, enabling: SI 2015/873, SI
2015/878, SI 2015/1839

Sch.21 para.8, enabling: SI 2015/725

Sch.21 para.9, enabling: SI 2015/674

Sch.33 Part 1 para.2, amended: 2015 c.11
s.73

Sch.33 Part 4 para.20, amended: 2015
c.11 s.73, 2015 c.33 Sch.8 para.42

30. Marriage (Same Sex Couples) Act 2013

see *MB v Secretary of State for Work and
Pensions* [2014] EWCA Civ 1112,
[2015] 1 All E.R. 920 (CA (Civ Div)),
Maurice Kay LJ

s.9, amended: 2015 c.20 s.99

32. Energy Act 2013

s.6, enabling: SI 2015/718, SI 2015/721,
SI 2015/981, SI 2015/1425

s.9, enabling: SI 2015/721

s.11, enabling: SI 2015/1425

s.12, enabling: SI 2015/981

s.13, enabling: SI 2015/981

s.14, enabling: SI 2015/1425

s.16, enabling: SI 2015/981

s.17, enabling: SI 2015/721

s.19, enabling: SI 2015/721, SI 2015/981,
SI 2015/1425

s.20, enabling: SI 2015/718, SI 2015/721

s.21, enabling: SI 2015/721

s.22, enabling: SI 2015/721

s.27, enabling: SI 2015/875, SI
2015/1974

s.28, enabling: SI 2015/875, SI 2015/1974
s.29, enabling: SI 2015/875
s.30, enabling: SI 2015/875, SI 2015/1974
s.31, enabling: SI 2015/875
s.32, enabling: SI 2015/875
s.33, enabling: SI 2015/875
s.36, enabling: SI 2015/875
s.40, enabling: SI 2015/875, SI 2015/1974
s.51, enabling: SI 2015/1412
s.57, enabling: SI 2015/933
s.60, enabling: SI 2015/933, SI 2015/1388
s.62, enabling: SI 2015/933, SI 2015/1388
s.84, amended: SI 2015/1682 Sch.1 para.4
s.89, amended: SI 2015/1682 Sch.1 para.4
s.90, amended: SI 2015/1682 Sch.1 para.4
s.101, enabling: SI 2015/363
s.113, enabling: SI 2015/363
s.150, enabling: SI 2015/1693
s.156, enabling: SI 2015/614, SI 2015/817
Sch.2 Part 2 para.11, enabling: SI 2015/718
Sch.2 Part 4 para.16, enabling: SI 2015/718, SI 2015/721
Sch.4, enabling: SI 2015/933
Sch.5, enabling: SI 2015/1388
Sch.9 Part 3 para.10, amended: SI 2015/1682 Sch.1 para.4
Sch.9 Part 3 para.14, repealed: 2015 c.20 Sch.13 para.6

33. Financial Services (Banking Reform) Act 2013
s.58, amended: 2015 c.26 s.14
s.81, varied: SI 2015/1911 Reg.14
s.83, varied: SI 2015/1911 Reg.14
s.90, varied: SI 2015/1911 Reg.14
s.91, varied: SI 2015/1911 Reg.14
s.93, varied: SI 2015/1911 Reg.14
s.98, amended: SI 2015/1911 Reg.19
s.108, amended: 2015 c.26 s.14
s.145, enabling: SI 2015/428, SI 2015/1864

s.146, enabling: SI 2015/492, SI 2015/1660, SI 2015/1865
s.148, enabling: SI 2015/428, SI 2015/490, SI 2015/2055
Sch.4 para.10, enabling: SI 2015/487

2014

1. Mesothelioma Act 2014
s.1, enabling: SI 2015/367
s.17, enabling: SI 2015/367

2. Local Audit and Accountability Act 2014
s.2, enabling: SI 2015/975
s.5, enabling: SI 2015/184
s.6, enabling: SI 2015/184
s.7, varied: SI 2015/184 Sch.1 para.3, SI 2015/192 Sch.1 para.2
s.8, varied: SI 2015/192 Sch.1 para.3
s.9, varied: SI 2015/192 Sch.1 para.4
s.10, varied: SI 2015/192 Sch.1 para.5
s.10, enabling: SI 2015/18
s.12, varied: SI 2015/192 Sch.1 para.6, Sch.1 para.7
s.17, enabling: SI 2015/192
s.32, varied: SI 2015/179 Art.3
s.32, enabling: SI 2015/234
s.43, enabling: SI 2015/184, SI 2015/192, SI 2015/234
s.46, enabling: SI 2015/184, SI 2015/192, SI 2015/234
s.49, enabling: SI 2015/179, SI 2015/223, SI 2015/841
Sch.2 para.24, amended: SI 2015/975 Reg.2
Sch.2 para.25, repealed: 2015 c.20 Sch.13 para.6
Sch.4 para.3, enabling: SI 2015/18
Sch.4 para.4, enabling: SI 2015/18
Sch.5 para.4A, varied: SI 2015/192 Sch.1 para.9
Sch.5 para.5, varied: SI 2015/192 Sch.1 para.10
Sch.5 para.6, varied: SI 2015/192 Sch.1 para.11
Sch.5 para.7, varied: SI 2015/192 Sch.1 para.12
Sch.5 para.16, varied: SI 2015/192 Sch.1 para.13
Sch.5 para.17, varied: SI 2015/192 Sch.1 para.14

Sch.6 para.1, varied: SI 2015/192 Sch.1
para.15
Sch.11 para.1, varied: SI 2015/192 Sch.1
para.16
Sch.13 para.2, enabling: SI 2015/972
Sch.13 para.3, amended: SI 2015/972
Art.2

4. Transparency of Lobbying, Non-Party Campaigning and Trade Union Administration Act 2014

s.4, enabling: SI 2015/379
s.9, enabling: SI 2015/379
s.22, enabling: SI 2015/379, SI 2015/1477, SI 2015/1998
s.23, enabling: SI 2015/379
s.24, enabling: SI 2015/379
s.25, amended: SI 2015/1376 Sch.2 para.17
s.33, amended: SI 2015/1376 Sch.2 para.17
s.45, enabling: SI 2015/717, SI 2015/954

6. Children and Families Act 2014

see *S (A Child) (Interim Care Order: Residential Assessment), Re* [2015] 1 W.L.R. 925 (CC (Bournemouth)), Sir James Munby PFD
s.10, enabling: SI 2015/1868
s.13, see *F (A Child) (Care Proceedings: Habitual Residence), Re* [2014] EWCA Civ 789, [2015] 1 F.C.R. 88 (CA (Civ Div)), Sir James Munby PFD; see *R (A Child) (Adoption: Judicial Approach), Re* [2014] EWCA Civ 1625, [2015] 1 W.L.R. 3273 (CA (Civ Div)), Sir James Munby PFD; see *S (A Child) (Interim Care Order: Residential Assessment), Re* [2015] 1 W.L.R. 925 (CC (Bournemouth)), Sir James Munby PFD
s.14, see *S (A Child) (Interim Care Order: Residential Assessment), Re* [2015] 1 W.L.R. 925 (CC (Bournemouth)), Sir James Munby PFD
s.27, see *R. (on the application of L) v Warwickshire CC* [2015] EWHC 203 (Admin), [2015] B.L.G.R. 81 (QBD (Admin)), Mostyn J
s.30, see *R. (on the application of L) v Warwickshire CC* [2015] EWHC 203 (Admin), [2015] B.L.G.R. 81 (QBD (Admin)), Mostyn J
s.31, enabling: SI 2015/62

s.36, enabling: SI 2015/62
s.37, amended: SI 2015/914 Sch.1 para.97
s.37, enabling: SI 2015/62, SI 2015/359
s.44, enabling: SI 2015/62, SI 2015/359
s.51, enabling: SI 2015/358, SI 2015/359
s.56, enabling: SI 2015/62
s.71, enabling: SI 2015/62
s.73, enabling: SI 2015/62
s.74, enabling: SI 2015/62
s.78, enabling: SI 2015/893
s.80, enabling: SI 2015/62
s.91, amended: SI 2015/895 Reg.2
s.92, enabling: SI 2015/895
s.93, enabling: SI 2015/895
s.94, enabling: SI 2015/829
s.135, enabling: SI 2015/62, SI 2015/358, SI 2015/359, SI 2015/829, SI 2015/895, SI 2015/914
s.136, enabling: SI 2015/914
s.137, enabling: SI 2015/505, SI 2015/1619
s.139, enabling: SI 2015/375

7. National Insurance Contributions Act 2014

s.2, amended: SI 2015/578 Reg.2
s.5, enabling: SI 2015/578

11. Offender Rehabilitation Act 2014

s.20, enabling: SI 2015/774
s.22, enabling: SI 2015/40

12. Anti-social Behaviour, Crime and Policing Act 2014

see *Bizunowicz v Poland* [2014] EWHC 3238 (Admin), [2015] 1 W.L.R. 2341 (QBD (Admin)), Aikens LJ
s.18, enabling: SI 2015/423
s.22, see *DPP v Bulmer* [2015] EWHC 2323 (Admin), [2015] 1 W.L.R. 5159 (DC), Beatson LJ
s.48, amended: SI 2015/664 Sch.4 para.45
s.53, enabling: SI 2015/749
s.71, enabling: SI 2015/858
s.116, amended: 2015 c.9 Sch.4 para.90
s.180, enabling: SI 2015/576
s.181, enabling: SI 2015/858, SI 2015/992, SI 2015/1321
s.182, enabling: SI 2015/992
s.185, enabling: SI 2015/373, SI 2015/987

14. Co-operative and Community Benefit Societies Act 2014

    Sch.4 Part 2 para.106, repealed: 2015 c.11 Sch.6 para.12

17. Gambling (Licensing and Advertising) Act 2014

    see *Gibraltar Betting & Gaming Association Ltd v Secretary of State for Culture, Media and Sport* [2014] EWHC 3236 (Admin), [2015] 1 C.M.L.R. 28 (QBD (Admin)), Green J

18. Intellectual Property Act 2014

    s.1, see *DKH Retail Ltd v H Young Operations Ltd* [2014] EWHC 4034 (IPEC), [2015] F.S.R. 21 (IPEC), Judge Hacon

    s.24, enabling: SI 2015/165

19. Pensions Act 2014

    s.2, enabling: SI 2015/173
    s.4, enabling: SI 2015/173
    s.8, enabling: SI 2015/173
    s.16, enabling: SI 2015/173
    s.17, enabling: SI 2015/173
    s.18, enabling: SI 2015/173
    s.19, enabling: SI 2015/173
    s.22, enabling: SI 2015/173
    s.24, varied: SI 2015/118 Reg.13, Reg.14, Reg.15
    s.24, enabling: SI 2015/118
    s.28, enabling: SI 2015/1529
    s.34, amended: 2015 c.8 Sch.4 para.45
    s.36, repealed: 2015 c.8 s.39
    s.43, enabling: SI 2015/879, SI 2015/889
    s.53, enabling: SI 2015/1985
    s.54, enabling: SI 2015/118, SI 2015/173, SI 2015/879, SI 2015/889, SI 2015/1985
    s.56, enabling: SI 2015/134, SI 2015/1475, SI 2015/1502, SI 2015/1670, SI 2015/2058
    Sch.8 para.4, enabling: SI 2015/173
    Sch.10 para.4, enabling: SI 2015/173
    Sch.14 para.2, varied: SI 2015/118 Reg.13, Reg.14, Reg.15
    Sch.14 para.2, enabling: SI 2015/118
    Sch.14 para.3, varied: SI 2015/118 Reg.13, Reg.15
    Sch.14 para.4, enabling: SI 2015/118
    Sch.14 para.6, enabling: SI 2015/118
    Sch.14 para.9, varied: SI 2015/118 Reg.13, Reg.15
    Sch.14 para.10, enabling: SI 2015/118

    Sch.14 para.12, enabling: SI 2015/118
    Sch.14 para.13, enabling: SI 2015/118
    Sch.14 para.14, enabling: SI 2015/118
    Sch.14 para.15, varied: SI 2015/118 Reg.13, Reg.15
    Sch.17 Part 1 para.1, amended: 2015 c.8 Sch.2 para.51, Sch.4 para.46
    Sch.17 Part 3 para.15, amended: 2015 c.8 Sch.2 para.51
    Sch.18 para.1, enabling: SI 2015/879, SI 2015/889
    Sch.18 para.2, enabling: SI 2015/879
    Sch.18 para.6, enabling: SI 2015/879
    Sch.18 para.7, enabling: SI 2015/879

20. Defence Reform Act 2014

    s.50, enabling: SI 2015/791

21. Water Act 2014

    s.64, enabling: SI 2015/1875, SI 2015/1902
    s.65, enabling: SI 2015/1875
    s.66, enabling: SI 2015/1902
    s.67, enabling: SI 2015/1902
    s.69, amended: SI 2015/1902 Reg.29
    s.69, enabling: SI 2015/1902
    s.82, enabling: SI 2015/1902
    s.84, enabling: SI 2015/1902
    s.91, enabling: SI 2015/773, SI 2015/1469, SI 2015/1786, SI 2015/1938
    s.94, enabling: SI 2015/773, SI 2015/1469, SI 2015/1786, SI 2015/1938, SSI 2015/360
    Sch.12, enabling: SSI 2015/360

22. Immigration Act 2014

    see *Secretary of State for the Home Department v Dube* [2015] UKUT 90 (IAC), [2015] Imm. A.R. 651 (UT (IAC)), Nicol J; see *YM (Uganda) v Secretary of State for the Home Department* [2014] EWCA Civ 1292, [2015] I.N.L.R. 405 (CA (Civ Div)), Aikens LJ

    s.38, enabling: SI 2015/792
    s.48, amended: SI 2015/395 Sch.4 para.2, SI 2015/396 Sch.4 para.2
    s.49, enabling: SI 2015/122
    s.50, amended: SI 2015/395 Sch.4 para.3, SI 2015/396 Sch.4 para.3
    s.50, enabling: SI 2015/397
    s.51, enabling: SI 2015/397
    s.53, enabling: SI 2015/395, SI 2015/396
    s.54, enabling: SI 2015/404

s.61, enabling: SI 2015/122
s.62, amended: SI 2015/395 Sch.4 para.4,
SI 2015/396 Sch.4 para.4
s.68, enabling: SI 2015/746, SI 2015/768,
SI 2015/1424
s.69, enabling: SI 2015/746, SI 2015/768,
SI 2015/1424
s.73, enabling: SI 2015/371, SI 2015/383,
SI 2015/874
s.74, enabling: SI 2015/122, SI 2015/383,
SI 2015/395, SI 2015/396, SI 2015/397,
SI 2015/404, SI 2015/746, SI 2015/768,
SI 2015/792
s.75, enabling: SI 2015/371, SI 2015/874
s.76, enabling: SI 2015/1532, SI
2015/1533, SI 2015/1765
Sch.5, enabling: SI 2015/404

23. Care Act 2014

see *R. (on the application of SG) v
Haringey LBC* [2015] EWHC 2579
(Admin), (2015) 18 C.C.L. Rep. 444
(QBD (Admin)), John Bowers QC
Part 1, varied: SI 2015/642 Art.2
Part 3 c.2, varied: SI 2015/642 Art.2
s.1, varied: SI 2015/642 Art.2
s.8, varied: SI 2015/305 Reg.4
s.9, see *R. (on the application of SG) v
Haringey LBC* [2015] EWHC 2579
(Admin), (2015) 18 C.C.L. Rep. 444
(QBD (Admin)), John Bowers QC
s.13, enabling: SI 2015/313
s.14, varied: SI 2015/305 Reg.5
s.14, enabling: SI 2015/644
s.17, varied: SI 2015/305 Reg.6
s.17, enabling: SI 2015/644
s.18, amended: SI 2015/993 Art.5
s.22, varied: SI 2015/305 Reg.7
s.23, varied: SI 2015/305 Reg.8
s.24, varied: SI 2015/305 Reg.9
s.25, varied: SI 2015/305 Reg.10
s.27, varied: SI 2015/305 Reg.11
s.33, enabling: SI 2015/644
s.34, enabling: SI 2015/644
s.37, amended: SI 2015/993 Art.5
s.38, amended: SI 2015/993 Art.5
s.39, amended: SI 2015/993 Art.6
s.39, enabling: SI 2015/644
s.52, enabling: SI 2015/301
s.53, enabling: SI 2015/314
s.62, enabling: SI 2015/305

s.67, see *R. (on the application of SG) v
Haringey LBC* [2015] EWHC 2579
(Admin), (2015) 18 C.C.L. Rep. 444
(QBD (Admin)), John Bowers QC
s.70, varied: SI 2015/305 Reg.12
s.75, amended: SI 2015/993 Art.7
s.75, enabling: SI 2015/644
s.92, enabling: SI 2015/988
s.123, enabling: SI 2015/137, SI
2015/643, SI 2015/914
s.124, enabling: SI 2015/993, SI
2015/995
s.125, enabling: SI 2015/301, SI
2015/305, SI 2015/313, SI 2015/314, SI
2015/643, SI 2015/644, SI 2015/914, SI
2015/995
s.127, enabling: SI 2015/993
s.128, enabling: SI 2015/642
Sch.1 para.1, enabling: SI 2015/644
Sch.1 para.2, enabling: SI 2015/644
Sch.1 para.4, enabling: SI 2015/644

24. House of Lords Reform Act 2014
s.6, amended: 2015 c.14 s.2

26. Finance Act 2014

see *R. (on the application of Rowe) v
Revenue and Customs Commissioners*
[2015] EWHC 2293 (Admin), [2015]
B.T.C. 27 (QBD (Admin)), Simler J
s.2, amended: 2015 c.11 s.3
s.18, enabling: SI 2015/931
s.32, amended: 2015 c.11 s.29
s.32, repealed: 2015 c.11 s.29
s.52, enabling: SI 2015/360
s.56, repealed: 2015 c.11 Sch.6 para.12
s.69, repealed: 2015 c.11 Sch.11 para.13
s.94, repealed: 2015 c.33 s.48
s.95, repealed: 2015 c.33 s.48
s.102, enabling: SI 2015/636
s.199, amended: 2015 c.11 Sch.18 para.2
s.220, amended: 2015 c.11 Sch.18 para.3
s.221, amended: 2015 c.11 Sch.18 para.4
s.222, amended: 2015 c.11 Sch.18 para.5
s.223, amended: 2015 c.11 Sch.18 para.6
s.225A, added: 2015 c.11 Sch.18 para.7
s.227, amended: 2015 c.11 Sch.18 para.8
s.227A, added: 2015 c.11 Sch.18 para.9
s.235, enabling: SI 2015/130
s.237, amended: 2015 c.11 Sch.19 para.2
s.249, enabling: SI 2015/549
s.253, enabling: SI 2015/549
s.257, enabling: SI 2015/549

s.259, enabling: SI 2015/549
s.260, enabling: SI 2015/549
s.261, enabling: SI 2015/549
s.268, enabling: SI 2015/549
s.282, enabling: SI 2015/549
s.283, amended: 2015 c.11 Sch.19 para.3
s.283, enabling: SI 2015/130, SI
2015/131, SI 2015/549
Sch.9 Part 4 para.49, enabling: SI
2015/360
Sch.9 Part 4 para.50, enabling: SI
2015/360
Sch.14, repealed: 2015 c.11 Sch.11
para.13
Sch.21 para.10, enabling: SI 2015/812
Sch.32 para.4, amended: 2015 c.11
Sch.18 para.10
Sch.32 para.5, amended: 2015 c.11
Sch.18 para.10
Sch.32 para.6, amended: 2015 c.11
Sch.18 para.10
Sch.32 para.6A, added: 2015 c.11 Sch.18
para.10
Sch.32 para.8, amended: 2015 c.11
Sch.18 para.10
Sch.34 Part 1 para.5, amended: 2015 c.11
Sch.19 para.6
Sch.34 Part 1 para.8, amended: 2015 c.11
Sch.19 para.7
Sch.34 Part 1 para.8, enabling: SI
2015/131
Sch.34 Part 1 para.9, enabling: SI
2015/131
Sch.34 Part 2, amended: 2015 c.11
Sch.19 para.4
Sch.34 Part 2 para.13, substituted: 2015
c.11 Sch.19 para.4
Sch.34 Part 3 para.14, amended: 2015
c.11 Sch.19 para.8
Sch.36 Part 1 para.4, repealed: 2015 c.11
Sch.19 para.5
Sch.36 Part 4 para.20, repealed: 2015
c.11 Sch.19 para.5
Sch.36 Part 4 para.21, amended: 2015
c.11 Sch.19 para.5

**27. Data Retention and Investigatory Powers
Act 2014**
s.2, amended: 2015 c.6 s.21
s.8, enabling: SI 2015/929
28. Childcare Payments Act 2014
s.2, enabling: SI 2015/448, SI 2015/522

s.3, enabling: SI 2015/448
s.4, enabling: SI 2015/522
s.5, enabling: SI 2015/522
s.7, enabling: SI 2015/448
s.8, enabling: SI 2015/448
s.9, enabling: SI 2015/448
s.10, enabling: SI 2015/448
s.11, varied: SI 2015/448 Reg.16
s.12, varied: SI 2015/448 Reg.17
s.14, enabling: SI 2015/448
s.15, enabling: SI 2015/522
s.16, see *Edenred (UK Group) Ltd v HM
Treasury* [2015] UKSC 45 (SC), Lord
Neuberger PSC
s.17, enabling: SI 2015/522
s.19, amended: SI 2015/537 Reg.2
s.19, enabling: SI 2015/522, SI 2015/537
s.24, enabling: SI 2015/522
s.25, enabling: SI 2015/522
s.26, enabling: SI 2015/522
s.32, enabling: SI 2015/448
s.33, enabling: SI 2015/448
s.49, enabling: SI 2015/522
s.62, enabling: SI 2015/522
s.69, enabling: SI 2015/448, SI 2015/522,
SI 2015/537
29. Wales Act 2014
s.13, amended: SI 2015/1376 Sch.2
para.18
Sch.1 para.15, amended: SI 2015/1376
Sch.2 para.18
30. Taxation of Pensions Act 2014
Sch.1 Part 1 para.31, repealed: 2015 c.33
s.22
Sch.2 Part 2 para.19, repealed: 2015 c.33
s.22

2015

1. Stamp Duty Land Tax Act 2015
Royal Assent, February 12, 2015
2. Criminal Justice and Courts Act 2015
Royal Assent, February 12, 2015
s.17, enabling: SI 2015/790, SI 2015/830
s.18, enabling: SI 2015/790, SI 2015/830
s.53, see *R. (on the application of DPP) v
South Tyneside Youth Court* [2015]
EWHC 1455 (Admin), [2015] 2 Cr. App.
R. (S.) 59 (DC), Sir Brian Leveson
PQBD

s.95, enabling: SI 2015/778, SI 2015/1463, SI 2015/1778

3. Social Action, Responsibility and Heroism Act 2015
Royal Assent, February 12, 2015
s.5, enabling: SI 2015/808

4. Insurance Act 2015
Royal Assent, February 12, 2015

5. National Insurance Contributions Act 2015
Royal Assent, February 12, 2015
s.3, enabling: SI 2015/478

6. Counter-Terrorism and Security Act 2015
Royal Assent, February 12, 2015
s.13, enabling: SI 2015/438
s.23, enabling: SI 2015/997
s.24, enabling: SI 2015/957
s.27, enabling: SI 2015/928
s.29, enabling: SI 2015/928, SI 2015/1697
s.30, amended: SI 2015/928 Reg.4
s.31, amended: SI 2015/928 Reg.5
s.32, amended: 2015 c.5 Sch.4 para.11
s.39, enabling: SI 2015/928
s.41, amended: SI 2015/928 Reg.6
s.52, enabling: SI 2015/956, SI 2015/1698, SI 2015/1729
Sch.1 para.19, enabling: SI 2015/217
Sch.3 para.7, enabling: SI 2015/406
Sch.4 para.2, amended: SSI 2015/338 Sch.2 para.15
Sch.4 para.4, amended: SSI 2015/338 Sch.2 para.15
Sch.6, substituted: SI 2015/928 Sch.1 para.2
Sch.6 Part 1, amended: 2015 c.5 Sch.4 para.11
Sch.6 Part 2, added: SI 2015/928 Sch.1 para.3
Sch.7, substituted: SI 2015/928 Sch.2 para.2
Sch.7 Part 1, amended: 2015 c.5 Sch.4 para.11
Sch.7 Part 2, added: SI 2015/928 Sch.2 para.3

7. Infrastructure Act 2015
Royal Assent, February 12, 2015
s.1, enabling: SI 2015/376
s.2, enabling: SI 2015/376
s.7, enabling: SI 2015/378

s.10, amended: SI 2015/1682 Sch.1 para.4
s.11, amended: SI 2015/1682 Sch.1 para.4
s.12, amended: SI 2015/1682 Sch.1 para.4
s.13, amended: SI 2015/1682 Sch.1 para.4
s.19, enabling: SI 2015/377
s.42, enabling: SI 2015/1661
s.57, enabling: SI 2015/481, SI 2015/758, SI 2015/990, SI 2015/1543, SI 2015/1576
Sch.1 Part 1 para.26, repealed: 2015 c.20 Sch.10 para.22
Sch.1 Part 2 para.148, repealed: 2015 c.20 Sch.10 para.12
Sch.7 para.3, enabling: SI 2015/1661
Sch.7 para.5, enabling: SI 2015/1661
Sch.7 para.6, enabling: SI 2015/1661
Sch.7 para.7, enabling: SI 2015/1661

8. Pension Schemes Act 2015
Royal Assent, March 03, 2015
s.48, enabling: SI 2015/742
s.49, enabling: SI 2015/742
s.51, enabling: SR 2015/165
s.52, enabling: SR 2015/165
s.83, enabling: SI 2015/498, SR 2015/164
s.86, enabling: SI 2015/498, SI 2015/742, SR 2015/164, SR 2015/165
s.89, enabling: SI 2015/742, SI 2015/1851, SR 2015/165

9. Serious Crime Act 2015
Royal Assent, March 03, 2015
s.85, enabling: SI 2015/800
s.88, enabling: SI 2015/820, SI 2015/1428, SI 2015/1809, SI 2015/1976, SR 2015/190
Sch.2 para.11, amended: 2015 c.9 (NI) Sch.1 para.144, (NI) Sch.9 Part 1

10. Supply and Appropriation (Anticipation and Adjustments) Act 2015
Royal Assent, March 26, 2015

11. Finance Act 2015
Royal Assent, March 26, 2015
s.4, amended: 2015 c.33 s.6
s.5, amended: 2015 c.33 s.5
s.23, enabling: SI 2015/2035
s.26, repealed: 2015 c.33 s.33
s.29, enabling: SI 2015/1741
s.79, amended: 2015 c.33 Sch.3 para.12
s.107, amended: 2015 c.33 Sch.3 para.13

Sch.2 Part 2 para.6, repealed: 2015 c.33
s.36
Sch.2 Part 3 para.8, repealed: 2015 c.33
s.36
Sch.4 Part 1 para.3, enabling: SI
2015/1454
Sch.6 Part 4 para.14, enabling: SI
2015/1836
Sch.21 para.4, enabling: SI 2015/866

**12. International Development (Official
Development Assistance Target) Act 2015**
Royal Assent, March 26, 2015

13. Mutuals Deferred Shares Act 2015
Royal Assent, March 26, 2015

**14. House of Lords (Expulsion and
Suspension) Act 2015**
Royal Assent, March 26, 2015

15. Consumer Rights Act 2015
Royal Assent, March 26, 2015
s.84, enabling: SI 2015/951
s.96, enabling: SI 2015/1629, SI
2015/1630, SI 2015/1726
s.97, enabling: SI 2015/1575, SI
2015/1605, SI 2015/1630
s.100, enabling: SI 2015/965, SI
2015/1333, SI 2015/1575, SI 2015/1584,
SI 2015/1605, SI 2015/1630, SI
2015/1831, SI 2015/1904
Sch.3 para.8, amended: SI 2015/1682
Sch.1 para.4
Sch.5 Part 2 para.10, amended: SI
2015/1640 Reg.15, SI 2015/1726 Sch.1
para.6
Sch.5 Part 2 para.12, enabling: SI
2015/1726

**16. Specialist Printing Equipment and
Materials (Offences) Act 2015**
Royal Assent, March 26, 2015

**17. Self-build and Custom Housebuilding
Act 2015**
Royal Assent, March 26, 2015

18. Lords Spiritual (Women) Act 2015
Royal Assent, March 26, 2015

**19. Armed Forces (Service Complaints and
Financial Assistance) Act 2015**
Royal Assent, March 26, 2015
s.6, enabling: SI 2015/1969
s.7, enabling: SI 2015/1957

20. Deregulation Act 2015
Royal Assent, March 26, 2015
s.104, enabling: SI 2015/1732

s.112, enabling: SI 2015/968, SI
2015/971, SI 2015/1637, SI 2015/1641,
SI 2015/1852
s.115, enabling: SI 2015/994, SI
2015/1402, SI 2015/1405, SI 2015/1732,
SI 2015/2074
Sch.1 Part 4, enabling: SI 2015/994
Sch.6 Part 6 para.23, amended: SI
2015/1732 Art.8

**21. Corporation Tax (Northern Ireland) Act
2015**
Royal Assent, March 26, 2015
Sch.2 Part 1 para.3, repealed: 2015 c.33
s.36

**22. Local Government (Review of Decisions)
Act 2015**
Royal Assent, March 26, 2015

23. Control of Horses Act 2015
Royal Assent, March 26, 2015

**24. House of Commons Commission Act
2015**
Royal Assent, March 26, 2015

25. Recall of MPs Act 2015
Royal Assent, March 26, 2015
s.22, amended: SI 2015/1376 Sch.2
para.19

**26. Small Business, Enterprise and
Employment Act 2015**
Royal Assent, March 26, 2015
s.4, enabling: SI 2015/1945
s.5, enabling: SI 2015/1946
s.6, enabling: SI 2015/1945, SI
2015/1946
s.7, enabling: SI 2015/1945, SI
2015/1946
s.10, enabling: SI 2015/2060
s.28, enabling: SI 2015/1864, SI
2015/1865, SI 2015/1945, SI 2015/1946
s.40, amended: SSI 2015/446 Sch.6
para.3
s.159, enabling: SI 2015/963, SI
2015/1651
s.160, enabling: SI 2015/1689
s.161, enabling: SI 2015/1329, SI
2015/1689, SI 2015/1945, SI 2015/1946,
SI 2015/2029
s.164, enabling: SI 2015/1329, SI
2015/1689, SI 2015/1710, SI 2015/2029

**27. Local Government (Religious etc
Observances) Act 2015**
Royal Assent, March 26, 2015

28. Health and Social Care (Safety and Quality) Act 2015
> Royal Assent, March 26, 2015
> s.6, enabling: SI 2015/1438

29. Health Service Commissioner for England (Complaint Handling) Act 2015
> Royal Assent, March 26, 2015

30. Modern Slavery Act 2015
> Royal Assent, March 26, 2015
> s.16, enabling: SI 2015/1478
> s.32, enabling: SI 2015/1478
> s.52, enabling: SI 2015/1743
> s.54, enabling: SI 2015/1833
> s.57, enabling: SI 2015/1472
> s.61, enabling: SI 2015/1476, SI 2015/1690, SI 2015/1816

31. Supply and Appropriation (Main Estimates) Act 2015
> Royal Assent, July 21, 2015

32. European Union (Finance) Act 2015
> Royal Assent, July 21, 2015

33. Finance (No.2) Act 2015
> Royal Assent, November 18, 2015
> Sch.8 Part 1 para.3, enabling: SI 2015/1986
> Sch.8 Part 1 para.8, enabling: SI 2015/1986
> Sch.8 Part 1 para.23, enabling: SI 2015/1986

34. Northern Ireland (Welfare Reform) Act 2015
> Royal Assent, November 25, 2015
> s.1, enabling: SI 2015/2006

35. National Insurance Contributions (Rate Ceilings) Act 2015
> Royal Assent, December 17, 2015

36. European Union Referendum Act 2015
> Royal Assent, December 17, 2015

37. European Union (Approvals) Act 2015
> Royal Assent, December 17, 2015

CURRENT LAW

STATUTORY INSTRUMENT CITATOR 2015

PART 4

This is Part 4 of the Statutory Instrument Citator 2015 and is up to date to March 10, 2016 (Orders and Acts received). It comprises in a single table:

    (i)   Statutory Instruments made between January 1, 2015 and March 10, 2016;

   (ii) Amendments, modifications and repeals made to existing Statutory Instruments during this period;

  (iii) Statutory Instruments judicially considered during this period;

  (iv) Statutory Instruments made under the powers of any Statutory Instrument issued during this period.

The material is arranged in numerical order under the relevant year.

Definitions of legislative effects:

"added" : new provisions are inserted by subsequent legislation

"amended" : text of legislation is modified by subsequent legislation

"applied" : brought to bear, or exercised by subsequent legislation

"consolidated" : used where previous legislation in the same subject area is brought together in subsequent legislation, with or without amendments

"disapplied" : an exception made to the application of an earlier enactment

"enabling" : giving power for the relevant SI to be made

"referred to" : direction from other legislation without specific effect or application

"repealed" : rescinded by subsequent legislation

"restored" : reinstated by subsequent legislation (where previously repealed/ revoked)

"substituted" : text of provision is completely replaced by subsequent legislation

"varied" : provisions modified in relation to their application to specified areas or circumstances, however the text itself remains unchanged

STATUTORY INSTRUMENTS ISSUED BY THE SCOTTISH PARLIAMENT

1992

1269. Aberdeen-Fraserburgh Trunk Road (A92) (Maconochie Road, Fraserburgh) (40mph Speed Limit) Order 1992
revoked: SSI 2015/267 Art.3

1999

1. Environmental Impact Assessment (Scotland) Regulations 1999
Reg.55, amended: SSI 2015/237 Reg.2
Reg.55, revoked: SSI 2015/237 Reg.2

2000

59. Disabled Persons (Badges for Motor Vehicles) (Scotland) Regulations 2000
Reg.9A, added: SSI 2015/9 Reg.3
Reg.10A, added: SSI 2015/9 Reg.4
Sch.1 Part IIIA para.1, amended: SSI 2015/9 Reg.5
Sch.1 Part IIIA para.1, revoked: SSI 2015/9 Reg.5
130. Foods for Special Medical Purposes (Scotland) Regulations 2000
Reg.3, amended: SSI 2015/100 Art.2
301. Human Rights Act 1998 (Jurisdiction) (Scotland) Rules 2000
r.4, amended: SSI 2015/338 Sch.1 para.2

2001

128. Limited Liability Partnerships (Scotland) Regulations 2001
Sch.2, amended: SI 2015/989 Sch.1 para.3
222. Education (Assisted Places) (Scotland) Regulations 2001
revoked: SSI 2015/318 Sch.1

2002

131. Adults with Incapacity (Public Guardian's Fees) (Scotland) Amendment Regulations 2002
revoked: SSI 2015/260 Sch.4
132. Act of Sederunt (Summary Cause Rules) 2002
Sch.1 Appendix, amended: SSI 2015/283 r.5, SSI 2015/419 r.11
Sch.1 Appendixa, amended: SSI 2015/419 r.11
Sch.1 Part 2 para.2_1, amended: SSI 2015/419 r.11
Sch.1 Part 8 para.8_15, revoked: SSI 2015/419 r.11
Sch.1 Part 8 para.8_16, revoked: SSI 2015/419 r.11
Sch.1 Part 16 para.16_2, substituted: SSI 2015/227 r.9
Sch.1 Part 16 para.16_3, amended: SSI 2015/227 r.9
Sch.1 Part 23 para.23_2, amended: SSI 2015/419 r.11
Sch.1 Part 23 para.23_3, amended: SSI 2015/419 r.11
Sch.1 Part 23 para.23_3, revoked: SSI 2015/419 r.11
Sch.1 Part 25 para.25_1, amended: SSI 2015/419 r.11
Sch.1 Part 25 para.25_1, substituted: SSI 2015/419 r.11
Sch.1 Part 25 para.25_2, revoked: SSI 2015/419 r.11
Sch.1 Part 25 para.25_4, amended: SSI 2015/419 r.11
Sch.1 Part 25 para.25_4, revoked: SSI 2015/419 r.11
Sch.1 Part 25 para.25_6, amended: SSI 2015/419 r.11
Sch.1 Part 25 para.25_7, revoked: SSI 2015/419 r.11
133. Act of Sederunt (Small Claim Rules) 2002
Sch.1 Appendix1, amended: SSI 2015/283 r.6, SSI 2015/419 r.12
Sch.1 Appendix2, amended: SSI 2015/419 r.12

Sch.1 Part 21 para.21_6, amended: SSI
2015/419 r.12
Sch.1 Part 21 para.21_6, revoked: SSI
2015/419 r.12
Sch.1 Part 23 para.23_1, amended: SSI
2015/419 r.12
Sch.1 Part 23 para.23_1, substituted: SSI
2015/419 r.12
Sch.1 Part 23 para.23_2, revoked: SSI
2015/419 r.12
Sch.1 Part 23 para.23_4, amended: SSI
2015/419 r.12
Sch.1 Part 23 para.23_4, revoked: SSI
2015/419 r.12
249. Education (Assisted Places) (Scotland)
Amendment Regulations 2002
    revoked: SSI 2015/318 Sch.1
270. Court of Session etc Fees Amendment
Order 2002
    revoked: SSI 2015/261 Sch.4
303. Community Care (Personal Care and
Nursing Care) (Scotland) Regulations 2002
    Reg.2, amended: SSI 2015/154 Reg.2
494. Civil Legal Aid (Scotland) Regulations
2002
    Reg.2, amended: SSI 2015/380 Reg.3
    Reg.4, amended: SSI 2015/380 Reg.3
    Reg.21, amended: SSI 2015/380 Reg.3
541. Genetically Modified Organisms
(Deliberate Release) (Scotland) Regulations
2002
    Reg.2, amended: SSI 2015/100 Art.2
    Reg.32, amended: SSI 2015/100 Art.2
560. Act of Sederunt (Debt Arrangement and
Attachment (Scotland) Act 2002) 2002
    Art.3, amended: SSI 2015/283 r.8
    Sch.1 Appendixa, amended: SSI
    2015/419 r.13
    Sch.1 Part CHAPTERb para.36A, added:
    SSI 2015/419 r.13
    Sch.2, amended: SSI 2015/283 r.8, Sch.2

2003

1. Cairngorms National Park Designation,
Transitional and Consequential Provisions
(Scotland) Order 2003
    Art.7, revoked: SSI 2015/181 Sch.9
176. Council Tax (Discounts) (Scotland)
Consolidation and Amendment Order 2003

Sch.2 Part 2 para.1, amended: SSI
2015/153 Sch.1 para.6
179. Advice and Assistance (Assistance by
Way of Representation) (Scotland)
Regulations 2003
    Reg.3, amended: SSI 2015/155 Reg.2
    Reg.3A, amended: SSI 2015/13 Reg.2
    Reg.6, amended: SSI 2015/402 Sch.1
    para.8
    Reg.9, amended: SSI 2015/279 Reg.2
    Reg.13, amended: SSI 2015/13 Reg.2
235. Landfill (Scotland) Regulations 2003
    Reg.2, amended: SSI 2015/188 Reg.4
281. Education (Assisted Places) (Scotland)
Amendment Regulations 2003
    revoked: SSI 2015/318 Sch.1
569. Honey (Scotland) Regulations 2003
    revoked: SSI 2015/208 Reg.19
593. End-of-Life Vehicles (Storage and
Treatment) (Scotland) Regulations 2003
    Reg.2, amended: SSI 2015/438 Art.3

2004

228. Community Right to Buy (Ballot)
(Scotland) Regulations 2004
    revoked: SSI 2015/400 Sch.13
229. Community Right to Buy
(Compensation) (Scotland) Regulations 2004
    revoked: SSI 2015/400 Sch.13
231. Community Right to Buy (Specification
of Plans) (Scotland) Regulations 2004
    revoked: SSI 2015/400 Sch.13
239. Education (Assisted Places) (Scotland)
Amendment Regulations 2004
    revoked: SSI 2015/318 Sch.1
276. Inshore Fishing (Prohibition of Fishing
and Fishing Methods) (Scotland) Order 2004
    Sch.1, amended: SSI 2015/435 Art.16,
    SSI 2015/436 Art.4
278. Common Agricultural Policy Non-IACS
Support Schemes (Appeals) (Scotland)
Regulations 2004
    Reg.2, amended: SSI 2015/167 Reg.3
    Reg.2, revoked: SSI 2015/167 Reg.3
    Reg.3, amended: SSI 2015/167 Reg.4
    Sch.1, substituted: SSI 2015/167 Reg.5
406. Building (Scotland) Regulations 2004
    Sch.5 Part 6 para.6_3, revoked: SSI
    2015/218 Reg.3

Sch.5 Part 6 para.6_9, amended: SSI
2015/218 Reg.2

**432. Genetically Modified Food (Scotland)
Regulations 2004**
Reg.3, amended: SSI 2015/100 Art.2

**433. Genetically Modified Animal Feed
(Scotland) Regulations 2004**
Reg.3, amended: SSI 2015/100 Art.2

2005

**157. Landfill Allowances Scheme (Scotland)
Regulations 2005**
Reg.2, amended: SSI 2015/188 Reg.5

**270. Education (Assisted Places) (Scotland)
Amendment Regulations 2005**
revoked: SSI 2015/318 Sch.1

**307. Honey (Scotland) Amendment
Regulations 2005**
revoked: SSI 2015/208 Reg.19

**325. Additional Support for Learning
(Appropriate Agencies) (Scotland) Order
2005**
Art.2, amended: SSI 2015/153 Sch.1
para.7, SSI 2015/157 Sch.1 para.16
Art.2, revoked: SSI 2015/157 Sch.1
para.16

**344. Fire (Scotland) Act 2005 (Consequential
Modifications and Amendments) (No.2)
Order 2005**
Sch.1 Part 1 para.14, revoked: SSI
2015/181 Sch.9

**377. A77 Trunk Road (Maybole) (Restricted
Road) Order 2005**
revoked: SSI 2015/332 Art.4

**494. Civil Contingencies Act 2004
(Contingency Planning) (Scotland)
Regulations 2005**
Reg.9, amended: SI 2015/483 Sch.6
para.1
Reg.29, amended: SSI 2015/100 Art.2

**608. Feed (Hygiene and Enforcement)
(Scotland) Regulations 2005**
Reg.2, amended: SSI 2015/100 Art.2

2006

**3. Food Hygiene (Scotland) Regulations
2006**

Reg.2, amended: SSI 2015/100 Art.2

**22. A830 Trunk Road (30mph Lochybridge
and Lochaber High School Part-time 20mph
Speed Limit) Order 2006**
revoked: SSI 2015/301 Art.3

**24. Crofting Counties Agricultural Grants
(Scotland) Scheme 2006**
varied: SSI 2015/105 Art.4
Part 3A, added: SSI 2015/105 Art.3
Art.2, amended: SSI 2015/105 Art.3
Art.6, substituted: SSI 2015/105 Art.3
Art.10, substituted: SSI 2015/105 Art.3
Art.11A, amended: SSI 2015/105 Art.3
Art.13, amended: SSI 2015/105 Art.3
Sch.1 para.1, substituted: SSI 2015/105
Art.3

**218. Charities Accounts (Scotland)
Regulations 2006**
Reg.1, amended: SSI 2015/153 Sch.1
para.8

**219. Charity Test (Specified Bodies)
(Scotland) Order 2006**
Sch.1, amended: SSI 2015/148 Art.2

**317. Education (Assisted Places) (Scotland)
Amendment Regulations 2006**
revoked: SSI 2015/318 Sch.1

**333. Education (Student Loans for Tuition
Fees) (Scotland) Regulations 2006**
Reg.3, amended: SSI 2015/212 Reg.2
Reg.3, revoked: SSI 2015/212 Reg.2

**338. Firefighters Compensation Scheme
(Scotland) Order 2006**
Sch.1, added: SSI 2015/143 Art.3, Art.6,
Art.10, Art.11, Art.12, Art.13
Sch.1, amended: SSI 2015/143 Art.3,
Art.4, Art.5, Art.6, Art.7, Art.8, Art.9,
Art.10, Art.11, Art.12, Art.13, Art.14,
Art.15
Sch.1, substituted: SSI 2015/143 Art.3,
Art.5, Art.8, Art.9, Art.14

456. Fire Safety (Scotland) Regulations 2006
Reg.2, amended: SI 2015/21 Reg.15
Reg.25, amended: SI 2015/1682 Sch.1
para.11

**458. Fire (Scotland) Act 2005
(Commencement No 3 and Savings) Order
2006**
Art.3, amended: SI 2015/483 Sch.6
para.5

2007

18. A77 Trunk Road (Maybole) (30mph Speed Limit) Variation and Maybole Schools (Part-time 20mph Speed Limit) Order 2007
revoked: SSI 2015/332 Art.4

83. A90 Trunk Road (Longhaven Primary School) (Part-time 20mph Speed Limit) Order 2007
revoked: SSI 2015/251 Art.3

105. Adults with Incapacity (Requirements for Signing Medical Treatment Certificates) (Scotland) Regulations 2007
Reg.2, amended: SSI 2015/153 Sch.1 para.11

114. Education (Assisted Places) (Scotland) Amendment Regulations 2007
revoked: SSI 2015/318 Sch.1

152. Education (Fees and Awards) (Scotland) Regulations 2007
Reg.3, amended: SSI 2015/153 Sch.1 para.12

154. Education (Student Loans) (Scotland) Regulations 2007
Reg.2, amended: SSI 2015/212 Reg.3
Reg.3, amended: SSI 2015/212 Reg.3

185. Inshore Fishing (Prohibited Methods of Fishing) (Loch Creran) Order 2007
revoked: SSI 2015/435 Art.16

199. Firefighters Pension Scheme (Scotland) Order 2007
Sch.1, added: SSI 2015/141 Reg.25, Reg.26, Reg.27, Reg.28, Reg.29, Reg.30, Reg.31, SSI 2015/143 Art.17, Art.18, Art.19
Sch.1, amended: SSI 2015/141 Reg.24, Reg.25, Reg.26, Reg.27, Reg.28, Reg.29, SSI 2015/143 Art.17, Art.18, Art.19, Art.20, Art.21, Art.22

307. European Fisheries Fund (Grants) (Scotland) Regulations 2007
revoked: SSI 2015/359 Reg.18

319. Court of Session etc Fees Amendment Order 2007
revoked: SSI 2015/261 Sch.4

320. Adults with Incapacity (Public Guardian's Fees) (Scotland) Amendment Regulations 2007
revoked: SSI 2015/260 Sch.4

321. High Court of Justiciary Fees Amendment Order 2007

revoked: SSI 2015/262 Sch.4

419. Housing (Scotland) Act 2006 (Repayment Charge and Discharge) Order 2007
Sch.1, amended: SSI 2015/144 Art.2

504. Club Gaming and Club Machine Permits (Scotland) Regulations 2007
Reg.19, amended: SSI 2015/338 Sch.2 para.17

505. Licensed Premises Gaming Machine Permits (Scotland) Regulations 2007
Reg.18, amended: SSI 2015/338 Sch.2 para.18

549. Infant Formula and Follow-on Formula (Scotland) Regulations 2007
Reg.2, amended: SSI 2015/100 Art.2

2008

52. Adults with Incapacity (Public Guardian's Fees) (Scotland) Regulations 2008
revoked: SSI 2015/260 Sch.4

64. Agricultural Processing, Marketing and Co-operation Grants (Scotland) Regulations 2008
revoked: SSI 2015/192 Sch.1

66. Leader Grants (Scotland) Regulations 2008
revoked: SSI 2015/192 Sch.1

101. Aquaculture and Fisheries (Scotland) Act 2007 (Fixed Penalty Notices) Order 2008
revoked: SSI 2015/113 Art.6

119. Act of Sederunt (Sheriff Court Bankruptcy Rules) 2008
Appendix 1., amended: SSI 2015/119 r.3, Sch.1
Sch.1 para.1, amended: SSI 2015/119 r.3
Sch.1 para.3, amended: SSI 2015/119 r.3
Sch.1 para.5, amended: SSI 2015/119 r.3
Sch.1 para.6, revoked: SSI 2015/119 r.3
Sch.1 para.8, amended: SSI 2015/119 r.3, SSI 2015/419 r.14
Sch.1 para.8, revoked: SSI 2015/419 r.14
Sch.1 para.8, substituted: SSI 2015/419 r.14
Sch.1 para.8A, added: SSI 2015/419 r.14
Sch.1 para.12, amended: SSI 2015/119 r.3
Sch.1 para.12, substituted: SSI 2015/119 r.3

Sch.1 para.15, amended: SSI 2015/119
r.3
**135. Forestry Challenge Funds (Scotland)
Regulations 2008**
revoked: SSI 2015/192 Sch.1
**162. Land Managers Skills Development
Grants (Scotland) Regulations 2008**
revoked: SSI 2015/192 Sch.1
Reg.5, amended: SSI 2015/153 Sch.1
para.13
**170. Bathing Waters (Scotland) Regulations
2008**
Reg.2, amended: SSI 2015/446 Sch.6
para.4
**184. Common Agricultural Policy (Single
Farm Payment and Support Schemes and
Cross-Compliance) (Scotland) Amendment
Regulations 2008**
revoked: SSI 2015/58 Reg.28
**213. Education (Assisted Places) (Scotland)
Amendment Regulations 2008**
revoked: SSI 2015/318 Sch.1
**230. Local Government Pension Scheme
(Benefits, Membership and Contributions)
(Scotland) Regulations 2008**
Reg.24A, added: SSI 2015/448 Reg.44
**236. Court of Session etc Fees Amendment
Order 2008**
revoked: SSI 2015/261 Sch.4
**237. High Court of Justiciary Fees
Amendment Order 2008**
revoked: SSI 2015/262 Sch.4
**238. Adults with Incapacity (Public
Guardian's Fees) (Scotland) Amendment
Regulations 2008**
revoked: SSI 2015/260 Sch.4
**268. Charity Test (Specified Bodies)
(Scotland) Order 2008**
Sch.1, substituted: SSI 2015/153 Sch.1
para.14
**298. Action Programme for Nitrate
Vulnerable Zones (Scotland) Regulations
2008**
Reg.3, amended: SSI 2015/376 Reg.5
**309. Energy Performance of Buildings
(Scotland) Regulations 2008**
Reg.12, amended: SSI 2015/386 Reg.2
Reg.12A, revoked: SSI 2015/386 Reg.2
Reg.13, revoked: SSI 2015/386 Reg.2
Reg.14, amended: SSI 2015/386 Reg.2
Reg.15, amended: SSI 2015/386 Reg.2

Reg.17, amended: SSI 2015/386 Reg.2
Reg.17A, amended: SSI 2015/386 Reg.2
Reg.17B, amended: SSI 2015/386 Reg.2
Sch.1 Part 1, amended: SSI 2015/386
Reg.2
Sch.1 Part 2, added: SSI 2015/386 Reg.2
Sch.1 Part 3, substituted: SSI 2015/386
Reg.2
**317. Inshore Fishing (Prohibition on Fishing)
(Lamlash Bay) (Scotland) Order 2008**
revoked: SSI 2015/437 Sch.4

2009

**44. International Organisations (Immunities
and Privileges) (Scotland) Order 2009**
Sch.16, added: SSI 2015/421 Sch.1
**85. Aquatic Animal Health (Scotland)
Regulations 2009**
Reg.46, amended: SSI 2015/100 Art.2
**87. High Court of Justiciary Fees
Amendment Order 2009**
revoked: SSI 2015/262 Sch.4
**88. Court of Session etc Fees Amendment
Order 2009**
revoked: SSI 2015/261 Sch.4
**156. Community Right to Buy (Prescribed
Form of Application and Notices) (Scotland)
Regulations 2009**
revoked: SSI 2015/400 Sch.13
**261. Food Irradiation (Scotland) Regulations
2009**
Reg.3, amended: SSI 2015/100 Art.2
**266. Environmental Liability (Scotland)
Regulations 2009**
Reg.2, amended: SSI 2015/214 Reg.3
Reg.4, amended: SSI 2015/214 Reg.4
Reg.5, amended: SSI 2015/214 Reg.5
Reg.7, amended: SSI 2015/214 Reg.6
Reg.11, amended: SSI 2015/214 Reg.7
Reg.16, amended: SSI 2015/214 Reg.8
**284. Act of Sederunt (Sheriff Court Rules
Amendment) (Adoption and Children
(Scotland) Act 2007) 2009**
Sch.1, amended: SSI 2015/5 r.2, SSI
2015/419 r.15
Sch.1, substituted: SSI 2015/5 r.2, SSI
2015/419 r.15
**380. Campbeltown Legalised Police Cells
(Declaration and Revocation) Rules 2009**

revoked: SSI 2015/324 r.6

382. Act of Sederunt (Money Attachment Rules) 2009
Sch.1, added: SSI 2015/419 r.16
Sch.1, revoked: SSI 2015/419 r.16

391. Common Agricultural Policy (Single Farm Payment and Support Schemes and Cross-Compliance) (Scotland) Amendment Regulations 2009
revoked: SSI 2015/58 Reg.28

427. Food for Particular Nutritional Uses (Addition of Substances for Specific Nutritional Purposes) (Scotland) Regulations 2009
Sch.1, amended: SSI 2015/100 Art.2

2010

216. Carbon Accounting Scheme (Scotland) Regulations 2010
Reg.2, amended: SSI 2015/189 Reg.2
Reg.8A, added: SSI 2015/189 Reg.2
Reg.9, amended: SSI 2015/189 Reg.2

273. Less Favoured Area Support Scheme (Scotland) Regulations 2010
Reg.2, amended: SSI 2015/185 Reg.3
Reg.3, amended: SSI 2015/185 Reg.4
Reg.4, substituted: SSI 2015/185 Reg.5
Reg.5, amended: SSI 2015/185 Reg.6
Reg.6, substituted: SSI 2015/185 Reg.7
Reg.7, amended: SSI 2015/185 Reg.8
Reg.9, amended: SSI 2015/185 Reg.9
Reg.10, amended: SSI 2015/185 Reg.10
Reg.11, amended: SSI 2015/185 Reg.11
Reg.12, amended: SSI 2015/185 Reg.12
Reg.12A, added: SSI 2015/185 Reg.13
Reg.13, amended: SSI 2015/185 Reg.14
Reg.15, amended: SSI 2015/185 Reg.15
Reg.17, substituted: SSI 2015/185 Reg.16
Reg.25, revoked: SSI 2015/194 Reg.11
Sch.2, substituted: SSI 2015/185 Reg.17
Sch.5 Part I, amended: SSI 2015/185 Reg.18
Sch.5 Part II, amended: SSI 2015/185 Reg.18
Sch.7 para.5, amended: SSI 2015/185 Reg.19
Sch.7 para.6, amended: SSI 2015/185 Reg.19

Sch.7 para.8, amended: SSI 2015/185 Reg.19

323. European Fisheries Fund (Grants) (Scotland) Amendment Regulations 2010
revoked: SSI 2015/359 Reg.18

373. Animal Feed (Scotland) Regulations 2010
Reg.5, amended: SSI 2015/100 Art.2

390. Cleaner Road Transport Vehicles (Scotland) Regulations 2010
Reg.2, amended: SSI 2015/446 Sch.6 para.5
Reg.6, amended: SSI 2015/446 Sch.6 para.5

2011

60. Aquaculture and Fisheries (Scotland) Act 2007 (Fixed Penalty Notices) Amendment Order 2011
revoked: SSI 2015/113 Art.6

141. Debt Arrangement Scheme (Scotland) Regulations 2011
Reg.3, amended: SSI 2015/216 Reg.3
Reg.30, amended: SSI 2015/216 Reg.4

146. Disclosure (Persons engaged in the Investigation and Reporting of Crime or Sudden Deaths) (Scotland) Regulations 2011
Sch.1, amended: SSI 2015/100 Art.2, SSI 2015/239 Art.23

213. A77 Trunk Road (Girvan) (Restricted Roads) Order 2011
revoked: SSI 2015/203 Art.3

375. Ancient Monuments and Archaeological Areas (Applications for Scheduled Monument Consent) (Scotland) Regulations 2011
revoked: SSI 2015/229 Reg.14

388. Act of Sederunt (Contempt of Court in Civil Proceedings) 2011
Art.1, amended: SSI 2015/419 r.17
Art.10, amended: SSI 2015/419 r.17

389. Education (Fees) (Scotland) Regulations 2011
Reg.2, amended: SSI 2015/153 Sch.1 para.17

416. Common Agricultural Policy Single Farm Payment and Support Schemes (Scotland) Regulations 2011
revoked: SSI 2015/58 Reg.28

2012

**162. Equality Act 2010 (Specific Duties)
(Scotland) Regulations 2012**
    Reg.2, amended: SSI 2015/254 Reg.3
    Reg.2A, added: SSI 2015/254 Reg.4
    Reg.9, amended: SSI 2015/446 Sch.6
    para.7
    Sch.1, amended: SSI 2015/254 Reg.5
**166. European Fisheries Fund (Grants)
(Scotland) Amendment Regulations 2012**
    revoked: SSI 2015/359 Reg.18
**182. Leader Grants (Scotland) Amendment
Regulations 2012**
    revoked: SSI 2015/192 Sch.1
**289. Adults with Incapacity (Public
Guardian's Fees) (Scotland) Amendment
Regulations 2012**
    revoked: SSI 2015/260 Sch.4
**290. Court of Session etc Fees Amendment
Order 2012**
    revoked: SSI 2015/261 Sch.4
**291. High Court of Justiciary Fees
Amendment Order 2012**
    revoked: SSI 2015/262 Sch.4
**292. Justice of the Peace Court Fees
(Scotland) Order 2012**
    revoked: SSI 2015/263 Art.4
**303. Council Tax Reduction (Scotland)
Regulations 2012**
    Reg.2, amended: SI 2015/971 Sch.3
    para.18, SSI 2015/46 Reg.3
    Reg.16, amended: SSI 2015/46 Reg.4
    Reg.19, amended: SSI 2015/46 Reg.5
    Reg.52, amended: SI 2015/971 Sch.3
    para.18
    Reg.67, amended: SSI 2015/46 Reg.6
    Reg.90C, amended: SSI 2015/46 Reg.7
    Reg.90D, amended: SSI 2015/46 Reg.8
    Sch.1 Part 1 para.1, amended: SSI
    2015/46 Reg.9
    Sch.1 Part 1 para.3, amended: SSI
    2015/46 Reg.9
    Sch.1 Part 3 para.10, amended: SI
    2015/1985 Art.36
    Sch.1 Part 4 para.17, amended: SSI
    2015/46 Reg.9
    Sch.1 Part 5 para.23, amended: SSI
    2015/46 Reg.9

    Sch.1 Part 5 para.24, amended: SSI
    2015/46 Reg.9
    Sch.2 para.1, amended: SSI 2015/46
    Reg.10
    Sch.3 para.1, amended: SI 2015/1985
    Art.36
    Sch.3 para.9, amended: SSI 2015/46
    Reg.11
    Sch.4 para.57, amended: SSI 2015/46
    Reg.12
    Sch.5 para.11A, added: SSI 2015/46
    Reg.13
**319. Council Tax Reduction (State Pension
Credit) (Scotland) Regulations 2012**
    Reg.2, amended: SI 2015/971 Sch.3
    para.19, SSI 2015/46 Reg.15
    Reg.16, amended: SSI 2015/46 Reg.16
    Reg.19, amended: SSI 2015/46 Reg.17
    Reg.38, amended: SI 2015/1985 Art.37
    Reg.48, amended: SSI 2015/46 Reg.18
    Reg.70C, amended: SSI 2015/46 Reg.19
    Sch.1 Part 1 para.2, amended: SSI
    2015/46 Reg.20
    Sch.1 Part 1 para.3, amended: SSI
    2015/46 Reg.20
    Sch.1 Part 4 para.13, amended: SSI
    2015/46 Reg.20
    Sch.2 para.3, amended: SSI 2015/46
    Reg.21
    Sch.4 Part 1 para.21, amended: SSI
    2015/46 Reg.22
    Sch.4 Part 1 para.22, amended: SSI
    2015/46 Reg.22
    Sch.4 Part 1 para.22, revoked: SSI
    2015/46 Reg.22
    Sch.4 Part 1 para.29, amended: SSI
    2015/46 Reg.22
    Sch.5 para.1, amended: SSI 2015/46
    Reg.23
**322. Court Fees (Miscellaneous
Amendments) Scotland Order 2012**
    revoked: SSI 2015/261 Sch.4
**335. Children's Hearings (Scotland) Act 2011
(Rights of Audience of the Principal
Reporter) Regulations 2012**
    Reg.2, amended: SSI 2015/402 Sch.1
    para.9
**345. Banchory and Crathes Light Railway
Order 2012**
    Art.3, amended: SI 2015/1682 Sch.1
    para.11

2013

3. Bovine Viral Diarrhoea (Scotland) Order 2013
Art.2, amended: SSI 2015/186 Art.3
Art.10, substituted: SSI 2015/186 Art.4
Art.11, substituted: SSI 2015/186 Art.5
Art.12, amended: SSI 2015/186 Art.6
Art.13, revoked: SSI 2015/186 Art.7
Art.14, amended: SSI 2015/186 Art.8
Art.14, revoked: SSI 2015/186 Art.8
Art.17, amended: SSI 2015/186 Art.9
Art.17, revoked: SSI 2015/186 Art.9
Art.21, amended: SSI 2015/186 Art.10
Art.23B, amended: SSI 2015/186 Art.11
Art.23C, amended: SSI 2015/186 Art.12
Art.23D, amended: SSI 2015/186 Art.13
Art.23E, added: SSI 2015/186 Art.14
Art.24, amended: SSI 2015/186 Art.15

21. Bovine Viral Diarrhoea (Scotland) Amendment Order 2013
Art.4, revoked: SSI 2015/186 Art.16

84. Food Safety (Sampling and Qualifications) (Scotland) Regulations 2013
Sch.2 Part 2 para.5, amended: SSI 2015/153 Sch.1 para.20

173. Animal Health (Miscellaneous Amendments) (Scotland) Order 2013
Art.8, revoked: SSI 2015/327 Art.23

177. European Union (Amendments in respect of the Accession of Croatia) (Scotland) Regulations 2013
Sch.1 para.10, revoked: SSI 2015/318 Sch.1

194. Children's Hearings (Scotland) Act 2011 (Rules of Procedure in Children's Hearings) Rules 2013
Part 7 r.29, amended: SSI 2015/21 r.3
Part 12 r.45, amended: SSI 2015/21 r.4
Part 12 r.46A, added: SSI 2015/21 r.4
Part 12 r.47, amended: SSI 2015/21 r.4
Part 12 r.49, substituted: SSI 2015/21 r.4
Part 12 r.49A, added: SSI 2015/21 r.4
Part 12 r.50, amended: SSI 2015/21 r.4
Part 12 r.52, amended: SSI 2015/21 r.4
Part 12 r.54, amended: SSI 2015/21 r.4
Part 15 r.59, amended: SSI 2015/21 r.5
Part 15 r.59, revoked: SSI 2015/21 r.5
Part 15 r.64, amended: SSI 2015/21 r.6

Part 17 r.77, amended: SSI 2015/21 r.7

256. Fish Labelling (Scotland) Regulations 2013
Reg.2, amended: SSI 2015/48 Reg.2
Reg.3, amended: SSI 2015/48 Reg.2
Reg.3, revoked: SSI 2015/48 Reg.2
Reg.5, amended: SSI 2015/48 Reg.2

265. Common Agricultural Policy Single Farm Payment and Support Schemes (Scotland) Amendment Regulations 2013
revoked: SSI 2015/58 Reg.28

266. Food Additives, Flavourings, Enzymes and Extraction Solvents (Scotland) Regulations 2013
Reg.13, amended: SSI 2015/100 Art.2

307. Animal By-Products (Enforcement) (Scotland) Regulations 2013
Reg.7A, added: SSI 2015/393 Reg.2
Reg.22, amended: SSI 2015/100 Art.2
Reg.25, amended: SSI 2015/393 Reg.2
Reg.28, amended: SSI 2015/100 Art.2
Reg.32, substituted: SSI 2015/393 Reg.2
Sch.1, amended: SSI 2015/393 Reg.2

337. Bovine Viral Diarrhoea (Scotland) Amendment (No.2) Order 2013
Art.5, revoked: SSI 2015/186 Art.16

363. Bovine Viral Diarrhoea (Scotland) Amendment (No.3) Order 2013
Art.10, revoked: SSI 2015/186 Art.16

2014

7. Less Favoured Area Support Scheme (Scotland) Amendment Regulations 2014
Reg.7, revoked: SSI 2015/194 Reg.11

36. Local Government Finance (Scotland) Order 2014
Art.2, revoked: SSI 2015/56 Art.5
Sch.1, amended: SSI 2015/56 Art.5

91. Community Care (Personal Care and Nursing Care) (Scotland) Amendment Regulations 2014
revoked: SSI 2015/154 Reg.3

102. Act of Sederunt (Fitness for Judicial Office Tribunal Rules) (No.2) 2014
revoked: SSI 2015/120 r.16

164. Local Government Pension Scheme (Scotland) Regulations 2014
Reg.22, amended: SSI 2015/87 Reg.13, SSI 2015/448 Reg.9

Reg.23, amended: SSI 2015/87 Reg.14

225. Bankruptcy (Scotland) Regulations 2014
Reg.19, amended: SSI 2015/80 Reg.2
Reg.24, amended: SSI 2015/80 Reg.2
Reg.25, added: SSI 2015/80 Reg.2
Sch.1, amended: SSI 2015/80 Reg.2,
Sch.1
Sch.1, substituted: SSI 2015/80 Reg.2
Sch.2, amended: SSI 2015/80 Reg.2

226. Bankruptcy (Applications and Decisions) (Scotland) Regulations 2014
Part 4, amended: SSI 2015/80 Reg.3
Reg.2A, added: SSI 2015/80 Reg.3
Reg.3, amended: SSI 2015/80 Reg.3
Reg.4, amended: SSI 2015/80 Reg.3
Reg.5, amended: SSI 2015/80 Reg.3
Reg.19, amended: SSI 2015/80 Reg.3
Reg.21A, added: SSI 2015/80 Reg.3
Sch.1, amended: SSI 2015/80 Reg.3,
Sch.2

227. Bankruptcy Fees (Scotland) Regulations 2014
Reg.13, amended: SSI 2015/80 Reg.4

261. Bankruptcy and Debt Advice (Scotland) Act 2014 (Commencement No 2, Savings and Transitionals) Order 2014
Art.4, amended: SSI 2015/54 Art.2

290. Common Financial Tool etc (Scotland) Regulations 2014
Reg.2, amended: SSI 2015/149 Reg.4
Reg.3, amended: SSI 2015/149 Reg.3,
Reg.4
Reg.3A, added: SSI 2015/149 Reg.3
Reg.4, amended: SSI 2015/149 Reg.4
Reg.7, amended: SSI 2015/149 Reg.4
Reg.8, amended: SSI 2015/149 Reg.4
Reg.9, amended: SSI 2015/149 Reg.4
Sch.1, amended: SSI 2015/149 Reg.4,
Sch.1

312. Food Information (Scotland) Regulations 2014
Reg.2, amended: SSI 2015/410 Reg.3
Reg.5, amended: SSI 2015/410 Reg.3
Reg.8, amended: SSI 2015/410 Reg.3
Sch.2 para.3, amended: SSI 2015/410
Reg.3
Sch.3, amended: SSI 2015/410 Reg.3
Sch.3 Part 1, amended: SSI 2015/410
Reg.3
Sch.3 Part 1, substituted: SSI 2015/410
Reg.3

Sch.4 Part 1, amended: SSI 2015/410
Reg.3
Sch.5 para.1, amended: SSI 2015/410
Reg.3
Sch.5 para.2, substituted: SSI 2015/410
Reg.3
Sch.5 para.4, amended: SSI 2015/410
Reg.3
Sch.5 para.5, substituted: SSI 2015/410
Reg.3
Sch.5 para.7, amended: SSI 2015/410
Reg.3
Sch.5 para.8, amended: SSI 2015/410
Reg.3
Sch.5 para.10, revoked: SSI 2015/208
Reg.20
Sch.5 para.11, amended: SSI 2015/410
Reg.3
Sch.5 para.12, amended: SSI 2015/410
Reg.3
Sch.5 para.13, amended: SSI 2015/410
Reg.3

325. Common Agricultural Policy (Cross-Compliance) (Scotland) Regulations 2014
Reg.9, revoked: SSI 2015/194 Reg.11
Sch.1 Part 1, amended: SSI 2015/58
Reg.27, SSI 2015/215 Reg.11
Sch.1 Part 2 para.1, amended: SSI
2015/58 Reg.27, SSI 2015/215 Reg.12
Sch.1 Part 2 para.7, amended: SSI
2015/58 Reg.27, SSI 2015/215 Reg.12

373. Designation of Nitrate Vulnerable Zones (Scotland) Regulations 2014
revoked: SSI 2015/376 Reg.6

377. Land and Buildings Transaction Tax (Transitional Provisions) (Scotland) Order 2014
Art.3, amended: SSI 2015/71 Art.2

2015

19. Firefighters Pension Scheme (Scotland) Regulations 2015
Reg.3, amended: SSI 2015/141 Reg.3
Reg.5A, added: SSI 2015/141 Reg.4
Reg.6, amended: SSI 2015/141 Reg.5
Reg.51, amended: SSI 2015/141 Reg.6
Reg.59, amended: SSI 2015/141 Reg.7
Reg.62, amended: SSI 2015/141 Reg.8
Reg.65, amended: SSI 2015/141 Reg.9

Reg.66, amended: SSI 2015/141 Reg.10
Reg.69, amended: SSI 2015/141 Reg.11
Reg.71A, added: SSI 2015/141 Reg.12
Reg.77, amended: SSI 2015/141 Reg.13
Reg.78, amended: SSI 2015/141 Reg.14
Reg.86, amended: SSI 2015/141 Reg.15
Reg.91, amended: SSI 2015/141 Reg.16
Reg.93, amended: SSI 2015/141 Reg.17
Reg.96, amended: SSI 2015/141 Reg.18
Reg.110, amended: SSI 2015/141 Reg.19
Reg.140A, added: SSI 2015/141 Reg.20
Reg.170, amended: SSI 2015/141 Reg.21
Sch.2 Part 1 para.3, amended: SSI 2015/141 Reg.22
Sch.2 Part 2 para.9, amended: SSI 2015/141 Reg.22
Sch.2 Part 3A, added: SSI 2015/141 Reg.22
Sch.2 Part 3 para.15, amended: SSI 2015/141 Reg.22

56. Local Government Finance (Scotland) Order 2015
Art.3, amended: SSI 2015/125 Art.2
Sch.1, substituted: SSI 2015/125 Sch.1
Sch.2, substituted: SSI 2015/125 Sch.2

58. Common Agricultural Policy (Direct Payments etc.) (Scotland) Regulations 2015
Reg.6, amended: SSI 2015/215 Reg.2
Reg.9, amended: SSI 2015/215 Reg.3
Reg.15, amended: SSI 2015/215 Reg.5
Reg.18, amended: SSI 2015/215 Reg.6
Reg.18A, added: SSI 2015/215 Reg.7
Reg.26, revoked: SSI 2015/194 Reg.11
Sch.1 Part 2 para.2, amended: SSI 2015/215 Reg.8
Sch.3, added: SSI 2015/215 Sch.1

77. Courts Reform (Scotland) Act 2014 (Commencement No 2, Transitional and Saving Provisions) Order 2015
Art.7, revoked: SSI 2015/338 Sch.1 para.4

87. Local Government Pension Scheme (Scotland) Amendment Regulations 2015
Reg.21, revoked: SSI 2015/448 Reg.47
Reg.44, amended: SSI 2015/448 Reg.48
Reg.45, amended: SSI 2015/448 Reg.49

111. A96 Trunk Road (Inveramsay Bridge Improvement) (Temporary Prohibitions on Traffic, Overtaking and Temporary Speed Restriction) Order 2015
revoked: SSI 2015/416 Art.6

227. Act of Sederunt (Rules of the Court of Session 1994 and Sheriff Court Rules Amendment) (No.2) (Personal Injury and Remits) 2015
r.5, substituted: SSI 2015/419 r.18
r.8, amended: SSI 2015/296 r.4

228. Act of Sederunt (Rules of the Court of Session 1994 Amendment) (No.3) (Courts Reform (Scotland) Act 2014) 2015
r.3, amended: SSI 2015/296 r.3
Sch.1, added: SSI 2015/296 r.3

241. Listed Buildings (Notification and Publication) (Scotland) Regulations 2015
Reg.3, amended: SSI 2015/328 Reg.5

245. Act of Adjournal (Criminal Procedure Rules 1996 Amendment) (No.4) (Sheriff Appeal Court) 2015
r.2, amended: SSI 2015/295 r.6
r.3, amended: SSI 2015/295 r.6
r.5, amended: SSI 2015/295 r.6
Sch.1, amended: SSI 2015/295 r.6

247. Courts Reform (Scotland) Act 2014 (Commencement No 3, Transitional and Saving Provisions) Order 2015
Art.8, amended: SSI 2015/378 Art.5

272. Housing (Scotland) Act 2014 (Commencement No 3 and Transitional Provision) Order 2015
Sch.1, amended: SSI 2015/349 Art.2

281. A96 Trunk Road (Aberdeen Western Peripheral Route, Blackburn to Bucksburn) (Temporary Prohibition of Traffic, Specified Turns, Overtaking and Speed Restrictions) Order 2015
revoked: SSI 2015/310 Art.7

356. Act of Sederunt (Sheriff Appeal Court Rules) 2015
Part 2 r.5.6, amended: SSI 2015/419 r.19
Part 3 r.6.1, amended: SSI 2015/419 r.19
Part 3 r.7.3, amended: SSI 2015/419 r.19
Part 3 r.7.9, substituted: SSI 2015/419 r.19
Part 5 r.13.4, amended: SSI 2015/419 r.19
Part 5 r.19.2A, added: SSI 2015/419 r.19
Part 6 r.24.6, amended: SSI 2015/419 r.19
Part 7 r.27.3, amended: SSI 2015/419 r.19
Part 7 r.28.2, amended: SSI 2015/419 r.19

Part 7 r.28.14, amended: SSI 2015/419
r.19
Part 7 r.30.1, amended: SSI 2015/419
r.19
Sch.1 para.3, amended: SSI 2015/419
r.19
Sch.1 para.5, amended: SSI 2015/419
r.19

Sch.2, amended: SSI 2015/419 r.19

418. A985 Trunk Road (Longannet Roundabout to Cairneyhill Roundabout) (Temporary Prohibition on Use of Road) Order 2015
revoked: SSI 2015/426 Art.4

STATUTORY RULES ISSUED BY THE UK PARLIAMENT

1994

428. Companies (1986 Order) (Insurance Companies Accounts) Regulations (Northern Ireland) 1994
Reg.6, amended: SI 2015/575 Sch.2
para.2

1998

105. Equal Pay (Complaints to Industrial Tribunals) (Armed Forces) Regulations (Northern Ireland) 1998
revoked: 2015 c.19 Sch.1 para.17

2002

147. Explosives (Fireworks) Regulations (Northern Ireland) 2002
Reg.2, amended: SI 2015/1553 Sch.11
para.2
Reg.4, amended: SI 2015/1553 Sch.11
para.3
Reg.7, amended: SI 2015/1553 Sch.11
para.4
Reg.11, amended: SI 2015/1553 Sch.11
para.5
Reg.12, amended: SI 2015/1553 Sch.11
para.6
Sch.1 para.1, amended: SI 2015/1553
Sch.11 para.7
Sch.2, revoked: SI 2015/1553 Sch.11
para.8

2003

358. Insolvent Companies (Disqualification of Unfit Directors) Proceedings Rules (Northern Ireland) 2003
r.1, amended: SI 2015/1651 Reg.3
r.4, amended: SI 2015/1651 Reg.3

2005

300. Hazardous Waste Regulations (Northern Ireland) 2005
Sch.10 Part 2 para.11, revoked: SI
2015/1640 Sch.6
482. Civil Partnership Regulations (Northern Ireland) 2005
Reg.3, amended: SI 2015/395 Sch.3
para.10
Reg.6, substituted: SI 2015/395 Sch.3
para.11

2010

184. Companies (Disqualification Orders) Regulations (Northern Ireland) 2010
Reg.2, amended: SI 2015/1651 Reg.5
Sch.1, amended: SI 2015/1651 Sch.2 Part
1
Sch.2, amended: SI 2015/1651 Sch.2 Part
2

2013

208. Electricity and Gas (Market Integrity and Transparency) (Enforcement etc.)

Regulations (Northern Ireland) 2013
Reg.10, amended: SI 2015/979 Reg.6

STATUTORY INSTRUMENTS ISSUED BY THE UK PARLIAMENT

1925

1178. Foot-and-Mouth Disease (Packing Materials) Order 1925
revoked: SI 2015/584 Art.2

1931

1140. Asbestos Industry Regulations 1931
see *McDonald v Department for Communities and Local Government* [2015] A.C. 1128 (SC), Lord Neuberger PSC
Reg.2, see *McDonald v Department for Communities and Local Government* [2015] A.C. 1128 (SC), Lord Neuberger PSC

1935

247. Cremation (Scotland) Regulations 1935
amended: SSI 2015/164 Art.3
Reg.6, revoked: SSI 2015/164 Art.4
Reg.8, revoked: SSI 2015/164 Art.4
Reg.8A, revoked: SSI 2015/164 Art.4
Reg.9, revoked: SSI 2015/164 Art.4
Reg.12, amended: SSI 2015/164 Art.5
Reg.13, amended: SSI 2015/164 Art.6
Reg.14, amended: SSI 2015/164 Art.7
Reg.15, amended: SSI 2015/164 Art.8
Reg.15A, revoked: SSI 2015/164 Art.4
Reg.16, amended: SSI 2015/164 Art.9
Sch.1, amended: SSI 2015/164 Art.10

1937

478. Grey Squirrels (Prohibition of Importation and Keeping) Order 1937
Art.1, amended: 2015 c.20 Sch.13 para.2
Art.1, substituted: 2015 c.20 Sch.13 para.2

1947

1. Statutory Instruments Regulations 1947
see *R. (on the application of Williams) v Secretary of State for Energy and Climate Change* [2015] EWHC 1202 (Admin), [2015] J.P.L. 1257 (QBD (Admin)), Lindblom J

1948

960. ICE CREAM (SCOTLAND) REGULATIONS, 1948
Reg.1, amended: SSI 2015/100 Art.2
2792. Greenwich Hospital School (Regulations) (Amendment) Order 1948
revoked: 2015 c.20 Sch.23 para.43

1956

1777. Coal and Other Mines (Horses) Order 1956
revoked: 2015 c.20 Sch.23 para.42

1957

1157. Landlord and Tenant (Notices) Regulations 1957
revoked: SI 2015/1 Reg.2

1958

2146. Coast Protection (Variation of Excluded Waters) Regulations 1958
revoked: SI 2015/523 Sch.1

1959

171. Agriculture (Miscellaneous Time-Limits) Regulations 1959
    revoked: SI 2015/950 Sch.2

1960

250. Cycle Racing on Highways Regulations, 1960
    Reg.5, amended: SI 2015/706 Reg.2
    Reg.5, revoked: SI 2015/706 Reg.2
    Reg.8, amended: SI 2015/706 Reg.2
543. Election Petition Rules 1960
    r.4, see *Erlam v Rahman* [2014] EWHC 2766 (QB), [2015] 1 W.L.R. 231 (QBD), Supperstone J

1961

342. Anglo-Norwegian Sea Fisheries Order 1961
    revoked: SI 2015/191 Sch.1

1963

596. Companies Registration Office (Fees) (No.2) Order 1963
    Art.2, revoked: SI 2015/971 Sch.5 para.1

1965

204. Coast Protection (Variation of Excluded Waters) Regulations 1965
    revoked: SI 2015/523 Sch.1
1000. Eggs (Marking and Storage) Regulations 1965
    revoked: 2015 c.20 Sch.23 para.33
1241. Fishing Boats (France) Designation Order 1965
    revoked: SI 2015/648 Sch.3
1448. Fishing Boats (Republic of Ireland) Designation Order 1965
    revoked: SI 2015/648 Sch.3
1569. Fishing Boats (Belgium) Designation Order 1965
    revoked: SI 2015/648 Sch.3

1776. Rules of the Supreme Court (Revision) 1965
    Ord.6 r.8, see *CDE SA v Sure Wind Marine Ltd* [2015] EWHC 720 (Admlty), [2015] 2 Lloyd's Rep. 268 (QBD (Admlty)), Jervis Kay QC, Admiralty Registrar
    Ord.12 r.7, see *PCL v Regional Government of X* [2015] EWHC 68 (Comm), [2015] 1 W.L.R. 3948 (QBD (Comm)), Hamblen J
    Ord.12 r.8, see *PCL v Regional Government of X* [2015] EWHC 68 (Comm), [2015] 1 W.L.R. 3948 (QBD (Comm)), Hamblen J
2040. Hares (Control of Importation) Order 1965
    revoked: SI 2015/751 Art.2

1967

1831. Landlord and Tenant (Notices) Regulations 1967
    revoked: SI 2015/1 Reg.2

1968

1728. Children (Performances) Regulations 1968
    revoked: SI 2015/1757 Sch.1

1970

318. Foreign Fishing Boats (Stowage of Gear) Order 1970
    revoked: SI 2015/648 Sch.3 , SSI 2015/320 Art.31
383. Commons Registration (Time Limits) (Amendment) Order 1970
    see *R. (on the application of Littlejohns) v Devon CC* [2015] EWHC 730 (Admin), [2015] Q.B. 869 (QBD (Admin)), Lang J

1971

218. Lands Tribunal for Scotland Rules 1971
    Sch.2, amended: SSI 2015/199 r.2

1253. Indictment Rules 1971
r.6, see *R. v Clarke (Dean)* [2015]
EWCA Crim 350, [2015] 2 Cr. App. R. 6
(CA (Crim Div)), Lord Thomas LCJ
**1861. Blood Tests (Evidence of Paternity)
Regulations 1971**
Reg.2, amended: SI 2015/1834 Reg.2
Reg.3, amended: SI 2015/1834 Reg.2
Reg.4, amended: SI 2015/1834 Reg.2
Reg.5, amended: SI 2015/1834 Reg.2
Reg.6, amended: SI 2015/1834 Reg.2
Reg.7, amended: SI 2015/1834 Reg.2
Reg.8, amended: SI 2015/1834 Reg.2
Reg.9, amended: SI 2015/1834 Reg.2
Reg.12, amended: SI 2015/1834 Reg.2
Sch.1, amended: SI 2015/1834 Reg.2
Sch.1, substituted: SI 2015/1834 Reg.2

1972

**1329. Brucellosis (Beef Incentives) Payments
Scheme 1972**
revoked: SI 2015/793 Art.2
**1613. Immigration (Exemption from Control)
Order 1972**
Art.7, added: SI 2015/1866 Art.2

1973

**1473. Agriculture (Maintenance, Repair and
Insurance of Fixed Equipment) Regulations
1973**
revoked: SI 2015/950 Sch.2
**1952. Crystal Glass (Descriptions)
Regulations 1973**
Reg.8, amended: SI 2015/1630 Sch.2
para.2
Reg.8, revoked: SI 2015/1630 Sch.2
para.3
**1998. Foreign Sea-Fishery Officers Order
1973**
revoked: SI 2015/191 Sch.1

1974

**540. Fire Services (Compensation)
Regulations 1974**

Sch.1 para.8A, added: SI 2015/643 Sch.1
para.2
**555. Family Allowances, National Insurance
and Industrial Injuries (Gibraltar) Order
1974**
Art.2, see *Secretary of State for Work
and Pensions v Garland* [2014] EWCA
Civ 1550, [2015] 1 C.M.L.R. 56 (CA
(Civ Div)), Richards LJ

1975

**1023. Rehabilitation of Offenders Act 1974
(Exceptions) Order 1975**
see *R. (on the application of T) v Chief
Constable of Greater Manchester* [2015]
A.C. 49 (SC), Lord Neuberger JSC
**1365. Coast Protection (Variation of
Excluded Waters) Regulations 1975**
revoked: SI 2015/523 Sch.1
**2211. Brucellosis (Beef Incentives) Payments
(Amendment) Scheme 1975**
revoked: SI 2015/793 Art.2

1976

117. Justices Allowances Regulations 1976
revoked: SI 2015/1423 Reg.4
**322. Employment Appeal Tribunal Rules
1976**
see *Birring v Rogers (t/a Charity Link)*
[2015] I.C.R. 1001 (EAT), Langstaff J
**919. Diseases of Animals (Local Authorities)
(Miscellaneous Provisions) Order 1976**
revoked: SI 2015/751 Art.2
**1572. Immigration (Variation of Leave)
Order 1976**
revoked: SI 2015/863 Art.2
**1606. Act of Sederunt (Expenses of Party
Litigants) 1976**
Art.2, amended: SSI 2015/419 r.2
Art.2, revoked: SSI 2015/419 r.2
**2118. Justices Allowances (Amendment)
Regulations 1976**
revoked: SI 2015/1423 Reg.4

1977

1303. Brucellosis Incentive Payments Scheme 1977
revoked: SI 2015/793 Art.2
1753. Alcoholometers and Alcohol Hydrometers (EEC Requirements) Regulations 1977
revoked: SI 2015/356 Sch.1 para.3
Reg.13, amended: SI 2015/1630 Sch.2 para.9
Reg.13, revoked: SI 2015/1630 Sch.2 para.9
Reg.14, revoked: SI 2015/1630 Sch.2 para.10
Reg.17, amended: SI 2015/1630 Sch.2 para.11

1978

809. Agriculture (Calculation of Value for Compensation) Regulations 1978
revoked: SI 2015/327 Reg.2
932. Control of Road-side Sales Orders (Procedure) Regulations 1978
Reg.2, amended: SI 2015/377 Sch.1 para.12
Reg.4, amended: SI 2015/377 Sch.1 para.12
Reg.7, amended: SI 2015/377 Sch.1 para.12
Reg.14, amended: SI 2015/377 Sch.1 para.12

1979

72. Isles of Scilly (Functions) Order 1979
Art.3, amended: SI 2015/968 Sch.1 para.2
132. Alcohol Tables Regulations 1979
revoked: SI 2015/356 Sch.1 para.3
642. Social Security (Widow's Benefit and Retirement Pensions) Regulations 1979
Reg.10, see *Secretary of State for Work and Pensions v Garland* [2014] EWCA Civ 1550, [2015] 1 C.M.L.R. 56 (CA (Civ Div)), Richards LJ

1980

751. Agriculture (Calculation of Value for Compensation) (Amendment) Regulations 1980
revoked: SI 2015/327 Reg.2
1094. European Communities (Definition of Treaties) (International Railway Tariffs Agreements) Order 1980
revoked: 2015 c.20 Sch.23 para.13

1981

644. Greater London Council (Transfer of Land and Housing Accommodation) (No.3) Order 1981
see *Tower Hamlets LBC v Bromley LBC* [2015] EWHC 1954 (Ch), [2015] B.L.G.R. 622 (Ch D), Norris J
Art.2, see *Tower Hamlets LBC v Bromley LBC* [2015] EWHC 1954 (Ch), [2015] B.L.G.R. 622 (Ch D), Norris J
677. Importation of Processed Animal Protein Order 1981
revoked: SI 2015/751 Art.2
822. Agriculture (Calculation of Value for Compensation) (Amendment) Regulations 1981
revoked: SI 2015/327 Reg.2
917. Health and Safety (First-Aid) Regulations 1981
Reg.5, substituted: SI 2015/1637 Sch.1 para.1
1388. Local Government (Allowances to Members) (Prescribed Bodies) (Scotland) Regulations 1981
revoked: SSI 2015/39 Sch.1 para.9
1473. Isles of Scilly (National Health Service) Order 1981
revoked: SI 2015/864 Art.2

1982

459. Importation of Processed Animal Protein (Amendment) Order 1982
revoked: SI 2015/751 Art.2
1686. Fishing Vessels (Temporary Financial Assistance) Scheme 1982
revoked: SI 2015/191 Sch.1

1983

125. Lerwick Harbour Revision Order 1983
Art.3, revoked: SSI 2015/4 Art.20

253. Fishing Boats (European Economic Community) Designation Order 1983
revoked: SI 2015/648 Sch.3

482. British Fishing Boats Order 1983
revoked: 2015 c.20 Sch.23 para.31

764. Dogs (Northern Ireland) Order 1983
Art.7, amended: SI 2015/2006 Art.133
Art.7, revoked: SI 2015/2006 Sch.12 Part 1

1168. Electrically Assisted Pedal Cycles Regulations 1983
Reg.2, revoked: SI 2015/24 Reg.2
Reg.3, amended: SI 2015/24 Reg.2
Reg.4, amended: SI 2015/24 Reg.2
Reg.4, revoked: SI 2015/24 Reg.2
Reg.5, added: SI 2015/24 Reg.2

1203. Coast Protection (Variation of Excluded Waters) (River Mersey) Regulations 1983
revoked: SI 2015/523 Sch.1

1475. Agriculture (Calculation of Value for Compensation) (Amendment) Regulations 1983
revoked: SI 2015/327 Reg.2

1503. Coast Protection (Variation of Excluded Waters) (River Wear) Regulations 1983
revoked: SI 2015/523 Sch.1

1553. Consumer Credit (Agreements) Regulations 1983
Reg.8, amended: SI 2015/910 Sch.1 para.3, SI 2015/1557 Art.3

1984

252. High Court of Justiciary Fees Order 1984
revoked: SSI 2015/262 Sch.4

341. Fish Farming (Financial Assistance) Scheme 1984
revoked: SI 2015/191 Sch.1

688. Increase of Fines (Plant Health) (Forestry) Order 1984
revoked: SI 2015/741 Art.2

887. Deeds of Arrangement Fees Order 1984
revoked: SI 2015/1641 Sch.3 para.3

1067. Great Yarmouth Port and Haven (Constitution) Revision Order 1984
revoked: SI 2015/1395 Art.12

1159. Industrial Training (Northern Ireland) Order 1984
Art.33, amended: SI 2015/2006 Art.72

1985

306. EEC Requirements (Amendment) Regulations 1985
Reg.4, revoked: SI 2015/356 Sch.1 para.3

454. Local Elections (Northern Ireland) Order 1985
Sch.2, amended: SI 2015/566 Art.3
Sch.2app001, amended: SI 2015/566 Sch.11

825. High Court of Justiciary Fees Amendment Order 1985
revoked: SSI 2015/262 Sch.4

960. Films Co-Production Agreements Order 1985
Sch.1, substituted: SI 2015/1886 Art.2

1203. British Fishing Boats Act 1983 (Guernsey) Order 1985
revoked: SI 2015/191 Sch.1

1204. Betting, Gaming, Lotteries and Amusements (Northern Ireland) Order 1985
see *Leisure Arcades Ltd's Application for Judicial Review, Re* [2015] NICA 36, [2015] L.L.R. 761 (CA (NI)), Morgan LCJ
Art.108, see *Leisure Arcades Ltd's Application for Judicial Review, Re* [2015] L.L.R. 110 (QBD (NI)), Gillen LJ

1516. Control of Pesticides (Advisory Committee on Pesticides) Order 1985
revoked: SI 2015/978 Sch.1 Part 2

1517. Control of Pesticides (Advisory Committee on Pesticides) (Terms of Office) Regulations 1985
revoked: SI 2015/978 Sch.1 Part 2

1876. Health Service Supply Council (Abolition) Regulations 1985
revoked: SI 2015/839 Reg.2

1877. Health Service Supply Council (Abolition) Order 1985
revoked: SI 2015/864 Art.2

1986

382. Fishing Boats (European Economic Community) Designation (Variation) Order 1986
revoked: SI 2015/648 Sch.3
449. High Court of Justiciary Fees Amendment Order 1986
revoked: SSI 2015/262 Sch.4
595. Mental Health (Northern Ireland) Order 1986
Art.2, see *MH v Mental Health Review Tribunal for Northern Ireland* [2015] M.H.L.R. 53 (QBD (NI)), Horner J; see *RS's Application for Judicial Review, Re* [2015] M.H.L.R. 61 (QBD (NI)), Treacy J
Art.4, see *MH v Mental Health Review Tribunal for Northern Ireland* [2015] M.H.L.R. 53 (QBD (NI)), Horner J; see *RS's Application for Judicial Review, Re* [2015] M.H.L.R. 61 (QBD (NI)), Treacy J
Art.12, see *RS's Application for Judicial Review, Re* [2015] M.H.L.R. 61 (QBD (NI)), Treacy J
Art.32, see *HM's Application for Judicial Review, Re* [2015] M.H.L.R. 326 (QBD (NI)), Treacy J
Art.36, see *HM's Application for Judicial Review, Re* [2015] M.H.L.R. 326 (QBD (NI)), Treacy J
Art.77, see *MH v Mental Health Review Tribunal for Northern Ireland* [2015] M.H.L.R. 53 (QBD (NI)), Horner J
952. Insolvency Practitioners Tribunal (Conduct of Investigations) Rules 1986
revoked: SI 2015/1641 Sch.1 para.1
1335. Costs in Criminal Cases (General) Regulations 1986
Reg.3, see *Quayum v DPP* [2015] EWHC 1660 (Admin), (2015) 179 J.P. 390 (DC), Sir Brian Leveson PQBD
Reg.14, amended: SI 2015/12 Reg.2
1764. Insolvency Practitioners (Recognised Professional Bodies) Order 1986
Sch.1, amended: SI 2015/2067 Art.2
1915. Insolvency (Scotland) Rules 1986
Part 4 r.4.84, amended: SI 2015/575 Sch.2 para.1

1925. Insolvency Rules 1986
see *Gate Gourmet Luxembourg IV Sarl v Morby* [2015] EWHC 1203 (Ch), [2015] B.P.I.R. 787 (Ch D), Registrar Briggs; see *Jervis v Pillar Denton Ltd* [2014] EWCA Civ 180, [2015] Ch. 87 (CA (Civ Div)), Patten LJ
Part 2 r.2.47, amended: SI 2015/443 r.2
Part 2 r.2.106, amended: SI 2015/443 r.3
Part 2 r.2.109AB, added: SI 2015/443 r.4
Part 2 r.2.109D, added: SI 2015/443 r.5
Part 4 r.4.49B, amended: SI 2015/443 r.6
Part 4 r.4.127, amended: SI 2015/443 r.7
Part 4 r.4.131AB, added: SI 2015/443 r.8
Part 4 r.4.131D, added: SI 2015/443 r.9
Part 6 r.6.78A, amended: SI 2015/443 r.10
Part 6 r.6.138, amended: SI 2015/443 r.11
Part 6 r.6.142AB, added: SI 2015/443 r.12
Part 7 r.7.11, amended: SI 2015/443 r.13
Part 13 r.13.13, amended: SI 2015/443 r.14
Pt 2., see *Eiffel Steel Works Ltd, Re* [2015] EWHC 511 (Ch), [2015] 2 B.C.L.C. 57 (Ch D), Andrew Hochhauser QC
Pt 5 r.5.22, see *Hope v Ireland* [2014] EWHC 3854 (Ch), [2015] B.P.I.R. 344 (Ch D), John Male QC
Pt 5 r.5.24, see *Forstater (In Bankruptcy), Re* [2015] B.P.I.R. 21 (Ch D), Registrar Derrett
r.2.67, see *Laverty v British Gas Trading Ltd* [2014] EWHC 2721 (Ch), [2015] 2 All E.R. 430 (Ch D (Companies Ct)), Sir Terence Etherton C
r.2.86, see *Lehman Brothers International (Europe) (In Administration), Re* [2015] EWHC 2270 (Ch), [2015] B.P.I.R. 1162 (Ch D (Companies Ct)), David Richards QC
r.2.88, see *Lehman Brothers International (Europe) (In Administration), Re* [2014] EWHC 704 (Ch), [2015] Ch. 1 (Ch D (Companies Ct)), David Richards J; see *Lehman Brothers International (Europe) (In Administration), Re* [2015] EWHC 2270

(Ch), [2015] B.P.I.R. 1162 (Ch D (Companies Ct)), David Richards QC
r.2.106, see *Maxwell v Brookes* [2015] B.C.C. 113 (Ch D (Companies Ct)), Registrar Jones; see *Pudsey Steel Services Ltd, Re* [2015] B.P.I.R. 1459 (Ch D), Judge Behrens QC
r.2.109, see *Calibre Solicitors Ltd, Re* [2015] B.P.I.R. 435 (Ch D (Companies Ct)), Registrar Jones
r.4.67, see *Kingstons Investments Ltd (In Liquidation), Re* [2015] EWHC 1619 (Ch), [2015] B.P.I.R. 959 (Ch D (Companies Ct)), Registrar Barber
r.4.70, see *Kingstons Investments Ltd (In Liquidation), Re* [2015] EWHC 1619 (Ch), [2015] B.P.I.R. 959 (Ch D (Companies Ct)), Registrar Barber
r.4.83, see *McCarthy v Tann* [2015] EWHC 2049 (Ch), [2015] B.P.I.R. 1224 (Ch D (Companies Ct)), Registrar Briggs
r.4.85, see *Mama Milla Ltd (In Liquidation), Re v Sharma* [2014] EWCA Civ 761, [2015] B.P.I.R. 590 (CA (Civ Div)), Vos LJ
r.4.90, see *Kingstons Investments Ltd (In Liquidation), Re* [2015] EWHC 1619 (Ch), [2015] B.P.I.R. 959 (Ch D (Companies Ct)), Registrar Barber
r.6.4, see *Maud v Libyan Investment Authority* [2015] EWHC 1625 (Ch), [2015] B.P.I.R. 858 (Ch D), Rose J
r.6.5, see *Clarke v Cognita Schools Ltd (t/a Hydesville Tower School)* [2015] EWHC 932 (Ch), [2015] 1 W.L.R. 3776 (Ch D (Birmingham)), Newey J; see *Ghadami v Donegan* [2014] EWHC 4448 (Ch), [2015] B.P.I.R. 494 (Ch D), Alan Steinfeld QC; see *Howell v Lerwick Commercial Mortgage Corp Ltd* [2015] EWHC 1177 (Ch), [2015] 1 W.L.R. 3554 (Ch D), Nugee J; see *Maud v Libyan Investment Authority* [2015] EWHC 1625 (Ch), [2015] B.P.I.R. 858 (Ch D), Rose J; see *Maud, Re* [2015] EWHC 1626 (Ch), [2015] B.P.I.R. 845 (Ch D), Rose J; see *Payne, Re* [2015] EWHC 968 (Ch), [2015] B.P.I.R. 933 (Ch D), John Male QC

r.6.29, see *Sekhon v Edginton* [2015] EWCA Civ 816, [2015] 1 W.L.R. 4435 (CA (Civ Div)), Lord Dyson MR
r.7.55, see *Eiffel Steel Works Ltd, Re* [2015] EWHC 511 (Ch), [2015] 2 B.C.L.C. 57 (Ch D), Andrew Hochhauser QC; see *Gate Gourmet Luxembourg IV Sarl v Morby* [2015] EWHC 1203 (Ch), [2015] B.P.I.R. 787 (Ch D), Registrar Briggs; see *Melodious Corp, Re* [2015] EWHC 621 (Ch), [2015] 2 All E.R. (Comm) 1139 (Ch D (Companies Ct)), Sir Terence Etherton C
r.9.2, see *Comet Group Ltd (In Liquidation), Re* [2014] EWHC 3477 (Ch), [2015] B.P.I.R. 1 (Ch D (Companies Ct)), John Baldwin QC
r.9.6, see *Harvest Finance Ltd (In Liquidation), Re* [2014] EWHC 4237 (Ch), [2015] 2 B.C.L.C. 240 (Ch D (Companies Ct)), Registrar Jones
r.12A.55, see *Calibre Solicitors Ltd, Re* [2015] B.P.I.R. 435 (Ch D (Companies Ct)), Registrar Jones
r.12.3, see *Laverty v British Gas Trading Ltd* [2014] EWHC 2721 (Ch), [2015] 2 All E.R. 430 (Ch D (Companies Ct)), Sir Terence Etherton C
r.13.12, see *Laverty v British Gas Trading Ltd* [2014] EWHC 2721 (Ch), [2015] 2 All E.R. 430 (Ch D (Companies Ct)), Sir Terence Etherton C; see *Welcome Financial Service Ltd, Re* [2015] EWHC 815 (Ch), [2015] 2 All E.R. (Comm) 992 (Ch D (Companies Ct)), Rose J

1992. Control of Pollution (Anglers Lead Weights) Regulations 1986
    revoked: SI 2015/815 Reg.6
1996. Insolvency Proceedings (Monetary Limits) Order 1986
    Sch.1 Part II, amended: SI 2015/26 Art.2
2194. Housing (Right to Buy) (Prescribed Forms) Regulations 1986
    revoked: SI 2015/1320 Sch.6
    Sch.1, amended: SI 2015/1542 Sch.1
2265. Importation of Salmonid Viscera Order 1986
    revoked: SI 2015/191 Sch.1
2297. Act of Sederunt (Sheriff Court Company Insolvency Rules) 1986

Part VI r.36, amended: SSI 2015/419 r.3
Part VI r.36, substituted: SSI 2015/419
r.3
Part VI r.36A, added: SSI 2015/419 r.3

1987

257. Police Pensions Regulations 1987
Pt A reg.19, see *Harrod v Chief*
Constable of the West Midlands [2015]
I.C.R. 1311 (EAT), Langstaff J

764. Town and Country Planning (Use
Classes) Order 1987
see *R. (on the application of Westminster*
City Council) v Secretary of State for
Communities and Local Government
[2015] EWCA Civ 482, [2015] L.L.R.
909 (CA (Civ Div)), Longmore LJ

772. High Court of Justiciary Fees
Amendment Order 1987
revoked: SSI 2015/262 Sch.4

1134. Fish Farming (Financial Assistance)
Scheme 1987
revoked: SI 2015/191 Sch.1

1135. Fishing Vessels (Acquisition and
Improvement) (Grants) Scheme 1987
revoked: SI 2015/191 Sch.1

1136. Fishing Vessels (Financial Assistance)
Scheme 1987
revoked: SI 2015/191 Sch.1

1967. Income Support (General) Regulations
1987
Reg.2, amended: SI 2015/67 Reg.2, SI
2015/389 Reg.2, SI 2015/971 Sch.3
para.2, SI 2015/1985 Art.8
Reg.16, amended: SI 2015/643 Sch.1
para.5
Reg.29, amended: SI 2015/389 Reg.2
Reg.39, amended: SI 2015/478 Reg.27
Reg.61, amended: SI 2015/971 Sch.3
para.2
Sch.1B para.28, amended: SI 2015/971
Sch.3 para.2
Sch.2 Part I para.1, amended: SI 2015/30
Sch.1
Sch.2 Part I para.2, amended: SI
2015/457 Sch.2
Sch.2 Part III para.12, amended: SI
2015/1985 Art.8

Sch.2 Part III para.13, amended: SI
2015/1754 Reg.14
Sch.2 Part IV para.15, amended: SI
2015/457 Sch.3
Sch.3 para.1, amended: SI 2015/1647
Reg.2
Sch.3 para.6, revoked: SI 2015/1647
Reg.2
Sch.3 para.7, revoked: SI 2015/1647
Reg.2
Sch.3 para.8, amended: SI 2015/1647
Reg.2
Sch.3 para.8, revoked: SI 2015/1647
Reg.2
Sch.3 para.8, substituted: SI 2015/1647
Reg.2
Sch.3 para.9, amended: SI 2015/1647
Reg.2
Sch.3 para.10, amended: SI 2015/1647
Reg.2
Sch.3 para.11, amended: SI 2015/1647
Reg.2
Sch.3 para.11, revoked: SI 2015/1647
Reg.2
Sch.3 para.13, amended: SI 2015/1647
Reg.2
Sch.3 para.14, amended: SI 2015/1647
Reg.2
Sch.3 para.14, revoked: SI 2015/1647
Reg.2
Sch.3 para.18, amended: SI 2015/457
Art.14
Sch.8 para.7, amended: SI 2015/389
Reg.2
Sch.8 para.15A, amended: SI 2015/389
Reg.2
Sch.9 para.27, amended: SI 2015/643
Sch.1 para.5
Sch.9 para.30, amended: SI 2015/643
Sch.1 para.5
Sch.9 para.30A, amended: SI 2015/643
Sch.1 para.5
Sch.9 para.58, amended: SI 2015/643
Sch.1 para.5
Sch.9 para.66, amended: SI 2015/643
Sch.1 para.5
Sch.10 para.44, see *R. (on the application*
of N) v Walsall MBC [2014] EWHC 1918
(Admin), [2015] 1 All E.R. 165 (QBD
(Admin)), Leggatt J

Sch.10 para.67, amended: SI 2015/643
Sch.1 para.5
1969. Income Support (Transitional) Regulations 1987
Reg.15, varied: SI 2015/457 Art.15
2023. Insolvent Companies (Disqualification of Unfit Directors) Proceedings Rules 1987
r.1, amended: SI 2015/1651 Reg.2
r.2, amended: SI 2015/1641 Sch.3 para.4
r.4, amended: SI 2015/1651 Reg.2

1988

120. Capacity Serving Measures (Intoxicating Liquor) Regulations 1988
revoked: SI 2015/356 Sch.1 para.1
281. Agriculture (Maintenance, Repair and Insurance of Fixed Equipment) (Amendment) Regulations 1988
revoked: SI 2015/950 Sch.2
282. Agriculture (Time-Limit) Regulations 1988
revoked: SI 2015/950 Sch.2
798. High Court of Justiciary Fees Amendment Order 1988
revoked: SSI 2015/262 Sch.4
809. Excise Warehousing (Etc.) Regulations 1988
Reg.15, amended: SI 2015/368 Reg.14
Reg.16, amended: SI 2015/368 Reg.15
Sch.2, amended: SI 2015/368 Reg.16
1241. Highways (Assessment of Environmental Effects) Regulations 1988
revoked: 2015 c.20 Sch.23 para.30
1324. Furniture and Furnishings (Fire) (Safety) Regulations 1988
Reg.12, revoked: SI 2015/1630 Sch.2 para.16
1478. Goods Vehicles (Plating and Testing) Regulations 1988
Reg.3, amended: SI 2015/971 Sch.2 para.1
Reg.12, amended: SI 2015/971 Sch.2 para.1
Reg.16, amended: SI 2015/971 Sch.2 para.1
2013. Act of Sederunt (Proceedings in the Sheriff Court under the Debtors (Scotland) Act 1987) 1988
Part VI r.72, amended: SSI 2015/419 r.4

Part VI r.72, revoked: SSI 2015/419 r.4
2157. Littlehampton (Pilotage) Harbour Revision Order 1988
Art.2, amended: SI 2015/1387 Art.3

1989

239. Housing (Right to Buy) (Prescribed Forms) (Amendment) Regulations 1989
revoked: SI 2015/1320 Sch.6
240. Housing (Right to Buy Delay Procedure) (Prescribed Forms) Regulations 1989
revoked: SI 2015/1320 Sch.6
258. High Court of Justiciary Fees Amendment Order 1989
revoked: SSI 2015/262 Sch.4
638. European Economic Interest Grouping Regulations 1989
Reg.5, amended: SI 2015/1695 Reg.8
Reg.10, amended: SI 2015/17 Sch.6 para.2
Sch.4 Part 2 para.32, amended: SI 2015/1695 Reg.8
Sch.4 Part 2 para.32A, added: SI 2015/1695 Reg.8
824. British Steel Act 1988 (Government Shareholding) Order 1989
revoked: 2015 c.20 Sch.23 para.11
947. Boards for Special Hospitals (Abolition) Order 1989
revoked: SI 2015/864 Art.2
1005. Immigration (Variation of Leave) (Amendment) Order 1989
revoked: SI 2015/863 Art.2
1339. Limitation (Northern Ireland) Order 1989
Art.2, amended: SI 2015/2006 Art.111
Art.51B, added: SI 2015/1392 Reg.8
Art.51B, amended: SI 2015/1972 Reg.6
1490. Civil Legal Aid (Scotland) (Fees) Regulations 1989
Reg.2, amended: SSI 2015/380 Reg.2
Reg.4, amended: SSI 2015/380 Reg.2
Reg.5, amended: SSI 2015/380 Reg.2
Reg.7A, added: SSI 2015/380 Reg.2
Reg.10, amended: SSI 2015/380 Reg.2
Reg.12, amended: SSI 2015/380 Reg.2
Sch.2 Part 002, amended: SSI 2015/380 Reg.2
Sch.4, substituted: SSI 2015/380 Reg.2

Sch.4 Part 003, amended: SSI 2015/337
Reg.2
Sch.4 Part 004, amended: SSI 2015/337
Reg.2, SSI 2015/380 Reg.2
Sch.4 Part 004, substituted: SSI 2015/380
Reg.2
Sch.4 para.13, amended: SSI 2015/380
Reg.2
Sch.5, substituted: SSI 2015/380 Reg.2
Sch.6, substituted: SSI 2015/380 Reg.2
Sch.6 Part II, amended: SSI 2015/380
Reg.2
Sch.6 Part II para.18, amended: SSI
2015/380 Reg.2
Sch.7, amended: SSI 2015/337 Reg.2

1491. Criminal Legal Aid (Scotland) (Fees)
Regulations 1989
Reg.2, amended: SSI 2015/337 Reg.3
Reg.11, amended: SSI 2015/337 Reg.3
Sch.1 para.8, amended: SSI 2015/337
Reg.3
Sch.2, amended: SSI 2015/337 Reg.3
Sch.2 Part 001, amended: SSI 2015/337
Reg.3
Sch.2 para.6, amended: SSI 2015/337
Reg.3

1737. Great Yarmouth Port Authority
Harbour Revision Order 1989
Art.4, revoked: SI 2015/1395 Art.12
Art.6, revoked: SI 2015/1395 Art.12
Art.8, revoked: SI 2015/1395 Art.12

1893. Health and Medicines Act 1988
(Superannuation) (Savings for Retired
Practitioners) Regulations 1989
revoked: SI 2015/839 Reg.2

1958. A55 Trunk Road (Penmaenmawr,
Gwynedd) (Derestriction) Order 1989
varied: SI 2015/1229 Art.16

2405. Insolvency (Northern Ireland) Order
1989
see *Bank of Ireland Mortgage Bank v*
Sheridan [2015] NICh 12, [2015]
B.P.I.R. 1001 (Ch D (NI)), Morgan LCJ
Art.5, amended: 2015 c.26 s.91
Art.9, amended: SI 2015/2006 Art.131
Art.106, amended: 2015 c.33 Sch.8
para.35
Art.108, substituted: 2015 c.33 Sch.8
para.36
Art.110, amended: 2015 c.33 Sch.8
para.37

Art.150, amended: 2015 c.33 Sch.8
para.38
Art.230A, see *Bank of Ireland Mortgage*
Bank v Sheridan [2015] NICh 12, [2015]
B.P.I.R. 1001 (Ch D (NI)), Morgan LCJ
Art.255A, see *Official Receiver v Gibson*
[2015] B.P.I.R. 717 (Ch D (NI)), Master
Kelly
Art.301, amended: 2015 c.33 Sch.8
para.39
Art.346, amended: SI 2015/486 Reg.15
Art.349, amended: 2015 c.26 s.116
Art.349, revoked: 2015 c.20 Sch.6
para.22
Sch.4, amended: SI 2015/486 Reg.15
Sch.4 para.17A, added: SI 2015/486
Reg.15
Sch.4 para.21, amended: SI 2015/486
Reg.15

2406. Education Reform (Northern Ireland)
Order 1989
Art.131, amended: SI 2015/2006 Sch.2
para.1, Sch.12 Part 1

1990

246. Employment (Miscellaneous Provisions)
(Northern Ireland) Order 1990
Art.13, amended: 2015 c.20 s.7
Art.13A, amended: 2015 c.20 s.7

304. Dangerous Substances (Notification and
Marking of Sites) Regulations 1990
Reg.8, amended: SI 2015/1682 Sch.1
para.10

470. High Court of Justiciary Fees
Amendment Order 1990
revoked: SSI 2015/262 Sch.4

685. Fishing Vessels (Acquisition and
Improvement) (Grants) (Amendment)
Scheme 1990
revoked: SI 2015/191 Sch.1

992. Football Spectators (Corresponding
Offences in Italy) Order 1990
revoked: SI 2015/212 Sch.1

993. Football Spectators (Corresponding
Offences in Scotland) Order 1990
revoked: SI 2015/212 Sch.1

1020. Public Service Vehicles (Conduct of
Drivers, Inspectors, Conductors and
Passengers) Regulations 1990

see *Paulley v First Group Plc* [2014]
EWCA Civ 1573, [2015] 1 W.L.R. 3384
(CA (Civ Div)), Arden LJ
1519. Planning (Listed Buildings and
Conservation Areas) Regulations 1990
see *Gerber v Wiltshire Council* [2015]
EWHC 524 (Admin), [2015] Env. L.R.
33 (QBD (Admin)), Dove J

1991

331. High Court of Justiciary Fees
Amendment Order 1991
revoked: SSI 2015/262 Sch.4
507. Environmental Protection (Applications,
Appeals and Registers) Regulations 1991
Reg.4, amended: SSI 2015/100 Art.2
513. Environmental Protection
(Authorisation of Processes) (Determination
Periods) Order 1991
revoked: 2015 c.20 Sch.13 para.11
682. Financial Assistance for Environmental
Purposes Order 1991
revoked: SI 2015/479 Sch.1
724. High Court and County Courts
Jurisdiction Order 1991
Art.2, revoked: SI 2015/1641 Sch.3
para.3
777. Agricultural, Fishery and Aquaculture
Products (Improvement Grant) Regulations
1991
revoked: SI 2015/191 Sch.1
891. Contact with Children Regulations 1991
revoked: SI 2015/1818 Sch.11
892. Definition of Independent Visitors
(Children) Regulations 1991
revoked: SI 2015/1818 Sch.11
980. Immigration (Variation of Leave)
(Revocation) Order 1991
revoked: SI 2015/863 Art.2
1083. Immigration (Variation of Leave)
(No.2) Order 1991
revoked: SI 2015/863 Art.2
1505. Children (Secure Accommodation)
Regulations 1991
Reg.1A, added: SI 2015/1988 Reg.17
Reg.6, amended: SI 2015/1883 Reg.2
1624. Controlled Waste (Registration of
Carriers and Seizure of Vehicles) Regulations
1991

revoked: SI 2015/426 Reg.26
1742. Dangerous Dogs Act 1991
(Commencement and Appointed Day) Order
1991
revoked: SI 2015/138 Sch.1
1744. Dangerous Dogs Compensation and
Exemption Schemes Order 1991
revoked: SI 2015/138 Sch.1
2034. Children (Secure Accommodation)
(No.2) Regulations 1991
revoked: SI 2015/1988 Reg.19
2297. Dangerous Dogs Compensation and
Exemption Schemes (Amendment) Order
1991
revoked: SI 2015/138 Sch.1
2628. Child Support (Northern Ireland)
Order 1991
Art.2, amended: SI 2015/2006 Sch.12
Part 1
Art.7, amended: SI 2015/2006 Art.127
Art.10, amended: SI 2015/2006 Sch.9
para.1, Sch.12 Part 8
Art.11, amended: SI 2015/2006 Art.126
Art.11A, added: SI 2015/2006 Art.128
Art.22, amended: SI 2015/2006 Sch.11
para.2, Sch.11 para.3
Art.29, amended: SI 2015/2006 Art.127
Art.40, amended: SI 2015/2006 Art.129
Art.47A, amended: SI 2015/2006 Sch.11
para.4
Art.48, amended: SI 2015/2006 Sch.11
para.5
Sch.1 Part I para.5, amended: SI
2015/2006 Sch.2 para.2
2636. Dangerous Dogs Compensation and
Exemption Schemes (Amendment) (No.2)
Order 1991
revoked: SI 2015/138 Sch.1
2872. Children and Young Persons
(Protection from Tobacco) (Northern
Ireland) Order 1991
Art.4, amended: SI 2015/829 Reg.19
2890. Social Security (Disability Living
Allowance) Regulations 1991
Reg.8, see *Mathieson v Secretary of State*
for Work and Pensions [2015] UKSC 47,
[2015] 1 W.L.R. 3250 (SC), Lady Hale
DPSC
Reg.12, see *Secretary of State for Work*
and Pensions v Robertson [2015] CSIH
82 (IH (Ex Div)), Lady Smith

1992

**17. Eastbourne Water Company
(Constitution and Regulation) Order 1992**
 revoked: 2015 c.20 Sch.23 para.27
**124. Lee Valley Water Plc (Constitution and
Regulation) Order 1992**
 revoked: 2015 c.20 Sch.23 para.27
129. Firemen's Pension Scheme Order 1992
 Part AI para.3, amended: SI 2015/579
 Art.2, SI 2015/1014 Art.2
 Part I, amended: SI 2015/589 Sch.3
 para.8, SI 2015/1016 Sch.3 para.8, SSI
 2015/141 Reg.40
 Part 1A para.3, amended: SSI 2015/140
 Art.4
 Part IIA, added: SI 2015/589 Sch.3
 para.9, SI 2015/1016 Sch.3 para.9, SSI
 2015/141 Reg.41
 Part VIA para.1, amended: SI 2015/589
 Sch.3 para.9, SI 2015/1016 Sch.3 para.9
 Part VIA para.3, added: SI 2015/589
 Sch.3 para.9, SI 2015/1016 Sch.3 para.9
 Sch.1 Part III, added: SSI 2015/140 Art.3
 Sch.2 Part A paraA.3, amended: SI
 2015/589 Sch.3 para.1, SI 2015/1016
 Sch.3 para.1, SSI 2015/141 Reg.33
 Sch.2 Part A paraA.13A, added: SI
 2015/589 Sch.3 para.1, SI 2015/1016
 Sch.3 para.1, SSI 2015/141 Reg.33
 Sch.2 Part B paraB.1, amended: SI
 2015/589 Sch.3 para.2, SI 2015/1016
 Sch.3 para.2, SSI 2015/141 Reg.34
 Sch.2 Part B paraB.1A, added: SI
 2015/589 Sch.3 para.2, SI 2015/1016
 Sch.3 para.2, SSI 2015/141 Reg.34
 Sch.2 Part B paraB.2, amended: SI
 2015/589 Sch.3 para.2, SI 2015/1016
 Sch.3 para.2, SSI 2015/141 Reg.34
 Sch.2 Part B paraB.2A, added: SI
 2015/589 Sch.3 para.2, SI 2015/1016
 Sch.3 para.2, SSI 2015/141 Reg.34
 Sch.2 Part B paraB.3, amended: SI
 2015/589 Sch.3 para.2, SI 2015/1016
 Sch.3 para.2, SSI 2015/141 Reg.34
 Sch.2 Part B paraB.5, amended: SI
 2015/589 Sch.3 para.2, SI 2015/1016
 Sch.3 para.2, SSI 2015/141 Reg.34
 Sch.2 Part B paraB.5A, amended: SI
 2015/589 Sch.3 para.2, SI 2015/1016
 Sch.3 para.2, SSI 2015/141 Reg.34

 Sch.2 Part B paraB.5D, amended: SI
 2015/589 Sch.3 para.2, SI 2015/1016
 Sch.3 para.2, SSI 2015/141 Reg.34
 Sch.2 Part B paraB.7, amended: SI
 2015/589 Sch.3 para.2, SI 2015/1016
 Sch.3 para.2, SSI 2015/141 Reg.34, SSI
 2015/173 Art.2
 Sch.2 Part B paraB.9, amended: SI
 2015/589 Sch.3 para.2, SI 2015/1016
 Sch.3 para.2, SSI 2015/141 Reg.34
 Sch.2 Part E paraE.1, amended: SI
 2015/589 Sch.3 para.5, SI 2015/1016
 Sch.3 para.5, SSI 2015/141 Reg.37
 Sch.2 Part E paraE.3, amended: SI
 2015/589 Sch.3 para.5, SI 2015/1016
 Sch.3 para.5, SSI 2015/141 Reg.37
 Sch.2 Part E paraE.4, amended: SI
 2015/589 Sch.3 para.5, SI 2015/1016
 Sch.3 para.5, SSI 2015/141 Reg.37
 Sch.2 Part E paraE.8A, amended: SI
 2015/589 Sch.3 para.5, SI 2015/1016
 Sch.3 para.5
 Sch.2 Part F paraF.2, amended: SI
 2015/589 Sch.3 para.6, SI 2015/1016
 Sch.3 para.6, SSI 2015/141 Reg.38
 Sch.2 Part F paraF.9, amended: SI
 2015/589 Sch.3 para.6, SI 2015/1016
 Sch.3 para.6, SSI 2015/141 Reg.38
 Sch.2 Part G, amended: SI 2015/589
 Sch.3 para.7, SI 2015/1016 Sch.3 para.7,
 SSI 2015/141 Reg.39
 Sch.2 Part C paraC.1, amended: SI
 2015/589 Sch.3 para.3, SI 2015/1016
 Sch.3 para.3, SSI 2015/141 Reg.35
 Sch.2 Part D paraD.1, amended: SI
 2015/589 Sch.3 para.4, SI 2015/1016
 Sch.3 para.4, SSI 2015/141 Reg.36
**223. Town and Country Planning (General
Permitted Development) (Scotland) Order
1992**
 see *MacKay v McGowan* 2015 S.L.T.
 (Lands Tr) 6 (Lands Tr (Scot)), R Smith
 QC
**231. Electricity (Northern Ireland) Order
1992**
 Sch.4 para.11, see *Brickkiln Waste Ltd v
 Northern Ireland Electricity* [2015]
 R.V.R. 197 (Lands Tr (NI)), Henry
 Spence
**412. High Court of Justiciary Fees
Amendment Order 1992**

revoked: SSI 2015/262 Sch.4

424. Colne Valley Water Company Plc (Constitution and Regulation) Order 1992
revoked: 2015 c.20 Sch.23 para.27

548. Council Tax (Discount Disregards) Order 1992
see *Rupp v Cambridge City Council* [2015] R.V.R. 310 (VT), S Rehman
Art.4, see *Rupp v Cambridge City Council* [2015] R.V.R. 310 (VT), S Rehman
Art.5, see *Rupp v Cambridge City Council* [2015] R.V.R. 310 (VT), S Rehman
Sch.1 Part IV para.8, amended: SI 2015/971 Sch.3 para.3

549. Council Tax (Chargeable Dwellings) Order 1992
Art.2, see *Dwelling in London N2, Re* [2015] R.V.R. 157 (VT), Graham Zellick QC; see *Ramdhun v Valuation Tribunal of England* [2014] EWHC 946 (Admin), [2015] R.V.R. 89 (QBD (Admin)), Haddon-Cave J
Art.3, see *Dwelling in London N2, Re* [2015] R.V.R. 157 (VT), Graham Zellick QC; see *Ramdhun v Valuation Tribunal of England* [2014] EWHC 946 (Admin), [2015] R.V.R. 89 (QBD (Admin)), Haddon-Cave J

550. Council Tax (Situation and Valuation of Dwellings) Regulations 1992
Reg.6, see *Pengelly v Listing Officer* [2014] EWHC 4142 (Admin), [2015] R.V.R. 194 (QBD (Admin)), Judge Worcester

551. Council Tax (Liability for Owners) Regulations 1992
Reg.2, amended: SI 2015/643 Sch.1 para.8

558. Council Tax (Exempt Dwellings) Order 1992
see *Rupp v Cambridge City Council* [2015] R.V.R. 310 (VT), S Rehman
Art.3, see *Ealing LBC v Notting Hill Housing Trust* [2015] EWHC 161 (Admin), [2015] P.T.S.R. 814 (QBD (Admin)), Mostyn J

613. Council Tax (Administration and Enforcement) Regulations 1992

see *Holdsworth v Bradford MDC* [2015] R.A. 559 (VT), Graham Zellick QC
Reg.24, see *Holdsworth v Bradford MDC* [2015] R.A. 559 (VT), Graham Zellick QC
Reg.34, see *R. (on the application of Nicolson) v Tottenham Magistrates* [2015] EWHC 1252 (Admin), [2015] P.T.S.R. 1045 (QBD (Admin)), Andrews J
Reg.57, see *Wiltshire Council v Piggin* [2014] EWHC 4386 (Admin), [2015] R.V.R. 45 (QBD (Admin)), Davis J

654. Financial Assistance for Environmental Purposes (England and Wales) Order 1992
revoked: SI 2015/479 Sch.1

708. Football Spectators (Corresponding Offences in Sweden) Order 1992
revoked: SI 2015/212 Sch.1

1214. Folkestone and District Water Company (Constitution and Regulation) Order 1992
revoked: 2015 c.20 Sch.23 para.27

1549. Coast Protection (Variation of Excluded Waters) (Chichester, Langstone and Portsmouth Harbours) Regulations 1992
revoked: SI 2015/523 Sch.1

1707. Housing (Right to Buy) (Prescribed Forms) (Amendment) Regulations 1992
revoked: SI 2015/1320 Sch.6

1724. Football Spectators (Corresponding Offences in Italy, Scotland and Sweden) (Amendment) Order 1992
revoked: SI 2015/212 Sch.1

1813. Child Support (Maintenance Assessment Procedure) Regulations 1992
Reg.17, amended: SI 2015/338 Reg.2
Reg.53A, added: SI 2015/338 Reg.2

1815. Child Support (Maintenance Assessments and Special Cases) Regulations 1992
see *Hakki v Secretary of State for Work and Pensions* [2014] EWCA Civ 530, [2015] 1 F.L.R. 547 (CA (Civ Div)), Longmore LJ
Reg.7, amended: SI 2015/1985 Art.14
Sch.1 Part I para.2A, amended: SI 2015/478 Reg.28
Sch.1 Part I para.3, amended: SI 2015/478 Reg.28

Sch.1 Part II para.6, amended: SI
2015/1985 Art.14
Sch.2 para.48G, added: SI 2015/338
Reg.3

1816. Child Support (Arrears, Interest and Adjustment of Maintenance Assessments) Regulations 1992
Reg.10A, amended: SI 2015/338 Reg.4

1988. Bournemouth and District Water Company (Constitution and Regulation) Order 1992
revoked: 2015 c.20 Sch.23 para.27

1989. Child Support (Collection and Enforcement) Regulations 1992
Reg.35, amended: SI 2015/583 Sch.2
para.9
Sch.1, amended: SI 2015/338 Reg.5
Sch.4, amended: SI 2015/583 Sch.2
para.9

2117. Children (Secure Accommodation) Amendment Regulations 1992
revoked: SI 2015/1988 Reg.19

2288. Education Assets Board (Transfers under the Further and Higher Education Act 1992) Regulations 1992
revoked: 2015 c.20 Sch.15 para.4

2633. Sea Fish Licensing Order 1992
Art.3, see *R. v JC* [2015] EWCA Crim
210, [2015] L.L.R. 380 (CA (Crim Div)),
Davis LJ

2645. Child Support (Maintenance Arrangements and Jurisdiction) Regulations 1992
see *D v R* [2014] EWHC 4306 (Fam),
[2015] 2 F.L.R. 978 (Fam Div), Holman
J

2726. Food Protection (Emergency Prohibitions) (Lead in Ducks and Geese) (England) Order 1992
revoked: SI 2015/300 Art.2

2793. Manual Handling Operations Regulations 1992
Reg.4, see *Sloan v Rastrick High School
Governors* [2014] EWCA Civ 1063,
[2015] P.I.Q.R. P1 (CA (Civ Div)),
Moore-Bick LJ

2966. Personal Protective Equipment at Work Regulations 1992
see *Kennedy v Cordia (Services) LLP*
2015 S.C. 154 (IH (Ex Div)), Lady Smith

Reg.4, see *Kennedy v Cordia (Services)
LLP* 2015 S.C. 154 (IH (Ex Div)), Lady
Smith

3004. Workplace (Health, Safety and Welfare) Regulations 1992
see *Coia v Portavadie Estates Ltd* [2015]
CSIH 3, 2015 S.C. 419 (IH (Ex Div)),
Lord Menzies; see *McShane v Burnwynd
Racing Stables Ltd* [2015] CSOH 70,
2015 Rep. L.R. 107 (OH), Lord Glennie
Reg.4, see *Wilkinson v Hjaltland
Housing Association Ltd* 2015 Rep. L.R.
62 (Sh Ct (Grampian) (Lerwick)), Sheriff
P Mann
Reg.12, see *Wilkinson v Hjaltland
Housing Association Ltd* 2015 Rep. L.R.
62 (Sh Ct (Grampian) (Lerwick)), Sheriff
P Mann

3108. Fishing Boats (European Economic Community) Designation (Variation) Order 1992
revoked: SI 2015/648 Sch.3

3122. Value Added Tax (Cars) Order 1992
see *Pendragon Plc v Revenue and
Customs Commissioners* [2015] UKSC
37, [2015] 1 W.L.R. 2838 (SC), Lord
Neuberger PSC
Art.8, see *Pendragon Plc v Revenue and
Customs Commissioners* [2015] UKSC
37, [2015] 1 W.L.R. 2838 (SC), Lord
Neuberger PSC

3135. Excise Goods (Holding, Movement, Warehousing and REDS) Regulations 1992
Reg.4, see *TDG (UK) Ltd v Revenue and
Customs Commissioners* [2015] UKUT
167 (TCC), [2015] S.T.C. 1954 (UT
(Tax)), Rose J
Reg.5, see *TDG (UK) Ltd v Revenue and
Customs Commissioners* [2015] UKUT
167 (TCC), [2015] S.T.C. 1954 (UT
(Tax)), Rose J

1993

12. Wildlife and Countryside (Definitive Maps and Statements) Regulations 1993
Reg.2, see *R. (on the application of Trail
Riders' Fellowship) v Dorset CC* [2015]
UKSC 18, [2015] 1 W.L.R. 1406 (SC),
Lord Neuberger PSC

Reg.8, see *R. (on the application of Trail Riders' Fellowship) v Dorset CC* [2015] UKSC 18, [2015] 1 W.L.R. 1406 (SC), Lord Neuberger PSC

49. Control of Pollution (Anglers Lead Weights) (Amendment) Regulations 1993
revoked: SI 2015/815 Reg.6

176. Motor Vehicles (Wearing of Seat Belts) Regulations 1993
Reg.5, see *Gordon v Murphy* [2015] HCJAC 36, 2015 S.L.T. 435 (HCJ), The Lord Justice Clerk (Carloway)

426. High Court of Justiciary Fees Amendment Order 1993
revoked: SSI 2015/262 Sch.4

465. Education (Further Education Corporations) (Designated Staff) Order 1993
revoked: 2015 c.20 Sch.15 para.4

570. Isles of Scilly (Community Care) Order 1993
Art.2, amended: SI 2015/642 Art.3
Art.2, revoked: SI 2015/642 Art.3

612. Education (Further Education Corporations) (Designated Staff) (Wales) Order 1993
revoked: 2015 c.20 Sch.15 para.4

901. Further Education (Exclusion of Land from Transfer) Order 1993
revoked: 2015 c.20 Sch.15 para.4

920. Act of Sederunt (Child Support Rules) 1993
Art.2, amended: SSI 2015/351 r.2
Art.4, amended: SSI 2015/351 r.2
Art.5, amended: SSI 2015/351 r.2
Art.5A, amended: SSI 2015/351 r.2
Art.5AC, amended: SSI 2015/351 r.2
Art.5B, amended: SSI 2015/351 r.2
Art.5D, amended: SSI 2015/351 r.2
Art.5E, amended: SSI 2015/351 r.2
Sch.1, substituted: SSI 2015/351 Sch.1

937. Further Education (Exclusion of Land from Transfer) (No.2) Order 1993
revoked: 2015 c.20 Sch.15 para.4

1062. Financial Assistance for Environmental Purposes Order 1993
revoked: SI 2015/479 Sch.1

1149. Coast Protection (Variation of Excluded Waters) Regulations 1993
revoked: SI 2015/523 Sch.1

1507. Value Added Tax (Supply of Services) Order 1993

Art.3, see *Associated Newspapers Ltd v Revenue and Customs Commissioners* [2015] UKUT 641 (TCC), [2015] B.V.C. 538 (UT (Tax)), David Richards LJ

1518. Financial Assistance for Environmental Purposes (No.2) Order 1993
revoked: SI 2015/479 Sch.1

1657. Immigration (Variation of Leave) (Amendment) Order 1993
revoked: SI 2015/863 Art.2

1813. Channel Tunnel (International Arrangements) Order 1993
Sch.3 Part I para.2, amended: SI 2015/856 Art.3
Sch.4 para.6, added: SI 2015/856 Art.4

1917. A43 Trunk Road (Ardley to Baynards Green) (Derestriction) Order 1993
revoked: SI 2015/1224 Art.5

1956. Act of Sederunt (Sheriff Court Ordinary Cause Rules) 1993
Sch.1, see *B v D* [2015] CSOH 24, 2015 S.L.T. 217 (OH), Lord Jones

2004. Income Tax (Manufactured Overseas Dividends) Regulations 1993
Reg.2B, see *Chappell v Revenue and Customs Commissioners* [2015] S.T.C. 271 (UT (Tax)), Simon J

2015. Fishing Boats (Marking and Documentation) (Enforcement) Order 1993
revoked: SI 2015/191 Sch.1 , SSI 2015/320 Art.31
Art.8, amended: SI 2015/664 Sch.4 para.51

2060. Capacity Serving Measures (Intoxicating Liquor) (Amendment) Regulations 1993
revoked: SI 2015/356 Sch.1 para.1

2245. Housing (Right to Buy Delay Procedure) (Prescribed Forms) (Amendment) Regulations 1993
revoked: SI 2015/1320 Sch.6

2246. Housing (Right to Buy) (Prescribed Forms) (Amendment) Regulations 1993
revoked: SI 2015/1320 Sch.6

2360. Clinical Thermometers (EEC Requirements) Regulations 1993
revoked: SI 2015/419 Reg.2

2854. Employment Appeal Tribunal Rules 1993
r.3, see *Carroll v Mayor's Office for Policing and Crime* [2015] I.C.R. 835

(EAT), Judge Hand QC; see *Martineau v Ministry of Justice* [2015] I.C.R. 1122 (EAT), Lewis J
r.18, see *Martineau v Ministry of Justice* [2015] I.C.R. 1122 (EAT), Lewis J
r.34, see *Goldwater v Sellafield Ltd (Costs)* [2015] I.R.L.R. 381 (EAT), Judge Shanks
r.34A, see *Goldwater v Sellafield Ltd (Costs)* [2015] I.R.L.R. 381 (EAT), Judge Shanks; see *Look Ahead Housing and Care Ltd v Chetty* [2015] I.C.R. 375 (EAT), Langstaff J

3053. Commercial Agents (Council Directive) Regulations 1993
Reg.17, see *Brand Studio Ltd v St Johns Knits Inc* [2015] EWHC 3143 (QB), [2015] Bus. L.R. 1421 (QBD (Merc)), Teare J; see *Warren (t/a On-line Cartons and Print) v Drukkerij Flach BV* [2014] EWCA Civ 993, [2015] 1 Lloyd's Rep. 111 (CA (Civ Div)), Longmore LJ

3080. Act of Sederunt (Fees of Solicitors in the Sheriff Court) (Amendment and Further Provisions) 1993
Sch.1 Part 1, amended: SSI 2015/246 r.3
Sch.1 Part 1, substituted: SSI 2015/246 r.3

3128. Act of Sederunt (Summary Suspension) 1993
Art.2, amended: SSI 2015/419 r.6
Art.4, amended: SSI 2015/419 r.6

1994

570. Channel Tunnel (Security) Order 1994
Art.11, amended: 2015 c.6 Sch.5 para.13
Art.13, amended: 2015 c.6 Sch.5 para.13, SI 2015/664 Sch.3 para.10
Art.14, amended: SI 2015/664 Sch.3 para.10
Art.15, amended: SI 2015/664 Sch.3 para.10
Art.16, amended: SI 2015/664 Sch.3 para.10
Art.23, amended: SI 2015/664 Sch.3 para.10
Art.36, amended: 2015 c.6 Sch.5 para.13

1002. Highways (Assessment of Environmental Effects) Regulations 1994

revoked: 2015 c.20 Sch.23 para.30

1405. Channel Tunnel (Miscellaneous Provisions) Order 1994
Art.7, amended: SI 2015/856 Art.6
Sch.3 para.3, amended: SI 2015/856 Art.7, Art.8

1443. Act of Sederunt (Rules of the Court of Session 1994) 1994
see *McGraddie v McGraddie* [2015] UKSC 1, [2015] 1 W.L.R. 560 (SC), Lord Neuberger PSC; see *Scottish Ministers v Mirza* 2015 S.C. 334 (IH (Ex Div)), Lady Clark of Calton
Appendix 1., amended: SSI 2015/26
Sch.1 Part 1, Sch.1 Part 2, SSI 2015/35
Sch.1, SSI 2015/227 r.4, Sch.1, SSI 2015/228 Sch.1, Sch.2, SSI 2015/283 r.2, SSI 2015/312 Sch.1
Sch.1, amended: SSI 2015/227 r.6
Sch.2, see *Drimsynie Estate Ltd v Ramsay* 2015 S.C.L.R. 58 (OH), Lord Malcolm; see *Perth and Kinross Council v Scottish Water Ltd* [2015] CSOH 138, 2015 S.L.T. 788 (OH), Lord Stewart
Sch.2 Part 1 para.1_3, amended: SSI 2015/227 r.2
Sch.2 para.1.3, see *Scottish Ministers v Mirza* 2015 S.C. 334 (IH (Ex Div)), Lady Clark of Calton
Sch.2 Part 2 para.3_2, amended: SSI 2015/419 r.7
Sch.2 Part 3, added: SSI 2015/228 r.2
Sch.2 Part 3, added: SSI 2015/35 r.2
Sch.2 Part 3, added: SSI 2015/228 r.5
Sch.2 Part 3 para.32_1, amended: SSI 2015/227 r.3
Sch.2 Part 3 para.32_2A, added: SSI 2015/227 r.3
Sch.2 Part 3 para.32_4, substituted: SSI 2015/227 r.3
Sch.2 Part 3 para.32_7, amended: SSI 2015/227 r.3
Sch.2 Part 3 para.37_2, amended: SSI 2015/227 r.2
Sch.2 Part 3 para.38_3, amended: SSI 2015/228 r.3
Sch.2 Part 3 para.38_8, amended: SSI 2015/228 r.3
Sch.2 Part 3 para.39_1A, added: SSI 2015/227 r.4

Sch.2 Part 3 para.39_2, amended: SSI
2015/227 r.4
Sch.2 Part 3 para.39_3, amended: SSI
2015/227 r.4
Sch.2 Part 3 para.39_4, amended: SSI
2015/227 r.4
Sch.2 Part 3 para.39_8, amended: SSI
2015/227 r.4
Sch.2 Part 3 para.39_9A, added: SSI
2015/227 r.4
Sch.2 Part 3 para.40_1, amended: SSI
2015/419 r.7
Sch.2 Part 3 para.40_21, amended: SSI
2015/419 r.7
Sch.2 Part 3 para.40_21, substituted: SSI
2015/419 r.7
Sch.2 Part 3 para.41_1, amended: SSI
2015/419 r.7
Sch.2 Part 3 para.41_37, amended: SSI
2015/419 r.7
Sch.2 Part 3 para.41_52, amended: SSI
2015/419 r.7
Sch.2 Pt 3 para.41.57, see *Murray Group
Holdings Ltd v Revenue and Customs
Commissioners* [2015] CSIH 77, 2015
S.L.T. 765 (IH (2 Div)), The Lord Justice
Clerk (Carloway)
Sch.2 Part 3 para.42_16, amended: SSI
2015/246 r.2
Sch.2 Part 4, substituted: SSI 2015/228
r.3
Sch.2 para.4.2, see *G, Petitioner* [2015]
CSIH 51, 2015 S.L.T. 461 (IH (Ex Div)),
Lady Dorrian
Sch.2 Part 4 para.42A_1, amended: SSI
2015/227 r.6
Sch.2 Part 4 para.42A_3, substituted: SSI
2015/227 r.6
Sch.2 Part 4 para.42A_4, substituted: SSI
2015/227 r.6
Sch.2 Part 4 para.42A_5, amended: SSI
2015/227 r.6
Sch.2 Part 4 para.42A_6, added: SSI
2015/227 r.6
Sch.2 Pt 4 para.43.1, see *Moran v
Freyssinet Ltd* 2015 Rep. L.R. 15 (OH),
Lord Boyd of Duncansby
Sch.2 Part 4 para.43_1A, substituted: SSI
2015/227 r.6
Sch.2 Pt 4 para.43.9, see *Moran v
Freyssinet Ltd* [2015] CSIH 76, 2015

S.L.T. 829 (IH (Ex Div)), Lady Paton;
see *Moran v Freyssinet Ltd* 2015 Rep.
L.R. 15 (OH), Lord Boyd of Duncansby
Sch.2 Part 4 para.43_10, substituted: SSI
2015/227 r.6
Sch.2 Pt 4 para.43.13, see *Fraser v
Kitsons Insulation Contractors Ltd*
[2015] CSOH 135, 2015 S.L.T. 753
(OH), Lord Doherty
Sch.2 Part 4 para.49_22, substituted: SSI
2015/312 r.2
Sch.2 Part 4 para.58A_1, substituted: SSI
2015/408 r.2
Sch.2 Part 4 para.58A_3, revoked: SSI
2015/408 r.2
Sch.2 Part 4 para.58A_4, amended: SSI
2015/408 r.2
Sch.2 Part 4 para.58_15, amended: SSI
2015/228 r.3
Sch.2 Part 5, substituted: SSI 2015/26 r.2
Sch.2 Part 5 para.62_26, amended: SSI
2015/26 r.2
Sch.2 Part 5 para.62_28, amended: SSI
2015/26 r.2
Sch.2 Part 5 para.62_28, revoked: SSI
2015/26 r.2
Sch.2 Part 5 para.62_28, substituted: SSI
2015/26 r.2
Sch.2 Part 5 para.62_30, amended: SSI
2015/26 r.2
Sch.2 Part 5 para.62_30, substituted: SSI
2015/26 r.2
Sch.2 Part 5 para.62_32, amended: SSI
2015/26 r.2
Sch.2 Part 5 para.62_32, substituted: SSI
2015/26 r.2
Sch.2 Part 5 para.62_33, substituted: SSI
2015/26 r.2
Sch.2 Part 5 para.62_34, amended: SSI
2015/26 r.2
Sch.2 Part 5 para.62_34, substituted: SSI
2015/26 r.2
Sch.2 Part 5 para.62_35, amended: SSI
2015/26 r.2
Sch.2 Part 5 para.62_35, substituted: SSI
2015/26 r.2
Sch.2 Part 5 para.62_36, amended: SSI
2015/26 r.2
Sch.2 Part 5 para.62_36, substituted: SSI
2015/26 r.2

Sch.2 Part 5 para.62_39, amended: SSI
2015/26 r.2
Sch.2 Part 5 para.62_39, substituted: SSI
2015/26 r.2
Sch.2 Part 5 para.62_40, amended: SSI
2015/26 r.2
Sch.2 Part 5 para.62_40, revoked: SSI
2015/26 r.2
Sch.2 Part 5 para.62_40, substituted: SSI
2015/26 r.2
Sch.2 Part 5 para.62_42A, added: SSI
2015/26 r.2
Sch.2 Part 5 para.69_1, amended: SSI
2015/425 Art.92
Sch.2 Part 5 para.70_1, amended: SSI
2015/419 r.7
Sch.2 Part 5 para.72_2, substituted: SSI
2015/119 r.2
Sch.2 Part 5 para.94_2, amended: SSI
2015/228 r.3
Sch.2 Part 5 para.102_1, substituted: SSI
2015/85 r.2
Sch.2 para.13.4, see *Hoe International
Ltd v Andersen* [2015] CSIH 24, 2015
S.C. 506 (IH (Ex Div)), Lord Menzies
Sch.2 para.16.5, see *Hoe International
Ltd v Andersen* [2015] CSIH 24, 2015
S.C. 506 (IH (Ex Div)), Lord Menzies
Sch.2 para.16.10, see *Hoe International
Ltd v Andersen* [2015] CSIH 24, 2015
S.C. 506 (IH (Ex Div)), Lord Menzies
Sch.2 para.21A_1, see *Abrahm v British
International Helicopters Ltd* 2015
S.C.L.R. 95 (IH (2 Div)), The Lord
Justice Clerk (Carloway)
Sch.2 para.29.1, see *Lord Advocate v
Mackie* [2015] CSIH 88 (IH (2 Div)),
The Lord Justice Clerk (Carloway)
Sch.2 para.29.3, see *Lord Advocate v
Mackie* [2015] CSIH 88 (IH (2 Div)),
The Lord Justice Clerk (Carloway)
Sch.2 para.38.1, see *Scottish Ministers v
Mirza* 2015 S.C. 334 (IH (Ex Div)), Lady
Clark of Calton
Sch.2 para.38.2, see *Scottish Ministers v
Mirza* 2015 S.C. 334 (IH (Ex Div)), Lady
Clark of Calton
Sch.2 para.38.9, see *Moran v Freyssinet
Ltd* [2015] CSIH 76, 2015 S.L.T. 829 (IH
(Ex Div)), Lady Paton

Sch.2 para.38.15, see *Hoblyn v Barclays
Bank Plc* 2015 S.C.L.R. 85 (IH (Ex
Div)), Lady Paton
Sch.2 para.40.7, see *Boyd v Fortune* 2015
S.C.L.R. 361 (IH), Lord Brodie
Sch.2 para.40.15, see *Boyd v Fortune*
2015 S.C.L.R. 361 (IH), Lord Brodie
Sch.2 para.40.16, see *Boyd v Fortune*
2015 S.C.L.R. 361 (IH), Lord Brodie
Sch.2 para.42.14, see *Phee v Gordon*
2015 S.C.L.R. 343 (IH (Ex Div)), Lord
Eassie
Sch.2 para.49.7, see *Moran v Freyssinet
Ltd* 2015 Rep. L.R. 15 (OH), Lord Boyd
of Duncansby
Sch.2 para.58.8, see *Hendrick v Chief
Constable of Strathclyde* 2015 S.C. 144
(IH (Ex Div)), Lady Paton
Sch.2 para.58.12, see *G v Watson* 2015
S.C. 222 (IH (Ex Div)), Lord Eassie
**1737. Aircraft Operators (Accounts and
Records) Regulations 1994**
Sch.1, amended: SI 2015/3 Reg.3, SI
2015/942 Reg.2
Sch.2 Part I para.1, amended: SI
2015/942 Reg.2
**1831. Authorities for London Post-Graduate
Teaching Hospitals (Abolition) Order 1994**
revoked: SI 2015/864 Art.2
2349. Countryside Access Regulations 1994
revoked: SI 2015/639 Reg.3
2421. Insolvent Partnerships Order 1994
Art.4, amended: SI 2015/989 Sch.1
para.1
Sch.1 Part I, amended: SI 2015/1641
Sch.2 para.1
**2716. Conservation (Natural Habitats,
&c.) Regulations 1994**
Reg.10, amended: SSI 2015/249 Reg.2
**2716. Conservation (Natural Habitats, &c.)
Regulations 1994**
Reg.8, see *Tummel Valley Leisure Ltd v
Scottish Natural Heritage* 2015 S.L.T.
(Land Ct) 117 (Land Ct), Lord Minginish
Reg.48, see *Tummel Valley Leisure Ltd v
Scottish Natural Heritage* 2015 S.L.T.
(Land Ct) 117 (Land Ct), Lord Minginish
**2931. Housing (Right to Buy Delay
Procedure) (Prescribed Forms) (Welsh
Forms) Regulations 1994**
revoked: SI 2015/1320 Sch.6

2932. Housing (Right to Buy) (Prescribed Forms) (Welsh Forms) Regulations 1994
revoked: SI 2015/1320 Sch.6

2974. Industry-Wide Mineworkers Pension Scheme Regulations 1994
Sch.1, amended: SI 2015/575 Sch.2 para.4

3087. A55 Trunk Road (Abergwyngregyn, Gwynedd) (Derestriction) Order 1994
varied: SI 2015/262 Art.7

3088. A55 Trunk Road (Penmaenbach Tunnel, Gwynedd) (Closure of Central Reservation Crossings) Order 1994
varied: SI 2015/1229 Art.13

3260. Electrical Equipment (Safety) Regulations 1994
Reg.18, amended: SI 2015/1630 Sch.2 para.21

3263. Highways (Inquiries Procedure) Rules 1994
Part I r.2, amended: SI 2015/377 Sch.1 para.33
Part I r.3, amended: SI 2015/377 Sch.1 para.33
Part III, amended: SI 2015/377 Sch.1 para.33
Part IV r.26, amended: SI 2015/377 Sch.1 para.33
Part IV r.27, amended: SI 2015/377 Sch.1 para.33

3266. High Court of Justiciary Fees Amendment Order 1994
revoked: SSI 2015/262 Sch.4

1995

150. Financial Assistance for Environmental Purposes Order 1995
revoked: SI 2015/479 Sch.1

418. Town and Country Planning (General Permitted Development) Order 1995
see *Mohamed v Secretary of State for Communities and Local Government* [2014] EWHC 4045 (Admin), [2015] J.P.L. 583 (QBD (Admin)), Gilbart J
Art.1, see *Evans v Secretary of State for Communities and Local Government* [2014] EWHC 4111 (Admin), [2015] J.P.L. 589 (QBD (Admin)), Neil Cameron QC

Art.3, see *Evans v Secretary of State for Communities and Local Government* [2014] EWHC 4111 (Admin), [2015] J.P.L. 589 (QBD (Admin)), Neil Cameron QC
Sch.2 Pt 1, see *Arnold v Secretary of State for Communities and Local Government* [2015] EWHC 1197 (Admin), [2015] J.P.L. 1053 (QBD (Admin)), Dove J; see *Evans v Secretary of State for Communities and Local Government* [2014] EWHC 4111 (Admin), [2015] J.P.L. 589 (QBD (Admin)), Neil Cameron QC
Sch.2 Pt 3 para.F, see *Valentino Plus Ltd v Secretary of State for Communities and Local Government* [2015] EWHC 19 (Admin), [2015] J.P.L. 707 (QBD (Admin)), Judge Sycamore

419. Town and Country Planning (General Development Procedure) Order 1995
Art.26, see *Sanger v Newham LBC* [2014] EWHC 1922 (Admin), [2015] 1 W.L.R. 332 (DC), Sir Brian Leveson PQBD

554. Financial Assistance for Environmental Purposes (No.2) Order 1995
revoked: SI 2015/479 Sch.1

572. Valuation Appeal Committee (Procedure in Appeals under the Valuation Acts) (Scotland) Regulations 1995
Reg.5, see *Old Golf Course Ltd v Assessor for Fife* 2015 S.L.T. (Lands Tr) 181 (Lands Tr (Scot)), Lord Minginish

632. Judicial Pensions (Miscellaneous) Regulations 1995
Sch.1, amended: SI 2015/533 Reg.2

755. Children (Northern Ireland) Order 1995
Art.2, amended: SI 2015/2006 Sch.12 Part 1
Art.18, amended: SI 2015/2006 Sch.2 para.28, Sch.12 Part 1
Art.18, revoked: SI 2015/2006 Sch.12 Part 1
Art.18C, amended: SI 2015/2006 Sch.2 para.28, Sch.12 Part 1
Art.24, amended: SI 2015/2006 Sch.2 para.28, Sch.12 Part 1
Art.39, amended: SI 2015/2006 Sch.2 para.28, Sch.12 Part 1

Art.183, amended: SI 2015/2006 Sch.12 Part 1
Art.183, revoked: SI 2015/2006 Sch.12 Part 1
Sch.9 para.186, revoked: SI 2015/2006 Sch.12 Part 7

1013. Contracting Out (Functions in relation to the Registration of Companies) Order 1995
Sch.1 para.4, revoked: SI 2015/971 Sch.5 para.2

1030. Antarctic Act 1994 (Overseas Territories) Order 1995
Sch.1 Part II para.3, amended: SI 2015/823 Sch.1 para.1
Sch.1 Part II para.7, amended: SI 2015/823 Sch.1 para.1, Sch.1 para.3
Sch.1 Part II para.8, amended: SI 2015/823 Sch.1 para.1, Sch.1 para.3
Sch.1 Part II para.8A, added: SI 2015/823 Sch.1 para.3
Sch.1 Part II para.8B, added: SI 2015/823 Sch.1 para.3
Sch.1 Part II para.9, amended: SI 2015/823 Sch.1 para.1
Sch.1 Part II para.10, amended: SI 2015/823 Sch.1 para.1, Sch.1 para.2
Sch.1 Part II para.11, amended: SI 2015/823 Sch.1 para.1
Sch.1 Part II para.12, amended: SI 2015/823 Sch.1 para.1, Sch.1 para.3
Sch.1 Part II para.15, amended: SI 2015/823 Sch.1 para.2
Sch.1 Part IV para.30, amended: SI 2015/823 Sch.1 para.2
Sch.1 Part IV para.31, amended: SI 2015/823 Sch.1 para.1, Sch.1 para.3
Sch.3, amended: SI 2015/823 Sch.1 para.1

1035. Antarctic Act 1994 (Isle of Man) Order 1995
Art.2, amended: SI 2015/1531 Art.2

1085. Financial Assistance for Environmental Purposes (No.3) Order 1995
revoked: SI 2015/479 Sch.1

1268. Value Added Tax (Special Provisions) Order 1995
Art.5, see *Pendragon Plc v Revenue and Customs Commissioners* [2015] UKSC 37, [2015] 1 W.L.R. 2838 (SC), Lord Neuberger PSC

1398. Children (Secure Accommodation) Amendment Regulations 1995
revoked: SI 2015/1988 Reg.19

1442. Credit Institutions (Protection of Depositors) Regulations 1995
Reg.46, revoked: SI 2015/486 Reg.17

1576. Fisheries and Aquaculture Structures (Grants) Regulations 1995
revoked: SI 2015/191 Sch.1

2015. Children (Short-term Placements) (Miscellaneous Amendments) Regulations 1995
revoked: SI 2015/1818 Sch.11

2489. Footwear (Indication of Composition) Labelling Regulations 1995
Reg.10, amended: SI 2015/1630 Sch.2 para.23
Reg.10, revoked: SI 2015/1630 Sch.2 para.24

2518. Value Added Tax Regulations 1995
see *Garrod v Revenue and Customs Commissioners* [2015] UKFTT 353 (TC), [2015] S.F.T.D. 952 (FTT (Tax)), Judge Barbara Mosedale
Reg.14, see *Revenue and Customs Commissioners v Infinity Distribution Ltd (In Administration)* [2015] UKUT 219 (TCC), [2015] S.T.C. 2374 (UT (Tax)), Peter Smith J
Reg.25A, see *Garrod v Revenue and Customs Commissioners* [2015] UKFTT 353 (TC), [2015] S.F.T.D. 952 (FTT (Tax)), Judge Barbara Mosedale
Reg.29, see *Perenco Holdings v Revenue and Customs Commissioners* [2015] UKFTT 65 (TC), [2015] S.F.T.D. 650 (FTT (Tax)), Judge Guy Brannan; see *Revenue and Customs Commissioners v GB Housley Ltd* [2015] UKUT 71 (TCC), [2015] S.T.C. 1403 (UT (Tax)), Warren J
Reg.134, see *Global Foods Ltd v Revenue and Customs Commissioners* [2015] S.F.T.D. 327 (FTT (Tax)), Judge Nicholas Aleksander
Reg.198, see *Global Foods Ltd v Revenue and Customs Commissioners* [2015] S.F.T.D. 327 (FTT (Tax)), Judge Nicholas Aleksander
Reg.201, see *Revenue and Customs Commissioners v Patel* [2015] S.T.C. 148 (UT (Tax)), Judge Colin Bishopp

2564. A5 Trunk Road (Various Roads, Corwen, Clwyd) (Restriction of Waiting) Order 1995
revoked: SI 2015/1925 Art.8

2587. Collective Redundancies and Transfer of Undertakings (Protection of Employment) (Amendment) Regulations 1995
see *United States v Nolan* [2015] UKSC 63, [2015] 3 W.L.R. 1105 (SC), Lord Neuberger PSC

2644. Statutory Nuisance (Appeals) Regulations 1995
Reg.2, see *R. (on the application of Bramford Royal British Legion) v Ipswich Magistrates' Court* [2014] EWHC 526 (Admin), [2015] Env. L.R. 1 (QBD (Admin)), Simler J

2705. Jobseekers (Northern Ireland) Order 1995
Art.2, amended: SI 2015/2006 Art.50, Art.55, Sch.7 para.2, Sch.12 Part 1, Sch.12 Part 3, Sch.12 Part 4
Art.3, amended: SI 2015/2006 Art.50, Art.66
Art.3, revoked: SI 2015/2006 Art.55 , Sch.12 Part 1
Art.4, amended: SI 2015/2006 Sch.2 para.29, Sch.12 Part 1
Art.4, revoked: SI 2015/2006 Sch.12 Part 1
Art.5, revoked: SI 2015/2006 Sch.12 Part 1
Art.6, amended: SI 2015/2006 Sch.5 para.5, Sch.12 Part 1
Art.6, revoked: SI 2015/2006 Sch.12 Part 1
Art.6A, revoked: SI 2015/2006 Sch.12 Part 1
Art.7, amended: SI 2015/2006 Sch.12 Part 1
Art.8, substituted: SI 2015/2006 Art.55
Art.10, amended: SI 2015/2006 Art.51, Sch.7 para.3
Art.10, revoked: SI 2015/2006 Sch.12 Part 3
Art.11, substituted: SI 2015/2006 Art.50
Art.12, substituted: SI 2015/2006 Art.50
Art.15, revoked: SI 2015/2006 Sch.12 Part 1
Art.17, revoked: SI 2015/2006 Sch.12 Part 1

Art.18, amended: SI 2015/2006 Sch.7 para.4
Art.19, amended: SI 2015/2006 Sch.7 para.4
Art.19A, amended: SI 2015/2006 Sch.7 para.5, Sch.12 Part 1
Art.19A, revoked: SI 2015/2006 Sch.12 Part 3 , Sch.12 Part 4
Art.20, revoked: SI 2015/2006 Sch.12 Part 1
Art.21, revoked: SI 2015/2006 Sch.12 Part 4
Art.21, substituted: SI 2015/2006 Art.52
Art.22, amended: SI 2015/2006 Sch.7 para.6
Art.22, revoked: SI 2015/2006 Sch.12 Part 3 , Sch.12 Part 4
Art.22A, revoked: SI 2015/2006 Sch.12 Part 3
Art.22C, revoked: SI 2015/2006 Sch.7 para.7
Art.22E, revoked: SI 2015/2006 Sch.12 Part 4
Art.24, amended: SI 2015/2006 Sch.7 para.8
Art.24, revoked: SI 2015/2006 Sch.12 Part 4
Art.25, revoked: SI 2015/2006 Sch.12 Part 1
Art.27, revoked: SI 2015/2006 Sch.12 Part 1
Art.30, revoked: SI 2015/2006 Sch.12 Part 1
Art.31, amended: SI 2015/2006 Art.55
Art.31, revoked: SI 2015/2006 Sch.12 Part 1
Art.32, revoked: SI 2015/2006 Sch.12 Part 1
Art.33, revoked: SI 2015/2006 Sch.12 Part 7 , Sch.12 Part 10
Art.36, amended: SI 2015/2006 Sch.7 para.9
Art.36, revoked: SI 2015/2006 Sch.12 Part 4
Art.37, amended: SI 2015/2006 Art.53, Sch.12 Part 3, Sch.12 Part 4
Art.37, revoked: SI 2015/2006 Sch.12 Part 1 , Sch.12 Part 4
Art.38, amended: SI 2015/2006 Sch.12 Part 1

Art.38, revoked: SI 2015/2006 Sch.12
Part 1
Art.39, revoked: SI 2015/2006 Sch.12
Part 1
Sch.1 para.6, amended: SI 2015/2006
Sch.12 Part 1
Sch.1 para.8, amended: SI 2015/2006
Sch.7 para.10
Sch.1 para.8, revoked: SI 2015/2006
Sch.12 Part 1
Sch.1 para.8A, revoked: SI 2015/2006
Sch.12 Part 1
Sch.1 para.8B, amended: SI 2015/2006
Sch.7 para.10
Sch.1 para.8B, revoked: SI 2015/2006
Sch.12 Part 4
Sch.1 para.8ZA, added: SI 2015/2006
Art.66
Sch.1 para.9, amended: SI 2015/2006
Art.109
Sch.1 para.9, revoked: SI 2015/2006
Sch.12 Part 1
Sch.1 para.10, amended: SI 2015/2006
Art.109, Sch.7 para.10
Sch.1 para.11, amended: SI 2015/2006
Sch.12 Part 1
Sch.1 para.14AA, added: SI 2015/2006
Art.52
Sch.1 para.14B, amended: SI 2015/2006
Art.52
Sch.1 para.16, amended: SI 2015/2006
Sch.12 Part 1
Sch.1 para.16, revoked: SI 2015/2006
Sch.12 Part 1
Sch.1 para.18, revoked: SI 2015/2006
Sch.12 Part 1
Sch.2 para.12, revoked: SI 2015/2006
Sch.12 Part 1
Sch.2 para.34, revoked: SI 2015/2006
Sch.12 Part 7
Sch.2 para.36, revoked: SI 2015/2006
Sch.12 Part 1
Sch.2 para.51, revoked: SI 2015/2006
Sch.12 Part 1
3099. Financial Assistance for Environmental Purposes (No.4) Order 1995
revoked: SI 2015/479 Sch.1
3213. Pensions (Northern Ireland) Order 1995

Art.75, see *Garvin Trustees Ltd v Pensions Regulator* [2015] Pens. L.R. 1 (UT (Tax)), Judge Timothy Herrington
3237. Insurance Companies (Overseas Life Assurance Business) (Compliance) Regulations 1995
Reg.2, amended: SI 2015/575 Sch.2
para.5
Reg.5, amended: SI 2015/575 Sch.2
para.5
Reg.7, amended: SI 2015/575 Sch.2
para.5
Reg.7A, amended: SI 2015/575 Sch.2
para.5
Reg.8, amended: SI 2015/575 Sch.2
para.5
Reg.13, amended: SI 2015/575 Sch.2
para.5
Reg.14, amended: SI 2015/575 Sch.2
para.5
Reg.14A, amended: SI 2015/575 Sch.2
para.5

1996

192. Equipment and Protective Systems Intended for Use in Potentially Explosive Atmospheres Regulations 1996
see *Weatherford Global Products Ltd v Hydropath Holdings Ltd* [2014] EWHC 2725 (TCC), [2015] B.L.R. 69 (QBD (TCC)), Akenhead J
207. Jobseeker's Allowance Regulations 1996
Reg.1, amended: SI 2015/67 Reg.2, SI 2015/336 Reg.2, SI 2015/389 Reg.3, SI 2015/971 Sch.3 para.4, SI 2015/1985 Art.16
Reg.11, amended: SI 2015/971 Sch.3 para.4
Reg.14, amended: SI 2015/336 Reg.2, SI 2015/339 Reg.2, SI 2015/389 Reg.3
Reg.14, revoked: SI 2015/339 Reg.2
Reg.15, amended: SI 2015/336 Reg.2
Reg.18, amended: SI 2015/389 Reg.3
Reg.19, amended: SI 2015/336 Reg.2, SI 2015/339 Reg.2, SI 2015/389 Reg.3
Reg.50, amended: SI 2015/389 Reg.3
Reg.53, amended: SI 2015/389 Reg.3
Reg.54, amended: SI 2015/336 Reg.2
Reg.54, revoked: SI 2015/336 Reg.2

Reg.55, amended: SI 2015/339 Reg.2
Reg.55ZA, added: SI 2015/339 Reg.2
Reg.57, amended: SI 2015/971 Sch.3
para.4
Reg.78, amended: SI 2015/643 Sch.1
para.9
Reg.79, amended: SI 2015/30 Art.8
Reg.94, amended: SI 2015/389 Reg.3
Reg.102, amended: SI 2015/478 Reg.29
Reg.130, amended: SI 2015/971 Sch.3
para.4
Reg.170, amended: SI 2015/971 Sch.3
para.4
Reg.172, amended: SI 2015/457 Art.20
Sch.A1 para.16, amended: SI 2015/971
Sch.3 para.4
Sch.1 Part I para.1, amended: SI 2015/30
Sch.3
Sch.1 Part I para.2, amended: SI
2015/457 Sch.9
Sch.1 Part III para.15, amended: SI
2015/1754 Reg.15
Sch.1 Part IV, amended: SI 2015/457
Sch.10
Sch.1 Part IVA para.20I, amended: SI
2015/1754 Reg.15
Sch.1 Part IVB para.20M, amended: SI
2015/457 Sch.11
Sch.2 para.1, amended: SI 2015/1647
Reg.3
Sch.2 para.6, revoked: SI 2015/1647
Reg.3
Sch.2 para.7, amended: SI 2015/1647
Reg.3
Sch.2 para.7, revoked: SI 2015/1647
Reg.3
Sch.2 para.7, substituted: SI 2015/1647
Reg.3
Sch.2 para.8, amended: SI 2015/1647
Reg.3
Sch.2 para.9, amended: SI 2015/1647
Reg.3
Sch.2 para.10, amended: SI 2015/1647
Reg.3
Sch.2 para.10, revoked: SI 2015/1647
Reg.3
Sch.2 para.12, amended: SI 2015/1647
Reg.3
Sch.2 para.13, amended: SI 2015/1647
Reg.3

Sch.2 para.13, revoked: SI 2015/1647
Reg.3
Sch.2 para.15, amended: SI 2015/1647
Reg.3
Sch.2 para.17, amended: SI 2015/457
Art.19
Sch.2 para.18, revoked: SI 2015/1647
Reg.3
Sch.6 para.1B, added: SI 2015/1985
Art.16
Sch.6 para.9, amended: SI 2015/389
Reg.3
Sch.6 para.19, amended: SI 2015/389
Reg.3
Sch.7 para.28, amended: SI 2015/643
Sch.1 para.9
Sch.7 para.31, amended: SI 2015/643
Sch.1 para.9
Sch.7 para.32, amended: SI 2015/643
Sch.1 para.9
Sch.7 para.56, amended: SI 2015/643
Sch.1 para.9
Sch.7 para.64, amended: SI 2015/643
Sch.1 para.9
Sch.8 para.60, amended: SI 2015/643
Sch.1 para.9

248. Fishing Boats (European Economic Community) Designation (Variation) Order 1996

revoked: SI 2015/648 Sch.3

252. Gas Act 1995 (Consequential Modifications of Subordinate Legislation) Order 1996

Sch.1, amended: SSI 2015/181 Sch.9

341. Health and Safety (Safety Signs and Signals) Regulations 1996

Reg.2, amended: SI 2015/21 Reg.3
Reg.3, amended: SI 2015/21 Reg.3
Sch.1 Part I para.12, substituted: SI
2015/21 Reg.3
Sch.1 Part II para.2, amended: SI
2015/21 Reg.3
Sch.1 Part II para.3, revoked: SI 2015/21
Reg.3
Sch.1 Part III para.1, substituted: SI
2015/21 Reg.3
Sch.1 Part III para.5, amended: SI
2015/21 Reg.3

439. Gas (Calculation of Thermal Energy) Regulations 1996

Reg.2, amended: SI 2015/953 Reg.2

505. Financial Assistance for Environmental Purposes Order 1996
revoked: SI 2015/479 Sch.1
511. Authorities for London Post-Graduate Teaching Hospitals (Abolition) Order 1996
revoked: SI 2015/864 Art.2
512. Authorities for London Post-Graduate Teaching Hospitals (Revocation) Regulations 1996
revoked: SI 2015/839 Reg.2
513. Act of Adjournal (Criminal Procedure Rules) 1996
Sch.2 Appendix, added: SSI 2015/443 r.2
Sch.2 Appendix, amended: SSI 2015/84 Sch.1, SSI 2015/121 Sch.1, SSI 2015/201 r.2, Sch.1, SSI 2015/245 r.5, Sch.1, SSI 2015/295 r.5, Sch.1, SSI 2015/375 Sch.1, SSI 2015/443 r.2
Sch.2 Appendix, substituted: SSI 2015/295 r.5
Sch.2 Part I para.2_3A, substituted: SSI 2015/295 r.2
Sch.2 Part II para.4_2, amended: SSI 2015/245 r.4
Sch.2 Part II para.7_9, amended: SSI 2015/245 r.4
Sch.2 Part IVA, added: SSI 2015/245 r.3
Sch.2 Part IV para.17_1, amended: SSI 2015/245 r.4
Sch.2 Part IV para.19A_1, amended: SSI 2015/295 r.3
Sch.2 Part IV para.19_1, amended: SSI 2015/245 r.2
Sch.2 Part IV para.19_5, amended: SSI 2015/245 r.2
Sch.2 Part IV para.19_6, amended: SSI 2015/245 r.2
Sch.2 Part IV para.19_8, amended: SSI 2015/245 r.2
Sch.2 Part IV para.19_9, amended: SSI 2015/245 r.2
Sch.2 Part IV para.19_10, amended: SSI 2015/245 r.2
Sch.2 Part IV para.19_10A, amended: SSI 2015/245 r.2
Sch.2 Part IV para.19_11, substituted: SSI 2015/245 r.2
Sch.2 Part IV para.19_12, amended: SSI 2015/245 r.2
Sch.2 Part IV para.19_14, amended: SSI 2015/245 r.2

Sch.2 Part IV para.19_15, amended: SSI 2015/245 r.2
Sch.2 Part IV para.19_16, amended: SSI 2015/245 r.2
Sch.2 Part IV para.19_17, amended: SSI 2015/245 r.2
Sch.2 Part IV para.19_18, amended: SSI 2015/245 r.2
Sch.2 Part IV para.19_18A, substituted: SSI 2015/245 r.2
Sch.2 Part IV para.19_19, amended: SSI 2015/245 r.2
Sch.2 Part VI para.22_1, substituted: SSI 2015/295 r.4
Sch.2 Part VI para.22_1ZA, added: SSI 2015/295 r.4
Sch.2 Part VI para.22_2, amended: SSI 2015/295 r.4
Sch.2 Part VI para.22_2, substituted: SSI 2015/295 r.4
Sch.2 Part VI para.22_2A, added: SSI 2015/295 r.4
Sch.2 Part VI para.22_3, amended: SSI 2015/295 r.4
Sch.2 Part VI para.22_7, amended: SSI 2015/295 r.4
Sch.2 Part VI para.22_9, substituted: SSI 2015/443 r.2
Sch.2 Part VI para.22_11, amended: SSI 2015/443 r.2
Sch.2 Part VI para.22_13, amended: SSI 2015/443 r.2
Sch.2 Part VI para.22_14, amended: SSI 2015/443 r.2
Sch.2 Part VI para.27A_1, amended: SSI 2015/245 r.4
Sch.2 Part VII, added: SSI 2015/121 r.2
Sch.2 Part VII, added: SSI 2015/375 r.2
Sch.2 Part VII para.29A_1, amended: SSI 2015/245 r.4
Sch.2 Part VII para.31_3A, added: SSI 2015/245 r.4
Sch.2 Part VII para.31_4, substituted: SSI 2015/245 r.4
Sch.2 Part VII para.38, amended: SSI 2015/245 r.4
Sch.2 Part VII para.56_1, substituted: SSI 2015/84 r.2
Sch.2 Part VII para.56_3, amended: SSI 2015/245 r.4

Sch.2 Part VII para.56_4, amended: SSI
2015/245 r.4
Sch.2 Part VII para.58_3, amended: SSI
2015/245 r.4
Sch.2 Part VII para.58_3, substituted: SSI
2015/245 r.4
Sch.2 Part VII para.61_9, amended: SSI
2015/201 r.2
Sch.2 para.40.12, see *HM Advocate v
Porch (Ross)* [2015] HCJAC 111 (HCJ),
Lady Paton
Sch.2 para.59.4, see *HM Advocate v
Sinclair (Angus Robertson)* 2015 J.C. 137
(HCJ), The Lord Justice Clerk
(Carloway)
**516. High Court of Justiciary Fees
Amendment Order 1996**
revoked: SSI 2015/262 Sch.4
**709. Health Authorities Act 1995
(Transitional Provisions) Order 1996**
revoked: SI 2015/864 Art.2
**713. Cambridge Water Company
(Constitution and Regulation) Order 1996**
revoked: 2015 c.20 Sch.23 para.27
**971. Health Authorities Act 1995
(Amendment of Transitional Provisions and
Modification of References) Order 1996**
revoked: SI 2015/864 Art.2
**1035. Fishing Boats (Specified Countries)
Designation Order 1996**
revoked: SI 2015/648 Sch.3
**1251. Hydrocarbon Oil (Designated Markers)
Regulations 1996**
Reg.2, amended: SI 2015/36 Reg.5
**1431. Financial Assistance for Environmental
Purposes (No.2) Order 1996**
revoked: SI 2015/479 Sch.1
**1462. Contracting-out (Transfer and
Transfer Payment) Regulations 1996**
Reg.1, amended: SI 2015/1452 Reg.31,
SI 2015/1677 Reg.30
Reg.13B, added: SI 2015/1452 Reg.31,
SI 2015/1677 Reg.30
**1507. Ancient Monuments (Class Consents)
(Scotland) Order 1996**
Sch.1, amended: SSI 2015/239 Art.20
1527. Landfill Tax Regulations 1996
Reg.2, amended: SI 2015/846 Reg.2, SI
2015/1453 Reg.2
Reg.16ZA, added: SI 2015/846 Reg.2

Reg.16ZA, amended: SI 2015/1453
Reg.2
Reg.31, amended: SI 2015/744 Reg.3
Reg.33, amended: SI 2015/599 Art.3
Reg.36, varied: SI 2015/599 Art.5
Reg.47, amended: SI 2015/1641 Sch.3
para.3
**1632. Deregulation and Contracting Out
(Northern Ireland) Order 1996**
Art.17, amended: SI 2015/2006 Sch.2
para.30
**1634. Football Spectators (Corresponding
Offences in Norway) Order 1996**
revoked: SI 2015/212 Sch.1
**1635. Football Spectators (Corresponding
Offences in the Republic of Ireland) Order
1996**
revoked: SI 2015/212 Sch.1
**1919. Employment Rights (Northern Ireland)
Order 1996**
Art.45, see *Patterson v Castlereagh BC*
[2015] NICA 47, [2015] I.R.L.R. 721
(CA (NI)), Morgan LCJ
**1974. Driving Licences (Community Driving
Licence) Regulations 1996**
Sch.1 para.32, revoked: SI 2015/583
Sch.1 Part 2
**2310. Health Authorities Act 1995
(Transitional Provisions) Amendment Order
1996**
revoked: SI 2015/864 Art.2
**2555. Criminal Legal Aid (Scotland)
Regulations 1996**
Reg.4, amended: SSI 2015/337 Reg.4
**2652. Housing (Right to Buy) (Prescribed
Forms) (Amendment) Regulations 1996**
revoked: SI 2015/1320 Sch.6
**2660. Duffield and Wirksworth Light
Railway Order 1996**
Art.3, revoked: SI 2015/1652 Art.7
Art.4, revoked: SI 2015/1652 Art.7
Art.5, revoked: SI 2015/1652 Art.7
Art.8, revoked: SI 2015/1652 Art.7
**2798. Civil Aviation (Investigation of Air
Accidents and Incidents) Regulations 1996**
Reg.18, see *Lord Advocate, Petitioner*
[2015] CSOH 80, 2015 S.L.T. 450 (OH),
Lord Jones
**2890. Housing Renewal Grants Regulations
1996**

Reg.41, amended: SI 2015/971 Sch.3
para.5
Sch.1 Part III para.12, amended: SI
2015/643 Sch.1 para.10, SI 2015/1985
Art.17
Sch.1 Part III para.13, amended: SI
2015/643 Sch.1 para.10
Sch.1 Part III para.14, amended: SI
2015/643 Sch.1 para.10
Sch.1A Part III para.7, amended: SI
2015/643 Sch.1 para.10
Sch.2 para.1, amended: SI 2015/1985
Art.17
Sch.3 para.24, amended: SI 2015/643
Sch.1 para.10
Sch.3 para.59, amended: SI 2015/643
Sch.1 para.10

**2907. Child Support Departure Direction and
Consequential Amendments Regulations 1996**
see *Hakki v Secretary of State for Work
and Pensions* [2014] EWCA Civ 530,
[2015] 1 F.L.R. 547 (CA (Civ Div)),
Longmore LJ

**2920. Dorset Fire Services (Combination
Scheme) Order 1996**
revoked: SI 2015/435 Art.3

**2991. Insurance Companies (Reserves) (Tax)
Regulations 1996**
revoked: SI 2015/1983 Reg.5

**3061. Code of Practice on Environmental
Procedures for Flood Defence Operating
Authorities (Environment Agency and
Natural Resources Body for Wales) Approval
Order 1996**
revoked: SI 2015/663 Art.5

**3111. Countryside Access (Amendment)
Regulations 1996**
revoked: SI 2015/639 Reg.3

**3122. Allocation of Housing and
Homelessness (Review Procedures and
Amendment) Regulations 1996**
revoked: SI 2015/1266 Reg.8

**3128. Occupational Pension Schemes
(Deficiency on Winding Up etc.) Regulations
1996**
see *Merchant Navy Ratings Pension
Fund, Re* [2015] EWHC 448 (Ch), [2015]
Pens. L.R. 239 (Ch D), Asplin J

**3158. Licensing (Northern Ireland) Order
1996**

Art.58, see *Morris v DPP* [2015] NICA
49, [2015] L.L.R. 772 (CA (NI)), Morgan
LCJ

**3204. Homelessness (Suitability of
Accommodation) Order 1996**
revoked: SI 2015/1268 Art.9
see *Samuels v Birmingham City Council*
[2015] EWCA Civ 1051, [2015] H.L.R.
47 (CA (Civ Div)), Richards LJ

**3205. Local Authorities (Contracting Out of
Allocation of Housing and Homelessness
Functions) Order 1996**
Art.3, amended: SI 2015/752 Reg.2
Sch.2, amended: SI 2015/752 Reg.2

1997

**194. Assured Tenancies and Agricultural
Occupancies (Forms) Regulations 1997**
revoked: SI 2015/620 Reg.4

**291. Act of Sederunt (Child Care and
Maintenance Rules) 1997**
Part 1 r.1.6, amended: SSI 2015/419 r.8
Part 2 r.2.60, substituted: SSI 2015/419
r.8
Part 3, substituted: SSI 2015/424 r.3
Part 3, added: SSI 2015/424 r.3
Part 3 r.3.1, amended: SSI 2015/424 r.3
Part 3 r.3.2, amended: SSI 2015/424 r.3
Part 3 r.3.3A, amended: SSI 2015/424 r.3
Part 3 r.3.5, amended: SSI 2015/424 r.3
Part 3 r.3.13, amended: SSI 2015/424 r.3
Part 3 r.3.59, amended: SSI 2015/419 r.8
Part 3 r.3.59, revoked: SSI 2015/419 r.8
Part 3 r.3.59, substituted: SSI 2015/419
r.8
Part 3 r.3.61, revoked: SSI 2015/419 r.8
Part 3 r.3.61A, revoked: SSI 2015/419 r.8
Part 3 r.3.66, amended: SSI 2015/419 r.8
Part 3 r.3.66, substituted: SSI 2015/424
r.3
Sch.1, amended: SSI 2015/283 r.4, SSI
2015/424 r.3, Sch.1

**302. Civil Jurisdiction and Judgments Act
1982 (Interim Relief) Order 1997**
Art.2, amended: SI 2015/1644 Reg.21

**569. Housing (Right to Acquire) (Discount)
(Wales) Order 1997**
Art.3, amended: SI 2015/1349 Art.2

631. Allocation of Housing and Homelessness (Amendment) Regulations 1997
revoked: SI 2015/1266 Reg.8

651. Financial Assistance for Environmental Purposes Order 1997
revoked: SI 2015/479 Sch.1

688. Court of Session etc Fees Order 1997
revoked: SSI 2015/261 Sch.4

813. Bovine Hides Regulations 1997
revoked: SI 2015/639 Reg.3

831. Lifts Regulations 1997
Sch.15 para.2, amended: SI 2015/1630 Sch.2 para.26
Sch.15 para.2, revoked: SI 2015/1630 Sch.2 para.26
Sch.15 para.3, amended: SI 2015/1630 Sch.2 para.27

873. Driving Standards Agency Trading Fund Order 1997
revoked: SI 2015/41 Sch.3

1160. Hedgerows Regulations 1997
Reg.6, amended: SI 2015/377 Sch.1 para.35
Reg.6, varied: SI 2015/318 Art.10

1630. Fishing Boats (Specified Countries) Designation (Variation) Order 1997
revoked: SI 2015/648 Sch.3

1729. Animals and Animal Products (Examination for Residues and Maximum Residue Limits) Regulations 1997
revoked: SI 2015/787 Sch.1

1741. Homelessness (Suitability of Accommodation) (Amendment) Order 1997
revoked: SI 2015/1268 Art.9

1924. Fishing Vessels (Decommissioning) Scheme 1997
revoked: SI 2015/191 Sch.1

2046. Allocation of Housing and Homelessness (Amendment) (No.2) Regulations 1997
Reg.1, revoked: SI 2015/1266 Reg.8

2196. Gaming Duty Regulations 1997
Reg.5, amended: SI 2015/1351 Reg.4

2675. Coast Protection (Variation of Excluded Waters) Regulations 1997
revoked: SI 2015/523 Sch.1

2751. Coypus (Special Licence) (Fees) Regulations 1997
revoked: SI 2015/613 Sch.1

2780. Civil Jurisdiction and Judgments Act 1982 (Provisional and Protective Measures) (Scotland) Order 1997
Art.2, amended: SI 2015/1644 Reg.22
Art.3, amended: SI 2015/1644 Reg.22

3032. Copyright and Rights in Databases Regulations 1997
see *Your Response Ltd v Datateam Business Media Ltd* [2014] EWCA Civ 281, [2015] Q.B. 41 (CA (Civ Div)), Moore-Bick LJ
Reg.16, see *Intercity Telecom Ltd v Solanki* [2015] 2 Costs L.R. 315 (QBD (Merc) (Birmingham)), Judge Simon Brown QC
Sch.1 para.3, amended: SI 2015/374 Art.10
Sch.1 para.6, amended: SI 2015/374 Art.10

1998

281. Chester Waterworks Company (Constitution and Regulation) Order 1998
revoked: 2015 c.20 Sch.23 para.27

378. A50 Trunk Road (Derby Southern Bypass) (Derestriction) Order 1998
Sch.1, varied: SI 2015/1072 Art.7

494. Health and Safety (Enforcing Authority) Regulations 1998
Reg.2, amended: SI 2015/21 Reg.6, SI 2015/51 Sch.5
Reg.2A, amended: SI 2015/51 Sch.5
Reg.3, amended: SI 2015/1682 Sch.1 para.10
Sch.1 para.1, amended: SI 2015/21 Reg.6
Sch.2 para.4, amended: SI 2015/51 Sch.5

538. Financial Assistance for Environmental Purposes Order 1998
revoked: SI 2015/479 Sch.1

562. Income-related Benefits (Subsidy to Authorities) Order 1998
Art.11, amended: SI 2015/1784 Art.5
Art.12, amended: SI 2015/1784 Art.2
Art.13, amended: SI 2015/1784 Art.2
Art.18, amended: SI 2015/1784 Art.3, Art.5
Art.19, amended: SI 2015/1784 Art.5
Art.20, amended: SI 2015/1784 Art.5
Sch.1, substituted: SI 2015/1784 Sch.1

Sch.1A, added: SI 2015/1784 Sch.2
Sch.4A Part II para.3, amended: SI
2015/1784 Art.4
Sch.4A Part III, substituted: SI
2015/1784 Sch.3
Sch.4A Part V, substituted: SI 2015/1784
Sch.4

**649. Scheme for Construction Contracts
(England and Wales) Regulations 1998**
   see *Khurana v Webster Construction Ltd*
[2015] EWHC 758 (TCC), [2015] B.L.R.
396 (QBD (TCC)), Judge Stephen
Davies; see *Purton (t/a Richwood
Interiors) v Kilker Projects Ltd* [2015]
EWHC 2624 (TCC), [2015] B.L.R. 754
(QBD (TCC)), Stuart-Smith J
   Sch.1, see *Aspect Contracts (Asbestos)
Ltd v Higgins Construction Plc* [2015]
UKSC 38, [2015] 1 W.L.R. 2961 (SC),
Lord Mance JSC
   Sch.1 Pt I, see *Ecovision Systems Ltd v
Vinci Construction UK Ltd* [2015]
EWHC 587 (TCC), [2015] 1 All E.R.
(Comm) 1110 (QBD (TCC)), Judge
Havelock-Allan QC
   Sch.1 para.23, see *Aspect Contracts
(Asbestos) Ltd v Higgins Construction
Plc* [2015] UKSC 38, [2015] 1 W.L.R.
2961 (SC), Lord Mance JSC

**1001. Financial Assistance for Environmental
Purposes (No.3) Order 1998**
   revoked: SI 2015/479 Sch.1

**1144. A50 Trunk Road (Derby Southern
Bypass) (50 Miles Per Hour Speed Limit and
Derestriction) Order 1998**
   revoked: SI 2015/1072 Art.6

**1266. Football Spectators (Corresponding
Offences in France) Order 1998**
   revoked: SI 2015/212 Sch.1

**1365. Fisheries and Aquaculture Structure
(Grants) Amendment Regulations 1998**
   revoked: SI 2015/191 Sch.1

**1449. Contracting Out (Functions Relating to
National Savings) Order 1998**
   Sch.1 para.3, varied: SI 2015/623 Reg.65

**1678. Children (Performances)
(Miscellaneous Amendments) Regulations
1998**
   revoked: SI 2015/1757 Sch.1

**1713. Faculty Jurisdiction (Appeals) Rules
1998**

revoked: SI 2015/1568 r.28_2

1833. Working Time Regulations 1998
   see *Benkharbouche v Embassy of Sudan*
[2015] EWCA Civ 33, [2015] 3 W.L.R.
301 (CA (Civ Div)), Lord Dyson MR;
   see *Lock v British Gas Trading Ltd*
[2015] I.R.L.R. 438 (ET), Judge Ahmed;
   see *Sash Window Workshop Ltd v King*
[2015] I.R.L.R. 348 (EAT), Simler J; see
*Shannon v Rampersad (t/a Clifton House
Residential Home)* [2015] I.R.L.R. 982
(EAT), Judge Peter Clark
   Reg.2, see *Edwards v Encirc Ltd* [2015]
I.R.L.R. 528 (EAT), Judge Eady QC
   Reg.10, see *Edwards v Encirc Ltd* [2015]
I.R.L.R. 528 (EAT), Judge Eady QC
   Reg.13, see *Lock v British Gas Trading
Ltd* [2015] I.R.L.R. 438 (ET), Judge
Ahmed; see *Sash Window Workshop Ltd
v King* [2015] I.R.L.R. 348 (EAT),
Simler J
   Reg.14, see *Sash Window Workshop Ltd
v King* [2015] I.R.L.R. 348 (EAT),
Simler J
   Reg.16, see *Bear Scotland Ltd v Fulton*
[2015] 1 C.M.L.R. 40 (EAT), Langstaff
J; see *Lock v British Gas Trading Ltd*
[2015] I.R.L.R. 438 (ET), Judge Ahmed;
   see *Sash Window Workshop Ltd v King*
[2015] I.R.L.R. 348 (EAT), Simler J

**1870. Individual Savings Account Regulations
1998**
   Reg.2, amended: SI 2015/575 Sch.2
para.8, SI 2015/869 Reg.3, SI 2015/1370
Reg.3
   Reg.2, revoked: SI 2015/1370 Reg.3
   Reg.2D, amended: SI 2015/869 Reg.4
   Reg.4, amended: SI 2015/869 Reg.5
   Reg.4ZA, amended: SI 2015/608 Reg.3
   Reg.4ZB, amended: SI 2015/608 Reg.3
   Reg.5D, amended: SI 2015/869 Reg.6, SI
2015/941 Reg.3
   Reg.5DDA, added: SI 2015/869 Reg.7
   Reg.5DF, amended: SI 2015/869 Reg.8
   Reg.5DFA, added: SI 2015/869 Reg.9
   Reg.7, amended: SI 2015/1370 Reg.4
   Reg.7, revoked: SI 2015/1370 Reg.4
   Reg.12A, amended: SI 2015/941 Reg.4
   Reg.21, amended: SI 2015/941 Reg.5
   Reg.21B, amended: SI 2015/941 Reg.6,
Reg.7

Reg.21B, revoked: SI 2015/941 Reg.6
Reg.31, amended: SI 2015/869 Reg.10,
SI 2015/941 Reg.7, SI 2015/1370 Reg.5

2306. Provision and Use of Work Equipment Regulations 1998

see *Coia v Portavadie Estates Ltd* [2015]
CSIH 3, 2015 S.C. 419 (IH (Ex Div)),
Lord Menzies; see *Gilchrist v Asda
Stores Ltd* [2015] CSOH 77, 2015 Rep.
L.R. 95 (OH), Lady Stacey
Reg.20, see *McLellan v Mitie Group Plc*
[2015] CSOH 151, 2015 S.L.T. 861
(OH), Lady Scott

2307. Lifting Operations and Lifting Equipment Regulations 1998

Reg.3, amended: SI 2015/1637 Sch.1
para.5

2451. Gas Safety (Installation and Use) Regulations 1998

Reg.2, amended: SI 2015/51 Sch.5

3132. Civil Procedure Rules 1998

see *Ashley v Tesco Stores Ltd* [2015]
EWCA Civ 414, [2015] 1 W.L.R. 5153
(CA (Civ Div)), Arden LJ; see *Chief
Constable of Warwickshire v MT* [2015]
EWHC 2303 (Admin), (2015) 179 J.P.
454 (QBD (Admin)), Hickinbottom J; see
*Clavis Liberty Fund 1 LP v Revenue and
Customs Commissioners* [2015] UKUT
72 (TCC), [2015] 1 W.L.R. 2949 (UT
(Tax)), Warren J; see *Daniels v Nursing
and Midwifery Council* [2015] EWCA
Civ 225, [2015] Med. L.R. 255 (CA (Civ
Div)), Sir Brian Leveson PQBD; see *G
(An Adult) (Costs), Re* [2015] EWCA Civ
446, [2015] C.P. Rep. 37 (CA (Civ Div)),
Sullivan LJ; see *Groupe Eurotunnel SA v
Competition and Markets Authority*
[2015] CAT 4, [2015] Comp. A.R. 163
(CAT), Roth J; see *Hague Plant Ltd v
Hague* [2014] EWCA Civ 1609, [2015]
C.P. Rep. 14 (CA (Civ Div)), Briggs LJ;
see *Harris v Academies Enterprise Trust*
[2015] I.C.R. 617 (EAT), Langstaff J; see
Kensington and Chelsea RLBC v CD
[2015] UKUT 396 (AAC), [2015] E.L.R.
493 (UT (AAC)), Judge Rowley; see *R v
R (Family Court: Procedural Fairness)*
[2015] 1 W.L.R. 2743 (Fam Ct), Peter
Jackson J; see *R. (on the application of
Bar Standards Board) v Disciplinary*

*Tribunal of the Council of the Inns of
Court* [2014] EWHC 1570 (Admin),
[2015] 1 W.L.R. 2778 (QBD (Admin)),
Moses LJ; see *TCT Mobile Europe SAS v
Telefonaktiebolaget LM Ericsson* [2015]
EWHC 938 (Pat), [2015] F.S.R. 31 (Ch
D (Patents Ct)), Birss J
Part .44 r.44, see *Crouch v King's
Healthcare NHS Trust* [2004] EWCA
Civ 1332, [2005] 1 W.L.R. 2015 (CA
(Civ Div)), Waller LJ
Part 1 r.1.2, amended: SI 2015/406 r.3
Part 3 r.3.1, amended: SI 2015/1569 r.4
Part 3 r.3.1A, added: SI 2015/1569 r.5
Part 5 r.5.4D, amended: SI 2015/1569 r.6
Part 6 r.6.31, amended: SI 2015/1644
Sch.1 para.1
Part 6 r.6.33, amended: SI 2015/1644
Sch.1 para.2
Part 7 r.7.4, amended: SI 2015/1569 r.7
Part 12 r.12.10, amended: SI 2015/1644
Sch.1 para.3
Part 12 r.12.11, amended: SI 2015/1644
Sch.1 para.4
Part 25 r.25.13, amended: SI 2015/1644
Sch.1 para.5
Part 26 r.26.2A, amended: SI 2015/1881
r.4
Part 46 r.46.4, amended: SI 2015/670 r.5
Part 46 r.46.15, added: SI 2015/670 r.6
Part 47 r.47.6, amended: SI 2015/1569
r.8
Part 52 r.52.15B, added: SI 2015/1569
r.10
Part 54 r.54.5, amended: SI 2015/102
Sch.6 para.11
Part 54 r.54.8, added: SI 2015/670 r.8
Part 54 r.54.8, amended: SI 2015/670 r.7
Part 54 r.54.11, amended: SI 2015/670
r.9
Part 54 r.54.11A, added: SI 2015/670
r.10
Part 63A, added: SI 2015/1569 Sch.1
Part 74 r.74.1, amended: SI 2015/1644
Sch.1 para.6
Part 74 r.74.3, amended: SI 2015/1644
Sch.1 para.7
Part 74 r.74.4, amended: SI 2015/1644
Sch.1 para.8
Part 74 r.74.10, amended: SI 2015/1644
Sch.1 para.9

Part 74 r.74.11, amended: SI 2015/1644
Sch.1 para.10
Part 76 r.76.29, amended: SI 2015/877
r.5
Part 79 r.79.21, amended: SI 2015/877
r.6
Part 80 r.80.25, amended: SI 2015/877
r.7
Part 82 r.82.14, amended: SI 2015/877
r.8
Part 88, added: SI 2015/406 Sch.1
Part 88 r.88.2, amended: SI 2015/877 r.9
Part 88 r.88.9, amended: SI 2015/877 r.9
Part 88 r.88.24, amended: SI 2015/877
r.9
Part 88 r.88.28, amended: SI 2015/877
r.9
Pt 1., see *CDE SA v Sure Wind Marine
Ltd* [2015] EWHC 720 (Admlty), [2015]
2 Lloyd's Rep. 268 (QBD (Admlty)),
Jervis Kay QC, Admiralty Registrar
Pt 11., see *Teekay Tankers Ltd v STX
Offshore & Shipping Co* [2014] EWHC
3612 (Comm), [2015] 2 All E.R. (Comm)
263 (QBD (Comm)), Hamblen J
Pt 12., see *S v Beach* [2014] EWHC 4189
(QB), [2015] 1 W.L.R. 2701 (QBD),
Warby J
Pt 13., see *Newland Shipping and
Forwarding Ltd v Toba Trading FZC*
[2014] EWHC 210 (Comm), [2015] 1 All
E.R. (Comm) 735 (QBD (Comm)),
Hamblen J; see *S v Beach* [2014] EWHC
4189 (QB), [2015] 1 W.L.R. 2701
(QBD), Warby J
Pt 18., see *Dowling v Bennett Griffin*
[2014] EWCA Civ 1545, [2015] Lloyd's
Rep. I.R. 522 (CA (Civ Div)), Sullivan
LJ
Pt 19., see *R. (on the application of
British American Tobacco UK Ltd) v
Secretary of State for Health* [2014]
EWHC 3515 (Admin), [2015] 1
C.M.L.R. 35 (QBD (Admin)), Turner J
Pt 20., see *Wagenaar v Weekend Travel
Ltd (t/a Ski Weekend)* [2014] EWCA Civ
1105, [2015] 1 W.L.R. 1968 (CA (Civ
Div)), Laws LJ; see *WH Newson
Holding Ltd v IMI Plc* [2015] EWHC
1676 (Ch), [2015] 1 W.L.R. 4881 (Ch D),
Rose J

Pt 25., see *Financial Services Authority v
Asset LI Inc (t/a Asset Land Investment
Inc)* [2014] EWCA Civ 435, [2015] 1 All
E.R. 1 (CA (Civ Div)), Rimer LJ
Pt 26., see *Akhtar v Boland* [2014]
EWCA Civ 872, [2015] 1 All E.R. 644
(CA (Civ Div)), Gloster LJ
Pt 29., see *Kershaw v Roberts* [2014]
EWHC 1037 (Ch), [2015] 1 All E.R. 734
(Ch D), Hickinbottom J
Pt 31., see *National Crime Agency v
Abacha* [2015] EWHC 357 (Admin),
[2015] Lloyd's Rep. F.C. 411 (QBD
(Admin)), Elisabeth Laing J
Pt 32., see *Central Trading & Exports
Ltd v Fioralba Shipping Co* [2014]
EWHC 2397 (Comm), [2015] 1 All E.R.
(Comm) 580 (QBD (Comm)), Males J
Pt 35., see *Green v Revenue and Customs
Commissioners* [2015] UKFTT 334 (TC),
[2015] S.F.T.D. 711 (FTT (Tax)), Judge
Anne Redston; see *Kensington and
Chelsea RLBC v CD* [2015] UKUT 396
(AAC), [2015] E.L.R. 493 (UT (AAC)),
Judge Rowley; see *Rogers v Hoyle*
[2014] EWCA Civ 257, [2015] Q.B. 265
(CA (Civ Div)), Arden LJ; see *Six
Continents Ltd v Inland Revenue
Commissioners* [2015] EWHC 2884
(Ch), [2015] B.T.C. 29 (Ch D),
Henderson J
Pt 36., see *Altus Group (UK) Ltd v Baker
Tilly Tax and Advisory Services LLP*
[2015] EWHC 411 (Ch), [2015] 2 Costs
L.R. 267 (Ch D), Judge Keyser QC; see
*Chief Constable of Hampshire v
Southampton City Council* [2014] EWCA
Civ 1541, [2015] C.P. Rep. 13 (CA (Civ
Div)), Jackson LJ; see *Coward v
Phaestos Ltd* [2014] EWCA Civ 1256,
[2015] C.P. Rep. 2 (CA (Civ Div)),
Moore-Bick LJ; see *Gulati v MGN Ltd*
[2015] EWHC 1805 (Ch), [2015] 4 Costs
L.R. 659 (Ch D), Mann J; see *Husky
Group Ltd, Re* [2014] EWHC 3003 (Ch),
[2015] 3 Costs L.O. 337 (Ch D
(Birmingham)), Judge Purle QC; see
RXDX v Northampton BC [2015] EWHC
2938 (QB), [2015] 5 Costs L.R. 897
(QBD), Sir Colin Mackay; see *Shaw v
Merthyr Tydfil County Borough* [2014]

EWCA Civ 1678, [2015] P.I.Q.R. P8
(CA (Civ Div)), Maurice Kay LJ
Pt 44., see *Coward v Phaestos Ltd* [2014]
EWCA Civ 1256, [2015] C.P. Rep. 2
(CA (Civ Div)), Moore-Bick LJ; see
McGraddie v McGraddie [2015] UKSC
1, [2015] 1 W.L.R. 560 (SC), Lord
Neuberger PSC; see *S (Children)
(Appeal from Care and Placement
Orders), Re* [2015] UKSC 20, [2015] 1
W.L.R. 1631 (SC), Lady Hale DPSC
Pt 45., see *Dalton v British
Telecommunications Plc* [2015] EWHC
616 (QB), [2015] 5 Costs L.R. 787 (QBD
(Cardiff)), Phillips J
Pt 47., see *McGraddie v McGraddie*
[2015] UKSC 1, [2015] 1 W.L.R. 560
(SC), Lord Neuberger PSC
Pt 52., see *Miaris v Secretary of State for
Communities and Local Government*
[2015] EWHC 2094 (Admin), [2015] 1
W.L.R. 4333 (QBD (Admin)), John
Howell QC
Pt 55., see *Akerman-Livingstone v Aster
Communities Ltd (formerly Flourish
Homes Ltd)* [2015] UKSC 15, [2015]
A.C. 1399 (SC), Lord Neuberger PSC
Pt 6., see *Ashley v Tesco Stores Ltd*
[2015] EWCA Civ 414, [2015] 1 W.L.R.
5153 (CA (Civ Div)), Arden LJ; see
*Clavis Liberty Fund 1 LP v Revenue and
Customs Commissioners* [2015] UKUT
72 (TCC), [2015] 1 W.L.R. 2949 (UT
(Tax)), Warren J; see *Gate Gourmet
Luxembourg IV Sarl v Morby* [2015]
EWHC 1203 (Ch), [2015] B.P.I.R. 787
(Ch D), Registrar Briggs; see *Omni
Trustees Ltd, Re* [2015] EWHC 2122
(Ch), [2015] B.C.C. 644 (Ch D), Judge
Pelling QC
Pt 7., see *Gotch v Enelco Ltd* [2015]
EWHC 1802 (TCC), [2015] T.C.L.R. 8
(QBD (TCC)), Edwards-Stuart J
Pt 71., see *Dar Al Arkan Real Estate
Development Co v Al-Refai* [2014]
EWCA Civ 715, [2015] 1 W.L.R. 135
(CA (Civ Div)), Richards LJ
Pt 8., see *Leeds City Council v Waco UK
Ltd* [2015] EWHC 1400 (TCC), [2015]
T.C.L.R. 5 (QBD (TCC)), Edwards-
Stuart J; see *NRAM Plc v McAdam*

[2014] EWHC 4174 (Comm), [2015] 2
All E.R. 340 (QBD (Comm)), Burton J
r.1.1, see *Ashley v Tesco Stores Ltd*
[2015] EWCA Civ 414, [2015] 1 W.L.R.
5153 (CA (Civ Div)), Arden LJ; see
Simpson v MGN Ltd [2015] EWHC 126
(QB), [2015] 1 Costs L.R. 139 (QBD),
Warby J; see *TCT Mobile Europe SAS v
Telefonaktiebolaget LM Ericsson* [2015]
EWHC 938 (Pat), [2015] F.S.R. 31 (Ch
D (Patents Ct)), Birss J; see *Walsham
Chalet Park Ltd (t/a Dream Lodge
Group) v Tallington Lakes Ltd* [2014]
EWCA Civ 1607, [2015] C.P. Rep. 15
(CA (Civ Div)), Richards LJ; see *Yeo v
Times Newspapers Ltd* [2014] EWHC
2853 (QB), [2015] 1 W.L.R. 971 (QBD),
Warby J
r.1.3, see *Owners and/or Bailees of the
Panamax Star v Owners of the Auk*
[2013] EWHC 4076 (Admlty), [2015] 1
All E.R. (Comm) 292 (QBD (Admlty)),
Hamblen J
r.2.3, see *R. (on the application of HS2
Action Alliance Ltd) v Secretary of State
for Transport* [2015] EWCA Civ 203,
[2015] P.T.S.R. 1025 (CA (Civ Div)),
Longmore LJ
r.3.1, see *Altomart Ltd v Salford Estates
(No.2) Ltd* [2014] EWCA Civ 1408,
[2015] 1 W.L.R. 1825 (CA (Civ Div)),
Moore-Bick LJ; see *Calibre Solicitors
Ltd, Re* [2015] B.P.I.R. 435 (Ch D
(Companies Ct)), Registrar Jones; see
Cole v Howlett [2015] EWHC 1697 (Ch),
[2015] B.P.I.R. 763 (Ch D), Peter Smith
J; see *Gregory v Commissioner of Police
of the Metropolis* [2014] EWHC 3922
(QB), [2015] 1 W.L.R. 4253 (QBD),
Cranston J; see *Lawal v Circle 33
Housing Trust* [2014] EWCA Civ 1514,
[2015] H.L.R. 9 (CA (Civ Div)), Sir
Terence Etherton; see *Michael Wilson &
Partners Ltd v Sinclair* [2015] EWCA
Civ 774, [2015] C.P. Rep. 45 (CA (Civ
Div)), Richards LJ; see *Newland
Shipping and Forwarding Ltd v Toba
Trading FZC* [2014] EWHC 210
(Comm), [2015] 1 All E.R. (Comm) 735
(QBD (Comm)), Hamblen J; see *R. (on
the application of Hysaj) v Secretary of*

State for the Home Department [2014]
EWCA Civ 1633, [2015] 1 W.L.R. 2472
(CA (Civ Div)), Moore-Bick LJ; see *R.
(on the application of Paolo) v City of
London Magistrates' Court* [2014]
EWHC 2011 (Admin), [2015] L.L.R. 298
(QBD (Admin)), Laws LJ; see *S v Beach*
[2014] EWHC 4189 (QB), [2015] 1
W.L.R. 2701 (QBD), Warby J; see *S v S*
[2015] EWHC 1005 (Fam), [2015] 1
W.L.R. 4592 (Fam Div), Sir James
Munby PFD; see *Salt v Stratstone
Specialist Ltd (t/a Stratstone Cadillac
Newcastle)* [2015] EWCA Civ 745,
[2015] C.T.L.C. 206 (CA (Civ Div)),
Longmore LJ; see *Thevarajah v Riordan*
[2015] UKSC 78 (SC), Lord Neuberger
PSC
r.3.3, see *Clarke v Cognita Schools Ltd
(t/a Hydesville Tower School)* [2015]
EWHC 932 (Ch), [2015] 1 W.L.R. 3776
(Ch D (Birmingham)), Newey J
r.3.4, see *Fairford Group Ltd Plc (In
Liquidation) v Revenue and Customs
Commissioners* [2015] S.T.C. 156 (UT
(Tax)), Simon J; see *Walsham Chalet
Park Ltd (t/a Dream Lodge Group) v
Tallington Lakes Ltd* [2014] EWCA Civ
1607, [2015] C.P. Rep. 15 (CA (Civ
Div)), Richards LJ
r.3.8, see *Altomart Ltd v Salford Estates
(No.2) Ltd* [2014] EWCA Civ 1408,
[2015] 1 W.L.R. 1825 (CA (Civ Div)),
Moore-Bick LJ
r.3.9, see *Altomart Ltd v Salford Estates
(No.2) Ltd* [2014] EWCA Civ 1408,
[2015] 1 W.L.R. 1825 (CA (Civ Div)),
Moore-Bick LJ; see *Avanesov v
Shymkentpivo* [2015] EWHC 394
(Comm), [2015] 1 All E.R. (Comm) 1260
(QBD (Comm)), Popplewell J; see *BPP
University College of Professional
Studies v Revenue and Customs
Commissioners* [2015] S.T.C. 415 (UT
(Tax)), Judge Colin Bishopp; see *British
Gas Trading Ltd v Oak Cash and Carry
Ltd* [2014] EWHC 4058 (QB), [2015] 1
All E.R. (Comm) 1000 (QBD),
McGowan J; see *Chadwick v Burling*
[2015] EWHC 1610 (Ch), [2015] 3 Costs
L.R. 589 (Ch D), Warren J; see *Elliott v*

Stobart Group Ltd [2015] EWCA Civ
449, [2015] C.P. Rep. 36 (CA (Civ Div)),
Laws LJ; see *Groupe Eurotunnel SA v
Competition and Markets Authority*
[2015] CAT 4, [2015] Comp. A.R. 163
(CAT), Roth J; see *H (Children) (Care
Proceedings: Appeals out of Time)*
[2015] EWCA Civ 583, [2015] 1 W.L.R.
5085 (CA (Civ Div)), McFarlane LJ; see
Home Group Ltd v Matrejek [2015]
EWHC 441 (QB), [2015] 2 Costs L.O.
267 (QBD), Sweeney J; see *Leeds City
Council v Revenue and Customs
Commissioners* [2015] S.T.C. 168 (UT
(Tax)), Judge Colin Bishopp; see *Long v
Value Properties Ltd* [2014] EWHC 2981
(Ch), [2015] 3 All E.R. 419 (Ch D),
Barling J; see *Michael Wilson &
Partners Ltd v Sinclair* [2015] EWCA
Civ 774, [2015] C.P. Rep. 45 (CA (Civ
Div)), Richards LJ; see *Newland
Shipping and Forwarding Ltd v Toba
Trading FZC* [2014] EWHC 210
(Comm), [2015] 1 All E.R. (Comm) 735
(QBD (Comm)), Hamblen J; see *R. (on
the application of Hysaj) v Secretary of
State for the Home Department* [2014]
EWCA Civ 1633, [2015] 1 W.L.R. 2472
(CA (Civ Div)), Moore-Bick LJ; see
*Walsham Chalet Park Ltd (t/a Dream
Lodge Group) v Tallington Lakes Ltd*
[2014] EWCA Civ 1607, [2015] C.P.
Rep. 15 (CA (Civ Div)), Richards LJ
r.3.10, see *Stoute v LTA Operations Ltd
(t/a Lawn Tennis Association)* [2014]
EWCA Civ 657, [2015] 1 W.L.R. 79 (CA
(Civ Div)), Rimer LJ
r.3.12, see *CIP Properties (AIPT) Ltd v
Galliford Try Infrastructure Ltd* [2014]
EWHC 3546 (TCC), [2015] 1 All E.R.
(Comm) 765 (QBD (TCC)), Coulson J;
see *Dowling v Bennett Griffin* [2014]
EWCA Civ 1545, [2015] Lloyd's Rep.
I.R. 522 (CA (Civ Div)), Sullivan LJ
r.3.13, see *CIP Properties (AIPT) Ltd v
Galliford Try Infrastructure Ltd* [2014]
EWHC 3546 (TCC), [2015] 1 All E.R.
(Comm) 765 (QBD (TCC)), Coulson J
r.3.15, see *Hegglin v Person(s) Unknown*
[2014] EWHC 3793 (QB), [2015] 1
Costs L.O. 65 (QBD), Edis J; see

Various Claimants v McAlpine [2015] EWHC 3543 (QB), [2015] 6 Costs L.R. 1085 (QBD), Supperstone J

r.3.16, see *Yeo v Times Newspapers Ltd* [2015] EWHC 209 (QB), [2015] 1 W.L.R. 3031 (QBD), Warby J

r.3.18, see *Capital For Enterprise Fund A LP v Bibby Financial Services Ltd* [2015] 6 Costs L.R. 1059 (Ch D (Manchester)), Judge Pelling QC; see *Simpson v MGN Ltd* [2015] EWHC 126 (QB), [2015] 1 Costs L.R. 139 (QBD), Warby J; see *Thomas Pink Ltd v Victoria's Secret UK Ltd* [2014] EWHC 3258 (Ch), [2015] 3 Costs L.R. 463 (Ch D), Birss J

r.3.19, see *Hegglin v Person(s) Unknown* [2014] EWHC 3793 (QB), [2015] 1 Costs L.O. 65 (QBD), Edis J

r.5.4C, see *Eurasian Natural Resources Corp Ltd v Dechert LLP* [2014] EWHC 3389 (Ch), [2015] 1 W.L.R. 4621 (Ch D), Roth J

r.6.1, see *Ashley v Tesco Stores Ltd* [2015] EWCA Civ 414, [2015] 1 W.L.R. 5153 (CA (Civ Div)), Arden LJ

r.6.2, see *Dar Al Arkan Real Estate Development Co v Al-Refai* [2014] EWCA Civ 715, [2015] 1 W.L.R. 135 (CA (Civ Div)), Richards LJ

r.6.3, see *Ashley v Tesco Stores Ltd* [2015] EWCA Civ 414, [2015] 1 W.L.R. 5153 (CA (Civ Div)), Arden LJ

r.6.4, see *Stoute v LTA Operations Ltd (t/a Lawn Tennis Association)* [2014] EWCA Civ 657, [2015] 1 W.L.R. 79 (CA (Civ Div)), Rimer LJ

r.6.7, see *Ashley v Tesco Stores Ltd* [2015] EWCA Civ 414, [2015] 1 W.L.R. 5153 (CA (Civ Div)), Arden LJ

r.6.9, see *Ashley v Tesco Stores Ltd* [2015] EWCA Civ 414, [2015] 1 W.L.R. 5153 (CA (Civ Div)), Arden LJ; see *Teekay Tankers Ltd v STX Offshore & Shipping Co* [2014] EWHC 3612 (Comm), [2015] 2 All E.R. (Comm) 263 (QBD (Comm)), Hamblen J

r.6.14, see *Heron Bros Ltd v Central Bedfordshire Council* [2015] EWHC 604 (TCC), [2015] P.T.S.R. 1146 (QBD (TCC)), Edwards-Stuart J

r.6.15, see *Gate Gourmet Luxembourg IV Sarl v Morby* [2015] EWHC 1203 (Ch), [2015] B.P.I.R. 787 (Ch D), Registrar Briggs; see *Omni Trustees Ltd, Re* [2015] EWHC 2122 (Ch), [2015] B.C.C. 644 (Ch D), Judge Pelling QC

r.6.36, see *Dar Al Arkan Real Estate Development Co v Al-Refai* [2014] EWCA Civ 715, [2015] 1 W.L.R. 135 (CA (Civ Div)), Richards LJ

r.6.40, see *Ashley v Tesco Stores Ltd* [2015] EWCA Civ 414, [2015] 1 W.L.R. 5153 (CA (Civ Div)), Arden LJ; see *Sloutsker v Romanova* [2015] EWHC 545 (QB), [2015] 2 Costs L.R. 321 (QBD), Warby J

r.7.2, see *Sands v Singh* [2015] EWHC 2219 (Ch), [2015] B.P.I.R. 1293 (Ch D (Birmingham)), Judge Purle QC

r.7.5, see *Ashley v Tesco Stores Ltd* [2015] EWCA Civ 414, [2015] 1 W.L.R. 5153 (CA (Civ Div)), Arden LJ; see *Heron Bros Ltd v Central Bedfordshire Council* [2015] EWHC 604 (TCC), [2015] P.T.S.R. 1146 (QBD (TCC)), Edwards-Stuart J

r.7.6, see *CDE SA v Sure Wind Marine Ltd* [2015] EWHC 720 (Admlty), [2015] 2 Lloyd's Rep. 268 (QBD (Admlty)), Jervis Kay QC, Admiralty Registrar; see *Stoute v LTA Operations Ltd (t/a Lawn Tennis Association)* [2014] EWCA Civ 657, [2015] 1 W.L.R. 79 (CA (Civ Div)), Rimer LJ

r.8.1, see *Gotch v Enelco Ltd* [2015] EWHC 1802 (TCC), [2015] T.C.L.R. 8 (QBD (TCC)), Edwards-Stuart J

r.8.2, see *Dellal v Dellal* [2015] EWHC 907 (Fam), [2015] W.T.L.R. 1137 (Fam Div), Mostyn J

r.11, see *Deutsche Bank AG London Branch v Petromena ASA* [2015] EWCA Civ 226, [2015] 1 W.L.R. 4225 (CA (Civ Div)), Longmore LJ; see *PCL v Regional Government of X* [2015] EWHC 68 (Comm), [2015] 1 W.L.R. 3948 (QBD (Comm)), Hamblen J; see *R. (on the application of Williams) v Secretary of State for Energy and Climate Change* [2015] EWHC 1202 (Admin), [2015] J.P.L. 1257 (QBD (Admin)), Lindblom J

r.12.4, see *S v Beach* [2014] EWHC 4189 (QB), [2015] 1 W.L.R. 2701 (QBD), Warby J

r.12.11, see *Thevarajah v Riordan* [2015] EWCA Civ 41, [2015] C.P. Rep. 19 (CA (Civ Div)), Richards LJ

r.13.3, see *Abdelmamoud v Egyptian Association in Great Britain Ltd* [2015] EWHC 1013 (Ch), [2015] Bus. L.R. 928 (Ch D), Edward Murray; see *Avanesov v Shymkentpivo* [2015] EWHC 394 (Comm), [2015] 1 All E.R. (Comm) 1260 (QBD (Comm)), Popplewell J

r.17.1, see *Gregory v Commissioner of Police of the Metropolis* [2014] EWHC 3922 (QB), [2015] 1 W.L.R. 4253 (QBD), Cranston J; see *Hertel v Saunders* [2015] EWHC 2848 (Ch), [2015] 5 Costs L.R. 825 (Ch D), Morgan J

r.19.5, see *American Leisure Group Ltd v Olswang LLP* [2015] EWHC 629 (Ch), [2015] P.N.L.R. 21 (Ch D), Judge Walden-Smith

r.19.6, see *Rendlesham Estates Plc v Barr Ltd* [2014] EWHC 3968 (TCC), [2015] 1 W.L.R. 3663 (QBD (TCC)), Edwards-Stuart J

r.21.4, see *Bradbury v Paterson* [2014] EWHC 3992 (QB), [2015] C.O.P.L.R. 425 (QBD), Foskett J

r.21.7, see *Bradbury v Paterson* [2014] EWHC 3992 (QB), [2015] C.O.P.L.R. 425 (QBD), Foskett J

r.23.5, see *Sands v Singh* [2015] EWHC 2219 (Ch), [2015] B.P.I.R. 1293 (Ch D (Birmingham)), Judge Purle QC

r.23.11, see *Carlton Advisory Services v Dorchester Holdings Ltd* [2014] EWHC 3341 (Comm), [2015] 1 Costs L.R. 1 (QBD (Merc)), Judge Mackie QC

r.24.2, see *Iliffe v Feltham Construction Ltd* [2015] EWCA Civ 715, [2015] C.P. Rep. 41 (CA (Civ Div)), Jackson LJ; see *Vince v Wyatt* [2015] UKSC 14, [2015] 1 W.L.R. 1228 (SC), Lady Hale DPSC

r.25.1, see *Wood v Baker* [2015] EWHC 2536 (Ch), [2015] B.P.I.R. 1524 (Ch D), Judge Hodge QC

r.25.12, see *Harlequin Property (SVG) Ltd v Wilkins Kennedy* [2015] EWHC

1122 (TCC), [2015] B.L.R. 469 (QBD (TCC)), Coulson J

r.25.13, see *GSM Export (UK) Ltd (In Administration) v Revenue and Customs Commissioners* [2015] S.T.C. 504 (UT (Tax)), Judge Roger Berner; see *Harlequin Property (SVG) Ltd v Wilkins Kennedy* [2015] EWHC 1122 (TCC), [2015] B.L.R. 469 (QBD (TCC)), Coulson J; see *Monde Petroleum SA v Westernzagros Ltd* [2015] EWHC 67 (Comm), [2015] 1 Lloyd's Rep. 330 (QBD (Comm)), Popplewell J; see *Peak Hotels and Resorts Ltd v Tarek Investments Ltd* [2015] EWHC 386 (Ch), [2015] 2 Costs L.R. 277 (Ch D), Henderson J

r.26.8, see *Akhtar v Boland* [2014] EWCA Civ 872, [2015] 1 All E.R. 644 (CA (Civ Div)), Gloster LJ

r.26.10, see *Conlon v Royal Sun Alliance Insurance Plc* [2015] EWCA Civ 92, [2015] C.P. Rep. 23 (CA (Civ Div)), Jackson LJ

r.26.11, see *Gregory v Commissioner of Police of the Metropolis* [2014] EWHC 3922 (QB), [2015] 1 W.L.R. 4253 (QBD), Cranston J

r.27.14, see *Chaplair Ltd v Kumari* [2015] EWCA Civ 798, [2015] C.P. Rep. 46 (CA (Civ Div)), Arden LJ; see *Conlon v Royal Sun Alliance Insurance Plc* [2015] EWCA Civ 92, [2015] C.P. Rep. 23 (CA (Civ Div)), Jackson LJ

r.31.5, see *Big Bus Co Ltd v Ticketogo Ltd* [2015] EWHC 1094 (Pat), [2015] Bus. L.R. 867 (Ch D (Patents Ct)), Arnold J

r.31.12, see *Dellal v Dellal* [2015] EWHC 907 (Fam), [2015] W.T.L.R. 1137 (Fam Div), Mostyn J; see *Stocker v Stocker* [2015] EWHC 1634 (QB), [2015] 4 Costs L.R. 651 (QBD), Warby J

r.31.14, see *National Crime Agency v Abacha* [2015] EWHC 357 (Admin), [2015] Lloyd's Rep. F.C. 411 (QBD (Admin)), Elisabeth Laing J

r.31.15, see *National Crime Agency v Abacha* [2015] EWHC 357 (Admin), [2015] Lloyd's Rep. F.C. 411 (QBD (Admin)), Elisabeth Laing J r.31.16, see *Big Bus Co Ltd v Ticketogo Ltd* [2015] EWHC 1094 (Pat), [2015] Bus. L.R. 867 (Ch D (Patents Ct)), Arnold J; see *Jet Airways (India) Ltd v Barloworld Handling Ltd* [2014] EWCA Civ 1311, [2015] C.P. Rep. 4 (CA (Civ Div)), Moore-Bick LJ

r.31.17, see *L v R* [2015] EWCA Civ 61, Times, April 7, 2015 (CA (Civ Div)), Aikens LJ

r.31.18, see *Simpson v MGN Ltd* [2015] EWHC 126 (QB), [2015] 1 Costs L.R. 139 (QBD), Warby J

r.31.19, see *Harlequin Property (SVG) Ltd v Wilkins Kennedy* [2015] EWHC 3050 (TCC), [2015] 6 Costs L.R. 925 (QBD (TCC)), Coulson J

r.31.20, see *Tchenguiz v Director of the Serious Fraud Office* [2014] EWCA Civ 1129, [2015] 1 W.L.R. 797 (CA (Civ Div)), Longmore LJ

r.31.22, see *AC Nielsen Co Ltd v Competition and Markets Authority* [2015] Comp. A.R. 32 (CAT), Sales J; see *Tchenguiz v Director of the Serious Fraud Office* [2014] EWHC 4199 (Comm), [2015] Lloyd's Rep. F.C. 180 (QBD (Comm)), Eder J; see *Tchenguiz v Serious Fraud Office* [2014] EWCA Civ 1471, [2015] C.P. Rep. 9 (CA (Civ Div)), Jackson LJ; see *Thomas Pink Ltd v Victoria's Secret UK Ltd* [2014] EWHC 3258 (Ch), [2015] 3 Costs L.R. 463 (Ch D), Birss J

r.32.10, see *Fouda v Southwark LBC* [2015] EWHC 1128 (QB), [2015] 3 Costs L.O. 397 (QBD), Cranston J; see *Walsham Chalet Park Ltd (t/a Dream Lodge Group) v Tallington Lakes Ltd* [2014] EWCA Civ 1607, [2015] C.P. Rep. 15 (CA (Civ Div)), Richards LJ

r.34.13, see *TCT Mobile Europe SAS v Telefonaktiebolaget LM Ericsson* [2015] EWHC 938 (Pat), [2015] F.S.R. 31 (Ch D (Patents Ct)), Birss J

r.35.1, see *British Airways Plc v Spencer* [2015] EWHC 2477 (Ch), [2015] Pens. L.R. 519 (Ch D), Warren J

r.36.1, see *Crouch v King's Healthcare NHS Trust* [2004] EWCA Civ 1332, [2005] 1 W.L.R. 2015 (CA (Civ Div)),

Waller LJ; see *Shaw v Merthyr Tydfil County Borough* [2014] EWCA Civ 1678, [2015] P.I.Q.R. P8 (CA (Civ Div)), Maurice Kay LJ

r.36.2, see *Hertel v Saunders* [2015] EWHC 2848 (Ch), [2015] 5 Costs L.R. 825 (Ch D), Morgan J; see *Shaw v Merthyr Tydfil County Borough* [2014] EWCA Civ 1678, [2015] P.I.Q.R. P8 (CA (Civ Div)), Maurice Kay LJ

r.36.3, see *Crouch v King's Healthcare NHS Trust* [2004] EWCA Civ 1332, [2005] 1 W.L.R. 2015 (CA (Civ Div)), Waller LJ; see *Dutton v Minards* [2015] EWCA Civ 984, [2015] 6 Costs L.R. 1047 (CA (Civ Div)), Lewison LJ; see *Shaw v Merthyr Tydfil County Borough* [2014] EWCA Civ 1678, [2015] P.I.Q.R. P8 (CA (Civ Div)), Maurice Kay LJ

r.36.4, see *Ted Baker Plc v AXA Insurance UK Plc* [2014] EWHC 4178 (Comm), [2015] 1 Costs L.R. 71 (QBD (Comm)), Eder J

r.36.10, see *Dutton v Minards* [2015] EWCA Civ 984, [2015] 6 Costs L.R. 1047 (CA (Civ Div)), Lewison LJ

r.36.11, see *Evans v Royal Wolverhampton Hospitals NHS Foundation Trust* [2014] EWHC 3185 (QB), [2015] 1 W.L.R. 4659 (QBD), Leggatt J

r.36.14, see *Cashman v Mid Essex Hospital Services NHS Trust* [2015] EWHC 1312 (QB), [2015] 3 Costs L.O. 411 (QBD), Slade J; see *Coward v Phaestos Ltd* [2014] EWCA Civ 1256, [2015] C.P. Rep. 2 (CA (Civ Div)), Moore-Bick LJ; see *Downing v Peterborough and Stamford Hospitals NHS Foundation Trust* [2014] EWHC 4216 (QB), [2015] 2 Costs L.O. 203 (QBD), Sir David Eady; see *Husky Group Ltd, Re* [2014] EWHC 3003 (Ch), [2015] 3 Costs L.O. 337 (Ch D (Birmingham)), Judge Purle QC; see *RXDX v Northampton BC* [2015] EWHC 2938 (QB), [2015] 5 Costs L.R. 897 (QBD), Sir Colin Mackay; see *Ted Baker Plc v AXA Insurance UK Plc* [2014] EWHC 4178 (Comm), [2015] 1 Costs L.R. 71 (QBD (Comm)), Eder J;

see *Webb v Liverpool Women's NHS
Foundation Trust* [2015] EWHC 449
(QB), [2015] 3 Costs L.O. 367 (QBD
(Leeds)), Judge Saffman
r.36.17, see *Altus Group (UK) Ltd v
Baker Tilly Tax and Advisory Services
LLP* [2015] EWHC 411 (Ch), [2015] 2
Costs L.R. 267 (Ch D), Judge Keyser
QC; see *Thai Airways International
Public Co Ltd v KI Holdings Co Ltd
(formerly Koito Industries Ltd)* [2015]
EWHC 1476 (Comm), [2015] 3 Costs
L.R. 545 (QBD (Comm)), Leggatt J; see
Yentob v MGN Ltd [2015] EWCA Civ
1292, [2015] 6 Costs L.R. 1103 (CA (Civ
Div)), Arden LJ
r.36.20, see *Crouch v King's Healthcare
NHS Trust* [2004] EWCA Civ 1332,
[2005] 1 W.L.R. 2015 (CA (Civ Div)),
Waller LJ
r.38.6, see *Adaptive Spectrum and Signal
Alignment Inc v British
Telecommunications Plc* [2014] EWHC
80 (Pat), [2015] F.S.R. 5 (Ch D (Patents
Ct)), Birss J
r.38.7, see *Hague Plant Ltd v Hague*
[2014] EWCA Civ 1609, [2015] C.P.
Rep. 14 (CA (Civ Div)), Briggs LJ
r.39.2, see *Eurasian Natural Resources
Corp Ltd v Dechert LLP* [2014] EWHC
3389 (Ch), [2015] 1 W.L.R. 4621 (Ch D),
Roth J; see *V v T* [2014] EWHC 3432
(Ch), [2015] W.T.L.R. 173 (Ch D),
Morgan J; see *X (A Child) v Dartford
and Gravesham NHS Trust* [2015]
EWCA Civ 96, [2015] 1 W.L.R. 3647
(CA (Civ Div)), Moore-Bick LJ
r.40.8, see *Involnert Management Inc v
Aprilgrange Ltd* [2015] EWHC 2834
(Comm), [2015] 5 Costs L.R. 813 (QBD
(Comm)), Leggatt LJ
r.40.9, see *Abdelmamoud v Egyptian
Association in Great Britain Ltd* [2015]
EWHC 1013 (Ch), [2015] Bus. L.R. 928
(Ch D), Edward Murray
r.40.20, see *JM (A Child), Re* [2015]
EWHC 2832 (Fam), [2015] Med. L.R.
544 (Fam Div), Mostyn J
r.43.2, see *Yeo v Times Newspapers Ltd*
[2014] EWHC 2853 (QB), [2015] 1
W.L.R. 971 (QBD), Warby J

r.44.2, see *Capital For Enterprise Fund
A LP v Bibby Financial Services Ltd*
[2015] 6 Costs L.R. 1059 (Ch D
(Manchester)), Judge Pelling QC; see
Coward v Phaestos Ltd [2014] EWCA
Civ 1256, [2015] C.P. Rep. 2 (CA (Civ
Div)), Moore-Bick LJ; see *French v
Carter Lemon Camerons LLP* [2015] 2
Costs L.O. 179 (QBD), Swift J; see
*Northrop Grumman Mission Systems
Europe Ltd v BAE Systems (Al Diriyah
C4I) Ltd* [2014] EWHC 3148 (TCC),
[2015] 3 All E.R. 782 (QBD (TCC)),
Ramsey J; see *S (Children) (Appeal from
Care and Placement Orders), Re* [2015]
UKSC 20, [2015] 1 W.L.R. 1631 (SC),
Lady Hale DPSC; see *Sugar Hut Group
Ltd v AJ Insurance* [2014] EWHC 3775
(Comm), [2015] 2 Costs L.R. 179 (QBD
(Comm)), Eder J; see *Ted Baker Plc v
AXA Insurance UK Plc* [2014] EWHC
4178 (Comm), [2015] 1 Costs L.R. 71
(QBD (Comm)), Eder J
r.44.3, see *CIP Properties (AIPT) Ltd v
Galliford Try Infrastructure Ltd* [2015]
EWHC 481 (TCC), [2015] B.L.R. 285
(QBD (TCC)), Coulson J; see *Crouch v
King's Healthcare NHS Trust* [2004]
EWCA Civ 1332, [2005] 1 W.L.R. 2015
(CA (Civ Div)), Waller LJ; see *Gulati v
MGN Ltd* [2015] EWHC 1805 (Ch),
[2015] 4 Costs L.R. 659 (Ch D), Mann J;
see *Yeo v Times Newspapers Ltd* [2015]
EWHC 209 (QB), [2015] 1 W.L.R. 3031
(QBD), Warby J
r.44.3B, see *Long v Value Properties Ltd*
[2014] EWHC 2981 (Ch), [2015] 3 All
E.R. 419 (Ch D), Barling J
r.44.4, see *Coventry v Lawrence* [2015]
UKSC 50, [2015] 1 W.L.R. 3485 (SC),
Lord Neuberger PSC; see *Kelly v Hays
Plc* [2015] EWHC 735 (QB), [2015] 5
Costs L.O. 595 (QBD), Jeremy Baker J
r.44.6, see *Transformers and Rectifiers
Ltd v Needs Ltd* [2015] EWHC 1687
(TCC), [2015] 3 Costs L.R. 611 (QBD
(TCC)), Coulson J
r.44.13, see *Wagenaar v Weekend Travel
Ltd (t/a Ski Weekend)* [2014] EWCA Civ
1105, [2015] 1 W.L.R. 1968 (CA (Civ
Div)), Laws LJ

r.44.14, see *Wagenaar v Weekend Travel Ltd (t/a Ski Weekend)* [2014] EWCA Civ 1105, [2015] 1 W.L.R. 1968 (CA (Civ Div)), Laws LJ

r.44.15, see *Yeo v Times Newspapers Ltd* [2014] EWHC 2853 (QB), [2015] 1 W.L.R. 971 (QBD), Warby J

r.44.16, see *Wagenaar v Weekend Travel Ltd (t/a Ski Weekend)* [2014] EWCA Civ 1105, [2015] 1 W.L.R. 1968 (CA (Civ Div)), Laws LJ

r.44.17, see *Wagenaar v Weekend Travel Ltd (t/a Ski Weekend)* [2014] EWCA Civ 1105, [2015] 1 W.L.R. 1968 (CA (Civ Div)), Laws LJ

r.45.15, see *James v Ireland* [2015] EWHC 1259 (QB), [2015] 3 Costs L.R. 511 (QBD), Slade J

r.45.16, see *James v Ireland* [2015] EWHC 1259 (QB), [2015] 3 Costs L.R. 511 (QBD), Slade J

r.45.17, see *James v Ireland* [2015] EWHC 1259 (QB), [2015] 3 Costs L.R. 511 (QBD), Slade J

r.45.31, see *Akhtar v Bhopal Productions (UK) Ltd* [2015] EWHC 154 (IPEC), [2015] F.S.R. 30 (IPEC), Judge Hacon

r.45.32, see *Akhtar v Bhopal Productions (UK) Ltd* [2015] EWHC 154 (IPEC), [2015] F.S.R. 30 (IPEC), Judge Hacon

r.45.41, see *R. (on the application of HS2 Action Alliance Ltd) v Secretary of State for Transport* [2015] EWCA Civ 203, [2015] P.T.S.R. 1025 (CA (Civ Div)), Longmore LJ; see *Venn v Secretary of State for Communities and Local Government* [2014] EWCA Civ 1539, [2015] 1 W.L.R. 2328 (CA (Civ Div)), Sullivan LJ

r.45.43, see *R. (on the application of HS2 Action Alliance Ltd) v Secretary of State for Transport* [2015] EWCA Civ 203, [2015] P.T.S.R. 1025 (CA (Civ Div)), Longmore LJ; see *R. (on the application of Luton BC) v Central Bedfordshire Council* [2015] EWCA Civ 537, [2015] 2 P. & C.R. 19 (CA (Civ Div)), Longmore LJ

r.46.5, see *Halborg v EMW Law LLP* [2015] EWHC 2005 (Ch), [2015] 4 Costs L.O. 427 (Ch D), Judge Purle QC

r.46.13, see *Conlon v Royal Sun Alliance Insurance Plc* [2015] EWCA Civ 92, [2015] C.P. Rep. 23 (CA (Civ Div)), Jackson LJ

r.47.6, see *Long v Value Properties Ltd* [2014] EWHC 2981 (Ch), [2015] 3 All E.R. 419 (Ch D), Barling J

r.47.7, see *Involnert Management Inc v Aprilgrange Ltd* [2015] EWHC 2834 (Comm), [2015] 5 Costs L.R. 813 (QBD (Comm)), Leggatt LJ

r.47.12, see *Edray Ltd v Canning* [2015] EWHC 2744 (Ch), [2015] 5 Costs L.R. 877 (Ch D), Stephen Jourdan QC

r.48.1, see *Wagenaar v Weekend Travel Ltd (t/a Ski Weekend)* [2014] EWCA Civ 1105, [2015] 1 W.L.R. 1968 (CA (Civ Div)), Laws LJ

r.48.2, see *Wagenaar v Weekend Travel Ltd (t/a Ski Weekend)* [2014] EWCA Civ 1105, [2015] 1 W.L.R. 1968 (CA (Civ Div)), Laws LJ

r.48.6, see *R. (on the application of Bar Standards Board) v Disciplinary Tribunal of the Council of the Inns of Court* [2014] EWHC 1570 (Admin), [2015] 1 W.L.R. 2778 (QBD (Admin)), Moses LJ

r.52.1, see *Miaris v Secretary of State for Communities and Local Government* [2015] EWHC 2094 (Admin), [2015] 1 W.L.R. 4333 (QBD (Admin)), John Howell QC

r.52.3, see *AB v CB (Financial Remedies: Variation of Trust)* [2015] EWCA Civ 447, [2015] C.P. Rep. 34 (CA (Civ Div)), Jackson LJ

r.52.4, see *R. (on the application of Hysaj) v Secretary of State for the Home Department* [2014] EWCA Civ 1633, [2015] 1 W.L.R. 2472 (CA (Civ Div)), Moore-Bick LJ

r.52.5, see *Altomart Ltd v Salford Estates (No.2) Ltd* [2014] EWCA Civ 1408, [2015] 1 W.L.R. 1825 (CA (Civ Div)), Moore-Bick LJ

r.52.9, see *Compania Sud Americana de Vapores SA v Hin-Pro International Logistics Ltd* [2015] EWCA Civ 401, [2015] 2 Lloyd's Rep. 1 (CA (Civ Div)), Elias LJ; see *Michael Wilson & Partners*

Ltd v Sinclair [2015] EWCA Civ 774,
[2015] C.P. Rep. 45 (CA (Civ Div)),
Richards LJ
r.52.11, see *JG (Jamaica) v Secretary of
State for the Home Department* [2015]
EWCA Civ 215, [2015] C.P. Rep. 24
(CA (Civ Div)), Jackson LJ; see *Uddin v
Islington LBC* [2015] EWCA Civ 369,
[2015] H.L.R. 28 (CA (Civ Div)),
Pitchford LJ
r.52.13, see *Miaris v Secretary of State
for Communities and Local Government*
[2015] EWHC 2094 (Admin), [2015] 1
W.L.R. 4333 (QBD (Admin)), John
Howell QC
r.52.14, see *Campbell v Thomas Cook
Tour Operations Ltd* [2014] EWCA Civ
1668, [2015] 1 W.L.R. 2007 (CA (Civ
Div)), Longmore LJ
r.52.17, see *Bishop v Chhokar* [2015]
EWCA Civ 24, [2015] C.P. Rep. 26 (CA
(Civ Div)), Aikens LJ; see *Lawal v
Circle 33 Housing Trust* [2014] EWCA
Civ 1514, [2015] H.L.R. 9 (CA (Civ
Div)), Sir Terence Etherton; see
McIntyre v United States [2014] EWHC
1886 (Admin), [2015] 1 W.L.R. 507
(DC), Lord Thomas LCJ; see *R. (on the
application of Harkins) v Secretary of
State for the Home Department* [2014]
EWHC 3609 (Admin), [2015] 1 W.L.R.
2975 (QBD (Admin)), Aikens LJ
r.54.2, see *R. (on the application of
Croydon Property Forum Ltd) v Croydon
LBC* [2015] EWHC 2403 (Admin),
[2015] L.L.R. 812 (QBD (Admin)), Sir
Stephen Silber
r.54.17, see *R. (on the application of
British American Tobacco UK Ltd) v
Secretary of State for Health* [2014]
EWHC 3515 (Admin), [2015] 1
C.M.L.R. 35 (QBD (Admin)), Turner J
r.57.7, see *Breslin v Bromley* [2015]
EWHC 3760 (Ch), [2015] 6 Costs L.R.
1115 (Ch D), Newey J; see *Randall v
Randall* [2014] EWHC 3134 (Ch), [2015]
W.T.L.R. 99 (Ch D), Deputy Master
Collaco Moraes
r.61.10, see *Bank of Tokyo-Mitsubishi
UFJ Ltd v Owners of the Sanko Mineral*
[2014] EWHC 3927 (Admlty), [2015] 2

All E.R. (Comm) 979 (QBD (Admlty)),
Teare J
r.62.5, see *Cruz City 1 Mauritius
Holdings v Unitech Ltd* [2014] EWHC
3704 (Comm), [2015] 1 All E.R. (Comm)
305 (QBD (Comm)), Males J; see
*Shipowners' Mutual Protection and
Indemnity Association (Luxembourg) v
Containerships Denizcilik Nakliyat ve
Ticaret AS* [2015] EWHC 258 (Comm),
[2015] 1 All E.R. (Comm) 966 (QBD
(Comm)), Teare J
r.62.18, see *Y v S* [2015] EWHC 612
(Comm), [2015] 2 All E.R. (Comm) 85
(QBD (Comm)), Eder J
r.63.10, see *Rovi Solutions Corp v Virgin
Media Ltd* [2014] EWHC 1793 (Pat),
[2015] R.P.C. 5 (Ch D), Mann J
r.63.26, see *Akhtar v Bhopal Productions
(UK) Ltd* [2015] EWHC 154 (IPEC),
[2015] F.S.R. 30 (IPEC), Judge Hacon
r.67.2, see *Birchall (A Bankrupt), Re*
[2015] EWHC 1541 (Ch), [2015]
B.P.I.R. 751 (Ch D (Manchester)), Judge
Pelling QC
r.73.8, see *National Bank of Greece
(Cyprus) Ltd v Christofi* [2015] EWHC
986 (QB), [2015] 1 W.L.R. 5405 (QBD),
Andrews J
r.74.8, see *National Bank of Greece
(Cyprus) Ltd v Christofi* [2015] EWHC
986 (QB), [2015] 1 W.L.R. 5405 (QBD),
Andrews J
r.81.4, see *Dar Al Arkan Real Estate
Development Co v Al-Refai* [2014]
EWCA Civ 715, [2015] 1 W.L.R. 135
(CA (Civ Div)), Richards LJ
r.81.10, see *Dar Al Arkan Real Estate
Development Co v Al-Refai* [2014]
EWCA Civ 715, [2015] 1 W.L.R. 135
(CA (Civ Div)), Richards LJ
Sch.1 Ord.54, see *Justice for Families
Ltd v Secretary of State for Justice* [2014]
EWCA Civ 1477, [2015] 2 F.L.R. 321
(CA (Civ Div)), Sir James Munby PFD
**3149. Health Service Commissioner for
England (London Post-Graduate Teaching
Hospitals Designation Orders) Revocation
Order 1998**
revoked: SI 2015/822 Art.2

3234. Financial Assistance for Environmental Purposes (No.4) Order 1998
revoked: SI 2015/479 Sch.1

1999

71. Allocation of Housing and Homelessness (Review Procedures) Regulations 1999
revoked: SI 2015/1266 Reg.8
see *Temur v Hackney LBC* [2014] EWCA
Civ 877, [2015] 1 All E.R. 311 (CA (Civ
Div)), Jackson LJ
Reg.2, see *Temur v Hackney LBC* [2014]
EWCA Civ 877, [2015] 1 All E.R. 311
(CA (Civ Div)), Jackson LJ
Reg.8, see *Mohamoud v Birmingham
City Council* [2014] EWCA Civ 227,
[2015] P.T.S.R. 17 (CA (Civ Div)),
Moore-Bick LJ; see *Temur v Hackney
LBC* [2014] EWCA Civ 877, [2015] 1
All E.R. 311 (CA (Civ Div)), Jackson LJ

292. Housing (Right to Buy) (Limits on Discount) (Wales) Order 1999
Art.3, amended: SI 2015/1349 Art.3

293. Town and Country Planning (Environmental Impact Assessment) (England and Wales) Regulations 1999
see *R. (on the application of Davies) v
Carmarthenshire CC* [2015] EWHC 230
(Admin), [2015] Env. L.R. 29 (QBD
(Admin)), Gilbart J
Sch.3, see *R. (on the application of
Davies) v Carmarthenshire CC* [2015]
EWHC 230 (Admin), [2015] Env. L.R.
29 (QBD (Admin)), Gilbart J

491. Criminal Legal Aid (Fixed Payments) (Scotland) Regulations 1999
see *Scottish Legal Aid Board v Lavery*
2015 S.L.T. (Sh Ct) 35 (Sh Ct
(Glasgow)), Sheriff A D Miller
Reg.2, amended: SSI 2015/337 Reg.5
Reg.4, see *Scottish Legal Aid Board v
Lavery* 2015 S.L.T. (Sh Ct) 35 (Sh Ct
(Glasgow)), Sheriff A D Miller
Sch.1 Part 1, amended: SSI 2015/337
Reg.5

503. Deregulation (Weights and Measures) Order 1999
Art.2, revoked: 2015 c.15 Sch.6 para.85

584. National Minimum Wage Regulations 1999
see *Revenue and Customs Commissioners
v Lorne Stewart Plc* [2015] I.C.R. 708
(EAT), Judge Shanks
Reg.4, see *Shannon v Rampersad (t/a
Clifton House Residential Home)* [2015]
I.R.L.R. 982 (EAT), Judge Peter Clark
Reg.12, see *Daler-Rowney Ltd v Revenue
and Customs Commissioners* [2015]
I.C.R. 632 (EAT), Langstaff J
Reg.16, see *Shannon v Rampersad (t/a
Clifton House Residential Home)* [2015]
I.R.L.R. 982 (EAT), Judge Peter Clark
Reg.33, see *Revenue and Customs
Commissioners v Lorne Stewart Plc*
[2015] I.C.R. 708 (EAT), Judge Shanks

614. Local Authorities Traffic Orders (Procedure) (Scotland) Regulations 1999
see *Hillhead Community Council v City
of Glasgow Council* [2015] CSOH 35,
2015 S.L.T. 239 (OH), Lord Bannatyne

728. Prison Rules 1999
r.45, see *R. (on the application of King) v
Secretary of State for Justice* [2015]
UKSC 54, [2015] 3 W.L.R. 457 (SC),
Lord Neuberger PSC

743. Control of Major Accident Hazards Regulations 1999
revoked: SI 2015/483 Reg.31

753. High Court of Justiciary Fees Amendment Order 1999
revoked: SSI 2015/262 Sch.4

755. Court of Session etc Fees Amendment Order 1999
revoked: SSI 2015/261 Sch.4

929. Act of Sederunt (Summary Applications, Statutory Applications and Appeals etc Rules) 1999
Part 2 r.2.21, revoked: SSI 2015/419 r.9
Part 2 r.2.25, amended: SSI 2015/419 r.9
Part 2 r.2.28, amended: SSI 2015/419 r.9
Part 2 r.2.42, amended: SSI 2015/419 r.9
Part 3, revoked: SSI 2015/419 r.9
Part 3, added: SSI 2015/283 r.7
Part 3 r.3.35.8, revoked: SSI 2015/419 r.9
Part 3 r.3.35.8, substituted: SSI 2015/419
r.9
Part 3 r.3.41.1, substituted: SSI 2015/85
r.4

Part 3 r.3.45.11, amended: SSI 2015/419
r.9
Pt 3., see *Dunn v Y* 2015 S.L.T. (Sh Ct)
113 (Sh Ct (Lothian) (Edinburgh)),
Sheriff T Welsh, QC
Sch.1, amended: SSI 2015/283 Sch.1

**1025. Highways (Road Humps) Regulations
1999**
Reg.3, amended: SI 2015/377 Sch.1
para.36

**1278. Warehousekeepers and Owners of
Warehoused Goods Regulations 1999**
see *CC&C Ltd v Revenue and Customs
Commissioners* [2014] EWCA Civ 1653,
[2015] 1 W.L.R. 4043 (CA (Civ Div)),
Arden LJ

**1347. Act of Sederunt (Proceedings for
Determination of Devolution Issues Rules)
1999**
Art.6, amended: SSI 2015/419 r.10
Art.7, amended: SSI 2015/419 r.10
Sch.1, amended: SSI 2015/419 r.10

**1441. Education (Inspection of Nursery
Education) (Wales) Regulations 1999**
revoked: SI 2015/1599 Reg.1

**1565. Excise Goods (Sales on Board Ships and
Aircraft) Regulations 1999**
Reg.6, amended: SI 2015/368 Reg.18
Reg.18, amended: SI 2015/368 Reg.19
Reg.19, amended: SI 2015/368 Reg.20

**1872. Feeding Stuffs (Establishments and
Intermediaries) Regulations 1999**
Reg.2, amended: SSI 2015/100 Art.2

**2083. Unfair Terms in Consumer Contracts
Regulations 1999**
see *Khurana v Webster Construction Ltd*
[2015] EWHC 758 (TCC), [2015] B.L.R.
396 (QBD (TCC)), Judge Stephen
Davies; see *Makdessi v Cavendish
Square Holdings BV* [2015] UKSC 67,
[2015] 3 W.L.R. 1373 (SC), Lord
Neuberger PSC; see *ParkingEye Ltd v
Beavis* [2015] EWCA Civ 402, [2015]
R.T.R. 27 (CA (Civ Div)), Moore-Bick
LJ; see *Welcome Financial Service Ltd,
Re* [2015] EWHC 815 (Ch), [2015] 2 All
E.R. (Comm) 992 (Ch D (Companies
Ct)), Rose J
Reg.5, see *Khurana v Webster
Construction Ltd* [2015] EWHC 758
(TCC), [2015] B.L.R. 396 (QBD (TCC)),

Judge Stephen Davies; see *ParkingEye
Ltd v Beavis* [2015] EWCA Civ 402,
[2015] R.T.R. 27 (CA (Civ Div)), Moore-
Bick LJ
Reg.7, see *AJ Building and Plastering
Ltd v Turner* [2013] EWHC 484 (QB),
[2015] T.C.L.R. 3 (QBD (Merc)
(Cardiff)), Judge Keyser QC

**2197. Countryside Access (Amendment)
(No.2) Regulations 1999**
revoked: SI 2015/639 Reg.3

**2325. Feeding Stuffs (Enforcement)
Regulations 1999**
Reg.2, amended: SSI 2015/100 Art.2

**2541. Health Act 1999 (Fund-holding
Practices) (Transfer of Assets, Savings,
Rights and Liabilities and Transitional
Provisions) Order 1999**
revoked: SI 2015/864 Art.2

**2979. Financial Markets and Insolvency
(Settlement Finality) Regulations 1999**
Reg.2, amended: SI 2015/347 Reg.2
Reg.4, amended: SI 2015/347 Reg.2

**3242. Management of Health and Safety at
Work Regulations 1999**
see *Gilchrist v Asda Stores Ltd* [2015]
CSOH 77, 2015 Rep. L.R. 95 (OH), Lady
Stacey; see *Kennedy v Cordia (Services)
LLP* 2015 S.C. 154 (IH (Ex Div)), Lady
Smith
Reg.3, see *Kennedy v Cordia (Services)
LLP* 2015 S.C. 154 (IH (Ex Div)), Lady
Smith

**3312. Maternity and Parental Leave etc
Regulations 1999**
Reg.10, see *Sefton BC v Wainwright*
[2015] I.C.R. 652 (EAT), Judge Eady QC

2000

**90. Health Act 1999 (Supplementary,
Consequential etc Provisions) Order 2000**
Art.2, amended: SI 2015/864 Art.3
Art.2, revoked: SI 2015/864 Art.3
Art.4, revoked: SI 2015/864 Art.3
Sch.1 para.1, revoked: SI 2015/864 Art.3
Sch.1 para.4, revoked: SI 2015/864 Art.3
Sch.1 para.6, revoked: SI 2015/864 Art.3
Sch.1 para.7, revoked: SI 2015/864 Art.3
Sch.1 para.9, revoked: SI 2015/864 Art.3

Sch.1 para.10, revoked: SI 2015/864 Art.3

Sch.1 para.11, revoked: SI 2015/864 Art.3

Sch.1 para.12, revoked: SI 2015/864 Art.3

Sch.1 para.14, revoked: SI 2015/864 Art.3

Sch.1 para.15, revoked: SI 2015/864 Art.3

Sch.1 para.16, revoked: SI 2015/864 Art.3

Sch.1 para.25, revoked: SI 2015/864 Art.3

Sch.1 para.26, revoked: SI 2015/864 Art.3

Sch.1 para.28, revoked: SI 2015/864 Art.3

Sch.1 para.30, revoked: SI 2015/864 Art.3

Sch.1 para.31, revoked: SI 2015/864 Art.3

Sch.1 para.33, revoked: SI 2015/864 Art.3

Sch.1 para.34, revoked: SI 2015/864 Art.3

Sch.1 para.35, revoked: SI 2015/864 Art.3

Sch.1 para.36, revoked: SI 2015/864 Art.3

Sch.2 Part I para.6, revoked: SI 2015/864 Art.3

179. Health Authorities Act 1995 (Rectification of Transitional Arrangements)Order 2000

revoked: SI 2015/864 Art.2

207. Financial Assistance for EnvironmentalPurposes Order 2000

revoked: SI 2015/479 Sch.1

221. Civil Procedure (Amendment) Rules 2000

see *Miaris v Secretary of State for Communities and Local Government* [2015] EWHC 2094 (Admin), [2015] 1 W.L.R. 4333 (QBD (Admin)), John Howell QC

249. A40 Trunk Road (Carmarthen Eastern Bypass, Carmarthenshire) (De-Restriction) (No.1) Order 2000

revoked: SI 2015/1446 Art.6

262. Competition Act 1998 (Small Agreements and Conduct of Minor Significance) Regulations 2000

Sch.1 para.1, amended: SI 2015/575 Sch.2 para.9

309. Competition Act 1998 (Determination of Turnover for Penalties) Order 2000

Sch.1 para.1, amended: SI 2015/575 Sch.2 para.10

516. Community Legal Service (Financial) Regulations 2000

Reg.19, amended: SI 2015/643 Sch.1 para.11, SI 2015/838 Reg.2

Reg.33, amended: SI 2015/643 Sch.1 para.11, SI 2015/838 Reg.2

604. Health Education Authority (Abolition) Order 2000

revoked: SI 2015/864 Art.2

656. Food Standards Act 1999 (Transitional and Consequential Provisions and Savings) (England and Wales) Regulations 2000

Reg.10, revoked: SI 2015/1782 Reg.47

Sch.8 Part III, revoked: SI 2015/1782 Reg.47

682. Disabled Persons (Badges for Motor Vehicles) (England) Regulations 2000

Reg.4, amended: SI 2015/643 Sch.1 para.12

694. Health Act 1999 (Supplementary, Consequential etc Provisions) (No.2) Order 2000

Art.2, revoked: SI 2015/864 Art.4

Sch.1 Part II para.2, revoked: SI 2015/864 Art.4

Sch.1 Part II para.3, revoked: SI 2015/864 Art.4

Sch.1 Part II para.4, revoked: SI 2015/864 Art.4

704. Asylum Support Regulations 2000

Reg.10, amended: SI 2015/645 Reg.2, SI 2015/944 Reg.3, SI 2015/1501 Reg.2

Reg.10, revoked: SI 2015/645 Reg.2 , SI 2015/1501 Reg.2

Reg.23, amended: SI 2015/643 Sch.1 para.14

738. European Communities (Designation) Order 2000

Sch.1, amended: SI 2015/1770 Art.4

824. Community Legal Service (Cost Protection) Regulations 2000

Reg.5, see *Rayner v Lord Chancellor*
[2015] EWCA Civ 1124, [2015] 6 Costs
L.R. 957 (CA (Civ Div)), McCombe LJ
874. Lobsters and Crawfish (Prohibition of
Fishing and Landing) Order 2000
revoked: SI 2015/2076 Art.7
1108. Football Spectators (Corresponding
Offences in Belgium) Order 2000
revoked: SI 2015/212 Sch.1
1109. Football Spectators (Corresponding
Offences in the Netherlands) Order 2000
revoked: SI 2015/212 Sch.1
1112. Deep Sea Mining (Temporary
Provisions) Act 1981 (Isle of Man) Order
2000
revoked: SI 2015/2012 Art.3
1119. European Communities (Lawyer's
Practice) Regulations 2000
Reg.2, amended: SI 2015/401 Sch.2
para.2, SI 2015/2059 Reg.73
Reg.29, amended: SI 2015/2059 Reg.73
Sch.1, amended: SI 2015/2059 Reg.73
Sch.4, amended: SI 2015/401 Sch.2
para.3
Sch.4 para.1, amended: SI 2015/401
Sch.2 para.3
Sch.4 para.7, amended: SI 2015/401
Sch.2 para.3
Sch.4 para.7, revoked: SI 2015/401 Sch.2
para.3
Sch.4 para.24, amended: SI 2015/401
Sch.2 para.3
1161. Immigration (Leave to Enter and
Remain) Order 2000
Art.1, amended: SI 2015/434 Art.2
Art.4, amended: SI 2015/434 Art.2
Art.13, amended: SI 2015/434 Art.2
Art.13A, added: SI 2015/434 Art.2
1300. Trade Union Recognition (Method of
Collective Bargaining) Order 2000
see *British Airline Pilots Association v*
Jet2.com Ltd [2015] EWHC 1110 (QB),
[2015] I.R.L.R. 543 (QBD), Supperstone
J
1551. Part-time Workers (Prevention of Less
Favourable Treatment) Regulations 2000
see *Barton v Secretary of State for*
Scotland [2015] CSIH 92 (IH (Ex Div)),
Lady Smith; see *Martineau v Ministry of*
Justice [2015] I.C.R. 1122 (EAT), Lewis
J

Reg.1, see *Barton v Secretary of State for*
Scotland [2015] CSIH 92 (IH (Ex Div)),
Lady Smith
Reg.2, see *Barton v Secretary of State for*
Scotland [2015] CSIH 92 (IH (Ex Div)),
Lady Smith; see *Moultrie v Ministry of*
Justice [2015] I.R.L.R. 264 (EAT), Lewis
J
Reg.5, see *Barton v Secretary of State for*
Scotland [2015] CSIH 92 (IH (Ex Div)),
Lady Smith
Reg.8, see *Barton v Secretary of State for*
Scotland [2015] CSIH 92 (IH (Ex Div)),
Lady Smith
1941. General Teaching Council for Wales
(Additional Functions) Order 2000
revoked: SI 2015/194 Sch.1
1979. General Teaching Council for Wales
(Functions) Regulations 2000
revoked: SI 2015/140 Sch.1 Part 1
Reg.9, revoked: SI 2015/195 Sch.1
2055. Brucellosis (England) Order 2000
revoked: SI 2015/364 Art.25
2211. Financial Assistance for Environmental
Purposes (No.2) Order 2000
revoked: SI 2015/479 Sch.1
2445. Immigration (Variation of Leave)
(Amendment) Order 2000
revoked: SI 2015/863 Art.2
2724. Immigration (Designation of Travel
Bans) Order 2000
Sch.1, substituted: SI 2015/1994 Sch.1
Sch.1 Part 1, substituted: SI 2015/388
Sch.1
2853. Local Authorities (Functions and
Responsibilities) (England) Regulations 2000
Sch.1, amended: SI 2015/968 Sch.1
para.4
3359. Environmental Protection (Disposal of
Polychlorinated Biphenyls and other
Dangerous Substances) (England and Wales)
(Amendment) Regulations 2000
revoked: SI 2015/639 Reg.4

2001

59. Federal Republic of Yugoslavia
(Freezing of Funds) Regulations 2001
revoked: SI 2015/81 Reg.2

155. Child Support (Maintenance Calculations and Special Cases) Regulations 2001

Reg.4, amended: SI 2015/1985 Art.19
Sch.Part III para.7, amended: SI 2015/478 Reg.32

493. Civil Aviation (Chargeable Air Services) (Detention and Sale of Aircraft) Regulations 2001

Reg.2, amended: SI 2015/912 Sch.5 para.2
Reg.7, amended: SI 2015/912 Sch.5 para.2
Sch.1 para.1, amended: SI 2015/912 Sch.5 para.2
Sch.1 para.2, amended: SI 2015/912 Sch.5 para.2

494. Civil Aviation (Chargeable Air Services) (Detention and Sale of Aircraft for Eurocontrol) Regulations 2001

Reg.2, amended: SI 2015/912 Sch.5 para.3
Reg.8, amended: SI 2015/912 Sch.5 para.3
Sch.1 para.1, amended: SI 2015/912 Sch.5 para.3
Sch.1 para.2, amended: SI 2015/912 Sch.5 para.3

544. Financial Services and Markets Act 2000 (Regulated Activities) Order 2001

Art.3, amended: SI 2015/489 Art.2, SI 2015/575 Sch.2 para.11, SI 2015/910 Sch.1 para.4
Art.4, amended: SI 2015/910 Sch.1 para.4
Art.11, amended: SI 2015/575 Sch.2 para.11
Art.25A, amended: SI 2015/910 Sch.1 para.4
Art.29, amended: SI 2015/910 Sch.1 para.4
Art.35B, added: SI 2015/489 Art.2
Art.36, amended: SI 2015/910 Sch.1 para.4
Art.36E, substituted: SI 2015/910 Sch.1 para.4
Art.36F, substituted: SI 2015/853 Art.3
Art.36G, amended: SI 2015/910 Sch.1 para.4
Art.39K, substituted: SI 2015/853 Art.3
Art.39KA, added: SI 2015/489 Art.2

Art.52C, added: SI 2015/489 Art.2
Art.53DA, added: SI 2015/910 Sch.1 para.4
Art.53E, added: SI 2015/731 Art.2
Art.54, amended: SI 2015/731 Art.2, SI 2015/910 Sch.1 para.4
Art.54A, amended: SI 2015/910 Sch.1 para.4
Art.54B, added: SI 2015/489 Art.2
Art.55, amended: SI 2015/910 Sch.1 para.4
Art.60B, amended: SI 2015/853 Art.3
Art.60C, amended: SI 2015/910 Sch.1 para.4, SI 2015/1863 Art.2
Art.60D, amended: SI 2015/910 Sch.1 para.4
Art.60E, amended: SI 2015/910 Sch.1 para.4
Art.60F, amended: SI 2015/352 Art.2, SI 2015/853 Art.3, SI 2015/910 Sch.1 para.4
Art.60G, amended: SI 2015/352 Art.2, SI 2015/910 Sch.1 para.4
Art.60H, amended: SI 2015/910 Sch.1 para.4
Art.60HA, added: SI 2015/910 Sch.1 para.4
Art.60K, amended: SI 2015/910 Sch.1 para.4
Art.60L, amended: SI 2015/853 Art.3
Art.61, amended: SI 2015/910 Sch.1 para.4, SI 2015/1863 Art.2
Art.61, revoked: SI 2015/910 Sch.1 para.4
Art.61A, added: SI 2015/910 Sch.1 para.4
Art.61A, amended: SI 2015/1863 Art.2
Art.63A, amended: SI 2015/910 Sch.1 para.4
Art.66, amended: SI 2015/910 Sch.1 para.4
Art.67, amended: SI 2015/910 Sch.1 para.4
Art.72, amended: SI 2015/910 Sch.1 para.4
Art.72A, amended: SI 2015/575 Sch.2 para.11, SI 2015/852 Art.3
Art.72A, revoked: SI 2015/575 Sch.2 para.11
Art.72G, amended: SI 2015/910 Sch.1 para.4
Art.72I, added: SI 2015/910 Sch.1 para.4

Art.82, amended: SI 2015/731 Art.2
Art.89, amended: SI 2015/731 Art.2
Art.89C, substituted: SI 2015/853 Art.3
Sch.1 Part II paraVIII, amended: SI
2015/575 Sch.2 para.11
Sch.1 Part II paraIX, amended: SI
2015/575 Sch.2 para.11
Sch.5, substituted: SI 2015/369 Art.3
824. Court of Protection Rules 2001
r.44, see *Public Guardian v M* [2015]
C.O.P.L.R. 107 (CP), Senior Judge
Denzil Lush
834. Broadmoor Hospital Authority
(Abolition) Order 2001
revoked: SI 2015/864 Art.2
838. Climate Change Levy (General)
Regulations 2001
Reg.11, amended: SI 2015/947 Reg.3
Reg.51A, amended: SI 2015/947 Reg.4
Sch.3 para.1, amended: SI 2015/947
Reg.5
Sch.3 para.2, amended: SI 2015/947
Reg.5
Sch.3 para.4, amended: SI 2015/947
Reg.5
Sch.3 para.5, amended: SI 2015/947
Reg.5
995. Financial Services and Markets Act
2000 (Recognition Requirements for
Investment Exchanges and Clearing Houses)
Regulations 2001
see *R. (on the application of United*
Company Rusal Plc) v London Metal
Exchange [2014] EWCA Civ 1271,
[2015] 1 W.L.R. 1375 (CA (Civ Div)),
Arden LJ
1002. Housing Benefit and Council Tax
Benefit (Decisions and Appeals) Regulations
2001
Reg.4, amended: SI 2015/1985 Art.20
Reg.7, amended: SI 2015/1985 Art.20
Reg.8, amended: SI 2015/1985 Art.20
1060. Financial Services and Markets Act
2000 (Promotion of Collective Investment
Schemes) (Exemptions) Order 2001
Art.16, amended: SI 2015/1882 Reg.6
1062. Financial Services and Markets Act
2000 (Collective Investment Schemes) Order
2001
Art.2, amended: SI 2015/754 Art.2
Sch.para.2, amended: SI 2015/754 Art.2

Sch.para.2A, added: SI 2015/754 Art.2
Sch.para.6A, added: SI 2015/2061 Art.2
1090. Limited Liability Partnerships
Regulations 2001
Sch.3, amended: SI 2015/1641 Sch.1
para.3
Sch.4, amended: SI 2015/989 Sch.1
para.2
Sch.6 Part II para.9, revoked: SI
2015/1641 Sch.1 para.3
1184. European Parliamentary Elections
(Franchise of Relevant Citizens of the Union)
Regulations 2001
Reg.8, amended: SI 2015/1376 Sch.2
para.22
1201. Financial Services and Markets Act
2000 (Exemption) Order 2001
Sch.Part II para.25, revoked: SI 2015/447
Art.2
Sch.Part IV para.48, amended: SI
2015/910 Sch.1 para.5
Sch.Part IV para.48, revoked: SI
2015/910 Sch.1 para.5
Sch.Part IV para.54, amended: SI
2015/352 Art.3
Sch.Part IV para.54A, added: SI
2015/352 Art.3
Sch.Part IV para.57, added: SI 2015/447
Art.2
1217. Financial Services and Markets Act
2000 (Appointed Representatives)
Regulations 2001
Reg.2, amended: SI 2015/910 Sch.1
para.7
Reg.3, amended: SI 2015/910 Sch.1
para.7
1424. General Teaching Council for Wales
(Disciplinary Functions) Regulations 2001
revoked: SI 2015/140 Sch.1 Part 1
1437. Criminal Defence Service (General)
(No.2) Regulations 2001
Reg.14, see *R. v Adebolajo (Michael)*
[2014] EWCA Crim 2779, [2015] 4 All
E.R. 194 (CA (Crim Div)), Lord Thomas
LCJ
Sch.1 para.8, amended: SI 2015/643
Sch.1 para.17, SI 2015/838 Reg.3
1633. A55 Trunk Road (Holyhead, Anglesey)
(50 mph Speed Limit &amp Prohibition of
Pedestrians) Order 2001
varied: SI 2015/691 Art.6

1653. A5 and A55 Trunk Roads (Llanfairpwllgwyngyll to Holyhead, Anglesey) (Deretsriction) Order 2001
    varied: SI 2015/691 Art.7

1783. Financial Services and Markets Act 2000 (Compensation Scheme Electing Participants) Regulations 2001
    Reg.1, amended: SI 2015/910 Sch.1 para.6, SI 2015/1882 Reg.7
    Reg.2, amended: SI 2015/910 Sch.1 para.6, SI 2015/1882 Reg.7
    Reg.3, amended: SI 2015/910 Sch.1 para.6, SI 2015/1882 Reg.7
    Reg.4, amended: SI 2015/910 Sch.1 para.6, SI 2015/1882 Reg.7

2188. Financial Services and Markets Act 2000 (Disclosure of Confidential Information) Regulations 2001
    Reg.2, amended: SI 2015/575 Sch.2 para.12, SI 2015/910 Sch.1 para.8
    Reg.9, amended: SI 2015/575 Sch.2 para.12, SI 2015/910 Sch.1 para.8
    Reg.9, revoked: SI 2015/575 Sch.2 para.12

2189. Children (Leaving Care) (Wales) Regulations 2001
    revoked: SI 2015/1820 Reg.11

2256. Financial Services and Markets Act 2000 (Rights of Action) Regulations 2001
    see *Connaught Income Fund Series 1 (In Liquidation) v Capita Financial Managers Ltd* [2014] EWHC 3619 (Comm), [2015] 1 All E.R. (Comm) 751 (QBD (Comm)), Judge Mackie QC
    Reg.6, see *Connaught Income Fund Series 1 (In Liquidation) v Capita Financial Managers Ltd* [2014] EWHC 3619 (Comm), [2015] 1 All E.R. (Comm) 751 (QBD (Comm)), Judge Mackie QC

2496. General Teaching Council for Wales (Functions) (Amendment) Regulations 2001
    revoked: SI 2015/140 Sch.1 Part 1

2497. General Teaching Council for Wales (Additional Functions) (Amendment) Order 2001
    revoked: SI 2015/194 Sch.1

2511. Financial Services and Markets Act 2000 (EEA Passport Rights) Regulations 2001
    Reg.1, amended: SI 2015/575 Sch.2 para.13, SI 2015/910 Sch.1 para.9

Reg.2, amended: SI 2015/575 Sch.2 para.13, SI 2015/910 Sch.1 para.9
Reg.3, amended: SI 2015/575 Sch.2 para.13, SI 2015/910 Sch.1 para.9
Reg.7B, added: SI 2015/910 Sch.1 para.9
Reg.9A, added: SI 2015/910 Sch.1 para.9
Reg.13, amended: SI 2015/575 Sch.2 para.13
Reg.15, amended: SI 2015/575 Sch.2 para.13
Reg.16, amended: SI 2015/575 Sch.2 para.13
Reg.17B, added: SI 2015/910 Sch.1 para.9
Reg.19, amended: SI 2015/575 Sch.2 para.13

2541. Capital Allowances (Energy-saving Plant and Machinery) Order 2001
    Art.2, amended: SI 2015/1508 Art.3

2635. Financial Services and Markets Act 2000 (Law Applicable to Contracts of Insurance) Regulations 2001
    Reg.6, amended: SI 2015/575 Sch.2 para.14

2678. Change of Category of Maintained Schools (Wales) Regulations 2001
    revoked: SI 2015/1521 Reg.1

2734. Foot-and-Mouth Disease (Ascertainment of Value) (No.5) Order 2001
    revoked: SI 2015/751 Art.2

3084. Financial Services and Markets Act 2000 (Gibraltar) Order 2001
    Art.2, amended: SI 2015/910 Sch.1 para.10
    Art.3, amended: SI 2015/910 Sch.1 para.10

3087. Federal Republic of Yugoslavia (Freezing of Funds) (Amendment) Regulations 2001
    revoked: SI 2015/81 Reg.2

3384. Local Authorities (Standing Orders) (England) Regulations 2001
    Reg.5, amended: SI 2015/881 Reg.2
    Reg.6, substituted: SI 2015/881 Reg.2
    Reg.7, revoked: SI 2015/881 Reg.2
    Reg.10, revoked: SI 2015/881 Reg.2
    Sch.1 Part I para.4, amended: SI 2015/881 Reg.2
    Sch.1 Part II para.4, amended: SI 2015/881 Reg.2

Sch.1 Part IV para.4, substituted: SI
2015/881 Reg.2
Sch.3, substituted: SI 2015/881 Sch.1
**3390. Fishing Vessels (Decommissioning)
Scheme 2001**
revoked: SI 2015/191 Sch.1
**3590. Animals and Animal Products
(Examination for Residues and Maximum
Residue Limits) (Amendment) Regulations
2001**
revoked: SI 2015/787 Sch.1
**3625. Financial Services and Markets Act
2000 (Control of Business Transfers)
(Requirements on Applicants) Regulations
2001**
Reg.2, amended: SI 2015/575 Sch.2
para.15
**3649. Financial Services and Markets Act
2000 (Consequential Amendments and
Repeals) Order 2001**
revoked: SI 2015/623 Sch.1
**3744. Abolition of the NHS Tribunal
(Consequential Provisions) Regulations 2001**
revoked: SI 2015/839 Reg.2
**3929. Civil Jurisdiction and Judgments Order
2001**
Sch.1 para.2B, added: SSI 2015/1 Reg.2
**3960. BSE Monitoring (England)
(Amendment) Regulations 2001**
revoked: SI 2015/639 Reg.3
3967. Children's Homes Regulations 2001
revoked: SI 2015/541 Reg.56
Reg.17A, see *Barnsley MBC v GS* [2015]
C.O.P.L.R. 51 (CP), Holman J
**4011. Electricity and Gas (Energy Efficiency
Obligations) Order 2001**
revoked: 2015 c.20 Sch.23 para.20
**4027. Aggregates Levy (Registration and
Miscellaneous Provisions) Regulations 2001**
Reg.3, amended: SI 2015/1487 Reg.3

2002

57. Fostering Services Regulations 2002
see *R. (on the application of
Cunningham) v Hertfordshire CC* [2015]
EWHC 1936 (Admin), (2015) 18 C.C.L.
Rep. 632 (QBD (Admin)), Hickinbottom
J

**253. Nursing and Midwifery Order (2001)
2002**
see *Daniels v Nursing and Midwifery
Council* [2015] EWCA Civ 225, [2015]
Med. L.R. 255 (CA (Civ Div)), Sir Brian
Leveson PQBD
Art.29, see *Daniels v Nursing and
Midwifery Council* [2015] EWCA Civ
225, [2015] Med. L.R. 255 (CA (Civ
Div)), Sir Brian Leveson PQBD
Art.38, see *D v Nursing and Midwifery
Council* 2015 S.C. 282 (IH (Ex Div)),
Lady Paton
**254. Health and Social Work Professions
Order 2002**
Art.3, amended: 2015 c.28 Sch.1 para.6
Art.7, enabled: SI 2015/93, SI 2015/1337
Art.9, enabled: SI 2015/93
Art.10, enabled: SI 2015/1337
Art.11A, enabled: SI 2015/93
Art.22, see *Ireland v Health and Care
Professions Council* [2015] EWHC 846
(Admin), [2015] 1 W.L.R. 4643 (QBD
(Admin)), Jay J
Art.26, amended: 2015 c.28 Sch.1 para.6
Art.26, see *Ireland v Health and Care
Professions Council* [2015] EWHC 846
(Admin), [2015] 1 W.L.R. 4643 (QBD
(Admin)), Jay J
Art.41, enabled: SI 2015/93, SI
2015/1337
Sch.1 Part II para.19, amended: 2015
c.28 Sch.1 para.6
**282. Health and Safety at Work etc Act 1974
(Application to Environmentally Hazardous
Substances) Regulations 2002**
Reg.2, amended: SI 2015/21 Reg.10
Reg.2, revoked: SI 2015/21 Reg.10
Reg.3, amended: SI 2015/21 Reg.10
324. Care Homes (Wales) Regulations 2002
Reg.18, see *R. (on the application of
Forge Care Homes Ltd) v Cardiff and
Vale University Health Board* [2015]
EWHC 601 (Admin), [2015] P.T.S.R.
945 (QBD (Admin)), Hickinbottom J
**326. General Teaching Council for Wales
(Fees) Regulations 2002**
revoked: SI 2015/195 Sch.1
**461. Control of Noise (Codes of Practice for
Construction and Open Sites) (England)
Order 2002**

revoked: SI 2015/227 Art.3

559. Ashworth Hospital Authority (Abolition) Order 2002
revoked: SI 2015/864 Art.2

676. Lobsters and Crawfish (Prohibition of Fishing and Landing) (Wales) Order 2002
revoked: SI 2015/2076 Art.7

1686. Financial Assistance for Environmental Purposes Order 2002
revoked: SI 2015/479 Sch.1

1773. Hydrocarbon Oil (Marking) Regulations 2002
Reg.2, amended: SI 2015/36 Reg.3
Reg.3, amended: SI 2015/36 Reg.3

1775. Electronic Commerce Directive (Financial Services and Markets) Regulations 2002
Part 3A, added: SI 2015/852 Art.2
Reg.12, amended: SI 2015/852 Art.2

1891. Agricultural or Forestry Tractors (Emission of Gaseous and Particulate Pollutants) Regulations 2002
Reg.2, amended: SI 2015/1350 Reg.2

1970. Exchange Gains and Losses (Bringing into Account Gains or Losses) Regulations 2002
Reg.4, amended: SI 2015/1960 Reg.2
Reg.13, amended: SI 2015/1960 Reg.2

2007. Child Tax Credit Regulations 2002
Reg.7, amended: SI 2015/451 Reg.2, SI 2015/567 Art.3

2021. Financial Assistance for Environmental Purposes (No.2) Order 2002
revoked: SI 2015/479 Sch.1

2034. Fixed-term Employees (Prevention of Less Favourable Treatment) Regulations 2002
Reg.20, amended: SI 2015/971 Sch.1 para.1

2676. Control of Lead at Work Regulations 2002
Sch.2, amended: SI 2015/21 Reg.11

2677. Control of Substances Hazardous to Health Regulations 2002
Reg.2, amended: SI 2015/21 Reg.12
Reg.3, amended: SI 2015/1637 Sch.1 para.7
Reg.7, amended: SI 2015/21 Reg.12
Reg.16A, amended: SI 2015/1682 Sch.1 para.10

Reg.20, amended: SI 2015/1637 Sch.1 para.7
Sch.2, amended: SI 2015/21 Reg.12
Sch.7, amended: SI 2015/21 Reg.12

2682. Town and Country Planning (Enforcement Notices and Appeals) (England) Regulations 2002
Reg.4, see *Silver v Secretary of State for Communities and Local Government* [2014] EWHC 2729 (Admin), [2015] J.P.L. 154 (QBD (Admin)), Supperstone J

2685. Town and Country Planning (Enforcement) (Determination by Inspectors) (Inquiries Procedure) (England) Rules 2002
r.16, see *Turner v Secretary of State for Communities and Local Government* [2015] EWHC 1895 (Admin), [2015] J.P.L. 1347 (QBD (Admin)), CMG Ockelton

2742. Road Vehicles (Registration and Licensing) Regulations 2002
Reg.27, see *R. (on the application of Duff) v Secretary of State for Transport* [2015] EWHC 1605 (Admin), [2015] R.T.R. 28 (QBD (Admin)), Edis J

2776. Dangerous Substances and Explosive Atmospheres Regulations 2002
Reg.2, amended: SI 2015/21 Reg.13
Sch.5, amended: SI 2015/21 Reg.13

2786. Air Navigation (Dangerous Goods) Regulations 2002
Reg.3, amended: SI 2015/970 Reg.2

2848. Double Taxation Relief (Taxes on Income) (The United States of America) Order 2002
see *Macklin v Revenue and Customs Commissioners* [2015] UKUT 39 (TCC), [2015] S.T.C. 1102 (UT (Tax)), Newey J

3150. Company Directors Disqualification (Northern Ireland) Order 2002
Art.2, amended: 2015 c.26 s.91, Sch.8 para.9
Art.3, amended: 2015 c.26 Sch.8 para.9
Art.4, amended: 2015 c.26 Sch.8 para.9
Art.5, amended: 2015 c.26 Sch.8 para.9
Art.6, amended: 2015 c.26 Sch.8 para.9
Art.8, amended: 2015 c.26 Sch.8 para.9
Art.8A, added: 2015 c.26 Sch.8 para.2
Art.9, amended: 2015 c.26 Sch.8 para.3, Sch.8 para.9

Art.10, amended: 2015 c.26 Sch.8 para.4,
Sch.8 para.9
Art.10, revoked: 2015 c.26 Sch.8 para.5
Art.10, substituted: 2015 c.26 Sch.8
para.5
Art.10A, added: 2015 c.26 Sch.8 para.5
Art.11, amended: 2015 c.26 Sch.8 para.3,
Sch.8 para.6
Art.11, revoked: 2015 c.26 Sch.8 para.6
Art.11, substituted: 2015 c.26 Sch.8
para.6
Art.11A, added: 2015 c.26 Sch.8 para.7
Art.12, amended: 2015 c.26 Sch.8 para.9
Art.13, revoked: 2015 c.26 Sch.8 para.3
Art.14, amended: 2015 c.26 Sch.8 para.9
Art.15, amended: 2015 c.26 s.114
Art.17A, added: 2015 c.26 Sch.8 para.3
Art.19A, added: 2015 c.26 Sch.8 para.8
Art.20, amended: 2015 c.26 Sch.8 para.9
Art.22, amended: 2015 c.26 Sch.8 para.9
Art.23, amended: 2015 c.26 Sch.8 para.9
Art.24, amended: 2015 c.26 Sch.8 para.9
Art.24D, revoked: 2015 c.26 Sch.8 para.9
Art.24E, revoked: 2015 c.26 Sch.8 para.9
Art.25, amended: 2015 c.26 Sch.8 para.9
Art.25, revoked: 2015 c.26 Sch.8 para.9
Art.25A, amended: 2015 c.26 Sch.8
para.9
Art.25A, revoked: 2015 c.26 Sch.8 para.9
Sch.1, substituted: 2015 c.26 Sch.8 para.3
**3154. Housing Support Services (Northern
Ireland) Order 2002**
    Art.8, revoked: SI 2015/2006 Sch.12 Part
    1

2003

**37. Motor Vehicles (Compulsory Insurance)
(Information Centre and Compensation
Body) Regulations 2003**
    Reg.13, see *Moreno v Motor Insurers'
    Bureau* [2015] EWHC 1002 (QB), [2015]
    Lloyd's Rep. I.R. 535 (QBD), Gilbart J
    Reg.16, see *Moreno v Motor Insurers'
    Bureau* [2015] EWHC 1002 (QB), [2015]
    Lloyd's Rep. I.R. 535 (QBD), Gilbart J
**74. Wireless Telegraphy (Exemption)
Regulations 2003**
    see *Recall Support Services Ltd v
    Secretary of State for Culture Media and*

Sport [2014] EWCA Civ 1370, [2015] 1
C.M.L.R. 38 (CA (Civ Div)), Richards
LJ
**260. Assured Tenancies and Agricultural
Occupancies (Forms) (Amendment)
(England) Regulations 2003**
    revoked: SI 2015/620 Reg.4
**418. Audit and Accountability (Northern
Ireland) Order 2003**
    Sch.2 para.4, revoked: SI 2015/2006
    Sch.12 Part 1
**435. Access to Justice (Northern Ireland)
Order 2003**
    Sch.2 para.2, amended: 2015 c.6 s.1
**480. A487 Trunk Road (Southern Approach
to Llanfarian, Aberystwyth, Ceredigion) (40
mph Speed Limit) Order 2003**
    varied: SI 2015/1287 Art.7
**503. General Teaching Council for Wales
(Disciplinary Functions) (Amendment)
Regulations 2003**
    revoked: SI 2015/140 Sch.1 Part 1
527. Police Regulations 2003
    Reg.25, see *Allard v Chief Constable of
    Devon and Cornwall* [2015] EWCA Civ
    42, [2015] I.C.R. 875 (CA (Civ Div)),
    Longmore LJ
    Reg.26, see *Allard v Chief Constable of
    Devon and Cornwall* [2015] EWCA Civ
    42, [2015] I.C.R. 875 (CA (Civ Div)),
    Longmore LJ
**548. British Nationality (General)
Regulations 2003**
    Part IIA, added: SI 2015/738 Reg.2
    Reg.2, amended: SI 2015/738 Reg.2, SI
    2015/1806 Reg.3
    Reg.4, revoked: SI 2015/1806 Reg.4
    Reg.5A, amended: SI 2015/681 Reg.3, SI
    2015/1806 Reg.5
    Reg.9, revoked: SI 2015/1806 Reg.6
    Sch.2A, amended: SI 2015/1806 Reg.8
    Sch.2 paraA.1, added: SI 2015/681 Reg.4
    Sch.2 para.7, amended: SI 2015/1806
    Reg.7
    Sch.2 para.11B, added: SI 2015/681
    Reg.4
    Sch.2 para.13, amended: SI 2015/1806
    Reg.7
    Sch.2 para.14, amended: SI 2015/1806
    Reg.7

Sch.2A para.1, amended: SI 2015/1806
Reg.8
Sch.2A para.1, revoked: SI 2015/1806
Reg.8
Sch.2A para.1, substituted: SI 2015/681
Reg.5
658. Immigration (Notices) Regulations 2003
Reg.4, see *JG (Jamaica) v Secretary of*
State for the Home Department [2015]
EWCA Civ 410, [2015] Imm. A.R. 1193
(CA (Civ Div)), Jackson LJ
Reg.5, see *JG (Jamaica) v Secretary of*
State for the Home Department [2015]
EWCA Civ 410, [2015] Imm. A.R. 1193
(CA (Civ Div)), Jackson LJ
714. Financial Assistance for Environmental
Purposes (England) Order 2003
revoked: SI 2015/479 Sch.1
757. Anglian Water Parks Byelaws
(Extension) Order 2003
revoked: SI 2015/924 Art.2
803. Housing (Right to Buy) (Limits of
Discount) (Amendment) (Wales) Order 2003
revoked: SI 2015/1349 Art.4
1034. Special Immigration Appeals
Commission (Procedure) Rules 2003
r.4, see *R. (on the application of*
Secretary of State for the Home
Department) v Special Immigration
Appeals Commission [2015] EWHC 681
(Admin), [2015] 1 W.L.R. 4799 (DC),
Sir Brian Leveson PQBD
1038. Education (National Curriculum) (Key
Stage 2 Assessment Arrangements) (England)
Order 2003
Art.1, amended: SI 2015/900 Art.12
Art.3, amended: SI 2015/900 Art.13
Art.4, amended: SI 2015/900 Art.14
Art.4A, added: SI 2015/900 Art.15
Art.5, amended: SI 2015/900 Art.16
Art.5B, amended: SI 2015/900 Art.17
Art.6B, amended: SI 2015/900 Art.18
Art.8, substituted: SI 2015/900 Art.19
Art.9, revoked: SI 2015/900 Art.20
Art.11, amended: SI 2015/900 Art.21
1039. Education (National Curriculum) (Key
Stage 3 Assessment Arrangements) (England)
Order 2003
Art.3, amended: SI 2015/900 Art.23
Art.5, substituted: SI 2015/900 Art.24
Art.6, revoked: SI 2015/900 Art.25

1180. Electricity and Gas (Energy Efficiency
Obligations) (Amendment) Order 2003
revoked: 2015 c.20 Sch.23 para.21
1196. Community Care (Delayed Discharges
etc.) Act (Qualifying Services) (England)
Regulations 2003
revoked: SI 2015/914 Sch.1 para.73
1370. Enterprise Act 2002 (Merger Fees and
Determination of Turnover) Order 2003
Art.3, amended: SI 2015/1936 Reg.23
Art.4, amended: SI 2015/1936 Reg.24
Sch.1 para.1, amended: SI 2015/575
Sch.2 para.16
1372. Competition Appeal Tribunal Rules
2003
revoked: SI 2015/1648 r.118
see *DSG Retail Ltd v Mastercard Inc*
[2015] CAT 7, [2015] Comp. A.R. 199
(CAT), Roth J
r.55, see *Skyscanner Ltd v Competition*
and Markets Authority [2015] Comp.
A.R. 91 (CAT), Peter Freeman QC
1374. Enterprise Act 2002 (Part 8
Community Infringements Specified UK
Laws) Order 2003
amended: SI 2015/1392 Reg.9
Art.3, amended: SI 2015/1392 Reg.9
Sch.1, amended: SI 2015/1392 Reg.9, SI
2015/1628 Art.2
1516. Iraq (United Nations Sanctions)
(Overseas Territories) Order 2003
revoked: SI 2015/1383 Art.1
1572. Health Professions Council
(Registration and Fees) Rules Order of
Council 2003
Sch.1, added: SI 2015/93 Sch.1
Sch.1, amended: SI 2015/1337 Sch.1
Sch.1, substituted: SI 2015/1337 Sch.1
1593. Enterprise Act 2002 (Part 8 Domestic
Infringements) Order 2003
Sch.1 Part I, amended: SI 2015/17 Sch.6
para.4
1596. Condensed Milk and Dried Milk
(England) Regulations 2003
revoked: SI 2015/675 Reg.8
1662. Education (School Teachers
Qualifications) (England) Regulations 2003
Sch.2 Part 1 para.8, amended: SI
2015/2059 Reg.74
1917. Education (Teacher Student Loans)
(Repayment etc.) Regulations 2003

Reg.2, amended: SI 2015/971 Sch.3
para.6
Reg.4, amended: SI 2015/971 Sch.3
para.6

2076. Capital Allowances (Environmentally Beneficial Plant and Machinery) Order 2003
Art.2, amended: SI 2015/1509 Art.3

2119. Financial Assistance for Environmental Purposes (England and Wales) Order 2003
revoked: SI 2015/479 Sch.1

2142. 487 Trunk Road (Brynhoffnant, Ceredigion) (40 MPH Speed Limit) Order 2003
varied: SI 2015/1284 Art.7

2243. Honey (England) Regulations 2003
revoked: SI 2015/1348 Reg.20

2276. Delayed Discharges (Mental Health Care) (England) Order 2003
revoked: SI 2015/643 Art.3

2277. Delayed Discharges (England) Regulations 2003
revoked: SI 2015/643 Art.3

2323. Care Standards Act 2000 (Domiciliary Care Agencies and Nurses Agencies) (Amendment) (England) Regulations 2003
revoked: SI 2015/839 Reg.2

2498. Copyright and Related Rights Regulations 2003
see *ITV Broadcasting Ltd v TV Catchup Ltd* [2015] EWCA Civ 204, [2015] E.C.D.R. 16 (CA (Civ Div)), Arden LJ

2613. Council Tax and Non-Domestic Rating (Demand Notices) (England) Regulations 2003
Sch.2 Part 1 para.7, substituted: SI 2015/427 Reg.3
Sch.2 Part 3 para.3, substituted: SI 2015/427 Reg.4

2627. Democratic Republic of the Congo (Restrictive Measures) (Overseas Territories) Order 2003
revoked: SI 2015/1382 Art.1

2669. Fishing Vessels (Decommissioning) Scheme 2003
revoked: SI 2015/191 Sch.1

2682. Income Tax (Pay As You Earn) Regulations 2003
Part 3, added: SI 2015/1927 Reg.6
Reg.2, amended: SI 2015/2 Reg.2, SI 2015/171 Reg.2, SI 2015/1667 Reg.3, SI 2015/1927 Reg.3

Reg.4, amended: SI 2015/1927 Reg.4
Reg.4, revoked: SI 2015/1927 Reg.4
Reg.5, revoked: SI 2015/1927 Reg.5
Reg.7, amended: SI 2015/1667 Reg.4
Reg.17, amended: SI 2015/2 Reg.2
Reg.19, amended: SI 2015/2 Reg.2
Reg.67F, revoked: SI 2015/2 Reg.2
Reg.70, amended: SI 2015/125 Reg.3
Reg.84E, added: SI 2015/171 Reg.2
Reg.85, amended: SI 2015/1927 Reg.7
Reg.87, revoked: SI 2015/1927 Reg.8
Reg.90, amended: SI 2015/1927 Reg.9
Reg.94, amended: SI 2015/1927 Reg.10
Reg.97, amended: SI 2015/1927 Reg.11
Reg.107, amended: SI 2015/1927 Reg.12
Reg.133A, amended: SI 2015/1667 Reg.5
Reg.211, amended: SI 2015/1927 Reg.13
Sch.A1 para.7, revoked: SI 2015/2 Reg.2
Sch.A1 para.22B, added: SI 2015/1927 Reg.14
Sch.A1 para.26, amended: SI 2015/1927 Reg.14

3044. Honey (Wales) Regulations 2003
revoked: SI 2015/1507 Reg.20

3108. Designation of Schools Having a Religious Character (Independent Schools) (England) Order 2003
Sch.1, amended: SI 2015/1636 Sch.2

3113. Customs (Contravention of a Relevant Rule) Regulations 2003
Reg.2, amended: SI 2015/636 Reg.3
Reg.3, amended: SI 2015/636 Reg.4
Sch.1, amended: SI 2015/636 Reg.5

3146. Local Authorities (Capital Finance and Accounting) (England) Regulations 2003
Reg.1, amended: SI 2015/341 Reg.2
Reg.30, substituted: SI 2015/341 Reg.2
Reg.30B, amended: SI 2015/341 Reg.2
Reg.30C, amended: SI 2015/341 Reg.2
Reg.30D, amended: SI 2015/341 Reg.2
Reg.30E, amended: SI 2015/341 Reg.2
Reg.30F, amended: SI 2015/341 Reg.2
Reg.30H, substituted: SI 2015/341 Reg.2
Reg.31, amended: SI 2015/341 Reg.2
Sch.1, amended: SI 2015/341 Sch.1
Sch.1 para.2, amended: SI 2015/341 Reg.2
Sch.1 para.9, substituted: SI 2015/341 Reg.2

3334. Extradition Act 2003 (Designation of Part 2 Territories) Order 2003

Art.2, amended: SI 2015/992 Art.2
Art.3, amended: SI 2015/992 Art.2
Art.4, amended: SI 2015/992 Art.2
3363. Insolvency Practitioners and Insolvency Services Account (Fees) Order 2003
Art.2, amended: SI 2015/1977 Art.2
Art.3, revoked: SI 2015/1641 Sch.1 para.4
Art.4, revoked: SI 2015/1641 Sch.1 para.4

2004

72. Designation of Schools Having a Religious Character (Independent Schools) (England) Order 2004
Sch.1, amended: SI 2015/2075 Sch.1
147. Animals and Animal Products (Examination for Residues and Maximum Residue Limits) (Amendment) Regulations 2004
revoked: SI 2015/787 Sch.1
293. European Parliamentary Elections Regulations 2004
Reg.17, amended: SI 2015/459 Reg.3
Reg.56, amended: SI 2015/664 Sch.5 para.17
Sch.2 Part 1 para.6, amended: SI 2015/459 Reg.4
Sch.2 Part 2 para.23, amended: SI 2015/643 Sch.1 para.22
Sch.2 Part 2 para.31C, added: SI 2015/459 Reg.5
347. Liberia (Restrictive Measures) (Overseas Territories) Order 2004
revoked: SI 2015/1899 Art.1
348. Liberia (United Nations Sanctions) Order 2004
Art.2, amended: SI 2015/2014 Art.3
353. Insurers (Reorganisation and Winding Up) Regulations 2004
Reg.2, amended: SI 2015/575 Sch.2 para.17
Reg.5, amended: SI 2015/575 Sch.2 para.17
Reg.6, amended: SI 2015/575 Sch.2 para.17
Reg.17, amended: SI 2015/575 Sch.2 para.17

Reg.50, amended: SI 2015/575 Sch.2 para.17
354. Designation of Schools Having a Religious Character (Independent Schools) (England) (No.2) Order 2004
Sch.1, amended: SI 2015/2075 Sch.1
400. High Court Enforcement Officers Regulations 2004
Reg.5, amended: SI 2015/1641 Sch.3 para.3
433. General Medical Services Transitional and Consequential Provisions Order 2004
revoked: SI 2015/1862 Sch.5 para.1
593. Insolvency Proceedings (Fees) Order 2004
Art.6, amended: SI 2015/1819 Art.2
Sch.2 para.2, amended: SI 2015/1819 Art.3
645. Police (Conduct) Regulations 2004
Reg.4, see *R. (on the application of Birks) v Commissioner of Police of the Metropolis* [2014] EWHC 3041 (Admin), [2015] I.C.R. 204 (QBD (Admin)), Lang J
692. Communications (Television Licensing) Regulations 2004
Sch.4 Part 2 para.5, amended: SI 2015/643 Sch.1 para.23
693. Enterprise Act 2002 (Part 9 Restrictions on Disclosure of Information) (Specification) Order 2004
Sch.1, amended: SI 2015/1640 Reg.13
696. Health and Social Care (Community Health and Standards) Act 2003 (Supplementary and Consequential Provision) (NHS Foundation Trusts) Order 2004
Sch.1 para.20, revoked: SI 2015/559 Sch.1
Sch.2, amended: SI 2015/570 Sch.3
702. Firearms (Northern Ireland) Order 2004
Art.30, amended: SI 2015/860 Reg.3
Art.38, amended: SI 2015/860 Reg.3
Art.38A, added: SI 2015/860 Reg.3
Sch.3 para.6, added: SI 2015/860 Reg.3
Sch.5, amended: SI 2015/860 Reg.3
756. Civil Aviation (Working Time) Regulations 2004
see *Bear Scotland Ltd v Fulton* [2015] 1 C.M.L.R. 40 (EAT), Langstaff J

**852. Fishguard to Bangor Trunk Road
(A487) (Pen-parc, Cardigan, Ceredigion) (40
mph Speed Limit) Order 2004**
  varied: SI 2015/1293 Art.7
**865. General Medical Services and Personal
Medical Services Transitional and
Consequential Provisions Order 2004**
  revoked: SI 2015/1862 Sch.5 para.1
  Sch.1 para.26, revoked: SI 2015/570
  Sch.3
**1031. Medicines for Human Use (Clinical
Trials) Regulations 2004**
  see *R. (on the application of Richmond
  Pharmacology Ltd) v Health Research
  Authority* [2015] EWHC 2238 (Admin),
  (2015) 146 B.M.L.R. 160 (QBD
  (Admin)), Jay J
  Reg.28, see *R. (on the application of
  Richmond Pharmacology Ltd) v Health
  Research Authority* [2015] EWHC 2238
  (Admin), (2015) 146 B.M.L.R. 160
  (QBD (Admin)), Jay J
  Sch.1, see *R. (on the application of
  Richmond Pharmacology Ltd) v Health
  Research Authority* [2015] EWHC 2238
  (Admin), (2015) 146 B.M.L.R. 160
  (QBD (Admin)), Jay J
  Sch.1 Pt 2 para.3, see *R. (on the
  application of Richmond Pharmacology
  Ltd) v Health Research Authority* [2015]
  EWHC 2238 (Admin), (2015) 146
  B.M.L.R. 160 (QBD (Admin)), Jay J
**1045. Credit Institutions (Reorganisation and
Winding up) Regulations 2004**
  see *Tchenguiz v Grant Thornton UK LLP*
  [2015] EWHC 1864 (Comm), [2015] 2
  B.C.L.C. 307 (QBD (Comm)), Carr J
  Reg.5, see *Tchenguiz v Grant Thornton
  UK LLP* [2015] EWHC 1864 (Comm),
  [2015] 2 B.C.L.C. 307 (QBD (Comm)),
  Carr J
**1106. Anglian Water Parks Byelaws
(Extension) Order 2004**
  revoked: SI 2015/924 Art.2
**1112. Liberia (Restrictive Measures)
(Overseas Territories) (Amendment) Order
2004**
  revoked: SI 2015/1899 Art.1
**1219. Accession (Immigration and Worker
Registration) Regulations 2004**

  see *Revenue and Customs Commissioners
  v Spiridonova* [2015] 1 C.M.L.R. 26 (CA
  (NI)), Morgan LCJ
**1267. European Parliamentary Elections
(Northern Ireland) Regulations 2004**
  Sch.1 Part VIII, amended: SI 2015/220
  Sch.1, Sch.2, Sch.3, Sch.4, Sch.5, Sch.6,
  Sch.7, Sch.8
  Sch.2 Part II para.32, amended: SI
  2015/220 Reg.3
  Sch.2 Part III, amended: SI 2015/220
  Sch.9, Sch.10
  Sch.6 para.17A, revoked: SI 2015/220
  Reg.4
  Sch.6 para.22, amended: SI 2015/220
  Sch.11
**1378. Designation of Schools Having a
Religious Character (Independent Schools)
(England) (No.4) Order 2004**
  Sch.1, amended: SI 2015/2075 Sch.1
**1425. Health and Social Care Act 2001 (Isles
of Scilly) Order 2004**
  revoked: SI 2015/864 Art.2
1450. Child Trust Funds Regulations 2004
  Reg.2, amended: SI 2015/575 Sch.2
  para.18, SI 2015/1371 Reg.3, Reg.4
  Reg.2, revoked: SI 2015/876 Reg.3 , SI
  2015/1371 Reg.4
  Reg.8, amended: SI 2015/876 Reg.4
  Reg.8, revoked: SI 2015/1371 Reg.5
  Reg.9, amended: SI 2015/600 Reg.3
  Reg.10, amended: SI 2015/876 Reg.5
  Reg.12, amended: SI 2015/1371 Reg.6
  Reg.13, amended: SI 2015/1371 Reg.7
  Reg.20A, added: SI 2015/876 Reg.6
  Reg.21, amended: SI 2015/876 Reg.7,
  Reg.8, SI 2015/1371 Reg.8
  Reg.21, revoked: SI 2015/876 Reg.8
  Reg.31, amended: SI 2015/876 Reg.9
  Reg.31, revoked: SI 2015/876 Reg.9
  Reg.32, amended: SI 2015/876 Reg.10
  Reg.33A, amended: SI 2015/1371 Reg.9
  Sch.1 para.2, amended: SI 2015/876
  Reg.11
**1481. Consumer Credit (Disclosure of
Information) Regulations 2004**
  Reg.2, amended: SI 2015/910 Sch.1
  para.11
**1490. Landfill Allowances Scheme (Wales)
Regulations 2004**
  Reg.2, amended: SI 2015/1417 Reg.2

Reg.6, amended: SI 2015/1417 Reg.2
Reg.7, amended: SI 2015/1417 Reg.2

1511. Human Fertilisation and Embryology Authority (Disclosure of Donor Information) Regulations 2004
Reg.1, amended: SI 2015/572 Reg.19

1633. Environmental Assessment of Plans and Programmes Regulations 2004
see *No Adastral New Town Ltd v Suffolk Coastal DC* [2014] EWHC 223 (Admin), [2015] Env. L.R. 3 (QBD (Admin)), Patterson J
Reg.5, see *R. (on the application of Larkfleet Homes Ltd) v Rutland CC* [2014] EWHC 4095 (Admin), [2015] P.T.S.R. 589 (QBD (Admin)), Collins J
Reg.12, see *IM Properties Development Ltd v Lichfield DC* [2015] EWHC 2077 (Admin), [2015] P.T.S.R. 1536 (QBD (Admin)), Cranston J
Sch.2, see *Satnam Millennium Ltd v Warrington BC* [2015] EWHC 370 (Admin), [2015] Env. L.R. 30 (QBD (Admin)), Stewart J

1662. Government Stock (Consequential and Transitional Provision) (No.2) Order 2004
revoked: SI 2015/623 Sch.1

1741. General Teaching Council for Wales (Functions) (Amendment) Regulations 2004
revoked: SI 2015/140 Sch.1 Part 1

1761. Nursing and Midwifery Council (Fitness to Practise) Rules Order of Council 2004
see *Daniels v Nursing and Midwifery Council* [2015] EWCA Civ 225, [2015] Med. L.R. 255 (CA (Civ Div)), Sir Brian Leveson PQBD

1771. Health Act 1999 (Consequential Amendments) (Nursing and Midwifery) Order 2004
Sch.1 Part 2 para.34, revoked: SI 2015/570 Sch.3

1836. Fireworks Regulations 2004
Reg.3, amended: SI 2015/1553 Sch.10 para.2
Reg.5, amended: SI 2015/1553 Sch.10 para.3
Reg.6, amended: SI 2015/1553 Sch.10 para.4
Reg.9, amended: SI 2015/1553 Sch.10 para.5

Reg.10, amended: SI 2015/1553 Sch.10 para.6
Reg.10, revoked: SI 2015/1553 Sch.10 para.6

1861. Employment Tribunals (Constitution and Rules of Procedure) Regulations 2004
Sch.1 para.27, see *Brindle v Flyde Motor Co Ltd* [2015] I.C.R. D4 (EAT), Judge Peter Clark
Sch.1 para.41, see *Flint v Coventry University* [2015] I.C.R. D1 (EAT), Judge Eady QC
Sch.1 para.54, see *Kiani v Secretary of State for the Home Department* [2015] EWCA Civ 776, [2015] C.P. Rep. 43 (CA (Civ Div)), Lord Dyson MR; see *Kiani v Secretary of State for the Home Department* [2015] I.C.R. 418 (EAT), Langstaff J

1862. Financial Conglomerates and Other Financial Groups Regulations 2004
Reg.1, amended: SI 2015/575 Sch.2 para.19
Reg.15, amended: SI 2015/575 Sch.2 para.19

1944. Community Radio Order 2004
Art.6, amended: SI 2015/1000 Art.2
Sch.1 Part 1 para.4, amended: SI 2015/1000 Art.4
Sch.1 Part 1 para.5, amended: SI 2015/1000 Art.5
Sch.1 Part 1 para.6, amended: SI 2015/1000 Art.6
Sch.1 Part 1 para.6A, amended: SI 2015/1000 Art.7
Sch.1 Part 2 para.10A, amended: SI 2015/1000 Art.8

1964. Fur Farming (Compensation Scheme) (England) Order 2004
revoked: SI 2015/663 Art.3

1983. Iraq (United Nations Sanctions) (Overseas Territories) (Amendment) Order 2004
revoked: SI 2015/1383 Art.1

2068. Competition Appeal Tribunal (Amendment and Communications Act Appeals) Rules 2004
revoked: SI 2015/1648 r.118

2326. European Public Limited-Liability Company Regulations 2004
Reg.10B, amended: SI 2015/1695 Reg.7

Reg.80C, amended: SI 2015/1695 Reg.7

Reg.85, amended: SI 2015/1695 Reg.7

2334. Genetically Modified Animal Feed (England) Regulations 2004

revoked: SI 2015/255 Sch.2

2607. General Medical Council (Fitness to Practise) (Disqualifying Decisions and Determinations by Regulatory Bodies) Procedure Rules Order of Council 2004

Sch.1, amended: SI 2015/1964 Sch.1

Sch.1, substituted: SI 2015/1964 Sch.1

2608. General Medical Council (Fitness to Practise) Rules Order of Council 2004

see *Soni v General Medical Council* [2015] EWHC 364 (Admin), (2015) 143 B.M.L.R. 113 (QBD (Admin)), Holroyde J

Sch.1, added: SI 2015/1964 Sch.1

Sch.1, amended: SI 2015/1964 Sch.1

Sch.1, revoked: SI 2015/1964 Sch.1

Sch.1, substituted: SI 2015/1964 Sch.1

Sch.1, see *R. (on the application of Chaudhuri) v General Medical Council* [2015] EWHC 6621 (Admin), [2015] Med. L.R. 440 (QBD (Admin)), Haddon-Cave J; see *R. (on the application of Squier) v General Medical Council* [2015] EWHC 299 (Admin), [2015] Med. L.R. 234 (QBD (Admin)), Ouseley J

2609. General Medical Council (Voluntary Erasure and Restoration following Voluntary Erasure) Regulations Order of Council 2004

Sch.1, amended: SI 2015/1964 Sch.1

Sch.1, substituted: SI 2015/1964 Sch.1

2611. General Medical Council (Constitution of Panels and Investigation Committee) Rules Order of Council 2004

revoked: SI 2015/1965 Art.3

Sch.1, revoked: SI 2015/1965 Sch.1

2612. General Medical Council (Restoration following Administrative Erasure) Regulations Order of Council 2004

Sch.1, amended: SI 2015/1964 Sch.1

Sch.1, substituted: SI 2015/1964 Sch.1

2625. General Medical Council (Legal Assessors) Rules 2004

revoked: SI 2015/1958 Art.3

2671. Iraq (United Nations Sanctions) (Overseas Territories) (Amendment) (No.2) Order 2004

revoked: SI 2015/1383 Art.1

2783. Education (National Curriculum) (Key Stage 1 Assessment Arrangements) (England) Order 2004

Art.1, amended: SI 2015/900 Art.3

Art.3, amended: SI 2015/900 Art.4

Art.4, amended: SI 2015/900 Art.5

Art.4A, added: SI 2015/900 Art.6

Art.5, amended: SI 2015/900 Art.7

Art.6, amended: SI 2015/900 Art.8

Art.7, revoked: SI 2015/900 Art.9

Art.9, amended: SI 2015/900 Art.10

2876. A55 Trunk Road (Penmaenmawr &mdash Conwy Morfa, Conwy) (Derestriction) Order 2004

varied: SI 2015/1229 Art.14

3256. Loan Relationships and Derivative Contracts (Disregard and Bringing into Account of Profits and Losses) Regulations 2004

Reg.2, amended: SI 2015/1961 Reg.3

Reg.5A, added: SI 2015/1961 Reg.4

Reg.6A, amended: SI 2015/1961 Reg.5

Reg.6B, substituted: SI 2015/1961 Reg.6

Reg.7, amended: SI 2015/1961 Reg.7

Reg.7, revoked: SI 2015/1961 Reg.7

Reg.9, amended: SI 2015/1961 Reg.8

Reg.9, revoked: SI 2015/1961 Reg.8

Reg.9A, revoked: SI 2015/1961 Reg.9

Reg.10, amended: SI 2015/1961 Reg.10

Reg.10, revoked: SI 2015/1961 Reg.10

3271. Loan Relationships and Derivative Contracts (Change Of Accounting Practice) Regulations 2004

Reg.3, amended: SI 2015/1962 Reg.3

Reg.3A, amended: SI 2015/1962 Reg.4

Reg.3A, revoked: SI 2015/1962 Reg.4

Reg.3B, amended: SI 2015/1962 Reg.5

Reg.3C, revoked: SI 2015/1962 Reg.6

Reg.4, amended: SI 2015/1541 Reg.2, SI 2015/1962 Reg.7

Reg.5, revoked: SI 2015/1962 Reg.8

3279. General Food Regulations 2004

Reg.2, amended: SSI 2015/433 Art.2

3391. Environmental Information Regulations 2004

see *Dransfield v Information Commissioner* [2015] EWCA Civ 454, [2015] 1 W.L.R. 5316 (CA (Civ Div)), Arden LJ

Reg.12, see *Dransfield v Information Commissioner* [2015] EWCA Civ 454, [2015] 1 W.L.R. 5316 (CA (Civ Div)), Arden LJ

Reg.17, amended: SI 2015/1897 Sch.1 para.3

3392. Electricity and Gas (Energy Efficiency Obligations) Order 2004

revoked: 2015 c.20 Sch.23 para.20

3426. Information and Consultation of Employees Regulations 2004

see *Moyer-Lee v Cofely Workplace Ltd* [2015] I.C.R. 1333 (EAT), Langstaff J

Reg.3, see *Moyer-Lee v Cofely Workplace Ltd* [2015] I.C.R. 1333 (EAT), Langstaff J

Reg.5, see *Moyer-Lee v Cofely Workplace Ltd* [2015] I.C.R. 1333 (EAT), Langstaff J

Reg.7, see *Moyer-Lee v Cofely Workplace Ltd* [2015] I.C.R. 1333 (EAT), Langstaff J

Reg.9, see *Moyer-Lee v Cofely Workplace Ltd* [2015] I.C.R. 1333 (EAT), Langstaff J

2005

17. Incidental Catches of Cetaceans in Fisheries (England) Order 2005

revoked: SI 2015/191 Sch.1

Art.5, amended: SI 2015/664 Sch.4 para.68

Art.11, amended: SI 2015/664 Sch.4 para.68

Sch.1, amended: SI 2015/664 Sch.4 para.68

36. General Teaching Council for Wales (Additional Functions) Order 2005

revoked: SI 2015/194 Sch.1

42. Licensing Act 2003 (Premises licences and club premises certificates) Regulations 2005

Reg.38, see *R. (on the application of Akin (t/a Efe's Snooker Club)) v Stratford Magistrates' Court* [2014] EWHC 4633 (Admin), [2015] 1 W.L.R. 4829 (DC), Beatson LJ

Reg.39, see *R. (on the application of Akin (t/a Efe's Snooker Club)) v Stratford*

Magistrates' Court [2014] EWHC 4633 (Admin), [2015] 1 W.L.R. 4829 (DC), Beatson LJ

68. General Teaching Council for Wales (Additional Functions) (Amendment) Order 2005

revoked: SI 2015/194 Sch.1

69. General Teaching Council for Wales (Functions) (Amendment) Regulations 2005

revoked: SI 2015/140 Sch.1 Part 1

122. A487 Trunk Road (Bow Street, Ceredigion) (30 mph Speed Limit) Order 2005

varied: SI 2015/1288 Art.7

255. Pensions (Northern Ireland) Order 2005

Art.34, see *Garvin Trustees Ltd v Pensions Regulator* [2015] Pens. L.R. 1 (UT (Tax)), Judge Timothy Herrington

402. General Medical Council (Constitution of Panels and Investigation Committee) (Amendment) Rules Order of Council 2005

revoked: SI 2015/1965 Art.3

Sch.1, revoked: SI 2015/1965 Sch.1

437. Armed Forces Early Departure Payments Scheme Order 2005

Art.3, amended: SI 2015/568 Reg.15

Art.3A, added: SI 2015/568 Reg.16

Art.4, amended: SI 2015/568 Reg.17

Art.8, amended: SI 2015/568 Reg.18

Art.10, amended: SI 2015/568 Reg.19

Art.12, amended: SI 2015/568 Reg.20

Art.14, amended: SI 2015/568 Reg.21

Art.16, amended: SI 2015/568 Reg.22

438. Armed Forces Pension Scheme Order 2005

Art.5, added: SI 2015/568 Reg.10

Sch.1, added: SI 2015/568 Reg.12

Sch.1, amended: SI 2015/568 Reg.11, Reg.12

Sch.2, added: SI 2015/568 Sch.2

448. Gangmasters (Licensing Authority) Regulations 2005

revoked: SI 2015/805 Reg.11

524. Insolvency Practitioners Regulations 2005

Reg.2, amended: SI 2015/1641 Sch.1 para.5

Reg.4, revoked: SI 2015/1641 Sch.1 para.5

Reg.5, amended: SI 2015/1641 Sch.3 para.3

Reg.5, revoked: SI 2015/1641 Sch.1 para.5

Reg.11, revoked: SI 2015/1641 Sch.1 para.5

Reg.12, amended: SI 2015/1641 Sch.1 para.5

Reg.13, amended: SI 2015/391 Reg.3

Reg.13, revoked: SI 2015/391 Reg.3

Reg.14, amended: SI 2015/391 Reg.4

Reg.14, revoked: SI 2015/1641 Sch.1 para.5

Reg.15, revoked: SI 2015/1641 Sch.1 para.5

Reg.16, revoked: SI 2015/1641 Sch.1 para.5

Sch.2 Part 3 para.9, amended: SI 2015/391 Reg.5

Sch.2 Part 3 para.9, revoked: SI 2015/1641 Sch.1 para.5

Sch.2 Part 3 para.10, revoked: SI 2015/1641 Sch.1 para.5

Sch.2 Part 3 para.11, amended: SI 2015/391 Reg.6

Sch.2 Part 3 para.13, revoked: SI 2015/1641 Sch.1 para.5

Sch.3, revoked: SI 2015/391 Reg.7

617. Courts Act 2003 (Consequential Provisions) (No.2) Order 2005

Art.2, revoked: SI 2015/191 Sch.1

Sch.1 para.179, revoked: SI 2015/191 Sch.1

Sch.1 para.180, revoked: SI 2015/191 Sch.1

Sch.1 para.183, revoked: SI 2015/191 Sch.1

Sch.1 para.187, revoked: SI 2015/191 Sch.1

Sch.1 para.212, revoked: SI 2015/191 Sch.1

Sch.1 para.235, revoked: SI 2015/191 Sch.1

648. Criminal Justice (Sentencing) (Licence Conditions) Order 2005

revoked: SI 2015/337 Art.2

678. Occupational Pension Schemes (Employer Debt) Regulations 2005

see *Merchant Navy Ratings Pension Fund, Re* [2015] EWHC 448 (Ch), [2015] Pens. L.R. 239 (Ch D), Asplin J

735. Work at Height Regulations 2005

see *Gilchrist v Asda Stores Ltd* [2015] CSOH 77, 2015 Rep. L.R. 95 (OH), Lady Stacey; see *McShane v Burnwynd Racing Stables Ltd* [2015] CSOH 70, 2015 Rep. L.R. 107 (OH), Lord Glennie

Reg.10, see *McLellan v Mitie Group Plc* [2015] CSOH 151, 2015 S.L.T. 861 (OH), Lady Scott

850. European Communities (Designation) Order 2005

Art.3, revoked: SI 2015/814 Art.5

Sch.1, amended: SI 2015/814 Art.5

890. Adoption Information and Intermediary Services (Pre-Commencement Adoptions) Regulations 2005

Reg.2, amended: SI 2015/1685 Reg.3

Reg.8, amended: SI 2015/1685 Reg.4

Reg.12, amended: SI 2015/1685 Reg.5

Reg.13, substituted: SI 2015/1685 Reg.6

Reg.14, amended: SI 2015/1685 Reg.7

Reg.14, revoked: SI 2015/1685 Reg.7

Reg.16, amended: SI 2015/1685 Reg.8

Reg.18, amended: SI 2015/1685 Reg.9

894. Hazardous Waste (England and Wales) Regulations 2005

Reg.2, amended: SI 2015/1360 Reg.3

Reg.3, amended: SI 2015/1360 Reg.3

Reg.4, amended: SI 2015/1360 Reg.3

Reg.8, amended: SI 2015/1360 Reg.3

Reg.9, amended: SI 2015/1360 Reg.3

Sch.3, revoked: SI 2015/1360 Reg.3

Sch.8, substituted: SI 2015/1360 Sch.1

Sch.11 Part 2 para.38, revoked: SI 2015/1640 Sch.6

895. List of Wastes (England) Regulations 2005

revoked: SI 2015/1360 Reg.10

896. General Medical Council (Legal Assessors) (Amendment) Rules 2005

revoked: SI 2015/1958 Art.3

1088. Control of Major Accident Hazards (Amendment) Regulations 2005

revoked: SI 2015/483 Reg.31

1093. Control of Vibration at Work Regulations 2005

Reg.2, amended: SI 2015/1682 Sch.1 para.10

Reg.3, amended: SI 2015/1637 Sch.1 para.9

1109. Special Guardianship Regulations 2005

Reg.21, see *R (A Child) (Child Arrangements Order: Best Interests), Re* [2015] EWCA Civ 405, [2015] 2 F.C.R. 385 (CA (Civ Div)), Laws LJ

1135. Gas (Standards of Performance) Regulations 2005

Part II, substituted: SI 2015/1544 Reg.12

Reg.3, amended: SI 2015/1544 Reg.12

Reg.4, revoked: SI 2015/1544 Reg.12

Reg.12, revoked: SI 2015/1544 Reg.12

Reg.13, amended: SI 2015/1544 Reg.12

Reg.14, revoked: SI 2015/1544 Reg.12

Reg.15, revoked: SI 2015/1544 Reg.12

Reg.16, revoked: SI 2015/1544 Reg.12

Sch.1 Part I, amended: SI 2015/1544 Reg.12

Sch.1 Part I, substituted: SI 2015/1544 Reg.12

1437. Education (Pupil Information) (England) Regulations 2005

Reg.2, amended: SI 2015/902 Reg.3, SI 2015/971 Sch.3 para.7

Sch.1 para.1, amended: SI 2015/902 Reg.4

Sch.1 para.2, amended: SI 2015/902 Reg.4

Sch.1 para.3, amended: SI 2015/902 Reg.4

Sch.2 para.6, amended: SI 2015/902 Reg.5

1455. Insolvency (Northern Ireland) Order 2005

Sch.2 para.64, revoked: 2015 c.26 Sch.8 para.5

Sch.2 para.65, revoked: 2015 c.26 Sch.8 para.10

Sch.6 para.4, revoked: 2015 c.26 s.116

1461. Democratic Republic of the Congo (United Nations Sanctions) (Overseas Territories) Order 2005

revoked: SI 2015/1382 Art.1

1529. Financial Services and Markets Act 2000 (Financial Promotion) Order 2005

Art.29, amended: SI 2015/1882 Reg.5

Art.55B, amended: SI 2015/853 Art.4

Art.59, amended: SI 2015/352 Art.4

Art.72F, amended: SI 2015/853 Art.4

Sch.1 Part I para.4B, amended: SI 2015/853 Art.4

Sch.1 Part I para.10BAA, added: SI 2015/910 Sch.1 para.12

Sch.1 Part II para.28, amended: SI 2015/910 Sch.1 para.12

1533. Children (Private Arrangements for Fostering) Regulations 2005

see *B v C (Surrogacy: Adoption)* [2015] EWFC 17, [2015] 1 F.L.R. 1392 (Fam Ct), Theis J

1622. Health and Social Care (Community Health and Standards) Act 2003 (Public Health Laboratory Service Board) (Consequential Provisions) Order 2005

revoked: SI 2015/864 Art.2

1643. Control of Noise at Work Regulations 2005

Reg.2, amended: SI 2015/1682 Sch.1 para.10

Reg.3, amended: SI 2015/1637 Sch.1 para.10

1673. List of Wastes (England) (Amendment) Regulations 2005

revoked: SI 2015/1360 Reg.10

1677. Export Control (Democratic Republic of Congo) Order 2005

revoked: SI 2015/1546 Sch.1

1803. General Product Safety Regulations 2005

Reg.21, revoked: SI 2015/1630 Sch.2 para.45

1805. Financial Assistance for Environmental Purposes Order 2005

revoked: SI 2015/479 Sch.1

1806. Hazardous Waste (Wales) Regulations 2005

Reg.2, amended: SI 2015/1417 Reg.3

Reg.3, amended: SI 2015/1417 Reg.3

Reg.4, amended: SI 2015/1417 Reg.3

Reg.6, amended: SI 2015/1417 Reg.3

Reg.8, amended: SI 2015/1417 Reg.3

Reg.9, amended: SI 2015/1417 Reg.3

Sch.3, revoked: SI 2015/1417 Reg.3

Sch.8, amended: SI 2015/1417 Sch.1

Sch.11 Part 2 para.41, revoked: SI 2015/1640 Sch.6

1820. List of Wastes (Wales) Regulations 2005

revoked: SI 2015/1417 Reg.7

1920. Honey (Amendment) (England) Regulations 2005

revoked: SI 2015/1348 Reg.20

1972. Children Act 2004 (Children's Services) Regulations 2005

Reg.2, amended: SI 2015/1792 Reg.5
Reg.2, revoked: SI 2015/1792 Reg.5
1973. Children Act 2004 (Joint Area Reviews)
Regulations 2005
revoked: SI 2015/1792 Reg.6
1988. Democratic Republic of the Congo
(Restrictive Measures) (Overseas Territories)
(Amendment) Order 2005
revoked: SI 2015/1382 Art.1
1998. Insurers (Reorganisation and Winding
Up) (Lloyd's) Regulations 2005
Reg.2, amended: SI 2015/575 Sch.2
para.23
2038. Education (School Inspection)
(England) Regulations 2005
Reg.2, amended: SI 2015/170 Reg.2
Reg.3, substituted: SI 2015/170 Reg.2
Reg.3A, added: SI 2015/1639 Reg.2
Reg.4, amended: SI 2015/170 Reg.2
Reg.6, amended: SI 2015/170 Reg.2
2041. Fishguard to Bangor Trunk Road
(A487) (Llanon, Ceredigion) (40 MPH Speed
Limit) Order 2005
varied: SI 2015/1285 Art.7
2042. Civil Contingencies Act 2004
(Contingency Planning) Regulations 2005
Reg.12, amended: SI 2015/483 Sch.6
para.3
2045. Income Tax (Construction Industry
Scheme) Regulations 2005
Reg.4, revoked: SI 2015/429 Reg.2
Reg.8, amended: SI 2015/125 Reg.4
Reg.56, amended: SI 2015/125 Reg.4, SI
2015/429 Reg.2
Reg.56, revoked: SI 2015/125 Reg.4
2339. Community Design Regulations 2005
Reg.2, see *Tech 21 UK Ltd v Logitech*
Europe S.A. [2015] EWHC 2614 (Ch),
[2015] Bus. L.R. 1276 (Ch D), Stephen
Jourdan QC
2701. Adoption Information and
Intermediary Services (Pre-Commencement
Adoptions) (Wales) Regulations 2005
Reg.2, amended: SI 2015/1802 Reg.3
Reg.2A, added: SI 2015/1802 Reg.4
Reg.4, amended: SI 2015/1802 Reg.5
Reg.5, amended: SI 2015/1802 Reg.6
Reg.5, revoked: SI 2015/1802 Reg.6
Reg.5, substituted: SI 2015/1802 Reg.6
Reg.5A, added: SI 2015/1802 Reg.7
Reg.8, amended: SI 2015/1802 Reg.8

Reg.8, revoked: SI 2015/1802 Reg.8
Reg.9, substituted: SI 2015/1802 Reg.9
Reg.10, amended: SI 2015/1802 Reg.10
Reg.11, amended: SI 2015/1802 Reg.11
Reg.12, amended: SI 2015/1802 Reg.12
Reg.13, amended: SI 2015/1802 Reg.13
Reg.14, amended: SI 2015/1802 Reg.14
Reg.14, revoked: SI 2015/1802 Reg.14
Reg.16, amended: SI 2015/1802 Reg.15
Reg.18, amended: SI 2015/1802 Reg.16
2876. Housing (Right to Buy) (Prescribed
Forms) (Amendment) (England) (No.3)
Regulations 2005
revoked: SI 2015/1542 Reg.3
2913. Education Act 2002 (Transitional
Provisions and Consequential Amendments)
(Wales) Regulations 2005
Reg.23, revoked: SI 2015/1599 Reg.1
2916. Change of Category of Maintained
Schools (Wales) (Amendment) Regulations
2005
revoked: SI 2015/1521 Reg.1
3052. Honey (Wales) (Amendment)
Regulations 2005
revoked: SI 2015/1507 Reg.20
3176. Civil Partnership (Registration
Provisions) Regulations 2005
Reg.3, substituted: SI 2015/177 Reg.4
Reg.5A, added: SI 2015/177 Reg.4
Sch.1, substituted: SI 2015/177 Reg.4
Sch.2, amended: SI 2015/177 Sch.1
Sch.3, added: SI 2015/177 Reg.4
3181. Proceeds of Crime Act 2002 (External
Requests and Orders) Order 2005
see *Blue Holding (1) Pte Ltd v United*
States [2014] EWCA Civ 1291, [2015] 1
W.L.R. 1917 (CA (Civ Div)), Rimer LJ;
see *National Crime Agency v Abacha*
[2015] EWHC 357 (Admin), [2015]
Lloyd's Rep. F.C. 411 (QBD (Admin)),
Elisabeth Laing J
3207. Channel Tunnel (International
Arrangements) Order 2005
revoked: SI 2015/785 Art.4
Art.2, amended: SI 2015/1682 Sch.1
para.10
Art.4A, amended: SI 2015/1682 Sch.1
para.10
3280. Feed (Hygiene and Enforcement)
(England) Regulations 2005
revoked: SI 2015/454 Sch.5

3320. Hydrocarbon Oil Duties (Reliefs for Electricity Generation) Regulations 2005
Reg.9, amended: SI 2015/943 Reg.3
Reg.10, amended: SI 2015/943 Reg.4
Sch.3, added: SI 2015/943 Reg.5
3422. Loan Relationships and Derivative Contracts (Exchange Gains and Losses using Fair Value Accounting) Regulations 2005
Reg.2, substituted: SI 2015/1963 Reg.2
Reg.3, amended: SI 2015/1963 Reg.2
Reg.5, amended: SI 2015/1963 Reg.2
Reg.6, amended: SI 2015/1963 Reg.2
Reg.7, amended: SI 2015/1963 Reg.2
Reg.9, amended: SI 2015/1963 Reg.2

2006

5. Public Contracts Regulations 2006
see *Nationwide Gritting Services Ltd v Scottish Ministers* 2015 S.C.L.R. 367 (OH), Lord Woolman; see *R. (on the application of Draper) v Lincolnshire CC* [2014] EWHC 2388 (Admin), [2015] P.T.S.R. 769 (QBD (Admin)), Collins J; see *Woods Building Services v Milton Keynes Council* [2015] EWHC 2011 (TCC), [2015] B.L.R. 571 (QBD (TCC)), Coulson J
Reg.14, see *Nationwide Gritting Services Ltd v Scottish Ministers* 2015 S.C.L.R. 367 (OH), Lord Woolman
Reg.47F, see *Heron Bros Ltd v Central Bedfordshire Council* [2015] EWHC 604 (TCC), [2015] P.T.S.R. 1146 (QBD (TCC)), Edwards-Stuart J
Reg.47G, see *Bristol Missing Link Ltd v Bristol City Council* [2015] EWHC 876 (TCC), [2015] P.T.S.R. 1470 (QBD (TCC)), Coulson J; see *Energy Solutions EU Ltd v Nuclear Decommissioning Authority* [2015] EWHC 73 (TCC), [2015] P.T.S.R. 1106 (QBD (TCC)), Edwards-Stuart J; see *Group M UK Ltd v Cabinet Office* [2014] EWHC 3659 (TCC), [2015] B.L.R. 258 (QBD (TCC)), Akenhead J; see *OpenView Security Solutions Ltd v Merton LBC* [2015] EWHC 2694 (TCC), [2015] B.L.R. 735 (QBD (TCC)), Stuart-Smith J

Reg.47H, see *Bristol Missing Link Ltd v Bristol City Council* [2015] EWHC 876 (TCC), [2015] P.T.S.R. 1470 (QBD (TCC)), Coulson J; see *Group M UK Ltd v Cabinet Office* [2014] EWHC 3659 (TCC), [2015] B.L.R. 258 (QBD (TCC)), Akenhead J; see *OpenView Security Solutions Ltd v Merton LBC* [2015] EWHC 2694 (TCC), [2015] B.L.R. 735 (QBD (TCC)), Stuart-Smith J
Reg.47I, see *Woods Building Services v Milton Keynes Council* [2015] EWHC 2172 (TCC), [2015] B.L.R. 591 (QBD (TCC)), Coulson J
Reg.47J, see *Energy Solutions EU Ltd v Nuclear Decommissioning Authority* [2015] EWHC 73 (TCC), [2015] P.T.S.R. 1106 (QBD (TCC)), Edwards-Stuart J
6. Utilities Contracts Regulations 2006
Reg.3, see *NATS (Services) Ltd v Gatwick Airport Ltd* [2014] EWHC 3133 (TCC), [2015] P.T.S.R. 566 (QBD (TCC)), Ramsey J
Reg.30, see *NATS (Services) Ltd v Gatwick Airport Ltd* [2014] EWHC 3728 (TCC), [2015] B.L.R. 19 (QBD (TCC)), Akenhead J
Reg.45G, see *NATS (Services) Ltd v Gatwick Airport Ltd* [2014] EWHC 3133 (TCC), [2015] P.T.S.R. 566 (QBD (TCC)), Ramsey J; see *NATS (Services) Ltd v Gatwick Airport Ltd* [2014] EWHC 3728 (TCC), [2015] B.L.R. 19 (QBD (TCC)), Akenhead J
213. Housing Benefit Regulations 2006
Reg.B13, see *R. (on the application of Hardy) v Sandwell MBC* [2015] EWHC 890 (Admin), [2015] P.T.S.R. 1292 (QBD (Admin)), Phillips J
Reg.2, amended: SI 2015/67 Reg.2, SI 2015/971 Sch.3 para.8, SI 2015/1985 Art.28
Reg.9, see *R. (on the application of Whapples) v Birmingham CrossCity Clinical Commissioning Group* [2015] EWCA Civ 435, [2015] P.T.S.R. 1398 (CA (Civ Div)), Underhill LJ
Reg.22, revoked: SI 2015/1857 Reg.2
Reg.23, revoked: SI 2015/1857 Reg.2
Reg.29, amended: SI 2015/6 Reg.2
Reg.29A, added: SI 2015/6 Reg.2

Reg.34, amended: SI 2015/478 Reg.33,
SI 2015/1985 Art.28
Reg.39, amended: SI 2015/478 Reg.33
Reg.52, amended: SI 2015/643 Sch.1
para.24
Reg.53, amended: SI 2015/971 Sch.3
para.8
Reg.59, amended: SI 2015/67 Reg.6
Reg.74, amended: SI 2015/457 Art.17
Reg.83, amended: SI 2015/1857 Reg.3
Sch.1 Part 1 para.2, amended: SI
2015/457 Art.17
Sch.1 Part 2 para.6, amended: SI
2015/457 Art.17
Sch.3 Part 1 para.1, amended: SI 2015/30
Sch.2
Sch.3 Part 1 para.2, amended: SI
2015/457 Sch.5
Sch.3 Part 2, revoked: SI 2015/1857
Reg.2
Sch.3 Part 3 para.13, amended: SI
2015/1985 Art.28
Sch.3 Part 3 para.14, amended: SI
2015/1754 Reg.17
Sch.3 Part 4, amended: SI 2015/457
Sch.6, SI 2015/1754 Reg.17
Sch.3 Part 6 para.25, amended: SI
2015/457 Art.17
Sch.3 Part 6 para.26, amended: SI
2015/457 Art.17
Sch.4 para.1, amended: SI 2015/1985
Art.28
Sch.4 para.17, amended: SI 2015/1857
Reg.2
Sch.5 para.27, amended: SI 2015/643
Sch.1 para.24
Sch.5 para.47, amended: SI 2015/1857
Reg.2
Sch.5 para.57, amended: SI 2015/643
Sch.1 para.24
Sch.6 para.58, amended: SI 2015/643
Sch.1 para.24

**214. Housing Benefit (Persons who have
attained the qualifying age for state pension
credit) Regulations 2006**
Reg.2, amended: SI 2015/67 Reg.2, SI
2015/971 Sch.3 para.9, SI 2015/1985
Art.29
Reg.22, revoked: SI 2015/1857 Reg.2
Reg.33, amended: SI 2015/6 Reg.3

Reg.34, amended: SI 2015/478 Reg.34,
SI 2015/1985 Art.29
Reg.38, amended: SI 2015/643 Sch.1
para.25
Reg.40, amended: SI 2015/478 Reg.34
Reg.41, amended: SI 2015/1985 Art.29
Reg.55, amended: SI 2015/457 Art.18
Sch.1 Part 1 para.2, amended: SI
2015/457 Art.18
Sch.1 Part 2 para.6, amended: SI
2015/457 Art.18
Sch.3 Part 1 para.1, amended: SI
2015/457 Sch.7
Sch.3 Part 1 para.2, amended: SI
2015/457 Sch.7
Sch.3 Part 2, revoked: SI 2015/1857
Reg.2
Sch.3 Part 3 para.6, amended: SI
2015/1754 Reg.18
Sch.3 Part 4, amended: SI 2015/457
Sch.8, SI 2015/1754 Reg.18
Sch.4 para.9, amended: SI 2015/1857
Reg.2
Sch.5 para.20, amended: SI 2015/1857
Reg.2
Sch.6 Part 1 para.26AA, added: SI
2015/1985 Art.29
Sch.6 Part 1 para.26D, amended: SI
2015/643 Sch.1 para.25

215. Council Tax Benefit Regulations 2006
Reg.2, amended: SI 2015/971 Sch.3
para.10
Reg.43, amended: SI 2015/971 Sch.3
para.10

**216. Council Tax Benefit (Persons who have
attained the qualifying age for state pension
credit) Regulations 2006**
Reg.2, amended: SI 2015/971 Sch.3
para.11

**223. Child Benefit (General) Regulations
2006**
Reg.1, amended: SI 2015/1512 Reg.2
Reg.1, revoked: SI 2015/1512 Reg.2
Reg.27, see *Revenue and Customs
Commissioners v Spiridonova* [2015] 1
C.M.L.R. 26 (CA (NI)), Morgan LCJ

**246. Transfer of Undertakings (Protection of
Employment) Regulations 2006**
see *Edie v HCL Insurance BPO Services
Ltd* [2015] I.C.R. 713 (EAT), Lewis J;
see *Ellis v Cabinet Office* [2015] EWCA

Civ 252, [2015] Pens. L.R. 379 (CA (Civ Div)), Moore-Bick LJ; see *Housing Maintenance Solutions Ltd v McAteer* [2015] I.C.R. 87 (EAT), Slade J; see *Jakowlew v Nestor Primecare Services Ltd (t/a Saga Care)* [2015] I.C.R. 1100 (EAT), Judge David Richardson; see *NHS Direct NHS Trust v Gunn* [2015] I.R.L.R. 799 (EAT), Langstaff J; see *Rynda (UK) Ltd v Rhijnsburger* [2015] EWCA Civ 75, [2015] I.C.R. 1300 (CA (Civ Div)), Jackson LJ

Reg.3, see *BT Managed Services Ltd v Edwards* [2015] I.R.L.R. 994 (EAT), Judge Serota QC; see *Ottimo Property Services Ltd v Duncan* [2015] I.C.R. 859 (EAT), Judge Eady QC; see *Rynda (UK) Ltd v Rhijnsburger* [2015] EWCA Civ 75, [2015] I.C.R. 1300 (CA (Civ Div)), Jackson LJ

Reg.4, see *BT Managed Services Ltd v Edwards* [2015] I.R.L.R. 994 (EAT), Judge Serota QC; see *Jakowlew v Nestor Primecare Services Ltd (t/a Saga Care)* [2015] I.C.R. 1100 (EAT), Judge David Richardson; see *Salmon v Castlebeck Care (Teesdale) Ltd (In Administration)* [2015] I.C.R. 735 (EAT), Langstaff J

373. Licensing and Management of Houses in Multiple Occupation and Other Houses (Miscellaneous Provisions) (England) Regulations 2006
Sch.1, amended: SI 2015/541 Reg.54

557. Health and Safety (Enforcing Authority for Railways and Other Guided Transport Systems) Regulations 2006
Reg.2, amended: SI 2015/51 Sch.5
Reg.3, amended: SI 2015/1682 Sch.1 para.10
Reg.4, amended: SI 2015/483 Sch.6 para.4, SI 2015/1682 Sch.1 para.10
Reg.5A, amended: SI 2015/1682 Sch.1 para.10
Reg.7, amended: SI 2015/1682 Sch.1 para.10

562. General Dental Services, Personal Dental Services and Abolition of the Dental Practice Board Transitional and Consequential Provisions Order 2006
Sch.1 para.9, revoked: SI 2015/570 Sch.3

602. Elections (Policy Development Grants Scheme) Order 2006
Sch.1, added: SI 2015/128 Sch.1 para.2, Sch.1 para.5, SI 2015/302 Sch.1 para.2, Sch.1 para.3, Sch.1 para.5
Sch.1, amended: SI 2015/128 Sch.1 para.3, Sch.1 para.4, Sch.1 para.6, SI 2015/302 Sch.1 para.3, Sch.1 para.4, Sch.1 para.6

623. Driving Standards Agency Trading Fund (Maximum Borrowing) Order 2006
revoked: SI 2015/41 Sch.3

650. Homelessness (Suitability of Accommodation) (Wales) Order 2006
revoked: SI 2015/1268 Art.9

755. Animals and Animal Products (Examination for Residues and Maximum Residue Limits) (Amendment) Regulations 2006
revoked: SI 2015/787 Sch.1

964. Authorised Investment Funds (Tax) Regulations 2006
Part 2, amended: SI 2015/485 Reg.2
Reg.12A, added: SI 2015/485 Reg.2
Reg.13, amended: SI 2015/485 Reg.2
Reg.17, revoked: SI 2015/485 Reg.2
Reg.108, revoked: SI 2015/616 Reg.4

965. Child Benefit (Rates) Regulations 2006
Reg.2, amended: SI 2015/567 Art.2

1003. Immigration (European Economic Area) Regulations 2006
see *R. (on the application of Byczek) v Secretary of State for the Home Department* [2014] EWHC 4298 (Admin), [2015] 2 C.M.L.R. 7 (QBD (Admin)), Jay J
Reg.2, amended: SI 2015/694 Sch.1 para.1
Reg.4, amended: SI 2015/694 Sch.1 para.2
Reg.4, revoked: SI 2015/694 Sch.1 para.2
Reg.6, see *Weldemichael v Secretary of State for the Home Department* [2015] UKUT 540 (IAC) (UT (IAC)), Judge Storey
Reg.7, see *Weldemichael v Secretary of State for the Home Department* [2015] UKUT 540 (IAC) (UT (IAC)), Judge Storey
Reg.8, see *AA (Algeria) v Secretary of State for the Home Department* [2014]

EWCA Civ 1741, [2015] 2 C.M.L.R. 14
(CA (Civ Div)), Sullivan LJ
Reg.9, see *AA (Nigeria) v Secretary of
State for the Home Department* [2015]
CSOH 158 (OH), Lord Glennie
Reg.10, see *Ahmed (Amos: Zambrano:
Reg. 15A(3)(c) 2006 EEA Regs), Re*
[2014] EWCA Civ 995, [2015] 1
C.M.L.R. 9 (CA (Civ Div)), Lord Dyson
MR
Reg.11, amended: SI 2015/694 Sch.1
para.3
Reg.13, amended: SI 2015/694 Sch.1
para.4
Reg.14, amended: SI 2015/694 Sch.1
para.5
Reg.15, amended: SI 2015/694 Sch.1
para.6
Reg.15, see *Weldemichael v Secretary of
State for the Home Department* [2015]
UKUT 540 (IAC) (UT (IAC)), Judge
Storey
Reg.15A, amended: SI 2015/694 Sch.1
para.7
Reg.15A, see *R. (on the application of
Mensah) v Salford City Council* [2014]
EWHC 3537 (Admin), [2015] P.T.S.R.
157 (QBD (Admin)), Lewis J
Reg.17, see *AA (Nigeria) v Secretary of
State for the Home Department* [2015]
CSOH 158 (OH), Lord Glennie
Reg.19, see *R. (on the application of
Byczek) v Secretary of State for the Home
Department* [2014] EWHC 4298
(Admin), [2015] 2 C.M.L.R. 7 (QBD
(Admin)), Jay J
Reg.20, amended: SI 2015/694 Sch.1
para.8
Reg.23A, added: SI 2015/694 Sch.1
para.9
Reg.24, amended: SI 2015/694 Sch.1
para.10
Reg.24, see *R. (on the application of
Byczek) v Secretary of State for the Home
Department* [2014] EWHC 4298
(Admin), [2015] 2 C.M.L.R. 7 (QBD
(Admin)), Jay J
Reg.24A, see *R. (on the application of
Byczek) v Secretary of State for the Home
Department* [2014] EWHC 4298

(Admin), [2015] 2 C.M.L.R. 7 (QBD
(Admin)), Jay J
Reg.25, amended: SI 2015/694 Sch.1
para.11
Reg.25, revoked: SI 2015/694 Sch.1
para.11
Reg.26, amended: SI 2015/694 Sch.1
para.12
Reg.26, see *Amirteymour (EEA Appeals:
Human Rights: United States)* [2015]
UKUT 466 (IAC), [2015] Imm. A.R.
1365 (UT (IAC)), McCloskey J
Reg.27, amended: SI 2015/694 Sch.1
para.13
Reg.27, revoked: SI 2015/694 Sch.1
para.13
Reg.27, see *R. (on the application of
Byczek) v Secretary of State for the Home
Department* [2014] EWHC 4298
(Admin), [2015] 2 C.M.L.R. 7 (QBD
(Admin)), Jay J
Reg.29, amended: SI 2015/694 Sch.1
para.14
Reg.29, see *R. (on the application of
Ahmed) v Secretary of State for the Home
Department* [2015] UKUT 436 (IAC),
[2015] Imm. A.R. 1320 (UT (IAC)),
Judge Storey
Sch.1, see *R. (on the application of
Ahmed) v Secretary of State for the Home
Department* [2015] UKUT 436 (IAC),
[2015] Imm. A.R. 1320 (UT (IAC)),
Judge Storey
Sch.1 para.1, amended: SI 2015/694
Sch.1 para.15
Sch.1 para.1, see *Amirteymour (EEA
Appeals: Human Rights: United States)*
[2015] UKUT 466 (IAC), [2015] Imm.
A.R. 1365 (UT (IAC)), McCloskey J
Sch.2 para.4, amended: SI 2015/694
Sch.1 para.16
Sch.2 para.4, revoked: SI 2015/694 Sch.1
para.16
**1028. Intellectual Property (Enforcement,
etc.) Regulations 2006**
Reg.3, see *DKH Retail Ltd v H Young
Operations Ltd* [2014] EWHC 4034
(IPEC), [2015] F.S.R. 21 (IPEC), Judge
Hacon
**1030. Cross-Border Insolvency Regulations
2006**

see *Bank of Tokyo-Mitsubishi UFJ Ltd v Owners of the Sanko Mineral* [2014] EWHC 3927 (Admlty), [2015] 2 All E.R. (Comm) 979 (QBD (Admlty)), Teare J

1031. Employment Equality (Age) Regulations 2006

Sch.6 para.2, see *Evbenata v South West London and St George's Mental Health NHS Trust* [2015] I.C.R. 483 (EAT), Simler J

Sch.6 para.4, see *Evbenata v South West London and St George's Mental Health NHS Trust* [2015] I.C.R. 483 (EAT), Simler J

Sch.6 para.5, see *Evbenata v South West London and St George's Mental Health NHS Trust* [2015] I.C.R. 483 (EAT), Simler J

1116. Criminal Justice Act 1988 (Reviews of Sentencing) Order 2006

Sch.1 para.2, amended: SI 2015/1472 Reg.3

Sch.1 para.3, amended: SI 2015/800 Reg.3

1260. Human Tissue Act 2004 (Ethical Approval, Exceptions from Licensing and Supply of Information about Transplants) Regulations 2006

Sch.2 para.10, amended: SI 2015/238 Sch.3 para.2

1341. General Teaching Council for Wales (Additional Functions) (Amendment) Order 2006

revoked: SI 2015/194 Sch.1

1343. General Teaching Council for Wales (Functions) (Amendment) Regulations 2006

revoked: SI 2015/140 Sch.1 Part 1

1496. British Nationality (Proof of Paternity) Regulations 2006

Reg.2, substituted: SI 2015/1615 Reg.3

Reg.3, amended: SI 2015/1615 Reg.4

1735. Financial Assistance for Environmental Purposes Order 2006

revoked: SI 2015/479 Sch.1

1743. Immigration (Provision of Physical Data) Regulations 2006

Reg.2, amended: SI 2015/737 Reg.3

Reg.4, amended: SI 2015/737 Reg.4

Reg.6, substituted: SI 2015/737 Reg.5

Reg.6A, added: SI 2015/737 Reg.6

Reg.8, substituted: SI 2015/737 Reg.7

1811. Firefighters Compensation Scheme (England) Order 2006

Sch.1, added: SI 2015/590 Sch.1 para.1, Sch.1 para.4, Sch.1 para.8, Sch.1 para.9, Sch.1 para.10, Sch.1 para.11

Sch.1, amended: SI 2015/590 Sch.1 para.1, Sch.1 para.2, Sch.1 para.3, Sch.1 para.4, Sch.1 para.5, Sch.1 para.6, Sch.1 para.7, Sch.1 para.8, Sch.1 para.9, Sch.1 para.10, Sch.1 para.11, Sch.1 para.12, Sch.1 para.13

Sch.1, substituted: SI 2015/590 Sch.1 para.1, Sch.1 para.3, Sch.1 para.6, Sch.1 para.7, Sch.1 para.12

2238. Environmental Noise (England) Regulations 2006

Reg.2, amended: SI 2015/377 Sch.1 para.38

2492. Criminal Defence Service (Financial Eligibility) Regulations 2006

Reg.2, amended: SI 2015/643 Sch.1 para.26, SI 2015/838 Reg.4

2986. Children (Secure Accommodation) (Amendment) (Wales) Regulations 2006

revoked: SI 2015/1988 Reg.18

3120. Feed (Specified Undesirable Substances) (England) Regulations 2006

revoked: SI 2015/454 Sch.5

3304. Local Elections (Principal Areas) (England and Wales) Rules 2006

Sch.2, amended: SI 2015/103 r.2, Sch.1

Sch.3, amended: SI 2015/103 r.3, Sch.2

3305. Local Elections (Parishes and Communities) (England and Wales) Rules 2006

Sch.2, amended: SI 2015/104 r.2, Sch.1

Sch.3, amended: SI 2015/104 r.3, Sch.2

3322. Compensation (Claims Management Services) Regulations 2006

Part 7, substituted: SI 2015/42 Reg.2

Reg.3, amended: SI 2015/42 Reg.2

Reg.12, amended: SI 2015/42 Reg.2

Reg.12, revoked: SI 2015/42 Reg.2

Reg.27, revoked: SI 2015/42 Reg.2

Reg.28, revoked: SI 2015/42 Reg.2

Reg.28A, added: SI 2015/42 Reg.2

Reg.29, amended: SI 2015/42 Reg.2

Reg.29, revoked: SI 2015/42 Reg.2

3332. Health Service Commissioner for England (Special Health Authorities) (Revocation) Order 2006

revoked: SI 2015/822 Art.2

3363. Enterprise Act 2002 (Amendment) Regulations 2006

Reg.15, revoked: 2015 c.15 Sch.6 para.85

Reg.24, revoked: 2015 c.15 Sch.6 para.85

3418. Electromagnetic Compatibility Regulations 2006

Reg.3, amended: SI 2015/1630 Sch.2 para.109

Reg.37A, added: SI 2015/1630 Sch.2 para.110

3432. Firefighters Pension Scheme (England) Order 2006

Sch.1, added: SI 2015/589 Sch.2 para.2, Sch.2 para.3, Sch.2 para.4, Sch.2 para.5, Sch.2 para.6, Sch.2 para.7, Sch.2 para.8, SI 2015/590 Sch.2 para.2, Sch.2 para.3

Sch.1, amended: SI 2015/589 Sch.2 para.1, Sch.2 para.2, Sch.2 para.3, Sch.2 para.5, Sch.2 para.6, SI 2015/590 Sch.2 para.1, Sch.2 para.2, Sch.2 para.3, Sch.2 para.4, Sch.2 para.5, Sch.2 para.6

2007

284. Liberia (Restrictive Measures) (Overseas Territories) (Amendment) Order 2007

revoked: SI 2015/1899 Art.1

312. Decommissioning of Fishing Vessels Scheme 2007

revoked: SI 2015/191 Sch.1

320. Construction (Design and Management) Regulations 2007

revoked: SI 2015/51 Reg.38

342. A43 Trunk Road (Ardley, Oxfordshire) (50 Miles Per Hour Speed Limit) Order 2007

revoked: SI 2015/1224 Art.5

399. Local Authorities (Executive Arrangements) (Functions and Responsibilities) (Wales) Regulations 2007

Sch.1, amended: SI 2015/968 Sch.1 para.6

529. Cattle Identification Regulations 2007

see *R. v Moss (Eric John)* [2015] EWCA Crim 713, [2015] Lloyd's Rep. F.C. 397 (CA (Crim Div)), Lord Thomas LCJ

Sch.5 para.1, amended: SI 2015/219 Reg.2

694. Her Majesty's Chief Inspector of Education, Children's Services and Skills (Fees and Frequency of Inspections) (Children's Homes etc.) Regulations 2007

revoked: SI 2015/551 Sch.1

722. Childcare (Supply and Disclosure of Information) (England) Regulations 2007

Reg.2, amended: SI 2015/357 Reg.3

Reg.10, amended: SI 2015/357 Reg.4

Sch.1 Part 2 para.6, amended: SI 2015/1562 Reg.2

Sch.1 Part 2 para.8, amended: SI 2015/1562 Reg.2

Sch.1 Part 3 para.19, added: SI 2015/357 Reg.5

736. Children (Performances) (Amendment)(Wales) Regulations 2007

revoked: SI 2015/1757 Sch.1

765. Smoke-free (Exemptions and Vehicles) Regulations 2007

Reg.5, see *R. (on the application of Black) v Secretary of State for Justice* [2015] EWHC 528 (Admin), [2015] 1 W.L.R. 3963 (QBD (Admin)), Singh J

779. Education (Fees and Awards) (England) Regulations 2007

Reg.9, amended: SI 2015/971 Sch.3 para.12

784. Housing (Right to Buy) (Prescribed Forms) (Amendment) (England) Regulations 2007

revoked: SI 2015/1542 Reg.3

797. Housing (Tenancy Deposits) (Prescribed Information) Order 2007

Art.2, amended: 2015 c.20 s.30

Art.3, added: 2015 c.20 s.30

798. Housing (Tenancy Deposits) (Specified Interest Rate) Order 2007

revoked: SI 2015/14 Art.3

848. Government of Wales Act 2006 (Designation of Receipts) Order 2007

Art.2, amended: SI 2015/640 Art.2

1028. Docking of Working Dogs Tails (Wales) Regulations 2007

Reg.5, amended: SI 2015/1990 Reg.16

1069. Education (Pupil Referral Units) (Application of Enactments) (Wales) Regulations 2007

Sch.1 Part 2 para.16, substituted: SI 2015/1793 Reg.2

1072. Firefighters Pension Scheme (Wales) Order 2007
    Sch.1, added: SI 2015/1013 Sch.2 para.2,
    Sch.2 para.3, SI 2015/1016 Sch.2 para.2,
    Sch.2 para.3, Sch.2 para.4, Sch.2 para.5,
    Sch.2 para.6, Sch.2 para.7, Sch.2 para.8
    Sch.1, amended: SI 2015/1013 Sch.2
    para.1, Sch.2 para.2, Sch.2 para.3, Sch.2
    para.4, Sch.2 para.5, Sch.2 para.6, SI
    2015/1016 Sch.2 para.1, Sch.2 para.2,
    Sch.2 para.3, Sch.2 para.5, Sch.2 para.6

1073. Firefighters Compensation Scheme (Wales) Order 2007
    Sch.1, added: SI 2015/1013 Sch.1 para.1,
    Sch.1 para.4, Sch.1 para.8, Sch.1 para.9,
    Sch.1 para.10, Sch.1 para.11
    Sch.1, amended: SI 2015/1013 Sch.1
    para.1, Sch.1 para.2, Sch.1 para.3, Sch.1
    para.4, Sch.1 para.5, Sch.1 para.6, Sch.1
    para.7, Sch.1 para.8, Sch.1 para.9, Sch.1
    para.10, Sch.1 para.11, Sch.1 para.12,
    Sch.1 para.13
    Sch.1, substituted: SI 2015/1013 Sch.1
    para.1, Sch.1 para.3, Sch.1 para.6, Sch.1
    para.7, Sch.1 para.12

1079. Criminal Justice Act 2003 (Surcharge)(No 2) Order 2007
    see *R. v Poole (Matthew Jason)* [2014]
    EWCA Crim 1641, [2015] 1 W.L.R. 522
    (CA (Crim Div)), Macur LJ

1115. Air Navigation (Isle of Man) Order 2007
    revoked: SI 2015/870 Art.2

1120. Docking of Working Dogs Tails (England) Regulations 2007
    Reg.4, amended: SI 2015/108 Reg.16

1167. Consumer Credit (Information Requirements and Duration of Licences and Charges) Regulations 2007
    see *NRAM Plc v McAdam* [2015] EWCA
    Civ 751, [2015] E.C.C. 30 (CA (Civ
    Div)), Longmore LJ

1174. Criminal Defence Service (Funding) Order 2007
    Sch.1 Part 6, amended: SI 2015/800
    Reg.4

1253. Lasting Powers of Attorney, Enduring Powers of Attorney and Public Guardian Regulations 2007

    see *Miles v Public Guardian* [2015]
    EWHC 2960 (Ch), [2015] C.O.P.L.R.
    676 (Ch D), Nugee J
    Reg.2, amended: SI 2015/899 Reg.4
    Reg.6, amended: SI 2015/899 Reg.5
    Reg.7, revoked: SI 2015/899 Reg.6
    Reg.9, amended: SI 2015/899 Reg.7
    Reg.9, revoked: SI 2015/899 Reg.7
    Reg.10, amended: SI 2015/899 Reg.8
    Reg.11, substituted: SI 2015/899 Reg.9
    Reg.14, amended: SI 2015/899 Reg.10
    Sch.1, substituted: SI 2015/899 Sch.1
    Sch.2, substituted: SI 2015/899 Sch.2
    Sch.3, substituted: SI 2015/899 Sch.3
    Sch.3A, revoked: SI 2015/899 Reg.14
    Sch.4, substituted: SI 2015/899 Sch.4
    Sch.6, substituted: SI 2015/899 Sch.5

1320. Health Service Medicines (Information Relating to Sales of Branded Medicines etc.) Regulations 2007
    Reg.2, amended: SI 2015/233 Reg.2
    Reg.3, amended: SI 2015/233 Reg.2
    Reg.3, revoked: SI 2015/233 Reg.2
    Reg.3A, added: SI 2015/233 Reg.2
    Reg.4, amended: SI 2015/233 Reg.2

1321. Collaboration Arrangements (Maintained Schools and Further Education Bodies) (England) Regulations 2007
    Reg.4, amended: SI 2015/883 Reg.4
    Reg.5, amended: SI 2015/883 Reg.4
    Reg.6, amended: SI 2015/883 Reg.4
    Reg.6, revoked: SI 2015/883 Reg.4
    Reg.8, amended: SI 2015/883 Reg.4

1621. Animals and Animal Products (Import and Export) (England) (Laboratories, Circuses and Avian Quarantine) Regulations 2007
    revoked: SI 2015/639 Reg.2

1671. Financial Assistance for Environmental Purposes Order 2007
    revoked: SI 2015/479 Sch.1

1744. Court of Protection Rules 2007
    see *PA, Re* [2015] EWCOP 38 (CP),
    Baker J; see *PD, Re* [2015] EWCOP 48,
    [2015] C.O.P.L.R. 544 (CP), Baker J; see
    Public Guardian v CT [2015] C.O.P.L.R.
    70 (CP), Senior Judge Denzil Lush; see
    X (Deprivation of Liberty), Re [2015] 1
    W.L.R. 2454 (CP), Sir James Munby
    PFD
    Part 2 r.3A, added: SI 2015/548 r.5

Part 2 r.4, substituted: SI 2015/548 r.6
Part 2 r.5, amended: SI 2015/548 r.7
Part 3 r.6, amended: SI 2015/548 r.8
Part 3 r.9, substituted: SI 2015/548 r.9
Part 4 r.10, revoked: SI 2015/548 r.10
Part 4 r.11, amended: SI 2015/548 r.11
Part 4 r.11, revoked: SI 2015/548 r.11
Part 4 r.11A, added: SI 2015/548 r.12
Part 4 r.12, amended: SI 2015/548 r.13
Part 5 r.25, revoked: SI 2015/548 r.14
Part 6 r.33, amended: SI 2015/548 r.15
Part 6 r.39, substituted: SI 2015/548 r.16
Part 7 r.40, amended: SI 2015/548 r.17
Part 7 r.41A, added: SI 2015/548 r.18
Part 7 r.44, amended: SI 2015/548 r.19
Part 7 r.46, amended: SI 2015/548 r.20
Part 7 r.48, substituted: SI 2015/548 r.21
Part 8 r.51, substituted: SI 2015/548 r.22
Part 8 r.52, revoked: SI 2015/548 r.23
Part 8 r.53, revoked: SI 2015/548 r.24
Part 8 r.54, substituted: SI 2015/548 r.25
Part 8 r.55, revoked: SI 2015/548 r.26
Part 8 r.59, amended: SI 2015/548 r.27
Part 8 r.60, amended: SI 2015/548 r.28
Part 9 r.61, revoked: SI 2015/548 r.29
Part 9 r.64, revoked: SI 2015/548 r.30
Part 9 r.65, substituted: SI 2015/548 r.31
Part 9 r.66, amended: SI 2015/548 r.32
Part 9 r.67, amended: SI 2015/548 r.33
Part 9 r.68, amended: SI 2015/548 r.34
Part 9 r.70, amended: SI 2015/548 r.35
Part 9 r.72, amended: SI 2015/548 r.36
Part 9 r.72, revoked: SI 2015/548 r.36
Part 10 r.77, amended: SI 2015/548 r.37
Part 10 r.81A, added: SI 2015/548 r.38
Part 12 r.84, amended: SI 2015/548 r.39
Part 12 r.85, amended: SI 2015/548 r.40
Part 12 r.85, revoked: SI 2015/548 r.40
Part 12 r.86, substituted: SI 2015/548 r.41
Part 12 r.87, amended: SI 2015/548 r.42
Part 12 r.87A, added: SI 2015/548 r.43
Part 12 r.88, amended: SI 2015/548 r.44
Part 12 r.89, amended: SI 2015/548 r.45
Part 13 r.91, amended: SI 2015/548 r.46
Part 14 r.95, amended: SI 2015/548 r.47
Part 15 r.120, amended: SI 2015/548 r.48
Part 17, substituted: SI 2015/548 Sch.1
Part 19 r.155, amended: SI 2015/548 r.50
Part 19 r.159, amended: SI 2015/548 r.51

Part 19 r.160, substituted: SI 2015/548 r.52
Part 19 r.166, amended: SI 2015/548 r.53
Part 20 r.169, substituted: SI 2015/548 r.54
Part 20 r.170, amended: SI 2015/548 r.55
Part 20 r.171, amended: SI 2015/548 r.56
Part 20 r.171A, added: SI 2015/548 r.57
Part 20 r.172, substituted: SI 2015/548 r.58
Part 20 r.173, amended: SI 2015/548 r.59
Part 20 r.174, substituted: SI 2015/548 r.60
Part 20 r.175, amended: SI 2015/548 r.61
Part 20 r.176, amended: SI 2015/548 r.62
Part 20 r.177, revoked: SI 2015/548 r.63
Part 20 r.180, revoked: SI 2015/548 r.64
Part 21 r.184, amended: SI 2015/548 r.65
Part 21 r.184, revoked: SI 2015/548 r.65
Pt 9., see *G (An Adult) (Costs), Re* [2015] EWCA Civ 446, [2015] C.P. Rep. 37 (CA (Civ Div)), Sullivan LJ
r.3, see *A (Court of Protection: Delay and Costs), Re* [2015] C.O.P.L.R. 1 (CP), Peter Jackson J
r.3A, see *P, Re* [2015] EWCOP 59, [2015] C.O.P.L.R. 690 (CP), Charles J; see *PD, Re* [2015] EWCOP 48, [2015] C.O.P.L.R. 544 (CP), Baker J
r.5, see *A (Court of Protection: Delay and Costs), Re* [2015] C.O.P.L.R. 1 (CP), Peter Jackson J
r.73, see *X (Deprivation of Liberty), Re* [2015] 1 W.L.R. 2454 (CP), Sir James Munby PFD
r.75, see *G (An Adult) (Costs), Re* [2015] EWCA Civ 446, [2015] C.P. Rep. 37 (CA (Civ Div)), Sullivan LJ
r.141, see *X (Deprivation of Liberty), Re* [2015] 1 W.L.R. 2454 (CP), Sir James Munby PFD
r.156, see *Public Guardian v CT* [2015] C.O.P.L.R. 70 (CP), Senior Judge Denzil Lush
r.157, see *G (An Adult) (Costs), Re* [2015] EWCA Civ 446, [2015] C.P. Rep. 37 (CA (Civ Div)), Sullivan LJ
r.159, see *G (An Adult) (Costs), Re* [2015] EWCA Civ 446, [2015] C.P. Rep. 37 (CA (Civ Div)), Sullivan LJ

1819. Community Drivers Hours and Recording Equipment Regulations 2007
  Sch.1 Part 1 para.1, amended: SI 2015/643 Sch.1 para.28

1884. General Dental Council (Overseas Registration Examination Regulations) Order of Council 2007
  Sch.1, revoked: SI 2015/735 Sch.1

1949. European Grouping of Territorial Cooperation Regulations 2007
  revoked: SI 2015/1493 Reg.13

2138. Liberia (Restrictive Measures) (Overseas Territories) (Amendment No 2) Order 2007
  revoked: SI 2015/1899 Art.1

2157. Money Laundering Regulations 2007
  see *Hunt v Revenue and Customs Commissioners* [2015] Lloyd's Rep. F.C. 140 (FTT (Tax)), Judge Timothy Herrington; see *RTA (Business Consultants) Ltd v Bracewell* [2015] EWHC 630 (QB), [2015] Bus. L.R. 800 (QBD), Judge Richard Seymour QC
  Reg.28, see *Hunt v Revenue and Customs Commissioners* [2015] Lloyd's Rep. F.C. 140 (FTT (Tax)), Judge Timothy Herrington
  Reg.33, see *RTA (Business Consultants) Ltd v Bracewell* [2015] EWHC 630 (QB), [2015] Bus. L.R. 800 (QBD), Judge Richard Seymour QC

2319. Gaming Machine (Circumstances of Use) Regulations 2007
  Reg.7, amended: SI 2015/121 Reg.2
  Reg.9, amended: SI 2015/121 Reg.2
  Reg.11, amended: SI 2015/121 Reg.2
  Reg.11A, added: SI 2015/121 Reg.2

2324. Education (School Performance Information) (England) Regulations 2007
  Reg.2, amended: SI 2015/902 Reg.7
  Sch.2 para.2, amended: SI 2015/902 Reg.8
  Sch.2 para.3, amended: SI 2015/902 Reg.8
  Sch.2 para.5, amended: SI 2015/902 Reg.8
  Sch.4 Part 1 para.2, amended: SI 2015/902 Reg.9, SI 2015/1566 Reg.3
  Sch.4 Part 2 para.1, substituted: SI 2015/1566 Reg.3

Sch.8 Part 1 para.1, amended: SI 2015/902 Reg.10

2325. Large Combustion Plants (National Emission Reduction Plan) Regulations 2007
  revoked: SI 2015/1973 Reg.11

2781. European Communities (Recognition of Professional Qualifications) Regulations 2007
  revoked: SI 2015/2059 Reg.79

2810. General Teaching Council for Wales (Additional Functions) (Amendment) Order 2007
  revoked: SI 2015/194 Sch.1

2974. Companies (Cross-Border Mergers) Regulations 2007
  Reg.16, see *International Game Technology Plc, Re* [2015] EWHC 717 (Ch), [2015] Bus. L.R. 844 (Ch D (Companies Ct)), Birss J; see *Livanova Plc, Re* [2015] EWHC 2865 (Ch), [2015] B.C.C. 915 (Ch D (Companies Ct)), Morgan J
  Reg.16, amended: SI 2015/180 Reg.2

3007. Feed (Corn Gluten Feed and Brewers Grains) (Emergency Control) (England) (Revocation) Regulations 2007
  revoked: SI 2015/255 Sch.2

3187. Asylum (Procedures) Regulations 2007
  Reg.5, amended: SI 2015/383 Art.2
  Reg.5, varied: SI 2015/383 Art.5

3284. Grants for Fishing and Aquaculture Industries Regulations 2007
  revoked: SI 2015/1711 Reg.15

3482. Civil Enforcement of Parking Contraventions (England) Representations and Appeals Regulations 2007
  Reg.2, amended: SI 2015/1001 Reg.3
  Reg.2, varied: SI 2015/969 Sch.1 para.1
  Reg.3, amended: SI 2015/1001 Reg.3
  Reg.7, varied: SI 2015/969 Sch.1 para.2
  Reg.8, varied: SI 2015/969 Sch.1 para.3
  Reg.11, amended: SI 2015/1001 Reg.3
  Reg.14, varied: SI 2015/969 Sch.1 para.4
  Reg.15, varied: SI 2015/969 Sch.1 para.5
  Sch.1 Part 1 para.1, varied: SI 2015/969 Sch.1 para.6
  Sch.1 Part 2 para.2, varied: SI 2015/969 Sch.1 para.6
  Sch.1 Part 2 para.3, varied: SI 2015/969 Sch.1 para.6
  Sch.1 Part 2 para.4, varied: SI 2015/969 Sch.1 para.6

Sch.1 Part 3 para.17, varied: SI 2015/969
Sch.1 para.6
Sch.1 Part 4, varied: SI 2015/969 Sch.1
para.6

**3483. Civil Enforcement of Parking
Contraventions (England) General
Regulations 2007**
Reg.3, amended: SI 2015/1001 Reg.2
Reg.4, substituted: SI 2015/561 Reg.2
Reg.8, amended: SI 2015/1001 Reg.2
Reg.9, substituted: SI 2015/1001 Reg.2
Reg.10, amended: SI 2015/1001 Reg.2
Reg.11, amended: SI 2015/1001 Reg.2
Reg.12, amended: SI 2015/1001 Reg.2
Reg.13, amended: SI 2015/1001 Reg.2
Reg.19, amended: SI 2015/1001 Reg.2
Reg.20, amended: SI 2015/1001 Reg.2
Sch.1 para.1, amended: SI 2015/1001
Reg.2
Sch.1 para.2, amended: SI 2015/1001
Reg.2

**3490. Childcare Act 2006 (Provision of
Information to Parents) (England)
Regulations 2007**
Sch.1 para.1, amended: SI 2015/1562
Reg.3

3531. Channel Tunnel (Safety) Order 2007
Art.4, amended: SI 2015/1682 Sch.1
para.10
Art.5, amended: SI 2015/1682 Sch.1
para.10

**3544. Legislative and Regulatory Reform
(Regulatory Functions) Order 2007**
Sch.1 Part 3, amended: SI 2015/21
Reg.17, SI 2015/968 Sch.1 para.7, SI
2015/1630 Sch.1 para.2, SI 2015/1640
Reg.14
Sch.1 Part 5, amended: SI 2015/968
Sch.1 para.7
Sch.1 Part 6, amended: SI 2015/1630
Sch.1 para.2

2008

**5. Immigration and Police (Passenger, Crew
and Service Information) Order 2008**
Art.1, amended: SI 2015/859 Art.2
Art.4, substituted: SI 2015/859 Art.2
Sch.1 para.1, amended: SI 2015/859
Art.2

Sch.1 para.2, amended: SI 2015/859
Art.2
Sch.3 para.1, amended: SI 2015/859
Art.2
Sch.3 para.2, amended: SI 2015/859
Art.2

**85. Condensed Milk and Dried Milk
(England) (Amendment) Regulations 2008**
revoked: SI 2015/675 Reg.8

**131. Export Control (Democratic Republic of
Congo) (Amendment) Order 2008**
revoked: SI 2015/1546 Sch.1

**373. Companies (Revision of Defective
Accounts and Reports) Regulations 2008**
Reg.2, amended: SI 2015/980 Reg.43
Reg.15, revoked: SI 2015/980 Reg.43

**377. Education (Budget Statements)
(England) Regulations 2008**
Reg.2, amended: SI 2015/971 Sch.3
para.13
Sch.1 Part 1, amended: SI 2015/971
Sch.3 para.13
Sch.1 Part 2, amended: SI 2015/971
Sch.3 para.13
Sch.1 Part 3, amended: SI 2015/971
Sch.3 para.13
Sch.1 Part 4, amended: SI 2015/971
Sch.3 para.13

**386. Non-Domestic Rating (Unoccupied
Property) (England) Regulations 2008**
Reg.4, see *PAG Management Services
Ltd, Re* [2015] EWHC 2404 (Ch), [2015]
B.C.C. 720 (Ch D), Norris J

**410. Large and Medium-sized Companies
and Groups (Accounts and Reports)
Regulations 2008**
Reg.4, amended: SI 2015/980 Reg.26
Reg.4, revoked: SI 2015/980 Reg.26
Sch.1 Part 1, amended: SI 2015/980
Reg.27
Sch.1 Part 1 para.1, amended: SI
2015/980 Reg.27
Sch.1 Part 1 para.1A, added: SI 2015/980
Reg.27
Sch.1 Part 1 para.6, amended: SI
2015/980 Reg.27
Sch.1 Part 1 para.9A, added: SI 2015/980
Reg.27
Sch.1 Part 2 para.12, amended: SI
2015/980 Reg.28

1

Sch.1 Part 2 para.13, amended: SI
2015/980 Reg.28
Sch.1 Part 2 para.15A, added: SI
2015/980 Reg.28
Sch.1 Part 2 para.19, amended: SI
2015/980 Reg.28
Sch.1 Part 2 para.20, amended: SI
2015/980 Reg.28, SI 2015/1672 Reg.4
Sch.1 Part 2 para.21, amended: SI
2015/980 Reg.28
Sch.1 Part 2 para.27, amended: SI
2015/980 Reg.28
Sch.1 Part 2 para.28, amended: SI
2015/980 Reg.28
Sch.1 Part 2 para.29A, added: SI
2015/980 Reg.28
Sch.1 Part 2 para.32, revoked: SI
2015/980 Reg.28
Sch.1 Part 2 para.34, amended: SI
2015/980 Reg.28
Sch.1 Part 2 para.35, amended: SI
2015/980 Reg.28
Sch.1 Part 2 para.36, amended: SI
2015/980 Reg.28
Sch.1 Part 2 para.39, substituted: SI
2015/980 Reg.28
Sch.1 Part 3 para.42, substituted: SI
2015/980 Reg.29
Sch.1 Part 3 para.55, substituted: SI
2015/980 Reg.29
Sch.1 Part 3 para.58, amended: SI
2015/980 Reg.29
Sch.1 Part 3 para.59, amended: SI
2015/980 Reg.29
Sch.1 Part 3 para.61, amended: SI
2015/980 Reg.29
Sch.1 Part 3 para.63, substituted: SI
2015/980 Reg.29
Sch.1 Part 3 para.67, amended: SI
2015/980 Reg.29
Sch.1 Part 3 para.69, amended: SI
2015/980 Reg.29
Sch.1 Part 3 para.72, amended: SI
2015/980 Reg.29
Sch.1 Part 3 para.72A, added: SI
2015/980 Reg.29
Sch.1 Part 4 para.73, revoked: SI
2015/980 Reg.30
Sch.2 Part 1 para.10A, added: SI
2015/980 Reg.31

Sch.2 Part 2 para.18, amended: SI
2015/980 Reg.32
Sch.2 Part 2 para.19, amended: SI
2015/980 Reg.32
Sch.2 Part 2 para.21A, added: SI
2015/980 Reg.32
Sch.2 Part 2 para.25, amended: SI
2015/980 Reg.32
Sch.2 Part 2 para.26, amended: SI
2015/980 Reg.32, SI 2015/1672 Reg.4
Sch.2 Part 2 para.27, substituted: SI
2015/980 Reg.32
Sch.2 Part 2 para.35, amended: SI
2015/980 Reg.32
Sch.2 Part 2 para.36, amended: SI
2015/980 Reg.32
Sch.2 Part 2 para.40, revoked: SI
2015/980 Reg.32
Sch.2 Part 2 para.42, amended: SI
2015/980 Reg.32
Sch.2 Part 2 para.43, amended: SI
2015/980 Reg.32
Sch.2 Part 2 para.44, amended: SI
2015/980 Reg.32
Sch.2 Part 2 para.47, substituted: SI
2015/980 Reg.32
Sch.2 Part 3 para.52, substituted: SI
2015/980 Reg.33
Sch.2 Part 3 para.66, substituted: SI
2015/980 Reg.33
Sch.2 Part 3 para.70, amended: SI
2015/980 Reg.33
Sch.2 Part 3 para.77, substituted: SI
2015/980 Reg.33
Sch.2 Part 3 para.91, amended: SI
2015/980 Reg.33
Sch.2 Part 3 para.92A, added: SI
2015/980 Reg.33
Sch.2 Part 4 para.96, amended: SI
2015/980 Reg.33
Sch.3 Part 1 para.8A, added: SI 2015/980
Reg.34
Sch.3 Part 2 para.17, amended: SI
2015/980 Reg.35
Sch.3 Part 2 para.18, amended: SI
2015/980 Reg.35
Sch.3 Part 2 para.20A, added: SI
2015/980 Reg.35
Sch.3 Part 2 para.30, amended: SI
2015/980 Reg.35

Sch.3 Part 2 para.33, substituted: SI 2015/980 Reg.35

Sch.3 Part 2 para.39, amended: SI 2015/1672 Reg.4

Sch.3 Part 2 para.41, substituted: SI 2015/980 Reg.35

Sch.3 Part 2 para.45, amended: SI 2015/980 Reg.35

Sch.3 Part 2 para.46, amended: SI 2015/980 Reg.35

Sch.3 Part 2 para.52, amended: SI 2015/575 Sch.2 para.26

Sch.3 Part 3 para.60, substituted: SI 2015/980 Reg.36

Sch.3 Part 3 para.73, substituted: SI 2015/980 Reg.36

Sch.3 Part 3 para.81, substituted: SI 2015/980 Reg.36

Sch.3 Part 3 para.89, amended: SI 2015/980 Reg.36

Sch.3 Part 3 para.90A, added: SI 2015/980 Reg.36

Sch.4 Part 1 para.1, amended: SI 2015/980 Reg.37

Sch.4 Part 1 para.5, amended: SI 2015/980 Reg.37

Sch.4 Part 1 para.7, amended: SI 2015/980 Reg.37

Sch.4 Part 1 para.7, revoked: SI 2015/980 Reg.37

Sch.4 Part 1 para.8, amended: SI 2015/980 Reg.37

Sch.4 Part 3 para.18, amended: SI 2015/980 Reg.38

Sch.4 Part 3 para.19, amended: SI 2015/980 Reg.38

Sch.4 Part 3 para.21, amended: SI 2015/980 Reg.38

Sch.6 Part 1 para.2, amended: SI 2015/980 Reg.39

Sch.6 Part 1 para.9, amended: SI 2015/980 Reg.39

Sch.6 Part 1 para.10, substituted: SI 2015/980 Reg.39

Sch.6 Part 1 para.16A, added: SI 2015/980 Reg.39

Sch.6 Part 1 para.17, substituted: SI 2015/980 Reg.39

Sch.6 Part 1 para.18, amended: SI 2015/980 Reg.39

Sch.6 Part 1 para.20, amended: SI 2015/980 Reg.39

Sch.6 Part 1 para.20, revoked: SI 2015/980 Reg.39

Sch.6 Part 1 para.22A, added: SI 2015/980 Reg.39

Sch.6 Part 2 para.24A, added: SI 2015/980 Reg.39

Sch.6 Part 2 para.25, substituted: SI 2015/980 Reg.39

Sch.6 Part 3 para.35A, added: SI 2015/980 Reg.39

Sch.6 Part 3 para.36, substituted: SI 2015/980 Reg.39

Sch.9 Part 1 para.2A, added: SI 2015/980 Reg.40

Sch.10 para.3, amended: SI 2015/980 Reg.41

495. Companies (Trading Disclosures) Regulations 2008
revoked: SI 2015/17 Sch.6 para.1

543. Honey (Wales) (Amendment) Regulations 2008
revoked: SI 2015/1507 Reg.20

563. Defence Support Group Trading Fund Order 2008
revoked: SI 2015/473 Art.2

565. Insurance Accounts Directive (Miscellaneous Insurance Undertakings) Regulations 2008
Reg.2, amended: SI 2015/575 Sch.2 para.27
Reg.2, revoked: SI 2015/575 Sch.2 para.27

618. Brucellosis (England) (Amendment) Order 2008
revoked: SI 2015/364 Art.25

629. Charities (Accounts and Reports) Regulations 2008
Reg.18, revoked: SI 2015/322 Reg.3
Reg.29, revoked: SI 2015/322 Reg.5

680. Immigration (Isle of Man) Order 2008
Art.2, amended: SI 2015/1765 Art.4
Art.22, added: SI 2015/1765 Art.5
Sch.9A, added: SI 2015/1765 Art.7
Sch.9 para.6, revoked: SI 2015/1765 Art.6
Sch.10 Part 7, revoked: SI 2015/1765 Art.8
Sch.10 Part 8, added: SI 2015/1765 Art.8

**696. Gas (Standards of Performance)
(Amendment) Regulations 2008**
    Reg.2, revoked: SI 2015/1544 Reg.13
    Reg.11, revoked: SI 2015/1544 Reg.13
    Reg.12, amended: SI 2015/1544 Reg.13
**728. European Grouping of Territorial
Cooperation (Amendment) Regulations 2008**
    revoked: SI 2015/1493 Reg.13
**794. Employment and Support Allowance
Regulations 2008**
    Reg.2, amended: SI 2015/67 Reg.2, SI
    2015/389 Reg.4, SI 2015/971 Sch.3
    para.14, SI 2015/1985 Art.31
    Reg.4, amended: SI 2015/339 Reg.4
    Reg.5, amended: SI 2015/339 Reg.4
    Reg.14, amended: SI 2015/971 Sch.3
    para.14
    Reg.14, revoked: SI 2015/971 Sch.3
    para.14
    Reg.30, amended: SI 2015/437 Reg.3
    Reg.43, amended: SI 2015/389 Reg.4
    Reg.91, amended: SI 2015/389 Reg.4
    Reg.99, amended: SI 2015/478 Reg.35
    Reg.131, amended: SI 2015/971 Sch.3
    para.14
    Reg.147A, amended: SI 2015/437 Reg.3
    Reg.156, amended: SI 2015/643 Sch.1
    para.29
    Sch.4 Part 1 para.1, amended: SI 2015/30
    Sch.4
    Sch.4 Part 2 para.6, amended: SI
    2015/1754 Reg.19
    Sch.4 Part 3 para.11, amended: SI
    2015/457 Sch.14
    Sch.4 Part 4 para.12, amended: SI
    2015/30 Art.11
    Sch.4 Part 4 para.13, amended: SI
    2015/457 Art.22
    Sch.6 para.1, amended: SI 2015/1647
    Reg.4
    Sch.6 para.8, revoked: SI 2015/1647
    Reg.4
    Sch.6 para.9, amended: SI 2015/1647
    Reg.4
    Sch.6 para.9, revoked: SI 2015/1647
    Reg.4
    Sch.6 para.9, substituted: SI 2015/1647
    Reg.4
    Sch.6 para.10, amended: SI 2015/1647
    Reg.4

    Sch.6 para.11, amended: SI 2015/1647
    Reg.4
    Sch.6 para.12, amended: SI 2015/1647
    Reg.4
    Sch.6 para.12, revoked: SI 2015/1647
    Reg.4
    Sch.6 para.14, amended: SI 2015/1647
    Reg.4
    Sch.6 para.15, amended: SI 2015/1647
    Reg.4
    Sch.6 para.15, revoked: SI 2015/1647
    Reg.4
    Sch.6 para.19, amended: SI 2015/457
    Art.22
    Sch.6 para.20, revoked: SI 2015/1647
    Reg.4
    Sch.7 para.3A, added: SI 2015/1985
    Art.31
    Sch.7 para.11A, amended: SI 2015/389
    Reg.4
    Sch.7 para.12, amended: SI 2015/389
    Reg.4
    Sch.8 para.29, amended: SI 2015/643
    Sch.1 para.29
    Sch.8 para.32, amended: SI 2015/643
    Sch.1 para.29
    Sch.8 para.34, amended: SI 2015/643
    Sch.1 para.29
    Sch.8 para.53, amended: SI 2015/643
    Sch.1 para.29
    Sch.8 para.56, amended: SI 2015/643
    Sch.1 para.29
    Sch.9 para.56, amended: SI 2015/643
    Sch.1 para.29
**974. Childcare (Early Years Register)
Regulations 2008**
    Reg.5, added: SI 2015/1562 Reg.4
    Sch.1 Part 1 para.10, amended: SI
    2015/1562 Reg.4
    Sch.1 Part 1 para.11A, added: SI
    2015/1562 Reg.4
    Sch.1 Part 2 para.19, amended: SI
    2015/1562 Reg.4
    Sch.1 Part 2 para.20, amended: SI
    2015/1562 Reg.4
    Sch.1 Part 2 para.23, added: SI
    2015/1562 Reg.4
    Sch.2 Part 1, amended: SI 2015/1562
    Reg.4
    Sch.2 Part 1 para.8, amended: SI
    2015/1562 Reg.4

Sch.2 Part 1 para.14, amended: SI 2015/1562 Reg.4

Sch.2 Part 1 para.14A, added: SI 2015/1562 Reg.4

Sch.2 Part 2, amended: SI 2015/1562 Reg.4

Sch.2 Part 2 para.24, amended: SI 2015/1562 Reg.4

Sch.2 Part 2 para.26, added: SI 2015/1562 Reg.4

975. Childcare (General Childcare Register) Regulations 2008

Reg.3A, added: SI 2015/1562 Reg.5

Sch.1 Part 1 para.7, amended: SI 2015/1562 Reg.5

Sch.1 Part 1 para.8A, added: SI 2015/1562 Reg.5

Sch.1 Part 2 para.12, amended: SI 2015/1562 Reg.5

Sch.1 Part 2 para.13, amended: SI 2015/1562 Reg.5

Sch.1 Part 2 para.16, added: SI 2015/1562 Reg.5

Sch.2 Part 1, amended: SI 2015/1562 Reg.5

Sch.2 Part 1 para.5, amended: SI 2015/1562 Reg.5

Sch.2 Part 1 para.11, amended: SI 2015/1562 Reg.5

Sch.2 Part 1 para.11A, added: SI 2015/1562 Reg.5

Sch.2 Part 2, amended: SI 2015/1562 Reg.5

Sch.2 Part 2 para.17, amended: SI 2015/1562 Reg.5

Sch.2 Part 2 para.19, added: SI 2015/1562 Reg.5

Sch.3 para.9, amended: SI 2015/1562 Reg.5

Sch.3 para.13ZA, added: SI 2015/1562 Reg.5

Sch.3 para.28, amended: SI 2015/1562 Reg.5

Sch.3 para.29, amended: SI 2015/1562 Reg.5

Sch.4 Part 1 para.7, amended: SI 2015/1562 Reg.5

Sch.4 Part 2 para.13, amended: SI 2015/1562 Reg.5

Sch.4 Part 2 para.14, amended: SI 2015/1562 Reg.5

Sch.4 Part 2 para.18, added: SI 2015/1562 Reg.5

Sch.5 Part 1, amended: SI 2015/1562 Reg.5

Sch.5 Part 1 para.9, amended: SI 2015/1562 Reg.5

Sch.5 Part 2, amended: SI 2015/1562 Reg.5

Sch.5 Part 2 para.17, amended: SI 2015/1562 Reg.5

Sch.5 Part 2 para.19, added: SI 2015/1562 Reg.5

Sch.6 para.11, amended: SI 2015/1562 Reg.5

Sch.6 para.14A, added: SI 2015/1562 Reg.5

Sch.6 para.31, amended: SI 2015/1562 Reg.5

Sch.6 para.32, amended: SI 2015/1562 Reg.5

976. Childcare (Early Years and General Childcare Registers) (Common Provisions) Regulations 2008

Part 3A, added: SI 2015/1562 Reg.6

Reg.2, amended: SI 2015/1562 Reg.6

Reg.3A, added: SI 2015/1562 Reg.6

Reg.6, substituted: SI 2015/1562 Reg.6

Reg.7, amended: SI 2015/1562 Reg.6

Reg.7A, amended: SI 2015/1562 Reg.6

Reg.8, amended: SI 2015/1562 Reg.6

Reg.10, amended: SI 2015/1562 Reg.6

Reg.12, amended: SI 2015/1562 Reg.6

979. Childcare (Exemptions from Registration) Order 2008

Art.2, amended: SI 2015/963 Reg.2

Art.9, revoked: SI 2015/963 Reg.2

1053. Civil Proceedings Fees Order 2008

Art.5, amended: SI 2015/576 Art.2

Sch.1, amended: SI 2015/576 Art.2

1054. Family Proceedings Fees Order 2008

Art.1, amended: SI 2015/687 Art.3

Art.3A, added: SI 2015/687 Art.4

Art.3A, amended: SI 2015/1419 Art.2

Sch.1, amended: SI 2015/576 Art.3, SI 2015/687 Art.5, SI 2015/1419 Art.2

Sch.2 para.1, amended: SI 2015/687 Art.6

1087. Control of Major Accident Hazard (Amendment) Regulations 2008

revoked: SI 2015/483 Reg.31

1184. Mental Health (Hospital, Guardianship and Treatment) (England) Regulations 2008

Reg.3, see *K v Kingswood Centre Hospital Managers* [2014] EWCA Civ 1332, [2015] P.T.S.R. 287 (CA (Civ Div)), Moore-Bick LJ; see *K v Kingswood Centre Hospital Managers* [2014] EWHC 2271 (Admin), [2015] M.H.L.R. 68 (QBD (Admin)), Burton J

1185. General Ophthalmic Services Contracts Regulations 2008

Reg.8, amended: SI 2015/416 Reg.10

Sch.1 Part 6 para.29, amended: SI 2015/416 Reg.11

Sch.1 Part 8 para.56, amended: SI 2015/137 Sch.2 para.19

1239. Air Navigation (Restriction of Flying) (Scottish Highlands) Regulations 2008

revoked: SI 2015/1589 Reg.2

1276. Business Protection from Misleading Marketing Regulations 2008

Reg.21, revoked: SI 2015/1630 Sch.2 para.112

Reg.28, revoked: SI 2015/1630 Sch.2 para.113

1277. Consumer Protection from Unfair Trading Regulations 2008

see *Hargreaves v Brecknock and Radnorshire Magistrates' Court* [2015] EWHC 1803 (Admin), (2015) 179 J.P. 399 (DC), Burnett LJ

Reg.5, amended: SI 2015/1630 Sch.1 para.3

Reg.6, see *Secretary of State for Business, Innovation and Skills v PLT Anti-Marketing Ltd* [2015] EWCA Civ 76, [2015] Bus. L.R. 959 (CA (Civ Div)), Richards LJ

Reg.20, revoked: SI 2015/1630 Sch.2 para.115

Reg.21, see *Hargreaves v Brecknock and Radnorshire Magistrates' Court* [2015] EWHC 1803 (Admin), (2015) 179 J.P. 399 (DC), Burnett LJ

Reg.22, see *Hargreaves v Brecknock and Radnorshire Magistrates' Court* [2015] EWHC 1803 (Admin), (2015) 179 J.P. 399 (DC), Burnett LJ

Reg.27I, amended: SI 2015/1629 Reg.9

Reg.28, revoked: SI 2015/1630 Sch.2 para.116

Sch.2 Part 1 para.63, revoked: 2015 c.15

Sch.6 para.85

Sch.2 Part 2 para.97, revoked: 2015 c.15

Sch.1 para.55

1409. Education (National Curriculum) (Attainment Targets and Programmes of Study) (Wales) Order 2008

Art.2, amended: SI 2015/1601 Art.2

Art.15, substituted: SI 2015/1601 Art.2

1487. Air Navigation (Isle of Man) (Amendment) Order 2008

revoked: SI 2015/870 Art.2

1660. Cross-border Railway Services (Working Time) Regulations 2008

Reg.9, amended: SI 2015/1682 Sch.1 para.10

Reg.10, amended: SI 2015/1682 Sch.1 para.10

Reg.15, amended: SI 2015/1682 Sch.1 para.10

Sch.2 para.1, amended: SI 2015/1682 Sch.1 para.10

Sch.2 para.2, amended: SI 2015/1682 Sch.1 para.10

Sch.2 para.7, amended: SI 2015/1682 Sch.1 para.10

Sch.2 para.8, amended: SI 2015/1682 Sch.1 para.10

1804. Childcare (Fees) Regulations 2008

Reg.2, amended: SI 2015/1562 Reg.7

Reg.2A, added: SI 2015/1562 Reg.7

Reg.4, amended: SI 2015/1562 Reg.7

Reg.6, amended: SI 2015/1562 Reg.7

Reg.8, amended: SI 2015/1562 Reg.7

Reg.10, amended: SI 2015/1562 Reg.7

Reg.12, amended: SI 2015/1562 Reg.7

Reg.15, amended: SI 2015/1562 Reg.7

1816. Cancellation of Contracts made in a Consumer's Home or Place of Work etc Regulations 2008

see *Cox v Woodlands Manor Care Home Ltd* [2015] EWCA Civ 415, [2015] 3 Costs L.O. 327 (CA (Civ Div)), Longmore LJ; see *RTA (Business Consultants) Ltd v Bracewell* [2015] EWHC 630 (QB), [2015] Bus. L.R. 800 (QBD), Judge Richard Seymour QC

Reg.2, see *RTA (Business Consultants) Ltd v Bracewell* [2015] EWHC 630 (QB), [2015] Bus. L.R. 800 (QBD), Judge Richard Seymour QC

Reg.5, see *Cox v Woodlands Manor Care Home Ltd* [2015] EWCA Civ 415, [2015] 3 Costs L.O. 327 (CA (Civ Div)), Longmore LJ

1879. Employment and Support Allowance (Consequential Provisions) (No.3) Regulations 2008
  Reg.3, revoked: SI 2015/621 Sch.1

1964. Export Control (Democratic Republic of Congo) (Amendment) (No.2) Order 2008
  revoked: SI 2015/1546 Sch.1

2164. Batteries and Accumulators (Placing on the Market) Regulations 2008
  Reg.2, amended: SI 2015/1360 Reg.4
  Reg.4, amended: SI 2015/63 Reg.4
  Reg.4, revoked: SI 2015/63 Reg.3
  Reg.7, amended: SI 2015/63 Reg.5

2252. Care Quality Commission (Membership) Regulations 2008
  revoked: SI 2015/1479 Reg.8

2366. Channel Tunnel (International Arrangements) (Amendment) Order 2008
  revoked: SI 2015/785 Art.4

2551. Child Support Information Regulations 2008
  Reg.14A, added: SI 2015/338 Reg.7

2682. Income Tax (Deposit-takers and Building Societies) (Interest Payments) Regulations 2008
  Reg.2, amended: SI 2015/653 Reg.3
  Reg.5, amended: SI 2015/653 Reg.4
  Reg.6, amended: SI 2015/653 Reg.5
  Reg.6, revoked: SI 2015/653 Reg.5
  Reg.9, amended: SI 2015/653 Reg.4
  Reg.10, amended: SI 2015/653 Reg.4
  Reg.11, amended: SI 2015/653 Reg.4
  Reg.12, amended: SI 2015/653 Reg.4

2698. Tribunal Procedure (Upper Tribunal) Rules 2008
  see *R. (on the application of Mahmood) v Secretary of State for the Home Department* [2015] Imm. A.R. 193 (UT (IAC)), McCloskey J; see *Raftopoulou v Revenue and Customs Commissioners* [2015] UKUT 630 (TCC), [2015] B.T.C. 535 (UT (Tax)), Judge Roger Berner
  r.2, see *Leeds City Council v Revenue and Customs Commissioners* [2015] S.T.C. 168 (UT (Tax)), Judge Colin Bishopp

r.10, see *Leeds City Council v Revenue and Customs Commissioners* [2015] S.T.C. 168 (UT (Tax)), Judge Colin Bishopp
  r.28, see *R. (on the application of Mahmood) v Secretary of State for the Home Department* [2015] Imm. A.R. 193 (UT (IAC)), McCloskey J
  r.42, see *AA (Pakistan) v Secretary of State for the Home Department* [2015] CSOH 10, 2015 S.L.T. 110 (OH), Lord Stewart; see *Tager v Revenue and Customs Commissioners* [2015] UKUT 663 (TCC), [2015] B.T.C. 538 (UT (Tax)), Judge Colin Bishopp
  r.43, see *Tager v Revenue and Customs Commissioners* [2015] UKUT 663 (TCC), [2015] B.T.C. 538 (UT (Tax)), Judge Colin Bishopp

2699. Tribunal Procedure (First-tier Tribunal) (Health, Education and Social Care Chamber) Rules 2008
  see *AF v Nottingham NHS Trust* [2015] UKUT 216 (AAC), [2015] M.H.L.R. 347 (UT (AAC)), Judge Wright
  r.2, see *Kensington and Chelsea RLBC v CD* [2015] UKUT 396 (AAC), [2015] E.L.R. 493 (UT (AAC)), Judge Rowley; see *LW v Norfolk CC* [2015] UKUT 65 (AAC), [2015] E.L.R. 167 (UT (AAC)), Judge Rowley
  r.7, see *AF v Nottingham NHS Trust* [2015] UKUT 216 (AAC), [2015] M.H.L.R. 347 (UT (AAC)), Judge Wright
  r.15, see *Kensington and Chelsea RLBC v CD* [2015] UKUT 396 (AAC), [2015] E.L.R. 493 (UT (AAC)), Judge Rowley
  r.24, see *Hammersmith and Fulham LBC v L* [2015] UKUT 523 (AAC), [2015] E.L.R. 528 (UT (AAC)), Judge Mitchell
  r.47, see *Essex CC v TB* [2015] E.L.R. 67 (UT (AAC)), Judge Rowland
  r.48, see *Essex CC v TB* [2015] E.L.R. 67 (UT (AAC)), Judge Rowland

2830. Immigration (Biometric Registration) (Objection to Civil Penalty) Order 2008
  Art.7, amended: SI 2015/564 Art.4
  Art.8, substituted: SI 2015/564 Art.5

2831. Housing and Regeneration Act 2008 (Consequential Provisions) (No.2) Order 2008

Sch.4 para.1, amended: SI 2015/316
Sch.1

2841. Cremation (England and Wales) Regulations 2008
Reg.29, amended: SI 2015/1360 Reg.5

2845. Home Loss Payments (Prescribed Amounts) (Wales) Regulations 2008
revoked: SI 2015/1878 Reg.3

3048. Immigration (Biometric Registration) Regulations 2008
Reg.2, amended: SI 2015/433 Reg.3
Reg.3, amended: SI 2015/433 Reg.4
Reg.3, revoked: SI 2015/433 Reg.4
Reg.3A, added: SI 2015/433 Reg.5
Reg.3A, amended: SI 2015/897 Reg.5
Reg.5, amended: SI 2015/433 Reg.6
Reg.6, amended: SI 2015/433 Reg.7
Reg.7, amended: SI 2015/433 Reg.8
Reg.8, substituted: SI 2015/433 Reg.9
Reg.9, substituted: SI 2015/433 Reg.10
Reg.13, amended: SI 2015/433 Reg.11
Reg.13A, added: SI 2015/433 Reg.12
Reg.15, amended: SI 2015/433 Reg.13
Reg.16, amended: SI 2015/433 Reg.14
Reg.17, amended: SI 2015/433 Reg.15
Reg.19, amended: SI 2015/433 Reg.16
Reg.20, amended: SI 2015/433 Reg.17
Reg.20, revoked: SI 2015/897 Reg.6
Reg.21, amended: SI 2015/433 Reg.18
Reg.23, amended: SI 2015/433 Reg.19
Sch.1, added: SI 2015/433 Sch.1
Sch.1, amended: SI 2015/897 Reg.3, Reg.4
Sch.1, revoked: SI 2015/897 Reg.6

3231. Export Control Order 2008
Art.4, amended: SI 2015/940 Art.2
Art.15, amended: SI 2015/940 Art.2
Art.16, amended: SI 2015/940 Art.2
Sch.1 Part 2 para.10A, added: SI 2015/940 Art.2
Sch.2, amended: SI 2015/940 Art.2
Sch.2, substituted: SI 2015/351 Sch.1
Sch.3, amended: SI 2015/940 Art.2
Sch.4 Part 2, amended: SI 2015/1546 Art.10
Sch.4 Part 3, amended: SI 2015/1546 Art.10, SI 2015/1586 Reg.7
Sch.4 Part 4, amended: SI 2015/1546 Art.10, SI 2015/1586 Reg.7

3243. Financial Assistance for Environmental Purposes (England and Wales) Order 2008

revoked: SI 2015/479 Sch.1

3258. Health Service Branded Medicines (Control of Prices and Supply of Information) (No.2) Regulations 2008
Reg.1, amended: SI 2015/233 Reg.3
Reg.2, amended: SI 2015/233 Reg.3

2009

153. Environmental Damage (Prevention and Remediation) Regulations 2009
revoked: SI 2015/810 Reg.36

212. Criminal Defence Service (Information Requests) (Prescribed Benefits) Regulations 2009
Reg.2, amended: SI 2015/838 Reg.5, SI 2015/1985 Art.32

214. Companies (Disclosure of Address) Regulations 2009
Sch.1, amended: SI 2015/842 Reg.2

218. Companies (Trading Disclosures) (Amendment) Regulations 2009
revoked: SI 2015/17 Sch.6 para.1

261. Fluorinated Greenhouse Gases Regulations 2009
revoked: SI 2015/310 Reg.34

263. General Osteopathic Council (Constitution) Order 2009
Art.2, amended: SI 2015/1906 Art.2
Art.11, amended: SI 2015/1906 Art.2

273. Tribunal Procedure (First-tier Tribunal) (Tax Chamber) Rules 2009
see *BPP University College of Professional Studies v Revenue and Customs Commissioners* [2015] S.T.C. 415 (UT (Tax)), Judge Colin Bishopp;
see *Clavis Liberty Fund 1 LP v Revenue and Customs Commissioners* [2015] UKUT 72 (TCC), [2015] 1 W.L.R. 2949 (UT (Tax)), Warren J
r.2, see *BPP University College of Professional Studies v Revenue and Customs Commissioners* [2015] S.T.C. 415 (UT (Tax)), Judge Colin Bishopp;
see *Wrottesley v Revenue and Customs Commissioners* [2015] UKUT 637 (TCC), [2015] B.T.C. 537 (UT (Tax)), Judge Timothy Herrington
r.8, see *BPP University College of Professional Studies v Revenue and*

Customs Commissioners [2015] S.T.C.
415 (UT (Tax)), Judge Colin Bishopp;
see *Enta Technologies Ltd, Re* [2015]
EWCA Civ 29, [2015] 1 W.L.R. 3911
(CA (Civ Div)), Longmore LJ; see
*Fairford Group Ltd Plc (In Liquidation)
v Revenue and Customs Commissioners*
[2015] S.T.C. 156 (UT (Tax)), Simon J
r.10, see *Market and Opinion Research
International Ltd v Revenue and Customs
Commissioners* [2015] UKUT 12 (TCC),
[2015] S.T.C. 1205 (UT (Tax)), Judge
Roger Berner
r.16, see *Clavis Liberty Fund 1 LP v
Revenue and Customs Commissioners*
[2015] UKUT 72 (TCC), [2015] 1
W.L.R. 2949 (UT (Tax)), Warren J

**275. Appeals (Excluded Decisions) Order
2009**
Art.3, amended: SI 2015/383 Art.3
Art.3, varied: SI 2015/383 Art.5

**309. Local Authority Social Services and
National Health Service Complaints
(England) Regulations 2009**
Reg.2, amended: SI 2015/1862 Sch.4
para.4, SI 2015/1879 Sch.3 para.2
Sch.1 para.3, revoked: SI 2015/1862
Sch.5 para.1
Sch.1 para.4, revoked: SI 2015/1879
Sch.4 para.1

**395. Independent Review of Determinations
(Adoption and Fostering) Regulations 2009**
Reg.13, amended: SI 2015/495 Reg.11

**469. Driving Standards Agency Trading
Fund (Maximum Borrowing etc.) Order 2009**
revoked: SI 2015/41 Sch.3

**669. Co-ordination of Regulatory
Enforcement (Regulatory Functions in
Scotland and Northern Ireland) Order 2009**
Sch.1 Part 1, amended: SI 2015/968
Sch.1 para.9
Sch.1 Part 2, amended: SI 2015/1630
Sch.1 para.4
Sch.1 Part 4, amended: SI 2015/21
Reg.19

**774. Financial Services and Markets Act
2000 (Controllers) (Exemption) Order 2009**
Art.2, amended: SI 2015/575 Sch.2
para.30

**883. Health Service Commissioner for
England (Authorities for the Ashworth,**

**Broadmoor and Rampton Hospitals)
(Revocation) Order 2009**
revoked: SI 2015/822 Art.2

**995. Environmental Damage (Prevention and
Remediation) (Wales) Regulations 2009**
Reg.2, amended: SI 2015/1394 Reg.2, SI
2015/1937 Reg.3
Reg.4, amended: SI 2015/1394 Reg.2
Reg.6, amended: SI 2015/1394 Reg.2
Reg.6, revoked: SI 2015/1394 Reg.2
Reg.8, amended: SI 2015/1394 Reg.2
Reg.10, amended: SI 2015/1394 Reg.2
Reg.11, amended: SI 2015/1394 Reg.2
Sch.1 para.5, substituted: SI 2015/1937
Reg.4
Sch.2 para.2, substituted: SI 2015/1937
Reg.5
Sch.2 para.3, amended: SI 2015/1937
Reg.5
Sch.2 para.5, amended: SI 2015/1937
Reg.5
Sch.2 para.7, amended: SI 2015/1937
Reg.5
Sch.2 para.8, substituted: SI 2015/1937
Reg.5
Sch.2 para.11, added: SI 2015/1937
Reg.5

**1085. Company and Business Names
(Miscellaneous Provisions) Regulations 2009**
revoked: SI 2015/17 Sch.6 para.1

**1117. Immigration (European Economic
Area) (Amendment) Regulations 2009**
see *R. (on the application of Byczek) v
Secretary of State for the Home
Department* [2014] EWHC 4298
(Admin), [2015] 2 C.M.L.R. 7 (QBD
(Admin)), Jay J

**1168. Armed Forces (Review of Court
Martial Sentence) Order 2009**
Sch.1 para.1, amended: SI 2015/800
Reg.5, SI 2015/1472 Reg.8

**1182. Health Care and Associated Professions
(Miscellaneous Amendments and Practitioner
Psychologists) Order 2009**
Art.4, revoked: SI 2015/2059 Sch.6
Art.7, enabled: SI 2015/991
Sch.4 Part 1 para.18, revoked: SI
2015/2059 Sch.6
Sch.4 Part 3 para.33, revoked: SI
2015/2059 Sch.6

1209. Armed Forces (Service Civilian Court) Rules 2009
    Part 1 r.3, amended: SI 2015/1812 r.14
    Part 3 r.21A, added: SI 2015/1812 r.15
    Part 3 r.22, amended: SI 2015/1812 r.16
    Part 12 r.74, amended: SI 2015/1472 Reg.9
    Part 12 r.76, amended: SI 2015/1472 Reg.9
    Part 12 r.79, amended: SI 2015/1472 Reg.9
    Part 14 r.96, amended: SI 2015/1812 r.17

1211. Armed Forces (Summary Appeal Court) Rules 2009
    Part 1 r.3, amended: SI 2015/1812 r.3
    Part 4 r.29A, added: SI 2015/1812 r.4
    Part 4 r.30, amended: SI 2015/1812 r.5
    Part 11, added: SI 2015/1812 r.6
    Part 12 r.86, amended: SI 2015/1812 r.7

1257. Carbon Accounting Regulations 2009
    Reg.2, amended: SI 2015/775 Reg.6
    Reg.9, amended: SI 2015/775 Reg.6

1348. Carriage of Dangerous Goods and Use of Transportable Pressure Equipment Regulations 2009
    Reg.32, amended: SI 2015/1682 Sch.1 para.10

1350. Education (Supply of Information) (Wales) Regulations 2009
    revoked: SI 2015/140 Sch.1 Part 1

1351. General Teaching Council for Wales (Additional Functions) (Amendment) Order 2009
    revoked: SI 2015/194 Sch.1

1353. General Teaching Council for Wales (Functions) (Amendment) Regulations 2009
    revoked: SI 2015/140 Sch.1 Part 1

1354. General Teaching Council for Wales (Disciplinary Functions) (Amendment) Regulations 2009
    revoked: SI 2015/140 Sch.1 Part 1

1506. Financial Assistance for Environmental Purposes (England and Wales) Order 2009
    revoked: SI 2015/479 Sch.1

1554. Childcare (Provision of Information About Young Children) (England) Regulations 2009
    Reg.2, amended: SI 2015/1696 Reg.3
    Sch.1 Part 2 para.14, added: SI 2015/1696 Reg.4

1582. Human Fertilisation and Embryology (Statutory Storage Period for Embryos and Gametes) Regulations 2009
    see *Warren v Care Fertility (Northampton) Ltd* [2014] EWHC 602 (Fam), [2015] Fam. 1 (Fam Div), Hogg J
    Reg.4, see *Warren v Care Fertility (Northampton) Ltd* [2014] EWHC 602 (Fam), [2015] Fam. 1 (Fam Div), Hogg J
    Reg.7, see *Warren v Care Fertility (Northampton) Ltd* [2014] EWHC 602 (Fam), [2015] Fam. 1 (Fam Div), Hogg J

1595. Control of Major Accident Hazards (Amendment) Regulations 2009
    revoked: SI 2015/483 Reg.31

1603. Supreme Court Rules 2009
    see *McGraddie v McGraddie* [2015] UKSC 1, [2015] 1 W.L.R. 560 (SC), Lord Neuberger PSC
    r.51, see *McGraddie v McGraddie* [2015] UKSC 1, [2015] 1 W.L.R. 560 (SC), Lord Neuberger PSC

1801. Overseas Companies Regulations 2009
    Reg.7, see *Teekay Tankers Ltd v STX Offshore & Shipping Co* [2014] EWHC 3612 (Comm), [2015] 2 All E.R. (Comm) 263 (QBD (Comm)), Hamblen J

1804. Limited Liability Partnerships (Application of Companies Act 2006) Regulations 2009
    Reg.9, amended: SI 2015/17 Sch.5 para.2
    Reg.10, amended: SI 2015/17 Sch.5 para.3
    Reg.11, amended: SI 2015/17 Sch.5 para.4
    Reg.14, amended: SI 2015/17 Sch.5 para.5
    Reg.15, amended: SI 2015/17 Sch.5 para.6
    Reg.18, amended: SI 2015/664 Sch.3 para.14
    Reg.19, amended: SI 2015/664 Sch.3 para.14
    Reg.31, amended: SI 2015/664 Sch.3 para.14
    Reg.50, amended: SI 2015/1695 Reg.5
    Reg.51, amended: SI 2015/1695 Reg.5
    Reg.58, amended: SI 2015/664 Sch.3 para.14
    Reg.66, added: SI 2015/1695 Reg.6

Reg.67, amended: SI 2015/664 Sch.3
para.14

1884. Lasting Powers of Attorney, Enduring Powers of Attorney and Public Guardian (Amendment) Regulations 2009
see *XZ v Public Guardian* [2015] EWCOP 35, [2015] C.O.P.L.R. 630 (CP), Judge Lush

1925. Animals and Animal Products (Examination for Residues and Maximum Residue Limits) (Amendment) Regulations 2009
revoked: SI 2015/787 Sch.1

2039. Lloyd's Underwriters (Equalisation Reserves) (Tax) Regulations 2009
revoked: SI 2015/1983 Reg.5

2041. Armed Forces (Court Martial) Rules 2009
Part 1 r.3, amended: SI 2015/1812 r.9
Part 3 r.22A, added: SI 2015/1812 r.10
Part 3 r.23, amended: SI 2015/1812 r.11
Part 12 r.89, amended: SI 2015/1472 Reg.10
Part 12 r.91, amended: SI 2015/1472 Reg.10
Part 12 r.94, amended: SI 2015/1472 Reg.10
Part 14 r.114, amended: SI 2015/1812 r.12

2081. Channel Tunnel (International Arrangements) (Amendment) Order 2009
revoked: SI 2015/785 Art.4

2100. Court Martial and Service Civilian Court (Youth Justice and Criminal Evidence Act 1999) Rules 2009
Part 1 r.3, amended: SI 2015/726 r.3
Part 4 r.9, substituted: SI 2015/726 r.4
Part 4 r.10, substituted: SI 2015/726 r.5
Part 4 r.11, substituted: SI 2015/726 r.6
Part 4 r.12, substituted: SI 2015/726 r.7
Part 4 r.13, amended: SI 2015/726 r.8
Part 4 r.14, amended: SI 2015/726 r.9

2108. Ecclesiastical Offices (Terms of Service) Regulations 2009
see *Sharpe v Worcester Diocesan Board of Finance Ltd* [2015] EWCA Civ 399, [2015] I.C.R. 1241 (CA (Civ Div)), Arden LJ
Reg.20, amended: SI 2015/1654 Reg.4
Reg.23, enabled: SI 2015/1612
Reg.27, amended: SI 2015/1654 Reg.2

Reg.29, amended: SI 2015/1654 Reg.3, Reg.4

2158. Assembly Learning Grant (Further Education) Regulations 2009
Reg.2, amended: SI 2015/971 Sch.3 para.15

2161. General Teaching Council for Wales (Disciplinary Functions) (Amendment No 2) Regulations 2009
revoked: SI 2015/140 Sch.1 Part 1

2231. Judiciary and Courts (Scotland) Act 2008 (Consequential Provisions and Modifications) Order 2009
Art.2, amended: SI 2015/700 Sch.1 para.14
Art.2, substituted: SI 2015/700 Sch.1 para.14
Art.3, amended: SI 2015/700 Sch.1 para.14

2264. Infrastructure Planning (Applications Prescribed Forms and Procedure) Regulations 2009
Sch.1, amended: SI 2015/377 Sch.1 para.42, SI 2015/1682 Sch.1 para.10

2268. Non-Domestic Rating (Alteration of Lists and Appeals) (England) Regulations 2009
see *R. (on the application of Reeves (Valuation Officer)) v Valuation Tribunal for England* [2015] EWHC 973 (Admin), [2015] R.A. 241 (QBD (Admin)), Holgate J

2269. Valuation Tribunal for England (Council Tax and Rating Appeals) (Procedure) Regulations 2009
see *R. (on the application of Reeves (Valuation Officer)) v Valuation Tribunal for England* [2015] EWHC 973 (Admin), [2015] R.A. 241 (QBD (Admin)), Holgate J
Reg.42, see *Wonder Investments Ltd v Jackson (Valuation Officer)* [2015] UKUT 335 (LC), [2015] R.A. 449 (UT (Lands)), Martin Rodger QC

2270. Council Tax (Alteration of Lists and Appeals) (England) Regulations 2009
see *Martin v Coll (Listing Officer)* [2015] R.V.R. 270 (VT), Graham Zellick QC
Reg.3, see *Martin v Coll (Listing Officer)* [2015] R.V.R. 270 (VT), Graham Zellick QC

2404. Company, Limited Liability Partnership and Business Names (Miscellaneous Provisions) (Amendment) Regulations 2009
revoked: SI 2015/17 Sch.6 para.1

2437. Companies (Companies Authorised to Register) Regulations 2009
Reg.7, amended: SI 2015/1695 Reg.10
Reg.7, revoked: SI 2015/1695 Reg.10

2471. Companies (Disqualification Orders) Regulations 2009
Reg.2, amended: SI 2015/1651 Reg.4
Sch.1, amended: SI 2015/1651 Sch.1 Part 1
Sch.2, amended: SI 2015/1651 Sch.1 Part 2

2657. Court Martial Appeal Court Rules 2009
Part 1 r.2, amended: SI 2015/1814 r.3
Part 3 r.16A, added: SI 2015/1814 r.4

2724. Her Majesty's Chief Inspector of Education, Children's Services and Skills (Fees and Frequency of Inspections) (Children's Homes etc) (Amendment) Regulations 2009
revoked: SI 2015/551 Sch.1

2751. General Medical Council (Constitution of Panels and Investigation Committee) (Amendment) Rules Order of Council 2009
revoked: SI 2015/1965 Art.3
Sch.1, revoked: SI 2015/1965 Sch.1

2969. Export Control (Amendment) (No.4) Order 2009
revoked: SI 2015/1546 Sch.1

2982. Company, Limited Liability Partnership and Business Names (Public Authorities) Regulations 2009
revoked: SI 2015/17 Sch.6 para.1

2999. Provision of Services Regulations 2009
Reg.14, see *R. (on the application of Lumsdon) v Legal Services Board* [2015] UKSC 41, [2015] 3 W.L.R. 121 (SC), Lord Neuberger PSC

3015. Air Navigation Order 2009
Art.7, amended: SI 2015/912 Sch.5 para.4
Art.8A, added: SI 2015/912 Sch.5 para.4
Art.37, see *Lord Advocate, Petitioner* [2015] CSOH 80, 2015 S.L.T. 450 (OH), Lord Jones
Art.132, enabled: SI 2015/970
Art.160, amended: SI 2015/1768 Art.10

Art.160, enabled: SI 2015/840
Art.161, enabled: SI 2015/144, SI 2015/146, SI 2015/257, SI 2015/259, SI 2015/261, SI 2015/263, SI 2015/264, SI 2015/265, SI 2015/266, SI 2015/267, SI 2015/269, SI 2015/270, SI 2015/510, SI 2015/511, SI 2015/513, SI 2015/514, SI 2015/515, SI 2015/1007, SI 2015/1008, SI 2015/1010, SI 2015/1073, SI 2015/1074, SI 2015/1075, SI 2015/1076, SI 2015/1077, SI 2015/1078, SI 2015/1079, SI 2015/1080, SI 2015/1097, SI 2015/1098, SI 2015/1099, SI 2015/1106, SI 2015/1117, SI 2015/1118, SI 2015/1281, SI 2015/1310, SI 2015/1311, SI 2015/1312, SI 2015/1318, SI 2015/1323, SI 2015/1324, SI 2015/1343, SI 2015/1345, SI 2015/1354, SI 2015/1355, SI 2015/1356, SI 2015/1364, SI 2015/1365, SI 2015/1372, SI 2015/1389, SI 2015/1589, SI 2015/1608, SI 2015/1609, SI 2015/1611, SI 2015/1664, SI 2015/1665, SI 2015/1676, SI 2015/1699, SI 2015/1700, SI 2015/1704, SI 2015/1721, SI 2015/1722, SI 2015/1734, SI 2015/1735, SI 2015/1747, SI 2015/1825, SI 2015/1845, SI 2015/1847, SI 2015/1900, SI 2015/1903, SI 2015/1918, SI 2015/1922
Art.226, revoked: SI 2015/1768 Art.3
Art.227, revoked: SI 2015/1768 Art.4
Art.246, amended: SI 2015/1768 Art.5
Art.246C, added: SI 2015/1768 Art.6
Art.252, amended: SI 2015/1768 Art.11
Art.255, amended: SI 2015/1768 Art.8
Sch.4, see *Lord Advocate, Petitioner* [2015] CSOH 80, 2015 S.L.T. 450 (OH), Lord Jones
Sch.12 para.7, amended: SI 2015/1768 Art.7
Sch.13 Part B, amended: SI 2015/1768 Art.9
Sch.13 Part C, added: SI 2015/1768 Art.9
Sch.13 Part C, amended: SI 2015/1768 Art.9

3029. Bournemouth-Swanage Motor Road and Ferry (Revision of Tolls) Order 2009
revoked: SI 2015/1105 Art.5

3075. Financial Services and Markets Act 2000 (Law Applicable to Contracts of Insurance) Regulations 2009

Reg.5, amended: SI 2015/575 Sch.2 para.31

3275. Environmental Damage (Prevention and Remediation) (Amendment) Regulations 2009

revoked: SI 2015/810 Reg.36

3328. Criminal Defence Service (Contribution Orders) Regulations 2009

Reg.2, amended: SI 2015/838 Reg.6

3420. A40/A48 Trunk Roads(Pensarn Roundabout, Carmarthen) (40 mph Speed Limit) Order 2009

revoked: SI 2015/1446 Art.5

2010

60. Criminal Procedure Rules 2010

r.69.5, see *Guardian News and Media Ltd v Incedal* [2014] EWCA Crim 1861, [2015] 1 Cr. App. R. 4 (CA (Crim Div)), Gross LJ

r.69.6, see *Guardian News and Media Ltd v Incedal* [2014] EWCA Crim 1861, [2015] 1 Cr. App. R. 4 (CA (Crim Div)), Gross LJ

102. Infrastructure Planning (Interested Parties) Regulations 2010

revoked: SI 2015/462 Sch.3

Sch.1, amended: SI 2015/377 Sch.1 para.43

104. Infrastructure Planning (Compulsory Acquisition) Regulations 2010

Reg.10, amended: SI 2015/462 Reg.10

Sch.2, amended: SI 2015/377 Sch.1 para.44, SI 2015/1682 Sch.1 para.10

105. Infrastructure Planning (Miscellaneous Prescribed Provisions) Regulations 2010

revoked: SI 2015/462 Sch.3

233. Health Professions (Hearing Aid Dispensers) Order 2010

Art.11, revoked: SI 2015/2059 Sch.6

234. General and Specialist Medical Practice (Education, Training and Qualifications) Order 2010

Sch.3 Part 2 para.10, revoked: SI 2015/1862 Sch.5 para.1

Sch.3 Part 2 para.13, revoked: SI 2015/1879 Sch.4 para.1

288. Community Health Councils (Constitution, Membership and Procedures) (Wales) Regulations 2010

Part VI, substituted: SI 2015/509 Reg.26

Reg.2, amended: SI 2015/509 Reg.3

Reg.3, amended: SI 2015/509 Reg.4

Reg.5, substituted: SI 2015/509 Reg.5

Reg.6, amended: SI 2015/509 Reg.6

Reg.9, amended: SI 2015/509 Reg.7

Reg.9A, added: SI 2015/509 Reg.8

Reg.10, amended: SI 2015/509 Reg.9

Reg.11, revoked: SI 2015/509 Reg.10

Reg.12, amended: SI 2015/137 Sch.2 para.9

Reg.13, amended: SI 2015/509 Reg.11

Reg.15, amended: SI 2015/509 Reg.12

Reg.15, revoked: SI 2015/509 Reg.12

Reg.16, revoked: SI 2015/509 Reg.13

Reg.17, amended: SI 2015/509 Reg.14

Reg.20, amended: SI 2015/509 Reg.15

Reg.20, revoked: SI 2015/509 Reg.15

Reg.21, amended: SI 2015/509 Reg.16

Reg.21, revoked: SI 2015/509 Reg.16

Reg.23, amended: SI 2015/509 Reg.17

Reg.26, amended: SI 2015/509 Reg.18

Reg.27, amended: SI 2015/509 Reg.19

Reg.29, amended: SI 2015/509 Reg.20

Reg.31, amended: SI 2015/509 Reg.21

Reg.32, amended: SI 2015/509 Reg.22

Reg.34, amended: SI 2015/509 Reg.23

Reg.34, revoked: SI 2015/509 Reg.23

Reg.35, amended: SI 2015/509 Reg.24

Reg.35, revoked: SI 2015/509 Reg.24

Reg.36, amended: SI 2015/509 Reg.25

Reg.36, revoked: SI 2015/509 Reg.25

Reg.41A, added: SI 2015/509 Reg.27

Sch.1, amended: SI 2015/509 Reg.28

Sch.2, amended: SI 2015/509 Reg.29

Sch.2, substituted: SI 2015/509 Reg.29

289. Community Health Councils (Establishment, Transfer of Functions and Abolition) (Wales) Order 2010

Art.2, amended: SI 2015/507 Art.2

Art.3A, added: SI 2015/507 Art.3

Art.4, amended: SI 2015/507 Art.4

Art.5A, added: SI 2015/507 Art.5

Art.6A, added: SI 2015/507 Art.6

Art.7A, added: SI 2015/507 Art.7

Art.8A, added: SI 2015/507 Art.8

Art.9A, added: SI 2015/507 Art.9
Art.10, revoked: SI 2015/507 Art.10
Art.11, revoked: SI 2015/507 Art.11
Sch.1A, added: SI 2015/507 Art.12
Sch.3, revoked: SI 2015/507 Art.13

304. Deposits in the Sea (Exemptions) (Amendment) (England and Wales) Order 2010
revoked: SI 2015/663 Art.4

364. Export Control (Guinea) Order 2010
revoked: SI 2015/1546 Sch.1

404. Building (Local Authority Charges) Regulations 2010
Reg.4, amended: SI 2015/643 Sch.1 para.31

473. Postgraduate Medical Education and Training Order of Council 2010
Art.8, see *General Medical Council v Nakhla* [2014] EWCA Civ 1522, (2015) 142 B.M.L.R. 35 (CA (Civ Div)), Longmore LJ

474. General Medical Council (Constitution of Panels and Investigation Committee) (Amendment) Rules Order of Council 2010
revoked: SI 2015/1965 Art.3
Sch.1, revoked: SI 2015/1965 Sch.1

490. Conservation of Habitats and Species Regulations 2010
see *Abbotskerswell Parish Council v Teignbridge DC* [2014] EWHC 4166 (Admin), [2015] Env. L.R. 10 (QBD (Admin)), Lang J; see *Cheshire East Council v Secretary of State for Communities and Local Government* [2014] EWHC 3536 (Admin), [2015] Env. L.R. 10 (QBD (Admin)), Lewis J; see *No Adastral New Town Ltd v Suffolk Coastal DC* [2014] EWHC 223 (Admin), [2015] Env. L.R. 3 (QBD (Admin)), Patterson J
Reg.9, see *Cheshire East Council v Secretary of State for Communities and Local Government* [2014] EWHC 3536 (Admin), [2015] Env. L.R. 10 (QBD (Admin)), Lewis J
Reg.84, amended: SI 2015/377 Sch.1 para.45
Reg.101, amended: SI 2015/2020 Reg.7
Reg.102, see *Abbotskerswell Parish Council v Teignbridge DC* [2014] EWHC

4166 (Admin), [2015] Env. L.R. 20 (QBD (Admin)), Lang J

587. Environmental Damage (Prevention and Remediation) (Amendment) Regulations 2010
revoked: SI 2015/810 Reg.36

593. Excise Goods (Holding, Movement and Duty Point) Regulations 2010
Reg.7, amended: SI 2015/368 Reg.22

617. Her Majesty's Chief Inspector of Education, Children's Services and Skills (Fees and Frequency of Inspections) (Children's Homes etc) (Amendment) Regulations 2010
revoked: SI 2015/551 Sch.1

671. Housing and Regeneration Act 2008 (Consequential Provisions) (No.2) Order 2010
Sch.1 para.23, revoked: SI 2015/621 Sch.1

675. Environmental Permitting (England and Wales) Regulations 2010
Reg.2, amended: SI 2015/324 Reg.2, SI 2015/1417 Reg.4
Reg.3, amended: SI 2015/918 Reg.2, SI 2015/1360 Reg.7, SI 2015/1417 Reg.4
Reg.35, amended: SI 2015/918 Reg.3
Reg.37, amended: SI 2015/1756 Reg.3
Reg.39, amended: SI 2015/664 Sch.4 para.78
Reg.42, substituted: SI 2015/1756 Reg.4
Reg.44A, added: SI 2015/324 Reg.2
Reg.57, amended: SI 2015/1756 Reg.5
Reg.66, amended: SI 2015/1973 Sch.2 para.1
Sch.1 Part 2 para.1A, added: SI 2015/918 Reg.4
Sch.3 Part 1 para.1, amended: SI 2015/1360 Reg.7, SI 2015/1417 Reg.4
Sch.3 Part 1 para.11, amended: SI 2015/1417 Reg.4
Sch.3 Part 1 para.15, amended: SI 2015/1360 Reg.7, SI 2015/1417 Reg.4
Sch.8A, added: SI 2015/918 Reg.6
Sch.8 para.1, amended: SI 2015/918 Reg.5
Sch.8A para.11, amended: SI 2015/934 Reg.2
Sch.12 para.2, amended: SI 2015/1360 Reg.7, SI 2015/1417 Reg.4
Sch.12 para.3, amended: SI 2015/1360 Reg.7, SI 2015/1417 Reg.4
Sch.23A, added: SI 2015/324 Sch.1

Sch.24 para.1, amended: SI 2015/324
Reg.2
698. Electricity (Standards of Performance)
Regulations 2010
revoked: SI 2015/699 Sch.1
733. Adult Skills (Specified Qualifications)
Regulations 2010
Reg.3, amended: SI 2015/971 Sch.3
para.16
Reg.9, amended: SI 2015/971 Sch.3
para.16
781. Health and Social Care Act 2008
(Regulated Activities) Regulations 2010
Reg.27, amended: SI 2015/664 Sch.4
para.79
825. Right to Manage (Prescribed
Particulars and Forms) (England)
Regulations 2010
Sch.2, see *Elim Court RTM Co Ltd v*
Avon Freeholds Ltd [2015] L. & T.R. 3
(UT (Lands)), Martin Rodger QC
828. Banking Act 2009 (Inter-Bank Payment
Systems) (Disclosure and Publication of
Specified Information) Regulations 2010
Sch.1, amended: SI 2015/488 Reg.2
832. Armed Forces (Redundancy,
Resettlement and Gratuity Earnings
Schemes) (No.2) Order 2010
Art.2, amended: SI 2015/568 Reg.36
Art.27, amended: SI 2015/568 Reg.37
Art.30, amended: SI 2015/568 Reg.38
Art.32, substituted: SI 2015/568 Reg.39
Art.35, amended: SI 2015/568 Reg.40
948. Community Infrastructure Levy
Regulations 2010
see *Smyth v Secretary of State for*
Communities and Local Government
[2015] EWCA Civ 174, [2015] P.T.S.R.
1417 (CA (Civ Div)), Richards LJ
Reg.2, amended: SI 2015/836 Reg.3
Reg.40, see *R. (on the application of*
Hourhope Ltd) v Shropshire Council
[2015] EWHC 518 (Admin), [2015]
P.T.S.R. 933 (QBD (Birmingham)),
Judge David Cooke
Reg.49, amended: SI 2015/836 Reg.4
Reg.53, amended: SI 2015/836 Reg.4
Reg.61, see *Oxfordshire CC v Secretary*
of State for Communities and Local
Government [2015] EWHC 186 (Admin),

[2015] J.P.L. 846 (QBD (Admin)), Lang
J
Reg.93, amended: SI 2015/664 Sch.4
para.80
Reg.110, amended: SI 2015/664 Sch.4
para.80
Reg.122, see *Oxfordshire CC v Secretary*
of State for Communities and Local
Government [2015] EWHC 186 (Admin),
[2015] J.P.L. 846 (QBD (Admin)), Lang
J; see *R. (on the application of Hampton*
Bishop PC) v Herefordshire Council
[2014] EWCA Civ 878, [2015] 1 W.L.R.
2367 (CA (Civ Div)), Sir Terence
Etherton C; see *R. (on the application of*
Midcounties Co-operative Ltd) v Forest
of Dean DC [2014] EWHC 3059
(Admin), [2015] J.P.L. 288 (QBD
(Admin)), Hickinbottom J
Reg.123, amended: SI 2015/377 Sch.1
para.46
959. Care Planning, Placement and Case
Review (England) Regulations 2010
see *M v Blackburn with Darwen BC*
[2014] EWCA Civ 1479, [2015] 1
W.L.R. 2441 (CA (Civ Div)), Beatson LJ
Reg.2, amended: SI 2015/495 Reg.3
Reg.22B, added: SI 2015/495 Reg.4
Reg.28, amended: SI 2015/495 Reg.5
Reg.36, amended: SI 2015/495 Reg.6
Reg.39, substituted: SI 2015/495 Reg.7
Reg.39ZA, revoked: SI 2015/495 Reg.8
Sch.2 para.3, amended: SI 2015/495
Reg.9
Sch.7 para.15, added: SI 2015/495
Reg.10
1013. Consumer Credit (Disclosure of
Information) Regulations 2010
Reg.2, amended: SI 2015/910 Sch.1
para.13
1014. Consumer Credit (Agreements)
Regulations 2010
Reg.2, amended: SI 2015/910 Sch.1
para.14
Sch.1, amended: SI 2015/910 Sch.1
para.14
1060. Additional Statutory Paternity Pay
(Weekly Rates) Regulations 2010
Reg.2, amended: SI 2015/30 Art.5
1085. Dairy (Specific Market Support
Measure) Regulations 2010

revoked: SI 2015/639 Reg.3

1140. Control of Artificial Optical Radiation at Work Regulations 2010

    Reg.1, amended: SI 2015/1682 Sch.1 para.10

1157. Environmental Civil Sanctions (England) Order 2010

    Sch.2 para.1, amended: SI 2015/664 Sch.5 para.19

    Sch.3 para.6, amended: SI 2015/664 Sch.4 para.81

1159. Environmental Civil Sanctions (Miscellaneous Amendments) (England) Regulations 2010

    Reg.10, revoked: SI 2015/668 Reg.44

1172. Local Education Authorities and Children's Services Authorities (Integration of Functions) (Local and Subordinate Legislation) Order 2010

    Sch.3 para.29, revoked: SI 2015/601 Sch.4

1174. Designation of Schools Having a Religious Character (Independent Schools) (England) Order 2010

    Sch.1, amended: SI 2015/1267 Art.2, SI 2015/1344 Art.2

1188. Building Societies (Financial Assistance) Order 2010

    Art.7, revoked: SI 2015/428 Art.3

    Art.11, amended: SI 2015/428 Art.3

1436. Education (Amendments Relating to the Intervals for the Inspection of Education and Training) (Wales) Regulations 2010

    Reg.2, revoked: SI 2015/1599 Reg.1

1513. Energy Act 2008 (Consequential Modifications) (Offshore Environmental Protection) Order 2010

    Art.11, revoked: SI 2015/310 Reg.33

1553. Education (Chief Inspector of Education and Training in Wales) (No.2) Order 2010

    revoked: SI 2015/205 Art.3

1821. Environmental Civil Sanctions (Wales) Order 2010

    Sch.2 para.1, amended: SI 2015/664 Sch.5 para.20

    Sch.3 para.6, amended: SI 2015/664 Sch.4 para.83

1881. Health and Social Care Act 2008 (Miscellaneous Consequential Amendments) Order 2010

Art.3, revoked: SI 2015/864 Art.2

Art.6, revoked: SI 2015/864 Art.2

Art.9, revoked: SI 2015/864 Art.2

Art.11, revoked: SI 2015/864 Art.2

Art.13, revoked: SI 2015/864 Art.2

1892. Common Agricultural Policy Single Payment and Support Schemes (Wales) Regulations 2010

    revoked: SI 2015/1252 Reg.17

1907. Employment and Support Allowance (Transitional Provisions, Housing Benefit and Council Tax Benefit) (Existing Awards) (No.2) Regulations 2010

    Sch.2 Part 3 para.10, substituted: SI 2015/437 Reg.7

1923. Ecclesiastical Offices (Terms of Service) Directions 2010

    Reg.1, amended: SI 2015/1612 Reg.2

2088. Electricity (Connection Standards of Performance) Regulations 2010

    revoked: SI 2015/698 Reg.1

2130. Care Standards Act 2000 (Registration)(England) Regulations 2010

    Reg.2, amended: SI 2015/541 Reg.53

    Sch.1 Part 2 para.13, amended: SI 2015/541 Reg.53

2131. Electricity (Standards of Performance) (Amendment) Regulations 2010

    revoked: SI 2015/699 Sch.1

2132. Equality Act 2010 (Sex Equality Rule) (Exceptions) Regulations 2010

    Reg.2, amended: SI 2015/1985 Art.34

2133. Equality Act (Age Exceptions for Pension Schemes) Order 2010

    Art.2, amended: SI 2015/1985 Art.35

    Sch.1 para.1, amended: SI 2015/1985 Art.35

    Sch.1 para.14, amended: SI 2015/1985 Art.35

    Sch.1 para.23, amended: SI 2015/1985 Art.35

2184. Town and Country Planning (Development Management Procedure) (England) Order 2010

    see *R. (on the application of HS2 Action Alliance Ltd) v Secretary of State for Transport* [2014] EWCA Civ 1578, [2015] P.T.S.R. 1025 (CA (Civ Div)), Longmore LJ

2214. Building Regulations 2010

    Reg.2, amended: SI 2015/767 Reg.2

Reg.4, amended: SI 2015/767 Reg.2
Reg.6, amended: SI 2015/767 Reg.2
Reg.13, amended: SI 2015/767 Reg.2
Reg.14, amended: SI 2015/767 Reg.2
Reg.35, amended: SI 2015/767 Reg.2
Reg.36, substituted: SI 2015/767 Reg.2
Reg.37, amended: SI 2015/767 Reg.2
Reg.43, amended: SI 2015/767 Reg.2, SI
2015/1486 Reg.4
Sch.1, amended: SI 2015/767 Reg.2
Sch.3, amended: SI 2015/767 Sch.1, SI
2015/1486 Sch.1

**2215. Building (Approved Inspectors etc.)
Regulations 2010**
Reg.2, amended: SI 2015/767 Reg.3
Sch.1, amended: SI 2015/767 Sch.2
Sch.2 para.4, amended: SI 2015/767
Reg.3
Sch.3 para.2A, added: SI 2015/767 Reg.3
Sch.4 para.2A, added: SI 2015/767 Reg.3
Sch.5 para.4, amended: SI 2015/767
Reg.3
Sch.6 para.2A, added: SI 2015/767 Reg.3
Sch.7 para.2A, added: SI 2015/767 Reg.3

**2280. Feed (Sampling and Analysis and
Specified Undesirable Substances) (England)
Regulations 2010**
Reg.4, revoked: SI 2015/454 Sch.5
Reg.21, revoked: SI 2015/454 Sch.5
Sch.1, revoked: SI 2015/454 Sch.5

**2435. Diocese of Guildford (Educational
Endowments) (Down Road Church of
England School) Order 2010**
Art.2, amended: SI 2015/1799 Art.3

**2484. Health and Social Care Act 2008
(Primary Dental Services, Private Ambulance
Services and Primary Medical Services)
(Regulated Activities) (Transitory and
Transitional Provisions) Order 2010**
revoked: SI 2015/864 Art.2

**2503. Animal Feed (England) Regulations
2010**
Reg.3, revoked: SI 2015/255 Sch.2
Reg.15, revoked: SI 2015/255 Sch.2
Sch.1, revoked: SI 2015/255 Sch.2

**2571. Care Leavers (England) Regulations
2010**
Reg.5, amended: SI 2015/495 Reg.14
Sch.1 para.11, amended: SI 2015/495
Reg.15

**2600. Tribunal Procedure (Upper Tribunal)
(Lands Chamber) Rules 2010**
r.2, see *Dickinson v Network Rail
Infrastructure Ltd* [2015] R.V.R. 19 (UT
(Lands)), Sir Keith Lindblom P
r.10, see *Dickinson v Network Rail
Infrastructure Ltd* [2015] R.V.R. 19 (UT
(Lands)), Sir Keith Lindblom P

**2617. Ecodesign for Energy-Related Products
Regulations 2010**
Sch.1 para.4, amended: SI 2015/469
Reg.2

**2655. First-tier Tribunal and Upper Tribunal
(Chambers) Order 2010**
Art.5A, amended: SI 2015/1563 Art.2
Art.6, amended: SI 2015/1563 Art.2

**2710. Education (Specified Work and
Registration) (Wales) Regulations 2010**
revoked: SI 2015/140 Sch.1 Part 1

2955. Family Procedure Rules 2010
see *AB v JJB (EU Maintenance
Regulation: Modification Application
Procedure)* [2015] EWHC 192 (Fam),
[2015] 2 F.L.R. 1143 (Fam Div), Sir
Peter Singer; see *Cooper-Hohn v Hohn*
[2014] EWHC 2314 (Fam), [2015] 1
F.L.R. 19 (Fam Div), Roberts J; see *JM
(A Child), Re* [2015] EWHC 2832 (Fam),
[2015] Med. L.R. 544 (Fam Div), Mostyn
J; see *L v R* [2015] EWCA Civ 61,
Times, April 7, 2015 (CA (Civ Div)),
Aikens LJ; see *N (An Adult) (Court of
Protection: Jurisdiction), Re* [2015]
EWCA Civ 411, [2015] 3 W.L.R. 1585
(CA (Civ Div)), Sir James Munby PFD;
see *R v R (Family Court: Procedural
Fairness)* [2015] 1 W.L.R. 2743 (Fam
Ct), Peter Jackson J; see *S v S* [2015]
EWHC 1005 (Fam), [2015] 1 W.L.R.
4592 (Fam Div), Sir James Munby PFD
Part 2 r.2.3, amended: SI 2015/913 r.3
Part 3 r.3.1, amended: SI 2015/1868 r.3
Part 5 r.5.5, added: SI 2015/1868 r.4
Part 6 r.6.23, amended: SI 2015/1868 r.5
Part 6 r.6.26, amended: SI 2015/1868 r.6
Part 7 r.7.1, amended: SI 2015/913 r.4
Part 7 r.7.11, amended: SI 2015/913 r.5
Part 7 r.7.12, amended: SI 2015/913 r.6
Part 7 r.7.20, amended: SI 2015/913 r.7
Part 7 r.7.21, amended: SI 2015/913 r.8
Part 7 r.7.32, amended: SI 2015/913 r.9

Part 9, added: SI 2015/1868 r.7

Part 11, amended: SI 2015/1420 r.3

Part 11 r.11.1, amended: SI 2015/1420 r.4

Part 11 r.11.2, amended: SI 2015/1420 r.5

Part 11 r.11.2A, added: SI 2015/1420 r.6

Part 11 r.11.3, amended: SI 2015/1420 r.7

Part 11 r.11.4, amended: SI 2015/1420 r.8

Part 11 r.11.4, revoked: SI 2015/1420 r.8

Part 11 r.11.6, amended: SI 2015/1420 r.9

Part 11 r.11.7, amended: SI 2015/1420 r.10

Part 11 r.11.8, amended: SI 2015/1420 r.11

Part 11 r.11.10, amended: SI 2015/1420 r.12

Part 11 r.11.11, revoked: SI 2015/913 r.10

Part 11 r.11.12, amended: SI 2015/1420 r.13

Part 11 r.11.12, substituted: SI 2015/913 r.11

Part 11 r.11.13, amended: SI 2015/1420 r.14

Part 11 r.11.14, amended: SI 2015/1420 r.15

Part 11 r.11.15, amended: SI 2015/1420 r.16

Part 11 r.11.19, amended: SI 2015/1420 r.17

Part 29 r.29.6, amended: SI 2015/913 r.12

Part 29 r.29.12, amended: SI 2015/1868 r.8

Part 33 r.33.9, amended: SI 2015/1420 r.18

Part 33 r.33.11, amended: SI 2015/1420 r.19

Part 33 r.33.13, substituted: SI 2015/1420 r.20

Part 33 r.33.14, substituted: SI 2015/1420 r.21

Part 33 r.33.14A, added: SI 2015/1420 r.22

Part 33 r.33.17, amended: SI 2015/1420 r.23

Part 34 r.34.35, substituted: SI 2015/1420 r.24

Part 34 r.34.36, amended: SI 2015/913 r.13, SI 2015/1420 r.25

Pt 16., see *S-W (Children) (Care Proceedings: Summary Disposal at Case Management Hearing), Re* [2015] EWCA Civ 27, [2015] 1 W.L.R. 4099 (CA (Civ Div)), Sir James Munby PFD

Pt 25., see *J-M (A Child) (Contact Proceedings: Balance of Harm), Re* [2014] EWCA Civ 434, [2015] 1 F.L.R. 838 (CA (Civ Div)), Maurice Kay LJ

Pt 28., see *S (Children) (Appeal from Care and Placement Orders), Re* [2015] UKSC 20, [2015] 1 W.L.R. 1631 (SC), Lady Hale DPSC

Pt 37., see *Newman, Re* [2014] EWHC 3136 (Fam), [2015] 1 F.L.R. 1359 (Fam Div), Sir James Munby PFD

Pt 4., see *N v N (Child Maintenance: Res Judicata and Strike Out)* [2015] EWHC 514 (Fam), [2015] 2 F.L.R. 1441 (Fam Div), Bodey J

r.1.1, see *A (A Child) (Financial Provision: Wealthy Parent), Re* [2014] EWCA Civ 1577, [2015] Fam. 277 (CA (Civ Div)), Lewison LJ; see *Q v Q* [2015] 1 W.L.R. 2040 (Fam Ct), Sir James Munby PFD

r.4.1, see *H (Children) (Care Proceedings: Appeals out of Time)* [2015] EWCA Civ 583, [2015] 1 W.L.R. 5085 (CA (Civ Div)), McFarlane LJ; see *S v S* [2015] EWHC 1005 (Fam), [2015] 1 W.L.R. 4592 (Fam Div), Sir James Munby PFD

r.4.4, see *Vince v Wyatt* [2015] UKSC 14, [2015] 1 W.L.R. 1228 (SC), Lady Hale DPSC

r.4.5, see *W (Children) (Strict Compliance with Court Orders), Re* [2015] 1 F.L.R. 1092 (Fam Ct), Sir James Munby PFD

r.4.6, see *H (Children) (Care Proceedings: Appeals out of Time)* [2015] EWCA Civ 583, [2015] 1 W.L.R. 5085 (CA (Civ Div)), McFarlane LJ; see *R v R (Family Court: Procedural Fairness)* [2015] 1 W.L.R. 2743 (Fam Ct), Peter Jackson J

r.4.8, see *Veluppillai v Veluppillai* [2015] EWHC 3095 (Fam), [2015] 6 Costs L.O. 735 (Fam Div), Mostyn J

r.6.36, see *G (Children) (Recognition of Brazilian Adoption), Re* [2014] EWHC 2605 (Fam), [2015] 1 F.L.R. 1402 (Fam Div), Cobb J

r.8.21, see *G (Children) (Recognition of Brazilian Adoption), Re* [2014] EWHC 2605 (Fam), [2015] 1 F.L.R. 1402 (Fam Div), Cobb J

r.12.37, see *X (Deprivation of Liberty), Re* [2015] 1 W.L.R. 2454 (CP), Sir James Munby PFD

r.14.3, see *G (A Child) (Non-relative Carer: Joinder to Adoption Proceedings), Re* [2014] EWCA Civ 432, [2015] Fam. 223 (CA (Civ Div)), Sullivan LJ; see *T (Children) (Placement Order: Revocation), Re* [2014] EWCA Civ 1369, [2015] 1 W.L.R. 3165 (CA (Civ Div)), Russell J

r.14.15, see *W (Children) (Adoption: Procedure: Conditions), Re* [2015] EWCA Civ 403, [2015] 3 F.C.R. 99 (CA (Civ Div)), Sir James Munby PFD

r.14.24, see *X (Adopted Child: Access to Court File), Re* [2015] 1 F.L.R. 375 (Fam Ct), Sir James Munby PFD

r.16.4, see *Haringey LBC v Musa* [2014] EWHC 962 (Fam), [2015] 1 F.C.R. 433 (Fam Div), Holman J

r.16.29, see *H (Children) (Care Orders: Evidence), Re* [2015] EWCA Civ 115, [2015] 2 F.C.R. 305 (CA (Civ Div)), Black LJ

r.20.2, see *Mann v Mann* [2014] EWCA Civ 1674, [2015] 2 F.L.R. 1116 (CA (Civ Div)), Patten LJ

r.21.1, see *L v R* [2015] EWCA Civ 61, Times, April 7, 2015 (CA (Civ Div)), Aikens LJ

r.21.2, see *L v R* [2015] EWCA Civ 61, Times, April 7, 2015 (CA (Civ Div)), Aikens LJ

r.21.3, see *L v R* [2015] EWCA Civ 61, Times, April 7, 2015 (CA (Civ Div)), Aikens LJ

r.22.10, see *R v R (Family Court: Procedural Fairness)* [2015] 1 W.L.R. 2743 (Fam Ct), Peter Jackson J

r.25.1, see *H (Children) (Care Orders: Evidence), Re* [2015] EWCA Civ 115, [2015] 2 F.C.R. 305 (CA (Civ Div)), Black LJ; see *S (A Child) (Interim Care Order: Residential Assessment), Re* [2015] 1 W.L.R. 925 (CC (Bournemouth)), Sir James Munby PFD

r.25.4, see *Wigan BC v M (Veracity Assessments)* [2015] EWFC 8 (Fam Ct), Peter Jackson J

r.27.3, see *Chai v Peng* [2014] EWHC 1519 (Fam), [2015] 1 F.L.R. 637 (Fam Div), Holman J

r.27.11, see *Cooper-Hohn v Hohn* [2014] EWHC 2314 (Fam), [2015] 1 F.L.R. 19 (Fam Div), Roberts J

r.28.3, see *Veluppillai v Veluppillai* [2015] EWHC 3095 (Fam), [2015] 6 Costs L.O. 735 (Fam Div), Mostyn J

r.29.12, see *Justice for Families Ltd v Secretary of State for Justice* [2014] EWCA Civ 1477, [2015] 2 F.L.R. 321 (CA (Civ Div)), Sir James Munby PFD

r.30.1, see *H (Children) (Care Proceedings: Appeals out of Time)* [2015] EWCA Civ 583, [2015] 1 W.L.R. 5085 (CA (Civ Div)), McFarlane LJ

r.33.3, see *EDG v RR (Enforcement of Foreign Maintenance Order)* [2014] EWHC 816 (Fam), [2015] 1 F.L.R. 270 (Fam Div), Mostyn J; see *Mann v Mann* [2014] EWCA Civ 1674, [2015] 2 F.L.R. 1116 (CA (Civ Div)), Patten LJ

r.37.9, see *Newman, Re* [2014] EWHC 3136 (Fam), [2015] 1 F.L.R. 1359 (Fam Div), Sir James Munby PFD

2011

99. Electronic Money Regulations 2011
   Reg.22, amended: SI 2015/575 Sch.2
   para.34

245. Investment Bank Special Administration Regulations 2011
   see *Hartmann Capital Ltd (In Special Administration), Re* [2015] EWHC 1514 (Ch), [2015] Bus. L.R. 983 (Ch D (Companies Ct)), Newey J
   Reg.15, amended: SI 2015/989 Sch.1
   para.5

Sch.6 Part 1 para.1, amended: SI 2015/17
Sch.6 para.6

517. Armed Forces and Reserve Forces (Compensation Scheme) Order 2011
Art.2, amended: SI 2015/413 Art.2
Art.12, amended: SI 2015/413 Art.3
Art.24A, amended: SI 2015/413 Art.4
Art.29, amended: SI 2015/413 Art.5
Art.35, amended: SI 2015/413 Art.6
Art.39, amended: SI 2015/413 Art.7
Sch.2 para.5, amended: SI 2015/413 Art.8
Sch.3 Part 1, amended: SI 2015/413 Art.9, Art.10

553. Her Majesty's Chief Inspector of Education, Children's Services and Skills (Fees and Frequency of Inspections) (Children's Homes etc.) (Amendment) Regulations 2011
revoked: SI 2015/551 Sch.1

558. Fire and Rescue Authorities (Performance Indicators) (Wales) Order 2011
revoked: SI 2015/604 Art.3

581. Fostering Services (England) Regulations 2011
Reg.25, amended: SI 2015/495 Reg.12

583. Children's Homes (Amendment) Regulations 2011
revoked: SI 2015/541 Reg.56

605. Libya (Asset-Freezing) Regulations 2011
see *Maud v Libyan Investment Authority* [2015] EWHC 1625 (Ch), [2015] B.P.I.R. 858 (Ch D), Rose J
Reg.3, see *Maud v Libyan Investment Authority* [2015] EWHC 1625 (Ch), [2015] B.P.I.R. 858 (Ch D), Rose J

723. Government Resources and Accounts Act 2000 (Estimates and Accounts) Order 2011
Sch.1, amended: SI 2015/971 Sch.3 para.17

817. Accounts and Audit (England) Regulations 2011
revoked: SI 2015/234 Sch.2

907. Asylum Support (Amendment) Regulations 2011
revoked: SI 2015/645 Reg.3, SI 2015/944 Reg.4

908. Greater Manchester Combined Authority Order 2011
Art.2, amended: SI 2015/960 Art.3

Sch.1 para.1A, added: SI 2015/960 Art.4
Sch.1 para.1i, amended: SI 2015/960 Art.4
Sch.1 para.2, amended: SI 2015/960 Art.4
Sch.1 para.2A, added: SI 2015/960 Art.4
Sch.1 para.3, amended: SI 2015/960 Art.4

917. Jobseeker's Allowance (Employment, Skills and Enterprise Scheme) Regulations 2011
see *R. (on the application of Reilly) v Secretary of State for Work and Pensions* [2014] EWHC 2182 (Admin), [2015] Q.B. 573 (QBD (Admin)), Lang J

968. Grants to the Churches Conservation Trust Order 2011
revoked: SI 2015/908 Art.4

1070. A11 Trunk Road (Fiveways to Thetford Improvement) (Detrunking) Order 2011
Sch.1, substituted: SI 2015/1581 Sch.1

1484. Civil Jurisdiction and Judgments (Maintenance) Regulations 2011
see *AB v JJB (EU Maintenance Regulation: Modification Application Procedure)* [2015] EWHC 192 (Fam), [2015] 2 F.L.R. 1143 (Fam Div), Sir Peter Singer; see *EDG v RR (Enforcement of Foreign Maintenance Order)* [2014] EWHC 816 (Fam), [2015] 1 F.L.R. 270 (Fam Div), Mostyn J
Sch.1 Pt 2 para.4, see *EDG v RR (Enforcement of Foreign Maintenance Order)* [2014] EWHC 816 (Fam), [2015] 1 F.L.R. 270 (Fam Div), Mostyn J
Sch.1 Pt 5, see *AB v JJB (EU Maintenance Regulation: Modification Application Procedure)* [2015] EWHC 192 (Fam), [2015] 2 F.L.R. 1143 (Fam Div), Sir Peter Singer
Sch.1 Part 5 para.11, amended: SI 2015/1489 Art.3
Sch.1 Part 5 para.11, revoked: SI 2015/1489 Art.3

1524. Energy Information Regulations 2011
Sch.1 para.1, amended: SI 2015/469 Reg.3

1543. Environmental Protection (Controls on Ozone-Depleting Substances) Regulations 2011
revoked: SI 2015/168 Reg.21

1556. National Health Service (Charges to Overseas Visitors) Regulations 2011

see *Ahmad v Secretary of State for the Home Department* [2014] EWCA Civ 988, [2015] 1 W.L.R. 593 (CA (Civ Div)), Arden LJ; see *R. (on the application of Cushnie) v Secretary of State for Health* [2014] EWHC 3626 (Admin), [2015] P.T.S.R. 384 (QBD (Admin)), Singh J

Reg.11, see *R. (on the application of Cushnie) v Secretary of State for Health* [2014] EWHC 3626 (Admin), [2015] P.T.S.R. 384 (QBD (Admin)), Singh J

1627. Education (Non-Maintained Special Schools) (England) Regulations 2011

revoked: SI 2015/728 Reg.8

Reg.2, amended: SI 2015/387 Reg.3

Sch.1 Part 1 para.4, amended: SI 2015/387 Reg.4

Sch.1 Part 1 para.5, amended: SI 2015/387 Reg.4

Sch.1 Part 1 para.6, amended: SI 2015/387 Reg.4

Sch.1 Part 1 para.7, substituted: SI 2015/387 Reg.4

Sch.1 Part 2 para.17, amended: SI 2015/387 Reg.4

1631. Cleaner Road Transport Vehicles Regulations 2011

Reg.2, amended: SI 2015/102 Sch.6 para.18

Reg.3, amended: SI 2015/102 Sch.6 para.18

Reg.6, amended: SI 2015/102 Sch.6 para.18

1709. Criminal Procedure Rules 2011

r.67.2, see *R. v Quillan (Gary)* [2015] EWCA Crim 538, [2015] 1 W.L.R. 4673 (CA (Crim Div)), Lord Thomas LCJ

1824. Town and Country Planning (Environmental Impact Assessment) Regulations 2011

see *Commercial Estates Group Ltd v Secretary of State for Communities and Local Government* [2014] EWHC 3089 (Admin), [2015] J.P.L. 350 (QBD (Admin)), Stuart-Smith J; see *R. (on the application of Champion) v North Norfolk DC* [2015] UKSC 52, [2015] 1 W.L.R. 3710 (SC), Lord Neuberger PSC;

see *R. (on the application of Larkfleet Ltd) v South Kesteven DC* [2014] EWHC 3760 (Admin), [2015] Env. L.R. 16 (QBD (Admin)), Lang J

Reg.3, see *Highland Council v Scottish Ministers* [2015] J.P.L. 166 (IH (1 Div)), The Lord President (Gill)

Reg.4, see *R. (on the application of Perry) v Hackney LBC* [2014] EWHC 3499 (Admin), [2015] J.P.L. 454 (QBD (Admin)), Patterson J

Sch.2, see *Gerber v Wiltshire Council* [2015] EWHC 524 (Admin), [2015] Env. L.R. 33 (QBD (Admin)), Dove J; see *R. (on the application of Larkfleet Ltd) v South Kesteven DC* [2014] EWHC 3760 (Admin), [2015] Env. L.R. 16 (QBD (Admin)), Lang J

Sch.3 para.1, see *Commercial Estates Group Ltd v Secretary of State for Communities and Local Government* [2014] EWHC 3089 (Admin), [2015] J.P.L. 350 (QBD (Admin)), Stuart-Smith J

1830. Disclosure of State Pension Credit Information (Warm Home Discount) Regulations 2011

Reg.1, amended: SI 2015/652 Reg.18

Reg.2, amended: SI 2015/652 Reg.19

Reg.3, amended: SI 2015/652 Reg.20

1848. Defence and Security Public Contracts Regulations 2011

Reg.2, amended: SI 2015/102 Sch.6 para.19

Reg.3, amended: SI 2015/102 Sch.6 para.19, SSI 2015/446 Sch.6 para.6

Reg.4, amended: SI 2015/102 Sch.6 para.19, SSI 2015/446 Sch.6 para.6

Reg.6, amended: SI 2015/102 Sch.6 para.19, SSI 2015/446 Sch.6 para.6

Reg.7, amended: SI 2015/102 Sch.6 para.19

Reg.12, amended: SI 2015/102 Sch.6 para.19

Reg.16, amended: SI 2015/102 Sch.6 para.19, SSI 2015/446 Sch.6 para.6

Reg.21, amended: SI 2015/102 Sch.6 para.19

Reg.21, revoked: SI 2015/102 Sch.6 para.19

Reg.31, amended: SI 2015/102 Sch.6
para.19, SSI 2015/446 Sch.6 para.6
Reg.33, amended: SI 2015/102 Sch.6
para.19, SSI 2015/446 Sch.6 para.6
Reg.46, amended: SI 2015/102 Sch.6
para.19, SSI 2015/446 Sch.6 para.6

1986. Education (Student Support)
Regulations 2011
 Reg.2, amended: SI 2015/1951 Reg.4
 Reg.2, revoked: SI 2015/1951 Reg.4
 Reg.4, revoked: SI 2015/1951 Reg.5
 Reg.5, amended: SI 2015/1951 Reg.6
 Reg.7, amended: SI 2015/1951 Reg.7
 Reg.9, amended: SI 2015/1951 Reg.8
 Reg.11, substituted: SI 2015/1951 Reg.9
 Reg.19, revoked: SI 2015/1951 Reg.10
 Reg.22, amended: SI 2015/1951 Reg.11
 Reg.23, amended: SI 2015/1951 Sch.1
 Reg.25, revoked: SI 2015/1951 Reg.12
 Reg.26, revoked: SI 2015/1951 Reg.13
 Reg.28, amended: SI 2015/1951 Reg.14
 Reg.29, amended: SI 2015/1951 Reg.15
 Reg.38, amended: SI 2015/1951 Reg.16
 Reg.38, revoked: SI 2015/1951 Reg.16
 Reg.41, amended: SI 2015/1951 Reg.17
 Reg.45, amended: SI 2015/1951 Reg.18
 Reg.56, amended: SI 2015/1951 Reg.19
 Reg.56, revoked: SI 2015/1951 Reg.19
 Reg.57, amended: SI 2015/1951 Reg.20
 Reg.57, revoked: SI 2015/1951 Reg.20
 Reg.58, amended: SI 2015/1951 Reg.21
 Reg.58, revoked: SI 2015/1951 Reg.21
 Reg.60, amended: SI 2015/1951 Reg.22
 Reg.60, revoked: SI 2015/1951 Reg.22
 Reg.60, substituted: SI 2015/1951 Reg.22
 Reg.61, amended: SI 2015/1951 Reg.23
 Reg.61, revoked: SI 2015/1951 Reg.23
 Reg.62, amended: SI 2015/1951 Reg.24
 Reg.62, revoked: SI 2015/1951 Reg.24
 Reg.63, amended: SI 2015/1951 Reg.25
 Reg.63, revoked: SI 2015/1951 Reg.25
 Reg.65, amended: SI 2015/1951 Reg.26
 Reg.65, revoked: SI 2015/1951 Reg.26
 Reg.65, substituted: SI 2015/1951 Reg.26
 Reg.66, amended: SI 2015/1951 Reg.27
 Reg.66, revoked: SI 2015/1951 Reg.27
 Reg.68, amended: SI 2015/1951 Reg.28
 Reg.69, amended: SI 2015/1951 Reg.29
 Reg.70, revoked: SI 2015/1951 Reg.30
 Reg.71, amended: SI 2015/1951 Reg.31

Reg.72, amended: SI 2015/1951 Reg.32,
Sch.1
Reg.73, revoked: SI 2015/1951 Reg.3
Reg.74, amended: SI 2015/1951 Reg.33,
Sch.1
Reg.74, revoked: SI 2015/1951 Reg.33
Reg.75, revoked: SI 2015/1951 Reg.3
Reg.76, amended: SI 2015/1951 Sch.1
Reg.77, amended: SI 2015/1951 Reg.34,
Sch.1
Reg.78, revoked: SI 2015/1951 Reg.3
Reg.80, amended: SI 2015/1951 Reg.35,
Sch.1
Reg.80, revoked: SI 2015/1951 Reg.35
Reg.80A, added: SI 2015/1951 Reg.36
Reg.81, amended: SI 2015/1951 Reg.37,
Sch.1
Reg.87, amended: SI 2015/1951 Reg.38,
Sch.1
Reg.88, amended: SI 2015/1951 Reg.39
Reg.91, revoked: SI 2015/1951 Reg.3
Reg.100, substituted: SI 2015/1951
Reg.40
Reg.101, substituted: SI 2015/1951
Reg.41
Reg.103, amended: SI 2015/1951 Reg.42
Reg.105, amended: SI 2015/1951 Reg.43,
Sch.1
Reg.106, revoked: SI 2015/1951 Reg.3
Reg.110, revoked: SI 2015/1951 Reg.44
Reg.113, amended: SI 2015/1951 Reg.45
Reg.115, revoked: SI 2015/1951 Reg.3
Reg.117, amended: SI 2015/1951 Reg.46
Reg.118, revoked: SI 2015/1951 Reg.3
Reg.119, amended: SI 2015/1951 Reg.47
Reg.119, revoked: SI 2015/1951 Reg.47
Reg.120, revoked: SI 2015/1951 Reg.48
Reg.135, amended: SI 2015/1951 Reg.49
Reg.137, revoked: SI 2015/1951 Reg.50
Reg.155, amended: SI 2015/1951 Reg.51
Reg.156, amended: SI 2015/1951 Reg.52
Reg.157, amended: SI 2015/1951 Reg.53
Reg.159, revoked: SI 2015/1951 Reg.54
Reg.168, amended: SI 2015/1951 Reg.55
Sch.4 para.5, amended: SI 2015/1951
Reg.56
Sch.4 para.9, amended: SI 2015/1951
Reg.56
Sch.4 para.9A, added: SI 2015/1951
Reg.56

2053. Public Procurement (Miscellaneous Amendments) Regulations 2011
> see *Heron Bros Ltd v Central Bedfordshire Council* [2015] EWHC 604 (TCC), [2015] P.T.S.R. 1146 (QBD (TCC)), Edwards-Stuart J

2055. Infrastructure Planning (Changes to, and Revocation of, Development Consent Orders) Regulations 2011
> Reg.4, amended: SI 2015/760 Reg.3
> Reg.5, substituted: SI 2015/760 Reg.3
> Reg.6, amended: SI 2015/760 Reg.3
> Reg.7, amended: SI 2015/760 Reg.3
> Reg.7A, added: SI 2015/760 Reg.3
> Reg.10, amended: SI 2015/760 Reg.5
> Reg.13, revoked: SI 2015/760 Reg.5
> Reg.14, amended: SI 2015/760 Reg.5
> Reg.14, revoked: SI 2015/760 Reg.5
> Reg.15, amended: SI 2015/760 Reg.5
> Reg.15, revoked: SI 2015/760 Reg.5
> Reg.16, amended: SI 2015/760 Reg.5
> Reg.19, amended: SI 2015/760 Reg.5
> Reg.21A, added: SI 2015/760 Reg.5
> Reg.22, amended: SI 2015/760 Reg.5
> Reg.36, amended: SI 2015/760 Reg.5
> Reg.42, amended: SI 2015/760 Reg.5
> Reg.43, amended: SI 2015/760 Reg.5
> Reg.49, amended: SI 2015/760 Reg.5
> Sch.1, amended: SI 2015/377 Sch.1 para.52, SI 2015/1682 Sch.1 para.10
> Sch.2 para.3, amended: SI 2015/760 Reg.7
> Sch.2 para.4, amended: SI 2015/760 Reg.7

2260. Equality Act 2010 (Specific Duties) Regulations 2011
> Sch.1, amended: SI 2015/137 Sch.2 para.20

2292. Alien and Locally Absent Species in Aquaculture (England and Wales) Regulations 2011
> Reg.29, revoked: SI 2015/88 Art.4

2547. Care Quality Commission (Membership) (Amendment) Regulations 2011
> revoked: SI 2015/1479 Reg.8

2598. Freedom of Information (Designation as Public Authorities) Order 2011
> see *University and Colleges Admissions Service v Information Commissioner*

> [2015] E.L.R. 112 (UT (AAC)), Judge Nicholas Wikeley

2775. Financial Restrictions (Iran) Order 2011
> see *Bank Mellat v HM Treasury* [2014] EWHC 3631 (Admin), [2015] H.R.L.R. 6 (QBD (Admin)), Collins J

2866. Legal Services Act 2007 (Designation as a Licensing Authority) (No.2) Order 2011
> Sch.2, amended: SI 2015/1641 Sch.1 para.7, Sch.3 para.3

2908. General Teaching Council for Wales (Disciplinary Functions) (Amendment) Regulations 2011
> revoked: SI 2015/140 Sch.1 Part 1

2935. Hydrocarbon Oil and Biofuels (Road Fuel in Defined Areas) (Reliefs) Regulations 2011
> Reg.2, amended: SI 2015/550 Reg.3
> Reg.6, amended: SI 2015/550 Reg.4
> Sch.1, substituted: SI 2015/550 Reg.6

2948. Health and Social Care Act 2008 (Primary Dental Services, Private Ambulance Services and Primary Medical Services) (Regulated Activities) (Transitory and Transitional Provisions) Order 2011
> revoked: SI 2015/864 Art.2

2012

8. School Admissions (Admission Arrangements and Co-ordination of Admission Arrangements) (England) Regulations 2012
> Reg.16, see *R. (on the application of London Oratory School Governors) v Schools Adjudicator* [2015] EWHC 1012 (Admin), [2015] E.L.R. 335 (QBD (Admin)), Cobb J

166. General Teaching Council for Wales (Functions) (Amendment) Regulations 2012
> revoked: SI 2015/140 Sch.1 Part 1

167. General Teaching Council for Wales (Additional Functions) (Amendment) Order 2012
> revoked: SI 2015/194 Sch.1

170. General Teaching Council for Wales (Disciplinary Functions) (Amendment) Regulations 2012
> revoked: SI 2015/140 Sch.1 Part 1

511. Her Majesty's Chief Inspector of Education, Children's Services and Skills (Fees and Frequency of Inspections) (Children's Homes etc.) (Amendment) Regulations 2012
    revoked: SI 2015/551 Sch.1

628. Localism Act 2011 (Commencement No 4 and Transitional, Transitory and Saving Provisions) Order 2012
    see *Charalambous v Ng* [2014] EWCA Civ 1604, [2015] 1 W.L.R. 3018 (CA (Civ Div)), Black LJ
    Art.16, see *Charalambous v Ng* [2014] EWCA Civ 1604, [2015] 1 W.L.R. 3018 (CA (Civ Div)), Black LJ

632. Control of Asbestos Regulations 2012
    Reg.2, amended: SI 2015/1682 Sch.1 para.10
    Sch.2 para.1, amended: SI 2015/21 Reg.21

700. Housing (Scotland) Act 2010 (Consequential Provisions and Modifications) Order 2012
    Sch.1 Part 2 para.11, revoked: SI 2015/621 Sch.1

717. Government Resources and Accounts Act 2000 (Estimates and Accounts) Order 2012
    Sch.1, amended: SI 2015/971 Sch.3 para.20

765. Education Act 2011 (Consequential Amendments to Subordinate Legislation) Order 2012
    Art.13, revoked: SI 2015/2059 Sch.6

767. Town and Country Planning (Local Planning) (England) Regulations 2012
    Reg.5, see *R. (on the application of Larkfleet Homes Ltd) v Rutland CC* [2014] EWHC 4095 (Admin), [2015] P.T.S.R. 589 (QBD (Admin)), Collins J; see *R. (on the application of Larkfleet Homes Ltd) v Rutland CC* [2015] EWCA Civ 597, [2015] P.T.S.R. 1369 (CA (Civ Div)), Moore-Bick LJ

811. Controlled Waste (England and Wales) Regulations 2012
    Sch.1 para.1, amended: SI 2015/1360 Reg.9, SI 2015/1417 Reg.6

847. Data-gathering Powers (Relevant Data) Regulations 2012
    Reg.8, amended: SI 2015/672 Reg.2

854. Government Resources and Accounts Act 2000 (Audit of Public Bodies) Order 2012
    Art.4, revoked: SI 2015/234 Sch.2

938. Early Years Foundation Stage (Welfare Requirements) Regulations 2012
    Reg.2A, added: SI 2015/1562 Reg.8
    Reg.3, amended: SI 2015/1562 Reg.8
    Reg.8A, added: SI 2015/1562 Reg.8
    Sch.1 para.11, amended: SI 2015/1562 Reg.8

979. Alternative Provision Academies and 16 to 19 Academies (Consequential Amendments to Subordinate Legislation) (England) Order 2012
    Sch.1 para.5, revoked: SI 2015/621 Sch.1

1115. Education (Induction Arrangements for School Teachers) (England) Regulations 2012
    see *Mosekari v Lewisham LBC* [2014] EWHC 3617 (Admin), [2015] E.L.R. 31 (QBD (Admin)), McGowan J
    Reg.7, see *Mosekari v Lewisham LBC* [2014] EWHC 3617 (Admin), [2015] E.L.R. 31 (QBD (Admin)), McGowan J
    Sch.1 para.10, amended: SI 2015/2059 Reg.77

1157. Further Education Corporations (Publication of Proposals) (England) Regulations 2012
    Reg.2, revoked: SI 2015/971 Sch.3 para.21
    Reg.3, revoked: SI 2015/971 Sch.3 para.21

1243. Export Control (Iran Sanctions) Order 2012
    Art.2, amended: SI 2015/1625 Art.2
    Art.4, amended: SI 2015/1625 Art.2
    Art.6, amended: SI 2015/1625 Art.2
    Art.6A, amended: SI 2015/1625 Art.2
    Art.7, amended: SI 2015/1625 Art.2
    Art.8, amended: SI 2015/1625 Art.2
    Art.8A, amended: SI 2015/1625 Art.2
    Art.9, amended: SI 2015/1625 Art.2
    Art.9A, amended: SI 2015/1625 Art.2
    Art.10, amended: SI 2015/1625 Art.2
    Art.11, amended: SI 2015/1625 Art.2
    Art.12, amended: SI 2015/1625 Art.2

1379. Cattle Compensation (England) Order 2012
    Sch.1 Part 1 para.4, amended: SI 2015/1838 Art.2

**1479. Health and Social Care Act 2012
(Consequential Provision-Social Workers)
Order 2012**
    Art.11, revoked: SI 2015/2059 Sch.6
    Sch.1 Part 1 para.18, revoked: SI
    2015/570 Sch.3
    Sch.1 Part 1 para.35, revoked: SI
    2015/1862 Sch.5 para.1
    Sch.1 Part 1 para.38, revoked: SI
    2015/1879 Sch.4 para.1
    Sch.1 Part 1 para.65, revoked: SSI
    2015/425 Sch.9 para.5
    Sch.1 Part 2 para.82, revoked: SI
    2015/2059 Sch.6
**1652. Health and Safety (Fees) Regulations
2012**
    revoked: SI 2015/363 Reg.26
**1696. Criminal Justice Act 2003 (Surcharge)
Order 2012**
    see *R. v George (Martin)* [2015] EWCA
    Crim 1096, [2015] 2 Cr. App. R. (S.) 58
    (CA (Crim Div)), Macur LJ
**1756. Iran (Restrictive Measures) (Overseas
Territories) Order 2012**
    Art.31A, amended: SI 2015/825 Art.2
    Art.32, amended: SI 2015/825 Art.2
    Art.43, amended: SI 2015/825 Art.2
    Art.43A, added: SI 2015/1772 Art.2
    Art.44, amended: SI 2015/1772 Art.2
**1796. Armed Forces (Enhanced Learning
Credit Scheme and Further and Higher
Education Commitment Scheme) Order 2012**
    Art.10, amended: SI 2015/497 Art.2
    Art.11, amended: SI 2015/497 Art.2
    Art.12, amended: SI 2015/497 Art.2
**1818. Further Education Loans Regulations
2012**
    Reg.11, substituted: SI 2015/181 Reg.3
    Reg.16, substituted: SI 2015/181 Reg.4
1916. Human Medicines Regulations 2012
    Reg.8, amended: SI 2015/1503 Reg.3
    Reg.38, amended: SI 2015/1503 Reg.4
    Reg.39, amended: SI 2015/1503 Reg.5
    Reg.44, amended: SI 2015/1503 Reg.6
    Reg.44, revoked: SI 2015/1503 Reg.6
    Reg.213, amended: SI 2015/323 Reg.3
    Reg.218, amended: SI 2015/903 Reg.3
    Reg.219, amended: SI 2015/903 Reg.4
    Reg.219, revoked: SI 2015/903 Reg.4
    Reg.219A, added: SI 2015/903 Reg.5
    Reg.229, amended: SI 2015/323 Reg.4

    Reg.233, amended: SI 2015/1503 Reg.7
    Reg.234, amended: SI 2015/323 Reg.5
    Reg.246, amended: SI 2015/903 Reg.6
    Reg.256E, amended: SI 2015/1503 Reg.8
    Reg.269, amended: SI 2015/903 Reg.7
    Reg.346, amended: SI 2015/323 Reg.6,
    SI 2015/903 Reg.8, SI 2015/1503 Reg.9
    Sch.16 Part 2, added: SI 2015/323 Reg.7
    Sch.16 Part 2, amended: SI 2015/323
    Reg.7
    Sch.16 Part 3, amended: SI 2015/323
    Reg.7
    Sch.17 Part 2, amended: SI 2015/1503
    Reg.10
    Sch.17 Part 5, amended: SI 2015/1503
    Reg.10
    Sch.22, amended: SI 2015/323 Reg.8
    Sch.22, substituted: SI 2015/323 Reg.8
    Sch.34 Part 5 para.73, revoked: SI
    2015/570 Sch.3
    Sch.34 Part 5 para.85, revoked: SI
    2015/1862 Sch.5 para.1
    Sch.34 Part 5 para.87, revoked: SI
    2015/1879 Sch.4 para.1
**2265. Designation of Schools Having a
Religious Character (Independent Schools)
(England) (No.2) Order 2012**
    Sch.1, amended: SI 2015/1636 Sch.2
**2601. Homelessness (Suitability of
Accommodation) (England) Order 2012**
    see *Nzolameso v Westminster City
    Council* [2014] EWCA Civ 1383, [2015]
    P.T.S.R. 211 (CA (Civ Div)), Moore-
    Bick LJ
**2677. Child Support Maintenance
Calculation Regulations 2012**
    Part 3, added: SI 2015/338 Reg.8
    Reg.14, amended: SI 2015/338 Reg.8
    Reg.44, amended: SI 2015/1985 Art.38
    Reg.64, amended: SI 2015/643 Sch.1
    para.35
**2685. General Medical Council (Licence to
Practise and Revalidation) Regulations Order
of Council 2012**
    Sch.1, added: SI 2015/1375 Sch.1
    Sch.1, amended: SI 2015/1375 Sch.1, SI
    2015/1964 Sch.1
    Sch.1, substituted: SI 2015/1964 Sch.1
**2748. Iraq (United Nations Sanctions)
(Overseas Territories) (Amendment) Order
2012**

revoked: SI 2015/1383 Art.1

**2749. Liberia (Restrictive Measures)
(Overseas Territories) (Amendment) Order
2012**

revoked: SI 2015/1899 Art.1

**2750. Democratic Republic of the Congo
(Restrictive Measures) (Overseas Territories)
(Amendment) Order 2012**

revoked: SI 2015/1382 Art.1

2782. Feed-in Tariffs Order 2012

Art.2, amended: SI 2015/35 Art.3, SI
2015/2045 Art.3

Art.4, substituted: SI 2015/2045 Art.4

Art.5, amended: SI 2015/2045 Art.5

Art.6, amended: SI 2015/2045 Art.6

Art.8A, added: SI 2015/2045 Art.7

Art.9, amended: SI 2015/35 Art.4, SI
2015/1659 Art.3, SI 2015/2045 Art.8

Art.10, amended: SI 2015/35 Art.5, SI
2015/2045 Art.9

Art.10, revoked: SI 2015/2045 Art.9

Art.11, amended: SI 2015/35 Art.6, SI
2015/1659 Art.4, SI 2015/2045 Art.10

Art.12, amended: SI 2015/2045 Art.11

Art.15, amended: SI 2015/35 Art.7

Art.15, revoked: SI 2015/2045 Art.12

Art.16, substituted: SI 2015/2045 Art.13

Art.18, amended: SI 2015/2045 Art.14

Art.19, amended: SI 2015/2045 Art.15

Art.24B, amended: SI 2015/2045 Art.16

Art.25, substituted: SI 2015/2045 Art.17

Art.27, amended: SI 2015/2045 Art.18

Art.27A, added: SI 2015/2045 Art.19

Art.38, amended: SI 2015/2045 Art.20

Sch.A1, added: SI 2015/2045 Sch.1

Sch.1A, added: SI 2015/2045 Sch.2

Sch.2, substituted: SI 2015/2045 Sch.3

Sch.2 para.5, amended: SI 2015/35 Art.8

**2814. International Recovery of Maintenance
(Hague Convention 2007 etc.) Regulations
2012**

Sch.1 para.7, amended: SI 2015/1489
Art.4

Sch.2 para.2, amended: SI 2015/1489
Art.5

Sch.2 para.2, revoked: SI 2015/583 Sch.2
para.17

**2885. Council Tax Reduction Schemes
(Prescribed Requirements) (England)
Regulations 2012**

Reg.2, amended: SI 2015/971 Sch.3
para.23, SI 2015/1985 Art.39, SI
2015/2041 Reg.2

Sch.1 Part 3 para.8, amended: SI
2015/643 Sch.1 para.36, SI 2015/2041
Reg.2

Sch.1 Part 6 para.17, amended: SI
2015/2041 Reg.2

Sch.1 Part 6 para.21, amended: SI
2015/643 Sch.1 para.36

Sch.1 Part 6 para.22, amended: SI
2015/1985 Art.39

Sch.1 Part 6 para.25, amended: SI
2015/643 Sch.1 para.36

Sch.1 Part 6 para.26, amended: SI
2015/643 Sch.1 para.36, SI 2015/1985
Art.39

Sch.1 Part 6 para.28, amended: SI
2015/1985 Art.39, SI 2015/2041 Reg.2

Sch.1 Part 6 para.30, amended: SI
2015/2041 Reg.2

Sch.2 Part 1 para.1, amended: SI
2015/2041 Reg.2

Sch.2 Part 2 para.3, substituted: SI
2015/2041 Reg.2

Sch.2 Part 3 para.6, amended: SI
2015/643 Sch.1 para.36, SI 2015/2041
Reg.2

Sch.2 Part 4, amended: SI 2015/2041
Reg.2

Sch.3 para.1, amended: SI 2015/2041
Reg.2

Sch.4 para.5, amended: SI 2015/643
Sch.1 para.36

Sch.4 para.10, amended: SI 2015/2041
Reg.2

Sch.5 para.20, amended: SI 2015/2041
Reg.2

Sch.6 Part 1 para.28A, added: SI
2015/1985 Art.39

Sch.6 Part 1 para.29, amended: SI
2015/643 Sch.1 para.36

Sch.6 Part 1 para.29B, added: SI
2015/2041 Reg.2

**2886. Council Tax Reduction Schemes
(Default Scheme) (England) Regulations 2012**

see *South Tyneside Council v Aitken*
[2014] EWHC 4163 (Admin), [2015]
R.V.R. 227 (QBD (Admin)), Ouseley J

Sch.1, added: SI 2015/1985 Art.40

Sch.1, amended: SI 2015/971 Sch.3
para.24, SI 2015/1985 Art.40

2897. Agriculture, Animals, Environment and Food etc (Miscellaneous Amendments) Order 2012

Art.2, revoked: SI 2015/787 Sch.1
Art.27, revoked: SI 2015/168 Reg.21
Art.29, revoked: SI 2015/310 Reg.33
Art.43, revoked: SI 2015/168 Reg.21

2904. Financial Restrictions (Iran) Order 2012

see *Bank Mellat v HM Treasury* [2014] EWHC 3631 (Admin), [2015] H.R.L.R. 6 (QBD (Admin)), Collins J

2994. Benefit Cap (Housing Benefit) Regulations 2012

see *R. (on the application of JS) v Secretary of State for Work and Pensions* [2015] UKSC 16, [2015] 1 W.L.R. 1449 (SC), Lady Hale DPSC

3038. Greenhouse Gas Emissions Trading Scheme Regulations 2012

Reg.3, amended: SI 2015/1849 Reg.2
Reg.13, amended: SI 2015/1849 Reg.3
Reg.15, amended: SI 2015/1849 Reg.4
Reg.16, amended: SI 2015/1849 Reg.5
Reg.46, amended: SI 2015/933 Reg.20, SI 2015/1388 Reg.14
Reg.58A, added: SI 2015/1849 Reg.6
Reg.67, amended: SI 2015/1849 Reg.7
Reg.70, amended: SI 2015/1849 Reg.8
Reg.73, amended: SI 2015/1849 Reg.9
Reg.76, amended: SI 2015/1849 Reg.10
Reg.80, amended: SI 2015/1849 Reg.11
Sch.4 para.2, amended: SI 2015/1849 Reg.12
Sch.6A, added: SI 2015/1849 Reg.14
Sch.6 para.1, amended: SI 2015/1849 Reg.13
Sch.6 para.1, revoked: SI 2015/1849 Reg.13
Sch.6 para.1A, added: SI 2015/1849 Reg.13
Sch.6 para.2, amended: SI 2015/1849 Reg.13
Sch.6 para.4, amended: SI 2015/1849 Reg.13
Sch.6 para.7, amended: SI 2015/1849 Reg.13
Sch.9 para.8, amended: SI 2015/912 Sch.5 para.5

3054. Air Navigation (Dangerous Goods) (Amendment) Regulations 2012

revoked: SI 2015/970 Reg.3

3093. Common Agricultural Policy Single Payment and Support Schemes (Wales) (Amendment) Regulations 2012

revoked: SI 2015/1252 Reg.17

3098. Civil Legal Aid (Procedure) Regulations 2012

Reg.2, amended: SI 2015/1416 Reg.2, SI 2015/1678 Reg.2
Reg.20, amended: SI 2015/1678 Reg.2
Reg.23, amended: SI 2015/1416 Reg.2, SI 2015/1678 Reg.2
Reg.30, amended: SI 2015/1416 Reg.2
Reg.31, amended: SI 2015/1416 Reg.2, SI 2015/1678 Reg.2
Reg.33, see *R. (on the application of Rights of Women) v Lord Chancellor* [2015] EWHC 35 (Admin), [2015] 2 F.L.R. 823 (QBD (Admin)), Fulford LJ
Reg.33, amended: SI 2015/1416 Reg.2
Reg.34, amended: SI 2015/1416 Reg.2
Reg.67, amended: SI 2015/1678 Reg.2

3112. Apprenticeships, Skills, Children and Learning Act 2009 (Consequential Amendments to Subordinate Legislation) (England and Wales) Order 2012

Art.2, revoked: SI 2015/621 Sch.1

3118. Energy Performance of Buildings (England and Wales) Regulations 2012

Reg.11, amended: SI 2015/609 Reg.2
Reg.18, amended: SI 2015/609 Reg.2
Reg.19, amended: SI 2015/609 Reg.2
Reg.28, amended: SI 2015/609 Reg.2
Reg.33, amended: SI 2015/609 Reg.2
Reg.33, revoked: SI 2015/609 Reg.2
Reg.34, amended: SI 2015/1681 Reg.2
Reg.34A, added: SI 2015/1681 Reg.2
Sch.2, amended: SI 2015/609 Reg.2
Sch.2 Part 1 para.2, amended: SI 2015/609 Reg.2
Sch.2 Part 1 para.3, amended: SI 2015/609 Reg.2
Sch.2 Part 2 para.4, amended: SI 2015/609 Reg.2
Sch.2 Part 3 para.5, amended: SI 2015/609 Reg.2

3174. Designation of Schools Having a Religious Character (Independent Schools) (England) (No.3) Order 2012
    Sch.1, amended: SI 2015/2075 Sch.1

2013

7. Scotland Act 2012 (Transitional and Consequential Provisions) Order 2013
    see *Macklin (Paul Alexander) v HM Advocate* [2015] UKSC 77 (SC), Lord Neuberger PSC
    Art.2, see *Rondos (Michal) v HM Advocate* 2015 S.C.L. 61 (HCJ), Lady Paton

9. Criminal Legal Aid (General) Regulations 2013
    Reg.2, amended: SI 2015/1369 Reg.4
    Reg.6, amended: SI 2015/1678 Reg.3
    Reg.8, amended: SI 2015/1369 Reg.4
    Reg.9, amended: SI 2015/326 Reg.2, SI 2015/838 Reg.7, SI 2015/1416 Reg.3
    Reg.9, revoked: SI 2015/326 Reg.2
    Reg.9, see *Brown v Haringey LBC* [2015] EWCA Civ 483, [2015] H.L.R. 30 (CA (Civ Div)), Richards LJ; see *King's Lynn and West Norfolk BC v Bunning* [2013] EWHC 3390 (QB), [2015] 1 W.L.R. 531 (QBD), Blake J
    Reg.10, see *Brown v Haringey LBC* [2015] EWCA Civ 483, [2015] H.L.R. 30 (CA (Civ Div)), Richards LJ
    Reg.11, amended: SI 2015/1369 Reg.4
    Reg.14, amended: SI 2015/1369 Reg.4
    Reg.15, amended: SI 2015/1369 Reg.4
    Reg.16, amended: SI 2015/1369 Reg.4
    Reg.17, amended: SI 2015/1369 Reg.4

77. Legal Aid, Sentencing and Punishment of Offenders Act 2012 (Commencement No 5 and Saving Provision) Order 2013
    Art.4, see *Hartmann Capital Ltd (In Special Administration), Re* [2015] EWHC 1514 (Ch), [2015] Bus. L.R. 983 (Ch D (Companies Ct)), Newey J

104. Civil Legal Aid (Merits Criteria) Regulations 2013
    Reg.2, amended: SI 2015/1414 Reg.2, SI 2015/2005 Reg.2
    Reg.5, amended: SI 2015/1571 Reg.2
    Reg.22, amended: SI 2015/1414 Reg.2

Reg.42, amended: SI 2015/1571 Reg.2
Reg.43, substituted: SI 2015/1571 Reg.2
Reg.56, amended: SI 2015/1571 Reg.2
Reg.60, amended: SI 2015/1414 Reg.2, SI 2015/1571 Reg.2
Reg.66, amended: SI 2015/1571 Reg.2
Reg.67, amended: SI 2015/1571 Reg.2
Reg.68, amended: SI 2015/1571 Reg.2
Reg.69, amended: SI 2015/1571 Reg.2, SI 2015/2005 Reg.2
Reg.75, amended: SI 2015/1571 Reg.2
Reg.75, revoked: SI 2015/1571 Reg.2

164. Belarus (Asset-Freezing) Regulations 2013
    Reg.2, amended: SI 2015/1850 Reg.3

175. Electricity (Competitive Tenders for Offshore Transmission Licences) Regulations 2013
    revoked: SI 2015/1555 Reg.1

218. Local Authority (Public Health, Health and Wellbeing Boards and Health Scrutiny) Regulations 2013
    Reg.1, amended: SI 2015/921 Reg.4
    Reg.19, amended: SI 2015/921 Reg.4

276. Jobseeker's Allowance (Schemes for Assisting Persons to Obtain Employment) Regulations 2013
    see *R. (on the application of Reilly) v Secretary of State for Work and Pensions* [2014] EWHC 2182 (Admin), [2015] Q.B. 573 (QBD (Admin)), Lang J
    Reg.3, revoked: SI 2015/336 Reg.3

339. Greater Manchester (Light Rapid Transit System) (Exemptions) Order 2013
    Art.19, added: SI 2015/1877 Art.3
    Sch.1, substituted: SI 2015/1877 Sch.1

351. Local Authorities (Public Health Functions and Entry to Premises by Local Healthwatch Representatives) Regulations 2013
    Reg.5A, added: SI 2015/921 Reg.2
    Reg.8A, added: SI 2015/921 Reg.3

378. Jobseeker's Allowance Regulations 2013
    Reg.2, amended: SI 2015/389 Reg.5, SI 2015/971 Sch.3 para.25
    Reg.3, amended: SI 2015/67 Reg.2
    Reg.16A, added: SI 2015/339 Reg.3
    Reg.41, amended: SI 2015/389 Reg.5
    Reg.44, amended: SI 2015/389 Reg.5
    Reg.45, amended: SI 2015/336 Reg.5
    Reg.46, amended: SI 2015/339 Reg.3

Reg.46A, added: SI 2015/339 Reg.3
Reg.49, amended: SI 2015/30 Art.10
Reg.54, amended: SI 2015/389 Reg.5
Reg.60, amended: SI 2015/643 Sch.1
para.41
Reg.62, amended: SI 2015/478 Reg.37
Sch.1 para.6, amended: SI 2015/389
Reg.5
Sch.1 para.12, amended: SI 2015/389
Reg.5

379. Employment and Support Allowance Regulations 2013
Reg.2, amended: SI 2015/971 Sch.3
para.26
Reg.5, amended: SI 2015/339 Reg.5
Reg.6, amended: SI 2015/339 Reg.5
Reg.26, amended: SI 2015/437 Reg.4
Reg.37, amended: SI 2015/643 Sch.1
para.42
Reg.62, amended: SI 2015/30 Art.12, SI
2015/457 Art.23
Reg.80, amended: SI 2015/67 Reg.2
Reg.84, amended: SI 2015/478 Reg.38
Reg.87, amended: SI 2015/437 Reg.4

419. Financial Services and Markets Act 2000 (Qualifying EU Provisions) Order 2013
Art.1, amended: SI 2015/1882 Reg.8
Art.2, amended: SI 2015/1882 Reg.8
Art.3, amended: SI 2015/1882 Reg.8
Art.5, amended: SI 2015/1882 Reg.8
Art.6, amended: SI 2015/1882 Reg.8

422. Civil Legal Aid (Remuneration) Regulations 2013
see *AB (A Child) (Temporary Leave to Remove from Jurisdiction: Expert Evidence), Re* [2014] EWHC 2758 (Fam), [2015] 1 F.C.R. 164 (Fam Div), Judge Clifford Bellamy
Reg.2, amended: SI 2015/325 Reg.2, SI
2015/1369 Reg.5, SI 2015/1678 Reg.4
Reg.5, amended: SI 2015/898 Reg.2
Reg.5A, added: SI 2015/898 Reg.2
Reg.5A, amended: SI 2015/1369 Reg.5,
SI 2015/1678 Reg.4
Reg.5A, revoked: SI 2015/1369 Reg.5
Reg.5A, see *R. (on the application of Ben Hoare Bell Solicitors) v Lord Chancellor* [2015] EWHC 523 (Admin), [2015] 1 W.L.R. 4175 (QBD (Admin)), Beatson LJ
Reg.6, amended: SI 2015/898 Reg.2

Reg.7, amended: SI 2015/898 Reg.2
Reg.8, amended: SI 2015/1416 Reg.4
Reg.12, amended: SI 2015/898 Reg.2
Sch.1 Part 1 para.3, amended: SI
2015/325 Reg.2
Sch.1 Part 3, amended: SI 2015/325
Reg.2

435. Criminal Legal Aid (Remuneration) Regulations 2013
Reg.2, amended: SI 2015/882 Reg.2
Reg.3, amended: SI 2015/325 Reg.3, SI
2015/1416 Reg.5
Reg.4, amended: SI 2015/882 Reg.2
Reg.5, amended: SI 2015/1678 Reg.5
Reg.8, amended: SI 2015/1369 Reg.6
Reg.10, amended: SI 2015/1678 Reg.5
Reg.13, amended: SI 2015/882 Reg.2
Reg.14, amended: SI 2015/1678 Reg.5
Reg.17A, amended: SI 2015/1369 Reg.6,
Sch.4, SI 2015/1678 Reg.5
Reg.18, amended: SI 2015/882 Reg.2
Reg.20, amended: SI 2015/1678 Reg.5
Reg.21, amended: SI 2015/882 Reg.2, SI
2015/1369 Reg.6
Reg.22, amended: SI 2015/882 Reg.2
Reg.23, amended: SI 2015/882 Reg.2
Reg.25, amended: SI 2015/882 Reg.2
Reg.28, amended: SI 2015/882 Reg.2, SI
2015/1369 Reg.6
Reg.31, amended: SI 2015/882 Reg.2
Sch.1 Part 1 para.1, amended: SI
2015/882 Reg.2, SI 2015/1678 Reg.5
Sch.1 Part 1 para.2, amended: SI
2015/1678 Reg.5
Sch.1 Part 1 para.2, revoked: SI
2015/1678 Reg.5
Sch.1 Part 3 para.6, amended: SI
2015/1678 Reg.5
Sch.1 Part 4 para.9, amended: SI
2015/1678 Reg.5
Sch.1 Part 5 para.12, amended: SI
2015/1678 Reg.5
Sch.1 Part 5 para.12, revoked: SI
2015/1678 Reg.5
Sch.1 Part 5 para.17, amended: SI
2015/882 Reg.2
Sch.1 Part 5 para.18, amended: SI
2015/882 Reg.2
Sch.1 Part 5 para.19, amended: SI
2015/1678 Reg.5

Sch.1 Part 5 para.22, amended: SI 2015/1678 Reg.5

Sch.1 Part 5 para.22, revoked: SI 2015/1678 Reg.5

Sch.1 Part 5 para.24, amended: SI 2015/1678 Reg.5

Sch.1 Part 6 para.25, amended: SI 2015/1678 Reg.5

Sch.1 Part 6 para.26, amended: SI 2015/882 Reg.2

Sch.1 Part 7, amended: SI 2015/325 Reg.3, SI 2015/800 Reg.6

Sch.1 Part 7, substituted: SI 2015/800 Reg.6

Sch.2, amended: SI 2015/1369 Reg.6

Sch.2 Part 1 para.1, amended: SI 2015/1369 Reg.6, SI 2015/1678 Reg.5

Sch.2 Part 1 para.2, amended: SI 2015/1678 Reg.5

Sch.2 Part 1 para.2, revoked: SI 2015/1678 Reg.5

Sch.2 Part 1A, added: SI 2015/1369 Sch.5

Sch.2 Part 2 para.4, amended: SI 2015/1369 Reg.6, SI 2015/1678 Reg.5

Sch.2 Part 2 para.5, substituted: SI 2015/1369 Sch.6

Sch.2 Part 2 para.6, amended: SI 2015/1369 Sch.1 para.1

Sch.2 Part 2 para.6, revoked: SI 2015/1369 Reg.6

Sch.2 Part 2 para.7, amended: SI 2015/1369 Reg.6, Sch.1 para.2

Sch.2 Part 2 para.8, amended: SI 2015/1369 Reg.6, Sch.1 para.3, Sch.7

Sch.2 Part 2 para.9, amended: SI 2015/1369 Reg.6, Sch.1 para.4, Sch.8

Sch.2 Part 3, amended: SI 2015/1369 Reg.6

Sch.2 Part 3 para.10, amended: SI 2015/1678 Reg.5

Sch.2 Part 3 para.11, amended: SI 2015/1369 Sch.1 para.5

Sch.2 Part 4 para.12, amended: SI 2015/1369 Reg.6

Sch.2 Part 4 para.12, revoked: SI 2015/1369 Reg.6

Sch.2 Part 4 para.13, amended: SI 2015/1369 Reg.6, SI 2015/1678 Reg.5

Sch.2 Part 5 para.14, amended: SI 2015/1369 Reg.6

Sch.2 Part 5 para.19, amended: SI 2015/1369 Sch.1 para.6

Sch.2 Part 5 para.20, amended: SI 2015/1369 Reg.6

Sch.2 Part 5 para.21, amended: SI 2015/1369 Sch.9, SI 2015/1678 Reg.5

Sch.2 Part 5 para.21, revoked: SI 2015/1678 Reg.5

Sch.2 Part 5 para.22, amended: SI 2015/1369 Reg.6

Sch.2 Part 5 para.22, revoked: SI 2015/1369 Reg.6

Sch.2 Part 5 para.23, amended: SI 2015/1369 Sch.10, SI 2015/1678 Reg.5

Sch.2 Part 6 para.25, substituted: SI 2015/1369 Sch.11

Sch.2 Part 6 para.27, amended: SI 2015/1369 Sch.1 para.7

Sch.3 para.7, amended: SI 2015/1369 Sch.2 para.1

Sch.4 para.1, amended: SI 2015/1369 Reg.6

Sch.4 para.1, substituted: SI 2015/325 Reg.3

Sch.4 para.2, amended: SI 2015/1369 Reg.6, Sch.3 para.2, Sch.12

Sch.4 para.3, amended: SI 2015/1369 Reg.6, Sch.3 para.1, Sch.3 para.3

Sch.4 para.4, amended: SI 2015/1369 Reg.6, Sch.3 para.4

Sch.4 para.5, amended: SI 2015/325 Reg.3, SI 2015/1369 Reg.6, Sch.3 para.5, Sch.13, SI 2015/1678 Reg.5

Sch.4 para.5, revoked: SI 2015/1678 Reg.5

Sch.4 para.5A, added: SI 2015/325 Reg.3

Sch.4 para.5A, amended: SI 2015/1369 Sch.3 para.6

Sch.4 para.6, amended: SI 2015/1369 Reg.6, Sch.3 para.7

Sch.4 para.6, revoked: SI 2015/1369 Reg.6

Sch.4 para.6, substituted: SI 2015/1369 Reg.6

Sch.4 para.7, amended: SI 2015/325 Reg.3, SI 2015/1369 Reg.6, Sch.3 para.1, Sch.3 para.8, SI 2015/1416 Reg.5

Sch.4 para.8, amended: SI 2015/1369 Reg.6, Sch.3 para.9

Sch.4 para.9, amended: SI 2015/1369 Sch.3 para.10

Sch.4 para.10, amended: SI 2015/325
Reg.3, SI 2015/1369 Reg.6, Sch.3 para.1,
Sch.3 para.11
Sch.4 para.11, amended: SI 2015/1369
Sch.3 para.12
Sch.4 para.12, amended: SI 2015/1369
Sch.3 para.13, SI 2015/1416 Reg.5

469. Functions of the National Health Service Commissioning Board and the NHS Business Services Authority (Awdurdod Gwasanaethau Busnes y GIG) (Primary Dental Services) (England) Regulations 2013
Reg.1, amended: SI 2015/1728 Reg.28
Sch.1, amended: SI 2015/1728 Reg.29

471. Criminal Legal Aid (Financial Resources) Regulations 2013
Reg.5, amended: SI 2015/1369 Reg.7
Reg.11, amended: SI 2015/643 Sch.1
para.43, SI 2015/838 Reg.8
Reg.20, amended: SI 2015/643 Sch.1
para.43, SI 2015/838 Reg.8
Reg.33, amended: SI 2015/643 Sch.1
para.43, SI 2015/838 Reg.8

479. Food Safety (Sampling and Qualifications) (Wales) Regulations 2013
Sch.1, amended: SI 2015/1867 Sch.13
para.4

480. Civil Legal Aid (Financial Resources and Payment for Services) Regulations 2013
Reg.5, see *D (A Child) (Non-availability of Legal Aid), Re* [2015] 1 F.L.R. 531 (Fam Ct), Sir James Munby PFD
Reg.6, amended: SI 2015/1416 Reg.6
Reg.8, amended: SI 2015/1416 Reg.6
Reg.12, amended: SI 2015/1416 Reg.6
Reg.16, amended: SI 2015/1416 Reg.6
Reg.24, amended: SI 2015/643 Sch.1
para.44, SI 2015/838 Reg.9
Reg.40, amended: SI 2015/643 Sch.1
para.44, SI 2015/838 Reg.9

483. Criminal Legal Aid (Contribution Orders) Regulations 2013
Reg.2, amended: SI 2015/710 Reg.2
Reg.10, amended: SI 2015/643 Sch.1
para.45, SI 2015/710 Reg.2, SI 2015/838
Reg.10
Reg.12, amended: SI 2015/1678 Reg.6
Reg.28, amended: SI 2015/710 Reg.2
Reg.32, amended: SI 2015/710 Reg.2

488. Government Resources and Accounts Act 2000 (Estimates and Accounts) Order 2013
Sch.1, amended: SI 2015/971 Sch.3
para.27

503. Civil Legal Aid (Statutory Charge) Regulations 2013
Reg.2, amended: SI 2015/1678 Reg.7

504. Financial Services and Markets Act 2000 (Over the Counter Derivatives, Central Counterparties and Trade Repositories) Regulations 2013
Reg.36, amended: SI 2015/348 Reg.2
Reg.52, amended: SI 2015/348 Reg.2

509. Animals (Scientific Procedures) Act 1986 (Fees) Order 2013
revoked: SI 2015/244 Art.3

520. Infrastructure Planning (Miscellaneous Prescribed Provisions) (Amendment) Regulations 2013
revoked: SI 2015/462 Sch.3

522. Infrastructure Planning (Prescribed Consultees and Interested Parties etc.) (Amendment) Regulations 2013
Reg.4, revoked: SI 2015/462 Sch.3

536. Copyright and Performances (Application to Other Countries) Order 2013
Sch.1, amended: SI 2015/216 Art.2

575. Apprenticeships (Modifications to the Specification of Apprenticeship Standards for England) Order 2013
revoked: 2015 c.20 Sch.1 para.12

614. Criminal Legal Aid (Determinations by a Court and Choice of Representative) Regulations 2013
see *R. (on the application of Sanjari) v Birmingham Crown Court* [2015] EWHC 2037 (Admin), [2015] 2 Cr. App. R. 30 (DC), Lord Thomas LCJ
Reg.4, see *King's Lynn and West Norfolk BC v Bunning* [2013] EWHC 3390 (QB), [2015] 1 W.L.R. 531 (QBD), Blake J
Reg.6, see *Brown v Haringey LBC* [2015] EWCA Civ 483, [2015] H.L.R. 30 (CA (Civ Div)), Richards LJ
Reg.7, see *Brown v Haringey LBC* [2015] EWCA Civ 483, [2015] H.L.R. 30 (CA (Civ Div)), Richards LJ; see *King's Lynn and West Norfolk BC v Bunning* [2013] EWHC 3390 (QB), [2015] 1 W.L.R. 531 (QBD), Blake J

Reg.8, see *Brown v Haringey LBC* [2015] EWCA Civ 483, [2015] H.L.R. 30 (CA (Civ Div)), Richards LJ
Reg.14, see *R. (on the application of Sanjari) v Birmingham Crown Court* [2015] EWHC 2037 (Admin), [2015] 2 Cr. App. R. 30 (DC), Lord Thomas LCJ
Reg.18, amended: SI 2015/1678 Reg.8
Reg.22, amended: SI 2015/1678 Reg.8

628. Legal Aid (Information about Financial Resources) Regulations 2013
Sch.1 para.9, amended: SI 2015/1985 Art.43
Sch.1 para.9A, added: SI 2015/1985 Art.43
Sch.1 para.10, amended: SI 2015/1985 Art.43
Sch.1 para.23, amended: SI 2015/643
Sch.1 para.46, SI 2015/838 Reg.11, SI 2015/1408 Reg.2, SI 2015/2005 Reg.3

637. Financial Services Act 2012 (Misleading Statements and Impressions) Order 2013
Art.3, substituted: SI 2015/369 Art.9

644. Bank of England Act 1998 (Macro-prudential Measures) Order 2013
Art.1, amended: SI 2015/575 Sch.2 para.35

647. Health Education England (Establishment and Constitution) Amendment Order 2013
revoked: SI 2015/137 Sch.1

648. Hinkley Point C (Nuclear Generating Station) Order 2013
Sch.1 Part 1, amended: SI 2015/1666 Art.3
Sch.1 Part 3, amended: SI 2015/1666 Sch.1
Sch.2 para.2, amended: SI 2015/1666 Art.5
Sch.2 para.4, amended: SI 2015/1666 Art.5

663. Children (Secure Accommodation) (Amendment) (Wales) Regulations 2013
revoked: SI 2015/1988 Reg.18

675. Lancashire County Council (Torrisholme to the M6 Link (A683 Completion of Heysham to M6 Link Road)) Order 2013
Sch.1, amended: SI 2015/571 Art.4
Sch.2 para.23, amended: SI 2015/571 Art.5

732. European Communities (Recognition of Professional Qualifications) (Amendment) Regulations 2013
revoked: SI 2015/2059 Sch.6

766. Environmental Permitting (England and Wales) (Amendment) (No.2) Regulations 2013
Reg.3, revoked: SI 2015/483 Reg.31

791. A5 Trunk Road (Bethesda, Gwynedd) (Prohibition and Restriction of Waiting) Order 2013
Art.5A, added: SI 2015/1950 Art.2
Art.6, amended: SI 2015/1950 Art.2
Sch.1, amended: SI 2015/1950 Art.2
Sch.3 para.3, amended: SI 2015/1950 Art.2
Sch.4, added: SI 2015/1950 Art.2

804. Animals and Animal Products (Examination for Residues and Maximum Residue Limits) (Amendment) Regulations 2013
revoked: SI 2015/787 Sch.1

815. General Medical Council (Fitness to Practise and Constitution of Panels and Investigation Committee) (Amendment) Rules Order of Council 2013
Sch.1, revoked: SI 2015/1965 Sch.1

817. Electronic Commerce Directive (Trafficking People for Exploitation) Regulations 2013
Reg.2, amended: SI 2015/1472 Reg.16
Reg.3, amended: SI 2015/1472 Reg.17

1037. Greenhouse Gas Emissions Trading Scheme (Amendment) Regulations 2013
see *R. (on the application of Swiss International Airlines AG) v Secretary of State for Climate Change and Energy* [2015] EWCA Civ 331, [2015] 3 C.M.L.R. 5 (CA (Civ Div)), Underhill LJ

1119. CRC Energy Efficiency Scheme Order 2013
Art.83, amended: SI 2015/664 Sch.4 para.84

1188. Tribunal Procedure (Amendment No 3) Rules 2013
see *Dickinson v Network Rail Infrastructure Ltd* [2015] R.V.R. 19 (UT (Lands)), Sir Keith Lindblom P

1191. Apprenticeships (Designation of Welsh Certifying Authority) Order 2013
Art.2, amended: SI 2015/1733 Art.2

**1197. Health Education England
(Establishment and Constitution)
Amendment (No.2) Order 2013**
    revoked: SI 2015/137 Sch.1
1203. Galloper Wind Farm Order 2013
    Sch.1 Part 3 para.8, amended: SI
    2015/1460 Art.2
**1237. Employment Tribunals (Constitution
and Rules of Procedure) Regulations 2013**
    see *Carroll v Mayor's Office for Policing
    and Crime* [2015] I.C.R. 835 (EAT),
    Judge Hand QC; see *EF v AB* [2015]
    I.R.L.R. 619 (EAT), Slade J
    Sch.1 para.1, see *Wolfe v North
    Middlesex University Hospital NHS Trust*
    [2015] I.C.R. 960 (EAT), Judge Serota
    QC
    Sch.1 para.11, see *Deangate Ltd v Hatley*
    [2015] I.C.R. 890 (EAT), Langstaff J
    Sch.1 para.37, see *Harris v Academies
    Enterprise Trust* [2015] I.C.R. 617
    (EAT), Langstaff J
    Sch.1 para.41, see *East of England
    Ambulance Service NHS Trust v Sanders*
    [2015] I.C.R. 293 (EAT), Langstaff J
    Sch.1 para.80, see *Hafiz and Haque
    Solicitors v Mullick* [2015] I.C.R. 1085
    (EAT), Langstaff J
    Sch.1 para.86, see *Carroll v Mayor's
    Office for Policing and Crime* [2015]
    I.C.R. 835 (EAT), Judge Hand QC
**1302. Dangerous Dogs (Fees) (England and
Wales) Order 2013**
    revoked: SI 2015/138 Sch.1
**1388. Collective Investment in Transferable
Securities (Contractual Scheme) Regulations
2013**
    Sch.2 Part 3, amended: SI 2015/1641
    Sch.2 para.2, SI 2015/1651 Reg.6
**1389. Electricity and Gas (Market Integrity
and Transparency) (Enforcement etc.)
Regulations 2013**
    Reg.2, amended: SI 2015/862 Reg.7
    Reg.4, amended: SI 2015/862 Reg.8
    Reg.6A, added: SI 2015/862 Reg.9
    Reg.10, amended: SI 2015/862 Reg.10,
    SI 2015/979 Reg.5
    Reg.20A, added: SI 2015/862 Reg.11
    Reg.21, amended: SI 2015/862 Reg.12
    Reg.26, amended: SI 2015/862 Reg.13
    Reg.27, amended: SI 2015/862 Reg.14

**1407. Family Proceedings Fees (Amendment)
Order 2013**
    Art.4, amended: SI 2015/687 Art.8
**1445. European Communities (Designation)
Order 2013**
    Art.2, amended: SI 2015/1530 Art.5
    Art.3, amended: SI 2015/1530 Art.5
**1460. Accession of Croatia (Immigration and
Worker Authorisation) Regulations 2013**
    Reg.1, amended: SI 2015/694 Sch.2
    para.1
    Reg.2, amended: SI 2015/694 Sch.2
    para.2
**1478. Cosmetic Products Enforcement
Regulations 2013**
    Reg.7, amended: SI 2015/1630 Sch.2
    para.133
    Sch.2, revoked: SI 2015/1630 Sch.2
    para.134
**1482. Justice and Security Act 2013
(Commencement, Transitional and Saving
Provisions) Order 2013**
    see *R. (on the application of K) v
    Secretary of State for the Home
    Department* [2014] EWCA Civ 151,
    [2015] 1 W.L.R. 125 (CA (Civ Div)),
    Richards LJ
**1506. Biocidal Products and Chemicals
(Appointment of Authorities and
Enforcement) Regulations 2013**
    Reg.9, amended: SI 2015/1682 Sch.1
    para.10
    Reg.18, amended: SI 2015/1682 Sch.1
    para.10
    Reg.36, amended: SI 2015/21 Reg.22
**1507. Biocidal Products (Fees and Charges)
Regulations 2013**
    revoked: SI 2015/363 Reg.26
1554. Criminal Procedure Rules 2013
    see *Abbas v Crown Prosecution Service*
    [2015] EWHC 579 (Admin), [2015] 2 Cr.
    App. R. 11 (DC), Hallett LJ
**1773. Alternative Investment Fund Managers
Regulations 2013**
    Part 3A, added: SI 2015/1882 Reg.4
    Reg.2, amended: SI 2015/1882 Reg.4
    Reg.30, amended: SI 2015/1882 Reg.4
    Reg.32, amended: SI 2015/1882 Reg.4
    Reg.52, amended: SI 2015/1882 Reg.4
    Reg.53, amended: SI 2015/1882 Reg.4

1819. Gaming Duty (Amendment) Regulations 2013
revoked: SI 2015/1351 Reg.3

1820. Life Insurance Qualifying Policies (Statement and Reporting Requirements) Regulations 2013
Reg.3, amended: SI 2015/544 Reg.2

1831. Cultural Test (Television Programmes) Regulations 2013
Reg.2, amended: SI 2015/1449 Reg.4
Reg.3, amended: SI 2015/1449 Reg.5
Reg.4A, added: SI 2015/1449 Reg.5
Reg.6, amended: SI 2015/1449 Reg.6
Reg.9, amended: SI 2015/1449 Reg.6
Reg.11, amended: SI 2015/1449 Reg.6
Reg.12, amended: SI 2015/1449 Reg.6
Sch.1, amended: SI 2015/1449 Reg.7, SI 2015/1941 Reg.2
Sch.2 para.2, amended: SI 2015/1449 Reg.8
Sch.2 para.11, amended: SI 2015/1449 Reg.8
Sch.2 para.14, amended: SI 2015/1449 Reg.8
Sch.2 para.15, substituted: SI 2015/1449 Reg.8
Sch.2 para.16, substituted: SI 2015/1449 Reg.8
Sch.2 para.17, amended: SI 2015/1449 Reg.8
Sch.2 para.18, amended: SI 2015/1449 Reg.8
Sch.2 para.19, amended: SI 2015/1449 Reg.8

1881. Financial Services and Markets Act 2000 (Regulated Activities) (Amendment) (No.2) Order 2013
Art.58, amended: SI 2015/910 Sch.1 para.15

1893. Employment Tribunals and the Employment Appeal Tribunal Fees Order 2013
Art.2, amended: SI 2015/414 Art.3
Art.11, amended: SI 2015/414 Art.4
Sch.1, amended: SI 2015/414 Art.5
Sch.2, amended: SI 2015/483 Sch.6 para.9
Sch.3 para.1, amended: SI 2015/414 Art.6

1916. Faculty Jurisdiction Rules 2013
revoked: SI 2015/1568 r.28_2

2012. Export Control (Syria Sanctions) Order 2013
Art.3, amended: SI 2015/97 Art.3, SI 2015/1546 Art.11
Art.8A, added: SI 2015/97 Art.3
Art.16, amended: SI 2015/97 Art.3
Art.17, amended: SI 2015/97 Art.3

2094. Education (Information About Individual Pupils) (England) Regulations 2013
Reg.2, amended: SI 2015/971 Sch.3 para.29

2157. Care Quality Commission (Membership) (Amendment) Regulations 2013
revoked: SI 2015/1479 Reg.8

2216. Gangmasters Licensing (Exclusions) Regulations 2013
Sch.1 Part 2 para.12, substituted: SI 2015/1782 Sch.6 para.5

2232. Education (National Curriculum)(Attainment Targets and Programmes of Study)(England) Order 2013
Art.2, amended: SI 2015/900 Art.26

2302. Courts and Tribunals Fee Remissions Order 2013
see *R. (on the application of Unison) v Lord Chancellor* [2014] EWHC 4198 (Admin), [2015] 2 C.M.L.R. 4 (QBD (Admin)), Elias LJ

2356. Local Government Pension Scheme Regulations 2013
Reg.3, amended: SI 2015/755 Reg.3, Reg.4
Reg.10, amended: SI 2015/755 Reg.5
Reg.15, amended: SI 2015/755 Reg.6
Reg.16, added: SI 2015/755 Reg.7
Reg.16, amended: SI 2015/755 Reg.7
Reg.17, amended: SI 2015/755 Reg.8
Reg.19, amended: SI 2015/755 Reg.9
Reg.21, amended: SI 2015/755 Reg.10
Reg.22, amended: SI 2015/755 Reg.11
Reg.32, amended: SI 2015/755 Reg.12
Reg.36, amended: SI 2015/755 Reg.13
Reg.39, amended: SI 2015/755 Reg.14
Reg.40, amended: SI 2015/755 Reg.15
Reg.41, amended: SI 2015/755 Reg.16
Reg.42, amended: SI 2015/755 Reg.17
Reg.44, amended: SI 2015/755 Reg.18
Reg.45, amended: SI 2015/755 Reg.19
Reg.53, revoked: SI 2015/57 Reg.3

Reg.55, amended: SI 2015/57 Reg.4
Reg.58, amended: SI 2015/755 Reg.20
Reg.62, amended: SI 2015/755 Reg.21
Reg.63, revoked: SI 2015/57 Reg.5
Reg.64, amended: SI 2015/755 Reg.22
Reg.65, revoked: SI 2015/57 Reg.6
Reg.66, amended: SI 2015/57 Reg.7
Reg.69, amended: SI 2015/755 Reg.23
Reg.83, amended: SI 2015/755 Reg.24
Reg.89, amended: SI 2015/755 Reg.25
Reg.89, revoked: SI 2015/755 Reg.25
Reg.94, amended: SI 2015/755 Reg.26
Reg.103, amended: SI 2015/755 Reg.27
Reg.105, added: SI 2015/57 Reg.9
Reg.106, added: SI 2015/57 Reg.9
Reg.107, added: SI 2015/57 Reg.9
Reg.109, added: SI 2015/57 Reg.9
Reg.111, added: SI 2015/57 Reg.9
Reg.113, added: SI 2015/57 Reg.9
Sch.1, amended: SI 2015/57 Reg.8, SI
2015/755 Reg.28
Sch.2 Part 1 para.24, substituted: SI
2015/755 Reg.29
Sch.2 Part 2 para.6, amended: SI
2015/755 Reg.30
Sch.3 Part 1 para.1, amended: SI
2015/755 Reg.31
Sch.3 Part 2 para.4, amended: SI
2015/755 Reg.32

**2571. Annual Tax on Enveloped Dwellings
Avoidance Schemes (Prescribed Descriptions
of Arrangements) Regulations 2013**
Reg.4, amended: SI 2015/464 Reg.2

**2870. Air Navigation (Overseas Territories)
Order 2013**
Art.19, amended: SI 2015/1769 Art.3
Art.26, amended: SI 2015/1769 Art.4
Art.39A, added: SI 2015/1769 Art.5
Art.185, substituted: SI 2015/1769 Art.6
Art.187, substituted: SI 2015/1769 Art.7
Sch.7, added: SI 2015/1769 Art.8

**2879. Growth and Infrastructure Act 2013
(Local Development Orders) (Consequential
Provisions) (England) Order 2013**
Art.2, revoked: SI 2015/595 Sch.9
Art.4, revoked: SI 2015/595 Sch.9

**2952. Animal By-Products (Enforcement)
(England) Regulations 2013**
Part 8, substituted: SI 2015/1980 Reg.7
Reg.2, amended: SI 2015/1980 Reg.2
Reg.7A, added: SI 2015/1980 Reg.3

Reg.9, amended: SI 2015/1980 Reg.4
Reg.10, amended: SI 2015/1980 Reg.5
Reg.23, amended: SI 2015/1980 Reg.6
Reg.23, revoked: SI 2015/1980 Reg.6
Reg.29, revoked: SI 2015/1980 Reg.8
Sch.1, amended: SI 2015/1980 Reg.9

**2996. Food Safety and Hygiene (England)
Regulations 2013**
see *R. (on the application of Association
of Independent Meat Suppliers) v Food
Standards Agency* [2015] EWHC 1896
(Admin), [2015] P.T.S.R. 1383 (QBD
(Admin)), Simon J

**3029. Council Tax Reduction Schemes and
Prescribed Requirements (Wales)
Regulations 2013**
Reg.2, amended: SI 2015/44 Reg.3, SI
2015/971 Sch.3 para.30
Reg.10, amended: SI 2015/44 Reg.4
Reg.18, amended: SI 2015/44 Reg.5
Reg.28, amended: SI 2015/44 Reg.6
Reg.28, revoked: SI 2015/44 Reg.6
Sch.1 Part 2 para.3, amended: SI 2015/44
Reg.7
Sch.1 Part 4 para.10, amended: SI
2015/44 Reg.7
Sch.1 Part 4 para.12, amended: SI
2015/44 Reg.7
Sch.1 Part 4 para.13, amended: SI
2015/44 Reg.7
Sch.1 Part 4 para.19, amended: SI
2015/44 Reg.7
Sch.2 Part 1 para.1, amended: SI 2015/44
Reg.8
Sch.2 Part 1 para.2, amended: SI 2015/44
Reg.8
Sch.2 Part 2 para.3, amended: SI 2015/44
Reg.8
Sch.2 Part 4, amended: SI 2015/44 Reg.8
Sch.3 para.5, amended: SI 2015/44 Reg.9
Sch.3 para.6, amended: SI 2015/44 Reg.9
Sch.6 Part 2 para.5, amended: SI 2015/44
Reg.10
Sch.6 Part 4 para.14, amended: SI
2015/44 Reg.10
Sch.6 Part 4 para.15, amended: SI
2015/44 Reg.10
Sch.6 Part 4 para.17, amended: SI
2015/44 Reg.10
Sch.6 Part 4 para.21, amended: SI
2015/44 Reg.10

Sch.7 Part 1 para.1, amended: SI 2015/44 Reg.11

Sch.7 Part 1 para.3, amended: SI 2015/44 Reg.11

Sch.7 Part 2 para.4, amended: SI 2015/44 Reg.11

Sch.7 Part 4, amended: SI 2015/44 Reg.11

Sch.7 Part 5 para.18, amended: SI 2015/44 Reg.11

Sch.7 Part 6 para.23, amended: SI 2015/44 Reg.11

Sch.7 Part 6 para.24, amended: SI 2015/44 Reg.11

Sch.7 Part 7 para.25, amended: SI 2015/44 Reg.11

Sch.7 Part 7 para.27, amended: SI 2015/44 Reg.11

Sch.8 para.12, amended: SI 2015/44 Reg.12

Sch.11 Part 1 para.1, amended: SI 2015/971 Sch.3 para.30

Sch.11 Part 1 para.3, amended: SI 2015/44 Reg.13

3035. Council Tax Reduction Schemes (Default Scheme) (Wales) Regulations 2013

Sch.1, added: SI 2015/44 Reg.17, Reg.18, Reg.19, Reg.20

Sch.1, amended: SI 2015/44 Reg.15, Reg.16, Reg.17, Reg.18, Reg.19, Reg.21, Reg.22, Reg.23, Reg.24, Reg.25, Reg.26, Reg.27, Reg.28, Reg.29, Reg.30, SI 2015/971 Sch.3 para.31

Sch.1, revoked: SI 2015/44 Reg.17

3104. School and Early Years Finance (England) Regulations 2013

Reg.11, see *Hammersmith and Fulham LBC v L* [2015] UKUT 523 (AAC), [2015] E.L.R. 528 (UT (AAC)), Judge Mitchell

Reg.13, see *Hammersmith and Fulham LBC v L* [2015] UKUT 523 (AAC), [2015] E.L.R. 528 (UT (AAC)), Judge Mitchell

3133. Feed (Hygiene and Enforcement) and the Animal Feed (England) (Amendment) Regulations 2013

revoked: SI 2015/454 Sch.5

3134. Consumer Contracts (Information, Cancellation and Additional Charges) Regulations 2013

Part 5, revoked: SI 2015/1629 Reg.8

Reg.6, amended: SI 2015/1629 Reg.3

Reg.9, amended: SI 2015/1629 Reg.4

Reg.9, revoked: SI 2015/1629 Reg.4

Reg.10, amended: SI 2015/1629 Reg.5

Reg.10, revoked: SI 2015/1629 Reg.5

Reg.13, amended: SI 2015/1629 Reg.6

Reg.13, revoked: SI 2015/1629 Reg.6

Reg.24, revoked: SI 2015/1726 Sch.1 para.7

Reg.34, amended: SI 2015/1629 Reg.7

3155. Fire and Rescue Services (Appointment of Inspector) (Wales) Order 2013

revoked: SI 2015/1524 Art.3

3156. Local Elections (Northern Ireland) Order 2013

Sch.1 para.23, amended: SI 2015/566 Sch.13

Sch.1 para.23, revoked: SI 2015/566 Art.5

3177. Education (Student Support) (Wales) Regulations 2013

Reg.1, revoked: SI 2015/54 Reg.3

Reg.2, amended: SI 2015/54 Reg.125

Reg.2, revoked: SI 2015/54 Reg.3

Reg.3, revoked: SI 2015/54 Reg.3

Reg.76, amended: SI 2015/54 Reg.125

Reg.76, revoked: SI 2015/54 Reg.3

Reg.77, revoked: SI 2015/54 Reg.3

Reg.78, amended: SI 2015/54 Reg.125

Reg.78, revoked: SI 2015/54 Reg.3

Reg.79, revoked: SI 2015/54 Reg.3

Reg.93, amended: SI 2015/54 Reg.125

Reg.93, revoked: SI 2015/54 Reg.3

Reg.94, revoked: SI 2015/54 Reg.3

Reg.95, amended: SI 2015/54 Reg.125

Reg.95, revoked: SI 2015/54 Reg.3

Reg.96, revoked: SI 2015/54 Reg.3

Reg.121, amended: SI 2015/54 Reg.125

Reg.121, revoked: SI 2015/54 Reg.3

Reg.122, revoked: SI 2015/54 Reg.3

3197. Electoral Registration and Administration Act 2013 (Transitional Provisions) Order 2013

Art.17, amended: SI 2015/1376 Sch.2 para.23

3220. Energy Efficiency (Eligible Buildings) Regulations 2013

Reg.2, amended: SSI 2015/446 Sch.6 para.9

2014

41. Agricultural Holdings (Units of Production) (Wales) Order 2014
    revoked: SI 2015/1020 Art.3
162. Heavy Fuel Oil (Amendment) Regulations 2014
    revoked: SI 2015/483 Reg.31
382. Employment Rights (Increase of Limits) Order 2014
    revoked: SI 2015/226 Art.2
469. Energy Act 2013 (Office for Nuclear Regulation) (Consequential Amendments, Transitional Provisions and Savings) Order 2014
    Sch.3 Part 5 para.183, revoked: SSI 2015/181 Sch.9
    Sch.3 Part 5 para.199, revoked: SI 2015/462 Sch.3
    Sch.3 Part 5 para.201, revoked: SI 2015/595 Sch.9
520. International Tax Compliance (Crown Dependencies and Gibraltar) Regulations 2014
    Reg.3, amended: SI 2015/873 Reg.2
    Reg.8, amended: SI 2015/873 Reg.2
    Reg.8, revoked: SI 2015/873 Reg.2
    Reg.8A, added: SI 2015/873 Reg.2
    Reg.10A, added: SI 2015/873 Reg.2
    Reg.12, amended: SI 2015/873 Reg.2
    Reg.13, amended: SI 2015/873 Reg.2
    Reg.14, amended: SI 2015/873 Reg.2
    Reg.15A, added: SI 2015/873 Reg.2
531. Government Resources and Accounts Act 2000 (Estimates and Accounts) Order 2014
    Sch.1, amended: SI 2015/971 Sch.3 para.32
533. Enterprise Act 2002 (Mergers) (Interim Measures Financial Penalties) (Determination of Control and Turnover) Order 2014
    Sch.1 para.1, amended: SI 2015/575 Sch.2 para.36
566. Emergency Ambulance Services Committee (Wales) Regulations 2014
    Reg.2, amended: SI 2015/137 Sch.2 para.12
603. Justices Clerks and Assistants Rules 2014
    Sch.1, amended: SI 2015/890 r.2

607. Civil Legal Aid (Remuneration) (Amendment) (No.3) Regulations 2014
    Reg.2, see *R. (on the application of Ben Hoare Bell Solicitors) v Lord Chancellor* [2015] EWHC 523 (Admin), [2015] 1 W.L.R. 4175 (QBD (Admin)), Beatson LJ
623. Automatic Enrolment (Earnings Trigger and Qualifying Earnings Band) Order 2014
    Art.3, revoked: SI 2015/468 Art.4
670. Her Majesty's Chief Inspector of Education, Children's Services and Skills (Fees and Frequency of Inspections) (Children's Homes etc.) (Amendment) Regulations 2014
    revoked: SI 2015/551 Sch.1
829. Contracting Out (Local Authorities Social Services Functions) (England) Order 2014
    Sch.1 para.1, revoked: SI 2015/643 Art.3
    Sch.1 para.14, revoked: SI 2015/643 Art.3
    Sch.1 para.20, revoked: SI 2015/643 Art.3
    Sch.1 para.23, revoked: SI 2015/643 Art.3
    Sch.1 para.25, revoked: SI 2015/643 Art.3
    Sch.1 para.27, revoked: SI 2015/643 Art.3
    Sch.1 para.29, revoked: SI 2015/643 Art.3
840. Family Court (Composition and Distribution of Business) Rules 2014
    Part 5 r.16, amended: SI 2015/1421 r.3
894. Capital Requirements (Capital Buffers and Macro-prudential Measures) Regulations 2014
    Part 5A, added: SI 2015/19 Reg.2
    Reg.1, amended: SI 2015/19 Reg.2
    Reg.2, amended: SI 2015/19 Reg.2
    Reg.34A, added: SI 2015/19 Reg.2
    Reg.34E, added: SI 2015/19 Reg.2
    Reg.34F, added: SI 2015/19 Reg.2
    Reg.34G, added: SI 2015/19 Reg.2
    Reg.34N, amended: SI 2015/19 Reg.2
    Reg.34O, added: SI 2015/19 Reg.2
    Reg.34P, added: SI 2015/19 Reg.2
895. Legal Officers (Annual Fees) Order 2014
    revoked: SI 2015/1613 Art.4

916. Diffuse Mesothelioma Payment Scheme Regulations 2014
Sch.4, amended: SI 2015/367 Reg.2

928. Domestic Renewable Heat Incentive Scheme Regulations 2014
Reg.2, amended: SI 2015/143 Reg.3, SI 2015/145 Reg.11, SI 2015/1459 Reg.12
Reg.3, amended: SI 2015/143 Reg.4
Reg.4, amended: SI 2015/143 Reg.5
Reg.5, amended: SI 2015/143 Reg.6
Reg.6, amended: SI 2015/143 Reg.7
Reg.8, amended: SI 2015/143 Reg.8, SI 2015/1459 Reg.13
Reg.12, amended: SI 2015/143 Reg.9
Reg.13, amended: SI 2015/143 Reg.10
Reg.17, amended: SI 2015/143 Reg.11
Reg.38, amended: SI 2015/143 Reg.12
Reg.39, amended: SI 2015/143 Reg.13
Reg.41, amended: SI 2015/145 Reg.12
Reg.42A, added: SI 2015/145 Reg.13
Reg.47, amended: SI 2015/143 Reg.14
Reg.50, amended: SI 2015/143 Reg.15
Reg.51, amended: SI 2015/143 Reg.16
Reg.56, amended: SI 2015/143 Reg.17
Sch.3 para.1, amended: SI 2015/143 Reg.18
Sch.4 Part 1 para.1, amended: SI 2015/143 Reg.19

1212. Education (Amendments Relating to the Inspection of Education and Training) (Wales) Regulations 2014
Reg.2, revoked: SI 2015/1599 Reg.1

1242. A1 Trunk Road (Elkesley, Nottinghamshire) (Temporary Restriction and Prohibition of Traffic) Order 2014
revoked: SI 2015/1199 Art.14

1368. Central African Republic (Sanctions) (Overseas Territories) Order 2014
Art.3, amended: SI 2015/1380 Art.2
Art.3, revoked: SI 2015/1380 Art.2
Art.5, amended: SI 2015/1380 Art.2
Art.5, revoked: SI 2015/1380 Art.2
Art.7, amended: SI 2015/1380 Art.2
Art.8, amended: SI 2015/1380 Art.2
Art.9, amended: SI 2015/1380 Art.2
Sch.3 para.8, amended: SI 2015/1380 Art.2

1506. International Tax Compliance (United States of America) Regulations 2014
revoked: SI 2015/878 Reg.25

1530. Special Educational Needs and Disability Regulations 2014
Sch.2, see *R. (on the application of L) v Warwickshire CC* [2015] EWHC 203 (Admin), [2015] B.L.G.R. 81 (QBD (Admin)), Mostyn J

1561. Films Co-Production Agreements (Amendment) Order 2014
revoked: SI 2015/1886 Art.3

1610. Criminal Procedure Rules 2014
revoked: SI 2015/1490
amended: SI 2015/13 r.15, SI 2015/646 r.9
see *West, Re* [2014] EWCA Crim 1480, [2015] 1 W.L.R. 109 (CA (Crim Div)), Sir Brian Leveson PQBD
Part 3 r.3.9, amended: SI 2015/13 r.4, SI 2015/646 r.3
Part 3 r.3.13, amended: SI 2015/13 r.4
Part 4 r.4.7, amended: SI 2015/646 r.4
Part 6, amended: SI 2015/13 r.5
Part 6 r.6.1, amended: SI 2015/13 r.5
Part 6 r.6.14, amended: SI 2015/13 r.5
Part 6 r.6.15, amended: SI 2015/13 r.5
Part 6 r.6.16, amended: SI 2015/13 r.5
Part 6 r.6.17, amended: SI 2015/13 r.5
Part 6 r.6.18, amended: SI 2015/13 r.5
Part 6 r.6.19, amended: SI 2015/13 r.5
Part 6 r.6.22, amended: SI 2015/13 r.5
Part 7 r.7.1, amended: SI 2015/646 r.5
Part 7 r.7.1, substituted: SI 2015/646 r.5
Part 7 r.7.2, amended: SI 2015/646 r.5
Part 7 r.7.4, amended: SI 2015/646 r.5
Part 9 r.9.9, amended: SI 2015/646 r.6
Part 9 r.9.11, amended: SI 2015/646 r.6
Part 9 r.9.13, amended: SI 2015/646 r.6
Part 14 r.14.1, amended: SI 2015/13 r.6
Part 14 r.14.1, revoked: SI 2015/13 r.6
Part 14 r.14.2, amended: SI 2015/13 r.6
Part 17 r.17.21, amended: SI 2015/13 r.7
Part 37 r.37.1, added: SI 2015/646 r.7
Part 37 r.37.1, amended: SI 2015/646 r.7
Part 37 r.37.2, amended: SI 2015/646 r.7
Part 37 r.37.3, amended: SI 2015/646 r.7
Part 37 r.37.8, substituted: SI 2015/646 r.7
Part 37 r.37.9, added: SI 2015/646 r.7
Part 37 r.37.9, substituted: SI 2015/646 r.7
Part 37 r.37.11, amended: SI 2015/646 r.7

Part 37 r.37.12, amended: SI 2015/646 r.7

Part 37 r.37.13, amended: SI 2015/646 r.7

Part 37 r.37.14, amended: SI 2015/646 r.7

Part 37 r.37.15, amended: SI 2015/646 r.7

Part 37 r.37.16, amended: SI 2015/646 r.7

Part 37 r.37.17, amended: SI 2015/646 r.7

Part 37 r.37.17, substituted: SI 2015/646 r.7

Part 39 r.39.1, amended: SI 2015/13 r.8

Part 42 r.42.1, amended: SI 2015/646 r.8

Part 42 r.42.4, amended: SI 2015/646 r.8

Part 50, amended: SI 2015/13 r.9

Part 50 r.50.1, amended: SI 2015/13 r.9

Part 50 r.50.1, revoked: SI 2015/13 r.9

Part 50 r.50.1, substituted: SI 2015/13 r.9

Part 50 r.50.2, amended: SI 2015/13 r.9

Part 50 r.50.2, revoked: SI 2015/13 r.9

Part 50 r.50.4, amended: SI 2015/13 r.9

Part 50 r.50.4, revoked: SI 2015/13 r.9

Part 50 r.50.5, amended: SI 2015/13 r.9

Part 52 r.52.1, amended: SI 2015/13 r.10

Part 52 r.52.7, amended: SI 2015/13 r.10

Part 52 r.52.8, substituted: SI 2015/13 r.10

Part 58 r.58.1, substituted: SI 2015/13 r.11

Part 58 r.58.2, substituted: SI 2015/13 r.11

Part 58 r.58.3, amended: SI 2015/13 r.11

Part 58 r.58.4, amended: SI 2015/13 r.11

Part 58 r.58.5, amended: SI 2015/13 r.11

Part 58 r.58.6, amended: SI 2015/13 r.11

Part 58 r.58.7, amended: SI 2015/13 r.11

Part 58 r.58.8, amended: SI 2015/13 r.11

Part 58 r.58.9, amended: SI 2015/13 r.11

Part 58 r.58.10, amended: SI 2015/13 r.11

Part 58 r.58.11, amended: SI 2015/13 r.11

Part 58 r.58.13, added: SI 2015/13 r.11

Part 59 r.59.1, amended: SI 2015/13 r.12

Part 59 r.59.7, added: SI 2015/13 r.12

Part 63 r.63.7, added: SI 2015/13 r.13

Part 63 r.63.7, substituted: SI 2015/13 r.13

Part 76 r.76.11, amended: SI 2015/13 r.14

Pt 3., see *West, Re* [2014] EWCA Crim 1480, [2015] 1 W.L.R. 109 (CA (Crim Div)), Sir Brian Leveson PQBD

r.1.1, see *R. v Boardman (David)* [2015] EWCA Crim 175, [2015] 1 Cr. App. R. 33 (CA (Crim Div)), Sir Brian Leveson PQBD

r.14.2, see *R. v A* [2015] EWCA Crim 177, [2015] 2 Cr. App. R. (S.) 12 (CA (Crim Div)), Fulford LJ; see *R. v Clarke (Dean)* [2015] EWCA Crim 350, [2015] 2 Cr. App. R. 6 (CA (Crim Div)), Lord Thomas LCJ

r.62.9, see *West, Re* [2014] EWCA Crim 1480, [2015] 1 W.L.R. 109 (CA (Crim Div)), Sir Brian Leveson PQBD

r.76.8, see *Quayum v DPP* [2015] EWHC 1660 (Admin), (2015) 179 J.P. 390 (DC), Sir Brian Leveson PQBD

1638. Explosives Regulations 2014

Sch.13 Part 2 para.14, revoked: SI 2015/627 Reg.28

1643. Energy Savings Opportunity Scheme Regulations 2014

Reg.16, amended: SI 2015/102 Sch.6 para.26, SSI 2015/446 Sch.6 para.11

Sch.1 para.1, amended: SI 2015/1731 Reg.2

Sch.2 para.12, revoked: SI 2015/1731 Reg.2

Sch.4 Part 1 para.6, amended: SI 2015/1731 Reg.2

Sch.4 Part 2 para.12, amended: SI 2015/1731 Reg.2

Sch.4 Part 2 para.13, amended: SI 2015/1731 Reg.2

1663. Genetically Modified Organisms (Contained Use) Regulations 2014

Reg.4, amended: SI 2015/1637 Sch.1 para.12

1777. Legal Aid, Sentencing and Punishment of Offenders Act 2012 (Alcohol Abstinence and Monitoring Requirements) Piloting Order 2014

Art.4, amended: SI 2015/1480 Art.2

1787. Criminal Justice Act 2003 (Alcohol Abstinence and Monitoring Requirement) (Prescription of Arrangement for Monitoring) Order 2014

Art.2, amended: SI 2015/1482 Art.2

1797. Housing (Right to Buy) (Prescribed Forms) (Amendment) (England) Regulations 2014
revoked: SI 2015/1542 Reg.3

1849. Immigration (Designation of Travel Bans) (Amendment) Order 2014
revoked: SI 2015/388 Sch.2

1855. Food Information Regulations 2014
Sch.5 Part 2, amended: SI 2015/1348
Sch.3 para.2
Sch.6 Part 1, amended: SI 2015/1348
Reg.20
Sch.7 Part 2 para.35, revoked: SI 2015/1348 Reg.20

1887. Health Care and Associated Professions (Indemnity Arrangements) Order 2014
Sch.2 para.1, revoked: SI 2015/1862
Sch.5 para.1
Sch.2 para.2, revoked: SI 2015/1879
Sch.4 para.1

1920. Childcare (Childminder Agencies) (Registration, Inspection and Supply and Disclosure of Information) Regulations 2014
Reg.14, amended: SI 2015/1562 Reg.9
Reg.15, amended: SI 2015/1562 Reg.9
Sch.2 para.7, amended: SI 2015/1562 Reg.9
Sch.2 para.19, amended: SI 2015/1562 Reg.9

1942. Control of Explosives Precursors Regulations 2014
revoked: SI 2015/968 Art.4

1966. Home Loss Payments (Prescribed Amounts) (England) Regulations 2014
revoked: SI 2015/1514 Reg.3

1996. Education (National Curriculum) (Foundation Phase) (Wales) Order 2014
Art.1, amended: SI 2015/1596 Art.4

2011. Contracts for Difference (Allocation) Regulations 2014
Reg.2, amended: SI 2015/981 Reg.3
Reg.4, amended: SI 2015/981 Reg.4
Reg.14A, added: SI 2015/981 Reg.5
Reg.51, amended: SI 2015/981 Reg.6

2012. Contracts for Difference (Standard Terms) Regulations 2014
Reg.3, amended: SI 2015/1425 Reg.2
Reg.9, amended: SI 2015/1425 Reg.3

2013. Electricity Market Reform (General) Regulations 2014

Part 5, added: SI 2015/718 Reg.2
Reg.2, amended: SI 2015/718 Reg.2
Reg.6, amended: SI 2015/718 Reg.2
Reg.7, amended: SI 2015/718 Reg.2

2014. Contracts for Difference (Electricity Supplier Obligations) Regulations 2014
Reg.2, amended: SI 2015/721 Reg.15
Reg.2, revoked: SI 2015/721 Reg.15
Reg.4, amended: SI 2015/721 Reg.16
Reg.5, amended: SI 2015/721 Reg.17
Reg.7, amended: SI 2015/721 Reg.18
Reg.8, amended: SI 2015/721 Reg.19
Reg.9, amended: SI 2015/721 Reg.20
Reg.10, amended: SI 2015/721 Reg.21
Reg.11, amended: SI 2015/721 Reg.22
Reg.13, amended: SI 2015/721 Reg.23
Reg.14, amended: SI 2015/721 Reg.24
Reg.16, amended: SI 2015/721 Reg.25
Reg.17, amended: SI 2015/721 Reg.26
Reg.19, amended: SI 2015/721 Reg.27
Reg.23, amended: SI 2015/721 Reg.28
Reg.24, amended: SI 2015/721 Reg.29
Reg.25, amended: SI 2015/721 Reg.30
Reg.25, revoked: SI 2015/721 Reg.30
Reg.26, amended: SI 2015/721 Reg.31
Reg.27, amended: SI 2015/721 Reg.32
Reg.29, amended: SI 2015/721 Reg.33
Reg.32, amended: SI 2015/721 Reg.34
Reg.35, amended: SI 2015/721 Reg.35
Sch.1 para.24, amended: SI 2015/721 Reg.36

2043. Electricity Capacity Regulations 2014
Reg.2, amended: SI 2015/875 Sch.1 para.1, Sch.1 para.12
Reg.4, amended: SI 2015/875 Sch.1 para.13
Reg.5A, added: SI 2015/875 Sch.1 para.2
Reg.7, amended: SI 2015/875 Sch.1 para.3
Reg.14, amended: SI 2015/875 Sch.1 para.4
Reg.15, amended: SI 2015/875 Sch.1 para.14
Reg.17, amended: SI 2015/1974 Reg.3
Reg.21, amended: SI 2015/875 Sch.1 para.5
Reg.23, amended: SI 2015/875 Sch.1 para.6
Reg.29, amended: SI 2015/875 Sch.1 para.15

Reg.30, amended: SI 2015/875 Sch.1
para.7
Reg.43A, added: SI 2015/875 Sch.1
para.8
Reg.43B, added: SI 2015/875 Sch.1
para.16
Reg.50, amended: SI 2015/875 Sch.1
para.17
Reg.59, amended: SI 2015/875 Sch.1
para.9, SI 2015/1974 Reg.4
Reg.60, amended: SI 2015/875 Sch.1
para.10
Reg.61, amended: SI 2015/875 Sch.1
para.11
Reg.69, amended: SI 2015/875 Sch.1
para.18
Reg.73, amended: SI 2015/875 Sch.1
para.19
Reg.87A, added: SI 2015/875 Sch.1
para.20
**2072. Ecclesiastical Judges, Legal Officers
and Others (Fees) Order 2014**
revoked: SI 2015/1954 Art.15
**2179. Education (Prescribed Courses of
Higher Education) (Information
Requirements) (England) Regulations 2014**
revoked: SI 2015/225 Reg.3
**2221. A1 Trunk Road (Derwenthaugh to
Eighton Lodge) (Temporary Restriction and
Prohibition of Traffic) Order 2014**
Art.3, amended: SI 2015/684 Art.2
**2270. Children and Families Act 2014
(Transitional and Saving Provisions) (No.2)
Order 2014**
Part 7, substituted: SI 2015/505 Art.8
Art.2, amended: SI 2015/505 Art.3
Art.14A, added: SI 2015/505 Art.4
Art.21, amended: SI 2015/505 Art.5, SI
2015/1619 Art.3
Art.22, amended: SI 2015/505 Art.6, SI
2015/1619 Art.4
Art.24, amended: SI 2015/1619 Art.5
Art.29A, added: SI 2015/505 Art.7
Art.34, amended: SI 2015/1619 Art.6
Art.35, amended: SI 2015/1619 Art.7
**2303. Food Information (Wales) Regulations
2014**
Sch.5 Part 2, amended: SI 2015/1507
Sch.3 para.2
Sch.6 Part 1, amended: SI 2015/1507
Reg.20

Sch.7 Part 2 para.32, revoked: SI
2015/1507 Reg.20
Sch.7 Part 2 para.49, revoked: SI
2015/1867 Sch.13 para.6
**2328. Armed Forces Early Departure
Payments Scheme Regulations 2014**
Reg.4, amended: SI 2015/466 Reg.20, SI
2015/568 Reg.42
Reg.8, amended: SI 2015/466 Reg.21
Reg.16, amended: SI 2015/466 Reg.22
Reg.19, amended: SI 2015/466 Reg.23
**2336. Armed Forces Pension Regulations
2014**
Reg.3, amended: SI 2015/466 Reg.3, SI
2015/568 Reg.41
Reg.32, amended: SI 2015/466 Reg.4
Reg.38, amended: SI 2015/466 Reg.5
Reg.43, amended: SI 2015/466 Reg.6
Reg.44, amended: SI 2015/466 Reg.7
Reg.45, amended: SI 2015/466 Reg.8
Reg.51, amended: SI 2015/466 Reg.9
Reg.52, amended: SI 2015/466 Reg.10
Reg.56, amended: SI 2015/466 Reg.11
Reg.74, amended: SI 2015/466 Reg.12
Reg.79, amended: SI 2015/466 Reg.13
Reg.81, amended: SI 2015/466 Reg.14
Reg.82, amended: SI 2015/466 Reg.15
Reg.91, amended: SI 2015/466 Reg.16
Reg.108, amended: SI 2015/466 Reg.17
Reg.114, amended: SI 2015/466 Reg.18
Reg.121, amended: SI 2015/466 Reg.19
**2353. A21 Trunk Road (Pembury Road,
40mph Speed) (Temporary Restriction of
Traffic) Order 2014**
revoked: SI 2015/1226 Art.8
**2357. Export Control (Russia, Crimea and
Sevastopol Sanctions) Order 2014**
Art.2, amended: SI 2015/97 Art.2, SI
2015/1933 Art.2
Art.4, amended: SI 2015/97 Art.2
Art.5, amended: SI 2015/1933 Art.2
Art.5A, see *R. (on the application of
OJSC Rosneft Oil Co) v HM Treasury*
[2014] EWHC 4002 (Admin), [2015]
Lloyd's Rep. F.C. 32 (QBD (Admin)),
Beatson LJ
Art.5A, substituted: SI 2015/97 Art.2
Art.7, substituted: SI 2015/97 Art.2
Art.9, amended: SI 2015/97 Art.2, SI
2015/1933 Art.2

Art.11, amended: SI 2015/97 Art.2, SI
2015/1933 Art.2

**2361. Copyright and Rights in Performances
(Personal Copies for Private Use) Regulations
2014**

see *R. (on the application of British
Academy of Songwriters, Composers and
Authors) v Secretary of State for
Business, Innovation and Skills* [2015]
EWHC 2041 (Admin), [2015] Bus. L.R.
1435 (QBD (Admin)), Green J

**2409. Corporation Tax (Instalment
Payments) (Amendment) Regulations 2014**

Reg.1, amended: 2015 c.33 s.39

**2478. A43 Trunk Road and M40 Motorway
(M40 Junction 10, Oxfordshire) (Temporary
Restriction and Prohibition of Traffic) Order
2014**

revoked: SI 2015/1009 Art.10

**2604. Tribunal Procedure (First-tier
Tribunal) (Immigration and Asylum
Chamber) Rules 2014**

see *R. (on the application of Detention
Action) v First-tier Tribunal
(Immigration and Asylum Chamber)*
[2015] EWCA Civ 840, [2015] 1 W.L.R.
5341 (CA (Civ Div)), Lord Dyson MR
r.19, see *R. (on the application of Ahmed)
v Secretary of State for the Home
Department* [2015] UKUT 436 (IAC),
[2015] Imm. A.R. 1320 (UT (IAC)),
Judge Storey
Sch.1 para.12, see *R. (on the application
of Detention Action) v First-tier Tribunal
(Immigration and Asylum Chamber)*
[2015] EWCA Civ 840, [2015] 1 W.L.R.
5341 (CA (Civ Div)), Lord Dyson MR
Sch.1 para.14, see *R. (on the application
of Detention Action) v First-tier Tribunal
(Immigration and Asylum Chamber)*
[2015] EWCA Civ 840, [2015] 1 W.L.R.
5341 (CA (Civ Div)), Lord Dyson MR

**2650. Designation of Rural Primary Schools
(England) Order 2014**

revoked: SI 2015/1748 Art.3

**2659. A40 Trunk Road (Llanwrda to
Llandovery, Carmarthenshire) (Temporary
Traffic Restrictions and Prohibitions) Order
2014**

revoked: SI 2015/1593 Art.8

**2671. Care and Support (Deferred Payment)
Regulations 2014**

Reg.6, amended: SI 2015/644 Reg.2

**2672. Care and Support (Charging and
Assessment of Resources) Regulations 2014**

Reg.2, varied: SI 2015/305 Reg.13
Reg.3, varied: SI 2015/305 Reg.13
Reg.6, amended: SI 2015/644 Reg.3
Reg.7, amended: SI 2015/644 Reg.3
Sch.1 Part 1 para.15, amended: SI
2015/644 Reg.3
Sch.1 Part 2 para.45, amended: SI
2015/644 Reg.3
Sch.1 Part 2 para.46, amended: SI
2015/644 Reg.3

**2699. A47 Trunk Road (Trowse Interchange
to Brundall, Norfolk) (Temporary Restriction
and Prohibition of Traffic and Pedestrians)
(No.2) Order 2014**

revoked: SI 2015/1003 Art.7

**2702. Immigration (Passenger Transit Visa)
Order 2014**

Art.2, amended: SI 2015/657 Art.2
Art.4, amended: SI 2015/657 Art.2, SI
2015/1534 Art.2
Art.4, substituted: SI 2015/657 Art.2
Sch.1, amended: SI 2015/657 Art.2

**2712. Agricultural Holdings (Units of
Production) (England) Order 2014**

revoked: SI 2015/1745 Art.3

**2771. Immigration Act 2014 (Commencement
No 3, Transitional and Saving Provisions)
Order 2014**

Art.9, amended: SI 2015/371 Art.7
Art.9, substituted: SI 2015/371 Art.8
Art.10, revoked: SI 2015/371 Art.8
Art.11, amended: SI 2015/371 Art.7
Art.11, revoked: SI 2015/371 Art.8
Art.13, revoked: SI 2015/371 Art.8

**2828. Care and Support (Ordinary
Residence) (Specified Accommodation)
Regulations 2014**

Reg.2, substituted: SI 2015/644 Reg.4

**2839. Care and Support (Cross-border
Placements) (Business Failure Duties of
Scottish Local Authorities) Regulations 2014**

Reg.1, amended: SI 2015/644 Reg.5
Reg.4, revoked: SI 2015/1641 Sch.3
para.3

**2840. Care and Support (Personal Budget
Exclusion of Costs) Regulations 2014**

Reg.1, varied: SI 2015/305 Reg.14

2848. Firefighters Pension Scheme (England) Regulations 2014

Reg.3, amended: SI 2015/465 Reg.3, SI 2015/589 Sch.1 para.1, SI 2015/871 Reg.2

Reg.4, amended: SI 2015/589 Sch.1 para.2

Reg.4A, added: SI 2015/465 Reg.4

Reg.6, amended: SI 2015/589 Sch.1 para.3

Reg.51, amended: SI 2015/589 Sch.1 para.4

Reg.59, amended: SI 2015/589 Sch.1 para.5

Reg.62, amended: SI 2015/589 Sch.1 para.5

Reg.65, amended: SI 2015/589 Sch.1 para.5, SI 2015/871 Reg.2

Reg.66, amended: SI 2015/589 Sch.1 para.5

Reg.69, amended: SI 2015/589 Sch.1 para.5

Reg.71A, added: SI 2015/589 Sch.1 para.5

Reg.77, amended: SI 2015/589 Sch.1 para.6

Reg.78, amended: SI 2015/589 Sch.1 para.6

Reg.86, amended: SI 2015/589 Sch.1 para.6

Reg.93, amended: SI 2015/589 Sch.1 para.6

Reg.96, amended: SI 2015/589 Sch.1 para.6

Reg.150A, added: SI 2015/465 Reg.5

Sch.2 Part 1 para.3, amended: SI 2015/589 Sch.1 para.7

Sch.2 Part 2 para.9, amended: SI 2015/589 Sch.1 para.7

Sch.2 Part 3A, added: SI 2015/589 Sch.1 para.7

Sch.2 Part 3C para.35, amended: SI 2015/871 Reg.2

Sch.2 Part 3 para.15, amended: SI 2015/589 Sch.1 para.7

2868. Drug Driving (Specified Limits) (England and Wales) Regulations 2014

Reg.2, amended: SI 2015/911 Reg.2

2871. Care and Support (Direct Payments) Regulations 2014

Sch.2, amended: SI 2015/644 Reg.6

2889. Care and Support (Independent Advocacy Support) (No.2) Regulations 2014

see *R. (on the application of SG) v Haringey LBC* [2015] EWHC 2579 (Admin), (2015) 18 C.C.L. Rep. 444 (QBD (Admin)), John Bowers QC

2908. Enterprise Act 2002 (Part 8 EU Infringements) Order 2014

Sch.1, amended: SI 2015/1628 Art.3

2926. Air Navigation (Overseas Territories) (Environmental Standards) Order 2014

Art.3, amended: SI 2015/236 Art.3

2928. Immigration Act 2014 (Transitional and Saving Provisions) Order 2014

revoked: SI 2015/371 Art.9

2936. Health and Social Care Act 2008 (Regulated Activities) Regulations 2014

Reg.1, amended: SI 2015/64 Reg.3

Reg.2, amended: SI 2015/64 Reg.4

Reg.4, amended: SI 2015/64 Reg.5

Reg.5, amended: SI 2015/64 Reg.6

Reg.6, amended: SI 2015/64 Reg.7

Reg.7, amended: SI 2015/64 Reg.8

Reg.8, amended: SI 2015/64 Reg.9

Reg.20, amended: SI 2015/64 Reg.10

Reg.20A, added: SI 2015/64 Reg.11

Reg.22, amended: SI 2015/64 Reg.12

Reg.22, revoked: SI 2015/64 Reg.12

Reg.23, amended: SI 2015/64 Reg.13, SI 2015/664 Sch.4 para.85

Reg.23, revoked: SI 2015/64 Reg.13 , SI 2015/664 Sch.4 para.85

Reg.25, substituted: SI 2015/64 Reg.14

Reg.26, revoked: SI 2015/64 Reg.15

Reg.27, amended: SI 2015/64 Reg.16

Reg.27, revoked: SI 2015/64 Reg.16

Sch.1 para.10, amended: SI 2015/643 Sch.1 para.48

Sch.5, amended: SI 2015/64 Reg.17

2972. A1(M) Motorway (Junction 4 to Junction 6) (Temporary Restriction and Prohibition of Traffic) Order 2014

revoked: SI 2015/1104 Art.8

3090. Health Research Authority (Transfer of Staff, Property and Liabilities) and Care Act 2014 (Consequential Amendments) Order 2014

Sch.1 para.1, revoked: SI 2015/559 Sch.1

3120. Heat Network (Metering and Billing) Regulations 2014

Reg.3, amended: SI 2015/855 Reg.3
Reg.4, revoked: SI 2015/855 Reg.4
Reg.5, substituted: SI 2015/855 Reg.5
Reg.6, amended: SI 2015/855 Reg.6
Reg.6, revoked: SI 2015/855 Reg.6
Reg.7, amended: SI 2015/855 Reg.7
Reg.8, amended: SI 2015/855 Reg.8
Reg.9, amended: SI 2015/855 Reg.9
Reg.13, amended: SI 2015/855 Reg.10
Reg.14, amended: SI 2015/855 Reg.11
Reg.15, amended: SI 2015/855 Reg.12

3178. Electoral Registration Pilot Scheme Order 2014
Art.6, amended: SI 2015/1376 Sch.2 para.24

3258. Export Control (Sudan, South Sudan and Central African Republic Sanctions) Regulations 2014
Reg.3, amended: SI 2015/1546 Art.9
Reg.5, amended: SI 2015/97 Art.4, SI 2015/1546 Art.9

3259. Common Agricultural Policy Basic Payment and Support Schemes (England) Regulations 2014
Reg.8, amended: SI 2015/1325 Reg.3
Reg.10, substituted: SI 2015/1997 Reg.3
Sch.1 Part 1, amended: SI 2015/1997 Reg.4
Sch.1 Part 2, substituted: SI 2015/1997 Reg.4

3263. Common Agricultural Policy (Control and Enforcement, Cross-Compliance, Scrutiny of Transactions and Appeals) Regulations 2014
Reg.3, amended: SI 2015/1325 Reg.2
Reg.5, amended: SI 2015/1325 Reg.2
Reg.9, amended: SI 2015/1997 Reg.7
Reg.10, amended: SI 2015/1997 Reg.8
Reg.14, revoked: SI 2015/1997 Reg.9
Reg.15, amended: SI 2015/1997 Reg.10
Reg.20, amended: SI 2015/1997 Reg.11
Reg.21, amended: SI 2015/1997 Reg.12
Reg.28, amended: SI 2015/1997 Reg.12
Sch.1, amended: SI 2015/1997 Sch.1 para.1
Sch.2 para.1, amended: SI 2015/1997 Reg.14
Sch.2 para.2, amended: SI 2015/1997 Reg.14
Sch.2 para.4, amended: SI 2015/1997 Reg.14

Sch.2 para.4, revoked: SI 2015/1997 Reg.14
Sch.2 para.5, amended: SI 2015/1997 Reg.14
Sch.2 para.5, revoked: SI 2015/1997 Reg.14

3299. Civil Procedure (Amendment No 8) Rules 2014
r.5, amended: SI 2015/670 r.11

3331. Hornsea One Offshore Wind Farm Order 2014
Art.2, amended: SI 2015/1280 Sch.1
Art.7, amended: SI 2015/1280 Sch.1
Art.10, substituted: SI 2015/1280 Sch.1
Art.14, amended: SI 2015/1280 Sch.1
Art.16, amended: SI 2015/1280 Sch.1
Art.24, amended: SI 2015/1280 Sch.1
Art.39, amended: SI 2015/1280 Sch.1
Sch.1 Part 3 para.3, amended: SI 2015/1280 Sch.1
Sch.1 Part 3 para.6, amended: SI 2015/1280 Sch.1
Sch.1 Part 3 para.22, amended: SI 2015/1280 Sch.1
Sch.12 Part 9 para.86, amended: SI 2015/1280 Sch.1
Sch.12 Part 10 para.103, amended: SI 2015/1280 Sch.1
Sch.12 Part 11 para.110, amended: SI 2015/1280 Sch.1

3354. Electricity Capacity (Supplier Payment etc.) Regulations 2014
Reg.2, amended: SI 2015/875 Sch.2 para.1
Reg.9, amended: SI 2015/875 Sch.2 para.2
Reg.34, revoked: SI 2015/875 Sch.2 para.3

3371. A12 Trunk Road (Junction 11 Brook Street Interchange to Junction 15 Webbs Farm Interchange) Essex (Temporary Restriction and Prohibition of Traffic) Order 2014
Art.3, varied: SI 2015/1274 Art.2

3434. A34 Trunk Road (East Ilsley Interchange Abingdon North Interchange) (Temporary Restriction and Prohibition of Traffic) Order 2014
Art.2, amended: SI 2015/1087 Art.2

3447. A12 Trunk Road (Junction 22 Coleman's Interchange, Witham to Junction

24 Kelvedon, Essex) (Temporary Prohibition of Traffic) Order 2014
revoked: SI 2015/1195 Art.6

2015

43. City of Birmingham (Scheme of Elections) Order 2015
Art.2, amended: SI 2015/666 Art.2
51. Construction (Design and Management) Regulations 2015
Reg.6, amended: SI 2015/1682 Sch.1 para.10
54. Education (Student Support) (Wales) Regulations 2015
Reg.3, amended: SI 2015/1505 Reg.3
Reg.10, amended: SI 2015/1505 Reg.4
Sch.5 para.2, amended: SI 2015/1505 Reg.5
Sch.5 para.4, amended: SI 2015/1505 Reg.5
Sch.5 para.6, amended: SI 2015/1505 Reg.5
Sch.6 para.4, amended: SI 2015/1505 Reg.6
102. Public Contracts Regulations 2015
Reg.72, see *Edenred (UK Group) Ltd v HM Treasury* [2015] UKSC 45 (SC), Lord Neuberger PSC
127. Delegation of Additional Functions to the NHS Business Services Authority (Awdurdod Gwasanaethau Busnes y GIG) Regulations 2015
Reg.2, amended: SI 2015/570 Sch.2 para.8
128. Elections (Policy Development Grants Scheme) (Amendment) Order 2015
revoked: SI 2015/302 Art.2
129. A160/A180 (Port of Immingham Improvement) Development Consent Order 2015
Art.38, amended: SI 2015/1231 Sch.1
Sch.2 para.3, amended: SI 2015/1231 Art.3
Sch.2 para.10, amended: SI 2015/1231 Art.3
Sch.2 para.11, amended: SI 2015/1231 Art.3
Sch.2 para.12, amended: SI 2015/1231 Art.3

Sch.2 para.14, amended: SI 2015/1231 Art.3
137. Care Act 2014 (Health Education England and the Health Research Authority) (Consequential Amendments and Revocations) Order 2015
Sch.2 Part 2 para.14, revoked: SI 2015/559 Sch.1
144. Air Navigation (Restriction of Flying) (The Solent, Hampshire) Regulations 2015
Reg.3, amended: SI 2015/146 Reg.3
147. Cornwall Council (A30 Temple to Higher Carblake Improvement) Order 2015
amended: SI 2015/243 Art.2
256. A494/A550 Trunk Road (Deeside Park Interchange, Flintshire) (Temporary Prohibition of Vehicles) Order 2015
revoked: SI 2015/1550 Art.5
264. Air Navigation (Restriction of Flying) (Northampton Sywell) Regulations 2015
Reg.3, amended: SI 2015/1117 Reg.3
267. Air Navigation (Restriction of Flying) (Balado) Regulations 2015
revoked: SI 2015/1008 Reg.2
318. Dogger Bank Creyke Beck Offshore Wind Farm Order 2015
Art.2, amended: SI 2015/1742 Sch.1
Art.23, amended: SI 2015/1742 Sch.1
334. A47 Trunk Road (Soke Parkway, Junction 15 Nene Parkway Interchange to Junction 20 Paston Parkway Interchange, City of Peterborough) (Temporary Restriction and Prohibition of Traffic) Order 2015
revoked: SI 2015/1278 Art.8
363. Health and Safety and Nuclear (Fees) Regulations 2015
Reg.14, amended: SI 2015/398 Sch.13 para.42, Sch.13 Part 2
Reg.20, amended: SI 2015/483 Sch.6 para.11
Reg.23, amended: SI 2015/483 Sch.6 para.11
Sch.10, amended: SI 2015/398 Sch.13 para.42
377. Infrastructure Act 2015 (Strategic Highways Companies) (Consequential, Transitional and Savings Provisions) Regulations 2015
Sch.1 para.47, revoked: SI 2015/595 Sch.9

387. Education (Non-Maintained Special Schools) (England) (Amendment) Regulations 2015
    revoked: SI 2015/728 Reg.8
388. Immigration (Designation of Travel Bans) (Amendment) Order 2015
    revoked: SI 2015/1994 Art.3
462. Infrastructure Planning (Interested Parties and Miscellaneous Prescribed Provisions) Regulations 2015
    Sch.1, amended: SI 2015/1682 Sch.1 para.10
483. Control of Major Accident Hazards Regulations 2015
    Reg.2, amended: SI 2015/1393 Reg.2
486. Deposit Guarantee Scheme Regulations 2015
    Reg.7, substituted: SI 2015/1456 Reg.2
    Reg.7A, added: SI 2015/1456 Reg.2
490. Financial Services (Banking Reform) Act 2013 (Commencement No 9) Order 2015
    Art.2, amended: SI 2015/2055 Art.2
492. Financial Services (Banking Reform) Act 2013 (Transitional and Savings Provisions) Order 2015
    Art.1, amended: SI 2015/1660 Art.3
    Art.10, substituted: SI 2015/1660 Art.4
    Art.10A, added: SI 2015/1660 Art.5
    Art.12, amended: SI 2015/1660 Art.6
    Art.22, amended: SI 2015/1660 Art.7
542. Alternative Dispute Resolution for Consumer Disputes (Competent Authorities and Information) Regulations 2015
    Reg.1, amended: SI 2015/1392 Reg.2
    Reg.2, amended: SI 2015/1392 Reg.2
    Reg.4, amended: SI 2015/1392 Reg.2
    Reg.5, amended: SI 2015/1392 Reg.2
    Reg.8, amended: SI 2015/1392 Reg.2
    Reg.8A, added: SI 2015/1972 Reg.7
    Reg.9, amended: SI 2015/1392 Reg.2
    Reg.9, revoked: SI 2015/1392 Reg.2
    Reg.14, substituted: SI 2015/1392 Reg.2
    Reg.14A, added: SI 2015/1392 Reg.2
    Reg.15, amended: SI 2015/1392 Reg.2, SI 2015/1972 Reg.7
    Reg.15A, added: SI 2015/1392 Reg.2
    Reg.18, amended: SI 2015/1392 Reg.2
    Reg.19, substituted: SI 2015/1392 Reg.2
    Reg.19A, added: SI 2015/1392 Reg.2
    Reg.20, revoked: SI 2015/1392 Reg.2

    Sch.3 para.1, amended: SI 2015/1392 Reg.2
    Sch.3 para.2, amended: SI 2015/1972 Reg.7
    Sch.3 para.3, amended: SI 2015/1392 Reg.2
    Sch.3 para.4, amended: SI 2015/1392 Reg.2
    Sch.3 para.6, amended: SI 2015/1392 Reg.2
    Sch.3 para.9, amended: SI 2015/1392 Reg.2
    Sch.3 para.10, amended: SI 2015/1392 Reg.2
    Sch.3 para.13, amended: SI 2015/1392 Reg.2
    Sch.3 para.13A, added: SI 2015/1392 Reg.2
    Sch.3 para.14, amended: SI 2015/1392 Reg.2
    Sch.3 para.14A, added: SI 2015/1392 Reg.2
    Sch.3 para.15, amended: SI 2015/1392 Reg.2
    Sch.3 para.15, substituted: SI 2015/1392 Reg.2
    Sch.3 para.16, substituted: SI 2015/1392 Reg.2
    Sch.3 para.17, added: SI 2015/1392 Reg.2
    Sch.8, revoked: SI 2015/1392 Reg.2
551. Her Majesty's Chief Inspector of Education, Children's Services and Skills (Fees and Frequency of Inspections) (Children's Homes etc.) Regulations 2015
    Reg.10, revoked: SI 2015/971 Sch.4 para.2
    Reg.17, revoked: SI 2015/971 Sch.4 para.2
620. Assured Tenancies and Agricultural Occupancies (Forms) (England) Regulations 2015
    Reg.3, amended: SI 2015/1646 Reg.4
    Reg.3A, added: SI 2015/1646 Reg.4
    Sch.1, amended: SI 2015/1646 Reg.4, Sch.1
622. Firefighters Pension Scheme (Wales) Regulations 2015
    Reg.3, amended: SI 2015/1016 Sch.1 para.1

Reg.4, amended: SI 2015/1016 Sch.1
para.2
Reg.15, amended: SI 2015/1016 Sch.1
para.3
Reg.60, amended: SI 2015/1016 Sch.1
para.4
Reg.68, amended: SI 2015/1016 Sch.1
para.5
Reg.71, amended: SI 2015/1016 Sch.1
para.5
Reg.74, amended: SI 2015/1016 Sch.1
para.5
Reg.75, amended: SI 2015/1016 Sch.1
para.5
Reg.78, amended: SI 2015/1016 Sch.1
para.5
Reg.80A, added: SI 2015/1016 Sch.1
para.5
Reg.86, amended: SI 2015/1016 Sch.1
para.6
Reg.87, amended: SI 2015/1016 Sch.1
para.6
Reg.95, amended: SI 2015/1016 Sch.1
para.6
Reg.102, amended: SI 2015/1016 Sch.1
para.6
Reg.105, amended: SI 2015/1016 Sch.1
para.6
Sch.2 Part 1 para.3, amended: SI
2015/1016 Sch.1 para.7
Sch.2 Part 2 para.9, amended: SI
2015/1016 Sch.1 para.7
Sch.2 Part 3A, added: SI 2015/1016
Sch.1 para.7
Sch.2 Part 3 para.15, amended: SI
2015/1016 Sch.1 para.7
**632. Government Resources and Accounts
Act 2000 (Estimates and Accounts) Order
2015**
Sch.1, amended: SI 2015/2062 Art.2,
Sch.1, Sch.2, Sch.3
**641. Enterprise and Regulatory Reform Act
2013 (Commencement No 8 and Saving
Provisions) Order 2015**
revoked: SI 2015/1558 Art.2
**645. Asylum Support (Amendment)
Regulations 2015**
revoked: SI 2015/944 Reg.2
**699. Electricity (Standards of Performance)
Regulations 2015**
Reg.3, amended: SI 2015/1544 Reg.14

Reg.14, revoked: SI 2015/1544 Reg.14
Reg.15, revoked: SI 2015/1544 Reg.14
Reg.17, amended: SI 2015/1544 Reg.14
Reg.17, revoked: SI 2015/1544 Reg.14
Reg.19, revoked: SI 2015/1544 Reg.14
Reg.20, amended: SI 2015/1544 Reg.14
Reg.21, amended: SI 2015/1544 Reg.14
Reg.22, revoked: SI 2015/1544 Reg.14
Reg.23, revoked: SI 2015/1544 Reg.14
Sch.2 Part 1, amended: SI 2015/1544
Reg.14
**700. Courts Reform (Scotland) Act 2014
(Consequential Provisions and Modifications)
Order 2015**
Art.5, enabled: SSI 2015/213
**768. Immigration and Nationality (Fees)
Regulations 2015**
Sch.2 para.1, amended: SI 2015/1424
Reg.2
Sch.2 para.1, revoked: SI 2015/1424
Reg.2
**785. Channel Tunnel (International
Arrangements) (Charging Framework and
Transfer of Economic Regulation Functions)
Order 2015**
Art.5, amended: SI 2015/1682 Sch.1
para.10
**790. Criminal Justice and Courts Act 2015
(Simple Cautions) (Specification of Either-
Way Offences) Order 2015**
Sch.1 para.54, added: SI 2015/1472
Reg.21
**794. General Medical Council (Fitness to
Practise and Over-arching Objective) and the
Professional Standards Authority for Health
and Social Care (References to Court) Order
2015**
Art.1, enabled: SI 2015/1579
**806. Health Care and Associated Professions
(Knowledge of English) Order 2015**
Art.1, enabled: SI 2015/1451
**810. Environmental Damage (Prevention and
Remediation) (England) Regulations 2015**
Reg.6, amended: SI 2015/1391 Reg.2
Reg.10, amended: SI 2015/1391 Reg.2
Reg.11, amended: SI 2015/1391 Reg.2
**832. Diocese of Ely (Educational
Endowments) (Shouldham Church of
England School) Order 2015**
amended: SI 2015/1429 Art.2
Art.2, amended: SI 2015/1429 Art.2

838. Legal Aid, Community Legal Service and Criminal Defence Service (Amendment) Regulations 2015
Reg.11, revoked: SI 2015/1408 Reg.3

857. Administrative Forfeiture of Cash (Forfeiture Notices) (England and Wales) Regulations 2015
Reg.3, amended: SI 2015/1854 Reg.2
Reg.4, amended: SI 2015/1854 Reg.2
Reg.5, amended: SI 2015/1854 Reg.2
Reg.8, added: SI 2015/1854 Reg.2

878. International Tax Compliance Regulations 2015
Reg.1, amended: SI 2015/1839 Reg.2
Reg.2, amended: SI 2015/1839 Reg.2
Reg.24, amended: SI 2015/1839 Reg.2
Sch.1, amended: SI 2015/1839 Reg.2
Sch.2 para.14, revoked: SI 2015/1839 Reg.2

899. Lasting Powers of Attorney, Enduring Powers of Attorney and Public Guardian (Amendment) Regulations 2015
see *XZ v Public Guardian* [2015] EWCOP 35, [2015] C.O.P.L.R. 630 (CP), Judge Lush

944. Asylum Support (Amendment No.2) Regulations 2015
revoked: SI 2015/1501 Reg.3

980. Companies, Partnerships and Groups (Accounts and Reports) Regulations 2015
Reg.2, amended: SI 2015/1672 Reg.5
Reg.3, amended: SI 2015/1672 Reg.5

994. Deregulation Act 2015 (Commencement No 1 and Transitional and Saving Provisions) Order 2015
Art.13, amended: SI 2015/1405 Art.2
Sch.1 Part 3A, added: SI 2015/1405 Art.2

995. Care Act 2014 (Transitional Provision) Order 2015
Art.2, see *R. (on the application of SG) v Haringey LBC* [2015] EWHC 2579 (Admin), (2015) 18 C.C.L. Rep. 444 (QBD (Admin)), John Bowers QC

1002. A45 Trunk Road (Wellingborough, Northamptonshire) (Temporary Restriction and Prohibition of Traffic) Order 2015
revoked: SI 2015/1100 Art.9

1007. Air Navigation (Restriction of Flying) (Bermondsey) Regulations 2015
revoked: SI 2015/1010 Reg.2

1011. A45 Trunk Road (Wilby Great Billing, Northamptonshire) (Temporary Prohibition of Traffic) Order 2015
revoked: SI 2015/1022 Art.7

1020. Agricultural Holdings (Units of Production) (Wales) Order 2015
revoked: SI 2015/1642 Art.3

1097. Air Navigation (Restriction of Flying) (Southport) Regulations 2015
Reg.3, amended: SI 2015/1664 Reg.3

1281. Air Navigation (Restriction of Flying) (Jet Formation Display Teams) (No.2) Regulations 2015
Sch.1, amended: SI 2015/1372 Reg.2

1320. Housing (Right to Buy) (Prescribed Forms) (Wales) Regulations 2015
Sch.1, amended: SI 2015/1795 Reg.2

1343. Air Navigation (Restriction of Flying) (Kensworth) Regulations 2015
revoked: SI 2015/1345 Reg.2

1365. Air Navigation (Restriction of Flying) (Overton) Regulations 2015
revoked: SI 2015/1665 Reg.2

1369. Criminal Legal Aid (Remuneration etc.) (Amendment) Regulations 2015
Part 3, amended: SI 2015/2049 Reg.2
Reg.1, amended: SI 2015/2049 Reg.2
Reg.2, amended: SI 2015/2049 Reg.2
Reg.4, amended: SI 2015/2049 Reg.3
Reg.5, amended: SI 2015/2049 Reg.3
Reg.6, amended: SI 2015/2049 Reg.3
Reg.7, substituted: SI 2015/2049 Reg.4
Sch.5, amended: SI 2015/1678 Reg.9
Sch.9, amended: SI 2015/1678 Reg.9
Sch.9, revoked: SI 2015/1678 Reg.9
Sch.10, amended: SI 2015/1678 Reg.9
Sch.13, revoked: SI 2015/1678 Reg.9

1389. Air Navigation (Restriction of Flying) (Jet Formation Display Teams) (No.3) Regulations 2015
Sch.1, amended: SI 2015/1676 Reg.3

1450. A470 Trunk Road (Bodnant, Conwy County Borough) (Temporary Speed Restrictions &amp No Overtaking) Order 2015
revoked: SI 2015/1746 Art.6

1574. Hirwaun Generating Station Order 2015
Art.2, amended: SI 2015/2070 Art.2

1608. Air Navigation (Restriction of Flying) (Bethnal Green) Regulations 2015

revoked: SI 2015/1611 Reg.2

1642. Agricultural Holdings (Units of Production) (Wales) (No.2) Order 2015
Art.1, amended: SI 2015/1975 Art.3

1646. Assured Shorthold Tenancy Notices and Prescribed Requirements (England) Regulations 2015
Sch.1, amended: SI 2015/1725 Sch.1

1699. Air Navigation (Restriction of Flying) (Shoreham) Regulations 2015
revoked: SI 2015/1721 Reg.2

1700. Air Navigation (Restriction of Flying) (Shoreham) (No.2) Regulations 2015
revoked: SI 2015/1722 Reg.2

1825. Air Navigation (Restriction of Flying) (Feltwell) Regulations 2015
revoked: SI 2015/1847 Reg.2
Reg.2, amended: SI 2015/1845 Reg.2
Sch.1, amended: SI 2015/1845 Reg.2

1831. Consumer Rights Act 2015 (Commencement No 2) (Wales) Order 2015
revoked: SI 2015/1904 Art.4

1834. Blood Tests (Evidence of Paternity) (Amendment) Regulations 2015
Reg.3, added: SI 2015/2048 Reg.2

1845. Air Navigation (Restriction of Flying) (Feltwell) (Amendment) Regulations 2015
revoked: SI 2015/1847 Reg.2

1900. Air Navigation (Restriction of Flying) (Tonbridge) (Emergency) Regulations 2015
revoked: SI 2015/1903 Reg.2

1918. Air Navigation (Restriction of Flying) (Tonbridge) (Emergency) (No.2) Regulations 2015
revoked: SI 2015/1922 Reg.2

1931. Fire and Rescue Services (National Framework) (Wales) (Revision) Order 2015
revoked: SI 2015/1991 Art.2

2021. Exclusivity Terms in Zero Hours Contracts (Redress) Regulations 2015
Reg.3, amended: SI 2015/2054 Art.3
Reg.3A, added: SI 2015/2054 Art.3